The
OXFORD
Study
German
DICTIONARY

Editorial Manager: Valerie Grundy
Editor: Neil and Roswitha Morris

CANCELLED 1 4 AUG 2024

OXFORD
UNIVERSITY PRESS

OXFORD

UNIVERSITY PRESS

Great Clarendon Street, Oxford OX2 6DP

Oxford University Press is a department of the University of Oxford.
It furthers the University's objective of excellence in research, scholarship,
and education by publishing worldwide in

Oxford New York

Athens Auckland Bangkok Bogotá Buenos Aires Calcutta
Cape Town Chennai Dar es Salaam Delhi Florence Hong Kong Istanbul
Karachi Kuala Lumpur Madrid Melbourne Mexico City Mumbai
Nairobi Paris São Paulo Singapore Taipei Tokyo Toronto Warsaw

with associated companies in Berlin Ibadan

Oxford is a registered trade mark of Oxford University Press
in the UK and in certain other countries

© Oxford University Press 1999

First published as *The Oxford School German Dictionary* 1998

British Library Cataloguing in Publication Data available

ISBN 0-19-910601-0

1 3 5 7 9 10 8 6 4 2

Typeset by Selwood Systems, Midsomer Norton
Printed in Spain

INTRODUCTION

Learning a new language is an exciting experience. It can also sometimes seem confusing and difficult. Feeling secure and at ease in using a bilingual dictionary is essential to the building of confidence in understanding and using a foreign language.

This dictionary has been specially written for students who are preparing for exams. We have paid particular attention to making the dictionary as user-friendly as possible. With the help of colour headwords, easy-to-follow signposts and simple example phrases, the right translation can quickly be found. The things students need to know about words in German are clearly shown. These include main parts of irregular verbs, noun plurals, and the case taken by prepositions.

We have adopted a simplified version of traditional bilingual entry layout. This means that the dictionary is ideal for learning basic dictionary skills, which can subsequently be built upon as the student moves towards larger, more complex dictionaries. We have done our best to make this dictionary a practical, easy-to-use tool for learning and understanding German.

Throughout the writing of this dictionary we have worked in close consultation with students, teachers, and examining boards. We gratefully acknowledge the examining boards AQA (NEAB and SEG), OCR, and EDEXCEL (ULEAC), who have read and commented on the dictionary text.

HOW A BILINGUAL DICTIONARY WORKS

A bilingual dictionary is a dictionary that has two languages in it. When you look up a word in one of the languages, the dictionary gives the translation for that word in the other language. The two languages in this dictionary are English and German. This dictionary is divided into two halves separated by red-edged pages in the middle. In the first half you look up German words to find out what they mean in English and in the second half you look up English words and find out how to say them in German.

The words you look up are in red and in the first half of the dictionary you will find **German** words in alphabetical order from a to z and in the second half **English** words from a to z. In a dictionary, these are called **headwords** because each one of them comes at the **head** of an **entry**. In the **entry** you can find **translations** but also other sorts of information which you can use to make sure you get the correct translation. The different sorts of information are typed in different ways to help you see clearly which is which. Here is a guide to the different things you will find in an entry:

headword	a word you look up in the dictionary
translation	translations are the only things that are in 'ordinary' type in an entry. They are always typed like this, and something that is typed in a different way can never be a translation
part of speech	tells you whether the word you are looking up is a verb, an adjective, or another part of speech. One headword can have more than one part of speech. **Book** can be a noun *(she was reading a book)* or a verb *(remember to book a table)*
(signpost)	helpful information to guide you to the right translation, to show you how to use the translation, or to give you essential information about either the headword or the translation
example	a phrase using the word you have looked up. If these appear in the entry you are looking at, you should read through them carefully to see if one of them is close to what you want to understand or say
der/die/das	gender: after a German noun to tell you whether it is masculine (*der*), feminine (*die*), or neuter (*das*)
(PL *die........*)	plural: shows the plural form of a German noun
●	indicates a phrasal verb such as *to carry on*
★	indicates an idiomatic expression such as *to look on the bright side*
✧	indicates an irregular German verb
SEP	indicates that a German verb is separable such as *ablenken* (PERF *lenkt ab*)
Δ	indicates a new spelling of a German word (see page xii)

vi

You can think of a dictionary entry as being made out of different sorts of building bricks. In the entries below you can see how they fit together to help you to find what you need. The more you use your dictionary the more confident you will feel about finding your way around it.

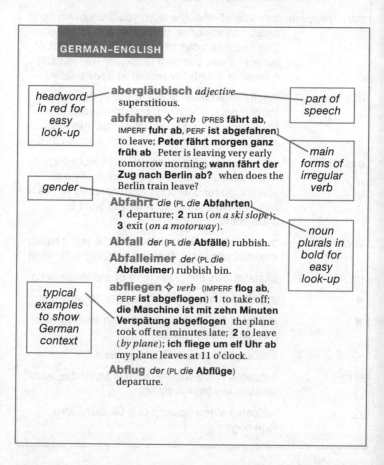

GERMAN–ENGLISH

headword in red for easy look-up

part of speech

abergläubisch *adjective* superstitious.

abfahren ✧ *verb* (PRES **fährt ab**, IMPERF **fuhr ab**, PERF **ist abgefahren**) to leave; **Peter fährt morgen ganz früh ab** Peter is leaving very early tomorrow morning; **wann fährt der Zug nach Berlin ab?** when does the Berlin train leave?

main forms of irregular verb

gender

Abfahrt *die* (PL *die* **Abfahrten**) **1** departure; **2** run (*on a ski slope*); **3** exit (*on a motorway*).

Abfall *der* (PL *die* **Abfälle**) rubbish.

noun plurals in bold for easy look-up

Abfalleimer *der* (PL *die* **Abfalleimer**) rubbish bin.

typical examples to show German context

abfliegen ✧ *verb* (IMPERF **flog ab**, PERF **ist abgeflogen**) **1** to take off; **die Maschine ist mit zehn Minuten Verspätung abgeflogen** the plane took off ten minutes late; **2** to leave (*by plane*); **ich fliege um elf Uhr ab** my plane leaves at 11 o'clock.

Abflug *der* (PL *die* **Abflüge**) departure.

ENGLISH–GERMAN

case governed by German preposition

based *adjective* **1 to be based on** basieren auf (+DAT); **the film is based on a true story** der Film basiert auf einer wahren Geschichte; **2 to be based in** wohnen in (+DAT); **he's based in Bristol** er wohnt in Bristol.

essential structures for expression in German

new spelling

basement *noun* Kellergeschoss △ *das* (PL *die* Kellergeschosse).

plural form

irregular verb

bear *noun* Bär *der* (PL *die* Bären). *verb* **1** ertragen ✧; **I can't bear the idea** ich kann den Gedanken nicht ertragen; **2 to bear something in mind** an etwas ←(ACC) denken; **I'll bear it in mind** ich denke daran.

case of 'etwas' shown in translation of example

perfect formed with 'sein'

blush *verb* erröten (PERF sein).

bolt *noun* (*on a door*) Riegel *der* (PL *die* Riegel). *verb* **1** (*lock*) verriegeln; **2** (*gobble down*) runterschlingen ✧ SEP (*informal*).

gender

separable verb

informal word or expression

✧ IRREGULAR VERB: *See the verb tables in the centre of the dictionary*

A STEP-BY-STEP GUIDE TO FINDING THE TRANSLATION YOU NEED

Finding a word in the dictionary

You will be using this dictionary to do one of the following things:

1 look up a German word or phrase to find out what it means
2 look up an English word or phrase to find out how to say it in German.

1 Finding out what a German word means

First of all, look for it in the first half of the dictionary where you can find the German words and expressions with their English translations. You will see that the top of every page is marked with this red box.

No matter what you are using the dictionary to find out, you will always start by looking up a headword. Here are the German headwords **Ampel**, **Amsel**, **Amt**, **amtlich**, and **amüsant** with their entries.

> **Ampel** *die* (PL *die* **Ampeln**) traffic lights.
>
> **Amsel** *die* (PL *die* **Amseln**) blackbird.
>
> **Amt** *das* (PL *die* **Ämter**) **1** office; **2** exchange (*telephone*).
>
> **amtlich** *adjective* official.
>
> **amüsant** *adjective* amusing.

Suppose you want to find out what the German word **Bürste** means. You will look through the first half of your dictionary until you come to the bit which has all the German words beginning with **b**. You now need to find the page or pages containing German words beginning with **bu**, then **bur**, then **burs**, then **burst**. The dictionary helps you to do this by showing you the alphabetical range of words that you can find on the two pages you can see when you have the dictionary open.

For instance, if you look at pages 52-53, you will see **Brühwürfel** and **campen** at the top of the pages. If you look down the first column on page 53, you will find **Bürste** between **Büroklammer** and **bürsten**. You will know that all German nouns start with a capital letter. Notice that this makes no difference to the alphabetical order, nor do accented letters like **ü**.

> **Büro** *das* (PL *die* **Büros**) office.
>
> **Büroklammer** *die* (PL *die* **Büroklammern**) paper clip.
>
> **Bürste** *die* (PL *die* **Bürsten**) brush.
>
> **bürsten** *verb* (PERF **hat gebürstet**) to brush.

When you look at the entry for **Bürste** you will find the translation you are looking for: **Bürste** means **brush**.

> **Bürste** *die* (PL *die* **Bürsten**) brush.

You can also see what the gender of **Bürste** is. Nouns in German are either masculine, feminine, or neuter. These are shown in the dictionary as *der*, *die*, or *das*. You can see that **Bürste** says *die*. **Bürste** is a feminine noun.

It often happens that a German word has more than one translation in English. If you look at the entry for **Tor** on page 235 you will see that it is divided into sections numbered **1** and **2**.

> **Tor** *das* (PL *die* **Tore**) **1** gate; **2** goal.

The first translation is **gate** and the second is **goal**. You will need to look at both translations and see which fits best in the German sentence you are trying to understand, so:

Uli hat das Tor geöffnet *means* Uli opened the gate

BUT

Uli steht im Tor *means* Uli's in goal

In English, the plural of most nouns is formed by adding **-s** (**book/books**). In German there are quite a lot of ways of forming the plural and these are not always easy to recognize. To help you with this, we show the plural form after every noun headword.

For instance, if you are trying to find out what the German word **Häuser** means, you can see immediately that it is the plural of **Haus** and so it means **houses**.

> **Haus** *das* (PL *die* **Häuser**) **1** house;
> **2 nach Hause** home; **zu Hause** at
> home.

German like English has certain words that you would use when chatting with friends but not in more formal situations. German words like this are marked (*informal*) like **flitzen** here:

> **flitzen** *verb* (*informal*) (PERF **ist**
> **geflitzt**) **1** to dash; **2** to whizz.

2 Finding an English word and how to say it in German

You can see that it is quite easy once you know how the dictionary works to look up a German word and find out what it means. Students usually find it harder to use the dictionary to find out how to say something in German. This dictionary is written specially to help you do this and to make it easy to find the right way of saying things in German.

ENGLISH–GERMAN

Suppose you want to know how to say garden in German. Look up the word in the second part of the dictionary where the top of every page is marked with this box framed in red.

If you follow the same way of going through the alphabetical order of the headwords as you did when you were looking up a German word, you will find **garden** on page 417.

Now you can see that the German word for garden is **Garten**. But
if you want to make a sentence using a noun like **Garten** you
need to know its gender. The dictionary shows you that it is *der*
Garten so **in the garden** will be **im Garten**.

It is not always as easy as this to know which German word you
need. Sometimes there will be more than one German word for
the English word you are looking up. When the dictionary entry
gives you more than just one translation, it is very important to
take the time to read through the whole entry. If you look up
plug the entry looks like this:

> **plug** *noun* **1** (*electrical*) Stecker *der*
> (PL *die* Stecker); **2** (*in a bath or sink*)
> Stöpsel *der* (PL *die* Stöpsel); **to pull
> out the plug** den Stöpsel
> herausziehen.

You can see that **1** tells you that the German word for an
electrical plug is **Stecker** and **2** tells you that the word for a plug
in a bath or a sink is **Stöpsel**.

Remember that information which is either in brackets or italics or
both is there to help you, but it *will never be* the translation itself.
Wherever there is more than one translation, depending on what
meaning of the English word you are looking for, the dictionary
will always help you to choose the right one.

Often it is not enough to find the translation of one word. In the
case of more common words the dictionary also gives you a
selection of phrases you will often want to use. In the entry for
hair below you can find out how to use the translation **Haare** in
different expressions:

> **hair** *noun* **1** Haare (*plural*); **to comb
> your hair** sich ←(DAT) die Haare
> kämmen; **to wash your hair** sich
> ←(DAT) die Haare waschen; **to have
> your hair cut** sich ←(DAT) die Haare
> schneiden lassen; **she's had her hair
> cut** sie hat sich die Haare schneiden
> lassen; **2 a hair** ein Haar.

THE GERMAN SPELLING REFORM

The German spelling reform was adopted by German-speaking countries in July 1996. It was agreed that both old and new spellings would be acceptable until 2005, by which time the new spellings should be included in all written texts.

The main changes to the spelling of German words include:
- After a short vowel, **ss** is used instead of **ß**. For example: **daß** becomes **dass**, **Schloß** becomes **Schloss**.
- Capital letters are now used more often, especially for adjectives used as nouns. For example: **recht haben** becomes **Recht haben**, **es tut mir leid** becomes **es tut mir Leid**.
- Words which were previously one word are now often spelt as two words. For example: **stehenlassen** becomes **stehen lassen**, **wieviel** becomes **wie viel**.

In the headword list of this dictionary you will find all the new spellings. They are marked Δ and there is a note at the foot of each page explaining that this symbol signals a new spelling. However, since you may come across old spellings if you are reading pre-reform German material, we have also given as headwords all the most frequent old spellings which could cause problems in looking up. These are cross-referred to the new spellings.

The same symbol Δ is used on the English-German side of the dictionary to signal new spellings in translations of English headwords.

A a

Aal *der* (PL *die* **Aale**) eel.

ab *preposition* ←(+DAT) from; **ab Montag** from Monday; **Kinder ab sechs Jahren** children from the age of six.
adverb 1 off; **der Henkel ist ab** the handle has come off; **ab ins Bett!** (*informal*) off (you go) to bed!; 2 **ab und zu** now and again.

abbiegen ✧ *verb* (IMPERF **bog ab**, PERF **ist abgebogen**) 1 to turn off; **nach rechts abbiegen** to turn off to the right; 2 **biegen Sie an der Ampel (nach) links ab** turn left at the lights.

Abbildung *die* (PL *die* **Abbildungen**) illustration.

abbrechen ✧ *verb* (PRES **bricht ab**, IMPERF **brach ab**, PERF **hat abgebrochen**) 1 to break off (*a branch, negotiations*); **Ruth brach ein paar Zweige ab** Ruth broke off a few branches; 2 to pull down (*a building*); 3 to cut short; **leider mussten wir unsere Ferien vorzeitig abbrechen** unfortunately we had to cut short our holidays; **er hat sein Studium aus finanziellen Gründen abgebrochen** he left university for financial reasons; 4 (PERF **ist abgebrochen**) **der Ast ist abgebrochen** the branch has broken off.

Abend *der* (PL *die* **Abende**) evening;

am Abend in the evening; **heute Abend** △ this evening, tonight; **gestern Abend** △ yesterday evening, last night; **wann esst ihr zu Abend?** when do you have dinner?

Abendessen *das* (PL *die* **Abendessen**) dinner (*in the evening*); **was gibt es zum Abendessen?** what are we having for dinner?

Abendbrot *das* evening meal.

Abendkurs *der* (PL *die* **Abendkurse**) evening course.

abends *adverb* in the evening.

Abenteuer *das* (PL *die* **Abenteuer**) adventure.

aber *conjunction* but; **es ist zwar nützlich, aber zu teuer** it's useful, but too expensive.
adverb really; **das ist aber sehr nett von dir** that's really nice of you; **du bist aber groß!** aren't you tall!; **aber ja!** but of course!; **jetzt ist aber Schluss!** that's it now!

abergläubisch *adjective* superstitious.

abfahren ✧ *verb* (PRES **fährt ab**, IMPERF **fuhr ab**, PERF **ist abgefahren**) to leave; **Peter fährt morgen ganz früh ab** Peter is leaving very early tomorrow morning; **wann fährt der Zug nach Berlin ab?** when does the Berlin train leave?

Abfahrt *die* (PL *die* **Abfahrten**) 1 departure; 2 run (*on a ski slope*); 3 exit (*on a motorway*).

Abfall *der* (PL *die* **Abfälle**) rubbish.

Abfalleimer der (PL die **Abfalleimer**) rubbish bin.

abfliegen ◇ verb (IMPERF **flog ab**, PERF **ist abgeflogen**) **1** to take off; **die Maschine ist mit zehn Minuten Verspätung abgeflogen** the plane took off ten minutes late; **2** to leave (by plane); **ich fliege um elf Uhr ab** my plane leaves at 11 o'clock.

Abflug der (PL die **Abflüge**) departure.

abfragen verb (PERF **hat abgefragt**) **1** to test; **sie fragt ihn Vokabeln ab** she's testing him on his vocabulary; **2** to call up (on a computer); **Adressen am Computer abfragen** to call up addresses on the computer.

Abgase (plural noun) exhaust fumes.

abgeben ◇ verb (PRES **gibt ab**, IMPERF **gab ab**, PERF **hat abgegeben**) **1** to hand in (homework, an application, lost property); **2** to pass (in football); **den Ball abgeben** to pass the ball; **3 sich mit etwas abgeben** to spend time on something; **mit solchen Typen würde ich mich nicht abgeben** I wouldn't associate with blokes like that; **4 jemandem etwas abgeben** to give someone something; **gib mir ein Stück von deiner Schokolade ab** give me a piece of your chocolate; **5 er wird einen guten Lehrer abgeben** he'll make a good teacher.

abgelegen adjective remote.

abgemacht adjective agreed.

Abgeordnete der/die (PL die **Abgeordneten**) member of parliament.

Abhang der (PL die **Abhänge**) slope.

abhängen[1] ◇ verb (IMPERF **hing ab**, PERF **hat abgehangen**) **von jemandem abhängen** to depend on somebody; **von etwas abhängen** to depend on something; **es hängt vom Wetter ab, ob wir am Wochenende nach Wales fahren** whether or not we are going to Wales at the weekend depends on the weather.

abhängen[2] verb (PERF **hat abgehängt**) **1** to unhitch (a trailer); **2** to uncouple (a train carriage); **3** (informal) to shake off; **die Einbrecher hängten die Polizei schnell ab** the burglars soon shook off the police.

abheben ◇ verb (IMPERF **hob ab**, PERF **hat abgehoben**) **1** to lift off; **2** to withdraw (money); **3** to answer the phone; **ich habe schon zweimal angerufen, aber niemand hat abgehoben** I've rung twice before, but nobody answered.

abholen verb (PERF **hat abgeholt**) **1** to collect; **2** to pick up; **ich hole dich am Bahnhof ab** I'll pick you up at the station.

Abitur das (PL die **Abiture**) A levels (German students usually take Abitur at 19, sitting exams in four subjects, which they have to pass to go on to university); **sein Abitur machen** to do your A levels.

Abiturient der (PL die **Abiturienten**) A-level student.

◇ IRREGULAR VERB: See the verb table in the centre of the dictionary

Abiturientin *die* (PL *die* **Abiturientinnen**) A-level student.

Abkommen *das* (PL *die* **Abkommen**) agreement.

abkürzen *verb* (PERF **hat abgekürzt**) 1 to abbreviate; **wie kürzt man das Wort ab?** how do you abbreviate that word?; 2 **den Weg abkürzen** to take a short cut.

Abkürzung *die* (PL *die* **Abkürzungen**) 1 abbreviation; **die Abkürzung für Europäische Union ist EU** the abbreviation for European Union is EU; 2 short cut.

abladen ✧ *verb* (PRES **lädt ab**, IMPERF **lud ab**, PERF **hat abgeladen**) to unload.

ablaufen ✧ *verb* (PRES **läuft ab**, IMPERF **lief ab**, PERF **ist abgelaufen**) 1 to expire (*passport, contract*); 2 to drain off; **das Badewasser ablaufen lassen** to let the bathwater out; 3 to go off; **wie ist die Besprechung abgelaufen?** how did the meeting go?

ablegen *verb* (PERF **hat abgelegt**) 1 to take off; 2 **abgelegte Kleidung** cast-offs.

ablehnen *verb* (PERF **hat abgelehnt**) 1 to turn down (*a position, money, an invitation*); 2 to reject (*an applicant, a suggestion*).

ablenken *verb* (PERF **hat abgelenkt**) 1 to distract; **jemanden von seiner Arbeit ablenken** to distract somebody from their work; 2 **jemanden von seinen Sorgen ablenken** to take somebody's mind off their worries; 3 to divert (*attention, suspicion*); **vom Thema ablenken** to change the subject.

abliefern *verb* (PERF **hat abgeliefert**) 1 to deliver; 2 to hand in (*an essay, a form, lost property*); 3 to drop off; **die Kinder abliefern** to drop the children off.

abmachen *verb* (PERF **hat abgemacht**) 1 to take off; **kannst du den Deckel abmachen?** can you take off the lid?; 2 to agree; **wir müssen noch einen Termin für unser nächstes Treffen abmachen** we still have to agree on a date for our next meeting; **abgemacht!** agreed!; 3 to sort out; **das müsst ihr untereinander abmachen** you'll have to sort that out amongst yourselves.

Abmachung *die* (PL *die* **Abmachungen**) agreement.

abnehmen ✧ *verb* (PRES **nimmt ab**, IMPERF **nahm ab**, PERF **hat abgenommen**) 1 to take off (*remove*); 2 **kann ich dir etwas abnehmen?** (*carry*) can I take something (for you)?; (*help*) can I do anything for you?; 3 **jemandem etwas abnehmen** to take something off somebody; **sie nehmen einem schnell zwanzig Mark ab** they'll soon take 20 marks off you; 4 to buy; 5 to decrease (*in number*); 6 to lose weight; **er hat schon vier Kilo abgenommen** he's already lost four kilos; 7 to answer the phone; 8 **das nehme ich dir nicht ab** (*informal*) I don't buy that.

Abonnement *das* (PL *die* **Abonnements**) subscription.

△ NEW SPELLING: *See page xii*

abonnieren *verb* (PERF **hat abonniert**) to subscribe to.

abraten ✧ *verb* (PRES **rät ab**, IMPERF **riet ab**, PERF **hat abgeraten**) **jemandem von etwas abraten** to advise somebody against something.

abräumen *verb* (PERF **hat abgeräumt**) to clear away.

abreagieren *verb* (PERF **hat abreagiert**) **1 seine Wut an jemandem abreagieren** to take your anger out on somebody; **2 sich abreagieren** to calm down.

Abreise *die* departure.

abreisen *verb* (PERF **ist abgereist**) to leave.

abreißen ✧ *verb* (IMPERF **riss ab** Δ, PERF **hat abgerissen**) **1** to tear down (*a poster, notice*); **2** (PERF **ist abgerissen**) to come off (*a button, for example*).

Absage *die* (PL *die* **Absagen**) refusal.

absagen *verb* (PERF **hat abgesagt**) **1** to cancel; **2 eine Einladung absagen** to turn down an invitation.

Absatz *der* (PL *die* **Absätze**) **1** heel (*of a shoe*); **2** paragraph.

abschaffen *verb* (PERF **hat abgeschafft**) **1** to abolish (*a regulation, capital punishment*); **2** to get rid of; **wir haben unseren Hund abgeschafft** we got rid of our dog.

abscheulich *adjective* horrible.

abschicken *verb* (PERF **hat abgeschickt**) to send off.

Abschied *der* (PL *die* **Abschiede**) **1** parting; **2** farewell; **3 Abschied nehmen** to say goodbye.

Abschleppdienst *der* breakdown service.

abschleppen *verb* (PERF **hat abgeschleppt**) **1** to tow away; **2 sich mit den Koffern abschleppen** (*informal*) to struggle along with the suitcases; **3 jemanden abschleppen** (*informal*) to pick somebody up.

abschließen ✧ *verb* (IMPERF **schloss ab** Δ, PERF **hat abgeschlossen**) to lock.

Abschlussprüfung Δ *die* (PL *die* **Abschlussprüfungen**) final exam.

abschneiden ✧ *verb* (IMPERF **schnitt ab**, PERF **hat abgeschnitten**) **1** to cut off; **ich schneide dir eine Scheibe Brot ab** I'll cut you a slice of bread; **2 gut/schlecht abschneiden** to do well/badly.

abschrecken *verb* (PERF **hat abgeschreckt**) to deter.

abschreiben ✧ *verb* (IMPERF **schrieb ab**, PERF **hat abgeschrieben**) to copy.

abseits *adverb* **1** far away; **etwas abseits** a little way away; **2** offside (*in soccer*).

Absender *der* (PL *die* **Absender**) sender.

absetzen *verb* (PERF **hat abgesetzt**) **1** to take off (*your hat, glasses*); **2** to put down (*a bag, suitcase*); **3** to drop off; **ich setze euch am Bahnhof ab** I'll drop you off at the station; **4 die**

✧ IRREGULAR VERB: *See the verb table in the centre of the dictionary*

Pille absetzen to stop taking the pill.

Absicht die (PL die **Absichten**) intention.

absichtlich adverb intentionally.

absolut adjective absolute. adverb absolutely; **das ist absolut unmöglich** that's absolutely impossible.

abspülen verb (PERF **hat abgespült**) 1 to rinse, to rinse off; 2 to do the washing up.

Abstand der (PL die **Abstände**) 1 distance; **in zwanzig Meter Abstand** at a distance of 20 metres; **Abstand halten** to keep your distance; 2 interval.

abstauben verb (PERF **hat abgestaubt**) to dust.

abstellen verb (PERF **hat abgestellt**) 1 to turn off (the radio, a tap); 2 to put down (a suitcase, the shopping); 3 to park (the car).

Abstimmung die (PL die **Abstimmungen**) vote.

abstreiten ✧ verb (IMPERF **stritt ab**, PERF **hat abgestritten**) to deny.

abstürzen verb (PERF **ist abgestürzt**) 1 to fall; 2 to crash (a plane).

Abteil das (PL die **Abteile**) compartment.

Abteilung die (PL die **Abteilungen**) department.

Abtreibung die (PL die **Abtreibungen**) abortion.

abtrocknen verb (PERF **hat abgetrocknet**) 1 to dry up; 2 sich **abtrocknen** to dry yourself.

abwägen verb (IMPERF **wog ab**, PERF **hat abgewogen**) to weigh up.

abwärts adverb down.

Abwasch der washing-up.

abwaschen ✧ verb (PRES **wäscht ab**, IMPERF **wusch ab**, PERF **hat abgewaschen**) 1 to wash up (the dishes); 2 to wash off (dirt, marks).

Abwasser das (PL die **Abwässer**) sewage.

Abwechslung die (PL die **Abwechslungen**) change; **zur Abwechslung** for a change.

abwerten verb (PERF **hat abgewertet**) to devalue.

abwertend adjective pejorative.

abwesend adjective absent.

Abwesenheit die absence.

abwischen verb (PERF **hat abgewischt**) to wipe.

abzählen verb (PERF **hat abgezählt**) to count.

Abzeichen das (PL die **Abzeichen**) badge.

abziehen ✧ verb (IMPERF **zog ab**, PERF **hat abgezogen**) 1 to take off (a sheet, backing); **die Betten abziehen** to strip the beds; 2 to take out (a key); 3 to deduct, to take away; 4 to withdraw (troops); 5 (PERF **ist abgezogen**) to escape (steam or smoke, for example); 6 (PERF **ist abgezogen**) sie sind

gleich nach dem Essen abgezogen (*informal*) they pushed off straight after the meal.

abzielen *verb* (PERF **hat abgezielt**) **etwas zielt auf etwas ab** something is aimed at something.

ach *exclamation* oh!

Achsel *die* (PL *die* **Achseln**) shoulder.

acht *number* eight; **um acht (Uhr)** at eight (o'clock); **um halb acht** at half past seven.

Acht¹ *die* (PL *die* **Achten**) eight; **eine Acht schreiben** to write an eight.

Acht² *die* **1 Acht geben** Δ to pay attention; **er sollte in der Schule besser Acht geben** he should pay more attention at school; **2 auf etwas/jemanden Acht geben** to look after something/somebody; **3 gib Acht!** watch out!; **4 sich in Acht nehmen** Δ to be careful; **5 etwas außer Acht lassen** Δ to disregard something.

Achtel *das* (PL *die* **Achtel**) eighth.

achten *verb* (PERF **hat geachtet**) **1** to respect (*a person, an opinion*); **2 auf etwas achten** to pay attention to something; **3 auf jemanden achten** to look after somebody; **4 achte nicht darauf!** don't take any notice of it!

achter, achte, achtes *adjective* eighth; **jede achte Kiste** every eighth crate; **mein achter Geburtstag** my eighth birthday; **sie ging als Achte durchs Ziel** she finished eighth.

Achterbahn *die* (PL *die* **Achterbahnen**) roller coaster.

achtgeben SEE **Acht²**.

achthundert *number* eight hundred.

achtmal *adverb* eight times.

Achtung *die* **1** respect; **Achtung vor jemandem haben** to have respect for somebody; **2 Achtung!** look out!; **Achtung, fertig, los!** on your marks, get set, go!; **'Achtung Stufe'** 'mind the step'.

achtzehn *number* eighteen.

achtzig *number* eighty.

Acker *der* (PL *die* **Äcker**) field.

addieren *verb* (PERF **hat addiert**) to add.

Ader *die* (PL *die* **Adern**) vein.

Adjektiv *das* (PL *die* **Adjektive**) adjective.

Adler *der* (PL *die* **Adler**) eagle.

adoptieren *verb* (PERF **hat adoptiert**) to adopt.

Adoption *die* (PL *die* **Adoptionen**) adoption.

Adoptiveltern *plural noun* adoptive parents.

Adoptivkind *das* (PL *die* **Adoptivkinder**) adopted child.

Adresse *die* (PL *die* **Adressen**) address.

adressieren *verb* (PERF **hat adressiert**) to address; **an wen soll ich den Brief adressieren?** who shall I address the letter to?

Δ IRREGULAR VERB: *See the verb table in the centre of the dictionary*

Advent der Advent.

Adventskalender der (PL die **Adventskalender**) Advent calendar.

Adventskranz der (PL die **Adventskränze**) Advent wreath.

Adverb das (PL die **Adverbien**) adverb.

Aerobic das aerobics.

Affe der (PL die **Affen**) 1 monkey; 2 ape.

Afrika das Africa; **aus Afrika** from Africa; **nach Afrika** to Africa.

Afrikaner der (PL die **Afrikaner**) African.

Afrikanerin die (PL die **Afrikanerinnen**) African.

afrikanisch adjective African.

Agentur die (PL die **Agenturen**) agency.

aggressiv adjective aggressive.

ähneln verb (PERF **hat geähnelt**) 1 to resemble; **er ähnelt seinem Vater sehr** he's very like his father; 2 **sich ähneln** to be alike.

ahnen verb (PERF **hat geahnt**) 1 to know; **das konnte ich wirklich nicht ahnen** I had no way of knowing that; **wer soll denn ahnen, dass …?** who would know that …?; 2 to suspect; **so etwas habe ich doch schon geahnt** I did suspect something like that.

ähnlich adjective 1 similar; 2 **jemandem ähnlich sein** to be like somebody; **jemandem ähnlich sehen** to look like somebody;

3 **ähnlich wie** like; 4 **das sieht dir ähnlich!** (informal) that's just like you!

Ähnlichkeit die (PL die **Ähnlichkeiten**) similarity.

Ahnung die 1 idea; **hast du eine Ahnung, wie er heißt?** have you got any idea what he's called?; 2 **keine Ahnung!** no idea!; **er hat von Mode absolut keine Ahnung** he doesn't know a thing about fashion; 3 premonition.

ahnungslos adjective unsuspecting.

Ahorn der (PL die **Ahorne**) maple.

Aids das Aids.

Akademiker der (PL die **Akademiker**) university graduate.

Akademikerin die (PL die **Akademikerinnen**) university graduate.

akademisch adjective academic.

Akkusativ der (PL die **Akkusative**) accusative.

Akne die acne.

Akte die (PL die **Akten**) file.

Aktentasche die (PL die **Aktentaschen**) briefcase.

Aktion die (PL die **Aktionen**) 1 action; **in Aktion treten** to go into action; 2 campaign.

aktiv adjective active.

Aktiv das active.

aktuell adjective 1 topical; **ein aktuelles Thema** a topical issue;

△ NEW SPELLING: See page xii

2 nicht mehr aktuell no longer relevant; **3** current; **eine aktuelle Sendung** a current-affairs programme.

Akzent *der* (PL *die* **Akzente**) **1** accent; **mit starkem Akzent sprechen** to speak with a strong accent; **2** accent (*on a letter*); **3** stress; **den Akzent auf etwas legen** to stress something.

albern *adjective* silly. *adverb* in a silly way.

Album *das* (PL *die* **Alben**) album.

Algebra *die* algebra.

Alkohol *der* alcohol.

alkoholfrei *adjective* non-alcoholic.

Alkoholiker *der* (PL *die* **Alkoholiker**) alcoholic.

Alkoholikerin *die* (PL *die* **Alkoholikerinnen**) alcoholic.

alkoholisch *adjective* alcoholic.

All *das* space; **einen Satelliten ins All schicken** to send a satellite into space.

alle SEE **aller**.

Allee *die* (PL *die* **Alleen**) avenue.

allein *adjective, adverb* **1** alone; **sie waren allein im Zimmer** they were alone in the room; **jemanden allein lassen** to leave somebody alone; **2** on your own; **sie hat das ganz allein gezeichnet** she drew it all on her own; **3 von allein** by yourself, by itself (*automatically*); **4 allein stehend** △ single; **5 eine allein**

erziehende Mutter △ a single mother; **der/die allein Erziehende** △ single parent; **6 nicht allein** not only; **7 allein der Gedanke** the mere thought.

alleinerziehend, alleinstehend SEE **allein**.

aller, alle, alles *pronoun* **1** all; **alle meine Freunde** all my friends; **alles Geld** all the money; **alle miteinander** all together; **2 alle Jungen in der Schule** all the boys in the school; **alle Bewohner der Stadt sind dagegen** all the people of the town are against it; **alles Gute!** all the best!; **Getränke aller Art** all kinds of drinks; **3 alle** (*plural*) all; **alle waren da** they were all there; **wir alle** we all, all of us; **wir haben alle gesehen** we saw all of them; **4 ohne allen Grund** without any reason; **5 alle beide** both of them; **6** every; **alle Tage** every day; **alle fünf Minuten** every five minutes; **7 alles** everything, everybody (*people*). *adjective* **alle sein** (*informal*) to be all gone.

allerbester, allerbeste, allerbestes *adjective* **1** very best; **2 am allerbesten** best of all.

allerdings *adverb* **1** though; **das Essen ist gut, allerdings ziemlich teuer** the food's good, though rather expensive; **2** certainly (*yes*); **'tut das weh?' – 'allerdings!'** 'does it hurt?' – 'it certainly does!'.

Allergie *die* (PL *die* **Allergien**) allergy.

allergisch *adjective* allergic.

✧ IRREGULAR VERB: *See the verb table in the centre of the dictionary*

Allerheiligen *das* All Saints' Day.

allerlei *adjective* all sorts of; **allerlei Ausreden** all sorts of excuses.

allerletzter, allerletzte, allerletztes *adjective* very last.

alles SEE **aller**.

allgemein *adjective* 1 general; 2 **im Allgemeinen** △ in general.
adverb 1 generally; 2 **es ist allgemein bekannt, dass** … it is common knowledge that …

allmählich *adjective* gradual.
adverb gradually; **wir sollten allmählich gehen** it's time we got going.

alltäglich *adjective* everyday (*event, sight*).

Alltag *der* 1 daily routine; 2 weekday.

alltags *adverb* on weekdays.

Alpen *plural noun* **die Alpen** the Alps.

Alphabet *das* (PL *die* **Alphabete**) alphabet.

alphabetisch *adjective* alphabetical.

Alptraum *der* (PL *die* **Alpträume**) nightmare.

als *conjunction* 1 when; **als meine Freundin hier war** when my friend was here; **erst als** only when; 2 than (*as a comparison*); **er ist jünger als sie** he's younger than her; 3 **lieber … als …** rather … than …; **ich ginge lieber ins Kino als zum Essen** I'd rather go to the cinema than for a

meal; 4 as; **als Frau kann ich das verstehen** as a woman, I can sympathize; **gerade als ich gehen wollte** just as I was about to leave; 5 **als ob** as if; **als ob ich das nicht wüsste!** as if I didn't know that!

also *adverb, conjunction* 1 so; **ich konnte ihn telefonisch nicht erreichen, also habe ich ihm ein Fax geschickt** I couldn't get through to him on the phone, so I sent him a fax; 2 then; **also kommst du mit?** you're coming too, then?; **also gut** all right then; 3 well; **also, wie gesagt** well, as I said before; 4 **na also!** there you are!

alt *adjective* 1 old; **wie alt bist du?** how old are you?; **alt werden** to grow old; 2 **alles beim Alten lassen** to leave everything as it was.

Altar *der* (PL *die* **Altäre**) altar.

Alter *das* (PL *die* **Alter**) 1 age; **in deinem Alter** at your age; **im Alter von zwanzig** at the age of twenty; 2 old age; **im Alter** in old age.

älter *adjective* 1 older; **mein Rad ist älter als deins** my bike is older than yours; 2 elder; **mein älterer Bruder** my elder brother; 3 elderly.

altern *verb* (PERF **ist gealtert**) to age.

Alternative *die* (PL *die* **Alternativen**) alternative.

Altersgrenze *die* (PL *die* **Altersgrenzen**) age limit.

Altersheim *das* (PL *die* **Altersheime**) old people's home.

△ NEW SPELLING: *See page xii*

ältester, älteste, ältestes
adjective 1 oldest; 2 eldest; **der älteste Sohn** the eldest son.

Altglas *das* used glass.

Altglascontainer *der* (PL *die* **Altglascontainer**) bottle bank.

altmodisch *adjective* old-fashioned.

Altpapier *das* waste paper.

Altstadt *die* (PL *die* **Altstädte**) old town.

Alufolie *die* tin foil.

Aluminium *das* aluminium.

am = **an dem**; 1 **am Freitag** on Friday; 2 **am besten** the best; 3 **am teuersten** (the) most expensive; 4 **am höchsten** the highest; 5 **am Abend** in the evening.

Ameise *die* (PL *die* **Ameisen**) ant.

Amerika *das* America.

Amerikaner *der* (PL *die* **Amerikaner**) American.

Amerikanerin *die* (PL *die* **Amerikanerinnen**) American.

amerikanisch *adjective* American.

Ampel *die* (PL *die* **Ampeln**) traffic lights.

Amsel *die* (PL *die* **Amseln**) blackbird.

Amt *das* (PL *die* **Ämter**) 1 office; 2 exchange (*telephone*).

amtlich *adjective* official.

amüsant *adjective* amusing.

amüsieren *verb* (PERF **hat amüsiert**) 1 to amuse; 2 **sich amüsieren** to enjoy oneself;

amüsier dich gut! enjoy yourself!; 3 **sich über etwas amüsieren** to find something funny.

an *preposition* ←(+DAT *or* +ACC) (*the dative is used when talking about position; the accusative shows movement or a change of place*) 1 at; **an der Spitze** at the top; **sich an den Tisch setzen** to sit down at the table; **er arbeitet an der Schule** he works at the school; 2 on (*attached to, when talking about time*); **das Bild hängt an der Wand** the picture is on the wall; **an dem Tag** on that day; **ich habe am fünften März Geburtstag** my birthday is on the fifth of March; 3 to; **einen Brief an jemanden schicken** to send a letter to somebody; 4 **an einer Krankheit sterben** to die of a disease; 5 **an jemanden denken** to think of somebody; 6 **sich an etwas erinnern** to remember something; 7 **an (und für) sich** actually; **an sich ist das kein Problem** actually, it's no problem; 8 **es liegt an dir, jetzt etwas zu unternehmen** it's up to you to do something now.
adverb 1 on; **das Licht ist an** the light's on; 2 **ohne etwas an** with nothing on; 3 **an die dreißig Mark** about thirty marks; 4 **von heute an** from today.

Ananas *die* (PL *die* **Ananas**) pineapple.

anbieten ✧ *verb* (IMPERF **bot an**, PERF **hat angeboten**) to offer; **Anna bot mir an, mich nach Hause zu bringen** Anna offered to take me home.

✧ IRREGULAR VERB: *See the verb table in the centre of the dictionary*

Anblick der (PL die **Anblicke**) sight.

anbrennen ✧ verb (IMPERF **brannte an**, PERF **ist angebrannt**) to burn; **das Essen ist angebrannt** the food's burnt.

Andenken das (PL die **Andenken**) 1 souvenir; 2 **zum Andenken an unsere Ferien** to remind us of our holiday.

anderer, andere, anderes adjective 1 other; **ich nehme das andere T-Shirt** I'll have the other T-shirt; 2 different; 3 **ein anderer/ eine andere/ein anderes** another; **ein anderes Mal** another time. pronoun 1 **der/die/das andere** the other one; **nicht dieses Buch, sondern das andere** not that book, but the other one; **die anderen** the others; **die anderen kommen später** the others are coming later; 2 other ones (things, toys, etc.); 3 **ein anderer/eine andere/ein anderes** a different one (thing); someone else (person); 4 **kein anderer** no one else; 5 **unter anderem** among other things; 6 **etwas anderes** something else; 7 **alles andere** everything else.

andererseits adverb on the other hand.

andermal adverb **ein andermal** another time.

ändern verb (PERF **hat geändert**) 1 to change; 2 to alter (a garment); 3 **sich ändern** to change; **sie hat sich sehr geändert** she's changed a lot.

anders adverb 1 differently;

2 **anders aussehen** to look different; 3 **niemand anders** nobody else; **jemand anders** somebody else; 4 **anders als** different from; **du bist ganz anders als ich** you're quite different from me; 5 **irgendwo anders** somewhere else.

anderthalb number one and a half.

Anerkennung die 1 appreciation; 2 recognition (of a king, state).

Anfall der (PL die **Anfälle**) fit.

Anfang der (PL die **Anfänge**) 1 beginning, start; **am Anfang** at the beginning; **von Anfang an** from the start; 2 **zu Anfang** at first.

anfangen ✧ verb (PRES **fängt an**, IMPERF **fing an**, PERF **hat angefangen**) 1 to begin, to start; **die Schule fängt um acht an** school starts at eight; **mit etwas anfangen** to start (on) something; 2 **bei einer Firma anfangen** to start working for a firm; 3 **was soll ich damit anfangen?** what am I supposed to do with that?; 4 **damit kann ich nichts anfangen** that's no good to me (it's no use); it doesn't mean anything to me (I don't understand it).

Anfänger der (PL die **Anfänger**) beginner.

Anfängerin die (PL die **Anfängerinnen**) beginner.

anfassen verb (PERF **hat angefasst** Δ) 1 to touch; 2 to tackle (a problem, a task); 3 to treat (a person); 4 **mit anfassen** to lend a

Δ NEW SPELLING: *See page xii*

hand; **5 sich anfassen** to feel; **es
fasst sich weich an** it feels soft;
6 jemanden anfassen to take
somebody's hand; **sie hat ihre
Mutter angefasst** she took her
mother's hand; **fasst euch an!** hold
hands!

anfragen *verb* (PERF **hat angefragt**)
to enquire, to ask.

anfreunden *verb* (PERF **hat sich
angefreundet**) **1 sich anfreunden**
to make friends; **sie freundet sich
mit allen möglichen Leuten an** she
makes friends with all sorts of
people; **2 sich anfreunden** to
become friends; **wir haben uns
angefreundet** we've become
friends.

Anführungszeichen *plural noun*
inverted commas.

Angabe *die* (PL *die* **Angaben**)
1 piece of information; **2** serve (*in
tennis*); **3** showing off; **das ist nur
Angabe** he is/she is/they are only
showing off.

angeben ✧ *verb* (PRES **gibt an**,
IMPERF **gab an**, PERF **hat angegeben**)
1 to give (*your name, a reason*); **2** to
show off; **3** to indicate (*on a map*);
4 to serve (*in tennis*).

Angeber *der* (PL *die* **Angeber**) show-
off.

Angeberin *die* (PL *die*
Angeberinnen) show-off.

Angebot *das* (PL *die* **Angebote**) offer.

angehen ✧ *verb* (IMPERF **ging an**,
PERF **ist angegangen**) **1** to come on
(*a radio, heating, a light*); **2** to

concern; **das geht auch dich etwas
an** it concerns you too; **das geht
dich nichts an** it's none of your
business; **3** (PERF **hat angegangen**)
to tackle (*problems, difficulty,
work*).

Angehörige *der/die* (PL *die*
Angehörigen) relative.

Angel *die* (PL *die* **Angeln**) fishing rod.

Angelegenheit *die* (PL *die*
Angelegenheiten) **1** matter;
2 business; **das ist meine
Angelegenheit** that's my business.

angeln *verb* (PERF **hat geangelt**) **1** to
fish; **angeln gehen** to go fishing;
2 to catch (*a fish*).

Angelrute *die* (PL *die* **Angelruten**)
fishing rod.

angenehm *adjective* pleasant.
exclamation pleased to meet you!
(*when introduced to somebody*).

Angestellte *der/die* (PL *die*
Angestellten) employee.

angewiesen *adjective* dependent;
auf etwas angewiesen sein to be
dependent on something; **auf
jemanden angewiesen sein** to be
dependent on somebody.

angewöhnen *verb* (PERF **hat
angewöhnt**) **1 jemandem etwas
angewöhnen** to get somebody used
to something; **2 sich etwas
angewöhnen** to get into the habit of
doing something; **ich habe es mir
angewöhnt, früh aufzustehen** I've
got into the habit of getting up early.

Angewohnheit *die* (PL *die*
Angewohnheiten) habit.

✧ IRREGULAR VERB: *See the verb table in the centre of the dictionary*

angreifen ✧ *verb* (IMPERF **griff an**, PERF **hat angegriffen**) **1** to attack; **2** to affect (*your health, voice*).

Angriff *der* (PL *die* **Angriffe**) attack.

Angst *die* (PL *die* **Ängste**) **1** fear; **2 Angst haben** to be afraid; **vor jemandem Angst haben** to be afraid of somebody; **mir ist Angst** I'm afraid; **3 jemandem Angst machen** to frighten somebody; **4 Angst vor einer Prüfung haben** to be worried about an exam; **Angst um jemanden haben** to be worried about somebody.

ängstlich *adjective* **1** nervous; **2** frightened; **3** anxious.

anhaben ✧ *verb* (*informal*) (PRES **hat an**, IMPERF **hatte an**, PERF **hat angehabt**) to have on; **sie hat heute das neue Kleid an** she's got her new dress on today.

anhalten ✧ *verb* (PRES **hält an**, IMPERF **hielt an**, PERF **hat angehalten**) **1** to stop; **2 den Atem anhalten** to hold your breath; **3** to last; **das schöne Wetter wird nicht lange anhalten** the nice weather won't last long; **4 jemanden zur Arbeit anhalten** to urge somebody to work.

Anhalter *der* (PL *die* **Anhalter**) hitchhiker; **per Anhalter fahren** to hitchhike.

Anhalterin *die* (PL *die* **Anhalterinnen**) hitchhiker.

Anhang *der* (PL *die* **Anhänge**) appendix.

Anhänger *der* (PL *die* **Anhänger**) **1** supporter; **2** trailer; **3** label (*on a suitcase*); **4** pendant; **5** loop (*for hanging up*).

Anhängerin *die* (PL *die* **Anhängerinnen**) supporter.

anhören *verb* (PERF **hat angehört**) **1** to listen to (*music, a CD*); **sich etwas anhören** to listen to something; **ich kann ihn mir nicht länger anhören** I can't listen to him any longer; **2 sich anhören** to sound; **sich gut anhören** to sound good; **3 jemandem etwas anhören** to hear something in somebody's voice; **man hörte ihr die Verzweifung an** you could hear the despair in her voice.

anklagen *verb* (PERF **hat angeklagt**) to accuse.

Ankleidekabine *die* (PL *die* **Ankleidekabinen**) changing cubicle.

ankommen ✧ *verb* (IMPERF **kam an**, PERF **ist angekommen**) **1** to arrive; **gut ankommen** to arrive safely; **2 (bei jemandem) ankommen** (*informal*) to go down well (with somebody); **3 ankommen auf** to depend on; **es kommt ganz darauf an** it all depends; **4 es drauf ankommen lassen** (*informal*) to take a chance; **5 auf ein paar Minuten kommt es nicht an** a few minutes don't matter.

ankündigen *verb* (PERF **hat angekündigt**) to announce.

Ankunft *die* (PL *die* **Ankünfte**) arrival.

Ankunftstafel *die* (PL *die* **Ankunftstafeln**) arrivals board.

△ NEW SPELLING: *See page xii*

Ankunftszeit *die* (PL *die* **Ankunftszeiten**) time of arrival.

Anlage *die* (PL *die* **Anlagen**)
1 gardens; 2 investment; **das Haus ist eine gute Anlage** the house is a good investment; 3 plant (*industrial, for recycling, for example*); 4 enclosure; **als Anlage** enclosed; 5 system (*music, loudspeakers, etc.*); 6 installation (*military*).

Anlass Δ *der* (PL *die* **Anlässe**)
1 cause; **der Anlass ihres Streits** the cause of their row; **Anlass zu etwas geben** to give cause for something; 2 occasion; **ein festlicher Anlass** a festive occasion; **aus Anlass ihres Geburtstags** on the occasion of her birthday.

Anleitung *die* (PL *die* **Anleitungen**) instructions.

anmachen *verb* (PERF **hat angemacht**) 1 to turn on (*the light, radio, TV*); 2 to light (*a fire*); 3 to dress (*salad*); 4 (*informal*) to chat up (*a person*).

Anmeldeformular *das* (PL *die* **Anmeldeformulare**) registration form.

anmelden *verb* (PERF **hat angemeldet**) 1 to register (*a car, change of address*); 2 **jemanden anmelden** to enrol somebody; 3 **jemanden anmelden** to make an appointment for somebody; **sind Sie angemeldet?** do you have an appointment?; 4 **ein Gespräch anmelden** to book a call (*on the phone*); 5 **sich anmelden** to say that you're coming; 6 **sich anmelden** to register your new address (*in Germany a change of address has to be registered at the 'Einwohnermeldeamt'*); **sich polizeilich anmelden** to register with the police; 7 **sich anmelden** to make an appointment; **sich beim Arzt anmelden** to make an appointment with the doctor; 8 **sich anmelden** to enrol; **sich zu einem Abendkurs anmelden** to enrol for an evening course.

Anmeldung *die* (PL *die* **Anmeldungen**) 1 registration; 2 appointment.

annehmen ✧ *verb* (PRES **nimmt an**, IMPERF **nahm an**, PERF **hat angenommen**) 1 to accept (*an invitation, help, a verdict*); 2 to take (*a call, name*); 3 to adopt (*a child, habit*); 4 to assume; **angenommen, dass …** assuming that …; 5 to suppose.

annehmbar *adjective* acceptable.

Annonce *die* (PL *die* **Annoncen**) (small) ad.

anordnen *verb* (PERF **hat angeordnet**) 1 to arrange; 2 to order.

anpassen *verb* (PERF **hat sich angepasst** Δ) **sich anpassen** to adapt.

anpassungsfähig *adjective* adaptable.

anprobieren *verb* (PERF **hat anprobiert**) to try on.

✧ IRREGULAR VERB: *See the verb table in the centre of the dictionary*

Anruf *der* (PL *die* **Anrufe**) (phone) call.

Anrufbeantworter *der* (PL *die* **Anrufbeantworter**) answering machine.

anrufen ✧ *verb* (IMPERF **rief an**, PERF **hat angerufen**) **1** to ring, to phone; **ich rufe schnell mal meine Mutter an** I'll just quickly ring my mother; **2** to call to (*a passer-by*).

ans = **an das**; **ans Telefon gehen** to answer the phone.

Ansage *die* (PL *die* **Ansagen**) announcement.

Ansager *der* (PL *die* **Ansager**) announcer.

Ansagerin *die* (PL *die* **Ansagerinnen**) announcer.

anschalten *verb* (PERF **hat angeschaltet**) to switch on.

anschauen *verb* (PERF **hat angeschaut**) **1** to look at; **2** **sich etwas anschauen** to look at something, to watch something (*on TV*); **sie schauten sich den neuen Film an** they saw the new film.

anscheinend *adverb* apparently.

Anschlag *der* (PL *die* **Anschläge**) **1** notice; **2** attack; **ein Anschlag auf den Präsidenten** an attack on the president.

Anschlagbrett *das* (PL *die* **Anschlagbretter**) notice board.

anschlagen ✧ *verb* (PRES **schlägt an**, IMPERF **schlug an**, PERF **hat angeschlagen**) **1** to put up (*a notice, an announcement*); **2** to chip.

anschließen ✧ *verb* (IMPERF **schloss an** △, PERF **hat angeschlossen**) **1** to connect; **2** **sich an etwas anschließen** to follow something; **an den Vortrag schließt sich eine Diskussion an** the talk will be followed by a discussion; **3** **sich jemandem anschließen** to join somebody; **sich einer Gruppe anschließen** to join a group.

anschließend *adverb* **1** afterwards; **2** **anschließend an das Essen** after the meal.

Anschluss △ *der* (PL *die* **Anschlüsse**) **1** connection; **2** **Anschluss finden** to make friends; **3** **den Anschluss verlieren** to lose contact; **4** **im Anschluss an** after.

anschnallen *verb* (PERF **hat sich angeschnallt**) **sich anschnallen** to fasten your seat belt.

Anschrift *die* (PL *die* **Anschriften**) address.

Anschuldigung *die* (PL *die* **Anschuldigungen**) accusation.

ansehen ✧ *verb* (PRES **sieht an**, IMPERF **sah an**, PERF **hat angesehen**) **1** to look at; **sie sah mich nicht an** she didn't look at me; **2** **sich etwas ansehen** to look at something; (*on TV*) to watch something; **sich einen Film ansehen** to see a film; **3** **sich eine Stadt ansehen** to look round a town; **4** to regard; **ich sehe ihn als meinen Freund an** I regard him as a friend.

△ NEW SPELLING: *See page xii*

Ansehen *das* 1 respect; 2 reputation.

Ansicht *die* (PL *die* **Ansichten**) view; **meiner Ansicht nach** in my view.

Ansichtskarte *die* (PL *die* **Ansichtskarten**) picture postcard.

ansprechen ✧ *verb* (PRES **spricht an**, IMPERF **sprach an**, PERF **hat angesprochen**) 1 to speak to; 2 to appeal to; **die Musik spricht mich an** the music appeals to me; 3 to mention; **er hat den Skandal, in den sie verwickelt war, angesprochen** he mentioned the scandal she was involved in; 4 **auf etwas ansprechen** to respond to something (*a treatment, for example*).

Anspruch *der* (PL *die* **Ansprüche**) 1 demand; **keine Ansprüche stellen** to make no demands; 2 claim; 3 **Anspruch auf etwas haben** to be entitled to something; 4 **viel Zeit in Anspruch nehmen** to take up a lot of time; 5 **etwas in Anspruch nehmen** to take advantage of something (*an offer, for example*).

anständig *adjective* 1 decent; 2 respectable.

anstarren *verb* (PERF **hat angestarrt**) to stare at.

anstatt *preposition* ←(+GEN) instead of.
conjunction **anstatt zu arbeiten** instead of working.

ansteckend *adjective* infectious.

anstelle *preposition* ←(+GEN) instead of.

anstellen *verb* (PERF **hat angestellt**) 1 to employ; 2 to turn on (*the TV, radio*); 3 to do; **was stellt ihr heute Abend noch an?** what are you doing tonight?; **wie kann ich es nur anstellen, dass ...?** what can I do to ...?; 4 **sich anstellen** to queue; 5 **sich anstellen** to make a fuss; **stell dich nicht so an!** don't make such a fuss!

anstreichen ✧ *verb* (IMPERF **strich an**, PERF **hat angestrichen**) to paint.

anstrengen *verb* (PERF **hat angestrengt**) 1 to tire; **ihr Besuch hat mich sehr angestrengt** their visit tired me out; 2 **sich anstrengen** to make an effort.

anstrengend *adjective* tiring.

Anstrengung *die* (PL *die* **Anstrengungen**) effort.

Antarktis *die* **die Antarktis** the Antarctic.

Anteil *der* (PL *die* **Anteile**) 1 share; **mein Anteil an dem Gewinn** my share of the profit; 2 **Anteil nehmen** to sympathize; 3 **Anteil nehmen an** to take an interest in.

Antenne *die* (PL *die* **Antennen**) aerial.

Antibiotikum *das* (PL *die* **Antibiotika**) antibiotic.

antik *adjective* antique.

Antiquitäten *plural noun* antiques.

Antrag *der* (PL *die* **Anträge**)

✧ IRREGULAR VERB: *See the verb table in the centre of the dictionary*

application; **einen Antrag stellen** to make an application.

Antragsformular *das* (PL *die* **Antragsformulare**) application form.

Antwort *die* (PL *die* **Antworten**) answer, reply; **jemandem eine Antwort geben** to give somebody an answer.

antworten *verb* (PERF **hat geantwortet**) to answer, to reply; **auf etwas antworten** to answer something; **jemandem antworten** to reply to somebody.

Anwalt *der* (PL *die* **Anwälte**) lawyer.

Anwältin *die* (PL *die* **Anwältinnen**) lawyer.

Anweisung *die* (PL *die* **Anweisungen**) instruction.

anwenden *verb* (PERF **hat angewendet**) 1 to use (*a method, process, medicine*); 2 to apply (*a rule, law*).

anwesend *adjective* present.

Anzahl *die* number.

anzahlen *verb* (PERF **hat angezahlt**) to pay a deposit; **hundert Mark anzahlen** to pay a hundred marks deposit; **ein Auto anzahlen** to pay a deposit on a car.

Anzahlung *die* (PL *die* **Anzahlungen**) deposit.

Anzeichen *das* (PL *die* **Anzeichen**) sign.

Anzeige *die* (PL *die* **Anzeigen**) 1 advertisement; 2 report (*to the police*); (**eine**) **Anzeige gegen jemanden erstatten** to report somebody to the police.

anzeigen *verb* (PERF **hat angezeigt**) 1 to report; **jemanden anzeigen** to report somebody to the police; 2 to show (*the time, a date*).

anziehen ✧ *verb* (IMPERF **zog an**, PERF **hat angezogen**) 1 to attract; 2 to put on (*clothes, the brakes*); 3 to dress (*a child or doll*); **gut angezogen** well dressed; 4 **sich anziehen** to get dressed; 5 **was soll ich anziehen?** what shall I wear?

Anzug *der* (PL *die* **Anzüge**) suit.

anzünden *verb* (PERF **hat angezündet**) to light.

Apfel *der* (PL *die* **Äpfel**) apple.

Apfelsaft *der* (PL *die* **Apfelsäfte**) apple juice.

Apfelsine *die* (PL *die* **Apfelsinen**) orange.

Apotheke *die* (PL *die* **Apotheken**) chemist's, pharmacy.

Apotheker *der* (PL *die* **Apotheker**) chemist, pharmacist.

Apothekerin *die* (PL *die* **Apothekerinnen**) chemist, pharmacist.

Apparat *der* (PL *die* **Apparate**) 1 set (*TV, radio*); 2 camera; 3 phone; **am Apparat!** speaking!; 4 gadget.

Appartement *das* (PL *die* **Appartements**) flat.

Appetit *der* appetite; **guten Appetit!** enjoy your meal!

△ NEW SPELLING: *See page xii*

Aprikose *die* (PL *die* **Aprikosen**) apricot.

April *der* April; **am ersten April** on the first of April; **April, April!** April fool!; **jemanden in den April schicken** to play an April fool trick on somebody.

Äquator *der* equator.

Araber *der* (PL *die* **Araber**) Arab.

Araberin *die* (PL *die* **Araberinnen**) Arab.

arabisch *adjective* 1 Arab; 2 Arabian; 3 Arabic (*number*); **die arabische Sprache** Arabic.

Arbeit *die* (PL *die* **Arbeiten**) 1 work; **viel Arbeit haben** to have a lot of work; **von der Arbeit kommen** to come from work; 2 job; 3 test (*at school*); 4 **sich viel Arbeit machen** to go to a lot of trouble.

arbeiten *verb* (PERF **hat gearbeitet**) to work.

Arbeiter *der* (PL *die* **Arbeiter**) worker.

Arbeiterin *die* (PL *die* **Arbeiterinnen**) worker.

Arbeitgeber *der* (PL *die* **Arbeitgeber**) employer.

Arbeitnehmer *der* (PL *die* **Arbeitnehmer**) employee.

Arbeitsamt *das* (PL *die* **Arbeitsämter**) job centre.

arbeitslos *adjective* unemployed.

Arbeitslose *der/die* (PL *die* **Arbeitslosen**) unemployed person; **die Arbeitslosen** the unemployed.

Arbeitslosigkeit *die* unemployment.

Arbeitspraktikum *das* (PL *die* **Arbeitspraktika**) work experience.

Arbeitsplatz *der* (PL *die* **Arbeitsplätze**) 1 job; 2 desk.

Architekt *der* (PL *die* **Architekten**) architect.

Architektin *die* (PL *die* **Architektinnen**) architect.

Architektur *die* architecture.

Ärger *der* 1 annoyance; 2 trouble; **Ärger mit dem Auto haben** to have trouble with the car.

ärgerlich *adjective* 1 annoying; 2 annoyed; **er war darüber sehr ärgerlich** he was very annoyed about it.

ärgern *verb* (PERF **hat geärgert**) 1 to annoy; 2 **sich ärgern** to be annoyed, to get annoyed; **ich habe mich darüber geärgert** I was annoyed about it; **sich über jemanden ärgern** to get annoyed with somebody.

artig *adjective* well-behaved.

Arktis *die* **die Arktis** the Arctic; **in der Arktis** in the Arctic.

arm *adjective* poor.

Arm *der* (PL *die* **Arme**) arm; **jemanden auf den Arm nehmen** (*informal*) to pull somebody's leg.

Armband *das* (PL *die* **Armbänder**) bracelet.

Armbanduhr *die* (PL *die* **Armbanduhren**) wrist-watch.

⬦ IRREGULAR VERB: *See the verb table in the centre of the dictionary*

Armee die (PL die **Armeen**) army.

Ärmel der (PL die **Ärmel**) sleeve.

Ärmelkanal der (English) Channel.

Armut die poverty.

arrangieren verb (PERF **hat arrangiert**) **1** to arrange; **2 sich arrangieren** to come to an arrangement.

Art die (PL die **Arten**) **1** way; **auf diese Art** in this way; **auf seine Art** in his own way; **2** kind; **diese Art (von) Buch** this kind of book; **Bücher aller Art** all kinds of books; **3** species; **4** nature; **es ist nicht seine Art, das zu tun** it's not (in) his nature to do that.

Artikel der (PL die **Artikel**) article.

Arznei die medicine.

Arzneimittel das (PL die **Arzneimittel**) drug.

Arzt der (PL die **Ärzte**) doctor.

Ärztin die (PL die **Ärztinnen**) doctor.

ärztlich adjective medical. adverb **sich ärztlich behandeln lassen** to have medical treatment.

As SEE **Ass**.

Asche die (PL die **Aschen**) ash.

Aschenbecher der (PL die **Aschenbecher**) ashtray.

Aschermittwoch der Ash Wednesday.

Asiat der (PL die **Asiaten**) Asian.

Asiatin die (PL die **Asiatinnen**) Asian.

asiatisch adjective Asian.

Asien das Asia; **nach Asien** to Asia.

aß SEE **essen**.

Ass △ das (PL die **Asse**) ace.

Assistent der (PL die **Assistenten**) assistant.

Assistentin die (PL die **Assistentinnen**) assistant.

Ast der (PL die **Äste**) branch.

Asthma das asthma.

Astrologie die astrology.

Astronaut der (PL die **Astronauten**) astronaut.

Astronomie die astronomy.

Asyl das (PL die **Asyle**) **1** asylum; **um politisches Asyl bitten** to apply for political asylum; **2** hostel (for the homeless).

Asylant der (PL die **Asylanten**) asylum-seeker.

Atelier das (PL die **Ateliers**) (artist's) studio.

Atem der breath; **außer Atem sein** to be out of breath.

atemlos adjective breathless.

Athlet der (PL die **Athleten**) athlete.

Athletin die (PL die **Athletinnen**) athlete.

Atlantik der **der Atlantik** the Atlantic (Ocean); **im Atlantik** in the Atlantic.

Atlas der (PL die **Atlanten**) atlas.

atmen verb (PERF **hat geatmet**) to breathe.

Atmosphäre *die* (PL *die* **Atmosphären**) atmosphere.

Atom *das* (PL *die* **Atome**) atom.

atomar *adjective* atomic.

Atomwaffen *plural noun* nuclear weapons.

atomwaffenfrei *adjective* nuclear-free.

attraktiv *adjective* attractive.

ätzend *adjective* 1 corrosive; 2 caustic (*wit, remark*).

au *exclamation* 1 ouch!; 2 oh! (*when surprised or enthusiastic*); **au ja!** oh yes!

auch *adverb* 1 also, too; **Sophie war auch dabei** Sophie was also there, Sophie was there too; **ich auch** me too; **nicht nur … sondern auch …** not only … but also …; 2 **'ich gehe jetzt' – 'ich auch'** 'I'm going now' – 'so am I'; **'er schläft' – 'sie auch'** 'he's asleep' – 'so is she'; 3 **'ich bin nicht müde' – 'ich auch nicht'** 'I'm not tired'-'neither am I'; **das weiß ich auch nicht** I don't know either; 4 **auch wenn** even if; 5 **wann auch** whenever; **was auch** whatever; **wo auch** wherever; **wer auch** whoever; 6 **wie dem auch sei** however that may be; 7 **lügst du auch nicht?** you're not lying, are you?

auf *preposition* ←(+DAT *or* +ACC) (*the dative is used when talking about position; the accusative shows movement or a change of place*) 1 on; **das Buch liegt auf dem Tisch** the book's on the table; **er hat das Buch auf den Tisch gelegt** he put the book on the table; 2 **ich war auf der Party** I was at the party; **ich gehe auf eine Party** I'm going to a party; **ich war auf der Post** I was at the post office; **er ist auf die Post gegangen** he went to the post office; 3 **auf der Straße** in the street; 4 **auf diese Art** in this way; **auf Deutsch** in German; 5 for (*indicating time or distance*); **er ist auf ein paar Tage verreist** he's gone away for a few days; 6 **auf seinen Rat hin** on his advice; 7 **auf Wiedersehen!** goodbye!
adverb 1 open; **die Tür ist auf** the door is open; **Mund auf!** open your mouth!; 2 up (*out of bed*); **auf sein** to be up; **er ist schon auf** he's already up; 3 **auf einmal** suddenly; 4 **auf einmal** at once (*at the same time*); 5 **auf und ab** up and down; 6 **sich auf und davon machen** to make off.

aufbekommen ◇ *verb* (IMPERF **bekam auf**, PERF **hat aufbekommen**) 1 to get open; 2 **Hausaufgaben aufbekommen** to be given homework.

aufbewahren *verb* (PERF **hat aufbewahrt**) to keep.

aufblasen ◇ *verb* (PRES **bläst auf**, IMPERF **blies auf**, PERF **hat aufgeblasen**) to blow up.

aufbleiben ◇ *verb* (IMPERF **blieb auf**, PERF **ist aufgeblieben**) 1 to stay open; **wie lange bleiben die Geschäfte auf?** how long do the shops stay open?; 2 to stay up (*not go to bed*).

◇ IRREGULAR VERB: *See the verb table in the centre of the dictionary*

aufbringen ◇ *verb* (IMPERF **brachte auf**, PERF **hat aufgebracht**) 1 to raise (*money*); 2 to find (*patience, strength*); 3 to open; **ich kann die Tür nicht aufbringen** I can't open the door; 4 **jemanden aufbringen** to make somebody angry; 5 **Verständnis für etwas aufbringen** to be able to understand something.

aufeinander *adverb* 1 one on top of the other; **die Bretter aufeinander legen** to put the planks one on top of the other; 2 **aufeinander liegen** △ to lie on top of each other; 3 **aufeinander folgen** △ to follow one another; 4 **aufeinander warten** to wait for each other; 5 **aufeinander schießen** to shoot at each other; 6 **aufeinander fahren** △ to collide with each other.

Aufenthalt *der* (PL *die* **Aufenthalte**) 1 stay; 2 stop (*pause in a journey*); **zehn Minuten Aufenthalt haben** to stop for ten minutes.

Auffahrt *die* (PL *die* **Auffahrten**) 1 drive; 2 slip road.

auffallend *adjective* striking.

auffangen ◇ *verb* (PRES **fängt auf**, IMPERF **fing auf**, PERF **hat aufgefangen**) to catch.

aufführen *verb* (PERF **hat aufgeführt**) 1 to perform (*a play*); 2 to list (*words, items*); 3 **sich aufführen** to behave.

Aufführung *die* (PL *die* **Aufführungen**) performance.

Aufgabe *die* (PL *die* **Aufgaben**)

1 task; 2 exercise (*at school*); 3 question (*in a test or an exam*); 4 **Aufgaben** homework.

aufgeben ◇ *verb* (PRES **gibt auf**, IMPERF **gab auf**, PERF **hat aufgegeben**) 1 to give up; **ich gebe auf!** I give up!; 2 to post; 3 to check in (*luggage*); 4 to place (*an advertisement, order*); 5 **Hausaufgaben aufgeben** to set homework.

aufgehen ◇ *verb* (IMPERF **ging auf**, PERF **ist aufgegangen**) 1 to open (*of a door or flower, for example*); 2 to come undone (*of a knot or zip, for example*); 3 to rise (*of the sun, moon*); 4 to realize; **es ist mir aufgegangen, dass** … I've realized that …; 5 to work out (*in maths*); **zehn durch drei geht nicht auf** three into ten won't go.

aufgeregt *adjective* excited.

aufgeschlossen *adjective* open-minded.

aufgrund *preposition* ←(+GEN) 1 because of; 2 on the strength of.

aufhaben ◇ *verb* (PRES **hat auf**, IMPERF **hatte auf**, PERF **hat aufgehabt**) 1 to have on (*a hat*); 2 **den Mund aufhaben** to have your mouth open; 3 **etwas aufhaben** to have homework to do; **viel aufhaben** to have a lot of homework; 4 to be open; **der Laden hat abends auf** the shop is open in the evening.

aufhalten ◇ *verb* (PRES **hält auf**, IMPERF **hielt auf**, PERF **hat aufgehalten**) 1 to hold open (*a*

△ NEW SPELLING: *See page xii*

door); **2** to hold up, to keep
(*somebody from doing something*);
3 die Hand aufhalten to hold out
your hand; **4 die Augen aufhalten**
to keep your eyes open; **5** to check
(*inflation, an advance,
unemployment*); **6 sich aufhalten**
to stay; **7 sich mit etwas aufhalten**
to spend your time on something.

aufhängen *verb* (PERF **hat
aufgehängt**) **1** to hang up
(*washing*); **2 sich aufhängen** to
hang yourself.

aufheben ✧ *verb* (IMPERF **hob auf**,
PERF **hat aufgehoben**) **1** to pick up
(*from the ground*); **2** to keep; **3** to
abolish (*a law*); **4 gut aufgehoben
sein** to be well looked after.

aufheitern *verb* (PERF **hat
aufgeheitert**) **1** to cheer up; **2 sich
aufheitern** to brighten up (*of the
weather*).

aufhören *verb* (PERF **hat aufgehört**)
to stop; **aufhören zu arbeiten** to
stop working.

aufklären *verb* (PERF **hat
aufgeklärt**) **1** to solve (*a crime*); **2** to
explain (*an event, incident*); **3 ein
Kind aufklären** to tell a child the
facts of life; **4 sich aufklären** to be
solved (*a misunderstanding or
mystery*); **5 sich aufklären** to clear
up; **das Wetter klärt sich auf** the
weather is clearing up.

Aufkleber *der* (PL *die* **Aufkleber**)
sticker.

auflegen *verb* (PERF **hat aufgelegt**)
1 to put on; **2** to hang up (*when

phoning); **3** to publish; **ein Buch
neu auflegen** to reprint a book.

auflösen *verb* (PERF **hat aufgelöst**)
1 to dissolve; **2** to close (*an
account*); **3 sich auflösen** to
dissolve; **4 sich auflösen** to break
up (*of a crowd, demonstration*);
5 der Nebel hat sich aufgelöst the
fog has lifted; **6 in Tränen aufgelöst
sein** to be in floods of tears.

aufmachen *verb* (PERF **hat
aufgemacht**) **1** to open;
2 jemandem aufmachen to open
the door to somebody; **3** to undo (*a
zip, knot*); **4 sich aufmachen** to set
out.

aufmerksam *adjective* **1** attentive;
2 auf etwas aufmerksam werden
to notice something; **3 jemanden
auf etwas aufmerksam machen** to
draw somebody's attention to
something.

aufmuntern *verb* (PERF **hat
aufgemuntert**) to cheer up.

Aufnahme *die* (PL *die* **Aufnahmen**)
1 photograph; **2** recording;
3 admission (*to hospital, to a club*);
4 welcome.

Aufnahmeprüfung *die* (PL *die*
Aufnahmeprüfungen) entrance
exam.

aufnehmen ✧ *verb* (PRES **nimmt
auf**, IMPERF **nahm auf**, PERF **hat
aufgenommen**) **1** to receive
(*guests*); **2** to take up (*an idea,
activity, a theme*); **3** to admit (*to
hospital, to a club*); **4** to photograph;
5 to film; **6** to record (*a song*); **7 es
mit jemandem aufnehmen können**

✧ IRREGULAR VERB: *See the verb table in the centre of the dictionary*

to be a match for somebody; **8** to take (*food, news*); **etwas gelassen aufnehmen** to take something calmly.

aufpassen *verb* (PERF **hat aufgepasst** Δ) **1** to pay attention; **2** to watch out; **3 auf jemanden aufpassen** to look after somebody; **4 auf etwas aufpassen** to keep an eye on something; **pass auf meine Tasche auf** keep an eye on my bag.

aufräumen *verb* (PERF **hat aufgeräumt**) to tidy up.

aufrecht *adjective* upright.

aufregen *verb* (PERF **hat aufgeregt**) **1** to excite; **2** to annoy; **3 sich aufregen** to get worked up.

aufregend *adjective* exciting.

aufs = **auf das.**

Aufsatz *der* (PL *die* **Aufsätze**) essay.

aufschieben ✧ *verb* (IMPERF **schob auf**, PERF **hat aufgeschoben**) **1** to put off (*an arrangement*); **2** to slide open.

aufschließen ✧ *verb* (IMPERF **schloss auf** Δ, PERF **hat aufgeschlossen**) to unlock.

Aufschnitt *der* sliced cold meat and cheese.

aufschreiben ✧ *verb* (IMPERF **schrieb auf**, PERF **hat aufgeschrieben**) to write down.

aufsehen ✧ *verb* (PRES **sieht auf**, IMPERF **sah auf**, PERF **hat aufgesehen**) to look up.

aufsetzen *verb* (PERF **hat aufgesetzt**) **1** to put on; **2** to draft; **3 sich aufsetzen** to sit up.

Aufsicht *die* **1** supervision; **2** supervisor.

Aufstand *der* (PL *die* **Aufstände**) rebellion.

aufstehen ✧ *verb* (IMPERF **stand auf**, PERF **ist aufgestanden**) **1** to get up; **2** (PERF **hat aufgestanden**) to be open.

aufstellen *verb* (PERF **hat aufgestellt**) **1** to put up; **2** to set up (*skittles, chess pieces*); **3 eine Mannschaft aufstellen** to pick a team; **4 eine Liste aufstellen** to draw up a list; **5 sich aufstellen** to line up.

auftauen *verb* (PERF **ist aufgetaut**) **1** to thaw; **2** to defrost; **die Erdbeeren sind aufgetaut** the strawberries have defrosted; **3** (PERF **hat aufgetaut**) to defrost; **ich habe die Erbeeren aufgetaut** I've defrosted the strawberries.

aufteilen *verb* (PERF **hat aufgeteilt**) to divide up.

Auftrag *der* (PL *die* **Aufträge**) **1** job; **2** order (*in business*); **etwas in Auftrag geben** to order something; **3** instructions; **einen Auftrag ausführen** to carry out an instruction; **4 im Auftrag von** on behalf of.

auftreten ✧ *verb* (PRES **tritt auf**, IMPERF **trat auf**, PERF **ist aufgetreten**) **1** to appear (*on stage*); **2** to arise (*a problem, difficulty*); **3** to behave; **4** to tread.

Δ NEW SPELLING: *See page xii*

aufwachen verb (PERF **ist aufgewacht**) to wake up.

aufwachsen ✧ verb (PRES **wächst auf**, IMPERF **wuchs auf**, PERF **ist aufgewachsen**) to grow up.

aufwecken verb (PERF **hat aufgeweckt**) to wake up.

aufziehen ✧ verb (IMPERF **zog auf**, PERF **hat aufgezogen**) 1 to wind up (*a clock or toy*); 2 to draw (*curtains*); 3 **jemanden aufziehen** (*informal*) to tease somebody; 4 to bring up (*a child*).

Aufzug der (PL die **Aufzüge**) lift; **ich fahre mit dem Aufzug runter** I'm going down in the lift.

Auge das (PL die **Augen**) 1 eye; 2 **unter vier Augen** in private.

Augenblick der (PL die **Augenblicke**) moment; **im Augenblick** at the moment.

Augenbraue die (PL die **Augenbrauen**) eyebrow.

August der August.

aus preposition ←(+DAT) 1 out of; **er hat es aus dem Fenster geworfen** he threw it out of the window; 2 from; **aus Spanien** from Spain; **aus Erfahrung** from experience; 3 made of; **aus Holz** made of wood; 4 **aus Spaß** for fun; 5 **aus der Mode** out of fashion; 6 **aus Versehen** by mistake; 7 **aus welchem Grund?** for what reason?; 8 **aus ihr ist eine gute Rechtsanwältin geworden** she made a good lawyer; **aus ihm ist nichts geworden** he never made anything of his life.
adverb 1 off (*of a TV, radio*); **das Licht ist aus** the light is off; **Licht aus!** lights out!; 2 finished; **wenn das Spiel aus ist** when the game has finished; 3 **von mir aus** as far as I'm concerned; 4 **von sich aus** of your own accord.

ausbeuten verb (PERF **hat ausgebeutet**) to exploit.

ausbilden verb (PERF **hat ausgebildet**) to train.

Ausbildung die 1 training; 2 education.

Ausdruck[1] der (PL die **Ausdrücke**) expression; **etwas zum Ausdruck bringen** to express something.

Ausdruck[2] der (PL die **Ausdrucke**) print-out.

ausdrucken verb (PERF **hat ausgedruckt**) to print out.

ausdrücken verb (PERF **hat ausgedrückt**) 1 to squeeze (*oranges, lemons*); 2 to express; 3 **sich ausdrücken** to express oneself.

auseinander adverb 1 apart; **etwas auseinander nehmen** Δ to take something apart; **auseinander halten** Δ to tell apart; 2 **auseinander gehen** Δ to part; 3 **auseinander schreiben** to write as separate words; 4 **sich mit einem Problem auseinander setzen** Δ to come to grips with a problem; 5 **sich mit jemandem auseinander setzen** Δ to have it out with somebody.

✧ IRREGULAR VERB: *See the verb table in the centre of the dictionary*

Ausfahrt *die* (PL *die* **Ausfahrten**)
1 exit; 2 **'Ausfahrt freihalten'** 'keep clear'.

ausfallen ◇ *verb* (PRES **fällt aus**, IMPERF **fiel aus**, PERF **ist ausgefallen**)
1 to be cancelled; **etwas ausfallen lassen** to cancel something; 2 to fall out (*hair*); 3 to fail (*an engine, brakes, a signal*); 4 to break down (*a machine, a car, heating*); 5 to turn out; **gut ausfallen** to turn out well.

Ausflug *der* (PL *die* **Ausflüge**) outing, trip; **einen Ausflug machen** to go on an outing.

Ausfuhr *die* export.

ausführen *verb* (PERF **hat ausgeführt**) 1 to carry out (*a plan*); 2 to export (*goods*); 3 to take out; **er hat seine Freundin zum Essen ausgeführt** he took his girlfriend out for a meal; 4 **den Hund ausführen** to take the dog for a walk.

ausführlich *adjective* detailed. *adverb* in detail.

ausfüllen *verb* (PERF **hat ausgefüllt**)
1 to fill in; 2 **ihr Beruf als Lehrerin füllt sie ganz aus** teaching gives her great satisfaction.

Ausgabe *die* (PL *die* **Ausgaben**)
1 edition; 2 issue; 3 **Ausgaben** expenditure.

Ausgang *der* (PL *die* **Ausgänge**)
1 exit; **'kein Ausgang'** 'no exit'; 2 end, ending; 3 result (*of a game, discussion*).

ausgeben ◇ *verb* (PRES **gibt aus**, IMPERF **gab aus**, PERF **hat ausgegeben**) 1 to spend; 2 to hand out; 3 **Fahrkarten ausgeben** to issue tickets; 4 to serve (*food*); 5 **sich ausgeben als** to pretend to be; 6 **einen ausgeben** (*informal*) to treat everybody (*to a round of drinks for example*).

ausgebucht *adjective* fully booked.

ausgehen ◇ *verb* (PRES **geht aus**, IMPERF **ging aus**, PERF **ist ausgegangen**) 1 to go out; 2 to run out (*of supplies*); 3 to end; **schlecht ausgehen** to end badly; 4 **davon ausgehen, dass** … to assume that …

ausgerechnet *adverb*
1 **ausgerechnet heute** today of all days; 2 **ausgerechnet sie** she of all people.

ausgeschlossen *adjective* out of the question.

ausgezeichnet *adjective* excellent.

aushalten ◇ *verb* (PRES **hält aus**, IMPERF **hielt aus**, PERF **hat ausgehalten**) 1 to stand; 2 **es ist nicht zum Aushalten** it's unbearable.

Aushilfe *die* (PL *die* **Aushilfen**) temporary assistant, temp.

auskennen ◇ *verb* (IMPERF **kannte sich aus**, PERF **hat sich ausgekannt**)
1 **sich auskennen** to know your way around; 2 **sich gut mit etwas auskennen** to know a lot about something.

auskommen ◇ *verb* (IMPERF **kam aus**, PERF **ist ausgekommen**) 1 to manage; **mit fünfzig Mark**

△ NEW SPELLING: *See page xii*

auskommen to manage on fifty marks; **2 mit jemandem gut auskommen** to get on well with somebody.

Auskunft die (PL die **Auskünfte**) 1 information; 2 information desk; 3 enquiries (*when phoning*).

auslachen verb (PERF **hat ausgelacht**) to laugh at.

ausladen ✧ verb (PRES **lädt aus**, IMPERF **lud aus**, PERF **hat ausgeladen**) 1 to unload; 2 **jemanden ausladen** (*informal*) to put somebody off.

Ausland das **im Ausland** abroad; **ins Ausland reisen** to travel abroad.

Ausländer der (PL die **Ausländer**) foreigner.

Ausländerin die (PL die **Ausländerinnen**) foreigner.

ausländisch adjective foreign.

Auslandsgespräch das (PL die **Auslandsgespräche**) international call.

ausleeren verb (PERF **hat ausgeleert**) to empty.

ausleihen ✧ verb (IMPERF **lieh aus**, PERF **hat ausgeliehen**) 1 to lend; 2 **sich etwas ausleihen** to borrow something.

ausmachen verb (PERF **hat ausgemacht**) 1 to turn off; 2 to put out; 3 to arrange; **wir haben ausgemacht, dass wir uns heute Abend treffen** we've arranged to meet up this evening; 4 **das macht mir nichts aus** I don't mind; **macht es Ihnen etwas aus, wenn …?**

would you mind if …?; **5 viel ausmachen** to make a great difference.

Ausnahme die (PL die **Ausnahmen**) exception.

ausnutzen verb (PERF **hat ausgenutzt**) 1 to use; 2 to take advantage of.

auspacken verb (PERF **hat ausgepackt**) to unpack.

Auspuff der (PL die **Auspuffe**) exhaust.

ausrechnen verb (PERF **hat ausgerechnet**) to work out.

Ausrede die (PL die **Ausreden**) excuse.

ausreichend adjective 1 sufficient 2 fair, pass (*as a mark at school*).

Ausreise die (PL die **Ausreisen**) departure (*from a country*).

ausrichten verb (PERF **hat ausgerichtet**) **jemandem etwas ausrichten** to tell somebody something.

Ausrufezeichen das (PL die **Ausrufezeichen**) exclamation mark.

ausruhen verb (PERF **hat sich ausgeruht**) **sich ausruhen** to have a rest.

Ausrüstung die equipment.

ausschalten verb (PERF **hat ausgeschaltet**) 1 to switch off; 2 to eliminate.

ausschneiden ✧ verb (IMPERF **schnitt aus**, PERF **hat ausgeschnitten**) to cut out.

✧ IRREGULAR VERB: *See the verb table in the centre of the dictionary*

Ausschuss △ *der* (PL *die* **Ausschüsse**) committee.

aussehen ◇ *verb* (PRES **sieht aus**, IMPERF **sah aus**, PERF **hat ausgesehen**) to look.

Aussehen *das* appearance.

außen *adverb* 1 (on the) outside; **von außen** from the outside; 2 **nach außen** outwards.

Außenminister *der* (PL *die* **Außenminister**) Foreign Secretary, Foreign Minister.

außer *preposition* ←(+DAT) 1 apart from, except (for); **alle außer ihm** everyone except (for) him; 2 out of; **außer Sicht** out of sight; **außer Betrieb** out of order; 3 **außer Haus** out; 4 **außer sich sein** to be beside yourself.
conjunction 1 except; **außer sonntags** except Sundays; 2 **außer wenn** unless.

außerdem *adverb* 1 as well; 2 besides.

äußerer, äußere, äußeres *adjective* 1 external (*injury, circumstances*); 2 outer (*layer, circle*); 3 outward (*appearance, effect*).

außergewöhnlich *adjective* unusual.

außerhalb *preposition* ←(+GEN) outside.
adverb **außerhalb wohnen** to live out of town.

äußerlich *adjective* 1 external; 2 outward (*appearance*).

außerordentlich *adjective* extraordinary.

äußerst *adverb* extremely.

Äußerung *die* (PL *die* **Äußerungen**) remark.

Aussicht *die* (PL *die* **Aussichten**) 1 prospect; **etwas in Aussicht haben** to have the prospect of something; **keine Aussichten auf Erfolg haben** to have no chance of success; 2 view; **ein Zimmer mit Aussicht aufs Meer** a room with a view of the sea.

Aussprache *die* (PL *die* **Aussprachen**) 1 pronunciation; 2 talk.

aussprechen ◇ *verb* (PRES **spricht aus**, IMPERF **sprach aus**, PERF **hat ausgesprochen**) 1 to pronounce; 2 to express; 3 **lassen Sie ihn aussprechen** let him finish (*speaking*); 4 **sich aussprechen** to talk; **sich mit jemandem aussprechen** to have a talk with somebody; 5 **sich gegen etwas aussprechen** to come out against something; **sich für etwas aussprechen** to come out in favour of something; 6 **sich lobend über jemanden aussprechen** to speak highly of somebody.

aussteigen ◇ *verb* (IMPERF **stieg aus**, PERF **ist ausgestiegen**) 1 to get out; 2 to get off.

ausstellen *verb* (PERF **hat ausgestellt**) 1 to display (*in a shop*); 2 to exhibit; 3 to make out (*a certificate, bill*); 4 to issue (*a passport*); 5 to switch off.

△ NEW SPELLING: *See page xii*

Ausstellung die (PL die
Ausstellungen) exhibition.

ausstreichen ✧ verb (IMPERF
strich aus, PERF **hat ausgestrichen**)
to cross out.

aussuchen verb (PERF **hat
ausgesucht**) 1 to choose; 2 **sich
etwas aussuchen** to choose
something.

Austausch der exchange.

austauschen verb (PERF **hat
ausgetauscht**) 1 to exchange; 2 to
replace; 3 to substitute (a player).

Auster die (PL die **Austern**) oyster.

austragen ✧ verb (PRES **trägt aus**,
IMPERF **trug aus**, PERF **hat
ausgetragen**) to deliver (post); to
hold (a race).

Australien das Australia; **aus
Australien** from Australia.

Australier der (PL die **Australier**)
Australian.

Australierin die (PL die
Australierinnen) Australian.

australisch adjective Australian.

austreten ✧ verb (PRES **tritt aus**,
IMPERF **trat aus**, PERF **hat
ausgetreten**) 1 to stamp out (a
cigarette or fire); 2 to wear out
(shoes); 3 (PERF **ist ausgetreten**) **aus
einem Klub austreten** to leave a
club; **ich trete aus** I'm leaving;
4 (informal) (PERF **ist ausgetreten**)
to go to the loo.

austrinken ✧ verb (IMPERF **trank
aus**, PERF **hat ausgetrunken**) to
drink up.

Ausverkauf der (PL die
Ausverkäufe) sale.

ausverkauft adjective 1 sold out;
2 **ein ausverkauftes Haus** a full
house (at the cinema or theatre).

Auswahl die (PL die **Auswahlen**)
choice, selection; **wenig Auswahl
haben** to have a limited selection.

auswärts adverb 1 away (in sport);
auswärts spielen to play away;
2 **auswärts essen** to eat out; 3 **sie
arbeitet auswärts** she doesn't work
locally.

Auswärtsspiel das (PL die
Auswärtsspiele) away game.

Ausweg der (PL die **Auswege**) way
out.

Ausweis der (PL die **Ausweise**)
1 identity card; 2 card (for students
or members); 3 pass.

auswendig adverb by heart.

auswirken verb (PERF **hat sich
ausgewirkt**) **sich auf etwas
auswirken** to have an effect on
something.

ausziehen ✧ verb (IMPERF **zog aus**,
PERF **hat ausgezogen**) 1 to take off
(clothes); 2 to undress; 3 **sich
ausziehen** to get undressed; 4 (PERF
ist ausgezogen) to move out (move
house).

Auto das (PL die **Autos**) car; **Auto
fahren** to drive.

Autobahn die (PL die **Autobahnen**)
motorway.

Autofahrer der (PL die **Autofahrer**)
motorist.

✧ IRREGULAR VERB: *See the verb table in the centre of the dictionary*

Autogramm das (PL die **Autogramme**) autograph.

Automat der (PL die **Automaten**) machine.

automatisch adjective automatic.

Autor der (PL die **Autoren**) author.

Autorin die (PL die **Autorinnen**) authoress.

Autorität die authority.

Autostopp der **per Autostopp fahren** to hitchhike.

Autotelefon das (PL die **Autotelefone**) car phone.

Autounfall der (PL die **Autounfälle**) car accident.

Autoverleih der (PL die **Autoverleihe**) car hire (firm).

Axt die (PL die **Äxte**) axe.

B b

Baby das (PL die **Babys**) baby.

Bach der (PL die **Bäche**) stream.

Backe die (PL die **Backen**) cheek.

backen ◇ verb (PRES **bäckt**, IMPERF **backte**, PERF **hat gebacken**) to bake.

Bäcker der (PL die **Bäcker**) 1 baker; 2 **beim Bäcker** at the baker's.

Bäckerei die (PL die **Bäckereien**) baker's.

Backofen der (PL die **Backöfen**) oven.

Backpflaume die (PL die **Backpflaumen**) prune.

Bad das (PL die **Bäder**) 1 bath; 2 bathroom; 3 pool (for swimming).

Badeanzug der (PL die **Badeanzüge**) swimsuit.

Badehose die (PL die **Badehosen**) swimming trunks.

Bademütze die (PL die **Bademützen**) bathing cap.

baden verb (PERF **hat gebadet**) 1 to have a bath; 2 to bathe (in the sea); 3 to bath (wash somebody).

Badetuch das (PL die **Badetücher**) bath towel.

Badewanne die (PL die **Badewannen**) bath (tub).

Badezimmer das (PL die **Badezimmer**) bathroom.

Bahn die (PL die **Bahnen**) 1 railway; 2 train; **mit der Bahn fahren** to go by train; 3 tram; 4 track (in sport); 5 lane (on a track); 6 path; **auf die schiefe Bahn geraten** to go off the rails.

Bahnhof der (PL die **Bahnhöfe**) (railway) station.

Bahnsteig der (PL die **Bahnsteige**) platform.

Bahnübergang der (PL die **Bahnübergänge**) level crossing.

bald adverb 1 soon; **bis bald!** see you soon!; 2 **wird's bald!** (informal) get a move on!; 3 almost; **ich hätte bald vergessen, ihn**

anzurufen I almost forgot to ring him.

Balken der (PL die **Balken**) beam.

Balkon der (PL die **Balkons**) balcony.

Ball der (PL die **Bälle**) 1 ball; **Ball spielen** to play ball; 2 ball; **auf dem Ball** at the ball.

Ballett das (PL die **Ballette**) ballet.

Balletttänzer ⚹ der (PL die **Balletttänzer**) ballet dancer.

Balletttänzerin ⚹ die (PL die **Balletttänzerinnen**) ballet dancer.

Ballon der (PL die **Ballons**) balloon.

Banane die (PL die **Bananen**) banana.

band SEE **binden**.

Band[1] das (PL die **Bänder**) 1 ribbon; 2 tape (for recording); **etwas auf Band aufnehmen** to tape something; 3 production line; **am Band arbeiten** to work on the production line; 4 **am laufenden Band** (informal) nonstop.

Band[2] der (PL die **Bände**) volume.

Band[3] die (PL die **Bands**) band.

Bank[1] die (PL die **Bänke**) bench.

Bank[2] die (PL die **Banken**) bank; **ich muss erst zur Bank gehen** I have to go to the bank first.

Bankkonto das (PL die **Bankkonten**) bank account.

Banknote die (PL die **Banknoten**) banknote.

bankrott adjective bankrupt;

bankrott gehen/machen to go bankrupt.

bar adjective (in) cash.

Bar die (PL die **Bars**) bar.

Bär der (PL die **Bären**) bear.

Bardame die (PL die **Bardamen**) barmaid.

barfuß adjective barefoot.

Bargeld das cash.

Barkeeper der (PL die **Barkeeper**) barman.

Barren der (PL die **Barren**) 1 bar; 2 parallel bars.

Bart der (PL die **Bärte**) beard.

bärtig adjective bearded.

Basel das Basle.

Basis die (PL die **Basen**) basis.

Bass ⚹ der (PL die **Bässe**) bass.

basta exclamation and that's that!

basteln verb (PERF **hat gebastelt**) 1 to make (things); 2 **sie bastelt gern** she likes making things.

bat SEE **bitten**.

Batterie die (PL die **Batterien**) battery.

Bau der (PL die **Bauten**) 1 construction; **im Bau sein** to be under construction; 2 building; 3 building site; **auf dem Bau arbeiten** to work on a building site.

Bauarbeiter der (PL die **Bauarbeiter**) builder.

Bauch der (PL die **Bäuche**) stomach, belly.

⬦ IRREGULAR VERB: See the verb table in the centre of the dictionary

Bauchschmerzen *plural noun* stomachache.

bauen *verb* (PERF **hat gebaut**) **1** to build; **2 einen Unfall bauen** (*informal*) to have an accident.

Bauer *der* (PL *die* **Bauern**) **1** farmer; **2** pawn (*in chess*).

Bäuerin *die* (PL *die* **Bäuerinnen**) **1** farmer; **2** farmer's wife.

Bauernhof *der* (PL *die* **Bauernhöfe**) farm.

Baum *der* (PL *die* **Bäume**) tree.

Baumwolle *die* cotton.

Bausparkasse *die* (PL *die* **Bausparkassen**) building society.

Baustelle *die* (PL *die* **Baustellen**) building site.

Bayer *der* (PL *die* **Bayern**) Bavarian.

Bayerin *die* (PL *die* **Bayerinnen**) Bavarian.

Bayern *das* Bavaria; **aus Bayern** from Bavaria.

bayrisch *adjective* Bavarian.

beabsichtigen *verb* (PERF **hat beabsichtigt**) to intend.

beachten *verb* (PERF **hat beachtet**) **1** to take notice of; **beachte ihn einfach nicht** just don't take any notice of him; **2** to observe; **3** to follow (*a rule, advice*); **4** to obey; **die Verkehrsregeln beachten** to obey traffic regulations.

Beamte *der* (PL *die* **Beamten**) **1** civil servant (*in Germany all public employees, such as teachers and policemen, are 'Beamte'*); **2** official.

Beamtin *die* (PL *die* **Beamtinnen**) **1** civil servant; **2** official.

beanspruchen *verb* (PERF **hat beansprucht**) **1** to claim (*benefit*); **2** to take up (*time, space*); **jemanden beanspruchen** to take up somebody's time; **3** to demand (*energy, attention*); **die Arbeit beansprucht sie sehr** her work is very demanding; **4** to take advantage of (*hospitality, services, help*); **ich möchte Ihre Geduld nicht zu sehr beanspruchen** I don't want to try your patience.

Beanstandung *die* (PL *die* **Beanstandungen**) complaint.

beantragen *verb* (PERF **hat beantragt**) to apply for.

beantworten *verb* (PERF **hat beantwortet**) to answer.

bearbeiten *verb* (PERF **hat bearbeitet**) **1** to deal with; **einen Antrag bearbeiten** to deal with an application; **2** to adapt (*a play*); **3** to treat (*wood, for example*); **er hat die Oberfläche mit Wachs bearbeitet** he's treated the surface with wax; **4 jemanden bearbeiten, dass er etwas macht** (*informal*) to work on somebody so that he does something (*persuade*).

beaufsichtigen *verb* (PERF **hat beaufsichtigt**) to supervise.

Becher *der* (PL *die* **Becher**) **1** beaker, mug; **2** pot, carton (*of yoghurt, cream*).

△ NEW SPELLING: *See page xii*

Becken *das* (PL **die Becken**)
1 basin; 2 pool (*for swimming*);
3 pelvis.

bedanken *verb* (PERF **hat sich bedankt**) **sich bedanken** to say thank you; **vergiss nicht, dich zu bedanken** don't forget to say thank you; **ich habe mich bei ihm bedankt** I thanked him.

Bedarf *der* 1 need; 2 **bei Bedarf** if required; 3 demand; **je nach Bedarf** according to demand.

bedauerlicherweise *adverb* unfortunately.

bedauern *verb* (PERF **hat bedauert**)
1 to regret; **ich bedaure kein Wort** I don't regret a single word; 2 **ich bedaure sehr, dass du nicht kommen kannst** I'm very sorry that you can't come; **bedaure!** sorry!;
3 **jemanden bedauern** to feel sorry for somebody.

bedecken *verb* (PERF **hat bedeckt**) to cover.

bedeckt *adjective* 1 covered;
2 overcast (*weather*); **gestern war es den ganzen Tag bedeckt** it was overcast all day yesterday.

bedenken ◇ *verb* (IMPERF **bedachte**, PERF **hat bedacht**) to consider.

Bedenken *plual noun* 1 doubts; **Bedenken haben** to have doubts;
2 **ohne Bedenken** without hesitation.

bedenklich *adjective* 1 worrying; **die Situation ist sehr bedenklich** the situation is very worrying;
2 dubious; **er hat bedenkliche Mittel angewendet, um sein Ziel zu**

erreichen he's used dubious methods to achieve his aims;
3 serious.

bedeuten *verb* (PERF **hat bedeutet**) to mean.

bedeutend *adjective* 1 important;
2 considerable.

Bedeutung *die* (PL **die Bedeutungen**) 1 meaning;
2 importance.

bedienen *verb* (PERF **hat bedient**)
1 to serve; **hier wird man sehr schnell bedient** you get served very quickly here; 2 to operate; 3 **sich bedienen** to help oneself.

Bedienung *die* (PL **die Bedienungen**) 1 service; **Bedienung inbegriffen** service included; 2 waiter, waitress; 3 shop assistant; 4 operation (*of a machine*).

Bedingung *die* (PL **die Bedingungen**) condition; **nur unter der Bedingung, dass du mitkommst** only on condition that you're coming with us.

bedrohen *verb* (PERF **hat bedroht**) to threaten.

Bedrohung *die* (PL **die Bedrohungen**) threat.

beeilen *verb* (PERF **hat sich beeilt**) **sich beeilen** to hurry (up); **beeilt euch!** hurry up!

beeindrucken *verb* (PERF **hat beeindruckt**) to impress.

beeinflussen *verb* (PERF **hat beeinflusst**) to influence.

◇ IRREGULAR VERB: *See the verb table in the centre of the dictionary*

beenden *verb* (PERF **hat beendet**) to end.

Beerdigung *die* (PL *die* **Beerdigungen**) funeral.

Beere *die* (PL *die* **Beeren**) berry.

Beet *das* (PL *die* **Beete**) 1 bed (*of flowers*); 2 patch (*of vegetables*).

befahl SEE **befehlen**.

Befehl *der* (PL *die* **Befehle**) 1 order; 2 command; **den Befehl über etwas haben** to be in command of something.

befehlen ✧ *verb* (PRES **befiehlt**, IMPERF **befahl**, PERF **hat befohlen**) 1 **jemandem etwas befehlen** to order somebody to do something; 2 to give orders.

befestigen *verb* (PERF **hat befestigt**) 1 to fix; **etwas an der Wand befestigen** to fix something to the wall; 2 to fasten.

befinden ✧ *verb* (IMPERF **befand sich**, PERF **hat sich befunden**) **sich befinden** to be; **sie befindet sich zur Zeit in Deutschland** she's in Germany at the moment.

befolgen *verb* (PERF **hat befolgt**) to follow.

befördern *verb* (PERF **hat befördert**) 1 to carry (*people by bus or train*); 2 to transport (*goods by train or lorry*); 3 to promote; **er ist zum Kommissar befördert worden** he's been promoted to superintendent.

befragen *verb* (PERF **hat befragt**) to question.

befreien *verb* (PERF **hat befreit**) 1 to free; 2 to exempt; **jemanden vom Wehrdienst befreien** to exempt somebody from military service; 3 **sich befreien** to free oneself.

Befreiung *die* liberation.

befreunden *verb* (PERF **hat sich befreundet**) **sich befreunden** to make friends.

befreundet *adjective* **mit jemandem befreundet sein** to be friends with somebody; **wir sind schon lange gut befreundet** we've been close friends for a long time.

befriedigen *verb* (PERF **hat befriedigt**) to satisfy.

befriedigend *adjective* satisfactory.

Befugnis *die* (PL *die* **Befugnisse**) authority.

begabt *adjective* gifted, talented.

Begabung *die* gift, talent.

begann SEE **beginnen**.

begegnen *verb* (PERF **ist begegnet**) 1 **jemandem begegnen** to meet somebody; **etwas begegnen** to meet something; 2 **sich begegnen** to meet (each other).

Begegnung *die* (PL *die* **Begegnungen**) meeting.

begehen ✧ *verb* (IMPERF **beging**, PERF **hat begangen**) to commit.

begeistern *verb* (PERF **hat begeistert**) 1 **jemanden für etwas begeistern** to fill somebody with enthusiasm for something; 2 **sich begeistern** to get enthusiastic.

△ NEW SPELLING: *See page xii*

begeistert *adjective* enthusiastic.

Begeisterung *die* enthusiasm.

Beginn *der* beginning; **zu Beginn** at the beginning.

beginnen ✧ *verb* (IMPERF **begann**, PERF **hat begonnen**) to begin, to start.

begleiten *verb* (PERF **hat begleitet**) to accompany; **er hat mich nach Hause begleitet** he took me home.

beglückwünschen *verb* (PERF **hat beglückwünscht**) to congratulate.

begonnen SEE **beginnen**.

begraben ✧ *verb* (PRES **begräbt**, IMPERF **begrub**, PERF **hat begraben**) to bury.

begreifen ✧ *verb* (IMPERF **begriff**, PERF **hat begriffen**) to understand.

Begriff *der* (PL *die* **Begriffe**) 1 concept; **davon kann ich mir keinen Begriff machen** I can't imagine that; 2 term; **ein Begriff aus der Malerei** a painting term; 3 **im Begriff sein, etwas zu tun** to be about to do something; 4 **für meine Begriffe** to my mind; 5 **schwer von Begriff** (*informal*) slow on the uptake.

Begründung *die* (PL *die* **Begründungen**) reason.

begrüßen *verb* (PERF **hat begrüßt**) 1 to greet; 2 to welcome.

Begrüßung *die* welcome.

begünstigen *verb* (PERF **hat begünstigt**) to favour.

behaglich *adjective* cosy.

behalten ✧ *verb* (PRES **behält**, IMPERF **behielt**, PERF **hat behalten**) 1 to keep; **du kannst die CD behalten** you can keep the CD; 2 to remember (*a name*).

Behälter *der* (PL *die* **Behälter**) container.

behandeln *verb* (PERF **hat behandelt**) 1 to treat; **er ist sehr schlecht behandelt worden** he's been treated very badly; **einen Patienten behandeln** to treat a patient; 2 to deal with (*a subject, question*).

Behandlung *die* (PL *die* **Behandlungen**) treatment.

behaupten *verb* (PERF **hat behauptet**) 1 to claim; 2 **sich behaupten** to assert oneself.

Behauptung *die* (PL *die* **Behauptungen**) claim.

beherrschen *verb* (PERF **hat beherrscht**) 1 to rule over (*a country, people*); 2 to control; 3 to know; 4 **sich beherrschen** to control oneself.

behilflich *adjective* **jemandem behilflich sein** to help somebody.

behindert *adjective* disabled, handicapped.

Behinderte *der/die* (PL *die* **Behinderten**) disabled person, handicapped person.

Behinderung *die* 1 obstruction; 2 handicap, disability.

Behörde *die* (PL *die* **Behörden**) authority, authorities.

✧ IRREGULAR VERB: *See the verb table in the centre of the dictionary*

behüten verb (PERF **hat behütet**) to protect.

bei preposition ←(+DAT) **1** near; **die Diskothek beim Bahnhof** the disco near the station; **2** at (indicating a place or time); **bei mir** at my place; **beim Arzt** at the doctor's; **bei Beginn** at the beginning; **3 bei seinen Eltern wohnen** to live with your parents; **4 bei uns in der Firma** in our firm; **bei guter Gesundheit** in good health; **5 bei einem Verlag arbeiten** to work for a publisher; **6 bei Regen** if it rains; **bei Nebel** in fog; **bei Tag** by day; **7 etwas bei sich haben** to have something on you; **8 bei Morris** c/o Morris; **9 sich bei jemandem entschuldigen** to apologize to somebody; **10 bei der hohen Miete** with the high rent; **11 beim Fahren** while driving; **beim Lesen sein** to be reading; **beim Frühstück** at breakfast; **12 bei der Ankunft** on arrival.

beibringen ✧ verb (PRES **bringt bei**, IMPERF **brachte bei**, PERF **hat beigebracht**) **jemandem etwas beibringen** to teach somebody something.

Beichte die (PL die **Beichten**) confession.

beichten verb (PERF **hat gebeichtet**) to confess.

beide adjective, pronoun **1** both; **ihr beide** both of you; **er hat seine beiden Eltern verloren** he has lost both his parents; **2 die ersten beiden** the first two; **eins von beiden** one of the two; **3 keiner von beiden** neither (of them); **4 beides** both; **er kann beides – Klavier und Gitarre spielen** he can do both – play the piano and the guitar; **5 dreißig beide** thirty all (in tennis).

beieinander adverb together.

Beifahrer der (PL die **Beifahrer**) passenger.

Beifahrerin die (PL die **Beifahrerinnen**) passenger.

Beifall der applause.

Beil das (PL die **Beile**) axe.

Beilage die (PL die **Beilagen**) **1** supplement (to a paper); **2** side-dish; **als Beilage Reis und Spinat** served with rice and spinach.

beiläufig adjective casual.

beilegen verb (PERF **hat beigelegt**) to enclose.

beiliegen ✧ verb (PRES **liegt bei**, IMPERF **lag bei**, PERF **hat beigelegen**) to be enclosed; **ein Scheck liegt bei** please find enclosed a cheque.

beiliegend adjective enclosed.

Beileid das condolences; **jemandem sein Beileid aussprechen** to offer your condolences to somebody.

beim = **bei dem**.

Bein das (PL die **Beine**) leg.

beinahe adverb almost.

Beinbruch der (PL die **Beinbrüche**) broken leg; **das ist doch kein Beinbruch** (informal) it's not the end of the world.

beisammen *adverb* together.

beiseite *adverb* 1 aside; **etwas beiseite schieben** to push something aside; 2 **etwas beiseite legen** to put something by; 3 **das Geld beiseite schaffen** to hide the money away.

Beispiel *das* (PL *die* **Beispiele**) example; **zum Beispiel** for example; **mit gutem Beispiel vorangehen** to set a good example.

beispielsweise *adverb* for example.

beißen ✧ *verb* (IMPERF **biss** △, PERF **hat gebissen**) 1 to bite; 2 to sting (*of smoke, for example*); 3 **sich beißen** to clash; **die Farben beißen sich** the colours clash.

Beitrag *der* (PL *die* **Beiträge**) 1 contribution; 2 subscription; 3 premium (*insurance fee*); 4 article (*in a newspaper*).

beitragen ✧ *verb* (PRES **trägt bei**, IMPERF **trug bei**, PERF **hat beigetragen**) **zu etwas beitragen** to contribute to something.

beitreten ✧ *verb* (PRES **tritt bei**, IMPERF **trat bei**, PERF **ist beigetreten**) to join; **ich trete dem Fußballverein bei** I'm joining the football club.

bekam SEE **bekommen**.

bekämpfen *verb* (PERF **hat bekämpft**) 1 to fight; 2 **sich bekämpfen** to fight.

bekannt *adjective* 1 well known; 2 familiar; **das kommt mir bekannt vor** that seems familiar; 3 **mit jemandem bekannt sein** to know

somebody; 4 **für etwas bekannt sein** to be (well) known for something; 5 **jemanden bekannt machen** to introduce somebody; 6 **das ist mir bekannt** I know that; 7 **etwas bekannt geben/machen** to announce something; 8 **bekannt werden** to become known.

Bekannte *der/die* (PL *die* **Bekannten**) 1 acquaintance; 2 friend.

bekanntlich *adverb* **Rauchen ist bekanntlich schädlich** as you know, smoking is bad for you.

beklagen *verb* (PERF **hat sich beklagt**) **sich beklagen** to complain.

Bekleidung *die* clothes, clothing.

bekommen ✧ *verb* (IMPERF **bekam**, PERF **hat bekommen**) 1 to get; **Angst bekommen** to get frightened; 2 to catch (*a cold, the train*); 3 **ein Kind bekommen** to have a baby; 4 **was bekommen Sie?** (*in a shop*) can I help you?; (*in a restaurant*) what would you like?; 5 **was bekommen Sie dafür?** how much is it?; 6 (PERF **ist bekommen**) **fettes Essen bekommt mir nicht** fatty food doesn't agree with me; 7 (PERF **ist bekommen**) **die Ferien sind mir gut bekommen** the holiday did me good.

Belag *der* (PL *die* **Beläge**) 1 covering; 2 coating; 3 topping (*on bread*); 4 lining (*of brakes*).

belasten *verb* (PERF **hat belastet**) 1 to burden; 2 to put weight on (*foot*); 3 to pollute (*the* *atmosphere*); **4** to debit (*an account*); **5** to incriminate.

belästigen *verb* (PERF **hat belästigt**) **1** to bother; **2** to harass.

Belastung *die* **1** strain; **2** load; **3** burden; **4** pollution.

belegen *verb* (PERF **hat belegt**) **1** to cover; **2 eine Scheibe Brot mit Käse belegen** to put some cheese on a slice of bread; **3** to enrol for (*a course*); **4** to reserve (*a seat*); **5 den ersten Platz belegen** to come first; **6** to prove (*facts*).

belegt *adjective* **1** occupied; **2 der Platz ist belegt** this seat is taken; **3 ein belegtes Brot** an open sandwich; **4 die Nummer ist belegt** (*when phoning*) the number's engaged.

beleidigen *verb* (PERF **hat beleidigt**) to insult.

Beleidigung *die* (PL *die* **Beleidigungen**) insult.

Beleuchtung *die* lighting.

Belgien *das* Belgium.

Belgier *der* (PL *die* **Belgier**) Belgian.

Belgierin *die* (PL *die* **Belgierinnen**) Belgian.

belgisch *adjective* Belgian.

Belichtung *die* exposure.

beliebig *adjective* any; **eine beliebige Zahl** any number you like.
adverb **beliebig lange** as long as you like; **beliebig viele** as many as you like.

beliebt *adjective* popular.

Beliebtheit *die* popularity.

bellen *verb* (PERF **hat gebellt**) to bark.

belohnen *verb* (PERF **hat belohnt**) to reward.

Belohnung *die* (PL *die* **Belohnungen**) reward.

belügen *verb* (IMPERF **belog**, PERF **hat belogen**) to lie to.

bemerkbar *adjective* **sich bemerkbar machen** to attract attention, to become noticeable.

bemerken *verb* (PERF **hat bemerkt**) **1** to notice; **2** to remark; **3 nebenbei bemerkt** by the way.

Bemerkung *die* (PL *die* **Bemerkungen**) remark.

bemitleiden *verb* (PERF **hat bemitleidet**) to pity.

bemühen *verb* (PERF **hat sich bemüht**) **1 sich bemühen** to try; **sich sehr bemühen** to try hard; **er bemüht sich um eine Stelle** he's trying to get a job; **2 sich um jemanden bemühen** to try to help somebody; **3 bitte, bemühen Sie sich nicht** please don't trouble yourself.

Bemühung *die* (PL *die* **Bemühungen**) effort.

benachrichtigen *verb* (PERF **hat benachrichtigt**) **1** to inform; **2** to notify (*officially*).

benachteiligt *adjective* disadvantaged.

△ NEW SPELLING: *See page xii*

benehmen ✧ *verb* (PRES **benimmt sich**, IMPERF **benahm sich**, PERF **hat sich benommen**) **sich benehmen** to behave; **benimm dich!** behave yourself!

Benehmen *das* behaviour.

beneiden *verb* (PERF **hat beneidet**) to envy; **jemanden um etwas beneiden** to envy somebody something.

benoten *verb* (PERF **hat benotet**) to mark.

benutzen *verb* (PERF **hat benutzt**) to use.

Benutzer *der* (PL *die* **Benutzer**) user.

Benutzung *die* use.

Benzin *das* petrol.

beobachten *verb* (PERF **hat beobachtet**) to observe, to watch.

bequem *adjective* **1** comfortable; **2 machen Sie es sich bequem** make yourself at home; **3** lazy; **4** easy; **eine bequeme Lösung finden** to find an easy way out.

beraten ✧ *verb* (PRES **berät**, IMPERF **beriet**, PERF **hat beraten**) **1** to advise; **2 jemanden gut/schlecht beraten** to give somebody good/bad advice; **3 sich beraten lassen** to get advice; **4 gut beraten sein** to be well advised; **5** to discuss (*a plan, matter*); **6 sich über etwas beraten** to discuss something.

Berater *der* (PL *die* **Berater**) adviser.

Beratung *die* (PL *die* **Beratungen**) **1** advice; **2** discussion; **3** consultation (*with a doctor*).

berauben *verb* (PERF **hat beraubt**) to rob.

berechnen *verb* (PERF **hat berechnet**) **1** to charge; **jemandem zehn Mark für etwas berechnen** to charge somebody ten marks for something; **2 jemandem zuviel berechnen** to overcharge somebody; **3** to calculate.

Bereich *der* (PL *die* **Bereiche**) **1** area; **2** field (*in a profession*).

bereit *adjective* ready.

bereiten *verb* (PERF **hat bereitet**) **1** to make (*coffee, tea*); **2** to cause (*trouble, difficulty*); **leider hat es uns Schwierigkeiten bereitet** unfortunately it caused us some trouble; **3** to give (*a surprise, pleasure*).

bereits *adverb* already.

bereuen *verb* (PERF **hat bereut**) to regret.

Berg *der* (PL *die* **Berge**) **1** mountain; **2** hill.

bergab *adverb* downhill.

Bergarbeiter *der* (PL *die* **Bergarbeiter**) miner.

bergauf *adverb* uphill.

bergen ✧ *verb* (PRES **birgt**, IMPERF **barg**, PERF **hat geborgen**) to rescue.

Bergsteigen *das* mountaineering.

Bergsteiger *der* (PL *die* **Bergsteiger**) mountaineer, climber.

Bergsteigerin *die* (PL *die* **Bergsteigerinnen**) mountaineer, climber.

✧ IRREGULAR VERB: *See the verb table in the centre of the dictionary*

Bergwacht *die* mountain rescue.

Bergwerk *das* (PL *die* **Bergwerke**) mine.

Bericht *der* (PL *die* **Berichte**) report.

berichten *verb* (PERF **hat berichtet**) 1 to report; **die Zeitungen haben nichts davon berichtet** the newspapers didn't report anything about it; 2 **jemandem über etwas berichten** to tell somebody about something; **er hat mir über seine Ferien in Amerika berichtet** he told me about his holiday in America.

berücksichtigen *verb* (PERF **hat berücksichtigt**) to take into account.

Beruf *der* (PL *die* **Berufe**) 1 occupation; 2 profession; **ich bin Lehrerin von Beruf** I'm a teacher by profession; 3 trade; 4 **was sind Sie von Beruf?** what do you do for a living?

beruflich *adjective* 1 professional; 2 vocational (*training*). *adverb* 1 **beruflich erfolgreich sein** to be successful in your career; 2 **viel beruflich unterwegs sein** to be away a lot on business.

Berufsberatung *die* careers advice.

Berufsschule *die* (PL *die* **Berufsschulen**) technical college.

berufstätig *adjective* working.

Berufsverkehr *der* rush-hour traffic.

beruhigen *verb* (PERF **hat beruhigt**) 1 to calm down; 2 to reassure; 3 **sich beruhigen** to calm down.

Beruhigungsmittel *das* (PL *die* **Beruhigungsmittel**) sedative, tranquillizer.

berühmt *adjective* famous.

berühren *verb* (PERF **hat berührt**) 1 to touch; 2 to touch on (*a topic, an issue*); 3 to affect; **ihre Geschichte berührte ihn seltsam** he was strangely affected by her story; 4 **sich berühren** to touch.

besaß SEE **besitzen**.

beschädigen *verb* (PERF **hat beschädigt**) to damage.

beschaffen[1] *verb* (PERF **hat beschafft**) to get; **kannst du mir nicht einen Job beschaffen?** can't you get me a job?

beschaffen[2] *adjective* **so beschaffen sein, dass …** to be such that …

beschäftigen *verb* (PERF **hat beschäftigt**) 1 to occupy (*keep busy*); 2 to employ (*people*); 3 **sich beschäftigen** to occupy yourself; 4 **ich beschäftige mich mit den Kindern** I'm busy with the children; 5 **sich mit einem Fall beschäftigen** to deal with a case; **sein Aufsatz beschäftigt sich mit der Umweltverschmutzung** his essay deals with environmental pollution.

beschäftigt *adjective* 1 busy; 2 employed.

Beschäftigung *die* (PL *die* **Beschäftigungen**) 1 occupation; 2 activity.

Bescheid *der* (PL *die* **Bescheide**) 1 information; 2 **jemandem**

△ NEW SPELLING: *See page xii*

bescheiden

Bescheid sagen to let somebody know; **3 über etwas Bescheid wissen** to know about something.

bescheiden *adjective* modest.

Bescheinigung *die* (PL *die* **Bescheinigungen**) 1 certificate; **eine Bescheinigung des Arztes** a doctor's certificate; **2** (written) confirmation.

beschimpfen *verb* (PERF **hat beschimpft**) to abuse.

beschlagnahmen *verb* (PERF **hat beschlagnahmt**) to confiscate.

beschleunigen *verb* (PERF **hat beschleunigt**) 1 to speed up; 2 to accelerate; **der Lastwagen hinter uns hat plötzlich beschleunigt** the lorry behind us suddenly accelerated.

beschließen ✧ *verb* (IMPERF **beschloss** ∆, PERF **hat beschlossen**) to decide.

Beschluss ∆ *der* (PL *die* **Beschlüsse**) decision.

beschreiben ✧ *verb* (IMPERF **beschrieb**, PERF **hat beschrieben**) to describe.

Beschreibung *die* (PL *die* **Beschreibungen**) description.

beschuldigen *verb* (PERF **hat beschuldigt**) to accuse.

beschützen *verb* (PERF **hat beschützt**) to protect.

Beschwerde *die* (PL *die* **Beschwerden**) complaint.

beschweren *verb* (PERF **hat sich beschwert**) **sich beschweren** to complain; **ich habe mich bei den Nachbarn über ihn beschwert** I've complained to the neighbours about him.

beschwipst *adjective* tipsy.

beseitigen *verb* (PERF **hat beseitigt**) to remove.

Besen *der* (PL *die* **Besen**) broom.

besetzen *verb* (PERF **hat besetzt**) 1 to occupy; 2 to fill (*a post, role*); 3 to trim, to edge (*with lace or fur*).

besetzt *adjective* 1 occupied; 2 **besetzt sein** to be engaged (*a phone, toilet*); 3 taken (*a table, seat*); **der Platz ist besetzt** this seat is taken; 4 full (*of a train, bus*); **der Zug ist voll besetzt** the train is full up.

Besetztzeichen *das* (PL *die* **Besetztzeichen**) engaged tone.

besichtigen *verb* (PERF **hat besichtigt**) 1 to look round (*a town, museum*); 2 to see (*sights, a house*).

Besichtigung *die* (PL *die* **Besichtigungen**) visit.

besinnungslos *adjective* unconscious.

Besitz *der* 1 property; 2 **im Besitz einer Sache sein** to be in possession of something.

besitzen ✧ *verb* (IMPERF **besaß**, PERF **hat besessen**) 1 to own; **sie besitzen ein Haus in Italien** they own a house in Italy; 2 to have (*talent, a quality*).

Besitzer *der* (PL *die* **Besitzer**) owner

Besitzerin die (PL die **Besitzerinnen**) owner.

besonderer, besondere, besonderes adjective 1 special; **unter besonderen Umständen** in special circumstances; 2 particular; **ohne besondere Begeisterung** without any particular enthusiasm; 3 **keine besonderen Kennzeichen** no distinguishing features.

Besonderheit die (PL die **Besonderheiten**) 1 special feature; 2 peculiarity.

besonders adverb particularly.

besorgen verb (PERF **hat besorgt**) to get; **ich kann dir Karten besorgen** I can get you tickets.

besorgt adjective worried.

besprechen ✧ verb (PRES **bespricht**, IMPERF **besprach**, PERF **hat besprochen**) 1 to discuss; **ich muss es erst mit meinen Eltern besprechen** I'll have to discuss it with my parents first; 2 to review (a book, film).

Besprechung die (PL die **Besprechungen**) 1 meeting (at work); 2 discussion; 3 review (of a film, play).

besser adjective, adverb better; **alles besser wissen** to know better.

Besserung die 1 improvement; 2 **gute Besserung!** get well soon!

beständig adjective 1 constant; 2 settled (weather).

Bestandteil der (PL die **Bestandteile**) component.

bestätigen verb (PERF **hat bestätigt**) 1 to confirm; 2 to acknowledge (receipt); 3 **sich bestätigen** to be confirmed, to prove to be true.

beste SEE **bester**.

Bestechung die (PL die **Bestechungen**) bribery.

Besteck das (PL die **Bestecke**) cutlery.

bestehen ✧ verb (IMPERF **bestand**, PERF **hat bestanden**) 1 to exist; 2 **es besteht die Gefahr, dass** ... there is a danger that ...; **noch besteht die Hoffnung, dass** ... there is still hope that ...; 3 to pass; **eine Prüfung bestehen** to pass an exam; 4 **auf etwas bestehen** to insist on something; 5 **aus etwas bestehen** to consist of something; 6 **aus etwas bestehen** to be made of something.

bestellen verb (PERF **hat bestellt**) 1 to order (goods); 2 to reserve (tickets); 3 to tell; **jemandem etwas bestellen** to tell somebody something; 4 **bestell ihm schöne Grüße** give him my regards; 5 **kann ich etwas bestellen?** can I take a message?; 6 to send for; **jemanden zu sich bestellen** to send for somebody.

Bestellung die (PL die **Bestellungen**) 1 order (for goods); 2 reservation (for tickets).

bestens adverb very well; **das hat ja bestens geklappt** that worked out very well.

△ NEW SPELLING: See page xii

bester, beste, bestes *adjective*
1 best; **sein bestes Buch** his best
book; 2 **ich halte es für das Beste** △,
wenn ... I think it would be best if
...; **sein Bestes tun** to do your best;
3 **einen Witz zum Besten geben** △
to tell a joke; 4 **jemanden zum
Besten halten** △ to pull somebody's
leg.
adverb **am besten** best; **du bleibst
am besten zu Hause** you'd best stay
at home; **es ist am besten, wenn wir
gleich anfangen** it's best if we get
started straight away.

bestimmen *verb* (PERF **hat
bestimmt**) 1 to fix (*a time, price*);
2 to decide (on); **etwas allein
bestimmen** to decide (on)
something on your own; **er bestimmt
immer, was wir machen** he always
decides what we're going to do; 3 to
be in charge; 4 **für jemanden
bestimmt sein** to be meant for
somebody; 5 **für etwas bestimmt
sein** to be intended for something
(*a donation for a good cause, for
example*).

bestimmt *adjective* 1 certain; **zu
einer bestimmten Zeit** at a certain
time; 2 particular; **suchen Sie
etwas Bestimmtes?** are you
looking for anything in particular?;
3 definite.
adverb 1 certainly, definitely; **ich
komme ganz bestimmt** I'm
definitely coming; 2 **er hat es
bestimmt vergessen** he's bound to
have forgotten; 3 **du weißt es doch
bestimmt noch** surely you must
remember it.

Bestimmung *die* (PL *die*
Bestimmungen) regulation.

bestrafen *verb* (PERF **hat bestraft**)
to punish.

bestreiten ♦ *verb* (IMPERF **bestritt**,
PERF **hat bestritten**) 1 to deny; 2 to
dispute; **das möchte ich nicht
bestreiten** I'm not disputing it; 3 to
pay for.

bestürzt *adjective* upset.

Besuch *der* (PL *die* **Besuche**) 1 visit;
2 attendance (*at school*); 3 **Besuch
haben** to have visitors/a visitor;
4 **bei Freunden zu Besuch sein** to
be staying with friends; **zu Besuch
kommen** to be visiting.

besuchen *verb* (PERF **hat besucht**)
1 to visit; 2 to go to (*an exhibition,
the theatre*); **die Schule besuchen**
to go to school; 3 to attend (*a
lecture*).

Besucher *der* (PL *die* **Besucher**)
visitor.

Besucherin *die* (PL *die*
Besucherinnen) visitor.

betätigen *verb* (PERF **hat betätigt**)
1 to operate; 2 **die Bremse
betätigen** to apply the brakes;
3 **sich politisch betätigen** to be
involved in politics; 4 **sich
künstlerisch betätigen** to do art;
5 **sich als Reporter betätigen** to
work as a reporter.

Betäubungsmittel *das* (PL *die*
Betäubungsmittel) anaesthetic.

Bete *die* **Rote Bete** △ beetroot.

beteiligen *verb* (PERF **hat beteiligt**)
1 to give a share to; **jemanden mit**

zehn Prozent an einem Geschäft beteiligen to give somebody a ten percent share of a business; **2 sich an etwas beteiligen** to take part in something; **3 kann ich mich an eurem Spiel beteiligen?** can I join in your game?

beten *verb* (PERF **hat gebetet**) to pray.

Beton *der* concrete.

betonen *verb* (PERF **hat betont**) to stress.

Betonung *die* (PL *die* **Betonungen**) stress.

Betrag *der* (PL *die* **Beträge**) amount.

betragen ◇ *verb* (PRES **beträgt**, IMPERF **betrug**, PERF **hat betragen**) **1** to amount to, to come to; **2 sich betragen** to behave; **haben sich die Kinder gut betragen?** did the children behave well?

Betragen *das* behaviour.

betreffen ◇ *verb* (PRES **betrifft**, IMPERF **betraf**, PERF **hat betroffen**) to concern; **was mich betrifft** as far as I'm concerned.

betreten ◇ *verb* (PRES **betritt**, IMPERF **betrat**, PERF **hat betreten**) **1** to enter; **2 'Betreten verboten'** 'keep out', 'keep off' (*the grass, for example*).

Betrieb *der* (PL *die* **Betriebe**) **1** business, firm; **2** activity; **es war viel Betrieb** it was very busy; **3 in Betrieb sein** to be working (*of a machine*); **4 außer Betrieb sein** to be out of order; **5 eine Maschine in**

Betrieb setzen to start up a machine.

Betriebsferien *plural noun* firm's holiday; **'Betriebsferien'** 'closed for the holidays'.

betrinken ◇ *verb* (IMPERF **betrank sich**, PERF **hat sich betrunken**) **sich betrinken** to get drunk.

betrog SEE **betrügen**.

Betrug *der* **1** deception; **2** fraud.

betrügen ◇ *verb* (IMPERF **betrog**, PERF **hat betrogen**) **1** to cheat; **jemanden um tausend Mark betrügen** to cheat somebody out of a thousand marks; **2** to be unfaithful to, to cheat on; **sie hat ihren Mann betrogen** she's been unfaithful to her husband.

betrunken *adjective* drunk.

Bett *das* (PL *die* **Betten**) bed; **ins Bett gehen** to go to bed.

Bettbezug *der* (PL *die* **Bettbezüge**) duvet cover.

betteln *verb* (PERF **hat gebettelt**) to beg.

Bettlaken *das* (PL *die* **Bettlaken**) sheet.

Bettler *der* (PL *die* **Bettler**) beggar.

Bettlerin *die* (PL *die* **Bettlerinnen**) beggar.

Bettwäsche *die* bed linen.

Bettzeug *das* bedding.

beugen *verb* (PERF **hat gebeugt**) **1** to bend; **2** to decline, to conjugate (*in grammar*); **3 sich nach vorn beugen** to bend forwards; **sich über**

etwas **beugen** to bend over something; **4 sich aus dem Fenster beugen** to lean out of the window; **5 sich beugen** to submit.

Beule die (PL die **Beulen**) **1** bump; **2** lump; **3** dent.

beurteilen verb (PERF **hat beurteilt**) to judge.

Beutel der (PL die **Beutel**) bag.

Bevölkerung die (PL die **Bevölkerungen**) population.

bevor conjunction **1** before; **2 bevor nicht** until; **bevor er nicht unterschrieben hat** until he has signed.

bevorzugen verb (PERF **hat bevorzugt**) to prefer.

bewachen verb (PERF **hat bewacht**) to guard.

bewaffnen verb (PERF **hat bewaffnet**) to arm.

bewaffnet adjective armed.

bewährt adjective **1** reliable; **2** proven (method, design); **3 ein bewährtes Rezept** a well-tried recipe.

bewegen¹ verb (PERF **hat bewegt**) **1** to move; **2 sich bewegen** to take exercise; **3 sich bewegen** to move.

bewegen² ✧ verb (IMPERF **bewog**, PERF **hat bewogen**) **jemanden dazu bewegen, etwas zu tun** to persuade somebody to do something.

bewegt adjective eventful.

Bewegung die (PL die **Bewegungen**) **1** movement;

2 exercise; **3 eine Maschine in Bewegung setzen** to start (up) a machine; **4 sich in Bewegung setzen** to start to move.

Beweis der (PL die **Beweise**) **1** proof; **2 belastende Beweise** incriminating evidence; **3** token, sign.

beweisen ✧ verb (IMPERF **bewies**, PERF **hat bewiesen**) **1** to prove; **2** to show.

bewerben ✧ verb (PRES **bewirbt sich**, IMPERF **bewarb sich**, PERF **sich beworben**) **sich bewerben** to apply; **sich um eine Stelle bewerben** to apply for a job.

Bewerber der (PL die **Bewerber**) applicant.

Bewerberin die (PL die **Bewerberinnen**) applicant.

Bewerbung die (PL die **Bewerbungen**) application.

bewohnen verb (PERF **hat bewohnt**) to live in.

Bewohner der (PL die **Bewohner**) **1** resident; **2** inhabitant (of a region).

Bewohnerin die (PL die **Bewohnerinnen**) **1** resident; **2** inhabitant (of a region).

bewölkt adjective cloudy.

Bewölkung die clouds.

bewundern verb (PERF **hat bewundert**) to admire.

Bewunderung die admiration.

bewusst Δ adjective **1** conscious;

✧ IRREGULAR VERB: See the verb table in the centre of the dictionary

2 deliberate; **3 sich etwas bewusst sein** to be aware of something; **ich war mir der Folgen bewusst** I was aware of the consequences.

bewusstlos ∆ *adjective* unconscious.

Bewusstsein ∆ *das*
1 consciousness; **2 bei vollem Bewusstsein sein** to be fully conscious; **3 mir kam zu(m) Bewusstsein, dass** … I realized that …

bezahlen *verb* (PERF **hat bezahlt**)
1 to pay; 2 to pay for (*goods, food*); **er hat das Essen bezahlt** he paid for the meal.

Bezahlung *die* payment.

bezeichnend *adjective* typical.

beziehen ◆ *verb* (IMPERF **bezog**, PERF **hat bezogen**) 1 to cover; **2 das Bett frisch beziehen** to put clean sheets on the bed; 3 to move into; **wann kannst du die neue Wohnung beziehen?** when will you be able to move into the new flat?; 4 to get (*goods, a pension*); 5 to take (*a newspaper*); **6 sich auf etwas/jemanden beziehen** to refer to something/somebody; **7 es bezieht sich** it's clouding over.

Beziehung *die* (PL *die* **Beziehungen**) 1 connection; 2 relationship; **3 Beziehungen** contacts; **Anna hat gute Beziehungen** Anna has good contacts; **4 diplomatische Beziehungen** diplomatic relations; **5 in dieser Beziehung** in this respect; **6 eine Beziehung zu etwas haben** to be able to relate to something (*to art, pop music, for example*).

beziehungsweise *conjunction*
1 or rather; 2 respectively.

Bezirk *der* (PL *die* **Bezirke**) district.

Bezug *der* (PL *die* **Bezüge**) 1 cover (*of a cushion, duvet, etc.*); 2 connection; **keinen Bezug zu etwas haben** to be unable to relate to something; **3 auf etwas Bezug nehmen** to refer to something; **4 in Bezug auf** regarding; **5 mit Bezug auf Ihr Angebot** with reference to your offer.

bezweifeln *verb* (PERF **hat bezweifelt**) to doubt.

BH *der* (PL *die* **BHs**) bra.

Bibel *die* (PL *die* **Bibeln**) bible; **die Bibel** the Bible.

Bibliothek *die* (PL *die* **Bibliotheken**) library.

biegen ◆ *verb* (IMPERF **bog**, PERF **hat gebogen**) 1 to bend; **2 sich biegen** to bend; 3 (PERF **ist gebogen**) to turn; **um die Ecke biegen** to turn the corner.

Biene *die* (PL *die* **Bienen**) bee.

Bier *das* (PL *die* **Biere**) beer.

Bierdeckel *der* (PL *die* **Bierdeckel**) beer mat.

bieten ◆ *verb* (IMPERF **bot**, PERF **hat geboten**) 1 to offer; 2 to bid (*at an auction*); **3 es bietet sich die Möglichkeit** there is a possibility; 4 to present (*a sight*); **5 das lasse**

∆ NEW SPELLING: *See page xii*

ich mir nicht bieten! I won't put up with it!

Bikini *der* (PL *die* **Bikinis**) bikini.

Bild *das* (PL *die* **Bilder**) 1 picture; **jemanden ins Bild setzen** to put somebody in the picture; 2 scene.

bilden *verb* (PERF **hat gebildet**) 1 to form; 2 **sich bilden** to form; 3 **sich bilden** to educate yourself.

Bildschirm *der* (PL *die* **Bildschirme**) screen.

bildschön *adjective* (very) beautiful.

Bildung *die* 1 formation; 2 education.

billig *adjective* cheap.

Billion *die* (PL *die* **Billionen**) billion (*a million million*).

bin SEE **sein**.

Binde *die* (PL *die* **Binden**) 1 bandage; 2 sanitary towel.

binden ✧ *verb* (IMPERF **band**, PERF **hat gebunden**) 1 to tie; 2 to bind (*a book*); 3 to make up (*a bouquet*); 4 to thicken (*a sauce*); 5 **sich binden** to commit oneself.

Bindestrich *der* (PL *die* **Bindestriche**) hyphen.

Bindfaden *der* (PL *die* **Bindfäden**) (piece of) string.

Bindung *die* (PL *die* **Bindungen**) 1 tie; 2 relationship; 3 binding (*on a ski*).

Biokost *die* health food.

Biologie *die* biology.

biologisch *adjective* biological.

Birke *die* (PL *die* **Birken**) birch tree.

Birne *die* (PL *die* **Birnen**) 1 pear; 2 bulb.

bis *preposition* ←(+ACC) 1 as far as; **dieser Zug fährt nur bis Passau** this train only goes as far as Passau; 2 up to; **Kinder bis zehn zahlen die Hälfte** children up to ten pay half; **bis jetzt** up to now; **bis zu** up to; 3 until, till (*with time*); 4 by; **bis dahin** by then; 5 **bis auf** except for; **alle sind durchgefallen bis auf die zwei Mädchen** everyone failed except for the two girls; 6 **bis bald!** see you soon!; 7 **von München bis Salzburg** from Munich to Salzburg; **von Montag bis Freitag** from Monday to Friday; **zwei bis drei Mark** two to three marks. *conjunction* until, till; **sie bleibt, bis es dunkel wird** she's staying until it gets dark.

Bischof *der* (PL *die* **Bischöfe**) bishop.

bisher *adverb* so far.

bisherig *adjective* previous.

biss ∆ SEE **beißen**.

Biss ∆ *der* (PL *die* **Bisse**) bite.

bisschen ∆ *pronoun* 1 **ein bisschen** a bit; **ein bisschen Brot** a bit of bread; 2 **kein bisschen** not a bit.

bissig *adjective* 1 vicious; **'Vorsicht bissiger Hund!'** 'beware of the dog!'; 2 cutting (*remark, tone*).

bist SEE **sein**.

bitte *adverb* 1 please; **'möchten Sie**

✧ IRREGULAR VERB: *See the verb table in the centre of the dictionary*

Kuchen?' – 'ja bitte' 'would you like some cake?' – 'yes please'; 2 you're welcome (*in reply to thanks*); 3 come in (*after a knock on the door*); 4 (*in a shop*) **bitte?** yes, please?; 5 **wie bitte?** sorry?

Bitte *die* (PL *die* **Bitten**) request.

bitten ✧ *verb* (IMPERF **bat**, PERF **hat gebeten**) to ask; **jemanden um etwas bitten** to ask somebody for something.

bitter *adjective* bitter.

blamieren *verb* (PERF **hat blamiert**) 1 to disgrace; 2 **jemanden blamieren** to embarrass somebody; 3 **sich blamieren** to make a fool of yourself.

Blase *die* (PL *die* **Blasen**) 1 bubble; 2 blister; 3 bladder.

blasen ✧ *verb* (PRES **bläst**, IMPERF **blies**, PERF **hat geblasen**) to blow.

Blasinstrument *das* (PL *die* **Blasinstrumente**) wind instrument.

Blaskapelle *die* (PL *die* **Blaskapellen**) brass band.

blass ∆ *adjective* pale.

Blatt *das* (PL *die* **Blätter**) 1 leaf; 2 sheet; **ein Blatt Papier** a sheet of paper; 3 page; 4 newspaper.

blau *adjective* 1 blue; **ein blau gestreiftes Kleid** a dress with blue stripes; 2 **ein blaues Auge haben** to have a black eye; 3 **ein blauer Fleck** a bruise; 4 **blau sein** (*informal*) to be tight; 5 **eine Fahrt ins Blaue** a mystery tour.

Blech *das* (PL *die* **Bleche**) 1 sheet metal; 2 tin; 3 baking tray; 4 brass (*in music*).

Blei *das* lead.

bleiben ✧ *verb* (IMPERF **blieb**, PERF **ist geblieben**) 1 to stay, to remain; 2 to be left; 3 **bleiben Sie am Apparat** hold the line; 4 **bei etwas bleiben** to stick to something; 5 **ruhig bleiben** to keep calm; 6 **wo bleibt er so lange?** where has he got to?; 7 **etwas bleiben lassen** to not do something; **wenn du nicht mitkommen willst, dann lass es eben bleiben** if you don't want to come, then don't.

bleich *adjective* pale.

Bleichmittel *das* (PL *die* **Bleichmittel**) bleach.

bleifrei *adjective* unleaded.

Bleistift *der* (PL *die* **Bleistifte**) pencil.

Bleistiftspitzer *der* (PL *die* **Bleistiftspitzer**) pencil sharpener.

blenden *verb* (PERF **hat geblendet**) 1 to dazzle; 2 to blind.

blendend *adjective* 1 marvellous; 2 **es geht mir blendend** I feel great; **wir haben uns blendend amüsiert** we had a great time.

Blick *der* (PL *die* **Blicke**) 1 look; 2 glance; 3 **auf den ersten Blick** at first sight; 4 view; **ein Zimmer mit Blick aufs Meer** a room with a sea view.

blicken *verb* (PERF **hat geblickt**) 1 to look; 2 **sich blicken lassen** to show your face.

blieb SEE **bleiben**.

∆ NEW SPELLING: *See page xii*

blies SEE **blasen**.

blind *adjective* blind.

Blinddarm *der* (PL *die* **Blinddärme**) appendix.

Blinddarmentzündung *die* (PL *die* **Blinddarmentzündungen**) appendicitis.

Blinde *der/die* (PL *die* **Blinden**) blind person, blind man/woman.

blinzeln *verb* (PERF **hat geblinzelt**) to blink.

blinken *verb* (PERF **hat geblinkt**) 1 to flash; 2 to indicate (*of a car*).

Blinker *der* (PL *die* **Blinker**) indicator.

Blitz *der* (PL *die* **Blitze**) 1 (flash of) lightning; 2 flash.

blitzen *verb* (PERF **hat geblitzt**) 1 to flash; 2 to sparkle; 3 **es hat geblitzt** there was a flash of lightning.

Block *der* (PL *die* **Blöcke**) 1 pad (*for writing on*); 2 (PL *die* **Blocks**) block (*of flats*).

Blockflöte *die* (PL *die* **Blockflöten**) recorder.

blöd *adjective* stupid.

Blödsinn *der* nonsense.

blond *adjective* blonde, fair-haired.

bloß *adverb* 1 only; **es kostet bloß fünf Mark** it's only five marks; 2 **warum hat er das bloß gemacht?** why on earth did he do it?; 3 **was mache ich bloß?** whatever shall I do?; 4 **fass das bloß nicht an!** don't touch it!
adjective 1 bare (*feet*); **mit bloßem Auge** with the naked eye; 2 mere (*words, suspicion*); **der bloße Gedanke daran** the mere thought of it.

Blume *die* (PL *die* **Blumen**) flower.

Blumenkohl *der* cauliflower.

Bluse *die* (PL *die* **Blusen**) blouse.

Blut *das* blood.

Blutdruck *der* blood pressure.

Blüte *die* (PL *die* **Blüten**) blossom.

bluten *verb* (PERF **hat geblutet**) to bleed.

Blutprobe *die* (PL *die* **Blutproben**) blood test.

Bock *der* (PL *die* **Böcke**) 1 buck; 2 billy-goat; 3 ram; 4 **Bock auf etwas haben** (*informal*) to fancy something; 5 **einen Bock schießen** (*informal*) to make a blunder.

Bockwurst *die* (PL *die* **Bockwürste**) frankfurter.

Boden *der* (PL *die* **Böden**) 1 ground; 2 floor; 3 bottom (*of a container*); 4 loft, attic.

Bodensee *der* Lake Constance.

bog SEE **biegen**.

Bogen *der* (PL *die* **Bögen**) 1 curve; 2 arch; 3 turn (*in skiing*).

Bohne *die* (PL *die* **Bohnen**) bean.

bohren *verb* (PERF **hat gebohrt**) to drill.

Bohrer *der* (PL *die* **Bohrer**) drill.

Bohrinsel *die* (PL *die* **Bohrinseln**) oil rig.

✧ IRREGULAR VERB: *See the verb table in the centre of the dictionary*

Bohrmaschine die (PL die **Bohrmaschinen**) electric drill.

Bombe die (PL die **Bomben**) bomb.

Bonbon der (PL die **Bonbons**) sweet.

Boot das (PL die **Boote**) boat.

Bord[1] das (PL die **Borde**) shelf.

Bord[2] der **an Bord** on board; **über Bord** overboard.

Bordkarte die (PL die **Bordkarten**) boarding card.

borgen (PERF **hat geborgt**) **1** to borrow; **2 sich etwas borgen** to borrow something; **ich habe es mir von ihr geborgt** I borrowed it from her; **3 jemandem etwas borgen** to lend somebody something; **Evi hat mir ihr Buch geborgt** Evi lent me her book.

Börse die (PL die **Börsen**) stock exchange.

Borste die (PL die **Borsten**) bristle.

böse adjective **1** bad; **2** wicked; **3** naughty (child); **4** angry; **böse werden** to get angry; **ich bin ihm böse** I'm angry with him; **5 auf jemanden böse sein** to be cross with somebody.

boshaft adjective malicious.

bot SEE **bieten**.

Bote der (PL die **Boten**) messenger.

Botin die (PL die **Botinnen**) messenger.

Botschaft die (PL die **Botschaften**) **1** message; **2** embassy.

Botschafter der (PL die **Botschafter**) ambassador.

Botschafterin die (PL die **Botschafterinnen**) ambassador.

Bowle die (PL die **Bowlen**) punch (for drinking).

boxen verb (PERF **hat geboxt**) **1** to box; **2** to punch.

Boxer der (PL die **Boxer**) boxer.

brach SEE **brechen**.

brachte SEE **bringen**.

Branche die (PL die **Branchen**) (line of) business.

Branchenverzeichnis das (PL die **Branchenverzeichnisse**) classified directory.

Brand der (PL die **Brände**) fire.

Brandung die surf.

brannte SEE **brennen**.

braten ✧ verb (PRES **brät**, IMPERF **briet**, PERF **hat gebraten**) **1** to fry; **2** to roast.

Braten der (PL die **Braten**) **1** roast; **2** joint.

Brathähnchen das (PL die **Brathähnchen**) roast chicken.

Bratkartoffeln plural noun fried potatoes.

Bratpfanne die (PL die **Bratpfannen**) frying pan.

Bratwurst die (PL die **Bratwürste**) fried sausage.

Brauch der (PL die **Bräuche**) custom.

brauchbar *adjective* **1** usable;
2 useful.

brauchen *verb* (PERF **hat gebraucht**) **1** need; **ich brauche eine neue Birne für meine Lampe** I need a new bulb for my light; **du brauchst nur auf den Knopf zu drücken** all you need to do is press the button; **du brauchst nicht zu gehen** you needn't go; **2 sie braucht es nur zu sagen** she only has to say; **3** to take (*time*); **wie lange brauchst du mit dem Auto?** how long does it take you by car?; **4 ich könnte es gut brauchen** I could do with it.

brauen *verb* (PERF **hat gebraut**) to brew.

Brauerei *die* (PL *die* **Brauereien**) brewery.

braun *adjective* **1** brown; **2 braun werden** to get a tan; **braun (gebrannt) sein** to be tanned.

Bräune *die* tan.

Brause *die* (PL *die* **Brausen**) fizzy drink.

Braut *die* (PL *die* **Bräute**) bride.

Bräutigam *der* (PL *die* **Bräutigame**) bridegroom.

Brautjungfer *die* (PL *die* **Brautjungfern**) bridesmaid.

Brautpaar *das* (PL *die* **Brautpaare**) bride and groom.

brav *adjective* good.

BRD *die* (*Bundesrepublik Deutschland*) FRG (*Federal Republic of Germany*).

brechen ◇ *verb* (PRES **bricht**, IMPERF **brach**, PERF **hat gebrochen**) **1** to break (*an agreement, a record*); **2 sich den Arm brechen** to break your arm; **3** to vomit; **4** (PERF **ist gebrochen**) to break; **der Ast ist gebrochen** the branch broke.

breit *adjective* **1** wide; **2** broad; **3 die breite Masse** the general public.

Breite *die* (PL *die* **Breiten**) width.

Bremse *die* (PL *die* **Bremsen**) **1** brake; **2** horsefly.

bremsen *verb* (PERF **hat gebremst**) **1** to brake; **2** to slow down (*development, production*); **3 jemanden bremsen** (*informal*) to stop somebody; **er ist nicht mehr zu bremsen** there's no stopping him.

Bremslicht *das* (PL *die* **Bremslichter**) brake light.

Bremspedal *das* (PL *die* **Bremspedale**) brake pedal.

brennen ◇ *verb* (IMPERF **brannte**, PERF **hat gebrannt**) **1** to burn; **2** to be on (*of a light*); **das Licht brennen lassen** to leave the light on; **3** to sting (*of a wound or sore*); **4 das Haus brennt** the house is on fire; **es brennt!** fire!; **5 darauf brennen, etwas zu tun** to be dying to do something.

Brennnessel △ *die* (PL *die* **Brennnesseln**) stinging nettle.

Brennpunkt *der* (PL *die* **Brennpunkte**) focus.

Brett *das* (PL *die* **Bretter**) **1** board; **2** plank; **3** shelf.

◇ IRREGULAR VERB: *See the verb table in the centre of the dictionary*

Brezel die (PL die **Brezeln**) pretzel.

bricht SEE **brechen**.

Brief der (PL die **Briefe**) letter.

Brieffreund der (PL die **Brieffreunde**) pen friend.

Brieffreundin die (PL die **Brieffreundinnen**) pen friend.

Briefkasten der (PL die **Briefkästen**) 1 letterbox; 2 postbox.

Briefmarke die (PL die **Briefmarken**) stamp.

Brieftasche die (PL die **Brieftaschen**) wallet.

Briefträger der (PL die **Briefträger**) postman.

Briefträgerin die (PL die **Briefträgerinnen**) postwoman.

Briefumschlag der (PL die **Briefumschläge**) envelope.

Briefwechsel der correspondence.

briet SEE **braten**.

Brillant der (PL die **Brillanten**) diamond.

Brille die (PL die **Brillen**) glasses, spectacles.

bringen ✧ verb (IMPERF **brachte**, PERF **hat gebracht**) 1 to bring; 2 to take; **Peter bringt dich nach Hause** Peter will take you home; 3 **die Kinder ins Bett bringen** to put the children to bed; 4 **einen Film im Fernsehen bringen** to show a film on television; 5 to publish (an article); 6 to yield (interest, a profit);

7 **jemanden dazu bringen, etwas zu tun** to get somebody to do something; 8 **mit sich bringen** to entail; 9 **etwas hinter sich bringen** to get something over and done with; 10 **es weit bringen** to go far; 11 **jemanden auf eine Idee bringen** to give somebody an idea; 12 **es zu nichts bringen** to get nowhere; 13 **das bringt's nicht!** (informal) that's no use!

Brise die (PL die **Brisen**) breeze.

Brite der (PL die **Briten**) Briton; **die Briten** the British.

Britin die (PL die **Britinnen**) Briton.

britisch adjective British.

Brokkoli der broccoli.

Brombeere die (PL die **Brombeeren**) blackberry.

Brosche die (PL die **Broschen**) brooch.

Broschüre die (PL die **Broschüren**) brochure.

Brot das (PL die **Brote**) 1 bread; **ein Brot** a loaf of bread; 2 **ein Brot** a slice of bread.

Brötchen das (PL die **Brötchen**) roll.

Bruch der (PL die **Brüche**) 1 break; 2 fracture; 3 hernia; 4 fraction.

Bruchteil der (PL die **Bruchteile**) fraction.

Brücke die (PL die **Brücken**) bridge.

Bruder der (PL die **Brüder**) brother.

Brühe die (PL die **Brühen**) 1 broth; 2 stock (for cooking).

△ NEW SPELLING: See page xii

Brühwürfel der (PL die **Brühwürfel**) stock cube.

brüllen verb (PERF **hat gebrüllt**) to roar.

brummen verb (PERF **hat gebrummt**) 1 to buzz; 2 to growl (of a bear); 3 to hum (of an engine).

Brunnen der (PL die **Brunnen**) 1 well; 2 fountain.

Brust die (PL die **Brüste**) 1 chest; 2 breast.

Brustschwimmen das breaststroke.

brutto adverb gross.

BSE das (bovine spongiforme Enzephalopathie) BSE.

Bub der (PL die **Buben**) boy.

Buch das (PL die **Bücher**) book.

Buche die (PL die **Buchen**) beech.

buchen verb (PERF **hat gebucht**) to book.

Bücherei die (PL die **Büchereien**) library.

Bücherregal das (PL die **Bücherregale**) bookcase.

Buchhalter der (PL die **Buchhalter**) accountant, bookkeeper.

Buchhalterin die (PL die **Buchhalterinnen**) accountant, bookkeeper.

Buchhandlung die (PL die **Buchhandlungen**) bookshop.

Büchse die (PL die **Büchsen**) tin, can.

Büchsenöffner der (PL die **Büchsenöffner**) tin opener.

Buchstabe der (PL die **Buchstaben**) letter (of the alphabet); **ein großer Buchstabe** a capital letter; **ein kleiner Buchstabe** a small letter.

buchstabieren verb (PERF **hat buchstabiert**) to spell.

Bucht die (PL die **Buchten**) bay.

bücken (PERF **hat sich gebückt**) **sich bücken** to bend down.

Buddhismus der Buddhism.

Bude die (PL die **Buden**) 1 hut; 2 stall; 3 **meine Bude** (informal) my room, my pad.

Büfett das (PL die **Büfetts**) buffet.

Bügel der (PL die **Bügel**) hanger.

Bügeleisen das (PL die **Bügeleisen**) iron.

bügeln verb (PERF **hat gebügelt**) to iron.

Bühne die (PL die **Bühnen**) stage.

Bulle der (PL die **Bullen**) 1 bull; 2 (informal) cop.

Bummel der (PL die **Bummel**) stroll (around town).

bummeln verb (PERF **ist gebummelt**) 1 to stroll; **wir sind durch die Stadt gebummelt** we strolled around town; 2 (PERF **hat gebummelt**) to dawdle.

Bund[1] der (PL die **Bünde**) 1 association; 2 waistband.

Bund[2] das (PL die **Bunde**) bunch.

◇ IRREGULAR VERB: See the verb table in the centre of the dictionary

Bundesbürger der (PL die **Bundesbürger**) German citizen.

Bundeskanzler der (PL die **Bundeskanzler**) Federal Chancellor.

Bundesland das (PL die **Bundesländer**) (federal) state.

Bundesliga die (PL die **Bundesligen**) (German) national league.

Bundesrat der Upper House (*of the German Parliament*).

Bundesrepublik die Federal Republic.

Bundesstraße die (PL die **Bundesstraßen**) A road, major road.

Bundestag der Lower House (*of the German Parliament*).

Bundeswehr die (German) Army.

bunt *adjective* colourful.

Buntstift der (PL die **Buntstifte**) coloured pencil.

Burg die (PL die **Burgen**) castle.

Bürger der (PL die **Bürger**) citizen.

Bürgerin die (PL die **Bürgerinnen**) citizen.

Bürgermeister der (PL die **Bürgermeister**) mayor.

Bürgersteig der (PL die **Bürgersteige**) pavement.

Büro das (PL die **Büros**) office.

Büroklammer die (PL die **Büroklammern**) paper clip.

Bürste die (PL die **Bürsten**) brush.

bürsten *verb* (PERF **hat gebürstet**) to brush.

Bus der (PL die **Busse**) bus; **ich fahre mit dem Bus** I'm going by bus.

Busbahnhof der (PL die **Busbahnhöfe**) bus station.

Busch der (PL die **Büsche**) bush.

Busen der (PL die **Busen**) bosom.

Busfahrer der (PL die **Busfahrer**) bus driver.

Busfahrerin die (PL die **Busfahrerinnen**) bus driver.

Busfahrkarte die (PL die **Busfahrkarten**) bus ticket.

Bushaltestelle die (PL die **Bushaltestellen**) bus stop.

Bußgeld das (PL die **Bußgelder**) fine.

Buslinie die (PL die **Buslinien**) bus route.

Büstenhalter der (PL die **Büstenhalter**) bra.

Butter die butter.

Butterbrot das (PL die **Butterbrote**) sandwich, bread and butter.

bzw. = **beziehungsweise**.

C c

Café das (PL die **Cafés**) café.

Cafeteria die (PL die **Cafeterias**) cafeteria.

campen *verb* (PERF **hat gecampt**) to camp.

△ NEW SPELLING: *See page xii*

Camping *das* camping.

Campingkocher *der* (PL *die* **Campingkocher**) camping stove.

Campingplatz *der* (PL *die* **Campingplätze**) campsite.

CD *die* (PL *die* **CDs**) CD.

CD-Spieler *der* (PL *die* **CD-Spieler**) CD player.

Cello *das* (PL *die* **Cellos**) cello.

Champignon *der* (PL *die* **Champignons**) mushroom.

Chance *die* (PL *die* **Chancen**) chance.

Chaos *das* chaos.

chaotisch *adjective* chaotic.

Charakter *der* (PL *die* **Charaktere**) character.

charmant *adjective* charming.

Charterflug *der* (PL *die* **Charterflüge**) charter flight.

Chauvinist *der* (PL *die* **Chauvinisten**) chauvinist.

Chef *der* (PL *die* **Chefs**) 1 head (*of a firm*); 2 boss.

Chefin *die* (PL *die* **Chefinnen**) 1 head (*of a firm*); 2 boss.

Chemie *die* chemistry.

Chemiker *der* (PL *die* **Chemiker**) chemist.

Chemikerin *die* (PL *die* **Chemikerinnen**) chemist.

chemisch *adjective* 1 chemical; 2 **chemische Reinigung** dry-cleaning; dry-cleaner's.

China *das* China.

Chinese *der* (PL *die* **Chinesen**) Chinese; **die Chinesen** the Chinese.

Chinesin *die* (PL *die* **Chinesinnen**) Chinese.

chinesisch *adjective* Chinese.

Chipkarte *die* (PL *die* **Chipkarten**) smart card.

Chips *plural noun* crisps.

Chirurg *der* (PL *die* **Chirurgen**) surgeon.

Chirurgin *die* (PL *die* **Chirurginnen**) surgeon.

Chlor *das* chlorine.

Chor *der* (PL *die* **Chöre**) choir.

Christ *der* (PL *die* **Christen**) Christian.

Christin *die* (PL *die* **Christinnen**) Christian.

christlich *adjective* Christian.

Christus *der* Christ.

circa *adverb* approximately.

Clown *der* (PL *die* **Clowns**) clown.

Cola™ *die* (PL *die* **Colas**) Coke™.

Comic *der* (PL *die* **Comics**) cartoon.

Comic-Heft *das* (PL *die* **Comic-Hefte**) comic.

Computer *der* (PL *die* **Computer**) computer.

Computerspiel *das* (PL *die* **Computerspiele**) computer game.

Container *der* (PL *die* **Container**) 1 container; 2 skip.

✧ IRREGULAR VERB: *See the verb table in the centre of the dictionary*

Cordsamt *der* corduroy.

Couch *die* (PL *die* **Couchs**) sofa.

Couchtisch *der* (PL *die* **Couchtische**) coffee table.

Cousin *der* (PL *die* **Cousins**) cousin.

Cousine *die* (PL *die* **Cousinen**) cousin.

Creme *die* (PL *die* **Cremes**) 1 cream; 2 cream dessert.

Curry *das* 1 curry; 2 curry powder.

Currywurst *die* (PL *die* **Currywürste**) curried sausage.

Cursor *der* (PL *die* **Cursors**) cursor.

D d

da *adverb* 1 there; **da draußen** out there; **da drüben** over there; **da sein** to be there; **man muss pünktlich da sein** you have to be there on time; 2 **ist noch Brot da?** is there any bread left?; 3 here; **sind alle da?** is everyone here?; **da sind deine Handschuhe** here are your gloves; 4 **ist Sabine da?** is Sabine about?; 5 **von da an** from then on; 6 **ich bin wieder da** I'm back; 7 so (*therefore*); **der Bus war weg, da bin ich gelaufen** the bus had gone, so I walked; 8 **da kann man nichts machen** there's nothing you can do about it; 9 **da, wo die Straße nach Stuttgart abzweigt** at the turning for Stuttgart.
conjunction as, since; **da es gerade regnet** as it's raining.

dabei *adverb* 1 (*included or next to*) with it/him/her/them; **sie hatten die Kinder dabei** they had the children with them; 2 **dicht dabei** close by; 3 (*referring to something already mentioned*) about it; **das Wichtigste dabei** the most important thing about it; 4 at the same time; **er malte ein Bild und sang dabei** he painted a picture and sang at the same time; 5 during this; 6 **jemandem helfen, etwas zu tun** to help somebody do something; 7 **was hast du dir denn dabei gedacht?** what were you thinking of?; 8 **dabei sein** △ to be there; **er ist dabei gewesen** he was there; 9 **was ist denn dabei?** so what?; 10 **dabei sein, etwas zu tun** to be just doing something; **ich war gerade dabei zu gehen** I was just about to leave; 11 **dabei bleiben** to stick with it (*an opinion, for example*); 12 and yet, even though.

dabeibleiben ◇ *verb* (IMPERF **blieb dabei**, PERF **ist dabeigeblieben**) 1 to stay on (*at an organisation*); 2 **er hat mit dem Training begonnen, ist aber nicht dabeigeblieben** he started training, but didn't keep it up.

dabeisein SEE **dabei**.

Dach *das* (PL *die* **Dächer**) roof.

Dachboden *der* (PL *die* **Dachböden**) loft, attic.

dachte SEE **denken**.

Dackel *der* (PL *die* **Dackel**) dachshund.

dadurch *adverb* 1 through it/them; **das Wasser muss dadurch**

△ NEW SPELLING: *See page xii*

gelaufen sein the water must have run through it; **2** as a result; **3** in this way; **ich nehme die U-Bahn, dadurch bin ich eine halbe Stunde eher da** I'll take the tube, that way I'll be there half an hour earlier. *conjunction* **dadurch, dass** because.

dafür *adverb* **1** for it/them; **dafür kriegt man nicht viel** you won't get much for it/them; **2** instead; **wenn er schon nicht auf die Party gehen will, kann er dich dafür zum Essen einladen** if he doesn't want to go to the party he can take you for a meal instead; **3** but then (*on the other hand*); **4** **dafür, dass** considering (that); **5 ich kann nichts dafür** it's not my fault.

dagegen *adverb* **1** against it/them; **ich bin dagegen** I'm against it; **2** for it/them (*when swapping*); **3** into it; **das Auto ist dagegen gefahren** the car drove into it; **4** by comparison; **5 hast du was dagegen?** do you mind?; **6** however.

daheim *adverb* at home.

daher *adverb* **1** from there; **2** that's why.

dahin *adverb* **1** there; **2 bis dahin** (*in the past*) until then; (*in the future*) by then; **3 jemanden dahin bringen, dass er etwas tut** to get somebody to do something.

dahinten *adverb* over there.

dahinter *adverb* **1** behind it/them; **2 dahinter kommen** △ to get to the bottom of it; **ich bin endlich dahinter**

gekommen I finally got to the bottom of it.

dalassen ✧ *verb* (PRES **lässt da** △, IMPERF **ließ da**, PERF **hat dagelassen**) to leave there.

damals *adverb* at that time; then; **wir wohnten damals in Berlin** we were then living in Berlin.

Dame *die* (PL *die* **Damen**) **1** lady; **2** queen (*in chess or cards*); **3** draughts.

Damenbinde *die* (PL *die* **Damenbinden**) sanitary towel.

damit *adverb* **1** with it/them; **ich will damit spielen** I want to play with it; **hör auf damit!** stop it!; **2** by it; **was meinst du damit?** what do you mean by that?; **3 damit hat es noch Zeit** there's no hurry (about that); **4** therefore, because of that; **sie hat den zweiten Satz verloren und damit das Spiel** she lost the second set and because of it the match. *conjunction* so that; **ich habe es aufgeschrieben, damit du es nicht vergisst** I wrote it down so that you won't forget.

Damm *der* (PL *die* **Dämme**) **1** dam; **2** embankment.

dämmern *verb* (PERF **hat gedämmert**) **es dämmert** it is getting light; it is getting dark.

Dämmerung *die* **1** dawn; **2** dusk.

Dampf *der* (PL *die* **Dämpfe**) steam.

dampfen *verb* (PERF **hat gedampft**) to steam.

dämpfen *verb* (PERF **hat gedämpft**)

✧ IRREGULAR VERB: *See the verb table in the centre of the dictionary*

1 to steam (*in cooking*); **2** to muffle (*a sound*); **3** to dampen (*somebody's enthusiasm*).

Dampfer *der* (PL *die* **Dampfer**) steamer.

danach *adverb* **1** after it/them; **2** afterwards; **kurz danach** shortly afterwards; **3 danach suchen** to look for it/them; **4 danach riechen** to smell of it; **5** accordingly; **6 es sieht danach aus** it looks like it.

Däne *der* (PL *die* **Dänen**) Dane.

daneben *adverb* **1** next to it/them; **2** by comparison.

Dänemark *das* Denmark.

Dänin *die* (PL *die* **Däninnen**) Dane.

dänisch *adjective* Danish.

dank *preposition* ←(+GEN *or* +DAT) thanks to.

Dank *der* **1** thanks; **mit Dank zurück** thanks for the loan; **2 vielen Dank** thank you very much.

dankbar *adjective* **1** grateful; **2** rewarding.

danke *exclamation* thank you, thanks; **danke schön** thank you very much; **(nein) danke** no thank you, no thanks.

danken *verb* (PERF **hat gedankt**) **1** to thank; **2 nichts zu danken** don't mention it.

dann *adverb* then.

daran *adverb* **1** on it/them; **2 daran denken** to think of it/them; **3 dicht daran** close to it/them; **4 nahe daran sein, etwas zu tun** to be on the point of doing something; **5** about it/them; **daran ist nichts zu machen** there is nothing you can do about it; **6 es liegt daran, dass** … it is because …; **7 er ist daran gestorben** he died of it.

darauf *adverb* **1** on it/them; **2 darauf warten** to wait for it; **3 darauf antworten** to reply to it; **4** after that; **kurz darauf** shortly after that; **5 am Tag darauf** the day after; **6 am darauf folgenden Tag** Δ the following day; **7 es kommt darauf an, ob** … it depends whether …

daraufhin *adverb* as a result.

daraus *adverb* **1** out of it/them, from it/them; **2 was ist daraus geworden?** what has become of it/them?; **3 mach dir nichts daraus** don't worry about it.

darf, darfst SEE **dürfen**.

darin *adverb* **1** in it/them; **2** in that respect; **der Unterschied liegt darin, dass** … the difference is that …

Darm *der* (PL *die* **Därme**) intestine(s).

darstellen *verb* (PERF **hat dargestellt**) **1** to represent; **2** to portray; **dieses Gemälde stellt Szenen aus dem Bürgerkrieg dar** this painting portrays scenes from the civil war; **3** to describe; **er stellt es so dar, als sei es meine Schuld** the way he describes it, it's all my fault; **4** to play (*in the theatre*).

Darsteller *der* (PL *die* **Darsteller**) actor.

Δ NEW SPELLING: *See page xii*

Darstellerin die (PL die Darstellerinnen) actress.

darüber adverb 1 over it/them; 2 about it; **darüber sprechen** to talk about it; 3 more; **dreißig Mark oder darüber** thirty marks or more.

darum adverb 1 round it/them; 2 **darum bitten** to ask for it; 3 that's why; **darum komme ich nicht** that's why I'm not coming; 4 **ich sorge mich darum** I worry about it; 5 **es geht darum, zu gewinnen** the main thing is to win; 6 **darum geht es nicht** that's not the point; 7 because of that; **darum, weil** because.

darunter adverb 1 under it/them; 2 **im Stock darunter** on the floor below; 3 among them; **mehrere Schüler, darunter zwei Zehnjährige** a number of pupils, among them two ten year olds; 4 less; **dreißig Mark oder darunter** thirty marks or less; 5 **was verstehen Sie darunter?** what do you understand by that?

das article (neuter) 1 the; **das Haus** the house; 2 that; **das Mädchen war es** it was that girl; **das da** that one. pronoun 1 which, that; **das Kleid, das ich im Schaufenster gesehen habe** the dress which I saw in the window; 2 **das mit der Spitze** the one with the lace; 3 who; **das Mädchen, das gegenüber wohnt** the girl who lives opposite; 4 that; **das wusste ich nicht** I didn't know that; **das geht** that's all right.

dasein SEE da.

Dasein das existence.

dass △ conjunction 1 that; **ich freue mich, dass …** I'm very pleased that …; 2 **ich verstehe nicht, dass Karin ihn mag** I don't understand why Karin likes him.

dasselbe pronoun the same, the same one.

Daten plural noun data.

Datenbank die (PL die Datenbanken) database.

Datenverarbeitung die data processing.

datieren verb (PERF hat datiert) to date.

Dativ der (PL die Dative) dative.

Datum das (PL die Daten) date.

Dauer die 1 duration; 2 length; 3 **für die Dauer von fünf Jahren** for (a period of) five years; 4 **von Dauer sein** to last; 5 **auf die Dauer** in the long run; **auf Dauer** permanently.

Dauerkarte die (PL die Dauerkarten) season ticket.

dauern verb (PERF hat gedauert) 1 to last; 2 **lange dauern** to take a long time; **es hat vier Wochen gedauert, bis der Brief hier ankam** it took four weeks for the letter to arrive.

dauernd adjective constant. adverb constantly.

Dauerwelle die (PL die Dauerwellen) perm.

Daumen der (PL die Daumen) thumb.

⬦ IRREGULAR VERB: *See the verb table in the centre of the dictionary*

Daunendecke *die* (PL *die* **Daunendecken**) duvet.

davon *adverb* **1** from it/them; **2** about it; **ich weiß nichts davon** I don't know anything about it; **3** of it/them; **die Hälfte davon** half of it/them; **4 das kommt davon** (*informal*) it serves you right; **5 was habe ich davon?** what's the point?; **6 abgesehen davon** apart from that.

davor *adverb* **1** in front of it/them; **2** beforehand; **3 Angst davor haben** to be frightened of it/them; **4 kurz davor sein, etwas zu tun** to be on the point of doing something.

dazu *adverb* **1** to it/them; **2** in addition; **noch dazu** in addition (to it); **3** with it; **was isst du dazu?** what are you having with it?; **4 ich habe keine Lust dazu** I don't feel like it; **5 jemanden dazu bringen, etwas zu tun** to get somebody to do something; **6 ich bin nicht dazu gekommen** I didn't get round to it; **7 er ist nicht dazu bereit** he's not prepared to do it.

dazugeben ✧ *verb* (PRES **gibt dazu**, IMPERF **gab dazu**, PERF **hat dazugegeben**) to add.

dazugehören *verb* (PERF **hat dazugehört**) **1** to belong to it/them; **2** to go with it/them (*of accessories*); **alles, was dazugehört** everything that goes with it.

dazukommen ✧ *verb* (IMPERF **kam dazu**, PERF **ist dazugekommen**) **1** to arrive; **2** to be added; **3 kommt noch etwas dazu?** would you like anything else?

dazwischen *adverb* **1** in between; **2** between them; **der Unterschied dazwischen** the difference between them.

dazwischenkommen ✧ *verb* (PRES **kommt dazwischen**, IMPERF **kam dazwischen**, PERF **ist dazwischengekommen**) to crop up.

DB *die* (*Deutsche Bundesbahn*) German railways.

DDR *die* (*Deutsche Demokratische Republik*) GDR, East Germany; **in der ehemaligen DDR** in the former East Germany.

Debatte *die* (PL *die* **Debatten**) debate.

Decke *die* (PL *die* **Decken**) **1** blanket, cover; **2** (table)cloth; **ich habe eine neue Decke aufgelegt** I've put on a new tablecloth; **3** ceiling.

Deckel *der* (PL *die* **Deckel**) **1** lid; **2** top.

decken *verb* (PERF **hat gedeckt**) **1** to cover; **2 ein Tuch über etwas decken** to spread a cloth over something; **3 den Tisch decken** to lay the table; **4 jemanden decken** to cover up for somebody; **5 einen Spieler decken** to mark a player (*in sport*).

definieren *verb* (PERF **hat definiert**) to define.

dehnbar *adjective* elastic.

dehnen *verb* (PERF **hat gedehnt**) to stretch.

dein *adjective* your.

△ NEW SPELLING: *See page xii*

deiner, deine, deins *pronoun*
yours; **meine Uhr ist kaputt, kann
ich deine haben?** my watch is
broken, can I take yours?

deinetwegen *adverb* **1** because of
you; **2** for your sake.

deins SEE **deiner**.

deklinieren *verb* (PERF **hat
dekliniert**) to decline.

Delle *die* (PL *die* **Dellen**) dent.

Delphin *der* (PL *die* **Delphine**)
dolphin.

dem *article* (*dative*) **1** (to) the; **2 es
liegt auf dem Tisch** it's on the table.
pronoun **1** to him; **gib es dem** give
it to him; **2** to it, to that one; **3** to
whom; **der Mann, dem ich das Geld
gegeben habe** the man I gave the
money to; **4** which; **das Messer, mit
dem ich Zwiebeln schneide** the
knife that I cut onions with.

demnächst *adverb* shortly.

Demokratie *die* (PL *die*
Demokratien) democracy.

demokratisch *adjective*
democratic.

Demonstrant *der* (PL *die*
Demonstranten) demonstrator.

Demonstrantin *die* (PL *die*
Demonstrantinnen) demonstrator.

Demonstration *die* (PL *die*
Demonstrationen) demonstration.

demonstrieren *verb* (PERF **hat
demonstriert**) to demonstrate.

den *article* (*accusative*) **1** the; **2 ich
habe mir den Arm gebrochen** I've
broken my arm.

pronoun **1** him; **kennst du den?** do
you know him?; **2** it, that one; **den
kannst du gerne haben** you're
welcome to it; **ich nehme den** I'll
take that one; **3** who(m); **4** which;
**der Mantel, den ich mir gekauft
habe** the coat I bought.

denen *pronoun* (*dative plural*)
1 (to) them; **2** that, (to) whom; **die
Menschen, denen sie geholfen hat**
the people she helped.

denkbar *adjective* conceivable.

denken ✧ *verb* (IMPERF **dachte**, PERF
hat gedacht) **1** to think; **ich denke
oft an dich** I often think of you;
2 das kann ich mir denken I can
imagine.

Denkmal *das* (PL *die* **Denkmäler**)
monument.

denn *conjunction* **1** because, for;
2 mehr denn je more than ever.
adverb **1 wo denn?** where?; **2 was
ist denn los?** so what's the matter?;
3 warum denn nicht? why ever
not?; **4 es sei denn** unless.

dennoch *conjunction* nevertheless.

deprimiert *adjective* depressed.

der *article* **1** (*masculine*) the; **der
Mann** the man; **2** (*feminine and
plural genitive*) of the; **die Katze der
Frau** the woman's cat; **der Ball der
Kinder** the children's ball; **3** (*dative*)
(to) the; **ich gab es der Frau** I gave
it to the woman.
pronoun **1** who; **der Mann, der hier
wohnt** the man who lives here;
2 which; **der Regenschirm, der mir**

✧ IRREGULAR VERB: *See the verb table in the centre of the dictionary*

gehört the umbrella which is mine;
3 der da that one; **4** him, he.

deren *pronoun* **1** their; **die Kinder
und deren Hund** the children and
their dog; **2** whose; **3** of which.

derselbe *pronoun* the same, the
same one.

des *article* **1** of the; **das Klingeln des
Telefons** the ringing of the phone;
2 der Ball des Jungen the boy's ball.

deshalb *adverb* **1** therefore; **2** that's
why.

desinfizieren *verb* (PERF **hat
desinfiziert**) to disinfect.

dessen *pronoun* **1** his; **2** its;
3 whose; **der Junge, dessen Mutter
weint** the boy whose mother is
crying; **4** of which.

desto *adverb* the; **je mehr, desto
besser** the more the better.

deswegen *conjunction*
1 therefore; **2** that's why.

Detektiv *der* (PL *die* **Detektive**)
detective.

deutlich *adjective* clear.
adverb **ich konnte ihn deutlich
sehen** I could clearly see him.

deutsch *adjective* German.

Deutsch *das* German; **auf Deutsch**
in German; **fließend Deutsch
sprechen** to speak fluent German.

Deutsche *der/die* (PL *die*
Deutschen) German; **er ist
Deutscher** he's German.

Deutschland *das* Germany; **nach
Deutschland** to Germany.

Devisen *plural noun* foreign
currency.

Dezember *der* December; **am
ersten Dezember** on the first of
December; **im Dezember** in
December.

Dezimalzahl *die* (PL *die*
Dezimalzahlen) decimal (number).

d.h. (*das heißt*) i.e.

Dia *das* (PL *die* **Dias**) slide.

diagonal *adjective* diagonal.

Diagramm *das* (PL *die* **Diagramme**)
diagram.

Dialekt *der* (PL *die* **Dialekte**) dialect.

Dialog *der* (PL *die* **Dialoge**) dialogue.

Diamant *der* (PL *die* **Diamanten**)
diamond.

Diät *die* (PL *die* **Diäten**) diet;
jemanden auf Diät setzen
(*informal*) to put somebody on a
diet.

dich *pronoun* **1** you; **2** yourself.

dicht *adjective* **1** thick (*fog*);
2 dense; **3** watertight; **4** airtight;
5 er ist nicht ganz dicht (*informal*)
he's off his head.
adverb **1** densely; **2** tightly; **3** close;
geh nicht so dicht an den Käfig
don't go so close to the cage; **dicht
bei** close to.

Dichter *der* (PL *die* **Dichter**) poet.

Dichterin *die* (PL *die* **Dichterinnen**)
poet.

Dichtung *die* (PL *die* **Dichtungen**)
1 poetry; **2** seal, washer.

△ NEW SPELLING: *See page xii*

dick *adjective* **1** thick; **2** swollen (*ankle, tonsils*); **3** fat (*person*).

Dickkopf *der* (PL *die* **Dickköpfe**) **1** stubborn person; **2 einen Dickkopf haben** to be stubborn.

die *article* (*feminine and plural*) the; **die Frau** the woman; **die Bücher** the books.
pronoun (*feminine and plural*) **1** who; **die Frau, die hier wohnt** the woman who lives here; **die Frau, die ich kenne** the woman I know; **die Kinder, die ich gefragt habe** the children I asked; **2** which; **die Tasche, die ich gekauft habe** the bag I bought; **3** she, her; **4** them; **ich meine die** I mean them; **5 die da** that one; (*plural*) those.

Dieb *der* (PL *die* **Diebe**) thief.

Diebin *die* (PL *die* **Diebinnen**) thief.

Diebstahl *der* (PL *die* **Diebstähle**) theft.

Diele *die* (PL *die* **Dielen**) **1** hall; **2** floorboard.

dienen *verb* (PERF **hat gedient**) to serve.

Dienst *der* (PL *die* **Dienste**) service; **Dienst haben** to work, to be on duty (*of a soldier or doctor*).

Dienstag *der* (PL *die* **Dienstage**) Tuesday; **am Dienstag** on Tuesday.

dienstags *adverb* on Tuesdays.

dienstfrei *adjective* **1 ein dienstfreier Tag** a day off; **2 dienstfrei haben** to have time off, to be off duty.

dienstlich *adverb* on business.

Dienstreise *die* (PL *die* **Dienstreisen**) business trip.

diese SEE **dieser**.

Diesel *der* diesel.

dieselbe *pronoun* the same, the same one.

dieser, diese, dieses *adjective* **1** this; **2** these; **diese Äpfel** these apples.
pronoun **1** this one; **mir gefällt dieses am besten** I like this one best; **2** these ones.

diesmal *adverb* this time.

Digitaluhr *die* (PL *die* **Digitaluhren**) **1** digital watch; **2** digital clock.

Diktat *das* (PL *die* **Diktate**) dictation.

Ding *das* (PL *die* **Dinge**) thing; **vor allen Dingen** above all; **das war ein Ding** (*informal*) that was quite something.

Dings *der/die/das* thingummy.

Dinosaurier *der* (PL *die* **Dinosaurier**) dinosaur.

Diplom *das* (PL *die* **Diplome**) diploma.

dir *pronoun* **1** you, to you; **sie hat es dir gegeben** she gave it to you; **ich verspreche dir, dass …** I promise you that …; **2 Freunde von dir** friends of yours; **3** yourself.

direkt *adjective* direct.

Direktor *der* (PL *die* **Direktoren**) **1** director; **2** headmaster, principal; **3** manager (*of a bank, theatre*).

Direktorin *die* (PL *die* **Direktorinnen**) **1** director;

2 headmistress, principal;
3 manager (*of a bank, theatre*).

Direktübertragung *die* (PL *die* **Direktübertragungen**) live transmission.

Dirigent *der* (PL *die* **Dirigenten**) conductor.

dirigieren *verb* (PERF **hat dirigiert**) to conduct.

Diskette *die* (PL *die* **Disketten**) floppy disk.

Diskothek *die* (PL *die* **Diskotheken**) disco, discotheque.

Diskriminierung *die* discrimination; **die Diskriminierung von Frauen** discrimination against women.

Diskussion *die* (PL *die* **Diskussionen**) discussion; **zur Diskussion stehen** to be under discussion.

diskutieren *verb* (PERF **hat diskutiert**) to discuss.

Disziplin *die* (PL *die* **Disziplinen**) discipline.

DJH *die* (*Deutsche Jugendherberge*) German youth hostel (association).

DM *die* (*Deutsche Mark*) DM, Deutschmark.

D-Mark *die* (PL *die* **D-Mark**) Deutschmark, German mark.

doch *adverb* 1 yes (*when you are contradicting somebody*); **'hast du keinen Hunger?' – 'doch!'** 'aren't you hungry?' – 'yes, I am!'; 2 after all; **sie hat ihn doch eingeladen** she invited him after all; **sie ist doch nicht gekommen** she hasn't come after all; 3 **er hat doch meinen Brief bekommen?** he did get my letter, didn't he?; **sie kommt doch?** she's coming, isn't she?; 4 anyway; **du hörst ja doch nicht auf mich** you won't listen to me anyway; 5 **pass doch auf!** do be careful! *conjunction* but.

Doktor *der* (PL *die* **Doktoren**) doctor; **den Doktor machen** to do a doctorate.

Dokument *das* (PL *die* **Dokumente**) document.

Dokumentarfilm *der* (PL *die* **Dokumentarfilme**) documentary.

Dokumentarsendung *die* (PL *die* **Dokumentarsendungen**) documentary (programme).

dolmetschen *verb* (PERF **hat gedolmetscht**) to interpret.

Dolmetscher *der* (PL *die* **Dolmetscher**) interpreter.

Dolmetscherin *die* (PL *die* **Dolmetscherinnen**) interpreter.

Dom *der* (PL *die* **Dome**) cathedral.

Donau *die* Danube.

Donner *der* thunder.

donnern *verb* (PERF **hat gedonnert**) to thunder.

Donnerstag *der* (PL *die* **Donnerstage**) Thursday; **am Donnerstag** on Thursday.

donnerstags *adverb* on Thursdays.

doof *adjective* (*informal*) stupid.

△ NEW SPELLING: *See page xii*

Doppel das (PL die **Doppel**)
1 duplicate; 2 doubles (*in sport*).

Doppelbett das (PL die
Doppelbetten) double bed.

Doppelfenster das (PL die
Doppelfenster) double-glazed
window; **wir haben Doppelfenster**
we've got double glazing.

Doppelhaus das (PL die
Doppelhäuser) semi-detached
house.

doppelt adjective 1 double; 2 in
doppelter Ausführung in
duplicate; 3 **die doppelte Menge**
twice the amount.
adverb 1 doubly; 2 twice; **doppelt
so viel** twice as much; **sich doppelt
anstrengen** to try twice as hard.

Doppelzimmer das (PL die
Doppelzimmer) double room.

Dorf das (PL die **Dörfer**) village.

Dorn der (PL die **Dornen**) thorn.

dort adverb there; **dort drüben** over
there.

dorther adverb from there.

dorthin adverb there; **geht ihr jetzt
dorthin?** are you going there now?

Dose die (PL die **Dosen**) tin, can.

Dosenöffner der (PL die
Dosenöffner) tin opener.

Dosis die (PL die **Dosen**) dose.

Dotter der (PL die **Dotter**) yolk.

Dozent der (PL die **Dozenten**)
lecturer.

Dozentin die (PL die **Dozentinnen**)
lecturer.

Drache der (PL die **Drachen**) dragon.

Drachen der (PL die **Drachen**) kite.

Drachenfliegen das hang-gliding.

Draht der (PL die **Drähte**) 1 wire; 2 **er
ist auf Draht** (*informal*) he's on the
ball.

Drama das (PL die **Dramen**) drama.

Dramatik die drama.

dran adverb SEE **daran**; 1 **ich bin
dran** it's my turn; **wer ist dran?**
whose turn is it?; 2 **gut dran sein** to
be well off; 3 **arm dran sein** to be
in a bad way; 4 **spät dran sein** to
be late.

drängen verb (PERF **hat gedrängt**)
1 to push; 2 to press, to urge
(*somebody*); 3 **sich drängen** to
crowd; **die Leute drängten sich vor
der Kasse** people crowded around
the box-office.

drankommen ✧ verb (IMPERF **kam
dran**, PERF **ist drangekommen**) to
have your turn; **wer kommt dran?**
whose turn is it?

drauf adverb SEE **darauf**; 1 **drauf
und dran sein, etwas zu tun** to be
on the point of doing something;
2 **gut drauf sein** (*informal*) to be in
a good mood.

draußen adverb outside.

Dreck der dirt.

dreckig adjective dirty, filthy.

Drehbuch das (PL die **Drehbücher**)
1 screenplay; 2 script.

drehen verb (PERF **hat gedreht**) 1 to
turn; **an etwas drehen** to turn

✧ IRREGULAR VERB: *See the verb table in the centre of the dictionary*

something; **2** to shoot (*a film*);
3 sich drehen to turn; **4 sich im
Kreis drehen** to rotate; **5 es dreht
sich um ihr Taschengeld** it's about
her pocket money.

drei *number* three.

Drei *die* (PL *die* **Dreien**) three.

Dreieck *das* (PL *die* **Dreiecke**)
triangle.

dreieckig *adjective* triangular.

dreifach *adjective* triple.

dreihundert *number* three
hundred.

dreimal *adverb* three times.

dreißig *number* thirty.

dreiviertel *number* three-quarters.

Dreiviertelstunde *die* (PL *die*
Dreiviertelstunden) three-quarters
of an hour.

dreizehn *number* thirteen.

drin *adverb* SEE **darin**; **drin sein** to
be inside.

dringend *adjective* urgent.

drinnen *adverb* **1** inside; **2** indoors.

dritt *adverb* **sie sind zu dritt** there
are three of them.

dritte SEE **dritter**.

Drittel *das* (PL *die* **Drittel**) third.

drittens *adverb* thirdly.

dritter, dritte, drittes *adjective*
third; **zum dritten Mal** for the third
time; **ein Dritter** a third person;
jeder Dritte, der mitwollte every

third person who wanted to come;
die Dritte Welt the Third World.

Droge *die* (PL *die* **Drogen**) drug.

drogenabhängig *adjective*
addicted to drugs.

Drogenabhängige *der/die* (PL *die*
Drogenabhängigen) drug addict.

Drogenabhängigkeit *die* drug
addiction.

drogensüchtig *adjective* addicted
to drugs.

Drogensüchtige *der/die* (PL *die*
Drogensüchtigen) drug addict.

Drogerie *die* (PL *die* **Drogerien**)
chemist's.

Drogist *der* (PL *die* **Drogisten**)
chemist.

Drogistin *die* (PL *die* **Drogistinnen**)
chemist.

drohen *verb* (PERF **hat gedroht**) to
threaten; **jemandem drohen** to
threaten somebody.

Drohung *die* (PL *die* **Drohungen**)
threat.

drüben *adverb* over there.

Druck *der* **1** pressure; **jemanden
unter Druck setzen** to put pressure
on somebody; **2** printing; **3** (PL *die*
Drucke) print.

drucken *verb* (PERF **hat gedruckt**) to
print.

drücken *verb* (PERF **hat gedrückt**)
1 to press; **2 an der Tür drücken** to
push the door; **'bitte drücken'**
'push'; **3** to hug; **4** to pinch (*of
shoes*); **5 die Preise drücken** to

△ NEW SPELLING: *See page xii*

Drucker

force down prices; **6 sich vor etwas drücken** (*informal*) to get out of something; **du hast dich mal wieder vor dem Aufräumen gedrückt** you've got out of tidying up again.

Drucker der (PL die **Drucker**) printer.

Druckknopf der (PL die **Druckknöpfe**) press stud.

Drucksache die (PL die **Drucksachen**) printed matter.

Druckschrift die (PL die **Druckschriften**) 1 block letters; 2 type; 3 pamphlet.

Drüse die (PL die **Drüsen**) gland.

Dschungel der (PL die **Dschungel**) jungle.

du pronoun 1 you; 2 **du sagen** to say 'du' (to each other); **per du sein** to be on familiar terms (*'du' is used when talking to family members, close friends, or people of your own age; otherwise 'Sie' is used*).

Dudelsack der (PL die **Dudelsäcke**) bagpipes.

Duft der (PL die **Düfte**) fragrance, scent.

duften verb (PERF **hat geduftet**) to smell; **nach Lavendel duften** to smell of lavender.

dumm adjective 1 stupid; 2 **das wird mir jetzt zu dumm** (*informal*) I've had enough of it; 3 **so etwas Dummes!** how annoying!; 4 **der Dumme sein** to draw the short straw.

dummerweise adverb stupidly.

Dummheit die (PL die **Dummheiten**) 1 stupidity; 2 stupid thing; **mach keine Dummheiten** don't do anything stupid.

Dummkopf der (PL die **Dummköpfe**) fool.

Dünger der (PL die **Dünger**) fertilizer.

dunkel adjective 1 dark; **ein dunkler Anzug** a dark suit; 2 **im Dunkeln** in the dark; 3 vague (*idea*); 4 shady (*business*); 5 deep (*voice*).

Dunkelheit die darkness, dark.

dünn adjective 1 thin; 2 weak (*coffee, tea*).

Dunst der (PL die **Dünste**) haze.

Duo das (PL die **Duos**) duet.

durch preposition ←(+ACC) 1 through; **er ist durch das Fernsehen bekannt geworden** he's become famous through television; 2 by; **durch Boten** by courier; 3 **acht durch zwei ist vier** eight divided by two is four; 4 due to. adverb 1 through; **die ganze Nacht durch** all through the night; 2 **den Winter durch** throughout the winter; 3 **durch und durch** completely; 4 **es war acht Uhr durch** (*informal*) it was gone eight o'clock.

durcharbeiten verb (PERF **hat durchgearbeitet**) 1 to work through; **die Nacht durcharbeiten** to work through the night; 2 **sich durch etwas durcharbeiten** to work your way through something.

durchaus adverb absolutely.

durchblicken verb (PERF **hat**

durchgeblickt) 1 (*informal*) to understand; 2 **durchblicken lassen, dass** ... to hint that ...

durchbrechen ◇ *verb* (PRES **bricht durch**, IMPERF **brach durch**, PERF **hat durchgebrochen**) 1 to snap, to break in two; 2 (PERF **ist durchgebrochen**) **das Brett ist durchgebrochen** the board has snapped.

durcheinander *adverb* 1 in a mess; **mein Zimmer ist durcheinander** my room is (in) a mess; 2 **die Akten durcheinander bringen** △ to muddle up the files; **Karl hat ihre Namen durcheinander gebracht** Karl got their names mixed up; 3 confused; **bring mich nicht durcheinander** don't confuse me; 4 **sie haben alle durcheinander geredet** they all talked at once.

Durcheinander *das* 1 muddle; 2 mess; **in der Wohnung herrschte ein fürchterliches Durcheinander** the flat was a terrible mess; 3 confusion; **im allgemeinen Durcheinander** in the general confusion.

durcheinanderbringen SEE **durcheinander**.

durchfahren ◇ *verb* (PRES **fährt durch**, IMPERF **fuhr durch**, PERF **ist durchgefahren**) 1 to drive through; 2 to go through; 3 **der Zug fährt (in Stuttgart) durch** the train doesn't stop (in Stuttgart).

Durchfall *der* diarrhoea.

durchfallen ◇ *verb* (PRES **fällt durch**, IMPERF **fiel durch**, PERF **ist**

durchgefallen) 1 to fall through; 2 to fail (*an exam*).

durchführen *verb* (PERF **hat durchgeführt**) to carry out.

Durchgang *der* (PL **die Durchgänge**) 1 passage; 2 'Durchgang verboten' 'no entry'; 3 round (*in sport*).

Durchgangsverkehr *der* through traffic.

durchgehen ◇ *verb* (IMPERF **ging durch**, PERF **ist durchgegangen**) 1 to go through; 2 (*informal*) to escape; 3 **jemandem etwas durchgehen lassen** to let somebody get away with something.

durchkommen ◇ *verb* (IMPERF **kam durch**, PERF **ist durchgekommen**) 1 to come through; 2 to get through (*on the phone, in an exam*); 3 to pull through (*after an illness*).

durchlassen ◇ *verb* (PRES **lässt durch** △, IMPERF **ließ durch**, PERF **hat durchgelassen**) 1 to let through; 2 to let in.

durchmachen *verb* (PERF **hat durchgemacht**) 1 to go through; 2 to work through (*your lunch break, for example*); 3 **wir haben die Nacht durchgemacht** we made a night of it.

Durchmesser *der* (PL **die Durchmesser**) diameter.

durchnehmen ◇ *verb* (PRES **nimmt durch**, IMPERF **nahm durch**, PERF **hat durchgenommen**) to do (*a topic at school*).

△ NEW SPELLING: *See page xii*

durchs = durch das.

Durchsage die (PL die **Durchsagen**) announcement.

Durchschnitt der (PL die **Durchschnitte**) average; **im Durchschnitt** on average.

durchschnittlich adjective average.
adverb on average.

durchsetzen verb (PERF hat durchgesetzt) 1 to carry through; 2 sich durchsetzen to assert yourself; 3 sich durchsetzen to catch on (of a fashion, an idea).

durchsichtig adjective transparent.

durchstreichen ◇ verb (IMPERF strich durch, PERF hat durchgestrichen) to cross out.

Durchzug der draught.

dürfen ◇ verb (PRES darf, IMPERF durfte, PERF hat gedurft or hat dürfen) 1 to be allowed; **sie darf das nicht** she's not allowed to do that; **er hat nicht gedurft** he wasn't allowed to; 2 **Klaus hat sie im Krankenhaus besuchen dürfen** Klaus was allowed to visit her in hospital; 3 **darf ich?** may I?; 4 **das dürfen Sie nicht vergessen** you mustn't forget that; **du darfst es nicht alles so ernst nehmen** you mustn't take it all so seriously; 5 **du darfst froh sein, dass sonst nichts passiert ist** you should be glad that nothing else happened; **das darf einfach nicht passieren** that just shouldn't happen; **das dürfte nicht schwierig sein** that shouldn't be

difficult; 6 **das darf nicht wahr sein!** I don't believe it!; 7 **was darf es sein?** can I help you?; 8 **das dürfte der Grund sein** that's probably the reason.

durfte, durften, durftest, durftet SEE **dürfen**.

Dürre die (PL die **Dürren**) drought.

Durst der thirst; **Durst haben** to be thirsty.

durstig adjective thirsty.

Dusche die (PL die **Duschen**) shower.

duschen verb (PERF hat geduscht) 1 to have a shower; 2 sich duschen to have a shower.

Düsenflugzeug das (PL die **Düsenflugzeuge**) jet (plane).

düster adjective 1 gloomy (future, thoughts); 2 dark.

Dutzend das (PL die **Dutzende**) dozen.

duzen verb (PERF hat geduzt) to call somebody 'du'; **wollen wir uns duzen?** shall we say 'du' to each other? ('du' is used when talking to family members, close friends, or people of your own age).

dynamisch adjective dynamic.

D-Zug der (PL die **D-Züge**) fast train, express.

◇ IRREGULAR VERB: See the verb table in the centre of the dictionary

E e

Ebbe die (PL die **Ebben**) low tide.

eben adjective **1** flat; **2** level.
adverb **1** just; **Gabi war eben hier** Gabi was just here; **eben noch** just now; **2 eben!** exactly!

Ebene die (PL die **Ebenen**) **1** plain; **2** level; **3** plane (in geometry).

ebenso adverb just as; **Ulla hat den Film ebenso oft gesehen wie du** Ulla's seen the film just as often as you; **ich habe ebenso viel Arbeit wie du** I've got just as much work as you.

Echo das (PL die **Echos**) echo.

echt adjective real, genuine; **die Kette ist aus echtem Gold** the necklace is real gold.
adverb (informal) really; **das ist echt gut** that's really good.

Eckball der (PL die **Eckbälle**) corner (kick).

Ecke die (PL die **Ecken**) corner; **um die Ecke** round the corner.

eckig adjective square.

Edelstein der (PL die **Edelsteine**) precious stone.

EDV die (elektronische Datenverarbeitung) electronic data processing, EDP.

Efeu der (PL die **Efeus**) ivy.

EG die (Europäische Gemeinschaft) EC.

egal adjective **1 das ist mir egal** it's all the same to me; **2 egal, wie groß** no matter how big; **egal, ob es will oder nicht** (it doesn't matter) whether he wants to or not.

egoistisch adjective selfish.

ehe conjunction before; **ehe ich nicht weiß, was er will, mache ich nichts** I won't do anything before I know what he wants.

Ehe die (PL die **Ehen**) marriage.

Ehefrau die (PL die **Ehefrauen**) wife.

ehemalig adjective former.

Ehemann der (PL die **Ehemänner**) husband.

Ehepaar das (PL die **Ehepaare**) married couple.

eher adverb **1** earlier, sooner; **je eher, desto besser** the sooner the better; **2** rather; **eher gehe ich zu Fuß, als Geld für ein Taxi auszugeben** I'd rather walk than pay for a taxi; **3** more; **das ist schon eher möglich** that's more likely.

Ehre die (PL die **Ehren**) honour.

Ehrgeiz der ambition.

ehrgeizig adjective ambitious.

ehrlich adjective honest.

Ehrlichkeit die honesty.

Ei das (PL die **Eier**) egg.

Eiche die (PL die **Eichen**) oak.

△ NEW SPELLING: See page xii

Eichhörnchen das (PL die **Eichhörnchen**) squirrel.

Eid der (PL die **Eide**) oath.

Eidechse die (PL die **Eidechsen**) lizard.

Eierbecher der (PL die **Eierbecher**) egg-cup.

Eierschale die (PL die **Eierschalen**) eggshell.

Eifer der eagerness.

Eifersucht die jealousy.

eifersüchtig adjective jealous; **auf jemanden eifersüchtig sein** to be jealous of somebody.

eifrig adjective eager.

Eigelb das (PL die **Eigelb(e)**) egg yolk.

eigen adjective own; **sie ist erst siebzehn und hat schon ihr eigenes Auto** she's only seventeen and she's already got her own car.

Eigenart die (PL die **Eigenarten**) peculiarity.

eigenartig adjective peculiar.

Eigenschaft die (PL die **Eigenschaften**) 1 quality; 2 characteristic.

eigensinnig adjective obstinate.

eigentlich adjective actual. adverb actually; **eigentlich habe ich keine Lust, heute ins Kino zu gehen** actually I don't fancy going to the cinema today.

Eigentum das property.

Eigentümer der (PL die **Eigentümer**) owner.

eignen verb (PERF **hat sich geeignet**) **sich eignen** to be suitable.

Eile die hurry.

eilen verb 1 (PERF **ist geeilt**) to hurry; 2 (PERF **hat geeilt**) to be urgent; **das eilt nicht** it's not urgent.

eilig adjective 1 urgent; 2 hurried; 3 **es eilig haben** to be in a hurry.

Eilzug der (PL die **Eilzüge**) fast stopping train.

Eimer der (PL die **Eimer**) bucket.

ein, eine, ein article a, an; **ein Haus** a house; **eine Allergie** an allergy; **ein bisschen mehr** a bit more; **was für ein Kleid hast du gekauft?** what sort of dress did you buy?
adjective 1 one; **sie haben nur ein Kind** they've got just one child; **eines Abends** one evening; 2 **einer Meinung sein** to be of the same opinion; 3 **ein für allemal** once and for all.

einander pronoun each other, one another.

Einbahnstraße die (PL die **Einbahnstraßen**) one-way street.

Einband der (PL die **Einbände**) cover.

einbauen verb (PERF **hat eingebaut**) 1 to fit; 2 to install.

Einbauküche die (PL die **Einbauküchen**) fitted kitchen.

einbiegen ⬦ verb (IMPERF **bog ein**, PERF **ist eingebogen**) to turn; **der Radfahrer bog langsam in die Seitenstraße ein** the cyclist turned slowly down the side street.

⬦ IRREGULAR VERB: *See the verb table in the centre of the dictionary*

einbilden *verb* (PERF **hat sich eingebildet**) **1 sich einbilden** to imagine; **das bildest du dir nur ein** you're only imagining it; **2 Till bildet sich viel ein** Till is very conceited.

Einbildung *die* imagination; **das ist alles nur Einbildung** it's all in the mind.

einbrechen ✧ *verb* (PRES **bricht ein**, IMPERF **brach ein**, PERF **ist eingebrochen**) to break in; **in unserem Haus sind Diebe eingebrochen** thieves broke into our house; **bei unseren Nachbarn ist eingebrochen worden** our neighbours have been burgled.

Einbrecher *der* (PL *die* **Einbrecher**) burglar.

Einbruch *der* (PL *die* **Einbrüche**) **1** burglary; **2 vor Einbruch der Dunkelheit** before it gets dark; **3 bei Einbruch der Nacht** at nightfall.

eindeutig *adjective* **1** clear; **2** definite (*proof*).

Eindruck *der* (PL *die* **Eindrücke**) impression.

eindrucksvoll *adjective* impressive.

eine SEE **ein, einer**.

eineinhalb *number* one and a half.

einer, eine, ein(e)s *pronoun* **1** one; **einer von uns** one of us; **wie soll das einer wissen?** how is one supposed to know?; **2** somebody; **3 kaum einer** hardly anyone; **4** you; **das macht einen müde** it makes you tired.

einerseits *adverb* on the one hand; **einerseits sagt sie, dass sie kein Geld hat, andererseits kauft sie sich dauernd neue Sachen** on the one hand she claims to have no money, on the other hand she's constantly buying new things.

eines SEE **einer**.

einfach *adjective* **1** simple; **2** easy; **3** single (*ticket, knot*). *adverb* simply.

Einfachheit *die* simplicity.

Einfahrt *die* (PL *die* **Einfahrten**) **1** entrance; **2** arrival (*of a train*); **3** slip road (*on a motorway*).

Einfall *der* (PL *die* **Einfälle**) idea.

einfallen ✧ *verb* (PRES **fällt ein**, IMPERF **fiel ein**, PERF **ist eingefallen**) **1 jemandem einfallen** to occur to somebody; **2 ihr Name fällt mir nicht ein** I can't think of her name; **3 was fällt dir eigentlich ein?** what do you think you're doing?; **4 sich etwas einfallen lassen** to think of something.

Einfamilienhaus *das* (PL *die* **Einfamilienhäuser**) detached family house.

Einfluss ∆ *der* (PL *die* **Einflüsse**) influence.

einfrieren ✧ *verb* (IMPERF **fror ein**, PERF **ist eingefroren**) **1** to freeze; **2** (PERF **hat eingefroren**) to freeze (*food in the freezer*).

Einfuhr *die* (PL *die* **Einfuhren**) import.

einführen *verb* (PERF **hat**

∆ NEW SPELLING: *See page xii*

eingeführt) 1 to import; **2** to introduce.

Einführung die (PL die **Einführungen**) introduction.

Eingabe die input (of data).

eingeben ✧ verb (PRES **gibt ein**, IMPERF **gab ein**, PERF **hat eingegeben**) **1** to hand in; **2** to input, to key in.

eingebildet adjective **1** conceited; **2** imaginary (illness).

Eingeborene der/die (PL die **Eingeborenen**) native.

eingehen ✧ verb (IMPERF **ging ein**, PERF **ist eingegangen**) **1** to shrink (of clothes); **2** to die (of plants); **3** to arrive (of goods); **4 auf etwas eingehen** to go into something; **sie ging näher darauf ein** she went into it in more detail; **5 auf etwas nicht eingehen** to ignore something; **6 auf etwas eingehen** to agree to something; **Oliver ist auf unseren Plan eingegangen** Oliver agreed to our plan; **7 ein Risiko eingehen** to take a risk.

eingeschrieben adjective registered; **ein eingeschriebener Brief** a registered letter.

eingestellt adjective **1 auf etwas eingestellt sein** to be prepared for something; **2 fortschrittlich eingestellt sein** to be progressively minded.

eingewöhnen verb (PERF **hat sich eingewöhnt**) **sich eingewöhnen** to settle in.

eingießen ✧ verb (IMPERF **goss ein** △, PERF **hat eingegossen**) to pour.

Eingriff der (PL die **Eingriffe**) **1** intervention; **2** operation (surgical).

einheimisch adjective **1** native; **2** local.

Einheit die (PL die **Einheiten**) **1** unity; **2** unit (of drink, soldiers).

Einheitspreis der (PL die **Einheitspreise**) **1** standard price; **2** flat fare.

einholen verb (PERF **hat eingeholt**) **1** to catch up with; **2** to make up (time, a delay); **3** to buy; **einholen gehen** to go shopping.

einhundert number one hundred.

einige SEE **einiger**.

einigen verb (PERF **hat sich geeinigt**) **sich einigen** to come to an agreement; **sich auf etwas einigen** to agree on something.

einiger, einige, einiges adjective, pronoun **1** some; **vor einiger Zeit** some time ago; **2** several; **3 nur einige waren noch da** there were only a few left; **4 einiges** quite a lot; **wir haben einiges gesehen** we saw quite a lot (of things); **5 einiges** some things; **einiges hat uns nicht gefallen** there were some things we didn't like.

einigermaßen adverb **1** fairly; **2** fairly well; **3 'wie geht es dir?' – 'einigermaßen'** 'how are you?' – 'so-so'.

einiges SEE **einiger**.

✧ IRREGULAR VERB: See the verb table in the centre of the dictionary

Einigung *die* agreement.

Einkauf *der* (PL *die* **Einkäufe**)
1 purchase; 2 shopping; **Einkäufe machen** to do some shopping.

einkaufen *verb* (PERF **hat eingekauft**) 1 to buy; **ich habe vergessen Milch einzukaufen** I forgot to buy milk; 2 to shop; **wir kaufen meist im Supermarkt ein** we usually shop at the supermarket; **einkaufen gehen** to go shopping.

Einkaufsbummel *der* (PL *die* **Einkaufsbummel**) shopping spree.

Einkaufswagen *der* (PL *die* **Einkaufswagen**) shopping trolley.

Einkaufszentrum *das* (PL *die* **Einkaufszentren**) shopping centre.

Einkommen *das* (PL *die* **Einkommen**) income.

einladen ✧ *verb* (PRES **lädt ein**, IMPERF **lud ein**, PERF **hat eingeladen**) 1 to invite; **jemanden zum Abendessen einladen** to invite somebody for dinner; 2 **jemanden ins Kino einladen** to take sombody to the cinema; 3 to treat; **ich lade euch ein** I'll treat you; 4 to load (*goods*).

Einladung *die* (PL *die* **Einladungen**) invitation.

einleben *verb* (PERF **hat sich eingelebt**) **sich einleben** to settle down.

Einleitung *die* (PL *die* **Einleitungen**) introduction.

einlösen *verb* (PERF **hat eingelöst**) to cash.

einmal *adverb* 1 once (*in the past*); **es war einmal** ... once upon a time ...; 2 one day (*in the future*); 3 **auf einmal** suddenly; 4 **auf einmal** at the same time; **sie kamen alle auf einmal** they all came at the same time; 5 **nicht einmal** not even; 6 **noch einmal** again; 7 **es geht nun einmal nicht** it's just not possible.

einmalig *adjective* 1 unique; 2 fantastic; 3 single, one-off (*payment*).

einmischen *verb* (PERF **hat sich eingemischt**) **sich einmischen** to interfere.

einordnen *verb* (PERF **hat eingeordnet**) 1 to put in order; 2 **sich einordnen** to fit in (*with other people*); 3 **sich einordnen** to get in lane (*when driving*).

einpacken *verb* (PERF **hat eingepackt**) 1 to pack; 2 to wrap.

einreichen *verb* (PERF **hat eingereicht**) to hand in.

Einreise *die* (PL *die* **Einreisen**) entry.

einreisen *verb* (PERF **ist eingereist**) to enter a country; **er reiste nach Italien ein** he entered Italy.

einrichten *verb* (PERF **hat eingerichtet**) 1 to furnish; 2 to set up (*an organisation*); 3 to arrange; **kannst du es so einrichten, dass du vormittags da bist?** can you arrange to be here in the morning?; 4 **sich einrichten** to furnish your home; 5 **sich einrichten** to economize; 6 **sich auf etwas**

△ NEW SPELLING: *See page xii*

einrichten to prepare for something.

Einrichtung *die* (PL *die* **Einrichtungen**) **1** furnishing; **2** furnishings; **3** setting up; **4** institution; **staatliche Einrichtungen** state institutions.

eins *number* one; **eins zu eins** one all; **es ist eins** it's one o'clock.
pronoun SEE **einer**.
adjective **mir ist alles eins** it's all the same to me.

Eins *die* (PL *die* **Einsen**) one.

einsam *adjective* lonely.

einsammeln *verb* (PERF **hat eingesammelt**) to collect.

Einsatz *der* **1** use; **2** stake (*when betting*).

einschalten *verb* (PERF **hat eingeschaltet**) **1** to switch on (*a radio, TV*); **2** **sich einschalten** to intervene.

einschlafen ✧ *verb* (PRES **schläft ein**, IMPERF **schlief ein**, PERF **ist eingeschlafen**) to go to sleep.

einschließen ✧ *verb* (IMPERF **schloss ein** Δ, PERF **hat eingeschlossen**) **1** to lock in; **2** to include; **3** **sich einschließen** to lock yourself in.

einschließlich *preposition* ←(+GEN) including; **einschließlich der Unkosten** including expenses.
adverb inclusive.

einschränken *verb* (PERF **hat eingeschränkt**) **1** to restrict; **2** to

cut back; **3** **sich einschränken** to economize.

einschreiben ✧ *verb* (IMPERF **schrieb sich ein**, PERF **hat sich eingeschrieben**) **1** **sich einschreiben** to enrol (*at university*); **2** **sich einschreiben** to put your name down.

Einschreiben *das* (PL *die* **Einschreiben**) registered letter, registered parcel; **per Einschreiben** registered.

einsehen ✧ *verb* (PRES **sieht ein**, IMPERF **sah ein**, PERF **hat eingesehen**) **1** to realize; **2** to see; **das sehe ich nicht ein** I don't see why.

einseitig *adjective* one-sided.

einsenden ✧ *verb* (IMPERF **sendete ein/sandte ein**, PERF **hat eingesendet/hat eingesandt**) to send in.

einsetzen *verb* (PERF **hat eingesetzt**) **1** to put in (*a missing part*), to insert; **2** to use; **während der Weltmeisterschaft wurden Sonderzüge eingesetzt** special train were put on during the World Cup; **3** to stake (*money*); **4** to start (*of rain, snow*); **5** **sich für jemanden einsetzen** to support somebody.

Einsicht *die* **1** insight; **2** sense; **3** **zu der Einsicht kommen, dass ...** to come to realize that ...

einsperren *verb* (PERF **hat eingesperrt**) to lock up.

Einspruch *der* (PL *die* **Einsprüche**) objection.

✧ IRREGULAR VERB: *See the verb table in the centre of the dictionary*

einst *adverb* **1** once; **2** one day (*in the future*).

einstecken *verb* (PERF **hat eingesteckt**) **1** to put in (*a coin*); **2 einen Brief einstecken** to post a letter; **3** to plug in; **4 etwas einstecken** to put something in your pocket or bag, to take something; **5** (*informal*) to take (*insults*).

einsteigen ✧ *verb* (IMPERF **stieg ein**, PERF **ist eingestiegen**) **1** to get in; **2** to get on (*a bus or train*).

einstellen *verb* (PERF **hat eingestellt**) **1** to employ (*in a job*); **2** to adjust (*a machine*); **3** to focus (*a camera*); **4** to tune into (*a radio station*); **5** to stop; **6 sich auf etwas einstellen** to prepare yourself for something; **7 sich schnell auf eine neue Situation einstellen** to adjust quickly to a new situation.

Einstellung *die* (PL *die* **Einstellungen**) **1** employment; **2** adjustment; **3** stopping; **4** take (*of a film*); **5** attitude; **seine politische Einstellung** his political views.

Einstieg *der* (PL *die* **Einstiege**) entrance.

einstürzen *verb* (PERF **ist eingestürzt**) to collapse.

einstweilen *adverb* **1** for the time being; **2** meanwhile.

eintausend *number* one thousand.

einteilen *verb* (PERF **hat eingeteilt**) **1** to divide up; **2 sich seine Zeit gut einteilen** to organize your time well.

Eintopf *der* (PL *die* **Eintöpfe**) stew.

Eintrag *der* (PL *die* **Einträge**) entry.

eintragen ✧ *verb* (PRES **trägt ein**, IMPERF **trug ein**, PERF **hat eingetragen**) **1** to enter, to write; **2 sich eintragen** to put your name down.

einträglich *adjective* profitable.

eintreffen ✧ *verb* (PRES **trifft ein**, IMPERF **traf ein**, PERF **ist eingetroffen**) **1** to arrive; **2** to come true.

eintreten ✧ *verb* (PRES **tritt ein**, IMPERF **trat ein**, PERF **ist eingetreten**) **1** to enter; **2 in einen Klub eintreten** to join a club; **für jemanden eintreten** to stand up for somebody.

Eintritt *der* **1** entrance; **2** admission; **'Eintritt frei'** 'admission free'.

Eintrittskarte *die* (PL *die* **Eintrittskarten**) (admission) ticket.

Eintrittspreis *der* (PL *die* **Eintrittspreise**) admission charge.

einverstanden *adjective* **1 einverstanden sein** to agree; **einverstanden!** okay!; **2 mit jemandem einverstanden sein** to approve of somebody.

Einwand *der* (PL *die* **Einwände**) objection.

Einwanderer *der* (PL *die* **Einwanderer**) immigrant.

Einwanderin *die* (PL *die* **Einwanderinnen**) immigrant.

einwandern *verb* (PERF **ist eingewandert**) to immigrate.

△ NEW SPELLING: *See page xii*

einweichen *verb* (PERF **hat eingeweicht**) to soak (*washing*).

einwerfen ◇ *verb* (PRES **wirft ein**, IMPERF **warf ein**, PERF **hat eingeworfen**) 1 to post; 2 to put in (*a coin, money*); 3 to throw in; 4 to smash.

Einwohner *der* (PL die **Einwohner**) inhabitant.

Einzahl *die* singular.

einzahlen *verb* (PERF **hat eingezahlt**) to pay in.

Einzel *das* (PL die **Einzel**) singles (*in sport*).

Einzelheit *die* (PL die **Einzelheiten**) detail.

Einzelkarte *die* (PL die **Einzelkarten**) single ticket.

Einzelkind *das* (PL die **Einzelkinder**) only child.

einzeln *adjective* 1 single; 2 individual; 3 odd (*sock, for example*).
adverb 1 individually; 2 separately, one at a time; **bitte einzeln eintreten** please enter one at a time.

Einzelne ∆ *der/die/das* (PL die **Einzelnen**) 1 **der/die Einzelne** the individual; 2 **Einzelne** some; 3 **ein Einzelner/eine Einzelne/ein Einzelnes** a single one; **jeder/jede/jedes Einzelne** every single one; 4 **im Einzelnen** in detail; **ins Einzelne gehen** to go into detail.

Einzelzimmer *das* (PL die **Einzelzimmer**) single room.

einziehen ◇ *verb* (IMPERF **zog ein**, PERF **hat eingezogen**) 1 to collect (*payment*); 2 to draw in (*its feelers, claws*); 3 **den Kopf einziehen** to duck; 4 (PERF **ist eingezogen**) to move in; **wann zieht ihr in die neue Wohnung ein?** when are you moving into your new flat?; 5 (PERF **ist eingezogen**) to soak in.

einzig *adjective* only; **ein einziges Mal** only once.

Einzige ∆ *der/die/das* (PL die **Einzigen**) 1 **der/die/das Einzige** the only one; 2 **ein Einziger/eine Einzige/ein Einziges** a single one; **kein Einziger/keine Einzige/kein Einziges** not a single one; 3 **das Einzige, was mich stört** the only thing that bothers me.

Eis *das* 1 ice; 2 ice cream.

Eisbahn *die* (PL die **Eisbahnen**) skating rink.

Eisbär *der* (PL die **Eisbären**) polar bear.

Eisbecher *der* (PL die **Eisbecher**) ice-cream sundae.

Eisdiele *die* (PL die **Eisdielen**) ice-cream parlour.

Eisen *das* iron.

Eisenbahn *die* (PL die **Eisenbahnen**) railway.

eisern *adjective* iron.

Eishockey *das* ice hockey.

eisig *adjective* icy.

eiskalt *adjective* 1 ice-cold (*drink*); 2 freezing cold.

Eislaufen *das* ice-skating.

◇ IRREGULAR VERB: *See the verb table in the centre of the dictionary*

Eiswürfel der (PL die **Eiswürfel**) ice cube.

Eiszapfen der (PL die **Eiszapfen**) icicle.

eitel adjective vain.

Eitelkeit die vanity.

Eiter der pus.

Eiweiß das 1 egg-white; 2 protein.

Ekel der disgust.

ekelhaft adjective disgusting.

ekeln verb (PERF **hat sich geekelt**) **sich vor etwas ekeln** to find something disgusting.

eklig adjective disgusting.

Ekzem das (PL die **Ekzeme**) eczema.

Elefant der (PL die **Elefanten**) elephant.

elegant adjective elegant.

Elektriker der (PL die **Elektriker**) electrician.

elektrisch adjective electrical.

Elektrizität die electricity.

Elektroherd der (PL die **Elektroherde**) electric cooker.

Elektronik die electronics.

elektronisch adjective electronic.

Elektrorasierer der (PL die **Elektrorasierer**) electric razor.

elend adjective 1 miserable; 2 terrible.

Elend das misery.

elf number eleven.

Elfe die (PL die **Elfen**) fairy.

Elfmeter der (PL die **Elfmeter**) penalty (in soccer).

Ellbogen der (PL die **Ellbogen**) elbow.

Eltern plural noun parents.

Email das (PL die **Emails**) enamel.

E-Mail die (PL die **E-Mails**) E-mail.

empfahl SEE **empfehlen**.

Empfang der (PL die **Empfänge**) 1 reception; 2 receipt (of goods or a letter).

empfangen ◇ verb (PRES **empfängt**, IMPERF **empfing**, PERF **hat empfangen**) to receive.

Empfängnisverhütung die contraception.

Empfangsdame die (PL die **Empfangsdamen**) receptionist.

empfehlen ◇ verb (PRES **empfiehlt**, IMPERF **empfahl**, PERF **hat empfohlen**) to recommend.

empfindlich adjective 1 sensitive; 2 delicate; 3 touchy.

empfing SEE **empfangen**.

empfohlen SEE **empfehlen**.

empört adjective indignant.

Ende das (PL die **Enden**) 1 end; Ende April at the end of April; am Ende der Straße at the end of the road; 2 am Ende in the end; 3 ending (of a film, novel); 4 zu Ende sein to be finished, to be over; 5 Ende gut, alles gut all's well that ends well.

△ NEW SPELLING: See page xii

enden *verb* (PERF **hat geendet**) to end.

endgültig *adjective* **1** final (*consent, decision*); **2** definite.

Endivie *die* (PL *die* **Endivien**) endive.

endlich *adverb* finally, at last; **na endlich!** at last!

endlos *adjective* endless.

Endspiel *das* (PL *die* **Endspiele**) final.

Endstation *die* (PL *die* **Endstationen**) terminus.

Endung *die* (PL *die* **Endungen**) ending.

Energie *die* energy.

energisch *adjective* energetic.

eng *adjective* **1** narrow; **2** tight; **3** close; **eng befreundet sein** to be close friends.

Engel *der* (PL *die* **Engel**) angel.

England *das* England; **aus England** from England.

Engländer *der* (PL *die* **Engländer**) Englishman.

Engländerin *die* (PL *die* **Engländerinnen**) Englishwoman.

englisch *adjective* English; **auf Englisch** in English.

Enkel *der* (PL *die* **Enkel**) grandson.

Enkelin *die* (PL *die* **Enkelinnen**) granddaughter.

Enkelkind *das* (PL *die* **Enkelkinder**) grandchild.

entdecken *verb* (PERF **hat entdeckt**) to discover.

Entdeckung *die* (PL *die* **Entdeckungen**) discovery.

Ente *die* (PL *die* **Enten**) duck.

entfernen *verb* (PERF **hat entfernt**) to remove.

entfernt *adjective* **1** distant; **2 zehn Kilometer entfernt** ten kilometres away.
adverb **entfernt verwandt sein** to be distantly related.

Entfernung *die* (PL *die* **Entfernungen**) distance.

entführen *verb* (PERF **hat entführt**) **1** to kidnap; **2** to hijack.

entgegen *preposition* ←(+DAT) contrary to.

entgegengesetzt *adjective* **1** opposite; **2** opposing (*views*).

entgegenkommen ◇ *verb* (IMPERF **kam entgegen**, PERF **ist entgegengekommen**) **1** to come towards; **2 jemandem entgegenkommen** to come to meet somebody; **3 jemandem auf halbem Wege entgegenkommen** to meet somebody halfway; **4 jemandem freundlich entgegenkommen** to be accommodating towards somebody.

entgegenkommend *adjective* **1** obliging; **2 der entgegen-kommende Verkehr** the oncoming traffic.

Entgelt *das* payment.

Enthaarungsmittel *das* (PL *die*

◇ IRREGULAR VERB: *See the verb table in the centre of the dictionary*

Enthaarungsmittel) hair remover, depilatory.

enthalten ✧ *verb* (PRES **enthält**, IMPERF **enthielt**, PERF **hat enthalten**) **1** to contain; **2 sich einer Sache enthalten** to abstain from something; **sich der Stimme enthalten** to abstain; **3** (PERF **ist enthalten sein**) **in etwas enthalten sein** to be included in something; **im Preis enthalten** included in the price.

entkommen ✧ *verb* (IMPERF **entkam**, PERF **ist entkommen**) to escape.

entlang *preposition* ←(+ACC *or* +DAT) along; **die Straße entlang** along the road; **am Fluss entlang** along the river.

entlanggehen ✧ *verb* (IMPERF **ging entlang**, PERF **ist entlanggegangen**) to walk along.

entlanglaufen ✧ *verb* (PRES **läuft entlang**, IMPERF **lief entlang**, PERF **ist entlanggelaufen**) to run along.

entlassen ✧ *verb* (PRES **entlässt** Δ, IMPERF **entließ**, PERF **hat entlassen**) **1** to dismiss (*from a job*); **2** to discharge (*from hospital*); **3** to release (*from prison*).

Entlassung *die* (PL *die* **Entlassungen**) **1** dismissal; **2** discharge; **3** release.

entmutigen *verb* (PERF **hat entmutigt**) to discourage.

entschädigen *verb* (PERF **hat entschädigt**) to compensate.

Entschädigung *die* compensation.

entscheiden ✧ *verb* (IMPERF **entschied**, PERF **hat entschieden**) **1** to decide (on); **2 sich entscheiden** to decide.

Entscheidung *die* (PL *die* **Entscheidungen**) decision.

entschließen ✧ *verb* (IMPERF **entschloss sich** Δ, PERF **hat sich entschlossen**) **1 sich entschließen** to decide; **2 sich anders entschließen** to change your mind; **Karl hat sich anders entschlossen** Karl has changed his mind.

entschlossen *adjective* determined.

Entschluss Δ *der* (PL *die* **Entschlüsse**) decision.

entschuldigen *verb* (PERF **hat entschuldigt**) **1** to excuse; **entschuldigen Sie bitte** excuse me; **2 sich entschuldigen** to apologize; **ich habe mich bei Michi entschuldigt** I apologized to Michi.

Entschuldigung *die* (PL *die* **Entschuldigungen**) **1** apology; **2 jemanden um Entschuldigung bitten** to apologize to somebody; **3 Entschuldigung!** sorry!; **4 Entschuldigung** (*with a question or request*) excuse me; **Entschuldigung, können Sie mir sagen, wie ich zum Bahnhof komme?** excuse me, could you tell me the way to the station?; **5** excuse.

Entsetzen *das* horror.

Δ NEW SPELLING: *See page xii*

entsetzlich *adjective* **1** horrible; **2** terrible.

entsetzt *adjective* horrified.

entspannen *verb* (PERF **hat sich entspannt**) **1 sich entspannen** to relax; **2 sich entspannen** to ease (*of a situation*).

entsprechen ◇ *verb* (PRES **entspricht**, IMPERF **entsprach**, PERF **hat entsprochen**) **1 den Anforderungen entsprechen** to meet the requirements; **2 einer Sache entsprechen** to correspond to something; **3** to agree with (*the truth, a description*); **4** to comply with (*certain standards*).

entsprechend *adjective* **1** corresponding; **2** appropriate. *preposition* ←(+DAT) in accordance with.

entstehen ◇ *verb* (IMPERF **entstand**, PERF **ist entstanden**) **1** to develop; **2** to result (*of damage*).

enttäuschen *verb* (PERF **hat enttäuscht**) to disappoint.

Enttäuschung *die* (PL *die* **Enttäuschungen**) disappointment.

entweder *conjunction* either; **entweder heute oder morgen** either today or tomorrow.

entwerten *verb* (PERF **hat entwertet**) **1** to devalue; **2** to punch (*a ticket in a machine found on trains, trams, buses, and on the platform; you have to punch your ticket before each journey*).

Entwerter *der* (PL *die* **Entwerter**) ticket-punching machine (*these machines are found on trains, trams, buses, and on the platform; you have to punch your ticket before each journey*).

entwickeln *verb* (PERF **hat entwickelt**) **1** to develop; **2** to display (*ability, a characteristic*); **3 sich entwickeln** to develop.

Entwicklung *die* (PL *die* **Entwicklungen**) **1** development; **2** developing.

Entwicklungsland *das* (PL *die* **Entwicklungsländer**) developing country.

Entwurf *der* (PL *die* **Entwürfe**) **1** design; **2** draft.

entzückend *adjective* delightful.

entzünden *verb* (PERF **hat entzündet**) **1** to light (*a fire, match*); **2 sich entzünden** to become inflamed; **3 sich entzünden** to ignite.

Entzündung *die* (PL *die* **Entzündungen**) inflammation.

Enzian *der* (PL *die* **Enziane**) gentian.

Epidemie *die* (PL *die* **Epidemien**) epidemic.

er *pronoun* **1** he; **2** it; **'wo ist mein Mantel?'** – **'er liegt auf dem Stuhl'** 'where's my coat?' – 'it's on the chair'; **3** him (*stressed*); **er war es** it was him.

erben *verb* (PERF **hat geerbt**) to inherit.

erblich *adjective* hereditary.

Erbschaft *die* (PL *die* **Erbschaften**) inheritance.

◇ IRREGULAR VERB: *See the verb table in the centre of the dictionary*

Erbse die (PL die **Erbsen**) pea.

Erdbeben das (PL die **Erdbeben**) earthquake.

Erdbeere die (PL die **Erdbeeren**) strawberry.

Erde die 1 earth, soil; 2 ground; **auf der Erde** on the ground; 3 Earth; 4 earth (*for electricity*).

Erdgeschoss △ das (PL die **Erdgeschosse**) ground floor; **im Erdgeschoss** on the ground floor.

Erdkunde die geography.

Erdnuss △ die (PL die **Erdnüsse**) peanut.

ereignen verb (PERF **hat sich ereignet**) **sich ereignen** to happen.

Ereignis das (PL die **Ereignisse**) event.

erfahren ✧ verb (PRES **erfährt**, IMPERF **erfuhr**, PERF **hat erfahren**) 1 to hear, to learn; 2 to experience. adjective experienced.

Erfahrung die (PL die **Erfahrungen**) experience.

erfinden ✧ verb (IMPERF **erfand**, PERF **hat erfunden**) to invent.

Erfindung die (PL die **Erfindungen**) invention.

Erfolg der (PL die **Erfolge**) 1 success; **Erfolg haben** to be successful; 2 **Erfolg versprechend** △ promising; 3 **viel Erfolg!** good luck!

erfolglos adjective unsuccessful.

erfolgreich adjective successful.

erfolgversprechend SEE **Erfolg**.

erforderlich adjective necessary.

erforschen verb (PERF **hat erforscht**) 1 to explore; 2 to investigate.

erfreulicherweise adverb happily.

erfreut adjective pleased.

Erfrischung die (PL die **Erfrischungen**) refreshment.

erfüllen verb (PERF **hat erfüllt**) to fulfil; **sich erfüllen** to come true.

Ergebnis das (PL die **Ergebnisse**) result.

ergreifen ✧ verb (IMPERF **ergriff**, PERF **hat ergriffen**) 1 to seize, to grab; 2 to take (*measures, an opportunity*); 3 to take up (*a job, career*); 4 to move; **die Nachricht von ihrem Tod hat uns tief ergriffen** the news of her death moved us deeply; 5 **die Flucht ergreifen** to flee.

ergreifend adjective moving.

erhalten ✧ verb (PRES **erhält**, IMPERF **erhielt**, PERF **hat erhalten**) 1 to receive; 2 to preserve.

erhältlich adjective obtainable.

erheben ✧ verb (IMPERF **erhob**, PERF **hat erhoben**) 1 to raise; 2 to charge (*a fee*); 3 **Protest erheben** to protest; 4 **sich erheben** to rise up (*in a rebellion*).

erheblich adjective considerable.

erheitern verb (PERF **hat erheitert**) to amuse.

△ NEW SPELLING: *See page xii*

erhitzen *verb* (PERF **hat erhitzt**) to heat.

erhöhen *verb* (PERF **hat erhöht**) **1** to increase; **2 sich erhöhen** to rise.

Erhöhung *die* (PL *die* **Erhöhungen**) increase.

erholen *verb* (PERF **hat sich erholt**) **1 sich erholen** to have a rest; **ich habe mich in den Ferien gut erholt** I had a good rest on holiday; **2 sich von einer Krankheit erholen** to recover from an illness.

erholsam *adjective* restful.

Erholung *die* rest; **Iris ist zur Erholung in die Berge gefahren** Iris went to the mountains for a rest.

erinnern *verb* (PERF **hat erinnert**) **1** to remind; **2 sich erinnern** to remember.

Erinnerung *die* (PL *die* **Erinnerungen**) **1** memory; **2** souvenir.

erkälten *verb* (PERF **hat sich erkältet**) **1 sich erkälten** to catch a cold; **2 erkältet sein** to have a cold; **Ben ist erkältet** Ben has a cold.

Erkältung *die* (PL *die* **Erkältungen**) cold.

erkennen ◇ *verb* (IMPERF **erkannte**, PERF **hat erkannt**) **1** to recognize; **2** to realize.

erklären *verb* (PERF **hat erklärt**) **1** to explain; **2** to declare; **3 sich zu etwas bereit erklären** to agree to something.

Erklärung *die* (PL *die* **Erklärungen**) **1** explanation; **2** declaration; **3 eine öffentliche Erklärung** a public statement.

erkundigen *verb* (PERF **hat sich erkundigt**) **1** to enquire; **2** to ask about; **Susi hat sich nach dir erkundigt** Susi was asking about you.

Erkundigung *die* (PL *die* **Erkundigungen**) enquiry.

erlauben *verb* (PERF **hat erlaubt**) **1** to allow; **jemandem etwas erlauben** to allow somebody to do something; **2 sich etwas erlauben** to allow yourself something; **3 sich alles erlauben** to do as you please; **4 erlauben Sie mal!** (*informal*) do you mind!

Erlaubnis *die* permission.

erleben *verb* (PERF **hat erlebt**) **1** to experience; **2** to have (*a disappointment, an experience*); **eine Überraschung erleben** to have a surprise; **3 er hat die Geburt seines Enkels nicht mehr erlebt** he didn't live to see the birth of his grandson.

Erlebnis *das* (PL *die* **Erlebnisse**) experience.

erledigen *verb* (PERF **hat erledigt**) to deal with, to do.

erledigt *adjective* **1** settled; **2** (*informal*) worn out.

Erleichterung *die* relief.

erleiden ◇ *verb* (IMPERF **erlitt**, PERF **hat erlitten**) to suffer.

Erlös *der* (PL *die* **Erlöse**) proceeds.

◇ IRREGULAR VERB: *See the verb table in the centre of the dictionary*

ermäßigen *verb* (PERF **hat ermäßigt**) to reduce.

Ermäßigung *die* (PL *die* **Ermäßigungen**) reduction.

ermorden *verb* (PERF **hat ermordet**) to murder.

ermutigen *verb* (PERF **hat ermutigt**) to encourage.

ernähren *verb* (PERF **hat ernährt**) 1 to feed; 2 **sich von Nudeln ernähren** to live on pasta; 3 to support (*a family*).

Ernährung *die* 1 diet; **eine gesunde Ernährung** a healthy diet; 2 nutrition.

erneuern *verb* (PERF **hat erneuert**) to renew.

erneut *adjective* renewed. *adverb* once again.

ernst *adjective* serious.

Ernst *der* 1 seriousness; 2 **im Ernst** seriously; 3 **ist das dein Ernst?** are you serious?

ernsthaft *adjective* serious.

ernstlich *adjective* serious.

Ernte *die* (PL *die* **Ernten**) harvest.

ernten *verb* (PERF **hat geerntet**) to harvest.

erobern *verb* (PERF **hat erobert**) to conquer.

Eroberung *die* (PL *die* **Eroberungen**) conquest.

eröffnen (PERF **hat eröffnet**) to open.

Eröffnung *die* (PL *die* **Eröffnungen**) opening.

erraten ✧ *verb* (PRES **errät**, IMPERF **erriet**, PERF **hat erraten**) to guess.

Erreger *der* (PL *die* **Erreger**) germ.

Erregung *die* excitement.

erreichen *verb* (PERF **hat erreicht**) 1 to reach; 2 **den Zug erreichen** to catch the train; 3 to achieve (*a goal, aim*); 4 **Irene ist telefonisch zu erreichen** Irene can be contacted by phone.

erröten *verb* (PERF **ist errötet**) to blush.

Ersatz *der* replacement, substitute.

Ersatzreifen *der* (PL *die* **Ersatzreifen**) spare tyre.

Ersatzteil *das* (PL *die* **Ersatzteile**) spare part.

erscheinen ✧ *verb* (IMPERF **erschien**, PERF **ist erschienen**) to appear.

erschöpft *adjective* exhausted.

erschrecken *verb* 1 (PERF **hat erschreckt**) to scare; 2 ✧ (PRES **erschrickt**, IMPERF **erschrak**, PERF **ist erschrocken**) to get a fright.

erschreckend *adjective* alarming.

erschrocken *adjective* 1 frightened; 2 startled.

ersetzen *verb* (PERF **hat ersetzt**) to replace; **jemandem einen Schaden ersetzen** to compensate somebody for damages.

Ersparnisse *plural noun* savings.

erst *adverb* 1 first; **erst einmal** first of all; 2 only; **eben erst** only just; 3 not until; **erst nächste Woche** not

△ NEW SPELLING: *See page xii*

until next week; **Oma war erst
zufrieden, als die ganze Familie da
war** granny was not happy until all
the family were there.

erstaunen *verb* (PERF **hat erstaunt**)
to astonish.

erstaunlich *adjective* astonishing.

erstaunt *adjective* amazed; **über
etwas erstaunt sein** to be amazed
about something.

Erste △ *der/die/das* (PL *die* **Ersten**)
1 **der/die Erste** the first (one); **das
Erste** the first (thing); 2 **Dirk kam
als Erster** Dirk arrived first;
Marianne ging als Erste Marianne
left first; 3 **als Erster/Erste etwas
tun** to be the first to do something;
4 **als Erstes** first of all; 5 **fürs Erste**
for the time being.

erstens *adverb* firstly.

erster, erste, erstes *adjective*
first; **mein erstes Rad war rot** my
first bike was red; **der erste April** the
first of April; **erste Hilfe** △ first aid.

erstklassig *adjective* first-class.

erstmals *adverb* for the first time.

erteilen *verb* (PERF **hat erteilt**) to
give (*advice, information*).

ertragen ✧ *verb* (PRES **erträgt**,
IMPERF **ertrug**, PERF **hat ertragen**) to
bear.

ertrinken ✧ *verb* (IMPERF **ertrank**,
PERF **ist ertrunken**) to drown.

erwachsen *adjective* grown-up.

Erwachsene *der/die* (PL *die*
Erwachsenen) adult, grown-up.

Erwachsenenbildung *die* adult
education.

erwähnen *verb* (PERF **hat erwähnt**)
to mention.

erwarten *verb* (PERF **hat erwartet**)
to expect.

Erwartung *die* (PL *die*
Erwartungen) expectation.

erzählen *verb* (PERF **hat erzählt**) to
tell.

Erzählung *die* (PL *die* **Erzählungen**)
story.

Erzeugnis *das* (PL *die* **Erzeugnisse**)
product.

erziehen ✧ *verb* (IMPERF **erzog**, PERF
hat erzogen) 1 to bring up; 2 to
educate.

Erziehung *die* 1 upbringing;
2 education.

es *pronoun* 1 it; **es regnet** it is
raining; 2 **es gibt** there is, there
are; 3 **'wo ist das Baby?'** – **'es
schläft'** 'where's the baby?' –
'he's/she's asleep'.

Esel *der* (PL *die* **Esel**) donkey.

essbar △ *adjective* edible.

essen ✧ *verb* (PRES **isst** △, IMPERF **aß**,
PERF **hat gegessen**) to eat.

Essen *das* 1 meal; 2 food.

Essig *der* vinegar.

Essiggurke *die* (PL *die*
Essiggurken) gherkin.

Esskastanie △ *die* (PL *die*
Esskastanien) sweet chestnut.

✧ IRREGULAR VERB: *See the verb table in the centre of the dictionary*

Esszimmer Δ *das* (PL *die* **Esszimmer**) dining room.

Etage *die* (PL *die* **Etagen**) floor; **in der zweiten Etage** on the second floor.

Etagenbett *das* (PL *die* **Etagenbetten**) bunk beds.

ethnisch *adjective* ethnic.

Etikett *das* (PL *die* **Etikette**) label.

Etui *das* (PL *die* **Etuis**) case.

etwa *adverb* **1** about; **er ist etwa so groß wie du** he's about as tall as you; **2** for example; **3 nicht etwa, dass** … not that …; **4 hat Klaus etwa Angst gehabt?** Klaus wasn't scared, was he?

etwas *pronoun, adverb* **1** something; **2** anything; **sonst noch etwas?** anything else?; **3** some; **etwas von dem Geld** some of the money; **noch etwas Kaffee?** (some) more coffee?; **4** a little; **nur etwas Zucker** only a little sugar; **etwas lauter singen** to sing a little louder.

EU *die* (*Europäische Union*) EU.

euch *pronoun* **1** you; **ich habe euch eingeladen** I've invited you; **2** to you; **Eva hat es euch geschenkt** Eva gave it to you; **3** (*reflexive*) yourselves.

euer *adjective* your.

Eule *die* (PL *die* **Eulen**) owl.

eurer, eure, eures *pronoun* yours.

Euro *der* (PL *die* **Euros**) (*European currency*) Euro.

Europa *das* Europe.

Europäer *der* (PL *die* **Europäer**) European.

Europäerin *die* (PL *die* **Europäerinnen**) European.

europäisch *adjective* European.

evangelisch *adjective* Protestant.

eventuell *adjective* possible. *adverb* possibly.

ewig *adjective* eternal. *adverb* forever.

Ewigkeit *die* eternity.

Examen *das* (PL *die* **Examen**) examination, exam.

Exemplar *das* (PL *die* **Exemplare**) **1** copy; **2** specimen.

existieren *verb* (PERF **hat existiert**) to exist.

explodieren *verb* (PERF **ist explodiert**) to explode.

Explosion *die* (PL *die* **Explosionen**) explosion.

extra *adverb* **1** separately; **2** extra; **3** specially; **4** (*informal*) on purpose.

extrem *adjective* extreme.

F f

fabelhaft *adjective* fabulous, fantastic.

Fabrik *die* (PL *die* **Fabriken**) factory.

Fach *das* (PL *die* **Fächer**) **1** compartment; **2** drawer; **3** subject (*at school*).

Δ NEW SPELLING: *See page xii*

Facharzt der (PL die **Fachärzte**) specialist.

Fachärztin die (PL die **Fachärztinnen**) specialist.

Fachfrau die (PL die **Fachfrauen**) expert.

Fachmann der (PL die **Fachleute**) expert.

Faden der (PL die **Fäden**) thread.

fähig adjective 1 capable; 2 able.

Fähigkeit die (PL die **Fähigkeiten**) ability.

Fahne die (PL die **Fahnen**) flag.

Fahrausweis der (PL die **Fahrausweise**) ticket.

Fahrbahn die (PL die **Fahrbahnen**) 1 carriageway; 2 road.

Fähre die (PL die **Fähren**) ferry.

fahren ◇ verb (PRES **fährt**, IMPERF **fuhr**, PERF **ist gefahren**) 1 to go; **mit dem Zug nach Wien fahren** to go to Vienna by train; **ich bin mit dem Auto gefahren** I went by car; 2 to drive; **Hanna ist sehr schnell gefahren** Hanna drove very fast; 3 to ride (of a cyclist); 4 to run (of a train, bus); **der Zug fährt nicht an Sonn- und Feiertagen** the train doesn't run on Sundays and public holidays; 5 to leave; **wann fahrt ihr?** when are you leaving?; 6 **was ist in sie gefahren?** (informal) what's got into her?; 7 (PERF **hat gefahren**) to drive; **er hat Doris nach Hause gefahren** he drove Doris home; **ich habe das Auto in die Garage gefahren** I drove the car into the garage.

Fahrer der (PL die **Fahrer**) driver.

Fahrerflucht die hit-and-run driving; **Fahrerflucht begehen** to be involved in a hit-and-run.

Fahrerin die (PL die **Fahrerinnen**) driver.

Fahrgast der (PL die **Fahrgäste**) passenger.

Fahrkarte die (PL die **Fahrkarten**) ticket.

Fahrkartenausgabe die ticket office.

Fahrkartenautomat der (PL die **Fahrkartenautomaten**) ticket machine.

Fahrkartenschalter der (PL die **Fahrkartenschalter**) ticket office.

fahrlässig adjective negligent.

Fahrlehrer der (PL die **Fahrlehrer**) driving instructor.

Fahrplan der (PL die **Fahrpläne**) timetable.

Fahrpreis der (PL die **Fahrpreise**) fare.

Fahrprüfung die (PL die **Fahrprüfungen**) driving test; **die Fahrprüfung machen** to take your driving test.

Fahrrad das (PL die **Fahrräder**) bicycle.

Fahrradweg der (PL die **Fahrradwege**) cycle lane.

◇ IRREGULAR VERB: See the verb table in the centre of the dictionary

Fahrschein der (PL die **Fahrscheine**) ticket.

Fahrschule die (PL die **Fahrschulen**) driving school.

Fahrstuhl der (PL die **Fahrstühle**) lift.

Fahrt die (PL die **Fahrten**) 1 journey; **gute Fahrt!** have a good journey!; 2 trip; 3 drive; 4 **in voller Fahrt** at full speed.

Fahrzeug das (PL die **Fahrzeuge**) vehicle.

fair adjective fair.

Faktor der (PL die **Faktoren**) factor.

Falke der (PL die **Falken**) falcon.

Fall der (PL die **Fälle**) 1 case; **in diesem Fall** in this case; **auf alle Fälle, auf jeden Fall** in any case; **für alle Fälle** just in case; 2 **auf jeden Fall** definitely; 3 **auf keinen Fall** on no account; 4 fall.

Falle die (PL die **Fallen**) trap.

fallen ◇ verb (PRES **fällt**, IMPERF **fiel**, PERF **ist gefallen**) 1 to fall; 2 **etwas fallen lassen** △ to drop something; **wir haben den Plan fallen lassen** we've dropped the idea; 3 **eine Bemerkung fallen lassen** △ to make a comment.

fallenlassen SEE **fallen**.

fällig adjective due.

falls conjunction 1 if; 2 in case.

Fallschirm der (PL die **Fallschirme**) parachute.

falsch adjective 1 wrong; **du hast ihn falsch verstanden** you got him

wrong; 2 false (teeth, etc.); 3 forged.

fälschen verb (PERF **hat gefälscht**) to forge.

Fälschung die (PL die **Fälschungen**) 1 fake; 2 forgery.

Falte die (PL die **Falten**) 1 fold; 2 crease; 3 pleat; 4 wrinkle.

falten verb (PERF **hat gefaltet**) to fold.

faltig adjective 1 wrinkled; 2 creased.

familiär adjective familiar.

Familie die (PL die **Familien**) family.

Familienname der (PL die **Familiennamen**) surname.

Fan der (PL die **Fans**) fan.

fand SEE **finden**.

fangen ◇ verb (PRES **fängt**, IMPERF **fing**, PERF **hat gefangen**) to catch.

fantastisch adjective fantastic.

Farbe die (PL die **Farben**) 1 colour; 2 paint; 3 dye; 4 suit (in playing cards).

farbecht adjective colour fast.

färben verb (PERF **hat gefärbt**) 1 to dye; 2 **sich die Haare färben** to dye your hair; 3 **das Sweatshirt färbt** this sweatshirt runs.

Farbfilm der (PL die **Farbfilme**) colour film.

farbig adjective coloured.

farblos adjective colourless.

Farbstift der (PL die **Farbstifte**) coloured pencil.

Farbstoff *der* (PL *die* **Farbstoffe**)
1 dye; 2 colouring (*for food*).

Farbton *der* (PL *die* **Farbtöne**) shade.

Fasan *der* (PL *die* **Fasane**) pheasant.

Fasching *der* (PL *die* **Faschinge**)
carnival.

Faser *die* (PL *die* **Fasern**) fibre.

Fass △ *das* (PL *die* **Fässer**) barrel; **Bier
vom Fass** draught beer.

fassen *verb* (PERF **hat gefasst** △) 1 to
grasp; 2 **einen Dieb fassen** to catch
a thief; 3 to hold (*of a container*);
4 to understand; 5 **nicht zu fassen**
unbelievable; 6 **sich fassen** to
compose yourself; 7 **einen
Entschluss fassen** to make a
decision; 8 **sich kurz fassen** to be
brief.

Fassung *die* (PL *die* **Fassungen**)
1 version; 2 composure;
3 **jemanden aus der Fassung
bringen** to throw somebody, to upset
somebody; 4 setting (*for gems*).

fassungslos *adjective* speechless.

fast *adverb* 1 almost; 2 **fast nie**
hardly ever.

Fastenzeit *die* (PL *die*
Fastenzeiten) Lent.

Fastnacht *die* carnival.

faul *adjective* 1 lazy; 2 rotten; 3 **eine
faule Ausrede** a lame excuse; 4 **an
der Sache ist etwas faul** (*informal*)
there's something fishy about it.

faulen *verb* (PERF **ist gefault**) to rot.

faulenzen *verb* (PERF **hat
gefaulenzt**) to laze about.

Faust *die* (PL *die* **Fäuste**) 1 fist; 2 **auf
eigene Faust** off your own bat.

Fax *das* (PL *die* **Fax(e)**) fax.

faxen *verb* (PERF **hat gefaxt**) to fax;
ich faxe Ihnen die Liste I'll fax you
the list.

Februar *der* February.

fechten ◇ *verb* (PRES **ficht**, IMPERF
focht, PERF **hat gefochten**) to fence.

Feder *die* (PL *die* **Federn**) 1 feather;
2 spring; 3 nib (*of a pen*).

Federball *der* (PL *die* **Federbälle**)
1 badminton; 2 shuttlecock.

Federmäppchen *das* (PL *die*
Federmäppchen) pencil case.

Fee *die* (PL *die* **Feen**) fairy.

fegen *verb* (PERF **hat gefegt**) to
sweep.

fehl *adjective* **fehl am Platz** out of
place.

fehlen *verb* (PERF **hat gefehlt**) 1 to
be missing; 2 to be lacking; 3 to be
absent (*from school*); 4 **mir fehlt die
Zeit** I haven't got the time; **es fehlt
ihnen einfach das Geld für ein
neues Auto** they simply haven't got
the money for a new car; 5 **was fehlt
dir?** what's the matter?; 6 **Rudi fehlt
mir** I miss Rudi.

Fehler *der* (PL *die* **Fehler**) 1 mistake;
2 fault.

Feier *die* (PL *die* **Feiern**) 1 party;
2 celebration.

Feierabend *der* (PL *die*
Feierabende) 1 finishing time;
2 **nach Feierabend** after work.

◇ IRREGULAR VERB: *See the verb table in the centre of the dictionary*

Feierlichkeiten *plural noun* festivities.

feiern *verb* (PERF **hat gefeiert**) to celebrate.

Feiertag *der* (PL *die* **Feiertage**) **1** holiday; **ein gesetzlicher Feiertag** a public holiday; **2 am ersten Feiertag** on Christmas Day; **der zweite Feiertag** Boxing Day.

feige *adjective* cowardly; **du bist feige** you're a coward.

Feige *die* (PL *die* **Feigen**) fig.

Feigling *der* (PL *die* **Feiglinge**) coward.

Feile *die* (PL *die* **Feilen**) file.

fein *adjective* **1** fine; **2** delicate; **3** refined; **4 sich fein machen** Δ to dress up.

Feind *der* (PL *die* **Feinde**) enemy.

feindlich *adjective* hostile.

Feld *das* (PL *die* **Felder**) **1** field; **2** pitch; **3** box (*on a form*); **4** square (*on a board game*).

Fell *das* (PL *die* **Felle**) fur, skin.

Fels *der* rock.

Felsen *der* (PL *die* **Felsen**) cliff.

feminin *adjective* feminine.

Feminist *der* (PL *die* **Feministen**) feminist.

Feministin *die* (PL *die* **Feministinnen**) feminist.

Fenster *das* (PL *die* **Fenster**) window.

Fensterladen *der* (PL *die* **Fensterläden**) shutter.

Ferien *plural noun* holidays; **Ferien haben** to be on holiday.

fern *adjective* **1** distant; **2 sich fern halten** Δ to keep away; **jemanden von etwas fern halten** Δ to keep somebody away from something. *adverb* far away.

Fernbedienung *die* remote control.

Ferngespräch *das* (PL *die* **Ferngespräche**) long-distance call.

fernhalten SEE **fern**.

Fernglas *das* (PL *die* **Ferngläser**) binoculars.

Fernsehapparat *der* (PL *die* **Fernsehapparate**) television set.

fernsehen ◇ *verb* (PRES **sieht fern**, IMPERF **sah fern**, PERF **hat ferngesehen**) to watch television.

Fernsehen *das* television; **im Fernsehen** on television.

Fernseher *der* (PL *die* **Fernseher**) television (set).

Fernsprecher *der* (PL *die* **Fernsprecher**) telephone.

Ferse *die* (PL *die* **Fersen**) heel.

fertig *adjective* **1** finished; **mit den Hausaufgaben fertig werden** to finish your homework; **fertig sein** to be finished; **2 mit jemandem fertig sein** (*informal*) to be through with somebody; **3 völlig fertig sein** to be completely worn out; **4 mit etwas fertig werden** to cope with something (*problems, for example*); **5** ready; **das Essen ist fertig** food's ready; **6 etwas fertig machen** Δ

Δ NEW SPELLING: *See page xii*

(*prepare*) to get something ready; (*complete*) to finish something; **sich fertig machen** △ to get ready; **7 jemanden fertig machen** △ to wear somebody out, to wear somebody down; **der ständige Stress macht mich fertig** this constant stress is wearing me down; **8 es fertig bringen** △, **etwas zu tun** to bring yourself to do something; **ich bringe es einfach nicht fertig** I just can't bring myself to do it. *adverb* **fertig essen** to finish eating.

fertigbringen SEE **fertig**.

Fertiggericht *das* (PL *die* **Fertiggerichte**) ready-to-serve meal.

fertigmachen SEE **fertig**.

Fest *das* (PL *die* **Feste**) **1** party; **2** celebration; **3** festival.

fest *adjective* **1** firm; **2** fixed (*salary, address*); **3** solid; **feste Nahrung** solids; **4 fest werden** to harden. *adverb* **1 fest schlafen** to be fast asleep; **2 fest befreundet sein** to be close friends; **3 fest angestellt sein** to be in permanent employment.

festbinden ✧ *verb* (IMPERF **band fest**, PERF **hat festgebunden**) to tie (up).

festhalten ✧ *verb* (PRES **hält fest**, IMPERF **hielt fest**, PERF **hat festgehalten**) **1** to hold on to; **2 sich festhalten** to hold on; **halt dich an mir fest** hold on to me.

Festigkeit *die* strength.

festlegen *verb* (PERF **hat**

festgelegt) **1** to fix; **2 sich auf etwas festlegen** to commit yourself to something.

festlich *adjective* festive.

festmachen *verb* (PERF **hat festgemacht**) **1** to fix; **ich mache gleich einen Termin fest** I'll fix a date straight away; **2** to fasten.

festnehmen ✧ *verb* (PRES **nimmt fest**, IMPERF **nahm fest**, PERF **hat festgenommen**) to arrest.

feststehen ✧ *verb* (IMPERF **stand fest**, PERF **hat festgestanden**) to be certain; **eins steht fest, Daniel lade ich nicht mehr ein** one thing's certain, I'm not going to invite Daniel again.

feststellen *verb* (PERF **hat festgestellt**) **1** to establish; **2** to notice.

Fett *das* (PL *die* **Fette**) **1** fat; **2** grease.

fett *adjective* **1** fat (*person*); **2** greasy, fatty (*food*); **3** bold (*type*).

fettarm *adjective* low-fat.

fettig *adjective* greasy.

Fetzen *der* (PL *die* **Fetzen**) **1** scrap; **2** rag.

feucht *adjective* **1** damp; **2** humid.

Feuchtigkeit *die* **1** moisture; **2** humidity.

Feuer *das* **1** fire; **2 hast du Feuer?** have you got a light?

Feuerlöscher *der* (PL *die* **Feuerlöscher**) fire extinguisher.

Feuermelder *der* (PL *die* **Feuermelder**) fire alarm.

✧ IRREGULAR VERB: *See the verb table in the centre of the dictionary*

Feuertreppe die (PL die **Feuertreppen**) fire escape.

Feuerwehr die (PL die **Feuerwehren**) fire brigade.

Feuerwehrauto das (PL die **Feuerwehrautos**) fire engine.

Feuerwehrmann der (PL die **Feuerwehrleute**) fireman.

Feuerwerk das fireworks.

Feuerzeug das (PL die **Feuerzeuge**) lighter.

ficht SEE **fechten**.

Fieber das (high) temperature, fever; **Fieber haben** to have a temperature.

fiel SEE **fallen**.

fies adjective (informal) nasty.

Figur die (PL die **Figuren**) 1 figure; 2 character.

Filiale die (PL die **Filialen**) branch.

Film der (PL die **Filme**) film.

filmen verb (PERF **hat gefilmt**) to film.

Filter der (PL die **Filter**) filter.

Filzstift der (PL die **Filzstifte**) felt pen.

finanziell adjective financial.

finanzieren verb (PERF **hat finanziert**) to finance.

finden ◇ verb (IMPERF **fand**, PERF **hat gefunden**) 1 to find; 2 to think; **wie findest du das?** what do you think of it?; **findest du?** do you think so?; 3 **ich finde nichts dabei** I don't mind.

fing SEE **fangen**.

Finger der (PL die **Finger**) finger.

Fingernagel der (PL die **Fingernägel**) fingernail.

Finne der (PL die **Finnen**) Finn.

Finnin die (PL die **Finninnen**) Finn.

Finnland das Finland.

finster adjective 1 dark; **im Finstern** in the dark; 2 sinister.

Finsternis die darkness.

Firma die (PL die **Firmen**) firm, company.

Fisch der (PL die **Fische**) 1 fish; 2 **Fische** Pisces; **Helmut ist Fisch** Helmut is Pisces.

Fischer der (PL die **Fischer**) fisherman.

fit adjective fit; **er hält sich durch Jogging fit** he keeps fit by jogging.

Fitnesstraining Δ das keep fit.

fix adjective 1 quick; 2 **fix und fertig** all finished, all ready; 3 **ich bin fix und fertig** (informal) I'm shattered.

flach adjective 1 flat; 2 low; 3 shallow; **die Erdbeeren kommen in die flache Schüssel** the strawberries go into the shallow bowl.

Fläche die (PL die **Flächen**) 1 surface; 2 area.

flackern verb (PERF **hat geflackert**) to flicker.

Flagge die (PL die **Flaggen**) flag.

Flamme die (PL die **Flammen**) flame.

Flasche die (PL die **Flaschen**) bottle.

Δ NEW SPELLING: *See page xii*

Flaschenöffner der (PL die **Flaschenöffner**) bottle opener.

flauschig adjective 1 fluffy; 2 fleecy.

Fleck der (PL die **Flecken**) 1 stain; 2 spot; 3 **ein blauer Fleck** a bruise.

fleckig adjective 1 stained; 2 blotchy (skin).

Fledermaus die (PL die **Fledermäuse**) bat.

Fleisch das 1 meat; 2 flesh.

Fleischer der (PL die **Fleischer**) butcher.

Fleischerei die (PL die **Fleischereien**) butcher's.

Fleiß der hard work.

fleißig adjective hard-working.

flicken verb (PERF **hat geflickt**) to mend.

Fliege die (PL die **Fliegen**) 1 fly; 2 bow tie.

fliegen ◇ verb (IMPERF **flog**, PERF **ist geflogen**) 1 to fly; 2 **ich bin geflogen** (informal) I fell; 3 **Manfred ist geflogen** (informal) Manfred has been fired; 4 (PERF **hat geflogen**) to fly (a plane).

fliehen ◇ verb (IMPERF **floh**, PERF **ist geflohen**) to flee.

Fliese die (PL die **Fliesen**) tile.

Fließband das (PL die **Fließbänder**) 1 conveyor belt; 2 assembly line.

fließen ◇ verb (IMPERF **floss** Δ, PERF **ist geflossen**) to flow.

fließend adjective 1 running;

2 fluent; **fließendes Deutsch** fluent German; 3 moving (traffic).

Flitterwochen plural noun honeymoon.

flitzen verb (informal) (PERF **ist geflitzt**) 1 to dash; 2 to whizz.

Flocke die (PL die **Flocken**) flake.

flog SEE **fliegen**.

floh SEE **fliehen**.

Floh der (PL die **Flöhe**) flee.

Flohmarkt der (PL die **Flohmärkte**) flea market.

floss Δ SEE **fließen**.

Flosse die (PL die **Flossen**) 1 fin; 2 flipper.

Flöte die (PL die **Flöten**) flute.

fluchen verb (PERF **hat geflucht**) to curse.

Flüchtling der (PL die **Flüchtlinge**) refugee.

Flug der (PL die **Flüge**) flight.

Flugblatt das (PL die **Flugblätter**) pamphlet.

Flügel der (PL die **Flügel**) 1 wing; 2 grand piano.

Fluggast der (PL die **Fluggäste**) (air) passenger.

Fluggesellschaft die (PL die **Fluggesellschaften**) airline.

Flughafen der (PL die **Flughäfen**) airport.

Flugplatz der (PL die **Flugplätze**) 1 airport; 2 airfield.

◇ IRREGULAR VERB: See the verb table in the centre of the dictionary

Flugzeug *das* (PL die **Flugzeuge**) aeroplane.

Fluor *das* fluoride.

Flur *der* (PL die **Flure**) 1 hall; 2 corridor.

Fluss Δ *der* (PL die **Flüsse**) river.

flüssig *adjective* liquid.

Flüssigkeit *die* (PL die **Flüssigkeiten**) liquid.

flüstern *verb* (PERF **hat geflüstert**) to whisper.

Flut *die* (PL die **Fluten**) 1 high tide; 2 flood (*of letters, complaints*).

Flutlicht *das* floodlight.

focht SEE **fechten**.

Föhn Δ *der* (PL die **Föhne**) hair drier.

föhnen Δ *verb* (PERF **hat geföhnt**) to blow-dry.

Folge *die* (PL die **Folgen**) 1 consequence; 2 episode; 3 **etwas zur Folge haben** to result in something; 4 **an den Folgen eines Unfalls sterben** to die as the result of an accident.

folgen *verb* (PERF **ist gefolgt**) 1 to follow; **daraus folgt, dass** ... it follows that ...; **ich kann dir nicht folgen** I can't follow what you're saying; 2 (PERF **hat gefolgt**) to obey.

folgend *adjective* 1 following; 2 **Folgendes** the following.

Folgerung *die* (PL die **Folgerungen**) conclusion.

folgsam *adjective* obedient.

Folie *die* (PL die **Folien**) foil.

Fön™ = **Föhn**.

fönen = **föhnen**.

fordern *verb* (PERF **hat gefordert**) to demand.

fördern *verb* (PERF **hat gefördert**) 1 to promote; 2 to sponsor.

Forderung *die* (PL die **Forderungen**) 1 demand; 2 claim.

Forelle *die* (PL die **Forellen**) trout.

Form *die* (PL die **Formen**) 1 shape; 2 form; **in Form sein** to be on form; 3 tin (*for baking*).

Format *das* (PL die **Formate**) format.

formatieren *verb* (PERF **hat formatiert**) to format.

formen *verb* (PERF **hat geformt**) 1 to form; 2 **sich formen** to take shape.

förmlich *adjective* formal. *adverb* 1 formally; 2 **jemanden förmlich zwingen, etwas zu tun** to positively force somebody to do something; **ich hätte förmlich schreien können** I really could have screamed.

Formular *das* (PL die **Formulare**) form.

Forscher *der* (PL die **Forscher**) 1 researcher, research scientist; 2 explorer.

Forschung *die* (PL die **Forschungen**) research.

Forst *der* (PL die **Forste**) forest.

Förster *der* (PL die **Förster**) forester.

fort *adverb* 1 away; 2 **fort sein** to have gone; 3 **und so fort** and so on; 4 **in einem fort** on and on.

fortbewegen verb (PERF **hat fortbewegt**) 1 to move; 2 **sich fortbewegen** to move.

fortfahren ◇ verb (PRES **fährt fort**, IMPERF **fuhr fort**, PERF **ist fortgefahren**) 1 to leave; **wann fahrt ihr fort?** when are you leaving?; 2 to continue.

fortgeschritten adjective advanced.

Fortschritt der (PL die **Fortschritte**) progress; **Fortschritte machen** to make progress.

fortsetzen verb (PERF **hat fortgesetzt**) to continue.

Fortsetzung die (PL die **Fortsetzungen**) 1 continuation; 2 instalment.

Foto das (PL die **Fotos**) photo.

Fotoapparat der (PL die **Fotoapparate**) camera.

Fotograf der (PL die **Fotografen**) photographer.

Fotografie die (PL die **Fotografien**) 1 photography; 2 photograph.

fotografieren verb (PERF **hat fotografiert**) 1 to photograph, to take a photograph of; 2 to take photographs.

Fotografin die (PL die **Fotografinnen**) photographer.

Fotokopie die (PL die **Fotokopien**) photocopy.

Fracht die (PL die **Frachten**) freight, cargo.

Frage die (PL die **Fragen**) question;

etwas in Frage stellen to question something; **das kommt nicht in Frage** that's out of the question.

Fragebogen der (PL die **Fragebogen**) questionnaire.

fragen verb (PERF **hat gefragt**) 1 to ask; 2 **sich fragen** to wonder.

Fragezeichen das (PL die **Fragezeichen**) question mark.

fraglich adjective doubtful.

Franken[1] der (PL die **Franken**) (Swiss) franc.

Franken[2] das Franconia.

Frankreich das France.

Franzose der (PL die **Franzosen**) Frenchman.

Französin die (PL die **Französinnen**) Frenchwoman.

französisch adjective French.

Französisch das French.

fraß SEE **fressen**.

Frau die (PL die **Frauen**) 1 woman; 2 wife; 3 Mrs, Ms ('Frau' is usually used to address both married and unmarried women).

Fräulein das (PL die **Fräulein**) 1 young lady; 2 Miss; **Fräulein Schmidt** Miss Schmidt.

frech adjective cheeky.

Frechheit die (PL die **Frechheiten**) 1 cheek; 2 cheeky remark.

frei adjective 1 free; 2 freelance; 3 **ist dieser Platz frei?** is this seat taken?; 4 **ein freier Tag** a day off;

◇ IRREGULAR VERB: *See the verb table in the centre of the dictionary*

sich frei nehmen to take a day off;
5 **'Zimmer frei'** 'vacancies'.

Freibad das (PL die **Freibäder**) open-air swimming pool.

Freie das im **Freien** in the open air.

freigebig *adjective* generous.

Freiheit die (PL die **Freiheiten**)
1 freedom; 2 liberty; **sich Freiheiten erlauben** to take liberties.

freimachen *verb* (PERF **hat freigemacht**) 1 to take time off;
2 **sich freimachen** to take time off.

Freistoß der (PL die **Freistöße**) free kick.

Freitag der (PL die **Freitage**) Friday.

freitags *adverb* on Fridays.

freiwillig *adjective* voluntary.

Freizeit die 1 spare time; 2 leisure.

fremd *adjective* 1 foreign; 2 strange;
fremde Leute strangers; **ich bin hier fremd** I'm a stranger here.

Fremde der/die (PL die **Fremden**)
1 foreigner; 2 stranger.

Fremdenverkehr der tourism.

Fremdenverkehrsbüro das (PL die **Fremdenverkehrsbüros**) tourist office.

Fremdenzimmer das (PL die **Fremdenzimmer**) room (to let).

Fremdsprache die (PL die **Fremdsprachen**) foreign language.

fressen ✧ *verb* (PRES **frisst** Δ, IMPERF **fraß**, PERF **hat gefressen**) to eat.

Freude die (PL die **Freuden**) 1 joy;
2 pleasure; **mit Freuden** with pleasure; 3 **an etwas Freude haben** to be delighted with something;
4 **jemandem eine Freude machen** to please somebody.

freuen *verb* (PERF **hat sich gefreut**)
1 **sich freuen** to be pleased; **sich über etwas freuen** to be pleased about something; 2 **sich auf etwas freuen** to look forward to something.

Freund der (PL die **Freunde**)
1 friend; 2 boyfriend.

Freundin die (PL die **Freundinnen**)
1 friend; 2 girlfriend.

freundlich *adjective* 1 friendly;
2 kind.

freundlicherweise *adverb* kindly.

Freundlichkeit die friendliness.

Freundschaft die (PL die **Freundschaften**) friendship.

Frieden der peace.

Friedhof der (PL die **Friedhöfe**) cemetery.

friedlich *adjective* peaceful.

frieren ✧ *verb* (IMPERF **fror**, PERF **hat gefroren**) 1 to be cold; **frierst du?** are you cold?; 2 **es friert** it's freezing, it's frosty; 3 (PERF **ist gefroren**) to freeze.

Frikadelle die (PL die **Frikadellen**) rissole.

frisch *adjective* fresh; **sich frisch machen** to freshen up.
adverb freshly; **'frisch gestrichen'** 'wet paint'.

Friseur *der* (PL *die* **Friseure**) hairdresser.

Friseuse *die* (PL *die* **Friseusen**) hairdresser.

frisieren *verb* (PERF **hat frisiert**) **1 jemanden frisieren** to do somebody's hair; **2 sich frisieren** to do your hair.

frisst △ SEE **fressen**.

Frisur *die* (PL *die* **Frisuren**) hairstyle, hairdo.

froh *adjective* **1** happy; **frohe Weihnachten!** happy Christmas!; **2 über etwas froh sein** to be glad about something.

fröhlich *adjective* cheerful.

Fröhlichkeit *die* cheerfulness.

fromm *adjective* devout.

fror SEE **frieren**.

Frosch *der* (PL *die* **Frösche**) frog.

Frost *der* (PL *die* **Fröste**) frost.

frostig *adjective* frosty.

Frottee *das* (PL *die* **Frottees**) towelling.

Frottiertuch *das* (PL *die* **Frottiertücher**) towel.

Frucht *die* (PL *die* **Früchte**) fruit.

fruchtbar *adjective* fertile.

Fruchtsaft *der* (PL *die* **Fruchtsäfte**) fruit juice.

früh *adjective, adverb* **1** early; **von früh auf** from an early age; **2 heute früh** this morning.

Frühe *die* **in aller Frühe** at the crack of dawn.

früher *adjective* **1** earlier; **2** former. *adverb* **1** earlier; **2** formerly; **3 früher war sie ganz anders** she used to be quite different; **das war früher ein Blumengeschäft** it used to be a florist's.

frühestens *adverb* at the earliest.

Frühjahr *das* (PL *die* **Frühjahre**) spring; **im Frühjahr** in spring.

Frühling *der* (PL *die* **Frühlinge**) spring; **im Frühling** in spring.

Frühstück *das* (PL *die* **Frühstücke**) breakfast.

frühstücken *verb* (PERF **hat gefrühstückt**) to have breakfast.

frühzeitig *adjective* early.

Fuchs *der* (PL *die* **Füchse**) fox.

fühlen *verb* (PERF **hat gefühlt**) **1** to feel; **2 sich krank fühlen** to feel ill.

fuhr SEE **fahren**.

führen *verb* (PERF **hat geführt**) **1** to lead; **sie führt mit fünf Punkten** she is five points in the lead; **unsere Mannschaft führt** our team's winning; **2** to run (*a shop or business*); **3** to show round; **4** to keep (*a diary, list*); **5 ein Telefongespräch führen** to make a phone call.

Führer *der* (PL *die* **Führer**) **1** leader; **2** guide.

Führerschein *der* (PL *die* **Führerscheine**) driving licence; **den Führerschein machen** to take your driving test.

✧ IRREGULAR VERB: *See the verb table in the centre of the dictionary*

Führung *die* (PL *die* **Führungen**)
1 leadership; 2 guided tour;
3 management (*of a shop*); 4 **in
Führung** in the lead.

füllen *verb* (PERF **hat gefüllt**) 1 to
fill; 2 to stuff (*a turkey, peppers*);
3 **sich füllen** to fill (up).

Füller *der* (PL *die* **Füller**) fountain
pen.

Füllfederhalter *der* (PL *die*
Füllfederhalter) fountain pen.

Füllung *die* (PL *die* **Füllungen**) filling.

Fundament *das* (PL *die*
Fundamente) foundations.

Fundbüro *das* (PL *die* **Fundbüros**)
lost property office.

fünf *number* five.

fünfhundert *number* five hundred.

Fünftel *das* (PL *die* **Fünftel**) fifth.

fünfter, fünfte, fünftes *adjective*
fifth.

fünfzehn *number* fifteen.

fünfzig *number* fifty.

Funke *der* (PL *die* **Funken**) spark.

funkeln *verb* (PERF **hat gefunkelt**)
1 to sparkle; 2 to twinkle (*of a star*).

funktionieren *verb* (PERF **hat
funktioniert**) to work.

für *preposition* ←(+ACC) 1 for; 2 **was
für ein ...?** what sort of ... ?; 3 **für
sich** by yourself; **jetzt habe ich das
Haus ganz für mich** now I've got
the house to myself; 4 **das Für und
Wider** the pros and cons.

Furcht *die* fear.

furchtbar *adjective* terrible.

fürchten *verb* (PERF **hat gefürchtet**)
1 to fear; 2 **sich fürchten** to be
afraid; **ich fürchte mich vor ihm** I'm
afraid of him; **ich fürchte, das geht
nicht** I'm afraid that's not possible.

fürchterlich *adjective* dreadful.

füreinander *adverb* for each other.

fürs = **für das.**

Fürsorge *die* 1 care; 2 welfare;
3 (*informal*) social security.

Fuß *der* (PL *die* **Füße**) 1 foot; **zu Fuß**
on foot; **zu Fuß gehen** to walk;
2 base.

Fußball *der* (PL *die* **Fußbälle**)
football.

Fußballplatz *der* (PL *die*
Fußballplätze) football pitch.

Fußballspiel *das* (PL *die*
Fußballspiele) football match.

Fußballspieler *der* (PL *die*
Fußballspieler) footballer.

Fußboden *der* (PL *die* **Fußböden**)
floor.

Fußgänger *der* (PL *die* **Fußgänger**)
pedestrian.

Fußgängerzone *die* (PL *die*
Fußgängerzonen) pedestrian
precinct.

Fußweg *der* (PL *die* **Fußwege**)
footpath.

Futter *das* 1 feed; **ich habe dem
Hund schon Futter gegeben** I've

Δ NEW SPELLING: *See page xii*

already given the dog his food;
2 lining (*of clothes*).

füttern *verb* (PERF **hat gefüttert**) **1** to
feed; **2** to line.

Futur *das* (PL *die* **Future**) future
(*tense*).

G g

gab SEE **geben**.

Gabel *die* (PL *die* **Gabeln**) fork.

gähnen *verb* (PERF **hat gegähnt**) to
yawn.

Galerie *die* (PL *die* **Galerien**) gallery.

galoppieren *verb* (PERF **ist
galoppiert**) to gallop.

Gammler *der* (PL *die* **Gammler**)
drop-out.

Gammlerin *die* (PL *die*
Gammlerinnen) drop-out.

Gang *der* (PL *die* **Gänge**) **1** walk;
2 errand; **3** corridor; **4** ein Platz am
Gang an aisle seat; **5** course (*of a
meal*); **6** gear (*of a car*); **7** in Gang
setzen to get going; **8** im Gange in
progress.

gängig *adjective* **1** common;
2 popular (*goods*).

Gans *die* (PL *die* **Gänse**) goose.

Gänseblümchen *das* (PL *die*
Gänseblümchen) daisy.

Gänsehaut *die* goose pimples.

ganz *adjective* whole; **1** ganz
Deutschland the whole of
Germany; **2** im Großen und Ganzen
on the whole; **3** eine ganze Menge
quite a lot; **4** all; **mein ganzes Geld**
all my money; **die ganzen Leute** all
the people; **5** etwas wieder ganz
machen to mend something.
adverb **1** quite; **es war ganz gut** it
was quite good; **2** ganz und gar
completely; **3** ganz und gar nicht
not at all.

ganztägig *adjective, adverb* **1** full-
time; **2** all-day; **ganztägig geöffnet**
open all day.

ganztags *adverb* **1** full time; **2** all
day.

gar *adjective* done, cooked.
adverb **1** gar nicht not at all; **gar
nichts** nothing; **2** oder gar or
even.

Garage *die* (PL *die* **Garagen**) garage.

Garantie *die* (PL *die* **Garantien**)
guarantee.

garantieren *verb* (PERF **hat
garantiert**) to guarantee.

Garderobe *die* (PL *die* **Garderoben**)
cloakroom; **wir können die Mäntel
an der Garderobe abgeben** we can
leave the coats in the cloakroom.

Gardine *die* (PL *die* **Gardinen**)
curtain.

Garn *das* (PL *die* **Garne**) thread.

Garnele *die* (PL *die* **Garnelen**)
1 shrimp; **2** prawn.

Garten *der* (PL *die* **Gärten**) garden.

Gärtner *der* (PL *die* **Gärtner**)
gardener.

✧ IRREGULAR VERB: See the verb table in the centre of the dictionary

Gärtnerin die (PL die **Gärtnerinnen**) gardener.

Gas das (PL die **Gase**) 1 gas; 2 **Gas geben** to accelerate.

Gasherd der (PL die **Gasherde**) gas cooker.

Gaspedal das (PL die **Gaspedale**) accelerator.

Gasse die (PL die **Gassen**) lane.

Gast der (PL die **Gäste**) 1 guest; **wir haben heute Abend Gäste** we've got guests tonight; 2 **bei jemandem zu Gast sein** to be staying with somebody.

Gastarbeiter der (PL die **Gastarbeiter**) foreign worker, guest worker.

Gästezimmer das (PL die **Gästezimmer**) 1 (hotel) room; 2 spare room.

gastfreundlich adjective hospitable.

Gastfreundschaft die hospitality.

Gastgeber der (PL die **Gastgeber**) host.

Gastgeberin die (PL die **Gastgeberinnen**) host.

Gasthaus das (PL die **Gasthäuser**) inn.

Gasthof der (PL die **Gasthöfe**) inn.

Gaststätte die (PL die **Gaststätten**) restaurant.

Gauner der (PL die **Gauner**) crook.

Gebäck das 1 pastries; 2 biscuits.

gebären ◇ verb (IMPERF **gebar**, PERF hat geboren) 1 to give birth to; 2 **geboren werden** to be born.

Gebäude das (PL die **Gebäude**) building.

geben ◇ verb (PRES **gibt**, IMPERF **gab**, PERF **hat gegeben**) 1 to give; 2 to deal (cards); 3 to teach (at school); 4 **geben Sie mir bitte Frau Scheck** please put me through to Mrs Scheck; 5 **es gibt** there is, there are; **es gibt viele gute Restaurants in München** there are lots of good restaurants in Munich; **was gibt's im Kino?** what's on at the cinema?; **was gibt es zum Mittagessen?** what are we having for lunch?; 6 **was gibt's Neues?** what's the news?, what's new?; 7 **sich geschlagen geben** to admit defeat; 8 **das gibt sich wieder** it'll get better; 9 **das gibt's doch nicht!** I don't believe it!

Gebet das (PL die **Gebete**) prayer.

gebeten SEE **bitten**.

Gebiet das (PL die **Gebiete**) 1 area; 2 field.

gebildet adjective educated.

Gebirge das (PL die **Gebirge**) mountain range; **im Gebirge** in the mountains.

Gebiss Δ das (PL die **Gebisse**) 1 teeth; 2 false teeth, dentures.

gebissen SEE **beißen**.

geblieben SEE **bleiben**.

geboren verb SEE **gebären**. adjective 1 born; 2 née; **Frau Hahn, geborene Müller** Mrs Hahn, née Müller.

Δ NEW SPELLING: *See page xii*

geborgen *adjective* safe.

geboten SEE **bieten**.

gebracht SEE **bringen**.

gebraten *adjective* fried.

Gebrauch *der* (PL *die* **Gebräuche**)
1 use; **vor Gebrauch schütteln**
shake before use; 2 custom.

gebrauchen *verb* (PERF **hat
gebraucht**) to use.

Gebrauchsanweisung *die* (PL *die*
Gebrauchsanweisungen)
instructions (for use).

gebraucht *adjective* used, secondhand.

Gebrauchtwagen *der* (PL *die*
Gebrauchtwagen) second-hand
car.

gebrochen SEE **brechen**.

Gebühr *die* (PL *die* **Gebühren**) fee,
charge.

gebührenfrei *adjective* free (of
charge).

gebührenpflichtig *adjective*
1 subject to a charge; 2 **eine
gebührenpflichtige Straße** a toll
road.

gebunden SEE **binden**.

Geburt *die* (PL *die* **Geburten**) birth.

Geburtenregelung *die* birth
control.

Geburtsdatum *das* (PL *die*
Geburtsdaten) date of birth.

Geburtsort *der* (PL *die*
Geburtsorte) place of birth.

Geburtstag *der* (PL *die*
Geburtstage) birthday.

Geburtsurkunde *die* (PL *die*
Geburtsurkunden) birth certificate.

gedacht SEE **denken**.

Gedächtnis *das* (PL *die*
Gedächtnisse) memory.

Gedanke *der* (PL *die* **Gedanken**)
1 thought; **in Gedanken versunken
sein** to be lost in thought; 2 **sich
Gedanken machen** to worry;
3 **jemanden auf andere Gedanken
bringen** to take somebody's mind
off things.

gedankenlos *adjective*
thoughtless.
adverb without thinking.

Gedeck *das* (PL *die* **Gedecke**)
1 place setting; 2 set meal.

Gedicht *das* (PL *die* **Gedichte**) poem.

Geduld *die* patience.

geduldig *adjective* patient.

gedurft SEE **dürfen**.

geehrt *adjective* 1 honoured;
2 **Sehr geehrte Frau Ross** Dear
Mrs Ross.

geeignet *adjective* 1 suitable;
2 right.

Gefahr *die* (PL *die* **Gefahren**)
1 danger; **außer Gefahr** out of
danger; 2 **auf eigene Gefahr** at your
own risk; **Gefahr laufen, etwas zu
tun** to run the risk of doing
something.

gefährlich *adjective* dangerous.

gefallen¹ SEE **fallen**.

✧ IRREGULAR VERB: *See the verb table in the centre of the dictionary*

gefallen² ⟡ *verb* (PRES **gefällt**, IMPERF **gefiel**, PERF **hat gefallen**) **1** **es gefällt mir** I like it; **es hat mir sehr gut gefallen** I liked it a lot; **2** **sich etwas gefallen lassen** to put up with something.

Gefallen¹ *der* (PL **die Gefallen**) favour.

Gefallen² *das* pleasure; **dir zu Gefallen** to please you.

Gefangene *der/die* (PL **die Gefangenen**) prisoner.

Gefängnis *das* (PL **die Gefängnisse**) prison.

Gefäß *das* (PL **die Gefäße**) container.

gefasst △ *adjective* **1** calm, composed; **2** **auf etwas gefasst sein** to be prepared for something.

gefiel SEE **gefallen**.

geflogen SEE **fliegen**.

geflossen SEE **fließen**.

Geflügel *das* poultry.

gefochten SEE **fechten**.

gefräßig *adjective* (*informal*) greedy.

gefrieren ⟡ *verb* (IMPERF **gefror**, PERF **ist gefroren**) to freeze.

Gefrierfach *das* (PL **die Gefrierfächer**) freezer (compartment).

gefroren *adjective* frozen.

Gefühl *das* (PL **die Gefühle**) **1** feeling; **2** **etwas im Gefühl haben** to have a feel for something.

gefüllt *adjective* stuffed (*peppers, for example*).

gefunden SEE **finden**.

gegangen SEE **gehen**.

gegeben SEE **geben**.

gegebenenfalls *adverb* if need be.

gegen *preposition* ←(+ACC)
1 against; **2** **gegen die Mauer fahren** to drive into the wall; **3** **ein Mittel gegen Grippe** a cure for flu; **4** towards; **gegen Abend** towards evening; **5** **gegen vier Uhr** around four o'clock; **6** compared with; **7** versus (*in sport*).

Gegend *die* (PL **die Gegenden**) **1** area; **2** neighbourhood.

gegeneinander *adverb* against each other, against one another.

Gegenmittel *das* (PL **die Gegenmittel**) **1** remedy; **2** antidote.

Gegensatz *der* (PL **die Gegensätze**) **1** contrast; **2** opposite; **3** **im Gegensatz zu mir** unlike me.

gegenseitig *adjective* mutual. *adverb* **sich gegenseitig helfen** to help each other.

Gegenstand *der* (PL **die Gegenstände**) **1** object; **2** subject (*in grammar or of a discussion*).

Gegenteil *das* (PL **die Gegenteile**) **1** opposite; **2** **im Gegenteil** on the contrary.

gegenüber *preposition* ←(+DAT)
1 opposite; **Susi saß mir gegenüber** Susi sat opposite me; **2** compared with; **3** towards; **jemandem gegenüber freundlich sein** to be friendly towards

△ NEW SPELLING: *See page xii*

somebody.
adverb opposite; **meine Freundin
wohnt gegenüber** my friend lives
opposite.

Gegenwart *die* **1** present;
2 presence.

gegessen SEE **essen**.

Gegner *der* (PL *die* **Gegner**)
opponent.

gegrillt *adjective* grilled.

Gehackte *das* mince.

Gehalt *das* (PL *die* **Gehälter**) salary.

gehässig *adjective* spiteful.

geheim *adjective* secret.

Geheimnis *das* (PL *die*
Geheimnisse) secret.

geheimnisvoll *adjective*
mysterious.

gehen ✧ *verb* (IMPERF **ging**, PERF **ist
gegangen**) **1** to go; **schlafen gehen**
to go to bed; **2** to walk; **3** **über die
Straße gehen** to cross the road;
4 **es geht ihr gut** she's well; **wie geht
es Ihnen?** how are you?; **es geht**
it's not too bad; **5** **das geht nicht**
that's impossible; **6** **um etwas
gehen** to be about something;
worum geht's hier? what's it all
about?; **7** **die Uhr geht falsch** the
clock's wrong.

Gehirn *das* (PL *die* **Gehirne**) brain.

Gehirnerschütterung *die* (PL *die*
Gehirnerschütterungen)
concussion.

gehoben SEE **heben**.

geholfen SEE **helfen**.

Gehör *das* hearing.

gehorchen *verb* (PERF **hat
gehorcht**) to obey.

gehören *verb* (PERF **hat gehört**) **1** to
belong; **es gehört mir** it belongs to
me; **2 dazu gehört Mut** that takes
courage; **3 es gehört sich nicht** it
isn't done.

gehorsam *adjective* obedient.

Gehsteig *der* (PL *die* **Gehsteige**)
pavement.

Geige *die* (PL *die* **Geigen**) violin.

Geisel *die* (PL *die* **Geiseln**) hostage.

Geist *der* (PL *die* **Geister**) **1** mind;
2 ghost; **3** wit.

geistesabwesend *adjective*
absent-minded.

Geisteskrankheit *die* (PL *die*
Geisteskrankheiten) mental illness.

Geisteswissenschaften (*plural
noun*) arts, humanities.

geistig *adjective* mental.

geizig *adjective* mean.

gekannt SEE **kennen**.

gekonnt SEE **können**.

Gel *das* (PL *die* **Gele**) gel.

Gelächter *das* (PL *die* **Gelächter**)
laughter.

geladen SEE **laden**.

gelähmt *adjective* paralysed.

Geländer *das* (PL *die* **Geländer**)
1 banister(s); **2** railing(s).

gelangweilt *adjective* bored.

✧ IRREGULAR VERB: *See the verb table in the centre of the dictionary*

gelassen *verb* SEE **lassen**.
adjective calm.

geläufig *adjective* 1 common; 2 **das
ist mir nicht geläufig** I'm not
familiar with it.

gelaunt *adjective* **gut gelaunt sein**
to be in a good mood.

gelb *adjective* yellow.

Geld *das* (PL *die* **Gelder**) money.

Geldautomat *der* (PL *die*
Geldautomaten) cash dispenser.

Geldbörse *die* (PL *die* **Geldbörsen**)
purse.

Geldschein *der* (PL *die*
Geldscheine) banknote.

Geldstrafe *die* (PL *die* **Geldstrafen**)
fine.

Geldwechsel *der* 1 bureau de
change; 2 currency exchange.

gelegen SEE **liegen**.

Gelegenheit *die* (PL *die*
Gelegenheiten) 1 opportunity;
2 occasion.

gelegentlich *adverb* occasionally.

Gelenk *das* (PL *die* **Gelenke**) joint.

Geliebte *der/die* (PL *die* **Geliebten**)
lover.

geliehen SEE **leihen**.

gelingen ◇ *verb* (IMPERF **gelang**,
PERF **ist gelungen**) to succeed; **es ist
mir gelungen, sie zu überreden** I
succeeded in persuading her.

gelten ◇ *verb* (PRES **gilt**, IMPERF **galt**,
PERF **hat gegolten**) 1 to be valid;
2 to apply (*of a rule*); 3 **jemandem**

gelten to be directed at somebody;
4 **sein Wort gilt viel** his word is
worth a lot; 5 **das gilt nicht** that
doesn't count; 6 **als etwas gelten**
to be regarded as something.

gelungen *verb* SEE **gelingen**.
adjective successful.

Gemälde *das* (PL *die* **Gemälde**)
painting.

gemein *adjective* mean.

Gemeinde *die* (PL *die* **Gemeinden**)
1 community; 2 congregation.

gemeinsam *adjective* 1 common;
2 joint.
adverb together; **gemeinsam
essen** to eat together.

Gemeinschaft *die* (PL *die*
Gemeinschaften) community.

gemischt *adjective* mixed.

gemocht SEE **mögen**.

Gemüse *das* (PL *die* **Gemüse**)
vegetables.

Gemüsehändler *der* (PL *die*
Gemüsehändler) greengrocer.

gemusst △ SEE **müssen**.

gemustert *adjective* patterned.

gemütlich *adjective* 1 cosy; 2 **mach
es dir gemütlich** make yourself
comfortable.

genannt SEE **nennen**.

genau *adjective* 1 exact; 2 accurate
(*scales, description*); 3 meticulous;
4 **ich weiß nichts Genaues** I don't
know any details.
adverb 1 exactly; 2 **genau
genommen** △ strictly speaking.

△ NEW SPELLING: *See page xii*

Genauigkeit *die* accuracy.

genauso *adverb* 1 just the same; 2 **genauso gut** just as good; **genauso viel** just as much, just as many; **genauso lange** just as long.

Genehmigung *die* (PL *die* **Genehmigungen**) 1 permission; 2 permit; 3 licence.

Generation *die* (PL *die* **Generationen**) generation.

generell *adjective* general.

Genetik *die* genetics.

Genf *das* Geneva.

Genfer See *der* Lake Geneva.

genial *adjective* brilliant.

Genick *das* (PL *die* **Genicke**) (back of the) neck.

Genie *das* (PL *die* **Genies**) genius.

genießbar *adjective* edible.

genießen ✧ *verb* (IMPERF **genoss** △, PERF **hat genossen**) to enjoy.

genommen SEE **nehmen**.

genug *adverb* enough.

genügen *verb* (PERF **hat genügt**) to be enough.

genügend *adjective* 1 enough; 2 sufficient.

Genuss △ *der* (PL *die* **Genüsse**) 1 enjoyment; 2 consumption (*of alcohol*).

geöffnet *adjective* open.

Geometrie *die* geometry.

Gepäck *das* luggage.

Gepäckausgabe *die* left-luggage office.

Gepäckaufbewahrung *die* left-luggage office.

Gepäckträger *der* (PL *die* **Gepäckträger**) 1 porter; 2 roof rack; 3 carrier (*on a bike*).

gerade *adjective* 1 straight; 2 **etwa gerade biegen** △ to straighten something; 3 upright; 4 **eine gerade Zahl** an even number. *adverb* 1 just; **gerade erst** only just; 2 **es war nicht gerade billig** wasn't exactly cheap.

geradeaus *adverb* straight ahead.

geradebiegen SEE **gerade**.

gerannt SEE **rennen**.

Gerät *das* (PL *die* **Geräte**) 1 appliance; 2 set (*TV or radio*); 3 tool; 4 gadget; 5 **die Geräte** apparatus (*in gymnastics*).

geraten ✧ *verb* (PRES **gerät**, IMPERF **geriet**, PERF **ist geraten**) 1 to get (*somewhere, the wrong side of the road etc.*); **in etwas geraten** to get into something; **in Wut geraten** to get angry; 2 **an den Richtigen geraten** to come to the right person; 3 **gut/schlecht geraten** to turn out well/badly; 4 **nach jemandem geraten** to take after somebody.

geräuchert *adjective* smoked.

geräumig *adjective* spacious.

Geräusch *das* (PL *die* **Geräusche**) noise.

gerecht *adjective* 1 just; 2 fair.

✧ IRREGULAR VERB: *See the verb table in the centre of the dictionary*

Gerechtigkeit *die* justice.

Gerede *das* gossip.

Gericht *das* (PL *die* **Gerichte**)
1 court; 2 dish.

gerieben SEE **reiben**.

gering *adjective* 1 small (*amount*);
2 low (*value*); 3 short (*time,
distance*).

Gerippe *das* (PL *die* **Gerippe**)
skeleton.

gerissen *adjective* crafty.

geritten SEE **reiten**.

gern(e) *adverb* 1 gladly;
2 **jemanden gern haben** to like
somebody; **etwas gern tun** to like
doing something; **ich tanze gern** I
like dancing; **ich hätte gerne einen
Kaffee** I'd like a coffee; 3 **ja, gern!**
yes, I'd love to!; 4 **das glaube ich
gern** I can well believe that.

Gerste *die* barley.

Geruch *der* (PL *die* **Gerüche**) smell.

Gerücht *das* (PL *die* **Gerüchte**)
rumour.

Gerümpel *das* junk.

gesalzen *verb* SEE **salzen**.
adjective 1 salted; 2 **gesalzene
Preise** (*informal*) steep prices.

gesamt *adjective* 1 whole; 2 **die
gesamten Kosten** the total cost;
3 **die gesamten Werke** the
complete works.

Gesamtschule *die* (PL *die*
Gesamtschulen) comprehensive
school.

gesandt SEE **senden**.

Geschäft *das* (PL *die* **Geschäfte**)
1 shop; 2 business; 3 deal.

Geschäftsführer *der* (PL *die*
Geschäftsführer) manager.

Geschäftsführerin *die* (PL *die*
Geschäftsführerinnen)
manageress.

Geschäftszeiten *plural noun*
business hours.

geschehen ◇ *verb* (PRES
geschieht, IMPERF **geschah**, PERF **ist
geschehen**) to happen.

gescheit *adjective* clever.

Geschenk *das* (PL *die* **Geschenke**)
present, gift.

Geschichte *die* (PL *die*
Geschichten) 1 story; 2 history;
3 **mach bloß keine große
Geschichte daraus** don't make such
a thing of it.

Geschick *das* 1 skill; 2 fate.

geschickt *adjective* 1 skilful;
2 clever.

geschieden *verb* SEE **scheiden**.
adjective divorced.

geschienen SEE **scheinen**.

Geschirr *das* 1 crockery; 2 dishes.

Geschirrspülmaschine *die* (PL
die **Geschirrspülmaschinen**)
dishwasher.

Geschirrtuch *das* (PL *die*
Geschirrtücher) tea towel.

Geschlecht *das* (PL *die*
Geschlechter) 1 sex; 2 gender.

△ NEW SPELLING: *See page xii*

geschlossen verb SEE **schließen**. *adjective* closed.

Geschmack der (PL die **Geschmäcke**) taste.

geschmacklos *adjective* 1 tasteless; 2 **geschmacklos sein** to be in bad taste.

geschnitten SEE **schneiden**.

geschossen SEE **schießen**.

geschrieben SEE **schreiben**.

geschrien SEE **schreien**.

Geschwätz das talk.

geschwätzig *adjective* talkative.

Geschwindigkeit die (PL die **Geschwindigkeiten**) speed.

Geschwindigkeits- beschränkung die (PL die **Geschwindigkeitsbeschränkungen**) speed limit.

Geschwister *plural noun* brothers and sisters, siblings.

geschwommen SEE **schwimmen**.

gesellig *adjective* sociable.

Gesellschaft die (PL die **Gesellschaften**) 1 society; 2 company; **ich leiste dir Gesellschaft** I'll keep you company; 3 party.

gesessen SEE **sitzen**.

Gesetz das (PL die **Gesetze**) law.

gesetzlich *adjective* legal; **ein gesetzlicher Feiertag** a public holiday.

Gesicht das (PL die **Gesichter**) face.

Gesichtsausdruck der (facial) expression.

gesollt SEE **sollen**.

gespannt *adjective* 1 eager; 2 **auf etwas gespannt sein** to look forward eagerly to something; **auf jemanden gespannt sein** to look forward to seeing somebody; 3 **ich bin gespannt, ob** … I wonder whether …; 4 tense; **in Südafrika is die Lage immer noch gespannt** th situation in South Africa is still tens

Gespenst das (PL die **Gespenster**) ghost.

Gespräch das (PL die **Gespräche**) 1 conversation; 2 call (*on the phone*).

gesprächig *adjective* talkative.

gesprochen SEE **sprechen**.

gesprungen SEE **springen**.

Gestalt die (PL die **Gestalten**) 1 figure; 2 form.

gestanden SEE **stehen**, **gestehen**.

Geständnis das (PL die **Geständnisse**) confession.

gestatten verb (PERF **hat gestattet** 1 to permit; 2 **nicht gestattet** prohibited; 3 **gestatten Sie?** may I?

Geste die (PL die **Gesten**) gesture.

gestehen ◇ verb (IMPERF **gestand**, PERF **hat gestanden**) to confess.

Gestell das (PL die **Gestelle**) 1 rack; 2 stand; 3 frame.

gestern *adverb* 1 yesterday; 2 **gestern Nacht** last night.

◇ IRREGULAR VERB: *See the verb table in the centre of the dictionary*

gestohlen SEE **stehlen**.

gestorben SEE **sterben**.

gestreift *adjective* striped.

gesund *adjective* 1 healthy;
2 **wieder gesund werden** to get
well again; 3 **Schwimmen ist
gesund** swimming is good for you.

Gesundheit die 1 health;
2 **Gesundheit!** bless you! (*said after
a sneeze*).

gesungen SEE **singen**.

getan SEE **tun**.

Getränk das (PL die **Getränke**) drink.

Getränkekarte die (PL die
Getränkekarten) wine list.

getrauen *verb* (PERF **hat sich
getraut**) **sich getrauen** to dare.

Getreide das grain.

Getriebe das (PL die **Getriebe**)
gearbox.

getrieben SEE **treiben**.

getroffen SEE **treffen**.

getrunken SEE **trinken**.

Getue das fuss.

geübt *adjective* 1 accomplished;
2 **mit geübtem Auge** with a
practised eye.

Gewächshaus das (PL die
Gewächshäuser) greenhouse.

Gewalt die 1 power; 2 force; **mit
Gewalt** by force; 3 violence.

gewaltig *adjective* enormous.

gewalttätig *adjective* violent.

gewann SEE **gewinnen**.

Gewebe das (PL die **Gewebe**)
1 fabric; 2 tissue.

Gewehr das (PL die **Gewehre**) rifle,
gun.

Gewerkschaft die (PL die
Gewerkschaften) trade union.

gewesen SEE **sein**.

Gewicht das (PL die **Gewichte**)
weight.

Gewinn der (PL die **Gewinne**)
1 profit; 2 winnings; 3 prize.

gewinnen ◇ *verb* (IMPERF **gewann**,
PERF **hat gewonnen**) 1 to win; 2 to
gain (*time or influence*); **an
Bedeutung gewinnen** to gain in
importance.

Gewinner der (PL die **Gewinner**)
winner.

Gewinnerin die (PL die
Gewinnerinnen) winner.

gewiss Δ *adjective* certain; **ein
gewisser Herr Schmidt möchte Sie
sprechen** a Mr Schmidt would like
to speak to you.
adverb certainly; **'darf ich?' 'aber
gewiss doch'** 'may I?' 'but of
course'.

Gewissen das (PL die **Gewissen**)
conscience.

gewissenhaft *adjective*
conscientious.

gewissermaßen *adverb* 1 more or
less; 2 as it were.

Gewitter das (PL die **Gewitter**)
thunderstorm.

Δ NEW SPELLING: *See page xii*

gewöhnen *verb* (PERF **hat gewöhnt**) 1 **jemanden an etwas gewöhnen** to get somebody used to something; 2 **an etwas gewöhnt sein** to be used to something; 3 **sich an etwas gewöhnen** to get used to something.

Gewohnheit *die* (PL *die* **Gewohnheiten**) habit.

gewöhnlich *adjective* 1 usual; 2 ordinary.
adverb usually; **wie gewöhnlich** as usual.

gewohnt *adjective* 1 usual; 2 **etwas gewohnt sein** to be used to something; **Renate ist es nicht gewohnt, früh aufzustehen** Renate isn't used to getting up early.

gewollt SEE **wollen**.

gewonnen SEE **gewinnen**.

geworden SEE **werden**.

geworfen SEE **werfen**.

Gewürz *das* (PL *die* **Gewürze**) spice.

gewusst ∆ SEE **wissen**.

Gezeiten *plural noun* tides.

gezogen SEE **ziehen**.

gezwungen SEE **zwingen**.

gibt SEE **geben**.

gierig *adjective* greedy.

gießen ✧ *verb* (IMPERF **goss** ∆, PERF **hat gegossen**) 1 to pour; **es gießt** it's pouring; 2 to water; **vergiss nicht, die Blumen zu gießen** don't forget to water the flowers.

Gießkanne *die* (PL *die* **Gießkannen**) watering can.

Gift *das* (PL *die* **Gifte**) poison.

giftig *adjective* 1 poisonous; 2 toxic.

ging SEE **gehen**.

Gipfel *der* (PL *die* **Gipfel**) 1 peak, summit; 2 **der Gipfel der Geschmacklosigkeit** the height of bad taste.

Gips *der* plaster.

Girokonto *das* (PL *die* **Girokonten**) current account.

Giraffe *die* (PL *die* **Giraffen**) giraffe.

Gitarre *die* (PL *die* **Gitarren**) guitar.

Gitter *das* (PL *die* **Gitter**) 1 grid; 2 bars.

glänzen *verb* (PERF **hat geglänzt**) to shine.

glänzend *adjective* 1 shining; 2 brilliant; **ein glänzender Erfolg** a brilliant success.

Glas *das* (PL *die* **Gläser**) 1 glass; 2 jar.

Glasscheibe *die* (PL *die* **Glasscheiben**) pane (of glass).

glatt *adjective* 1 smooth; 2 slippery; 3 **eine glatte Absage** a flat refusal.
adverb 1 smoothly; 2 flatly; **etwas glatt ablehnen** to flatly reject something; 3 **das ist glatt gelogen** that's a downright lie; 4 **ich habe ihren Geburtstag glatt vergessen** I totally forgot about her birthday.

Glatteis *das* (black) ice.

Glatze *die* (PL *die* **Glatzen**) **eine Glatze haben** to be bald; **eine Glatze bekommen** to go bald.

✧ IRREGULAR VERB: *See the verb table in the centre of the dictionary*

glauben *verb* (PERF **hat geglaubt**) **1** to believe; **an Gott glauben** to believe in God; **2** to think; **3 nicht zu glauben!** incredible!

gleich *adjective* **1** same; **2** identical; **3 gleich bleibend** △ constant; **4 das ist mir gleich** it's all the same to me; **ganz gleich, wer anruft** no matter who calls.
adverb **1** the same; **2** equally; **3** immediately; **4 gleich neben** right next to; **5 er ist gleich fertig** he'll be ready in a minute.

gleichartig *adjective* similar.

gleichberechtigt *adjective* equal.

Gleichberechtigung *die* equality.

gleichbleibend SEE **gleich**.

gleichen ◇ *verb* (IMPERF **glich**, PERF **hat geglichen**) **1** to be like; **2 sich gleichen** to be alike.

gleichfalls *adverb* **1** also; **2 danke gleichfalls!** the same to you!

Gleichgewicht *das* balance.

gleichgültig *adjective* indifferent; **das ist doch gleichgültig** it's not important.

gleichzeitig *adverb* at the same time.

Gleis *das* (PL *die* **Gleise**) **1** track, line; **2** platform; **Gleis vier** platform four.

glich SEE **gleichen**.

Glied *das* (PL *die* **Glieder**) **1** limb; **2** link.

glitschig *adjective* slippery.

glitzern *verb* (PERF **hat geglitzert**) to glitter.

Glocke *die* (PL *die* **Glocken**) bell.

Glück *das* **1** luck; **viel Glück!** good luck!; **Glück haben** to be lucky; **zum Glück** luckily; **2** happiness.

glücklich *adjective* **1** lucky; **es war ein glücklicher Zufall, dass ich ihn heute in der Stadt getroffen habe** it was a lucky coincidence that I met him in town today; **2** happy.

glücklicherweise *adverb* luckily, fortunately.

Glückwunsch *der* (PL *die* **Glückwünsche**) congratulations; **herzlichen Glückwunsch zum Geburtstag!** happy birthday!

Glückwunschkarte *die* (PL *die* **Glückwunschkarten**) greetings card.

Glühbirne *die* (PL *die* **Glühbirnen**) light bulb.

glühen *verb* (PERF **hat geglüht**) to glow.

Gold *das* gold.

golden *adjective* **1** gold; **2** golden.

Goldfisch *der* (PL *die* **Goldfische**) goldfish.

Golf[1] *der* (PL *die* **Golfe**) gulf.

Golf[2] *das* golf.

Golfplatz *der* (PL *die* **Golfplätze**) golf course.

Golfschläger *der* (PL *die* **Golfschläger**) golf club.

goss △ SEE **gießen**.

Gott *der* (PL *die* **Götter**) god.

△ NEW SPELLING: *See page xii*

Gottesdienst der (PL die **Gottesdienste**) service.

Göttin die (PL die **Göttinnen**) goddess.

Grab das (PL die **Gräber**) grave.

graben △ verb (PRES **gräbt**, IMPERF **grub**, PERF **hat gegraben**) to dig.

Grad der (PL die **Grade**) degree.

Gramm das (PL die **Gramme**) gram.

Grammatik die (PL die **Grammatiken**) grammar.

grantig adjective grumpy.

Gras das (PL die **Gräser**) grass.

grässlich △ adjective horrible.

Gräte die (PL die **Gräten**) (fish)bone.

gratis adverb free of charge.

gratulieren verb (PERF **hat gratuliert**) 1 to congratulate; 2 **ich habe Gabi zum Geburtstag gratuliert** I wished Gabi happy birthday; 3 **wir gratulieren!** congratulations!

grau adjective grey.

Gräuel △ der horror.

grauen verb (PERF **hat gegraut**) **mir graut es davor** I dread it.

grauhaarig adjective grey-haired.

grausam adjective cruel.

Grausamkeit die cruelty.

graziös adjective graceful.

greifen ◇ verb (IMPERF **griff**, PERF **hat gegriffen**) 1 to take hold of; 2 to catch; 3 **nach etwas greifen** to

reach for something; 4 **um sich greifen** to spread (of fire).

grell adjective 1 glaring; 2 garish; 3 shrill.

Grenze die (PL die **Grenzen**) 1 border; 2 boundary; 3 limit.

grenzen verb (PERF **hat gegrenzt**) **an etwas grenzen** to border on something.

Greuel SEE **Gräuel**.

Grieche der (PL die **Griechen**) Greek.

Griechenland das Greece.

Griechin die (PL die **Griechinnen**) Greek.

griechisch adjective Greek.

griff SEE **greifen**.

Griff der (PL die **Griffe**) 1 grasp; 2 handle.

griffbereit adjective handy; **sie hat den Korkenzieher immer griffbereit** she always keeps the corkscrew handy.

Grill der (PL die **Grills**) 1 grill; 2 barbecue.

Grille die (PL die **Grillen**) cricket (the insect).

grillen verb (PERF **hat gegrillt**) 1 to grill; 2 to have a barbecue.

Grillfest das (PL die **Grillfeste**) barbecue.

grinsen verb (PERF **hat gegrinst**) to grin.

Grippe die (PL die **Grippen**) flu.

grob adjective 1 coarse; 2 rough;

◇ IRREGULAR VERB: See the verb table in the centre of the dictionary

3 rude; **4 ein grober Fehler** a bad mistake.

Groschen der (PL die **Groschen**)
1 (*Austrian money*) groschen;
2 (*informal*) ten-pfennig piece;
3 **der Groschen ist gefallen** the penny's dropped.

groß *adjective* 1 big; 2 great; **Gisela hatte große Angst** Gisela was very frightened; 3 tall; **4 ein großer Buchstabe** a capital letter; **5 groß werden** to grow up; **6 die großen Ferien** the summer holidays; **7 im Großen und Ganzen** △ on the whole; **8 Groß und Klein** △ young and old.
adverb **was soll man da schon groß machen?** what are you supposed to do?

großartig *adjective* great.

Großbritannien *das* Great Britain.

Großbuchstabe der (PL die **Großbuchstaben**) capital (letter).

Größe die (PL die **Größen**) 1 size; 2 height; 3 greatness.

Großeltern *plural noun* grandparents.

großenteils *adverb* largely.

Großmarkt der (PL die **Großmärkte**) hypermarket.

Großmutter die (PL die **Großmütter**) grandmother.

Großstadt die (PL die **Großstädte**) city.

großschreiben ◇ *verb* (IMPERF **schrieb groß**, PERF **hat großgeschrieben**) **ein Wort**

großschreiben to write a word with a capital.

Großvater der (PL die **Großväter**) grandfather.

großzügig *adjective* generous.

grub SEE **graben**.

grün *adjective* 1 green; **2 im Grünen** in the country; **3 die Grünen** the Greens.

Grund der (PL die **Gründe**) 1 ground; 2 bottom; 3 reason; **aus diesem Grund** for this reason; **4 im Grunde genommen** basically.

gründen *verb* (PERF **hat gegründet**) 1 to set up, to found; **2 sich auf etwas gründen** to be based on something.

Grundlage die (PL die **Grundlagen**) basis.

gründlich *adjective* thorough.

grundsätzlich *adjective* 1 fundamental; 2 basic.
adverb 1 basically; 2 on principle.

Grundschule die (PL die **Grundschulen**) primary school.

Grundstück *das* (PL die **Grundstücke**) plot (of land).

Gruppe die (PL die **Gruppen**) group.

Gruß der (PL die **Grüße**) greeting; **einen schönen Gruß an Lars** give my regards to Lars; **mit herzlichen Grüßen** with best wishes.

grüßen *verb* (PERF **hat gegrüßt**) 1 to greet; 2 to say hello; **3 grüß Gott!** hello; **4 grüße Thomas von mir** give Thomas my regards; **Gisela lässt grüßen** Gisela sends her regards.

△ NEW SPELLING: *See page xii*

gucken *verb* (PERF **hat geguckt**) to look.

gültig *adjective* valid.

Gummi *der* (PL *die* **Gummis**) rubber.

Gummiband *das* (PL *die* **Gummibänder**) rubber band.

Gummistiefel *der* (PL *die* **Gummistiefel**) wellington (boot).

günstig *adjective* 1 favourable; 2 convenient.

Gurgel *die* (PL *die* **Gurgeln**) throat.

gurgeln *verb* (PERF **hat gegurgelt**) to gargle.

Gurke *die* (PL *die* **Gurken**) 1 cucumber; 2 gherkin.

Gürtel *der* (PL *die* **Gürtel**) belt.

Gürteltasche *die* (PL *die* **Gürteltaschen**) bum bag.

gut *adjective* 1 good; 2 **guten Appetit!** enjoy your meal!; 3 **schon gut** that's all right; **also gut** all right; 4 **im Guten** △ amicably; 5 **alles Gute!** all the best!
adverb 1 well; 2 **gut schmecken** to taste good; 3 **gut zwei Stunden** a good two hours; 4 **uns geht's gut** we're fine; **ihm geht es nicht gut** he's not well.

Güte *die* 1 goodness; **du meine Güte!** my goodness!; 2 quality.

Güterzug *der* (PL *die* **Güterzüge**) goods train.

gutgehen SEE **gut**.

gutmütig *adjective* good-natured.

Gutschein *der* (PL *die* **Gutscheine**) 1 voucher; 2 coupon.

Gymnasium *das* (PL *die* **Gymnasien**) grammar school.

Gymnastik *die* 1 gymnastics; 2 keep-fit (exercises).

H h

Haar *das* (PL *die* **Haare**) 1 hair; **sich die Haare waschen** to wash your hair; 2 **um ein Haar** (*informal*) very nearly.

Haarbürste *die* (PL *die* **Haarbürsten**) hairbrush.

haarig *adjective* hairy.

Haarschnitt *der* (PL *die* **Haarschnitte**) haircut.

Haarwaschmittel *das* (PL *die* **Haarwaschmittel**) shampoo.

haben ◇ *verb* (PRES **hat**, IMPERF **hatte**, PERF **hat gehabt**) 1 to have (got); **ich habe ein neues Auto** I have (*or* I've got) a new car; **etwas gegen jemanden haben** to have something against somebody; 2 (*used with another verb, like 'have' in English, to form past tenses*) **ich habe Werners Adresse verloren** I've lost Werner's address; **ich habe deine Mutter gestern angerufen** I rang your mother yesterday; 3 **Angst haben** to be frightened; **Hunger haben** to be hungry; 4 **heute haben wir Mittwoch** it's Wednesday today; 5 **die Kinder haben Ferien** the children are on holiday; 6 **was hat sie?** what's the

matter with her?; **7 ich hätte gern
... I'd like ...; ich hätte ihr geholfen
I** would have helped her; **8 sich
haben** (*informal*) to make a fuss.

acken *verb* (PERF **hat gehackt**) **1** to
chop (up); **2** to peck (*of a bird*).

ackfleisch *das* minced meat.

afen *der* (PL *die* **Häfen**) harbour.

aferflocken *plural noun*
porridge oats.

aftbar *adjective* **für etwas haftbar
sein** to be liable for something.

aften *verb* (PERF **hat gehaftet**) **1** to
stick; **2 für etwas haften** to be
responsible for something.

agel *der* hail.

ageln *verb* (PERF **hat gehagelt**) to
hail.

agelschauer *der* (PL *die*
Hagelschauer) hailstorm.

ahn *der* (PL *die* **Hähne**) **1** cock;
2 tap.

ähnchen *das* (PL *die* **Hähnchen**)
chicken.

ai *der* (PL *die* **Haie**) shark.

aken *der* (PL *die* **Haken**) **1** hook;
2 tick; **3** catch; **da muss ein Haken
dran sein** there must be a catch.

alb *adjective* half; **zum halben
Preis** at half price; **halb eins** half
past twelve.

albfinale *das* (PL *die* **Halbfinale**)
semi-final.

albieren *verb* (PERF **hat halbiert**)
to halve.

Halbkreis *der* (PL *die* **Halbkreise**)
semicircle.

Halbpension *die* half board.

halbtags *adverb* part-time.

halbwegs *adverb* **1** half-way;
2 more or less.

Halbzeit *die* (PL *die* **Halbzeiten**)
1 half; **2** half-time; **während der
Halbzeit** during half-time.

half SEE **helfen**.

Hälfte *die* (PL *die* **Hälften**) half; **zur
Hälfte** half.

Halle *die* (PL *die* **Hallen**) **1** hall;
2 foyer.

Hallenbad *das* (PL *die* **Hallenbäder**)
indoor swimming pool.

hallo *exclamation* hello!

Hals *der* (PL *die* **Hälse**) **1** neck;
2 throat; **mir tut der Hals weh** I've
got a sore throat; **3 aus vollem Hals
schreien** to shout at the top of your
voice; **4 Hals über Kopf** in a rush.

Halsband *das* (PL *die* **Halsbänder**)
collar.

Halsschmerzen *plural noun* sore
throat; **Paul hat Halsschmerzen**
Paul's got a sore throat.

Halstuch *das* (PL *die* **Halstücher**)
scarf.

halt *exclamation* stop!

Halt *der* **1** hold; **jetzt hat es einen
besseren Halt** it holds better now;
2 Halt machen △ to stop.

haltbar *adjective* **1** hard-wearing;

2 durable; 3 **mindestens haltbar
bis ...** best before ...

halten ◇ *verb* (PRES **hält,** IMPERF
hielt, PERF **hat gehalten**) 1 to hold;
2 to keep; **sein Versprechen halten**
to keep your promise; **warm
halten** ∆ to keep warm; 3 to stop;
**der Bus hält direkt vor seiner
Haustür** the bus stops right outside
his door; 4 to save (*in sport*); 5 to
take (*a paper, magazine*); 6 **ich habe
ihn für deinen Bruder gehalten** I
took him for your brother; 7 **viel von
jemandem halten** to think a lot of
somebody; **jemanden für ehrlich
halten** to think somebody is
honest; 8 **zu jemandem halten** to
stand by somebody; 9 **eine Rede
halten** to make a speech; 10 **sich
halten** to keep (*of milk, fruit, etc.*);
11 **sich links/rechts halten** to keep
left/right; 12 **sich gut halten** to do
well; 13 **sich an etwas halten** to
keep to something.

Haltestelle *die* (PL *die* **Haltestellen**)
stop.

haltmachen SEE **Halt**.

Haltung *die* (PL *die* **Haltungen**)
1 posture; 2 attitude; 3 composure.

Hammelfleisch *das* mutton.

Hammer *der* (PL *die* **Hämmer**)
hammer.

hämmern *verb* (PERF **hat
gehämmert**) to hammer.

Hamster *der* (PL *die* **Hamster**)
hamster.

Hand *die* (PL *die* **Hände**) hand;
jemandem die Hand geben to
shake hands with somebody.

Handarbeit *die* (PL *die*
Handarbeiten) 1 handicraft;
2 hand-made article.

Handball *der* handball.

Handbremse *die* (PL *die*
Handbremsen) handbrake; **die
Handbremse ziehen** to pull the
handbrake.

Handbuch *das* (PL *die* **Handbücher**)
manual.

Handel *der* 1 trade; 2 deal; 3 **in den
Handel kommen** to come on the
market.

handeln *verb* (PERF **hat gehandelt**)
1 to trade, to deal; 2 **mit jemandem
handeln** to bargain with somebody;
3 to act; 4 **von etwas handeln** to
be about something; 5 **es handelt
sich um ...** it's about ...; **worum
handelt es sich?** what's it about?

Handelsschule *die* (PL *die*
Handelsschulen) business school,
vocational college.

Handfläche *die* (PL *die*
Handflächen) palm.

Handgelenk *das* (PL *die*
Handgelenke) wrist.

Handgepäck *das* hand luggage.

handhaben *verb* (PERF **hat
gehandhabt**) to handle.

Händler *der* (PL *die* **Händler**) dealer.

handlich *adjective* handy.

Handlung *die* (PL *die* **Handlungen**)
1 act; 2 action; 3 plot.

◇ IRREGULAR VERB: *See the verb table in the centre of the dictionary*

Handschellen (*plural noun*) handcuffs.

Handschrift die (PL die **Handschriften**) handwriting.

Handschuh der (PL die **Handschuhe**) glove.

Handtasche die (PL die **Handtaschen**) bag.

Handtuch das (PL die **Handtücher**) towel.

Handwerker der (PL die **Handwerker**) 1 craftsman; 2 workman.

Handwerkszeug das tools.

Handy das (PL die **Handys**) mobile (phone).

Hang der (PL die **Hänge**) slope.

Hängematte die (PL die **Hängematten**) hammock.

hängen[1] *verb* (PERF **hat gehängt**) 1 to hang; **Florian hat das Bild an die Wand gehängt** Florian hung the picture on the wall; **sie hängte ihren Mantel in den Schrank** she hung her coat up in the cupboard; 2 **sie haben den Wohnwagen an das Auto gehängt** they attached the caravan to the car; 3 **sich an jemanden hängen** to latch on to somebody.

hängen[2] ◇ *verb* (IMPERF **hing**, PERF **hat gehangen**) 1 to hang; **mein Bild hat immer hier gehangen** my picture used to hang here; 2 **an seinen Eltern hängen** to be attached to your parents; **sie hängt sehr an ihrer Mutter** she's very attached to her mother; 3 **an etwas**

hängen bleiben Δ to catch on something, to stick to something; **ich bin mit dem Ärmel am Zaun hängen geblieben** I got my sleeve caught on the fence.

hängenbleiben SEE **hängen**[2].

Hansaplast™ das plaster.

Happen der (PL die **Happen**) mouthful; **ich habe heute keinen Happen gegessen** I haven't had a bite to eat all day.

Harfe die (PL die **Harfen**) harp.

Harke die (PL die **Harken**) rake.

harmlos *adjective* harmless.

hart *adjective* 1 hard; 2 harsh.

hartgekocht *adjective* hard-boiled.

Hase der (PL die **Hasen**) hare.

Haselnuss Δ die (PL die **Hasselnüsse**) hazelnut.

Hass Δ der hatred.

hassen *verb* (PERF **hat gehasst** Δ) to hate.

hässlich Δ *adjective* 1 ugly; **sie hat ein hässliches Gesicht** she's got an ugly face; 2 nasty; **das war sehr hässlich von dir** that was very nasty of you.

hast SEE **haben**.

hastig *adjective* hasty.

hat, hatte, hatten, hattest, hattet SEE **haben**.

Haube die (PL die **Hauben**) 1 bonnet; 2 cap.

hauen ♦ *verb* (PRES **haut**, IMPERF **haute**, PERF **hat gehauen**) **1** to beat; **2** to thump, to bang; **3 sich hauen** to fight; **4 jemanden übers Ohr hauen** (*informal*) to cheat somebody.

Haufen der (PL **die Haufen**) **1** heap; **2** crowd (*of people*); **3 ein Haufen** (*informal*) heaps of; **ein Haufen Geld** heaps of money.

haufenweise *adverb* heaps of; **Gabi hat haufenweise CDs** Gabi has heaps of CDs.

häufig *adjective* frequent.

Hauptbahnhof der (PL **die Hauptbahnhöfe**) main station.

Hauptrolle die (PL **die Hauptrollen**) lead.

Hauptsache die (PL **die Hauptsachen**) main thing.

hauptsächlich *adjective* main. *adverb* mainly.

Hauptschule die secondary school.

Hauptstadt die (PL **die Hauptstädte**) capital.

Hauptstraße die (PL **die Hauptstraßen**) main road.

Hauptverkehrszeit die (PL **die Hauptverkehrszeiten**) rush hour.

Hauptwort das (PL **die Hauptwörter**) noun.

Haus das (PL **die Häuser**) **1** house; **2 nach Hause** home; **zu Hause** at home.

Hausarbeit die (PL **die Hausarbeiten**) **1** housework; **die Kinder müssen bei der Hausarbeit helfen** the children have to help with the housework; **2** homework.

Hausaufgaben *plural noun* homework; **hast du deine Hausaufgaben gemacht?** have you done your homework?

Hausfrau die (PL **die Hausfrauen**) housewife.

Haushalt der (PL **die Haushalte**) **1** household; **2 den Haushalt machen** to do the housework; **3** budget.

Haushaltswarengeschäft das (PL **die Haushaltswarengeschäfte**) hardware shop.

Hausmeister der (PL **die Hausmeister**) caretaker.

Hausnummer die house number.

Hausschlüssel der (PL **die Hausschlüssel**) front-door key.

Hausschuh der (PL **die Hausschuhe**) slipper.

Haustier das (PL **die Haustiere**) pet.

Haustür die (PL **die Haustüren**) front door.

Haut die (PL **die Häute**) skin; **aus der Haut fahren** (*informal*) to go up the wall.

Hebamme die (PL **die Hebammen**) midwife.

Hebel der (PL **die Hebel**) lever.

heben ♦ *verb* (IMPERF **hob**, PERF **hat gehoben**) **1** to lift; **2 sich heben** to rise.

Hecke die (PL **die Hecken**) hedge.

♦ IRREGULAR VERB: *See the verb table in the centre of the dictionary*

Heer das (PL die **Heere**) army.

Hefe die (PL die **Hefen**) yeast.

Heft das (PL die **Hefte**) 1 exercise book; 2 issue (*of a magazine*).

heften verb (PERF **hat geheftet**) 1 to pin; 2 to tack (*by sewing*); 3 to clip; 4 to staple.

heftig adjective 1 violent; 2 heavy (*snow, rain*).

Heftklammer die (PL die **Heftklammern**) staple.

Heftpflaster das (PL die **Heftpflaster**) sticking plaster.

Heftzwecke die (PL die **Heftzwecken**) drawing pin.

Heide die heath.

Heidekraut das heather.

Heidelbeere die (PL die **Heidelbeeren**) bilberry.

heilen verb (PERF **hat geheilt**) 1 to cure; 2 to heal.

heilig adjective 1 holy; 2 **heilig halten** to hold sacred; 3 **der heilige Franz von Assisi** Saint Francis of Assisi.

Heiligabend der (PL die **Heiligabende**) Christmas Eve.

Heilige der/die (PL die **Heiligen**) saint.

Heilmittel das (PL die **Heilmittel**) remedy.

heim adverb home.

Heim das (PL die **Heime**) 1 home; 2 hostel.

Heimat die (PL die **Heimaten**) 1 home; 2 native land.

Heimatstadt die home town.

Heimfahrt die (PL die **Heimfahrten**) 1 journey home; 2 way home.

heimgehen ✧ verb (IMPERF **ging heim**, PERF **ist heimgegangen**) to go home.

heimlich adjective secret. adverb secretly.

Heimspiel das (PL die **Heimspiele**) home game.

Heimweg der (PL die **Heimwege**) way home.

Heimweh das homesickness; **Heimweh haben** to be homesick.

Heirat die (PL die **Heiraten**) marriage.

heiraten verb (PERF **hat geheiratet**) to marry.

heiser adjective hoarse.

heiß adjective hot.

heißen ✧ verb (IMPERF **hieß**, PERF **hat geheißen**) 1 to be called; **wie heißt du?** what's your name?; 2 to mean; 3 **das heißt** that is; 4 **es heißt** it is said; 5 **wie heißt 'dog' auf Deutsch?** what's the German for 'dog'?

heiter adjective 1 bright; 2 cheerful.

heizen verb (PERF **hat geheizt**) 1 to heat (*a room*); 2 to put the heating on; 3 to have the heating on.

Heizung die heating.

hektisch adjective hectic.

Held der (PL die **Helden**) hero.

△ NEW SPELLING: See page xii

Heldin *die* (PL *die* **Heldinnen**)
heroine.

helfen ✧ *verb* (PRES **hilft**, IMPERF **half**,
PERF **hat geholfen**) **1** to help; **Lisa
hilft mir** Lisa is helping me; **2 es
hilft nichts** it's no good; **3 sich zu
helfen wissen** to know what to do;
ich weiß mir nicht zu helfen I don't
know what to do.

Helfer *der* (PL *die* **Helfer**) **1** helper;
2 assistant.

Helferin *die* (PL *die* **Helferinnen**)
1 helper; **2** assistant.

hell *adjective* **1** light (*colour*);
2 bright; **3 eine helle Stimme** a
clear voice; **4 helles Bier** lager;
5 da ist heller Wahnsinn
(*informal*) that's sheer madness.

hellwach *adjective* wide awake.

Helm *der* (PL *die* **Helme**) helmet.

Hemd *das* (PL *die* **Hemden**) **1** shirt;
2 vest.

Henkel *der* (PL *die* **Henkel**) handle.

Henne *die* (PL *die* **Hennen**) hen.

her *adverb* **1** here; **komm her** come
here; **2 vor jemandem her** in front
of somebody; **3 hinter etwas her
sein** to be after something; **4 von
der Farbe her** as far as the colour is
concerned; **5 wo bist du her?**
where do you come from?; **6 wo hat
Klaus das her?** where did Klaus get
it from?; **7 her damit!** (*informal*)
give it to me!; **8** ago; **das ist schon
lange her** it was a long time ago; **das
ist drei Tage her** it was three days
ago.

herab *adverb* down.

herablassend *adjective*
condescending.

herabsetzen *verb* (PERF **hat
herabgesetzt**) **1** to reduce; **2** to
belittle.

heran *adverb* **1 an etwas heran**
close to something, right up to
something; **bis an die Wand heran**
up to the wall; **2 immer heran!**
come closer!

herankommen ✧ *verb* (IMPERF
kam heran, PERF **ist
herangekommen**) **1** to come near;
2 herankommen an to come up to;
3 ich komme nicht heran I can't get
at it.

herauf *adverb* up.

heraufkommen ✧ *verb* (IMPERF
kam herauf, PERF **ist
heraufgekommen**) to come up.

heraus *adverb* out.

herausbekommen ✧ *verb* (IMPERF
bekam heraus, PERF **hat
herausbekommen**) **1** to get out;
2 to find out; **3** to solve; **4 Geld
herausbekommen** to get change.

herausfinden ✧ *verb* (IMPERF **fand
heraus**, PERF **hat herausgefunden**)
1 to find out; **2** to find your way out.

herausgeben ✧ *verb* (PRES **gibt
heraus**, IMPERF **gab heraus**, PERF **hat
herausgegeben**) **1** to hand over;
2 to bring out.

herauskommen ✧ *verb* (IMPERF
kam heraus, PERF **ist
herausgekommen**) to come out.

herausnehmen ✧ *verb* (PRES

✧ IRREGULAR VERB: *See the verb table in the centre of the dictionary*

nimmt heraus, IMPERF **nahm heraus**, PERF **hat herausgenommen**) **1** to take out; **sie hat ihren Lippenstift aus der Tasche herausgenommen** she took her lipstick out of the bag; **2 sich die Mandeln herausnehmen lassen** to have your tonsils out; **3 es sich herausnehmen, etwas zu tun** to have the nerve to do something; **du nimmst dir zu viel heraus** you're going too far.

herausstellen verb (PERF **hat herausgestellt**) **1** to put out; **2 sich herausstellen** to turn out; **es stellte sich heraus, dass …** it turned out that …

herausziehen ✧ verb (IMPERF **zog heraus**, PERF **hat herausgezogen**) to pull out.

herb adjective **1** sharp; **2** dry (wine).

herbei adverb over (here); **kommt herbei!** come over here!

Herberge die (PL die **Herbergen**) hostel.

Herbergsmutter die (PL die **Herbergsmütter**) warden (in a youth hostel).

Herbergsvater der (PL die **Herbergsväter**) warden (in a youth hostel).

herbringen ✧ verb (IMPERF **brachte her**, PERF **hat hergebracht**) to bring (here).

Herbst der (PL die **Herbste**) autumn; **im Herbst** in autumn.

Herd der (PL die **Herde**) cooker.

Herde die (PL die **Herden**) **1** herd; **2** flock.

herein adverb in; **herein!** come in!

hereinfallen ✧ verb (PRES **fällt herein**, IMPERF **fiel herein**, PERF **ist hereingefallen**) to be taken in; **auf einen Betrüger hereinfallen** to be taken in by a swindler.

hereinkommen ✧ verb (IMPERF **kam herein**, PERF **ist hereingekommen**) to come in.

hereinlassen ✧ verb (PRES **lässt herein** △, IMPERF **ließ herein**, PERF **hat hereingelassen**) to let in; **Max lässt mich nicht ins Zimmer herein** Max won't let me into the room.

Herfahrt die (PL die **Herfahrten**) **1** journey here; **2** way here.

hergeben ✧ verb (PRES **gibt her**, IMPERF **gab her**, PERF **hat hergegeben**) **1** to hand over; **gib die Tasche her!** hand over the bag!; **2** to give away; **3 sich für etwas hergeben** to get involved in something; **dazu gebe ich mich nicht her** I won't have anything to do with it.

Hering der (PL die **Heringe**) herring.

herkommen ✧ verb (IMPERF **kam her**, PERF **ist hergekommen**) to come (here); **wo kommt das her?** where does it come from?

Herkunft die (PL die **Herkünfte**) **1** origin; **2** background.

Heroin das heroin.

Herr der (PL die **Herren**) **1** gentleman; **2 Herr Huber** Mr Huber; **3 Sehr geehrte Herren** Dear Sirs (in a letter); **4 meine Herren!**

△ NEW SPELLING: See page xii

gentlemen!; **5** master; **6 der Herr** the Lord.

herrichten *verb* (PERF **hat hergerichtet**) to get ready, to prepare; **sie richtet die Betten für die Gäste her** she's getting the beds for the guests ready.

herrlich *adjective* marvellous.

herrschen *verb* (PERF **hat geherrscht**) **1** to rule; **2** to be; **es herrschte große Aufregung** there was great excitement.

herstellen *verb* (PERF **hat hergestellt**) to manufacture, to make; **in Deutschland hergestellt** made in Germany.

Herstellung *die* (PL *die* **Herstellungen**) manufacture, production.

herüber *adverb* over (here).

herum *adverb* **um ... herum** round; **falsch herum** the wrong way round; **im Kreis herum** in a circle.

herumdrehen *verb* (PERF **hat herumgedreht**) **1** to turn (over or round); **2 sich herumdrehen** to turn round.

herumführen *verb* (PERF **hat herumgeführt**) to show around.

herumgehen ✧ *verb* (IMPERF **ging herum**, PERF **ist herumgegangen**) **1** to go round; **2** to walk around; **im Park herumgehen** to walk around the park; **3** to pass (*of time*).

herunter *adverb* down; **die Treppe herunter** down the stairs.

herunterfallen ✧ *verb* (PRES **fällt herunter**, IMPERF **fiel herunter**, PERF **ist heruntergefallen**) **1** to fall down; **2** to fall off.

herunterkommen ✧ *verb* (IMPERF **kam herunter**, PERF **ist heruntergekommen**) **1** to come down; **2** (*informal*) to go to rack and ruin.

herunterlassen ✧ *verb* (PRES **läss¹ herunter** ∆, IMPERF **ließ herunter**, PERF **hat heruntergelassen**) to let down, to lower.

hervor *adverb* out.

hervorragend *adjective* outstanding.
adverb outstandingly well.

hervorrufen ✧ *verb* (IMPERF **rief hervor**, PERF **hat hervorgerufen**) to cause.

Herz *das* (PL *die* **Herzen**) **1** heart; **2** hearts (*in cards*).

Herzanfall *der* (PL *die* **Herzanfälle**) heart attack.

herzlich *adjective* **1** warm; **2** sincere; **3 herzlichen Dank** many thanks; **4 herzliche Grüße** best wishes; **5 herzlichen Glückwunsch!** congratulations!; **6 herzlich willkommen in Passau!** welcome to Passau!

herzlos *adjective* heartless.

Herzschlag *der* (PL *die* **Herzschläge**) **1** heartbeat; **2** heart failure; **er hat einen Herzschlag bekommen** he had a heart attack.

heterosexuell *adjective* heterosexual.

✧ **IRREGULAR VERB:** *See the verb table in the centre of the dictionary*

Heterosexuelle *der/die* (PL *die* **Heterosexuellen**) heterosexual.

Heu *das* hay.

heulen *verb* (PERF **hat geheult**) 1 to howl; 2 (*informal*) to cry.

Heuschnupfen *der* hay fever.

heute *adverb* today; **heute Abend** this evening; **heute Morgen** this morning.

heutig *adjective* 1 today's; 2 **in der heutigen Zeit** nowadays.

heutzutage nowadays.

Hexe *die* (PL *die* **Hexen**) witch.

Hexenschuss ∆ *der* lumbago.

hielt SEE **halten**.

hier *adverb* here.

hierher *adverb* here; **komm sofort hierher!** come here immediately!

hierhin *adverb* here.

hiesig *adjective* local.

hieß SEE **heißen**.

Hilfe *die* (PL *die* **Hilfen**) 1 help; 2 aid.

hilflos *adjective* helpless.

hilfsbereit *adjective* helpful.

hilft SEE **helfen**.

Himbeere *die* (PL *die* **Himbeeren**) raspberry.

Himmel *der* (PL *die* **Himmel**) 1 sky; 2 heaven.

himmlisch *adjective* heavenly.

hin *adverb* 1 there; **hin und zurück** there and back; 2 **hin und wieder** now and again; 3 **hin und her** back and forth, to and fro; 4 **auf meinen Rat hin** on my advice; **auf Ihren Brief hin** in reply to your letter; 5 **wo ist Dominik hin?** where's Dominik gone?; 6 **es ist nicht mehr lange hin** it's not long to go; 7 **ich bin hin** (*informal*) I'm worn out.

hinauf *adverb* up; **die Straße hinauf** up the road.

hinaufgehen ✧ *verb* (IMPERF **ging hinauf**, PERF **ist hinaufgegangen**) to go up.

hinaus *adverb* 1 out; 2 **auf Jahre hinaus** for years to come.

hinausgehen ✧ *verb* (IMPERF **ging hinaus**, PERF **ist hinausgegangen**) 1 to go out; 2 **über etwas hinausgehen** to exceed something; 3 **das Zimmer geht nach Norden hinaus** the room faces north.

hindern *verb* (PERF **hat gehindert**) to stop; **jemanden daran hindern, etwas zu tun** to stop somebody from doing something.

Hindernis *das* (PL *die* **Hindernisse**) obstacle.

hinduistisch *adjective* Hindu.

hindurch *adverb* 1 through it/them; 2 **das ganze Jahr hindurch** throughout the year.

hinein *adverb* 1 in; 2 **in etwas hinein** into something.

hineingehen ✧ *verb* (IMPERF **ging hinein**, PERF **ist hineingegangen**) 1 to go in; 2 **in etwas hineingehen** to go into something.

∆ NEW SPELLING: *See page xii*

hinfahren ◇ *verb* (PRES **fährt hin**, IMPERF **fuhr hin**, PERF **ist hingefahren**) 1 to go/drive there; 2 (PERF **hat hingefahren**) to take/drive there.

Hinfahrt *die* (PL *die* **Hinfahrten**) 1 journey there, way there; 2 outward journey.

hinfallen ◇ *verb* (PRES **fällt hin**, IMPERF **fiel hin**, PERF **ist hingefallen**) to fall over.

hing SEE **hängen**.

hingehen ◇ *verb* (IMPERF **ging hin**, PERF **ist hingegangen**) 1 to go there; **wo geht ihr hin?** where are you going?; 2 to go by (*of time*).

hinken *verb* (PERF **hat/ist gehinkt**) to limp.

hinkommen ◇ *verb* (IMPERF **kam hin**, PERF **ist hingekommen**) 1 to get there; 2 to go; **wo kommt das Buch hin?** where does the book go?; 3 **mit etwas hinkommen** (*informal*) to manage (with something).

hinlegen *verb* (PERF **hat hingelegt**) 1 to put down; **leg die Zeitung unten hin** put the paper down there; 2 **sich hinlegen** to lie down.

hinsetzen *verb* (PERF **hat sich hingesetzt**) **sich hinsetzen** to sit down; **Petra setzte sich neben ihm hin** Petra sat down next to him.

hinten *adverb* at the back; **von hinten** from behind.

hinter *preposition* ←(+DAT *or* +ACC) 1 behind; 2 **etwas hinter sich bringen** to get something over with.

hintere SEE **hinterer**.

hintereinander *adverb* 1 one behind the other; 2 one after the other; **dreimal hintereinander** three times in a row.

hinterer, hintere, hinteres *adjective* 1 back; 2 **am hinteren Ende** at the far end.

Hintergrund *der* (PL *die* **Hintergründe**) background.

hinterher *adverb* afterwards.

Hintern *der* (PL *die* **Hintern**) bottom.

Hinterrad *das* (PL *die* **Hinterräder**) back wheel.

hinters = **hinter das.**

hinüber *adverb* 1 over (there), across (there); 2 **das Radio ist hinüber** (*informal*) the radio has had it.

hinübergehen ◇ *verb* (IMPERF **ging hinüber**, PERF **ist hinübergegangen**) to go over, to go across.

hinunter *adverb* down.

Hinweg *der* (PL *die* **Hinwege**) way there; **auf dem Hinweg** on the way there.

Hinweis *der* (PL *die* **Hinweise**) 1 hint; **das war ein deutlicher Hinweis, dass er lieber allein fährt** it was an obvious hint that he prefers to go on his own; 2 reference; 3 **Hinweise zur Bedienung** operating instructions.

hinweisen ◇ *verb* (IMPERF **wies hin**, PERF **hat hingewiesen**) to point; **jemanden auf etwas hinweisen** to point something out to somebody.

Hirn *das* (PL *die* **Hirne**) brain.

◇ IRREGULAR VERB: *See the verb table in the centre of the dictionary*

Hirsch der (PL die **Hirsche**) 1 deer; 2 stag; 3 venison.

historisch adjective historical.

Hitze die heat.

hitzefrei adjective **hitzefrei haben** to have the day off school because of hot weather.

Hitzewelle die (PL die **Hitzewellen**) heatwave.

Hitzschlag der (PL die **Hitzschläge**) heatstroke.

hob SEE **heben**.

Hobby das (PL die **Hobbys**) hobby.

hoch adjective (with endings 'hoch' becomes 'hoher/hohe/hohes') 1 high; **der Zaun ist zu hoch** the fence is too high; **ein hoher Zaun** a high fence; 2 deep (snow); 3 great (age, weight).
adverb 1 highly; **hoch begabt** highy gifted; 2 **die Treppe hoch** up the stairs.

Hoch das (PL die **Hochs**) 1 cheer; **ein dreifaches Hoch für das Geburtstagskind** three cheers for the birthday girl/boy; 2 high (pressure).

hochachtungsvoll adverb **Hochachtungsvoll** Yours faithfully.

hochhackig adjective high-heeled; **hochhackige Schuhe** high-heeled shoes.

Hochhaus das (PL die **Hochhäuser**) high-rise building.

hochheben ✧ verb (IMPERF **hob hoch**, PERF **hat hochgehoben**) to lift up; **sie hob das Kind hoch** she lifted up the child.

hochnäsig adjective stuck-up.

Hochschule die (PL die **Hochschulen**) university, college.

Hochsprung der (PL die **Hochsprünge**) high jump.

höchst adverb extremely.

höchstens adverb 1 at most; 2 except perhaps.

höchster, höchste, höchstes adjective highest; **Mount Everest ist der der höchste Berg der Welt** Mount Everest is the highest mountain in the world; **es ist höchste Zeit** it is high time.

Höchstgeschwindigkeit die maximum speed.

Höchsttemperatur die (PL die **Höchsttemperaturen**) maximum temperature.

Hochzeit die (PL die **Hochzeiten**) wedding.

Hochzeitstag der (PL die **Hochzeitstage**) 1 wedding day; 2 wedding anniversary.

Hocker der (PL die **Hocker**) stool.

Hockey das hockey.

Hockeyschläger der (PL die **Hockeyschläger**) hockey stick.

Hof der (PL die **Höfe**) 1 yard; 2 farm.

hoffen verb (PERF **hat gehofft**) to hope; **auf etwas hoffen** to hope for something.

hoffentlich adverb hopefully; **hoffentlich nicht** I hope not.

Hoffnung die (PL die **Hoffnungen**) hope.

△ NEW SPELLING: See page xii

hoffnungslos *adjective* hopeless.

höflich *adjective* polite.

Höflichkeit *die* (PL *die* **Höflichkeiten**) politeness, courtesy.

Höhe *die* (PL *die* **Höhen**) 1 height; 2 **das ist die Höhe!** (*informal*) that's the limit!

hoher, hohe, hohes SEE **hoch**.

höher *adjective* 1 higher; 2 deeper.

hohl *adjective* hollow.

Höhle *die* (PL *die* **Höhlen**) 1 cave; 2 den.

holen *verb* (PERF **hat geholt**) 1 to get, to fetch; 2 **jemanden holen lassen** to send for somebody; 3 **sich etwas holen** to get something.

Holland *das* Holland.

Holländer *der* (PL *die* **Holländer**) Dutchman.

Holländerin *die* (PL *die* **Holländerinnen**) Dutchwoman.

holländisch *adjective* Dutch.

Hölle *die* (PL *die* **Höllen**) hell.

Holz *das* (PL *die* **Hölzer**) wood.

Holzkohle *die* charcoal.

homöopathisch *adjective* homeopathic.

homosexuell *adjective* homosexual.

Homosexuelle *der/die* (PL *die* **Homosexuellen**) homosexual.

Honig *der* (PL *die* **Honige**) honey.

horchen *verb* (PERF **hat gehorcht**) 1 to listen; 2 to eavesdrop.

hören *verb* (PERF **hat gehört**) 1 to hear; 2 to listen (to).

Hörer *der* (PL *die* **Hörer**) 1 listener; 2 receiver (*of a phone*).

Hörerin *die* (PL *die* **Hörerinnen**) listener.

Horizont *der* (PL *die* **Horizonte**) horizon.

Horn *das* (PL *die* **Hörner**) horn.

Horoskop *das* (PL *die* **Horoskope**) horoscope.

Hose *die* (PL *die* **Hosen**) trousers.

Hosenträger *plural noun* braces.

Hotel *das* (PL *die* **Hotels**) hotel.

Hotelverzeichnis *das* (PL *die* **Hotelverzeichnisse**) list of hotels.

hübsch *adjective* 1 pretty; 2 nice.

Hubschrauber *der* (PL *die* **Hubschrauber**) helicopter.

Huf *der* (PL *die* **Hufe**) hoof.

Hufeisen *das* (PL *die* **Hufeisen**) horseshoe.

Hüfte *die* (PL *die* **Hüften**) hip.

Hügel *der* (PL *die* **Hügel**) hill.

Huhn *das* (PL *die* **Hühner**) 1 chicken; 2 hen.

Hummel *die* (PL *die* **Hummeln**) bumble-bee.

Hummer *der* (PL *die* **Hummer**) lobster.

Humor *der* humour; **Humor haben** to have a sense of humour.

Hund *der* (PL *die* **Hunde**) dog.

◇ IRREGULAR VERB: *See the verb table in the centre of the dictionary*

Hundehütte die (PL die **Hundehütten**) kennel.

hundemüde adjective (informal) dog-tired.

hundert number a hundred, one hundred.

Hunger der hunger; **Hunger haben** to be hungry.

hungrig adjective hungry.

Hupe die (PL die **Hupen**) horn.

hurra exclamation hooray!

husten verb (PERF **hat gehustet**) to cough.

Husten der cough.

Hut der (PL die **Hüte**) hat.

hüten verb (PERF **hat gehütet**) 1 to look after (a child, children); 2 **sich hüten** to be on your guard; 3 **sich hüten, etwas zu tun** to take care not to do something.

Hütte die (PL die **Hütten**) hut.

hygienisch adjective hygienic.

hypnotisieren verb (PERF **hat hypnotisiert**) to hypnotize.

Hypothek die (PL die **Hypotheken**) mortgage.

hysterisch adjective hysterical.

I i

ich pronoun I.

IC-Zug der (PL die **IC-Züge**) (Intercityzug) intercity train.

ideal adjective ideal.

Idee die (PL die **Ideen**) idea.

identifizieren verb (PERF **hat identifiziert**) to identify.

identisch adjective identical.

Idiot der (PL die **Idioten**) idiot.

idiotisch adjective idiotic.

idyllisch adjective idyllic.

Igel der (PL die **Igel**) hedgehog.

ihm pronoun 1 him, to him; 2 it, to it.

ihn pronoun 1 him; 2 it.

ihnen pronoun them, to them.

ihr pronoun 1 you (plural); 2 her, to her; 3 (standing for an object) it, to it.
adjective 1 her; 2 its; 3 their; **sie haben ihr Auto verkauft** they sold their car.

Ihr adjective your; **Ihr Sohn hat mir geschrieben** your son wrote to me.

ihrer, ihre, ihr(e)s pronoun 1 hers; **mein Rad ist rot, ihrs ist blau** my bike is red, hers is blue; 2 theirs; **das ist nicht ihre Katze, ihre ist**

△ NEW SPELLING: See page xii

schwarz that's not their cat, theirs is black.

Ihrer, Ihre, Ihr(e)s *pronoun* yours; **mein Job ist nicht so interessant wie Ihrer** my job's not as interesting as yours.

ihretwegen *adverb* 1 for her sake; 2 for their sake; 3 because of her; 4 because of them.

Ihretwegen *adverb* 1 for your sake; 2 because of you.

Illusion *die* (PL *die* **Illusionen**) illusion.

Illustration *die* (PL *die* **Illustrationen**) illustration.

Illustrierte *die* (PL *die* **Illustrierten**) magazine.

im = **in dem; was läuft im Kino?** what's on at the cinema?; **im August** in August.

Imbiss Δ *der* (PL *die* **Imbisse**) 1 snack; 2 snack bar.

Imbissstube Δ *die* (PL *die* **Imbissstuben**) snack bar.

imitieren *verb* (PERF **hat imitiert**) to imitate.

immer *adverb* 1 always; 2 **immer wieder** again and again; 3 **immer mehr** more and more; **immer dunkler** darker and darker; 4 **immer noch** still; 5 **immer, wenn er anruft** every time he rings; 6 **wo/wer/wann immer** wherever/whoever/whenever; 7 **für immer** for ever.

immerhin *adverb* at least.

immerzu *adverb* all the time.

impfen *verb* (PERF **hat geimpft**) to vaccinate.

Impfung *die* (PL *die* **Impfungen**) vaccination.

imponieren *verb* (PERF **hat imponiert**) to impress; **jemandem imponieren** to impress somebody.

Import *der* (PL *die* **Importe**) import.

importieren *verb* (PERF **hat importiert**) to import.

imprägniert *adjective* waterproof.

imstande *adverb* **imstande sein, etwas zu tun** to be able to do something; **er ist nicht imstande, seine Hausaufgaben allein zu machen** he's not able to do his homework on his own.

in *preposition* ←(+DAT *or* +ACC) (*the dative is used when talking about position; the accusative shows movement towards something*) 1 in; **es ist in der Küche** it's in the kitchen; 2 into, in; **ich habe es in meine Tasche gesteckt** I've put it in my bag; 3 **in die Schule gehen** to go to school; 4 **Susi ist in der Schule** Susi is at school; 5 **in diesem Jahr** this year; 6 **in sein** to be in; **der Rap ist in** rap is in.

inbegriffen *adjective* included; **Essen ist inbegriffen** food is included.

indem *conjunction* 1 while; 2 by.

Inder *der* (PL *die* **Inder**) Indian.

Inderin *die* (PL *die* **Inderinnen**) Indian.

Indianer *der* (PL *die* **Indianer**)

✧ IRREGULAR VERB: See the verb table in the centre of the dictionary

(American) Indian, native American.

Indianerin *die* (PL *die* **Indianerinnen**) (American) Indian, native American.

indianisch *adjective* (American) Indian, native American.

Indien *das* India.

indisch *adjective* Indian.

indiskutabel *adjective* out of the question.

individuell *adjective* individual.

Individuum *das* (PL *die* **Individuen**) individual.

Industrie *die* (PL *die* **Industrien**) industry.

industriell *adjective* industrial.

Infektion *die* (PL *die* **Infektionen**) infection.

Infinitiv *der* (PL *die* **Infinitive**) infinitive.

infizieren *verb* (PERF **hat infiziert**) 1 to infect; 2 **sich bei jemandem infizieren** to be infected by somebody.

infolge *preposition* ←(+GEN) as a result of.

infolgedessen *adverb* consequently.

Informatik *die* computer science.

Informatiker *der* (PL *die* **Informatiker**) computer scientist.

Informatikerin *die* (PL *die* **Informatikerinnen**) computer scientist.

Information *die* (PL *die* **Informationen**) (piece of) information.

Informationsbüro *das* (PL *die* **Informationsbüros**) (tourist) information office.

informieren *verb* (PERF **hat informiert**) 1 to inform; 2 **informiert sein** to be aware; **da bist du falsch informiert** you've been wrongly informed; 3 **sich über etwas informieren** to find out about something; **ich habe mich darüber genau informieren lassen** I found out all about it.

Ingenieur *der* (PL *die* **Ingenieure**) engineer.

Ingenieurin *die* (PL *die* **Ingenieurinnen**) engineer.

Ingwer *der* ginger.

Inhaber *der* (PL *die* **Inhaber**) 1 owner (*of a shop*); 2 holder (*of an office*).

Inhaberin *die* (PL *die* **Inhaberinnen**) 1 owner (*of a shop*); 2 holder (*of a position*).

Inhalt *der* (PL *die* **Inhalte**) 1 contents; **den Inhalt der Dose mit etwas Wasser verdünnen** dilute the contents of the tin with a little water; 2 content (*of a story, film*); **er hat uns eine kurze Zusammenfassung des Inhalts der Geschichte gegeben** he gave us a quick summary of the content of the story; 3 volume; 4 area (*of a rectangle, circle, etc.*).

△ NEW SPELLING: *See page xii*

inklusive *preposition* ←(+GEN) including.
adverb inclusive.

innen *adverb* inside; **nach innen** inwards.

Innenstadt *die* (PL *die* **Innenstädte**) town centre, city centre.

Innere *das* **1** interior; **2** inside.

innerer, innere, inneres *adjective* **1** inner; **2** inside; **3** internal (*injuries*).

innerhalb *preposition* ←(+GEN) **1** within; **2** during.
adverb **innerhalb von** within.

innerlich *adjective* **1** internal; **2** inner.
adverb **1** internally; **2** inwardly.

ins = **in das**; **ins Theater gehen** to go to the theatre.

Insekt *das* (PL *die* **Insekten**) insect.

Insel *die* (PL *die* **Inseln**) island.

Inserat *das* (PL *die* **Inserate**) advertisement.

inserieren *verb* (PERF **hat inseriert**) to advertise.

insgesamt *adverb* in all.

Instinkt *der* (PL *die* **Instinkte**) instinct.

instinktiv *adjective* instinctive.

Instrument *das* (PL *die* **Instrumente**) instrument.

intelligent *adjective* intelligent.

Intelligenz *die* intelligence.

Intercityzug *der* (PL *die* **Intercityzüge**) intercity train.

interessant *adjective* interesting.

Interesse *das* (PL *die* **Interessen**) interest.

interessieren *verb* (PERF **hat interessiert**) **1** to interest; **2 sich für etwas interessieren** to be interested in something.

Internat *das* (PL *die* **Internate**) boarding school.

international *adjective* international.

Internet *das* internet.

Interview *das* (PL *die* **Interviews**) interview.

inzwischen *adverb* in the meantime, meanwhile.

Ire *der* (PL *die* **Iren**) Irishman; **die Iren** the Irish.

irgend *adverb* **1** at all; **wenn irgend möglich** if at all possible; **wenn du irgend kannst** if you could possibly manage it; **2 irgend so ein Idiot** some such idiot.

irgendein *adjective* **1** some; **2** any; **3 irgendein anderer** someone else, anyone else.

irgendeiner, irgendeine, irgendein(e)s *pronoun* **1** any one; **'welche möchten Sie?'** – **'irgendeine'** 'which one would you like?' – 'any one'; **2** somebody, someone; **3** anybody, anyone; **hat irgendeiner angerufen?** has anybody phoned?

✧ IRREGULAR VERB: *See the verb table in the centre of the dictionary*

irgendetwas ∆ *pronoun*
1 something; **2** anything.

irgendjemand ∆ *pronoun*
1 somebody; **2** anybody, anyone.

irgendwann *adverb* **1** some time, at
some time; **2** any time, at any time.

irgendwas (*informal*) =
irgendetwas.

irgendwie *adverb* somehow.

irgendwo *adverb* **1** somewhere;
2 anywhere.

Irin *die* (PL *die* **Irinnen**) Irishwoman.

irisch *adjective* Irish.

Irland *das* Ireland.

ironisch *adjective* ironic.

irre *adjective* **1** mad; **2** (*informal*)
incredible, fantastic (*party, song*).
adverb **irre gut** incredibly good.

irren *verb* (PERF **ist geirrt**) **1** to
wander (about) (*when lost*); **2** (PERF
hat sich geirrt) **sich irren** to be
mistaken, to be wrong.

irrsinnig *adjective* **1** mad;
2 (*informal*) incredible.

Irrtum *der* (PL *die* **Irrtümer**) mistake.

Islam *der* Islam.

isst ∆ SEE **essen**.

ist SEE **sein**.

Italien *das* Italy.

Italiener *der* (PL *die* **Italiener**)
Italian.

Italienerin *die* (PL *die*
Italienerinnen) Italian.

italienisch *adjective* Italian.

J j

ja *adverb* **1** yes; **2** **ich glaube ja** I
think so; **3** **du kommst doch, ja?**
you'll come, won't you?; **es passt
doch, ja?** it fits, doesn't it?; **4** **sag's
ihm ja nicht!** don't (you dare) tell
him, whatever you do!; **seid ja
vorsichtig!** do be careful!; **5** **es ist
ja noch früh** it's still early; **ich kann
ihn ja mal fragen, ob er mitkommen
will** I could always ask him if he
wants to come.

Jacht *die* (PL *die* **Jachten**) yacht.

Jacke *die* (PL *die* **Jacken**) **1** jacket;
2 cardigan.

Jackett *das* (PL *die* **Jacketts**) jacket.

Jagd *die* (PL *die* **Jagden**) **1** hunt;
2 hunting.

jagen *verb* (PERF **hat gejagt**) **1** to
hunt; **2** to chase; **drei Polizisten
jagten den Einbrecher, aber er
hängte sie schnell ab** three
policemen chased the burglar, but he
soon shook them off; **meine Mutter
hat mich aus dem Bett gejagt**
(*informal*) my mother chased me
out of bed; **3** **jemanden aus dem
Haus jagen** to throw somebody out
of the house; **4** **damit kannst du
mich jagen** (*informal*) I can't stand
that.

Jahr *das* (PL *die* **Jahre**) year; **in den
sechziger Jahren** in the sixties;

∆ NEW SPELLING: *See page xii*

Kinder bis zu zwölf Jahren children up to the age of twelve.

jahrelang *adverb* for years.

Jahrestag *der* (PL *die* **Jahrestage**) anniversary.

Jahreszeit *die* (PL *die* **Jahreszeiten**) season.

Jahrgang *der* (PL *die* **Jahrgänge**) 1 year; 2 vintage.

Jahrhundert *das* (PL *die* **Jahrhunderte**) century.

jährlich *adjective, adverb* yearly; **zweimal jährlich** twice a year.

Jahrmarkt *der* (PL *die* **Jahrmärkte**) fair.

Jahrtausend *das* (PL *die* **Jahrtausende**) millennium.

Jahrzehnt *das* (PL *die* **Jahrzehnte**) decade.

jähzornig *adjective* hot-tempered.

jammern *verb* (PERF **hat gejammert**) to moan.

Januar *der* January.

Japan *das* Japan.

Japaner *der* (PL *die* **Japaner**) Japanese.

Japanerin *die* (PL *die* **Japanerinnen**) Japanese.

japanisch *adjective* Japanese.

jawohl *adverb* 1 yes; 2 certainly.

je *adverb* 1 ever; **besser denn je** better than ever; 2 each; **sie kosten je zwanzig Mark** they are twenty marks each; 3 **seit eh und je** always; 4 **je nach** depending on.

preposition ←(+ACC) per.
conjunction 1 **je mehr, desto besser** the more the better; 2 **je nachdem** it depends.

Jeans *plural noun* jeans.

jede SEE **jeder**.

jedenfalls *adverb* in any case.

jeder, jede, jedes *adjective* 1 every; **jedes Mal** △ every time; 2 each; 3 any; **ohne jeden Grund** without any reason.
pronoun 1 everybody, everyone; 2 each one; 3 anybody, anyone; **das kann jeder** anybody can do that.

jedermann *pronoun* everybody, everyone.

jederzeit *adverb* at any time.

jedes SEE **jeder**.

jedesmal SEE **jeder**.

jedoch *adverb* however.

jemals *adverb* ever.

jemand *pronoun* 1 somebody, someone; **jemand hat das für dich abgegeben** sombody left this for you; 2 anybody, anyone; **hat jemand angerufen?** did anybody call?

jener, jene, jenes *adjective* (*used in elevated language and in literature*) 1 that; 2 those (*plural*).
pronoun 1 that one; 2 those (*plural*).

jenseits *preposition* ←(+GEN) (on) the other side of.

jetzt *adverb* now.

✧ IRREGULAR VERB: *See the verb table in the centre of the dictionary*

Job der (PL die **Jobs**) job.

jobben verb (informal) (PERF **hat gejobbt**) to work.

joggen verb (PERF **ist gejoggt**) to jog.

Jogginganzug der (PL die **Jogginganzüge**) tracksuit.

Joghurt der (PL die **Joghurt**) yoghurt.

Johannisbeere die (PL die **Johannisbeeren**) **1 rote Johannisbeeren** redcurrants; **2 schwarze Johannisbeeren** blackcurrants.

Journalist der (PL die **Journalisten**) journalist.

Journalistin die (PL die **Journalistinnen**) journalist.

jubeln verb (PERF **hat gejubelt**) **1** to cheer; **2 Beifall jubeln** to applaud.

Jubiläum das (PL die **Jubiläen**) **1** anniversary; **2** jubilee.

Jude der (PL die **Juden**) Jew.

Jüdin die (PL die **Jüdinnen**) Jew.

jüdisch adjective Jewish.

Jugend die youth.

Jugendherberge die (PL die **Jugendherbergen**) youth hostel.

Jugendklub der (PL die **Jugendklubs**) youth club.

Jugendliche der/die (PL die **Jugendlichen**) **1** young man/woman; **2 die Jugendlichen** youth, young people.

Jugoslawien das Yugoslavia.

jugoslawisch adjective Yugoslavian.

Juli der July.

jung adjective **1** young; **2 Jung und Alt** △ young and old.

Junge[1] der (PL die **Jungen**) boy.

Junge[2] das (PL die **Jungen**) young (animal).

Jungfrau die (PL die **Jungfrauen**) **1** virgin; **2** Virgo.

jüngster, jüngste, jüngstes adjective **1** youngest; **2** latest (news, developments); **3 in jüngster Zeit** recently.

Juni der June.

Jury die (PL die **Jurys**) **1** jury; **2** judges (in sport).

Juwelier der (PL die **Juweliere**) jeweller.

Jux der (informal) laugh; **aus Jux** for a laugh.

K k

Kabel das (PL die **Kabel**) **1** cable; **2** wire.

Kabelfernsehen das cable television.

Kabeljau der (PL die **Kabeljaus**) cod.

Kabine die (PL die **Kabinen**) **1** cabin; **2** cubicle (for changing); **3** car (of a cable car).

Kachel die (PL die **Kacheln**) tile.

△ NEW SPELLING: See page xii

Käfer *der* (PL *die* **Käfer**) beetle.

Kaffee *der* (PL *die* **Kaffee(s)**) coffee; **zwei Kaffee mit Milch bitte** two white coffees please.

Kaffeekanne *die* (PL *die* **Kaffeekannen**) coffee-pot.

Käfig *der* (PL *die* **Käfige**) cage.

kahl *adjective* **1** bald (*head*); **2** bare (*tree, walls*).

Kaiser *der* (PL *die* **Kaiser**) emperor.

Kaiserin *die* (PL *die* **Kaiserinnen**) empress.

Kakao *der* (PL *die* **Kakao(s)**) cocoa; **zwei Kakao bitte** two cups of cocoa please.

Kakerlak *der* (PL *die* **Kakerlaken**) cockroach.

Kaktus *der* (PL *die* **Kakteen**) cactus.

Kalb *das* (PL *die* **Kälber**) **1** calf; **2** veal.

Kalbfleisch *das* veal.

Kalender *der* (PL *die* **Kalender**) **1** calendar; **2** diary.

Kalk *der* **1** lime; **2** limescale; **3** calcium.

Kalorie *die* (PL *die* **Kalorien**) calorie.

kalorienarm *adjective* low-calorie.

kalt *adjective* cold; **ist dir kalt?** are you cold?; **stell die Heizung an, den Kindern ist kalt** put on the heating, the children are cold; **abends essen wir kalt** we have a cold meal in the evening; **den Wein kalt stellen** to chill the wine.

Kälte *die* **1** cold; **2** coldness; **3** fünf

Grad Kälte five degrees below zero.

kam SEE **kommen**.

Kamel *das* (PL *die* **Kamele**) camel.

Kamera *die* (PL *die* **Kameras**) camera.

Kamerad *der* (PL *die* **Kameraden**) friend.

Kameramann *der* (PL *die* **Kameramänner**) cameraman.

Kamin *der* (PL *die* **Kamine**) fireplace; **wir saßen am Kamin** we sat by the fire.

Kamm *der* (PL *die* **Kämme**) **1** comb; **2** ridge (*of a mountain*).

kämmen *verb* (PERF **hat gekämmt**) **1** to comb; **2** sich kämmen to comb your hair.

Kammer *die* (PL *die* **Kammern**) **1** store room; **2** chamber.

Kampf *der* (PL *die* **Kämpfe**) **1** fight; **2** contest; **3** struggle.

kämpfen *verb* (PERF **hat gekämpft**) to fight.

Kanada *das* Canada.

Kanadier *der* (PL *die* **Kanadier**) Canadian.

Kanadierin *die* (PL *die* **Kanadierinnen**) Canadian.

kanadisch *adjective* Canadian.

Kanal *der* (PL *die* **Kanäle**) **1** canal; **2** channel (*radio, TV*); **3** der Kanal the (English) Channel; **4** sewer, drain.

Kanalinseln *plural noun* Channel Islands.

◈ IRREGULAR VERB: *See the verb table in the centre of the dictionary*

Kanalisation *die* sewers, drains.

Kanarienvogel *der* (PL *die* **Kanarienvögel**) canary.

Kandidat *der* (PL *die* **Kandidaten**) candidate.

Kandidatin *die* (PL *die* **Kandidatinnen**) candidate.

Känguru Δ *das* (PL *die* **Kängurus**) kangaroo.

Kaninchen *das* (PL *die* **Kaninchen**) rabbit.

kann SEE **können**.

Kännchen *das* (PL *die* **Kännchen**) 1 pot; **ein Kännchen Kaffee bitte** a pot of coffee please; 2 jug (*of milk*).

Kanne *die* (PL *die* **Kannen**) 1 pot (*for coffee, tea*); 2 jug (*for water*); 3 can (*for oil*); 4 churn (*for milk*); 5 watering can.

kannst SEE **können**.

kannte SEE **kennen**.

Kante *die* (PL *die* **Kanten**) edge.

Kantine *die* (PL *die* **Kantinen**) canteen; **wir essen immer in der Kantine zu Mittag** we always have lunch in the canteen.

Kanu *das* (PL *die* **Kanus**) canoe; **Kanu fahren** to go canoeing.

Kapelle *die* (PL *die* **Kapellen**) chapel.

kapieren *verb* (*informal*) (PERF **hat kapiert**) to understand; **er hat es mir schon dreimal erklärt, aber ich kapier es einfach nicht** he's already explained it to me three times, but I still don't get it.

Kapital *das* capital.

Kapitalismus *der* capitalism.

Kapitän *der* (PL *die* **Kapitäne**) captain.

Kapitel *das* (PL *die* **Kapitel**) chapter.

Kappe *die* (PL *die* **Kappen**) cap.

kaputt *adjective* 1 broken; 2 **an meinem Computer ist etwas kaputt** there's something wrong with my computer; 3 **ich bin kaputt** (*informal*) I'm shattered.

kaputtgehen ◆ *verb* (IMPERF **ging kaputt**, PERF **ist kaputtgegangen**) 1 to break; 2 to pack up; **mein Fernseher ist mitten im Fußballspiel kaputtgegangen** the television packed up in the middle of the football match; 3 to wear out (*of clothing*); 4 to break up (*of a marriage or friendship*).

kaputtmachen *verb* (PERF **hat kaputtgemacht**) 1 to break; **er macht alle seine Spielsachen kaputt** he breaks all his toys; 2 to ruin (*clothes, furniture*); 3 to finish off (*a person*); **die viele Arbeit macht mich ganz kaputt** all this work is wearing me out; 4 **sich kaputtmachen** to wear yourself out.

Kapuze *die* (PL *die* **Kapuzen**) hood.

Karamell Δ *der* (PL *die* **Karamells**) caramel.

Karfreitag *der* Good Friday.

Karibik *die* **die Karibik** the Caribbean.

karibisch *adjective* Caribbean.

kariert *adjective* 1 check; **ein**

karierter Rock a check skirt;
2 squared (*paper*).

Karneval der (PL die **Karnevale**)
carnival.

Karo das (PL die **Karos**) **1** square;
2 diamonds (*in cards*).

Karotte die (PL die **Karotten**) carrot.

Karriere die (PL die **Karrieren**)
career; **Karriere machen** to get to
the top.

Karte die (PL die **Karten**) **1** card; **ich
schicke euch eine Karte aus
Italien** I'll send you a card from
Italy; **2** card (*for playing*); **wir haben
den ganzen Abend Karten gespielt**
we played cards all evening;
gute/schlechte Karten haben to
have a good/bad hand; **3** ticket; **gibt
es noch Karten für das
Popfestival?** can you still get tickets
for the pop festival?; **4** menu; **5** map;
**ich kann Oberammergau nicht auf
der Karte finden** I can't find
Oberammergau on the map; **6** alles
auf eine Karte setzen to put all your
eggs in one basket.

Kartenspiel das (PL die
Kartenspiele) **1** card game; **2** pack
of cards.

Kartoffel die (PL die **Kartoffeln**)
potato.

Kartoffelbrei der mashed
potatoes.

Karton der (PL die **Kartons**)
1 cardboard; **2** cardboard box.

Karussell das (PL die **Karussells**)
merry-go-round; **Karussell fahren**
to go on the merry-go-round.

Käse der cheese.

Käsekuchen der (PL die
Käsekuchen) cheesecake.

Kasse die (PL die **Kassen**) **1** till;
2 checkout; **an der Kasse zahlen**
pay at the checkout; **3** cash desk (*in
a bank*); **4** box-office; **Sie können
die Karten an der Kasse abholen**
you can collect the tickets from the
box office; **5** ticket office (*at a sports
stadium*); **Sie müssen sich an der
Kasse anstellen** you have to queue
at the ticket office; **6** health
insurance; **7** knapp bei Kasse sein
(*informal*) to be short of money; **gut
bei Kasse sein** (*informal*) to be in
the money.

Kassenzettel der (PL die
Kassenzettel) receipt.

Kassette die (PL die **Kassetten**)
1 cassette, tape; **ich habe den neuen
Song auf Kassette aufgenommen**
I've taped the new song; **2** box (*for
money, jewellery*).

Kassettenrekorder der (PL die
Kassettenrekorder) cassette
recorder.

kassieren verb (PERF **hat kassiert**)
1 to collect the money; **2** to collect
the fares; **3** wie viel hat er kassiert?
how much did he charge you?;
4 darf ich bei Ihnen kassieren?
would you like to pay now? (*your bill
in a restaurant*); **5** (*informal*) to take
away (*a driving licence, for
example*).

Kassierer der (PL die **Kassierer**)
cashier.

✧ IRREGULAR VERB: *See the verb table in the centre of the dictionary*

Kassiererin die (PL die **Kassiererinnen**) cashier.

Kastanie die (PL die **Kastanien**) chestnut.

Kasten der (PL die **Kästen**) 1 box; 2 crate; **ein Kasten Bier** a crate of beer; 3 bin; 4 letter-box; 5 **was auf dem Kasten haben** (*informal*) to be brainy.

Katalog der (PL die **Kataloge**) catalogue.

Katalysator der (PL die **Katalysatoren**) catalytic converter.

Katastrophe die (PL die **Katastrophen**) catastrophe.

katastrophal *adjective, adverb* 1 catastrophic; 2 **sie hat katastrophal schlecht abgeschnitten** she came out terribly badly.

Kategorie die (PL die **Kategorien**) category.

Kater der (PL die **Kater**) 1 tom-cat; 2 **einen Kater haben** (*informal*) to have a hangover.

Kathedrale die (PL die **Kathedralen**) cathedral.

Katholik der (PL die **Katholiken**) Catholic.

Katholikin die (PL die **Katholikinnen**) Catholic.

katholisch *adjective* Catholic.

Kätzchen das (PL die **Kätzchen**) kitten.

Katze die (PL die **Katzen**) cat.

kauen *verb* (PERF **hat gekaut**) to chew.

Kauf der (PL die **Käufe**) 1 purchase; 2 **ein guter Kauf** a bargain; 3 **etwas in Kauf nehmen** to put up with something.

kaufen *verb* (PERF **hat gekauft**) to buy.

Käufer der (PL die **Käufer**) buyer.

Käuferin die (PL die **Käuferinnen**) buyer.

Kauffrau die (PL die **Kauffrauen**) businesswoman.

Kaufhaus das (PL die **Kaufhäuser**) department store.

Kaufmann der (PL die **Kaufleute**) businessman.

Kaugummi der (PL die **Kaugummis**) chewing gum.

kaum *adverb* hardly, scarcely.

kauern *verb* (PERF **hat gekauert**) to crouch.

Kaution die (PL die **Kautionen**) 1 deposit; 2 bail.

Kegel der (PL die **Kegel**) 1 cone; 2 skittle.

Kegelbahn die skittle alley.

kegeln *verb* (PERF **hat gekegelt**) to play skittles.

Kehle die (PL die **Kehlen**) throat.

Keim der (PL die **Keime**) 1 shoot; 2 germ.

kein *adjective* 1 no; **auf keinen Fall** on no account; 2 **ich habe keine Zeit** I haven't got any time; **er hat**

△ NEW SPELLING: *See page xii*

kein Geld he hasn't got any money; **3 keine zehn Minuten** less than ten minutes.

keiner, keine, kein(e)s *pronoun* **1** nobody, no one; **2** none, not one; **3 von diesen Kleidern gefällt mir keins** I don't like any of these dresses; **4 keiner von beiden** neither (of them).

keinesfalls *adverb* on no account.

keineswegs *adverb* by no means.

keinmal *adverb* not once.

keins SEE **keiner**.

Keks der (PL die **Kekse**) biscuit.

Keller der (PL die **Keller**) cellar.

Kellergeschoss △ das (PL die **Kellergeschosse**) basement.

Kellner der (PL die **Kellner**) waiter.

Kellnerin die (PL die **Kellnerinnen**) waitress.

kennen ✧ *verb* (IMPERF **kannte**, PERF **hat gekannt**) **1** to know; **2 kennen lernen** △ to get to know; **sich kennen lernen** to get to know each other; **3 kennen lernen** △ to meet; **ich habe Ulrike in London kennen gelernt** I met Ulrike in London; **wo habt ihr euch kennen gelernt?** where did you meet?

kennenlernen SEE **kennen**.

Kenntnis die (PL die **Kenntnisse**) **1** knowledge; **2 etwas zur Kenntnis nehmen** to take note of something.

Kennzeichen das (PL die **Kennzeichen**) **1** mark;

2 characteristic; **3** registration (number) (*of a vehicle*).

Kerl der (PL die **Kerle**) **1** bloke; **2 Eva ist ein netter Kerl** Eva's a nice girl.

Kern der (PL die **Kerne**) **1** pip; **2** stone (*of an apricot, peach*); **3** kernel (*of a nut*).

Kernenergie die nuclear power.

Kernkraftwerk das (PL die **Kernkraftwerke**) nuclear power station.

Kernwaffen *plural noun* nuclear weapons.

Kerze die (PL die **Kerzen**) candle.

Kerzenhalter der (PL die **Kerzenhalter**) candlestick.

Kessel der (PL die **Kessel**) **1** kettle; **2** boiler.

Kette die (PL die **Ketten**) chain.

Keule die (PL die **Keulen**) **1** club; **2** leg (*of lamb*); **3** drumstick (*of chicken*).

kichern *verb* (PERF **hat gekichert**) to giggle.

Kiefer[1] der (PL die **Kiefer**) jaw.

Kiefer[2] die (PL die **Kiefern**) pine tree.

Kieselstein der (PL die **Kieselsteine**) pebble.

Kilo das (PL die **Kilo(s)**) kilo.

Kilogramm das (PL die **Kilogramme**) kilogram.

Kilometer der (PL die **Kilometer**) kilometre.

Kind das (PL die **Kinder**) child.

✧ IRREGULAR VERB: *See the verb table in the centre of the dictionary*

Kindergarten *der* (PL *die* **Kindergärten**) nursery school.

Kindergeld *das* child benefit.

kinderleicht *adjective* very easy; **das ist kinderleicht** it's child's play.

Kindertagesstätte *die* (PL *die* **Kindertagesstätten**) day nursery.

Kinderwagen *der* (PL *die* **Kinderwagen**) pram.

Kindheit *die* childhood.

kindisch *adjective* childish.

Kinn *das* (PL *die* **Kinne**) chin.

Kino *das* (PL *die* **Kinos**) cinema.

kippen *verb* (PERF **hat gekippt**) **1** to tip; **2** (PERF **ist gekippt**) to topple.

Kirche *die* (PL *die* **Kirchen**) church.

Kirsche *die* (PL *die* **Kirschen**) cherry.

Kissen *das* (PL *die* **Kissen**) **1** cushion; **2** pillow.

Kiste *die* (PL *die* **Kisten**) **1** crate; **2** box.

kitzeln *verb* (PERF **hat gekitzelt**) to tickle.

kitzlig *adjective* ticklish.

Kiwi *die* (PL *die* **Kiwis**) kiwi fruit.

klagen *verb* (PERF **hat geklagt**) to complain.

Klammer *die* (PL *die* **Klammern**) **1** peg (*for washing*); **2** grip (*for hair*); **3** bracket.

klang SEE **klingen**.

Klang *der* (PL *die* **Klänge**) sound.

Klappe *die* (PL *die* **Klappen**) **1** flap;

2 clapperboard; **3** (*informal*) trap (*mouth*); **halt die Klappe!** shut up!

klappen *verb* (PERF **hat geklappt**) **1 nach vorne klappen** to tilt forward; **2 nach hinten klappen** to tip back; **3 nach oben klappen** to lift up; **4 nach unten klappen** to put down; **5** to work out; **hoffentlich klappt es** I hope it'll work out.

Klappstuhl *der* (PL *die* **Klappstühle**) folding chair.

klar *adjective* **1** clear (*water, answer*); **klar werden** △ to become clear; **2 jetzt ist mir alles klar** now I understand; **3 sich klar werden** △ to make up your mind; **4 sich über etwas im Klaren sein** △ to realize something.
adverb clearly; **na klar!** (*informal*) of course!

klären *verb* (PERF **hat geklärt**) **1** to clarify; **2** to sort out; **3** to purify (*sewage*); **4 sich klären** to clear (*of the weather or the sky*); **5 sich klären** to resolve itself, to be settled.

Klarinette *die* (PL *die* **Klarinetten**) clarinet.

klarwerden SEE **klar**.

klasse *adjective* (*informal*) great, smashing.

Klasse *die* (PL *die* **Klassen**) **1** class; **erster Klasse reisen** to travel first class; **2** year; **in die sechste Klasse gehen** to be in year six.

Klassenarbeit *die* (PL *die* **Klassenarbeiten**) (written) test.

Klassenbuch *das* register (*kept by*

△ NEW SPELLING: *See page xii*

the teacher, it also contains notes about students' achievements).

Klassenkamerad *der* (PL *die* **Klassenkameraden**) class-mate.

Klassenkameradin *die* (PL *die* **Klassenkameradinnen**) class-mate.

Klassensprecher *der* (PL *die* **Klassenprecher**) class representative.

Klassensprecherin *die* (PL *die* **Klassensprecherinnen**) class representative.

Klassenzimmer *das* (PL *die* **Klassenzimmer**) classroom.

klassisch *adjective* classical.

Klatsch *der* gossip.

klatschen *verb* (PERF **hat geklatscht**) 1 to clap; **jemandem Beifall klatschen** to clap somebody, to applaud somebody; 2 to slap; 3 to gossip.

klauen *verb* (*informal*) (PERF **hat geklaut**) to pinch.

Klavier *das* (PL *die* **Klaviere**) piano.

kleben *verb* (PERF **hat geklebt**) 1 to stick; 2 to glue; 3 **jemandem eine kleben** (*informal*) to belt somebody one.

klebrig *adjective* sticky.

Klebstoff *der* (PL *die* **Klebstoffe**) glue.

Klebstreifen *der* (PL *die* **Klebstreifen**) sticky tape.

Klecks *der* (PL *die* **Kleckse**) stain.

Kleid *das* (PL *die* **Kleider**) 1 dress;

Uschi hat sich zwei neue Kleider gekauft Uschi bought two new dresses; 2 **Kleider** clothes.

Kleiderbügel *der* (PL *die* **Kleiderbügel**) coat hanger.

Kleiderschrank *der* (PL *die* **Kleiderschränke**) wardrobe.

Kleidung *die* clothes, clothing.

klein *adjective* 1 small, little; **etwas klein schneiden** △ to cut something up small; 2 short; **Peter ist kleiner als Klaus** Peter is shorter than Klaus.

Kleingeld *das* change.

Klempner *der* (PL *die* **Klempner**) plumber.

klettern *verb* (PERF **ist geklettert**) to climb.

Klima *das* (PL *die* **Klimas**) climate.

Klimaanlage *die* (PL *die* **Klimaanlagen**) air conditioning.

Klinge *die* (PL *die* **Klingen**) blade.

Klingel *die* (PL *die* **Klingeln**) bell.

klingeln *verb* (PERF **hat geklingelt**) to ring; **es klingelt** there's a ring at the door.

klingen ◇ *verb* (IMPERF **klang**, PERF **hat geklungen**) to sound.

Klinik *die* (PL *die* **Kliniken**) clinic.

Klinke *die* (PL *die* **Klinken**) handle.

Klippe *die* (PL *die* **Klippen**) rock.

Klo *das* (*informal*) (PL *die* **Klos**) loo.

klopfen *verb* (PERF **hat geklopft**) 1 to knock; 2 to beat.

◇ IRREGULAR VERB: *See the verb table in the centre of the dictionary*

Klosett das (PL die **Klosetts**) lavatory.

Kloster das (PL die **Kloster**) 1 monastery; 2 convent.

Klotz der (PL die **Klötze**) block.

Klub der (PL die **Klubs**) club.

klug adjective 1 clever; 2 **ich werde daraus nicht klug** I don't understand it.

Klugheit die cleverness.

Klumpen der (PL die **Klumpen**) lump.

knabbern verb (PERF **hat geknabbert**) to nibble.

Knäckebrot das (PL die **Knäckebrote**) crispbread.

knacken verb (PERF **hat geknackt**) to crack.

Knall der (PL die **Knalle**) bang.

knallen verb (PERF **hat geknallt**) 1 to go bang; 2 to pop (of a cork); 3 to slam (of a door); 4 to crack (of a whip).

knapp adjective 1 scarce; 2 tight (skirt, top); 3 **knapp bei Kasse sein** to be short of money; 4 **mit knapper Mehrheit** by a narrow majority; 5 just; **eine knappe Stunde** just under an hour; **sie haben knapp verloren** they only just lost; 6 **das war knapp** (informal) that was a close shave.

knarren verb (PERF **hat geknarrt**) to creak.

Knauf der (PL die **Knäufe**) knob.

knautschen verb (PERF **hat geknautscht**) 1 to crumple; 2 to crease.

kneifen ✧ verb (IMPERF **kniff**, PERF **hat gekniffen**) 1 to pinch; 2 (informal) to chicken out; **sie hat mal wieder gekniffen und nichts gesagt** she's chickened out yet again and didn't say anything.

Kneipe die (PL die **Kneipen**) pub.

kneten verb (PERF **hat geknetet**) to knead.

knicken verb (PERF **hat geknickt**) 1 to bend; 2 to fold.

Knie das (PL die **Knie**) knee.

knien verb (PERF **hat gekniet**) 1 to kneel; 2 **sich knien** to kneel down.

kniff SEE **kneifen**.

knipsen verb (PERF **hat geknipst**) (to photograph) to take a snap, to take snaps.

Knoblauch der garlic.

Knoblauchzehe die (PL die **Knoblauchzehen**) clove of garlic.

Knöchel der (PL die **Knöchel**) 1 ankle; 2 knuckle; **Mario hat sich beim Jogging den Knöchel verstaucht** Mario sprained his ankle when jogging.

Knochen der (PL die **Knochen**) bone.

Knopf der (PL die **Knöpfe**) button.

Knoten der (PL die **Knoten**) 1 knot; 2 bun (as a hairstyle); 3 lump.

knurren verb (PERF **hat geknurrt**) 1 to growl; 2 to rumble; 3 to grumble.

knusprig adjective crisp, crusty (bread).

△ NEW SPELLING: See page xii

Koch der (PL die **Köche**) 1 cook;
2 chef.

Kochbuch das (PL die **Kochbücher**)
cookery book.

kochen verb (PERF **hat gekocht**) 1 to
cook; 2 to boil; **das Wasser kocht**
the water's boiling.

Köchin die (PL die **Köchinnen**) cook.

Kochtopf der (PL die **Kochtöpfe**)
saucepan.

Koffer der (PL die **Koffer**) suitcase.

Kofferkuli der (PL die **Kofferkulis**)
baggage trolley.

Kofferraum der (PL die
Kofferräume) boot.

Kohl der 1 cabbage; 2 (informal)
rubbish; **rede keinen Kohl** don't
talk rubbish.

Kohle die (PL die **Kohlen**) coal.

Kokosnuss Δ die (PL die
Kokosnüsse) coconut.

Kollege der (PL die **Kollegen**)
colleague.

Kollegin die (PL die **Kolleginnen**)
colleague.

Köln das Cologne.

Kölnischwasser das eau de
cologne.

Kombination die (PL die
Kombinationen) combination.

Komfort der comfort.

Komiker der (PL die **Komiker**)
comedian.

komisch adjective funny.

Komma das (PL die **Kommas**)
1 comma; 2 decimal point; **zwei
Komma fünf** two point five.

kommen ✧ verb (IMPERF **kam**, PERF
ist gekommen) 1 to come; 2 to get;
wie komme ich zur U-Bahn? how
do I get to the tube station?; **kommt
gut nach Hause!** have a safe
journey home!; 3 **etwas kommen
lassen** to send for something; 4 **wie
kommst du darauf?** what gave you
that idea?; 5 **hinter etwas kommen**
to find out about something; 6 **zur
Schule kommen** to start school;
7 to go; **die Gabeln kommen in die
Schublade** the forks go in the
drawer; **ins Krankenhaus kommen**
to go to hospital; 8 **wer kommt
zuerst?** who's first?; **du kommst an
die Reihe** it's your turn; 9 **wie
kommt das?** why is that?; 10 **zu
etwas kommen** to acquire
something; 11 **wieder zu sich
kommen** to come round (after
fainting or anaesthetic); 12 **dazu
kommen, etwas zu tun** to get round
to doing something; **ich komme
einfach nicht zum Einkaufen** I just
can't get round to doing the
shopping; 13 **das kommt davon!**
see what happens!

Kommissar der (PL die
Kommissare) superintendent.

Kommode die (PL die **Kommoden**)
chest of drawers.

Kommunismus der communism.

Kommunist der (PL die
Kommunisten) communist.

Kommunistin die (PL die
Kommunistinnen) communist.

✧ IRREGULAR VERB: See the verb table in the centre of the dictionary

Komödie *die* (PL *die* **Komödien**) comedy.

Kompass Δ *der* (PL *die* **Kompasse**) compass.

komplett *adjective* complete.

Kompliment *das* (PL *die* **Komplimente**) compliment.

kompliziert *adjective* complicated.

Komponist *der* (PL *die* **Komponisten**) composer.

Komponistin *die* (PL *die* **Komponistinnen**) composer.

Kompott *das* (PL *die* **Kompotte**) stewed fruit.

Kompromiss Δ *der* (PL *die* **Kompromisse**) compromise; **einen Kompromiss schließen** to compromise.

Konditorei *die* (PL *die* **Konditoreien**) patisserie, cake shop.

Kondom *das* (PL *die* **Kondome**) condom.

Konfektion *die* ready-made clothes.

Konferenz *die* (PL *die* **Konferenzen**) conference.

Konflikt *der* (PL *die* **Konflikte**) conflict.

König *der* (PL *die* **Könige**) king.

Königin *die* (PL *die* **Königinnen**) queen.

königlich *adjective* royal.

Königreich *das* (PL *die* **Königreiche**) kingdom.

Konjunktion *die* (PL *die* **Konjunktionen**) conjunction.

Konkurrent *der* (PL *die* **Konkurrenten**) competitor.

Konkurrentin *die* (PL *die* **Konkurrentinnen**) competitor.

Konkurrenz *die* competition.

können ✧ *verb* (PRES **kann**, IMPERF **konnte**, PERF **hat gekonnt**) **1** can; **kann ich Ihnen helfen?** can I help you?; **kannst du Auto fahren?** can you drive?; **kannst du Deutsch?** can you speak German?; **ich konnte nicht früher kommen** I couldn't come any earlier; **das kann ich nicht** I can't do that; **2** **etwas können** to be able to do something; **er wird es vor Dienstag nicht machen können** he won't be able to do it before Tuesday; **3** **das kann gut sein** that may well be so; **es kann sein, dass …** it may be that …; **4** **ich kann nichts dafür** it's not my fault.

Können *das* ability.

Könner *der* (PL *die* **Könner**) expert.

könnt SEE **können**.

konnte, konnten, konntest, konntet SEE **können**.

Konserven *plural noun* tinned food.

Konsonant *der* (PL *die* **Konsonanten**) consonant.

Korsika *das* Corsica.

Kontakt *der* (PL *die* **Kontakte**) contact.

Kontaktlinse *die* (PL *die* **Kontaktlinsen**) contact lens.

Kontinent der (PL die **Kontinente**) continent.

Konto das (PL die **Konten**) account.

Kontrolle die (PL die **Kontrollen**) 1 check; 2 control.

Kontrolleur der (PL die **Kontrolleure**) inspector.

kontrollieren verb (PERF **hat kontrolliert**) 1 to check; 2 to control.

konzentrieren verb (PERF **hat konzentriert**) 1 to concentrate; 2 sich konzentrieren to concentrate.

Konzert das (PL die **Konzerte**) 1 concert; 2 concerto.

Kopf der (PL die **Köpfe**) 1 head; 2 sich den Kopf zerbrechen to rack your brains; 3 seinen Kopf durchsetzen to get your own way; 4 sich den Kopf waschen to wash your hair; 5 auf dem Kopf upside down; 6 ein Kopf Salat a lettuce.

köpfen verb (PERF **hat geköpft**) 1 to head (in football); 2 to behead.

Kopfhörer der (PL die **Kopfhörer**) headphones.

Kopfkissen das (PL die **Kopfkissen**) pillow.

Kopfsalat der (PL die **Kopfsalate**) lettuce.

Kopfschmerzen plural noun headache.

Kopie die (PL die **Kopien**) copy.

kopieren verb (PERF **hat kopiert**) to copy.

Kopiergerät das (PL die **Kopiergeräte**) photocopier.

Korb der (PL die **Körbe**) 1 basket; 2 jemandem einen Korb geben to turn somebody down.

Kork der (PL die **Korke**) cork.

Korken der (PL die **Korken**) cork.

Korkenzieher der (PL die **Korkenzieher**) corkscrew.

Korn das (PL die **Körner**) corn.

Körper der (PL die **Körper**) body.

körperbehindert adjective disabled.

körperlich adjective physical.

Korrektur die (PL die **Korrekturen**) correction.

korrigieren verb (PERF **hat korrigiert**) to correct.

koscher adjective kosher.

Kosmetik die (PL die **Kosmetika**) 1 cosmetics; 2 beauty care.

Kost die food.

kostbar adjective precious.

kosten verb (PERF **hat gekostet**) 1 to cost; 2 wie viel kostet es? how much is it?; 3 to taste.

Kosten plural noun 1 cost; 2 expenses.

kostenlos adjective free (of charge).

köstlich adjective 1 delicious; 2 funny.

Kostüm das (PL die **Kostüme**) 1 suit; 2 costume.

Kotelett das (PL die **Koteletts**) chop.

✧ IRREGULAR VERB: *See the verb table in the centre of the dictionary*

Krabbe die (PL die **Krabben**) 1 crab;
2 shrimp.

krabbeln verb (PERF **ist gekrabbelt**)
to crawl.

Krach der 1 row; 2 noise; 3 crash.

krachen verb (PERF **hat gekracht**)
1 to crash; 2 (PERF **ist gekracht**) to
crack; **er ist gegen die Mauer
gekracht** he crashed into the wall.

krächzen verb (PERF **hat gekrächzt**)
to croak.

Kraft die (PL die **Kräfte**) 1 strength;
er hat nicht viel Kraft he's not very
strong; 2 force; **in Kraft treten** to
come into force; 3 **geistige Kräfte**
mental powers; 4 worker.

kräftig adjective 1 strong;
2 nourishing.
adverb 1 strongly; 2 hard; **kräftig
schütteln** shake hard.

Kraftwerk das (PL die **Kraftwerke**)
power station.

Kragen der (PL die **Kragen**) collar.

Krähe die (PL die **Krähen**) crow.

Kralle die (PL die **Krallen**) claw.

Kram der stuff; **mach deinen Kram
allein!** (informal) do it yourself!

kramen verb (PERF **hat gekramt**) to
rummage about.

Krampf der (PL die **Krämpfe**) cramp.

Kran der (PL die **Kräne**) crane
(machine).

Kranich der (PL die **Kraniche**) crane
(bird).

krank adjective ill, sick; **krank
werden** to fall ill.

Kranke der/die (PL die **Kranken**)
patient.

kränken verb (PERF **hat gekränkt**) to
hurt.

Krankenhaus das (PL die
Krankenhäuser) hospital; **sie
haben ihn gestern ins Krankenhaus
eingeliefert** he was taken to
hospital yesterday.

Krankenkasse die health
insurance; **bei welcher
Krankenkasse sind Sie versichert?**
what health insurance have you got?

Krankenpfleger der (PL die
Krankenpfleger) (male) nurse.

Krankenpflegerin die (PL die
Krankenpflegerinnen) nurse.

Krankenschwester die (PL die
Krankenschwestern) nurse; **Ulrike
ist Krankenschwester** Ulrike is a
nurse.

Krankenwagen der (PL die
Krankenwagen) ambulance.

Krankheit die (PL die **Krankheiten**)
illness, disease.

kratzen verb (PERF **hat gekratzt**) to
scratch.

Kratzer der (PL die **Kratzer**) scratch.

kraus adjective frizzy.

Kraut das (PL die **Kräuter**) 1 herb;
2 sauerkraut; 3 cabbage.

Krawall der (PL die **Krawalle**) 1 riot;
2 row.

Krawatte die (PL die **Krawatten**) tie.

kreativ adjective creative.

△ NEW SPELLING: See page xii

Krebs der (PL die **Krebse**) 1 crab;
2 cancer; 3 Cancer.

Kredit der (PL die **Kredite**) credit; **auf
Kredit** on credit.

Kreditkarte die (PL die
Kreditkarten) credit card.

Kreide die (PL die **Kreiden**) chalk.

kreieren verb (PERF **hat kreiert**) to
create.

Kreis der (PL die **Kreise**) 1 circle;
2 district.

Kreislauf der 1 cycle;
2 circulation.

Kreuz das (PL die **Kreuze**) 1 cross;
2 (small of the) back; 3 intersection
(of a motorway); 4 clubs (in cards).

kreuzen verb (PERF **hat gekreuzt**)
1 to cross; 2 **sich kreuzen** to cross.

Kreuzung die (PL die **Kreuzungen**)
1 crossroads; 2 cross (of plants,
animals).

Kreuzfahrt die (PL die
Kreuzfahrten) 1 cruise; **eine
Kreuzfahrt machen** to go on a
cruise; 2 crusade.

Kreuzworträtsel das (PL die
Kreuzworträtsel) crossword
(puzzle).

kriechen ✧ verb (IMPERF **kroch**, PERF
ist gekrochen) to crawl.

Krieg der (PL die **Kriege**) war.

kriegen verb (informal) (PERF **hat
gekriegt**) 1 to get; 2 **ein Kind
kriegen** to have a baby.

Krimi der (PL die **Krimis**) thriller.

Kriminalroman der (PL die
Kriminalromane) crime novel.

kriminell adjective criminal.

Kriminelle der/die (PL die
Kriminellen) criminal.

Krippe die (PL die **Krippen**)
1 manger; 2 crib; 3 crèche.

Krise die (PL die **Krisen**) crisis.

Kristall[1] der (PL die **Kristalle**) crystal.

Kristall[2] das (glass) crystal.

kritisch adjective critical.

kritisieren verb (PERF **hat kritisiert**)
1 to criticize; 2 to review.

kroch SEE **kriechen**.

Krokodil das (PL die **Krokodile**)
crocodile.

Krone die (PL die **Kronen**) crown.

Kröte die (PL die **Kröten**) toad.

Krücke die (PL die **Krücken**) crutch.

Krug der (PL die **Krüge**) 1 jug; 2 mug.

Krümel der (PL die **Krümel**) crumb.

krümelig adjective crumbly.

krumm adjective 1 bent; 2 crooked.

Kruste die (PL die **Krusten**) crust.

Küche die (PL die **Küchen**)
1 kitchen; 2 cooking; **die
italienische Küche** Italian cooking;
3 **warme Küche** hot food.

Kuchen der (PL die **Kuchen**) cake.

Kuckuck der (PL die **Kuckucke**)
cuckoo.

Kugel die (PL die **Kugeln**) 1 ball;
2 bullet; 3 sphere.

✧ IRREGULAR VERB: See the verb table in the centre of the dictionary

Kugelschreiber der (PL die **Kugelschreiber**) ballpoint pen, biro™.

Kuh die (PL die **Kühe**) cow.

kühl adjective cool.

kühlen verb (PERF **hat gekühlt**) **1** to cool, to chill; **2** to refrigerate.

Kühler der (PL die **Kühler**) radiator.

Kühlerhaube die (PL die **Kühlerhauben**) bonnet.

Kühlschrank der (PL die **Kühlschränke**) fridge.

Kühltruhe die (PL die **Kühltruhen**) freezer.

Küken das (PL die **Küken**) chick.

Kuli der (PL die **Kulis**) biro™.

Kultur die (PL die **Kulturen**) **1** culture; **2** civilization.

Kulturbeutel der (PL die **Kulturbeutel**) toilet bag.

kulturell adjective cultural.

Kummer der **1** sorrow; **2** worry; **3** trouble.

kümmern verb (PERF **hat gekümmert**) **1** to concern; **2 sich um jemanden kümmern** to look after somebody; **sich um den Garten kümmern** to look after the garden; **3 sich darum kümmern, dass ...** to see to it that ...; **4 kümmere dich um deine eigenen Angelegenheiten** mind your own business.

Kunde der (PL die **Kunden**) **1** customer; **2** client.

kündigen verb (PERF **hat gekündigt**) **1** to cancel; **2** to give notice; **die Firma hat ihm gekündigt** the company gave him his notice; **3 seine Stellung kündigen** to hand in your notice.

Kundin die (PL die **Kundinnen**) **1** customer; **2** client.

Kundschaft die customers.

Kunst die (PL die **Künste**) **1** art; **2** skill.

Künstler der (PL die **Künstler**) artist.

Künstlerin die (PL die **Künstlerinnen**) artist.

künstlerisch adjective artistic.

künstlich adjective artificial.

Kunststoff der (PL die **Kunststoffe**) plastic.

Kunststück das (PL die **Kunststücke**) **1** trick; **2** feat.

Kunstwerk das (PL die **Kunstwerke**) work of art.

Kupfer das copper.

Kupplung die (PL die **Kupplungen**) **1** clutch (of a car); **2** coupling.

Kürbis der (PL die **Kürbisse**) pumpkin.

Kurort der (PL die **Kurorte**) health resort.

Kurs der (PL die **Kurse**) **1** course; **2** exchange rate; **3** price (of shares).

Kurve die (PL die **Kurven**) **1** curve; **2** bend.

kurz adjective **1** short; **vor kurzem** a short time ago; **2 zu kurz kommen**

△ NEW SPELLING: See page xii

to get less than your fair share, to come off badly.
adverb 1 shortly; 2 briefly; 3 **kurz gesagt** in a word.

Kurzarbeit *die* short-time working.

kurzärmelig *adjective* short-sleeved.

kürzen *verb* (PERF **hat gekürzt**) 1 to shorten; 2 to cut.

kurzfristig *adjective* short-term. *adverb* at short notice.

kürzlich *adverb* recently.

kurzsichtig *adjective* short-sighted.

Kurzwaren *plural noun* haberdashery.

Kusine *die* (PL *die* **Kusinen**) cousin.

Kuss Δ *der* (PL *die* **Küsse**) kiss.

küssen *verb* (PERF **hat geküsst** Δ) 1 to kiss; 2 **sich küssen** to kiss.

Küste *die* (PL *die* **Küsten**) coast.

Kuvert *das* (PL *die* **Kuverts**) envelope.

L l

Labor *das* (PL *die* **Labors**) laboratory.

Lache *die* (PL *die* **Lachen**) pool.

lächeln *verb* (PERF **hat gelächelt**) to smile.

lachen *verb* (PERF **hat gelacht**) to laugh.

lächerlich *adjective* ridiculous.

Lachs *der* (PL *die* **Lachse**) salmon.

Lack *der* (PL *die* **Lacke**) 1 varnish; 2 paint.

lackieren *verb* (PERF **hat lackiert**) 1 to varnish; 2 to spray (*with paint*)

laden ✧ *verb* (PRES **lädt**, IMPERF **lud**, PERF **hat geladen**) 1 to load; **wir haben die Möbel in den Möbelwagen geladen** we loaded the furniture into the removal van; 2 **eine Batterie laden** to charge a battery; 3 to summon; **mein Bruder wurde als Zeuge geladen** my brother was summoned as a witness

Laden *der* (PL *die* **Läden**) 1 shop; **wann macht der Laden zu?** when does the shop close?; 2 shutter; **wenn es heiß ist, lassen wir die Läden den ganzen Tag zu** when it hot we keep the shutters closed all day.

Ladendieb *der* (PL *die* **Ladendiebe**) shoplifter.

Ladung *die* (PL *die* **Ladungen**) 1 cargo; 2 charge (*of dynamite or shot*); 3 summons; 4 load.

lag SEE **liegen**.

Lage *die* (PL *die* **Lagen**) 1 situation; **nicht in der Lage sein, etwas zu tun** not be in a position to do something; 2 layer.

Lager *das* (PL *die* **Lager**) 1 camp; 2 warehouse; 3 stock; **etwas auf Lager haben** to have something in stock; 4 stock-room; 5 bearing (*in a machine*).

lagern *verb* (PERF **hat gelagert**) 1 to store; 2 to camp.

✧ IRREGULAR VERB: *See the verb table in the centre of the dictionary*

ahm *adjective* lame.

ähmen *verb* (PERF **hat gelähmt**) to paralyse.

ähmung *die* paralysis.

aib *der* (PL *die* **Laibe**) loaf.

aken *das* (PL *die* **Laken**) sheet.

akritze *die* liquorice.

amm *das* (PL *die* **Lämmer**) lamb.

ampe *die* (PL *die* **Lampen**) lamp.

ampenschirm *der* (PL *die* **Lampenschirme**) lampshade.

and *das* (PL *die* **Länder**) 1 country; **auf dem Land** in the country; 2 land; 3 state (*there are 16 Länder in Germany*).

andebahn *die* (PL *die* **Landebahnen**) runway.

anden *verb* (PERF **ist gelandet**) 1 to land; 2 **im Krankenhaus landen** (*informal*) to end up in hospital.

andkarte *die* (PL *die* **Landkarten**) map.

andkreis *der* (PL *die* **Landkreise**) district.

ändlich *adjective* rural.

andschaft *die* (PL *die* **Landschaften**) 1 countryside; 2 landscape.

andstraße *die* (PL *die* **Landstraßen**) country road.

andtag *der* state parliament.

andwirtschaft *die* agriculture, farming.

ang *adjective* 1 long; **seit langem** for a long time; 2 tall. *adverb* **eine Woche lang** for a week.

langärmelig *adjective* long-sleeved.

lange *adverb* 1 a long time; **lange nicht** not for a long time; 2 **so lange wie möglich** as long as possible; 3 **er ist lange nicht so reich** he's nowhere near as rich.

Länge *die* (PL *die* **Längen**) 1 length; 2 longitude.

langen *verb* (PERF **hat gelangt**) 1 to be enough; **das Geld langt nicht** it's not enough money; **mir langt's** (*informal*) I've had enough; 2 to reach; **nach etwas langen** to reach for something; 3 **jemandem eine langen** (*informal*) to slap somebody's face.

Langlauf *der* cross-country (*in skiing*).

langsam *adjective, adverb* slow; **die Musik geht mir langsam auf die Nerven** the music is slowly getting on my nerves.

längst *adverb* 1 a long time ago; **das habe ich schon längst gemacht** I did it a long time ago; 2 for a long time; **er weiß es schon längst** he's known it for a long time; 3 **längst nicht** nowhere near, not nearly.

längster, längste, längstes *adjective* longest; **Marion hat den längsten Aufsatz geschrieben** Marion wrote the longest essay.

langweilen *verb* (PERF **hat gelangweilt**) 1 to bore; 2 **sich langweilen** to be bored.

△ NEW SPELLING: *See page xii*

langweilig *adjective* boring.

Lappen *der* (PL *die* **Lappen**) cloth, rag.

Laptop *der* (PL *die* **Laptops**) laptop.

Lärm *der* noise.

las SEE **lesen**

Laser *der* (PL *die* **Laser**) laser.

Laserdrucker *der* (PL *die* **Laserdrucker**) laser printer.

lassen ⬦ *verb* (PRES **lässt** Δ, IMPERF **ließ**, PERF **hat gelassen**) 1 to let; **jemanden schlafen lassen** to let somebody sleep; **lass uns jetzt gehen** let's go now; 2 **jemandem etwas lassen** to let somebody have something; 3 to leave; **die Kinder zu Hause lassen** to leave the children at home; **lass mich!** leave me!; 4 **jemanden warten lassen** to keep somebody waiting; 5 **etwas reparieren lassen** to have something repaired; 6 **lass das!** stop it!; 7 **die Tür lässt sich leicht öffnen** the door opens easily; **das lässt sich alles machen** that can all be arranged.

lässig *adjective* casual.

Last *die* (PL *die* **Lasten**) 1 load; 2 **jemandem zur Last fallen** to be a burden on somebody.

lästig *adjective* troublesome.

Lastwagen *der* (PL *die* **Lastwagen**) lorry, truck.

Latein *das* Latin.

Laterne *die* (PL *die* **Laternen**) 1 lantern; 2 street lamp.

Laub *das* leaves.

Lauch *der* leek(s).

Lauf *der* (PL *die* **Läufe**) 1 run; 2 course; **im Laufe der Zeit** in the course of time; **im Laufe der Jahre** over the years; 3 race; 4 barrel (*of a gun*).

Laufbahn *die* (PL *die* **Laufbahnen**) career.

laufen ⬦ *verb* (PRES **läuft**, IMPERF **lief** PERF **ist gelaufen**) 1 to run; **sie kann viel schneller laufen als ihr Bruder** she can run much faster than her brother; 2 to walk; **du kannst nach Hause laufen oder mit dem Bus fahren** you can walk home or go on the bus; 3 to be valid; 4 **Ski laufen** to ski; 5 to be on (*of a film, programme, or machine*).

laufend *adjective* 1 running; 2 current (*issue, month*); 3 **auf dem Laufenden sein** Δ to be up to date; **Anita hält mich auf dem Laufenden** Δ Anita keeps me up to date.
adverb continually, constantly.

Läufer *der* (PL *die* **Läufer**) 1 runner; 2 rug; 3 bishop (*in chess*).

Läuferin *die* (PL *die* **Läuferinnen**) runner.

Laufmasche *die* (PL *die* **Laufmaschen**) ladder (*in your tights*).

Laufwerk *das* (PL *die* **Laufwerke**) drive (*on a computer*).

Laune *die* (PL *die* **Launen**) mood.

launisch *adjective* moody.

⬦ IRREGULAR VERB: *See the verb table in the centre of the dictionary*

Laus *die* (PL *die* **Läuse**) louse.

laut *adjective* **1** loud; **2** noisy.
adverb **1** loudly; **2** **laut lesen** to read aloud; **3** **lauter stellen** to turn up.
preposition ←(+GEN *or* +DAT) according to.

Laut *der* (PL *die* **Laute**) sound.

lauten *verb* (PERF **hat gelautet**) **1** to be; **2** to go.

läuten *verb* (PERF **hat geläutet**) to ring.

lauter *adjective* nothing but.

Lautsprecher *der* (PL *die* **Lautsprecher**) (loud)speaker.

Lautstärke *die* volume.

lauwarm *adjective* lukewarm.

Lavendel *der* lavender.

Lawine *die* (PL *die* **Lawinen**) avalanche.

leben *verb* (PERF **hat gelebt**) **1** to live; **2** to be alive; **3** **leb wohl!** farewell!

Leben *das* (PL *die* **Leben**) life; **am Leben sein** to be alive; **ums Leben kommen** to lose your life.

lebend *adjective* living.

lebendig *adjective* **1** living; **2** **lebendig sein** to be alive; **3** lively.

Lebensgefahr *die* mortal danger; **sein Vater ist in Lebensgefahr** his father is critically ill.

lebensgefährlich *adjective* **1** extremely dangerous; **2** critical;

lebensgefährlich verletzt critically injured.

Lebenshaltungskosten *plural noun* cost of living.

lebenslänglich *adjective* life.
adverb for life.

Lebenslauf *der* (PL *die* **Lebensläufe**) CV.

Lebensmittel *plural noun* food, groceries.

Lebensmittelgeschäft *das* (PL *die* **Lebensmittelgeschäfte**) grocer's (shop).

Lebensunterhalt *der* livelihood; **seinen Lebensunterhalt verdienen** to earn one's living.

Leber *die* (PL *die* **Lebern**) liver.

Leberfleck *der* (PL *die* **Leberflecke**) mole.

Leberwurst *die* liver sausage.

Lebewesen *das* (PL *die* **Lebewesen**) living being, living thing.

lebhaft *adjective* **1** lively; **2** vivid (*idea, colour*).

Lebkuchen *der* (PL *die* **Lebkuchen**) gingerbread.

leblos *adjective* lifeless.

Leck *das* (PL *die* **Lecks**) leak.

lecken *verb* (PERF **hat geleckt**) **1** to lick; **die Katze leckte ihre Jungen** the cat licked the kittens; **an etwas lecken** to lick something; **2** to leak.

lecker *adjective* delicious.

Leder *das* (PL *die* **Leder**) leather.

△ NEW SPELLING: *See page xii*

ledig *adjective* single.

lediglich *adverb* merely.

leer *adjective* empty; **leer machen** to empty.

leeren *verb* (PERF **hat geleert**) 1 to empty; 2 **ein leeres Blatt Papier** a blank sheet of paper; 3 **sich leeren** to empty.

Leerlauf *der* neutral (*gear*).

Leerung *die* (PL die **Leerungen**) collection.

legal *adjective* legal.

legen *verb* (PERF **hat gelegt**) 1 to put; 2 to lay; 3 **sich legen** to lie down; 4 **sich legen** to die down (*of a storm, noise*); **unsere Begeisterung hat sich gelegt** our enthusiasm has worn off.

leger *adjective, adverb* casual; **leger gekleidet sein** to be casually dressed.

Lehm *der* clay.

Lehne *die* (PL die **Lehnen**) 1 back (*of a chair*); 2 arm (*of a sofa or chair*).

lehnen *verb* (PERF **hat gelehnt**) 1 to lean; 2 **sich an etwas lehnen** to lean against something.

Lehrbuch *das* (PL die **Lehrbücher**) textbook.

lehren *verb* (PERF **hat gelehrt**) to teach.

Lehrer *der* (PL die **Lehrer**) 1 teacher; 2 instructor.

Lehrerin *die* (PL die **Lehrerinnen**) 1 teacher; 2 instructor.

Lehrerzimmer *das* (PL die **Lehrerzimmer**) staffroom.

Lehrling *der* (PL die **Lehrlinge**) 1 apprentice; 2 trainee.

Lehrplan *der* (PL die **Lehrpläne**) syllabus.

Lehrstelle *die* (PL die **Lehrstellen**) apprenticeship.

Leibwächter *der* (PL die **Leibwächter**) bodyguard.

Leiche *die* (PL die **Leichen**) (dead) body, corpse.

leicht *adjective* 1 light; 2 easy; **jemandem leicht fallen** Δ to be easy for somebody; **es ist ihm nicht leicht gefallen** it wasn't easy for him; **Markus macht es sich immer leicht** Markus always takes the easy way out; 3 **ein leichter Akzent** a slight accent.

Leichtathletik *die* athletics.

leichtfallen SEE **leicht**.

Leichtsinn *der* 1 carelessness; 2 recklessness.

leichtsinnig *adjective* 1 careless; 2 reckless.

leid *adjective* **jemanden leid sein** Δ to be fed up with somebody; **etwas leid sein** Δ to be fed up with something.

Leid *das* 1 sorrow; 2 harm; 3 **es tut mir Leid** Δ I'm sorry; **Andreas tut mir Leid** Δ I feel sorry for Andreas.

leiden ♦ *verb* (IMPERF **litt**, PERF **hat gelitten**) 1 to suffer; 2 **jemanden gut leiden können** to like

♦ IRREGULAR VERB: *See the verb table in the centre of the dictionary*

somebody; **3 ich kann Erika nicht leiden** I can't stand Erika.

leider *adverb* **1** unfortunately; **2 leider ja** I'm afraid so; **leider nicht** I'm afraid not.

leihen ✧ *verb* (IMPERF **lieh**, PERF **hat geliehen**) **1** to lend; **2 sich etwas leihen** to borrow something; **ich habe mir das Buch von Alex geliehen** I borrowed the book from Alex.

Leihwagen *der* (PL *die* **Leihwagen**) hire car.

Leim *der* (PL *die* **Leime**) glue.

Leine *die* (PL *die* **Leinen**) **1** rope; **2** line (*for washing*); **3** lead (*for a dog*).

Leinen *das* (PL *die* **Leinen**) linen.

Leinwand *die* screen (*in a cinema*).

leise *adjective* quiet.
adverb **1** quietly; **2 die Musik leiser stellen** to turn the music down.

leisten *verb* (PERF **hat geleistet**) **1** to achieve; **2 jemandem Hilfe leisten** to help somebody; **3 jemandem Gesellschaft leisten** to keep somebody company; **4 sich etwas leisten** to treat yourself to something; **5 sich etwas leisten können** to be able to afford something; **ich kann mir kein neues Auto leisten** I can't afford a new car.

Leistung *die* (PL *die* **Leistungen**) **1** achievement; **2** performance; **3 Leistungen** payment.

leiten *verb* (PERF **hat geleitet**) **1** to lead; **2** to direct; **3** to manage, run (*a business*); **4** to conduct.

Leiter[1] *die* (PL *die* **Leitern**) ladder.

Leiter[2] *der* (PL *die* **Leiter**) **1** leader; **2** head; **3** manager; **4** director; **5** conductor (*of an orchestra or electricity*).

Leiterin *die* (PL *die* **Leiterinnen**) **1** leader; **2** head; **3** manageress; **4** director.

Leitung *die* (PL *die* **Leitungen**) **1** direction; **2** management; **3** (*phone*) line; **4** (*electric*) lead; **5** cable; **6** pipe; **7 unter der Leitung von** conducted by.

Leitungswasser *das* tap water.

Lektion *die* (PL *die* **Lektionen**) lesson.

lenken *verb* (PERF **hat gelenkt**) **1** to steer; **2** to guide; **3 den Verdacht auf jemanden lenken** to throw suspicion on somebody.

Lenkrad *das* (PL *die* **Lenkräder**) steering wheel.

Lenkstange *die* (PL *die* **Lenkstangen**) handlebars.

lernen *verb* (PERF **hat gelernt**) **1** to learn; **schwimmen lernen** to learn to swim; **2** to study.

lesen ✧ *verb* (PRES **liest**, IMPERF **las**, PERF **hat gelesen**) to read.

Leser *der* (PL *die* **Leser**) reader.

Leserin *die* (PL *die* **Leserinnen**) reader.

letzte SEE **letzter**.

Letzte ⚠ *der/die/das* (PL *die* **Letzten**) **1 der/die Letzte** the last (one); **das**

Letzte the last (thing); **2 Boris kam als Letzter** Boris arrived last.

letztens *adverb* **1** recently; **2** lastly.

letzter, letzte, letztes *adjective* **1** last; **zum letzten Mal** for the last time; **das letzte Mal** the last time; **2** latest (*news, information*); **3 in letzter Zeit** recently.

leuchten *verb* (PERF **hat geleuchtet**) to shine.

Leuchter *der* (PL *die* **Leuchter**) candlestick.

Leuchtreklame *die* neon sign.

Leuchtturm *der* (PL *die* **Leuchttürme**) lighthouse.

leugnen *verb* (PERF **hat geleugnet**) to deny.

Leute *plural noun* people.

Lexikon *das* (PL *die* **Lexika**) **1** encyclopedia; **2** dictionary.

Licht *das* (PL *die* **Lichter**) light.

Lichtbild *das* (PL *die* **Lichtbilder**) photograph.

Lichtschalter *der* (PL *die* **Lichtschalter**) light switch.

Lid *das* (PL *die* **Lider**) (eye)lid.

Lidschatten *der* (PL *die* **Lidschatten**) eye shadow.

lieb *adjective* **1** dear; **liebe Gabi** dear Gabi; **2** nice; **das ist lieb von euch** that's nice of you; **3 jemanden lieb haben** △ to be fond of somebody; **4 es wäre mir lieber, wenn** … I'd prefer it if …; **5 ihr liebstes Spielzeug** her favourite toy.

Liebe *die* (PL *die* **Lieben**) love.

lieben *verb* (PERF **hat geliebt**) to love.

liebenswürdig *adjective* kind.

lieber *adverb* **1** rather; **2 lieber mögen** to like better; **3 lass das lieber** you'd better not do that; **4 ich trinke lieber Kaffee** I prefer coffee.

Liebesbrief *der* (PL *die* **Liebesbriefe**) love letter.

Liebeskummer *der* **Liebeskummer haben** to be lovesick.

liebevoll *adjective* loving.

liebhaben SEE **lieb**.

Liebling *der* (PL *die* **Lieblinge**) **1** darling; **2** favourite.

Lieblings- *prefix* favourite.

liebster, liebste, liebstes *adjective* **1** dearest; **2** favourite. *adverb* **am liebsten** best (of all); **ich mag Max am liebsten** I like Max best.

Lied *das* (PL *die* **Lieder**) song.

lief SEE **laufen**.

liefern *verb* (PERF **hat geliefert**) **1** to deliver; **2** to supply.

Lieferung *die* (PL *die* **Lieferungen**) delivery.

Lieferwagen *der* (PL *die* **Lieferwagen**) (delivery) van.

liegen ◇ *verb* (IMPERF **lag**, PERF **hat gelegen**) **1** to lie; **der Brief liegt auf dem Tisch** the letter is on the table; **es liegt viel Schnee** there's lots of snow; **2** to be, to be situated; **3 liegen bleiben** △ to stay (*in bed*); **er ist liegen geblieben** he didn't get

up; **4 etwas bleibt liegen**
something is left behind; **die Arbeit
ist liegen geblieben** the job was left
undone; **5 der Schnee bleibt liegen**
the snow is settling; **6 liegen
lassen** △ to leave; **7 es liegt mir
nicht** it doesn't suit me; **8 an etwas
liegen** to be due to something;
9 das liegt an ihm it's up to him.

liegenbleiben, liegenlassen
SEE **liegen**.

Liegestuhl der (PL die **Liegestühle**)
deckchair.

Liegewagen der (PL die
Liegewagen) couchette (car).

ließ SEE **lassen**.

liest SEE **lesen**.

Lift der (PL die **Lifte**) lift.

Liga die (PL die **Ligen**) league.

lila adjective **1** purple; **2** mauve.

Limo die (PL die **Limo(s)**) = **Limonade**.

Limonade die (PL die **Limonaden**)
1 fizzy drink; **2** lemonade.

Limone die (PL die **Limonen**) lime.

Lineal das (PL die **Lineale**) ruler.

Linie die (PL die **Linien**) **1** line;
2 route (of a bus); **Linie 6**
number 6.

Linke die **1** left; **zu meiner Linken**
on my left; **2** left hand; **3** left side;
4 die Linke the left (in politics).

linker, linke, linkes adjective
1 left; **2** left-wing.

links adverb **1** on the left; **links
fahren** to drive on the left; **links

abbiegen** to turn left; **nach links**
left; **von links** from the left; **2 links
sein** to be left-wing; **3 zwei links,
zwei rechts stricken** to purl two,
knit two; **4** (clothing) inside out.

Linkshänder der (PL die
Linkshänder) left-hander.

Linkshänderin die (PL die
Linkshänderinnen) left-hander.

Linse die (PL die **Linsen**) **1** lens;
2 lentil.

Lippe die (PL die **Lippen**) lip.

Lippenstift der (PL die **Lippenstifte**)
lipstick.

Liste die (PL die **Listen**) list.

listig adjective cunning.

Liter der (PL die **Liter**) litre.

Literatur die literature.

litt SEE **leiden**.

Livesendung △ die (PL die
Livesendungen) live programme.

Lizenz die (PL die **Lizenzen**) licence.

Lkw der (PL die **Lkws**)
(Lastkraftwagen) lorry, truck.

Lob das praise.

loben verb (PERF **hat gelobt**) to
praise.

Loch das (PL die **Löcher**) hole.

Locke die (PL die **Locken**) curl.

locken verb (PERF **hat gelockt**) **1** to
tempt; **2** to curl.

locker adjective **1** loose; **2** slack
(rope); **3** relaxed (atmosphere,
person).

△ NEW SPELLING: See page xii

lockerlassen ✧ *verb* (PRES **lässt locker** Δ, IMPERF **ließ locker**, PERF **hat lockergelassen**) (*informal*) not to let up.

lockig *adjective* curly.

Löffel *der* (PL *die* **Löffel**) 1 spoon; 2 **ein Löffel Mehl** a spoonful of flour.

log SEE **lügen**.

Logik *die* logic.

logisch *adjective* 1 logical; 2 **ja, logisch!** yes, of course!

Lohn *der* (PL *die* **Löhne**) 1 wages; 2 reward.

lohnen *verb* (PERF **hat sich gelohnt**) **sich lohnen** to be worth it.

Lokal *das* (PL *die* **Lokale**) 1 bar; 2 restaurant.

Lokomotive *die* (PL *die* **Lokomotiven**) locomotive, engine.

Lorbeerblatt *das* (PL *die* **Lorbeerblätter**) bay leaf.

los *adjective* 1 **der Hund ist los** the dog is off the lead; 2 **die Schraube ist los** the screw's loose; 3 **es ist viel los** there's a lot going on; 4 **etwas los sein** to be rid of something; 5 **was ist los?** what's the matter?
adverb 1 **los!** go on!; 2 **Achtung, fertig, los!** ready, steady, go!

Los *das* (PL *die* **Lose**) 1 (lottery) ticket; 2 **das große Los ziehen** to hit the jackpot; 3 lot.

losbinden ✧ *verb* (IMPERF **band los**, PERF **hat losgebunden**) to untie.

löschen *verb* (PERF **hat gelöscht**) 1 to put out; 2 **seinen Durst löschen** to quench your thirst; 3 to delete, to cancel; 4 to erase.

lose *adjective* loose.

lösen *verb* (PERF **hat gelöst**) 1 to solve; 2 to undo; 3 **eine Fahrkarte lösen** to buy a ticket; 4 **sich lösen** to come undone; 5 **sich lösen** to be solved (*of a puzzle or mystery*); **sich von selbst lösen** to be resolved (*of a problem*); 6 **sich in Wasser lösen** to dissolve in water.

losfahren ✧ *verb* (PRES **fährt los**, IMPERF **fuhr los**, PERF **ist losgefahren**) 1 to set off; 2 to drive off.

losgehen ✧ *verb* (IMPERF **ging los**, PERF **ist losgegangen**) 1 to set off; 2 to start; 3 to come off (*of a button*); 4 to go off (*of a bomb*); 5 **auf jemanden losgehen** to go for somebody.

loslassen ✧ *verb* (PRES **lässt los** Δ, IMPERF **ließ los**, PERF **hat losgelassen**) 1 to let go of; 2 to let go.

Lösung *die* (PL *die* **Lösungen**) solution.

loswerden ✧ *verb* (PRES **wird los**, IMPERF **wurde los**, PERF **ist losgeworden**) to get rid of.

Lotterie *die* (PL *die* **Lotterien**) lottery.

Lotto *das* (PL *die* **Lottos**) (national) lottery.

Löwe *der* (PL *die* **Löwen**) 1 lion; 2 Leo.

✧ IRREGULAR VERB: *See the verb table in the centre of the dictionary*

Lücke *die* (PL *die* **Lücken**) gap.

Luft *die* (PL *die* **Lüfte**) **1** air; **2 die Luft anhalten** to hold your breath; **3 in die Luft gehen** (*informal*) to blow your top; **4 jemanden wie Luft behandeln** to ignore somebody.

Luftballon *der* (PL *die* **Luftballons**) balloon.

Luftdruck *der* air pressure.

Luftmatratze *die* (PL *die* **Luftmatratzen**) air-bed.

Luftpost *die* airmail; **per Luftpost** by airmail.

Luftverschmutzung *die* air pollution.

Luftwaffe *die* air force.

Lüge *die* (PL *die* **Lügen**) lie.

lügen ◇ *verb* (IMPERF **log**, PERF **hat gelogen**) to lie.

Lügner *der* (PL *die* **Lügner**) liar.

Lügnerin *die* (PL *die* **Lügnerinnen**) liar.

Lunge *die* (PL *die* **Lungen**) lungs.

Lungenentzündung *die* pneumonia.

Lupe *die* (PL *die* **Lupen**) magnifying glass.

Lust *die* **1** pleasure; **2 Lust haben, etwas zu tun** to feel like doing something; **ich habe keine Lust** I don't feel like it; **Lust auf etwas haben** to feel like something.

lustig *adjective* **1** jolly; **2** funny; **3 Dieter hat sich über mich lustig gemacht** Dieter made fun of me.

lutschen *verb* (PERF **hat gelutscht**) to suck.

Lutscher *der* (PL *die* **Lutscher**) lollipop.

Luxemburg *das* Luxembourg.

Luxus *der* luxury.

M m

machen *verb* (PERF **hat gemacht**) **1** to make; **2** to do; **was machst du da?** what are you doing?; **3 was macht die Arbeit?** how's work?; **was macht Karin?** how's Karin?; **4 sich an die Arbeit machen** to get down to work; **5 schnell machen** to hurry; **6 das macht nichts** it doesn't matter; **7 das macht fünf Mark** that's five marks; **8 sich nichts aus etwas machen** to not be very keen on something; **Roswitha macht sich nichts aus Schokolade** Roswitha isn't keen on chocolate.

Macht *die* (PL *die* **Mächte**) power; **an die Macht kommen** to come to power.

Mädchen *das* (PL *die* **Mädchen**) girl.

Made *die* (PL *die* **Maden**) maggot.

Mädchenname *der* (PL *die* **Mädchennamen**) maiden name.

mag SEE **mögen**.

Magazin *das* (PL *die* **Magazine**) magazine.

Magen *der* (PL *die* **Mägen**) stomach.

△ NEW SPELLING: *See page xii*

Magenschmerzen *plural noun* stomach-ache.

mager *adjective* 1 thin; 2 lean; 3 low-fat.

Magie *die* magic.

Magnet *der* (PL *die* **Magneten**) magnet.

magnetisch *adjective* magnetic.

magst SEE **mögen**.

Mahagoni *das* mahogany.

mähen *verb* (PERF **hat gemäht**) to mow; **den Rasen mähen** to mow the lawn.

mahlen ✧ *verb* (PERF **hat gemahlen**) to grind.

Mahlzeit *die* (PL *die* **Mahlzeiten**) meal; **Mahlzeit!** enjoy your meal!

Mai *der* May; **der Erste Mai** May Day.

Maiglöckchen *das* (PL *die* **Maiglöckchen**) lily of the valley.

Mais *der* maize.

Majonäse Δ *die* mayonnaise.

Majoran *der* marjoram.

Makkaroni (*plural noun*) macaroni.

Makler *der* (PL *die* **Makler**) estate agent.

Makrele *die* (PL *die* **Makrelen**) mackerel.

mal *adverb* 1 times; **zwei mal drei** two times three; 2 by (*with measurements*); 3 sometime (*in the future*); **ich möchte mal nach Brasilien fahren** I'd like to go to Brazil sometime; 4 **schon mal** ever; 5 **ich war schon mal da** I've been once before; 6 **nicht mal** not even; 7 **komm mal her!** come here

Mal *das* (PL *die* **Male**) 1 time; **nächstes Mal** next time; **zum ersten Mal** for the first time; 2 mark; 3 mole.

malen *verb* (PERF **hat gemalt**) to paint.

Maler *der* (PL *die* **Maler**) painter.

Malerei *die* painting.

Malerin *die* (PL *die* **Malerinnen**) painter.

Mallorca *das* Majorca.

Mama *die* (PL *die* **Mamas**) mum.

Mami *die* (PL *die* **Mamis**) mummy.

man *pronoun* 1 you, one; **wie macht man das?** how do you do it?; **man kann ja nie wissen** one can never tell; 2 they, people; **man sagt** they say; 3 **man hat mir gesagt** I was told.

mancher, manche, manches *adjective* 1 many a; **so manchen Tag** many a day; 2 **manche** (*plural*) some; **an manchen Tagen** some days. *pronoun* 1 many a person; 2 **manche** (*plural*) some people; 3 **manches** some things.

manchmal *adverb* sometimes.

Mandarine *die* (PL *die* **Mandarinen**) mandarin.

Mandel *die* (PL *die* **Mandeln**) 1 almond; 2 tonsil.

✧ IRREGULAR VERB: *See the verb table in the centre of the dictionary*

Mandelentzündung die tonsillitis.

Mangel der (PL die **Mängel**) 1 lack; 2 shortage; 3 defect, fault.

mangelhaft adjective 1 faulty; 2 unsatisfactory (school mark).

Manie die (PL die **Manien**) mania.

Manieren plural noun manners; **er hat keine Manieren** he's got no manners.

Mann der (PL die **Männer**) 1 man; 2 husband.

Männchen das (PL die **Männchen**) male (animal).

Mannequin das (PL die **Mannequins**) model.

männlich adjective 1 male; 2 manly; 3 masculine.

Mannschaft die (PL die **Mannschaften**) 1 team; 2 crew.

Manschette die (PL die **Manschetten**) cuff.

Mantel der (PL die **Mäntel**) coat.

Mappe die (PL die **Mappen**) 1 folder; 2 briefcase; 3 bag.

Märchen das (PL die **Märchen**) fairy tale.

Margarine die margarine.

Marienkäfer der (PL die **Marienkäfer**) ladybird.

Marine die (PL die **Marinen**) navy.

Mark die (PL die **Mark**) mark.

Marke die (PL die **Marken**) 1 make, brand; **meine Mutter fährt seit**

Jahren die gleiche Marke my mother has been driving the same make of car for years; **Adidas ist eine führende Marke** Adidas is a leading brand; 2 tag; 3 stamp (for letters); 4 coupon.

markieren verb (PERF **hat markiert**) 1 to mark; 2 to fake.

Markstück das (PL die **Markstücke**) one-mark piece.

Markt der (PL die **Märkte**) market.

Marktplatz der (PL die **Marktplätze**) market-place.

Marmelade die (PL die **Marmeladen**) jam.

Marmor der marble.

Marokko das Morocco.

Marsch der (PL die **Märsche**) march.

März der March.

Masche die (PL die **Maschen**) 1 stitch; 2 mesh; 3 (informal) trick; **die Masche raushaben** to know how to do it; **das is die neueste Masche** that's the latest thing.

Maschine die (PL die **Maschinen**) 1 machine; 2 plane; 3 typewriter; **Maschine schreiben** △ to type.

Masern plural noun measles.

Maske die (PL die **Masken**) mask.

maskieren verb (PERF **hat sich maskiert**) 1 **sich maskieren** to dress up; 2 **sich maskieren** to disguise yourself.

maß SEE **messen**.

Maß[1] das (PL die **Maße**) 1 measure; 2 measurement; 3 extent; **in hohem**

Maße to a high degree; **4 Maß halten** to show moderation.

Maß² die (PL die **Maß**) litre (of beer).

Masse die (PL die **Massen**) 1 mass; **eine Masse Arbeit** masses of work; 2 crowd; 3 mixture (in cooking).

massenhaft adjective masses of.

massieren verb (PERF **hat massiert**) to massage.

mäßig adjective moderate.

Maßnahme die (PL die **Maßnahmen**) measure.

Maßstab der (PL die **Maßstäbe**) 1 standard; 2 scale.

Mast der (PL die **Masten**) 1 mast; 2 pole; 3 pylon.

Material das (PL die **Materialien**) 1 material; 2 materials.

Mathe die (informal) maths.

Mathematik die mathematics.

Matratze die (PL die **Matratzen**) mattress.

Matrose der (PL die **Matrosen**) sailor.

Matsch der 1 mud; 2 slush.

matschig adjective 1 muddy; 2 slushy.

matt adjective 1 weak; 2 matt; 3 dull; 4 **matt!** checkmate!

Matte die (PL die **Matten**) mat.

Mauer die (PL die **Mauern**) wall.

Maul das (PL die **Mäuler**) mouth; **halt's Maul!** (informal) shut up!

Maulkorb der (PL die **Maulkörbe**) muzzle.

Maulwurf der (PL die **Maulwürfe**) mole.

Maurer der (PL die **Maurer**) bricklayer.

Maus die (PL die **Mäuse**) mouse.

Mayonnaise die mayonnaise.

Mechaniker der (PL die **Mechaniker**) mechanic.

mechanisch adjective mechanical.

meckern verb (PERF **hat gemeckert**) 1 to bleat; 2 to grumble.

Medaille die (PL die **Medaillen**) medal.

Medien plural noun media.

Medikament das (PL die **Medikamente**) medicine, drug.

Medizin die (PL die **Medizinen**) medicine.

Meer das (PL die **Meere**) sea.

Meeresfrüchte plural noun seafood.

Meerschweinchen das (PL die **Meerschweinchen**) guinea pig.

Mehl das flour.

mehr adverb, pronoun more; **nichts mehr** no more; **nie mehr** never again.

mehrere pronoun several.

mehreres pronoun several things.

mehrfach adjective 1 multiple, many; 2 repeated.
adverb several times.

✧ IRREGULAR VERB: *See the verb table in the centre of the dictionary*

Mehrheit die (PL die **Mehrheiten**) majority.

mehrmalig adjective repeated.

mehrmals adverb several times.

Mehrwertsteuer die value added tax.

Mehrzahl die 1 majority; 2 plural.

meiden ✧ verb (IMPERF **mied**, PERF **hat gemieden**) to avoid.

Meile die (PL die **Meilen**) mile.

mein adjective my.

meine SEE **meiner**.

meinen verb (PERF **hat gemeint**) 1 to think; 2 to mean; **es gut meinen** to mean well; 3 to say.

meiner, meine, mein(e)s pronoun mine.

meinetwegen adverb 1 for my sake; 2 because of me; 3 as far as I'm concerned; **'kann ich das Auto haben?' – 'meinetwegen'** 'can I take the car?' – 'I don't mind'.

meins SEE **meiner**.

Meinung die (PL die **Meinungen**) opinion.

meist adverb 1 mostly; 2 usually.

meiste adjective, pronoun **der/die/das meiste** most; **die meisten** most; **am meisten** most, the most.

meistens adverb 1 mostly; 2 usually.

Meister der (PL die **Meister**) 1 master; 2 champion.

Meisterin die (PL die **Meisterinnen**) champion.

Meisterschaft die (PL die **Meisterschaften**) championship.

Meisterwerk das (PL die **Meisterwerke**) masterpiece.

melden verb (PERF **hat gemeldet**) 1 to report; 2 to register; 3 **sich melden** to report; (on the phone) to answer; **Luise hat sich gemeldet** (in school) Luise put up her hand; 4 **sich bei jemandem melden** to get in touch with somebody.

Melodie die (PL die **Melodien**) melody, tune.

Melone die (PL die **Melonen**) 1 melon; 2 bowler (hat).

Menge die (PL die **Mengen**) 1 quantity; **eine Menge Geld** a lot of money; 2 crowd; 3 set (in maths).

Mensch der (PL die **Menschen**) 1 human being; 2 person; **kein Mensch** nobody; **jeder Mensch** everybody; 3 **die Menschen** people; **wie viele Menschen?** how many people?; 4 (as an exclamation) **Mensch!** (informal) wow!, hey!; **Mensch, hab ich mich geärgert!** (informal) I was damn annoyed.

menschenleer adjective deserted.

Menschenverstand der **gesunder Menschenverstand** common sense.

Menschheit die mankind.

menschlich adjective 1 human; 2 humane.

△ NEW SPELLING: See page xii

Mentalität die (PL die **Mentalitäten**) mentality.

Menü das (PL die **Menüs**) 1 menu; 2 set meal.

merken verb (PERF **hat gemerkt**) 1 to notice; 2 **sich etwas merken** to remember something.

Merkmal das (PL die **Merkmale**) feature.

merkwürdig adjective strange, odd.

Messe die (PL die **Messen**) 1 mass; 2 trade fair.

messen ✧ verb (PRES **misst** Δ, IMPERF **maß**, PERF **hat gemessen**) 1 to measure; (bei jemandem) **Fieber messen** to take somebody's temperature; 2 **sich mit jemandem messen können** to be as good as somebody.

Messer das (PL die **Messer**) knife.

Messing das brass.

Metall das (PL die **Metalle**) metal.

Meter der (PL die **Meter**) metre.

Metermaß das (PL die **Metermaße**) tape measure.

Methode die (PL die **Methoden**) method.

metrisch adjective metric.

Metzger der (PL die **Metzger**) butcher.

Metzgerei die (PL die **Metzgereien**) butcher's (shop).

Mexiko das Mexico.

miauen verb (PERF **hat miaut**) to miaow.

mich pronoun 1 me; 2 myself.

mied SEE **meiden**.

Miete die (PL die **Mieten**) 1 rent; **zur Miete wohnen** to live in rented accommodation; 2 hire charge.

mieten verb (PERF **hat gemietet**) 1 to rent; 2 to hire.

Mieter der (PL die **Mieter**) tenant.

Mieterin die (PL die **Mieterinnen**) tenant.

Mietshaus das (PL die **Mietshäuser**) block of rented flats.

Mietvertrag der (PL die **Mietverträge**) lease.

Mietwagen der (PL die **Mietwagen**) hire car.

Mikrofon das (PL die **Mikrofone**) microphone.

Mikroskop das (PL die **Mikroskope**) microscope.

Mikrowellenherd der (PL die **Mikrowellenherde**) microwave oven.

Milch die milk.

mild adjective mild.

Militär das army.

militärisch adjective military.

Milliarde die (PL die **Milliarden**) thousand million, billion.

Millimeter der (PL die **Millimeter**) millimetre.

Million die (PL die **Millionen**) million.

✧ IRREGULAR VERB: *See the verb table in the centre of the dictionary*

Millionär der (PL die **Millionäre**) millionaire.

Millionärin die (PL die **Millionärinnen**) millionairess.

Minderheit die (PL die **Minderheiten**) minority.

minderjährig adjective under age.

mindestens adverb at least.

mindester, mindeste, mindestes adjective least. pronoun **1 der/die/das Mindeste** △ the least; **zum Mindesten** △ at least; **2 nicht im Mindesten** △ not in the least.

Mine die (PL die **Minen**) **1** mine; **2** lead (in a pencil); **3** refill (for a ball-point).

Mineralwasser das (PL die **Mineralwasser**) mineral water.

Minirock der (PL die **Miniröcke**) miniskirt.

Minister der (PL die **Minister**) minister.

Ministerin die (PL die **Ministerinnen**) minister.

Ministerium das (PL die **Ministerien**) ministry, department.

minus adverb minus.

Minute die (PL die **Minuten**) minute.

mir pronoun **1** me, to me; **2** myself.

mischen verb (PERF **hat gemischt**) **1** to mix; **2 die Karten mischen** to shuffle the cards; **3 sich mischen** to mix.

Mischung die (PL die **Mischungen**) **1** mixture; **2** blend.

miserabel adjective (informal) **1** hopeless; **2** dreadful.

missbilligen △ verb (PERF **hat missbilligt**) to disapprove.

Missbrauch △ der abuse.

missbrauchen △ verb (PERF **hat missbraucht**) to abuse.

Misserfolg △ der (PL die **Misserfolge**) failure.

Missgeschick △ das (PL die **Missgeschicke**) **1** misfortune; **2** mishap.

misshandeln △ verb (PRES **hat misshandelt**) to ill-treat.

misslingen △ ✧ verb (IMPERF **misslang**, PERF **ist misslungen**) to fail; **es misslang ihr** she failed.

misst △ SEE **messen**.

Misstrauen △ das **1** mistrust; **2** distrust.

misstrauen △ verb (PERF **hat misstraut**) **jemandem misstrauen** to mistrust somebody.

misstrauisch △ adjective suspicious.

Missverständnis △ das (PL die **Missverständnisse**) misunderstanding.

missverstehen △ ✧ verb (IMPERF **missverstand**, PERF **hat missverstanden**) to misunderstand.

Mist der **1** manure; **2** (informal) rubbish.

Mistel die (PL die **Misteln**) mistletoe.

△ NEW SPELLING: *See page xii*

mit *preposition* ←(+DAT) **1** with; **2 mit der Bahn fahren** to go by train; **3 mit sechs Jahren** at the age of six; **4 mit jemandem sprechen** to speak to somebody; **5 mit Bleistift** in pencil; **6 mit lauter Stimme** in a loud voice. *adverb* as well, too; **warst du mit dabei?** were you there too?

Mitarbeiter *der* (PL *die* **Mitarbeiter**) **1** colleague; **2** employee.

Mitarbeiterin *die* (PL *die* **Mitarbeiterinnen**) **1** colleague; **2** employee.

mitbringen ✧ *verb* (IMPERF **brachte mit**, PERF **hat mitgebracht**) to bring, to bring along; **ich bringe den Kindern Schokolade mit** I'm taking the children some chocolate.

miteinander *adverb* with each other, with one another.

Mitesser *der* (PL *die* **Mitesser**) blackhead.

mitfahren ✧ *verb* (PRES **fährt mit**, IMPERF **fuhr mit**, PERF **ist mitgefahren**) **1 mit jemandem mitfahren** to go with somebody; **die Kinder fahren mit uns mit** the children are coming with us; **2 bei jemandem mitfahren** to get a lift with somebody; **jemanden mitfahren lassen** to give somebody a lift.

mitgeben ✧ *verb* (PRES **gibt mit**, IMPERF **gab mit**, PERF **hat mitgegeben**) to give.

Mitglied *das* (PL *die* **Mitglieder**) member.

mithalten ✧ *verb* (PRES **hält mit**, IMPERF **hielt mit**, PERF **hat mitgehalten**) to keep up.

mitkommen ✧ *verb* (IMPERF **kam mit**, PERF **ist mitgekommen**) **1** to come too; **2** to keep up.

Mitleid *das* pity; **kein Mitleid mit jemandem haben** not to feel any sympathy for somebody.

mitmachen *verb* (PERF **hat mitgemacht**) **1** to join in; **hast du Lust, bei dem Spiel mitzumachen?** do you want to join in the game? **2** to take part in; **3** to go through (*experiences, troubles*); **sie hat viel mitgemacht** she's gone through a lot.

mitnehmen ✧ *verb* (PRES **nimmt mit**, IMPERF **nahm mit**, PERF **hat mitgenommen**) **1** to take, to take along; **Anni hat die Kinder auf den Spielplatz mitgenommen** Anni has taken the children to the playground; **2** to give a lift to; **3** to affect (badly); **4 zum Mitnehmen** to take away.

Mitschüler *der* (PL *die* **Mitschüler**) schoolfriend.

Mitschülerin *die* (PL *die* **Mitschülerinnen**) schoolfriend.

mitspielen *verb* (PERF **hat mitgespielt**) **1** to play; **wer spielt bei dem Fußballspiel mit?** who's playing in the football match?; **willst du mitspielen?** do you want to join in?; **2 in einem Film mitspielen** to be in a film.

Mittag *der* (PL *die* **Mittage**) **1** midday; **2** lunch; **zu Mittag essen** to have lunch; **3** lunch-break.

✧ IRREGULAR VERB: *See the verb table in the centre of the dictionary*

Mittagessen *das* (PL *die* **Mittagessen**) lunch; **beim Mittagessen** at lunch.

mittags *adverb* **1** at lunchtime, at midday; **2 um zwölf Uhr mittags** at noon.

Mittagspause *die* (PL *die* **Mittagspausen**) lunch-break.

Mitte *die* (PL *die* **Mitten**) **1** middle; **2** centre.

Mitteilung *die* (PL *die* **Mitteilungen**) **1** announcement; **2** communication.

Mittel *das* (PL *die* **Mittel**) **1** means; **2 ein Mittel gegen Husten** a cough remedy; **3 öffentliche Mittel** public funds.

Mittelalter *das* Middle Ages.

mittelgroß *adjective* medium-sized.

mittelmäßig *adjective* mediocre.

Mittelmeer *das* Mediterranean.

Mittelpunkt *der* (PL *die* **Mittelpunkte**) centre; **im Mittelpunkt stehen** to be the centre of attention.

Mittelstand *der* middle class.

Mittelstürmer *der* (PL *die* **Mittelstürmer**) centre-forward.

mitten *adverb* **mitten in/auf** in the middle of; **mitten in der Nacht** in the middle of the night.

Mitternacht *die* midnight.

mittlerer, mittlere, mittleres *adjective* **1** middle; **2** medium (*quality, size*); **3** average.

mittlerweile *adverb* **1** meanwhile; **2** by now.

Mittwoch *der* (PL *die* **Mittwoche**) Wednesday.

mittwochs *adverb* on Wednesdays.

Möbel *plural noun* furniture.

Möbelwagen *der* (PL *die* **Möbelwagen**) removal van.

Mobiltelefon *das* (PL *die* **Mobiltelefone**) mobile phone.

möbliert *adjective* furnished.

mochte, möchte SEE **mögen**.

Mode *die* (PL *die* **Moden**) fashion.

Modell *das* (PL *die* **Modelle**) model.

Moderator *der* (PL *die* **Moderatoren**) presenter (*on TV*).

Moderatorin *die* (PL *die* **Moderatorinnen**) presenter (*on TV*).

modern *adjective* modern.

modernisieren *verb* (PERF **hat modernisiert**) to modernize.

modisch *adjective* fashionable.

Mofa *die* (PL *die* **Mofas**) moped.

mogeln *verb* (PERF **hat gemogelt**) to cheat.

mögen ◇ *verb* (PRES **mag**, IMPERF **mochte**, PERF **hat gemocht**) **1** to like; **ich mag ihn nicht** I don't like him; **ich möchte** I'd like; **ich möchte gern wissen** I'd like to know; **möchtest du nach Hause?** would you like to go home?; **2 lieber mögen** to prefer; **ich möchte lieber Tee** I would prefer tea; **3 etwas nicht tun mögen** not to want to do

△ NEW SPELLING: *See page xii*

something; **ich mag nicht fragen** I don't want to ask; **ich mag nicht mehr** I've had enough; **4 das mag sein** maybe; **5 was mag das sein?** whatever can it be?

möglich *adjective* possible; **alles Mögliche** all sorts of things.

möglicherweise *adverb* possibly.

Möglichkeit *die* (PL *die* **Möglichkeiten**) possibility.

möglichst *adverb* if possible; **möglichst früh** as early as possible.

Möhre *die* (PL *die* **Möhren**) carrot.

Molekül *das* (PL *die* **Moleküle**) molecule.

Moment *der* (PL *die* **Momente**) moment; **im Moment** at the moment; **Moment (mal)!** just a moment!

Monat *der* (PL *die* **Monate**) month.

monatelang *adverb* for months.

monatlich *adjective, adverb* monthly.

Mönch *der* (PL *die* **Mönche**) monk.

Mond *der* (PL *die* **Monde**) moon.

Mondschein *der* moonlight; **im Mondschein** by moonlight.

Montag *der* (PL *die* **Montage**) Monday.

montags *adverb* on Mondays.

Moped *das* (PL *die* **Mopeds**) moped.

Moral *die* **1** moral; **2** morale; **3** morals.

moralisch *adjective* moral.

Mord *der* (PL *die* **Morde**) murder.

Mörder *der* (PL *die* **Mörder**) murderer.

Mörderin *die* (PL *die* **Mörderinnen**) murderer.

morgen *adverb* tomorrow; **morgen Abend** tomorrow evening.

Morgen *der* (PL *die* **Morgen**) morning; **am Morgen** in the morning; **heute Morgen** △ this morning; **guten Morgen!** good morning!

morgens *adverb* in the morning.

Moschee *die* (PL *die* **Moscheen**) mosque.

Mosel *die* (River) Moselle.

Moslem *der* (PL *die* **Moslems**) Muslim.

moslemisch *adjective* Muslim.

Moskau *das* Moscow.

Moslime *die* (PL *die* **Moslimen**) Muslim.

Motiv *das* (PL *die* **Motive**) **1** motive; **2** motif.

Motor *der* (PL *die* **Motoren**) engine, motor.

Motorrad *das* (PL *die* **Motorräder**) motorcycle, motorbike.

Möwe *die* (PL *die* **Möwen**) seagull.

Mücke *die* (PL *die* **Mücken**) **1** midge; **2** mosquito.

müde *adjective* tired.

Müdigkeit *die* tiredness.

Mühe *die* (PL *die* **Mühen**) **1** effort;

◇ **IRREGULAR VERB: See the verb table in the centre of the dictionary**

sich Mühe geben to make an effort; **2** trouble; **machen Sie sich keine Mühe** don't go to any trouble; **3 mit Müh und Not** only just.

Mühle *die* (PL *die* **Mühlen**) **1** mill; **2** grinder (*for coffee*).

mühsam *adjective* laborious.

Müll *der* rubbish.

Müllabfuhr *die* refuse collection.

Mülleimer *der* (PL *die* **Mülleimer**) rubbish bin.

Mülltonne *die* (PL *die* **Mülltonnen**) dustbin.

Mumps *der* mumps.

München *das* Munich.

Mund *der* (PL *die* **Münder**) mouth; **halt den Mund!** (*informal*) shut up!

Mundharmonika *die* (PL *die* **Mundharmonikas**) mouth organ.

mündlich *adjective* oral.

Münster *das* (PL *die* **Münster**) cathedral.

Münze *die* (PL *die* **Münzen**) coin.

Münzfernsprecher *der* (PL *die* **Münzfernsprecher**) payphone.

murmeln *verb* (PERF **hat gemurmelt**) to mumble.

mürrisch *adjective* surly.

Muschel *die* (PL *die* **Muscheln**) **1** mussel; **2** (sea) shell; **3** mouthpiece (*of a phone*).

Museum *das* (PL *die* **Museen**) museum.

Musik *die* music.

musikalisch *adjective* musical.

Musiker *der* (PL *die* **Musiker**) musician.

Musikerin *die* (PL *die* **Musikerinnen**) musician.

Muskat *der* nutmeg.

Muskel *der* (PL *die* **Muskeln**) muscle.

Müsli *das* muesli.

muss △ SEE **müssen**.

müssen ✧ *verb* (PRES **muss** △, IMPERF **musste** △, PERF **hat gemusst** △) **1 etwas tun müssen** to have to do something; **sie muss es tun** she's got to do it, she must do it; **muss ich?** do I have to?; **muss das sein?** is that necessary?; **2 Sie müssten es mal versuchen** you should try it; **3 sie müssen gleich hier sein** they'll be here at any moment; **4 ich muss mal** (*informal*) I need (to go to) the loo.

Muster *das* (PL *die* **Muster**) **1** pattern; **2** sample.

Mut *der* courage; **jemandem Mut machen** to encourage somebody.

mutig *adjective* courageous.

Mutter[1] *die* (PL *die* **Mütter**) mother.

Mutter[2] *die* (PL *die* **Muttern**) nut.

Muttersprache *die* (PL *die* **Muttersprachen**) mother tongue, native language.

△ NEW SPELLING: *See page xii*

Muttertag der (PL die **Muttertage**)
Mother's Day.

Mutti die (PL die **Muttis**) mum.

Mütze die (PL die **Mützen**) cap.

MwSt. (*Mehrwertsteuer*) VAT.

Mythos der (PL die **Mythen**) myth.

N n

na *exclamation* well; **na und?** so
what?; **na gut** all right then.

Nabel der (PL die **Nabel**) navel.

nach *preposition* ←(+DAT) **1** to; **nach
Hause gehen** to go home; **nach
oben** up; **nach hinten** back; **nach
rechts abbiegen** to turn right;
2 after; **nach Ihnen** after you; **zehn
nach eins** ten past one; **nach etwas
greifen** to reach for something;
3 according to; **meiner Meinung
nach** in my opinion.
adverb **nach und nach** bit by bit,
gradually; **nach wie vor** still.

nachahmen *verb* (PERF **hat
nachgeahmt**) to imitate.

Nachbar der (PL die **Nachbarn**)
neighbour.

Nachbarin die (PL die
Nachbarinnen) neighbour.

Nachbarschaft die
neighbourhood.

nachdem *conjunction* **1** after; **2 je
nachdem** it depends; **je nachdem,
wie schnell du damit fertig wirst** it

depends on how quicky you can
finish it.

nachdenken ✧ *verb* (IMPERF
dachte nach, PERF **hat
nachgedacht**) to think; **über etwas
nachdenken** to think about
something; **ich habe lange über ihr
Angebot nachgedacht und mich
schließlich dagegen entschieden**
I've thought a long time about her
offer and finally decided against it.

nachdenklich *adjective*
thoughtful.

nacheinander *adverb* one after the
other; **die Bewerber kamen
nacheinander herein** the
applicants came in one after the
other.

Nachfrage die (PL die **Nachfragen**)
demand; **es besteht keine
Nachfrage** there's no demand for it.

nachgehen ✧ *verb* (IMPERF **ging
nach**, PERF **ist nachgegangen**) **1** to
be slow; **meine Uhr geht nach** my
watch is slow; **2 jemandem
nachgehen** to follow somebody;
einer Sache nachgehen to look
into something.

nachher *adverb* afterwards; **erst
gehen wir ins Kino und nachher
könnten wir essen gehen** we go to
the cinema first and afterwards we
could go for a meal; **bis nachher!**
see you later!

nachholen *verb* (PERF **hat
nachgeholt**) **1** to catch up on; **ich
hatte Grippe und muss jetzt viel
Mathe nachholen** I've had flu and
now I've got a lot of maths to catch
up on; **2** to make up for (*something*

✧ IRREGULAR VERB: *See the verb table in the centre of the dictionary*

missed); **3 eine Prüfung nachholen** to do an exam at a later date.

Nachtklub *der* (PL *die* **Nachtklubs**) night club.

nachkommen ◇ *verb* (IMPERF **kam nach**, PERF **ist nachgekommen**) **1** to come later, to follow; **2 ich komme nicht nach** I can't keep up; **3 einem Versprechen nachkommen** to carry out a promise; **seinen Verpflichtungen nachkommen** to meet your commitments.

nachlassen ◇ *verb* (PRES **lässt nach** △, IMPERF **ließ nach**, PERF **hat nachgelassen**) **1** to ease; **meine Zahnschmerzen lassen langsam nach** my toothache is getting better; **2** to let up; **sobald die Kälte nachlässt** as soon as it gets warmer; **3** to deteriorate; **4 etwas vom Preis nachlassen** to take something off the price; **jemandem zwanzig Mark nachlassen** to give somebody twenty marks off.

nachlässig *adjective* careless.

nachlaufen ◇ *verb* (PRES **läuft nach**, IMPERF **lief nach**, PERF **ist nachgelaufen**) **jemandem nachlaufen** to run after somebody; **Philipp läuft allen Mädchen nach** (*informal*) Philipp chases all the girls.

nachmachen *verb* (PERF **hat nachgemacht**) to copy.

Nachmittag *der* (PL *die* **Nachmittage**) afternoon.

nachmittags *adverb* in the afternoon.

Nachnahme *die* **per Nachnahme** cash on delivery.

Nachname *der* (PL *die* **Nachnamen**) surname.

nachprüfen *verb* (PERF **hat nachgeprüft**) to check; **er prüft nach, ob es stimmt** he's going to check if it is correct.

Nachricht *die* (PL *die* **Nachrichten**) **1** news; **ich warte noch immer auf eine Nachricht von ihm** I'm still waiting for news of him; **eine Nachricht hinterlassen** to leave a message; **2 die Nachrichten** the news; **das kam in den Nachrichten** it was on the news.

Nachrichtensprecher *der* (PL *die* **Nachrichtensprecher**) newsreader.

Nachrichtensprecherin *der* (PL *die* **Nachrichtensprecherinnen**) newsreader.

nachschlagen ◇ *verb* (PRES **schlägt nach**, IMPERF **schlug nach**, PERF **hat nachgeschlagen**) to look up.

nachsehen ◇ *verb* (PRES **sieht nach**, IMPERF **sah nach**, PERF **hat nachgesehen**) **1** to check; **sieh nach, wer da ist** go and see who's there; **2** to look up; **3 jemandem etwas nachsehen** to let somebody get away with something.

nachsitzen ◇ *verb* (IMPERF **saß nach**, PERF **hat nachgesessen**) to be in detention; **Jan muss nachsitzen** Jan has detention.

Nachspeise *die* (PL *die* **Nachspeisen**) dessert, pudding.

△ NEW SPELLING: *See page xii*

nächste SEE **nächster**.

nächstens *adverb* shortly.

nächster, nächste, nächstes
adjective 1 next; 2 nearest; **am
nächsten sein** to be nearest; 3 **in
nächster Nähe** close by.
pronoun **der/die/das Nächste** △
(the) next; **als Nächstes** △ next.

Nacht *die* (PL *die* **Nächte**) night.

Nachteil *der* (PL *die* **Nachteile**)
disadvantage.

Nachtfalter *der* (PL *die* **Nachtfalter**)
moth.

Nachthemd *das* (PL *die*
Nachthemden) nightdress,
nightshirt.

Nachtigall *die* (PL *die* **Nachtigallen**)
nightingale.

Nachtisch *der* (PL *die* **Nachtische**)
dessert, pudding.

Nachtleben *das* nightlife.

nachträglich *adjective*
1 subsequent; 2 belated.
adverb 1 later; 2 belatedly.

nachts *adverb* at night; **um zwei Uhr
nachts** at two o'clock in the
morning.

Nacken *der* (PL *die* **Nacken**) neck.

nackt *adjective* 1 naked; 2 bare.

Nadel *die* (PL *die* **Nadeln**) 1 needle;
2 pin.

Nagel *der* (PL *die* **Nägel**) nail.

Nagelbürste *die* (PL *die*
Nagelbürsten) nailbrush.

Nagelfeile *die* (PL *die* **Nagelfeilen**)
nailfile.

Nagellack *der* (PL *die* **Nagellacke**)
nail varnish.

nagelneu *adjective* brand-new.

Nagelschere *die* (PL *die*
Nagelscheren) nail scissors.

nahe, nah *adjective, adverb* 1 near,
nearby; **der Nahe Osten** the Middle
East; **nahe daran sein, etwas zu tun**
to nearly do something; 2 close;
nahe bei close to; **nahe verwandt
sein** to be closely related;
3 **jemandem nahe legen** △, **etwas zu
tun** to urge somebody to do
something; 4 **nahe liegend** △
obvious.
preposition ←(+DAT) near, close to.

Nähe *die* 1 proximity; 2 **in der Nähe
der Kirche** near the church; **ganz
in der Nähe** nearby; 3 **aus der
Nähe** close up.

nahelegen, naheliegend SEE
nahe.

nähen *verb* (PERF **hat genäht**) 1 to
sew; 2 to stitch (*a wound*).

näher *adjective* 1 closer; 2 **nähere
Einzelheiten** further details;
3 shorter (*way, road*).
adverb 1 closer; **näher kommen** to
come closer; 2 more closely;
3 **Näheres** further details.

nähern *verb* (PERF **hat sich
genähert**) **sich nähern** to
approach.

Nähgarn *das* cotton.

nahm SEE **nehmen**.

✧ IRREGULAR VERB: *See the verb table in the centre of the dictionary*

Nähmaschine *die* (PL *die* **Nähmaschinen**) sewing machine.

Nahrung *die* food.

Naht *die* (PL *die* **Nähte**) seam.

Nahverkehrszug *der* (PL *die* **Nahverkehrszüge**) local train.

Name *der* (PL *die* **Namen**) name.

nämlich *adverb* 1 because; 2 namely; 3 **das war nämlich ganz anders** it was quite different actually.

nannte SEE **nennen**.

nanu *exclamation* well, well!

Narbe *die* (PL *die* **Narben**) scar.

Narr *der* (PL *die* **Narren**) fool.

Närrin *die* (PL *die* **Närrinnen**) fool.

Nase *die* (PL *die* **Nasen**) nose; **die Nase voll haben** (*informal*) to have had enough.

Nasenbluten *das* nosebleed.

Nashorn *das* (PL *die* **Nashörner**) rhinoceros.

nass Δ *adjective* wet.

Nation *die* (PL *die* **Nationen**) nation.

Nationalhymne *die* (PL *die* **Nationalhymnen**) national anthem.

Nationalität *die* (PL *die* **Nationalitäten**) nationality.

Natur *die* 1 nature; **von Natur aus** by nature; 2 **die freie Natur** the open countryside.

natürlich *adjective* natural. *adverb* of course, naturally.

Naturschutzgebiet *das* (PL *die* **Naturschutzgebiete**) nature reserve.

Naturwissenschaft *die* natural science.

Nebel *der* (PL *die* **Nebel**) 1 fog; 2 mist.

nebelig *adjective* = **neblig**.

neben *preposition* ←(+DAT, *or* +ACC *with movement towards a place*) 1 next to; **er hat neben mir gesessen** he sat next to me; **er hat sich neben mich gesetzt** he sat down next to me; 2 apart from.

nebenan *adverb* next door.

nebenbei *adverb* 1 as well, at the same time; **er liest die Zeitung und hört nebenbei Musik** he reads the newspaper and listens to music at the same time; 2 on the side; **nebenbei arbeite ich noch in einem Blumengeschäft** I work in a florist's on the side; **das mache ich so nebenbei** (*informal*) that's just a sideline; 3 in passing; **nebenbei bemerkt** by the way.

nebeneinander *adverb* next to each other.

nebenhergehen ◇ *verb* (IMPERF **ging nebenher**, PERF **ist nebenhergegangen**) to walk alongside.

neblig *adjective* 1 foggy; 2 misty.

necken *verb* (PERF **hat geneckt**) to tease.

Neffe *der* (PL *die* **Neffen**) nephew.

negativ *adjective* negative.

Negativ das (PL die **Negative**) negative.

nehmen ✧ verb (PRES **nimmt**, IMPERF **nahm**, PERF **hat genommen**) 1 to take; 2 **ich nehme eine Suppe** I'll have soup; 3 **was nehmen Sie dafür?** how much do you want for it?; 4 **jemanden zu sich nehmen** to have somebody live with you; 5 **sich etwas nehmen** to take something; **nimm dir ein Stück Kuchen** help yourself to a piece of cake.

Neid der envy, jealousy.

neidisch adjective envious, jealous.

nein adverb no.

Nelke die (PL die **Nelken**) carnation.

nennen ✧ verb (IMPERF **nannte**, PERF **hat genannt**) 1 to call; 2 to name; 3 **ihr Name wurde nicht genannt** her name wasn't mentioned; 4 **sich nennen** to call yourself.

Nerv der (PL die **Nerven**) nerve; **Gabi geht mir auf die Nerven** Gabi gets on my nerves.

nervös adjective nervous.

Nervosität die nervousness.

Nessel die (PL die **Nesseln**) nettle.

Nest das (PL die **Nester**) 1 nest; 2 little place (a village).

nett adjective nice.

netto adverb net.

Netz das (PL die **Netze**) 1 net; 2 network; 3 string bag; 4 (spider's) web.

neu adjective 1 new; **wie neu** as good as new; **neue Sprachen** modern languages; 2 **seit neuestem** recently; 3 **die neueste Mode** the latest fashion; **das Neueste** the latest news; 4 **das ist mir neu** that's news to me.
adverb 1 newly; 2 only just; **es ist neu eingetroffen** it has only just come in; 3 **etwas neu schreiben** to rewrite something.

neuartig adjective new; **ein neuartiger Flaschenöffner** a new kind of bottle opener.

neuerdings adverb recently.

Neugier die curiosity.

neugierig adjective curious, inquisitive.

Neuigkeit die (PL die **Neuigkeiten**) piece of news; **gibt es irgendwelche Neuigkeiten?** is there any news?

Neujahr das New Year, New Year's Day.

neulich adverb the other day.

neun number nine.

neunter, neunte, neuntes adjective ninth.

neunzehn number nineteen.

neunzig number ninety.

Neuseeland das New Zealand.

nicht adverb 1 not; **ich kann nicht** I can't; **Iris hat nicht angerufen** Iris didn't ring; **bitte nicht** please don't; **nicht!** don't!; **nicht berühren!** don't touch!; 2 **'ich mag das nicht'** – **'ich auch nicht'** 'I don't like it' – 'neither do I'; 3 **nicht (wahr)?** isn't he/she/it?; **du kennst ihn doch,**

nicht? you know him, don't you?;
4 gar nicht not at all; **5 nicht mehr**
no more.

Nichte die (PL die **Nichten**) niece.

Nichtraucher der (PL die
Nichtraucher) non-smoker.

nichts pronoun **1** nothing; **2 ich
habe nichts gewusst** I didn't know
anything; **3 nichts mehr** no more;
4 das macht nichts it doesn't
matter; **5 nichts ahnend** △
unsuspecting.

nichtsahnend SEE **nichts**.

nicken verb (PERF **hat genickt**) to
nod.

Nickerchen das (PL die
Nickerchen) nap; **ein Nickerchen
machen** to have a nap.

nie adverb never.

nieder adjective low.
adverb down.

Niederlage die (PL die **Niederlagen**)
defeat.

Niederlande plural noun **die
Niederlande** the Netherlands.

Niederländer der (PL die
Niederländer) Dutchman; **die
Niederländer** the Dutch.

Niederländerin die (PL die
Niederländerinnen) Dutchwoman.

niederländisch adjective Dutch.

niedlich adjective sweet.

niedrig adjective **1** low; **2** base.

niemals adverb never.

niemand pronoun nobody; **wir**

haben niemand or **niemanden
gesehen** we didn't see anybody.

Niere die (PL die **Nieren**) kidney.

nieseln verb (PERF **hat genieselt**) to
drizzle; **es nieselt** it's drizzling.

niesen verb (PERF **hat geniest**) to
sneeze.

Nilpferd das (PL die **Nilpferde**)
hippopotamus.

nimmt SEE **nehmen**.

nirgends, nirgendwo adverb
nowhere.

Niveau das (PL die **Niveaus**) **1** level;
2 standard.

noch adverb **1** still; **immer noch**
still; **2** even; **noch besser** even
better; **3 noch nicht** not yet; **noch
nie** never; **4 gerade noch** only
just; **5 wer war noch da?** who else
was there?; **was noch?** what else?;
6 noch einmal again; **7 noch ein
Bier** another beer; **noch etwas
Kaffee?** (would you like some) more
coffee?; **8 noch gestern** only
yesterday; **9 noch und noch Geld**
loads of money.
conjunction nor; **weder ... noch**
neither ... nor

nochmals adverb again.

Nominativ der (PL die **Nominative**)
nominative.

Nordamerika das North America.

Norden der north.

Nordirland das Northern Ireland.

nördlich adjective **1** northern;
2 northerly (direction).

adverb, preposition ←(+GEN)
nördlich von Wien to the north of
Vienna; **nördlich der Stadt** north of
the town.

Nordosten *der* north-east.

Nordpol *der* North Pole.

Nordsee *die* North Sea.

Nordwesten *der* north-west.

nörgeln *verb* (PERF **hat genörgelt**) to
grumble.

Norm *die* (PL *die* **Normen**) 1 norm;
2 standard.

normal *adjective* normal.

normalerweise *adverb* normally.

Norwegen *das* Norway.

Norweger *der* (PL *die* **Norweger**)
Norwegian.

Norwegerin *die* (PL *die*
Norwegerinnen) Norwegian.

norwegisch *adjective* Norwegian.

Not *die* (PL *die* **Nöte**) 1 need; **zur Not**
if necessary, at a pinch; **mit knapper
Not** only just; 2 hardship.

Notausgang *der* (PL *die*
Notausgänge) emergency exit.

Notdienst *der* **Notdienst haben** to
be on call.

Note *die* (PL *die* **Noten**) 1 note; **Noten
lesen** to read music; 2 mark.

Notfall *der* (PL *die* **Notfälle**)
emergency.

notfalls *adverb* if need be.

notieren *verb* (PERF **hat notiert**) 1 to

note down; 2 **sich etwas notieren**
to make a note of something.

nötig *adjective* necessary.
adverb urgently.

Notiz *die* (PL *die* **Notizen**) 1 note;
2 **keine Notiz von etwas nehmen**
to take no notice of something;
3 item (*in a newspaper*).

Notizblock *der* (PL *die* **Notizblöcke**)
notepad.

Notizbuch *das* (PL *die* **Notizbücher**)
notebook.

Notlage *die* (PL *die* **Notlagen**) crisis.

Notruf *der* (PL *die* **Notrufe**)
1 emergency call; 2 emergency
number.

notwendig *adjective* necessary.

November *der* November.

nüchtern *adjective* 1 sober; **wieder
nüchtern werden** to sober up;
2 **auf nüchternen Magen** on an
empty stomach; 3 down-to-earth.

Nudeln *plural noun* 1 noodles;
2 pasta.

null *number* 1 nought; **unter null**
below zero; 2 nil; **zwei zu null** two
nil; 3 love (*in tennis*); 4 **null Fehler
haben** to have no mistakes; **ich habe
null Ahnung** (*informal*) I haven't
got a clue; 5 **in null Komma nichts**
(*informal*) in less than no time.

Null *die* (PL *die* **Nullen**) 1 zero,
nought; 2 failure.

numerieren = **nummerieren**.

Nummer *die* (PL *die* **Nummern**)
1 number; 2 issue (*of a magazine*);

✧ IRREGULAR VERB: *See the verb table in the centre of the dictionary*

3 size (*of clothing*); **4** act; **5 auf Nummer sicher gehen** to play safe.

nummerieren Δ *verb* (PERF **hat nummeriert**) to number.

Nummernschild *das* (PL *die* **Nummernschilder**) number plate.

nun *adverb* now.
exclamation well; **nun ja ...** well, yes ...

nur *adverb* **1** only; **2 was sollen wir nur tun?** what on earth are we going to do?; **sie soll es nur versuchen!** just let her try!; **3 nur zu!** go ahead!

Nürnberg *das* Nuremberg.

Nuss Δ *die* (PL *die* **Nüsse**) nut.

Nutzen *der* benefit; **von Nutzen sein** to be useful.

nutzen, nützen *verb* (PERF **hat genutzt/genützt**) **1** to use; **etwas nutzen** to take advantage of something; **2** to be useful; **3 nichts nutzen** to be no use; **das nutzt mir nichts** that won't help me; **4 das nutzt ja doch nichts** it's pointless.

nützlich *adjective* useful.

nutzlos *adjective* useless.

O o

ob *conjunction* **1** whether; **wissen Sie, ob heute noch ein Zug nach Freising fährt?** do you know if there is another train to Freising today?; **2 ob Alex noch anruft?** I wonder if Alex will ring; **3 und ob!** you bet!

obdachlos *adjective* homeless.

Obdachlose *der/die* (PL *die* **Obdachlosen**) homeless person; **die Obdachlosen** the homeless.

oben *adverb* **1** on top; **oben auf** on top of; **die Vase steht oben auf dem Schrank** the vase is on top of the cupboard; **2** at the top; **von oben bis unten** from top to bottom; **er hat uns von oben bis unten gemustert** he looked us up and down; **3** upstairs; **4 nach oben** up, upstairs; **er ist nach oben in sein Zimmer gegangen** he went up into his room; **geht der Fahrstuhl nach oben?** is the lift going up?; **hier oben** up here; **da oben** up there; **5 siehe oben** see above (*on a page*); **oben erwähnt** Δ above mentioned; **6 oben ohne** (*informal*) topless.

obenerwähnt SEE **oben**.

Ober *der* (PL *die* **Ober**) waiter; **Herr Ober!** waiter!

oberer, obere, oberes *adjective* upper, top.

Oberfläche *die* (PL *die* **Oberflächen**) surface.

oberflächlich *adjective* superficial.

Oberhaupt *das* (PL *die* **Oberhäupter**) head.

Oberhemd *das* (PL *die* **Oberhemden**) shirt.

Oberschenkel *der* (PL *die* **Oberschenkel**) thigh.

Oberschule *die* (PL *die* **Oberschulen**) secondary school.

Δ NEW SPELLING: *See page xii*

oberster, oberste, oberstes *adjective* top.

Oberstufe *die* (PL *die* **Oberstufen**) upper school.

Oberweite *die* (PL *die* **Oberweiten**) chest size, bust measurement.

Objekt *das* (PL *die* **Objekte**) object.

objektiv *adjective* objective.

Objektiv *das* (PL *die* **Objektive**) lens.

Obst *das* fruit.

Obstbaum *der* (PL *die* **Obstbäume**) fruit tree.

Obstsalat *der* (PL *die* **Obstsalate**) fruit salad.

obszön *adjective* obscene.

obwohl *conjunction* although.

öde *adjective* 1 desolate; 2 dreary; **das ist so ein furchtbar öder Job** it's such terribly dull job.

oder *conjunction* 1 or; 2 **du kennst sie doch, oder?** you know her, don't you?

Ofen *der* (PL *die* **Öfen**) 1 oven; 2 stove; 3 heater.

offen *adjective* 1 open; **offen haben** to be open; **Tag der offenen Tür** open day; 2 frank; 3 vacant; **eine offene Stelle** a vacancy; 4 **offen bleiben** ⬦ to stay open; 5 **offen bleiben** ⬦ to remain open (*of a question, possibility*). *adverb* 1 openly; 2 frankly; **offen gesagt** frankly.

offenbar *adjective* obvious. *adverb* 1 apparently; 2 **da hast du dich offenbar geirrt** you seem to have made a mistake; **sie hat offenbar den Zug verpasst** she must have missed the train.

offenbleiben SEE **offen**.

offensichtlich *adjective* obvious.

öffentlich *adjective* public.

Öffentlichkeit *die* public; **in aller Öffentlichkeit** in public.

offiziell *adjective* official.

Offizier *der* (PL *die* **Offiziere**) officer.

öffnen *verb* (PERF **hat geöffnet**) to open; **jemandem die Tür öffnen** to open the door for somebody.

Öffner *der* (PL *die* **Öffner**) opener.

Öffnung *die* (PL *die* **Öffnungen**) opening.

Öffnungszeiten *plural noun* opening times.

oft *adverb* often.

öfter, öfters *adverb* quite often; **ich habe ihn öfters mal getroffen** I used to meet him quite often.

ohne *preposition* ←(+ACC) 1 without; **ohne mich** count me out; 2 **ohne weiteres** easily; 3 **oben ohne** (*informal*) topless; 4 **das ist nicht ohne** (*informal*) it's not bad. *conjunction* without; **ohne zu überlegen** without thinking.

Ohnmacht *die* **in Ohnmacht fallen** to faint.

ohnmächtig *adjective* 1 unconscious; 2 **ohnmächtig werden** to faint; **Roswitha ist ohnmächtig** Roswitha's fainted.

⬦ IRREGULAR VERB: *See the verb table in the centre of the dictionary*

Ohr das (PL die **Ohren**) ear.

Ohrenschmerzen plural noun earache.

Ohrring der (PL die **Ohrringe**) earring.

oje exclamation oh dear!

Ökoladen der (PL die **Ökoläden**) health-food shop.

Ökologie die ecology.

ökologisch adjective ecological.

Oktober der October.

Öl das (PL die **Öle**) oil.

Ölfarbe die (PL die **Ölfarben**) oil-paint.

Ölgemälde das (PL die **Ölgemälde**) oil painting.

ölig adjective oily.

Olive die (PL die **Oliven**) olive.

Olivenöl das (PL die **Olivenöle**) olive oil.

Olympiade die (PL die **Olympiaden**) Olympic Games; **die Olympiade findet alle vier Jahre statt** the Olympic Games take place every four years.

olympisch adjective Olympic.

Oma die (PL die **Omas**) granny.

Omelett das (PL die **Omeletts**) omelette.

Omi die (PL die **Omis**) granny.

Onkel der (PL die **Onkel**) uncle.

Opa der (PL die **Opas**) grandpa.

Oper die (PL die **Opern**) opera.

Operation die (PL die **Operationen**) operation.

Operationssaal der (PL die **Operationssäle**) operating theatre.

operieren verb (PERF **hat operiert**) 1 to operate on; **sich operieren lassen** to have an operation; **sie wurde am Magen operiert** she had a stomach operation; 2 to operate.

Opfer das (PL die **Opfer**) 1 sacrifice; 2 victim; **das Erdbeben forderte viele Opfer** the earthquake claimed many victims.

Optiker der (PL die **Optiker**) optician.

Optikerin die (PL die **Optikerinnen**) optician.

Optimist der (PL die **Optimisten**) optimist.

optimistisch adjective optimistic.

orange adjective orange.

Orange die (PL die **Orangen**) orange.

Orangensaft der (PL die **Orangensäfte**) orange juice.

Orchester das (PL die **Orchester**) orchestra.

ordentlich adjective 1 tidy; 2 respectable; 3 proper (meal, job, salary); 4 **eine ordentliche Tracht Prügel** (informal) a good hiding. adverb 1 tidily; **ordentlich schreiben** to write neatly; 2 respectably; 3 properly; 4 **ordentlich feiern** (informal) to have a really good celebration; **wir sind ordentlich nass geworden** (informal) we got soaked.

ordinär adjective vulgar.

△ NEW SPELLING: See page xii

ordnen *verb* (PERF **hat geordnet**)
1 to arrange; 2 to put in order.

Ordner *der* (PL *die* **Ordner**) file.

Ordnung *die* 1 order; **Ordnung halten** to keep order; 2 **Ordnung machen** to tidy up; **die Wohnung in Ordnung bringen** to tidy up the flat;
3 **mit der Waschmaschine ist etwas nicht in Ordnung** there's something wrong with the washing machine;
4 **etwas in Ordnung bringen** to put something right; **die Waschmaschine in Ordnung bringen** to repair the washing machine; 5 **in Ordnung!** okay!;
6 **er ist in Ordnung** he's all right.

Organ *das* (PL *die* **Organe**) 1 organ; 2 (*informal*) voice.

Organisation *die* (PL *die* **Organisationen**) organization.

organisch *adjective* organic.

organisieren *verb* (PERF **hat organisiert**) 1 to organize; 2 (*informal*) to get (hold of).

Orgel *die* (PL *die* **Orgeln**) organ.

orientieren *verb* (PERF **hat sich orientiert**) 1 **sich orientieren** to get your bearings; 2 **sich über etwas orientieren** to inform yourself about something.

Orientierung *die* 1 orientation; **die Orientierung verlieren** to lose your bearings; 2 **zu Ihrer Orientierung** for your information.

Orientierungssinn *der* sense of direction.

originell *adjective* original.

Orkan *der* (PL *die* **Orkane**) hurricane

Ort *der* (PL *die* **Orte**) 1 place; **an Ort und Stelle** on the spot; 2 (small) town.

Orthografie Δ, **Orthographie** *die* spelling.

örtlich *adjective* local.

Ortschaft *die* (PL *die* **Ortschaften**) village.

Ortsgespräch *das* (PL *die* **Ortsgespräche**) local call.

Ossi *der* (*informal*) (PL *die* **Ossis**) East German.

Osten *der* east.

Osterei *das* (PL *die* **Ostereier**) Easter egg.

Ostern *das* Easter.

Österreich *das* Austria.

Österreicher *der* (PL *die* **Österreicher**) Austrian.

Österreicherin *die* (PL *die* **Österreicherinnen**) Austrian.

österreichisch *adjective* Austrian.

östlich *adjective* 1 eastern; 2 easterly.
adverb, preposition ←(+GEN) **östlich von Wien** to the east of Vienna; **östlich der Stadt** east of the town.

Ostsee *die* Baltic (Sea).

oval *adjective* oval.

Ozean *der* (PL *die* **Ozeane**) ocean.

Ozon *das* ozone.

Ozonschicht *die* ozone layer.

✧ IRREGULAR VERB: *See the verb table in the centre of the dictionary*

P p

paar *pronoun* **ein paar** a few; **ein paar Mal** △ a few times; **alle paar Tage** every few days.

Paar das (PL die **Paare**) 1 pair; **ein Paar Schuhe** a pair of shoes; 2 couple.

paarmal SEE **paar**.

paarweise *adjective* in pairs; **die Kinder stellten sich paarweise auf** the children lined up in pairs.

Päckchen das (PL die **Päckchen**) 1 package, packet; 2 small parcel.

packen *verb* (PERF **hat gepackt**) 1 to pack; **ich muss jetzt meinen Koffer packen** I must pack my case now; 2 to grab (hold of); **von Furcht gepackt** seized with fear.

Packung die (PL die **Packungen**) packet, pack.

Pädagoge der (PL die **Pädagogen**) 1 educationalist; 2 teacher.

pädagogisch *adjective* educational.

Paddel das (PL die **Paddel**) paddle.

Paket das (PL die **Pakete**) 1 parcel; **Gabi hat mir ein Paket geschickt** Gabi sent me a parcel; 2 packet; **kaufe bitte ein Paket Waschpulver für mich** can you please buy a packet of washing powder for me.

Palast der (PL die **Paläste**) palace.

Palme die (PL die **Palmen**) palm (tree).

Pampelmuse die (PL die **Pampelmusen**) grapefruit.

Panik die panic; **in Panik geraten** to panic.

Panne die (PL die **Pannen**) 1 breakdown; **wir haben auf dem Rückweg eine Panne gehabt** we had a breakdown on the way back; 2 mishap; **uns ist eine Panne passiert** we had a mishap.

Papa der (PL die **Papas**) daddy.

Papagei der (PL die **Papageien**) parrot.

Papier das (PL die **Papiere**) paper.

Papierkorb der (PL die **Papierkörbe**) waste-paper basket.

Papiertüte die (PL die **Papiertüten**) paper bag.

Pappe die (PL die **Pappen**) cardboard.

Paprika der (PL die **Paprikas**) 1 pepper; 2 paprika.

Papst der (PL die **Päpste**) pope.

Parabolantenne die (PL die **Parabolantennen**) satellite dish.

Paradies das paradise.

Paragraph der (PL die **Paragraphen**) 1 section; 2 clause.

parallel *adjective* parallel.

Pärchen das (PL die **Pärchen**) couple.

Parfüm das (PL die **Parfüms**) perfume.

△ NEW SPELLING: *See page xii*

Park der (PL die **Parks**) park.

Parkanlage die (PL die **Parkanlagen**) park.

parken verb (PERF **hat geparkt**) to park.

Parkett das (PL die **Parkette**) 1 (in a theatre) stalls; 2 parquet floor.

Parkhaus das (PL die **Parkhäuser**) multi-storey car park.

Parklücke die (PL die **Parklücken**) parking space.

Parkplatz der (PL die **Parkplätze**) 1 car park; 2 parking space.

Parkschein der (PL die **Parkscheine**) car-park ticket.

Parkuhr die (PL die **Parkuhren**) parking meter.

Parkverbot das 'Parkverbot' 'no parking'; **in der Innenstadt ist Parkverbot** you can't park in the town centre.

Parlament das (PL die **Parlamente**) parliament.

Parole die (PL die **Parolen**) slogan.

Partei die (PL die **Parteien**) 1 party; 2 **für jemanden Partei ergreifen** to side with somebody.

Parterre das (PL die **Parterres**) ground floor.

Partie die (PL die **Partien**) 1 part; 2 game (of tennis, chess).

Partner der (PL die **Partner**) partner.

Partnerin die (PL die **Partnerinnen**) partner.

Partnerstadt die (PL die **Partnerstädte**) twin town.

Party die (PL die **Partys**) party.

Pass Δ der (PL die **Pässe**) 1 passport; 2 pass.

Passagier der (PL die **Passagiere**) passenger.

Passant der (PL die **Passanten**) passer-by.

Passantin die (PL die **Passantinnen**) passer-by.

passen (PERF **hat gepasst** Δ) 1 to fit; **jemandem passen** to fit somebody; 2 to suit; **jemandem passen** to suit somebody; **Freitag passt mir nicht** Friday doesn't suit me; **seine Art passt mir nicht** I don't like his manner; 3 **zu etwas passen** to go with something; **zu jemandem passen** to be right for somebody.

passend adjective 1 suitable; 2 matching.

passieren verb (PERF **ist passiert**) to happen.

passiv adjective passive.

Passiv das passive.

Passkontrolle Δ die passport control.

Paste die (PL die **Pasten**) paste.

Pastete die (PL die **Pasteten**) pie.

Pate der (PL die **Paten**) godfather.

Patenkind das (PL die **Patenkinder**) godchild.

patent adjective capable, clever.

✧ IRREGULAR VERB: See the verb table in the centre of the dictionary

Patentante der (PL die **Patentanten**) godmother.

Patient der (PL die **Patienten**) patient.

Patientin die (PL die **Patientinnen**) patient.

Patin die (PL die **Patinnen**) godmother.

patschnass Δ adjective soaking wet.

pauken verb (informal) (PERF **hat gepaukt**) to swot.

Pauschalreise die (PL die **Pauschalreisen**) package tour.

Pause die (PL die **Pausen**) 1 break; 2 pause; 3 interval.

Pazifik der **der Pazifik** the Pacific (Ocean).

PC der (PL die **PCs**) PC.

Pech das 1 bad luck; **Pech haben** to be unlucky; 2 pitch.

Pedal das (PL die **Pedale**) pedal.

peinlich adjective 1 embarrassing; **es war mir sehr peinlich** I felt very embarrassed about it; 2 awkward; 3 meticulous.

Peitsche die (PL die **Peitschen**) whip.

Pelle die skin.

Pelz der (PL die **Pelze**) fur.

pendeln verb 1 (PERF **ist gependelt**) to commute; 2 (PERF **hat gependelt**) to swing.

Pendler der (PL die **Pendler**) commuter.

penetrant adjective 1 overpowering (odour, perfume); 2 pushy (person).

Penis der (PL die **Penisse**) penis.

pennen verb (informal) (PERF **hat gepennt**) to sleep, to kip.

Pension die (PL die **Pensionen**) 1 guesthouse; **2 bei voller Pension** with full board; 3 pension; **eine schöne Pension haben** to get a good pension; **in Pension gehen** to retire.

pensioniert adjective retired.

per preposition ←(+ACC) 1 by; **per Luftpost** by airmail; 2 per.

perfekt adjective perfect.

Perfekt das (PL die **Perfekte**) perfect.

Periode die (PL die **Perioden**) period.

Perle die (PL die **Perlen**) 1 pearl; 2 bead.

Person die (PL die **Personen**) person; **für vier Personen** for four people; **ich für meine Person** personally.

Personal das staff, personnel.

Personenzug der (PL die **Personenzüge**) stopping train.

Personalausweis der (PL die **Personalausweise**) identity card.

persönlich adjective personal. adverb 1 personally; 2 in person.

Perücke die (PL die **Perücken**) wig.

Pessimist der (PL die **Pessimisten**) pessimist.

Δ NEW SPELLING: See page xii

pessimistisch *adjective*
pessimistic.

Petersilie *die* parsley.

Petroleum *das* paraffin.

Pfad *der* (PL *die* **Pfade**) path.

Pfadfinder *der* (PL *die* **Pfadfinder**)
(Boy) Scout.

Pfadfinderin *die* (PL *die*
Pfadfinderinnen) (Girl) Guide.

Pfand *das* (PL *die* **Pfänder**) **1** forfeit;
2 deposit (*on a bottle*); **3** pledge.

Pfanne *die* (PL *die* **Pfannen**) (frying)
pan.

Pfannkuchen *der* (PL *die*
Pfannkuchen) pancake.

Pfarrer *der* (PL *die* **Pfarrer**) **1** vicar;
2 priest.

Pfau *der* (PL *die* **Pfauen**) peacock.

Pfeffer *der* pepper.

Pfefferkorn *das* (PL *die*
Pfefferkörner) peppercorn.

Pfefferkuchen *der* gingerbread.

Pfefferminzbonbon *der* (PL *die*
Pfefferminzbonbons) mint.

Pfefferminze *die* peppermint.

Pfeffermühle *die* (PL *die*
Pfeffermühlen) peppermill.

Pfeife *die* (PL *die* **Pfeifen**) **1** whistle;
2 pipe.

pfeifen ◇ *verb* (IMPERF **pfiff**, PERF **hat
gepfiffen**) to whistle.

Pfeil *der* (PL *die* **Pfeile**) arrow.

Pfeiler *der* (PL *die* **Pfeiler**) **1** pillar;
2 pier.

Pfennig *der* (PL *die* **Pfennige**)
pfennig; **ein Kaugummi kostet
zwanzig Pfennig** a chewing gum is
twenty pfennigs; **ich habe keinen
Pfennig mehr** I haven't got a penny
left.

Pferd *das* (PL *die* **Pferde**) horse.

Pferdeschwanz *der* (PL *die*
Pferdeschwänze) ponytail.

pfiff SEE **pfeifen**.

Pfingsten *das* (PL *die* **Pfingsten**)
Whitsun.

Pfirsich *der* (PL *die* **Pfirsiche**) peach.

Pflanze *die* (PL *die* **Pflanzen**) plant.

pflanzen *verb* (PERF **hat gepflanzt**)
to plant.

Pflaster *das* (PL *die* **Pflaster**)
1 pavement; **2** plaster.

Pflaume *die* (PL *die* **Pflaumen**) plum.

Pflege *die* **1** care; **2** nursing; **3 ein
Kind in Pflege nehmen** to foster a
child.

Pflegeeltern *plural noun* foster
parents.

Pflegeheim *das* (PL *die*
Pflegeheime) nursing home.

Pflegekind *das* (PL *die*
Pflegekinder) foster child.

pflegeleicht *adjective* easy-care
(*fabric*).

pflegen *verb* (PERF **hat geflegt**) **1** to
look after, to care for; **eine
Freundschaft pflegen** to foster a
friendship; **2** to nurse.

◇ IRREGULAR VERB: *See the verb table in the centre of the dictionary*

Pfleger der (PL die **Pfleger**) (male) nurse.

Pflicht die (PL die **Pflichten**) duty; **Pflicht sein** to be compulsory.

pflichtbewusst △ adjective conscientious.

Pflichtfach das (PL die **Pflichtfächer**) compulsory subject.

pflücken verb (PERF **hat gepflückt**) to pick.

Pflug der (PL die **Pflüge**) plough.

Pforte die (PL die **Pforten**) gate.

Pförtner der (PL die **Pförtner**) porter.

Pfosten der (PL die **Pfosten**) post.

Pfote die (PL die **Pfoten**) paw.

pfui exclamation ugh!

Pfund das (PL die **Pfund(e)**) pound.

Pfütze die (PL die **Pfützen**) puddle.

Phantasie die 1 imagination; 2 **Phantasien** (plural) fantasies.

phantasievoll adjective imaginative.

phantastisch adjective fantastic.

Philosoph der (PL die **Philosophen**) philosopher.

Philosophie die (PL die **Philosophien**) philosophy.

Photo das (PL die **Photos**) photo.

Physik die physics.

Physiker der (PL die **Physiker**) physicist.

Physikerin die (PL die **Physikerinnen**) physicist.

Pickel der (PL die **Pickel**) spot, pimple.

Picknick das (PL die **Picknicks**) picnic.

Pik das spades (in cards).

pikant adjective spicy.

Pille die (PL die **Pillen**) pill.

Pilot der (PL die **Piloten**) pilot.

Pilz der (PL die **Pilze**) 1 mushroom; 2 fungus.

Pinguin der (PL die **Pinguine**) penguin.

pinkeln verb (informal) (PERF **hat gepinkelt**) to pee.

Pinnwand die (PL die **Pinnwände**) noticeboard.

Pinsel der (PL die **Pinsel**) brush.

Pinzette die (PL die **Pinzetten**) tweezers.

Pirat der (PL die **Piraten**) pirate.

Piste die (PL die **Pisten**) 1 run, piste; 2 track; 3 runway.

Pizza die (PL die **Pizzas**) pizza.

Pkw der (PL die **Pkws**) (Personenkraftwagen) car.

plagen verb (PERF **hat geplagt**) 1 to bother, to torment; 2 to pester; 3 **sich plagen** to struggle; **sich in der Schule plagen** to struggle at school; **er muss sich plagen** he has to work hard.

Plakat das (PL die **Plakate**) poster.

Plan der (PL die **Pläne**) 1 plan; 2 map.

△ NEW SPELLING: See page xii

planen

GERMAN–ENGLISH

planen *verb* (PERF **hat geplant**) to plan.

planmäßig *adjective* scheduled. *adverb* 1 according to plan; **alles läuft planmäßig** everything is going according to plan; **2** on schedule; **der Zug ist planmäßig abgefahren** the train left on schedule.

Plastik¹ *das* plastic.

Plastik² *die* (PL *die* **Plastiken**) sculpture.

Plastiktüte *die* (PL *die* **Plastiktüten**) plastic bag.

platt *adjective* flat; **platt sein** (*informal*) to be flabbergasted.

plattdeutsch *adjective* low German.

Platte *die* (PL *die* **Platten**) 1 plate; **2** dish; **kalte Platte** cold meats and cheeses; **3** hotplate; **4** record; **5** board (*made of wood*); **6** slab (*made of stone*); **7** sheet (*made of metal or glass*); **8** top (*of a table*).

Plattenspieler *der* (PL *die* **Plattenspieler**) record player.

Platz *der* (PL *die* **Plätze**) 1 place; **viel Platz haben** to have a lot of room; **Platz lassen** to leave room; **auf die Plätze, fertig, los!** on your marks, get set, go!; **2** seat; **Platz nehmen** to take a seat; **3** square (*in a town*); **4** ground, pitch; **einen Spieler vom Platz stellen** to send a player off; **5** court (*for tennis*); **6** course (*for golf*).

Plätzchen *das* (PL *die* **Plätzchen**) 1 biscuit; **2** spot.

platzen *verb* (PERF **ist geplatzt**) 1 to burst; **2 der Plan ist geplatzt** (*informal*) the plan fell through; **3 vor Neugier platzen** to be bursting with curiosity.

plaudern *verb* (PERF **hat geplaudert**) to chat.

pleite *adjective* (*informal*) broke.

Plombe *die* (PL *die* **Plomben**) filling.

plombieren *verb* (PERF **hat plombiert**) to fill.

plötzlich *adjective* sudden. *adverb* suddenly.

plump *adjective* 1 plump; **2** clumsy.

Plural *der* (PL *die* **Plurale**) plural.

plus *adverb* plus.

Plus *das* 1 plus; **2** profit; **3** advantage.

PLZ = **Postleitzahl**.

Po *der* (*informal*) (PL *die* **Pos**) bottom.

Poesie *die* poetry.

Pokal *der* (PL *die* **Pokale**) 1 cup; **2** goblet.

Pokalspiel *das* (PL *die* **Pokalspiele**) cup-tie.

Pole *der* (PL *die* **Polen**) Pole.

Polen *das* Poland.

polieren *verb* (PERF **hat poliert**) to polish.

Polin *die* (PL *die* **Polinnen**) Pole.

Politik *die* 1 politics; **2** policy.

Politiker *der* (PL *die* **Politiker**) politician.

⬦ IRREGULAR VERB: *See the verb table in the centre of the dictionary*

Politikerin die (PL die **Politikerinnen**) politician.

politisch adjective political.

Politur die (PL die **Polituren**) polish.

Polizei die police.

polizeilich adjective police. adverb by the police; **sich polizeilich anmelden** to register with the police.

Polizeiwache die (PL die **Polizeiwachen**) police station.

Polizist der (PL die **Polizisten**) policeman.

Polizistin die (PL die **Polizistinnen**) policewoman.

polnisch adjective Polish.

Pommes frites plural noun chips, French fries.

Pony[1] das (PL die **Ponys**) pony.

Pony[2] der (PL die **Ponys**) fringe.

Popmusik die pop music.

poppig adjective bright; **Natalie hat immer poppige Socken an** Natalie always wears bright socks.

Porree der leeks; **eine Stange Porree** a leek.

Portemonnaie das = **Portmonee**.

Portier der (PL die **Portiers**) porter.

Portion die (PL die **Portionen**) portion.

Portmonee Δ das (PL die **Portmonees**) purse.

Porto das postage.

Porträt das (PL die **Porträts**) portrait.

Portugal das Portugal.

Portugiese der (PL die **Portugiesen**) Portuguese.

Portugiesin die (PL die **Portugiesinnen**) Portuguese.

portugiesisch adjective Portuguese.

Posaune die (PL die **Posaunen**) trombone.

Post die 1 post; **mit der Post** by post; 2 post office.

Postamt das (PL die **Postämter**) post office.

Postbote der (PL die **Postboten**) postman.

Poster das (PL die **Poster**) poster.

Postkarte die (PL die **Postkarten**) postcard.

Postleitzahl die (PL die **Postleitzahlen**) postcode.

prächtig adjective splendid.

prahlen verb (PERF **hat geprahlt**) to boast.

praktisch adjective 1 practical; **praktische Erfahrung** practical experience; 2 handy; 3 **ein praktischer Arzt** a general practitioner. adverb 1 practically; 2 in practice.

Praline die (PL die **Pralinen**) chocolate.

Präposition die (PL die **Präpositionen**) preposition.

Präsens das present (tense).

Präservativ das (PL die **Präservative**) condom.

Präsident der (PL die **Präsidenten**) president.

Präsidentin die (PL die **Präsidentinnen**) president.

Praxis die (PL die **Praxen**) 1 practice; 2 practical experience; 3 surgery.

Preis der (PL die **Preise**) 1 price; **um keinen Preis** not at any price; 2 prize.

Preisausschreiben das (PL die **Preisausschreiben**) competition.

Preiselbeere die (PL die **Preiselbeeren**) cranberry.

preiswert adjective reasonable, cheap.

Prellung die (PL die **Prellungen**) bruise.

Premierminister der (PL die **Premierminister**) prime minister.

Presse die press.

Priester der (PL die **Priester**) priest.

prima adjective (informal) brilliant.

Prinz der (PL die **Prinzen**) prince.

Prinzessin die (PL die **Prinzessinnen**) princess.

Prise die (PL die **Prisen**) pinch; **eine Prise Salz** a pinch of salt.

privat adjective private.

Privileg das (PL die **Privilegien**) privilege.

pro preposition ←(+ACC) per.

Probe die (PL die **Proben**) 1 test; **jemanden auf die Probe stellen** to test somebody; **ein Auto Probe fahren** △ to test-drive a car; 2 sample; 3 rehearsal.

probefahren SEE **Probe**.

probieren verb (PERF **hat probiert**) 1 to try; 2 to taste.

Problem das (PL die **Probleme**) problem.

Produkt das (PL die **Produkte**) product.

Produzent der (PL die **Produzenten**) producer.

produzieren verb (PERF **hat produziert**) to produce.

Profi der (PL die **Profis**) pro.

Profil das (PL die **Profile**) 1 profile; 2 tread (of a tyre).

Programm das (PL die **Programme**) 1 programme; 2 program (in computing); 3 channel (on TV).

programmieren verb (PERF **hat programmiert**) to program.

Programmierer der (PL die **Programmierer**) programmer.

Projekt das (PL die **Projekte**) project.

Promille das alcohol level; **zuviel Promille haben** to be over the limit.

Pronomen das (PL die **Pronomen** or **Pronomina**) pronoun.

Prospekt der (PL die **Prospekte**) brochure.

prost exclamation cheers!

✧ IRREGULAR VERB: See the verb table in the centre of the dictionary

Protein das (PL die **Proteine**)
protein.

Protest der (PL die **Proteste**) protest.

protestantisch adjective
Protestant.

protestieren verb (PERF **hat
protestiert**) to protest.

Protokoll das (PL die **Protokolle**)
1 minutes, transcript; 2 record (in
court); 3 protocol.

protzen verb (PERF **hat geprotzt**) to
show off; **Klaus protzt mit seinem
neuen Auto** Klaus is showing off
with his new car.

Proviant der provisions.

Prozent das (PL die **Prozente**) 1 per
cent; **zehn Prozent** ten per cent;
2 **Prozente bekommen** (informal)
to get a discount.

Prozentsatz der (PL die
Prozentsätze) percentage.

Prozess Δ der (PL die **Prozesse**)
1 court case; **einen Prozess
gewinnen** to win a case; 2 trial;
3 process.

prüfen verb (PERF **hat geprüft**) 1 to
test, to examine (at school); 2 to
check; **hast du die Reifen geprüft?**
have you checked the tyres?

Prüfung die (PL die **Prüfungen**)
1 examination, exam; **eine Prüfung
bestehen** to pass an examination;
sie ist durch die Prüfung gefallen
she failed the exam; 2 check.

Prügel der (PL die **Prügel**) 1 stick;
2 **Prügel bekommen** to get a
beating.

Prügelei die (PL die **Prügeleien**)
fight.

prügeln verb (PERF **hat geprügelt**)
1 to beat; 2 **sich prügeln** to fight;
sich um etwas prügeln to fight for
something.

Psychiater der (PL die **Psychiater**)
psychiatrist.

Psychiaterin die (PL die
Psychiaterinnen) psychiatrist.

psychisch adjective psychological.

Psychologe der (PL die
Psychologen) psychologist.

Psychologie die psychology.

Psychologin die (PL die
Psychologinnen) psychologist.

Publikum das 1 audience, crowd;
2 public.

Pudding der (PL die **Puddings**)
1 blancmange; 2 pudding
(steamed).

Pudel der (PL die **Pudel**) poodle.

Puder der (PL die **Puder**) powder.

Puffmais der popcorn.

Pulli der (PL die **Pullis**) pullover.

Pullover der (PL die **Pullover**)
pullover.

Puls der (PL die **Pulse**) pulse.

Pult das (PL die **Pulte**) desk.

Pulver das (PL die **Pulver**) powder.

Pulverkaffee der instant coffee.

Pumpe die (PL die **Pumpen**) pump.

pumpen verb (PERF **hat gepumpt**)
1 to pump; 2 (informal) to lend;

jemandem Geld pumpen to lend somebody money; **3** (*informal*) to borrow; **sich etwas pumpen** to borrow something.

Punker *der* (PL die **Punker**) punk.

Punkerin *die* (PL die **Punkerinnen**) punk.

Punkt *der* (PL die **Punkte**) **1** dot, spot; **Punkt sechs Uhr** at six o'clock on the dot; **2** full stop; **3** point; **nach Punkten siegen** to win on points.

pünktlich *adjective* punctual.

Puppe *die* (PL die **Puppen**) **1** doll; **2** puppet.

pur *adjective* **1** pure; **2 Whisky pur** neat whisky.

Purzelbaum *der* (PL die **Purzelbäume**) somersault.

pusten *verb* (PERF **hat gepustet**) to blow.

Pute *die* (PL die **Puten**) turkey.

putzen *verb* (PERF **hat geputzt**) **1** to clean; **putz dir die Zähne** clean your teeth; **putzen gehen** to work as a cleaner; **2 sich die Nase putzen** to blow your nose.

Putzfrau *die* (PL die **Putzfrauen**) cleaning lady, cleaner.

putzig *adjective* cute.

Puzzle *das* (PL die **Puzzles**) jigsaw (puzzle).

Pyjama *der* (PL die **Pyjamas**) pyjamas.

Pyramide *die* (PL die **Pyramiden**) pyramid.

Pyrenäen (*plural noun*) **die Pyrenäen** the Pyrenees.

Q q

Quadrat *das* (PL die **Quadrate**) square.

quadratisch *adjective* square.

Quadratmeter *der* (PL die **Quadratmeter**) square metre.

quaken *verb* (PERF **hat gequakt**) **1** to quack; **2** to croak (*of a frog*).

Qual *die* (PL die **Qualen**) **1** torment; **2** agony; **es war eine Qual, das ansehen zu müssen** it was agony to watch.

quälen *verb* (PERF **hat gequält**) **1** to torment; **2** to torture; **3** to pester; **4 sich quälen** to suffer; **5 sich mit etwas quälen** to struggle with something; **sich durch ein Buch quälen** to struggle (your way) through a book.

Quälgeist *der* (*informal*) (PL die **Quälgeister**) pest.

Qualifikation *die* (PL die **Qualifikationen**) qualification.

Qualität *die* (PL die **Qualitäten**) quality.

Qualle *die* (PL die **Quallen**) jellyfish.

Qualm *der* thick smoke.

qualmen *verb* (PERF **hat gequalmt**) to give off clouds of smoke; **sie**

✧ IRREGULAR VERB: *See the verb table in the centre of the dictionary*

qualmt wie ein Schlot (*informal*) she smokes like a chimney.

Quarantäne *die* quarantine.

Quark *der* (*curd cheese*) quark.

Quartett *das* (PL *die* **Quartette**) quartet.

Quartier *das* (PL *die* **Quartiere**) 1 accommodation; 2 quarters.

quasseln *verb* (*informal*) (PERF **hat gequasselt**) to natter.

Quatsch *der* (*informal*) rubbish.

quatschen *verb* (*informal*) (PERF **hat gequatscht**) to chat.

Quelle *die* (PL *die* **Quellen**) 1 source; 2 spring.

quer *adverb* 1 across; 2 crosswise; 3 diagonally; **quer gestreift** Δ with diagonal stripes; 4 **quer durch** straight through.

quergestreift SEE **quer**.

Querstraße *die* (PL *die* **Querstraßen**) side street; **die erste Querstraße rechts** the first turning on the right.

quetschen *verb* (PERF **hat gequetscht**) 1 to crush; 2 to squash; 3 **ich habe mich in meine Jeans gequetscht** I squeezed into my jeans.

Quetschung *die* (PL *die* **Quetschungen**) bruise.

quietschen *verb* (PERF **hat gequietscht**) to squeak.

quitt *adjective* quits.

Quittung *die* (PL *die* **Quittungen**) receipt.

Quiz *das* (PL *die* **Quiz**) quiz.

R r

Rabatt *der* (PL *die* **Rabatte**) discount.

Rache *die* revenge.

rächen *verb* (PERF **hat gerächt**) 1 to avenge; 2 **sich an jemandem rächen** to take revenge on somebody; 3 **das wird sich rächen** you'll have to pay for it.

Rad *das* (PL *die* **Räder**) 1 wheel; 2 bike; **Julia ist mit dem Rad gekommen** Julia came by bike; 3 **Rad fahren** Δ to cycle.

Radar *der* radar.

Radarschirm *der* (PL *die* **Radarschirme**) radar screen.

radfahren SEE **Rad**.

Radfahrer *der* (PL *die* **Radfahrer**) cyclist.

Radfahrerin *die* (PL *die* **Radfahrerinnen**) cyclist.

Radfahrweg *der* (PL *die* **Radfahrwege**) cycle lane.

radeln *verb* (PERF **ist geradelt**) to cycle; **Max ist ins Dorf geradelt** Max cycled into the village.

Radiergummi *der* (PL *die* **Radiergummis**) rubber.

Radieschen *das* (PL *die* **Radieschen**) radish.

Δ NEW SPELLING: *See page xii*

Radio das (PL die **Radios**) radio.

radioaktiv adjective radioactive.

Radler der (PL die **Radler**) cyclist.

Radlerin die (PL die **Radlerinnen**) cyclist.

Radrennen das **1** cycle race; **Maria hat das Radrennen gewonnen** Maria won the cycle race; **2** cycle racing.

raffiniert adjective crafty.

Rahm der cream.

Rahmen der (PL die **Rahmen**) **1** frame; **2** framework; **3** limits; **im Rahmen des Möglichen** within the bounds of possibility.

rahmen verb (PERF **hat gerahmt**) to frame (a picture).

Rakete die (PL die **Raketen**) rocket.

ran (informal) SEE **heran**.

Rand der (PL die **Ränder**) **1** edge; **2** rim; **der Rand der Tasse war angeschlagen** the rim of the cup was chipped; **3** ring, mark; **4** margin (of a page); **du musst einen Rand für die Korrekturen lassen** you must leave a margin for the corrections; **5** outskirts (of a town); **6 etwas am Rande erwähnen** to mention something in passing; **7 am Rande der Pleite sein** to be on the verge of bankruptcy; **8 außer Rand und Band geraten** (informal) to go wild.

Randstreifen der (PL die **Randstreifen**) hard shoulder.

Rang der (PL die **Ränge**) **1** rank; **2** (in a theatre) circle.

rannte SEE **rennen**.

rasch adjective quick.

Rasen der (PL die **Rasen**) lawn, grass.

rasen verb (PERF **ist gerast**) to tear along, to rush; **gegen eine Mauer rasen** to career into a wall.

Rasenmäher der (PL die **Rasenmäher**) lawnmower.

Rasierapparat der (PL die **Rasierapparate**) **1** shaver; **2** razor.

Rasiercreme die (PL die **Rasiercremes**) shaving cream.

rasieren verb (PERF **hat rasiert**) **1** to shave; **2 sich rasieren** to shave.

Rasierklinge die (PL die **Rasierklingen**) razor blade.

Rasierwasser das aftershave.

Rasse die (PL die **Rassen**) **1** race; **2** breed; **ich weiß nicht, was für eine Rasse unser Hund ist** I don't know what breed our dog is.

Rassenhass △ der racial hatred.

rassisch adjective racial.

Rassismus der racism.

Rassist der (PL die **Rassisten**) racist.

Rassistin die (PL die **Rassistinnen**) racist.

rassistisch adjective racist.

rasten verb (PERF **hat gerastet**) to rest.

Rastplatz der (PL die **Rastplätze**) picnic area (on a motorway).

Raststätte die (PL die **Raststätten**) services (on a motorway).

✧ IRREGULAR VERB: *See the verb table in the centre of the dictionary*

Rat *der* **1** advice; **ein Rat** a piece of advice; **jemanden zu Rate ziehen** to ask somebody's advice; **2 sich keinen Rat wissen** not to know what to do; **3** council.

Rate *die* (PL *die* **Raten**) instalment; **in monatlichen Raten abzahlen** to pay in monthly instalments.

raten ✧ *verb* (PRES **rät**, IMPERF **riet**, PERF **hat geraten**) **1 jemandem raten** to advise somebody; **was rätst du mir?** what do you advise me to do?; **2** to guess; **richtig raten** to guess right.

Rathaus *das* (PL *die* **Rathäuser**) town hall.

rationell *adjective* efficient.

ratlos *adjective* helpless; **Emma hat mich ratlos angesehen** Emma gave me a helpless look; **ratlos sein** not to know what to do.

ratsam *adjective* advisable; **es wäre ratsam, früher zu fahren** it would be advisable to leave earlier.

Ratschlag *der* (PL *die* **Ratschläge**) piece of advice, advice; **deine klugen Ratschläge kannst du dir sparen** you can keep your advice to yourself.

Rätsel *das* (PL *die* **Rätsel**) **1** puzzle; **2** mystery.

rätselhaft *adjective* mysterious.

Ratte *die* (PL *die* **Ratten**) rat.

rau △ *adjective* **1** rough; **2** harsh; **3 eine raue Stimme** a husky voice; **4 einen rauen Hals haben** to have a sore throat.

Raub *der* robbery.

Räuber *der* (PL *die* **Räuber**) robber.

Rauch *der* smoke.

rauchen *verb* (PERF **hat geraucht**) to smoke; **'Rauchen verboten'** 'no smoking'.

Raucher *der* (PL *die* **Raucher**) smoker.

Raucherin *die* (PL *die* **Raucherinnen**) smoker.

räuchern *verb* (PERF **hat geräuchert**) to smoke (*fish, meat*).

rauf (*informal*) SEE **herauf, hinauf**.

rauh *adjective* = **rau**.

Raum *der* (PL *die* **Räume**) **1** room; **das Haus hat sehr große Räume** the house has very big rooms; **2** space; **wir brauchen mehr Raum** we need more space; **3 die Rakete ist im Raum explodiert** the rocket exploded in space; **4** area; **im Raum Berlin** in the area of Berlin.

räumen *verb* (PERF **hat geräumt**) **1** to clear; **das Geschirr vom Tisch räumen** to clear away the dishes; **2 die Hemden in den Schrank räumen** to put the shirts in the cupboard; **seine Sachen beiseite räumen** to put your things to one side; **die Akten aus dem Schrank räumen** to take the files out of the cabinet; **3** to vacate.

Raumfahrt *die* space travel.

Raumschiff *das* (PL *die* **Raumschiffe**) space ship.

Raupe *die* (PL *die* **Raupen**) caterpillar.

raus (*informal*) SEE **heraus**, **hinaus**.

Rauschgift *das* (PL *die* **Rauschgifte**) drug; **Rauschgift nehmen** to take drugs.

Rauschgiftsüchtige *der/die* (PL *die* **Rauschgiftsüchtigen**) drug addict.

rauskriegen *verb* (*informal*) (PERF **hat rausgekriegt**) 1 to get out; 2 **ein Geheimnis rauskriegen** to find out a secret; 3 **ich kann die Aufgabe nicht rauskriegen** I can't do the exercise.

räuspern *verb* (PERF **hat sich geräuspert**) **sich räuspern** to clear your throat.

reagieren *verb* (PERF **hat reagiert**) to react.

Reaktion *die* (PL *die* **Reaktionen**) reaction.

realisieren *verb* (PERF **hat realisiert**) 1 to realize; 2 to implement.

Realschule *die* (PL *die* **Realschulen**) secondary school.

rebellieren *verb* (PERF **hat rebelliert**) to rebel.

rechnen *verb* (PERF **hat gerechnet**) 1 to do arithmetic; **Peter kann gut rechnen** Peter's good at arithmetic, Peter's good at figures; 2 to reckon; **mit etwas rechnen** to reckon with something; 3 **er wird zu den besten Schauspielern gerechnet** he's reckoned to be one of the best actors; 4 to count; **jemanden zu seinen Freunden rechnen** to count somebody as a friend; 5 **mit etwas**

rechnen to expect something; 6 **auf jemanden rechnen** to count on somebody.

Rechner *der* (PL *die* **Rechner**) 1 calculator; 2 computer.

Rechnung *die* (PL *die* **Rechnungen**) 1 bill; 2 invoice; **die Rechnung liegt bei** the invoice is enclosed; 3 calculation.

recht *adjective* 1 right; **jemandem recht sein** to be all right with somebody; **wenn es dir recht ist** if it's all right with you; 2 **der/die Rechte** the right man/woman; 3 **das Rechte** the right thing; **etwas Rechtes** something proper; **ich habe nichts Rechtes gegessen** I haven't had a proper meal; **etwas Rechtes lernen** to learn something useful; 4 real; **ich habe keine rechte Lust** I don't really feel like it. *adverb* 1 correctly; 2 quite; **recht einfach** quite simple; 3 really; 4 **recht vielen Dank** many thanks; 5 **das geschieht dir recht!** (it) serves you right!; 6 **man kann es nicht allen recht machen** you can't please everyone.

Recht *das* (PL *die* **Rechte**) 1 law; **nach deutschem Recht** under German law; 2 right; **Recht haben** △ to be right; **im Recht sein** to be in the right; **Recht bekommen** △ to be proved right; **Recht geben** △ to agree with somebody; 4 **mit Recht** rightly; **du hast dich mit Recht beschwert** you were right to complain.

rechte SEE **rechter**.

Rechte *die* 1 right (side); **zu meiner**

Rechten on my right; **2** right hand; **3 die Rechte** the right (*in politics*).

rechteckig *adjective* rectangular.

Rechteck *das* (PL *die* **Rechtecke**) rectangle.

rechter, rechte, rechtes *adjective* **1** right; **auf der rechten Seite** on the right; **2** right-wing.

rechtfertigen *verb* **1** (PERF **hat gerechtfertigt**) to justify; **2 sich rechtfertigen** to justify yourself.

rechtlich *adjective* legal.

rechts *adverb* **1** on the right; **von rechts** from the right; **rechts abbiegen** to turn right; **2 rechts sein** to be right-wing; **3 zwei rechts, zwei links stricken** to knit two, purl two.

Rechtsanwalt *der* (PL *die* **Rechtsanwälte**) lawyer.

Rechtsanwältin *die* (PL *die* **Rechtsanwältinnen**) lawyer.

Rechtschreibung *die* spelling.

Rechtshänder *der* (PL *die* **Rechtshänder**) **Klaus ist Rechtshänder** Klaus is right-handed.

Rechtshänderin *die* (PL *die* **Rechtshänderinnen**) **Beate ist Rechtshänderin** Beate is right-handed.

rechtzeitig *adjective* timely. *adverb* in time; **wir sind gerade noch rechtzeitig angekommen** we got there just in time.

Redakteur *der* (PL *die* **Redakteure**) editor.

Redakteurin *die* (PL *die* **Redakteurinnen**) editor.

Rede *die* (PL *die* **Reden**) **1** speech; **eine Rede halten** to make a speech; **2 nicht der Rede wert** not worth mentioning; **davon kann keine Rede sein** it's out of the question; **jemanden zur Rede stellen** to take somebody to task.

reden *verb* (PERF **hat geredet**) **1** to talk; **2** to speak; **mit jemandem reden** to speak to somebody; **3 sie hat kein Wort geredet** she didn't say a word; **4 mir ist egal, was über mich geredet wird** I don't care what people say about me.

reduzieren *verb* (PERF **hat reduziert**) to reduce.

reflexiv *adjective* reflexive.

Reformhaus *das* (PL *die* **Reformhäuser**) health-food shop.

Regal *das* (PL *die* **Regale**) **1** shelf; **2** shelves, bookcase.

Regel *die* (PL *die* **Regeln**) **1** rule; **in der Regel** as a rule; **2** period (*menstruation*).

regelmäßig *adjective* regular.

regeln *verb* (PERF **hat geregelt**) **1** to regulate; **2** to direct (*the traffic*); **3** to settle (*a matter*); **wir haben die Sache so geregelt, dass …** we've arranged things so that …; **4 sich von selbst regeln** to sort itself out.

Regelung *die* (PL *die* **Regelungen**) **1** regulation; **2** settlement.

Regen *der* rain.

Δ NEW SPELLING: *See page xii*

Regenbogen der (PL die **Regenbogen**) rainbow.

Regenmantel der (PL die **Regenmäntel**) raincoat.

Regenschirm der (PL die **Regenschirme**) umbrella.

Regenwurm der (PL die **Regenwürmer**) earthworm.

regieren verb (PERF **hat regiert**) 1 to govern; 2 to rule, to reign.

Regierung die (PL die **Regierungen**) 1 government; 2 reign.

Regisseur der (PL die **Regisseure**) director.

Regisseurin die (PL die **Regisseurinnen**) director.

regnen verb (PERF **hat geregnet**) to rain.

regnerisch adjective rainy.

Reh das (PL die **Rehe**) deer.

reiben ◇ verb (IMPERF **rieb**, PERF **hat gerieben**) 1 to rub; 2 to grate.

reibungslos adjective smooth.

reich adjective rich.

Reich das (PL die **Reiche**) 1 empire; 2 kingdom, realm.

reichen verb (PERF **hat gereicht**) 1 to hand, to pass; 2 to be enough; **mit dem Geld reichen** to have enough money; 3 **bis zu etwas reichen** to reach up to something; **er reicht seinem Vater bis zur Schulter** he comes up to his father's shoulder; **die Felder reichen bis zum Wald** the fields extend as far as or go right up to the forest; 4 **mir reicht's!** (informal) I've had enough!

reichlich adjective 1 large; 2 ample (space).
adverb plenty of.

Reichtum der (PL die **Reichtümer**) wealth.

Reichweite die 1 reach; **außer Reichweite** out of reach; 2 range.

reif adjective 1 ripe; 2 mature.

Reifen der (PL die **Reifen**) 1 tyre; 2 hoop.

Reifenpanne die (PL die **Reifenpannen**) puncture.

Reifendruck der tyre pressure.

Reihe die (PL die **Reihen**) 1 row; 2 series; 3 **der Reihe nach** in turn; **außer der Reihe** out of turn; **du bist an der Reihe** it's your turn.

Reihenfolge die (PL die **Reihenfolgen**) order.

Reihenhaus das (PL die **Reihenhäuser**) terraced house.

Reim der (PL die **Reime**) rhyme.

reimen verb (PERF **hat gereimt**) 1 to rhyme; 2 **sich reimen** to rhyme.

rein¹ adjective 1 pure; 2 clean; 3 sheer (madness); 4 **etwas ins Reine schreiben** △ to make a fair copy of something; **etwas ins Reine bringen** △ to sort something out.
adverb 1 purely; 2 absolutely; **rein gar nichts** absolutely nothing.

rein² (informal) SEE **herein**, **hinein**.

◇ IRREGULAR VERB: See the verb table in the centre of the dictionary

reinigen *verb* (PERF **hat gereinigt**) to clean.

Reinigung *die* (PL *die* **Reinigungen**) 1 cleaning; 2 cleaner's.

Reis *der* rice.

Reise *die* (PL *die* **Reisen**) 1 journey, trip; **gute Reise!** have a good journey!; **auf meinen Reisen** on my travels; 2 voyage.

Reiseandenken *das* (PL *die* **Reiseandenken**) souvenir.

Reisebüro *das* (PL *die* **Reisebüros**) travel agency.

Reisebus *der* (PL *die* **Reisebusse**) coach.

Reiseführer *der* (PL *die* **Reiseführer**) 1 guidebook; 2 (travel) guide.

Reiseleiter *der* (PL *die* **Reiseleiter**) (travel) guide.

reisen *verb* (PERF **ist gereist**) to travel.

Reisende *der/die* (PL *die* **Reisenden**) traveller.

Reisepass △ *der* (PL *die* **Reisepässe**) passport.

Reisescheck *der* (PL *die* **Reiseschecks**) traveller's cheque.

Reiseziel *das* (PL *die* **Reiseziele**) destination.

reißen ◇ *verb* (IMPERF **riss** △, PERF **hat gerissen**) 1 to tear; 2 to snatch; 3 to pull; **an etwas reißen** to pull at something; 4 **mit sich reißen** to sweep away; 5 **etwas an sich reißen** to snatch something; **die Macht an**

sich reißen to seize power; 6 **Witze reißen** to crack jokes; 7 **sich um etwas reißen** to fight for something; 8 **hin und her gerissen sein** to be torn; 9 (PERF **ist gerissen**) to tear, to break.

Reißverschluss △ *der* (PL *die* **Reißverschlüsse**) zip.

Reißzwecke *die* (PL *die* **Reißzwecken**) drawing pin.

reiten ◇ *verb* (IMPERF **ritt**, PERF **hat/ist geritten**) to ride.

Reiter *der* (PL *die* **Reiter**) rider.

Reiterin *die* (PL *die* **Reiterinnen**) rider.

Reitschule *die* (PL *die* **Reitschulen**) riding school.

Reiz *der* (PL *die* **Reize**) 1 attraction, appeal; 2 charm.

reizen *verb* (PERF **hat gereizt**) 1 to appeal to, to tempt; **das reizt mich sehr** it's very tempting; 2 to annoy; **jemanden zum Zorn reizen** to provoke somebody to anger; 3 to irritate (*the skin, eyes*); 4 to bid (*when playing cards*).

reizend *adjective* charming.

reizvoll *adjective* attractive.

Reklame *die* (PL *die* **Reklamen**) 1 advertisement, advert; **für etwas Reklame machen** to advertise something; 2 commercial (*on TV*).

Rekord *der* (PL *die* **Rekorde**) record.

Rektor *der* (PL *die* **Rektoren**) 1 head (*of a school*); 2 vice-chancellor (*of a university*).

△ NEW SPELLING: *See page xii*

Religion die (PL die **Religionen**)
religion.

religiös adjective religious.

Rendezvous das (PL die
Rendezvous) date.

Rennbahn die (PL die **Rennbahnen**)
racetrack.

rennen ✧ verb (IMPERF **rannte**, PERF
ist gerannt) to run.

Rennen das (PL die **Rennen**) race.

Rennfahrer der (PL die **Rennfahrer**)
racing driver.

Rennwagen der (PL die
Rennwagen) racing car.

renovieren verb (PERF **hat
renoviert**) to renovate, to redecorate.

rentabel adjective profitable.

Rente die (PL die **Renten**) pension; **in
Rente gehen** to retire.

Rentner der (PL die **Rentner**)
pensioner.

Rentnerin die (PL die **Rentnerinnen**)
pensioner.

Reparatur die (PL die **Reparaturen**)
repair.

reparieren verb (PERF **hat repariert**)
to repair.

Reportage die (PL die **Reportagen**)
1 report; 2 live commentary.

Reporter der (PL die **Reporter**)
reporter.

Reporterin die (PL die
Reporterinnen) reporter.

Reptil das (PL die **Reptile**) reptile.

Republik die (PL die **Republiken**)
republic.

Reservat das (PL die **Reservate**)
reservation.

Reserverad das (PL die
Reserveräder) spare wheel.

reservieren verb (PERF **hat
reserviert**) to reserve.

Reservierung die (PL die
Reservierungen) reservation.

Respekt der respect.

respektieren verb (PERF **hat
respektiert**) to respect.

Rest der (PL die **Reste**) 1 rest,
remainder; 2 left-over; **zum
Mittagessen gibt's die Reste** we're
having the leftovers for lunch; 3 **die
Reste** the remains.

Restaurant das (PL die
Restaurants) restaurant.

restlich adjective remaining.

restlos adjective complete.

Resultat das (PL die **Resultate**)
result.

retten verb (PERF **hat gerettet**) 1 to
save, to rescue; **jemandem das
Leben retten** to save somebody's
life; 2 **sich retten** to escape.

Rettich der (PL die **Rettiche**) radish.

Rettung die rescue.

Rettungsring der (PL die
Rettungsringe) lifebelt.

Rettungswagen der (PL die
Rettungswagen) ambulance.

✧ IRREGULAR VERB: *See the verb table in the centre of the dictionary*

Rezept *das* (PL *die* **Rezepte**)
1 prescription; 2 recipe.

Rezeption *die* (PL *die* **Rezeptionen**)
reception; **bitte geben Sie Ihren
Schlüssel an der Rezeption ab**
please leave your key at reception.

R-Gespräch *das* (PL *die* **R-
Gespräche**) reverse-charge call.

Rhabarber *der* rhubarb.

Rhein *der* Rhine.

Rheuma *das* rheumatism.

Rhythmus *der* (PL *die* **Rhythmen**)
rhythm.

richten *verb* (PERF **hat gerichtet**)
1 to direct, to point (*a torch,
telescope, gun*); 2 **eine Frage an
jemanden richten** to put a question
to somebody; 3 to address (*a letter,
remarks*); 4 to prepare (*a meal,
room*); 5 **sich auf etwas richten** to
be directed towards something;
6 **sich nach jemandem richten** to
fit in with somebody's wishes; **sich
nach den Vorschriften richten** to
follow the rules; 7 **sich nach etwas
richten** to depend on something.

Richter *der* (PL *die* **Richter**) judge.

richtig *adjective* 1 right; 2 **das
Richtige** the right thing; **der/die
Richtige** the right man/woman;
3 real, proper.
adverb 1 correctly; 2 really;
3 **richtig stellen** △ to put right; **die
Uhr geht richtig** the clock is right.

Richtung *die* (PL *die* **Richtungen**)
1 direction; 2 trend.

rieb SEE **reiben**.

riechen ✧ *verb* (IMPERF **roch**, PERF
hat gerochen) 1 to smell; 2 **ich
kann ihn nicht riechen** (*informal*)
I can't stand him.

rief SEE **rufen**.

Riegel *der* (PL *die* **Riegel**) 1 bolt;
2 **ein Riegel Schokolade** a bar of
chocolate.

Riemen *der* (PL *die* **Riemen**) strap.

Riese *der* (PL *die* **Riesen**) giant.

riesengroß *adjective* gigantic.

riesig *adjective* huge.

riet SEE **raten**.

Rind *das* (PL *die* **Rinder**) 1 ox; 2 cow;
Rinder cattle; 3 beef.

Rinde *die* (PL *die* **Rinden**) 1 bark;
2 rind; 3 crust.

Rindfleisch *das* beef.

Ring *der* (PL *die* **Ringe**) ring.

Ringbuch *das* (PL *die* **Ringbücher**)
ring binder.

Ringen *das* wrestling.

Rippe *die* (PL *die* **Rippen**) rib.

Risiko *das* (PL *die* **Risiken**) risk.

riskant *adjective* risky.

riskieren *verb* (PERF **hat riskiert**) to
risk.

riss △ SEE **reißen**.

Riss △ *der* (PL *die* **Risse**) 1 tear;
2 crack.

ritt SEE **reiten**.

Rivale *der* (PL *die* **Rivalen**) rival.

Rivalin *die* (PL *die* **Rivalinnen**) rival.

△ NEW SPELLING: *See page xii*

Robbe *die* (PL *die* **Robben**) seal.

Roboter *der* (PL *die* **Roboter**) robot.

roch SEE **riechen**.

Rock *der* (PL *die* **Röcke**) skirt.

Roggen *der* rye.

roh *adjective* **1** raw; **2** rough;
3 brutal.

Rohr *das* (PL *die* **Rohre**) **1** pipe;
2 reed; **3** cane.

Rolladen = **Rollladen**.

Rolle *die* (PL *die* **Rollen**) **1** roll;
2 reel; **3** role, part; **4 es spielt keine
Rolle** it doesn't matter.

rollen *verb* (PERF **hat gerollt**) **1** to
roll; **2** (PERF **ist gerollt**) to roll.

Roller *der* (PL *die* **Roller**) scooter.

Rollkragen *der* (PL *die* **Rollkrägen**)
polo neck.

Rollladen Δ *der* (PL *die* **Rollläden**)
shutter.

Rollschuh *der* (PL *die* **Rollschuhe**)
roller-skate.

Rollschuhlaufen *das* roller-
skating.

Rollstuhl *der* (PL *die* **Rollstühle**)
wheelchair.

Rolltreppe *die* (PL *die* **Rolltreppen**)
escalator.

Rom *das* Rome.

Roman *der* (PL *die* **Romane**) novel.

romantisch *adjective* romantic.

röntgen *verb* (PERF **hat geröntgt**) to
X-ray.

rosa *adjective* pink.

Rose *die* (PL *die* **Rosen**) rose.

Rosenkohl *der* (Brussels) sprouts.

Rosine *die* (PL *die* **Rosinen**) raisin.

Rosmarin *der* rosemary.

Rosskastanie Δ *die* (PL *die*
Rosskastanien) horse-chestnut.

Rost *der* (PL *die* **Roste**) **1** rust;
2 grate, grill.

rosten *verb* (PERF **ist gerostet**) to
rust.

rösten (PERF **hat geröstet**) **1** to roast;
2 to toast.

rostig *adjective* rusty.

rot *adjective* red.

Röteln *plural noun* German
measles.

rothaarig *adjective* red-haired.

Rotkehlchen *das* (PL *die*
Rotkehlchen) robin.

Rotwein *der* (PL *die* **Rotweine**) red
wine.

rüber *adverb* (*informal*) over;
komm zu uns rüber come over to
us.

rücken *verb* (PERF **hat gerückt**) to
move; **kannst du ein wenig
rücken?** can you move over a bit?

Rücken *der* (PL *die* **Rücken**) **1** back;
2 spine (*of a book*).

Rückfahrkarte *die* (PL *die*
Rückfahrkarten) return ticket; **eine
Rückfahrkarte nach München** a
return ticket to Munich.

✧ IRREGULAR VERB: *See the verb table in the centre of the dictionary*

Rückfahrt *die* return journey; **auf der Rückfahrt** on the way back.

Rückgabe *die* (PL *die* **Rückgaben**) return.

rückgängig *adjective* **etwas rückgängig machen** to cancel something.

Rückkehr *die* return.

Rückreise *die* return journey.

Rucksack *der* (PL *die* **Rucksäcke**) rucksack.

Rückseite *die* (PL *die* **Rückseiten**) back.

Rücksicht *die* consideration.

rücksichtslos *adjective* **1** inconsiderate; **ein rücksichtsloser Fahrer** a reckless driver; **2** ruthless.

rücksichtsvoll *adjective* considerate.

Rücksitz *der* (PL *die* **Rücksitze**) back seat.

rückwärts *adverb* backwards.

Rückwärtsgang *der* (PL *die* **Rückwärtsgänge**) reverse (gear).

Rückweg *der* (PL *die* **Rückwege**) **1** way back; **2** return journey.

Rückzahlung *die* (PL *die* **Rückzahlungen**) refund, repayment.

Ruder *das* (PL *die* **Ruder**) **1** oar; **2** rudder.

Ruderboot *das* (PL *die* **Ruderboote**) rowing boat.

rudern *verb* (PERF **ist gerudert**) **1** to row; **ich bin über den See gerudert** I rowed across the lake; **2** (PERF **hat gerudert**) to row; **ich habe Monika über den See gerudert** I rowed Monika across the lake.

Ruf *der* (PL *die* **Rufe**) **1** call, shout; **2** reputation; **3** phone number.

rufen ◇ *verb* (IMPERF **rief**, PERF **hat gerufen**) to call; **den Arzt rufen** to send for the doctor.

Rufnummer *die* (PL *die* **Rufnummern**) phone number.

Ruhe *die* **1** silence; **Ruhe bitte!** quiet please!; **2** rest; **3** peace; **jemanden in Ruhe lassen** to leave somebody in peace; **in aller Ruhe** calmly; **4** **sich nicht aus der Ruhe bringen lassen** to not get worked up; **5** **sich zur Ruhe setzen** to retire.

ruhen *verb* (PERF **hat geruht**) to rest; **hier ruht …** here lies …

Ruhestand *der* **im Ruhestand** retired.

Ruhetag *der* (PL *die* **Ruhetage**) closing day; **'Dienstag Ruhetag'** 'closed on Tuesdays'.

ruhig *adjective* **1** quiet; **2** peaceful; **3** calm.
adverb **1** quietly; **sich ruhig verhalten** to keep quiet; **2** calmly; **ruhig bleiben** to remain calm; **3** **sehen Sie sich ruhig um** you're welcome to look around; **du kannst es ihm ruhig sagen** it's OK, you can tell him.

Ruhm *der* fame.

Rührei *das* scrambled eggs.

Δ NEW SPELLING: *See page xii*

rühren *verb* (PERF **hat gerührt**) **1** to move; **2** to stir; **3 sich rühren** to move; **4 an etwas rühren** to touch, to touch on.

Ruine *die* (PL *die* **Ruinen**) ruin.

ruinieren *verb* (PERF **hat ruiniert**) to ruin.

rülpsen *verb* (PERF **hat gerülpst**) to belch.

Rumänien *das* Romania.

rumänisch *adjective* Romanian.

Rummel *der* **1** hustle and bustle; **2** fuss; **3** fair.

Rummelplatz *der* (PL *die* **Rummelplätze**) fairground.

rund *adjective* round.
adverb about; **rund um** around.

Runde *die* (PL *die* **Runden**) **1** round; **2** lap; **3** circle, group; **4 über die Runden kommen** (*informal*) to get by.

Rundfahrt *die* (PL *die* **Rundfahrten**) tour.

Rundfrage *die* (PL *die* **Rundfragen**) poll.

Rundfunk *der* radio; **im Rundfunk** on the radio.

rundherum *adverb* all around.

runter *adverb* (*informal*) SEE **herunter, hinunter**; **runter da!** get off!

runzlig *adjective* wrinkled.

Rüsche *die* (PL *die* **Rüschen**) frill.

Russe *der* (PL *die* **Russen**) Russian.

Rüssel *der* (PL *die* **Rüssel**) trunk.

Russin *die* (PL *die* **Russinnen**) Russian.

russisch *adjective* Russian.

Russland Δ *das* Russia.

Rüstung *die* (PL *die* **Rüstungen**) **1** armament; **2** arms; **3** (suit of) armour.

Rutschbahn *die* (PL *die* **Rutschbahnen**) slide.

rutschen *verb* (PERF **ist gerutscht**) **1** to slide; **2** to slip; **3 rutsch mal!** move over!

rutschig *adjective* slippery.

rütteln *verb* (PERF **hat gerüttelt**) to shake; **an der Tür rütteln** to rattle a the door.

S s

Saal *der* (PL *die* **Säle**) hall.

Sabbat *der* (PL *die* **Sabbate**) Sabbath.

Sache *die* (PL *die* **Sachen**) **1** matter; **das ist eine andere Sache** that's a different matter; **2** business; **das ist seine Sache** that's his business; **3** thing; **meine Sachen** my things (*clothing*); **sie räumt nie ihre Sacher weg** she never puts away her things; **4 zur Sache kommen** to get to the point; **5 das ist so'ne Sache** (*informal*) it's a bit tricky.

Sachgebiet *das* (PL *die* **Sachgebiete**) field, area.

◇ IRREGULAR VERB: *See the verb table in the centre of the dictionary*

sachlich *adjective* **1** objective; **2** factual.

sächlich *adjective* neuter.

Sachsen *das* Saxony.

Sack *der* (PL *die* **Säcke**) **1** sack; **2** bag.

Sackgasse *die* (PL *die* **Sackgassen**) cul-de-sac.

Saft *der* (PL *die* **Säfte**) **1** juice; **2** sap.

saftig *adjective* juicy.

Säge *die* (PL *die* **Sägen**) saw.

Sägemehl *das* sawdust.

sagen *verb* (PERF **hat gesagt**) **1** to say; **man sagt, dass …** it's said that …; **2 was ich noch sagen wollte** by the way; **unter uns gesagt** between you and me; **3** to tell; **jemandem etwas sagen** to tell somebody something; **sag mal** tell me; **was sagen Sie dazu?** what do you think about it?; **4** to mean; **das hat nichts zu sagen** it doesn't mean anything; **5 zu jemandem Tante sagen** to call somebody aunt; **6 ihr Gesicht sagte alles** it was written all over her face.

sägen *verb* (PERF **hat gesägt**) to saw.

sagenhaft *adjective* **1** legendary; **2** (*informal*) brilliant.

sah SEE **sehen**.

Sahne *die* cream.

Saison *die* (PL *die* **Saisons**) season.

Saite *die* (PL *die* **Saiten**) string.

Sakko *das* (PL *die* **Sakkos**) jacket.

Salat *der* (PL *die* **Salate**) **1** lettuce; **2** salad.

Salatsoße *die* (PL *die* **Salatsoßen**) salad dressing.

Salbe *die* (PL *die* **Salben**) ointment.

Salbei *der* sage.

salopp *adjective* casual, informal.

Salz *das* salt.

salzen *verb* (PERF **hat gesalzen**) to salt.

salzig *adjective* salty.

Salzkartoffeln *plural noun* boiled potatoes.

Salzwasser *das* **1** salt water; **2** salted water (*for cooking*).

Samen *der* (PL *die* **Samen**) **1** seed; **2** sperm, semen.

sammeln *verb* (PERF **hat gesammelt**) **1** to collect; **Martin sammelt Briefmarken** Martin collects stamps; **2** to gather; **3 sich sammeln** to gather; **seine Gedanken sammeln** to gather your thoughts.

Sammlung *die* (PL *die* **Sammlungen**) collection; **eine Sammlung für einen guten Zweck** a collection for charity.

Samstag *der* (PL *die* **Samstage**) Saturday.

samstags *adverb* on Saturdays.

samt *preposition* ←(+DAT) (together) with; **Mimi kam samt Puppen und Katze** Mimi arrived with her dolls and cat.

△ NEW SPELLING: *See page xii*

Samt der (PL die **Samte**) velvet.

sämtlicher, sämtliche, sämtliches adjective all the; **meine sämtlichen Bücher** all my books.

Sand der sand.

Sandale die (PL die **Sandalen**) sandal.

sandig adjective sandy.

sandte SEE **senden**.

sanft adjective gentle; **eine sanfte Stimme** a soft voice.

sang SEE **singen**.

Sänger der (PL die **Sänger**) singer.

Sängerin die (PL die **Sängerinnen**) singer.

sank SEE **sinken**.

Sardelle die (PL die **Sardellen**) anchovy.

Sardine die (PL die **Sardinen**) sardine.

Sarg der (PL die **Särge**) coffin.

Sarkasmus der sarcasm.

sarkastisch adjective sarcastic.

saß SEE **sitzen**.

Satellit der (PL die **Satelliten**) satellite.

Satellitenfernsehen das satellite television.

satt adjective 1 full (up); **bist du satt geworden?** have you had enough to eat?; **sich satt essen** to eat as much as one wants; **satt machen** to be filling; 2 **etwas satt haben** (informal) to be fed up with something.

Sattel der (PL die **Sättel**) saddle.

Satz der (PL die **Sätze**) 1 sentence; 2 set (of things or in tennis); **ein Satz Reifen** a set of tyres; 3 movement (in music); 4 rate (of tax, interest); 5 leap.

sauber adjective 1 clean; 2 neat; 3 (informal) fine (expressing irony); 4 **sauber machen** △ to clean.

Sauberkeit die cleanliness, cleanness.

saubermachen SEE **sauber**.

Sauce die (PL die **Saucen**) = **Soße**.

sauer adjective 1 sour; 2 pickled; 3 acid; **saurer Regen** acid rain; 4 **sauer sein** (informal) to be annoyed; **ich bin sauer auf Eva** I'm annoyed with Eva.

Sauerei die (informal) (PL die **Sauereien**) 1 mess; 2 disgrace, scandal; 3 obscenity.

Sauerstoff der oxygen.

saufen ◇ verb (informal) (PRES **säuft**, IMPERF **soff**, PERF **hat gesoffen**) to drink, to booze.

saugen verb (PERF **hat gesaugt**) 1 to suck; 2 to vacuum, to hoover.

Säugetier das (PL die **Säugetiere**) mammal.

Säugling der (PL die **Säuglinge**) baby, infant.

Säule die (PL die **Säulen**) column.

Säure die (PL die **Säuren**) acid.

◇ IRREGULAR VERB: See the verb table in the centre of the dictionary

axofon △ das (PL die **Saxofone**) saxophone.

-Bahn die (PL die **S-Bahnen**) city and suburban railway.

chäbig adjective shabby.

chach das chess; **Schach!** check!

chachbrett das (PL die **Schachbretter**) chessboard.

chachfigur die (PL die **Schachfiguren**) chess piece.

chachtel die (PL die **Schachteln**) box.

chade adjective **1 schade sein** to be a pity; **schade!** (what a) pity!; **2 zu schade für jemanden sein** to be too good for somebody.

chaden verb (PERF **hat geschadet**) **1** to damage; **das hat seinem Ruf geschadet** it damaged his reputation; **2 jemandem schaden** to harm somebody; **3 das schadet nichts** it doesn't matter.

chaden der (PL die **Schäden**) **1** damage; **2** disadvantage.

chädlich adjective harmful.

chaf das (PL die **Schafe**) sheep.

chäfer der (PL die **Schäfer**) shepherd.

chäferhund der (PL die **Schäferhunde**) sheepdog.

chaffen¹ ◇ verb (IMPERF **schuf**, PERF **hat geschaffen**) to create; **wie geschaffen für** made for.

chaffen² verb (PERF **hat geschafft**) **1** to manage; **es schaffen, etwas zu tun** to manage to do something;

2 eine Prüfung schaffen to pass an exam; **3 jemandem zu schaffen machen** to cause somebody trouble; **4 geschafft sein** (informal) to be worn out.

Schaffner der (PL die **Schaffner**) **1** conductor; **2** (ticket) inspector.

Schaffnerin die (PL die **Schaffnerinnen**) **1** conductress; **2** (ticket) inspector.

Schal der (PL die **Schals**) scarf.

Schale die (PL die **Schalen**) **1** skin; **2** peel; **3** shell; **4** dish, bowl; **eine Schale Obst** a bowl of fruit.

schälen verb (PERF **hat geschält**) **1** to peel; **er hat ihr eine Orange geschält** he peeled an orange for her; **2 sich schälen** to peel; **mein Rücken schält sich** my back's peeling.

Schall der sound.

Schallplatte die (PL die **Schallplatten**) record.

schalten verb (PERF **hat geschaltet**) **1** to switch; **auf etwas schalten** to turn to something; **2** to change gear; **3 schnell schalten** (informal) to catch on quickly.

Schalter der (PL die **Schalter**) **1** switch; **2** counter.

Schaltjahr das (PL die **Schaltjahre**) leap year.

schämen verb (PERF **hat sich geschämt**) **sich schämen** to be ashamed.

Schampon das (PL die **Schampons**) shampoo.

△ NEW SPELLING: *See page xii*

Schande die 1 disgrace; 2 shame.

scharf *adjective* 1 sharp; 2 hot
(*food*); **ein scharfer Wind** a biting
wind; 3 fierce (*dog, frost*); 4 **scharf
nachdenken** to think hard; 5 (*in
photography*) **scharf sein** to be in
focus; **scharf einstellen** to focus;
6 **scharf schießen** to fire live
ammunition; 7 **scharf auf etwas
sein** (*informal*) to be really keen on
something; **sie ist scharf auf Bernd**
(*informal*) she fancies Bernd.

Schaschlik der (PL die **Schaschliks**)
kebab.

Schatten der (PL die **Schatten**)
1 shadow; 2 shade.

schattig *adjective* shady.

Schatz der (PL die **Schätze**)
1 treasure; 2 darling.

Schätzchen das (PL die
Schätzchen) darling.

schätzen *verb* (PERF **hat geschätzt**)
1 to estimate; 2 to value; 3 to
reckon, to guess; **schätz mal!**
guess!; 4 **etwas zu schätzen
wissen** to appreciate something.

Schau die (PL die **Schauen**) show.

schauen *verb* (PERF **hat geschaut**)
to look.

Schauer der (PL die **Schauer**)
shower.

Schauergeschichte die (PL die
Schauergeschichten) horror story.

Schaufel die (PL die **Schaufeln**)
1 shovel; 2 dustpan.

Schaufenster das (PL die
Schaufenster) shop window.

Schaukel die (PL die **Schaukeln**)
swing.

schaukeln *verb* (PERF **hat
geschaukelt**) to swing.

Schaukelstuhl der (PL die
Schaukelstühle) rocking chair.

Schaum der 1 foam; 2 froth;
3 lather.

schäumen *verb* (PERF **hat
geschäumt**) 1 to foam; 2 to froth
(up).

Schauplatz der (PL die
Schauplätze) scene.

Schauspiel das (PL die
Schauspiele) 1 play; 2 spectacle.

Schauspieler der (PL die
Schauspieler) actor.

Schauspielerin die (PL die
Schauspielerinnen) actress.

Scheck der (PL die **Schecks**) chequ

Scheckbuch das (PL die
Scheckbücher) chequebook.

Scheckkarte die (PL die
Scheckkarten) cheque card.

Scheibe die (PL die **Scheiben**)
1 pane (*of a window, car*); 2 slice;
eine Scheibe Schinken a slice of
ham; **die Salami in Scheiben
schneiden** to slice the salami; **du
könntest dir eine Scheibe von ihr
abschneiden** (*informal*) you coul
take a leaf out of her book; 3 disc.

Scheibenwischer der (PL die

◇ IRREGULAR VERB: *See the verb table in the centre of the dictionary*

Scheibenwischer) windscreen wiper.

cheiden ✧ *verb* (IMPERF **schied**, PERF **hat geschieden**) **1** to separate; **sich scheiden lassen** to get divorced; **2 geschieden sein** to be divorced.

cheidung *die* (PL *die* **Scheidungen**) divorce.

chein *der* (PL *die* **Scheine**) **1** light; **2** appearance; **etwas nur zum Schein machen** to only pretend to do something; **3** certificate; **4** note (*money*).

cheinbar *adverb* apparently.

cheinen ✧ *verb* (IMPERF **schien**, PERF **hat geschienen**) **1** to shine; **2** to seem; **mir scheint** it seems to me.

cheinwerfer *der* (PL *die* **Scheinwerfer**) **1** headlamp, headlight; **2** floodlight, spotlight.

cheitern *verb* (PERF **ist gescheitert**) to fail.

chenkel *der* (PL *die* **Schenkel**) thigh.

chenken *verb* (PERF **hat geschenkt**) **1** to give; **etwas geschenkt bekommen** to be given something; **2 sich etwas schenken** to give something a miss; **3 das ist ja geschenkt!** (*informal*) it's a gift!

chere *die* (PL *die* **Scheren**) **1** (pair of) scissors; **2** shears; **3** claw (*of a crab*).

cheren *verb* (*informal*) (PERF **hat geschert**) to bother; **sich nicht um etwas scheren** not to care about

something; **scher dich um deine eigenen Angelegenheiten!** mind your own business!; **scher dich zum Teufel!** go to hell!

Scherz *der* (PL *die* **Scherze**) joke.

scheu *adjective* shy.

scheuern *verb* (PERF **hat gescheuert**) **1** to scrub; **2** to rub.

Scheune *die* (PL *die* **Scheunen**) barn.

scheußlich *adjective* horrible.

Schi *der* (PL *die* **Schi(er)**) = **Ski**.

Schicht *die* (PL *die* **Schichten**) **1** layer; **2** class; **3** shift.

schick *adjective* **1** stylish, smart; **2** (*informal*) great.

schicken *verb* (PERF **hat geschickt**) to send.

Schicksal *das* (PL *die* **Schicksale**) fate.

schieben ✧ *verb* (IMPERF **schob**, PERF **hat geschoben**) **1** to push; **2 etwas auf etwas schieben** to blame something for something; **die Schuld auf jemanden schieben** to put the blame on somebody.

schied SEE **scheiden**.

Schiedsrichter *der* (PL *die* **Schiedsrichter**) referee, umpire.

schief *adjective* crooked; **ein schiefer Blick** a funny look. *adverb* **1 das Bild hängt schief** the picture is not straight; **2 schief gehen**△ to go wrong.

Schiefer *der* slate.

schiefgehen SEE **schief**.

schielen verb (PERF **hat geschielt**) to squint.

schien SEE **scheinen**.

Schienbein das (PL die **Schienbeine**) shin.

Schiene die (PL die **Schienen**) 1 rail; 2 splint.

schießen ✧ verb (IMPERF **schoss** Δ, PERF **hat geschossen**) 1 to shoot; **auf jemanden schießen** to shoot at somebody; **ein Tor schießen** to score a goal; 2 (PERF **ist geschossen**) to shoot (along); **Andrea ist in die Höhe geschossen** Andrea's shot up (has got a lot taller).

Schiff das (PL die **Schiffe**) ship.

schikanieren verb (PERF **hat schikaniert**) to bully.

Schikoree Δ der chicory.

Schild das (PL die **Schilder**) 1 sign; 2 badge; 3 label.

Schildkröte die (PL die **Schildkröten**) 1 tortoise; 2 turtle.

Schilling der (PL die **Schilling(e)**) Schilling.

Schimmel der (PL die **Schimmel**) 1 mould; 2 white horse.

Schimpanse der (PL die **Schimpansen**) chimpanzee.

schimpfen verb (PERF **hat geschimpft**) 1 to tell off; 2 to grumble.

Schinken der (PL die **Schinken**) ham.

Schirm der (PL die **Schirme**)

1 umbrella; 2 sunshade; 3 shade (a lamp); 4 peak (of a cap).

Schlaf der sleep.

Schlafanzug der (PL die **Schlafanzüge**) pyjamas.

schlafen ✧ verb (PRES **schläft**, IMPERF **schlief**, PERF **hat geschlafen**) 1 to sleep; 2 to be asleep; 3 **schlafen gehen** to go to bed.

Schlafcouch die (PL die **Schlafcouchs**) sofa bed.

schlaff adjective 1 slack (rope); 2 limp (handshake, body); 3 lethargic.

Schlafsaal der (PL die **Schlafsäle**) dormitory.

Schlafsack der (PL die **Schlafsäcke**) sleeping bag.

Schlafzimmer das (PL die **Schlafzimmer**) bedroom.

Schlafwagen der (PL die **Schlafwagen**) sleeper.

Schlag der (PL die **Schläge**) 1 blow, punch; **Schläge kriegen** to get a beating; 2 stroke; 3 (electric) shock; 4 **Schlag auf Schlag** in quick succession; **auf einen Schlag** all at once.

schlagen ✧ verb (PRES **schlägt**, IMPERF **schlug**, PERF **hat geschlagen**) 1 to hit; **einen Nagel in die Wand schlagen** to knock a nail into the wall; 2 to beat; 3 to bang; **mit dem Kopf gegen etwas schlagen** to bang your head against something; 4 to strike (of a clock); 5 to whip (cream); 6 **sich schlagen** to fight;

✧ IRREGULAR VERB: See the verb table in the centre of the dictionary

7 sich geschlagen geben to admit defeat.

chlager der (PL die **Schlager**) hit.

chläger der (PL die **Schläger**) 1 racket (in tennis); 2 bat (in baseball); 3 club (in golf); 4 stick (in hockey); 5 thug.

chlägerei die (PL die **Schlägereien**) fight.

chlagsahne die 1 whipping cream; 2 whipped cream.

chlagzeile die (PL die **Schlagzeilen**) headline.

chlagzeug das (PL die **Schlagzeuge**) drums.

chlagzeuger der (PL die **Schlagzeuger**) drummer.

chlamm der mud.

chlampen verb (PERF **hat geschlampt**) to be sloppy.

chlamperei die (PL die **Schlampereien**) 1 sloppiness; 2 mess.

chlampig adjective sloppy.

chlange die (PL die **Schlangen**) 1 snake; 2 queue; **Schlange stehen** to queue.

chlank adjective slim.

chlankheitskur die (PL die **Schlankheitskuren**) diet; **eine Schlankeitskur machen** to be on a diet.

chlapp adjective worn out, tired out.

chlau adjective 1 crafty; 2 clever;

ich werde nicht schlau daraus I can't make head nor tail of it.

Schlauch der (PL die **Schläuche**) hose.

schlecht adjective 1 bad; **schlecht werden** to go bad; 2 **mir ist schlecht** I feel sick; 3 **jemanden schlecht machen** △ to run somebody down.
adverb 1 badly; **schlecht gelaunt** in a bad mood; 2 **es geht ihm schlecht** he's not well.

schleichen ♦ verb (IMPERF **schlich**, PERF **ist geschlichen**) 1 to creep; 2 to crawl (in traffic); 3 **sich schleichen** to creep.

Schleife die (PL die **Schleifen**) 1 bow; 2 loop.

Schleuder die (PL die **Schleudern**) 1 catapult; 2 spin-dryer.

schleudern verb (PERF **hat geschleudert**) 1 to hurl; 2 to spin (washing); 3 (PERF **ist geschleudert**) to skid.

schlich SEE **schleichen**.

schlicht adjective plain, simple.

schlief SEE **schlafen**.

schließen ♦ verb (IMPERF **schloss** △, PERF **hat geschlossen**) 1 to close, to shut; 2 to close down; 3 to lock; 4 to conclude; **aus etwas schließen, dass** … to conclude from something that …; 5 **einen Vertrag schließen** to enter into a contract; 6 **Freundschaft mit jemandem schließen** to make friends with somebody; 7 **sich schließen** to close.

△ NEW SPELLING: See page xii

Schließfach das (PL die **Schließfächer**) locker.

schließlich adverb 1 finally; 2 after all; **er hat sie schließlich doch eingeladen** he's invited her after all.

schlimm adjective bad.

schlimmstenfalls adverb if the worst comes to the worst.

Schlips der (PL die **Schlipse**) tie.

Schlitten der (PL die **Schlitten**) sledge; **Schlitten fahren gehen** to go sledging.

Schlittschuh der (PL die **Schlittschuhe**) skate; **Schlittschuh laufen** to skate.

Schlittschuhlaufen das ice-skating.

Schlitz der (PL die **Schlitze**) 1 slit; 2 flies (in trousers); 3 slot.

schloss△ SEE **schließen**.

Schloss△ das (PL die **Schlösser**) 1 lock; 2 castle.

Schluck der (PL die **Schlucke**) 1 mouthful; 2 gulp.

Schluckauf der hiccups.

schlucken verb (PERF **hat geschluckt**) to swallow.

schlug SEE **schlagen**.

Schlüpfer der (PL die **Schlüpfer**) knickers.

Schluss△ der (PL die **Schlüsse**) 1 end, ending; **zum Schluss** in the end; **Schluss machen** to stop; **mit jemandem Schluss machen** to finish with somebody; 2 conclusion.

Schlüssel der (PL die **Schlüssel**) 1 key; 2 spanner.

Schlussverkauf△ der sales.

schmal adjective 1 narrow; 2 thin (face, nose); 3 **sie ist schmäler geworden** she's lost weight.

schmecken verb (PERF **hat geschmeckt**) to taste; **die Suppe schmecht gut** the soup tastes goo〈 **das schmeckt mir nicht** I don't lik〈 it; **das Eis schmeckt nacht Zitrone** the ice cream tastes of lemon.

schmeicheln verb (PERF **hat geschmeichelt**) to flatter; **jemandem schmeicheln** to flatter somebody.

schmeißen✧ verb (informal) (IMPERF **schmiss**△, PERF **hat geschmissen**) to chuck; **mit etwas schmeißen** to chuck something.

schmelzen✧ verb (PRES **schmilzt** IMPERF **schmolz**, PERF **ist geschmolzen**) 1 to melt; **der Schnee ist geschmolzen** the snow has melted; 2 (PERF **hat geschmolzen**) to melt (snow, ice); 3 (PERF **hat geschmolzen**) to smelt (ore).

Schmerz der (PL die **Schmerzen**) 1 pain; 2 grief.

schmerzen verb (PERF **hat geschmerzt**) to hurt.

schmerzhaft adjective painful.

Schmerzmittel das (PL die **Schmerzmittel**) painkiller.

Schmetterling der (PL die **Schmetterlinge**) butterfly.

✧ IRREGULAR VERB: See the verb table in the centre of the dictionary

schmieren *verb* (PERF **hat geschmiert**) **1** to lubricate; **2** to spread (*butter, jam*); **Brote schmieren** to spread slices of bread; **jemandem eine schmieren** (*informal*) to clout somebody; **3** to crawl; **4** to smudge.

schmilzt SEE **schmelzen**.

Schminke *die* make-up.

schminken *verb* (PERF **hat geschminkt**) **1** to make up; **2 sich schminken** to put on make-up.

schmiss Δ SEE **schmeißen**.

schmolz SEE **schmelzen**.

Schmuck *der* **1** jewellery; **2** decoration.

schmücken *verb* (PERF **hat geschmückt**) to decorate.

schmuggeln *verb* (PERF **hat geschmuggelt**) to smuggle.

schmusen *verb* (PERF **hat geschmust**) to cuddle; **Gabi hat mit Max geschmust** Gabi cuddled Max.

Schmutz *der* dirt.

schmutzig *adjective* dirty.

Schnabel *der* (PL *die* **Schnäbel**) beak.

Schnalle *die* (PL *die* **Schnallen**) buckle.

schnarchen *verb* (PERF **hat geschnarcht**) to snore.

Schnauze *die* (PL *die* **Schnauzen**) **1** muzzle; **eine kalte Schnauze** a cold nose; **2 die Schnauze halten** (*informal*) to keep your mouth shut.

schnäuzen Δ (PERF **hat sich geschnäuzt**) **sich schnäuzen** to blow your nose.

Schnecke *die* (PL *die* **Schnecken**) snail.

Schnee *der* snow.

Schneeregen *der* sleet.

schneiden ✧ *verb* (IMPERF **schnitt**, PERF **hat geschnitten**) **1** to cut; **ich kann dir die Haare schneiden** I can cut your hair; **Evi hat sich die Haare kurz schneiden lassen** Evi had her hair cut short; **in Scheiben schneiden** to slice; **2 sich schneiden** to cut yourself; **ich habe mich in den Finger geschnitten** I've cut my finger; **3 sich schneiden** to intersect; **4 Gesichter schneiden** to pull faces.

Schneider *der* (PL *die* **Schneider**) tailor.

Schneiderin *die* (PL *die* **Schneiderinnen**) dressmaker.

schneien *verb* (PERF **hat geschneit**) to snow; **es schneit** it's snowing.

schnell *adjective* quick, fast. *adverb* quickly; **mach schnell!** hurry up!

Schnelligkeit *die* speed.

Schnellimbiss Δ *der* (PL *die* **Schnellimbisse**) snack bar.

schnellstens *adverb* as quickly as possible.

Schnellzug *der* (PL *die* **Schnellzüge**) express (train).

schneuzen = **schnäuzen**.

schnitt SEE schneiden.

Schnitt der (PL die Schnitte) 1 cut; er hat einen tiefen Schnitt im Finger he's got a deep cut in his finger; das Kostüm hat einen sehr guten Schnitt the suit is well cut; 2 cutting (of a film); 3 im Schnitt on average; 4 pattern.

Schnittlauch der chives.

Schnitzel das (PL die Schnitzel) 1 escalope; 2 scrap.

schnitzen verb (PERF hat geschnitzt) to carve.

Schnorchel der (PL die Schnorchel) snorkel.

schnüffeln verb (PERF hat geschnüffelt) 1 to sniff; 2 to snoop around.

Schnuller der (PL die Schnuller) dummy.

Schnupfen der (PL die Schnupfen) cold.

Schnur die (PL die Schnüre) 1 (piece of) string; 2 flex; 3 cord.

Schnurrbart der (PL die Schnurrbärte) moustache.

schnurren verb (PERF hat geschnurrt) to purr.

Schnürsenkel der (PL die Schnürsenkel) shoelace.

schob SEE schieben.

Schock der (PL die Schocks) shock.

schockieren verb (PERF hat schockiert) to shock.

Schokolade die (PL die Schokoladen) chocolate.

schon adverb 1 already ('schon' is often not translated); schon wied« again; schon oft often; du wirst schon sehen you'll see; ja schon aber … well yes, but …; nun geh schon! go on then!; 2 yet; hast d sie schon gesehen? have you se« her yet?; du weißt schon you kno 3 even; 4 komm schon! come or 5 schon deshalb for that reason alone; 6 das ist schon möglich that's quite possible; 7 er war sch mal da he's been there before.

schön adjective 1 beautiful; 2 nic« schönes Wochenende! have a ni weekend!; 3 good; na schön all right then; 4 schönen Dank than you very much; schöne Grüße be wishes.

schonen verb (PERF hat geschon« 1 to look after; 2 sich schonen t« take things easy.

Schönheit die (PL die Schönheite« beauty.

Schornstein der (PL die Schornsteine) chimney, funnel.

schoss △ SEE schießen.

Schoß der (PL die Schöße) lap.

Schotte der (PL die Schotten) Scot Scotsman.

Schottin die (PL die Schottinnen) Scot, Scotswoman.

schottisch adjective Scottish.

Schottland das Scotland.

schräg adjective 1 diagonal;

✧ IRREGULAR VERB: See the verb table in the centre of the dictionary

2 sloping.
adverb **etwas schräg halten** to tilt something; **etwas schräg stellen** to put something at an angle.

Schrank *der* (PL *die* **Schränke**) **1** cupboard; **2** wardrobe.

Schranke *die* (PL *die* **Schranken**) barrier.

Schraube *die* (PL *die* **Schrauben**) screw.

schrauben *verb* (PERF **hat geschraubt**) to screw.

Schraubenschlüssel *der* (PL *die* **Schraubenschlüssel**) spanner.

Schraubenzieher *der* (PL *die* **Schraubenzieher**) screwdriver.

Schreck *der* fright; **jemandem einen Schreck einjagen** to give somebody a fright; **ich habe einen Schreck bekommen** I got a fright.

schrecklich *adjective* terrible.

Schrei *der* (PL *die* **Schreie**) **1** cry, shout; **2** scream; **3 der letzte Schrei** (*informal*) the latest thing.

Schreibblock *der* (PL *die* **Schreibblöcke**) writing pad.

schreiben ◇ *verb* (IMPERF **schrieb**, PERF **hat geschrieben**) **1** to write; **David hat mir einen Brief geschrieben** David wrote a letter to me; **einen Test schreiben** to do a test; **2** to spell; **wie schreibt man das?** how is it spelt?; **3** to type.

Schreibmaschine *die* (PL *die* **Schreibmaschinen**) typewriter.

Schreibpapier *das* writing paper.

Schreibtisch *der* (PL *die* **Schreibtische**) desk.

Schreibwaren *plural noun* stationery.

schreien ◇ *verb* (IMPERF **schrie**, PERF **hat geschrien**) **1** to cry, to shout; **das Baby schreit** the baby's crying; **2** to scream; **vor Lachen schreien** to scream with laughter; **zum Schreien sein** (*informal*) to be a scream.

Schreiner *der* (PL *die* **Schreiner**) joiner.

schrie SEE **schreien**.

schrieb SEE **schreiben**.

Schrift *die* (PL *die* **Schriften**) **1** writing; **2** type; **3** script.

schriftlich *adjective* written.
adverb in writing; **das lasse ich mir schriftlich geben** I'll get that in writing; **jemanden schriftlich einladen** to send somebody a written invitation.

Schriftsteller *der* (PL *die* **Schriftsteller**) writer.

Schriftstellerin *die* (PL *die* **Schriftstellerinnen**) writer.

Schritt *der* (PL *die* **Schritte**) step.

schrumpfen *verb* (PERF **ist geschrumpft**) **1** to shrink; **2** to shrivel.

Schublade *die* (PL *die* **Schubladen**) drawer.

schubsen *verb* (PERF **hat geschubst**) to shove.

schüchtern *adjective* shy.

schuf SEE **schaffen**.

△ NEW SPELLING: *See page xii*

Schuh der (PL die **Schuhe**) shoe.

Schuhgröße die (PL die **Schuhgrößen**) shoe size.

Schularbeiten plural noun homework.

Schulaufgaben plural noun homework.

Schulbuch das (PL die **Schulbücher**) schoolbook.

Schuld die (PL die **Schulden**) 1 blame; **Schuld haben**△ to be to blame; **jemandem Schuld geben** to blame somebody; 2 fault; **es war seine Schuld** it was his fault; 3 guilt; 4 debt; **Schulden haben** to be in debt; **Schulden machen** to get into debt.

schuld adjective **schuld sein** to be to blame; **du bist schuld daran** it's your fault.

schulden verb (PERF **hat geschuldet**) to owe.

schuldig adjective 1 guilty; 2 **jemandem etwas schuldig sein** to owe somebody something.

Schule die (PL die **Schulen**) school.

schulen verb (PERF **hat geschult**) to train.

Schüler der (PL die **Schüler**) pupil, student.

Schülerin die (PL die **Schülerinnen**) pupil, student.

Schulferien plural noun school holidays.

schulfrei adjective **ein schulfreier Tag** a day off school; **wir haben**

heute schulfrei there's no school today.

Schulfreund der (PL die **Schulfreunde**) schoolfriend.

Schulfreundin die (PL die **Schulfreundinnen**) schoolfriend.

Schulhof der (PL die **Schulhöfe**) playground.

Schulstunde die (PL die **Schulstunden**) period.

Schultasche die (PL die **Schultaschen**) schoolbag.

Schulter die (PL die **Schultern**) shoulder.

schummeln verb (PERF **hat geschummelt**) to cheat.

Schuppe die (PL die **Schuppen**) 1 scale; 2 **Schuppen** dandruff.

Schuppen der (PL die **Schuppen**) shed.

Schürze die (PL die **Schürzen**) apron.

Schuss△ der (PL die **Schüsse**) 1 shot; 2 dash (of brandy, vinegar); 3 schuss (in skiing).

Schüssel die (PL die **Schüsseln**) bowl, dish.

Schuster der (PL die **Schuster**) shoemaker.

schütten verb (PERF **hat geschüttet**) 1 to pour; **es schüttet** (informal) it's pouring (down); 2 to tip; 3 to spill.

schütteln verb (PERF **hat geschüttelt**) 1 to shake; 2 **sich**

✧ IRREGULAR VERB: See the verb table in the centre of the dictionary

schütteln to shake yourself; **sich vor Ekel schütteln** to shudder.

Schutz *der* 1 protection; 2 shelter.

Schütze *der* (PL *die* **Schützen**) 1 marksman; 2 Sagittarius; **Daniel ist Schütze** Daniel's Sagittarius.

schützen *verb* (PERF **hat geschützt**) 1 to protect; **die meisten Cremes schützen die Haut gegen Sonnenbrand** most creams protect the skin from sunburn; 2 **gesetzlich geschützt** registered (*as a trademark*).

schwach *adjective* 1 weak; 2 poor (*performance, memory*).

Schwäche *die* (PL *die* **Schwächen**) weakness.

schwachsinnig *adjective* idiotic.

Schwager *der* (PL *die* **Schwäger**) brother-in-law.

Schwägerin *die* (PL *die* **Schwägerinnen**) sister-in-law.

Schwalbe *die* (PL *die* **Schwalben**) swallow.

schwamm SEE **schwimmen**.

Schwamm *der* (PL *die* **Schwämme**) sponge.

Schwan *der* (PL *die* **Schwäne**) swan.

schwanger *adjective* pregnant.

schwanken *verb* (PERF **hat geschwankt**) 1 to sway; 2 to fluctuate; 3 to waver; 4 (PERF **ist geschwankt**) to stagger.

Schwanz *der* (PL *die* **Schwänze**) tail.

schwänzen *verb* (PERF **hat geschwänzt**) to skip, to skive off; **die Schule schwänzen** to play truant.

Schwarm *der* (PL *die* **Schwärme**) swarm.

schwarz *adjective, adverb* 1 black; **schwarz gekleidet** dressed in black; **ein schwarz gestreiftes Kleid** a dress with black stripes; **das habe ich schwarz auf weiß** I have it in black and white; 2 **ins Schwarze treffen** to hit the nail on the head, to score a bull's eye; 3 **schwarz sehen** △ to be pessimistic; 4 **etwas schwarz machen** to do something illegally.

Schwarze *der/die* (PL *die* **Schwarzen**) black.

schwarzsehen SEE **schwarz**.

Schwarzwald *der* Black Forest.

schwätzen *verb* (PERF **hat geschwätzt**) to chatter.

Schwede *der* (PL *die* **Schweden**) Swede.

Schweden *das* Sweden.

Schwedin *die* (PL *die* **Schwedinnen**) Swede.

schwedisch *adjective* Swedish.

schweigen ◇ *verb* (IMPERF **schwieg**, PERF **hat geschwiegen**) to be silent; **ganz zu schweigen von …** not to mention …

Schwein *das* (PL *die* **Schweine**) 1 pig; 2 pork; 3 **du Schwein!** (*informal*) you swine!; **Schwein haben** (*informal*) to be lucky.

Schweinefleisch *das* pork.

△ NEW SPELLING: *See page xii*

Schweiß *der* sweat.

Schweiz *die* **die Schweiz** Switzerland.

Schweizer *der* (PL *die* **Schweizer**) Swiss.

Schweizerin *die* (PL *die* **Schweizerinnen**) Swiss.

schweizerisch *adjective* Swiss.

schwer *adjective* 1 heavy; **zwei Pfund schwer sein** to weigh two pounds; 2 difficult; 3 serious. *adverb* 1 heavily; 2 seriously; **schwer krank** seriously ill; 3 **schwer arbeiten** to work hard; **jemandem schwer fallen** △ to be hard for somebody; 4 **sich mit etwas schwer tun** △ to have difficulty with something.

schwerfallen SEE **schwer**.

schwerhörig *adjective* hard of hearing.

Schwert *das* (PL *die* **Schwerter**) sword.

schwertun SEE **schwer**.

Schwester *die* (PL *die* **Schwestern**) sister.

schwieg SEE **schweigen**.

Schwiegereltern *plural noun* parents-in-law.

Schwiegermutter *die* (PL *die* **Schwiegermütter**) mother-in-law.

Schwiegersohn *der* (PL *die* **Schwiegersöhne**) son-in-law.

Schwiegertochter *die* (PL *die* **Schwiegertöchter**) daughter-in-law.

Schwiegervater *der* (PL *die* **Schwiegerväter**) father-in-law.

schwierig *adjective* difficult.

Schwierigkeit *die* (PL *die* **Schwierigkeiten**) difficulty.

Schwimmbad *das* (PL *die* **Schwimmbäder**) swimming baths.

Schwimmbecken *das* (PL *die* **Schwimmbecken**) swimming pool.

schwimmen ✧ (IMPERF **schwamm**, PERF **ist/hat geschwommen**) 1 to swim; 2 to float.

Schwimmweste *die* (PL *die* **Schwimmwesten**) life-jacket.

schwindlig *adjective* dizzy; **mir ist schwindlig** I feel dizzy.

Schwips *der* (PL *die* **Schwipse**) **einen Schwips haben** to be tipsy.

schwitzen *verb* (PERF **hat geschwitzt**) to sweat.

schwören ✧ *verb* (IMPERF **schwor**, PERF **hat geschworen**) to swear.

schwul *adjective* gay.

schwül *adjective* close.

Schwule *der* (PL *die* **Schwulen**) gay.

Schwung *der* (PL *die* **Schwünge**) 1 swing; 2 drive; **die Party in Schwung bringen** to get the party going.

sechs *number* six.

sechster, sechste, sechstes *adjective* sixth.

sechzehn *number* sixteen.

sechzig *number* sixty.

✧ IRREGULAR VERB: *See the verb table in the centre of the dictionary*

See[1] *der* (PL *die* **Seen**) lake.

See[2] *die* sea.

Seehund *der* (PL *die* **Seehunde**) seal.

seekrank *adjective* seasick.

Seele *die* (PL *die* **Seelen**) soul.

Seemann *der* (PL *die* **Seeleute**) seaman, sailor.

Seetang *der* seaweed.

Segel *das* (PL *die* **Segel**) sail.

Segelboot *das* (PL *die* **Segelboote**) sailing boat.

Segelfliegen *das* gliding.

Segelflugzeug *das* (PL *die* **Segelflugzeuge**) glider.

segeln *verb* (PERF **ist gesegelt**) to sail.

sehen ◇ *verb* (PRES **sieht**, IMPERF **sah**, PERF **hat gesehen**) 1 to see; **jemanden wieder sehen** △ to see somebody again; **mal sehen, ob …** let's see if …; 2 to look; 3 **eine Fernsehsendung sehen** to watch a television programme; 4 **gut/schlecht sehen** to have good/bad eyesight; 5 **nach jemandem sehen** to look after somebody.

sehenswert *adjective* worth seeing.

Sehenswürdigkeiten *plural noun* sights.

Sehnsucht *die* longing; **Sehnsucht nach jemandem haben** to long to see somebody.

sehr *adverb* 1 very; **sehr gut** very good; 2 **danke sehr** thank you very much; 3 **ich habe Karin sehr gern** I like Karin a lot; 4 **Sehr geehrte Frau Huber** Dear Mrs Huber.

seid SEE **sein**.

Seide *die* (PL *die* **Seiden**) silk.

Seife *die* (PL *die* **Seifen**) soap.

Seil *das* (PL *die* **Seile**) 1 rope; 2 cable.

Seilbahn *die* (PL *die* **Seilbahnen**) cable railway.

sein[1] ◇ *verb* (PRES **ist**, IMPERF **war**, PERF **ist gewesen**) 1 to be; **wir sind in der Küche** we're in the kitchen; **Rosi ist krank** Rosi is ill; **mir ist schlecht** I feel sick; **mir ist kalt** I'm cold; 2 **sie ist Lehrerin** she's a teacher; 3 **es ist drei Uhr** it's three o'clock; **Karl ist aus München** Karl's from Munich; **es war viel zu tun** there was a lot to be done; 4 **aus Seide sein** to be made of silk; 5 **etwas sein lassen** △ to stop something; **lass das sein!** stop it!; 6 **es sei denn, dass …** unless …; 7 (*used with certain verbs to form past tenses*) **ich bin nach Berlin gefahren** I went to Berlin; **wir sind kurz vor acht nach Hause gekommen** we got home shortly before eight o'clock; **er ist abgeholt worden** he's been collected.

sein[2] *adjective* 1 his; 2 (*of a thing or animal*) its; **der Hund ist in seiner Hütte** the dog is in its kennel; 3 (*after the pronoun 'man'*) your, one's; **wenn man sich seine Eltern aussuchen könnte** if you could choose your parents.

△ NEW SPELLING: *See page xii*

seiner, seine, sein(e)s *pronoun*
1 his; **das ist nicht meine CD, das
ist seine** it's not my CD, it's his; **du
kannst seins nehmen** you can take
his; 2 (*after the pronoun 'man'*) your
own, one's own; **das Seine tun** to
do one's share.

seinetwegen *adverb* 1 for his sake;
2 because of him; 3 on his account.

seinlassen SEE **sein**.

seins SEE **seiner**.

seit *preposition* ←(+DAT),
conjunction 1 since; **seit etwa einer
Woche** since about a week; **seit du
hier wohnst** since you've been
living here; **seit wann?** since
when?; 2 **ich bin seit zwei Wochen
hier** I've been here for two weeks;
seit einiger Zeit for some time.

seitdem *adverb* since then; **ich
habe sie seitdem nicht mehr
gesehen** I haven't seen her since.
conjunction since.

Seite *die* (PL *die* **Seiten**) 1 side; **auf
der einen Seite** on the one hand;
2 page; **das steht auf Seite zwanzig**
it's on page twenty.

Seitenstechen *das* stich; **ich habe
Seitenstechen** I've got a stitch.

Seitenstraße *die* (PL *die*
Seitenstraßen) side street.

seither *adverb* since then.

Sekretärin *die* (PL *die*
Sekretärinnen) secretary.

Sekt *der* (PL *die* **Sekte**) sparkling
wine.

Sekte *die* (PL *die* **Sekten**) sect.

Sekunde *die* (PL *die* **Sekunden**)
second.

selbst *pronoun* 1 **ich selbst** I
myself; **er selbst** he himself; **wir
selbst** we ourselves; **Sie selbst** you
yourself, you yourselves; 2 **von
selbst** by itself; 3 **sie schneidet
sich die Haare selbst** she cuts her
own hair; 4 on one's own; **ich kann
es selbst machen** I can do it on my
own; 5 **selbst gemacht** Δ homemade.
adverb even; **selbst wenn** even if.

selbständig = **selbstständig**.

Selbstbedienung *die* self-service.

selbstbewusst Δ *adjective* self-
confident.

Selbstbewusstsein Δ *das*
self-confidence.

selbstgemacht SEE **selbst**.

Selbstmord *der* (PL *die*
Selbstmorde) suicide; **Selbstmord
begehen** to commit suicide.

selbstständig Δ *adjective*
1 independent; 2 self-employed;
sich selbstständig machen to set
up on your own.

selbstverständlich *adjective*
natural; **etwas für
selbstverständlich halten** to take
something for granted; **das ist
selbstverständlich** it goes without
saying.
adverb naturally, of course; **wir
haben ihn selbstverständlich auf
die Party eingeladen** of course we
invited him to the party.

✧ IRREGULAR VERB: *See the verb table in the centre of the dictionary*

selten *adjective* rare.
adverb rarely.

seltsam *adjective* strange, odd.

Semester *das* (PL *die* **Semester**)
semester, term.

Semikolon *das* (PL *die* **Semikolons**)
semicolon.

Semmel *die* (PL *die* **Semmeln**) roll.

senden *verb* (PERF **hat gesendet**)
1 to send; **etwas an jemanden
senden** to send something to
somebody; 2 to broadcast; **seine
Rede wird im ersten Programm
gesendet** his speech will be
broadcast on channel one; 3 to
transmit.

Sendung *die* (PL *die* **Sendungen**)
1 programme; 2 consignment.

Senf *der* (PL *die* **Senfe**) mustard.

Senior *der* (PL *die* **Senioren**)
1 senior; 2 **Senioren** senior
citizens.

sensationell *adjective* sensational.

sensibel *adjective* sensitive.

September *der* September.

Serie *die* (PL *die* **Serien**) 1 series;
2 serial.

Service[1] *das* (PL *die* **Service**) set (*of
china, for example*).

Service[2] *der* service; **das Essen im
Hotel ist gut, aber der Service ist
furchtbar** the food in the hotel is
good but the service is appalling.

servieren *verb* (PERF **hat serviert**) to
serve.

Serviette *die* (PL *die* **Servietten**)
napkin.

Sessel *der* (PL *die* **Sessel**) armchair.

Sessellift *der* (PL *die* **Sessellifte**)
chair-lift.

setzen *verb* (PERF **hat gesetzt**) 1 to
put; **ein Komma setzen** to put a
comma; **vergiss nicht, deinen
Namen auf die Liste zu setzen**
don't forget to put your name on the
list; 2 to move (*a counter in games*);
3 **auf etwas setzen** to bet on
something; **auf ein Pferd setzen** to
back a horse; 4 **sich setzen** to sit
down; **sich auf einen Stuhl setzen**
to sit down on a chair.

seufzen *verb* (PERF **hat geseufzt**) to
sigh.

Seufzer *der* (PL *die* **Seufzer**) sigh.

Sex *der* sex.

Sexismus *der* sexism.

sexistisch *adjective* sexist.

sexuell *adjective* sexual.

Shampoo *das* (PL *die* **Shampoos**)
shampoo.

sich *pronoun* 1 (*with 'er/sie/es'*)
himself/herself/itself; **sie hat sich
eingeschlossen** she locked herself
in; 2 (*with plural 'sie'*) themselves;
3 (*with 'Sie'*) yourself, yourselves
(*plural*); 4 each other, one another;
sich kennen to know each other;
Petra und Werner lieben sich Petra
and Werner love each other; 5 (*not
translated with certain verbs*) **sich
freuen** to be pleased; **sich wundern**
to be surprised; 6 **Anita wäscht sich**

△ NEW SPELLING: *See page xii*

die Haare Anita is washing her hair; **sich den Arm brechen** to break your arm; **7 sich gut verkaufen** to sell well; **8 von sich aus** of your own accord.

sicher *adjective* 1 safe; 2 certain; **bist du sicher?** are you sure? *adverb* 1 safely; 2 certainly, surely; **sicher!** certainly!

Sicherheit *die* 1 safety; **zur Sicherheit** for safety's sake; **schnallen Sie sich zur Ihrer eigenen Sicherheit an** fasten your seat belt for your own safety; **etwas in Sicherheit bringen** to rescue something; **in Sicherheit sein** to be safe; 2 security; **die Sicherheit der Arbeitsplätze** job security; 3 certainty; **mit Sicherheit!** certainly! (*as a reply*).

Sicherheitsgurt *der* (PL *die* **Sicherheitsgurte**) seatbelt.

Sicherheitsnadel *die* (PL *die* **Sicherheitsnadeln**) safety pin.

sicherlich *adverb* certainly.

sichern *verb* (PERF **hat gesichert**) to secure; **jemandem etwas sichern** to secure something for somebody.

Sicherung *die* (PL *die* **Sicherungen**) 1 fuse; **die Sicherung is durchgebrannt** the fuse has blown; 2 safeguard; **die Sicherung der Arbeitsplätze** safeguarding jobs; 3 safety catch.

Sicht *die* 1 view; **ich hatte eine gute Sicht auf den See** I had a good view of the lake; **auf lange Sicht** in the long term; 2 **aus meiner Sicht** as I see it; 3 visibility; **gute/schlechte Sicht** good/poor visibility.

sichtbar *adjective* visible.

sie *pronoun* 1 she; 2 her; **ich kenne sie** I know her; 3 it; **so eine hübsche Bluse, war sie teuer?** what a pretty blouse, was it expensive?; 4 they; **sie sind in der Küche** they're in the kitchen; 5 them; **ich habe sie gestern abgeschickt** I posted them yesterday.

Sie *pronoun* you; **kommen Sie herein!** come in!

Sieb *das* (PL *die* **Siebe**) 1 sieve; 2 strainer.

sieben *number* seven.

siebter, siebte, siebtes *adjective* seventh.

siebzehn *number* seventeen.

siebzig *number* seventy.

Siedlung *die* (PL *die* **Siedlungen**) 1 (housing) estate; 2 settlement.

Sieg *der* (PL *die* **Siege**) victory, win.

Siegel *das* (PL *die* **Siegel**) seal.

siegen *verb* (PERF **hat gesiegt**) to win.

Sieger *der* (PL *die* **Sieger**) winner.

Siegerin *die* (PL *die* **Siegerinnen**) winner.

sieht SEE **sehen**.

Silbe *die* (PL *die* **Silben**) syllable.

Silber *das* silver.

silbern *adjective* silver.

✧ IRREGULAR VERB: *See the verb table in the centre of the dictionary*

Silvester *das* New Year's Eve.

sind SEE **sein**.

Sinfonie *die* (PL *die* **Sinfonien**) symphony.

singen ✧ *verb* (IMPERF **sang**, PERF **hat gesungen**) to sing.

sinken ✧ *verb* (IMPERF **sank**, PERF **ist gesunken**) 1 to sink; 2 to go down.

Sinn *der* (PL *die* **Sinne**) 1 sense; 2 meaning; 3 point; **das hat keinen Sinn** there's no point.

sinnlos *adjective* pointless.

sinnvoll *adjective* 1 sensible; 2 meaningful.

Situation *die* (PL *die* **Situationen**) situation.

Sitz *der* (PL *die* **Sitze**) 1 seat; 2 fit (*of clothes*).

sitzen ✧ *verb* (IMPERF **saß**, PERF **hat gesessen**) 1 to sit; **sitzen bleiben** △ to remain seated; 2 **sitzen bleiben** △ to have to repeat a year, to stay down (*at school*); 3 **er sitzt** (*informal*) he's in jail; 4 **jemanden sitzen lassen** △ to leave somebody in the lurch; 5 to fit (*of clothes*); **der Mantel sitzt gut** the coat fits well.

Sitzplatz *der* (PL *die* **Sitzplätze**) seat.

Sitzung *die* (PL *die* **Sitzungen**) 1 meeting; 2 session.

Sizilien *das* Sicily.

Skandal *der* (PL *die* **Skandale**) scandal.

Skandinavien *das* Scandinavia.

skandinavisch *adjective* Scandinavian.

Skelett *das* (PL *die* **Skelette**) skeleton.

Ski *der* (PL *die* **Ski(er)**) ski; **Ski fahren/laufen** to ski.

Skifahren *das* skiing.

Skifahrer *der* (PL *die* **Skifahrer**) skier.

Skifahrerin *die* (PL *die* **Skifahrerinnen**) skier.

Skilaufen *das* skiing.

Skiläufer *der* (PL *die* **Skiläufer**) skier.

Skiläuferin *die* (PL *die* **Skiläuferinnen**) skier.

Skilehrer *der* (PL *die* **Skilehrer**) ski instructor.

Skizze *die* (PL *die* **Skizzen**) sketch.

Skorpion *der* (PL *die* **Skorpione**) 1 scorpion; 2 Scorpio.

Skulptur *die* (PL *die* **Skulpturen**) sculpture.

Slip *der* (PL *die* **Slips**) briefs, pants.

Slowake *der* (PL *die* **Slowaken**) Slovak.

Slowakei *die* Slovakia.

Slowakin *die* (PL *die* **Slowakinnen**) Slovak.

slowakisch *adjective* Slovak.

Smoking *der* (PL *die* **Smokings**) dinner jacket.

so *adverb* 1 so; **nicht so viel** not so much; **und so weiter** and so on; 2 like this, like that; **so nicht** not like

that; **3** as; **so bald wie** as soon as;
4 such; **so ein Zufall!** what a
coincidence!; **5 das kriegst du so**
(*informal*) you get it for nothing;
6 so um zwanzig Mark (*informal*)
about twenty marks.
conjunction **so dass** so that.
exclamation right!, well!; **so?**
really?

sobald *conjunction* as soon as.

Socke *die* (PL *die* **Socken**) sock.

Sofa *das* (PL *die* **Sofas**) sofa.

sofort *adverb* immediately.

sogar *adverb* even.

sogleich *adverb* at once.

Sohle *die* (PL *die* **Sohlen**) sole.

Sohn *der* (PL *die* **Söhne**) son.

solange *conjunction* as long as.

solch *pronoun* such; **solch
einer/eine/eins** one like that,
somebody like that.

solcher, solche, solches
adjective, pronoun **1** such; **ich habe
solche Angst** I'm so frightened;
2 ein solcher Mann a man like that;
eine solche Frage a question like
that; **ein solches Haus** a house like
that; **3 solche** (*plural*) those;
solche wie die people like that.

Soldat *der* (PL *die* **Soldaten**) soldier.

solide *adjective* **1** solid;
2 respectable.

Solist *der* (PL *die* **Solisten**) soloist.

Solistin *die* (PL *die* **Solistinnen**)
soloist.

sollen ✧ *verb* (PRES **soll**, IMPERF
sollte, PERF **hat gesollt**) **1** should;
sollte es regnen if it should rain;
2 to be supposed to; **was soll das
heißen?** what's that supposed to
mean?; **3 sagen Sie ihr, sie soll
anrufen** tell her to ring; **4 was soll
ich machen?** what shall I do?; **soll
ich?** shall I?; **5 was soll's!** so what

sollte, sollten, solltest, solltet
SEE **sollen**.

Sommer *der* (PL *die* **Sommer**)
summer.

sommerlich *adjective* summery,
summer.

Sommersprossen *plural noun*
freckles.

Sonderangebot *das* (PL *die*
Sonderangebote) special offer; **im
Sonderangebot** on special offer.

sonderbar *adjective* strange, odd.

sondern *conjunction* but; **nicht nur
..., sondern auch ...** not only ..., but
also ...

Song *der* (PL *die* **Songs**) song.

Sonnabend *der* (PL *die*
Sonnabende) Saturday.

sonnabends *adverb* on Saturdays.

Sonne *die* (PL *die* **Sonnen**) sun.

sonnen *verb* (PERF **hat sich gesonnt**)
sich sonnen to sun yourself.

Sonnenaufgang *der* sunrise.

Sonnenbrand *der* sunburn.

Sonnenbrille *die* (PL *die*
Sonnenbrillen) sunglasses.

✧ IRREGULAR VERB: *See the verb table in the centre of the dictionary*

Sonnencreme *die* (PL *die* **Sonnencremes**) suntan lotion.

Sonnenenergie *die* solar energy.

Sonnenmilch *die* suntan lotion.

Sonnenöl *das* suntan oil.

Sonnenschein *der* sunshine.

Sonnenstich *der* sunstroke.

sonnig *adjective* sunny.

Sonntag *der* (PL *die* **Sonntage**) Sunday.

sonntags *adverb* on Sundays.

sonst *adverb* 1 usually; 2 else; **wer sonst?** who else?; **was sonst?** what else?; 3 **sonst noch etwas?** anything else?; **sonst noch jemand?** anybody else?; 4 **sonst wo** △ somewhere; **es kann sonst wo sein** it could be anywhere; 5 otherwise; **geh jetzt, sonst verpasst du den Bus** go now, otherwise you'll miss the bus.

sonstwo SEE **sonst**.

sooft *conjunction* whenever.

Sorge *die* (PL *die* **Sorgen**) worry; **sich Sorgen machen** to worry.

sorgen *verb* (PERF **hat gesorgt**) 1 **für etwas sorgen** to take care of something; **für die Musik sorgen** to see to the music; **für jemanden sorgen** to look after somebody; 2 **dafür sorgen, dass …** to make sure that …; 3 **sich sorgen** to worry; **ich sorge mich um meine Eltern** I worry about my parents.

sorgfältig *adjective* careful.

Sorte *die* (PL *die* **Sorten**) 1 kind; 2 brand.

Soße *die* (PL *die* **Soßen**) 1 sauce; 2 gravy; 3 dressing.

Souvenir *das* (PL *die* **Souvenirs**) souvenir.

soviel *conjunction* as far as; **soviel ich weiß** as far as I know. *adverb* SEE **viel**.

soweit *conjunction* as far as; **soweit ich weiß, ist er in Ferien** as far as I know, he's on holiday. *adverb* SEE **weit**.

sowenig SEE **wenig**.

sowie *conjunction* 1 as well as; 2 as soon as.

sowieso *adverb* anyway.

sowohl *adverb* **sowohl … als auch …** both … and …; **sowohl er wie auch sein Freund** both he and his friend.

sozial *adjective* social.

Sozialarbeiter *der* (PL *die* **Sozialarbeiter**) social worker.

Sozialarbeiterin *die* (PL *die* **Sozialarbeiterinnen**) social worker.

Sozialhilfe *die* social security.

Sozialismus *der* socialism.

sozialistisch *adjective* socialist.

Sozialkunde *die* social studies.

Sozialwohnung *die* (PL *die* **Sozialwohnungen**) council flat.

Soziologie *die* sociology.

sozusagen *adverb* so to speak.

△ NEW SPELLING: *See page xii*

Spalte die (PL die **Spalten**) 1 crack;
2 column (in text).

spalten verb (PERF **hat gespalten**) to
split.

Spanien das Spain.

Spanier der (PL die **Spanier**)
Spaniard.

Spanierin die (PL die **Spanierinnen**)
Spaniard.

spanisch adjective Spanish.

spann SEE **spinnen**.

spannend adjective exciting.

Spannung die (PL die **Spannungen**)
1 tension; 2 suspense (in a film or
novel, for example); **ich erwarte
seine Antwort mit Spannung** I can't
wait for his answer; 3 voltage.

sparen verb (PERF **hat gespart**) 1 to
save; **auf etwas sparen** to save up
for something; 2 **sich etwas sparen**
not to bother with something; **sich
die Mühe sparen** to save yourself
the trouble; 3 **an etwas sparen** to
economize on something.

Spargel der asparagus.

Sparkasse die savings bank.

sparsam adjective 1 economical;
2 thrifty.

Spaß der (PL die **Späße**) 1 fun;
zum/aus Spaß for fun; **das macht
Spaß** it's fun; **Segeln macht mir
keinen Spaß** I don't like sailing;
2 **viel Spaß!** have a good time!;
3 joke; **er macht nur Spaß** he's only
joking.

spät adjective, adverb late; **zu spät**

kommen to be late; **wie spät ist
es?** what time is it?

Spaten der (PL die **Spaten**) spade.

später adjective later.

spätestens adverb at the latest.

Spatz der (PL die **Spatzen**) sparrow.

spazieren verb (PERF **ist spaziert**)
1 to stroll; 2 **spazieren gehen** Δ to
go for a walk; **hast du Lust,
spazieren zu gehen?** would you
like to go for a walk?

spazierengehen SEE **spazieren**.

Spaziergang der (PL die
Spaziergänge) walk; **einen
Spaziergang machen** to go for a
walk.

Speck der bacon.

Speiche die (PL die **Speichen**) spoke

Speicher der (PL die **Speicher**)
1 loft, attic; 2 memory (in
computing).

speichern verb (PERF **hat
gespeichert**) 1 to store; 2 to save
(in computing).

Speise die (PL die **Speisen**) 1 food;
2 dish.

Speisekarte die (PL die
Speisekarten) menu.

Speisesaal der (PL die **Speisesäle**)
1 dining hall; 2 dining room.

Speisewagen der (PL die
Speisewagen) dining car.

Spende die (PL die **Spenden**)
donation.

✧ IRREGULAR VERB: See the verb table in the centre of the dictionary

spenden *verb* (PERF **hat gespendet**) **1** to donate; **2** to give.

spendieren *verb* (PERF **hat spendiert**) **jemandem etwas spendieren** to treat somebody to something.

Sperre *die* (PL *die* **Sperren**) **1** barrier; **2** ban.

sperren *verb* (PERF **hat gesperrt**) **1** to close; **2** to block (*an entrance, access*); **3 den Strom sperren** to cut off the electricity; **4 einen Scheck sperren** to stop a cheque; **5 ein Tier in einen Käfig sperren** to shut an animal (up) in a cage.

Spezialität *die* (PL *die* **Spezialitäten**) speciality.

speziell *adjective* special.

Spiegel *der* (PL *die* **Spiegel**) mirror.

Spiegelbild *das* (PL *die* **Spiegelbilder**) reflection.

Spiegelei *das* (PL *die* **Spiegeleier**) fried egg.

spiegeln *verb* (PERF **hat gespiegelt**) **1** to reflect; **2 sich spiegeln** to be reflected.

Spiel *das* (PL *die* **Spiele**) **1** game; **2 ein Spiel Karten** a pack of cards; **3 es steht viel auf dem Spiel** there's a lot at stake.

spielen *verb* (PERF **hat gespielt**) **1** to play; **wir spielen morgen Tennis** we're going to play tennis tomorrow; **2** to gamble; **3** to act; **das Stück war gut gespielt** the play was well acted; **4 der Film spielt in Rom** the film is set in Rome.

spielend *adverb* easily.

Spieler *der* (PL *die* **Spieler**) **1** player; **2** gambler.

Spielerin *die* (PL *die* **Spielerinnen**) **1** player; **2** gambler.

Spielfeld *das* (PL *die* **Spielfelder**) pitch, field.

Spielhalle *die* (PL *die* **Spielhallen**) amusement arcade.

Spielplatz *der* (PL *die* **Spielplätze**) playground.

Spielverderber *der* (PL *die* **Spielverderber**) spoilsport.

Spielverderberin *die* (PL *die* **Spielverderberinnen**) spoilsport.

Spielwaren *plural noun* toys.

Spielzeug *das* **1** toy; **2** toys.

Spinat *der* spinach.

Spinne *die* (PL *die* **Spinnen**) spider.

spinnen ◇ *verb* (IMPERF **spann**, PERF **hat gesponnen**) **1** to spin; **2 du spinnst!** (*informal*) you're mad!

Spinnennetz *das* (PL *die* **Spinnennetze**) cobweb.

Spion *der* (PL *die* **Spione**) spy.

Spionage *die* spying, espionage.

spionieren *verb* (PERF **hat spioniert**) to spy.

Spirituosen *plural noun* spirits (*alcohol*).

spitz *adjective* pointed.

Spitze *die* (PL *die* **Spitzen**) **1** point; **2** top; **Schalke liegt jetzt an der Spitze** Schalke is top of the league

△ NEW SPELLING: *See page xii*

at the moment; **3** peak; **von hier kann man die schneebedeckten Spitzen sehen** you can see the snow-covered peaks from here; **4** front; **an der Spitze liegen** to be in the lead; **5** lace; **6 Spitze sein** (*informal*) to be great.

spitzen *verb* (PERF **hat gespitzt**) **1** to sharpen; **2 sich auf etwas spitzen** (*informal*) to look forward to something.

Spitzname *der* (PL die **Spitznamen**) nickname.

Splitter *der* (PL die **Splitter**) splinter.

sponsern *verb* (PERF **hat gesponsert**) to sponsor.

Sport *der* sport.

Sporthalle *die* (PL die **Sporthallen**) sports hall.

Sportler *der* (PL die **Sportler**) sportsman.

Sportlerin *die* (PL die **Sportlerinnen**) sportswoman.

sportlich *adjective* **1** sporting; **2** sporty.

Sportplatz *der* (PL die **Sportplätze**) sports field, sports ground.

Sportschuh *der* (PL die **Sportschuhe**) trainer.

Sportverein *der* (PL die **Sportvereine**) sports club.

Sportwagen *der* (PL die **Sportwagen**) **1** sports car; **2** pushchair.

Sportzentrum *das* (PL die **Sportzentren**) sports centre.

spotten *verb* (PERF **hat gespottet**) to mock.

sprach SEE **sprechen**.

Sprache *die* (PL die **Sprachen**) **1** language; **2** speech; **etwas zur Sprache bringen** to bring something up.

sprachlos *adjective* speechless.

sprang SEE **springen**.

sprechen ✧ *verb* (PRES **spricht**, IMPERF **sprach**, PERF **hat gesprochen**) **1** to speak; **Deutsch sprechen** to speak German; **mit wem spreche ich?** who's speaking? (*on the phone*); **jemanden sprechen** to speak to somebody; **2 Frau Hahn ist nicht zu sprechen** Mrs Hahn is not available; **3** to talk; **mit jemandem über etwas sprechen** to talk to somebody about something; **4** to say (*a word, sentence*).

Sprecher *der* (PL die **Sprecher**) **1** spokesman; **2** (*on TV*) announcer; **3** (*in a film*) narrator; **4** speaker.

Sprecherin *die* (PL die **Sprecherinnen**) **1** spokeswoman; **2** (*on TV*) announcer; **3** (*in a film*) narrator; **4** speaker.

Sprechstunde *die* (PL die **Sprechstunden**) surgery.

spricht SEE **sprechen**.

Sprichwort *das* (PL die **Sprichwörter**) proverb.

springen ✧ *verb* (IMPERF **sprang**, PERF **ist gesprungen**) **1** to jump;

✧ IRREGULAR VERB: *See the verb table in the centre of the dictionary*

2 to bounce (*of a ball*); **3** to dive; **4** to crack.

Spritze die (PL die **Spritzen**)
1 syringe; **2** injection; **3** hose.

spritzen verb (PERF **hat gespritzt**)
1 to inject; **2** to splash; **du hast mich nass gespritzt** you've splashed me; **3** to spray; **4** to spit (*of fat*); **5** (PERF **ist gespritzt**) to splash up.

Sprudel der (PL die **Sprudel**) sparkling mineral water.

sprühen verb (PERF **hat gesprüht**)
1 to spray; **2** to sparkle (*of eyes*); **3** (PERF **ist gesprüht**) to fly (*of sparks*); **die Funken sind in alle Richtungen gesprüht** sparks flew in all directions.

Sprung der (PL die **Sprünge**)
1 jump; **2** dive; **3** crack (*in china, glass*).

Sprungbrett das (PL die **Sprungbretter**) diving board.

spucken verb (PERF **hat gespuckt**) to spit.

Spülbecken das (PL die **Spülbecken**) sink.

spülen verb (PERF **hat gespült**) **1** to rinse; **2** to wash up; **3** to flush.

Spülmaschine die (PL die **Spülmaschinen**) dishwasher.

Spülmittel das (PL die **Spülmittel**) washing-up liquid.

Spur die (PL die **Spuren**) **1** track; **auf der falschen Spur sein** to be on the wrong track; **jemandem auf die Spur kommen** to get on to somebody;

2 lane; **in der Spur bleiben** to keep in lane; **3** trail; **4** trace.

spüren verb (PERF **hat gespürt**) **1** to feel; **2** to sense.

Staat der (PL die **Staaten**) state.

staatlich adjective state; **eine staatliche Schule** a state school. adverb by the state.

Staatsangehörigkeit die (PL die **Staatsangehörigkeiten**) nationality.

stabil adjective **1** stable; **2** sturdy.

stach SEE **stechen**.

Stachel der (PL die **Stacheln**)
1 spine; **2** spike; **3** sting.

Stachelbeere die (PL die **Stachelbeeren**) gooseberry.

Stacheldraht der barbed wire.

Stadion das (PL die **Stadien**) stadium.

Stadium das (PL die **Stadien**) stage.

Stadt die (PL die **Städte**) town, city.

städtisch adjective **1** urban; **2** municipal.

Stadtmitte die town centre.

Stadtplan der (PL die **Stadtpläne**) street map.

Stadtrand der outskirts (of town); **am Stadtrand** on the outskirts.

Stadtrundfahrt die (PL die **Stadtrundfahrten**) sightseeing tour (*of a town*).

Stadtteil der (PL die **Stadtteile**) district.

stahl SEE **stehlen**.

△ NEW SPELLING: *See page xii*

Stahl *der* steel.

Stall *der* (PL *die* **Ställe**) 1 stable;
2 cowshed; 3 pigsty.

Stamm *der* (PL *die* **Stämme**)
1 trunk; 2 tribe; 3 stem (*of a word*).

stammen *verb* (PERF **hat gestammt**)
aus Deutschland stammen to
come from Germany.

Stammgast *der* (PL *die*
Stammgäste) regular customer (*in
a pub or restaurant*).

stand SEE **stehen**.

Stand *der* (PL *die* **Stände**) 1 state;
**etwas auf den neuesten Stand
bringen** to bring something up to
date; 2 score (*in a game*); 3 stall;
4 level.

ständig *adjective* constant.

Standort *der* (PL *die* **Standorte**)
position, location; **von ihrem
Standort aus konnte sie nichts
sehen** she couldn't see anything
from where she was standing.

Stange *die* (PL *die* **Stangen**) 1 bar;
2 pole.

stank SEE **stinken**.

starb SEE **sterben**.

stark *adjective* 1 strong; 2 heavy
(*rain, traffic*); 3 severe (*frost, pain*);
4 (*informal*) great; **das ist stark!**
that's great!

Stärke *die* (PL *die* **Stärken**)
1 strength; 2 starch.

starrsinnig *adjective* obstinate.

Start *der* (PL *die* **Starts**) 1 start;
2 take-off.

Startbahn *die* (PL *die* **Startbahnen**)
runway.

starten *verb* (PERF **ist gestartet**)
1 (*of a plane*) to take off; 2 (PERF **hat
gestartet**) to start, to launch (*a
campaign*).

Station *die* (PL *die* **Stationen**)
1 station; 2 stop; **Station machen**
to stop over; 3 ward.

statt *conjunction, preposition*
←(+GEN) instead of; **statt zu
arbeiten** instead of working; **sie
ging statt ihrer Schwester** she went
instead of her sister.

stattdessen Δ *conjunction* instead.

stattfinden ◇ *verb* (IMPERF **fand
statt**, PERF **hat stattgefunden**) to
take place.

Stau *der* (PL *die* **Staus**) 1 congestion;
2 traffic jam.

Staub *der* dust.

staubig *adjective* dusty.

staubsaugen *verb* (PERF **hat
staubgesaugt**) to vacuum.

Staubsauger *der* (PL *die*
Staubsauger) vacuum cleaner.

staunen *verb* (PERF **hat gestaunt**) to
be amazed.

stechen ◇ *verb* (PRES **sticht**, IMPERF
stach, PERF **hat gestochen**) 1 to
prick; **sich in den Finger stechen** to
prick your finger; 2 to sting, to bite
(*of an insect*); 3 **mit etwas in etwas
stechen** to jab something into
something.

◇ IRREGULAR VERB: *See the verb table in the centre of the dictionary*

Steckdose die (PL die **Steckdosen**) socket.

stecken verb (PERF **hat gesteckt**) 1 to put; **du musst die Münze in den Schlitz stecken** put the coin into the slot; 2 to pin; 3 **wo steckt er?** where is he?; 4 **stecken bleiben** Δ to get stuck; **den Schlüssel stecken lassen** Δ to leave the key in the lock.

Stecker der (PL die **Stecker**) plug.

Stecknadel die (PL die **Stecknadeln**) pin.

stehen ◇ verb (IMPERF **stand**, PERF **hat gestanden**) 1 to stand; 2 to be; **es steht zwei zu zwei** the score is two all; **wie steht's?** what's the score?; 3 to have stopped (of a clock or a machine); 4 **es steht schlecht um ihn** he's in a bad way; **na, wie steht's?** how are you?; 5 **stehen bleiben** Δ to stop; **die Uhr ist stehen geblieben** the clock has stopped; 6 **in der Zeitung steht, dass …** it says in the paper that …; 7 **jemandem (gut) stehen** to suit somebody; 8 **zu jemandem stehen** to stand by somebody; 9 **sich gut stehen** to be on good terms; 10 **zum Stehen kommen** to come to a standstill.

stehenbleiben SEE **stehen**.

stehlen ◇ verb (PRES **stiehlt**, IMPERF **stahl**, PERF **hat gestohlen**) to steal.

steif adjective stiff.

steigen verb (IMPERF **stieg**, PERF **ist gestiegen**) 1 to climb; **auf eine Leiter steigen** to climb up a ladder; **auf ein Fahrrad steigen** to get on a bike; **in den Bus steigen** to get on the bus; 2 to rise.

steil adjective steep.

Stein der (PL die **Steine**) stone.

Steinbock der (PL die **Steinböcke**) 1 ibex; 2 Capricorn; **Petra ist Steinbock** Petra's Capricorn.

Stelle die (PL die **Stellen**) 1 place; **an deiner Stelle** in your place; 2 job; 3 authority; 4 **auf der Stelle** immediately.

stellen verb (PERF **hat gestellt**) 1 to put; 2 to set (a watch, task); 3 **zur Verfügung stellen** to provide; 4 **lauter stellen** to turn up; **leiser stellen** to turn down; **die Heizung höher stellen** to turn the heating up; 5 **sich krank stellen** to pretend to be ill; 6 **sich stellen** to give yourself up; 7 **die Kinder stellten sich an die Wand** the children stood against the wall.

Stellenanzeige die (PL die **Stellenanzeigen**) job advertisement.

Stellung die (PL die **Stellungen**) position.

Stempel der (PL die **Stempel**) 1 stamp; 2 postmark.

stempeln verb (PERF **hat gestempelt**) to stamp.

Steppdecke die (PL die **Steppdecken**) quilt.

sterben ◇ verb (PRES **stirbt**, IMPERF **starb**, PERF **ist gestorben**) to die.

Stereoanlage die (PL die **Stereoanlagen**) stereo (system).

Δ NEW SPELLING: See page xii

Stern der (PL die **Sterne**) star.

Sternzeichen das (PL die **Sternzeichen**) star sign; **was ist dein Sternzeichen?** what star sign are you?

Steuer[1] das (PL die **Steuer**) 1 (steering) wheel; 2 helm.

Steuer[2] die (PL die **Steuern**) tax.

steuern verb (PERF **hat gesteuert**) 1 to steer; 2 to control; 3 (PERF **ist gesteuert**) to head.

Stewardess Δ die (PL die **Stewardessen**) stewardess, air hostess.

Stich der (PL die **Stiche**) 1 prick; 2 stab; 3 sting, bite (of an insect); 4 stitch; 5 trick (when playing cards); 6 engraving; 7 **jemanden im Stich lassen** to leave somebody in the lurch.

sticht SEE **stechen**.

sticken verb (PERF **hat gestickt**) to embroider.

Stickstoff der nitrogen.

Stiefbruder der (PL die **Stiefbrüder**) stepbrother.

Stiefel der (PL die **Stiefel**) boot.

Stiefkind das (PL die **Stiefkinder**) stepchild.

Stiefmutter die (PL die **Stiefmütter**) stepmother.

Stiefschwester die (PL die **Stiefschwestern**) stepsister.

Stiefvater der (PL die **Stiefväter**) stepfather.

stieg SEE **steigen**.

stiehlt SEE **stehlen**.

Stiel der (PL die **Stiele**) 1 handle; 2 stem.

Stier der (PL die **Stiere**) 1 bull; 2 Taurus; **Andrea ist Stier** Andrea's Taurus.

stieß SEE **stoßen**.

Stift der (PL die **Stifte**) 1 pencil; 2 crayon; 3 tack (nail).

Stil der (PL die **Stile**) style.

still adjective 1 quiet; 2 still.

stillen verb (PERF **hat gestillt**) 1 to quench; 2 to breast-feed.

stillhalten ◇ verb (PRES **hält still**, IMPERF **hielt still**, PERF **hat stillgehalten**) to keep still.

Stimme die (PL die **Stimmen**) 1 voice; 2 vote.

stimmen verb (PERF **hat gestimmt**) 1 to be right; **stimmt das?** is that right?; 2 to vote; 3 to tune.

Stimmung die (PL die **Stimmungen**) 1 mood; 2 atmosphere.

stinken ◇ verb (IMPERF **stank**, PERF **hat gestunken**) to smell, to stink.

Stipendium das (PL die **Stipendien**) 1 scholarship; 2 grant.

stirbt SEE **sterben**.

Stirn die (PL die **Stirnen**) forehead.

Stock[1] der (PL die **Stöcke**) stick.

Stock[2] der (PL die **Stock**) floor.

Stockwerk das (PL die **Stockwerke**) floor.

◇ IRREGULAR VERB: See the verb table in the centre of the dictionary

Stoff *der* (PL *die* **Stoffe**) **1** material, fabric; **2** substance.

stöhnen *verb* (PERF **hat gestöhnt**) to groan.

stolpern *verb* (PERF **ist gestolpert**) **1** to stumble; **2** to trip; **ich bin über einen Stein gestolpert** I tripped on a stone.

stolz *adjective* proud.

stoppen *verb* (PERF **hat gestoppt**) to stop.

Stöpsel *der* (PL *die* **Stöpsel**) **1** plug; **2** stopper.

stören *verb* (PERF **hat gestört**) **1** to disturb; **2** to bother; **das stört mich nicht** that doesn't bother me; **3** stört es Sie, wenn ich das Fenster aufmache? do you mind if I open the window?; **der Empfang ist gestört** there's interference (*on a TV*).

Störung *die* (PL *die* **Störungen**) **1** disturbance, interruption; **entschuldigen Sie die Störung** I'm sorry to bother you; **2** interference; **eine technische Störung** a technical fault.

Stoß *der* (PL *die* **Stöße**) **1** push; **2** pile; **ein Stoß Handtücher** a pile of towels.

stoßen ♦ *verb* (PRES **stößt**, IMPERF **stieß**, PERF **hat gestoßen**) **1** to push; **2** to kick; **3** sich den Kopf stoßen to hit your head; **ich habe mir den Kopf an dem Balken gestoßen** I hit my head on the beam; **sich stoßen** to bump yourself; **4** sich an etwas stoßen to object to something;

5 (PERF **ist gestoßen**) **gegen etwas stoßen** to bump into something; **6** (PERF **ist gestoßen**) **auf etwas stoßen** to come across something.

Stoßstange *die* (PL *die* **Stoßstangen**) bumper.

Stoßzeit *die* (PL *die* **Stoßzeiten**) rush hour.

stottern *verb* (PERF **hat gestottert**) to stutter.

Strafe *die* (PL *die* **Strafen**) **1** punishment; **2** fine; **3** penalty.

Straftat *die* (PL *die* **Straftaten**) crime.

Strahl *der* (PL *die* **Strahlen**) **1** ray, beam; **2** jet.

strahlen *verb* (PERF **hat gestrahlt**) **1** to shine; **2** to beam.

Strand *der* (PL *die* **Strände**) beach.

Straße *die* (PL *die* **Straßen**) street, road; **in welcher Straße ist der Supermarkt?** which street is the supermarket in?; **über die Straße gehen** to cross the road; **jemanden auf die Straße setzen** (*informal*) to give somebody the sack; **mein Wirt hat mich einfach auf die Straße gesetzt** (*informal*) my landlord just turned me out (*of a flat or room*).

Straßenbahn *die* (PL *die* **Straßenbahnen**) tram; **mit der Straßenbahn fahren** to go by tram.

Strauch *der* (PL *die* **Sträucher**) bush.

Strauß[1] *der* (PL *die* **Sträuße**) bunch of flowers, bouquet.

Strauß[2] *der* (PL *die* **Strauße**) ostrich.

△ NEW SPELLING: *See page xii*

Streber der (PL die **Streber**) swot.

Strecke die (PL die **Strecken**)
1 distance; 2 route; 3 line (*rail*).

strecken verb (PERF **hat gestreckt**)
1 to stretch (*your arms, legs*); 2 **sich strecken** to stretch.

Streich der (PL die **Streiche**) trick.

streicheln verb (PERF **hat gestreichelt**) to stroke.

streichen ✧ verb (IMPERF **strich**, PERF **hat gestrichen**) 1 to paint; **'frisch gestrichen'** 'wet paint'; 2 to spread (*with butter*); 3 to delete; 4 to cancel (*a flight*); 5 **jemandem über den Kopf streichen** to stroke somebody's head.

Streichholz das (PL die **Streichhölzer**) match.

Streifen der (PL die **Streifen**)
1 stripe; 2 strip.

Streik der (PL die **Streiks**) strike.

streiken verb (PERF **hat gestreikt**) to strike.

Streit der (PL die **Streite**) quarrel, argument.

streiten ✧ verb (IMPERF **stritt**, PERF **hat gestritten**) 1 to quarrel, to argue; 2 **sich streiten** to quarrel, to argue.

streng adjective strict.

Stress ∆ der stress.

stressig adjective stressful.

streuen verb (PERF **hat gestreut**)
1 to spread; **die Straßen streuen** to grit the roads; 2 to sprinkle.

strich SEE **streichen**.

Strich der (PL die **Striche**) 1 line; 2 stroke.

Strichpunkt der (PL die **Strichpunkte**) semicolon.

stricken verb (PERF **hat gestrickt**) to knit.

Strickjacke die (PL die **Strickjacken**) cardigan.

stritt SEE **streiten**.

Stroh das straw.

Strohhalm der (PL die **Strohhalme**) straw (*for drinking*).

Strom der (PL die **Ströme**) 1 river; 2 stream (*of people or blood*); **es regnet in Strömen** it's pouring with rain; 3 current.

strömen verb (PERF **ist geströmt**) to stream.

Strömung die (PL die **Strömungen**) current.

Strumpf der (PL die **Strümpfe**)
1 stocking; 2 sock.

Strumpfhose die (PL die **Strumpfhosen**) tights.

Stube die (PL die **Stuben**) room.

Stück das (PL die **Stücke**) 1 piece; 2 item; **eine Mark das Stück** one mark each; 3 play.

Stückchen das (PL die **Stückchen**) little piece.

Student der (PL die **Studenten**) student.

Studentin die (PL die **Studentinnen**) student.

✧ IRREGULAR VERB: See the verb table in the centre of the dictionary

studieren *verb* (PERF **hat studiert**) to study; **Horst studiert Mathematik** Horst is studying mathematics.

Studium *das* (PL *die* **Studien**) studies.

Stufe *die* (PL *die* **Stufen**) 1 step; **'Vorsicht Stufe'** 'mind the step'; 2 stage (*of development*).

Stuhl *der* (PL *die* **Stühle**) chair.

stumm *adjective* 1 dumb; 2 silent.

stumpf *adjective* 1 blunt; 2 dull; 3 **ein stumpfer Winkel** an obtuse angle.

Stunde *die* (PL *die* **Stunden**) 1 hour; 2 lesson.

stundenlang *adverb* for hours.

Stundenplan *der* (PL *die* **Stundenpläne**) timetable.

stündlich *adjective* hourly.

stur *adjective* stubborn.

Sturm *der* (PL *die* **Stürme**) storm.

stürmisch *adjective* stormy.

Sturz *der* (PL *die* **Stürze**) 1 fall; 2 overthrow.

stürzen *verb* (PERF **ist gestürzt**) 1 to fall; 2 to rush (*into a room*); 3 (PERF **hat gestürzt**) to overthrow; 4 (PERF **hat sich gestürzt**) **er hat sich aus dem Fenster gestürzt** he threw himself out of the window; **sich auf jemanden stürzen** to pounce on somebody.

Sturzhelm *der* (PL *die* **Sturzhelme**) crash helmet.

stützen *verb* (PERF **hat gestützt**) to support; **sich auf jemanden stützen** to lean on somebody.

Subjekt *das* (PL *die* **Subjekte**) subject.

Substantiv *das* (PL *die* **Substantive**) noun.

subventionieren *verb* (PERF **hat subventioniert**) to subsidize.

Suche *die* (PL *die* **Suchen**) search.

suchen *verb* (PERF **hat gesucht**) 1 to look for; **'Zimmer gesucht'** 'room wanted'; 2 to search.

süchtig *adjective* addicted.

Süchtige *der/die* (PL *die* **Süchtigen**) addict.

Südafrika *das* South Africa.

Südamerika *das* South America.

Süden *der* south.

südlich *adjective* 1 southern; 2 southerly.
adverb, preposition ←(+GEN) **südlich von Wien** south of Vienna; **südlich der Stadt** to the south of the town.

Südosten *der* south-east.

Südpol *der* South Pole.

Südwesten *der* south-west.

Summe *die* (PL *die* **Summen**) sum.

summen *verb* (PERF **hat gesummt**) 1 to hum; 2 to buzz.

super *adjective* (*informal*) great.

Supermarkt *der* (PL *die* **Supermärkte**) supermarket.

Suppe *die* (PL *die* **Suppen**) soup.

△ NEW SPELLING: *See page xii*

surfen *verb* (PERF **hat gesurft**) to surf.

süß *adjective* sweet.

Süßigkeit *die* (PL *die* **Süßigkeiten**) sweet.

sympathisch *adjective* likeable.

Synagoge *die* (PL *die* **Synagogen**) synagogue.

synthetisch *adjective* synthetic.

System *das* (PL *die* **Systeme**) system.

Szene *die* (PL *die* **Szenen**) scene.

T t

Tabak *der* (PL *die* **Tabake**) tobacco.

Tabelle *die* (PL *die* **Tabellen**) table.

Tablett *das* (PL *die* **Tabletts**) tray.

Tablette *die* (PL *die* **Tabletten**) tablet.

Tafel *die* (PL *die* **Tafeln**) **1** board, blackboard; **ein Wort an die Tafel schreiben** to write a word on the blackboard; **2 eine Tafel Schokolade** a bar of chocolate.

Tag *der* (PL *die* **Tage**) day; **guten Tag** hello; **am Tag** in the daytime.

Tagebuch *das* (PL *die* **Tagebücher**) diary.

tagelang *adverb* for days.

Tagesanbruch *der* dawn.

Tageskarte *die* (PL *die* **Tageskarten**) **1** today's menu; **2** day ticket.

Tageslicht *das* daylight.

Tageslichtprojektor *der* (PL *die* **Tageslichtprojektoren**) overhead projector.

Tagesmutter *die* (PL *die* **Tagesmütter**) childminder.

Tagesschau *die* (PL *die* **Tagesschauen**) news (*on television*).

Tageszeitung *die* (PL *die* **Tageszeitungen**) daily paper.

täglich *adverb, adjective* daily; **zweimal täglich** twice a day.

tagsüber *adverb* during the day.

Taille *die* (PL *die* **Taillen**) waist.

Takt *der* (PL *die* **Takte**) **1** tact; **2** time; **im Takt** in time to the music; **3** rhythm.

taktlos *adjective* tactless.

taktvoll *adjective* tactful.

Tal *das* (PL *die* **Täler**) valley.

Talent *das* (PL *die* **Talente**) talent.

Tampon *der* (PL *die* **Tampons**) tampon.

Tank *der* (PL *die* **Tanks**) tank.

tanken *verb* (PERF **hat getankt**) to fill up (*with petrol*), to get petrol.

Tankstelle *die* (PL *die* **Tankstellen**) petrol station.

Tankwart *der* (PL *die* **Tankwarte**) petrol-pump attendant.

Tanne *die* (PL *die* **Tannen**) fir.

Tannenbaum *der* (PL *die* **Tannenbäume**) **1** fir tree; **2** Christmas tree.

✧ IRREGULAR VERB: *See the verb table in the centre of the dictionary*

Tante die (PL die **Tanten**) aunt.

Tanz der (PL die **Tänze**) dance.

tanzen verb (PERF **hat getanzt**) to dance.

Tänzer der (PL die **Tänzer**) dancer.

Tänzerin die (PL die **Tänzerinnen**) dancer.

Tapete die (PL die **Tapeten**) wallpaper.

tapezieren verb (PERF **hat tapeziert**) to (wall)paper.

tapfer adjective brave.

Tarif der (PL die **Tarife**) 1 tariff; 2 rate.

Tasche die (PL die **Taschen**) 1 bag; 2 pocket; **er hat es aus eigener Tasche bezahlt** he paid for it out of his own pocket; **Max hat mir fünf Mark aus der Tasche gezogen** (informal) Max wangled five marks out of me.

Taschenbuch das (PL die **Taschenbücher**) paperback.

Taschendieb der (PL die **Taschendiebe**) pickpocket.

Taschengeld das pocket money.

Taschenlampe die (PL die **Taschenlampen**) torch.

Taschenmesser das (PL die **Taschenmesser**) penknife.

Taschenrechner der (PL die **Taschenrechner**) pocket calculator.

Taschentuch das (PL die **Taschentücher**) handkerchief.

Tasse die (PL die **Tassen**) cup.

Tastatur die (PL die **Tastaturen**) keyboard.

Taste die (PL die **Tasten**) 1 key; 2 button (on a phone or a machine).

tasten verb (PERF **hat getastet**) 1 to feel; 2 **sich tasten** to feel your way.

tat SEE **tun**.

Tat die (PL die **Taten**) 1 action; 2 **eine gute Tat** a good deed; 3 crime; 4 **in der Tat** indeed.

Täter der (PL die **Täter**) 1 culprit; 2 offender.

Täterin die (PL die **Täterinnen**) 1 culprit; 2 offender.

Tätigkeit die (PL die **Tätigkeiten**) 1 activity; 2 job.

Tätowierung die (PL die **Tätowierungen**) tattoo.

Tatsache die (PL die **Tatsachen**) fact.

tatsächlich adjective actual. adverb 1 actually; 2 really.

Tau[1] der dew.

Tau[2] das (PL die **Taue**) rope.

taub adjective deaf.

Taube die (PL die **Tauben**) 1 pigeon; 2 dove.

tauchen verb (PERF **hat getaucht**) 1 to dip; 2 (PERF **ist getaucht**) ('ist getaucht' is used when movement is described) to dive.

Taucher der (PL die **Taucher**) diver.

Taucherin die (PL die **Taucherinnen**) diver.

△ NEW SPELLING: See page xii

tauen verb (PERF **ist getaut**) **1** to melt; **2 es taut** it's thawing.

Taufe die (PL die **Taufen**) christening.

taufen verb (PERF **hat getauft**) **1** to christen; **2** to baptize.

taugen verb (PERF **hat getaugt**) **nichts taugen** to be no good.

tauschen verb (PERF **hat getauscht**) to exchange, to swap.

tausend number a thousand.

Taxi das (PL die **Taxis**) taxi.

Taxifahrer der (PL die **Taxifahrer**) taxi driver.

Taxifahrerin die (PL die **Taxifahrerinnen**) taxi driver.

Taxistand der (PL die **Taxistände**) taxi rank.

Technik die (PL die **Techniken**) **1** technology; **2** technique.

Techniker der (PL die **Techniker**) technician.

Technikerin die (PL die **Technikerinnen**) technician.

technisch adjective **1** technical; **2** technological.

Technologie die technology.

technologisch adjective technological.

Teddybär der (PL die **Teddybären**) teddy bear.

Tee der (PL die **Tee(s)**) tea; **Tee mit Zitrone** lemon tea.

Teebeutel der (PL die **Teebeutel**) tea bag.

Teekanne die (PL die **Teekannen**) teapot.

Teelöffel der (PL die **Teelöffel**) teaspoon.

Teenager der (PL die **Teenager**) teenager.

Teich der (PL die **Teiche**) pond.

Teig der (PL die **Teige**) **1** dough; **2** pastry; **3** mixture.

Teigwaren plural noun pasta.

Teil[1] der (PL die **Teile**) **1** part; **der zweite Teil** the second part; **zum größten Teil** for the most part; **2 zum Teil** partly; **3** share; **mein Teil am Gewinn** my share of the profit.

Teil[2] das (PL die **Teile**) **1** spare part; **2** part (of a car, machine); **3** unit (of furniture).

teilen verb (PERF **hat geteilt**) **1** to divide; **2 sich etwas mit jemandem teilen** to share something with somebody.

teilnehmen ◇ verb (PRES **nimmt teil**, IMPERF **nahm teil**, PERF **hat teilgenommen**) **an etwas teilnehmen** to take part in something.

Teilnehmer der (PL die **Teilnehmer**) **1** participant; **2** competitor.

Teilnehmerin die (PL die **Teilnehmerinnen**) **1** participant; **2** competitor.

teils adverb partly.

Teilung die (PL die **Teilungen**) division.

◇ IRREGULAR VERB: *See the verb table in the centre of the dictionary*

Teilzeitarbeit *die* part-time work.

Telefax *das* (PL *die* **Telefax(e)**) fax.

Telefon *das* (PL *die* **Telefone**) telephone.

Telefonanruf *der* (PL *die* **Telefonanrufe**) phone call.

Telefonbuch *das* (PL *die* **Telefonbücher**) telephone directory, phone book.

Telefongespräch *das* (PL *die* **Telefongespräche**) telephone call.

Telefonhörer *der* (PL *die* **Telefonhörer**) receiver.

telefonieren *verb* (PERF **hat telefoniert**) to telephone, to make a phone call.

telefonisch *adjective* telephone. *adverb* by telephone; **er ist telefonisch nicht erreichbar** he can't be contacted by phone.

Telefonkarte *die* (PL *die* **Telefonkarten**) phone card.

Telefonnummer *die* (PL *die* **Telefonnummern**) telephone number.

Telefonzelle *die* (PL *die* **Telefonzellen**) phone box, call box.

Teller *der* (PL *die* **Teller**) plate.

Temperatur *die* (PL *die* **Temperaturen**) temperature.

Tempo *das* (PL *die* **Tempos**) speed; **Tempo Tempo!** (*informal*) hurry up!

Tendenz *die* (PL *die* **Tendenzen**) 1 trend; 2 tendency.

tendieren *verb* (PERF **hat tendiert**) **zu etwas tendieren** to tend towards something.

Tennis *das* tennis.

Tennisplatz *der* (PL *die* **Tennisplätze**) tennis court.

Tennisschläger *der* (PL *die* **Tennisschläger**) tennis racket.

Tennisspieler *der* (PL *die* **Tennisspieler**) tennis player.

Tennisspielerin *die* (PL *die* **Tennisspielerinnen**) tennis player.

Teppich *der* (PL *die* **Teppiche**) 1 carpet; 2 rug.

Termin *der* (PL *die* **Termine**) 1 date; **einen Termin vereinbaren** to fix a date; 2 appointment; 3 **der letzte Termin** the deadline.

Terminal[1] *der* (PL *die* **Terminals**) terminal.

Terminal[2] *das* (PL *die* **Terminals**) (computer) terminal.

Terrasse *die* (PL *die* **Terrassen**) terrace.

Terror *der* terror.

Terrorismus *der* terrorism.

Terrorist *der* (PL *die* **Terroristen**) terrorist.

Terroristin *die* (PL *die* **Terroristinnen**) terrorist.

Tesafilm™ *der* Sellotape™.

Test *der* (PL *die* **Tests**) test.

testen *verb* (PERF **hat getestet**) to test.

△ NEW SPELLING: *See page xii*

teuer *adjective* expensive; **wie teuer?** how much?

Teufel *der* (PL *die* **Teufel**) devil.

Text *der* (PL *die* **Texte**) 1 text; 2 lyrics; 3 caption.

Textverarbeitung *die* word processing.

Theater *das* (PL *die* **Theater**) 1 theatre; 2 (*informal*) fuss.

Theaterstück *das* (PL *die* **Theaterstücke**) play.

Theke *die* (PL *die* **Theken**) 1 bar; 2 counter.

Thema *das* (PL *die* **Themen**) subject, topic.

Themse *die* Thames.

theoretisch *adjective* theoretical. *adverb* in theory.

Theorie *die* (PL *die* **Theorien**) theory.

Therapie *die* (PL *die* **Therapien**) therapy.

Thermometer *das* (PL *die* **Thermometer**) thermometer.

Thron *der* (PL *die* **Throne**) throne.

Thunfisch *der* (PL *die* **Thunfische**) tuna.

Thymian *der* thyme.

tief *adjective* 1 deep; 2 low.

Tiefe *die* (PL *die* **Tiefen**) depth.

Tiefgarage *die* (PL *die* **Tiefgaragen**) underground car park.

Tiefkühlfach *das* (PL *die* **Tiefkühlfächer**) freezer compartment.

Tiefkühlkost *die* frozen food.

Tiefkühltruhe *die* (PL *die* **Tiefkühltruhen**) freezer.

Tiefsttemperatur *die* (PL *die* **Tiefsttemperaturen**) minimum temperature.

Tier *das* (PL *die* **Tiere**) animal.

Tierarzt *der* (PL *die* **Tierärzte**) vet.

Tierärztin *die* (PL *die* **Tierärztinnen**) vet.

Tiergarten *der* (PL *die* **Tiergärten**) zoo.

Tierkreis *der* zodiac.

Tiger *der* (PL *die* **Tiger**) tiger.

Tinte *die* (PL *die* **Tinten**) ink.

Tintenfisch *der* (PL *die* **Tintenfische**) 1 octopus; 2 squid.

Tipp △ *der* (PL *die* **Tipps**) tip.

tippen *verb* (PERF **hat getippt**) 1 to type; 2 to tap; 3 **auf etwas tippen** to bet on something; **ich tippe auf ihn** I'm tipping him to win; **im Lotto tippen** to do the lottery.

Tisch *der* (PL *die* **Tische**) 1 table; 2 **nach Tisch** after the meal.

Tischdecke *die* (PL *die* **Tischdecken**) tablecloth.

Tischler *der* (PL *die* **Tischler**) joiner, carpenter.

Tischtennis *das* table tennis.

Tischtuch *das* (PL *die* **Tischtücher**) tablecloth.

Titel *der* (PL *die* **Titel**) title.

Toast *der* (PL *die* **Toasts**) toast.

✧ IRREGULAR VERB: *See the verb table in the centre of the dictionary*

toben *verb* (PERF **hat getobt**) **1** to rage; **2** to go mad; **3** to charge about.

Tochter *die* (PL *die* **Töchter**) daughter.

Tod *der* (PL *die* **Tode**) death.

Todesstrafe *die* death penalty.

tödlich *adjective* **1** fatal; **2** deadly.

todmüde *adjective* dead tired.

todschick *adjective* trendy.

Toilette *die* (PL *die* **Toiletten**) toilet; **auf die Toilette gehen** to go to the toilet.

Toilettenpapier *das* toilet paper.

toll *adjective* (*informal*) brilliant.

Tollwut *die* rabies.

Tomate *die* (PL *die* **Tomaten**) tomato.

Tomatenmark *das* tomato purée.

Ton[1] *der* (PL *die* **Töne**) **1** sound; **er hat keinen Ton gesagt** he didn't make a sound; **2 große Töne spucken** (*informal*) to talk big; **3** tone; **einen frechen Ton anschlagen** to adopt a cheeky tone; **4** note; **5** shade (*of colour*); **6** stress (*in pronunciation*).

Ton[2] *der* clay.

Tonband *das* (PL *die* **Tonbänder**) tape.

Tonbandgerät *das* (PL *die* **Tonbandgeräte**) tape recorder.

Tonne *die* (PL *die* **Tonnen**) **1** barrel; **2** bin (*for rubbish*); **3** tonne, ton.

Topf *der* (PL *die* **Töpfe**) **1** pot; **2** pan.

Töpferei *die* (PL *die* **Töpfereien**) pottery.

Tor *das* (PL *die* **Tore**) **1** gate; **2** goal.

Torte *die* (PL *die* **Torten**) **1** gateau; **2** cake.

Torwart *der* (PL *die* **Torwarte**) goalkeeper.

tot *adjective* dead.

total *adjective* complete. *adverb* completely; **du bist total verrückt** you're totally mad.

Tote *der/die* (PL *die* **Toten**) **1** dead man/woman; **die Toten** the dead; **2** fatality.

töten *verb* (PERF **hat getötet**) to kill.

totlachen *verb* (*informal*) (PERF **hat sich totgelacht**) **sich totlachen** to laugh your head off.

Tour *die* (PL *die* **Touren**) **1** tour; **2** trip; **3 auf diese Tour** (*informal*) in this way.

Tourismus *der* tourism.

Tourist *der* (PL *die* **Touristen**) tourist.

Touristin *die* (PL *die* **Touristinnen**) tourist.

Tournee *die* (PL *die* **Tournees**) tour.

traben *verb* (PERF **ist getrabt**) to trot.

Tradition *die* (PL *die* **Traditionen**) tradition.

traditionell *adjective* traditional.

traf SEE **treffen**.

tragbar *adjective* **1** portable; **2** wearable.

tragen ◇ *verb* (PRES **trägt**, IMPERF **trug**, PERF **hat getragen**) **1** to carry; **2** to wear; **sie trug ein weißes Kleid** she wore a white dress; **man trägt**

wieder kurz short skirts are in fashion again; **3** to bear; **die Verantwortung für etwas tragen** to be responsible for something; **4** to support; **die Organisation trägt sich selbst** the organization is self-supporting.

Träger der (PL die **Träger**) **1** porter; **2** bearer (of a name, title); **3** strap (of a dress); **4** girder.

Tragetasche die (PL die **Tragetaschen**) carrier bag.

tragisch adjective tragic.

Tragödie die (PL die **Tragödien**) tragedy.

Trainer der (PL die **Trainer**) coach, trainer.

trainieren verb (PERF **hat trainiert**) **1** to coach; **2** to train.

Training das training.

Trainingsanzug der (PL die **Trainingsanzüge**) tracksuit.

Traktor der (PL die **Traktoren**) tractor.

trampen verb (PERF **ist getrampt**) to hitchhike.

Tramper der (PL die **Tramper**) hitchhiker.

Tramperin die (PL die **Tramperinnen**) hitchhiker.

Träne die (PL die **Tränen**) tear.

trank SEE **trinken**.

Transport der (PL die **Transporte**) **1** transport; **2** consignment.

transportieren verb (PERF **hat transportiert**) to transport.

trat SEE **treten**.

Traube die (PL die **Trauben**) grape.

trauen verb (PERF **hat getraut**) **1** to trust; **jemandem trauen** to trust somebody; **2 sich trauen** to dare; **Ich trau mich nicht** I don't dare; **3** to marry.

Trauer die **1** grief; **2** mourning.

Traum der (PL die **Träume**) dream.

träumen verb (PERF **hat geträumt**) to dream.

traumhaft adjective fabulous.

traurig adjective sad.

Traurigkeit die sadness.

Trauung die (PL die **Trauungen**) wedding.

treffen ◆ verb (PRES **trifft**, IMPERF **traf**, PERF **hat getroffen**) **1** to hit; **2** to meet; **3** to make (arrangements, a decision); **4 sich mit jemandem treffen** to meet somebody; **5 sich gut treffen** to be convenient; **6** (PERF **ist getroffen**) **auf etwas treffen** to meet with (resistance, difficulties).

Treffen das (PL die **Treffen**) meeting.

Treffer der (PL die **Treffer**) **1** hit; **2** winner; **3** goal.

Treffpunkt der (PL die **Treffpunkte**) meeting place.

treiben ◆ verb (IMPERF **trieb**, PERF **hat getrieben**) **1** to drive; **2** to do; **viel Sport treiben** to do a lot of sport;

◆ IRREGULAR VERB: See the verb table in the centre of the dictionary

Handel treiben to trade;
3 jemanden zur Eile treiben to
hurry somebody up; **4 Unsinn
treiben** to mess about; **5** (PERF **ist
getrieben**) to drift.

Treibhaus das (PL die **Treibhäuser**)
hothouse.

Treibhauseffekt der greenhouse
effect.

Treibstoff der fuel.

trennen verb (PERF **hat getrennt**)
1 to separate; **2** to divide (words,
parts of a room); **3 sich trennen** to
separate; **wir haben uns getrennt**
we've separated; **Jutta hat sich von
ihm getrennt** Jutta has left him;
4 sich von etwas trennen to part
with something.

Trennung die (PL die **Trennungen**)
1 separation; **2** division.

Treppe die (PL die **Treppen**) stairs;
eine Treppe a flight of stairs.

Treppenhaus das stairwell; **im
Treppenhaus** on the stairs.

treten ◇ verb (PRES **tritt**, IMPERF **trat**,
PERF **ist getreten**) **1** to step; **2** to
tread; **3** to kick; **4 mit jemandem in
Verbindung treten** to get in touch
with somebody.

treu adjective faithful.

Tribüne die (PL die **Tribünen**)
1 stand (in a stadium); **2** platform.

Trick der (PL die **Tricks**) trick.

Trickfilm der (PL die **Trickfilme**)
cartoon.

trieb SEE **treiben**.

trifft SEE **treffen**.

Trimm-dich-Pfad der (PL die
Trimm-dich-Pfade) keep-fit trail.

trimmen verb (PERF **hat getrimmt**)
1 to trim; **2 sich trimmen** to keep
fit.

trinken ◇ verb (IMPERF **trank**, PERF
hat getrunken) to drink.

Trinkgeld das (PL die **Trinkgelder**)
tip.

Trinkwasser das drinking water.

tritt SEE **treten**.

Tritt der (PL die **Tritte**) **1** step; **2** kick.

Triumph der (PL die **Triumphe**)
triumph.

trocken adjective dry.

trocknen verb (PERF **hat
getrocknet**) to dry.

Trockner der (PL die **Trockner**) drier.

Trödel der (informal) junk.

Trödelmarkt der (PL die
Trödelmärkte) flea market.

Trommel die (PL die **Trommeln**)
drum.

trommeln verb (PERF **hat
getrommelt**) to drum.

Trompete die (PL die **Trompeten**)
trumpet.

Tropen (plural noun) **die Tropen**
the tropics.

tropfen verb (PERF **hat getropft**) to
drip.

Tropfen der (PL die **Tropfen**) drop.

△ NEW SPELLING: See page xii

Trophäe die (PL die **Trophäen**) trophy.

tropisch adjective tropical.

trösten verb (PERF **hat getröstet**) to console, to comfort.

trotz preposition ←(+GEN) despite, in spite of.

trotzdem adverb nevertheless.

trüb adjective 1 dull, dismal; 2 cloudy (liquid).

trübsinnig adjective gloomy.

trug SEE **tragen**.

Truhe die (PL die **Truhen**) chest.

Trümmer plural noun ruins.

Trumpf der (PL die **Trümpfe**) 1 trump (card); 2 trumps.

Trunkenheit die drunkenness; **Trunkenheit am Steuer** drink-driving.

Truppen plural noun troops.

Truthahn der (PL die **Truthähne**) turkey.

Tscheche der (PL die **Tschechen**) Czech.

Tschechin die (PL die **Tschechinnen**) Czech.

tschechisch adjective Czech.

Tschechische Republik die Czech Republic.

tschüss △ exclamation bye!

T-Shirt das (PL die **T-Shirts**) T-shirt.

Tube die (PL die **Tuben**) tube.

Tuberkulose die tuberculosis.

Tuch das (PL die **Tücher**) 1 cloth; 2 scarf.

tüchtig adjective 1 competent; 2 big.

Tulpe die (PL die **Tulpen**) tulip.

Tumor der (PL die **Tumoren**) tumour.

tun ✧ verb (PRES **tut**, IMPERF **tat**, PERF **hat getan**) 1 to do; **das tut man nicht** it isn't done; **das tut's** (informal) that'll do; **das tut's** (informal) that'll do; **die Butter in den Kühlschrank tun** to put the butter in the fridge; 3 to pretend; **er tut nur so** he's only pretending; 4 to act; **freundlich tun** to act friendly; 5 **jemandem etwas tun** to hurt somebody; 6 **mit jemandem etwas zu tun haben** to have dealings with somebody; **das hat nichts damit zu tun** it's got nothing to do with it; 7 **das tut nichts** it doesn't matter; **es hat sich viel getan** lots has happened.

Tunfisch △ der (PL die **Tunfische**) tuna.

Tunesien das Tunisia.

Tunesier der (PL die **Tunesier**) Tunisian.

Tunesierin die (PL die **Tunesierinnen**) Tunisian.

tunesisch adjective Tunisian.

Tunnel der (PL die **Tunnel**) tunnel.

tupfen verb (PERF **hat getupft**) to dab.

Tupfen der (PL die **Tupfen**) dot.

Tür die (PL die **Türen**) door.

Türke der (PL die **Türken**) Turk.

✧ IRREGULAR VERB: See the verb table in the centre of the dictionary

Türkei *die* Turkey.

Türkin *die* (PL *die* **Türkinnen**) Turk.

türkis *adjective* turquoise.

türkisch *adjective* Turkish.

Turm *der* (PL *die* **Türme**) 1 tower; 2 steeple; 3 rook, castle (*in chess*).

turnen *verb* (PERF **hat geturnt**) to do gymnastics.

Turnen *das* 1 gymnastics; 2 physical education, PE.

Turnhalle *die* (PL *die* **Turnhallen**) gymnasium, gym.

Turnier *das* (PL *die* **Turniere**) tournament.

Turnschuh *der* (PL *die* **Turnschuhe**) 1 trainer; 2 gym shoe.

Turnverein *der* (PL *die* **Turnvereine**) gymnastics club.

tuscheln *verb* (PERF **hat getuschelt**) to whisper.

tut SEE **tun**.

Tüte *die* (PL *die* **Tüten**) bag.

Typ *der* (PL *die* **Typen**) 1 type; 2 (*informal*) bloke.

typisch *adjective* typical.

U u

U-Bahn *die* (PL *die* **U-Bahnen**) underground.

übel *adjective* 1 bad; 2 **mir ist übel** I feel sick; 3 **etwas übel nehmen** Δ to take offence at something; **jemandem etwas übel nehmen** Δ to hold something against somebody.

Übelkeit *die* nausea.

übelnehmen SEE **übel**.

üben *verb* (PERF **hat geübt**) to practise.

über *preposition* ←(+DAT, *or* +ACC *with movement towards a place*) 1 over; **über Weihnachten** over Christmas; 2 above; **er wohnt über uns** he lives above us; **fünf Grad über Null** five degrees above zero; 3 about; **über etwas schreiben** to write about something; 4 for; **ein Scheck über hundert Mark** a cheque for one hundred marks; 5 across (*a field, the street*); 6 **über Frankfurt fahren** to go via Frankfurt; 7 **über die Straße gehen** to cross the road.
adverb 1 **über und über** over and over; 2 **jemandem über sein** to be better than somebody; 3 **über sein** (*informal*) to be left over; 4 **jemandem ist etwas über** (*informal*) somebody is fed up with something; 5 **etwas über haben** Δ (*informal*) to be fed up with something; **Nudeln habe ich über** I'm getting fed up with pasta.

überall *adverb* everywhere.

Überblick *der* (PL die **Überblicke**) **1 einen guten Überblick über etwas haben** to have a good view of something; **2** overall view; **den Überblick verlieren** to lose track of things; **3** summary.

überblicken *verb* (PERF **hat überblickt**) **1** to overlook; **2** to assess.

Überdruss△ *der* **bis zum Überdruss** ad nauseam.

übereinander *adverb* **1** one on top of the other; **2 übereinander sprechen** to talk about each other.

übereinstimmen *verb* (PERF **hat übereingestimmt**) to agree.

überempfindlich *adjective* hypersensitive.

überfahren◇ *verb* (PRES **überfährt**, IMPERF **überfuhr**, PERF **hat überfahren**) to run over; **das Kind ist von einem Auto überfahren worden** the child was run over by a car.

Überfahrt *die* (PL die **Überfahrten**) crossing.

Überfall *der* (PL die **Überfälle**) **1** attack; **2** raid.

überfallen◇ *verb* (PRES **überfällt**, IMPERF **überfiel**, PERF **hat überfallen**) **1** to attack, to mug; **2** to raid; **3 jemanden mit Fragen überfallen** to bombard somebody with questions.

überfällig *adjective* overdue.

überflüssig *adjective* superfluous.

Überführung *die* (PL die **Überführungen**) **1** transfer; **2** flyover; **3** footbridge.

überfüllt *adjective* **1** crowded; **2** oversubscribed.

Übergang *der* (PL die **Übergänge**) **1** crossing; **2** transition.

übergeben◇ *verb* (PRES **übergibt**, IMPERF **übergab**, PERF **hat übergeben**) **1** to hand over; **2 sich übergeben** to be sick.

überhaben SEE **über**.

überhaupt *adverb* **1** in general; **2** anyway; **was will er überhaupt?** what does he want anyway?; **3 überhaupt nicht** not at all; **überhaupt nichts** nothing at all; **überhaupt keine Zeit haben** to have no time at all.

überholen *verb* (PERF **hat überholt**) **1** to overtake; **2** to overhaul.

überholt *adjective* out-of-date.

überlassen◇ *verb* (PRES **überlässt** △, IMPERF **überließ**, PERF **hat überlassen**) **1 jemandem etwas überlassen** to let somebody have something; **2 etwas jemandem überlassen** to leave something up to somebody (*a decision, for example*); **das bleibt dir überlassen** it's up to you.

überlaufen◇ *verb* (PRES **läuft über**, IMPERF **lief über**, PERF **ist übergelaufen**) to overflow.

überleben *verb* (PERF **hat überlebt**) to survive.

überlegen[1] *verb* (PERF **hat**

◇ IRREGULAR VERB: *See the verb table in the centre of the dictionary*

überlegt) 1 to think; **sich etwas überlegen** to think something over; **ohne zu überlegen** without thinking; **2 ich habe es mir anders überlegt** I've changed my mind.

überlegen² *adjective* **1** superior; **jemandem überlegen sein** to be superior to somebody; **2** convincing (*victory*).

überm = **über dem.**

übermäßig *adjective* excessive.

übermorgen *adverb* the day after tomorrow.

übernächster, übernächste, übernächstes *adjective* next but one; **übernächstes Jahr** the year after next.

übernachten *verb* (PERF **hat übernachtet**) to stay the night; **bei jemandem übernachten** to stay the night at somebody's house.

übernehmen ✧ *verb* (PRES **übernimmt**, IMPERF **übernahm**, PERF **hat übernommen**) **1** to take over; **2** to take on; **3 sich übernehmen** to take on too much.

überqueren *verb* (PERF **hat überquert**) to cross.

überraschen *verb* (PERF **hat überrascht**) to surprise.

Überraschung *die* (PL *die* **Überraschungen**) surprise.

überreden *verb* (PERF **hat überredet**) to persuade.

übers = **über das.**

Überschrift *die* (PL *die* **Überschriften**) heading.

überschüssig *adjective* surplus.

überschütten *verb* (PERF **hat überschüttet**) **jemanden mit etwas überschütten** to shower somebody with something.

Überschwemmung *die* (PL *die* **Überschwemmungen**) flood.

übersehen¹ ✧ *verb* (PRES **übersieht**, IMPERF **übersah**, PERF **hat übersehen**) **1** to overlook; **einen Fehler übersehen** to overlook a mistake; **2** to assess (*consequences, damages*).

übersehen² ✧ *verb* (PRES **sieht sich über**, IMPERF **sah sich über**, PERF **hat sich übergesehen**) **sich etwas übersehen** to get fed up of seeing something.

übersetzen *verb* (PERF **hat übersetzt**) to translate.

Übersetzer *der* (PL *die* **Übersetzer**) translator.

Übersetzerin *die* (PL *die* **Übersetzerinnen**) translator.

Übersetzung *die* (PL *die* **Übersetzungen**) translation.

Übersicht *die* **1** overall view; **2** summary.

überspringen ✧ *verb* (IMPERF **übersprang**, PERF **hat übersprungen**) **1** to jump (over); **2** to skip (*a chapter*).

überstehen ✧ *verb* (IMPERF **überstand**, PERF **hat überstanden**) **1** to get over; **2** to survive.

△ NEW SPELLING: *See page xii*

Überstunden *plural noun* overtime; **Überstunden machen** to work overtime.

übertragen ✧ *verb* (PRES **überträgt**, IMPERF **übertrug**, PERF **hat übertragen**) 1 to transfer; 2 to transmit; 3 to broadcast; 4 **etwas ins Reine übertragen** to make a fair copy of something; 5 **sich auf jemanden übertragen** to communicate itself to somebody (*of enthusiasm or nervousness*).

Übertragung *die* (PL *die* **Übertragungen**) 1 broadcast; 2 transmission.

übertreiben ✧ *verb* (IMPERF **übertrieb**, PERF **hat übertrieben**) 1 to exaggerate; 2 to overdo.

Übertreibung *die* (PL *die* **Übertreibungen**) exaggeration.

überwältigend *adjective* overwhelming.

überweisen ✧ *verb* (IMPERF **überwies**, PERF **hat überwiesen**) 1 to transfer; 2 to refer (*a patient*).

überzeugen *verb* (PERF **hat überzeugt**) 1 to convince; 2 **sich selbst überzeugen** to satisfy yourself.

überzeugend *adjective* convincing.

Überzeugung *die* (PL *die* **Überzeugungen**) conviction.

überziehen¹ ✧ *verb* (IMPERF **zog über**, PERF **hat übergezogen**) to put on (*a cardigan, jacket*).

überziehen² ✧ *verb* (IMPERF **überzog**, PERF **hat überzogen**) 1 to overdraw; 2 to cover (*with icing, for example*).

üblich *adjective* usual.

übrig *adjective* 1 remaining; 2 **übrig sein** to be left over; 3 **etwas übrig lassen** △ to leave something (over); 4 **uns blieb nichts anderes übrig** we had no other choice; 5 **alles Übrige** the rest; **die Übrigen** the others; 6 **im Übrigen** besides.

übrigens *adverb* by the way.

übriglassen SEE **übrig**.

Übung *die* (PL *die* **Übungen**) 1 exercise; 2 practice; **aus der Übung sein** to be out of practice.

Ufer *das* (PL *die* **Ufer**) 1 bank (*of a river*); 2 shore.

Uhr *die* (PL *die* **Uhren**) 1 clock; 2 watch; 3 (*in time phrases*) **es ist ein Uhr** it's one o'clock; **wie viel Uhr ist es?** what's the time?; **um sechzehn Uhr** at four o'clock (in the afternoon).

Uhrzeiger *der* (PL *die* **Uhrzeiger**) hand (*of a clock or watch*).

Uhrzeigersinn *der* **im Uhrzeigersinn** clockwise; **entgegen dem Uhrzeigersinn** anti-clockwise.

Uhrzeit *die* time; **jemanden nach der Uhrzeit fragen** to ask somebody the time.

ulkig *adjective* funny.

um *preposition* ←(+ACC) 1 round, around; **um das Haus herum** around the house; 2 at; **um fünf Uhr**

✧ IRREGULAR VERB: *See the verb table in the centre of the dictionary*

at five o'clock; **3** around (about); **4** for; **um etwas bitten** to ask for something; **um seinetwillen** for his sake; **5 sich um jemanden sorgen** to worry about somebody; **6** by (*indicating difference*); **um vieles besser** better by far; **um so besser** so much the better.
adverb **1** about, around; **um die dreihundert Mark herum** about three hundred marks; **um Weihnachten** around Christmas; **2 um sein** (*informal*) to be over.
conjunction **um zu** (in order) to; **er ist noch zu klein, um in die Schule zu gehen** he's too young to go to school.

umarmen *verb* (PERF **hat umarmt**) to hug.

Umbau *der* (PL *die* **Umbauten**) **1** renovation; **2** conversion.

umbinden ◇ *verb* (IMPERF **band um**, PERF **hat umgebunden**) to put on.

umblättern *verb* (PERF **hat umgeblättert**) to turn over.

umbringen ◇ *verb* (IMPERF **brachte um**, PERF **hat umgebracht**) to kill.

umdrehen *verb* (PERF **hat umgedreht**) **1** to turn (round); **2 sich umdrehen** to turn round, to turn over.

umfallen ◇ *verb* (PRES **fällt um**, IMPERF **fiel um**, PERF **ist umgefallen**) to fall down.

Umfrage *die* (PL *die* **Umfragen**) survey.

umgänglich *adjective* sociable.

Umgangsformen *plural noun* manners.

Umgangssprache *die* slang, colloquial language.

umgeben ◇ *verb* (PRES **umgibt**, IMPERF **umgab**, PERF **hat umgeben**) to surround.

Umgebung *die* (PL *die* **Umgebungen**) **1** surroundings; **2** neighbourhood.

umgehen[1] ◇ *verb* (IMPERF **ging um**, PERF **ist umgegangen**) **1** to go round (*of a rumour, an illness*); **2 mit jemandem streng umgehen** to treat somebody strictly; **3 er kann mit Geld nicht umgehen** he can't handle money; **mit seinen Sachen sorgfältig umgehen** to handle one's things carefully.

umgehen[2] ◇ *verb* (IMPERF **umging**, PERF **hat umgangen**) to avoid.

umgekehrt *adjective* **1** opposite; **2** reverse (*order*); **3 es war umgekehrt** it was the other way round.
adverb **1 und umgekehrt** and vice versa; **2** the other way round; **warum machst du es nicht umgekehrt?** why don't you do it the other way round?

umkehren *verb* (PERF **ist umgekehrt**) **1** to turn back; **nach zehn Minuten sind wir wieder umgekehrt** ten minutes later we turned back again; **2** to turn round (*a picture, book*); **3** to turn inside out (*a bag, for example*); **4 sie hat das ganze Zimmer umgekehrt**

(*informal*) she turned the whole room upside down.

Umkleidekabine die (PL die **Umkleidekabinen**) changing cubicle.

Umkleideraum der (PL die **Umkleideräume**) changing room.

umkommen ✧ *verb* (IMPERF **kam um**, PERF **ist umgekommen**) to be killed.

Umlaut der (PL die **Umlaute**) umlaut.

umlegen *verb* (PERF **hat umgelegt**) 1 to put on (*a scarf*); 2 to transfer (*a patient, call*); 3 **jemanden umlegen** (*informal*) to bump somebody off.

Umleitung die (PL die **Umleitungen**) diversion.

umrechnen *verb* (PERF **hat umgerechnet**) to convert.

Umrechnung die conversion.

Umrechnungskurs der exchange rate.

Umriss Δ der (PL die **Umrisse**) outline.

umrühren *verb* (PERF **hat umgerührt**) to stir.

ums = **um das**.

umschalten *verb* (PERF **hat umgeschaltet**) 1 to turn over; **vom ersten aufs zweite Programm umschalten** to turn from channel one to channel two; 2 **auf Rot umschalten** to change to red.

Umschlag der (PL die **Umschläge**) 1 envelope; 2 cover.

umsehen ✧ *verb* (PRES **sieht sich um**, IMPERF **sah sich um**, PERF **hat sich umgesehen**) **sich umsehen** to look round.

umso Δ *adverb* **umso besser** all the better; **je mehr, umso besser** the more the better.

umsonst *adverb* 1 in vain; 2 free, for nothing.

Umstand der (PL die **Umstände**) 1 circumstance; 2 **unter Umständen** possibly; 3 **jemandem Umstände machen** to put somebody to trouble; **das macht gar keine Umstände** it's no trouble at all; 4 **in anderen Umständen sein** to be pregnant.

umständlich *adjective* 1 laborious; 2 complicated.

umsteigen ✧ *verb* (IMPERF **stieg um**, PERF **ist umgestiegen**) to change.

umstellen[1] *verb* (PERF **hat umgestellt**) 1 to rearrange; 2 to reset; 3 to change over; 4 **sich umstellen** to adjust.

umstellen[2] *verb* (PERF **hat umstellt**) to surround.

Umtausch der exchange.

umtauschen *verb* (PERF **hat umgetauscht**) to change, to exchange.

Umweg der (PL die **Umwege**) detour.

Umwelt die environment.

umweltfreundlich *adjective* environmentally friendly.

Umweltschützer der (PL die **Umweltschützer**) environmentalist.

✧ IRREGULAR VERB: *See the verb table in the centre of the dictionary*

Umweltverschmutzung *die*
pollution.

umwerfen ✧ *verb* (PRES **wirft um**,
IMPERF **warf um**, PERF **hat
umgeworfen**) 1 to knock over; 2 to
upset (*a plan*); **das hat mich
umgeworfen** it's thrown me.

umwerfend *adjective* fantastic.

umziehen ✧ *verb* (IMPERF **zog um**,
PERF **ist umgezogen**) 1 to move; **sie
ziehen nächste Woche um** they're
moving next week; 2 (PERF **hat
umgezogen**) to change; 3 (PERF **hat
sich umgezogen**) **sich umziehen**
to get changed.

Umzug *der* (PL *die* **Umzüge**) move.

unabhängig *adjective*
independent.

Unabhängigkeit *die*
independence.

unangenehm *adjective*
1 unpleasant; 2 embarrassing
(*question, situation*).

unartig *adjective* naughty.

unbedeutend *adjective*
insignificant.
adverb slightly.

unbedingt *adjective* absolute.
adverb really; **ich muss ihn
unbedingt sprechen** I really must
talk to him; **nicht unbedingt** not
necessarily.

unbefriedigend *adjective*
unsatisfactory.

unbefriedigt *adjective* unsatisfied.

unbehaglich *adjective*
1 uncomfortable; 2 uneasy.

unbekannt *adjective* unknown.

unbeliebt *adjective* unpopular.

unbequem *adjective*
uncomfortable.

unbestimmt *adjective* 1 indefinite;
auf unbestimmte Zeit for an
indefinite period; 2 uncertain.
adverb vaguely; **etwas unbestimmt
lassen** to leave something open.

unbewusst △ *adjective*
unconscious.

und *conjunction* and; **und so weiter**
and so on; **na und?** so what?

undankbar *adjective* ungrateful.

undeutlich *adjective* unclear.

undicht *adjective* leaking, leaky;
eine undichte Stelle a leak.

uneben *adjective* uneven.

unempfindlich *adjective* 1 hard-
wearing, easy-care; 2 immune;
gegen Kälte unempfindlich sein
not to feel the cold.

unentbehrlich *adjective*
indispensable.

unentschieden *adjective*
undecided; **unentschieden spielen**
to draw.

unerträglich *adjective* unbearable.

unerwartet *adjective* unexpected.

unfähig *adjective* 1 incompetent;
2 **unfähig sein, etwas zu tun** to be
incapable of doing something.

△ NEW SPELLING: *See page xii*

unfair *adjective* unfair.

Unfall *der* (PL *die* **Unfälle**) accident.

unfreundlich *adjective* unfriendly.

Unfug *der* 1 nonsense; 2 mischief; **Unfug machen** to get up to mischief.

Ungar *der* (PL *die* **Ungarn**) Hungarian.

Ungarin *die* (PL *die* **Ungarinnen**) Hungarian.

ungarisch *adjective* Hungarian.

Ungarn *das* Hungary.

Ungeduld *die* impatience.

ungeduldig *adjective* impatient.

ungeeignet *adjective* unsuitable.

ungefähr *adjective* approximate. *adverb* approximately, about.

ungefährlich *adjective* safe, harmless.

ungeheuer *adjective* enormous.

Ungeheuer *das* (PL *die* **Ungeheuer**) monster.

ungehorsam *adjective* disobedient.

ungelegen *adjective* inconvenient.

ungemütlich *adjective* uncomfortable.

ungenau *adjective* 1 inaccurate; 2 vague.

ungenießbar *adjective* 1 inedible; 2 undrinkable; **3 Bernd ist heute aber ungenießbar** (*informal*) Bernd is quite unbearable today.

ungenügend *adjective* 1 insufficient; 2 unsatisfactory (*mark at school*).

ungerade *adjective* **eine ungerade Zahl** an odd number.

ungerecht *adjective* unjust.

ungern *adverb* reluctantly.

ungeschickt *adjective* clumsy.

ungesund *adjective* unhealthy.

ungewöhnlich *adjective* unusual.

Ungeziefer *das* vermin.

ungezwungen *adjective* 1 informal; 2 natural.

unglaublich *adjective* incredible.

Unglück *das* (PL *die* **Unglücke**) 1 accident; 2 misfortune; 3 bad luck; **das bringt Unglück** that's unlucky.

unglücklich *adjective* 1 unhappy; 2 unfortunate.

unglücklicherweise *adverb* unfortunately.

unheilbar *adjective* incurable.

unheimlich *adjective* eerie. *adverb* 1 eerily; 2 (*informal*) incredibly; **unheimlich viel** an incredible amount.

unhöflich *adjective* impolite.

Uniform *die* (PL *die* **Uniformen**) uniform.

uninteressant *adjective* uninteresting.

Universität *die* (PL *die* **Universitäten**) university.

Unkenntnis *die* ignorance.

✧ IRREGULAR VERB: See the verb table in the centre of the dictionary

unklar *adjective* unclear.

Unkosten *plural noun* expenses.

Unkraut *das* weed.

unmodern *adjective* old-fashioned.

unleserlich *adjective* illegible.

unlogisch *adjective* illogical.

unmittelbar *adjective* immediate, direct.

unmöglich *adjective* impossible.

Unmöglichkeit *die* impossibility.

unnötig *adjective* unnecessary.

unordentlich *adjective* untidy.

Unordnung *die* 1 disorder; 2 mess.

unpraktisch *adjective* impractical.

unpünktlich *adjective* unpunctual; **unpünktlich sein** to be late.

unrecht *adjective* wrong; **jemandem unrecht tun** to do somebody an injustice.

Unrecht *das* 1 wrong; **zu Unrecht** wrongly; **Unrecht haben** △ to be wrong; 2 **jemandem Unrecht geben** △ to disagree with somebody.

unregelmäßig *adjective* irregular.

unreif *adjective* 1 unripe; 2 immature.

Unruhe *die* (PL *die* **Unruhen**) 1 restlessness; 2 agitation; 3 **Unruhen** unrest.

Unruhestifter *der* (PL *die* **Unruhestifter**) troublemaker.

unruhig *adjective* restless.

uns *pronoun* 1 us; **gib es uns** give it to us; **sie kommen mit uns** they're coming with us; 2 ourselves; **wir waschen uns die Hände** we are washing our hands; 3 each other; **wir kennen uns** we know each other.

unschuldig *adjective* innocent.

unser our.

unserer, unsere, unser(e)s *pronoun* ours.

unsertwegen *adverb* 1 for our sake; 2 because of us; 3 as far as we're concerned.

unsicher *adjective* 1 uncertain; 2 insecure.
adverb unsteadily.

unsichtbar *adjective* invisible.

Unsinn *der* nonsense.

unsrer SEE **unserer**.

unsympathisch *adjective* unpleasant; **Tobias ist mir unsympathisch** I don't like Tobias.

unten *adverb* 1 at the bottom; 2 underneath; 3 downstairs; **hier unten** down here; **nach unten** down.

unter *preposition* ←(+DAT *or* +ACC *with movement towards a place*) 1 under, below; 2 among; **unter anderem** among other things; 3 **unter sich** by themselves; **unter uns gesagt** between ourselves; 4 **unter der Woche** during the week.

Unterbewusstsein △ *das* subconscious.

unterbrechen ✧ *verb* (PRES **unterbricht**, IMPERF **unterbrach**, PERF **hat unterbrochen**) to interrupt.

△ NEW SPELLING: *See page xii*

Unterbrechung *die* (PL *die* **Unterbrechungen**) interruption.

unterbringen ✧ *verb* (IMPERF **brachte unter**, PERF **hat untergebracht**) **1** to put; **2** to put up (*a guest*).

untere SEE **unterer**.

untereinander *adverb* **1** among ourselves/yourselves/themselves; **2** one below the other.

unterer, untere, unteres *adjective* lower.

Unterführung *die* (PL *die* **Unterführungen**) subway.

untergehen ✧ *verb* (IMPERF **ging unter**, PERF **ist untergegangen**) **1** to set (*of the sun*); **2** to sink, to drown; **3** to come to an end.

Untergrundbahn *die* (PL *die* **Untergrundbahnen**) underground.

unterhalb *preposition* ←(+GEN) below.

unterhalten ✧ *verb* (PRES **unterhält**, IMPERF **unterhielt**, PERF **hat unterhalten**) **1** to support; **2** to run (*a hotel, leisure centre*); **3** to entertain; **4** **sich über etwas unterhalten** to talk about something; **5** **sich unterhalten** to enjoy yourself.

unterhaltsam *adjective* entertaining.

Unterhaltung *die* (PL *die* **Unterhaltungen**) **1** conversation; **2** entertainment.

Unterhemd *das* (PL *die* **Unterhemden**) vest.

Unterhose *die* (PL *die* **Unterhosen**) underpants.

Unterkunft *die* (PL *die* **Unterkünfte**) accommodation.

Unterlagen *plural noun* documents, papers.

Untermieter *der* (PL *die* **Untermieter**) lodger.

Untermieterin *die* (PL *die* **Untermieterinnen**) lodger.

unternehmen ✧ *verb* (PRES **unternimmt**, IMPERF **unternahm**, PERF **hat unternommen**) **1** to undertake; **2** **nichts unternehmen** to do nothing; **was unternehmt ihr heute?** what are you doing today?

Unternehmen *das* (PL *die* **Unternehmen**) **1** enterprise; **2** concern.

Unterricht *der* **1** lessons; **heute haben wir keinen Unterricht** we've got no lessons today; **2** teaching.

unterrichten *verb* (PERF **hat unterrichtet**) **1** to teach; **2** to inform; **3** **sich unterrichten** to inform yourself.

Unterrichtsfach *das* (PL *die* **Unterrichtsfächer**) subject.

Unterrock *der* (PL *die* **Unterröcke**) slip.

unterscheiden ✧ *verb* (IMPERF **unterschied**, PERF **hat unterschieden**) **1** to distinguish, to tell apart; **2** **sich unterscheiden** to differ.

Unterschied *der* (PL *die* **Unterschiede**) difference.

✧ IRREGULAR VERB: *See the verb table in the centre of the dictionary*

unterschiedlich *adjective* different; **das ist unterschiedlich** it varies.

unterschreiben ✧ *verb* (IMPERF **unterschrieb**, PERF **hat unterschrieben**) to sign.

Unterschrift *die* (PL *die* **Unterschriften**) signature.

unterster, unterste, unterstes *adjective* bottom, lowest.

unterstreichen ✧ *verb* (IMPERF **unterstrich**, PERF **hat unterstrichen**) to underline.

unterstützen *verb* (PERF **hat unterstüzt**) to support.

Unterstützung *die* support.

untersuchen *verb* (PERF **hat untersucht**) 1 to examine; 2 to investigate.

Untersuchung *die* (PL *die* **Untersuchungen**) 1 examination, check-up; 2 investigation.

Untertasse *die* (PL *die* **Untertassen**) saucer.

Untertitel *der* (PL *die* **Untertitel**) subtitle.

Unterwäsche *die* underwear.

unterwegs *adverb* on the way; **den ganzen Tag unterwegs sein** to be out all day.

untreu *adjective* 1 unfaithful; 2 disloyal.

ununterbrochen *adjective* uninterrupted.

unverbleit *adjective* unleaded.

unvergleichlich *adjective* incomparable.

unverheiratet *adjective* unmarried.

unverkäuflich *adjective* not for sale; **ein unverkäufliches Muster** a free sample.

unverschämt *adjective* impertinent.

unverständlich *adjective* incomprehensible.

unvorsichtig *adjective* careless.

unwahr *adjective* untrue.

unwahrscheinlich *adjective* 1 unlikely; 2 incredible. *adverb* (*informal*) incredibly; **unwahrscheinlich schön** incredibly beautiful.

Unwetter *das* storm.

unwichtig *adjective* unimportant.

unzählig *adjective* countless.

unzerbrechlich *adjective* unbreakable.

unzertrennlich *adjective* inseparable.

unzufrieden *adjective* dissatisfied.

üppig *adjective* lavish.

uralt *adjective* ancient.

Urenkel *der* (PL *die* **Urenkel**) great-grandson; **die Urenkel** the great-grandchildren.

Urenkelin *die* (PL *die* **Urenkelinnen**) great-granddaughter.

△ NEW SPELLING: *See page xii*

Urkunde *die* (PL *die* **Urkunden**) certificate.

Urlaub *der* (PL *die* **Urlaube**) holiday; **Urlaub haben** to be on holiday; **auf/im Urlaub** on holiday.

Urlauber *der* (PL *die* **Urlauber**) holidaymaker.

Ursache *die* (PL *die* **Ursachen**) cause; **keine Ursache!** don't mention it!

Urprung *der* (PL *die* **Ursprünge**) origin.

ursprünglich *adjective* original. *adverb* originally.

Urteil *das* (PL *die* **Urteile**) 1 judgement; 2 opinion; 3 verdict.

urteilen *verb* (PERF **hat geurteilt**) to judge.

Urwald *der* (PL *die* **Urwälder**) jungle.

USA *plural noun* USA.

usw. (*und so weiter*) etc.

V v

vage *adjective* vague.

Vagina *die* (PL *die* **Vaginen**) vagina.

Valentinstag *der* Valentine's Day.

Vanille *die* vanilla.

Vase *die* (PL *die* **Vasen**) vase.

Vater *der* (PL *die* **Väter**) father.

Vaterunser *das* Lord's Prayer.

Vati *der* (PL *die* **Vatis**) dad.

Veganer *der* (PL *die* **Veganer**) vegan.

Vegetarier *der* (PL *die* **Vegetarier**) vegetarian.

Vegetarierin *die* (PL *die* **Vegetarierinnen**) vegetarian.

vegetarisch *adjective* vegetarian.

Veilchen *das* (PL *die* **Veilchen**) violet.

Vene *die* (PL *die* **Venen**) vein.

Ventil *das* (PL *die* **Ventile**) valve.

Ventilator *der* (PL *die* **Ventilatoren**) fan.

verabreden *verb* (PERF **hat verabredet**) 1 to arrange; **was habt ihr verabredet?** what did you arrange?; **mit jemandem verabredet sein** to have arranged to meet somebody; 2 **sich mit jemandem verabreden** to arrange to meet somebody; **ich habe mich mit Oliver zum Tennis verabredet** I've arranged to play tennis with Oliver.

Verabredung *die* (PL *die* **Verabredungen**) 1 appointment; 2 date; 3 arrangement.

verabschieden *verb* (PERF **hat verabschiedet**) 1 to say goodbye to; 2 **sich verabschieden** to say goodbye.

Verachtung *die* contempt.

verallgemeinern *verb* (PERF **hat verallgemeinert**) to generalize.

veralten *verb* (PERF **ist veraltet**) to become obsolete.

veränderlich *adjective* changeable.

✧ IRREGULAR VERB: *See the verb table in the centre of the dictionary*

verändern verb (PERF **hat verändert**) 1 to change; 2 **sich verändern** to change.

Veränderung die (PL die **Veränderungen**) change.

veranstalten verb (PERF **hat veranstaltet**) to organize.

Veranstalter der (PL die **Veranstalter**) organizer.

Veranstaltung die (PL die **Veranstaltungen**) event.

verantwortlich adjective responsible.

Verantwortung die responsibility.

verantwortungsbewusst △ adjective responsible.

verantwortungslos adjective irresponsible.

verarbeiten verb (PERF **hat verarbeitet**) 1 to process; **etwas zu etwas verarbeiten** to make something into something; 2 to digest (food, information).

verärgern verb (PERF **hat verärgert**) to annoy.

Verb das (PL die **Verben**) verb.

verband SEE **verbinden**.

Verband der (PL die **Verbände**) 1 association; **sich zu einem Verband zusammenschließen** to form an associaton; 2 bandage, dressing; **einen Verband anlegen** to apply a dressing.

verbergen ◇ verb (PRES **verbirgt**, IMPERF **verbarg**, PERF **hat verborgen**) 1 to hide; 2 **sich verbergen** to hide.

verbessern verb (PERF **hat verbessert**) 1 to improve; 2 to correct; 3 **sich verbessern** to improve.

Verbesserung die (PL die **Verbesserungen**) 1 improvement; 2 correction.

verbiegen ◇ verb (IMPERF **verbog**, PERF **hat verbogen**) 1 to bend; 2 **sich verbiegen** to bend.

verbieten ◇ verb (IMPERF **verbot**, PERF **hat verboten**) 1 to forbid; **sie hat ihm verboten, das Haus zu betreten** she forbade him to enter the house; **meine Eltern verbieten mir, am Abend wegzugehen** my parents don't allow me to go out in the evening; 2 to ban.

verbilligt adjective reduced.

verbinden ◇ verb (IMPERF **verband**, PERF **hat verbunden**) 1 to connect, to join; 2 to combine; 3 to bandage, to dress (a wound); **jemandem die Augen verbinden** to blindfold somebody; 4 **jemanden verbinden** to put somebody through (on the phone); **ich verbinde** I'm putting you through.

verbindlich adjective 1 friendly; 2 binding (agreement, decision).

Verbindung die (PL die **Verbindungen**) 1 connection; 2 **gute Verbindungen haben** to have good contacts; **sich mit jemandem in Verbindung setzen** to get in touch with somebody; 3 combination; 4 **eine chemische Verbindung** a chemical compound.

verbirgt SEE **verbergen**.

△ NEW SPELLING: See page xii

verbleit *adjective* leaded.

verblüffen *verb* (PERF **hat verblüfft**) to amaze.

verbog SEE **verbiegen**.

verbogen *adjective* hidden.

verbot SEE **verbieten**.

Verbot *das* (PL *die* **Verbote**) ban.

verboten *adjective* forbidden; **'Rauchen verboten'** 'no smoking'.

verbracht, verbrachte SEE **verbringen**.

verbrannt, verbrannte SEE **verbrennen**.

Verbrauch *der* consumption.

verbrauchen *verb* (PERF **hat verbraucht**) to use, to use up; **die Waschmaschine verbraucht nicht viel Strom** the washing machine doesn't use up much electricity.

Verbraucher *der* (PL *die* **Verbraucher**) consumer.

Verbrechen *das* (PL *die* **Verbrechen**) crime.

Verbrecher *der* (PL *die* **Verbrecher**) criminal.

verbreiten *verb* (PERF **hat verbreitet**) 1 to spread; **eine Krankheit verbreiten** to spread an illness; 2 **eine Meldung über den Rundfunk verbreiten** to broadcast a message; 3 **sich verbreiten** to spread; **die Neuigkeit hat sich schnell verbreitet** the news spread quickly.

verbreitet *adjective* widespread.

verbrennen ✧ *verb* (IMPERF **verbrannte**, PERF **ist verbrannt**) 1 to burn; 2 (PERF **hat verbrannt**) to burn (*rubbish, leaves*); 3 to cremate; 4 **sich die Hand verbrennen** to burn your hand.

verbringen ✧ *verb* (IMPERF **verbrachte**, PERF **hat verbracht**) to spend; **wir haben schöne Ferien in Bayern verbracht** we spent a nice holiday in Bavaria.

verbunden SEE **verbinden**.

Verdacht *der* suspicion.

verdächtig *adjective* suspicious.

verdächtigen *verb* (PERF **hat verdächtigt**) to suspect.

verdammt *adjective, adverb* (*informal*) damned; **verdammt!** damn!

verdarb SEE **verderben**.

Verdauung *die* digestion.

verderben ✧ *verb* (PRES **verdirbt**, IMPERF **verdarb**, PERF **hat verdorben**) 1 to spoil, to ruin; **das hat mir den Abend verdorben** it ruined the evening for me; **ich habe mir den Magen verdorben** I have an upset stomach; 2 **es sich mit jemandem verderben** to get into somebody's bad books; 3 (PERF **ist verdorben**) to go off; **die Milch verdirbt, wenn du sie nicht in den Kühlschrank stellst** the milk will go off if you don't put it in the fridge.

verdienen *verb* (PERF **hat verdient**) 1 to earn; 2 to deserve.

✧ IRREGULAR VERB: *See the verb table in the centre of the dictionary*

Verdienst der (PL die **Verdienste**)
1 salary; 2 achievement.

verdirbt SEE **verderben**.

verdoppeln verb (PERF **hat
verdoppelt**) 1 to double; 2 sich
verdoppeln to double.

verdorben SEE **verderben**.

verdünnen verb (PERF **hat
verdünnt**) to dilute.

verehren verb (PERF **hat verehrt**) to
worship.

Verehrer der (PL die **Verehrer**)
admirer.

Verehrerin die (PL die
Verehrerinnen) admirer.

Verein der (PL die **Vereine**) 1 society;
2 organization; 3 club.

vereinbaren verb (PERF **hat
vereinbart**) to arrange.

Vereinbarung die (PL die
Vereinbarungen) 1 agreement;
2 arrangement.

vereinfachen verb (PERF **hat
vereinfacht**) to simplify.

vereinigen verb (PERF **hat vereinigt**)
to unite; **ein Land wieder
vereinigen** △ to reunify a country.

Vereinigte Staaten plural noun
United States.

Vereinigung die (PL die
Vereinigungen) organization.

erfahren ✧ verb (PRES **verfährt**,
IMPERF **verfuhr**, PERF **ist verfahren**)
1 to proceed; 2 **ich habe mich
verfahren** I've lost my way.

verfallen ✧ verb (PRES **verfällt**,
IMPERF **verfiel**, PERF **ist verfallen**) 1 to
decay; 2 to expire (of a passport or
ticket).

Verfassung die (PL die
Verfassungen) 1 constitution;
2 state (of a person).

verfaulen verb (PERF **ist verfault**) to
rot.

verfiel SEE **verfallen**.

verfolgen verb (PERF **hat verfolgt**)
1 to follow; 2 to persecute.

Verfolgung die (PL die
Verfolgungen) 1 pursuit, hunt;
2 persecution.

verfügbar adjective available.

Verfügung die **jemandem etwas
zur Verfügung stellen** to put
something at somebody's disposal;
jemandem zur Verfügung stehen
to be at somebody's disposal.

verfuhr SEE **verfahren**.

verführen verb (PERF **hat verführt**)
1 to tempt; 2 to seduce.

Verführung die (PL die
Verführungen) 1 temptation;
2 seduction.

vergab SEE **vergeben**.

vergangen verb SEE **vergehen**.
adjective last.

Vergangenheit die 1 past; 2 past
tense.

vergaß SEE **vergessen**.

vergeben ✧ verb (PRES **vergibt**,
IMPERF **vergab**, PERF **hat vergeben**)
1 to forgive; **jemandem etwas
vergeben** to forgive somebody for

something; **2** to give away, to award;
3 vergeben sein to be taken; **das Zimmer ist schon vergeben** the room's already taken.

vergeblich *adverb* in vain.

vergehen ✧ *verb* (IMPERF **verging**, PERF **ist vergangen**) to pass.

vergessen ✧ *verb* (PRES **vergisst** △, IMPERF **vergaß**, PERF **hat vergessen**) to forget.

vergesslich △ *adjective* forgetful.

vergewaltigen *verb* (PERF **hat vergewaltigt**) to rape.

Vergewaltigung *die* (PL *die* **Vergewaltigungen**) rape.

vergibt SEE **vergeben**.

vergiften *verb* (PERF **hat vergiftet**) to poison.

verging SEE **vergehen**.

vergisst △ SEE **vergessen**.

Vergleich *der* (PL *die* **Vergleiche**) comparison.

vergleichen ✧ *verb* (IMPERF **verglich**, PERF **hat verglichen**) to compare.

Vergnügen *das* (PL *die* **Vergnügen**) pleasure; **viel Vergnügen!** have fun!

vergnügt *adjective* cheerful.

vergrößern *verb* (PERF **hat vergrößert**) **1** to enlarge; **2** to increase; **3** to magnify; **4** to extend (*a room, building*); **5 sich vergrößern** to expand, to grow bigger.

Vergrößerung *die* (PL *die* **Vergrößerungen**) **1** expansion; **2** enlargement (*of a photograph*).

verhaften *verb* (PERF **hat verhaftet**) to arrest; **er ist verhaftet worden** he was arrested.

verhalten ✧ *verb* (PRES **verhält sich**, IMPERF **verhielt sich**, PERF **hat sich verhalten**) **sich verhalten** to behave.

Verhalten *das* behaviour.

Verhältnis *das* (PL *die* **Verhältnisse**) **1** relationship; **sie hat ein gutes Verhältnis zu ihren Eltern** she has good relationship with her parents; **2** affair; **Gabi hat ein Verhältnis mit einem verheirateten Mann** Gabi is having an affair with a married man; **3** ratio (*in maths*); **4 in keinem Verhältnis zu etwas stehen** to be out of all proportion to something; **5 Verhältnisse** conditions; **über seine Verhältnisse leben** to live beyond your means.

verhältnismäßig *adverb* relatively.

verhandeln *verb* (PERF **hat verhandelt**) to negotiate; **über etwas verhandeln** to negotiate something.

Verhandlung *die* (PL *die* **Verhandlungen**) **1** negotiation; **2** hearing; **3** trial.

verhauen *verb* (PERF **hat verhauen**) **1** to beat up; **2 die Prüfung verhauen** (*informal*) to make a mess of the exam.

verheimlichen *verb* (PERF **hat verheimlicht**) to keep secret.

✧ IRREGULAR VERB: *See the verb table in the centre of the dictionary*

verheiratet *adjective* married.

verhielt SEE **verhalten**.

verhindern *verb* (PERF **hat verhindert**) 1 to prevent; 2 **verhindert sein** to be unable to make it; **Petra ist verhindert** Petra won't be able to make it.

verhungern *verb* (PERF **ist verhungert**) to starve.

Verhütungsmittel *das* (PL *die* **Verhütungsmittel**) contraceptive.

verirren *verb* (PERF **hat sich verirrt**) **sich verirren** to get lost.

verkam SEE **verkommen**.

Verkauf *der* (PL *die* **Verkäufe**) sale; **zum Verkauf** for sale.

verkaufen *verb* (PERF **hat verkauft**) to sell; **zu verkaufen** for sale.

Verkäufer *der* (PL *die* **Verkäufer**) 1 seller; 2 sales assistant.

Verkäuferin *die* (PL *die* **Verkäuferinnen**) 1 seller; 2 sales assistant.

Verkehr *der* traffic.

Verkehrsampel *die* (PL *die* **Verkehrsampeln**) traffic lights.

Verkehrsamt *das* (PL *die* **Verkehrsämter**) tourist office.

Verkehrsunfall *der* (PL *die* **Verkehrsunfälle**) road accident.

Verkehrszeichen *das* (PL *die* **Verkehrszeichen**) traffic sign, road sign.

verkehrt *adjective* 1 wrong;

2 **verkehrt herum** inside out, the wrong way round.

verklagen *verb* (PERF **hat verklagt**) to sue.

verkleiden *verb* (PERF **hat sich verkleidet**) **sich verkleiden** to dress up.

Verkleidung *die* (PL *die* **Verkleidungen**) disguise, fancy dress.

verkommen ✧ *verb* (IMPERF **verkam**, PERF **ist verkommen**) 1 to go off (*of food*); 2 to become dilapidated (*of a house*); 3 to go to the bad.

verkratzt *adjective* scratched.

Verlag *der* (PL *die* **Verlage**) publisher's.

verlangen *verb* (PERF **hat verlangt**) 1 to ask for, to require; **am Telefon verlangt werden** to be wanted on the phone; 2 to demand; 3 to charge.

verlängern *verb* (PERF **hat verlängert**) 1 to extend; 2 to lengthen; 3 to renew (*a passport, driving licence*).

Verlängerung *die* (PL *die* **Verlängerungen**) 1 extension; 2 renewal; 3 extra time (*in sport*).

verlassen[1] ✧ *verb* (PRES **verlässt** Δ, IMPERF **verließ**, PERF **hat verlassen**) 1 to leave; **jemanden verlassen** to leave somebody; 2 **sich auf etwas verlassen** to rely on something; **du kannst dich auf ihn verlassen** you can rely on him.

verlassen[2] *adjective* deserted.

Δ NEW SPELLING: See page xii

verlaufen ⬦ *verb* (PRES **verläuft**, IMPERF **verlief**, PERF **ist verlaufen**) **1** to go; **es ist gut verlaufen** it went well; **2 sich verlaufen** to lose your way; **3 die Menge verlief sich schnell** the crowd quickly dispersed.

verlegen¹ *adjective* embarrassed.

verlegen² *verb* (PERF **hat verlegt**) **1** to mislay; **2** to postpone; **3** to publish; **4** to lay (*a carpet, cable*).

Verlegenheit *die* embarrassment.

Verleih *der* (PL *die* **Verleihe**) **1** renting out, hiring out; **2** rental firm, hire shop.

verleihen ⬦ *verb* (IMPERF **verlieh**, PERF **hat verliehen**) **1** to hire out; **2** to lend; **3** to award.

verlernen *verb* (PERF **hat verlernt**) to forget.

verletzen *verb* (PERF **hat verletzt**) **1** to injure; **2** to hurt; **3** to violate (*a law*); **4 sich verletzen** to hurt yourself.

Verletzte *der/die* (PL *die* **Verletzten**) **1** injured person; **2** casualty.

Verletzung *die* (PL *die* **Verletzungen**) injury.

verlieben *verb* (PERF **hat sich verliebt**) **sich verlieben** to fall in love.

verlief SEE **verlaufen**.

verlieh SEE **verleihen**.

verlieren ⬦ *verb* (IMPERF **verlor**, PERF **hat verloren**) to lose.

verließ SEE **verlassen**.

verloben *verb* (PERF **hat sich verlobt**) **sich verloben** to get engaged.

Verlobte *der/die* (PL *die* **Verlobten**) fiancé, fiancée.

Verlobung *die* (PL *die* **Verlobungen**) engagement.

verlor, verloren SEE **verlieren**.

Verlosung *die* (PL *die* **Verlosungen**) prize draw.

Verlust *der* (PL *die* **Verluste**) loss.

vermeiden ⬦ *verb* (IMPERF **vermied**, PERF **hat vermieden**) to avoid.

vermieten *verb* (PERF **hat vermietet**) **1** to rent out, to hire out; **2** to let; **Zimmer zu vermieten** rooms to let.

Vermieter *der* (PL *die* **Vermieter**) landlord.

Vermieterin *die* (PL *die* **Vermieterinnen**) landlady.

vermissen *verb* (PERF **hat vermisst** Δ) to miss.

Vermittlung *die* (PL *die* **Vermittlungen**) **1** arrangement; **2** agency; **3** switchboard; **4** telephone exchange; **5** mediation

Vermögen *das* (PL *die* **Vermögen**) fortune.

vermuten *verb* (PERF **hat vermutet**) to suspect.

vermutlich *adjective* probable. *adverb* probably.

vernichten *verb* (PERF **hat vernichtet**) **1** to destroy; **2** to exterminate.

⬦ IRREGULAR VERB: *See the verb table in the centre of the dictionary*

Vernunft *die* reason.

vernünftig *adjective* sensible.

verpacken *verb* (PERF **hat verpackt**) **1** to pack; **2** to wrap up.

Verpackung *die* (PL *die* **Verpackungen**) packaging.

verpassen *verb* (PERF **hat verpasst** Δ) to miss.

Verpflegung *die* food; **Unterkunft und Verpflegung** board and lodging.

verpflichten *verb* (PERF **hat verpflichtet**) **1** sich verpflichten to promise; **2** sich vertraglich verpflichten to sign a contract; **3** verpflichtet sein, etwas zu tun to be obliged to do something; **jemandem zu Dank verpflichtet sein** to be obliged to somebody; **4** verpflichtend binding.

Verpflichtung *die* (PL *die* **Verpflichtungen**) **1** obligation; **2** commitment.

verprügeln *verb* (PERF **hat verprügelt**) to beat up.

verraten ◇ *verb* (PRES **verrät**, IMPERF **verriet**, PERF **hat verraten**) **1** to betray; **2** to give away; **3** to tell; **4** sich verraten to give yourself away.

verrechnen *verb* (PERF **hat sich verrechnet**) sich verrechnen to make a mistake.

verregnet *adjective* rainy.

verreisen *verb* (PERF **ist verreist**) to go away; **verreist sein** to be away.

verriet SEE **verraten**.

verrosten *verb* (PERF **ist verrostet**) to rust.

verrostet *adjective* rusty.

verrückt *adjective* mad, crazy.

Verrückte *der/die* (PL *die* **Verrückten**) maniac.

versagen *verb* (PERF **hat versagt**) to fail.

versammeln *verb* (PERF **hat versammelt**) **1** to assemble; **2** sich versammeln to assemble.

Versammlung *die* (PL *die* **Versammlungen**) meeting.

versäumen *verb* (PERF **hat versäumt**) to miss; **es versäumen, etwas zu tun** to fail to do something.

verschenken *verb* (PERF **hat verschenkt**) to give away.

verschieben ◇ *verb* (IMPERF **verschob**, PERF **hat verschoben**) to postpone.

verschieden *adjective* **1** different; **2** various.

verschlafen ◇ *verb* (PRES **verschläft**, IMPERF **verschlief**, PERF **hat verschlafen**) **1** to oversleep; **2** to sleep through (*the day*); **3** to miss (*a date, the train*).

verschlechtern *verb* (PERF **hat verschlechtert**) **1** to make worse; **2** sich verschlechtern to get worse.

verschlief SEE **verschlafen**.

verschließen ◇ *verb* (IMPERF **verschloss** Δ, PERF **hat verschlossen**) **1** to close (*a tin,* *package*); **2** to lock (*a door, drawer*).

verschlimmern *verb* (PERF **hat verschlimmert**) **1** to make worse; **2 sich verschlimmern** to get worse.

verschloss △ SEE **verschließen**.

verschlucken *verb* (PERF **hat verschluckt**) **1** to swallow; **2 sich verschlucken** to choke.

Verschluss △ *der* (PL *die* **Verschlüsse**) **1** fastener, clasp; **2** top (*of a bottle*).

verschmutzen *verb* (PERF **hat verschmutzt**) to soil; **die Umwelt verschmutzen** to pollute the environment.

Verschmutzung *die* pollution.

verschob SEE **verschieben**.

verschreiben ◇ *verb* (IMPERF **verschrieb**, PERF **hat verschrieben**) **1** to prescribe; **2 sich verschreiben** to make a mistake.

verschütten *verb* (PERF **hat verschüttet**) to spill.

verschwand SEE **verschwinden**.

verschwenden *verb* (PERF **hat verschwendet**) to waste.

Verschwendung *die* waste.

verschwinden ◇ *verb* (IMPERF **verschwand**, PERF **ist verschwunden**) to disappear.

Versehen *das* (PL *die* **Versehen**) oversight; **aus Versehen** by mistake.

versehentlich *adverb* by mistake.

versetzen *verb* (PERF **hat versetzt**) **1** to move, to transfer (*a person*);

2 to move up (*into the next class at school*); **3 jemanden versetzen** to stand somebody up; **4 jemandem einen Schreck versetzen** to give somebody a fright; **jemandem einen Tritt versetzen** to kick somebody; **5 sich in jemandes Lage versetzen** to put yourself in somebody's position.

versichern *verb* (PERF **hat versichert**) **1** to insure; **2** to assert; **jemandem versichern, dass …** to assure somebody that …

Versicherung *die* (PL *die* **Versicherungen**) **1** insurance; **2** assurance.

versöhnen *verb* (PERF **hat sich versöhnt**) **sich versöhnen** to make up; **sich mit jemandem versöhnen** to make it up with somebody.

versorgen *verb* (PERF **hat versorgt**) **1** to supply; **2** to provide for; **3** to look after.

verspäten *verb* (PERF **hat sich verspätet**) **sich verspäten** to be late.

Verspätung *die* lateness, delay; **Verspätung haben** to be late.

versprechen ◇ *verb* (PRES **verspricht**, IMPERF **versprach**, PERF **hat versprochen**) **1** to promise; **2 sich viel von etwas versprechen** to have high hopes of something; **3 sich versprechen** to make a slip of the tongue.

Versprechen *das* (PL *die* **Versprechen**) promise.

verstand SEE **verstehen**.

◇ IRREGULAR VERB: See the verb table in the centre of the dictionary

Verstand *der* 1 mind; **den Verstand verlieren** to go out of your mind; 2 reason.

verstanden SEE **verstehen**.

verständigen *verb* (PERF **hat verständigt**) 1 to notify; 2 **sich verständigen** to communicate, to make yourself understood; 3 **sich über etwas verständigen** to agree on something.

verständlich *adjective* 1 understandable; **jemandem etwas verständlich machen** to make something clear to somebody; 2 comprehensible.

Verständigung *die* 1 communication; 2 notification.

Verstärker *der* (PL *die* **Verstärker**) amplifier.

verstauchen *verb* (PERF **hat verstaucht**) to sprain; **sich den Fuß verstauchen** to sprain your ankle.

Versteck *das* (PL *die* **Verstecke**) hiding place.

verstecken *verb* (PERF **hat versteckt**) 1 to hide; 2 **sich verstecken** to hide.

verstehen ⬦ *verb* (IMPERF **verstand**, PERF **hat verstanden**) 1 to understand; **etwas falsch verstehen** to misunderstand something; 2 **sich gut verstehen** to get on well; 3 **das versteht sich von selbst** that goes without saying.

verstellbar *adjective* adjustable.

verstellen *verb* (PERF **hat verstellt**) 1 to adjust; 2 to block; 3 to disguise; 4 **sich verstellen** to pretend.

verstimmt *adjective* 1 out of tune; 2 peeved; 3 **ein verstimmter Magen** an upset stomach.

Versuch *der* (PL *die* **Versuche**) 1 attempt; 2 experiment.

versuchen *verb* (PERF **hat versucht**) to try.

verteidigen *verb* (PERF **hat verteidigt**) to defend.

Verteidiger *der* (PL *die* **Verteidiger**) 1 defender; 2 defence counsel.

Verteidigung *die* defence.

verteilen *verb* (PERF **hat verteilt**) to distribute.

Vertrag *der* (PL *die* **Verträge**) 1 contract; 2 treaty.

vertragen ⬦ *verb* (PRES **verträgt**, IMPERF **vertrug**, PERF **hat vertragen**) 1 to stand, to take; 2 **ich vertrage keinen Kaffee** coffee disagrees with me; 3 **sich vertragen** to get on; **sich wieder vertragen** to make it up.

vertrat SEE **vertreten**.

vertrauen *verb* (PERF **hat vertraut**) to trust.

Vertrauen *das* trust; **im Vertrauen** in confidence.

vertraulich *adjective* 1 confidential; 2 familiar.

vertreten ⬦ *verb* (PRES **vertritt**, IMPERF **vertrat**, PERF **hat vertreten**) 1 to stand in for; 2 to represent; 3 **eine Meinung vertreten** to hold an opinion; 4 **sich die Beine vertreten** to stretch your legs.

△ NEW SPELLING: *See page xii*

Vertreter der (PL die **Vertreter**)
1 representative; 2 deputy.

Vertreterin die (PL die
Vertreterinnen) 1 representative;
2 deputy.

vertritt SEE **vertreten**.

vertrug SEE **vertragen**.

verunglücken verb (PERF **ist
verunglückt**) to have an accident.

verursachen verb (PERF **hat
verursacht**) to cause.

verurteilen verb (PERF **hat
verurteilt**) 1 to sentence; 2 to
condemn.

Verwaltung die (PL die
Verwaltungen) administration.

verwandt adjective related.

Verwandte der/die (PL die
Verwandten) relative.

Verwandtschaft die relatives.

verwechseln verb (PERF **hat
verwechselt**) to mix up, to confuse;
**jemanden mit jemandem
verwechseln** to mistake somebody
for somebody.

verwenden verb (PERF **hat
verwendet**) to use.

Verwendung die use.

verwickelt adjective complicated.

verwirren verb (PERF **hat verwirrt**)
1 to confuse; 2 to tangle up.

verwirrt adjective confused.

verwöhnen verb (PERF **hat
verwöhnt**) to spoil.

verwunden verb (PERF **hat
verwundet**) to wound.

Verwundete der/die (PL die
Verwundeten) casualty, injured
person.

Verwundung die (PL die
Verwundungen) injury, wound.

verzählen verb (PERF **hat sich
verzählt**) sich verzählen to
miscount.

Verzeichnis das (PL die
Verzeichnisse) 1 list; 2 index.

verzeihen verb (IMPERF **verzieh**, PERF
hat verziehen) to forgive; **verzeihen
Sie, können Sie mir sagen ...?**
excuse me, could you tell me ...?

Verzeihung die forgiveness;
jemanden um Verzeihung bitten to
apologize to somebody;
Verzeihung! sorry!

verzieh, verziehen SEE **verzeihen**.

verzichten verb (PERF **hat
verzichtet**) 1 to do without; **ich
verzichte auf deine Hilfe** I can do
without your help; 2 **auf etwas
verzichten** to give up something
(smoking or your share of
something); to relinquish something
(a right or privilege).

verzögern verb (PERF **hat
verzögert**) 1 to delay; 2 **sich
verzögern** to be delayed.

Verzögerung die (PL die
Verzögerungen) delay.

verzollen verb (PERF **hat verzollt**) to
pay duty on; **haben Sie etwas zu**

⬦ IRREGULAR VERB: See the verb table in the centre of the dictionary

verzollen? have you anything to declare?

verzweifeln *verb* (PERF **ist verzweifelt**) to despair.

verzweifelt *adjective* desperate.

Verzweiflung *die* despair.

Vetter *der* (PL *die* **Vettern**) cousin.

Video *das* (PL *die* **Videos**) video.

Videokamera *die* (PL *die* **Videokameras**) video camera.

Videokassette *die* (PL *die* **Videokassetten**) video cassette.

Videorekorder *der* (PL *die* **Videorekorder**) video recorder.

Videospiel *das* (PL *die* **Videospiele**) video game.

Videothek *die* (PL *die* **Videotheken**) video shop.

Vieh *das* cattle.

viel *adjective, pronoun* **1** a lot of; **Erika hat viel Arbeit** Erika's got a lot of work; **2 viele** (*plural*) many, a lot of; **viele Leute** many people; **3** much, a lot; **wie viel?** how much?, how many?; **zu viel** too much; **vielen Dank** thank you very much; **viel Spaß !** have fun!; **viel Glück !** good luck!; **4 das viele Geld** all that money.
adverb **1** much, a lot; **viel weniger** much less; **so viel wie möglich** as much as possible; **sie redet viel** she talks a lot; **2 viel zu groß** far too big, much too big; **das dauert viel zu lange** it'll take far too long.

vielleicht *adverb* perhaps.

vielmals *adverb* **danke vielmals** thanks a lot.

vier *number* four.

Viereck *das* (PL *die* **Vierecke**) **1** rectangle; **2** square.

viereckig *adjective* **1** rectangular; **2** square.

vierte SEE **vierter**.

Viertel *das* (PL *die* **Viertel**) quarter; **es ist Viertel vor acht** it's quarter to eight.

viertel *adjective* quarter; **wir treffen uns um viertel acht** △ we'll meet at quarter past seven; **um drei viertel acht** △ at quarter to eight.

Viertelstunde *die* (PL *die* **Viertelstunden**) quarter of an hour.

vierter, vierte, viertes *adjective* fourth.

vierzehn *number* fourteen.

vierzig *number* forty.

Villa *die* (PL *die* **Villen**) villa.

virtuell *adjective* virtual; **virtuelle Realität** virtual reality.

Virus *das* (PL *die* **Viren**) virus.

visuell *adjective* visual.

Visum *das* (PL *die* **Visa**) visa.

Vitamin *das* (PL *die* **Vitamine**) vitamin.

Vogel *der* (PL *die* **Vögel**) bird.

Vokabel *die* (PL *die* **Vokabeln**) word; **Vokabeln** vocabulary.

Vokal *der* (PL *die* **Vokale**) vowel.

Volk *das* (PL *die* **Völker**) people.

△ NEW SPELLING: *See page xii*

Volkshochschule *die* adult education centre; **ein Kurs an der Volkshochschule** an adult education class.

Volkslied *das* (PL *die* **Volkslieder**) folk song.

Volkswirtschaft *die* economics.

voll *adjective* **1** full; **ein Korb voll Äpfel** a basket full of apples; **die volle Wahrheit** the whole truth; **2 etwas voll machen** △ to fill something up; **voll tanken** △ to fill up with petrol.
adverb **1** fully, completely; **voll und ganz** completely; **2 jemanden nicht für voll nehmen** (*informal*) not to take somebody seriously.

völlig *adjective* complete.
adverb completely.

vollkommen *adjective* **1** perfect; **2** complete.
adverb completely.

Vollkornbrot *das* wholemeal bread.

vollmachen SEE **voll**.

Vollpension *die* full board.

vollständig *adjective* complete.

volltanken SEE **voll**.

vom = **von dem**.

von *preposition* ←(+DAT) **1** from; **von heute an** from today; **von hier bis …** from here to …; **2** of; **eine Freundin von mir** a friend of mine; **3** about; **Peter hat mir von dem neuen Haus erzählt** Peter told me about the new house; **4** by; **ein**

Theaterstück von Brecht a play by Brecht; **5 von mir aus** I don't mind.

voneinander *adverb* from each other; **sie sind voneinander abhängig** they depend on each other.

vor *preposition* ←(+DAT *or* +ACC *with movement towards a place*) **1** in front of; **2** before; **Manfred war vor euch da** Manfred arrived before you; **kurz vor der Ampel** shortly before the lights; **3** with; **vor Angst zittern** to tremble with fear; **4** (*with clock time*) **zehn vor fünf** ten to five; **5** ago; **vor zwei Jahren** two years ago; **6 sich vor jemandem fürchten** to be frightened of somebody; **7 vor allen Dingen** above all; **8 vor sich hin summen** to hum to yourself.
adverb forward; **vor und zurück** backwards and forwards.

voraus *adverb* **1** ahead; **2 im Voraus** △ in advance.

vorausgehen ◇ *verb* (IMPERF **ging voraus**, PERF **ist vorausgegangen**) **1** to go on ahead; **2** to precede.

voraussetzen *verb* (PERF **hat vorausgesetzt**) **1** to take for granted; **2** to require; **3 vorausgesetzt, dass …** provided that …

Voraussetzung *die* (PL *die* **Voraussetzungen**) **1** condition; **2** assumption.

vorbei *adverb* **1** past; **2** over; **vorbei sein** to be over.

vorbeifahren ◇ *verb* (PRES **fährt vorbei**, IMPERF **fuhr vorbei**, PERF **ist**

◇ IRREGULAR VERB: *See the verb table in the centre of the dictionary*

vorbeigefahren) to drive past, to pass.

vorbeigehen ⟡ *verb* (IMPERF **ging vorbei**, PERF **ist vorbeigegangen**) 1 to go past, to pass; 2 to drop in; **ich gehe bei Anne vorbei** I'll drop in on Anne.

vorbeikommen ⟡ *verb* (IMPERF **kam vorbei**, PERF **ist vorbeigekommen**) 1 to pass; 2 to get past; 3 to drop in.

vorbereiten *verb* (PERF **hat vorbereitet**) 1 to prepare; 2 **sich vorbereiten** to prepare.

Vorbereitung *die* (PL *die* **Vorbereitungen**) preparation.

vorbeugen *verb* (PERF **hat vorgebeugt**) 1 to prevent; 2 **sich vorbeugen** to lean forward.

Vorbild *das* (PL *die* **Vorbilder**) example.

vorderer, vordere, vorderes *adjective* front.

Vorderseite *die* front.

vorderster, vorderste, vorderstes *adjective* front.

Vorfahrt *die* right of way; **'Vorfahrt beachten/gewähren'** 'give way'.

Vorfall *der* (PL *die* **Vorfälle**) incident.

Vorführung *die* (PL *die* **Vorführungen**) 1 performance; 2 demonstration.

Vorgänger *der* (PL *die* **Vorgänger**) predecessor.

Vorgängerin *die* (PL *die* **Vorgängerinnen**) predecessor.

vorgehen ⟡ *verb* (IMPERF **ging vor**, PERF **ist vorgegangen**) 1 to go on ahead; 2 to go forward; 3 to proceed; 4 **die Uhr geht vor** the clock is fast; 5 **was geht hier vor?** what's going on here?

vorgestern *adverb* the day before yesterday.

vorhaben ⟡ *verb* (PRES **hat vor**, IMPERF **hatte vor**, PERF **hat vorgehabt**) 1 to intend; 2 **etwas vorhaben** to have something planned.

Vorhang *der* (PL *die* **Vorhänge**) curtain.

vorher *adverb* beforehand, before.

Vorhersage *die* (PL *die* **Vorhersagen**) 1 forecast; 2 prediction.

vorhin *adverb* just now.

voriger, vorige, voriges *adjective* last.

vorkommen ⟡ *verb* (IMPERF **kam vor**, PERF **ist vorgekommen**) 1 to happen; 2 to occur; 3 to come forward; 4 to come out (*from behind somewhere*); 5 to seem; **jemandem bekannt vorkommen** to seem familiar to somebody; 6 **sich alt vorkommen** to feel old.

vorlesen ⟡ *verb* (PRES **liest vor**, IMPERF **las vor**, PERF **hat vorgelesen**) 1 to read (out); 2 **jemandem vorlesen** to read to somebody.

vorletzter, vorletzte, vorletztes *adjective* last but one; **vorletztes Jahr** the year before last.

△ NEW SPELLING: *See page xii*

Vormittag *der* (PL *die* **Vormittage**) morning.

vormittags *adverb* in the morning.

vorn *adverb* **1** at the front; **nach vorn** to the front; **2 von vorn** from the beginning; **wieder von vorn anfangen** to start again at the beginning; **da vorn** over there.

Vorname *der* (PL *die* **Vornamen**) first name.

vorne = **vorn**.

vornehm *adjective* **1** elegant; **2** distinguished.

vornehmen ✧ *verb* (PRES **nimmt vor**, IMPERF **nahm vor**, PERF **hat vorgenommen**) **1** to carry out; **2 sich vornehmen, etwas zu tun** to plan to do something.

Vorort *der* (PL *die* **Vororte**) suburb.

Vorrat *der* (PL *die* **Vorräte**) supply, stock.

Vorsatz *der* (PL *die* **Vorsätze**) intention.

Vorschau *die* **1** preview; **2** trailer (*of a film*).

Vorschlag *der* (PL *die* **Vorschläge**) suggestion.

vorschlagen ✧ *verb* (PRES **schlägt vor**, IMPERF **schlug vor**, PERF **hat vorgeschlagen**) to suggest.

Vorschrift *die* (PL *die* **Vorschriften**) **1** regulation; **2** instruction.

Vorschule *die* (PL *die* **Vorschulen**) infant school.

vorsehen ✧ *verb* (PRES **sieht sich vor**, IMPERF **sah sich vor**, PERF **hat sich vorgesehen**) **sich vorsehen** to be careful.

Vorsicht *die* care; **Vorsicht!** careful!; (*on a sign*) caution!

vorsichtig *adjective* careful.

vorsichtshalber *adverb* to be on the safe side.

Vorspeise *die* (PL *die* **Vorspeisen**) starter.

Vorsprung *der* (PL *die* **Vorsprünge**) **1** ledge (*of a rock*); **2** lead (*over somebody*).

vorstellen *verb* (PERF **hat vorgestellt**) **1** to introduce; **darf ich Ihnen Herrn Schulz vorstellen?** may I introduce Mr Schulz?; **2 die Uhr vorstellen** to put the clock forward; **3 sich vorstellen** to introduce yourself; **4 sich beim Personalchef vorstellen** to go for an interview with the personnel manager; **5 sich etwas vorstellen** to imagine something; **stell dir vor!** can you imagine?

Vorstellung *die* (PL *die* **Vorstellungen**) **1** performance; **2** introduction; **3** interview (*for a job*); **4** idea; **5** imagination.

Vorteil *der* (PL *die* **Vorteile**) advantage.

Vortrag *der* (PL *die* **Vorträge**) talk.

vorüber *adverb* **vorüber sein** to be over.

vorübergehend *adjective* temporary. *adverb* temporarily.

✧ IRREGULAR VERB: *See the verb table in the centre of the dictionary*

Vorurteil *das* (PL *die* **Vorurteile**) prejudice.

Vorwahl *die* (PL *die* **Vorwahlen**) dialling code.

vorwärts *adverb* forward(s).

vorwiegend *adverb* predominantly.

Vorwurf *der* (PL *die* **Vorwürfe**) reproach; **jemandem Vorwürfe machen** to reproach somebody.

vorzeigen *verb* (PERF **hat vorgezeigt**) to show.

vorziehen ✧ *verb* (PRES **zieht vor**, IMPERF **zog vor**, PERF **hat vorgezogen**) **1** to prefer; **2** to pull up (*a chair*); **3** **den Vorhang vorziehen** to draw the curtain.

vorzüglich *adjective* excellent.

vulgär *adjective* vulgar.

Vulkan *der* (PL *die* **Vulkane**) volcano.

W w

Waage *die* (PL *die* **Waagen**) **1** scales; **2** Libra; **Gabi ist Waage** Gabi's Libra.

waagerecht *adjective* horizontal.

wach *adjective* awake; **wach sein** to be awake; **wach werden** to wake up.

Wache *die* (PL *die* **Wachen**) **1** guard; **2** (police) station.

Wachhund *der* (PL *die* **Wachhunde**) guard dog.

Wachs *das* wax.

wachsen ✧ *verb* (PRES **wächst**, IMPERF **wuchs**, PERF **ist gewachsen**) to grow.

Wachstum *das* growth.

wackelig *adjective* wobbly.

wackeln *verb* (PERF **hat gewackelt**) to wobble.

Wade *die* (PL *die* **Waden**) calf.

Waffe *die* (PL *die* **Waffen**) weapon.

Waffel *die* (PL *die* **Waffeln**) waffle.

wagen *verb* (PERF **hat gewagt**) **1** to risk; **2** **es wagen, etwas zu tun** to dare to do something; **sich nicht irgendwohin wagen** not dare to go somewhere.

Wagen *der* (PL *die* **Wagen**) **1** car; **nimmst du den Wagen?** are you going by car?; **2** carriage (*of a train*); **3** cart.

Wagenheber *der* (PL *die* **Wagenheber**) jack.

Wahl *die* (PL *die* **Wahlen**) **1** choice; **er hat die Wahl** it's his choice; **2** election; **die nächsten Wahlen sind im Herbst** the next election is in autumn.

wählen *verb* (PERF **hat gewählt**) **1** to choose; **zwischen zwei Möglichkeiten wählen** to choose between two possibilities; **2** **haben Sie schon gewählt?** are you ready to order? (*in a restaurant*); **3** to elect; **4** to vote; **wählt Schröder!** vote for Schröder!; **5** to dial; **ich muss die falsche Nummer gewählt**

△ NEW SPELLING: *See page xii*

haben I must have dialled the wrong number.

Wahlfach *das* (PL *die* **Wahlfächer**) optional subject, option.

Wahnsinn *der* madness.

wahnsinnig *adjective* 1 mad; **wahnsinnig werden** to go mad; 2 **wahnsinnigen Durst haben** to be terribly thirsty; **der Film war wahnsinnig gut** the film was incredibly good.

wahr *adjective* 1 true; 2 **du kommst doch, nicht wahr?** you're coming, aren't you?

während *preposition* ←(+GEN) during.
conjunction 1 while; 2 whereas.

Wahrheit *die* (PL *die* **Wahrheiten**) truth.

Wahrsager *der* (PL *die* **Wahrsager**) fortune-teller.

Wahrsagerin *die* (PL *die* **Wahrsagerinnen**) fortune-teller.

wahrscheinlich *adjective* probable, likely.
adverb probably.

Währung *die* (PL *die* **Währungen**) currency.

Waise *die* (PL *die* **Waisen**) orphan.

Wal *der* (PL *die* **Wale**) whale.

Wald *der* (PL *die* **Wälder**) wood, forest.

Waliser *der* (PL *die* **Waliser**) Welshman.

Waliserin *die* (PL *die* **Waliserinnen**) Welshwoman.

walisisch *adjective* Welsh.

Walkman™ *der* (PL *die* **Walkmen**) walkman™.

Walnuss△ *die* (PL *die* **Walnüsse**) walnut.

Wand *die* (PL *die* **Wände**) wall.

wandern *verb* (PERF **ist gewandert**) 1 to hike; 2 to go walking.

Wanderung *die* (PL *die* **Wanderungen**) 1 hike; 2 walking tour.

wann *adverb* when.

Wanne *die* (PL *die* **Wannen**) 1 tub; 2 bath.

war SEE **sein**.

warb SEE **werben**.

Ware *die* (PL *die* **Waren**) 1 article; 2 **Waren** goods.

waren SEE **sein**.

Warenhaus *das* (PL *die* **Warenhäuser**) department store.

warf SEE **werfen**.

warm *adjective* warm; **eine warme Mahlzeit** a hot meal; **das Essen warm machen** to heat up the food.

Wärme *die* warmth.

wärmen *verb* (PERF **hat gewärmt**) to warm, to heat.

Warndreieck *das* (PL *die* **Warndreiecke**) warning triangle.

warnen *verb* (PERF **hat gewarnt**) to warn; **jemanden vor etwas warnen** to warn somebody of something.

⬦ IRREGULAR VERB: *See the verb table in the centre of the dictionary*

Warnung die (PL die **Warnungen**) warning.

warst, wart SEE **sein**.

Warteliste die (PL die **Wartelisten**) waiting list.

warten verb (PERF **hat gewartet**) 1 to wait; **auf jemanden warten** to wait for somebody; 2 **auf sich warten lassen** to take your time.

Wärter der (PL die **Wärter**) 1 keeper; 2 attendant; 3 warder.

Warteraum der (PL die **Warteräume**) waiting room.

Wärterin die (PL die **Wärterinnen**) 1 keeper; 2 attendant; 3 warder.

Wartezeit die wait; **eine Stunde Wartezeit** an hour's wait.

Wartezimmer das (PL die **Wartezimmer**) waiting room.

warum adverb why.

was pronoun 1 what; **was für ein/eine …?** what kind of …?; **was für ein Fahrrad hast du?** what kind of bike do you have?; **was für ein Glück!** what luck!; **was kostet das?** how much is it?; 2 that; **alles, was wir brauchen** all (that) we need; **alles, was du willst** all (that) you want; 3 (short for 'etwas') something; **heute gibt's was Gutes im Fernsehen** there's something good on television today; 4 (short for 'etwas' in questions and negatives) anything; **hast du was für mich?** have you got anything for me?

Waschbecken das (PL die **Waschbecken**) washbasin.

Wäsche die 1 washing; 2 underwear.

waschen ◇ verb (PRES **wäscht**, IMPERF **wusch**, PERF **hat gewaschen**) 1 to wash; 2 **sich waschen** to have a wash; **sich die Hände waschen** to wash your hands.

Wäscherei die (PL die **Wäschereien**) laundry.

Waschlappen der (PL die **Waschlappen**) flannel.

Waschmaschine die (PL die **Waschmaschinen**) washing machine.

Waschsalon der (PL die **Waschsalons**) launderette.

Waschpulver das (PL die **Waschpulver**) washing powder.

Wasser das water.

wasserdicht adjective waterproof.

Wasserfall der (PL die **Wasserfälle**) waterfall.

Wasserfarbe die (PL die **Wasserfarben**) watercolour.

Wasserhahn der (PL die **Wasserhähne**) tap.

Wassermann der Aquarius; **Lisa ist Wasserman** Lisa's Aquarius.

Wasserskifahren das water-skiing.

Watte die cotton wool.

wattiert adjective padded.

WC das (PL die **WCs**) WC, toilet.

weben verb (PERF **hat gewebt**) to weave.

△ NEW SPELLING: See page xii

Wechselkurs der (PL die Wechselkurse) exchange rate.

wechseln verb (PERF hat gewechselt) 1 to change; **kannst du mir zehn Mark wechseln?** have you got change for ten marks?; 2 to exchange (glances, letters).

Wechselstube die (PL die Wechselstuben) bureau de change.

wecken verb (PERF hat geweckt) to wake (up).

Wecker der (PL die Wecker) alarm clock; **Max geht mir auf den Wecker** (informal) Max gets on my nerves.

weder conjunction **weder … noch** neither … nor.

weg adverb 1 away; **geh weg!** go away!; **Hände weg!** hands off!; 2 gone; **der Ring ist weg** the ring's gone; **Heidi ist schon weg** Heidi's already gone.

Weg der (PL die Wege) 1 way; **auf dem Weg nach Hause** on the way home; 2 path; 3 **sich auf den Weg machen** to set off; 4 **im Weg sein** to be in the way.

wegen preposition ←(+GEN) because of.

wegfahren ◇ verb (PRES fährt weg, IMPERF fuhr weg, PERF ist weggefahren) 1 to leave; **sie fahren gerade weg** they are leaving just now; 2 (PERF hat weggefahren) to drive away (a car or things).

weggehen ◇ verb (IMPERF ging weg, PERF ist weggegangen) 1 to go away; 2 to leave; 3 to go out; **wir**

gehen heute Abend weg we're going out tonight; 4 to come out (of a stain).

weglassen ◇ verb (PRES lässt weg △, IMPERF ließ weg, PERF hat weggelassen) 1 to let go; 2 to leave out.

weglaufen ◇ verb (PRES läuft weg, IMPERF lief weg, PERF ist weggelaufen) to run away.

weglegen verb (PERF hat weggelegt) 1 to put down; 2 to put away.

wegmachen verb (PERF hat weggemacht) to get rid of (a stain or wart, for example).

wegmüssen ◇ verb (informal) (PRES muss weg △, IMPERF musste weg △, PERF hat weggemusst △) to have to go.

wegnehmen ◇ verb (PRES nimmt weg, IMPERF nahm weg, PERF hat weggenommen) to take away.

wegräumen verb (PERF hat weggeräumt) to clear away.

wegschicken verb (PERF hat weggeschickt) 1 to send away; 2 to send off.

wegtun ◇ verb (IMPERF tat weg, PERF hat weggetan) to put away.

Wegweiser der (PL die Wegweiser) signpost.

wegwerfen ◇ verb (PRES wirft weg, IMPERF warf weg, PERF hat weggeworfen) to throw away.

◇ IRREGULAR VERB: *See the verb table in the centre of the dictionary*

weh *adjective* **1** sore; **2 oh weh!** oh dear!; **3 es tut weh** it hurts.

wehen *verb* (PERF **hat geweht**) to blow.

Wehrdienst *der* military service.

wehren *verb* (PERF **hat sich gewehrt**) **sich wehren** to defend yourself.

wehrlos *adjective* defenceless.

wehtun △ ✧ *verb* (PRES **tut weh**, IMPERF **tat weh**, PERF **hat wehgetan**) **1** to hurt; **mein Arm tut weh** my arm hurts; **jemandem wehtun** to hurt somebody; **2 sich wehtun** to hurt yourself.

Weibchen *das* (PL *die* **Weibchen**) female.

weiblich *adjective* **1** female; **2** feminine (*noun*).

weich *adjective* soft.

Weide *die* (PL *die* **Weiden**) **1** willow; **2** pasture.

weigern *verb* (PERF **hat sich geweigert**) **sich weigern** to refuse.

Weihnachten *das* (PL *die* **Weihnachten**) Christmas; **Frohe Weihnachten!** Merry Christmas!

Weihnachtslied *das* (PL *die* **Weihnachtslieder**) Christmas carol.

Weihnachtsmann *der* (PL *die* **Weihnachtsmänner**) Father Christmas.

Weihnachtstag *der* (PL *die* **Weihnachtstage**) Christmas Day; **zweiter Weihnachtstag** Boxing Day.

weil *conjunction* because.

Weile *die* while.

Wein *der* (PL *die* **Weine**) wine.

Weinberg *der* (PL *die* **Weinberge**) vineyard.

Weinbergschnecke *die* (PL *die* **Weinbergschnecken**) snail.

Weinbrand *der* brandy.

weinen *verb* (PERF **hat geweint**) to cry.

Weinkarte *die* (PL *die* **Weinkarten**) wine list.

Weinkeller *der* (PL *die* **Weinkeller**) wine cellar.

Weinstube *die* (PL *die* **Weinstuben**) wine bar.

Weintraube *die* (PL *die* **Weintrauben**) grape.

weise *adjective* wise.

Weise *die* (PL *die* **Weisen**) way; **auf diese Weise** in this way.

Weisheit *die* (PL *die* **Weisheiten**) wisdom.

weiß¹ SEE **wissen**.

weiß² *adjective* white.

Weißwein *der* (PL *die* **Weißweine**) white wine.

weit *adjective, adverb* **1** wide, loose (*clothes*); **2** long; **eine weite Reise** a long journey; **3** far; **wie weit ist es?** how far is it?; **ist es noch weit?** is it much further?; **so weit wie möglich** as far as possible; **bei weitem** by far; **4 von weitem** from a distance; **5 ich bin so weit** I'm ready; **6 weit verbreitet**

△ NEW SPELLING: *See page xii*

widespread; **7 zu weit gehen** to go too far.

weiten *verb* (PERF **hat sich geweitet**) **sich weiten** to stretch.

weiter *adjective, adverb* **1** further; **2** in addition; **3 etwas weiter tun** to go on doing something; **weiter nichts** nothing else; **weiter niemand** nobody else; **4 und so weiter** and so on.

weiterer, weitere, weiteres *adjective* **1** further; **2 ohne weiteres** just like that, easily; **3 bis auf weiteres** for the time being.

weiterfahren ◇ *verb* (PRES **fährt weiter**, IMPERF **fuhr weiter**, PERF **ist weitergefahren**) to go on.

weitergehen ◇ *verb* (IMPERF **ging weiter**, PERF **ist weitergegangen**) to go on.

weiterhin *adverb* **1** still; **2** in future; **3 etwas weiterhin tun** to go on doing something.

weitermachen *verb* (PERF **hat weitergemacht**) to carry on.

Weitsprung *der* long jump.

Weizen *der* wheat.

welcher, welche, welches *adjective* which; **welches Kleid?** which dress?; **um welche Zeit?** at what time? *pronoun* **1** which (one); **2** some; **brauchst du Briefmarken? ich habe welche** do you need stamps? I've got some; **3** any; **hast du welche?** have you got any?

Welle *die* (PL *die* **Wellen**) wave.

Wellensittich *der* (PL *die* **Wellensittiche**) budgerigar.

wellig *adjective* wavy.

Welt *die* (PL *die* **Welten**) world; **auf der ganzen Welt** in the whole world.

Weltall *das* universe.

Weltkrieg *der* (PL *die* **Weltkriege**) world war.

Weltmeister *der* (PL *die* **Weltmeister**) world champion.

Weltmeisterin *die* (PL *die* **Weltmeisterinnen**) world champion.

Weltmeisterschaft *die* (PL *die* **Weltmeisterschaften**) **1** world championship; **2 die Weltmeisterschaft** (*football*) the World Cup.

Weltraum *der* space.

wem *pronoun* to whom; **wem hat er das Geld gegeben?** who did he give the money to?

wen *pronoun* whom, who; **wen hast du eingeladen?** who did you invite?

Wende *die* **1** change; **2** reunification (*of Germany*).

wenig *pronoun, adjective* **1** little; **zu wenig** too little, not enough; **2 wenige** few; **in wenigen Wochen** in a few weeks. *adverb* little; **so wenig wie möglich** as little as possible.

weniger *pronoun, adjective* less, fewer; **sie hat weniger Geschenke bekommen** she got fewer presents;

◇ IRREGULAR VERB: *See the verb table in the centre of the dictionary*

immer weniger Geld less and less money; **immer weniger Häuser** fewer and fewer houses. *adverb, conjunction* less; **zehn weniger fünf** ten minus five.

wenigste SEE **wenigster**.

wenigstens *adverb* at least.

wenigster, wenigste, wenigstes *adjective, pronoun* least; **am wenigsten** least; **sein Geschenk hat mir am wenigsten gefallen** I liked his present least.

wenn *conjunction* 1 when; **wenn ich in München bin, schreibe ich dir** I'll write to you when I'm in Munich; **immer, wenn** whenever; 2 if; **wenn es regnet** if it rains; 3 **außer wenn** unless.

wer *pronoun* who.

werben ◇ *verb* (PRES **wirbt**, IMPERF **warb**, PERF **hat geworben**) 1 to advertise; 2 to recruit (*members*).

Werbespot *der* (PL die **Werbespots**) advert, commercial.

Werbung *die* 1 advertising; **in der Werbung arbeiten** to work in advertising; 2 advert; **im Fernsehen kommt viel Werbung** there are many adverts on television; **Werbung für etwas machen** to advertise something.

werden ◇ *verb* (PRES **wird**, IMPERF **wurde**, PERF **ist geworden**) 1 to become; **Arzt werden** to become a doctor; 2 **müde werden** to get tired; **alt werden** to get old; **mir wird kalt** I'm getting cold; 3 **mir wurde schlecht** I felt sick; **blass werden** to turn pale; 4 **wach werden** to wake up; 5 (*used to form the future tense*) will, shall; **sie wird anrufen** she'll ring; **sie wird gleich da sein** she'll be here in a minute; 6 (*used to form the passive*) to be; **gerufen werden** to be called; **er wurde gefragt** he was asked; 7 (*used to form the conditional*) **sie würde kommen** she would come; **ich würde gern kommen, aber ...** I'd like to come but ...

werfen ◇ *verb* (PRES **wirft**, IMPERF **warf**, PERF **hat geworfen**) to throw.

Werk *das* (PL die **Werke**) 1 work; 2 works (*a factory*).

Werken *das* handicraft.

Werkstatt *die* (PL die **Werkstätten**) workshop.

Werktag *der* (PL die **Werktage**) weekday.

werktags *adverb* on weekdays.

Werkzeug *das* (PL die **Werkzeuge**) tool.

wert *adjective* **viel wert sein** to be worth a lot; **nichts wert sein** to be worthless.

Wert *der* (PL die **Werte**) 1 value; **im Wert von hundert Mark** worth one hundred marks; 2 **auf etwas Wert legen** to attach importance to something; 3 **es hat doch keinen Wert** there's no point.

wertlos *adjective* worthless.

wertvoll *adjective* valuable.

Wesen *das* (PL die **Wesen**) 1 nature, manner; 2 creature.

△ NEW SPELLING: *See page xii*

wesentlich *adjective* essential; **im Wesentlichen** △ essentially. *adverb* considerably.

weshalb *adverb* why.

Wespe *die* (PL *die* **Wespen**) wasp.

wessen *pronoun* whose.

Wessi *der* (*informal*) (PL *die* **Wessis**) West German.

Weste *die* (PL *die* **Westen**) waistcoat.

Westen *der* west.

Westinder *der* (PL *die* **Westinder**) West Indian.

Westinderin *die* (PL *die* **Westinderinnen**) West Indian.

westlich *adjective* 1 western; 2 westerly. *adverb, preposition* ←(+GEN) **westlich von Wien** west of Vienna; **westlich der Stadt** to the west of the town.

weswegen *adverb* why.

Wettbewerb *der* (PL *die* **Wettbewerbe**) competition, contest.

Wette *die* (PL *die* **Wetten**) bet; **mit jemandem um die Wette laufen** to race somebody.

wetten *verb* (PERF **hat gewettet**) to bet; **mit jemandem um etwas wetten** to bet somebody something.

Wetter *das* weather.

Wetterbericht *der* (PL *die* **Wetterberichte**) weather report.

Wettervorhersage *die* weather forecast.

Wettkampf *der* (PL *die* **Wettkämpfe**) contest.

Wettlauf *der* race.

wichtig *adjective* important.

wickeln *verb* (PERF **hat gewickelt**) 1 to wind; 2 **ein Kind wickeln** to change a baby.

Widder *der* (PL *die* **Widder**) 1 ram; 2 Aries; **Jan ist Widder** Jan's Aries.

widerlich *adjective* disgusting.

widersprechen ✧ *verb* (PRES **widerspricht**, IMPERF **widersprach**, PERF **hat widersprochen**) to contradict.

Widerspruch *der* (PL *die* **Widersprüche**) contradiction.

Widerstand *der* resistance.

widerstehen ✧ *verb* (IMPERF **widerstand**, PERF **hat widerstanden**) to resist.

widmen *verb* (PERF **hat gewidmet**) 1 to dedicate; 2 to devote; 3 **sich einer Sache widmen** to devote yourself to something.

wie *adverb* 1 how; **wie geht's?** how are you?; **wie viel?** △ how much?, how many?; **um wie viel** △ **Uhr kommst du?** (at) what time are you coming?; 2 **wie ist Ihr Name?** what is your name?; **wie ist das Wetter?** what's the weather like?; 3 **wie bitte?** sorry? *conjunction* 1 as; **so schnell wie möglich** as quickly as possible; 2 like; **wie du** like you; 3 **wie zum Beispiel** such as.

wieder *adverb* 1 again; **sie ist**

✧ IRREGULAR VERB: *See the verb table in the centre of the dictionary*

wieder da she's back again;
2 **jemanden wieder erkennen** Δ to
recognize somebody; **etwas wieder
finden** Δ to find something (again);
etwas wieder verwerten Δ to
recycle something.

wiederbekommen ◇ *verb* (IMPERF
bekam wieder, PERF **hat
wiederbekommen**) to get back.

wiedererkennen SEE **wieder**.

wiederfinden SEE **wieder**.

wiederholen *verb* (PERF **hat
wiederholt**) 1 to repeat; 2 to revise
(*work at school*); 3 **sich
wiederholen** to recur; **er hat sich
wiederholt** he's repeated himself.

Wiederholung *die* (PL *die*
Wiederholungen) 1 repetition;
2 repeat; 3 revision (*at school*).

Wiederhören *das* **auf
Wiederhören!** (*said on the phone*)
goodbye!

wiederkommen ◇ *verb* (IMPERF
kam wieder, PERF **ist
wiedergekommen**) 1 to come back;
2 to come again.

wiedersehen SEE **sehen**.

Wiedersehen *das* (PL *die*
Wiedersehen) 1 reunion; 2 **auf
Wiedersehen!** goodbye!

wiedervereinigen SEE **vereinigen**.

Wiedervereinigung *die*
reunification.

wiederverwerten SEE **wieder**.

Wiege *die* (PL *die* **Wiegen**) cradle.

wiegen ◇ *verb* (IMPERF **wog**, PERF **hat
gewogen**) to weigh.

Wiegenlied *das* (PL *die*
Wiegenlieder) lullaby.

Wien *das* Vienna.

Wiese *die* (PL *die* **Wiesen**) meadow.

wieso *adverb* why.

wieviel SEE **wie**.

wievielmal *adverb* how often.

**wievielter, wievielte,
wievieltes** *adjective* 1 which;
2 **die wievielte Querstraße ist das
von hier aus?** how many roads is
that from here?; **der Wievielte ist
heute?** what's the date today?

wild *adjective* wild.

Wildleder *das* suede.

Wildpark *der* (PL *die* **Wildparks**)
wildlife park.

will SEE **wollen**.

Wille *der* will; **seinen Willen
durchsetzen** to get your own way.

willkommen *adjective* welcome.

willst SEE **wollen**.

Wimper *die* (PL *die* **Wimpern**)
eyelash.

Wimperntusche *die* (PL *die*
Wimperntuschen) mascara.

Wind *der* (PL *die* **Winde**) wind.

Windel *die* (PL *die* **Windeln**) nappy.

Windhund *der* (PL *die* **Windhunde**)
greyhound.

windig *adjective* windy.

Δ NEW SPELLING: *See page xii*

Windmühle *die* (PL *die* **Windmühlen**) windmill.

Windpocken *plural noun* chickenpox.

Windschutzscheibe *die* (PL *die* **Windschutzscheiben**) windscreen.

Winkel *der* (PL *die* **Winkel**) 1 angle; 2 corner.

winken *verb* (PERF **hat gewinkt**) to wave.

Winter *der* (PL *die* **Winter**) winter.

winzig *adjective* tiny.

wir *pronoun* we; **wir sind es** it's us; **wir alle** all of us.

Wirbelsäule *die* (PL *die* **Wirbelsäulen**) spine.

wirbt SEE **werben**.

wird SEE **werden**.

wirft SEE **werfen**.

wirken *verb* (PERF **hat gewirkt**) 1 to have an effect; 2 **gegen etwas wirken** to be effective against something; 3 to seem (*sad, happy*).

wirklich *adjective* real. *adverb* really.

Wirklichkeit *die* reality.

wirksam *adjective* effective.

Wirkung *die* (PL *die* **Wirkungen**) effect.

wirst SEE **werden**.

Wirt *der* (PL *die* **Wirte**) landlord.

Wirtin *die* (PL *die* **Wirtinnen**) landlady.

Wirtschaft *die* (PL *die* **Wirtschaften**) 1 economy; 2 pub.

wirtschaftlich *adjective* economic.

Wirtshaus *das* (PL *die* **Wirtshäuser**) pub.

wischen *verb* (PERF **hat gewischt**) to wipe.

wissen ✧ *verb* (PRES **weiß**, IMPERF **wusste** Δ, PERF **hat gewusst** Δ) to know; **ich weiß, dass er in London wohnt** I know he lives in London; **ich wüsste gern ...** I'd like to know ...; **von etwas wissen** to know about something; **weißt du was?** you know what?

Wissen *das* knowledge.

Wissenschaft *die* (PL *die* **Wissenschaften**) science.

Wissenschaftler *der* (PL *die* **Wissenschaftler**) scientist.

Wissenschaftlerin *die* (PL *die* **Wissenschaftlerinnen**) scientist.

wissenschaftlich *adjective* scientific.

Witwe *die* (PL *die* **Witwen**) widow.

Witwer *der* (PL *die* **Witwer**) widower.

Witz *der* (PL *die* **Witze**) joke.

witzig *adjective* funny.

wo *adverb* where; **wo seid ihr gewesen?** where have you been?; **in München, wo Markus seit einem Jahr lebt** in Munich, where Markus has been living for a year; **wo immer** wherever. *conjunction* 1 seeing that;

✧ IRREGULAR VERB: *See the verb table in the centre of the dictionary*

2 although; **jetzt ist sie mir böse, wo ich doch so nett zu ihr war** now she's angry with me, although I've been so nice to her.

woanders *adverb* elsewhere.

Woche *die* (PL *die* **Wochen**) week.

Wochenende *das* (PL *die* **Wochenenden**) weekend.

wochenlang *adverb* for weeks.

Wochentag *der* (PL *die* **Wochentage**) weekday.

wochentags *adverb* on weekdays.

wöchentlich *adjective* weekly.

wofür *adverb* what … for; **wofür brauchst du das Geld?** what do you need the money for?

wog SEE **wiegen**.

woher *adverb* where … from; **woher ist er?** where does he come from?; **woher weißt du das?** how do you know?

wohin *adverb* where … (to); **wohin geht ihr?** where are you going?

wohl *adverb* **1** well; **sich wohl fühlen** to feel well; **ich fühle mich heute nicht wohl** I don't feel well today; **2 sich wohl fühlen** to be happy; **Anni fühlt sich in London wohl** Anni is happy in London; **3 jemandem wohl tun** △ to do somebody good; **4** probably; **er hat den Zug wohl verpasst** he probably missed the train; **du bist wohl verrückt!** you must be mad!; **5 wohl kaum** hardly.

Wohl *das* **1** welfare, well-being; **2 zu**

seinem Wohl for his benefit; **3 zum Wohl!** cheers!

wohlhabend *adjective* well-off.

wohltun SEE **wohl**.

wohnen *verb* (PERF **hat gewohnt**) **1** to live; **2** to stay (*for a short time*).

Wohngemeinschaft *die* (PL *die* **Wohngemeinschaften**) people sharing a flat/house; **wir wohnen in einer Wohngemeinschaft** we share a flat.

wohnhaft *adjective* resident.

Wohnheim *das* (PL *die* **Wohnheime**) **1** hostel; **2** home (*for old people*).

Wohnort *der* (PL *die* **Wohnorte**) place of residence.

Wohnsitz *der* (PL *die* **Wohnsitze**) place of residence.

Wohnung *die* (PL *die* **Wohnungen**) flat.

Wohnwagen *der* (PL *die* **Wohnwagen**) caravan.

Wohnzimmer *das* (PL *die* **Wohnzimmer**) living room.

Wolf *der* (PL *die* **Wölfe**) wolf.

Wolke *die* (PL *die* **Wolken**) cloud.

Wolkenkratzer *der* (PL *die* **Wolkenkratzer**) skyscraper.

wolkig *adjective* cloudy.

Wolldecke *die* (PL *die* **Wolldecken**) blanket.

Wolle *die* wool.

wollen ◇ *verb* (PRES **will**, IMPERF **wollte**, PERF **hat gewollt**) **1** to want; **Anne will einen Hund** Anne wants a dog; **ich will nach Hause** I want to go home; **2 sie wollte gerade gehen** she was just about to go; **3 ganz wie du willst** as you like.

womit *adverb* **1** what … with; **womit hast du das gewaschen?** what did you wash it with?; **2** with which.

womöglich *adverb* possibly.

wonach *adverb* **1** what … for; **wonach suchst du?** what are you looking for?; **wonach riecht es?** what does it smell of?; **2** after which, according to which; **eine Regelung, wonach wir eine Stunde mehr arbeiten müssen** a rule according to which we have to work an extra hour.

woran *adverb* what … of; **1 woran denkst du?** what are you thinking of?; **woran hast du ihn erkannt?** how did you recognize him?; **2** on which, of which; **nichts, woran man sich verletzen könnte** nothing you could hurt yourself on.

worauf *adverb* **1** what … on, what … for; **worauf hast du die Vase gestellt?** what did you put the vase on?; **worauf wartet ihr?** what are you waiting for?; **2** on which, for which; **das Regal, worauf das Radio steht** the shelf the radio is on; **das Einzige, worauf ich mich freue** the only thing I'm looking forward to.

woraus *adverb* **1** what … from, what … of; **woraus ist das?** what's it made of?; **2** from which; **es gibt nichts, woraus wir trinken können** there isn't anything we can drink out of.

worin *adverb* **1** what … in, in what; **2** in which; **die Punkte, worin ich mit dir übereinstimme** the points I agree with you on.

Wort *das* (PL *die* **Worte/Wörter**) word; **mir fehlen die Worte** I'm lost for words; **ich habe heute zwanzig neue Wörter gelernt** I've learnt twenty new words today.

Wörterbuch *das* (PL *die* **Wörterbücher**) dictionary.

wörtlich *adjective* word for word.

Wortschatz *der* vocabulary.

Wortspiel *das* (PL *die* **Wortspiele**) pun.

worüber *adverb* **1** what … over, what … about; **worüber lacht ihr?** what are you laughing about?; **2** over which, about which.

worum *adverb* **1** about what; **worum geht es?** what's it about?; **worum hat sie dich gebeten?** what did she ask you for?; **2** for which; **3** round which.

wovon *adverb* **1** what … from, what … about; **wovon redet ihr?** what are you talking about?; **2** from which, about which; **der Geruch, wovon mir schlecht geworden ist** the smell which made me feel sick.

wovor *adverb* **1** what … of; **wovor hast du Angst?** what are you frightened of?; **2** in front of what; **3** of which; **4** in front of which; **der Turm, wovor wir stehen** the tower we are standing in front of.

wozu *adverb* **1** what … for, why; **wozu brauchst du das?** what do

you need it for?; **wozu?** what for?;
2 to which, for which; **wozu ich dir
raten würde** which I would advise.

Wrack *das* (PL *die* **Wracks**) wreck.

wuchs SEE **wachsen**.

Wuchs *der* growth.

wund *adjective* sore.

Wunde *die* (PL *die* **Wunden**) wound.

Wunder *das* (PL *die* **Wunder**) miracle;
kein Wunder! no wonder!

wunderbar *adjective* wonderful.

wundern *verb* (PERF **hat sich
gewundert) sich wundern** to be
surprised.

wunderschön *adjective* beautiful.

wundervoll *adjective* wonderful.

Wunsch *der* (PL *die* **Wünsche**) wish;
auf Wunsch on request; **haben Sie
sonst noch einen Wunsch?** will
there be anything else?

wünschen *verb* (PERF **hat
gewünscht) 1** to wish; **ich wünsche
dir alles Gute zum Geburtstag** I
wish you a happy birthday; **ich
wünschte, ich könnte …** I wish I
could …; **was wünschen Sie?** can I
help you?; **2 sich etwas wünschen**
to want something.

wünschenswert *adjective*
desirable.

**wurde, würde, wurden,
würden, wurdest, würdest,
wurdet, würdet** SEE **werden**.

Wurf *der* (PL *die* **Würfe**) throw.

Würfel *der* (PL *die* **Würfel**) **1** dice (*in
games*); **2** cube.

würfeln *verb* (PERF **hat gewürfelt**) to
throw the dice.

Wurm *der* (PL *die* **Würmer**) worm.

Wurst *die* (PL *die* **Würste**) **1** sausage;
2 das ist mir Wurst (*informal*) I
couldn't care less.

Würstchen *das* (PL *die* **Würstchen**)
(little) sausage.

Wurzel *die* (PL *die* **Wurzeln**) root.

würzen *verb* (PERF **hat gewürzt**) to
season.

würzig *adjective* spicy.

wusch SEE **waschen**.

wusste △ SEE **wissen**.

Wüste *die* (PL *die* **Wüsten**) desert.

Wut *die* rage; **eine Wut auf jemanden
haben** to be furious with somebody.

wütend *adjective* furious.

X x

x-beliebig *adjective* (*informal*)
any; **eine x-beliebige Zahl** any
number (you like).

x-mal *adverb* (*informal*) umpteen
times; **zum x-ten Mal** for the
umpteenth time.

Xylophon *das* (PL *die* **Xylophone**)
xylophone.

△ NEW SPELLING: *See page xii*

Y y

Yoga *das* yoga.

Ypsilon *das* (PL *die* **Ypsilons**) Y.

Z z

zaghaft *adjective* **1** timid;
2 tentative.

zäh *adjective* tough.

Zahl *die* (PL *die* **Zahlen**) **1** number;
2 figure.

zahlen *verb* (PERF **hat gezahlt**) **1** to
pay; **hast du schon gezahlt?** have
you paid?; **2** to pay for; **bitte zahlen!**
the bill please!

zählen *verb* (PERF **hat gezählt**) **1** to
count; **auf jemanden zählen** to
count on somebody; **jemanden zu
seinen Freunden zählen** to count
somebody among your friends;
2 zählen zu to be one of.

Zähler *der* (PL *die* **Zähler**) meter.

zahlreich *adjective* numerous.

Zahlung *die* (PL *die* **Zahlungen**)
payment.

Zählung *die* (PL *die* **Zählungen**)
1 count; **2** census.

zahm *adjective* tame.

Zahn *der* (PL *die* **Zähne**) tooth.

Zahnarzt *der* (PL *die* **Zahnärzte**)
dentist.

Zahnärztin *die* (PL *die*
Zahnärztinnen) dentist.

Zahnbürste *die* (PL *die*
Zahnbürsten) toothbrush.

Zahnfleisch *das* gums.

Zahnpasta *die* (PL *die* **Zahnpasten**)
toothpaste.

Zahnschmerzen *plural noun*
toothache.

Zange *die* (PL *die* **Zangen**) pliers.

zanken *verb* (PERF **hat sich gezankt**)
sich zanken to squabble.

zappeln *verb* (PERF **hat gezappelt**)
1 to wriggle; **2** to fidget.

zart *adjective* **1** delicate, soft;
2 gentle; **3** tender.

zärtlich *adjective* affectionate.

Zauber *der* **1** magic; **2** spell.

Zauberer *der* (PL *die* **Zauberer**)
magician, conjurer.

zauberhaft *adjective* enchanting.

zaubern *verb* (PERF **hat gezaubert**)
to do magic.

Zaun *der* (PL *die* **Zäune**) fence.

z.B. (*zum Beispiel*) e.g.

Zebra *das* (PL *die* **Zebras**) zebra.

Zebrastreifen *der* (PL *die*
Zebrastreifen) zebra crossing.

Zeh *der* (PL *die* **Zehen**) toe.

Zehe *die* (PL *die* **Zehen**) **1** toe;
2 clove (*of garlic*).

✧ IRREGULAR VERB: *See the verb table in the centre of the dictionary*

zehn *number* ten.

Zehntel *das* (PL *die* **Zehntel**) tenth.

zehnter, zehnte, zehntes *adjective* tenth.

Zeichen *das* (PL *die* **Zeichen**) 1 sign; 2 signal.

zeichnen *verb* (PERF **hat gezeichnet**) to draw.

Zeichnung *die* (PL *die* **Zeichnungen**) drawing.

Zeigefinger *der* (PL *die* **Zeigefinger**) index finger.

zeigen *verb* (PERF **hat gezeigt**) 1 to show; **Peter hat uns sein neues Auto gezeigt** Peter showed us his new car; 2 to point; **auf jemanden zeigen** to point at somebody; 3 **sich zeigen** to appear; 4 **es hat sich gezeigt, dass** … it has become clear that …; **es wird sich zeigen** time will tell.

Zeiger *der* (PL *die* **Zeiger**) hand.

Zeile *die* (PL *die* **Zeilen**) line.

Zeit *die* (PL *die* **Zeiten**) 1 time; **sich Zeit lassen** to take your time; **ich habe keine Zeit mehr** I haven't got any more time; **eine Zeit lang** △ for a time; 2 **es hat Zeit** there's no hurry; **die erste Zeit** at first; **in nächster Zeit** in the near future.

Zeitalter *das* (PL *die* **Zeitalter**) age.

Zeitlang *die* SEE **Zeit**.

Zeitlupe *die* slow motion; **in Zeitlupe** in slow motion.

Zeitraum *der* (PL *die* **Zeiträume**) period.

Zeitschrift *die* (PL *die* **Zeitschriften**) magazine.

Zeitung *die* (PL *die* **Zeitungen**) newspaper.

Zeitverschwendung *die* waste of time.

zeitweise *adverb* at times.

Zeitungshändler *der* (PL *die* **Zeitungshändler**) newsagent.

Zelle *die* (PL *die* **Zellen**) 1 cell; 2 booth.

Zelt *das* (PL *die* **Zelte**) tent.

zelten *verb* (PERF **hat gezeltet**) to camp.

Zeltplatz *der* (PL *die* **Zeltplätze**) campsite.

Zement *der* cement.

Zentimeter *der* (PL *die* **Zentimeter**) centimetre.

Zentimetermaß *das* (PL *die* **Zentimetermaße**) tape measure.

zentral *adjective* central.

Zentrale *die* (PL *die* **Zentralen**) 1 central office, head office; 2 headquarters; 3 (telephone) exchange, switchboard.

Zentralheizung *die* central heating.

Zentrum *das* (PL *die* **Zentren**) centre.

zerbrechen ◇ *verb* (PRES **zerbricht**, IMPERF **zerbrach**, PERF **hat zerbrochen**) 1 to break; **Irene hat meine Vase zerbrochen** Irene broke my vase; 2 (PERF **ist zerbrochen**) to break; **die**

△ NEW SPELLING: *See page xii*

Untertasse ist zerbrochen the saucer broke.

zerbrechlich *adjective* fragile.

Zeremonie *die* (PL *die* **Zeremonien**) ceremony.

zerreißen ✧ *verb* (IMPERF **zerriss** △, PERF **hat zerrissen**) 1 to tear; **sie hat sich das Kleid zerrissen** she tore her dress; 2 to tear up; **Anna hat seinen Brief zerrissen** Anna tore up his letter; 3 (PERF **ist zerrissen**) to tear; **das Hemd ist in der Wäsche zerrissen** the shirt got torn in the washing.

zerschlagen ✧ *verb* (PRES **zerschlägt**, IMPERF **zerschlug**, PERF **hat zerschlagen**) 1 to smash, to smash up; 2 **sich zerschlagen** to fall through (*of plans*); **meine Hoffnungen haben sich zerschlagen** my hopes were dashed.

zerschneiden ✧ *verb* (IMPERF **zerschnitt**, PERF **hat zerschnitten**) to cut, to cut up.

zerstören *verb* (PERF **hat zerstört**) to destroy.

Zerstörung *die* destruction.

zerstreuen *verb* (PERF **hat zerstreut**) 1 to scatter; 2 **jemanden zerstreuen** to entertain somebody; 3 **sich zerstreuen** to take your mind off things; 4 **die Menge hat sich zerstreut** the crowd's dispersed.

zerstreut *adjective* absent-minded.

Zettel *der* (PL *die* **Zettel**) 1 piece of paper; 2 note; 3 leaflet.

Zeug *das* (*informal*) 1 stuff; 2 things, gear; 3 **dummes Zeug** nonsense.

Zeuge *der* (PL *die* **Zeugen**) witness.

Zeugin *die* (PL *die* **Zeuginnen**) witness.

Zeugnis *das* (PL *die* **Zeugnisse**) 1 certificate; 2 report (*at school*).

Zickzack *der* (PL *die* **Zickzacke**) zigzag; **im Zickzack laufen** to zigzag.

Ziege *die* (PL *die* **Ziegen**) goat.

Ziegel *der* (PL *die* **Ziegel**) 1 brick; 2 tile.

ziehen ✧ *verb* (IMPERF **zog**, PERF **hat gezogen**) 1 to pull; **an etwas ziehen** to pull on something; **einen Zahn ziehen** to pull out a tooth; 2 to draw; **einen Strich ziehen** to draw a line; **eine Niete ziehen** to draw a blank; 3 **die Bremse ziehen** to put on the brakes; 4 to grow (*vegetables, flowers*); 5 **sich ziehen** to run (*of a path, road*); 6 (PERF **ist gezogen**) to move; **sie sind nach Berlin gezogen** they've moved to Berlin.

Ziel *das* (PL *die* **Ziele**) 1 destination; 2 goal, aim; 3 finish (*in sport*).

zielen *verb* (PERF **hat gezielt**) to aim; **auf etwas zielen** to aim at something.

Zielscheibe *die* (PL *die* **Zielscheiben**) target.

ziemlich *adjective* fair. *adverb* 1 quite; **ziemlich viel** quite a lot; 2 fairly; **ihre Eltern haben ein**

✧ IRREGULAR VERB: *See the verb table in the centre of the dictionary*

ziemlich großes Haus her parents have a fairly large house.

zierlich *adjective* dainty.

Ziffer *die* (PL *die* **Ziffern**) figure.

Zifferblatt *das* (PL *die* **Zifferblätter**) face, dial.

zig *adjective* (*informal*) umpteen.

Zigarette *die* (PL *die* **Zigaretten**) cigarette.

Zigarre *die* (PL *die* **Zigarren**) cigar.

Zigeuner *der* (PL *die* **Zigeuner**) gypsy.

Zigeunerin *die* (PL *die* **Zigeunerinnen**) gypsy.

Zimmer *das* (PL *die* **Zimmer**) room; **Zimmer mit Frühstück** bed and breakfast; **'Zimmer frei'** 'vacancies'.

Zimmermädchen *das* (PL *die* **Zimmermädchen**) chambermaid.

Zimt *der* cinnamon.

Zink *das* zinc.

zirka *adverb* about.

Zirkel *der* (PL *die* **Zirkel**) pair of compasses.

Zirkus *der* (PL *die* **Zirkusse**) circus.

zischen *verb* (PERF **hat gezischt**) to hiss.

Zitat *das* (PL *die* **Zitate**) quotation.

zitieren *verb* (PERF **hat zitiert**) to quote.

Zitrone *die* (PL *die* **Zitronen**) lemon.

Zitronensaft *der* (PL *die* **Zitronensäfte**) lemon juice.

zittern *verb* (PERF **hat gezittert**) to tremble; **vor Kälte zittern** to shiver.

Zivildienst *der* community service.

Zivilisation *die* (PL *die* **Zivilisationen**) civilization.

zog SEE **ziehen**.

zögern *verb* (PERF **hat gezögert**) to hesitate.

Zoll *der* (PL *die* **Zölle**) **1** customs; **am Zoll** at customs; **2** duty; **Zoll auf etwas bezahlen** to pay duty on something.

Zollbeamte *der* (PL *die* **Zollbeamten**) customs officer.

Zollbeamtin *die* (PL *die* **Zollbeamtinnen**) customs officer.

zollfrei *adjective* duty-free.

Zollkontrolle *die* (PL *die* **Zollkontrollen**) customs check.

Zone *die* (PL *die* **Zonen**) zone.

Zoo *der* (PL *die* **Zoos**) Zoo.

Zoomobjektiv *das* (PL *die* **Zoomobjektive**) zoom lens.

Zopf *der* (PL *die* **Zöpfe**) plait.

Zorn *der* anger.

zornig *adjective* angry.

zu *preposition* ←(+DAT) **1** to; **ich gehe zum Arzt** I'm going to the doctor's; **zu einer Party eingeladen sein** to be invited to a party; **2 zu … hin** towards; **zum Fenster hin** towards the window; **er kam zu dieser Tür herein** he came in through this door; **3** with; **das passt nicht zu meinem Mantel** it doesn't go with

△ NEW SPELLING: *See page xii*

my coat; **es gab Wein zum Käse** there was wine with the cheese; **4** at; **zu Weihnachten** at Christmas; **zu Hause** at home; **5 zu etwas werden** to turn into something; **6 zu diesem Zweck** for this purpose; **was schenkst du Karin zum Geburtstag?** what are you giving Karin for her birthday?; **zum Spaß** for fun; **zum ersten Mal** for the first time; **7 sich zu etwas äußern** to comment on something; **Papier zum Schreiben** paper to write on; **8 nett zu jemandem sein** to be nice to somebody; **9 sie waren zu zweit** there were two of them; **eine Marke zu achtzig Pfennig** an 80-pfennig stamp; **es steht drei zu zwei** the score is 3–2; **10 zu Fuß** on foot.
adverb **1** too; **zu groß** too big; **2** closed; **zu haben** ∆ to be closed; **Tür zu!** (*informal*) shut the door!; **3 zu sein** ∆ to be closed; **alle Läden sind zu gewesen** the shops were all closed; **4** towards (*indicating direction*); **5 mach zu!** (*informal*) hurry up!
conjunction to; **nichts zu essen** nothing to eat; **zu verkaufen** for sale.

zuallererst *adverb* first of all.

zuallerletzt *adverb* last of all.

Zubehör *das* accessories.

zubereiten *verb* (PERF **hat zubereitet**) to prepare; **sie bereitet das Essen zu** she's preparing the meal.

zubinden ✧ *verb* (IMPERF **band zu**, PERF **hat zugebunden**) to tie, to tie up.

zubringen ✧ *verb* (IMPERF **brachte zu**, PERF **hat zugebracht**) to spend; **sie bringt viel Zeit bei ihrem Freund zu** she spends a lot of time with her boyfriend.

Zucchini *plural noun* courgettes.

züchten *verb* (PERF **hat gezüchtet**) to breed.

zucken *verb* (PERF **hat gezuckt**) to twitch.

Zucker *der* sugar.

Zuckerguss ∆ *der* icing.

zuckerkrank *adjective* diabetic.

zudecken *verb* (PERF **hat zugedeckt**) **1** to cover up, to cover; **2** to tuck up (*in bed*).

zueinander *adverb* **1** to one another; **lieb zueinander sein** to be nice to one another; **2** together; **zueinander passen** to go together; **zueinander halten** ∆ to stick together.

zuerst *adverb* **1** first; **2** at first.

Zufahrt *die* (PL *die* **Zufahrten**) **1** access; **2** drive(way).

Zufall *der* (PL *die* **Zufälle**) **1** chance; **durch Zufall** by chance; **2** coincidence; **so ein komischer Zufall** such a strange coincidence; **per Zufall traf ich ihn in der U-Bahn** I happened to meet him on the tube.

zufällig *adjective* chance; **das war rein zufällig** it was purely by chance.
adverb by chance; **kannst du mir zufällig zehn Mark leihen?** could

✧ IRREGULAR VERB: *See the verb table in the centre of the dictionary*

you lend me ten marks by any chance?

zufrieden *adjective* **1** content; **2** satisfied; **mit etwas zufrieden sein** to be satisfied with something. *adverb* **jemanden zufrieden lassen** Δ to leave somebody in peace; **jemanden zufrieden stellen** Δ to satisfy somebody.

zufriedenlassen, zufriedenstellen SEE **zufrieden**.

Zug *der* (PL *die* **Züge**) **1** train; **2** procession; **3** characteristic, trait; **4** move (*in games*); **5** swig (*when drinking*); **6** drag (*when smoking*); **7 in einem Zug** in one go.

Zugabe *die* (PL *die* **Zugaben**) **1** free gift; **2** encore.

Zugang *der* (PL *die* **Zugänge**) access.

zugeben ◇ *verb* (PRES **gibt zu**, IMPERF **gab zu**, PERF **hat zugegeben**) **1** to add; **2** to admit.

zugehen ◇ *verb* (IMPERF **ging zu**, PERF **ist zugegangen**) **1** to close, to shut; **die Tür geht nicht zu** the door won't shut; **2 auf etwas zugehen** to go towards something; **auf jemanden zugehen** to walk up to somebody; **3 jemandem zugehen** to be sent to somebody; **4 auf der Party ging es lustig zu** the party was good fun; **5 dem Ende zugehen** to be nearing the end.

zügig *adjective* quick.

zugreifen ◇ *verb* (IMPERF **griff zu**, PERF **hat zugegriffen**) **1** to grab it/them; **2** to help yourself; **3** to lend a hand.

zugunsten *preposition* ←(+GEN) in favour of.

zuhaben SEE **zu**.

Zuhause *das* home.

zuhören *verb* (PERF **hat zugehört**) to listen.

Zuhörer *der* (PL *die* **Zuhörer**) listener.

Zuhörerin *die* (PL *die* **Zuhörerinnen**) listener.

zukommen ◇ *verb* (IMPERF **kam zu**, PERF **ist zugekommen**) **1 auf jemanden zukommen** to come up to somebody; **nächstes Jahr kommt eine Menge Arbeit auf mich zu** I'm in for a lot of work next year; **2 jemandem etwas zukommen lassen** to give somebody something; **3 etwas auf sich zukommen lassen** to take things as they come.

Zukunft *die* future.

zukünftig *adjective* future.

zulassen ◇ *verb* (PRES **lässt zu** Δ, IMPERF **ließ zu**, PERF **hat zugelassen**) **1** to allow; **2** to register (*a car*); **3** to leave closed.

Zulassung *die* (PL *die* **Zulassungen**) **1** registration; **2** admission.

zuletzt *adverb* **1** last; **2** in the end.

zum = **zu dem**; **1 etwas zum Lesen** something to read; **2 spätestens zum fünften März** by 5 March at the latest; **3 er hat es zum Fenster hinausgeworfen** he threw it out of the window.

zumachen *verb* (PERF **hat zugemacht**) **1** to close, to shut; **2** to fasten.

zumindest *adverb* at least.

zunächst *adverb* **1** first (of all); **2** at first.

Zuname *der* (PL *die* **Zunamen**) surname.

zunehmen ◇ *verb* (PRES **nimmt zu**, IMPERF **nahm zu**, PERF **hat zugenommen**) **1** to increase; **2** to put on weight.

Zunge *die* (PL *die* **Zungen**) tongue.

zur = **zu der.**

zurechtkommen ◇ *verb* (IMPERF **kam zurecht**, PERF **ist zurechtgekommen**) to cope, to manage.

zurechtlegen *verb* (PERF **hat zurechtgelegt**) **1** to put out ready; **2 sich eine Ausrede zurechtlegen** to think up an excuse.

zurück *adverb* **1** back; **2 Hamburg, hin und zurück** a return to Hamburg.

zurückbekommen ◇ *verb* (IMPERF **bekam zurück**, PERF **hat zurückbekommen**) to get back; **zehn Pfennig zurückbekommen** to get 10 pfennigs change.

zurückbringen ◇ *verb* (IMPERF **brachte zurück**, PERF **hat zurückgebracht**) **1** to bring back; **2** to take back.

zurückfahren ◇ *verb* (PRES **fährt zurück**, IMPERF **fuhr zurück**, PERF **ist zurückgefahren**) **1** to go back; **2** to drive back; **3** (PERF **hat zurückgefahren**) to drive back; **jemanden zurückfahren** to drive somebody back.

zurückgeben ◇ *verb* (PRES **gibt zurück**, IMPERF **gab zurück**, PERF **hat zurückgegeben**) to give back.

zurückgehen ◇ *verb* (IMPERF **ging zurück**, PERF **ist zurückgegangen**) **1** to go back; **zurückgehen auf** to go back to; **2** to go down; **3** to decrease.

zurückhalten ◇ *verb* (PRES **hält zurück**, IMPERF **hielt zurück**, PERF **hat zurückgehalten**) **1** to hold back; **2 sich zurückhalten** to restrain yourself.

zurückkommen ◇ *verb* (IMPERF **kam zurück**, PERF **ist zurückgekommen**) **1** to come back; **2** to get back.

zurücklassen ◇ *verb* (PRES **lässt zurück** Δ, IMPERF **ließ zurück**, PERF **hat zurückgelassen**) to leave behind.

zurücklegen *verb* (PERF **hat zurückgelegt**) **1** to put back; **2** to keep, to put aside; **3 Geld für etwas zurücklegen** to put money by for something; **4** to cover (*a distance*); **5 sich zurücklegen** to lie back.

zurücknehmen ◇ *verb* (PRES **nimmt zurück**, IMPERF **nahm zurück**, PERF **hat zurückgenommen**) to take back.

zurückrufen ◇ *verb* (IMPERF **rief zurück**, PERF **hat zurückgerufen**) to call back.

zurücktreten ◇ *verb* (PRES **tritt zurück**, IMPERF **trat zurück**, PERF **ist**

◇ IRREGULAR VERB: *See the verb table in the centre of the dictionary*

zurückgetreten) 1 to step back; **2** to resign.

zurückzahlen *verb* (PERF **hat zurückgezahlt**) to pay back.

zurückziehen ✧ *verb* (IMPERF **zog zurück**, PERF **hat zurückgezogen**) **1** to draw back; **2** to withdraw (*an offer*); **3 sich zurückziehen** to withdraw, to retire.

zurzeit Δ *adverb* at the moment.

Zusage *die* (PL *die* **Zusagen**) acceptance.

zusammen *adverb* **1** together; **zusammen sein** to be together; **2** altogether.

Zusammenarbeit *die* co-operation.

zusammenarbeiten *verb* (PERF **hat zusammengearbeitet**) to co-operate.

zusammenbleiben ✧ *verb* (IMPERF **blieb zusammen**, PERF **ist zusammengeblieben**) to stay together.

zusammenbrechen ✧ *verb* (PRES **bricht zusammen**, IMPERF **brach zusammen**, PERF **ist zusammengebrochen**) to collapse.

zusammenfassen *verb* (PERF **hat zusammengefasst** Δ) to summarize.

Zusammenfassung *die* (PL *die* **Zusammenfassungen**) summary.

zusammenhalten ✧ *verb* (PRES **hält zusammen**, IMPERF **hielt zusammen**, PERF **hat zusammengehalten**) **1** to hold together; **2** to keep together; **3 die**

Kinder haben zusammengehalten the children stuck together.

Zusammenhang *der* (PL *die* **Zusammenhänge**) **1** context; **2** connection.

zusammenkommen ✧ *verb* (IMPERF **kam zusammen**, PERF **ist zusammengekommen**) **1** to meet; **2** to accumulate.

Zusammenkunft *die* (PL *die* **Zusammenkünfte**) meeting.

zusammenlegen *verb* (PERF **hat zusammengelegt**) **1** to put together; **2** to fold up; **3** to club together.

zusammennehmen ✧ *verb* (PRES **nimmt zusammen**, IMPERF **nahm zusammen**, PERF **hat zusammengenommen**) **1** to gather up; **2** to summon up, to collect; **3 sich zusammennehmen** to pull yourself together.

zusammenpassen *verb* (PERF **hat zusammengepasst** Δ) **1** to match; **2** to be well matched (*of people*); **3** to fit together.

Zusammensein *das* get-together.

Zusammenstoß *der* (PL *die* **Zusammenstöße**) collision, crash.

zusammenstoßen ✧ *verb* (PRES **stößt zusammen**, IMPERF **stieß zusammen**, PERF **ist zusammengestoßen**) to collide, to crash.

zusammenzählen *verb* (PERF **hat zusammengezählt**) to add up.

Δ NEW SPELLING: *See page xii*

zusätzlich *adjective* additional, extra.
adverb in addition, extra.

zuschauen *verb* (PERF **hat zugeschaut**) to watch.

Zuschauer *der* (PL *die* **Zuschauer**) 1 spectator; 2 viewer; 3 *die* **Zuschauer** the audience.

Zuschauerin *die* (PL *die* **Zuschauerinnen**) 1 spectator; 2 viewer.

Zuschlag *der* (PL *die* **Zuschläge**) 1 surcharge; 2 supplement.

Zuschuss △ *der* (PL *die* **Zuschüsse**) 1 contribution; 2 grant.

zusehen ✧ *verb* (PRES **sieht zu**, IMPERF **sah zu**, PERF **hat zugesehen**) 1 to watch; 2 **zusehen, dass …** to see (to it) that …

zusein SEE **zu**.

zusenden *verb* (PERF **hat zugesendet**) to send; **jemandem etwas zusenden** to send something to somebody.

Zustand *der* (PL *die* **Zustände**) 1 condition; 2 state.

zustande *adverb* **zustande bringen** to bring about; **zustande kommen** to come about.

zuständig *adjective* responsible.

Zustellung *die* (PL *die* **Zustellungen**) delivery.

zustimmen *verb* (PERF **hat zugestimmt**) to agree.

Zustimmung *die* (PL *die* **Zustimmungen**) 1 agreement; 2 approval.

zustoßen ✧ *verb* (PRES **stößt zu**, IMPERF **stieß zu**, PERF **ist zugestoßen**) to happen.

Zutat *die* (PL *die* **Zutaten**) ingredient.

zutreffen ✧ *verb* (PRES **trifft zu**, IMPERF **traf zu**, PERF **hat zugetroffen**) **auf etwas zutreffen** to apply to something.

Zutritt *der* entry; **Zutritt haben** to have access.

zuverlässig *adjective* reliable.

zuviel SEE **viel**.

zuvor *adverb* 1 before; **der Tag zuvor** the day before; 2 first.

zuwenig SEE **wenig**.

zuzahlen *verb* (PERF **hat zugezahlt**) to pay extra.

zuziehen ✧ *verb* (IMPERF **zog zu**, PERF **hat zugezogen**) 1 to pull tight; 2 to draw (*curtains*); 3 to call in (*an expert etc.*); 4 (PERF **ist zugezogen**) to move into an area; 5 **sich eine Verletzung zuziehen** to sustain an injury; **sich eine Erkältung zuziehen** to catch a cold.

zuzüglich *preposition* ←(+GEN) plus.

zwang SEE **zwingen**.

Zwang *der* (PL *die* **Zwänge**) 1 compulsion; 2 urge; 3 obligation.

zwängen *verb* (PERF **hat gezwängt**) to squeeze.

zwanglos *adjective* casual, informal.

✧ IRREGULAR VERB: *See the verb table in the centre of the dictionary*

zwar *adverb* **1** admittedly; **2 ich war zwar dabei, habe aber nichts gesehen** I was there, but I didn't see anything; **3 und zwar** to be exact.

Zweck *der* (PL *die* **Zwecke**) **1** purpose; **2** point; **es hat keinen Zweck** there's no point.

zwecklos *adjective* pointless.

zwei *number* two.

zweideutig *adjective* ambiguous.

zweifach *adjective* twice.

Zweifel *der* (PL *die* **Zweifel**) doubt.

zweifelhaft *adjective* **1** doubtful; **2** dubious.

zweifellos *adverb* undoubtedly.

zweifeln *verb* (PERF **hat gezweifelt**) to doubt; **an etwas zweifeln** to doubt something.

Zweig *der* (PL *die* **Zweige**) branch.

zweihundert *number* two hundred.

zweimal *adverb* twice.

zweisprachig *adjective* bilingual.

zweit *adverb* **zu zweit** in twos; **wir sind zu zweit** there are two of us.

zweite SEE **zweiter**.

zweitens *adverb* secondly.

zweiter, zweite, zweites *adjective* second; **Mario kam als Zweiter** Mario was the second to arrive.

Zwerg *der* (PL *die* **Zwerge**) dwarf.

Zwiebel *die* (PL *die* **Zwiebeln**) **1** onion; **2** bulb.

Zwilling *der* (PL *die* **Zwillinge**) **1** twin; **2 Zwillinge** Gemini; **Markus ist Zwilling** Markus is Gemini.

zwingen ◇ *verb* (IMPERF **zwang**, PERF **hat gezwungen**) **1** to force; **2 sich zwingen** to force yourself.

zwinkern *verb* (PERF **hat gezwinkert**) to wink.

zwischen *preposition* ←(+DAT, *or* +ACC *with movement towards a place*) **1** between; **2** among (*a crowd*).

zwischendurch *adverb* **1** in between; **2** now and again.

Zwischenfall *der* (PL *die* **Zwischenfälle**) incident.

Zwischenlandung *die* (PL *die* **Zwischenlandungen**) stop-over.

Zwischenraum *der* (PL *die* **Zwischenräume**) gap, space.

Zwischenzeit *die* **in der Zwischenzeit** in the meantime.

zwo *number* two.

zwölf *number* twelve.

zwoter, zwote, zwotes *adjective* second.

△ NEW SPELLING: *See page xii*

VERB TABLES AND FORMS

On the following pages you will find forms for a regular German verb **machen** followed by the forms for a reflexive verb **sich waschen** and then the forms for the twelve most important irregular verbs in alphabetical order: **dürfen, essen, fahren, gehen, haben, kommen, können, müssen, sein, sollen, werden, wissen**.

After these are given the main forms for other irregular verbs. Note that the forms for separable verbs such as **aufstehen** are not given as they can be looked up under the base form (**stehen**).

machen
to do *or* to make

Imperative	Past participle
mach!	hat gemacht
macht!	
machen Sie!	

Present
ich mache
du machst
er* macht
wir machen
ihr macht
sie machen

Present subjunctive
ich mache
du machest
er mache
wir machen
ihr machet
sie machen

Perfect
ich habe gemacht
du hast gemacht
er hat gemacht
wir haben gemacht
ihr habt gemacht
sie haben gemacht

Imperfect
ich machte
du machtest
er machte
wir machten
ihr machtet
sie machten

Future
ich werde machen
du wirst machen
er wird machen
wir werden machen
ihr werdet machen
sie werden machen

Conditional
ich würde machen
du würdest machen
er würde machen
wir würden machen
ihr würdet machen
sie würden machen

* er *should be read as* er/sie/es

2

sich waschen
to wash (oneself)

Imperative

wasch dich!
wascht euch!
waschen Sie sich!

Past participle

hat sich
gewaschen

Present

ich wasche mich
du wäschst dich
er wäscht sich
wir waschen uns
ihr wascht euch
sie waschen sich

Present subjunctive

ich wasche mich
du waschest dich
er wasche sich
wir waschen uns
ihr waschet euch
sie waschen sich

Perfect

ich habe mich gewaschen
du hast dich gewaschen
er hat sich gewaschen
wir haben uns gewaschen
ihr habt euch gewaschen
sie haben sich gewaschen

Imperfect

ich wusch mich
du wuschst dich
er wusch sich
wir wuschen uns
ihr wuscht euch
sie wuschen sich

Future

ich werde mich waschen
du wirst dich waschen
er wird sich waschen
wir werden uns waschen
ihr werdet euch waschen
sie werden sich waschen

Conditional

ich würde mich waschen
du würdest dich waschen
er würde sich waschen
wir würden uns waschen
ihr würdet euch waschen
sie würden sich waschen

Note: New German spellings are
used throughout this verb table.
For a general note on the
German spelling reform see
page xii.

dürfen
to be allowed

Imperative	Past participle
—	hat gedurft

Present

ich darf
du darfst
er darf
wir dürfen
ihr dürft
sie dürfen

Present subjunctive

ich dürfe
du dürfest
er dürfe
wir dürfen
ihr dürfet
sie dürfen

Perfect

ich habe gedurft
du hast gedurft
er hat gedurft
wir haben gedurft
ihr habt gedurft
sie haben gedurft

Imperfect

ich durfte
du durftest
er durfte
wir durften
ihr durftet
sie durften

Future

ich werde dürfen
du wirst dürfen
er wird dürfen
wir werden dürfen
ihr werdet dürfen
sie werden dürfen

Conditional

ich würde dürfen
du würdest dürfen
er würde dürfen
wir würden dürfen
ihr würdet dürfen
sie würden dürfen

Imperative	Past participle	**essen**
iss!	hat gegessen	to eat
esst!		
essen Sie!		

Present

ich esse
du isst
er isst
wir essen
ihr esst
sie essen

Perfect

ich habe gegessen
du hast gegessen
er hat gegessen
wir haben gegessen
ihr habt gegessen
sie haben gegessen

Future

ich werde essen
du wirst essen
er wird essen
wir werden essen
ihr werdet essen
sie werden essen

Present subjunctive

ich esse
du essest
er esse
wir essen
ihr esset
sie essen

Imperfect

ich aß
du aßest
er aß
wir aßen
ihr aßt
sie aßen

Conditional

ich würde essen
du würdest essen
er würde essen
wir würden essen
ihr würdet essen
sie würden essen

fahren
to drive *or* to go

Imperative	Past participle
fahr! fahrt! fahren Sie!	ist gefahren

Present

ich fahre
du fährst
er fährt
wir fahren
ihr fahrt
sie fahren

Perfect

ich bin gefahren
du bist gefahren
er ist gefahren
wir sind gefahren
ihr seid gefahren
sie sind gefahren

Future

ich werde fahren
du wirst fahren
er wird fahren
wir werden fahren
ihr werdet fahren
sie werden fahren

Present subjunctive

ich fahre
du fahrest
er fahre
wir fahren
ihr fahret
sie fahren

Imperfect

ich fuhr
du fuhrst
er fuhr
wir fuhren
ihr fuhrt
sie fuhren

Conditional

ich würde fahren
du würdest fahren
er würde fahren
wir würden fahren
ihr würdet fahren
sie würden fahren

Imperative	**Past participle**	**gehen**
geh!	ist gegangen	to go
geht!		
gehen Sie!		

Present

ich gehe
du gehst
er geht
wir gehen
ihr geht
sie gehen

Present subjunctive

ich gehe
du gehest
er gehe
wir gehen
ihr gehet
sie gehen

Perfect

ich bin gegangen
du bist gegangen
er ist gegangen
wir sind gegangen
ihr seid gegangen
sie sind gegangen

Imperfect

ich ging
du gingst
er ging
wir gingen
ihr gingt
sie gingen

Future

ich werde gehen
du wirst gehen
er wird gehen
wir werden gehen
ihr werdet gehen
sie werden gehen

Conditional

ich würde gehen
du würdest gehen
er würde gehen
wir würden gehen
ihr würdet gehen
sie würden gehen

haben
to have

Imperative
hab!
habt!
haben Sie!

Past participle
hat gehabt

Present
ich habe
du hast
er hat
wir haben
ihr habt
sie haben

Present subjunctive
ich habe
du habest
er habe
wir haben
ihr habet
sie haben

Perfect
ich habe gehabt
du hast gehabt
er hat gehabt
wir haben gehabt
ihr habt gehabt
sie haben gehabt

Imperfect
ich hatte
du hattest
er hatte
wir hatten
ihr hattet
sie hatten

Future
ich werde haben
du wirst haben
er wird haben
wir werden haben
ihr werdet haben
sie werden haben

Imperfect subjunctive
ich hätte
du hättest
er hätte
wir hätten
ihr hättet
sie hätten

Conditional
ich würde haben
du würdest haben
er würde haben
wir würden haben
ihr würdet haben
sie würden haben

Imperative	Past participle	**kommen**
komm!	ist gekommen	to come
kommt!		
kommen Sie!		

Present

ich komme
du kommst
er kommt
wir kommen
ihr kommt
sie kommen

Present subjunctive

ich komme
du kommest
er komme
wir kommen
ihr kommet
sie kommen

Perfect

ich bin gekommen
du bist gekommen
er ist gekommen
wir sind gekommen
ihr seid gekommen
sie sind gekommen

Imperfect

ich kam
du kamst
er kam
wir kamen
ihr kamt
sie kamen

Future

ich werde kommen
du wirst kommen
er wird kommen
wir werden kommen
ihr werdet kommen
sie werden kommen

Conditional

ich würde kommen
du würdest kommen
er würde kommen
wir würden kommen
ihr würdet kommen
sie würden kommen

können
can *or* to be able to

Imperative	Past participle
——	hat gekonnt *or* hätte können

Present
ich kann
du kannst
er kann
wir können
ihr könnt
sie können

Perfect
ich habe gekonnt
du hast gekonnt
er hat gekonnt
wir haben gekonnt
ihr habt gekonnt
sie haben gekonnt

Future
ich werde können
du wirst können
er wird können
wir werden können
ihr werdet können
sie werden können

Present subjunctive
ich könne
du könnest
er könne
wir können
ihr könnet
sie können

Imperfect
ich konnte
du konntest
er konnte
wir konnten
ihr konntet
sie konnten

Imperfect subjunctive
ich könnte
du könntest
er könnte
wir könnten
ihr könntet
sie könnten

Conditional
ich würde können
du würdest können
er würde können
wir würden können
ihr würdet können
sie würden können

Imperative	Past participle	**müssen**
—	hat gemusst *or* hätte müssen	must *or* to have to

Present

ich muss
du musst
er muss
wir müssen
ihr müsst
sie müssen

Perfect

ich habe gemusst
du hast gemusst
er hat gemusst
wir haben gemusst
ihr habt gemusst
sie haben gemusst

Future

ich werde müssen
du wirst müssen
er wird müssen
wir werden müssen
ihr werdet müssen
sie werden müssen

Present subjunctive

ich müsse
du müssest
er müsse
wir müssen
ihr müsset
sie müssen

Imperfect

ich musste
du musstest
er musste
wir mussten
ihr musstet
sie mussten

Imperfect subjunctive

ich müsste
du müsstest
er müsste
wir müssten
ihr müsstet
sie müssten

Conditional

ich würde müssen
du würdest müssen
er würde müssen
wir würden müssen
ihr würdet müssen
sie würden müssen

sein
to be

Imperative
sei!
seid!
seien Sie!

Past participle
ist gewesen

Present	**Present subjunctive**
ich bin	ich sei
du bist	du sei(e)st
er ist	er sei
wir sind	wir seien
ihr seid	ihr seiet
sie sind	sie seien

Perfect	**Imperfect**
ich bin gewesen	ich war
du bist gewesen	du warst
er ist gewesen	er war
wir sind gewesen	wir waren
ihr seid gewesen	ihr wart
sie sind gewesen	sie waren

Future	**Imperfect subjunctive**
ich werde sein	ich wäre
du wirst sein	du wär(e)st
er wird sein	er wäre
wir werden sein	wir wären
ihr werdet sein	ihr wär(e)t
sie werden sein	sie wären

Conditional
ich würde sein
du würdest sein
er würde sein
wir würden sein
ihr würdet sein
sie würden sein

Imperative	Past participle	**sollen**
—	hat gesollt	should

Present

ich soll
du sollst
er soll
wir sollen
ihr sollt
sie sollen

Perfect

ich habe gesollt
du hast gesollt
er hat gesollt
wir haben gesollt
ihr habt gesollt
sie haben gesollt

Future

ich werde sollen
du wirst sollen
er wird sollen
wir werden sollen
ihr werdet sollen
sie werden sollen

Present subjunctive

ich solle
du sollest
er solle
wir sollen
ihr sollet
sie sollen

Imperfect

ich sollte
du solltest
er sollte
wir sollten
ihr solltet
sie sollten

Imperfect subjunctive

ich sollte
du solltest
er sollte
wir sollten
ihr solltet
sie sollten

Conditional

ich würde sollen
du würdest sollen
er würde sollen
wir würden sollen
ihr würdet sollen
sie würden sollen

werden
to become *or* to get

Imperative
werde!
werdet!
werden Sie!

Past participle
ist geworden

Present
ich werde
du wirst
er wird
wir werden
ihr werdet
sie werden

Perfect
ich bin geworden
du bist geworden
er ist geworden
wir sind geworden
ihr seid geworden
sie sind geworden

Future
ich werde werden
du wirst werden
er wird werden
wir werden werden
ihr werdet werden
sie werden werden

Present subjunctive
ich werde
du werdest
er werde
wir werden
ihr werdet
sie werden

Imperfect
ich wurde
du wurdest
er wurde
wir wurden
ihr wurdet
sie wurden

Conditional
ich würde werden
du würdest werden
er würde werden
wir würden werden
ihr würdet werden
sie würden werden

Imperative	**Past participle**	**wissen**
wisse!	hat gewusst	to know
wisst!		
wissen Sie!		

Present

ich weiß
du weißt
er weiß
wir wissen
ihr wisst
sie wissen

Present subjunctive

ich wisse
du wissest
er wisse
wir wissen
ihr wisset
sie wissen

Perfect

ich habe gewusst
du hast gewusst
er hat gewusst
wir haben gewusst
ihr habt gewusst
sie haben gewusst

Imperfect

ich wusste
du wusstest
er wusste
wir wussten
ihr wusstet
sie wussten

Future

ich werde wissen
du wirst wissen
er wird wissen
wir werden wissen
ihr werdet wissen
sie werden wissen

Conditional

ich würde wissen
du würdest wissen
er würde wissen
wir würden wissen
ihr würdet wissen
sie würden wissen

German irregular verb forms

This list shows the main forms of other irregular verbs.

Infinitive	Present ich, du, er/sie/es	Imperfect er/sie/es	Perfect er/sie/es
bekommen	bekomme, bekommst, bekommt	bekam	hat bekommen
bergen	berge, birgst, birgt	barg	hat geborgen
besitzen	besitze, besitzst, besitzt	besaß	hat besessen
betrügen	betrüge, betrügst, betrügt	betrog	hat betrogen
biegen	biege, biegst, biegt	bog	hat *or* ist gebogen
bieten	biete, bietest, bietet	bot	hat geboten
binden	binde, bindest, bindet	band	hat gebunden
bitten	bitte, bittest, bittet	bat	hat gebeten
blasen	blase, bläst, bläst	blies	hat geblasen
bleiben	bleibe, bleibst, bleibt	blieb	ist geblieben
braten	brate, brätst, brät	briet	hat gebraten
brechen	breche, brichst, bricht	brach	hat *or* ist gebrochen
brennen	brenne, brennst, brennt	brannte	hat gebrannt
bringen	bringe, bringst, bringt	brachte	hat gebracht
denken	denke, denkst, denkt	dachte	hat gedacht
dürfen	darf, darfst, darf	durfte	hat gedurft
einladen	lade ein, lädst ein, lädt ein	lud ein	hat eingeladen
empfangen	empfange, empfängst, empfängt	empfing	hat empfangen
empfehlen	empfehle, empfiehlst, empfiehlt	empfahl	hat empfohlen
entscheiden	entscheide, entscheidest, entscheidet	entschied	hat entschieden

Infinitive	Present ich, du, er/sie/es	Imperfect er/sie/es	Perfect er/sie/es
erfahren	erfahre, erfährst, erfährt	erfuhr	hat erfahren
erfinden	erfinde, erfindest, erfindet	erfand	hat erfunden
erschrecken	erschrecke, erschrickst, erschrickt	erschrak	ist erschrocken
ertrinken	ertrinke, ertrinkst, ertrinkt	ertrank	ist ertrunken
essen	esse, isst, isst	aß	hat gegessen
fahren	fahre, fährst, fährt	fuhr	ist *or* hat gefahren
fallen	falle, fällst, fällt	fiel	ist gefallen
fangen	fange, fängst, fängt	fing	hat gefangen
fechten	fechte, fichtst, ficht	focht	hat gefochten
finden	finde, findest, findet	fand	hat gefunden
fliegen	fliege, fliegst, fliegt	flog	ist *or* hat geflogen
fliehen	fliehe, fliehst, flieht	floh	ist geflohen
fließen	fließe, fließt, fließt	floss	ist geflossen
fressen	fresse, frisst, frisst	fraß	hat gefressen
frieren	friere, frierst, friert	fror	hat *or* ist gefroren
geben	gebe, gibst, gibt	gab	hat gegeben
gefallen	gefalle, gefällst, gefällt	gefiel	hat gefallen
gehen	gehe, gehst, geht	ging	ist gegangen
gelingen	es gelingt mir/dir/ihm/ihr/ihm	gelang	ist gelungen
gelten	gelte, giltst, gilt	galt	hat gegolten
genießen	genieße, genießt, genießt	genoss	hat genossen
geraten	gerate, gerätst, gerät	geriet	ist geraten
geschehen	es geschieht	geschah	ist geschehen
gewinnen	gewinne, gewinnst, gewinnt	gewann	hat gewonnen
gießen	gieße, gießt, gießt	goss	hat gegossen
gleichen	gleiche, gleichst, gleicht	glich	hat geglichen
graben	grabe, gräbst, gräbt	grub	hat gegraben
greifen	greife, greifst, greift	griff	hat gegriffen

Infinitive	Present ich, du, er/sie/es	Imperfect er/sie/es	Perfect er/sie/es
haben	habe, hast, hat	hatte	hat gehabt
halten	halte, hältst, hält	hielt	hat gehalten
hängen	hänge, hängst, hängt	hing	hat gehangen
heben	hebe, hebst, hebt	hob	hat gehoben
heißen	heiße, heißt, heißt	hieß	hat geheißen
helfen	helfe, hilfst, hilft	half	hat geholfen
hinweisen	weise hin, weist hin, weist hin	wies hin	hat hingewiesen
kennen	kenne, kennst, kennt	kannte	hat gekannt
klingen	klinge, klingst, klingt	klang	hat geklungen
kneifen	kneife, kneifst, kneift	kniff	hat gekniffen
kommen	komme, kommst, kommt	kam	ist gekommen
können	kann, kannst, kann	konnte	hat gekonnt
kriechen	krieche, kriechst, kriecht	kroch	ist gekrochen
lassen	lasse, lässt, lässt	ließ	hat gelassen
laufen	laufe, läufst, läuft	lief	ist gelaufen
leiden	leide, leidest, leidet	litt	hat gelitten
leihen	leihe, leihst, leiht	lieh	hat geliehen
lesen	lese, liest, liest	las	hat gelesen
liegen	liege, liegst, liegt	lag	hat gelegen
lügen	lüge, lügst, lügt	log	hat gelogen
mahlen	mahle, mahlst, mahlt	mahlte	hat gemahlen
meiden	meide, meidest, meidet	mied	hat gemieden
messen	messe, mißt, mißt	maß	hat gemessen
misslingen Δ	misslinge, misslingst, misslingt	misslang	ist misslungen
mögen	mag, magst, mag	mochte	hat gemocht
müssen	muss, musst, muss	musste	hat gemusst

Infinitive	Present ich, du, er/sie/es	Imperfect er/sie/es	Perfect er/sie/es
nehmen	nehme, nimmst, nimmt	nahm	hat genommen
nennen	nenne, nennst, nennt	nannte	hat genannt
pfeifen	pfeife, pfeifst, pfeift	pfiff	hat gepfiffen
raten	rate, rätst, rät	riet	hat geraten
reiben	reibe, reibst, reibt	rieb	hat gerieben
reißen	reiße, reißt, reißt	riss	hat or ist gerissen
reiten	reite, reitest, reitet	ritt	hat or ist geritten
rennen	renne, rennst, rennt	rannte	ist gerannt
riechen	rieche, riechst, riecht	roch	hat gerochen
rufen	rufe, rufst, ruft	rief	hat gerufen
saufen	saufe, säufst, säuft	soff	hat gesoffen
schaffen	schaffe, schaffst, schafft	schuf	hat geschaffen
scheiden	scheide, scheidest, scheidet	schied	hat or ist geschieden
scheinen	scheine, scheinst, scheint	schien	hat geschienen
schieben	schiebe, schiebst, schiebt	schob	hat geschoben
schießen	schieße, schießt, schießt	schoss	hat or ist geschossen
schlafen	schlafe, schläfst, schläft	schlief	hat geschlafen
schlagen	schlage, schlägst, schlägt	schlug	hat geschlagen
schleichen	schleiche, schleichst, schleicht	schlich	ist geschlichen
schließen	schließe, schließt, schließt	schloss	hat geschlossen
schmeißen	schmeiße, schmeißt, schmeißt	schmiss	hat geschmissen
schmelzen	schmelze, schmilzt, schmilzt	schmolz	ist geschmolzen
schneiden	schneide, schneidest, schneidet	schnitt	hat geschnitten

Infinitive	Present ich, du, er/sie/es	Imperfect er/sie/es	Perfect er/sie/es
schreiben	schreibe, schreibst, schreibt	schrieb	hat geschrieben
schreien	schreie, schreist, schreit	schrie	hat geschrien
schweigen	schweige, schweigst, schweigt	schwieg	hat geschwiegen
schwimmen	schwimme, schwimmst, schwimmt	schwamm	ist *or* hat geschwommen
schwören	schwöre, schwörst, schwört	schwor	hat geschworen
sehen	sehe, siehst, sieht	sah	hat gesehen
sein	bin, bist, ist	war	ist gewesen
singen	singe, singst, singt	sang	hat gesungen
sinken	sinke, sinkst, sinkt	sank	ist gesunken
sitzen	sitze, sitzt, sitzt	saß	hat gesessen
sollen	soll, sollst, soll	sollte	hat gesollt
spinnen	spinne, spinnst, spinnt	spann	hat gesponnen
sprechen	spreche, sprichst, spricht	sprach	hat gesprochen
springen	springe, springst, springt	sprang	ist gesprungen
stechen	steche, stichst, sticht	stach	hat gestochen
stehen	stehe, stehst, steht	stand	hat gestanden
stehlen	stehle, stiehlst, stiehlt	stahl	hat gestohlen
steigen	steige, steigst, steigt	stieg	ist gestiegen
sterben	sterbe, stirbst, stirbt	starb	ist gestorben
stinken	stinke, stinkst, stinkt	stank	hat gestunken
stoßen	stoße, stößt, stößt	stieß	hat *or* ist gestoßen
streichen	streiche, streichst, streicht	strich	hat gestrichen
streiten	streite, streitest, streitet	stritt	hat gestritten
tragen	trage, trägst, trägt	trug	hat getragen
treffen	treffe, triffst, trifft	traf	hat getroffen
treiben	treibe, treibst, treibt	trieb	hat getrieben
treten	trete, trittst, tritt	trat	hat *or* ist getreten
trinken	trinke, trinkst, trinkt	trank	hat getrunken
tun	tue, tust, tut	tat	hat getan

Infinitive	Present ich, du, er/sie/es	Imperfect er/sie/es	Perfect er/sie/es
überweisen	überweise, überweist, überweist	überwies	hat überwiesen
umziehen	ziehe um, ziehst um, zieht um	zog um	ist *or* hat umgezogen
verbieten	verbiete, verbietest, verbietet	verbot	hat verboten
verderben	verderbe, verdirbst, verdirbt	verdarb	hat *or* ist verdorben
vergessen	vergesse, vergißt, vergißt	vergaß	hat vergessen
verlieren	verliere, verlierst, verliert	verlor	hat verloren
verschwinden	verschwinde, verschwindest, verschwindet	verschwand	ist verschwunden
verstehen	verstehe, verstehst, versteht	verstand	hat verstanden
verzeihen	verzeihe, verzeihst, verzeiht	verzieh	hat verziehen
wachsen	wachse, wächst, wächst	wuchs	ist gewachsen
waschen	wasche, wäscht, wäscht	wusch	hat gewaschen
werben	werbe, wirbst, wirbt	warb	hat geworben
werden	werde, wirst, wird	wurde	ist geworden
werfen	werfe, wirfst, wirft	warf	hat geworfen
wiegen	wiege, wiegst, wiegt	wog	hat gewogen
wissen	weiß, weißt, weiß	wusste	hat gewusst
wollen	will, willst, will	wollte	hat gewollt
ziehen	ziehe, ziehst, zieht	zog	hat *or* ist gezogen
zwingen	zwinge, zwingst, zwingt	zwang	hat gezwungen

Note: New German spellings are used throughout this verb table. For a general note on the German spelling reform see page xii.

A a

a *indefinite article* **1** (*before a noun which is masculine in German*) ein; **a tree** ein Baum; **2** (*before a noun which is feminine in German*) eine; **a story** eine Geschichte; **3** (*before a noun which is neuter in German*) ein; **a dress** ein Kleid; **4** not a kein; **the party was not a success** die Party war kein Erfolg; **he didn't say a word** er hat kein Wort gesagt; **5** six marks **a kilo** sechs Mark das Kilo; **6** fifty kilometres an hour fünfzig Stundenkilometer; **7** three times a **day** dreimal täglich.

abandon *verb* **1** aufgeben ◇ SEP; **they abandoned the plan** sie gaben den Plan auf; **2** verlassen ◇; **they abandoned the city** sie verließen die Stadt.

abbey *noun* Abtei *die* (PL *die* Abteien).

abbreviation *noun* Abkürzung *die* (PL *die* Abkürzungen).

ability *noun* Fähigkeit *die* (PL *die* Fähigkeiten); **to have the ability to do something** etwas tun können.

about *preposition* **1** über (+ACC); **a film about space** ein Film über den Weltraum; **to talk about something/somebody** über etwas/jemanden reden; **what is she talking about?** worüber redet sie?; **2** um (+ACC); **to be about something**

um etwas gehen; **what's it about?** worum geht es?; **3** to know about **something** von etwas ←(DAT) wissen; **she didn't know about the party** sie wusste nichts von der Party; **he knows nothing about it** er weiß nichts davon; **4** to think about **something/somebody** an etwas/jemanden ←(ACC) denken; **I'm thinking about you** ich denke an dich.

adverb **1** (*approximately*) ungefähr; **about sixty people** ungefähr sechzig Leute; **in about a week** in ungefähr einer Woche; **2** (*when talking about time*) gegen; **about three o'clock** gegen drei Uhr; **3** to **be about to do something** gerade etwas tun wollen; **I was (just) about to leave** ich wollte gerade gehen.

above *preposition* **1** über (+DAT); **the lamp above the table** die Lampe über dem Tisch; **2** above all vor allem.

abroad *adverb* im Ausland; **to live abroad** im Ausland leben; **to go abroad** ins Ausland fahren.

absent *adjective* abwesend; **to be absent from school** in der Schule fehlen.

absent-minded *adjective* zerstreut.

absolute *adjective* absolut; **an absolute disaster** eine absolute Katastrophe.

absolutely *adverb* **1** wirklich; **it's absolutely dreadful** das ist wirklich furchtbar; **2** völlig; **you're**

absolutely right du hast völlig recht.

abuse noun **1** Missbrauch △ der; **drug abuse** Missbrauch von Drogen; **2** (insults) Beschimpfungen (plural). verb **1 to abuse somebody** jemanden missbrauchen; **2** (to insult) beschimpfen.

accelerator noun Gaspedal das (PL die Gaspedale).

accent noun Akzent der (PL die Akzente); **to speak with a German accent** mit deutschem Akzent sprechen.

accept verb annehmen ✧ SEP; **he accepted the invitation** er nahm die Einladung an.

acceptable adjective annehmbar.

access noun Zugang der. verb **to access data** auf Daten zugreifen.

accessory noun **1** Zubehörteil das; **accessories** Zubehör das; **2 accessories** (fashion items) Accessoires (plural).

accident noun **1** Unfall der (PL die Unfälle); **to have an accident** einen Unfall haben; **road accident** der Verkehrsunfall; **car accident** der Autounfall; **2** Zufall der (PL die Zufälle); **by accident** zufällig; **I found it by accident** ich habe es zufällig gefunden.

accidental adjective zufällig; **an accidental discovery** eine zufällige Entdeckung.

accidentally adverb **1** (without meaning to) versehentlich; **I accidentally threw it away** ich habe es versehentlich weggeworfen; **2** (by chance) zufällig; **I accidentally discovered that ...** ich habe zufällig herausgefunden, dass ...

accommodation noun Unterkunft die; **accommodation is free** Unterkunft ist kostenlos; **I'm looking for accommodation** (when looking for a room) ich suche ein Zimmer.

according in phrase **according to** laut (+DAT); **according to Sophie** laut Sophie.

accordion noun Akkordeon das (PL die Akkordeons).

account noun **1** (in a bank, shop, or post office) Konto das (PL die Konten); **bank account** das Bankkonto; **to open an account** ein Konto eröffnen; **I have fifty pounds in my account** ich habe fünfzig Pfund auf meinem Konto; **2** (an explanation) Darstellung die (PL die Darstellungen); **I want to hear his account of what happened** ich möchte seine Darstellung der Ereignisse hören; **3 on account of** wegen (+GEN); **4 to take something into account** etwas berücksichtigen.

accountant noun Buchhalter der (PL die Buchhalter), Buchhalterin die (PL die Buchhalterinnen); **she's an accountant** sie ist Buchhalterin.

accurate adjective genau.

accurately adverb genau.

accuse *verb* beschuldigen; **she accused me of stealing her pen** sie beschuldigte mich, ihren Kugelschreiber gestohlen zu haben.

ace *noun* Ass△ *das* (PL *die* Asse); **the ace of hearts** das Herzass. *adjective* klasse (*informal*); **he's an ace drummer** er spielt klasse Schlagzeug.

achieve *verb* **1** leisten; **she's achieved a great deal** sie hat eine Menge geleistet; **2** erreichen (*an aim*); **he achieved what he wanted** er hat erreicht, was er wollte.

achievement *noun* Leistung *die* (PL *die* Leistungen); **it's a great achievement** das ist eine große Leistung.

acid *noun* Säure *die* (PL *die* Säuren).

acne *noun* Akne *die*.

across *preposition* **1** (*over to the other side of*) über (+ACC); **to run across the road** über die Straße laufen; **we walked across the park** wir sind durch den Park gegangen; **2** (*on the other side of*) auf der anderen Seite (+GEN); **he lives across the river** er wohnt auf der anderen Seite des Flusses; **3 they live across the street** sie wohnen gegenüber.

act *noun* (*deed*) Tat *die* (PL *die* Taten). *verb* (*in a play or film*) spielen; **to act the part of the hero** die Rolle des Helden spielen.

action *noun* **1** Handlung *die* (PL *die* Handlungen); **2 to take action** etwas unternehmen.

active *adjective* aktiv.

activity *noun* Aktivität *die* (PL *die* Aktivitäten).

actor *noun* Schauspieler *der* (PL *die* Schauspieler).

actress *noun* Schauspielerin *die* (PL *die* Schauspielerinnen).

actual *adjective* **what were his actual words?** was genau hat er gesagt?; **in actual fact** eigentlich.

actually *adverb* **1** (*in fact, as it happens*) eigentlich; **actually, I've changed my mind** ich habe mich eigentlich anders entschlossen; **2** (*really and truly*) wirklich; **did she actually say that?** hat sie das wirklich gesagt?

ad *noun* **1** (*on TV*) Werbespot *der* (PL *die* Werbespots); **2** (*in a newspaper*) Anzeige *die* (PL *die* Anzeigen); **to put an ad in the paper** eine Anzeige in die Zeitung setzen; **the small ads** die Kleinanzeigen.

AD (*Anno Domini*) n.Chr. (*nach Christus*); **in 400 AD** 400 n.Chr.

adapt *verb* **1 to adapt something** (*a book or film*) etwas bearbeiten; **2 to adapt to** sich anpassen SEP (+DAT); **she's adapted to her new surroundings** sie hat sich der neuen Umgebung angepasst.

adaptor *noun* **1** Adapter *der* (PL *die* Adapter); **2** (*for two plugs*) Doppelstecker *der* (PL *die* Doppelstecker).

add *verb* **1** hinzufügen SEP; **to add an introduction to something** etwas ←(DAT) eine Einleitung hinzufügen; **2** dazugeben ◇ SEP; **add three eggs** geben Sie drei Eier dazu.

● **to add up** zusammenzählen SEP.

△ NEW SPELLING: *See page xii*

addict noun 1 (*drug addict*)
Süchtige *der/die* (PL *die* Süchtigen);
2 **she's a telly addict** sie ist
fernsehsüchtig; **he's a football
addict** er hat die Fußballsucht.

addicted *adjective* 1 **to become
addicted to drugs** drogensüchtig
werden; 2 **he's addicted to football**
Fußball ist bei ihm zur Sucht
geworden; 3 **I'm addicted to
sweets** ich bin nach Süßigkeiten
süchtig.

addition noun 1 (*adding up*)
Addition *die*; 2 **in addition**
außerdem; 3 **in addition to**
zusätzlich zu (+DAT).

additional *adjective* zusätzlich.

additive noun Zusatz *der* (PL *die*
Zusätze).

address noun Adresse *die* (PL *die*
Adressen); **do you know his
address?** weißt du seine Adresse?;
to change address die Adresse
wechseln.

address book noun
Adressbuch △ *das* (PL *die*
Adressbücher).

adhesive noun Klebstoff *der*.
adjective **adhesive tape** *der*
Klebstreifen.

adjective noun Adjektiv *das* (PL *die*
Adjektive).

adjust verb 1 **to adjust something**
etwas einstellen SEP; **he adjusted the
set** er stellte das Gerät ein; **to adjust
the distance** auf die richtige
Entfernung einstellen; 2 **to adjust
to something** sich an etwas ←(ACC)
gewöhnen.

adjustable *adjective* verstellbar.

administration noun
Verwaltung *die*.

admiration noun
Bewunderung *die*.

admire verb bewundern.

admission noun Eintritt *der*;
'admission free' 'Eintritt frei'.

admit verb 1 (*confess, concede*)
zugeben ◇ SEP; **she admits she lied**
sie gibt zu, dass sie gelogen hat;
2 (*allow to enter*) hereinlassen ◇
SEP; **to admit somebody to a
restaurant** jemanden in ein
Restaurant hereinlassen; 3 **to be
admitted to hospital** ins
Krankenhaus eingeliefert werden.

adolescence noun Jugend *die*.

adolescent noun
Jugendliche *der/die* (PL *die*
Jugendlichen).

adopt verb adoptieren.

adopted *adjective* adoptiert.

adoption noun Adoption *die* (PL *die*
Adoptionen).

adore verb lieben.

adult noun Erwachsene *der/die* (PL
die Erwachsenen).
adjective **the adult population**
Erwachsene (*plural*).

Adult Education noun
Erwachsenenbildung *die*.

advance noun Fortschritt *der* (PL
die Fortschritte); **advances in**

technology technologische Fortschritte.
verb 1 (*make progress*) Fortschritte machen; 2 (*move forward*) (*of a group or an army*) vorrücken SEP (PERF *sein*).

advanced *adjective* fortgeschritten (*student, age*).

advantage *noun* 1 Vorteil *der* (PL *die* Vorteile); **there are several advantages** es gibt verschiedene Vorteile; 2 **to take advantage of something** etwas ausnutzen SEP; **I always take advantage of the sales to buy myself some shoes** ich nutze immer den Ausverkauf aus, um mir Schuhe zu kaufen; 3 **to take advantage of somebody** (*unfairly*) jemanden ausnutzen SEP.

Advent *noun* Advent *der*.

adventure *noun* Abenteuer *das* (PL *die* Abenteuer).

adverb *noun* Adverb *das* (PL *die* Adverbien).

advert, advertisement *noun* 1 (*at the cinema or on television*) Werbespot *der* (PL *die* Werbespots); 2 (*in a newspaper for a job, article for sale, etc.*) Anzeige *die* (PL *die* Anzeigen); **she answered a job advertisement** sie meldete sich auf eine Stellenanzeige.

advertise *verb* **to advertise something in the newspaper** (*in the small ads*) etwas in der Zeitung inserieren; **I saw a bike advertised in the paper** ich habe ein Rad in der Zeitung inseriert gesehen.

advertising *noun* Werbung *die*.

advice *noun* Rat *der*; **to ask somebody's advice** jemanden um Rat fragen; **a piece of advice** ein Ratschlag.

advise *verb* raten ✧ (+DAT); **to advise somebody to do something** jemandem raten, etwas zu tun; **I advised him to stop** ich riet ihm anzuhalten; **I advised her not to buy the car** ich habe ihr geraten, das Auto nicht zu kaufen.

aerial *noun* Antenne *die* (PL *die* Antennen).

aerobics *noun* Aerobic *das*; **to do aerobics** Aerobic machen.

aeroplane *noun* Flugzeug *das* (PL *die* Flugzeuge).

aerosol *noun* **an aerosol can** eine Spraydose.

affair *noun* 1 Angelegenheit *die* (PL *die* Angelegenheiten); **international affairs** internationale Angelegenheiten; **current affairs** *die* Tagespolitik; 2 **love affair** *das* Liebesverhältnis.

affect *verb* beeinflussen.

affectionate *adjective* liebevoll.

afford *verb* **to be able to afford something** sich ←(DAT) etwas leisten können; **we can't afford to go out much** wir können es uns nicht leisten, oft auszugehen; **I can't afford a new bike** ich kann mir kein neues Rad leisten.

afraid *adjective* 1 **to be afraid of something** Angst vor etwas ←(DAT) haben; **she's afraid of dogs** sie hat vor Hunden Angst; 2 **I'm afraid I**

can't help you ich kann dir leider nicht helfen; **I'm afraid so** leider ja; **I'm afraid not** leider nicht.

Africa *noun* Afrika *das*; **to Africa** nach Afrika.

African *noun* Afrikaner *der* (PL *die* Afrikaner), Afrikanerin *die* (PL *die* Afrikanerinnen).
adjective afrikanisch; **she is African** sie ist Afrikanerin.

after *preposition, adverb* **1** nach (+DAT); **after 10 o'clock** nach zehn Uhr; **after lunch** nach dem Mittagessen; **after school** nach der Schule; **2 the day after tomorrow** übermorgen; **soon after** kurz danach; **3 to run after somebody** jemandem hinterherlaufen ◇ SEP.
conjunction nachdem; **after I'd finished my homework** nachdem ich meine Hausaufgaben gemacht hatte.

after all *adverb* schließlich; **after all, she's only six** sie ist schließlich erst sechs.

afternoon *noun* **1** Nachmittag *der* (PL *die* Nachmittage); **in the afternoon** am Nachmittag; **every afternoon** jeden Nachmittag; **2 this afternoon** heute Nachmittag; **on Sunday afternoon** am Sonntagnachmittag; **3 on Saturday afternoons** samstagsnachmittags; **at four o' clock in the afternoon** um vier Uhr nachmittags.

after-shave *noun* Rasierwasser *das*.

afterwards *adverb* danach; **shortly afterwards** kurz danach.

again *adverb* **1** wieder; **she's ill again** sie ist wieder krank; **2 I saw her again yesterday** ich habe sie gestern wieder gesehen; **3 never again!** nie wieder!; **again and again** immer wieder; **4** (*one more time*) noch einmal; **try again** versuche es noch einmal; **you should ask her again** du solltest sie noch einmal fragen.

against *preposition* gegen (+ACC); **against the wall** gegen die Wand; **to lean against the wall** sich gegen die Wand lehnen; **I'm against the idea** ich bin gegen die Idee.

age *noun* **1** Alter *das*; **at the age of fifty** im Alter von fünfzig; **she's the same age as me** sie ist genauso alt wie ich; **to be under age** minderjährig sein; **2 I haven't seen Johnny for ages** ich habe Johnny schon ewig nicht mehr gesehen; **I haven't been to London for ages** ich bin schon ewig nicht mehr in London gewesen.

agent *noun* Vertreter *der* (PL *die* Vertreter); **an estate agent** ein Immobilienmakler; **a travel agent's** ein Reisebüro.

aggressive *adjective* aggressiv.

ago *adverb* vor (+DAT); **an hour ago** vor einer Stunde; **three days ago** vor drei Tagen; **a long time ago** vor langer Zeit; **not long ago** vor kurzem; **how long ago was it?** wie lange ist das her?

agree *verb* **1 to agree with somebody** mit jemandem übereinstimmen SEP; **I agree with**

◇ IRREGULAR VERB: *See the verb table in the centre of the dictionary*

Laura ich stimme mit Laura überein; **2 I agree** ich bin der gleichen Meinung; **I don't agree** ich bin anderer Meinung; **3 to agree that …** zugeben ◇ SEP, dass …; **I agree that it's too late now** ich gebe zu, dass es jetzt zu spät ist; **4 to agree to something** mit etwas einverstanden sein; **Steve's agreed to help me** Steve war damit einverstanden, mir zu helfen; **5 coffee doesn't agree with me** Kaffee bekommt mir nicht.

agreement noun **1** (when sharing an opinion) Übereinstimmung die; **2** (contract) Abkommen das (PL die Abkommen).

agriculture noun Landwirtschaft die.

ahead adverb **1 go ahead!** bitte!; **2 straight ahead** geradeaus; **keep going straight ahead until you get to the crossroads** gehen Sie immer geradeaus bis zur Kreuzung; **3 our team was ten points ahead** unsere Mannschaft hatte zehn Punkte Vorsprung; **4 ahead of time** früher als geplant; **5 the people ahead of me** die Leute vor mir.

aid noun **1** Hilfe die; **aid to developing countries** die Entwicklungshilfe; **2 in aid of** zugunsten (+GEN); **in aid of the homeless** zugunsten der Obdachlosen.

Aids noun Aids das; **to have Aids** Aids haben.

aim noun Ziel das (PL die Ziele); **their aim is to control pollution** ihr Ziel ist es, die Verschmutzung unter Kontrolle zu bringen.
verb **1 to aim to do something** beabsichtigen, etwas zu tun; **we're aiming to finish it today** wir beabsichtigen, es heute fertig zu machen; **2 the campaign is aimed at young people** die Kampagne ist auf junge Leute abgezielt.

air noun **1** Luft die; **in the open air** im Freien; **to go out for a breath of air** frische Luft schöpfen gehen; **2 to travel by air** fliegen ◇ (PERF sein).

air-conditioned adjective klimatisiert.

air conditioning noun Klimaanlage die.

Air Force noun Luftwaffe die.

air hostess noun Stewardess △ die (PL die Stewardessen); **she's an air hostess** sie ist Stewardess.

airline noun Fluggesellschaft die (PL die Fluggesellschaften).

airmail noun **by airmail** per Luftpost.

airport noun Flughafen der (PL die Flughäfen).

alarm noun Alarm der (PL die Alarme); **fire alarm** der Feuermelder; **burglar alarm** die Alarmanlage.

alarm clock noun Wecker der (PL die Wecker).

album noun Album das (PL die Alben).

alcohol noun Alkohol der.

△ NEW SPELLING: See page xii

alcoholic noun Alkoholiker der (PL die Alkoholiker), Alkoholikerin die (PL die Alkoholikerinnen).
adjective alkoholisch.

A levels noun Abitur das (Students who want to go on to university do Abitur at the end of secondary school; they are examined in four subjects).

alike adjective 1 gleich; 2 they're all alike sie sind alle gleich; 3 to look alike sich ←(DAT) ähnlich sehen; the two brothers look alike die beiden Brüder sehen sich ähnlich.

alive adjective 1 to be alive leben; to stay alive am Leben bleiben; 2 (lively) lebendig.

all adjective 1 (with a singular noun) ganz; all the time die ganze Zeit; all day den ganzen Tag; 2 (with a plural noun) alle; all the knives alle Messer; all our friends alle unsere Freunde.
pronoun 1 (everything) alles; they've eaten it all sie haben alles aufgegessen; 2 (everybody) alle; all of us wir alle; they're all there sie sind alle da; 3 not at all gar nicht.
adverb 1 ganz; all alone ganz allein; 2 three all drei zu drei.

all along adverb die ganze Zeit; I knew it all along ich habe es die ganze Zeit gewusst.

allergic adjective allergisch; to be allergic to something gegen etwas ←(ACC) allergisch sein.

allow verb 1 to allow somebody to do something jemandem erlauben, etwas zu tun; the teacher allowed them to go home der Lehrer

erlaubte ihnen, nach Hause zu gehen; 2 to be allowed to dürfen ✧; I'm not allowed to go to the cinema during the week ich darf während der Woche nicht ins Kino gehen.

all right adverb 1 (yes) ist gut, okay (informal); 'come round to my house around six' – 'all right' 'komm um sechs bei mir vorbei' – 'okay'; 2 (fine) in Ordnung, okay (informal); is everything all right? ist alles okay?; she's all right now sie ist jetzt okay; it's all right by me das geht in Ordnung; is it all right if I come later? geht es in Ordnung, wenn ich später komme?; 3 (not bad) gut, okay (informal); the meal was all right das Essen war okay; 4 'how are you?' – 'I'm all right' 'wie geht's dir?' – 'mir geht's gut'.

almost adverb fast; almost every day fast jeden Tag; almost everybody fast alle.

alone adjective 1 allein; he lives alone er lebt allein; 2 leave me alone! lass mich in Ruhe!

along preposition 1 entlang (+ACC, or +DAT); there are trees all along the river den ganzen Fluss entlang stehen Bäume; to go for a walk along the beach am Strand entlang spazieren gehen; 2 (there is often no direct translation for 'along', so the sentence has to be expressed differently) she lives along the road from me sie wohnt in der gleichen Straße wie ich; I'll bring it along ich bringe es mit.

✧ IRREGULAR VERB: See the verb table in the centre of the dictionary

aloud *adverb* laut; **to read something aloud** etwas vorlesen ✧ SEP.

alphabet *noun* Alphabet *das* (PL *die* Alphabete).

Alps *plural noun* **the Alps** die Alpen.

already *adverb* schon; **they've already left** sie sind schon weggefahren; **it's six o'clock already** es ist schon sechs Uhr.

Alsatian *noun* Schäferhund *der* (PL *die* Schäferhunde).

also *adverb* auch; **I've also invited Karen** ich habe Karen auch eingeladen.

alternative *noun* **1** Alternative *die* (PL *die* Alternativen); **there are several alternatives** es gibt mehrere Alternativen; **2 we have no alternative** wir haben keine andere Wahl.
adjective anderer/andere/anderes (*masculine/feminine/neuter*); **to find an alternative solution** eine andere Lösung finden.

alternative medicine *noun* Alternativmedizin *die*.

although *conjunction* obwohl; **although she's ill, she wants to help us** obwohl sie krank ist, will sie uns helfen.

altogether *adverb* **1** insgesamt; **I've spent thirty pounds altogether** insgesamt habe ich dreißig Pfund ausgegeben; **2** (*completely*) ganz; **I'm not altogether convinced** ich bin nicht ganz überzeugt.

always *adverb* immer; **I always leave at five** ich gehe immer um fünf weg.

am *verb* SEE **be**.

a.m. *abbreviation* vormittags; **at 8 a.m.** um acht Uhr morgens.

amateur *noun* **1** Amateur *der* (PL *die* Amateure); **2 amateur dramatics** *das* Laientheater.

amaze *verb* erstaunen; **what amazes me is…** was mich erstaunt, ist…

amazed *adjective* erstaunt; **I was amazed to see her** ich war erstaunt, sie zu sehen.

amazing *adjective* **1** (*terrific*) fantastisch △; **they've got an amazing house** sie haben ein fantastisches Haus; **2** (*extraordinary*) erstaunlich; **she has an amazing number of friends** sie hat erstaunlich viele Freunde.

ambition *noun* Ehrgeiz *der*.

ambitious *adjective* ehrgeizig.

ambulance *noun* Krankenwagen *der* (PL *die* Krankenwagen).

America *noun* Amerika *das*; **in America** in Amerika; **to America** nach Amerika.

American *noun* Amerikaner *der* (PL *die* Amerikaner), Amerikanerin *die* (PL *die* Amerikanerinnen).
adjective amerikanisch; **she's American** sie ist Amerikanerin.

among, amongst *preposition* **1** unter (+DAT); **I found it amongst my books** ich habe das unter

meinen Büchern gefunden;
amongst other things unter
anderem; **2** (*between*) **among
yourselves** untereinander.

amount *noun* **1** Menge *die* (PL *die*
Mengen); **a huge amount of work**
eine Menge Arbeit; **2** (*of money*)
Betrag *der* (PL *die* Beträge); **a large
amount of money** ein sehr hoher
Betrag.

amp *noun* (*amplifier*)
Verstärker *der* (PL *die* Verstärker).

amplifier *noun* Verstärker *der* (PL
die Verstärker).

amuse *verb* amüsieren.

amusement arcade *noun*
Spielhalle *die* (PL *die* Spielhallen).

amusing *adjective* amüsant.

an *article* SEE **a**.

anchovy *noun* Sardelle *die* (PL *die*
Sardellen).

ancient *adjective* **1** alt; **ancient
Greece** *das* alte Griechenland;
2 (*very old*) uralt; **an ancient pair of
jeans** uralte Jeans.

and *conjunction* **1** und; **Rosie and I**
Rosie und ich; **girls and boys**
Mädchen und Jungen; **2 louder and
louder** immer lauter; **3 try and
come** versuche zu kommen.

angel *noun* Engel *der* (PL *die* Engel).

anger *noun* Zorn *der*.

angle *noun* Winkel *der* (PL *die*
Winkel).

angrily *adverb* wütend.

angry *adjective* **to be angry** böse
sein; **she was angry with me** sie
war böse auf mich; **to get angry**
böse werden.

animal *noun* Tier *das* (PL *die* Tiere).

ankle *noun* Knöchel *der* (PL *die*
Knöchel).

anniversary *noun* **1** Jahrestag *der*
(PL *die* Jahrestage); **2 our wedding
anniversary** unser Hochzeitstag.

annoy *verb* **to be annoyed** verärgert
sein; **to get annoyed with
somebody** sich über jemanden
ärgern; **she got annoyed about it**
sie hat sich darüber geärgert.

annoying *adjective* ärgerlich.

annual *adjective* jährlich.

anorak *noun* Anorak *der* (PL *die*
Anoraks).

anorexia *noun* Magersucht *die*.

another *adjective* **1** (*additional*)
noch ein/noch eine/noch ein;
would you like another cup of tea?
möchtest du noch eine Tasse Tee?;
we need another three chairs wir
brauchen noch drei Stühle;
2 (*different*) ein anderer/eine
andere/ein anderes; **we saw
another film** wir haben einen
anderen Film gesehen; **3 in another
two years** in zwei weiteren Jahren.

answer *noun* **1** Antwort *die* (PL *die*
Antworten); **the right answer** die
richtige Antwort; **the wrong answer**
die falsche Antwort; **2 the answer
to a problem** die Lösung eines
Problems.
verb **1** antworten (+DAT); **why don't
you answer him?** warum

antwortest du ihm nicht?;
2 beantworten (*a letter, a question*);
he hasn't answered our letter er
hat unseren Brief nicht beantwortet.

answering machine *noun*
Anrufbeantworter *der* (PL *die*
Anrufbeantworter).

anthem *noun* **the national anthem**
die Nationalhymne.

antibiotic *noun* Antibiotikum *das*
(PL *die* Antibiotika).

antique *noun* **antiques**
Antiquitäten (*plural*).
adjective antik; **an antique table**
ein antiker Tisch.

antique shop *noun*
Antiquitätengeschäft *das* (PL *die*
Antiquitätengeschäfte).

anxious *adjective* **1** (*worried*)
besorgt; **2** (*keen*) **she was anxious
to see him** sie wollte ihn unbedingt
sehen.

anxiously *adverb* ängstlich.

any *adjective* **1** irgendein; **if they had
any plan** wenn sie irgendeinen Plan
hätten; **2** (*with plural nouns*)
irgendwelche; **if they had any plans**
wenn sie irgendwelche Pläne hätten;
3 (*in questions 'any' is often not
translated*) **have you got any
stamps?** haben Sie Briefmarken?;
have we got any milk? haben wir
Milch?; **4 not any** kein; **they
haven't made any plans** sie haben
keine Pläne gemacht; **we haven't
got any milk** wir haben keine Milch;
5 (*no matter which*) jeder
beliebige/jede beliebige/jedes

beliebige; **you can have any colour**
du kannst jede beliebige Farbe
haben.
pronoun **1** (*in questions, replacing
the noun*) welcher/welche/welches;
(*replacing a plural noun*) welche;
**I need some flour, have you got
any?** ich brauche Mehl, hast du
welches?; **2 not any** keiner/keine/
keins; (*replacing a plural noun*)
keine; **I don't want any** ich will
keins haben; **there aren't any** es gibt
keine; **3** (*no matter which one*)
irgendein; **'which chair can I take?'**
– **'take any of them'** 'welchen
Stuhl kann ich nehmen?' – 'nimm
irgendeinen'.
adverb **1** (*in questions*) noch; **would
you like any more?** möchtest du
noch etwas?; **2** (*with negatives*) **I
can't see him any more** ich kann
ihn nicht mehr sehen.

anybody, anyone *pronoun* **1** (*in
questions*) jemand; **does anybody
want some tea?** möchte jemand
Tee?; **is anybody in?** ist
irgendjemand da?; **2 not anybody**
niemand; **there isn't anybody in the
office** niemand ist im Büro; **3** (*absolutely anybody*) jeder;
anybody can do it das kann jeder.

anyhow *adverb* SEE **anyway**.

anyone *pronoun* SEE **anybody**.

anything *pronoun* **1** (*in questions*)
irgendetwas △; **is there anything I
can do to help?** kann ich irgendwie
helfen?; **2 not anything** nichts;
there isn't anything on the table
auf dem Tisch liegt nichts;
3 (*anything at all*) alles; **I'll do**

△ NEW SPELLING: *See page xii*

anything to help him ich werde alles tun, um ihm zu helfen.

anyway, anyhow *adverb*
1 jedenfalls; **anyway, I'll ring you before I leave** jedenfalls ruf ich dich an, bevor ich fahre; **2** sowieso.

anywhere *adverb* **1** (*in questions*) irgendwo; **have you seen my keys anywhere?** hast du meine Schlüssel irgendwo gesehen?; **2** *not anywhere* nirgends; **I can't find my keys anywhere** ich kann meine Schlüssel nirgends finden; **3** (*to any place*) irgendwohin; **are you going anywhere tomorrow?** fahrt ihr morgen irgendwohin?; **put your cases down anywhere** stell deine Koffer irgendwohin; **4** (*in any place*) überall; **you can get that anywhere** das kann man überall kriegen.

apart *adjective, adverb* **1** (*separate*) auseinander; **they've been apart for some time** sie sind schon lange auseinander; **2** **to be two metres apart** zwei Meter auseinander liegen; **3** *apart from* außer (+DAT); **apart from my brother everybody was there** außer meinem Bruder waren alle da.

apologize *verb* sich entschuldigen; **he apologized for his mistake** er enschuldigte sich für seinen Fehler; **he apologized to Sam** er hat sich bei Sam entschuldigt.

apology *noun* Entschuldigung *die* (PL *die* Entschuldigungen).

apostrophe *noun* Apostroph *der* (PL *die* Apostrophe).

apparent *adjective* offensichtlich.

apparently *adverb* offensichtlich.

appeal *noun* Appell *der* (PL *die* Appelle).
verb **1** **to appeal for something** um etwas ←(ACC) bitten ✧; **2** **to appeal to somebody** sich an jemanden wenden ✧; **horror films don't appeal to me** Horrorfilme sind nicht mein Geschmack.

appear *verb* **1** erscheinen ✧ (PERF *sein*); **Mick appeared at breakfast** Mick erschien zum Frühstück; **2** **to appear on television** im Fernsehen auftreten ✧ SEP (PERF *sein*); **3** (*seem*) scheinen ✧; **it appears that somebody has stolen the key** es scheint, dass jemand den Schlüssel gestohlen hat.

appendicitis *noun* Blinddarmentzündung *die*.

appetite *noun* Appetit *der*; **it'll spoil your appetite** das verdirbt dir den Appetit.

applaud *verb* Beifall klatschen.

applause *noun* Beifall *der*.

apple *noun* Apfel *der* (PL *die* Äpfel).

apple tree *noun* Apfelbaum *der* (PL *die* Apfelbäume).

applicant *noun* Bewerber *der* (PL *die* Bewerber), Bewerberin *die* (PL *die* Bewerberinnen).

application *noun* Bewerbung *die* (PL *die* Bewerbungen).

application form *noun* (*for a job*) Bewerbungsformular *das* (PL *die* Bewerbungsformulare).

✧ IRREGULAR VERB: *See the verb table in the centre of the dictionary*

apply *verb* **1 to apply for a job** sich um eine Stellung bewerben ✧; **2 to apply for university** sich um einen Studienplatz bewerben ✧; **3 to apply for a passport** einen Pass beantragen; **4 to apply to** zutreffen ✧ SEP auf (+ACC); **that doesn't apply to students** das trifft nicht auf Studenten zu.

appointment *noun* Termin *der* (PL *die* Termine); **to make a dental appointment** einen Termin mit dem Zahnarzt vereinbaren; **I've got a hair appointment at four** ich bin um vier beim Friseur angemeldet.

appreciate *verb* **I appreciate your advice** ich bin dir für deinen Rat dankbar; **I'd appreciate it if you could tidy up afterwards** es wäre nett von dir, wenn du danach aufräumen würdest.

apprentice *noun* Lehrling *der* (PL *die* Lehrlinge).

apprenticeship *noun* Lehre *die* (PL *die* Lehren).

approve *verb* **to approve of something** mit etwas ←(DAT) einverstanden sein; **they don't approve of her friends** sie sind nicht mit ihren Freunden einverstanden.

approximate *adjective* ungefähr.

approximately *adverb* ungefähr; **approximately fifty people** ungefähr fünfzig Personen.

apricot *noun* Aprikose *die* (PL *die* Aprikosen).

April *noun* April *der*; **in April** im April.

April Fool *noun* (*trick*) Aprilscherz *der* (PL *die* Aprilscherze); **April fool!** April, April!

April Fool's Day *noun* der erste April.

apron *noun* Schürze *die* (PL *die* Schürzen).

Aquarius *noun* Wassermann *der*; **Sharon's Aquarius** Sharon ist Wassermann.

archaeologist *noun* Archäologe *der* (PL *die* Archäologen), Archäologin *die* (PL *die* Archäologinnen); **she's an archaeologist** sie ist Archäologin.

archaeology *noun* Archäologie *die*.

architect *noun* Architekt *der* (PL *die* Architekten), Architektin *die* (PL *die* Architektinnen); **he's an architect** er ist Architekt.

architecture *noun* Architektur *die*.

are *verb* SEE **be**.

area *noun* **1** (*part of a town, a region*) Gegend *die* (PL *die* Gegenden); **a nice area** eine nette Gegend; **in the Leeds area** in der Gegend von Leeds; **2 picnic area** *der* Picknickplatz.

argue *verb* sich streiten ✧; **to argue about something** sich über etwas ←(ACC) streiten; **they're arguing about the result** sie streiten sich über das Ergebnis.

argument *noun* Streit *der* (PL *die* Streite); **to get into an argument with somebody** mit jemandem in

Streit geraten ◇; **to have an
argument** sich streiten ◇.

Aries *noun* Widder *der*; **Pauline's
Aries** Pauline ist Widder.

arm *noun* Arm *der* (PL *die* Arme);
arm in arm Arm in Arm; **to break
your arm** sich ←(DAT) den Arm
brechen.

armchair *noun* Sessel *der* (PL *die*
Sessel).

armed *adjective* bewaffnet.

army *noun* **1** Heer *das* (PL *die*
Heere); **2** (*profession*) Militär *das*;
to join the army zum Militär gehen.

around *preposition, adverb* **1** (*with
time of day*) gegen (+ACC); **we'll be
there around ten** wir werden gegen
zehn da sein; **2** (*with ages or
amounts*) etwa; **she's around
fifteen** sie ist etwa fünfzehn; **we
need around six kilos** wir brauchen
etwa sechs Kilo; **3** (*with dates*) um
(+ACC); **around 10 August** um den
10. August; **4** (*surrounding*) um …
herum; **the countryside around
Edinburgh** die Landschaft um
Edinburgh herum; **5** (*near*) **is there
a post office around here?** gibt es
hier in der Gegend eine Post?; **is Phil
around?** ist Phil da?

arrange *verb* **to arrange
something** etwas vereinbaren;
**we've arranged to go to the cinema
on Saturday** wir haben vereinbart,
am Samstag ins Kino zu gehen.

arrest *noun* **to be under arrest**
verhaftet sein.
verb verhaften.

arrival *noun* Ankunft *die* (PL *die*
Ankünfte).

arrive *verb* ankommen ◇ SEP (PERF
sein); **they arrived at 3 p.m.** sie
kamen um fünfzehn Uhr an.

art *noun* **1** Kunst *die* (PL *die* Künste);
modern art moderne Kunst;
2 (*school subject*)
Kunsterziehung *die*.

art gallery *noun* Kunstgalerie *die*
(PL *die* Kunstgalerien).

article *noun* **1** (*in a newspaper or
magazine*) Artikel *der* (PL *die*
Artikel); **2** (*object*) Stück *das* (PL *die*
Stücke).

artificial *adjective* künstlich.

artist *noun* Künstler *der* (PL *die*
Künstler), Künstlerin *die* (PL *die*
Künstlerinnen); **he's an artist** er ist
Künstler.

artistic *adjective* künstlerisch.

art school *noun*
Kunsthochschule *die* (PL *die*
Kunsthochschulen).

as *conjunction, adverb* **1** wie; **as you
know** wie du weißt; **as usual** wie
üblich; **as I told you** wie ich dir
gesagt habe; **2** (*because*) da; **as
there was no bus, we took a taxi**
da es keinen Bus gab, nahmen wir
ein Taxi; **3 as … as** so … wie; **he's
as tall as his brother** er ist so groß
wie sein Bruder; **come as quickly as
possible** komm so schnell wie
möglich; **4 as much … as** so viel
… wie; **you have as much time as I
do** du hast so viel Zeit wie ich; **5 as
many … as** so viele … wie; **we have**

◇ IRREGULAR VERB: *See the verb table in the centre of the dictionary*

as many problems as he does wir haben so viele Probleme wie er; **6 as long as** vorausgesetzt; **we'll go tomorrow, as long as it's a nice day** wir gehen morgen, vorausgesetzt es ist schönes Wetter; **7 for as long as** solange; **you can stay for as long as you like** du kannst bleiben, solange du willst; **8 as soon as possible** so bald wie möglich; **9 to work as** arbeiten als; **he works as a waiter in the evenings** abends arbeitet er als Kellner; **as well** auch.

ash *noun* **1** Asche *die* (PL *die* Aschen). **2** (*tree*) Esche *die* (PL *die* Eschen).

ashamed *adjective* **to be ashamed of something** sich über etwas ←(ACC) schämen; **you should be ashamed of yourself!** du solltest dich schämen!

ashtray *noun* Aschenbecher *der* (PL *die* Aschenbecher).

Asia *noun* Asien *das*; **in Asia** in Asien.

ask *verb* **1** fragen; **to ask somebody something** jemanden nach etwas ←(DAT) fragen; **I asked him the way** ich fragte ihn nach dem Weg; **2 to ask something** um etwas ←(ACC) bitten; **to ask somebody a favour** jemanden um einen Gefallen bitten; **to ask somebody to do something** jemanden bitten, etwas zu tun; **ask Danny to give you a hand** bitte Danny, dir zu helfen; **3 to ask somebody a question** jemandem eine Frage stellen; **I asked him a few questions** ich habe ihm ein paar Fragen gestellt; **4** einladen ✧ SEP;

they've asked us to a party sie haben uns auf eine Party eingeladen; **Paul's asked Janie out on Friday** Paul hat Janie Freitag eingeladen; **5 to ask for** verlangen; **how much are they asking for the car?** wieviel verlangen sie für das Auto?

asparagus *noun* Spargel *der* (PL *die* Spargel).

aspirin *noun* Aspirin *das*.

assembly *noun* (*at school*) Morgenandacht *die* (PL *die* Morgenandachten).

assignment *noun* (*at school*) Aufgabe *die* (PL *die* Aufgaben).

assistance *noun* Hilfe *die*.

assistant *noun* **1** Helfer *der* (PL *die* Helfer), Helferin *die* (PL *die* Helferinnen); **2** (*in school*) Assistent *der* (PL *die* Assistenten), Assistentin *die* (PL *die* Assistentinnen); **3 shop assistant** *der* Verkäufer, *die* Verkäuferin.

association *noun* Verband *der* (PL *die* Verbände).

assorted *adjective* gemischt.

assortment *noun* Auswahl *die*.

assume *verb* annehmen ✧ SEP; **I assume** ich nehme an.

asthma *noun* Asthma *das*.

astrology *noun* Astrologie *die*.

astronaut *noun* Astronaut *der* (PL *die* Astronauten), Astronautin *die* (PL *die* Astronautinnen).

astronomy *noun* Astronomie *die*.

△ NEW SPELLING: *See page xii*

at *preposition* **1** in (+DAT); **at school** in der Schule; **at my office** in meinem Büro; **at the supermarket** im Supermarkt; **2** an (+DAT); **at the station** am Bahnhof; **at the bus stop** an der Bushaltestelle; **3** bei (+DAT); **at the dentist** beim Zahnarzt; **at discussions** bei Besprechungen; **at Emma's** bei Emma; **she's at her brother's this evening** sie ist heute Abend bei ihrem Bruder; **at the hairdresser's** beim Friseur; **4** at **a party** auf einer Party; **5 at home** zu Hause; **6** (*talking about the time*) um; **at eight o'clock** um acht Uhr; **7 at night** nachts; **at Christmas** zu Weihnachten; **at the weekend** am Wochenende; **8 at last** endlich; **she's found a job at last** sie hat endlich einen Job gefunden.

athlete *noun* Athlet *der* (PL *die* Athleten), Athletin *die* (PL *die* Athletinnen).

athletic *adjective* sportlich.

athletics *noun* Leichtathletik *die*.

Atlantic *noun* **the Atlantic (Ocean)** der Atlantik.

atlas *noun* Atlas *der* (PL *die* Atlanten).

atmosphere *noun* Atmosphäre *die* (PL *die* Atmosphären).

attach *verb* befestigen.

attached *adjective* (*emotionally*) **to be attached to somebody/ something** an jemandem/ etwas ←(DAT) hängen ✧.

attack *noun* Angriff *der* (PL *die* Angriffe).
verb **1** angreifen ✧ SEP; **2** (*mug or raid*) überfallen ✧.

attempt *noun* Versuch *der* (PL *die* Versuche); **at the first attempt** beim ersten Versuch.
verb **to attempt to do something** versuchen, etwas zu tun.

attend *verb* teilnehmen ✧ SEP an (+DAT); **to attend a meeting** an einer Besprechung teilnehmen; **to attend an evening class** einen Abendkurs besuchen.

attention *noun*
1 Aufmerksamkeit *die*; **to pay attention** aufpassen SEP; **I wasn't paying attention** ich habe nicht aufgepasst; **2 he wasn't paying attention to the teacher** er hörte dem Lehrer nicht zu.

attic *noun* Dachboden *der* (PL *die* Dachböden); **in the attic** auf dem Dachboden.

attitude *noun* **1** (*way of thinking*) Einstellung *die*; **2** (*way of acting*) Haltung *die*.

attract *verb* anziehen ✧ SEP.

attraction *noun* **1** Anziehung *die*; **2** (*a thing that attracts*) Attraktion *die* (PL *die* Attraktionen); **the whale was a big attraction** der Wal war eine große Attraktion.

attractive *adjective* attraktiv.

aubergine *noun* Aubergine *die* (PL *die* Auberginen).

audience *noun* Publikum *das*; **the television audience** die Fernsehzuschauer (*plural*).

✧ IRREGULAR VERB: *See the verb table in the centre of the dictionary*

August *noun* August *der*; **in August** im August.

aunt, auntie *noun* Tante *die* (PL *die* Tanten).

au pair *noun* Aupairmädchen △ *das* (PL *die* Aupairmädchen); **I'm looking for a job as an au pair** ich suche eine Aupair-Stelle.

Australia *noun* Australien *das*; **to Australia** nach Australien.

Australian *noun* Australier *der* (PL *die* Australier), Australierin *die* (PL *die* Australierinnen).
adjective australisch; **she's Australian** sie ist Australierin.

Austria *noun* Österreich *das*; **in Austria** in Österreich.

Austrian *noun* Österreicher *der* (PL *die* Österreicher), Österreicherin *die* (PL *die* Österreicherinnen).
adjective österreichisch; **he's Austrian** er ist Österreicher.

author *noun* Autor *der* (PL *die* Autoren), Autorin *die* (PL *die* Autorinnen).

autograph *noun* Autogramm *das* (PL *die* Autogramme).

automatic *adjective* automatisch.

automatically *adverb* automatisch.

autumn *noun* Herbst *der* (PL *die* Herbste); **in autumn** im Herbst.

available *adjective* (*on sale*) erhältlich.

average *noun* Durchschnitt *der* (PL *die* Durchschnitte); **on average** im Durchschnitt; **above average** über dem Durchschnitt.
adjective durchschnittlich; **the average height** die durchschnittliche Größe.

avocado *noun* Avocado *die* (PL *die* Avocados).

avoid *verb* 1 vermeiden ✧; **to avoid doing something** es vermeiden, etwas zu tun; **I avoid speaking to him** ich vermeide es, mit ihm zu reden; 2 (*keep away from somebody or a place*) meiden ✧; **she avoids me** sie meidet mich.

awake *adjective* **to be awake** wach sein; **are you still awake?** bist du noch wach?

award *noun* Preis *der* (PL *die* Preise); **to win an award** einen Preis gewinnen.

aware *adjective* **to be aware of a problem** sich ←(DAT) eines Problems bewusst △ sein; **I'm aware of the danger** ich bin mir der Gefahr bewusst; **as far as I'm aware** soweit ich weiß.

away *adverb* 1 **to be away** nicht da sein; **I'll be away next week** ich bin nächste Woche nicht da; 2 **to go away** verreisen (PERF *sein*); **Laura's gone away for a week** Laura ist auf eine Woche verreist; **go away!** geh weg!; 3 **to run away** weglaufen ✧ SEP (PERF *sein*); **the thieves ran away** die Diebe liefen weg; 4 **the school is two kilometres away** die Schule ist zwei Kilometer entfernt; **how far away is it?** wie weit entfernt ist es?; **not far away** nicht weit entfernt; 5 **to put something away** etwas wegräumen SEP; **I'm just putting my**

books away ich räume gerade meine Bücher weg; **6 to give something away** etwas weggeben ✧ SEP; (*as a present*) etwas verschenken; **she's given away all her cassettes** sie hat alle ihre Kassetten verschenkt.

awful *adjective* furchtbar; **the film was awful** der Film war furchtbar; **I feel awful** (*ill*) ich fühle mich furchtbar; **I feel awful about it** es ist mir furchtbar unangenehm; **an awful lot of mistakes** furchtbar viele Fehler.

awkward *adjective* **1** schwierig; **it's an awkward situation** das ist eine schwierige Situation; **it's a bit awkward** das ist ein bisschen schwierig; **an awkward child** ein schwieriges Kind; **2 an awkward question** eine peinliche Frage.

B b

baby *noun* Baby *das* (PL *die* Babys).

babysit *verb* babysitten.

babysitter *noun* Babysitter *der* (PL *die* Babysitter).

babysitting *noun* Babysitten *das*.

back *noun* **1** (*of a person or animal*) Rücken *der* (PL *die* Rücken); **he did it behind my back** er hat es hinter meinem Rücken getan; **2** (*of a piece of paper, cheque, or building*) Rückseite *die* (PL *die* Rückseiten); **on the back** auf der Rückseite; **3 the**

back of your hand der Handrücken; **4 at the back** hinten; **at the back of the room** hinten im Zimmer; **we sat at the back** wir saßen hinten; **a garden at the back of the house** ein Garten hinter dem Haus; **5** (*of a chair or sofa*) Rückenlehne *die* (PL *die* Rückenlehnen); **6** (*in football or hockey*) Verteidiger *der* (PL *die* Verteidiger); **left back** *der* Linksverteidiger.

adjective **1 the back seat** (*of a car*) der Rücksitz; **2 the back door** die Hintertür; **the back garden** der Garten hinter dem Haus.

adverb **1** zurück; **there and back** hin und zurück; **to go back** (*on foot*) zurückgehen ✧ SEP (PERF *sein*) (*in a vehicle*) zurückfahren ✧ SEP (PERF *sein*); **2 to come back** zurückkommen ✧ SEP (PERF *sein*); **they've come back from Italy** sie sind aus Italien zurückgekommen; **I'll be back at 8 o'clock** ich bin um acht Uhr zurück; **Sue's not back yet** Sue ist noch nicht zurück; **3 to phone back** zurückrufen ✧ SEP; **I'll ring back later** ich rufe dich später zurück; **4 to give something back to somebody** jemandem etwas zurückgeben ✧ SEP; **give it back!** gib es zurück!

verb (*bet on*) setzen auf (+ACC).

● **to back up** (*computing*) sichern; **to back up a file** eine Sicherungsdatei machen.

● **to back somebody up** jemanden unterstützen.

backache *noun* Rückenschmerzen (*plural*).

✧ IRREGULAR VERB: *See the verb table in the centre of the dictionary*

background *noun* **1** (*of a person*) Verhältnisse (*plural*); **she comes from a poor background** sie kommt aus ärmlichen Verhältnissen; **2** (*in a picture, view, or situation*) Hintergrund *der* (PL *die* Hintergründe); **background noise** Hintergrundgeräusche (*plural*); **3** (*to events or problems*) Hintergründe (*plural*).

backing *noun* **1** (*on sticky-back plastic, for example*) Verstärkung *die* (PL *die* Verstärkungen); **2** (*moral support*) Unterstützung *die*; **3** (*in music*) Begleitung *die*; **a backing group** eine Begleitband.

backpack *noun* Rucksack *der* (PL die Rucksäcke). *verb* **to go backpacking** trampen (PERF *sein*).

back seat *noun* Rücksitz *der* (PL die Rücksitze).

backstroke *noun* Rückenschwimmen *das*.

back to front *adverb* verkehrt herum; **your jumper's back to front** du hast deinen Pullover verkehrt herum an.

backup *noun* **1** (*support*) Unterstützung *die*; **2** (*in computing*) Sicherungskopie *die* (PL die Sicherungskopien); **a backup disk** eine Sicherungsdiskette.

backwards *adverb* **1** rückwärts; **2 to lean backwards** sich nach hinten lehnen; **to fall backwards** nach hinten fallen.

bacon *noun* Speck *der*; **bacon and eggs** Eier mit Speck.

bad *adjective* **1** (*not good*) schlecht; **a bad idea** eine schlechte Idee; **a bad meal** ein schlechtes Essen; **his new film's not bad** sein neuer Film ist nicht schlecht; **it's bad for your health** das ist ungesund; **I'm bad at physics** ich bin schlecht in Physik; **2** (*serious*) schlimm; **a bad mistake** ein schlimmer Fehler; **a bad cold** eine schlimme Erkältung; **3 a bad accident** ein schwerer Unfall; **4** (*rotten*) schlecht; **to go bad** schlecht werden; **5 a bad apple** ein fauler Apfel; **6 bad language** Kraftausdrücke (*plural*); ★ **too bad!** schade!, so ein Pech!

badge *noun* Abzeichen *das* (PL die Abzeichen).

badly *adverb* **1** (*poorly*) schlecht; **he writes badly** er schreibt schlecht; **I slept badly** ich habe schlecht geschlafen; **2** (*seriously*) schwer; **they were badly injured** sie waren schwer verletzt; **3** (*very much*) dringend; **to need something badly** etwas dringend brauchen.

bad-mannered *adjective* **to be bad-mannered** schlechte Manieren haben.

badminton *noun* Badminton *das*.

bad-tempered *adjective* schlecht gelaunt Δ; **a bad-tempered old man** ein schlecht gelaunter alter Mann.

bag *noun* **1** Tasche *die* (PL die Taschen); **2** (*made of paper or plastic*) Tüte *die* (PL die Tüten).

Δ NEW SPELLING: *See page xii*

baggage noun Gepäck das.

bagpipes plural noun Dudelsack der.

bags plural noun Gepäck das; **to pack your bags** sein Gepäck packen; ★ **to have bags under your eyes** Ringe unter den Augen haben (informal).

bake verb 1 backen; **to bake a cake** einen Kuchen backen; 2 **to bake vegetables** Gemüse backen.

baked adjective 1 (fish or fruit) überbacken; **baked apples** Bratäpfel; 2 **a baked potato** eine (in der Schale) gebackene Kartoffel.

baked beans plural noun Bohnen in Tomatensoße.

baker noun Bäcker der (PL die Bäcker); **to go to the baker's** zum Bäcker gehen.

balance noun 1 Gleichgewicht das; **to lose your balance** das Gleichgewicht verlieren; 2 (in a bank account) Kontostand der.

balanced adjective ausgeglichen.

balcony noun Balkon der (PL die Balkons).

bald adjective 1 kahl; 2 (of a person) kahlköpfig; **to go bald** eine Glatze bekommen.

ball noun 1 (for tennis, football, or golf) Ball der (PL die Bälle); 2 (for billiards, croquet) Kugel die (PL die Kugeln); 3 (of string or wool) Knäuel das (PL die Knäuel).

ballet noun Ballett das (PL die Ballette).

ballet dancer noun Balletttänzer △ der (PL die Balletttänzer), Balletttänzerin △ die (PL die Balletttänzerinnen).

balloon noun 1 Luftballon der (PL die Luftballons); 2 (hot-air) Ballon der (PL die Ballons).

ballpoint (pen) noun Kugelschreiber der (PL die Kugelschreiber).

ban noun Verbot das (PL die Verbote); **a ban on smoking** ein Rauchverbot.
verb verbieten ◇; **to ban someone from smoking** jemandem verbieten zu rauchen.

banana noun 1 Banane die (PL die Bananen); 2 **a banana yoghurt** ein Bananenjoghurt.

band noun 1 (playing music) Band die (PL die Bands); **rock band** die Rockband; **brass band** die Blaskapelle; 2 **rubber band** das Gummiband.

bandage noun Verband der (PL die Verbände).
verb verbinden ◇.

bang noun (noise) Knall der (PL die Knalle).
verb 1 (hit, knock) schlagen ◇; **he banged his fist on the table** er hat mit der Faust auf den Tisch geschlagen; **to bang on the door** gegen die Tür schlagen; 2 **I banged my head on the door** ich habe mir den Kopf an der Tür gestoßen; 3 **to bang into something** gegen etwas ←(ACC) knallen; 4 (shut loudly) zuknallen SEP; **he banged the door**

◇ IRREGULAR VERB: See the verb table in the centre of the dictionary

er knallte die Tür zu.
exclamation peng!

bank *noun* 1 (*for money*) Bank *die*
(PL *die* Banken); **I'm going to the**
bank ich gehe auf die Bank; 2 (*of a*
river or lake) Ufer *das* (PL *die* Ufer).

bank account *noun*
Bankkonto *das* (PL *die* Bankkonten).

bank balance *noun*
Kontostand *der* (PL *die*
Kontostände).

bank card *noun* Scheckkarte *die*
(PL *die* Scheckkarten).

bank holiday *noun* gesetzliche
Feiertag *der* (PL *die* gesetzlichen
Feiertage).

banknote *noun* Geldschein *der* (PL
die Geldscheine).

bank statement *noun*
Kontoauszug *der* (PL *die*
Kontoauszüge).

bar *noun* 1 (*selling drinks*) Bar *die*
(PL *die* Bars); **Janet works in a bar**
Janet arbeitet in einer Bar;
2 (*counter*) Theke *die* (PL *die*
Theken); **on the bar** auf der Theke;
3 **a bar of chocolate** eine Tafel
Schokolade; 4 **a bar of soap** ein
Stück Seife; 5 (*made of wood or*
metal) Stange *die* (PL *die* Stangen);
an iron bar eine Eisenstange;
6 (*in music*) Takt *der* (PL *die* Takte).

barbecue *noun* 1 (*apparatus*)
Grill *der* (PL *die* Grills); 2 (*party*)
Grillfest *das* (PL *die* Grillfeste).
verb **to barbecue a chicken** ein
Hühnchen grillen; **barbecued**
chicken gegrilltes Hühnchen.

bare *adjective* nackt.

barefoot *adjective* **to be barefoot**
barfuß sein; **to walk barefoot**
barfuß gehen.

bargain *noun* (*a good buy*) gute
Kauf *der* (PL *die* guten Käufe); **I got**
a bargain ich habe einen guten Kauf
gemacht; **it's a bargain!** ein guter
Kauf!

bark *noun* 1 (*of a tree*) Rinde *die* (PL
die Rinden); 2 (*of a dog*) Bellen *das*.
verb bellen.

barmaid *noun* Bardame *die* (PL *die*
Bardamen).

barman *noun* Barkeeper *der* (PL *die*
Barkeeper).

barn *noun* Scheune *die* (PL *die*
Scheunen).

barrel *noun* Fass △ *das* (PL *die*
Fässer).

barrier *noun* Absperrung *die* (PL *die*
Absperrungen).

base *noun* (*bottom part*) Fuß *der*
(PL *die* Füße).

baseball *noun* Baseball *der*.

based *adjective* 1 **to be based on**
basieren auf (+DAT); **the film is**
based on a true story der Film
basiert auf einer wahren
Geschichte; 2 **to be based in**
wohnen in (+DAT); **he's based in**
Bristol er wohnt in Bristol.

basement *noun*
Kellergeschoss △ *das* (PL *die*
Kellergeschosse).

bash *noun* **1** Schlag *der* (PL *die* Schläge); **2 I'll have a bash** ich probier's mal.
verb **I bashed my head** ich habe mir den Kopf angehauen.

basic *adjective* **1** grundlegend, Grund-; **basic knowledge** Grundkenntnisse (*plural*); **her basic salary** ihr Grundgehalt; **2 the basic problem** das Hauptproblem; **3** (*not luxurious*) einfach.

basically *adverb* **1** grundsätzlich; **it's basically all right** grundsätzlich ist es okay; **2 basically, I don't want to come** eigentlich will ich nicht kommen.

basics *plural noun* **the basics** das Wesentliche.

basin *noun* Becken *das* (PL *die* Becken).

basis *noun* **1** Basis *die*; **2 on a regular basis** regelmäßig.

basket *noun* Korb *der* (PL *die* Körbe); **a basket of apples** ein Korb Äpfel; **waste-paper basket** *der* Papierkorb.

basketball *noun* Basketball *der*.

bass *noun* **1** Bass △ *der* (PL *die* Bässe); **2 double bass** *der* Kontrabass △.

bass guitar *noun* Bassgitarre △ *die* (PL *die* Bassgitarren).

bassoon *noun* Fagott *das* (PL *die* Fagotte).

bat *noun* **1** (*for games*) Schläger *der* (PL *die* Schläger); **2** (*animal*) Fledermaus *die* (PL *die* Fledermäuse).

bath *noun* **1** Bad *das* (PL *die* Bäder); **to have a bath** baden; **2** (*tub*) Badewanne *die* (PL *die* Badewannen).

bathroom *noun* Badezimmer *das* (PL *die* Badezimmer).

baths *plural noun* Badeanstalt *die* (PL *die* Badeanstalten).

bath towel *noun* Badetuch *das* (PL *die* Badetücher).

batter *noun* Teig *der* (PL *die* Teige); **fish in batter** ausgebackener Fisch.

battery *noun* Batterie *die* (PL *die* Batterien).

battle *noun* **1** (*in war*) Schlacht *die* (PL *die* Schlachten); **2** (*contest*) Kampf *der* (PL *die* Kämpfe).

Bavaria *noun* Bayern *das*.

bay *noun* Bucht *die* (PL *die* Buchten).

BC (*before Christ*) v.Chr. (*vor Christus*).

be *verb* **1** sein ✧ (PERF *sein*); **Melanie is in the kitchen** Melanie ist in der Küche; **where is the butter?** wo ist die Butter?; **I'm tired** ich bin müde; **when we were in Germany** als wir in Deutschland waren; **2** (*with jobs and professions*) sein ✧ (PERF *sein*); **she's a teacher** sie ist Lehrerin; **he's a taxi driver** er ist Taxifahrer; **3** (*in clock times, days of the week, dates, and age*) sein ✧ (PERF *sein*); **it's three o'clock** es ist drei Uhr; **it's half past five** es ist halb sechs; **what day is it today?** welcher Tag ist heute?; **it's Tuesday today** heute ist Dienstag; **it's the twentieth of May** heute ist der zwanzigste Mai; **what's**

✧ IRREGULAR VERB: *See the verb table in the centre of the dictionary*

the date today? der Wievielte ist heute?; **how old are you?** wie alt bist du?; **I'm fifteen** ich bin fünfzehn; **4** (*cold, hot, ill*) sein ✧ (PERF *sein*); **I'm hot** mir ist heiß; **I'm cold** mir ist kalt; **to be ill** krank sein; **5** (*weather*) sein ✧ (PERF *sein*); **it's cold today** heute ist es kalt; **it's a nice day** es ist schönes Wetter; **it's raining** es regnet; **6 I'm hungry** ich habe Hunger; **she's thirsty** sie hat Durst; **7** (*saying how much something costs*) kosten; **how much are the bananas?** wie viel kosten die Bananen?; **8** (*go, come, or visit*) sein ✧ (PERF *sein*); **I've never been to Berlin** ich bin noch nie in Berlin gewesen; **have you been to England before?** bist du schon einmal in England gewesen?; **has the postman been?** war der Briefträger schon da?; **9** (*forming the passive*) werden ✧ (PERF *sein*); **to be loved** geliebt werden; **he has been promoted** er ist befördert worden; **10 there is/are** es gibt; **are there any shops near here?** gibt es hier in der Nähe Geschäfte?

beach *noun* Strand *der* (PL die Strände); **to go to the beach** zum Strand gehen; **on the beach** am Strand.

bead *noun* Perle *die* (PL die Perlen).

beam *noun* **1** (*of light*) Strahl *der* (PL die Strahlen); **2** (*for a roof*) Balken *der* (PL die Balken).

bean *noun* Bohne *die* (PL die Bohnen); **green beans** grüne Bohnen.

bear *noun* Bär *der* (PL die Bären). *verb* **1** ertragen ✧; **I can't bear the idea** ich kann den Gedanken nicht ertragen; **2 to bear something in mind** an etwas ←(ACC) denken; **I'll bear it in mind** ich denke daran.

beard *noun* Bart *der* (PL die Bärte).

bearded *adjective* bärtig.

bearings *plural noun* **to get one's bearings** sich orientieren.

beast *noun* **1** (*animal*) Tier *das* (PL die Tiere); **2 you beast!** du Biest!

beat *noun* (*in music*) Takt *der*. *verb* **1** schlagen ✧; (*defeat*) **we beat them!** wir haben sie geschlagen; **2 you can't beat a good meal** es geht doch nichts über ein gutes Essen.
● **to beat somebody up** jemanden verprügeln.

beautiful *adjective* schön.

beauty *noun* **1** Schönheit *die* (PL die Schönheiten); **2 the beauty of it is that …** das Schöne daran ist, dass …

because *conjunction* **1** weil; **because it's cold** weil es kalt ist; **2 because of** wegen (+GEN); **because of the accident** wegen des Unfalls; **because of you** deinetwegen.

become *verb* werden ✧ (PERF *sein*); **she's become a painter** sie ist Malerin geworden.

bed *noun* **1** Bett *das* (PL die Betten); **double bed** *das* Doppelbett; **in bed** im Bett; **to go to bed** ins Bett gehen; **2** (*flower bed*) Beet *das* (PL die Beete).

△ NEW SPELLING: *See page xii*

bedclothes *plural noun*
Bettwäsche *die*.

bedding *noun* Bettzeug *das*.

bedroom *noun* Schlafzimmer *das*
(PL *die* Schlafzimmer); **bedroom
furniture** Schlafzimmermöbel
(*plural*); **my bedroom window**
mein Schlafzimmerfenster.

bedside table *noun* Nachttisch
der.

bedsit, bedsitter *noun* möblierte
Zimmer *das* (PL *die* möblierten
Zimmer).

bedspread *noun* Tagesdecke *die*
(PL *die* Tagesdecken).

bedtime *noun* Schlafenszeit *die*; **at
bedtime** vor dem Schlafengehen.

bee *noun* Biene *die* (PL *die* Bienen).

beech *noun* Buche *die* (PL *die*
Buchen).

beef *noun* Rindfleisch *das*; **we had
roast beef** wir haben Rinderbraten
gegessen.

beefburger *noun* Hamburger *der*
(PL *die* Hamburger).

beer *noun* Bier *das* (PL *die* Biere);
two beers please zwei Bier bitte;
beer can *die* Bierdose.

beetle *noun* Käfer *der* (PL *die* Käfer).

beetroot *noun* Rote Bete △ *die*.

before *preposition* 1 vor (+DAT);
before Monday vor Montag; **he left
before me** er ist vor mir gegangen;
the day before the wedding am Tag
vor der Hochzeit; **2 the day before**
am Tag zuvor; **the day before**
yesterday vorgestern; **the week
before** in der Woche zuvor;
3 (*already*) schon einmal; **I've seen
him before somewhere** ich habe
ihn schon einmal irgendwo gesehen;
I had seen the film before ich hatte
den Film schon einmal gesehen.
conjunction bevor; **I closed the
windows before leaving** (*or* before
I left) ich habe die Fenster
zugemacht, bevor ich wegging;
before the train leaves bevor der
Zug abfährt; **oh, before I forget** …
bevor ich es vergesse …

beforehand *adverb* (*ahead of time*)
vorher; **phone beforehand** rufe
vorher an.

beg *verb* 1 betteln; **to beg for money**
um Geld betteln; **2** (*ask*) bitten ✧;
he begged her not to say anything
er bat sie, nichts zu sagen; **3 I beg
your pardon** entschuldigen Sie
bitte.

begin *verb* anfangen ✧ SEP,
beginnen ✧; **the meeting begins at
ten** die Besprechung fängt um zehn
an; **the words beginning with P** die
Wörter, die mit P anfangen; **to begin
to do something** anfangen, etwas
zu tun; beginnen, etwas zu tun; **I'm
beginning to understand why** …
ich beginne zu verstehen, warum …

beginner *noun* Anfänger *der* (PL *die*
Anfänger), Anfängerin *die* (PL *die*
Anfängerinnen).

beginning *noun* Anfang *der* (PL *die*
Anfänge); **at the beginning** am
Anfang; **at the beginning of the
holidays** am Anfang der Ferien.

✧ IRREGULAR VERB: *See the verb table in the centre of the dictionary*

behave *verb* **1** sich benehmen ✧; **he behaved badly** er hat sich schlecht benommen; **2 to behave oneself** sich benehmen ✧; **behave yourself!** benimm dich!

behaviour *noun* Benehmen *das*.

behind *noun* Hintern *der* (*informal*) (PL *die* Hintern). *preposition, adverb* **1** hinter (+DAT, *or* +ACC *when there is movement towards a place*); **behind the sofa** hinter dem Sofa; **behind them** hinter ihnen; **the car behind** das Auto hinter ihnen/uns; **2 to leave something behind** (*belongings*) etwas vergessen.

beige *adjective* beige.

Belgian *noun* Belgier *der* (PL *die* Belgier), Belgierin *die* (PL *die* Belgierinnen). *adjective* belgisch; **he's Belgian** er ist Belgier.

Belgium *noun* Belgien *das*; **to Belgium** nach Belgien.

belief *noun* Glaube *der* (PL *die* Glauben); **his political beliefs** seine politische Überzeugung.

believe *verb* **1** glauben; **I believe so** ich glaube schon; **they believed what I said** sie glaubten, was ich sagte; **I don't believe you** das glaube ich dir nicht; **2 to believe in something** an etwas ←(ACC) glauben; **to believe in God** an Gott glauben.

bell *noun* **1** (*in a church*) Glocke *die* (PL *die* Glocken); **2** (*on a door*) Klingel *die* (PL *die* Klingeln); **to ring the bell** klingeln; **3** (*for a cat or toy*)

Glöckchen *das* (PL *die* Glöckchen); ★ **that name rings a bell** der Name sagt mir etwas (*literally: says something to me*).

belong *verb* **1 to belong to** gehören (+DAT); **that belongs to my mother** das gehört meiner Mutter; **2 to belong to a club** einem Klub angehören; **3** (*go*) gehören; **where does this vase belong?** wo gehört diese Vase hin?

belongings *plural noun* Sachen (*plural*); **all my belongings** alle meine Sachen.

below *preposition* unter (+DAT, *or* +ACC *when there is movement towards a place*); **below the window** unter dem Fenster; **the flat below yours** die Wohnung unter dir. *adverb* **1** (*further down*) unten; **he called from below** er rief von unten; **2 the flat below** die Wohnung darunter.

belt *noun* Gürtel *der* (PL *die* Gürtel).

bench *noun* Bank *die* (PL *die* Bänke).

bend *noun* **1** (*in a road*) Kurve *die* (PL *die* Kurven); **2** (*in a river*) Biegung *die* (PL *die* Biegungen). *verb* **1** (*make a bend in*) biegen ✧ (*a pipe or wire*), beugen (*your knee, arm, or head*); **2** (*curve*) eine Biegung machen; **3 to bend down** sich bücken.

beneath *preposition* unter (+DAT).

benefit *noun* **1** Vorteil *der* (PL *die* Vorteile); **2 unemployment benefit** *die* Arbeitslosenunterstützung.

bent *adjective* verbogen.

beret noun Baskenmütze die (PL die Baskenmützen).

beside preposition (next to) neben (+DAT, or +ACC when there is movement towards a place); **she was sitting beside me** sie saß neben mir; **she sat down beside me** sie hat sich neben mich gesetzt; ★ **that's beside the point** das hat nichts damit zu tun.

besides adverb (anyway) außerdem; **besides, it's too late** außerdem ist es zu spät; (as well) **four dogs, and six cats besides** vier Hunde und außerdem sechs Katzen.

best adjective 1 bester/beste/bestes; **she's my best friend** sie ist meine beste Freundin; 2 **she's the best at tennis** im Tennis ist sie die Beste; **it's best to wait** das Beste ist zu warten.
adverb am besten; **he plays best** er spielt am besten; **I like Munich best** München gefällt mir am besten; **best of all** am allerbesten; **I like grapes best** ich mag Weintrauben am liebsten; ★ **all the best!** alles Gute!; ★ **to make the best of it** das Beste daraus machen; ★ **to do your best** sein Bestes tun; **I did my best to help her** ich habe mein Bestes getan, um ihr zu helfen.

bet noun Wette die (PL die Wetten).
verb wetten; **to bet on a horse** auf ein Pferd wetten; **I bet you he'll forget it** ich wette mit dir, dass er es vergisst.

better adjective, adverb 1 besser; **she's found a better flat** sie hat eine bessere Wohnung gefunden; 2 **it works better than the other one** dieser geht besser als der andere; **even better** noch besser; **it's even better than before** das ist noch besser als vorher; 3 (less ill) **I'm better** es geht mir besser; **he's a bit better today** es geht ihm heute ein bisschen besser; **I feel better** ich fühle mich besser; 4 **to get better** besser werden; **my German is getting better** mein Deutsch wird besser; 5 **so much the better** umso besser; **the sooner the better** je eher, desto besser.
adverb **it's better to phone at once** es wäre besser, sofort anzurufen; **he'd better not go** er sollte besser nicht gehen; **I'd better go now** ich gehe jetzt besser.

better off adjective 1 (richer) besser gestellt; **they're better off than us** sie sind besser gestellt als wir; 2 (more comfortable) **to be better off** besser dran sein; **you'd be better off in bed** du wärst im Bett besser dran.

between preposition 1 zwischen (+DAT, or +ACC when there is movement towards a place); **between London and Dover** zwischen London und Dover; **between Monday and Friday** zwischen Montag und Freitag; 2 (sharing) unter (+DAT); **between ourselves** unter uns; **between the two of them** unter sich.

beyond preposition 1 (in space)

✧ IRREGULAR VERB: See the verb table in the centre of the dictionary

jenseits (+GEN); **beyond the border**
jenseits der Grenze; **2** (*in time*) nach
(+DAT); **beyond midnight** nach
Mitternacht; **3 it's beyond me!** das
ist mir unverständlich.

bicycle *noun* Fahrrad *das* (PL *die*
Fahrräder); **she rides a bicycle** sie
fährt Rad.

big *adjective* groß; **a big house** ein
großes Haus; **my big sister** meine
große Schwester; **a big mistake** ein
großer Fehler; **it's too big for me**
das ist mir zu groß.

big toe *noun* große Zehe *die* (PL *die*
großen Zehen).

bike *noun* Rad *das* (PL *die* Räder); **by
bike** mit dem Rad.

bilingual *adjective* zweisprachig.

bill *noun* Rechnung *die* (PL *die*
Rechnungen); **can we have the bill,
please?** die Rechnung bitte.

billiards *noun* Billard *das*; **to play
billiards** Billard spielen.

bin *noun* Mülleimer *der* (PL *die*
Mülleimer).

biochemistry *noun*
Biochemie *die*.

biology *noun* Biologie *die*.

bird *noun* Vogel *der* (PL *die* Vögel).

bird sanctuary *noun*
Vogelschutzgebiet *das* (PL *die*
Vogelschutzgebiete).

Biro™ *noun* Kugelschreiber *der* (PL
die Kugelschreiber).

birth *noun* Geburt *die* (PL *die*
Geburten).

birth certificate *noun*
Geburtsurkunde *die* (PL *die*
Geburtsurkunden).

birthday *noun* Geburtstag *der* (PL
die Geburtstage); **happy birthday!**
herzlichen Glückwunsch zum
Geburtstag!

birthday party *noun*
Geburtstagsfeier *die* (PL *die*
Geburtstagsfeiern).

biscuit *noun* Keks *der* (PL *die*
Kekse).

bit *noun* **1** (*piece*) Stückchen *das*; **a
bit of chocolate** ein Stückchen
Schokolade; **2** (*a small amount*) **a
bit of** ein bisschen △; **a bit of sugar**
ein bisschen Zucker; **3** (*in a book,
film, etc.*) Teil *der* (PL *die* Teile); **this
bit is brilliant** dieser Teil ist
glänzend; **4 a bit** ein bisschen △; **a
bit too early** ein bisschen zu früh;
wait a bit! warte ein bisschen!;
5 he's a bit of a show-off er ist ein
ziemlicher Angeber; **6 bit by bit**
nach und nach.

bite *noun* **1** (*snack*) Happen *der* (PL
die Happen); **we'll just have a bite
before we go** wir essen noch einen
kleinen Happen, bevor wir gehen;
2 (*from an insect*) Stich *der* (PL *die*
Stiche); **mosquito bite** *der*
Mückenstich; **3** (*from a dog*)
Biss △ *der* (PL *die* Bisse).
verb **1** (*person or dog*) beißen ◇;
2 (*insect*) stechen ◇.

bitter *adjective* (*taste*) bitter.

black *adjective* **1** schwarz; **my black
jacket** meine schwarze Jacke; **2 a
black man** ein Schwarzer; **a black
woman** eine Schwarze.

△ NEW SPELLING: *See page xii*

blackberry noun Brombeere die
(PL die Brombeeren).

blackbird noun Amsel die (PL die
Amseln).

blackboard noun Tafel die (PL die
Tafeln).

blackcurrant noun schwarze
Johannisbeere die (PL die schwarzen
Johnannisbeeren).

blame noun Schuld die; **to take the
blame for something** die Schuld für
etwas ←(ACC) auf sich ←(ACC) nehmen;
to put the blame on somebody die
Schuld auf jemanden schieben.
verb **to blame somebody for
something** jemandem die Schuld
an etwas ←(DAT) geben; **they blamed
him for the accident** sie haben ihm
die Schuld an dem Unfall gegeben;
she is to blame for it sie ist daran
schuld; **I blame the parents** ich
gebe den Eltern Schuld; **I don't
blame you** ich kann es dir nicht
verdenken.

blank noun Lücke die (PL die
Lücken).
adjective 1 (page) leer; (tape or
disk) unbespielt; 2 **blank cheque**
der Blankoscheck.

blanket noun Decke die (PL die
Decken).

blaze noun Feuer das (PL die Feuer).
verb brennen ✧.

bleach noun Bleichmittel das (PL
die Bleichmittel).

bleed verb bluten; **my nose is
bleeding** meine Nase blutet.

blend verb mischen.

blender noun Mixer der (PL die
Mixer).

bless verb segnen; **bless you!** (afte
a sneeze) Gesundheit!

blind noun (in a window) Rollo das
(PL die Rollos).
adjective blind.

blister noun Blase die (PL die
Blasen).

block noun (a building or buildings)
Block der (PL die Blocks); **block of
flats** der Wohnblock; **office block**
das Bürohaus; **to drive round the
block** um den Block fahren.
verb 1 sperren (an exit or a road);
2 **the sink's blocked** das
Spülbecken ist verstopft.

blonde adjective blond.

blood noun Blut das.

blood test noun Blutprobe die (PL
die Blutproben).

blouse noun Bluse die (PL die
Blusen).

blow noun Schlag der (PL die
Schläge).
verb 1 (a person) blasen ✧; 2 (the
wind) wehen; 3 **the bomb blew the
bridge to pieces** die Bombe hat die
Brücke in die Luft gesprengt; 4 **to
blow your nose** sich ←(DAT) die Nase
putzen.
● **to blow something out** etwas
ausblasen ✧ SEP.
● **to blow up** (explode) explodieren
(PERF sein).
● **to blow something up** (a tyre or
balloon) etwas aufblasen ✧ SEP;
(with explosives) etwas sprengen.

✧ IRREGULAR VERB: *See the verb table in the centre of the dictionary*

blow-dry *noun* Föhnen △ *das*; **a cut and blow-dry** Schneiden und Föhnen.

blue *adjective* blau; **blue eyes** blaue Augen.

blunder *noun* Fehler *der* (PL *die* Fehler).

blunt *adjective* **1** (*a knife, pencil, or scissors*) stumpf; **2** (*a person or question*) direkt.

blush *verb* erröten (PERF *sein*).

board *noun* **1** (*plank, notice board, game*) Brett *das* (PL *die* Bretter); **chess board** *das* Schachbrett; **2** (*blackboard*) Tafel *die* (PL *die* Tafeln); **3** (*accommodation in a hotel*) **full board** *die* Vollpension; **half board** *die* Halbpension; **board and lodging** Unterkunft und Verpflegung.

boarder *noun* (*in a school*) Internatsschüler *der* (PL *die* Internatsschüler), Internatsschülerin *die* (PL *die* Internatsschülerinnen).

board game *noun* Brettspiel *das* (PL *die* Brettspiele).

boarding *noun* (*on a plane, train*) Einsteigen *das*.

boarding card *noun* Bordkarte *die* (PL *die* Bordkarten).

boarding school *noun* Internat *das* (PL *die* Internate).

boast *verb* prahlen; **he was boasting about his new bike** er prahlte mit seinem neuen Rad.

boat *noun* **1** Boot *das* (PL *die* Boote); **rowing boat** *das* Ruderboot; **2** (*larger boat*) Schiff *das* (PL *die* Schiffe); **to go by boat** mit dem Schiff fahren.

body *noun* **1** Körper *der* (PL *die* Körper); **2** (*corpse*) Leiche *die* (PL *die* Leichen).

bodybuilding *noun* Bodybuilding *das*.

bodyguard *noun* Leibwächter *der* (PL *die* Leibwächter).

boil *noun* **1** **to bring the water to the boil** das Wasser zum Kochen bringen; **2** (*swelling*) Furunkel *der* (PL *die* Furunkel).
verb **1** kochen; **the water's boiling** das Wasser kocht; **to boil vegetables** Gemüse kochen; **2** (*put the kettle on*) **to boil some water** Wasser aufsetzen SEP.
● **to boil over** überkochen SEP (PERF *sein*).

boiled egg *noun* gekochte Ei *das* (PL *die* gekochten Eier).

boiled potato *noun* Salzkartoffel *die* (PL *die* Salzkartoffeln).

boiler *noun* (*for central heating*) Heizkessel *der* (PL *die* Heizkessel).

boiling *adjective* **1** (*water*) kochend; **2** **it's boiling hot today** heute ist es wahnsinnig heiß.

bolt *noun* (*on a door*) Riegel *der* (PL *die* Riegel).
verb **1** (*lock*) verriegeln; **2** (*gobble down*) runterschlingen ◇ SEP (*informal*).

△ NEW SPELLING: *See page xii*

bomb noun Bombe die (PL die Bomben).
verb bombardieren.

bombing noun 1 (in war) Bombardierung die (PL die Bombardierungen); 2 (a terrorist attack) Bombenattentat das (PL die Bombenattentate).

bone noun 1 Knochen der (PL die Knochen); 2 (of a fish) Gräte die (PL die Gräten).

bonfire noun Feuer das (PL die Feuer).

book noun 1 Buch das (PL die Bücher); **a book about dinosaurs** ein Buch über Dinosaurier; **my biology book** mein Biologiebuch; 2 (of stamps, tickets) Heft das (PL die Hefte); 3 **exercise book** das Heft; **cheque book** das Scheckbuch.
verb 1 buchen (holiday, flight); 2 bestellen (a table, theatre, or cinema tickets); **I booked a table for 8 p.m.** ich habe einen Tisch für zwanzig Uhr bestellt.

bookcase noun Bücherregal das (PL die Bücherregale).

booking noun (for a flight or a holiday, for example) Buchung die (PL die Buchungen).

booking office noun 1 (at a train station) Fahrkartenschalter der (PL die Fahrkartenschalter); 2 (in a theatre or cinema) Kasse die (PL die Kassen).

booklet noun Broschüre die (PL die Broschüren).

bookshelf noun Bücherregal das (PL die Bücherregale).

bookshop noun Buchhandlung die (PL die Buchhandlungen).

boot noun 1 Stiefel der (PL die Stiefel); 2 (for football, walking, climbing, or skiing) Schuh der (PL die Schuhe); **football boots** Fußballschuhe; 3 (of a car) Kofferraum der (PL die Kofferräume).

border noun (between countries) Grenze die (PL die Grenzen); **at the border** an der Grenze.

bore noun 1 (a boring person) langweilige Mensch der (PL die langweiligen Menschen); 2 (a nuisance) **what a bore!** wie ärgerlich!

bored adjective **to be bored** sich langweilen; **I'm bored** ich langweile mich.

boring adjective langweilig.

born adjective geboren; **to be born** geboren werden; **she was born in Germany** sie ist in Deutschland geboren.

borrow verb sich ←(DAT) borgen; **can I borrow your bike?** kann ich mir dein Rad borgen?; **to borrow something from somebody** sich etwas von jemandem borgen; **I borrowed some money from Dad** ich habe mir Geld von Vati geborgt.

boss noun Chef der (PL die Chefs), Chefin die (PL die Chefinnen).

bossy adjective herrisch.

◇ IRREGULAR VERB: See the verb table in the centre of the dictionary

both *pronoun* beide; **they both came** sie kamen beide; **both my sisters were there** meine beiden Schwestern waren da; **both of us** wir beide; **they are both sold** beide sind verkauft.
adverb **both at home and at school** sowohl zu Hause als auch in der Schule; **both in summer and in winter** sowohl im Sommer als auch im Winter.

bother *noun* **1** (*minor trouble*) Ärger *der*; **I've had a lot of bother with the car** ich hatte viel Ärger mit dem Auto; **2 if it isn't too much bother** wenn es nicht zuviel Mühe macht; **it's no bother** das ist kein Problem; **the children were no bother** die Kinder waren kein Problem; **without any bother** ohne irgendwelche Schwierigkeiten.
verb **1** (*disturb*) stören; **I'm sorry to bother you** es tut mir leid, dich zu stören; **2** (*worry*) stören; **what's bothering you?** was stört dich?; **it doesn't bother me at all** das stört mich überhaupt nicht; **3** (*take trouble*) **don't bother to write** du brauchst nicht zu schreiben; **she didn't even bother to wait** sie hat nicht einmal gewartet; **don't bother!** lass es! (*informal*); **I can't be bothered** ich habe keine Lust.

bottle *noun* Flasche *die* (PL *die* Flaschen).

bottle bank *noun* Altglascontainer *der* (PL *die* Altglascontainer).

bottle opener *noun* Flaschenöffner *der* (PL *die* Flaschenöffner).

bottom *noun* **1** (*of a bag, bottle, hole, or stretch of water*) Boden *der* (PL *die* Böden); **at the bottom of the lake** am Boden des Sees; **2** (*of a hill or building*) Fuß *der* (PL *die* Füße); **at the bottom of the tower** am Fuß des Turms; **3** (*of a garden, street, list*) Ende *das* (PL *die* Enden); **at the bottom of the street** am Ende der Straße; **4 at the bottom of the page** unten auf der Seite; **5** (*buttocks*) Hintern *der* (*informal*) (PL *die* Hintern).
adjective **1** unterster/unterste/unterstes; **the bottom shelf** das unterste Regal; **2 the bottom flat** die Wohnung im Erdgeschoss.

bounce *verb* (*jump*) springen ✧ (PERF *sein*).

bouncer *noun* Rausschmeißer *der* (PL *die* Rausschmeißer).

bound *adjective* (*certain*) **he's bound to be late** er kommt ganz bestimmt zu spät; **that was bound to happen** das musste ja kommen.

bow *noun* **1** (*in a shoelace or ribbon*) Schleife *die* (PL *die* Schleifen); **2** (*for a violin or with arrows*) Bogen *der* (PL *die* Bogen); **with bow and arrow** mit Pfeil und Bogen.

bowl *noun* **1** (*large, for salad, mixing, or washing up*) Schüssel *die* (PL *die* Schüsseln); **2** (*smaller*) Schale *die* (PL *die* Schalen).

bowler *noun* (*in cricket*) Werfer *der* (PL *die* Werfer), Werferin *die* (PL *die* Werferinnen).

bowling *noun* (*tenpin*) Bowling *das*; **to go bowling** bowlen gehen.

△ NEW SPELLING: *See page xii*

bow tie noun Fliege die (PL die Fliegen).

box noun 1 Schachtel die (PL die Schachteln); **a box of chocolates** eine Schachtel Pralinen; 2 **cardboard box** der Karton; 3 (on a form) Kästchen das (PL die Kästchen).

boxer noun Boxer der (PL die Boxer).

boxing noun 1 Boxen das; 2 **boxing match** der Boxkampf.

Boxing Day noun zweite Weihnachtsfeiertag der.

boy noun Junge der (PL die Jungen); **a little boy** ein kleiner Junge.

boyfriend noun Freund der (PL die Freunde).

bra noun BH der (PL die BHs).

brace noun (for teeth) Spange die (PL die Spangen).

bracelet noun Armband das (PL die Armbänder).

bracket noun Klammer die (PL die Klammern); **in brackets** in Klammern.

brain noun Gehirn das (PL die Gehirne).

brainwave noun Geistesblitz der (PL die Geistesblitze).

brake noun Bremse die (PL die Bremsen).
verb bremsen.

branch noun 1 (of a tree) Ast der (PL die Äste); 2 (of a shop) Filiale die (PL die Filialen); 3 (of a bank) Zweigstelle die (PL die Zweigstellen).

brand noun Marke die (PL die Marken).

brand new adjective nagelneu.

brass noun 1 (metal) Messing das; 2 (in an orchestra) **the brass** das Blech.

brass band noun Blaskapelle die (PL die Blaskapellen).

brave adjective tapfer.

bread noun Brot das (PL die Brote); **a slice of bread** eine Scheibe Brot; **a piece of bread and butter** ein Butterbrot.

break noun 1 (a short rest or at school) Pause die (PL die Pausen); **ten minutes' break** eine Pause von zehn Minuten; **to take a break** Pause machen; **at break** in der Pause; 2 **the Christmas break** die Weihnachtsferien (plural): verb 1 zerbrechen ✧, kaputtmachen SEP (informal); **he broke a glass** er hat ein Glas zerbrochen; **don't break the doll** mach die Puppe nicht kaputt; 2 (get damaged) zerbrechen ✧ (PERF sein), kaputtgehen ✧ SEP (informal) (PERF sein); **the glass broke** das Glas zerbrach; **the eggs broke** die Eier sind kaputtgegangen; 3 **to break your arm** sich ←(DAT) den Arm brechen; 4 brechen ✧ (rules, promise); **to break one's promise** sein Versprechen brechen; 5 **to break the record** den Rekord brechen ✧; 6 **to break the news that** … melden, dass …
● **to break down** 1 (car) eine Panne haben; **the car broke down** das

Auto hatte eine Panne; **2** (*talks, negotiations*) scheitern (PERF *sein*).

● **to break in** einbrechen ⬦ SEP (PERF *sein*).

● **to break up 1** (*couple*) sich trennen; **2** (*crowd*) sich auflösen SEP; **3 we break up on Thursday** die Ferien fangen Donnerstag an.

breakdown *noun* **1** (*of a vehicle*) Panne *die* (PL *die* Pannen); **we had a breakdown on the motorway** wir hatten eine Panne auf der Autobahn; **2** (*in talks or negotiations*) Scheitern *das*; **3** (*a nervous collapse*) Zusammenbruch *der* (PL *die* Zusammenbrüche); **to have a nervous breakdown** einen Nervenzusammenbruch haben.

breakfast *noun* Frühstück *das* (PL *die* Frühstücke); **we have breakfast at eight** wir frühstücken um acht Uhr.

break-in *noun* Einbruch *der* (PL *die* Einbrüche).

breast *noun* Brust *die* (PL *die* Brüste).

breath *noun* Atem *der*; **out of breath** außer Atem; **to hold your breath** den Atem anhalten; **to get your breath back** wieder zu Atem kommen; **to take a deep breath** tief einatmen.

breathe *verb* atmen.

breed *noun* (*of animal*) Rasse *die* (PL *die* Rassen).

breeze *noun* Brise *die* (PL *die* Brisen).

brew *verb* **1** brauen (*beer*); **2** aufbrühen SEP (*tea*); **the tea's brewing** der Tee zieht noch.

brick *noun* Ziegel *der* (PL *die* Ziegel); **a brick wall** eine Ziegelmauer.

bride *noun* Braut *die* (PL *die* Bräute); **the bride and groom** das Brautpaar.

bridegroom *noun* Bräutigam *der* (PL *die* Bräutigame).

bridesmaid *noun* Brautjungfer *die* (PL *die* Brautjungfern).

bridge *noun* **1** (*over a river*) Brücke *die* (PL *die* Brücken); **2** (*card game*) Bridge *das*.

brief *adjective* kurz.

briefcase *noun* Aktentasche *die* (PL *die* Aktentaschen).

briefly *adverb* kurz.

briefs *plural noun* Slip *der* (PL *die* Slips).

bright *adjective* **1** (*colour*) leuchtend; **bright green socks** leuchtend grüne Socken; **2** (*eyes, sunshine*) strahlend; **3** (*light*) hell; **4** (*clever*) intelligent; **she's not very bright** sie ist nicht sehr intelligent; ★ **to look on the bright side** die Sache positiv sehen (*literally: to see things positively*).

brilliant *adjective* **1** (*very clever*) glänzend; **he's a brilliant surgeon** er ist ein glänzender Chirurg; **2** (*wonderful*) toll; **the party was brilliant!** die Party war toll!

bring *verb* **1** mitbringen ⬦ SEP; **he brought a present** er brachte ein Geschenk mit; **bring your camera**

bring deinen Fotoapparat mit; **2** (*to a place*) bringen ✧; **she's bringing the children home** sie bringt die Kinder nach Hause.

● **to bring somebody up** jemanden großziehen ✧ SEP; **he was brought up by his aunt** er wurde von seiner Tante großgezogen.

Britain *noun* Großbritannien *das*; **to Britain** nach Großbritannien.

British *plural noun* **the British** die Briten.
adjective **1** britisch; **the British Isles** die Britischen Inseln; **2 he's British** er ist Brite; **she's British** sie ist Britin.

broad *adjective* **1** (*wide*) breit; **2** (*extensive*) weit.

broad bean *noun* dicke Bohne *die* (PL *die* dicken Bohnen).

broadcast *noun* Sendung *die* (PL *die* Sendungen).
verb senden.

broccoli *noun* Brokkoli *der* (PL *die* Brokkoli).

brochure *noun* Broschüre *die* (PL *die* Broschüren).

broke *adjective* **to be broke** pleite sein (*informal*).

broken *adjective* zerbrochen, kaputt (*informal*); **the window's broken** das Fenster ist kaputt; **to have a broken leg** ein gebrochenes Bein haben.

bronchitis *noun* Bronchitis *die*.

brooch *noun* Brosche *die* (PL *die* Broschen).

brother *noun* Bruder *der* (PL *die* Brüder); **my mother's brother** der Bruder meiner Mutter.

brother-in-law *noun* Schwager *der* (PL *die* Schwäger).

brown *adjective* braun; **my brown shoes** meine braunen Schuhe; **light brown** hellbraun; **dark brown** dunkelbraun; **to go brown** (*suntanned*) braun werden.

brown bread *noun* Mischbrot *das* (PL *die* Mischbrote).

bruise *noun* **1** (*on a person*) blaue Fleck *der* (PL *die* blauen Flecken); **2** (*on fruit*) Druckstelle *die* (PL *die* Druckstellen).

brush *noun* **1** (*for your hair, clothes, nails, or shoes*) Bürste *die* (PL *die* Bürsten); **my hair brush** meine Haarbürste; **2** (*for sweeping*) Besen *der* (PL *die* Besen); **3** (*for paint*) Pinsel *der* (PL *die* Pinsel).
verb **1** bürsten; **to brush your hair** sich ←(DAT) die Haare bürsten; **I brushed my hair** ich habe mir die Haare gebürstet; **2 to brush your teeth** sich ←(DAT) die Zähne putzen.

Brussels *noun* Brüssel *das*.

Brussels sprout *noun* Rosenkohl *der*; **he likes Brussels sprouts** er mag Rosenkohl.

bubble *noun* Blase *die* (PL *die* Blasen).

bubble bath *noun* Badeschaum *der*.

bucket *noun* Eimer *der* (PL *die* Eimer).

✧ IRREGULAR VERB: *See the verb table in the centre of the dictionary*

buckle *noun* Schnalle *die* (PL *die* Schnallen).

Buddhism *noun* Buddhismus *der*.

Buddhist *noun* Buddhist *der* (PL *die* Buddhisten), Buddhistin *die* (PL *die* Buddhistinnen).

budget *noun* Budget *das* (PL *die* Budgets).

buffet car *noun* Speisewagen *der* (PL *die* Speisewagen).

bug *noun* 1 (*insect*) Wanze *die* (PL *die* Wanzen); 2 (*germ*) Bazillus *der* (PL *die* Bazillen); **a stomach bug** eine Magengrippe; 3 **a computer bug** ein Programmierfehler.

build *verb* bauen.

builder *noun* Bauarbeiter *der* (PL *die* Bauarbeiter).

building *noun* Gebäude *das* (PL *die* Gebäude).

building site *noun* Baustelle *die* (PL *die* Baustellen).

built-up *adjective* 1 bebaut; 2 **built-up area** das Wohngebiet.

bulb *noun* 1 (*lightbulb*) Birne *die* (PL *die* Birnen); 2 (*flower bulb*) Zwiebel *die* (PL *die* Zwiebeln).

bull *noun* Bulle *der* (PL *die* Bullen).

bullet *noun* Kugel *die* (PL *die* Kugeln).

bulletin *noun* 1 (*written*) Bulletin *das* (PL *die* Bulletins); 2 (*on TV, radio*) **news bulletin** die Kurzmeldung.

bully *noun* 1 (*in school*) Rabauke *der* (PL *die* Rabauken);

2 (*adult*) Tyrann *der* (PL *die* Tyrannen).
verb schikanieren.

bum *noun* Hintern *der* (*informal*) (PL *die* Hintern).

bump *noun* 1 (*on a surface*) Unebenheit *die* (PL *die* Unebenheiten); **there are lots of bumps in the road** die Straße hat viele Unebenheiten; 2 (*swelling*) Beule *die* (PL *die* Beulen); **a bump on the head** eine Beule am Kopf; 3 (*jolt*) Stoß *der* (PL *die* Stöße); 4 (*noise*) Bums *der* (PL *die* Bumse).
verb 1 (*bang*) stoßen ◇; **I bumped my head** ich habe mir den Kopf gestoßen; **to bump into something** gegen etwas ←(ACC) stoßen; 2 **to bump into somebody** (*meet by chance*) jemanden zufällig treffen.

bumper *noun* Stoßstange *die* (PL *die* Stoßstangen).

bumpy *adjective* holperig.

bun *noun* 1 (*for a burger*) Brötchen *das* (PL *die* Brötchen), Semmel *die* (PL *die* Semmeln); 2 (*sweet*) süße Brötchen *das* (PL *die* süßen Brötchen), süße Semmel *die* (PL *die* süßen Semmeln).

bunch *noun* 1 (*of flowers*) Strauß *der* (PL *die* Sträuße); 2 (*of carrots, radishes, or keys*) Bund *das* (PL *die* Bunde); 3 **a bunch of grapes** eine ganze Weintraube.

bundle *noun* Bündel *das* (PL *die* Bündel).

bunk *noun* 1 (*on a boat*) Koje *die* (PL *die* Kojen); 2 (*on a train*) Bett *das* (PL *die* Betten).

△ NEW SPELLING: *See page xii*

bunk beds *plural noun*
Etagenbett *das* (*singular*).

burger *noun* Hamburger *der* (PL *die* Hamburger).

burglar *noun* Einbrecher *der* (PL *die* Einbrecher).

burglar alarm *noun*
Alarmanlage *die* (PL *die* Alarmanlagen).

burglary *noun* Einbruch *der* (PL *die* Einbrüche).

burn *noun* 1 (*on the skin*)
Verbrennung *die* (PL *die* Verbrennungen); 2 (*on fabric, object*) Brandstelle *die* (PL *die* Brandstellen).
verb 1 verbrennen ✧; **she burnt his letters** sie hat seine Briefe verbrannt; 2 (*fire, candle*) brennen ✧; 3 (*injure*) verbrennen ✧; **to burn yourself** sich verbrennen; **you'll burn your fingers!** du verbrennst dir die Finger!; 4 (*cake, meat, etc.*) anbrennen ✧ SEP; **Mum's burnt the cake** Mutti hat den Kuchen anbrennen lassen.

burnt *adjective* 1 (*papers, rubbish*) verbrannt; 2 (*cake, meat, etc.*) angebrannt.

burst *verb* 1 platzen lassen (*a balloon*); **the tyre has burst** der Reifen ist geplatzt; 2 **to burst out laughing** in Lachen ausbrechen ✧ SEP (PERF *sein*); **to burst into tears** in Tränen ausbrechen ✧ SEP (PERF *sein*); 3 **to burst into flames** in Flammen aufgehen ✧ SEP (PERF *sein*).

bury *verb* 1 begraben ✧ (*a dead person*); 2 vergraben ✧ (*a treasure or a bone*).

bus *noun* Bus *der* (PL *die* Busse); **on the bus** im Bus; **by bus** mit dem Bus.

bus driver *noun* Busfahrer *der* (PL *die* Busfahrer), Busfahrerin *die* (PL *die* Busfahrerinnen).

bush *noun* Busch *der* (PL *die* Büsche).

business *noun* 1 (*commercial dealings*) Geschäfte (*plural*); **business is bad** die Geschäfte gehen schlecht; **he's in Leeds on business** er ist geschäftlich in Leeds; 2 (*a line of business or profession*) Branche *die* (PL *die* Branchen); **he's in the insurance business** er ist in der Versicherungsbranche; 3 (*firm or company*) Betrieb *der* (PL *die* Betriebe); **small businesses** kleine Betriebe; 4 (*personal concern*) Angelegenheit *die* (PL *die* Angelegenheiten); **mind your own business!** kümmere dich um deine eigenen Angelegenheiten!

businessman *noun*
Geschäftsmann *der* (PL *die* Geschäftsleute).

business trip *noun*
Geschäftsreise *die* (PL *die* Geschäftsreisen).

businesswoman *noun*
Geschäftsfrau *die* (PL *die* Geschäftsfrauen).

bus pass *noun* Zeitkarte *die* (PL *die* Zeitkarten).

✧ IRREGULAR VERB: *See the verb table in the centre of the dictionary*

bus route *noun* Buslinie *die* (PL *die* Buslinien).

bus shelter *noun* Wartehäuschen *das* (PL *die* Wartehäuschen).

bus station *noun* Busbahnhof *der* (PL *die* Busbahnhöfe).

bus stop *noun* Bushaltestelle *die* (PL *die* Bushaltestellen).

bus ticket *noun* Busfahrkarte *die* (PL *die* Busfahrkarten).

busy *adjective* **1** beschäftigt; **he's busy** er ist beschäftigt; **she was busy packing** sie war mit Packen beschäftigt; **2 to have a busy day** viel zu tun haben; **3 the shops were busy** die Läden waren sehr voll; **4** (*phone*) besetzt.

but *conjunction* **1** aber; **small but strong** klein aber stark; **2** (*after a negative statement*) sondern; **not Thursday but Friday** nicht Donnerstag, sondern Freitag; **not only … but also** nicht nur … sondern auch.
preposition **1** außer (+DAT); **everyone but Winston** alle außer Winston; **anything but that!** nur das nicht!; **2 the last but one** der/die/das Vorletzte.

butcher *noun* **1** Fleischer *der* (PL *die* Fleischer), Metzger *der* (PL *die* Metzger); **he's a butcher** er ist Fleischer, er ist Metzger; **2 the butcher's** die Fleischerei, die Metzgerei.

butter *noun* Butter *die*.
verb buttern.

butterfly *noun* Schmetterling *der* (PL *die* Schmetterlinge).

button *noun* Knopf *der* (PL *die* Knöpfe).

buttonhole *noun* Knopfloch *das* (PL *die* Knopflöcher).

buy *noun* Kauf *der* (PL *die* Käufe); **a bad buy** ein schlechter Kauf.
verb kaufen; **I bought the tickets** ich habe die Karten gekauft; **to buy something for somebody** jemandem etwas kaufen; **Sarah bought him a sweater** Sarah hat ihm einen Pullover gekauft.

buzz *verb* (*a fly or bee*) summen.

buzzer *noun* Summer *der* (PL *die* Summer).

by *preposition* **1** von (+DAT); **I was bitten by a dog** ich bin von einem Hund gebissen worden; **by Mozart** von Mozart; **2 by mistake** versehentlich; **3** (*travel*) mit (+DAT); **to come by bus** mit dem Bus kommen; **to go by train** mit dem Zug fahren; **by bike** mit dem Rad; **4** (*near*) an (+DAT); **by the sea** am Meer; **the stop by the school** die Haltestelle an der Schule; **5** (*before*) bis; **it'll be ready by Monday** es wird bis Montag fertig sein; **I'll be back by four** ich bin bis vier Uhr zurück; **6 by now** inzwischen; **7 by yourself** ganz allein; **I was by myself in the house** ich war ganz allein im Haus; **she did it by herself** sie hat es ganz allein gemacht; **8 by the way** übrigens; **9 to go by** vorbeigehen ✧ SEP (PERF *sein*).

bye *exclamation* tschüs! (*informal*).

△ NEW SPELLING: *See page xii*

C c

cab noun 1 Taxi das (PL die Taxis); **to call a cab** ein Taxi rufen; 2 (on a lorry) Führerhaus das (PL die Führerhäuser).

cabbage noun Kohl der.

café noun Café das (PL die Cafés).

cage noun Käfig der (PL die Käfige).

cake noun Kuchen der (PL die Kuchen); **would you like a piece of cake?** möchtest du ein Stück Kuchen?

calculate verb berechnen.

calculation noun Rechnung die (PL die Rechnungen).

calculator noun Taschenrechner der (PL die Taschenrechner).

calendar noun Kalender der (PL die Kalender).

calf noun 1 (animal) Kalb das (PL die Kälber); 2 (of your leg) Wade die (PL die Waden).

call noun (telephone) Anruf der (PL die Anrufe); **I had several calls this morning** ich erhielt heute Morgen mehrere Anrufe; **thank you for your call** danke für deinen Anruf; **a phone call** ein Telefonanruf. verb 1 rufen ◇; **to call a taxi** ein Taxi rufen; **to call the doctor** einen Arzt rufen; **they called the police** sie riefen die Polizei; 2 (phone)

anrufen ◇ SEP; **call me later** ruf mich später an; **thank you for calling** danke für deinen Anruf; **I'll call you back later** ich rufe dich später zurück; 3 nennen ◇; **they've called the baby Julie** sie haben das Baby Julie genannt; 4 **to be called** heißen ◇; **her brother is called Dan** ihr Bruder heißt Dan; **what's he called?** wie heißt er?

call box noun Telefonzelle die (PL die Telefonzellen).

calm adjective ruhig. verb beruhigen.
● **to calm down** sich beruhigen; **he's calmed down a bit** er hat sich etwas beruhigt.
● **to calm somebody down** jemanden beruhigen; **I tried to calm her down** ich habe versucht, sie zu beruhigen.

calmly adverb ruhig.

camcorder noun Camcorder der (PL die Camcorder).

camera noun 1 Fotoapparat der (PL die Fotoapparate); 2 (film or video camera) Kamera die (PL die Kameras).

camp noun Lager das (PL die Lager). verb campen, zelten.

camper van noun Camper der (PL die Camper).

camping noun Camping das; **to go camping** zelten; **we're going camping in Bavaria this summer** diesen Sommer zelten wir in Bayern.

campsite noun Campingplatz der (PL die Campingplätze).

can¹ noun 1 Dose die (PL die Dosen);

a can of tomatoes eine Dose Tomaten; **2** (*for petrol or oil*) Kanister *der* (PL *die* Kanister).

can[2] *verb* **1** können ✧; **I can't be there before ten** ich kann vor zehn Uhr nicht da sein; **can you open the door, please?** kannst du die Tür bitte aufmachen?; **can I help you?** kann ich Ihnen helfen?; **they couldn't come** sie konnten nicht kommen; **you could have told me** das hättest du mir wirklich sagen können; **I can't see him** ich kann ihn nicht sehen; **I can't remember it** ich kann mich nicht daran erinnern; **she can't drive** sich kann nicht Auto fahren; **2** (*be allowed*) dürfen ✧; **you can't smoke here** Sie dürfen hier nicht rauchen.

Canada *noun* Kanada *das*; **to Canada** nach Kanada.

Canadian *noun* Kanadier *der* (PL *die* Kanadier), Kanadierin *die* (PL *die* Kanadierinnen).
adjective kanadisch; **he is Canadian** er ist Kanadier.

canal *noun* Kanal *der* (PL *die* Kanäle).

cancel *verb* absagen SEP; **the concert's been cancelled** das Konzert ist abgesagt worden.

cancer *noun* Krebs *der*; **to have lung cancer** Lungenkrebs haben.

Cancer *noun* Krebs *der* (PL *die* Krebse); **I'm Cancer** ich bin Krebs.

candidate *noun* Kandidat *der* (PL *die* Kandidaten), Kandidatin *die* (PL *die* Kandidatinnen).

candle *noun* Kerze *die* (PL *die* Kerzen).

candlestick *noun* Kerzenhalter *der* (PL *die* Kerzenhalter).

canned *adjective* in Dosen; **canned tomatoes** Tomaten in Dosen.

canoe *noun* Kanu *das* (PL *die* Kanus).

canoeing *noun* **to go canoeing** Kanu fahren ✧ (PERF *sein*); **I like canoeing** ich fahre gerne Kanu.

can-opener *noun* Dosenöffner *der* (PL *die* Dosenöffner).

canteen *noun* Kantine *die* (PL *die* Kantinen).

canvas *noun* **1** (*of a tent or bag*) Segeltuch *das*; **2** (*for painting on*) Leinwand *die*.

cap *noun* **1** (*hat*) Kappe *die* (PL *die* Kappen); **baseball cap** *die* Baseballkappe; **2** (*on a bottle or tube*) Verschluss △ *der* (PL *die* Verschlüsse).

capable *adjective* fähig.

capital *noun* **1** (*city*) Hauptstadt *die* (PL *die* Hauptstädte); **Berlin is the capital of Germany** Berlin ist die Hauptstadt von Deutschland; **2** (*letter*) Großbuchstabe *der* (PL *die* Großbuchstaben); **in capitals** mit Großbuchstaben.

capitalism *noun* Kapitalismus *der*.

△ NEW SPELLING: *See page xii*

Capricorn noun Steinbock der (PL die Steinböcke); **Linda's Capricorn** Linda ist Steinbock.

captain noun Kapitän der (PL die Kapitäne).

car noun Auto das (PL die Autos); **to park the car** das Auto einparken; **we're going by car** wir fahren mit dem Auto; **car crash** der Autounfall.

caramel noun Karamell∆ der (PL die Karamells).

caravan noun Wohnwagen der (PL die Wohnwagen).

card noun Karte die (PL die Karten); **card game** das Kartenspiel; **to have a game of cards** Karten spielen.

cardboard noun Pappe die.

cardigan noun Strickjacke die (PL die Strickjacken).

cardphone noun Kartentelefon das (PL die Kartentelefone).

care noun 1 Vorsicht die; **to take care crossing the road** vorsichtig beim Überqueren der Straße sein; **take care!** (be careful) sei vorsichtig!; (when saying goodbye) mach's gut!; 2 **to take care to do something** aufpassen SEP, dass man etwas tut; **to take care of somebody** auf jemanden aufpassen.
verb 1 **to care about something** sich um etwas ←(ACC) kümmern; **she cares about the environment** sie kümmert sich um die Umwelt; 2 **she doesn't care** es ist ihr egal; **I couldn't care less!** das ist mir völlig egal!

careful adjective vorsichtig; **a careful driver** ein vorsichtiger Fahrer, eine vorsichtige Fahrerin; **be careful!** sei vorsichtig!

carefully adverb 1 sorgfältig; **to read the instructions carefully** die Anweisungen sorgfältig lesen; 2 vorsichtig; **she put the vase down carefully** sie stellte die Vase vorsichtig hin; **drive carefully!** fahr vorsichtig!; 3 **listen carefully!** hören Sie gut zu!

careless adjective 1 **he's very careless** er ist sehr nachlässig; **this is careless work** das ist eine nachlässige Arbeit; 2 **a careless mistake** ein Flüchtigkeitsfehler; 3 **a careless driver** ein leichtsinniger Fahrer.

car ferry noun Autofähre die (PL die Autofähren).

car hire noun Autovermietung die.

Caribbean noun **the Caribbean (islands)** die Karibik (singular).

carnation noun Nelke die (PL die Nelken).

carnival noun Karneval der (PL die Karnevale).

car park noun Parkplatz der (PL die Parkplätze); (multi-storey) Parkhaus das (PL die Parkhäuser).

carpenter noun Tischler der (PL die Tischler).

carpentry noun Tischlerhandwerk das.

carpet noun Teppich der (PL die Teppiche).

◇ IRREGULAR VERB: See the verb table in the centre of the dictionary

car phone noun Autotelefon das (PL die Autotelefone).

car radio noun Autoradio das (PL die Autoradios).

carriage noun (of a train) Abteil das (PL die Abteile).

carrier bag noun Tragetasche die (PL die Tragetaschen).

carrot noun Karotte die (PL die Karotten), Möhre die (PL die Möhren).

carry verb tragen; **she was carrying a case** sie trug einen Koffer.
● **to carry on** weitermachen SEP; **they carried on working** sie machten ihre Arbeit weiter.

carrycot noun Babytragetasche die (PL die Babytragetaschen).

carsick adjective **he gets carsick** ihm wird beim Autofahren schlecht.

carton noun 1 (of cream or yoghurt) Becher der (PL die Becher); 2 (of milk or orange) Tüte die (PL die Tüten).

cartoon noun 1 (a film) Zeichentrickfilm der (PL die Zeichentrickfilme); 2 (a comic strip) Cartoon der (PL die Cartoons); 3 (a drawing) Karikatur die (PL die Karikaturen).

cartridge noun (for a pen) Patrone die (PL die Patronen).

case¹ noun 1 (suitcase) Koffer der (PL die Koffer); **to pack a case** einen Koffer packen; 2 (a large wooden box) Kiste die (PL die Kisten); 3 (for spectacles or small things) Etui das (PL die Etuis).

case² noun 1 Fall der (PL die Fälle); **in that case** in dem Fall; **that's not the case** das ist nicht der Fall; **in case of fire** bei Feuer; 2 **in case** falls; **in case he comes** falls er kommt; 3 **just in case** für alle Fälle; 4 **in any case** sowieso; **in any case, it's too late** es ist sowieso zu spät.

cash noun 1 (money in general) Geld das; **I haven't any cash on me** ich habe kein Geld dabei; 2 (money rather than a cheque) Bargeld das; **to pay in cash** bar zahlen; **£50 in cash** fünfzig Pfund in bar.

cash card noun Bankkarte die (PL die Bankkarten).

cash desk noun Kasse die (PL die Kassen); **to pay at the cash desk** an der Kasse zahlen.

cash dispenser noun Geldautomat der (PL die Geldautomaten).

cashier noun Kassierer der (PL die Kassierer), Kassiererin die (PL die Kassiererinnen).

cash point noun Geldautomat der (PL die Geldautomaten).

cassette noun Kassette die (PL die Kassetten).

cassette recorder noun Kassettenrekorder der (PL die Kassettenrekorder).

cast noun (of a play) Besetzung die.

castle noun 1 Burg die (PL die Burgen); 2 (in chess) Turm der (PL die Türme).

casual adjective zwanglos.

casualty *noun* 1 (*in an accident*)
Verletzte *der/die* (PL *die* Verletzten);
2 (*hospital department*)
Unfallstation *die* (PL *die*
Unfallstationen); **he's in casualty** er
ist auf der Unfallstation.

cat *noun* Katze *die* (PL *die* Katzen);
(*tomcat*) Kater *der* (PL *die* Kater);
★ **it's raining cats and dogs** es
regnet in Strömen (*literally: it's
raining in streams*).

catalogue *noun* Katalog *der* (PL *die*
Kataloge).

catastrophe *noun*
Katastrophe *die* (PL *die*
Katastrophen).

catch *noun* 1 (*on a door*)
Schnapper *der* (PL *die* Schnapper);
2 (*a drawback*) Haken *der* (PL *die*
Haken); **where's the catch?** wo ist
der Haken?
verb 1 fangen ✧; **Tom caught the
ball** Tom hat den Ball gefangen; **she
caught a fish** sie hat einen Fisch
gefangen; **catch me!** fang mich!;
2 **to catch somebody doing
something** jemanden bei etwas
←(DAT) erwischen; **he was caught
stealing money** er wurde beim
Geldstehlen erwischt; 3 (*be in time
for*) noch erreichen; **did Tim catch
his plane?** hat Tim sein Flugzeug
noch erreicht?; 4 (*become ill with*)
bekommen ✧; **she's caught
chickenpox** sie hat die
Windpocken bekommen;
5 verstehen ✧ (*what somebody
says*); **I didn't catch your name** ich
habe Ihren Namen nicht verstanden.
● **to catch up with somebody**
jemanden einholen SEP.

catering *noun* 1 (*trade*)
Gastronomie *die*; 2 **who's doing the
catering?** wer liefert das Essen und
die Getränke?

cathedral *noun* Kathedrale *die* (PL
die Kathedralen); **Cologne
cathedral** der Kölner Dom.

Catholic *noun* Katholik *der* (PL *die*
Katholiken), Katholikin *die* (PL *die*
Katholikinnen).
adjective katholisch.

cattle *plural noun* Vieh *das*.

cauliflower *noun* Blumenkohl *der*;
cauliflower cheese *der*
Blumenkohlauflauf.

cause *noun* 1 Ursache *die* (PL *die*
Ursachen); **the cause of the
accident** die Unfallursache; 2 **for a
good cause** für eine gute Sache.
verb verursachen; **to cause
difficulties** Schwierigkeiten
verursachen.

cave *noun* Höhle *die* (PL *die*
Höhlen).

caving *noun* Höhlenforschung *die*;
to go caving auf Höhlenforschung
gehen.

CD *noun* CD *die* (PL *die* CDs).

CD player *noun* CD-Spieler *der* (PL
die CD-Spieler).

CD-ROM *noun* CD-ROM *die* (PL *die*
CD-ROMs).

ceiling *noun* Decke *die* (PL *die*
Decken); **on the ceiling** an der
Decke.

✧ IRREGULAR VERB: *See the verb table in the centre of the dictionary*

celebrate *verb* feiern; **he's celebrating his birthday** er feiert seinen Geburtstag.

celebrity *noun* Berühmtheit die (PL die Berühmtheiten).

celery *noun* Sellerie der (PL die Sellerie).

cell *noun* Zelle die (PL die Zellen).

cellar *noun* Keller der (PL die Keller).

cello *noun* Cello das (PL die Cellos); **to play the cello** Cello spielen.

cement *noun* Zement der.

cemetery *noun* Friedhof der (PL die Friedhöfe).

centigrade *adjective* Celsius; **ten degrees centigrade** zehn Grad Celsius.

centimetre *noun* Zentimeter der (PL die Zentimeter).

central *adjective* 1 zentral; **the office is very central** das Büro ist sehr zentral gelegen; 2 **in central London** im Zentrum von London.

central heating *noun* Zentralheizung die.

centre *noun* Zentrum das (PL die Zentren); **in the centre of** im Zentrum von (+DAT); **in the town centre** im Stadtzentrum; **a shopping centre** ein Einkaufszentrum.

century *noun* Jahrhundert das (PL die Jahrhunderte); **in the twentieth century** im zwanzigsten Jahrhundert.

cereal *noun* **breakfast cereal** Frühstücksflocken (*plural*).

certain *adjective* 1 (*definite*) bestimmt; **a certain number of** eine bestimmte Zahl von (+DAT); 2 (*confident*) sicher; **to be certain** sich ←(DAT) sicher sein; **are you certain of the address?** bist du dir der Adresse sicher?; **I'm absolutely certain** ich bin mir ganz sicher; **to be certain that** … sicher sein, dass …; 3 **nobody knows for certain** niemand weiß es genau.

certainly *adverb* bestimmt; **certainly not** bestimmt nicht.

certificate *noun* 1 Bescheinigung die (PL die Bescheinigungen); 2 **birth certificate** die Geburtsurkunde; 3 (*at school*) Zeugnis das (PL die Zeugnisse).

chain Kette die (PL die Ketten).

chair *noun* 1 (*upright*) Stuhl der (PL die Stühle); **a kitchen chair** ein Küchenstuhl; 2 (*with arms*) Sessel der (PL die Sessel).

chair lift *noun* Sessellift der (PL die Sessellifte).

chalet *noun* 1 (*in the mountains*) Chalet das (PL die Chalets); 2 (*in a holiday camp*) Ferienhaus das (PL die Ferienhäuser).

challenge *noun* Herausforderung die (PL die Herausforderungen).

champion *noun* Meister der (PL die Meister), Meisterin die (PL die Meisterinnen); **the world slalom champion** der Weltmeister im Slalom, die Weltmeisterin im Slalom.

chance noun 1 (opportunity) Gelegenheit die (PL die Gelegenheiten); **to have the chance to do something** die Gelegenheit haben, etwas zu tun; **if you have the chance to go to New York** wenn du die Gelegenheit hast, nach New York zu fahren; **I had no chance to speak to him** ich hatte keine Gelegenheit, mit ihm zu reden; 2 (likelihood) Aussicht die (PL die Aussichten); **he's got no chance of winning** er hat keine Aussicht zu gewinnen; 3 (luck) **by chance** zufällig; **do you have her address, by any chance?** hast du zufällig ihre Adresse?

change noun 1 (from one thing to another) Änderung die (PL die Änderungen); **a change of address** eine Adressenänderung; **there's been a change of plan** der Plan ist geändert worden; 2 (alteration) Veränderung die (PL die Veränderungen); **they've made some changes to the house** sie haben im Haus ein paar Veränderungen vorgenommen; **a change in the weather** eine Wetterveränderung; 3 (for the sake of variety) **for a change, we could go to a restaurant** zur Abwechslung könnten wir in ein Restaurant gehen; **it makes a change from hamburgers** das ist mal etwas anderes als Hamburger; **a change of clothes** etwas anderes zum Anziehen; 4 (cash) Wechselgeld das; **I haven't any change** ich habe kein Wechselgeld. verb 1 (make different) ändern; **you can't change her** du kannst sie nicht ändern; **to change your address** seine Adresse ändern; 2 (become different) sich verändern; **Liz has changed a lot** Liz hat sich sehr verändert; 3 (transform completely) verwandeln; **the prince changed into a frog** der Prinz hat sich in einen Frosch verwandelt; 4 (exchange in a shop) umtauschen SEP; **just change it for a larger size** tauschen Sie es einfach gegen eine größere Größe um; 5 (change clothes) sich umziehen ♦ SEP; **Mike's just changing** Mike zieht sich gerade um; 6 (switch from one train or bus to another) umsteigen ♦ SEP (PERF sein); **we changed trains at Crewe** wir sind in Crewe umgestiegen; 7 (switch one thing for another) wechseln; **I want to change my job** ich möchte meine Stellung wechseln; **they changed places** sie haben die Plätze gewechselt; 8 **to change your mind** sich anders entschließen ♦.

changing room noun (for sport or swimming) Umkleideraum der (PL die Umkleideräume).

channel noun 1 (on TV) Kanal der (PL die Kanäle); **to change channels** auf einen anderen Kanal schalten; 2 **the Channel** der Kanal.

Channel Tunnel noun Eurotunnel der.

chaos noun Chaos das; **it was chaos!** das war ein Chaos!

chapel noun Kapelle die (PL die Kapellen).

♦ IRREGULAR VERB: See the verb table in the centre of the dictionary

chapter *noun* Kapitel *das* (PL *die* Kapitel); **in chapter two** im zweiten Kapitel.

character *noun* 1 (*personality*) Charakter *der*; 2 (*somebody in a book*) Charakter *der* (PL *die* Charaktere); 3 (*part in a play or film*) Rolle *die* (PL *die* Rollen); **the main character** die Hauptrolle.

charcoal *noun* 1 (*for burning*) Holzkohle *die*; 2 (*for drawing*) Kohlestift *der* (PL *die* Kohlestifte).

charge *noun* 1 (*what you pay*) Gebühr *die* (PL *die* Gebühren); **a booking charge** Buchungskosten (*plural*); **an extra or additional charge** eine zusätzliche Gebühr; **there's no charge** das ist kostenlos; **2 to be in charge** für etwas ←(ACC) verantwortlich sein; **who's in charge of the children?** wer ist für die Kinder verantwortlich?; **3 to be on a charge of theft** wegen Diebstahls angeklagt sein.
verb 1 (*ask to pay*) berechnen; **they charge us fifteen pounds an hour** sie berechnen uns fünfzehn Pfund pro Stunde; **they didn't charge for delivery** sie haben die Lieferung nicht berechnet; **we won't charge you for it** wir berechnen Ihnen nichts dafür; **2 to charge somebody with something** jemanden wegen etwas ←(GEN) anklagen SEP.

charity *noun* Wohltätigkeitsverein *der* (PL *die* Wohltätigkeitsvereine).

charming *adjective* reizend.

chart *noun* 1 (*table*) Tabelle *die* (PL *die* Tabellen); 2 **the weather chart** die Wetterkarte; 3 **the charts** die Hitparade.

charter flight *noun* Charterflug *der* (PL *die* Charterflüge).

chase *noun* Verfolgungsjagd *die* (PL *die* Verfolgungsjagden); **a car chase** eine Verfolgungsjagd im Auto.
verb jagen.

chat *noun* Plauderei *die* (PL *die* Plaudereien); **to have a chat with somebody** mit jemandem plaudern.

chat show *noun* Talkshow *die* (PL *die* Talkshows).

chatter *verb* 1 (*talk*) schwatzen; **2 my teeth were chattering** ich habe mit den Zähnen geklappert.

cheap *adjective* billig; **cheap shoes** billige Schuhe; **that's very cheap** das ist sehr billig.

cheaply *adverb* billig; **to eat cheaply** billig essen.

cheap-rate *adjective* verbilligt; **a cheap-rate phone call** ein Gespräch zum Spartarif.

cheat *noun* 1 Betrüger *der* (PL *die* Betrüger), Betrügerin *die* (PL *die* Betrügerinnen); 2 (*in games*) Mogler *der* (PL *die* Mogler), Moglerin *die* (PL *die* Moglerinnen).
verb 1 betrügen ✧; 2 (*in games*) mogeln.

check *noun* 1 (*in a factory or at a border control*) Kontrolle *die* (PL *die* Kontrollen); **passport check** die

Passkontrolle; **2** (*in chess*) **check!** Schach!
verb **1** (*make sure*) prüfen; **he checked their statements** er prüfte ihre Aussage; **2** (*make sure by looking*) nachsehen ✧ SEP; **to check the time** nachsehen, wie viel Uhr es ist; **check they're all back** sieh nach, ob alle wieder da sind; **3** (*inspect*) kontrollieren; **to check the tickets** die Fahrkarten kontrollieren.

check in *verb* (*for a flight*) einchecken SEP.

check-in *noun* Abfertigungsschalter *der* (PL *die* Abfertigungsschalter).

checkout *noun* Kasse *die* (PL *die* Kassen); **at the checkout** an der Kasse.

check-up *noun* Untersuchung *die* (PL *die* Untersuchungen).

cheek *noun* **1** (*part of face*) Backe *die* (PL *die* Backen); **2** (*nerve*) Frechheit *die*; **what a cheek!** so eine Frechheit!

cheer *noun* **1 three cheers for Tom!** ein dreifaches Hurra für Tom!; **2** (*when drinking*) **cheers!** prost!
verb (*shout hurray*) Hurra schreien ✧.

● **to cheer somebody up** jemanden aufmuntern SEP; **your visits always cheer me up** dein Besuch muntert mich immer auf; **cheer up!** Kopf hoch!

cheerful *adjective* fröhlich.

cheese *noun* Käse *der*; **a cheese sandwich** ein Käsebrot.

chef *noun* Koch *der* (PL *die* Köche), Köchin *die* (PL *die* Köchinnen).

chemist *noun* **1** (*in a pharmacy*) Apotheker *der* (PL *die* Apotheker), Apothekerin *die* (PL *die* Apothekerinnen); **2 chemist's** (*dispensing*) Apotheke *die* (PL *die* Apotheken); **at the chemist's** in der Apotheke; **3** (*scientist*) Chemiker *der* (PL *die* Chemiker), Chemikerin *die* (PL *die* Chemikerinnen).

chemistry *noun* Chemie *die*.

cheque *noun* Scheck *der* (PL *die* Schecks); **to pay by cheque** mit Scheck bezahlen; **to write a cheque** einen Scheck austellen.

cheque book *noun* Scheckbuch *das* (PL *die* Scheckbücher).

cherry *noun* Kirsche *die* (PL *die* Kirschen).

chess *noun* Schach *das*; **to play chess** Schach spielen.

chessboard *noun* Schachbrett *das* (PL *die* Schachbretter).

chest *noun* **1** (*part of the body*) Brust *die* (PL *die* Brüste); **2** (*box*) Truhe *die* (PL *die* Truhen); **3 a chest of drawers** eine Kommode.

chestnut *noun* Esskastanie △ *die* (PL *die* Esskastanien).

chestnut tree *noun* **1** (*horse-chestnut*) Rosskastanie △ *die* (PL *die* Rosskastanien); **2** (*sweet chestnut*)

✧ IRREGULAR VERB: *See the verb table in the centre of the dictionary*

Edelkastanie *die* (PL *die* Edelkastanien).

chew *verb* kauen.

chewing gum *noun* Kaugummi *der* (PL *die* Kaugummis).

chicken *noun* Huhn *das* (PL *die* Hühner); **roast chicken** *das* Brathähnchen; **chicken breast** *die* Hühnerbrust.

chickenpox *noun* Windpocken (*plural*).

child *noun* Kind *das* (PL *die* Kinder); **when I was a child** ... als Kind ...

childish *adjective* kindisch.

childminder *noun* Tagesmutter *die* (PL *die* Tagesmütter).

chill *noun* 1 Kälte *die*; 2 **to have a chill** eine Erkältung haben.

chilled *adjective* gekühlt.

chilli *noun* Chili *der*.

chimney *noun* Schornstein *der* (PL *die* Schornsteine).

chimpanzee *noun* Schimpanse *der* (PL *die* Schimpansen).

chin *noun* Kinn *das* (PL *die* Kinne).

china *noun* Porzellan *das*; **china bowl** die Porzellanschüssel.

China *noun* China *das*.

Chinese *noun* 1 **the Chinese** (*people*) die Chinesen; 2 (*language*) Chinesisch *das*. *adjective* 1 chinesisch; **a Chinese man** ein Chinese; **a Chinese**

woman eine Chinesin; 2 **to have a Chinese meal** chinesisch essen.

chip *noun* 1 (*fried potato*) **chips** Pommes frites (*plural*); **fish and chips** ausgebackener Fisch mit Pommes frites; 2 (*microchip*) Chip *der* (PL *die* Chips); 3 (*in glass or china*) angeschlagene Stelle *die* (PL *die* angeschlagenen Stellen).

chipped *adjective* angeschlagen.

chocolate *noun* 1 Schokolade *die*; **a box of chocolates** eine Schachtel Pralinen; 2 **chocolate ice cream** *das* Schokoladeneis; 3 **a cup of hot chocolate** eine Tasse Kakao.

choice *noun* 1 Wahl *die* (PL *die* Wahlen); **to make a good choice** eine gute Wahl treffen; 2 (*variety*) Auswahl *die*; **you have a choice of two flights** du hast zwei Flüge zur Auswahl.

choir *noun* Chor *der* (PL *die* Chöre).

choke *noun* (*on a car*) Choke *der* (PL *die* Chokes). *verb* (*by yourself*) sich verschlucken; **she choked on a bone** sie hat sich an einer Gräte verschluckt.

choose *verb* 1 wählen; **you chose well** du hast gut gewählt; **it's hard to choose from all these colours** es ist schwer, unter allen diesen Farben zu wählen; 2 (*select from a group of things*) sich ←(DAT) aussuchen SEP; **Cathy chose the red skirt** Cathy suchte sich den roten Rock aus.

chop *noun* Kotelett *das* (PL *die* Koteletts); **a pork chop** ein

Schweinekotelett.
verb hacken.

chord *noun* Akkord *der* (PL *die* Akkorde).

chorus *noun* **1** (*when you all join in the song*) Refrain *der* (PL *die* Refrains); **2** (*a group of singers*) Chor *der* (PL *die* Chöre).

Christ *noun* Christus *der*.

christening *noun* Taufe *die* (PL *die* Taufen).

Christian *noun* Christ *der* (PL *die* Christen), Christin *die* (PL *die* Christinnen).
adjective christlich.

Christian name *noun* Vorname *der* (PL *die* Vornamen).

Christmas *noun* Weihnachten *das* (PL *die* Weihnachten); **at Christmas** zu Weihnachten; **what did you get for Christmas?** was hast du zu Weihnachten bekommen?; **Happy Christmas!** Frohe Weihnachten!

Christmas card *noun* Weihnachtskarte *die* (PL *die* Weihnachtskarten).

Christmas carol *noun* Weihnachtslied *das* (PL *die* Weihnachtslieder).

Christmas cracker *noun* Knallbonbon *der* (PL *die* Knallbonbons).

Christmas Day *noun* erste Weihnachtstag *der*.

Christmas Eve *noun* Heiligabend *der*; **on Christmas Eve** Heiligabend.

Christmas present *noun* Weihnachtsgeschenk *das* (PL *die* Weihnachtsgeschenke).

Christmas tree *noun* Weihnachtsbaum *der* (PL *die* Weihnachtsbäume).

church *noun* Kirche *die* (PL *die* Kirchen); **to go to church** in die Kirche gehen.

chute *noun* (*in a swimming pool or playground*) Rutsche *die* (PL *die* Rutschen).

cider *noun* Apfelwein *der* (PL *die* Apfelweine).

cigar *noun* Zigarre *die* (PL *die* Zigarren).

cigarette *noun* Zigarette *die* (PL *die* Zigaretten).

cinema *noun* Kino *das* (PL *die* Kinos); **to go to the cinema** ins Kino gehen.

circle *noun* Kreis *der* (PL *die* Kreise); **to sit in a circle** im Kreis sitzen; **to go round in circles** sich im Kreis drehen.

circus *noun* Zirkus *der* (PL *die* Zirkusse).

citizen *noun* Bürger *der* (PL *die* Bürger), Bürgerin *die* (PL *die* Bürgerinnen).

city *noun* Stadt *die* (PL *die* Städte); **the city of Berlin** die Stadt Berlin.

city centre *noun* Stadtzentrum *das* (PL *die* Stadtzentren); **in the city centre** im Stadtzentrum.

ivilization *noun* Zivilisation *die* (PL *die* Zivilisationen).

ivil servant *noun* Beamte *der* (PL *die* Beamten), Beamtin *die* (PL *die* Beamtinnen); **she's a civil servant** sie ist Beamtin.

laim *verb* behaupten; **he claims to know who …** er behauptet zu wissen, wer …

lap *verb* 1 klatschen; **everyone clapped** alle klatschten; 2 **to clap your hands** in die Hände klatschen.

larinet *noun* Klarinette *die* (PL *die* Klarinetten); **to play the clarinet** Klarinette spielen.

lash *noun* (*between two groups*) Zusammenstoß *der* (PL *die* Zusammenstöße). *verb* 1 (*rival groups*) zusammenstoßen ◆ SEP; 2 (*colours*) sich beißen ◆; **the curtains clash with the wallpaper** die Vorhänge beißen sich mit der Tapete.

lass *noun* 1 (*a group of students or pupils*) Klasse *die* (PL *die* Klassen); **she's in my class** sie geht in meine Klasse; 2 (*a lesson*) Stunde *die* (PL *die* Stunden); **history class** die Geschichtsstunde; **in class** im Unterricht; 3 (*category*) Klasse *die* (PL *die* Klassen); **social class** die gesellschaftliche Klasse.

lassical *adjective* klassisch; **classical music** die klassische Musik.

lassroom *noun* Klassenzimmer *das* (PL *die* Klassenzimmer).

lay *noun* Ton *der*.

clean *adjective* sauber; **a clean shirt** ein sauberes Hemd; **my hands are clean** ich habe saubere Hände. *verb* 1 putzen; **I cleaned the windows** ich habe die Fenster geputzt; 2 **to clean your teeth** sich ←(DAT) die Zähne putzen; **I'm going to clean my teeth** ich putze mir jetzt die Zähne.

cleaner *noun* 1 (*cleaning lady*) Putzfrau *die* (PL *die* Putzfrauen); 2 (*in a public place*) Reinigungskraft *die* (PL *die* Reinigungskräfte); 3 **dry cleaner's** die chemische Reinigung.

cleaning *noun* **to do the cleaning** putzen.

cleanser *noun* 1 (*for the house*) Reinigungsmittel *das* (PL *die* Reinigungsmittel); 2 (*for your face*) Reinigungsmilch *die*.

clear *adjective* 1 (*that you can see through*) klar; **clear water** klares Wasser; 2 (*cloudless*) klar; 3 (*easy to understand*) klar; **clear instructions** klare Anweisungen; **is that clear?** ist das klar? (*informal*); **to make something clear** etwas klarmachen. *verb* 1 räumen; **have you cleared your stuff out of your room?** hast du deine Sachen aus deinem Zimmer geräumt?; 2 **can I clear the table?** kann ich den Tisch abräumen SEP?; 3 **to clear your throat** sich räuspern.
● **to clear up** 1 (*tidy up*) aufräumen SEP; 2 (*the weather*) sich aufklären SEP; **the weather's clearing up a bit**

das Wetter klärt sich ein bisschen
auf.

clearly adverb **1** (*to think, speak, or
hear*) deutlich; **2** (*obviously*)
eindeutig; **she was clearly better**
sie war eindeutig besser.

clementine noun Klementine die
(PL die Klementinen).

clever adjective **1** klug; **their
children are all very clever** ihre
Kinder sind alle sehr klug;
2 (*ingenious*) clever; **a clever idea**
eine clevere Idee.

cliff noun Klippe die (PL die
Klippen).

climate noun Klima das (PL die
Klimas).

climb verb **1** (*the stairs, a hill*)
hinaufgehen ✧ SEP (PERF *sein*); **to
climb a mountain** auf einen Berg
steigen ✧ (PERF *sein*); **2** (*a wall, tree,
or rock*) klettern (PERF *sein*) auf
(+ACC); **to climb a tree** auf einen
Baum klettern.

climber noun Bergsteiger der (PL die
Bergsteiger), Bergsteigerin die (PL
die Bergsteigerinnen).

climbing noun Bergsteigen das;
they go climbing in Italy sie gehen
in Italien bergsteigen.

clinic noun Klinik die (PL die
Kliniken).

clip noun **1** (*from a film*)
Ausschnitt der (PL die Ausschnitte);
2 (*for your hair*) Klammer die (PL die
Klammern).

cloakroom noun (*for coats*)
Garderobe die (PL die Garderoben).

clock noun **1** Uhr die (PL die Uhren)
to put the clocks forward an hour
die Uhr eine Stunde vorstellen; **to
put the clocks back** die Uhr
zurückstellen; **2 an alarm clock** e
Wecker.

close¹ adjective, adverb **1** (*result*)
knapp; **2** (*friend, connection*) eng;
3 (*relation or acquaintance*) nahe;
4 (*near*) in der Nähe; **the station's
very close** der Bahnhof ist ganz in
der Nähe; **she lives close by** sie
wohnt in der Nähe; **5 close to** nah
nah (*informal*) (+DAT); **close to the
cinema** nahe am Kino; **not very
close** nicht sehr nah.

close² noun Ende das; **at the clos**
am Ende.
verb zumachen SEP, schließen ✧;
close your eyes! mach die Augen
zu!; **she closed the door** sie macht
die Tür zu; **the post office closes a
six** die Post macht um sechs zu, di
Post schließt um sechs.

closed adjective geschlossen;
'closed on Mondays' 'Montags
geschlossen'.

closing date noun **the closing
date for entries** (*for a competition*
der Einsendeschluss △; (*for a sportin
event*) der Meldeschluss △.

closing time noun
1 Ladenschluss △ der; **2** (*of a pub*)
Polizeistunde die.

cloth noun **1** (*for drying up and
polishing*) Tuch das (PL die Tücher)
2 (*for the floor*) Lappen der (PL die

✧ IRREGULAR VERB: See the verb table in the centre of the dictionary

Lappen); 3 (*fabric*) Stoff der (PL die Stoffe).

clothes *plural noun* 1 Kleider (*plural*); 2 **to put your clothes on** sich anziehen ✧ SEP; **to take your clothes off** sich ausziehen ✧ SEP; **to change your clothes** sich umziehen ✧ SEP.

clothes peg *noun* Wäscheklammer die (PL die Wäscheklammern).

clothing *noun* Kleidung die.

cloud *noun* Wolke die (PL die Wolken).

cloudy *adjective* bewölkt.

clown *noun* Clown der (PL die Clowns).

club *noun* 1 (*association, for tennis-players, golfers*) Klub der (PL die Klubs); (*for footballers*) Verein der (PL die Vereine); **a football club** ein Fußballverein; 2 (*in cards*) Kreuz das (PL die Kreuze); **the four of clubs** die Kreuz-Vier; 3 (*golfing iron*) Schläger der (PL die Schläger).

clue *noun* 1 Anhaltspunkt der (PL die Anhaltspunkte); **they have a few clues** sie haben ein paar Anhaltspunkte; 2 (*in a crossword*) Frage die (PL die Fragen); ★ **I haven't a clue** ich habe keine Ahnung.

clumsy *adjective* ungeschickt.

clutch *noun* (*in a car*) Kupplung die (PL die Kupplungen). *verb* **to clutch something** etwas festhalten ✧ SEP.

coach *noun* 1 (*bus*) Bus der (PL die Busse); **on the coach** im Bus; **to travel by coach** mit dem Bus fahren; 2 (*sports trainer*) Trainer der (PL die Trainer), Trainerin die (PL die Trainerinnen); 3 (*railway carriage*) Wagen der (PL die Wagen).

coach station *noun* Busbahnhof der (PL die Busbahnhöfe).

coach trip *noun* Busausflug der (PL die Busausflüge); **to go on a coach trip** einen Busausflug machen.

coal *noun* Kohle die (PL die Kohlen).

coarse *adjective* grob.

coast *noun* Küste die (PL die Küsten); **on the east coast** an der Ostküste.

coat *noun* 1 Mantel der (PL die Mäntel); 2 **coat of paint** der Anstrich.

coat hanger *noun* Kleiderbügel der (PL die Kleiderbügel).

cock *noun* Hahn der (PL die Hähne).

cocoa *noun* Kakao der.

coconut *noun* Kokosnuss △ die (PL die Kokosnüsse).

cod *noun* Kabeljau der (PL die Kabeljaue).

code *noun* 1 (*in law*) Gesetzbuch das; **the highway code** die Straßenverkehrsordnung; 2 **the dialling code for Hull** die Vorwahl für Hull.

coffee *noun* Kaffee der (PL die Kaffees); **a cup of coffee** eine Tasse

△ NEW SPELLING: *See page xii*

Kaffee; **a black coffee, please** einen Kaffee ohne Milch bitte; **a white coffee, please** einen Kaffee mit Milch bitte.

coffee break *noun* Kaffeepause *die* (PL *die* Kaffeepausen).

coffee cup *noun* Kaffeetasse *die* (PL *die* Kaffeetassen).

coffee machine *noun* Kaffeemaschine *die* (PL *die* Kaffeemaschinen).

coin *noun* **1** Münze *die* (PL *die* Münzen); **2 a pound coin** ein Einpfundstück.

coincidence *noun* Zufall *der* (PL *die* Zufälle).

Coke™ *noun* Cola *die*; **two Cokes™ please** zwei Cola bitte.

cold *noun* **1** (*cold weather*) Kälte *die*; **to be out in the cold** draußen in der Kälte sein; **2** (*illness*) Schnupfen *der* (PL *die* Schnupfen), Erkältung *die* (PL *die* Erkältungen); **to have a cold** Schnupfen haben; **Carol's got a cold** Carol hat Schnupfen; **a bad cold** eine schlimme Erkältung.
adjective **1** kalt; **your hands are cold** du hast kalte Hände; **cold milk** kalte Milch; **2** (*weather, temperature*) **it's cold today** heute ist es kalt; **3** (*feeling*) **I'm cold** mir ist kalt.

collapse *verb* **1** (*a roof or wall*) einstürzen SEP (PERF *sein*); **2** (*a person*) zusammenbrechen ◇ SEP (PERF *sein*); **he collapsed in his office** er brach in seinem Büro zusammen.

collar *noun* **1** (*on a garment*) Kragen *der* (PL *die* Kragen); **2** (*for an animal*) Halsband *das* (PL *die* Halsbänder).

colleague *noun* Kollege *der* (PL *die* Kollegen), Kollegin *die* (PL *die* Kolleginnen).

collect *verb* **1** (*as a hobby*) sammeln; **do you collect stamps?** sammelst du Briefmarken?; **2** (*fetch*) abholen SEP; **she collects the children from school** sie holt die Kinder von der Schule ab; **3 to collect up the exercise books** die Hefte einsammeln SEP.

collection *noun* (*of stamps, CDs, money, etc.*) Sammlung *die* (PL *die* Sammlungen).

college *noun* **1** (*for higher education*) Hochschule *die* (PL *die* Hochschulen); **to go to college** studieren; **2** (*a school*) College *das* (PL *die* Colleges).

Cologne *noun* Köln *das*.

colour *noun* Farbe *die* (PL *die* Farben); **what colour is it?** welche Farbe hat es?; **do you have it in a different colour?** haben Sie es in einer anderen Farbe?
verb **1** (*with paints or crayons*) anmalen SEP; **to colour something red** etwas rot anmalen; **2** (*with dye*) färben.

colour film *noun* Farbfilm *der* (PL *die* Farbfilme).

colourful *adjective* bunt.

◇ IRREGULAR VERB: *See the verb table in the centre of the dictionary*

olumn *noun* **1** (*of a building*) Säule *die* (PL *die* Säulen); **2** (*on a page*) Spalte *die* (PL *die* Spalten).

omb *noun* Kamm *der* (PL *die* Kämme).
verb kämmen; **to comb your hair** sich ←(DAT) die Haare kämmen; **I'll just comb my hair** ich kämme mir nur die Haare.

ome *verb* **1** kommen ✧ (PERF *sein*); **come quick!** komm schnell!; **come here!** komm mal her!; **Nick came by car** Nick kam mit dem Auto; **can you come over for a coffee?** kannst du auf eine Tasse Kaffe kommen?; **did Jess come to school yesterday?** war Jess gestern in der Schule?; **2** (*arrive*) **coming!** ich komme schon!; **the bus is coming** der Bus kommt gerade; **come along!** komm schon!
to come back zurückkommen ✧ SEP (PERF *sein*); **he's coming back to collect us** er kommt zurück, um uns abzuholen.
to come down herunterkommen ✧ SEP (PERF *sein*).
to come for (*collect*) abholen SEP; **my father's coming for me** mein Vater holt mich ab.
to come in hereinkommen ✧ SEP (PERF *sein*); **come in!** herein!; **she came into the kitchen** sie kam in die Küche.
to come off (*a button*) abgehen ✧ SEP (PERF *sein*).
to come out herauskommen ✧ SEP (PERF *sein*); **they came out when I called** als ich rief, kamen sie heraus; **the new CD's coming out soon** die neue CD kommt bald heraus.
● **to come up** heraufkommen ✧ SEP (PERF *sein*); **can you come up a moment?** kannst du eine Sekunde heraufkommen?
● **to come up to somebody** auf jemanden zukommen ✧ SEP (PERF *sein*).

comedian *noun* Komiker *der* (PL *die* Komiker), Komikerin *die* (PL *die* Komikerinnen).

comedy *noun* Komödie *die* (PL *die* Komödien), Komikerin *die* (PL *die* Komikerinnen).

comfortable *adjective* **1** bequem; **this chair's really comfortable** dieser Sessel ist wirklich bequem; **2 to feel comfortable** (*a person*) sich wohl fühlen.

comfortably *adverb* bequem.

comic *noun* (*magazine*) Comic-Heft *das* (PL *die* Comic-Hefte).

comic strip *noun* Comic *der* (PL *die* Comics).

comma *noun* Komma *das* (PL *die* Kommas).

comment *noun* (*remark*) Bemerkung *die* (PL *die* Bemerkungen); **he made some rude comments about my friends** er hat ein paar unhöfliche Bemerkungen über meine Freunde gemacht.

commentary *noun* Reportage *die* (PL *die* Reportagen); **the commentary on the soccer match** die Reportage über das Fußballspiel.

commentator *noun* Reporter *der* (PL *die* Reporter), Reporterin *die* (PL

△ NEW SPELLING: *See page xii*

die Reporterinnen); **sports commentator** *der* Sportreporter.

commercial *noun* Werbespot *der* (PL *die* Werbespots).
adjective kommerziell.

committee *noun* Ausschuss △ *der* (PL *die* Ausschüsse).

common *adjective* **1** häufig; **it's a common problem** das Problem kommt häufig vor; **2 in common** gemeinsam; **they have nothing in common** sie haben nichts gemeinsam.

common sense *noun* gesunde Menschenverstand *der*.

communication *noun* Verständigung *die*.

communion *noun* (*in a Catholic church*) Kommunion *die*; (*in a Protestant church*) Abendmahl *das*.

communism *noun* Kommunismus *der*.

community *noun* Gemeinschaft *die* (PL *die* Gemeinschaften); **the European Community** die Europäische Gemeinschaft.

commute *verb* **to commute between Oxford and London** zwischen Oxford und London pendeln (PERF *sein*).

commuter *noun* Pendler *der* (PL *die* Pendler), Pendlerin *die* (PL *die* Pendlerinnen).

compact disc *noun* Compactdisc △ *die* (PL *die* Compactdiscs).

compact disc player *noun* Compactdisc Spieler △ *der* (PL *die* Compactdisc Spieler).

company *noun* **1** (*business*) Gesellschaft *die* (PL *die* Gesellschaften); **an airline company** eine Fluggesellschaft; **she's set up a company** sie hat eine Firma gegründet; **2** (*group*) Truppe *die* (PL *die* Truppen); **a theatre company** eine Theatertruppe; **3 to keep somebody company** jemandem Gesellschaft leisten; **the dog keeps me company** der Hund leistet mir Gesellschaft.

compare *verb* vergleichen ✧; **if you compare the German phrase with the English** wenn man den deutschen mit dem englischen Ausdruck vergleicht; **our house is small compared with yours** unser Haus ist klein verglichen mit eurem.

compass *noun* Kompass △ *der* (PL *die* Kompasse).

compatible *adjective* **1** zueinander passend; **2** (*in computing*) kompatibel.

compete *verb* **1 to compete in something** (*race, event*) an etwas ←(DAT) teilnehmen ✧ SEP; **2 to compete with each other** miteinander konkurrieren; **3 to compete for something** um etwas ←(ACC) kämpfen; **thirty people are competing for one job** dreißig Leute kämpfen um eine Stelle.

competent *adjective* fähig.

✧ **IRREGULAR VERB:** *See the verb table in the centre of the dictionary*

competition noun 1 (*a contest*)
Wettbewerb der (PL die
Wettbewerbe); 2 (*in a magazine*)
Preisausschreiben das (PL die
Preisausschreiben).

competitor noun Konkurrent der
(PL die Konkurrenten), Konkurrentin
die (PL die Konkurrentinnen).

complain verb sich beschweren; **we
complained about the meals** wir
haben uns über das Essen beschwert.

complete adjective 1 (*whole*)
vollständig; **the complete
collection** die vollständige
Sammlung; 2 (*absolute*) völlig; **a
complete idiot** ein völliger Idiot
(*informal*).
verb (*to finish*) beenden.

completely adverb völlig.

complexion noun Teint der (PL die
Teints).

complicated adjective
kompliziert.

compliment noun
Kompliment das (PL die
Komplimente); **to pay somebody a
compliment** jemandem ein
Kompliment machen.

composer noun Komponist der (PL
die Komponisten), Komponistin die
(PL die Komponistinnen).

comprehensive school noun
Gemeinschaftsschule die (PL die
Gemeinschaftsschulen).

compulsory adjective
1 obligatorisch; 2 (*at school*)
compulsory subject das Pflichtfach.

computer noun Computer der (PL
die Computer); **to work on a**
computer mit einem Computer
arbeiten; **to have something on
computer** etwas im Computer
gespeichert haben.

computer engineer noun
Computeringenieur der (PL die
Computeringenieure),
Computeringenieurin die (PL die
Computeringenieurinnen).

computer game noun
Computerspiel das (PL die
Computerspiele).

computer programmer noun
Programmierer der (PL die
Programmierer), Programmiererin
die (PL die Programmiererinnen).

computer science noun
Informatik die.

computing noun
Computertechnik die.

concentrate verb sich
konzentrieren; **I can't concentrate**
ich kann mich nicht konzentrieren;
I was concentrating on the film ich
konzentrierte mich auf den Film.

concentration noun
Konzentration die.

concern verb (*to affect*)
betreffen ◇; **this doesn't concern
you** das betrifft Sie nicht; **as far as
I'm concerned** was mich betrifft.

concert noun 1 Konzert das (PL die
Konzerte); **to go to a concert** ins
Konzert gehen; 2 **concert ticket** die
Konzertkarte.

conclusion noun Schluss △ der (PL
die Schlüsse).

△ NEW SPELLING: *See page xii*

concrete noun Beton der; **concrete floor** der Betonboden.

condemn verb verurteilen; **to condemn somebody to death** jemanden zum Tode verurteilen.

condition noun 1 Zustand der (PL die Zustände); **in good condition** in gutem Zustand; **weather conditions** die Wetterlage; 2 (something you insist on) Bedingung die (PL die Bedingungen); **on condition that you let me pay** unter der Bedingung, dass du mich zahlen lässt.

conditioner noun (for your hair) Spülung die (PL die Spülungen).

condom noun Kondom das (PL die Kondome).

conduct noun Benehmen das. verb dirigieren (an orchestra or a piece of music).

conductor noun (of an orchestra) Dirigent der (PL die Dirigenten), Dirigentin die (PL die Dirigentinnen).

cone noun 1 (for ice-cream) Eistüte die (PL die Eistüten); 2 (for traffic) Kegel der (PL die Kegel).

conference noun Konferenz die (PL die Konferenzen).

confess verb gestehen ✧.

confession noun Geständnis das (PL die Geständnisse).

confidence noun 1 (self-confidence) Selbstvertrauen das; **to be lacking in confidence** kein Selbstvertrauen haben; 2 (faith in somebody else) Vertrauen das; **to**

have confidence in somebody zu jemandem Vertrauen haben.

confident adjective 1 (sure of yourself) selbstbewusst ∆; 2 (sure that something will happen) zuversichtlich.

confirm verb bestätigen; **he confirmed the date** er bestätigte das Datum.

confused adjective 1 wirr; **a confused story** eine wirre Geschichte; 2 durcheinander; **I'm confused about the holiday plans** ich bin mit den Ferienplänen durcheinander; **now I'm completely confused** jetzt bin ich völlig durcheinander.

confusing adjective verwirrend; **the instructions are confusing** die Anweisungen sind verwirrend.

confusion noun Verwirrung die.

congratulate verb gratulieren; **I congratulated Tim on passing his exam** ich gratulierte Tim zur bestandenen Prüfung.

congratulations plural noun Glückwünsche (plural); **congratulations on the baby!** herzlichen Glückwunsch zum Baby!

connect verb (to plug in to the mains) anschließen ✧ SEP (a dishwasher or TV, for example).

connection noun 1 (between two ideas or events) Zusammenhang der (PL die Zusammenhänge); **there's no connection between his letter and my decision** es besteht kein Zusammenhang zwischen

---

✧ IRREGULAR VERB: See the verb table in the centre of the dictionary

seinem Brief und meiner Entscheidung; **2** (*between trains, planes, on phone, and electrical*) Anschluss Δ *der* (PL *die* Anschlüsse); **Sally missed her connection** Sally hat ihren Anschluss verpasst.

onscience *noun* Gewissen *das*; **to have a guilty conscience** ein schlechtes Gewissen haben.

onservation *noun* (*of nature*) Schutz *der*; **environmental conservation** *der* Umweltschutz.

onservative *noun* Konservative *der/die* (PL *die* Konservativen). *adjective* konservativ.

onservatory *noun* Wintergarten *der* (PL *die* Wintergärten).

onsider *verb* **1** sich ←(DAT) überlegen; (*a suggestion or idea*) **all things considered** alles in allem; **2** (*think about (doing)*) erwägen ◇; **we are considering buying a flat** wir erwägen, eine Wohnung zu kaufen.

onsiderate *adjective* rücksichtsvoll.

onsidering *preposition* wenn man bedenkt; **considering her age** wenn man ihr Alter bedenkt; **considering he did it all himself** wenn man bedenkt, dass er es ganz allein gemacht hat.

onsist *verb* **to consist of** bestehen ◇ aus (+DAT).

onstant *adjective* ständig.

construct *verb* bauen.

consumer *noun* Verbraucher *der* (PL *die* Verbraucher), Verbraucherin *die* (PL *die* Verbraucherinnen).

contact *noun* Kontakt *der* (PL *die* Kontakte); **to be in contact with somebody** mit jemandem in Kontakt sein; **we've lost contact** wir haben den Kontakt verloren; **Rob has contacts in the music business** Rob hat Kontakte zur Musikindustrie. *verb* sich in Verbindung setzen mit (+DAT); **I'll contact you tomorrow** ich setze mich morgen mit dir in Verbindung.

contact lens *noun* Kontaktlinse *die* (PL *die* Kontaktlinsen).

contain *verb* enthalten ◇.

container *noun* Behälter *der* (PL *die* Behälter).

contemporary *adjective* **1** (*around today*) zeitgenössisch; **2** (*modern*) modern.

contents *plural noun* Inhalt *der*; **the contents of my suitcase** der Inhalt meines Koffers.

contest *noun* Wettbewerb *der* (PL *die* Wettbewerbe).

contestant *noun* Teilnehmer *der* (PL *die* Teilnehmer), Teilnehmerin *die* (PL *die* Teilnehmerinnen).

continent *noun* Kontinent *der* (PL *die* Kontinente).

continue *verb* **1** fortsetzen SEP; **we continued (with) our journey** wir setzten unsere Reise fort; **2 to**

Δ NEW SPELLING: *See page xii*

continue to do something etwas weiter tun; **Jill continued talking** Jill redete weiter; **3 'to be continued'** 'Fortsetzung folgt'.

continuous *adjective* ununterbrochen.

contraceptive *noun* Verhütungsmittel *das* (PL *die* Verhütungsmittel).

contract *noun* Vertrag *der* (PL *die* Verträge).

contradict *verb* widersprechen ✧ (+DAT).

contradiction *noun* Widerspruch *der* (PL *die* Widersprüche).

contrary *noun* Gegenteil *das*; **on the contrary** im Gegenteil.

contrast *noun* Kontrast *der* (PL *die* Kontraste).

contribute *verb* beisteuern SEP (*money*).

contribution *noun* (*to charity or an appeal*) Spende *die* (PL *die* Spenden).

control *noun* (*of a crowd or animals*) Kontrolle *die*; **the police are in control of the situation** die Polizei hat die Situation unter Kontrolle; **keep your dogs under control** halten Sie Ihre Hunde unter Kontrolle; **everything's under control** alles ist unter Kontrolle; **to get out of control** außer Kontrolle geraten.
verb **to control yourself** sich beherrschen.

convenient *adjective* **1** praktisch; **frozen food is very convenient** Tiefkühlkost ist sehr praktisch; **2 to be convenient for somebody** jemandem passen; **whenever's convenient for you** wann immer es dir passt.

conventional *adjective* konventionell.

conversation *noun* Gespräch *das* (PL *die* Gespräche).

convert *verb* **1** umwandeln SEP; **2** (*adapt a building*) umbauen SEP; **we're going to convert the garage into a workshop** wir wollen die Garage zu einer Werkstatt umbauen.

convince *verb* überzeugen; **I'm convinced he's wrong** ich bin davon überzeugt, dass er sich irrt.

convincing *adjective* überzeugend.

cook *noun* Koch *der* (PL *die* Köche), Köchin *die* (PL *die* Köchinnen). *verb* **1** kochen; **who's cooking tonight?** wer kocht heute Abend?; **I like cooking** ich koche gern; **to cook vegetables and pasta** Gemüse und Nudeln kochen; **cook the cabbage for five minutes** lass den Kohl fünf Minuten kochen; **2** (*prepare food or a meal*) machen; **Fran's busy cooking supper** Fran macht gerade Abendessen; **how do you cook duck?** wie macht man Ente?; **3** (*boil*) kochen; (*fry or roast*) braten ✧; **the potatoes are cooking** die Kartoffeln kochen; **the sausages are cooking** die Würstchen braten.

cooker *noun* Herd *der* (PL *die* Herde); **electric cooker** *der*

Elektroherd; **gas cooker** *der* Gasherd.

cookery *noun* Kochen *das*.

cookery book *noun* Kochbuch *das* (PL *die* Kochbücher).

cooking *noun* 1 (*preparing food*) Kochen *das*; **cooking is fun** Kochen macht Spaß; **who's doing the cooking?** wer kocht?; 2 (*food*) Küche *die*; **Italian cooking** die italienische Küche.

cool *noun* 1 (*coldness*) Kühle *die*; 2 (*calm*) **to lose one's cool** durchdrehen SEP (PERF *sein*) (*informal*); **don't lose your cool!** dreh nicht durch!; **he kept his cool** er blieb gelassen.
adjective 1 (*cold*) kühl; **it's cool inside** es ist kühl drinnen; 2 (*laid back*) gelassen; **to stay cool** gelassen bleiben (PERF *sein*).
verb abkühlen SEP (PERF *sein*).

cop *noun* Polizist *der* (PL *die* Polizisten).

cope *verb* zurechtkommen ✧ SEP (PERF *sein*); **she copes well** sie kommt gut zurecht; **to cope with the children** mit den Kindern zurechtkommen; **she's had a lot to cope with** sie musste mit viel zurechtkommen.

copy *noun* 1 (*photocopy*) Kopie *die* (PL *die* Kopien); 2 (*of a book*) Exemplar *das* (PL *die* Exemplare).
verb 1 (*imitate*) kopieren; 2 (*make a copy of*) abschreiben ✧ SEP; **I copied (down) the address** ich habe die Adresse abgeschrieben; (*in*

an exam) **to copy from somebody** bei jemandem abschreiben.

cord *noun* (*for a blind, for example*) Schnur *die* (PL *die* Schnüre).

cordless telephone *noun* schnurlose Telefon *das* (PL *die* schnurlosen Telefone).

core *noun* (*of an apple or a pear*) Kerngehäuse *das* (PL *die* Kerngehäuse).

cork *noun* 1 (*in a bottle*) Korken *der* (PL *die* Korken); 2 (*material*) Kork *der*.

corkscrew *noun* Korkenzieher *der* (PL *die* Korkenzieher).

corn *noun* 1 (*wheat*) Korn *das*; 2 (*sweetcorn*) Mais *der*.

corner *noun* 1 Ecke *die* (PL *die* Ecken); **at the corner of the street** an der Straßenecke; **it's just round the corner** es ist gleich um die Ecke; 2 (*of mouth, eye*) Winkel *der* (PL *die* Winkel); **out of the corner of your eye** aus dem Augenwinkel heraus; 3 (*bend in the road*) Kurve *die* (PL *die* Kurven); 4 (*in football*) Eckball *der* (PL *die* Eckbälle).

corpse *noun* Leiche *die* (PL *die* Leichen).

correct *adjective* 1 richtig; **the correct answer** die richtige Antwort; **2 yes, that's correct** ja, das stimmt.
verb 1 verbessern; 2 (*teacher*) korrigieren; **the teacher has already corrected our homework**

△ NEW SPELLING: *See page xii*

der Lehrer hat unsere Hausaufgaben schon korrigiert.

correction *noun* Verbesserung *die* (PL *die* Verbesserungen).

corridor *noun* Korridor *der* (PL *die* Korridore).

cosmetics *plural noun* Kosmetik *die*.

cost *noun* 1 Kosten (*plural*); **the cost of living** die Lebenshaltungskosten (*plural*); 2 **the cost of a new computer** der Preis für einen neuen Computer. *verb* kosten; **how much does it cost?** was kostet es?; **the tickets cost £10** die Karten kosten zehn Pfund; **it costs too much** das ist zu teuer.

costume *noun* Kostüm *das* (PL *die* Kostüme).

cosy *adjective* (*a room*) gemütlich.

cot *noun* Kinderbett *das* (PL *die* Kinderbetten).

cottage *noun* Häuschen *das* (PL *die* Häuschen).

cotton *noun* 1 (*fabric*) Baumwolle *die*; **cotton shirt** das Baumwollhemd; 2 (*thread*) Nähgarn *das* (PL *die* Nähgarne).

cotton wool *noun* Watte *die*.

couch *noun* Couch *die* (PL *die* Couchs).

cough *noun* Husten *der*; **a nasty cough** ein schlimmer Husten; **to have a cough** Husten haben. *verb* husten.

could *verb* 1 (*the past tense of können is used to translate 'was able to'*) **I couldn't open it** ich konnte es nicht aufmachen; **they couldn't come** sie konnten nicht kommen; **she did all she could** sie hat getan, was sie konnte; **he couldn't drive** er konnte nicht Auto fahren; **she couldn't see anything** sie konnte überhaupt nichts sehen; 2 (*the past tense of dürfen is used to translate 'was allowed to'*) **they couldn't smoke there** sie durften da nicht rauchen; 3 (*might*) (*the subjunctive of können is used to translate a wish or suggestion*) **could I speak to David?** könnte ich David sprechen?; **you could try phoning** du könntest versuchen anzurufen; **if he could pay** wenn er zahlen könnte; **he could be right** er könnte recht haben.

count *verb* 1 (*reckon up*) zählen; **I counted my money** ich habe mein Geld gezählt; 2 (*include*) mitzählen SEP; **thirty-five not counting the children** fünfunddreißig, die Kinder nicht mitgezählt.

counter *noun* 1 (*in a shop*) Ladentisch *der* (PL *die* Ladentische); 2 (*in a post office or bank*) Schalter *der* (PL *die* Schalter); 3 (*in a bar or café*) Theke *die* (PL *die* Theken); 4 (*for board games*) Spielmarke *die* (PL *die* Spielmarken).

country *noun* 1 (*Germany, England, etc.*) Land *das* (PL *die* Länder); **a foreign country** ein fremdes Land; **from another country** aus einem anderen Land; 2 (*not town*)

Land *das*; **in the country** auf dem Land; **country road** *die* Landstraße.

country dancing *noun*
Volkstanz *der*.

countryside *noun* 1 (*not town*) Land *das*; 2 (*scenery*) Landschaft *die*.

county *noun* Grafschaft *die* (PL *die* Grafschaften).

couple *noun* 1 (*a pair*) Paar *das* (PL *die* Paare); 2 **a couple of** ein paar; **a couple of times** ein paar Mal; **I've got a couple of things to do** ich habe ein paar Sachen zu tun.

courage *noun* Mut *der*.

course *noun* 1 (*lessons*) Kurs *der* (PL *die* Kurse); **computer course** *der* Computerkurs; **to go on a course** einen Kurs machen; 2 (*part of a meal*) Gang *der* (PL *die* Gänge); **the main course** der Hauptgang; 3 **golf course** *der* Golfplatz; 4 **of course** natürlich; **yes, of course!** ja, natürlich!; **he's forgotten, of course** er hat es natürlich vergessen.

court *noun* 1 (*for playing sports*) Platz *der* (PL *die* Plätze); 2 (*lawcourt*) Gericht *das*; **to go to court** vor Gericht gehen.

cousin *noun* Vetter *der* (PL *die* Vettern), Kusine *die* (PL *die* Kusinen); **my cousin Sonia** meine Kusine Sonia.

cover *noun* 1 (*of a book*) Einband *der* (PL *die* Einbände); 2 (*for a duvet or cushion*) Bezug *der* (PL *die* Bezüge).

verb 1 (*to cover up*) zudecken SEP; **he covered her with a blanket** er hat sie mit einer Decke zugedeckt; 2 **he was covered in spots** er war völlig verpickelt; **the room was covered in dust** das Zimmer war völlig verstaubt; 3 (*with leaves, snow, or for protection*) bedecken; **the ground was covered with snow** der Boden war mit Schnee bedeckt; 4 (*with fabric*) beziehen ✧.

cow *noun* Kuh *die* (PL *die* Kühe); **mad cow disease** *der* Rinderwahn.

coward *noun* Feigling *der* (PL *die* Feiglinge).

cowboy *noun* Cowboy *der* (PL *die* Cowboys).

crack *noun* 1 (*in a glass or cup*) Sprung *der* (PL *die* Sprünge); 2 (*in wood or a wall*) Riss △ *der* (PL *die* Risse); 3 (*a cracking noise*) Knack *der* (PL *die* Knacke). *verb* 1 (*to make a crack in*) anschlagen ✧ SEP; 2 (*to break*) zerbrechen ✧; 3 (*to make a noise*) (*a twig*) knacken.

cracker *noun* 1 (*biscuit*) Cracker *der* (PL *die* Cracker); 2 (*Christmas cracker*) Knallbonbon *der* (PL *die* Knallbonbons).

craft *noun* (*at school*) Werken *das*.

cramp *noun* Krampf *der* (PL *die* Krämpfe); **to have cramp in your leg** einen Krampf im Bein haben.

crash *noun* 1 (*an accident*) Unfall *der* (PL *die* Unfälle); **car crash** *der* Autounfall; 2 (*a noise*) Krachen *das*.

verb 1 (*a plane*) abstürzen SEP (PERF *sein*); **the plane crashed** das Flugzeug ist abgestürzt; 2 (*have a collision in a car*) einen Unfall haben; 3 **to crash into something** gegen etwas ←(ACC) krachen (PERF *sein*); **the car crashed into a tree** das Auto krachte gegen einen Baum.

crash course *noun* Schnellkurs *der* (PL *die* Schnellkurse).

crash helmet *noun* Sturzhelm *der* (PL *die* Sturzhelme).

crate *noun* Kiste *die* (PL *die* Kisten).

crawl *noun* (*in swimming*) Kraul *das*.
verb 1 (*a person*) kriechen ✧ (PERF *sein*); (*a baby*) krabbeln (PERF *sein*); 2 (*cars in a jam*) im Schneckentempo fahren ✧ (PERF *sein*); **we were crawling along** wir fuhren im Schneckentempo.

crayon *noun* 1 (*wax*) Wachsstift *der* (PL *die* Wachsstifte); 2 (*coloured pencil*) Buntstift *der* (PL *die* Buntstifte).

craze *noun* Mode *die*; **the craze for rollerblades** die Inlinermode.

crazy *adjective* verrückt; **to be crazy for something** verrückt auf etwas ←(ACC) sein.

cream *noun* Sahne *die*; **strawberries and cream** Erdbeeren mit Sahne.

cream cheese *noun* Frischkäse *der*.

creased *adjective* zerknittert.

creative *adjective* kreativ.

creature *noun* Geschöpf *das* (PL *die* Geschöpfe).

credit *noun* Kredit *der*; **to buy something on credit** etwas auf Kredit kaufen.

credit card *noun* Kreditkarte *die* (PL *die* Kreditkarten).

cress *noun* Kresse *die*.

crew *noun* 1 (*on a ship or plane*) Besatzung *die*; 2 **camera crew** das Kamerateam; 3 (*in water sports*) Mannschaft *die* (PL *die* Mannschaften).

crew cut *noun* Bürstenschnitt *der* (PL *die* Bürstenschnitte).

cricket *noun* 1 (*game*) Kricket *das*; **to play cricket** Kricket spielen; 2 (*insect*) Grille *die* (PL *die* Grillen).

cricket bat *noun* Kricketschläger *der*.

crime *noun* 1 Verbrechen *das* (PL *die* Verbrechen); **theft is a crime** Diebstahl ist ein Verbrechen; 2 (*criminality*) Kriminalität *die*; **to fight crime** die Kriminalität bekämpfen.

criminal *noun* Kriminelle *der/die* (PL *die* Kriminellen).
adjective kriminell.

crisis *noun* Krise *die* (PL *die* Krisen).

crisp *noun* Chip *der* (PL *die* Chips); **a packet of potato crisps** eine Tüte Kartoffelchips.
adjective 1 (*biscuit*) knusprig; 2 (*apple*) knackig.

criticism noun Kritik die (PL die Kritiken).

criticize verb kritisieren.

crocodile noun Krokodil das (PL die Krokodile).

crook noun (criminal) Schwindler der (PL die Schwindler).

crop noun Ernte die.

cross noun Kreuz das (PL die Kreuze).
adjective ärgerlich; **she was very cross** sie war sehr ärgerlich; **I'm cross with you** ich bin sehr ärgerlich auf dich.
verb 1 (to cross over) überqueren; **to cross the road** die Straße überqueren; 2 **to cross your legs** die Beine übereinanderschlagen ✧ SEP; 3 (to cross each other) sich kreuzen; **the two roads cross here** die beiden Straßen kreuzen sich hier.
to cross out ausstreichen ✧ SEP.

cross-Channel adjective **a cross-Channel ferry** eine Fähre über den Kanal.

cross-country noun 1 Cross der; 2 **cross-country skiing** der Langlauf.

crossing noun 1 (from one place to another) Überquerung die (PL die Überquerungen); 2 (a sea journey) Überfahrt die (PL die Überfahrten); **Channel crossing** die Überfahrt über den Kanal; 3 **pedestrian crossing** der Fußgängerübergang; **level crossing** der Bahnübergang.

crossroads noun Kreuzung die (PL die Kreuzungen); **at the crossroads** an der Kreuzung.

crossword noun Kreuzworträtsel das (PL die Kreuzworträtsel); **to do the crossword** ein Kreuzworträtsel machen.

crow noun Krähe die (PL die Krähen).
verb (a cock) krähen.

crowd noun 1 Menschenmenge die (PL die Menschenmengen); **in the crowd** in der Menschenmenge; 2 (spectators) **a crowd of five thousand** fünftausend Zuschauer (plural).
verb **to crowd into or onto something** sich in etwas ←(ACC) drängen; **we all crowded into the train** wir drängten uns alle in den Zug.

crowded adjective überfüllt.

crown noun Krone die (PL die Kronen).

crude adjective 1 (rough and ready) primitiv; 2 (vulgar) ordinär.

cruel adjective grausam.

crumb noun Krümel der (PL die Krümel).

crumpled adjective zerknittert.

crunchy adjective knusprig.

crush verb zerquetschen.

crust noun Kruste die (PL die Krusten).

crusty adjective knusprig.

△ NEW SPELLING: See page xii

crutch noun Krücke die (PL die Krücken); **to be on crutches** an Krücken gehen.

cry noun Schrei der (PL die Schreie). verb 1 (*weep*) weinen; 2 (*call out*) schreien ✧.

cub noun 1 (*animal*) Junge das (PL die Jungen); 2 (*boy scout*) Wölfling der (PL die Wölflinge).

cube noun Würfel der (PL die Würfel); **ice cube** der Eiswürfel.

cubic adjective (*in measurements*) Kubik-; **three cubic metres** drei Kubikmeter.

cubicle noun 1 (*in a changing room*) Kabine die; 2 (*in a public lavatory*) Toilette die (PL die Toiletten).

cuckoo noun Kuckuck der (PL die Kuckucke).

cucumber noun Gurke die (PL die Gurken).

cuddle noun **to give somebody a cuddle** jemanden in den Arm nehmen. verb schmusen.

cue noun (*billiards, pool, snooker*) Queue das (PL die Queues).

cuff noun (*on a shirt*) Manschette die (PL die Manschetten).

cul-de-sac noun Sackgasse die (PL die Sackgassen).

culture noun Kultur die (PL die Kulturen).

cunning adjective listig.

cup noun 1 (*for drinking*) Tasse die (PL die Tassen); **a cup of tea** eine Tasse Tee; 2 (*a trophy*) Pokal der (PL die Pokale).

cupboard noun Schrank der (PL die Schränke); **in the kitchen cupboard** im Küchenschrank.

cup tie noun Pokalspiel das (PL die Pokalspiele).

cure noun Heilmittel das (PL die Heilmittel). verb heilen.

curiosity noun Neugier die.

curious adjective neugierig.

curl noun Locke die (PL die Locken). verb 1 locken (*hair*); 2 (*of hair*) sich locken.

currant noun Korinthe die (PL die Korinthen).

currency noun Währung die (PL die Währungen); **the Japanese currency** die japanische Währung; **foreign currencies** Devisen (*plural*).

current noun 1 (*electricity*) Strom der; 2 (*in water or air*) Strömung die (PL die Strömungen). adjective aktuell.

current affairs noun Tagespolitik die.

curriculum noun Lehrplan der (PL die Lehrpläne).

curry noun Curry das; **vegetable curry** das Gemüse in Currysoße.

curtain noun Vorhang der (PL die Vorhänge).

cushion noun Kissen das (PL die Kissen).

✧ IRREGULAR VERB: *See the verb table in the centre of the dictionary*

custard *noun* Vanillesoße *die* (PL *die* Vanillesoßen).

custom *noun* Brauch *der* (PL *die* Bräuche).

customer *noun* Kunde *der* (PL *die* Kunden), Kundin *die* (PL *die* Kundinnen).

customs *plural noun* Zoll *der*; **to go through customs** durch den Zoll gehen.

customs hall *noun* Zollabfertigung *die*.

customs officer *noun* Zollbeamte *der* (PL *die* Zollbeamten), Zollbeamtin *die* (PL *die* Zollbeamtinnen).

cut *noun* 1 (*injury*) Schnittwunde *die* (PL *die* Schnittwunden); 2 (*haircut*) Schnitt *der* (PL *die* Schnitte). *verb* 1 schneiden ✧; **can you cut the bread please?** kannst du bitte Brot schneiden?; **you'll cut yourself!** du schneidest dich!; **Kevin's cut his finger** Kevin hat sich in den Finger geschnitten; 2 **to cut the grass** den Rasen mähen; 3 **to get your hair cut** sich ←(DAT) die Haare schneiden lassen; **I had my hair cut** ich habe mir die Haare schneiden lassen; 4 **to cut prices** die Preise senken.

● **to cut down** 1 fällen (*a tree*); 2 **to cut down on cigarettes** seinen Zigarettenkonsum einschränken SEP.

● **to cut out something** 1 etwas ausschneiden ✧ SEP (*a shape, a newspaper article*); 2 etwas streichen ✧ (*sugar, fatty food, holidays, for example*).

● **to cut something up** etwas zerschneiden ✧ (*food*).

cutlery *noun* Besteck *das* (PL *die* Bestecke).

CV *noun* Lebenslauf *der* (PL *die* Lebensläufe).

cycle *noun* (*bike*) Rad *das* (PL *die* Räder). *verb* Rad fahren ✧ Δ (PERF *sein*); **do you like cycling?** fährst du gerne Rad?; **we cycle to school** wir fahren mit dem Rad zur Schule.

cycle lane *noun* Fahrradspur *die* (PL *die* Fahrradspuren).

cycle race *noun* Radrennen *das* (PL *die* Radrennen).

cycling *noun* Radfahren *das*.

cycling shorts *noun* Radlerhose *die* (PL *die* Radlerhosen).

cyclist *noun* Radfahrer *der* (PL *die* Radfahrer), Radfahrerin *die* (PL *die* Radfahrerinnen).

D d

dad *noun* Vati *der* (PL *die* Vatis).

daffodil *noun* Osterglocke *die* (PL *die* Osterglocken).

daily *adjective* täglich.

dairy products *plural noun* Milchprodukte (*plural*).

daisy *noun* Gänseblümchen *das* (PL *die* Gänseblümchen).

Δ NEW SPELLING: *See page xii*

damage noun Schaden der (PL die Schäden); **to do a lot of damage** großen Schaden anrichten. verb beschädigen.

damn noun **I don't give a damn** das ist mir piepegal (informal). exclamation **damn!** verdammt!

damp adjective feucht. noun Feuchtigkeit die.

dance noun Tanz der (PL die Tänze); **a folk dance** ein Volkstanz. verb tanzen; **I like dancing** ich tanze gerne.

dancer noun Tänzer der (PL die Tänzer), Tänzerin die (PL die Tänzerinnen).

dancing noun Tanzen das.

dancing class noun Tanzstunde die (PL die Tanzstunden); **to go to dancing classes** in die Tanzstunde gehen.

dandruff noun Schuppen (plural).

danger noun Gefahr die (PL die Gefahren); **to be in danger** in Gefahr sein.

dangerous adjective gefährlich; **it's dangerous to drive too fast** es ist gefährlich, zu schnell zu fahren.

Danish noun Dänisch das. adjective dänisch; **he's Danish** er ist Däne; **she's Danish** sie ist Dänin.

dare verb 1 wagen; **to dare to do something** es wagen, etwas zu tun; **I didn't dare suggest it** ich habe es nicht gewagt, das vorzuschlagen; 2 **don't you dare tell her I'm here!** untersteh dich, ihr zu sagen, dass ich da bin!; 3 **I dare you!** trau dich!; **I**

dare you to tell him! sag's ihm, trau dich doch!

daring adjective gewagt; **that was a bit daring** das war etwas gewagt.

dark noun **in the dark** im Dunkeln; **after dark** nach Einbruch der Dunkelheit; **to be afraid of the dark** Angst im Dunkeln haben. adjective 1 (colour) dunkel (adjectives ending in -el drop the e when followed by a vowel, which means that dunkel becomes dunkler/dunkle/dunkles); **a dark colour** eine dunkle Farbe; **it gets dark around five** es wird gegen fünf dunkel; 2 **a dark blue skirt** ein dunkelblauer Rock; **she has dark brown hair** sie hat dunkelbraune Haare.

darkness noun Dunkelheit die; **in darkness** in der Dunkelheit.

darling noun Liebling der (PL die Lieblinge); **see you later, darling!** bis später, Liebling!

dart noun 1 Wurfpfeil der (PL die Wurfpfeile); 2 (game) **darts** Darts das; **to play darts** Darts spielen.

data plural noun Daten (plural).

database noun Datenbank die (PL die Datenbanken).

date noun 1 Datum das (PL die Daten); **what's the date today?** welches Datum haben wir heute?; **the date of the meeting** das Datum für das Treffen; **what date is he coming?** wann kommt er?; 2 Termin der (PL die Termine); **the**

last date for payment der letzte Zahlungstermin; **3 out of date** ungültig; **my passport's out of date** mein Pass ist ungültig; **4** (*fruit*) Dattel *die* (PL *die* Datteln).

date of birth *noun* Geburtsdatum *das* (PL *die* Geburtsdaten).

daughter *noun* Tochter *die* (PL *die* Töchter); **Tina's daughter** Tinas Tochter.

daughter-in-law *noun* Schwiegertochter *die* (PL *die* Schwiegertöchter).

dawn *noun* Morgendämmerung *die* (PL *die* Morgendämmerungen).

day *noun* **1** Tag *der* (PL *die* Tage); **three days later** drei Tage später; **a few days ago** vor ein paar Tagen; **the day I went to London** an dem Tag, an dem ich nach London gefahren bin; **we spent the day in London** wir haben den Tag in London verbracht; **it rained all day** es hat den ganzen Tag geregnet; **the day after** am Tag danach; **the day after the wedding** am Tag nach der Hochzeit; **the day before** am Tag davor; **the day before the wedding** am Tag vor der Hochzeit; **2 the day after tomorrow** übermorgen; **my sister's arriving the day after tomorrow** meine Schwester kommt übermorgen an; **3 the day before yesterday** vorgestern; **my brother arrived the day before yesterday** mein Bruder kam vorgestern an; **4 during the day** tagsüber.

dead *adjective* tot; **her father's dead** ihr Vater ist tot.

adverb (*really*) irre (*informal*); **he's dead nice** er ist irre nett; **it was dead good** es war irre gut; **it was dead easy** es war kinderleicht; **you're dead right** du hast völlig Recht; **she arrived dead on time** sie kam auf die Minute pünktlich an.

deadline *noun* letzte Termin *der* (PL *die* letzten Termine).

deaf *adjective* taub.

deafening *adjective* ohrenbetäubend.

deal *noun* **1** (*involving money*) Geschäft *das* (PL *die* Geschäfte); **it's a good deal** das ist ein gutes Geschäft; **2** (*agreement*) Vereinbarung *die* (PL *die* Vereinbarungen); **to make a deal with somebody** mit jemandem eine Vereinbarung treffen; **it's a deal!** abgemacht!; **3 a great deal of** viel; **I don't have a great deal of time** ich habe nicht viel Zeit.
verb (*in cards*) geben; **it's you to deal** du gibst.
● **to deal with something** sich um etwas ←(ACC) kümmern; **Linda deals with the accounts** Linda kümmert sich um die Buchführung; **I'll deal with it as soon as possible** ich kümmere mich so schnell wie möglich darum.

dear *adjective* **1** lieb; **Dear Franz** Lieber Franz; **Dear Mr Smith** Sehr geehrter Herr Smith; **2** (*expensive*) teuer.

death *noun* Tod *der*; **after his father's death** nach dem Tod seines Vaters; **three deaths** drei

Todesfälle; ★ **I was bored to death** ich habe mich zu Tode gelangweilt; ★ **I'm sick to death of it** ich habe es gründlich satt.

death penalty noun Todesstrafe die.

debate noun Debatte die (PL die Debatten).
verb debattieren.

debt noun (money owed) Schulden (plural); **to get into debt** in Schulden geraten.

decaffeinated adjective koffeinfrei.

deceive verb betrügen ✧.

December noun Dezember der (PL die Dezember); **in December** im Dezember.

decent adjective anständig; **a decent salary** ein anständiges Gehalt; **a decent meal** ein anständiges Essen.

decide verb 1 entscheiden ✧; **to decide on something** sich für etwas ←(ACC) entscheiden; **he's decided against buying a new car** er hat sich entschieden, kein neues Auto zu kaufen; 2 **to decide to do something** sich entschließen ✧, etwas zu tun; **they've decided to buy a house** sie haben sich entschlossen, ein Haus zu kaufen.

decimal adjective Dezimal-; **decimal number** die Dezimalzahl.

decimal point noun Komma das (PL die Kommas).

decision noun Entscheidung die (PL die Entscheidungen); **to make a**

decision eine Entscheidung treffen

deckchair noun Liegestuhl der (PL die Liegestühle).

declare verb 1 erklären; 2 (at customs) **nothing to declare** nichts zu verzollen.

decorate verb 1 schmücken; **to decorate the Christmas tree** den Weihnachtsbaum schmücken; 2 (with paint) streichen ✧; (with wallpaper) tapezieren; **we're decorating the kitchen this weekend** wir streichen dieses Wochenende die Küche.

decoration noun Verzierung die (PL die Verzierungen); **Christmas decorations** der Weihnachtsschmuck.

deep adjective tief; **a deep feeling of gratitude** ein tiefes Dankbarkeitsgefühl; **how deep is the swimming pool?** wie tief ist das Schwimmbecken?; **a hole two metres deep** ein zwei Meter tiefes Loch.

deep freeze noun Tiefkühltruhe die (PL die Tiefkühltruhen); (upright) Tiefkühlschrank der (PL die Tiefkühlschränke).

deeply adverb tief.

deer noun 1 Hirsch der (PL die Hirsche); 2 (roe deer) Reh das (PL die Rehe).

defeat noun Niederlage die (PL die Niederlagen).
verb schlagen ✧.

defence noun Verteidigung die.

✧ IRREGULAR VERB: See the verb table in the centre of the dictionary

defend *verb* verteidigen.

defender *noun* Verteidiger *der* (PL *die* Verteidiger), Verteidigerin *die* (PL *die* Verteidigerinnen).

definite *adjective* **1** eindeutig; **a definite improvement** eine eindeutige Besserung; **2** (*certain*) sicher; **it's not definite yet** es ist noch nicht sicher; **3** (*exact*) klar; **a definite answer** eine klare Antwort.

definitely *adverb* **1** (*when giving your opinion about something*) eindeutig; **your German is definitely better than mine** dein Deutsch ist eindeutig besser als meins; **2** (*without doubt*) bestimmt; **she's definitely going to be there** sie wird bestimmt dort sein; **I'm definitely not coming** ich komme ganz bestimmt nicht; **3** '**are you sure you like this one better?**' – '**definitely!**' 'gefällt dir diese wirklich besser?' – 'klar!' (*informal*).

degree *noun* **1** Grad *der* (PL *die* Grade); **thirty degrees** dreißig Grad; **2 a university degree** ein akademischer Grad.

delay *noun* Verspätung *die* (PL *die* Verspätungen); **a two-hour delay** eine zweistündige Verspätung.
verb **1** (*hold up*) aufhalten ◇ SEP; **she was delayed in the office** sie ist im Büro aufgehalten worden; **2** (*train, plane*) **to be delayed** Verspätung haben; **the flight was delayed by bad weather** der Flug hatte wegen des schlechten Wetters Verspätung; **3** (*postpone*) aufschieben ◇ SEP; **the decision has been delayed until Thursday** die

Entscheidung wurde bis Donnerstag aufgeschoben.

delete *verb* **1** streichen ◇; **2** (*in computing*) löschen.

deliberate *adjective* absichtlich.

deliberately *adverb* absichtlich; **she did it deliberately** sie hat das absichtlich getan.

delicate *adjective* **1** (*fabric, health*) zart; **2** (*situation, question*) heikel; **3** (*taste, smell*) fein.

delicatessen *noun* Feinkostgeschäft *das* (PL *die* Feinkostgeschäfte).

delicious *adjective* köstlich.

delighted *adjective* hocherfreut; **to be delighted** begeistert sein; **they're delighted with their new flat** sie sind von ihrer neuen Wohnung begeistert; **I'm delighted that you can come** ich freue mich sehr, dass ihr kommen könnt.

deliver *verb* **1** liefern; **they're delivering the washing machine tomorrow** die Waschmaschine wird morgen geliefert; **2** (*mail, newspapers*) zustellen SEP.

delivery *noun* **1** Lieferung *die* (PL *die* Lieferungen); **2** (*of mail, newspapers*) Zustellung *die* (PL *die* Zustellungen).

demand *noun* Nachfrage *die* (PL *die* Nachfragen); **much in demand** sehr gefragt.
verb verlangen.

demo *noun* (*protest*) Demo *die* (*informal*) (PL *die* Demos).

△ NEW SPELLING: *See page xii*

democracy noun Demokratie die (PL die Demokratien).

democratic adjective demokratisch.

demonstrate verb 1 (a machine, product, or technique) vorführen SEP; 2 (protest) demonstrieren; **to demonstrate against something** gegen etwas ←(ACC) demonstrieren.

demonstration noun 1 (of a machine, product, or technique) Vorführung die (PL die Vorführungen); 2 (protest) Demonstration die (PL die Demonstrationen).

demonstrator noun Demonstrant der (PL die Demonstranten), Demonstrantin die (PL die Demonstrantinnen).

denim noun Jeansstoff der (PL die Jeansstoffe); **a denim jacket** eine Jeansjacke.

Denmark noun Dänemark das.

dental adjective 1 Zahn-; **dental floss** die Zahnseide; **dental hygiene** die Zahnpflege; 2 **to have a dental appointment** beim Zahnarzt angemeldet sein.

dentist noun Zahnarzt der (PL die Zahnärzte), Zahnärztin die (PL die Zahnärztinnen); **my mum's a dentist** meine Mutter ist Zahnärztin.

deny verb bestreiten ✧.

deodorant noun Deodorant das (PL die Deodorants).

depart verb 1 (set out on a journey) abreisen SEP (PERF sein); 2 (train, coach) abfahren ✧ SEP (PERF sein); 3 (plane) abfliegen ✧ SEP (PERF sein).

department noun 1 (in a shop, firm, or hospital) Abteilung die (PL die Abteilungen); **the men's department** die Herrenabteilung; 2 (of a university) Seminar das (PL die Seminare); **the history department** das Seminar für Geschichte; 3 (in school) Fachbereich der (PL die Fachbereiche).

department store noun Kaufhaus das (PL die Kaufhäuser).

departure noun 1 (of a person) Abreise die; 2 (of a car, train) Abfahrt die; 3 (of a plane) Abflug der.

departure lounge noun Abflughalle die (PL die Abflughallen).

depend verb 1 **to depend on** abhängen ✧ SEP von (+DAT); **it depends on the price** das hängt vom Preis ab; **it depends on what you want** das hängt davon ab, was du willst; 2 **it depends** es kommt darauf an.

deposit noun 1 (when renting or hiring) Kaution die (PL die Kautionen); 2 (when booking a holiday or hotel room) Anzahlung die (PL die Anzahlungen); **to pay a deposit** eine Anzahlung leisten; 3 (on a bottle) Pfand das.

depressed adjective deprimiert.

depressing adjective deprimierend.

✧ IRREGULAR VERB: See the verb table in the centre of the dictionary

depth *noun* Tiefe *die*.

deputy *noun* Stellvertreter *der* (PL *die* Stellvertreter), Stellvertreterin *die* (PL *die* Stellvertreterinnen).

describe *verb* beschreiben ✧.

description *noun* Beschreibung *die* (PL *die* Beschreibungen).

desert *noun* Wüste *die* (PL *die* Wüsten).

desert island *noun* verlassene Insel *die* (PL *die* verlassenen Inseln).

deserve *verb* verdienen.

design *noun* 1 Konstruktion *die* (PL *die* Konstruktionen); **the design of the plane** die Flugzeugkonstruktion; 2 (*artistic design*) Design *das* (PL *die* Designs); **modern design** modernes Design; 3 (*pattern*) Muster *das* (PL *die* Muster); **a floral design** ein Blumenmuster; 4 (*sketch*) Entwurf *der* (PL *die* Entwürfe). *verb* 1 konstruieren (*a machine, plane, system*); 2 entwerfen ✧ (*costumes, fabric, scenery*).

designer *noun* Designer *der* (PL *die* Designer), Designerin *die* (PL *die* Designerinnen).

desk *noun* 1 (*in an office or at home*) Schreibtisch *der* (PL *die* Schreibtische); 2 (*pupil's*) Pult *das* (PL *die* Pulte); 3 **the reception desk** die Rezeption; **the information desk** die Auskunft.

despair *noun* Verzweiflung *die*. *verb* **to despair of doing something** alle Hoffnung aufgeben ✧ SEP, etwas zu tun.

desperate *adjective* 1 verzweifelt; **a desperate attempt** ein verzweifelter Versuch; 2 **to be desperate to do something** etwas dringend tun müssen; **I'm desperate to speak to you** ich muss dich dringend sprechen; **to be desperate for something** etwas dringend brauchen.

dessert *noun* Nachtisch *der* (PL *die* Nachtische); **what's for dessert?** was gibt's zum Nachtisch?

destination *noun* Ziel *das* (PL *die* Ziele).

destroy *verb* zerstören.

destruction *noun* Zerstörung *die*.

detached house *noun* Einzelhaus *das* (PL *die* Einzelhäuser).

detail *noun* Einzelheit *die* (PL *die* Einzelheiten).

detailed *adjective* ausführlich.

detective *noun* 1 (*in the police*) Kriminalbeamte *der* (PL *die* Kriminalbeamten), Kriminalbeamtin *die* (PL *die* Kriminalbeamtinnen); 2 **private detective** der Detektiv, die Detektivin.

detective story *noun* Detektivgeschichte *die* (PL *die* Detektivgeschichten).

detention *noun* 1 (*at school*) Nachsitzen *das*; 2 (*in prison*) Haft *die*.

detergent *noun* Waschmittel *das*
(PL *die* Waschmittel).

determined *adjective*
entschlossen; **he's determined to
leave** er ist fest entschlossen zu
gehen.

detour *noun* Umweg *der* (PL *die*
Umwege).

develop *verb* 1 entwickeln; **to get a
film developed** einen Film
entwickeln lassen; 2 sich
entwickeln; **how children develop**
wie Kinder sich entwickeln.

developing country *noun*
Entwicklungsland *das* (PL *die*
Entwicklungsländer).

development *noun*
Entwicklung *die* (PL *die*
Entwicklungen).

devil *noun* Teufel *der* (PL *die* Teufel).

devoted *adjective* treu.

diabetes *noun*
Zuckerkrankheit *die*.

diabetic *noun* Diabetiker *der* (PL *die*
Diabetiker), Diabetikerin *die* (PL *die*
Diabetikerinnen).
adjective zuckerkrank; **to be
diabetic** zuckerkrank sein.

diagonal *adjective* diagonal.

diagram *noun* Diagramm *das* (PL
die Diagramme).

dial *verb* wählen; **I dialled the wrong
number** ich habe die falsche
Nummer gewählt.

dialling tone *noun*
Freizeichen *das*.

dialogue *noun* Dialog *der* (PL *die*
Dialoge).

diamond *noun* 1 Diamant *der* (PL
die Diamanten); (*gemstone*)
Brillant *der* (PL *die* Brillanten); 2 (*in
cards*) Karo *das*; **the jack of
diamonds** der Karobube; 3 (*shape*)
Raute *die* (PL *die* Rauten).

diarrhoea *noun* Durchfall *der*.

diary *noun* 1 (*for appointments*)
Terminkalender *der* (PL *die*
Terminkalender); 2 Tagebuch *das*
(PL *die* Tagebücher); **to keep a diary**
ein Tagebuch führen.

dice *noun* Würfel *der* (PL *die* Würfel)
to throw the dice würfeln.

dictation *noun* Diktat *das* (PL *die*
Diktate).

dictionary *noun* Wörterbuch *das*
(PL *die* Wörterbücher).

did *verb* SEE **do**.

die *verb* 1 sterben ✧ (PERF *sein*); **my
grannie died in January** meine
Oma starb im Januar; 2 **to be dying
to do something** darauf brennen,
etwas zu tun; **I'm dying to meet her**
ich brenne darauf, sie kennen zu
lernen.

diesel *noun* 1 Dieselöl *das*; 2 **diesel
engine** *der* Dieselmotor; **diesel car**
der Diesel.

diet *noun* 1 Ernährung *die*; **a
healthy diet** eine gesunde
Ernährung; 2 (*slimming or special*)
Diät *die* (PL *die* Diäten); **to be on a
diet** Diät machen.

✧ IRREGULAR VERB: *See the verb table in the centre of the dictionary*

difference *noun* **1** Unterschied *der* (PL *die* Unterschiede); **I can't see any difference between the two** ich finde, es besteht kein Unterschied zwischen den beiden; **what's the difference between …?** was ist der Unterschied zwischen …?; **2 it makes a difference** es ist ein Unterschied; **it makes no difference** es ist egal; **it makes no difference what I say** es ist egal, was ich sage.

different *adjective* **1** verschieden; **the two sisters are very different** die beiden Schwestern sind sehr verschieden; **2 to be different from** anders sein als; **she's very different from her sister** sie ist ganz anders als ihre Schwester; **3** (*separate*) anderer/andere/anderes; **she reads a different book every day** sie liest jeden Tag ein anderes Buch.

difficult *adjective* schwer; **it's really difficult** es ist sehr schwer; **he finds it difficult** es fällt ihm schwer.

difficulty *noun* Schwierigkeit *die* (PL *die* Schwierigkeiten); **to have difficulty doing something** Schwierigkeiten haben, etwas zu tun; **I had difficulty finding your house** ich hatte Schwierigkeiten, dein Haus zu finden.

dig *verb* graben ✧; **to dig a hole** ein Loch graben.

digital *adjective* digital; **digital watch** *die* Digitaluhr; **digital recording** *die* Digitalaufnahme.

din *noun* Lärm *der*; **stop making such a din!** hör auf, so einen Lärm zu machen!

dinghy *noun* **1 sailing dinghy** *das* Dingi; **2 rubber dinghy** *das* Schlauchboot.

dining room *noun* Esszimmer ∆ *das* (PL *die* Esszimmer); **in the dining room** im Esszimmer.

dinner *noun* **1** (*evening*) Abendessen *das* (PL *die* Abendessen); **to invite somebody to dinner** jemanden zum Abendessen einladen; **2** (*midday*) Mittagessen *das* (PL *die* Mittagessen); **to have school dinner** in der Schulkantine zu Mittag essen.

dinner party *noun* Abendessen *das* (PL *die* Abendessen).

dinner time *noun* Essenszeit *die*.

dinosaur *noun* Dinosaurier *der* (PL *die* Dinosaurier).

diploma *noun* Diplom *das* (PL *die* Diplome).

direct *adjective* direkt. *verb* **1 to direct a film or a play** bei einem Film oder einem Theaterstück Regie führen; **2** regeln (*traffic*).

direction *noun* **1** Richtung *die* (PL *die* Richtungen); **to go in the other direction** in die andere Richtung gehen; **2 to ask somebody for directions** jemanden nach dem Weg fragen; **3 directions for use** *die* Gebrauchsanweisung (*singular*).

director *noun* **1** (*of a company*) Direktor *der* (PL *die* Direktoren), Direktorin *die* (PL *die* Direktorinnen); **2** (*of a programme,* *play, or film*) Regisseur *der* (PL *die* Regisseure), Regisseurin *die* (PL *die* Regisseurinnen).

directory *noun* Telefonbuch *das* (PL *die* Telefonbücher); **he's ex-directory** seine Nummer steht nicht im Telefonbuch.

dirt *noun* Schmutz *der*.

dirty *adjective* schmutzig; **my hands are dirty** ich habe schmutzige Hände; **to get something dirty** etwas schmutzig machen; **you'll get your dress dirty** du machst dir das Kleid schmutzig; **to get dirty** schmutzig werden; **the curtains get dirty quickly** die Vorhänge werden sehr schnell schmutzig.

disabled *adjective* behindert; **disabled people** Behinderte (*plural*).

disadvantage *noun* **1** Nachteil *der* (PL *die* Nachteile); **2 to be at a disadvantage** im Nachteil sein.

disagree *verb* **1 I disagree** ich bin anderer Meinung; **2 to disagree with somebody** mit jemandem nicht übereinstimmen SEP; **I disagree with James** ich stimme mit James nicht überein.

disappear *verb* verschwinden ✧ (PERF *sein*).

disappearance *noun* Verschwinden *das*.

disappointed *adjective* enttäuscht; **I'm disappointed with my marks** ich bin über meine Noten enttäuscht.

disappointment *noun* Enttäuschung *die* (PL *die* Enttäuschungen).

disaster *noun* Katastrophe *die* (PL *die* Katastrophen); **it was a complete disaster** es war eine komplette Katastrophe.

disastrous *adjective* katastrophal.

disc *noun* **1 compact disc** *die* Compact disc; **2 tax disc** (*for a vehicle*) die Steuerplakette; **3 slipped disc** *der* Bandscheibenvorfall.

discipline *noun* Disziplin *die*.

disc-jockey *noun* Diskjockey *der* (PL *die* Diskjockeys).

disco *noun* **1** Diskoparty *die* (PL *die* Diskopartys); **they're having a disco** sie machen eine Diskoparty; **2** (*club*) Disko *die* (PL *die* Diskos); **to go to a disco** in eine Disko gehen.

discount *noun* Rabatt *der* (PL *die* Rabatte).

discover *verb* entdecken.

discovery *noun* Entdeckung *die* (PL *die* Entdeckungen).

discreet *adjective* diskret.

discrimination *noun* Diskriminierung *die*; **discrimination against women** die Diskriminierung von Frauen; **racial discrimination** *die* Rassendiskriminierung.

discuss *verb* **to discuss something** etwas besprechen ✧; **we'll discuss the problem tomorrow** wir besprechen das Problem morgen;

✧ IRREGULAR VERB: *See the verb table in the centre of the dictionary*

I'm going to discuss it with Phil ich werde es mit Phil besprechen.

discussion *noun* Gespräch *das* (PL die Gespräche).

disease *noun* Krankheit *die* (PL die Krankheiten).

disguise *noun* Verkleidung *die* (PL die Verkleidungen); **to be in disguise** verkleidet sein. *verb* verkleiden; **disguised as a woman** als Frau verkleidet.

disgust *noun* Ekel *der*.

disgusted *adjective* 1 (*filled with indignation*) empört; 2 (*nauseated*) angeekelt.

disgusting *adjective* eklig.

dish *noun* 1 Schüssel *die* (PL die Schüsseln); **a large white dish** eine große weiße Schüssel; **satellite dish** *die* Satellitenschüssel; 2 (*type of food*) Gericht *das* (PL die Gerichte); **risotto is my favourite dish** Risotto ist mein Lieblingsgericht; 3 (*crockery*) **the dishes** das Geschirr; **to do the dishes** Geschirr spülen.

dishonest *adjective* unehrlich.

dishonesty *noun* Unehrlichkeit *die*.

dishwasher *noun* Geschirrspülmaschine *die* (PL die Geschirrspülmaschinen).

disinfectant *noun* Desinfektionsmittel *das*.

disk *noun* Diskette *die* (PL die Disketten); **floppy disk** *die* Diskette; **hard disk** *die* Festplatte.

diskette *noun* Diskette *die* (PL die Disketten).

dismiss *verb* entlassen ✧ (*an employee*).

disobedient *adjective* ungehorsam.

display *noun* 1 Ausstellung *die* (PL die Ausstellungen); **handicrafts display** *die* Handarbeitsausstellung; **to be on display** ausgestellt sein; 2 **window display** *die* Auslage; 3 **firework display** *das* Feuerwerk. *verb* ausstellen SEP.

disposable *adjective* Wegwerf-; **disposable towel** *das* Wegwerfhandtuch.

disqualify *verb* disqualifizieren.

dissolve *verb* auflösen SEP.

distance *noun* Entfernung *die* (PL die Entfernungen); **from this distance** aus dieser Entfernung; **from a distance** von weitem; **in the distance** in der Ferne; **it's within walking distance** es ist zu Fuß erreichbar.

distant *adjective* fern.

distinct *adjective* deutlich.

distinctly *adverb* 1 deutlich; 2 **it's distinctly odd** es ist äußerst komisch.

distract *verb* ablenken SEP.

distribute *verb* verteilen.

district *noun* 1 (*of a town*) Stadtteil *der* (PL die Stadtteile); **a poor district of Berlin** ein ärmlicher Stadtteil von Berlin; 2 (*in the country*) Gebiet *das* (PL die Gebiete).

△ NEW SPELLING: *See page xii*

disturb *verb* stören; **sorry to disturb you** Entschuldigung, dass ich störe.

dive *noun* Kopfsprung *der* (PL *die* Kopfsprünge).
verb 1 einen Kopfsprung machen; 2 (*swim underwater*) tauchen (PERF *sein*).

diver *noun* 1 (*underwater*) Taucher *der* (PL *die* Taucher), Taucherin *die* (PL *die* Taucherinnen); 2 (*from a diving board*) Springer *der* (PL *die* Springer), Springerin *die* (PL *die* Springerinnen).

diversion *noun* (*of traffic*) Umleitung *die* (PL *die* Umleitungen).

divide *verb* teilen.

diving *noun* 1 (*underwater*) Tauchen *das*; 2 (*from a diving board*) Kopfspringen *das*.

diving board *noun* Sprungbrett *das* (PL *die* Sprungbretter).

division *noun* 1 Teilung *die* (PL *die* Teilungen); 2 (*in maths*) Division *die* (PL *die* Divisionen); 3 (*sports league*) Liga *die* (PL *die* Ligen).

divorce *noun* Scheidung *die* (PL *die* Scheidungen).

divorced *adjective* geschieden.

DIY *noun* 1 Heimwerken *das*; 2 **to do DIY** heimwerken; 3 **DIY shop** *der* Baumarkt (PL *die* Baumärkte).

dizzy *adjective* **I feel dizzy** mir ist schwindlig.

DJ *noun* DJ *der* (PL *die* DJs).

do *verb* 1 tun ✧, machen; **what are you doing?** was machst du?; **I'm doing my homework** ich mache meine Hausaufgaben; **what have you done with the hammer?** was hast du mit dem Hammer gemacht?; **can you do me a favour?** kannst du mir einen Gefallen tun?; **do as I say** tu was ich sage; 2 **she's doing the cleaning** sie putzt; **I'll do the washing up** ich wasche ab; **I must do the shopping** ich muss einkaufen gehen; 3 (*in questions*) **do you like it?** gefällt es dir?; **when does the film start?** wann fängt der Film an?; **how do you open the door?** wie macht man die Tür auf?; **do you know him?** kennst du ihn?; 4 (*in negative sentences*) **I don't like mushrooms** ich mag keine Pilze; **Rosie doesn't like spinach** Rosie mag keinen Spinat; **you didn't shut the door** du hast die Tür nicht zugemacht; **it doesn't matter** das macht nichts; 5 (*when it refers back to another verb, 'do' is not translated*) **'do you live here?' – 'yes, I do'** 'wohnst du hier?' -'ja'; **she has more money than I do** sie hat mehr Geld als ich; **'I live in Oxford' – 'so do I'** 'ich wohne in Oxford' – 'ich auch'; **'I didn't phone Gemma' – 'neither did I'** 'ich habe Gemma nicht angerufen' – 'ich auch nicht'; 6 **don't you?, doesn't he?,** *etc.* nicht wahr?; **you know Helen, don't you?** du kennst Helen, nicht wahr?; **she left on Thursday, didn't she?** sie ist Donnerstag abgefahren, nicht

---

✧ IRREGULAR VERB: *See the verb table in the centre of the dictionary*

wahr?; **7 that'll do** das reicht; **it'll do like that** das geht so.

● **to do something up 1** etwas zubinden ✧ SEP (*shoes*); **2** etwas zumachen SEP (*a cardigan, jacket*); **3** etwas renovieren (*a house*).

● **to do without something** ohne etwas ←(ACC) auskommen ✧ SEP (PERF *sein*); **we can do without knives** wir können ohne Messer auskommen.

doctor *noun* Arzt *der* (PL *die* Ärzte), Ärztin *die* (PL *die* Ärztinnen); **her mother's a doctor** ihre Mutter ist Ärztin.

documentary *noun* Dokumentarfilm *der* (PL *die* Dokumentarfilme).

dog *noun* Hund *der* (PL *die* Hunde).

do-it-yourself *noun* Heimwerken *das*.

dole *noun* Stempelgeld *das*; **to be on the dole** stempeln gehen (*informal*).

doll *noun* Puppe *die* (PL *die* Puppen).

dollar *noun* Dollar *der* (PL *die* Dollars).

domino *noun* **1** Dominostein *der* (PL *die* Dominosteine); **2** (*game*) **dominoes** Domino *das*; **to play dominoes** Domino spielen.

donkey *noun* Esel *der* (PL *die* Esel).

don't SEE **do**.

door *noun* Tür *die* (PL *die* Türen); **to open the door** die Tür aufmachen; **to shut the door** die Tür zumachen.

doorbell *noun* Türklingel *die* (PL *die* Türklingeln); **to ring the doorbell** klingeln.

dot *noun* **1** Punkt *der* (PL *die* Punkte); **at ten on the dot** Punkt zehn Uhr; **2** (*small dot on fabric*) Pünktchen *das* (PL *die* Pünktchen).

double *adjective, adverb* **1** doppelt; **a double helping** eine doppelte Portion; **double the size** doppelt so groß; **double the time** doppelt so viel Zeit; **at double the price** zum doppelten Preis; **2 double room** *das* Doppelzimmer; **3 double bed** *das* Doppelbett.

double bass *noun* Kontrabass △ *der* (PL *die* Kontrabässe).

double-decker bus *noun* Doppeldeckerbus *der* (PL *die* Doppeldeckerbusse).

doubles *noun* (*in tennis*) Doppel *das* (PL *die* Doppel).

doubt *noun* Zweifel *der* (PL *die* Zweifel); **there's no doubt about it** es besteht kein Zweifel daran; **I have my doubts** ich habe gewisse Zweifel.
verb **to doubt something** etwas bezweifeln; **I doubt it** das bezweifle ich; **I doubt that …** ich bezweifle, dass …; **I doubt they'll buy it** ich bezweifle, dass sie es kaufen.

doubtful *adjective* **1** fraglich; **it's doubtful** es ist fraglich; **2 to be doubtful about doing something** Bedenken haben, ob man etwas tun soll; **I'm doubtful about inviting them together** ich habe Bedenken, ob ich sie zusammen einladen soll.

dough noun Teig der.

doughnut noun Krapfen der (PL die Krapfen).

down adverb, preposition 1 unten; **he's down in the cellar** er ist unten im Keller; **it's down there** es ist da unten; 2 **down the road** (nearby) in der Nähe; **there's a chemist's just down the road** eine Apotheke ist ganz in der Nähe; 3 **to go down** nach unten gehen; **I went down to open the door** ich bin nach unten gegangen, um die Tür aufzumachen; **to walk down the street** die Straße entlanggehen ✧ SEP (PERF sein); **to run down the stairs** die Treppe runterrennen SEP (PERF sein) (informal); 4 **to come down** herunterkommen ✧ SEP (PERF sein); **she came down into the kitchen** sie kam in die Küche herunter; 5 **to sit down** sich setzen; **she sat down on the chair** sie setzte sich auf den Stuhl; 6 **to write something down** etwas aufschreiben ✧ SEP.

downstairs adverb 1 unten; **she's downstairs** sie ist unten; 2 (with movement) nach unten; **to go downstairs** nach unten gehen; 3 im Erdgeschoss △; **the flat downstairs** die Wohnung im Erdgeschoss.

dozen noun Dutzend das (PL die Dutzende).

drag noun 1 **what a drag!** so'n Mist! (informal); 2 **what a drag she is!** Mann, ist die langweilig! (informal). verb schleppen.

drama noun 1 (play) Drama das (PL die Dramen); **he made a big drama out of it** er hat ein großes Drama daraus gemacht (informal); 2 (dramatic nature) Dramatik die.

dramatic adjective dramatisch.

draught noun Luftzug der; **there's a draught in here** hier zieht es.

draughts noun Damespiel das; **to play draughts** Dame spielen.

draw noun 1 (in a match) Unentschieden das; **to end in a draw** mit einem Unentschieden enden; 2 (lottery) Ziehung die (PL die Ziehungen). verb 1 zeichnen; **she can draw really well** sie kann wirklich sehr gut zeichnen; 2 **to draw the curtains** (open) die Vorhänge aufziehen ✧ SEP; (close) die Vorhänge zuziehen ✧ SEP; 3 (in a match) unentschieden spielen; **we drew three all** wir haben drei zu drei unentschieden gespielt.

drawer noun Schublade die (PL die Schubladen).

drawing noun Zeichnung die (PL die Zeichnungen).

drawing pin noun Reißzwecke die (PL die Reißzwecken).

dreadful adjective furchtbar.

dreadfully adverb furchtbar; **I'm dreadfully late** ich habe mich furchtbar verspätet; **I'm dreadfully sorry** es tut mir furchtbar Leid.

dream noun Traum der (PL die Träume); **to have a dream** einen Traum haben. verb träumen; **to dream about something** von etwas ←(DAT) träumen.

✧ IRREGULAR VERB: See the verb table in the centre of the dictionary

dress *noun* Kleid *das* (PL *die* Kleider).
verb **to dress a child** ein Kind anziehen ✧ SEP.
▸ **to dress up** sich verkleiden; **to dress up as a vampire** sich als Vampir verkleiden.

dressed *adjective* **1** angezogen; **is Tom dressed yet?** ist Tom schon angezogen?; **2 she was dressed in black trousers and a yellow shirt** sie trug schwarze Hosen und ein gelbes Hemd; **3 to get dressed** sich anziehen ✧ SEP; **I got dressed quickly** ich zog mich schnell an.

dressing gown *noun* Morgenrock *der* (PL *die* Morgenröcke).

dressing table *noun* Frisierkommode *die* (PL *die* Frisierkommoden).

drier *noun* **hair drier** *der* Föhn △; **tumble drier** *der* Wäschetrockner.

drill *noun* Bohrer *der* (PL *die* Bohrer).

drink *noun* Getränk *das* (PL *die* Getränke); **1 to have a drink** etwas trinken; **would you like a drink of water?** möchtest du etwas Wasser trinken?; **2** (*an alcoholic drink*) Drink *der* (PL *die* Drinks); **they've invited us round for drinks** sie haben uns auf einen Drink eingeladen; **let's have a drink!** trinken wir einen! (*informal*).
verb trinken ✧; **he drank a glass of water** er trank ein Glas Wasser.

drive *noun* **1 to go for a drive** eine Autofahrt machen; **2** (*in front of a house*) Einfahrt *die* (PL *die* Einfahrten).

verb **1** fahren ✧ (PERF *sein*); **she drives very fast** sie fährt sehr schnell; **to drive a car** Auto fahren; **I'd like to learn to drive** ich möchte Autofahren lernen; **can you drive?** kannst du Auto fahren?; **2 we drove to Berlin** wir sind mit dem Auto nach Berlin gefahren; **3 to drive somebody (to a place)** jemanden (irgendwohin) fahren (PERF *haben*); **Mum drove me to the station** Mutti hat mich zum Bahnhof gefahren; **to drive somebody home** jemanden nach Hause fahren; ★ **she drives me mad!** sie macht mich verrückt!

driver *noun* **1** Fahrer *der* (PL *die* Fahrer), Fahrerin *die* (PL *die* Fahrerinnen); **2** (*of a locomotive*) Führer *der* (PL *die* Führer), Führerin *die* (PL *die* Führerinnen).

driving instructor *noun* Fahrlehrer *der* (PL *die* Fahrlehrer), Fahrlehrerin *die* (PL *die* Fahrlehrerinnen).

driving lesson *noun* Fahrstunde *die* (PL *die* Fahrstunden).

driving licence *noun* Führerschein *der*.

driving test *noun* Fahrprüfung *die*; **to take your driving test** die Fahrprüfung machen; **Jenny's passed her driving test** Jenny hat den Führerschein gemacht.

drop *noun* Tropfen *der* (PL *die* Tropfen).
verb **1 to drop something** etwas fallen lassen; **I dropped my glasses**

△ NEW SPELLING: *See page xii*

ich habe meine Brille fallen lassen;
2 drop it! lass das !; **3 I'm going to
drop history next year** nächstes
Jahr lege ich Geschichte ab;
4 absetzen SEP (*a person*); **could you
drop me at the station?** könntest
du mich am Bahnhof absetzen?

drug *noun* **1** (*medicine*)
Medikament *das* (PL *die*
Medikamente); **2** (*illegal*) **drugs**
Drogen (*plural*).

drug abuse *noun*
Drogenmissbrauch △ *der*.

drug addict *noun*
Drogenabhängige *der/die* (PL *die*
Drogenabhängigen).

drug addiction *noun*
Drogenabhängigkeit *die*.

drum *noun* **1** Trommel *die* (PL *die*
Trommeln); **2 drums** *das*
Schlagzeug; **to play drums**
Schlagzeug spielen.

drummer *noun* Schlagzeuger *der*
(PL *die* Schlagzeuger).

drunk *noun* Betrunkene *der/die* (PL
die Betrunkenen).
adjective betrunken; **to get drunk**
sich betrinken ◇.

dry *adjective* trocken.
verb **1** trocknen; **to let something
dry** etwas trocknen lassen; **to dry
your hair** sich ←(DAT) die Haare
trocknen; **to dry the washing** die
Wäsche trocknen; **2 to dry your
hands** sich ←(DAT) die Hände
abtrocknen SEP; **I dried my feet** ich
trocknete mir die Füße ab; **to dry the
dishes** das Geschirr abtrocknen .

dry cleaner's *noun* chemische
Reinigung *die*.

dryer *noun* SEE **drier**.

dubbed *adjective* **a dubbed film** ein
synchronisierter Film.

duck *noun* Ente *die* (PL *die* Enten).

due *adjective, adverb* **1 to be due to
do something** etwas tun müssen;
Paul's due back soon Paul muss
bald zurück sein; **we're due to leave
on Thursday** wir müssen
Donnerstag abfahren; **2 due to**
wegen (+GEN); **due to bad weather**
wegen schlechten Wetters.

dull *adjective* **1 dull weather** trübes
Wetter; **it's a dull day today** heute
ist ein trüber Tag; **2** (*boring*)
langweilig.

dumb *adjective* **1** stumm; **2** (*stupid*)
dumm; **he asked some dumb
questions** er hat ein paar dumme
Fragen gestellt.

dump *verb* **1** abladen ◇ SEP
(*rubbish*); **2** (*put down*)
hinwerfen ◇ SEP; **he dumped it in the
rubbish** er hat es in den Müll
geworfen; **3** abschieben ◇ SEP (*a
person*) (*informal*); **she's dumped
her boyfriend** sie hat ihren Freund
abgeschoben.

dungarees *plural noun*
Latzhose *die* (PL *die* Latzhosen).

during *preposition* während (+GEN);
during the night während der
Nacht; **I saw her during the
holidays** ich habe sie während der
Ferien gesehen.

◇ IRREGULAR VERB: *See the verb table in the centre of the dictionary*

dust *noun* Staub *der*.
verb **1** abstauben SEP (*furniture, objects*); **2** (*in a room*) Staub wischen; **she's dusting** sie wischt Staub.

dustbin *noun* Mülltonne *die* (PL *die* Mülltonnen).

dustman *noun* Müllmann *der* (PL *die* Müllmänner).

dusty *adjective* staubig.

Dutch *noun* **1** (*language*) Holländisch *das*; **2 the Dutch** (*people*) die Holländer.
adjective holländisch; **he's Dutch** er ist Holländer; **she's Dutch** sie ist Holländerin.

duty *noun* **1** Pflicht *die* (PL *die* Pflichten); **to have a duty to do something** die Pflicht haben, etwas zu tun; **you have a duty to inform us** du hast die Pflicht, uns zu benachrichtigen; **2 to be on duty** Dienst haben; **to be on night duty** Nachtdienst haben; **I'm off duty tonight** ich habe heute Abend keinen Dienst.

duty-free *adjective* zollfrei; **duty-free shop** *der* Dutyfreeshop; **duty-free goods** zollfreie Waren (*plural*).

duvet *noun* Federbett *das* (PL *die* Federbetten).

duvet cover *noun* Bettbezug *der* (PL *die* Bettbezüge).

dye *noun* Farbe *die* (PL *die* Farben).
verb färben; **to dye your hair** sich ←(DAT) die Haare färben; **I'm going to have my hair dyed pink** ich lasse mir die Haare rosa färben.

dynamic *adjective* dynamisch.

dyslexia *noun* Legasthenie *die*.

dyslexic *adjective* legasthenisch; **to be dyslexic** Legastheniker sein, Legasthenikerin sein.

E e

each *adjective, pronoun*
1 jeder/jede/jedes; **each Sunday** jeden Sonntag; **each time** jedes Mal; **at the beginning of each year** am Anfang jedes Jahres; **we each have an invitation** jeder von uns hat eine Einladung; **my sisters each have a computer** meine Schwestern haben alle einen Computer; **she gave us an apple each** sie hat jedem von uns einen Apfel gegeben; **each of you** jeder von euch/jede von euch; **we each got a present** jeder Einzelne hat ein Geschenk bekommen; **2 the tickets cost ten pounds each** die Karten kosten je zehn Pfund; **£5 each** (*per person*) fünf Pfund pro Person; (*per item*) fünf Pfund pro Stück.

each other *pronoun* (*'each other' is usually translated using a reflexive pronoun*) **they love each other** sie lieben sich; **we know each other** wir kennen uns; **do you see each other often?** seht ihr euch oft?

ear *noun* Ohr *das* (PL *die* Ohren).

earache *noun* **to have earache** Ohrenschmerzen haben.

△ NEW SPELLING: *See page xii*

earlier *adverb* 1 (*a while ago*) vor kurzem; **your brother phoned earlier** dein Bruder hat vor kurzem angerufen; 2 (*not as late*) früher; **we should have started earlier** wir hätten früher anfangen sollen.

early *adverb* 1 (*in the morning*) früh; **to get up early** früh aufstehen; **it's too early** es ist zu früh; 2 (*for an appointment*) **to be early** früh dran sein; **we're early, the train doesn't leave until ten** wir sind früh dran, der Zug fährt erst um zehn Uhr ab. *adjective* 1 (*one of the first*) **in the early months** während der ersten Monate; **I'm getting the early train** ich nehme den früheren Zug; 2 **to have an early lunch** früh zu Mittag essen; **Jan's having an early night** Jan geht früh zu Bett; 3 **in the early afternoon** am frühen Nachmittag; **in the early hours** in den frühen Morgenstunden.

earn *verb* verdienen; **Richard earns four pounds an hour** Richard verdient vier Pfund die Stunde.

earring *noun* Ohrring *der* (PL *die* Ohrringe).

earth *noun* Erde *die*; **life on earth** das Leben auf der Erde; ★ **what on earth are you doing?** was in aller Welt machst du da?

easily *adverb* leicht; **he's easily the best** er ist mit Abstand der Beste.

east *noun* Osten *der*; **in the east** im Osten.
adjective, adverb östlich, Ost-; **the east side** die Ostseite; **an east**

wind ein Ostwind; **east of Munich** östlich von München.

Easter *noun* Ostern *das* (PL *die* Ostern); **they're coming at Easter** sie kommen zu Ostern; **Happy Easter** Frohe Ostern.

Easter Day *noun* Ostersonntag *de* (PL *die* Ostersonntage).

Easter egg *noun* Osterei *das* (PL *die* Ostereier).

Eastern Europe *noun* Osteuropa *das*.

easy *adjective* leicht; **it's easy!** das ist leicht!; **it was easy to decide** es war leicht zu entscheiden.

eat *verb* 1 essen ✧; **he was eating a banana** er aß eine Banane; **we're going to have something to eat** wir essen jetzt etwas; 2 **to eat your breakfast** frühstücken.

EC *noun* EG *die* (*Europäische Gemeinschaft*).

ecological *adjective* ökologisch.

ecology *noun* Ökologie *die*.

economical *adjective* sparsam.

economics *noun* Wirtschaftswissenschaften (*plural*).

economy *noun* Wirtschaft *die*.

edge *noun* 1 Kante *die* (PL *die* Kanten); **the edge of the table** die Tischkante; 2 (*of a road, sheet of paper, or cliff*) Rand *der* (PL *die* Ränder); **at the edge of the forest** am Waldrand.

editor *noun* 1 (*of a newspaper or magazine*) Chefredakteur *der* (PL

die Chefredakteure),
Chefredakteurin *die* (PL *die*
Chefredakteurinnen); **2** (*of a book*)
Redakteur *der* (PL *die* Redakteure),
Redakteurin *die* (PL *die*
Redakteurinnen).

educate *verb* erziehen ◇.

education *noun* Ausbildung *die*.

effect *noun* **1** Wirkung *die* (PL *die*
Wirkungen); **the effect of the
explosion was horrific** die Wirkung
der Explosion war entsetzlich; **2 to
have an effect on something** eine
Auswirkung auf etwas ←(ACC) haben;
**it had a good effect on the whole
family** es hatte eine gute
Auswirkung auf die ganze Familie;
3 (*in a film*) Effekt *der* (PL *die*
Effekte); **special effects** besondere
Effekte.

efficient *adjective* **1** (*person*)
tüchtig; **2** (*machine or
organization*) leistungsfähig.

effort *noun* **1** Mühe *die* (PL *die*
Mühen); **2 to make an effort** sich
bemühen; **Toya made an effort to
help us** Toya hat sich bemüht, uns
zu helfen; **he didn't even make the
effort to apologize** er hat sich nicht
einmal die Mühe gemacht, sich zu
entschuldigen.

e.g. *abbreviation* z.B. (*zum Beispiel*)

egg *noun* Ei *das* (PL *die* Eier); **a fried
egg** ein Spiegelei; **a hard-boiled
egg** ein hart gekochtes Ei.

egg-cup *noun* Eierbecher *der* (PL
die Eierbecher).

eggshell *noun* Eierschale *die* (PL *die*
Eierschalen).

egg-white *noun* Eiweiß *das* (PL *die*
Eiweiße).

egg-yolk *noun* Eigelb *das* (PL *die*
Eigelbe).

eight *number* acht; **Maya's eight**
Maya ist acht; **at eight o'clock** um
acht Uhr.

eighteen *number* achtzehn;
Jason's eighteen Jason ist
achtzehn.

eighth *number* achter/achte/
achtes; **on the eighth of July** am
achten Juli.

eighty *number* achtzig; **eighty-five**
fünfundachtzig.

either *pronoun* **1** (*one or the other*)
einer von beiden/eine von
beiden/eins von beiden; **take either
(of them)** nimm einen von
beiden/eine von beiden/eins von
beiden; **I don't like either (of them)**
ich mag keinen von beiden/keine
von beiden/keins von beiden;
2 (*both*) beide (*plural*); **either is
possible** beide sind möglich; **on
either side** auf beiden Seiten.
conjunction **1 either … or** entweder
… oder; **either Susie or Judy**
entweder Susie oder Judy; **2 either
… or** (*with a negative*) weder …
noch; **he didn't ring either Sam or
Emma** er hat weder Sam noch
Emma angerufen; **3 I don't know
them either** ich kenne sie auch
nicht.

elastic *noun* Gummiband *das* (PL
die Gummibänder).

elastic band *noun*
Gummiband *das* (PL *die*
Gummibänder).

△ NEW SPELLING: *See page xii*

elbow *noun* Ellbogen *der* (PL *die* Ellbogen).

elder *adjective* älterer/ältere/älteres; **her elder brother** ihr älterer Bruder.

elderly *adjective* alt; **the elderly** ältere Menschen (*plural*).

eldest *adjective* ältester/älteste/ältestes; **her eldest brother** ihr ältester Bruder.

elect *verb* wählen; **she has been elected** sie ist gewählt worden.

election *noun* Wahl *die* (PL *die* Wahlen); **in the election** bei den Wahlen.

electric *adjective* elektrisch.

electrical *adjective* elektrisch, Elektro-; **electrical equipment** Elektrogeräte (*plural*).

electrician *noun* Elektriker *der* (PL *die* Elektriker), Elektrikerin *die* (PL *die* Elektrikerinnen).

electricity *noun* Strom *der*.

electronic *adjective* elektronisch.

electronics *noun* Elektronik *die*.

elephant *noun* Elefant *der* (PL *die* Elefanten).

eleven *number* elf; **Josh is eleven** Josh ist elf; **at eleven o'clock** um elf Uhr; **a football eleven** eine Fußballelf.

eleventh *number* elfter/elfte/elftes; **the eleventh of May** der elfte Mai; **on the eleventh floor** im elften Stock.

else *adverb* 1 (*in addition*) sonst; **who else?** wer sonst?; **did you see anyone else?** hast du sonst noch jemanden gesehen?; **nothing else** sonst nichts; **I don't want anything else** ich will sonst nichts; 2 **would you like something else?** möchten Sie sonst noch etwas?; 3 (*instead or different*) anderer/andere/anderes; **somewhere else** irgendwo anders; **everyone else** alle anderen; **somebody else** jemand anders; **something else** etwas anderes; 4 **or else** sonst; **hurry up, or else we'll be late** beeil dich, sonst kommen wir zu spät.

E-mail *noun* E-Mail *die* (PL *die* E-Mails).

embarrassed *adjective* verlegen; **he was very embarrassed** er war ganz verlegen.

embarrassing *adjective* peinlich.

emergency *noun* Notfall *der* (PL *die* Notfälle).

emergency exit *noun* Notausgang *der* (PL *die* Notausgänge).

emotion *noun* Gefühl *das* (PL *die* Gefühle).

emotional *adjective* 1 (*person*) empfindsam; 2 (*speech or occasion*) emotionsgeladen.

emphasize *verb* betonen; **he emphasized that it was voluntary** er betonte, dass es freiwillig war.

employ *verb* 1 (*have working for you*) beschäftigen; 2 (*take on a worker*) einstellen SEP.

✧ IRREGULAR VERB: *See the verb table in the centre of the dictionary*

employee *noun*
Angestellte *der/die* (PL *die*
Angestellten).

employer *noun* Arbeitgeber *der* (PL
die Arbeitgeber), Arbeitgeberin *die*
(PL *die* Arbeitgeberinnen).

employment *noun* Arbeit *die*.

empty *adjective* leer; **an empty
bottle** eine leere Flasche.
verb **1** (*empty out*) ausleeren SEP;
2 (*pour*) schütten.

enclose *verb* (*in a letter*) beilegen
SEP; **please find enclosed a cheque**
ein Scheck liegt bei.

encourage *verb* ermutigen; **to
encourage somebody to do
something** jemanden dazu
ermutigen, etwas zu tun; **Mum
encouraged me to try again** Mutti
hat mich dazu ermutigt, es noch
einmal zu versuchen.

encouragement *noun*
Ermutigung *die* (PL *die*
Ermutigungen).

encouraging *adjective*
ermutigend.

encyclopedia *noun* Lexikon *das*
(PL *die* Lexika).

end *noun* **1** Ende *das* (PL *die* Enden);
'The End' 'Ende'; **at the end of the
film** am Ende des Films; **by the end
of the lesson** als die Stunde zu Ende
war; **in the end I went home**
schließlich bin ich nach Hause
gegangen; **Sally's coming at the end
of June** Sally kommt Ende Juni; **I
read to the end of the page** ich
habe die Seite zu Ende gelesen; **hold

the other end** halte das andere Ende
fest; **at the end of the street** am
Ende der Straße; **2** (*in sports*)
Spielfeldhälfte *die* (PL *die*
Spielfeldhälften); **to change ends**
die Seiten wechseln.
verb **1** (*to put an end to*) beenden;
they've ended the strike sie haben
den Streik beendet; **2** (*to come to an
end*) enden; **the day ended with a
meal** der Tag endete mit einem
Essen.

• **to end up 1 to end up doing
something** am Ende etwas tun; **we
ended up taking a taxi** am Ende
haben wir ein Taxi genommen; **2 to
end up somewhere** irgendwo
landen (PERF *sein*) (*informal*); **Rob
ended up in Berlin** Rob ist in Berlin
gelandet.

ending *noun* **1** Ende *das* (PL *die*
Enden); **2** (*in grammar*)
Endung *die* (PL *die* Endungen).

endless *adjective* endlos (*day or
journey, for example*).

enemy *noun* Feind *der* (PL *die*
Feinde); **to make enemies** sich
←(DAT) Feinde machen.

energetic *adjective*
energiegeladen.

energy *noun* Energie *die*.

engaged *adjective* **1** (*to be married*)
verlobt; **they're engaged** sie sind
verlobt; **to get engaged** sich
verloben; **2** (*a phone or toilet*)
besetzt; **it's engaged, I'll ring later**
es ist besetzt, ich rufe später an.

engagement *noun* (*to marry*)
Verlobung *die* (PL *die* Verlobungen).

△ NEW SPELLING: *See page xii*

engagement ring *noun*
Verlobungsring *der* (PL *die*
Verlobungsringe).

engine *noun* 1 (*in a car*) Motor *der*
(PL *die* Motoren); 2 (*pulling a train*)
Lokomotive *die* (PL *die*
Lokomotiven).

engineer *noun* 1 (*who comes for
repairs*) Techniker *der* (PL *die*
Techniker), Technikerin *die* (PL *die*
Technikerinnen); 2 (*who builds
roads and bridges*) Ingenieur *der* (PL
die Ingenieure), Ingenieurin *die* (PL
die Ingenieurinnen).

England *noun* England *das*; **I'm
from England** ich bin Engländer,
ich bin Engländerin.

English *noun* 1 (*the language*)
Englisch *das*; **do you speak
English?** sprechen Sie Englisch?; **he
answered in English** er hat auf
Englisch geantwortet; 2 (*the people*)
the English die Engländer.
adjective 1 (*of or from England*)
englisch; **the English team** die
englische Mannschaft; **he's English**
er ist Engländer; **she's English** sie
ist Engländerin; 2 **an English
lesson** eine Englischstunde; **our
English teacher** unser
Englischlehrer.

English Channel *noun* **the
English Channel** der Ärmelkanal.

Englishman *noun* Engländer *der*
(PL *die* Engländer).

Englishwoman *noun*
Engländerin *die* (PL *die*
Engländerinnen).

enjoy *verb* 1 **did you enjoy the
party?** hat dir die Party gefallen?; **we
really enjoyed the concert** das
Konzert hat uns wirklich gut
gefallen; 2 **to enjoy doing
something** etwas gerne tun ✧; **I
enjoy reading** ich lese gerne; **do you
enjoy living in York?** wohnst du
gerne in York?; 3 **to enjoy oneself**
sich gut amüsieren; **we really
enjoyed ourselves** wir haben uns
richtig gut amüsiert; **enjoy
yourselves!** viel Vergnügen!; **did
you enjoy yourself?** hast du dich
gut amüsiert?

enjoyable *adjective* nett.

enormous *adjective* riesig.

enough *adverb, adjective, pronoun*
1 genug; **there's enough for
everyone** es gibt genug für alle; **big
enough** groß genug; **have we got
enough bread?** haben wir genug
Brot?; 2 **that's enough** das reicht.

enrol *verb* sich anmelden SEP; **I want
to enrol on the course** ich möchte
mich zu dem Kurs anmelden.

enter *verb* 1 (*to go inside*) gehen ✧
(PERF *sein*) in (+ACC) (*a room or a
building*); **we all entered the
church** wir gingen alle in die
Kirche; 2 (*in computing*)
eingeben ✧ SEP; 3 **to enter for** sich
anmelden SEP zu (+DAT) (*an exam or
a race*); **to enter for a competition**
an einem Preisausschreiben
teilnehmen ✧ SEP.

entertain *verb* 1 (*to keep amused*)
unterhalten ✧; 2 (*to have people
round*) Gäste haben ✧; **they don't
entertain much** sie haben selten
Gäste.

✧ IRREGULAR VERB: *See the verb table in the centre of the dictionary*

entertainment *noun* (*fun*)
Unterhaltung *die*; **there wasn't
much entertainment in the
evenings** abends wurde wenig
Unterhaltung geboten.

enthusiasm *noun*
Begeisterung *die*.

enthusiast *noun* **1** Enthusiast *der*
(PL *die* Enthusiasten), Enthusiastin
die (PL *die* Enthusiastinnen); **2** (*for
sports*) Fan *der* (PL *die* Fans); **he's a
rugby enthusiast** er ist ein
Rugbyfan.

enthusiastic *adjective* begeistert.

entire *adjective* ganz; **the entire
class** die ganze Klasse.

entirely *adverb* ganz.

entrance *noun* **1** (*fee*) Eintritt *der*;
2 (*way in*) Eingang *der* (PL *die*
Eingänge).

entry *noun* **1** (*way in*) Eingang *der*
(PL *die* Eingänge); (*for cars*)
Einfahrt *die* (PL *die* Einfahrten);
2 'no entry' 'Zutritt verboten'; (*to
cars*) 'Einfahrt verboten'.

entry phone *noun*
Sprechanlage *die* (PL *die*
Sprechanlagen).

envelope *noun* Briefumschlag *der*
(PL *die* Briefumschläge).

environment *noun* Umwelt *die*.

environmental *adjective* Umwelt-;
environmental pollution die
Umweltverschmutzung.

environment-friendly *adjective*
umweltfreundlich.

epidemic *noun* Epidemie *die* (PL
die Epidemien).

epileptic *adjective* epileptisch.

episode *noun* **1** (*an event*)
Episode *die* (PL *die* Episoden);
2 (*on TV or radio*) Folge *die* (PL *die*
Folgen).

equal *adjective* gleich; **milk and
water in equal quantities** gleich
viel Milch und Wasser.
verb gleichen ◇ (+DAT).

equality *noun*
Gleichberechtigung *die*.

equally *adverb* (*to share*)
gleichmäßig; **we divided it equally**
wir haben es gleichmäßig verteilt.

equator *noun* Äquator *der*.

equip *verb* ausrüsten SEP; **well
equipped for the hike** für die
Wanderung gut ausgerüstet;
equipped with rucksacks mit
Rucksäcken ausgerüstet.

equipment *noun* **1** (*for sport*)
Ausrüstung *die* (PL *die*
Ausrüstungen); **2** Ausstattung *die*
(PL *die* Ausstattungen); **laboratory
equipment** die Laborausstattung;
3 (*something needed for an activity*)
Geräte (*plural*); **recording
equipment** Aufnahmegeräte.

error *noun* **1** (*in spelling, typing, on
a computer, or in maths*) Fehler *der*
(PL *die* Fehler); **spelling error** *der*
Schreibfehler; **2** (*wrong opinion*)
Irrtum *der* (PL *die* Irrtümer).

error message *noun*
Fehlermeldung *die* (PL *die*
Fehlermeldungen).

△ NEW SPELLING: *See page xii*

escalator *noun* Rolltreppe *die* (PL die Rolltreppen).

escape *noun* (*from prison*) Ausbruch *der* (PL die Ausbrüche). *verb* 1 (*from prison*) ausbrechen ⬦ SEP (PERF *sein*); 2 entkommen ⬦ (PERF *sein*); **to escape from somebody** jemandem entkommen.

especially *adverb* besonders.

essay *noun* Aufsatz *der* (PL die Aufsätze); **an essay on German reunification** ein Aufsatz über die deutsche Wiedervereinigung.

essential *adjective* unbedingt erforderlich; **it's essential to reply quickly** es ist unbedingt erforderlich, sofort zu antworten.

estate *noun* 1 (*a housing estate*) Wohnsiedlung *die* (PL die Wohnsiedlungen); 2 (*a big house and grounds*) Landsitz *der* (PL die Landsitze).

estate agent *noun* Immobilienmakler *der* (PL die Immobilienmakler).

estate car *noun* Kombiwagen *der* (PL die Kombiwagen).

estimate *noun* 1 (*a quote for work*) Kostenvoranschlag *der* (PL die Kostenvoranschläge); 2 (*a rough guess*) Schätzung *die* (PL die Schätzungen). *verb* schätzen.

etc. *abbreviation* usw. (*und so weiter*).

ethnic *adjective* ethnisch; **an ethnic minority** eine ethnische Minderheit.

EU *noun* EU *die* (*Europäische Union*).

Europe *noun* Europa *das*.

European *noun* Europäer *der* (PL die Europäer), Europäerin *die* (PL die Europäerinnen). *adjective* europäisch.

European Union *noun* Europäische Union *die*.

even¹ *adverb* 1 sogar; **even Lisa is coming** sogar Lisa kommt; 2 **not even** nicht einmal; **I don't like animals, not even dogs** ich mag keine Tiere, nicht einmal Hunde; 3 **without even asking** ohne wenigstens zu fragen; 4 **even if** selbst wenn; **even if they arrive late** selbst wenn sie spät ankommen; 5 (*with a comparison*) (sogar) noch; **even bigger** sogar noch größer; **even faster** noch schneller; **even better than** sogar noch besser als; **the song is even better than their last one** das Lied ist sogar noch besser als ihr letztes; 6 **even so** trotzdem; **even so, we had a good time** trotzdem haben wir uns amüsiert.

even² *adjective* 1 (*surface or layer*) eben; 2 (*number*) gerade; **six is an even number** sechs ist eine gerade Zahl; 3 (*equal*) gleich (*distance, value*); **the score is even** die Punktzahl ist gleich; 4 **to get even with somebody** es jemandem heimzahlen.

evening *noun* 1 Abend *der* (PL die Abende); **in the evening** am Abend; **this evening** heute Abend;

⬦ IRREGULAR VERB: *See the verb table in the centre of the dictionary*

tomorrow evening morgen Abend; **on Monday evening** am Montagabend; **every Thursday evening** jeden Donnerstagabend; **the evening before** am Abend zuvor; **the evening meal** das Abendessen; **2 at six o'clock in the evening** um sechs Uhr abends; **the other evening** neulich abends; **I work in the evening(s)** ich arbeite abends.

evening class noun
Abendkurs der (PL die Abendkurse).

event noun **1** (a happening) Ereignis das (PL die Ereignisse); **2** (in athletics) Disziplin die (PL die Disziplinen).

eventually adverb schließlich.

ever adverb **1** (at any time) je; **have you ever noticed that?** hast du das je bemerkt?; **more than ever** mehr denn je; **colder than ever** kälter denn je; **he drove more slowly than ever** er fuhr langsamer als je zuvor; **2 not ever** nie; **nobody ever came** es kam nie jemand; **hardly ever** fast nie; **3** (always) immer; **as cheerful as ever** so vergnügt wie immer; **the same as ever** so wie immer; **4 ever since** seitdem; **and it's been raining ever since** und seitdem regnet es.

every adjective **1** jeder/jede/jedes; **every house has a garden** jedes Haus hat einen Garten; **every day** jeden Tag; **every Monday** jeden Montag; **every time** jedes Mal; **2 every few days** alle paar Tage; **every ten kilometres** alle zehn Kilometer; **3 every one** jeder Einzelne/jede Einzelne/jedes Einzelne/jede Einzelne △; **I've seen every one of his films** ich habe jeden Einzelnen seiner Filme gesehen; **4 every now and then** ab und zu.

everybody, everyone pronoun **1** alle (plural); **everybody knows that …** alle wissen, dass …; **everyone else** alle anderen; **2** (each one) jeder; **not everybody can afford it** das kann sich nicht jeder leisten.

everything pronoun alles; **everything is ready** es ist alles fertig; **everything's fine** alles ist okay (informal); **everything else** alles andere; **he gets everything he wants** er bekommt alles, was er will.

everywhere adverb **1** überall; **there was dirt everywhere** überall war Dreck; **she went everywhere** sie ist überall hingegangen; **everywhere else** sonst überall; **2 everywhere she went** wohin sie auch ging.

evidently adverb offensichtlich.

exact adjective genau; **the exact fare** das genaue Fahrgeld; **it's the exact opposite** das ist genau das Gegenteil.

exactly adverb genau; **they're exactly the right age** sie sind genau im richtigen Alter; **yes, exactly!** ja, genau!

exaggerate verb übertreiben ◈.

exaggeration noun Übertreibung die (PL die Übertreibungen).

exam noun Prüfung die (PL die Prüfungen); **history exam** die Geschichtsprüfung; **to sit an exam** eine Prüfung machen; **to pass an exam** eine Prüfung bestehen; **to fail an exam** durch eine Prüfung fallen.

examination noun Prüfung die (PL die Prüfungen).

examine verb **1** (at school or university) prüfen; **2** (at the doctor's) untersuchen.

examiner noun Prüfer der (PL die Prüfer), Prüferin die (PL die Prüferinnen).

example noun Beispiel das (PL die Beispiele); **for example** zum Beispiel; **to set a good example** ein gutes Beispiel geben.

excellent adjective ausgezeichnet.

except preposition **1** außer (+DAT); **every day except Tuesday** täglich außer Dienstag; **we play except when it rains** wir spielen, außer wenn es regnet; **except in March** außer März; **2 except for** außer (+DAT); **except for the children** außer den Kindern.

exception noun Ausnahme die (PL die Ausnahmen); **without exception** ohne Ausnahme; **with the exception of** mit Ausnahme von (+DAT).

exchange noun **1** Austausch der; **the students are coming to London on an exchange** die Studenten kommen im Austausch nach London; **exchange student** der Austauschstudent, die Austauschstudentin; **an exchange of**

pupils ein Schüleraustausch; **2 in exchange for his help** für seine Hilfe.
verb umtauschen SEP; **can I exchange this shirt for a smaller one?** kann ich dieses Hemd gegen ein kleineres umtauschen?

exchange rate noun Wechselkurs der (PL die Wechselkurse).

excite verb **1** (thrill) begeistern; **2** (agitate) aufregen SEP.

excited adjective **1** aufgeregt; **the children are excited** die Kinder sind aufgeregt; **the dogs get excited when they hear the car** die Hunde sind aufgeregt, wenn sie das Auto hören; **2** (annoyed or angry) **to get excited** sich aufregen SEP.

exciting adjective aufregend; **a very exciting film** ein sehr aufregender Film.

exclamation mark noun Ausrufezeichen das (PL die Ausrufezeichen).

excursion noun Ausflug der (PL die Ausflüge).

excuse noun Entschuldigung die (PL die Entschuldigungen).
verb (apologizing) **excuse me!** Entschuldigung!

exercise noun **1** Übung die (PL die Übungen); **a maths exercise** eine Übung in Mathe; **2 physical exercise** körperliche Bewegung; **to get exercise** Bewegung haben.

exercise bike noun Heimtrainer der (PL die Heimtrainer).

✧ IRREGULAR VERB: See the verb table in the centre of the dictionary

exercise book *noun* Heft *das* (PL die Hefte); **my German exercise book** mein Deutschheft.

exhausted *adjective* erschöpft.

exhaust fumes *noun* Abgase (*plural*).

exhaust (pipe) *noun* Auspuff *der* (PL die Auspuffe).

exhibition *noun* Ausstellung *die* (PL die Ausstellungen); **the Dürer exhibition** die Dürer-Ausstellung.

exist *verb* existieren.

exit *noun* **1** Ausgang *der* (PL die Ausgänge); **2** (*from a motorway*) Ausfahrt *die* (PL die Ausfahrten).

expect *verb* **1** erwarten (*guests or a baby*); **we're expecting thirty visitors** wir erwarten dreißig Besucher; **2** (*require something*) **to expect somebody to do something** von jemandem erwarten, dass er etwas tut; **3** rechnen mit (+DAT) (*something to happen*); **I didn't expect that** damit habe ich nicht gerechnet; **I didn't expect it at all** damit habe ich überhaupt nicht gerechnet; **4** (*suppose*) glauben; **I expect she'll bring her boyfriend** ich glaube, sie bringt ihren Freund mit; **yes, I expect so** ich glaube ja.

expel *verb* **to be expelled** (*from school*) von der Schule verwiesen werden.

expensive *adjective* teuer; **those shoes are too expensive for me** diese Schuhe sind mir zu teuer; **the most expensive CDs** die teuersten CDs.

experience *noun* **1** Erfahrung *die* (PL die Erfahrungen); **2** (*an event*) Erlebnis *das* (PL die Erlebnisse).

experienced *adjective* erfahren.

experiment *noun* Experiment *das* (PL die Experimente); **to do an experiment** ein Experiment machen.

expert *noun* Experte *der* (PL die Experten), Expertin *die* (PL die Expertinnen); **he's a computer expert** er ist ein Computerexperte.

expire *verb* ablaufen ◇ SEP (PERF sein).

explain *verb* erklären.

explanation *noun* Erklärung *die* (PL die Erklärungen).

explode *verb* explodieren (PERF sein).

explore *verb* erforschen.

explosion *noun* Explosion *die* (PL die Explosionen).

exposure *noun* (*of a film*) Belichtung *die*; **a 24-exposure film** ein Film mit 24 Aufnahmen.

express *noun* (*train*) Schnellzug *der* (PL die Schnellzüge). *verb* **1** ausdrücken SEP; **2 to express yourself** sich ausdrücken.

expression *noun* Ausdruck *der* (PL die Ausdrücke).

extension *noun* **1** (*to a house*) Anbau *der* (PL die Anbauten); **2** (*telephone*) Apparat *der* (PL die Apparate); **can I have extension 2347 please?** bitte verbinden Sie mich mit Apparat 2347 (*note that in*

△ NEW SPELLING: *See page xii*

spoken German telephone numbers are usually broken down into groups of two figures); **3** (*electrical*) Verlängerung *die* (PL *die* Verlängerungen).

extension number *noun* Apparatnummer *die* (PL *die* Apparatnummern).

exterior *adjective* äußerer/äußere/äußeres.

extinguish *verb* **1** löschen (*a fire*); **2 to extinguish a cigarette** eine Zigarette ausmachen SEP.

extinguisher *noun* Feuerlöscher *der* (PL *die* Feuerlöscher).

extra *adjective* **1** zusätzlich, extra (*informal*) (*extra never has an ending*); **extra homework** zusätzliche Hausaufgaben; **wine is extra** Wein ist extra; **you have to pay extra** das wird extra berechnet; **2 at no extra charge** ohne Aufschlag. *adverb* **1** besonders; **he was extra careful** er war besonders vorsichtig; **2 extra large** extragroß.

extraordinary *adjective* außerordentlich.

extra time *noun* (*in football*) Verlängerung *die* (PL *die* Verlängerungen); **to go into extra time** in die Verlängerung gehen.

extravagant *adjective* verschwenderisch (*person*).

extreme *noun* Extrem *das* (PL *die* Extreme); **to go from one extreme to another** von einem Extrem ins

andere fallen. *adjective* extrem.

extremely *adverb* äußerst; **extremely fast** äußerst schnell.

eye *noun* Auge *das* (PL *die* Augen); **a girl with blue eyes** ein Mädchen mit blauen Augen; **shut your eyes!** mach die Augen zu!; ★ **to keep an eye on something** auf etwas ←(ACC) aufpassen SEP.

eyebrow *noun* Augenbraue *die* (PL *die* Augenbrauen).

eyelash *noun* Augenwimper *die* (PL *die* Augenwimpern).

eyelid *noun* Augenlid *das* (PL *die* Augenlider).

eyeliner *noun* Eyeliner *der* (PL *die* Eyeliner).

eye shadow *noun* Lidschatten *der* (PL *die* Lidschatten).

eyesight *noun* **to have good eyesight** gute Augen haben; **to have bad eyesight** schlechte Augen haben.

F f

fabric *noun* (*cloth*) Stoff *der* (PL *die* Stoffe).

fabulous *adjective* phantastisch.

face *noun* **1** (*of a person*) Gesicht *das* (PL *die* Gesichter); **to pull a face** ein Gesicht machen; **2** (*of a clock or watch*) Zifferblatt *das* (PL *die* Zifferblätter).

verb **1** gegenüberstehen ✧ SEP (PERF *sein*) (+DAT); **she was facing him** sie stand ihm gegenüber; **2 the house faces the park** das Haus ist gegenüber dem Park; **3** (*to stand the idea of*) verkraften; **I can't face going back** ich kann es nicht verkraften zurückzugehen; **4 to face up to something** sich etwas ←(DAT) stellen.

facilities *plural noun* **1 the school has good sports facilities** die Schule hat gute Sportanlagen; **2 the flat has no cooking facilities** die Wohnung hat keine Kochgelegenheit.

fact *noun* Tatsache *die* (PL *die* Tatsachen); **the fact is that …** Tatsache ist, dass …; **in fact** tatsächlich; **is that a fact?** Tatsache?

factory *noun* Fabrik *die* (PL *die* Fabriken).

fade *verb* **1** (*fabric*) verbleichen ✧ (PERF *sein*); **faded jeans** ausgeblichene Jeans; **2** (*a colour or memory*) verblassen (PERF *sein*); **the colours have faded** die Farben sind verblasst.

fail *verb* **1** nicht bestehen ✧ (*a test or an exam*); **I failed my driving test** ich habe meine Fahrprüfung nicht bestanden; **2** (*in a test or an exam*) durchfallen ✧ SEP (PERF *sein*); **three students failed** drei Studenten sind durchgefallen; **3 to fail to do something** etwas nicht tun; **he failed to inform us** er hat uns nicht benachrichtigt; ★ **without fail** auf

jeden Fall; **ring me without fail** ruf mich auf jeden Fall an.

faint *adjective* **1** (*slight*) leicht; **a faint smell of gas** ein leichter Gasgeruch; **I haven't the faintest idea** ich habe keine blasse Ahnung (*informal*); **2** (*voice or sound*) leise. *verb* ohnmächtig werden; **Lisa fainted** Lisa wurde ohnmächtig.

fair *noun* Jahrmarkt *der* (PL *die* Jahrmärkte). *adjective* **1** (*not unfair*) gerecht; **2** (*hair*) blond; **he's fair-haired** er ist blond; **3** (*skin*) hell; **fair-skinned** hellhäutig; **4** (*fairly good*) ganz gut (*chance, condition, or performance*); **5** (*weather*) schön; **if it's fair tomorrow** wenn es morgen schön ist.

fairground *noun* Jahrmarkt *der* (PL *die* Jahrmärkte).

fairly *adverb* (*quite*) ziemlich.

fairy *noun* Fee *die* (PL *die* Feen).

fairy tale *noun* Märchen *das* (PL *die* Märchen).

faith *noun* **1** (*trust*) Vertrauen *das*; **to have faith in somebody** Vertrauen zu jemandem haben; **2** (*religious belief*) Glaube *der* (PL *die* Glauben).

faithful *adjective* treu; **to be faithful to somebody** jemandem treu sein.

faithfully *adverb* **Yours faithfully** Hochachtungsvoll.

fake *noun* **1** Imitation *die* (PL *die* Imitationen); **the diamonds were fakes** die Brillanten waren eine Imitation; **2** (*a painting or money*)

△ NEW SPELLING: *See page xii*

Fälschung *die* (PL *die* Fälschungen). *adjective* gefälscht; **a fake passport** ein gefälschter Pass.

fall *noun* Fall *der* (PL *die* Fälle); **to have a fall** stürzen (PERF *sein*). *verb* **1** fallen ✧ (PERF *sein*); **mind, you'll fall** pass auf, dass du nicht hinfällst; **Tony fell off his bike** Tony ist vom Rad gefallen; **she fell down the stairs** sie ist die Treppe heruntergefallen; **2** (*of temperature, prices*) sinken ✧ (PERF *sein*).

false *adjective* falsch; **a false alarm** ein falscher Alarm.

fame *noun* Ruhm *der*.

familiar *adjective* bekannt; **his face is familiar** sein Gesicht kommt mir bekannt vor.

family *noun* Familie *die* (PL *die* Familien); **a family of six** eine sechsköpfige Familie; **Ben's one of the family** Ben gehört zur Familie; **the Morris family** Familie Morris.

famous *adjective* berühmt.

fan *noun* **1** (*a supporter*) Fan *der* (PL *die* Fans); **Will's a Chelsea fan** Will ist ein Fan von Chelsea; **2** (*electric, for cooling*) Ventilator *der* (PL *die* Ventilatoren); **3** (*hand-held*) Fächer *der* (PL *die* Fächer).

fanatic *noun* Fanatiker *der* (PL *die* Fanatiker), Fanatikerin *die* (PL *die* Fanatikerinnen).

fancy *noun* **to take somebody's fancy** jemandem gefallen ✧; **the picture took his fancy** das Bild hat es ihm angetan. *adjective* (*equipment*) ausgefallen.

verb **1** (*to want*) **(do you) fancy a coffee?** hast du Lust auf einen Kaffee?; **do you fancy going to the cinema?** hast du Lust, ins Kino zu gehen?; **2 I really fancy him** ich mag ihn wirklich sehr gern; **3** (*just*) **fancy that!** stell dir vor!; **fancy you being here!** na so was, dich hier zu treffen!

fancy dress *noun* **in fancy dress** verkleidet; **fancy-dress party** *das* Kostümfest.

fantastic *adjective* fantastisch Δ; **really? that's fantastic!** wirklich? das ist ja fantastisch!; **a fantastic holiday** fantastische Ferien.

far *adverb, adjective* **1** weit; **it's not far** es ist nicht weit; **is it far to Carlisle?** ist Carlisle weit von hier?; **how far is it to Bristol?** wie weit ist es bis nach Bristol?; **2 he took us as far as Newport** er hat uns bis Newport mitgenommen; **3 by far** bei weitem; **the prettiest by far** bei weitem das hübscheste; **4** (*much*) viel; **far better** viel besser; **far faster** viel schneller; **far too many people** viel zu viele Leute; **5 so far** bis jetzt; **so far everything's going well** bis jetzt läuft alles gut; **6 as far as I know** soweit ich weiß.

fare *noun* **1** (*on a bus, train, or the underground*) Fahrpreis *der* (PL *die* Fahrpreise); **2** (*on a plane*) Flugpreis *der* (PL *die* Flugpreise); **half fare** *der* halbe Fahrpreis; **full fare** *der* volle Fahrpreis.

farm *noun* Bauernhof *der* (PL *die* Bauernhöfe).

farmer *noun* Bauer *der* (PL *die* Bauern), Bäuerin *die* (PL *die* Bäuerinnen).

fascinating *adjective* faszinierend.

fashion *noun* Mode *die* (PL *die* Moden); **in fashion** in Mode; **to go out of fashion** aus der Mode kommen.

fashionable *adjective* modisch.

fashion model *noun* Mannequin *das* (PL *die* Mannequins).

fashion show *noun* Modenschau *die* (PL *die* Modenschauen).

fast *adjective* **1** schnell; **a fast car** ein schnelles Auto; **2** (*of a clock or watch*) **to be fast** vorgehen ✧ SEP (PERF *sein*); **my watch is fast** meine Uhr geht vor; **you're ten minutes fast** deine Uhr geht zehn Minuten vor.
adverb **1** schnell; **he swims fast** er schwimmt schnell; **2 to be fast asleep** fest schlafen.

fat *noun* Fett *das* (PL *die* Fette). *adjective* **1** (*meat*) fett; **2** (*person*) dick, fett (*informal*); **a fat man** ein dicker Mann; **to get fat** fett werden (*informal*).

father *noun* Vater *der* (PL *die* Väter); **my father's office** das Büro von meinem Vater.

Father Christmas *noun* der Weihnachtsmann.

father-in-law *noun* Schwiegervater *der* (PL *die* Schwiegerväter).

fault *noun* **1** (*when you are responsible*) Schuld *die*; **it's Stephen's fault** Stephen ist Schuld; **it's not my fault** es ist nicht meine Schuld; **2** (*in tennis*) **double fault** *der* Doppelfehler.

favour *noun* **1** (*a kindness*) Gefallen *der* (PL *die* Gefallen); **to do somebody a favour** jemandem einen Gefallen tun; **can you do me a favour?** kannst du mir einen Gefallen tun?; **to ask a favour of somebody** jemanden um einen Gefallen bitten; **2 to be in favour of something** für etwas ←(ACC) sein.

favourite *adjective* Lieblings-; **my favourite band** meine Lieblingsband.

fax *noun* Fax *das* (PL *die* Faxe). *verb* faxen.

fear *noun* Angst *die* (PL *die* Ängste). *verb* fürchten.

feather *noun* Feder *die* (PL *die* Federn).

feature *noun* **1** (*of your face*) Gesichtszug *der* (PL *die* Gesichtszüge); **to have delicate features** feine Gesichtszüge haben; **2** (*of a car or a machine*) Merkmal *das* (PL *die* Merkmale).

February *noun* Februar *der*; **in February** im Februar.

fed up *adjective* **1 I'm fed up** ich habe die Nase voll (*informal*); **he's fed up with her** er hat die Nase voll von ihr; **2 to be fed up with something** etwas ←(ACC) satt haben (*informal*); **I'm fed up with working**

△ NEW SPELLING: *See page xii*

every day ich habe es satt, jeden Tag zu arbeiten.

feed verb füttern; **have you fed the dog?** hast du den Hund gefüttert?

feel verb 1 sich fühlen; **I don't feel well** ich fühle mich nicht gut; 2 spüren; **I didn't feel a thing** ich habe nichts gespürt; 3 **I feel tired** ich bin müde; **I feel cold** mir ist kalt; 4 **to feel afraid** Angst haben; **to feel thirsty** Durst haben; 5 **to feel like doing something** Lust haben, etwas zu tun; **I feel like going to the cinema** ich habe Lust, ins Kino zu gehen; 6 (touch) fühlen; 7 (to the touch) sich anfühlen SEP; **to feel soft** sich weich anfühlen SEP.

feeling noun 1 Gefühl das (PL die Gefühle); **to show your feelings** seine Gefühle zeigen; **a dizzy feeling** ein Schwindelgefühl; **I have the feeling James doesn't like me** ich habe das Gefühl, dass James mich nicht mag; 2 **to hurt somebody's feelings** jemanden verletzen.

felt-tip (pen) noun Filzstift der (PL die Filzstifte).

female noun (animal) Weibchen das (PL die Weibchen). adjective weiblich.

feminine adjective weiblich.

feminist noun Feministin die (PL die Feministinnen), Feminist der (PL die Feministen). adjective feministisch.

fence noun Zaun der (PL die Zäune).

ferry noun Fähre die (PL die Fähren).

festival noun (of films, art, or music) Festspiele (plural).

fetch verb 1 (collect) abholen SEP; **Tom's fetching the children** Tom holt die Kinder ab; 2 holen; **fetch me the other knife** hol mir das andere Messer.

fever noun Fieber das.

few adjective, pronoun 1 wenige; **few people know that …** wenige Leute wissen, dass …; 2 **a few** (several) ein paar (ein paar never changes); **a few weeks** ein paar Wochen; **in a few minutes** in ein paar Minuten; **have you got any tomatoes? we want a few for the salad** haben Sie Tomaten? wir brauchen ein paar für den Salat; 3 **quite a few** eine ganze Menge; **there were quite a few questions** es gab eine ganze Menge Fragen.

fewer adjective weniger; **there are fewer mosquitoes this year** dieses Jahr gibt es weniger Mücken.

field noun 1 (with grass or crops) Feld das (PL die Felder); **a field of wheat** ein Kornfeld; 2 (for sport) Spielfeld das (PL die Spielfelder).

fierce adjective 1 wild (animal or person); 2 heftig (storm or battle).

fifteen number fünfzehn.

fifth number fünfter/fünfte/fünftes; **the fifth of January** der fünfte Januar; **on the fifth floor** im fünften Stock.

fifty number fünfzig.

fight *noun* 1 (*a scuffle*) Schlägerei *die* (PL *die* Schlägereien); 2 (*in boxing or against illness*) Kampf *der* (PL *die* Kämpfe).
verb 1 (*to have a fight*) sich prügeln; **they were fighting** sie haben sich geprügelt; 2 (*to quarrel*) sich streiten ✧; **they're always fighting** sie streiten sich immer; 3 (*struggle against*) kämpfen gegen (+ACC) (*poverty or a disease*).

figure *noun* 1 (*number*) Zahl *die* (PL *die* Zahlen); **a four-figure number** eine vierstellige Zahl; 2 (*body shape*) Figur *die*; **good for your figure** gut für die Figur; 3 (*a person*) Gestalt *die* (PL *die* Gestalten).
verb **to figure something out** etwas herausfinden ✧ SEP (*the answer or reason*).

file *noun* 1 (*for records of a person or case*) Akte *die* (PL *die* Akten); 2 (*ring binder or folder*) Ordner *der* (PL *die* Ordner); 3 (*on a computer*) Datei *die* (PL *die* Dateien); 4 **a nail file** eine Nagelfeile.
verb 1 ablegen SEP (*documents*); 2 **to file your nails** sich ←(DAT) die Nägel feilen.

fill *verb* 1 füllen (*a container*); **she filled my glass** sie füllte mein Glas; 2 **to be filled with people** voller Menschen sein; **filled with smoke** voller Rauch.
● **to fill in** ausfüllen SEP (*a form*).

film *noun* (*in a cinema and for a camera*) Film *der* (PL *die* Filme); **shall we go and see the new film about Freud?** wollen wir uns den neuen Film über Freud ansehen?; **to make a film** einen Film drehen; **a**

24-exposure colour film ein Farbfilm mit 24 Aufnahmen.

film star *noun* Filmstar *der* (PL *die* Filmstars).

filter *noun* Filter *der* (PL *die* Filter).

filthy *adjective* dreckig.

final *noun* (*in sport*) Endspiel *das* (PL *die* Endspiele).
adjective letzter/letzte/letztes; **the final instalment** die letzte Folge; **the final result** das Endergebnis.

finally *adverb* schließlich.

find *verb* finden ✧; **did you find your passport?** hast du deinen Pass gefunden?; **I can't find my keys** ich kann meine Schlüssel nicht finden.
● **to find out** 1 (*to enquire*) sich informieren; **I don't know, I'll find out** das weiß ich nicht, ich werde mich informieren; 2 **to find something out** etwas ←(ACC) herausfinden ✧ SEP (*the facts or an answer*); **when she found out the truth** als sie die Wahrheit herausfand.

fine *noun* Bußgeld *das* (PL *die* Bußgelder) (*for parking or speeding*).
adjective 1 (*in good health*) gut; **'how are you?' – 'fine, thanks'** 'wie geht's?' – 'danke, gut'; **I'm fine** mir geht es gut; 2 (*convenient*) in Ordnung; **ten o'clock? yes, that's fine** zehn Uhr? ja, in Ordnung!; **Friday will be fine** Freitag geht in Ordnung; 3 (*sunny*) schön; (*weather or day*) **if it's fine** wenn es schön ist; **in fine weather** bei schönem Wetter; 4 (*not coarse or thick*) fein.

△ NEW SPELLING: *See page xii*

finely *adverb* fein (*chopped or grated*).

finger *noun* Finger *der* (PL *die* Finger); ★ **I'll keep my fingers crossed for you** ich drücke dir den Daumen.

fingernail *noun* Fingernagel *der* (PL *die* Fingernägel).

finish *noun* 1 (*end*) Schluss △ *der* (PL *die* Schlüsse); 2 (*in a race*) Ziel *das* (PL *die* Ziele).
verb 1 beenden (*a conversation or quarrel*); **to finish a discussion** ein Gespräch beenden; **to be finished with something** mit etwas ←(DAT) fertig sein (*work or a project*); **have you finished your homework?** bist du mit den Hausaufgaben fertig?; **wait, I haven't finished!** warte, ich bin noch nicht fertig!; 2 (*to finish off*) **to finish doing something** etwas zu Ende tun; **have you finished (reading) the letter?** hast du den Brief zu Ende gelesen?; **he hasn't yet finished (writing) the report** er hat den Bericht noch nicht zu Ende geschrieben; 3 (*come to an end*) zu Ende sein, aus sein △ (*informal*) (*a meeting or performance*); **the film finishes at ten o'clock** der Film ist um zehn Uhr zu Ende; **when does school finish?** wann ist die Schule aus?
• **to finish with** (*complete your use of*) nicht mehr brauchen; **when you've finished with these clothes, give them back to me** wenn du die Sachen nicht mehr brauchst, gib sie mir zurück; **have you finished with**

the computer? brauchen Sie den Computer noch?

Finland *noun* Finnland *das*.

Finnish *noun* (*the language*) Finnisch *das*.
adjective finnisch; **he's Finnish** er ist Finne; **she's Finnish** sie ist Finnin.

fire *noun* 1 (*in a grate*) Kaminfeuer *das* (PL *die* Kaminfeuer); **to light the fire** das Feuer im Kamin anmachen; 2 (*accidental*) Feuer *das* (PL *die* Feuer); **to catch fire** (*fabric, furnishings*) Feuer fangen; 3 (*in a building or forest*) Brand *der* (PL *die* Brände); **to set fire to a factory** eine Fabrik in Brand stecken; 4 **to be on fire** brennen ✧.
verb 1 (*with a gun*) schießen ✧; **to fire at somebody** auf jemanden schießen; 2 abfeuern SEP (*a gun*).

fire alarm *noun* Feuermelder *der* (PL *die* Feuermelder).

fire brigade *noun* Feuerwehr *die*.

fire engine *noun* Feuerwehrauto *das* (PL *die* Feuerwehrautos).

fire escape *noun* Feuertreppe *die* (PL *die* Feuertreppen).

fire extinguisher *noun* Feuerlöscher *der* (PL *die* Feuerlöscher).

firefighter *noun* Feuerwehrmann *der* (PL *die* Feuerwehrleute).

fireplace *noun* Kamin *der* (PL *die* Kamine).

✧ IRREGULAR VERB: *See the verb table in the centre of the dictionary*

fire station noun Feuerwache die (PL die Feuerwachen).

firework noun Feuerwerkskörper der (PL die Feuerwerkskörper); **firework display** das Feuerwerk.

firm noun (business) Firma die (PL die Firmen).
adjective **1** fest; **2** (strict) streng.

first adjective erster/erste/erstes; **the first of May** der erste Mai; **for the first time** zum ersten Mal; **I was the first to arrive** ich kam als Erster/Erste an; **Susan was first** Susan war die Erste; **to come first in the 100 metres** beim Hundertmeterlauf Erster/Erste werden.
adverb **1** (to begin with) zuerst; **first, I'm going to make some tea** zuerst mache ich Tee; **2 at first** zuerst; **at first he was shy** er war zuerst schüchtern.

first aid noun erste Hilfe Δ die.

first class adjective (ticket, carriage, or hotel) erster Klasse (goes after the noun); **a first-class hotel** ein Hotel erster Klasse; **he always travels first class** er reist immer erster Klasse; **a first-class compartment** ein Erste-Klasse-Abteil.

first floor noun erste Stock der; **on the first floor** im ersten Stock.

first name noun Vorname der (PL die Vornamen).

fir tree noun Tanne die (PL die Tannen).

fish noun Fisch der (PL die Fische).
verb fischen; (with a rod) angeln.

fish and chips noun ausgebackener Fisch mit Pommes frites.

fishing noun Fischen das; (with a rod) Angeln das; **to go fishing** fischen/angeln gehen.

fishing rod noun Angel die (PL die Angeln).

fishing tackle noun Angelgeräte (plural).

fist noun Faust die (PL die Fäuste).

fit noun **1** (of rage) Anfall der (PL die Anfälle); **your dad'll have a fit when he sees your hair** dein Vater kriegt bestimmt einen Anfall, wenn er deine Haare sieht; **2 an epileptic fit** ein epileptischer Anfall.
adjective (healthy) fit; **I feel really fit** ich fühle mich richtig fit; **to keep fit** fit bleiben.
verb **1** (be the right size for) (of shoes or a garment) passen (+DAT); **this skirt doesn't fit me** der Rock passt mir nicht; **2** (be able to be put into) passen in (+ACC); **will my cases all fit in the car?** passen meine Koffer alle in das Auto?; **the key doesn't fit in the lock** der Schlüssel passt nicht ins Schloss; **3** (install) einbauen SEP.

fitted carpet noun Teppichboden der (PL die Teppichböden).

fitted kitchen noun Einbauküche die (PL die Einbauküchen).

five *number* fünf; **it's five o'clock** es ist fünf Uhr.

fix *verb* **1** (*repair*) reparieren; **Mum's fixed the computer** Mutti hat den Computer repariert; **2** (*decide on*) festlegen ✧ SEP; **to fix a date** einen Termin festlegen; **3** machen (*a meal*); **I'll fix supper** ich mache Abendessen.

fizzy *adjective* sprudelnd; **fizzy water** das Sprudelwasser.

flag *noun* Fahne *die* (PL *die* Fahnen).

flame *noun* Flamme *die* (PL *die* Flammen).

flan *noun* Torte *die* (PL *die* Torten); **fruit flan** *die* Obsttorte.

flap *verb* (*of a bird*) **to flap its wings** mit den Flügeln schlagen ✧.

flash *noun* (*on a camera*) Blitz *der* (PL *die* Blitze); **flash of lightning** *der* Blitz.
verb **1** (*a light*) aufleuchten SEP; (*repeatedly*) blinken; **2 to flash by** *or* **past** vorbeiflitzen SEP (*informal*).

flat *noun* Wohnung *die* (PL *die* Wohnungen); **a third-floor flat** eine Wohnung im dritten Stock.
adjective **1** flach; **flat shoes** flache Schuhe; **a flat landscape** eine flache Landschaft; **2 a flat tyre** ein platter Reifen.

flatmate *noun* Mitbewohner *der* (PL *die* Mitbewohner), Mitbewohnerin *die* (PL *die* Mitbewohnerinnen).

flavour *noun* **1** Geschmack *der* (PL *die* Geschmäcke); **the sauce has a bitter flavour** die Soße hat einen bitteren Geschmack; **strawberry flavour** Erdbeergeschmack; **2** (*of drinks, coffee, or tea*) Aroma *das* (PL *die* Aromen).
verb abschmecken SEP; **vanilla-flavoured** mit Vanillegeschmack.

flea *noun* Floh *der* (PL *die* Flöhe).

flight *noun* **1** Flug *der* (PL *die* Flüge); **the flight was delayed** der Flug hatte Verspätung; **charter flight** *der* Charterflug; **the flight from Munich to London takes an hour and a half** die Flugzeit von München nach London beträgt eineinhalb Stunden; **2 flight of stairs** *die* Treppe.

flipper *noun* Flosse *die* (PL *die* Flossen).

flirt *verb* flirten.

float *verb* **1** (*on water*) treiben ✧; **2** (*in the air*) schweben.

flood *noun* **1** (*of water*) Überschwemmung *die* (PL *die* Überschwemmungen); **2 to be in floods of tears** in Tränen aufgelöst sein; **3** (*of letters or complaints*) Flut *die*.
verb überschwemmen.

floodlight *noun* Flutlicht *das*.

floor *noun* **1** Boden *der* (PL *die* Böden); **your glasses are on the floor** deine Brille liegt auf dem Boden; **2 to sweep the floor** ausfegen SEP; **to sweep the kitchen floor** die Küche ausfegen; **3** (*a storey*) Stock *der* (PL *die* Stock); **on the second floor** im zweiten Stock.

floppy disk *noun* Diskette *die* (PL *die* Disketten).

✧ **IRREGULAR VERB:** *See the verb table in the centre of the dictionary*

florist *noun* Blumenhändler *der* (PL die Blumenhändler), Blumenhändlerin *die* (PL die Blumenhändlerinnen).

flour *noun* Mehl *das*.

flower *noun* Blume *die* (PL die Blumen); **bunch of flowers** *der* Blumenstrauß.
verb blühen.

flu *noun* Grippe *die* (PL die Grippen); **to have flu** die Grippe haben.

fluent *adjective* **she speaks fluent Italian** sie spricht fließend Italienisch.

fluently *adverb* fließend.

flute *noun* Flöte *die* (PL die Flöten); **to play the flute** Flöte spielen.

fly *noun* Fliege *die* (PL die Fliegen).
verb **1** fliegen ◇ (PERF *sein*); **we flew to Berlin** wir sind nach Berlin geflogen; **2** steigen lassen (*a kite*); **3** fliegen ◇ (PERF *haben*) (*a plane or helicopter*); **4** (*to pass quickly*) schnell vergehen ◇ (PERF *sein*).

foam *noun* **1** (*foam rubber*) Schaumgummi *der*; **foam mattress** *die* Schaumgummimatratze; **2** (*on a drink*) Schaum *der*.

fog *noun* Nebel *der*.

foggy *adjective* neblig.

foil *noun* (*kitchen foil*) Alufolie *die*.

fold *noun* **1** (*in fabric or skin*) Falte *die* (PL die Falten); **2** (*in paper*) Kniff *der* (PL die Kniffe).
verb falten; **to fold something up** etwas zusammenfalten SEP.

folder *noun* Mappe *die* (PL die Mappen).

follow *verb* **1** folgen (PERF *sein*) (+DAT); **follow me!** folgen Sie mir!; **2 do you follow me?** verstehst du, was ich meine?

following *adjective* folgend; **the following evening** am folgenden Abend.

fond *adjective* **to be fond of somebody** jemanden gern haben; **I'm very fond of him** ich habe ihn sehr gern.

food *noun* **1** Essen *das*; **I have to buy some food** ich muss noch etwas zu essen einkaufen; **2 I like German food** ich mag die deutsche Küche; **3** (*stocks*) Lebensmittel (*plural*); **we bought food for the holiday** wir haben Lebensmittel für die Ferien eingekauft.

fool *noun* Dummkopf *der* (PL die Dummköpfe).

foot *noun* Fuß *der* (PL die Füße); **Lucy came on foot** Lucy ist zu Fuß gekommen.

football *noun* Fußball *der* (PL die Fußbälle); **to play football** Fußball spielen.

footballer *noun* Fußballspieler *der* (PL die Fußballspieler), Fußballspielerin *die* (PL die Fußballspielerinnen).

footpath *noun* Fußweg *der* (PL die Fußwege).

for *preposition* **1** für (+ACC); **a present for my mother** ein Geschenk für

△ NEW SPELLING: See page xii

meine Mutter; **what's it for?** wofür
ist das?; **2** (*for a particular occasion
or event*) zu (+DAT); **sausages for
lunch** Würstchen zum Mittagessen;
Sam got a bike for Christmas Sam
hat ein Rad zu Weihnachten
bekommen; **what for?** wozu?;
3 (*time expressions in the past but
continuing in the present*) seit
(+DAT); **I've been waiting here for an
hour** (*and I'm still waiting*) ich
warte hier seit einer Stunde; **my
brother's been living in Berlin for
three years** (*and he still lives there*)
mein Bruder wohnt seit drei Jahren
in Berlin; **4** (*time expressions in the
past or the future*) **I studied French
for six years** (*but I no longer do*) ich
habe sechs Jahre lang Französisch
gelernt; **I'll be away for four days**
ich werde vier Tage nicht da sein;
5 (*with a price*) für (+ACC); **I sold my
bike for fifty pounds** ich habe mein
Rad für fünfzig Pfund verkauft;
6 what's the German for 'bee'? wie
heißt 'bee' auf Deutsch?

forbid *verb* verbieten ✧; **to forbid
somebody to do something**
jemandem verbieten, etwas zu tun.

forbidden *adjective* verboten.

force *noun* Kraft *die* (PL *die* Kräfte).
verb zwingen ✧; **to force
somebody to do something**
jemanden zwingen, etwas zu tun.

forecast *noun* Vorhersage *die* (PL
die Vorhersagen).

forehead *noun* Stirn *die* (PL *die*
Stirnen).

foreign *adjective* **1** ausländisch; **in a**
foreign country im Ausland; **from
a foreign country** aus dem Ausland;
2 foreign language *die*
Fremdsprache.

foreigner *noun* Ausländer *der* (PL
die Ausländer), Ausländerin *die* (PL
die Ausländerinnen).

forest *noun* Wald *der* (PL *die*
Wälder).

forever *adverb* **1** immer; **I'd like to
stay here forever** ich möchte
immer hier bleiben; **2** (*non-stop*)
ständig; **he's forever asking
questions** er fragt ständig.

forget *verb* vergessen ✧; **to forget
about something** etwas vergessen;
we've forgotten the bread wir
haben Brot vergessen; **to forget to
do something** vergessen, etwas zu
tun; **I forgot to phone** ich habe
vergessen anzurufen.

forgive *verb* verzeihen ✧ (+DAT); **to
forgive somebody** jemandem
verzeihen; **I forgave him** ich habe
ihm verziehen; **to forgive
somebody for doing something**
jemandem verzeihen, dass er/sie
etwas getan hat; **I forgave her for
losing my ring** ich habe ihr
verziehen, dass sie meinen Ring
verloren hat.

fork *noun* Gabel *die* (PL *die* Gabeln).

form *noun* **1** Formular *das* (PL *die*
Formulare); **to fill in a form** ein
Formular ausfüllen; **2** (*shape or
kind*) Form *die* (PL *die* Formen); **in
the form of** in Form von; **to be on
form** gut in Form sein; **3** (*in school*)

Klasse *die* (PL *die* Klassen).
verb bilden.

formal *adjective* formell (*invitation, event*).

format *noun* Format *das* (PL *die* Formate).

former *adjective* ehemalig; **a former pupil** ein ehemaliger Schüler, eine ehemalige Schülerin.

fortnight *noun* vierzehn Tage (*plural*); **we're going to Spain for a fortnight** wir fahren vierzehn Tage nach Spanien.

fortunately *adverb* glücklicherweise.

forty *number* vierzig.

forward *noun* (*in sport*) Stürmer *der* (PL *die* Stürmer). *adverb* (*to the front*) nach vorn; **to move forward** vorrücken SEP (PERF *sein*); **a seat further forward** ein Platz weiter vorn.

foster child *noun* Pflegekind *das* (PL *die* Pflegekinder).

foul *noun* (*in sport*) Foul *das* (PL *die* Fouls). *adjective* scheußlich; **the weather's foul** das Wetter ist scheußlich.

fountain *noun* Brunnen *der* (PL *die* Brunnen).

fountain pen *noun* Füllfederhalter *der* (PL *die* Füllfederhalter).

four *number* vier; **it's four o'clock** es ist vier Uhr; ★ **on all fours** auf allen vieren.

fourteen *number* vierzehn.

fourth *number* vierter/vierte/viertes; **the fourth of July** der vierte Juli; **on the fourth floor** im vierten Stock.

fox *noun* Fuchs *der* (PL *die* Füchse).

frame *noun* 1 Rahmen *der* (PL *die* Rahmen); 2 (*of spectacles*) Gestell *das* (PL *die* Gestelle).

franc *noun* 1 Franc *der* (PL *die* Francs); **a fifty-franc note** ein Fünfzig-Franc-Schein; 2 (*Swiss*) Franken *der* (PL *die* Franken).

France *noun* Frankreich *das*; **to France** nach Frankreich.

frantic *adjective* 1 (*very upset*) **to be frantic** außer sich ←(DAT) sein; **I was frantic with worry** ich war außer mir vor Sorge; 2 (*desperate*) hektisch (*effort or search*).

freckle *noun* Sommersprosse *die* (PL *die* Sommersprossen).

free *adjective* 1 (*when you don't pay*) kostenlos; **a free ride** eine kostenlose Fahrt; **a free ticket** eine Freikarte; 2 (*without charge*) umsonst; **to do something for free** etwas umsonst machen; 3 (*not occupied*) frei; **are you free on Thursday?** sind Sie am Donnerstag frei?; 4 **sugar-free** ohne Zucker; **lead-free** bleifrei. *verb* befreien.

freedom *noun* Freiheit *die*.

free gift *noun* Werbegeschenk *das* (PL *die* Werbegeschenke).

freeze *verb* 1 (*in a freezer*) einfrieren ◇ SEP; **to freeze raspberries** Himbeeren einfrieren;

△ NEW SPELLING: *See page xii*

2 (*in cold weather*) frieren ✧; **it's freezing** es friert; **3** (*become covered with ice*) zufrieren ✧ SEP (PERF *sein*); **the pond is frozen** der Teich ist zugefroren.

freezer *noun* Gefrierschrank *der* (PL *die* Gefrierschränke).

freezing *noun* **below freezing** unter Null; **three degrees above freezing** drei Grad über Null. *adjective* **1 I'm freezing** ich friere sehr; **2 it's freezing outside** es ist eiskalt draußen.

French *noun* **1** (*the language*) Französisch *das*; **2** (*the people*) **the French** die Franzosen. *adjective* **1** französisch; **Jean-Marc is French** Jean-Marc ist Franzose; **2** (*teacher or lesson*) Französisch-; **the French class** der Französischunterricht.

French bean *noun* grüne Bohne *die* (PL *die* grünen Bohnen).

French dressing *noun* Vinaigrette *die*.

French fries *plural noun* Pommes frites (*plural*).

Frenchman *noun* Franzose *der* (PL *die* Franzosen).

French window *noun* Verandatür *die* (PL *die* Verandatüren).

Frenchwoman *noun* Französin *die* (PL *die* Französinnen).

fresh *adjective* frisch; **fresh eggs** frische Eier; **I'm going out for some fresh air** ich gehe ein bisschen frische Luft schnappen.

Friday *noun* **1** Freitag *der* (PL *die* Freitage); **next Friday** nächsten Freitag; **last Friday** letzten Freitag; **on Friday** (am) Freitag; **I'll phone you on Friday evening** ich rufe dich Freitagabend an; **every Friday** jeden Freitag; **Good Friday** Karfreitag; **2 on Fridays** freitags; **closed on Fridays** freitags geschlossen.

fridge *noun* Kühlschrank *der* (PL *die* Kühlschränke); **put it in the fridge** stell es in den Kühlschrank.

friend *noun* **1** Freund *der* (PL *die* Freunde), Freundin *die* (PL *die* Freundinnen); **a friend of mine** ein Freund von mir; **2 to make friends** sich anfreunden; **he made friends with Danny** er hat sich mit Danny angefreundet; **he is friends with Danny** er ist mit Danny befreundet.

friendly *adjective* freundlich.

fries *plural noun* Pommes frites (*plural*).

fright *noun* **1** Schreck *der* (PL *die* Schrecke); **to have** or **get a fright** einen Schreck bekommen; **2 you gave me a fright!** du hast mich erschreckt!

frighten *verb* **1** (*of an explosion or shot*) erschrecken; **2** (*scare or threaten*) **to frighten somebody** jemandem Angst machen.

frightened *adjective* **to be frightened** Angst haben; **Martin's frightened of snakes** Martin hat Angst vor Schlangen.

frightening *adjective* beängstigend.

✧ IRREGULAR VERB: *See the verb table in the centre of the dictionary*

fringe noun 1 (hairstyle) Pony der (PL die Ponys); 2 (on clothes or a curtain) Fransen (plural).

frog noun Frosch der (PL die Frösche).

from preposition 1 von (+DAT); **ten metres from the cinema** zehn Meter vom Kino; **a letter from Tom** ein Brief von Tom; **from Monday to Friday** von Montag bis Freitag; **from now on** von jetzt an; 2 aus (+DAT); **he comes from Dublin** er kommt aus Dublin; **the train from London** der Zug aus London; 3 **from seven o'clock onwards** ab sieben Uhr; **from then on** von da ab.

front noun 1 (of a building) Vorderfront die (PL die Vorderfronten); (of a cupboard, card, or envelope) Vorderseite die (PL die Vorderseiten); 2 (of a garment or in an interior) Vorderteil das (PL die Vorderteile); 3 (at the seaside) Strandpromenade die (PL die Strandpromenaden); 4 (of a car) **to sit in (the) front** vorne sitzen; 5 (of a train or queue) vordere Ende das; 6 (of a procession or in a race) Spitze die; 7 **in/at the front** vorne; **in/at the front of** vorne in (+DAT, or +ACC with movement towards a place); **there are still seats at the front of the train** es gibt noch Plätze vorne im Zug; **we got on at the front of the train** wir sind vorne in den Zug eingestiegen; 8 **in front of** vor (+DAT, or +ACC with movement towards a place); **in front of the TV** vor dem Fernseher; **in front of me** vor mir. adjective 1 vorderer/vordere/

vorderes; **in the front rows** in den vorderen Reihen; 2 Vorder-; **front seat** (of a car) der Vordersitz; **front wheel** das Vorderrad.

front door noun Haustür die (PL die Haustüren).

frontier noun Grenze die (PL die Grenzen).

frost noun Frost der.

frosty adjective frostig.

frown verb die Stirn runzeln; **he frowned at us** er runzelte die Stirn.

frozen adjective (in a freezer) tiefgekühlt; **a frozen pizza** eine tiefgekühlte Pizza.

fruit noun 1 (a single fruit or type of fruit) Frucht die (PL die Früchte); 2 (various fruits) Obst das; **we bought cheese and fruit** wir haben Käse und Obst gekauft.

fruit juice noun Fruchtsaft der (PL die Fruchtsäfte).

fruit machine noun Spielautomat der (PL die Spielautomaten).

fruit salad noun Obstsalat der (PL die Obstsalate).

frustrated adjective frustriert.

fry verb braten ◇; **we fried fish** wir haben Fisch gebraten; **fried potatoes** Bratkartoffeln; **fried egg** das Spiegelei.

frying pan noun Bratpfanne die (PL die Bratpfannen).

fuel noun (for a car) Kraftstoff der.

full *adjective* 1 voll; **the glass is full** das Glas ist voll; **I'm full** ich bin voll (*informal*); 2 **full of** voller (+GEN); **the train was full of tourists** der Zug war voller Touristen; 3 **at full speed** in voller Fahrt; 4 **to write something out in full** etwas voll ausschreiben.

full stop *noun* Punkt *der* (PL *die* Punkte).

full-time *adjective* **a full-time job** eine Ganztagsstelle.

fully *adverb* voll.

fun *noun* 1 Spaß *der*; **have fun!** viel Spaß!; **we had fun catching the ponies** wir hatten Spaß daran, die Ponys einzufangen; **skiing is fun** Skifahren macht Spaß; **I do it for fun** ich mache es aus Spaß; 2 **to have fun** sich amüsieren; ★ **to make fun of somebody** sich über jemanden lustig machen.

funds *plural noun* Geldmittel (*plural*).

funeral *noun* Beerdigung *die* (PL *die* Beerdigungen).

funfair *noun* Jahrmarkt *der* (PL *die* Jahrmärkte).

funny *adjective* 1 (*amusing*) lustig; **he's so funny** er ist so lustig; **a funny story** eine lustige Geschichte; 2 (*strange*) komisch; **a funny noise** ein komisches Geräusch; **that's funny, I'm sure I paid** das ist komisch, ich bin mir sicher, dass ich gezahlt habe.

fur *noun* 1 (*on an animal*) Fell *das* (PL *die* Felle); 2 (*for a coat*) Pelz *der* (PL *die* Pelze); **fur coat** *der* Pelzmantel.

furious *adjective* wütend; **she was furious with Steve** sie war wütend auf Steve.

furniture *noun* Möbel (*plural*); **to buy some furniture** Möbel kaufen; **piece of furniture** *das* Möbelstück.

further *adverb* weiter; **further than the station** weiter als der Bahnhof; **ten kilometres further on** zehn Kilometer weiter; **further off** weiter entfernt; **further forward** weiter vorn; **further back** weiter hinten.

fuse *noun* Sicherung *die* (PL *die* Sicherungen).

fuss *noun* Theater *das*; **to make a fuss** ein Theater machen; **to make a big fuss about the bill** ein großes Theater um die Rechnung machen.

fussy *adjective* **to be fussy about something** wählerisch in etwas ←(DAT) sein (*food, for example*).

future *noun* Zukunft *die*; **in future** in Zukunft.

G g

gadget *noun* Gerät *das* (PL *die* Geräte).

gain *verb* 1 gewinnen ✧; **in order to gain time** um Zeit zu gewinnen; 2 profitieren; **to gain by something** von etwas profitieren.

✧ IRREGULAR VERB: *See the verb table in the centre of the dictionary*

gale *noun* Sturm *der* (PL *die* Stürme).

gallery *noun* Galerie *die* (PL *die* Galerien).

gamble *verb* spielen (*for money*).

game *noun* 1 Spiel *das* (PL *die* Spiele); **game of chance** *das* Glücksspiel; **board game** *das* Brettspiel; 2 **to have a game of cards** eine Partie Karten spielen; 3 **to have a game of football** Fußball spielen; 4 **games** (*at school*) Sport *der*.

gang *noun* Bande *die* (PL *die* Banden); **all the gang were there** die ganze Bande war da.

gap *noun* 1 (*hole*) Lücke *die* (PL *die* Lücken); 2 (*in time*) Pause *die* (PL *die* Pausen); **a two-hour gap** eine zweistündige Pause; 3 **age gap** *der* Altersunterschied.

garage *noun* 1 (*for keeping your car*) Garage *die* (PL *die* Garagen); 2 (*for repairing cars*) Autowerkstatt *die* (PL *die* Autowerkstätten); 3 (*for petrol*) Tankstelle *die* (PL *die* Tankstellen).

garden *noun* Garten *der* (PL *die* Gärten).

gardener *noun* Gärtner *der* (PL *die* Gärtner), Gärtnerin *die* (PL *die* Gärtnerinnen).

gardening *noun* Gartenarbeit *die*.

garlic *noun* Knoblauch *der*.

garment *noun* Kleidungsstück *das* (PL *die* Kleidungsstücke).

gas *noun* Gas *das*.

gas cooker *noun* Gasherd *der* (PL *die* Gasherde).

gas fire *noun* Gasofen *der* (PL *die* Gasöfen).

gas meter *noun* Gaszähler *der* (PL *die* Gaszähler).

gate *noun* 1 (*in garden*) Pforte *die* (PL *die* Pforten); 2 (*in field*) Gatter *das* (PL *die* Gatter); 3 (*at an airport*) Flugsteig *der* (PL *die* Flugsteige).

gather *verb* 1 (*of people*) sich versammeln; 2 sammeln (*fruit, vegetables, flowers*); 3 **as far as I can gather** soweit ich weiß.

gay *adjective* (*homosexual*) schwul (*informal*).

gaze *verb* **to gaze at something** etwas anstarren SEP.

gear *noun* 1 (*in a car*) Gang *der* (PL *die* Gänge); **to change gear** schalten; 2 (*equipment*) Ausrüstung *die*; **camping gear** *die* Campingausrüstung; 3 (*things*) Sachen (*plural*); **I've left all my gear at Gary's** ich habe alle meine Sachen bei Gary gelassen.

gear lever *noun* Schalthebel *der* (PL *die* Schalthebel).

gel *noun* Gel *das* (PL *die* Gele).

Gemini *noun* Zwillinge (*plural*); **Steph's Gemini** Steph ist Zwilling.

gender *noun* (*of a word*) Geschlecht *das* (PL *die* Geschlechter); **what is the gender of 'Haus'?** welches Geschlecht hat 'Haus'?

△ NEW SPELLING: *See page xii*

general noun General der (PL die Generäle).
adjective allgemein; **in general** im Allgemeinen; **the general election** die allgemeinen Wahlen.

general knowledge noun Allgemeinwissen das.

generally adverb im Allgemeinen Δ.

generation noun Generation die (PL die Generationen).

generous adjective großzügig.

genetics noun Genetik die.

Geneva noun Genf das; **Lake Geneva** der Genfer See.

genius noun Genie das (PL die Genies); **Lisa, you're a genius!** Lisa, du bis ein Genie!

gentle adjective sanft.

gentleman noun Herr der (PL die Herren); **ladies and gentlemen!** meine Damen und Herren!

gently adverb sanft.

gents noun (lavatory) Herrentoilette die (PL die Herrentoiletten); (on a sign) **'Gents'** 'Herren'; **where's the gents?** wo ist die Toilette?

genuine adjective 1 (real, authentic) echt; **a genuine diamond** ein echter Brillant; 2 aufrichtig (person); **she's very genuine** sie ist sehr aufrichtig.

geography noun Geographie die; (at school) Erdkunde die.

germ noun 1 Keim der (PL die Keime); 2 (causing a cold) **germs** Bazillen (plural).

German noun (person)
1 Deutsche der/die (PL die Deutschen); 2 (language) Deutsch das; **in German** auf Deutsch.
adjective deutsch; **he is German** er ist Deutscher; **she is German** sie ist Deutsche; **our German teacher** unser Deutschlehrer, unsere Deutschlehrerin.

Germany Deutschland das; **to Germany** nach Deutschland; **from Germany** aus Deutschland.

get verb 1 (obtain, receive) bekommen ✧, kriegen (informal); **I got a bike for my birthday** ich habe ein Rad zum Geburtstag bekommen; **Fred got the job** Fred hat die Stelle bekommen; **she got a shock** sie hat einen Schreck gekriegt; **I got a good mark for my German homework** ich habe eine gute Note für meine Deutschhausaufgaben gekriegt; 2 **he's got lots of money** er hat viel Geld; **she's got long hair** sie hat lange Haare; **I've got a headache** ich habe Kopfschmerzen; 3 (fetch) holen; **I'll get some bread** ich hole Brot; **I'll get your bag for you** ich hole dir deine Tasche; 4 **to have got to do something** etwas tun müssen ✧; **I've got to phone before midday** ich muss vor Mittag anrufen; 5 **to get (to) somewhere** irgendwo ankommen ✧ SEP (PERF sein); **when I got to London** als ich in London ankam; **we got here this morning** wir sind heute Morgen angekommen; **what time did they get there?** wann sind sie angekommen?; 6 (become) werden ✧ (PERF sein); **it's getting**

✧ IRREGULAR VERB: See the verb table in the centre of the dictionary

late es wird spät; **it's getting dark** es wird dunkel; **7 to get something done** etwas machen lassen ✧; **I'm getting my hair cut today** ich lasse mir heute die Haare schneiden.

● **to get back** zurückkommen ✧ SEP (PERF *sein*); **Mum gets back at six** Mutti kommt um sechs zurück.

● **to get something back** etwas zurückbekommen ✧ SEP, etwas zurückkriegen SEP (*informal*); **did you get your books back?** hast du deine Bücher zurückbekommen?

● **to get into something** (*a vehicle*) in etwas ←(ACC) einsteigen ✧ SEP (PERF *sein*); **he got into the car** er ist ins Auto eingestiegen.

● **to get off something** (*a vehicle*) aus etwas ←(DAT) aussteigen ✧ SEP (PERF *sein*); **I got off the train at Banbury** ich bin in Banbury aus dem Zug ausgestiegen.

● **to get on: how's Amanda getting on?** wie geht's Amanda?

● **to get on something** (*a vehicle*) in etwas ←(ACC) einsteigen ✧ SEP (PERF *sein*); **she got on the train at Reading** sie ist in Reading in den Zug eingestiegen.

● **to get on with somebody** sich mit jemandem verstehen ✧; **she doesn't get on with her brother** sie versteht sich nicht mit ihrem Bruder.

● **to get out of something** (*a vehicle*) aus etwas ←(DAT) austeigen ✧ SEP (PERF *sein*); **Laura got out of the car** Laura ist aus dem Auto ausgestiegen.

● **to get together** sich wieder sehen ✧ SEP Δ; **we must get together soon** wir müssen uns bald mal wieder sehen.

● **to get up** aufstehen ✧ SEP (PERF *sein*); **I get up at seven** ich stehe um sieben auf.

ghost *noun* Geist *der* (PL *die* Geister).

gift *noun* **1** Geschenk *das* (PL *die* Geschenke); **a Christmas gift** ein Weihnachtsgeschenk; **2** Begabung *die*; **to have a gift for something** für etwas ←(ACC) begabt sein; **Jo has a real gift for languages** Jo ist richtig sprachbegabt.

gigantic *adjective* riesig.

gin *noun* Gin *der* (PL *die* Gins).

ginger *noun* Ingwer *der* (PL *die* Ingwer).

girl *noun* Mädchen *das* (PL *die* Mädchen); **three boys and four girls** drei Jungen und vier Mädchen; **when I was a little girl I had …** als kleines Mädchen hatte ich …

girlfriend *noun* Freundin *die* (PL *die* Freundinnen).

give *verb* **1** geben ✧; **to give something to somebody** jemandem etwas geben; **I'll give you my address** ich gebe dir meine Adresse; **give me the key** gib mir den Schlüssel; **Yasmin's dad gave her the money** Yasmins Vater hat ihr das Geld gegeben; **2** (*give as a gift*) schenken; **to give somebody a present** jemandem etwas schenken.

● **to give something away** etwas weggeben ✧ SEP; **she's given away all her books** sie hat alle ihre Bücher weggegeben.

- **to give something back to somebody** jemandem etwas zurückgeben ✧ SEP; **I gave her back the keys** ich habe ihr die Schlüssel zurückgegeben.

- **to give in** nachgeben ✧ SEP; **my mum said no but she gave in in the end** meine Mutti hat nein gesagt, aber schließlich hat sie nachgegeben.

- **to give up** aufgeben ✧ SEP; **I give up!** ich gebe auf!

- **to give up doing something** etwas aufgeben ✧SEP; **she's given up smoking** sie hat das Rauchen aufgegeben.

glad adjective froh; **I'm glad to hear he's better** ich bin froh, dass es ihm besser geht; **I'm glad to be back** ich bin froh, dass ich wieder zurück bin.

glass noun Glas das (PL die Gläser); **a glass of water** ein Glas Wasser; **a glass table** ein Glastisch.

glasses plural noun Brille die (PL die Brillen); **to wear glasses** eine Brille tragen.

glove noun Handschuh der (PL die Handschuhe); **a pair of gloves** ein Paar Handschuhe.

glove compartment noun Handschuhfach das (PL die Handschuhfächer).

glue noun Klebstoff der (PL die Klebstoffe).

go noun 1 (in a game) **whose go is it?** wer ist dran?; **it's my go** ich bin dran; 2 **to have a go at doing something** versuchen, etwas zu tun; **I'll have a go at mending it** ich versuche, es zu reparieren.

verb 1 (on foot) gehen ✧ (PERF sein); **to go to school** in die Schule gehen; **Mark's gone to the dentist's** Mark ist zum Zahnarzt gegangen; **to go shopping** einkaufen gehen; 2 (in a vehicle) fahren ✧ (PERF sein); **we're going to London** wir fahren nach London; **we're planning to go early** wir wollen früh fahren; **to go on holiday** in die Ferien fahren; 3 (by plane) fliegen ✧ (PERF sein); 4 **to go for a walk** spazieren gehen △ ✧ SEP (PERF sein); 5 (with another verb) **I'm going to do it** ich werde es tun; **I'm going to make some tea** ich mache Tee; **he was going to phone you** er wollte dich anrufen; 6 (leave) gehen ✧ (PERF sein); **Pauline's already gone** Pauline ist schon gegangen; 7 (on a journey) abfahren ✧ SEP (PERF sein); **when does the train go?** wann fährt der Zug ab?; 8 (turn out) verlaufen ✧ (PERF sein) (event); **how did your evening go?** wie ist dein Abend verlaufen?; **the party went well** die Party war gut.

- **to go away** 1 weggehen ✧ SEP (PERF sein); **go away!** geh weg!; 2 (on holiday) verreisen (PERF sein).

- **to go back** 1 zurückgehen ✧ SEP (PERF sein); **I'm going back to Germany in March** ich gehe im März nach Deutschland zurück; **I'm not going back there again!** ich gehe da nicht wieder zurück!; 2 **I went back home** ich bin nach Hause gegangen.

- **to go down** 1 hinuntergehen ✧ SEP (PERF sein); **she's gone down to the kitchen** sie ist in die Küche

✧ IRREGULAR VERB: See the verb table in the centre of the dictionary

hinuntergegangen; **to go down the stairs** die Treppe hinuntergehen; **2** (*price, temperature*) fallen ◇ (PERF *sein*); **3** (*tyre, balloon, airbed*) Luft verlieren ◇.

- **to go in** hineingehen ◇ SEP (PERF *sein*); **he went in and shut the door** er ist hineingegangen und hat die Tür zugemacht.

- **to go into 1** (*person*) gehen in (+ACC) (PERF *sein*); **Fran went into the kitchen** Fran ging in die Küche; **2** (*object*) passen in (+ACC); **this book won't go into my bag** dieses Buch passt nicht in meine Tasche.

- **to go off 1** (*bomb*) hochgehen ◇ SEP (PERF *sein*); **2** (*alarm clock*) klingeln; **my alarm clock went off at six** mein Wecker hat um sechs geklingelt; **3** (*fire or burglar alarm*) losgehen ◇ SEP (PERF *sein*); **the fire alarm went off** der Feuermelder ging los.

- **to go on 1 what's going on?** was ist los?; **2 to go on doing something** weiter etwas tun; **she went on talking** sie hat weiter geredet; **3 to go on about something** stundenlang von etwas ←(DAT) reden; **he's always going on about his dog** er redet stundenlang von seinem Hund.

- **to go out 1** (*for an evening*) ausgehen ◇ SEP, weggehen ◇ SEP (PERF *sein*) (*informal*); **we're going out tonight** wir gehen heute Abend aus; **2** (*leave*) **she went out of the kitchen** sie ist aus der Küche gegangen; **3 to be going out with somebody** mit jemandem gehen ◇ (PERF *sein*) (*informal*); **she's going out with my brother** sie geht mit

meinem Bruder; **4** (*light, fire*) ausgehen ◇ SEP (PERF *sein*); **the light went out** das Licht ist ausgegangen.

- **to go past something** an etwas ←(DAT) vorbeigehen ◇ SEP; **we went past your house** wir sind an eurem Haus vorbeigegangen.

- **to go round: to go round to somebody's house** jemanden besuchen; **we went round to Fred's last night** wir haben gestern Abend Fred besucht.

- **to go round something 1** um etwas ←(ACC) herumgehen ◇ SEP (PERF *sein*) (*building, park, garden*); **2** besichtigen (*museum, monument*).

- **to go through 1 the train goes through Cologne** der Zug fährt durch Köln; **2 to go through a room** durch ein Zimmer gehen; **3** (*search*) durchsuchen.

- **to go up 1** (*person*) hinaufgehen ◇ SEP (PERF *sein*); **she's gone up to her room** sie ist in ihr Zimmer hinaufgegangen; **to go up the stairs** die Treppe hinaufgehen; **2** (*prices*) steigen ◇ (PERF *sein*); **the price of petrol has gone up** die Benzinpreise sind gestiegen.

goal *noun* Tor *das* (PL *die* Tore); **to score a goal** ein Tor schießen.

goalkeeper *noun* Torwart *der* (PL *die* Torwarte).

goat *noun* Ziege *die* (PL *die* Ziegen).

god *noun* Gott *der* (PL *die* Götter).

God *noun* Gott *der*; **to believe in God** an Gott glauben.

godchild noun Patenkind das (PL die Patenkinder).

goddaughter noun Patentochter die (PL die Patentöchter).

goddess noun Göttin die (PL die Göttinnen).

godfather noun Pate der (PL die Paten).

godmother noun Patin die (PL die Patinnen).

godson noun Patensohn der (PL die Patensöhne).

gold noun Gold das; **a gold bracelet** ein Goldarmband.

goldfish noun Goldfisch der (PL die Goldfische).

golf noun Golf das; **to play golf** Golf spielen.

golf club noun 1 (place) Golfklub der (PL die Golfklubs); 2 (iron) Golfschläger der (PL die Golfschläger).

golf course noun Golfplatz der (PL die Golfplätze).

good adjective 1 gut; **she's a good teacher** sie ist eine gute Lehrerin; **the cherries are very good** die Kirschen sind sehr gut; 2 **to be good for you** gesund sein; **tomatoes are good for you** Tomaten sind gesund; 3 **good at** gut in (+DAT); **she's good at maths** sie ist gut in Mathe; **he's good at drawing** er ist gut im Zeichnen; 4 (well-behaved) brav; **be good!** sei brav!; 5 (kind) nett; **she's been very good to me** sie ist sehr nett zu mir gewesen; 6 **for**

good endgültig; **I've stopped smoking for good** ich habe das Rauchen endgültig aufgegeben.

good afternoon exclamation guten Tag!

goodbye exclamation auf Wiedersehen!

good evening exclamation guten Abend!

Good Friday noun Karfreitag der (PL die Karfreitage).

good-looking adjective gut aussehend △.

good morning exclamation guten Morgen!

goodness exclamation meine Güte!; **for goodness sake!** um Himmels willen!

good night exclamation gute Nacht!

goods plural noun Waren (plural).

goods train noun Güterzug der (PL die Güterzüge).

goose noun Gans die (PL die Gänse).

gorgeous adjective herrlich; **it's a gorgeous day** es ist ein herrlicher Tag.

gorilla noun Gorilla der (PL die Gorillas).

gosh exclamation Mensch!

gossip noun 1 (person) Klatschbase die (PL die Klatschbasen); 2 (scandal) Klatsch der. verb klatschen.

✧ IRREGULAR VERB: *See the verb table in the centre of the dictionary*

government noun Regierung die (PL die Regierungen).

grab verb **1** packen; **she grabbed my arm** sie packte mich am Arm; **2 to grab something from somebody** jemandem etwas ←(ACC) entreißen ✧; **he grabbed the book from me** er hat mir das Buch entrissen.

grade noun (mark) Note die (PL die Noten); **to get good grades** gute Noten bekommen.

gradual adjective allmählich.

gradually adverb allmählich; **the weather got gradually better** das Wetter wurde allmählich besser.

graffiti plural noun Graffiti (plural).

gram noun Gramm das; **100 grams of salami** hundert Gramm Salami.

grammar noun Grammatik die.

grammar school noun Gymnasium das (PL die Gymnasien).

gran noun Oma die (PL die Omas).

grandchildren plural noun Enkelkinder (plural).

granddad noun Opa der (PL die Opas).

granddaughter noun Enkelin die (PL die Enkelinnen).

grandfather noun Großvater der (PL die Großväter).

grandma noun Oma die (PL die Omas).

grandmother noun Großmutter die (PL die Großmütter).

grandpa noun Opa der (PL die Opas).

grandparents plural noun Großeltern (plural).

grandson noun Enkel der (PL die Enkel).

granny noun Omi die (PL die Omis).

grape noun Weintraube die (PL die Weintrauben); **a grape** eine Weintraube; **to buy some grapes** Weintrauben kaufen; **do you like grapes?** magst du Weintrauben?; **a bunch of grapes** eine ganze Weintraube.

grapefruit noun Grapefruit die (PL die Grapefruits).

grasp verb festhalten ✧ SEP.

grass noun **1** Gras das; **to lie on the grass** im Gras liegen; **2** (lawn) Rasen der (PL die Rasen); **to cut the grass** den Rasen mähen.

grasshopper noun Heuschrecke die (PL die Heuschrecken).

grate verb reiben ✧; **grated cheese** geriebener Käse.

grateful adjective dankbar; **to be grateful to somebody** jemandem dankbar sein.

grater noun Reibe die (PL die Reiben).

grave noun Grab das (PL die Gräber).

△ NEW SPELLING: See page xii

graveyard noun Friedhof der (PL die Friedhöfe).

gravy noun Soße die (PL die Soßen).

grease noun Fett das.

greasy adjective 1 fettig; **to have greasy skin** fettige Haut haben; 2 (food) fett.

great adjective 1 groß; **a great poet** ein großer Dichter; 2 (terrific) großartig; **it was a great party** das war eine großartige Party; **great!** großartig!, prima! (informal); 3 **a great deal of** sehr viel; **a great many** sehr viele.

Great Britain noun Großbritannien das.

Greece noun Griechenland das.

greedy adjective gierig; (with food) gefräßig.

Greek noun 1 (person) Grieche der (PL die Griechen), Griechin die (PL die Griechinnen); 2 (language) Griechisch das.
adjective griechisch; **she's Greek** sie ist Griechin.

green noun 1 (colour) Grün das; **a pale green** ein Hellgrün; 2 **the Greens** (ecologists) die Grünen.
adjective 1 grün; **a green door** eine grüne Tür; 2 **the Green Party** die Grünen (plural).

greengrocer noun Obst- und Gemüsehändler der (PL die Obst- und Gemüsehändler).

greenhouse noun Gewächshaus das (PL die Gewächshäuser).

greenhouse effect noun Treibhauseffekt der.

greetings plural noun Grüße (plural); **Season's Greetings** fröhliche Weihnachten und ein glückliches neues Jahr.

greetings card noun Glückwunschkarte die (PL die Glückwunschkarten).

grey adjective grau.

grief noun Trauer die.

grill noun Grill der (PL die Grills).
verb grillen; **I'm going to grill the sausages** ich grille die Würstchen.

grin verb grinsen.

grind verb mahlen.

grip verb (hold on to) festhalten ✧ SEP.

groan noun Stöhnen das.
verb stöhnen.

grocer noun Lebensmittelhändler der (PL die Lebensmittelhändler).

groceries plural noun Lebensmittel (plural).

grocer's noun Lebensmittelgeschäft das (PL die Lebensmittelgeschäfte).

groom noun Bräutigam der (PL die Bräutigame); **the bride and groom** das Brautpaar.

gross adjective 1 **a gross injustice** ein schreiendes Unrecht; 2 grob; **a gross error** ein grober Fehler; 3 (disgusting) ekelhaft; **the food was gross!** das Essen war ekelhaft!

✧ IRREGULAR VERB: See the verb table in the centre of the dictionary

ground noun 1 Boden der; **to sit on the ground** auf dem Boden sitzen; 2 (for sport) Sportplatz der (PL die Sportplätze); **football ground** der Fußballplatz.
adjective gemahlen; **ground coffee** gemahlener Kaffee.

ground floor noun Erdgeschoss △ das; **they live on the ground floor** sie wohnen im Erdgeschoss.

group noun Gruppe die (PL die Gruppen).

grow verb (get bigger) 1 wachsen ✧ (PERF sein); **your hair grows very quickly** deine Haare wachsen sehr schnell; **my little sister's grown quite a bit this year** meine kleine Schwester ist dieses Jahr ein ganzes Stück gewachsen; **the number of students is still growing** die Zahl der Studenten wächst noch; 2 anbauen SEP (fruit, vegetables); 3 **to grow a beard** sich ←(DAT) einen Bart wachsen lassen; 4 (become) werden ✧ (PERF sein); **to grow old** alt werden.

to grow up 1 erwachsen werden; **the children are growing up** die Kinder werden erwachsen; 2 aufwachsen ✧ SEP (PERF sein); **she grew up in Scotland** sie ist in Schottland aufgewachsen.

growl verb knurren.

grown-up noun Erwachsene der/die (PL die Erwachsenen).

growth noun Wachstum das.

grudge noun **to bear a grudge against somebody** etwas gegen jemanden haben; **she bears me a grudge** sie hat etwas gegen mich.

grumble verb 1 murren; **he's always grumbling** er murrt immer; 2 **to grumble about something** sich über etwas ←(ACC) beklagen; **what's she grumbling about?** worüber beklagt sie sich?

guarantee noun Garantie die (PL die Garantien); **a year's guarantee** ein Jahr Garantie.
verb garantieren.

guard noun 1 **prison guard** der Gefängniswärter, die Gefängniswärterin; 2 (on a train) Zugführer der (PL die Zugführer), Zugführerin die (PL die Zugführerinnen); 3 **security guard** der Wächter, die Wächterin.
verb bewachen.

guard dog noun Wachhund der (PL die Wachhunde).

guess noun **have a guess!** rate mal!; **it's a good guess** gut geraten.
verb 1 raten ✧; **guess who I saw last night** rate mal, wen ich gestern Abend gesehen habe; 2 (guess something correctly) es erraten ✧; **you'll never guess!** du errätst es nie!

guest noun Gast der (PL die Gäste); **we've got guests coming tonight** wir haben heute Abend Gäste; **a paying guest** ein zahlender Gast.

guide noun 1 (person) Führer der (PL die Führer), Führerin die (PL die Führerinnen); 2 (book) Reiseführer der (PL die Reiseführer);

3 (*girl guide*) Pfadfinderin *die* (PL *die* Pfadfinderinnen).

guidebook *noun* **1** Reiseführer *der* (PL *die* Reiseführer); **2** (*to a museum or monument*) Handbuch *das* (PL *die* Handbücher).

guide dog *noun* Blindenhund *der* (PL *die* Blindenhunde).

guilty *adjective* **1** schuldig; **2 to feel guilty** ein schlechtes Gewissen haben; **I felt guilty about the noise** ich hatte ein schlechtes Gewissen wegen des Lärms.

guinea pig *noun* **1** (*pet*) Meerschweinchen *das* (PL *die* Meerschweinchen); **2** (*in an experiment*) Versuchskaninchen *das* (PL *die* Versuchskaninchen).

guitar *noun* Gitarre *die* (PL *die* Gitarren); **to play the guitar** Gitarre spielen.

gum *noun* **1** (*in your mouth*) Zahnfleisch *das*; **2** (*chewing gum*) Kaugummi *der* (PL *die* Kaugummi).

gun *noun* **1** Pistole *die* (PL *die* Pistolen); **2** (*rifle*) Gewehr *das* (PL *die* Gewehre).

guy *noun* Typ *der* (PL *die* Typen) (*informal*); **he's a nice guy** er ist ein netter Typ; **that guy from Newcastle** der Typ aus Newcastle.

gym *noun* **1** (*school lesson*) Turnen *das*; **2** (*building*) Turnhalle *die* (PL *die* Turnhallen); **3** (*health club*) Fitnesscenter △ *das* (PL *die* Fitnesscenter); **to go to the gym** ins Fitnesscenter gehen.

gymnasium *noun* Turnhalle *die* (PL *die* Turnhallen).

gymnast *noun* Turner *der* (PL *die* Turner), Turnerin *die* (PL *die* Turnerinnen).

gymnastics *noun* Turnen *das*.

gym shoe *noun* Turnschuh *der* (PL *die* Turnschuhe).

H h

habit *noun* Gewohnheit *die* (PL *die* Gewohnheiten); **it's a bad habit** es ist eine schlechte Gewohnheit.

haddock *noun* Schellfisch *der*; **smoked haddock** *der* Haddock.

hail *noun* Hagel *der*.

hailstone *noun* Hagelkorn *das* (PL *die* Hagelkörner).

hailstorm *noun* Hagelschauer *der* (PL *die* Hagelschauer).

hair *noun* **1** Haare (*plural*); **to comb your hair** sich ←(DAT) die Haare kämmen; **to wash your hair** sich ←(DAT) die Haare waschen; **to have your hair cut** sich ←(DAT) die Haare schneiden lassen; **she's had her hair cut** sie hat sich die Haare schneiden lassen; **2 a hair** ein Haar.

hairbrush *noun* Haarbürste *die* (PL *die* Haarbürsten).

haircut *noun* **1** Haarschnitt *der* (PL *die* Haarschnitte); **2 to have a haircut** sich ←(DAT) die Haare schneiden lassen.

✧ IRREGULAR VERB: *See the verb table in the centre of the dictionary*

hairdresser noun Friseur der (PL die Friseure), Friseuse die (PL die Friseusen); **at the hairdresser's** beim Friseur.

hair drier noun Föhn△ der (PL die Föhne).

hair gel noun Haargel das (PL die Haargele).

hairgrip noun Haarklemme die (PL die Haarklemmen).

hairslide noun Haarspange die (PL die Haarspangen).

hairspray noun Haarspray das (PL die Haarsprays).

hairstyle noun Frisur die (PL die Frisuren).

half noun 1 Hälfte die (PL die Hälften); **half of** die Hälfte von (+DAT); **I gave him half of the money** ich habe ihm die Hälfte von dem Geld gegeben; **half of it** die Hälfte davon; 2 **half an apple** ein halber Apfel; 3 **to cut something in half** etwas halbieren; 4 (as a fraction) halb; **three and a half** dreieinhalb; 5 (in time) halb; **half an hour** eine halbe Stunde; **an hour and a half** anderthalb Stunden; **it's half past three** es ist halb vier (literally: half on the way to four); 6 (in weights and measures) halb; **half a litre** ein halber Liter.

half hour noun halbe Stunde die; **every half hour** jede halbe Stunde.

half price adjective, adverb zum halben Preis; **half-price CDs** CDs zum halben Preis.

half-time noun Halbzeit die; **at half-time the score is 0–0** zur Halbzeit steht es null zu null.

halfway adverb 1 auf halbem Weg; **halfway to Frankfurt** auf halbem Weg nach Frankfurt; 2 **to be halfway through doing something** halb fertig mit etwas sein; **I'm halfway through my homework** ich bin halb fertig mit meinen Hausaufgaben.

hall noun 1 (in a house) Diele die (PL die Dielen); 2 (public) Saal der (PL die Säle); **village hall** der Gemeindesaal; **concert hall** der Konzertsaal.

Hallowe'en noun der Tag vor Allerheiligen (in Germany there are no particular customs for this date).

ham noun Schinken der; **a ham sandwich** ein Schinkenbrot.

hamburger noun Hamburger der (PL die Hamburger).

hammer noun Hammer der (PL die Hammer).

hamster noun Hamster der (PL die Hamster).

hand noun 1 Hand die (PL die Hände); **to have something in your hand** etwas in der Hand haben; **to hold somebody's hand** jemandes Hand halten; 2 **to give somebody a hand** jemandem helfen ✧; **can you give me a hand to move the table into the corner?** kannst du mir helfen, den Tisch in die Ecke zu rücken?; **do you need a hand?** kann ich dir helfen?; 3 **on the other hand** ... andererseits ...; 4 (of a watch or clock) Zeiger der (PL die Zeiger); **the**

hour hand der Stundenzeiger.
verb **to hand something to somebody** jemandem etwas geben ✧; **I handed him the keys** ich gab ihm die Schlüssel.

● **to hand something in** etwas abgeben ✧ SEP; **hand in your homework** gebt eure Hausaufgaben ab.

● **to hand something out** etwas austeilen SEP.

handbag *noun* Handtasche *die* (PL *die* Handtaschen).

handcuffs *plural noun* Handschellen (*plural*).

handful *noun* **a handful of** eine Hand voll Δ.

handicapped *adjective* behindert.

handkerchief *noun* Taschentuch *das* (PL *die* Taschentücher).

handle *noun* **1** (*of a door, drawer, bag, or knife*) Griff *der* (PL *die* Griffe); **2** (*on a cup, jug, or basket*) Henkel *der* (PL *die* Henkel); **3** (*of a frying pan or broom*) Stiel *der* (PL *die* Stiele).
verb **1** erledigen; **Gina handles the correspondence** Gina erledigt die Korrespondenz; **2** umgehen ✧ SEP (PERF *sein*) mit; **she's good at handling people** sie kann gut mit Menschen umgehen; **3** fertig werden Δ ✧ (PERF *sein*) mit; **he can't handle problems** er kann mit Problemen nicht fertig werden.

handlebars *plural noun* Lenkstange *die* (PL *die* Lenkstangen).

hand luggage *noun* Handgepäck *das*.

handmade *adjective* handgemacht

handsome *adjective* gut aussehend Δ; **he's a handsome guy** er ist ein gut aussehender Typ.

handwriting *noun* Handschrift *die* (PL *die* Handschriften).

handy *adjective* **1** praktisch; **this little knife's very handy** dieses kleine Messer ist sehr praktisch; **2** griffbereit; **I always keep a notebook handy** ich habe immer ein kleines Notizbuch griffbereit.

hang *verb* **1** hängen ✧; **there was a mirror hanging on the wall** an der Wand hing ein Spiegel; **2** aufhängen SEP; **to hang a mirror on the wall** einen Spiegel an der Wand aufhängen.

● **to hang around** rumhängen ✧ SEP (PERF *sein*) (*informal*); **we were hanging around outside the cinema** wir haben vor dem Kino rumgehangen.

● **to hang on** warten; **hang on a second!** warten Sie einen Moment!

● **to hang up** (*on the phone*) auflegen SEP; **she hung up on me** sie hat einfach aufgelegt.

● **to hang something up** etwas aufhängen SEP.

hangover *noun* Kater *der* (PL *die* Kater).

happen *verb* **1** passieren (PERF *sein*); **what happened?** was ist passiert?; **it happened in June** es ist im Juni passiert; **2 what's happening?** was ist los?; **what's happened to Jill?** was ist mit Jill los?; **3 what's happened to the can-opener?** wo ist der Dosenöffner?; **4 if you happen to see him** wenn du ihn

✧ IRREGULAR VERB: *See the verb table in the centre of the dictionary*

zufällig triffst; **Leila happened to be there** Leila war zufällig da.

happily *adverb* 1 glücklich; 2 (*willingly*) gerne; **I'll happily do it for you** ich tu es gerne für dich.

happiness *noun* Glück *das*.

happy *adjective* glücklich; **a happy child** ein glückliches Kind; **Happy Birthday** herzlichen Glückwunsch zum Geburtstag.

harbour *noun* Hafen *der* (PL die Häfen).

hard *adjective* 1 hart; 2 (*difficult*) schwer; **a hard question** eine schwere Frage; **it's hard to know …** es ist schwer zu wissen … *adverb* 1 **to work hard** hart arbeiten; 2 **to try hard** sich sehr bemühen.

hard disk *noun* Festplatte *die* (PL die Festplatten).

hardly *adverb* 1 kaum; **I can hardly hear him** ich kann ihn kaum hören; **there was hardly anybody there** es war kaum jemand da; **we've got hardly any milk** wir haben kaum Milch; **hardly anything** kaum etwas; **he ate hardly anything** er hat kaum etwas gegessen; 2 **hardly ever** fast nie; **I hardly ever see him** ich sehe ihn fast nie.

hard up *adjective* **to be hard up** knapp bei Kasse sein.

harm *noun* **it won't do any harm** es kann nichts schaden. *verb* 1 **to harm somebody** jemandem etwas tun; **they didn't harm him** sie haben ihm nichts

getan; 2 schaden (+DAT) (*health, environment, reputation*); **a cup of coffee won't harm you** eine Tasse Kaffee schadet nicht.

harmful *adjective* schädlich.

harmless *adjective* unschädlich.

hat *noun* Hut *der* (PL die Hüte).

hate *verb* hassen; **I hate geography** ich hasse Erdkunde.

hatred *noun* Hass △ *der*.

have *verb* 1 haben ♦; **Anna has three brothers** Anna hat drei Brüder; **how many sisters do you have?** wie viele Schwestern hast du?; 2 **what have you got in your hand?** was hast du in der Hand?; **he has (got) flu** er hat die Grippe; 3 (*to form past tenses, some verbs in German take 'haben' and others 'sein'*) **I've finished** ich bin fertig; **have you seen the film?** hast du den Film gesehen?; **Rosie hasn't arrived yet** Rosie ist noch nicht angekommen; 4 **to have to do something** etwas tun müssen ♦; **I have to phone my mum** ich muss meine Mutter anrufen; 5 (*'have' is often translated by a more specific German verb*) **we had a coffee** wir haben einen Kaffee getrunken; **what will you have?** was nehmen Sie?; **I'll have an omelette** ich nehme ein Omelett; **I'm going to have a shower** ich dusche jetzt; **to have lunch** zu Mittag essen; **to have dinner** (*in the evening*) zu Abend essen; 6 (*get*) bekommen ♦; **Emma had a letter from Sam yesterday**

△ NEW SPELLING: *See page xii*

gestern bekam Emma einen Brief von Sam; **she had a baby** sie hat ein Baby bekommen; **7 to have something done** etwas machen lassen ✧; **I'm going to have my hair cut** ich lasse mir die Haare schneiden; **8 to have on** (*be wearing*) anhaben ✧ SEP; **to have nothing on** nichts anhaben.

hay fever *noun* Heuschnupfen *der*.

hazelnut *noun* Haselnuss △ *die* (PL *die* Haselnüsse).

he *pronoun* er; **he lives in Manchester** er wohnt in Manchester.

head *noun* 1 Kopf *der* (PL *die* Köpfe); **he shook his head** er schüttelte den Kopf; 2 (*of a school*) Direktor *der* (PL *die* Direktoren), Direktorin *die* (PL *die* Direktorinnen); 3 (*of a firm*) Chef *der* (PL *die* Chefs), Chefin *die* (PL *die* Chefinnen); 4 (*when tossing a coin*) **'heads or tails?'** 'Kopf oder Zahl?'.
● **to head for something** auf etwas ←(ACC) zusteuern SEP (PERF *sein*); **Liz headed for the door** Liz steuerte auf die Tür zu.

headache *noun* Kopfschmerzen (*plural*); **I've got a headache** ich habe Kopfschmerzen.

headlight *noun* Scheinwerfer *der* (PL *die* Scheinwerfer).

headline *noun* Schlagzeile *die* (PL *die* Schlagzeilen).

headmaster *noun* Direktor *der* (PL *die* Direktoren).

headmistress *noun* Direktorin *die* (PL *die* Direktorinnen).

headphones *noun* Kopfhörer *der* (PL *die* Kopfhörer).

headteacher *noun* Direktor *der* (PL *die* Direktoren), Direktorin *die* (PL *die* Direktorinnen).

health *noun* Gesundheit *die*.

health centre *noun* Ärztezentrum *das* (PL *die* Ärztezentren).

healthy *adjective* gesund.

heap *noun* Haufen *der* (PL *die* Haufen); **I've got heaps of work** ich habe einen Haufen Arbeit (*informal*).

hear *verb* hören; **I can't hear anything** ich kann überhaupt nichts hören; **I hear you've bought a dog** ich habe gehört, dass ihr einen Hund gekauft habt.
● **to hear about something** von etwas ←(DAT) hören; **have you heard about the concert?** hast du von dem Konzert gehört?
● **to hear from somebody** von jemandem hören.

heart *noun* 1 Herz *das* (PL *die* Herzen); 2 **to learn something by heart** etwas auswendig lernen; 3 (*in cards*) Herz *das*; **the jack of hearts** der Herzbube.

heat *noun* Hitze *die*.
verb 1 **to heat something** etwas heiß machen; **I'll go and heat the soup** ich mache die Suppe heiß; 2 **the soup's heating** die Suppe wird warm; 3 heizen (*a room*);

✧ IRREGULAR VERB: *See the verb table in the centre of the dictionary*

to heat something up etwas aufwärmen SEP; **I'm heating the sauce up** ich wärme die Soße auf.

heater noun Heizgerät das (PL die Heizgeräte).

heather noun Heidekraut das.

heating noun Heizung die.

heatwave noun Hitzewelle die (PL die Hitzewellen).

heaven noun Himmel der.

heavy adjective **1** schwer; **my rucksack's really heavy** mein Rucksack ist sehr schwer; **2** (busy) **I've got a heavy day tomorrow** ich habe morgen viel zu tun; **3** (in quantity) stark; **heavy rain** starker Regen.

hectic adjective hektisch; **a hectic day** ein hektischer Tag.

hedge noun Hecke die (PL die Hecken).

hedgehog noun Igel der (PL die Igel).

heel noun **1** (of foot or sock) Ferse die (PL die Fersen); **2** (of a shoe) Absatz der (PL die Absätze).

height noun **1** (of a person) Größe die; **what height are you?** wie groß bist du?; **2** (of a building, mountain) Höhe die; **what height is it?** wie hoch ist es?

helicopter noun Hubschrauber der (PL die Hubschrauber).

hell noun Hölle die; **hell!** verdammt! (informal).

hello exclamation **1** (polite) guten Tag!; **2** (informal, and on the phone) hallo!

helmet noun Helm der (PL die Helme).

help noun Hilfe die; **do you need any help?** kann ich dir helfen?; (in a shop) kann ich Ihnen behilflich sein?
verb **1** helfen ✧ (+DAT); **to help somebody (to) do something** jemandem helfen, etwas zu tun; **can you help me lay the table?** kannst du mir helfen, den Tisch zu decken?; **2 to help yourself to something** sich ←(DAT) etwas nehmen ✧; **help yourself to vegetables** nimm dir Gemüse; **help yourself!** greif zu!; **3 help!** Hilfe!; **4 he can't help it** er kann nichts dafür.

helpful adjective (person) hilfsbereit.

hen noun Henne die (PL die Hennen).

her pronoun (in German this pronoun changes according to the function it has in the sentence or the preposition it follows) **1** (as a direct object in the accusative) sie; **I know her** ich kenne sie; **I saw her last week** ich habe sie letzte Woche gesehen; **2** (after prepositions +ACC) sie; **without her** ohne sie; **we've heard a lot about her** wir haben viel über sie gehört; **3** (as an indirect object or after verbs that take the dative) ihr; **I gave her my address** ich habe ihr meine Adresse gegeben; **we helped her** wir haben ihr

△ NEW SPELLING: *See page xii*

geholfen; **4** (*after prepositions* +DAT) ihr; **with her** mit ihr; **5** (*in comparisons*) sie; **he's older than her** er ist älter als sie; **6** (*in the nominative*) sie; **it was her** sie war es.

adjective **1** (*before a masculine noun*) ihr; **her brother** ihr Bruder; **2** (*before a feminine noun*) ihre; **her sister** ihre Schwester; **3** (*before a neuter noun*) ihr; **her house** ihr Haus; **4** (*before a plural noun*) ihre; **her children** ihre Kinder; **5** (*with parts of the body*) der/die/das, die (*plural*); **she had a glass in her hand** sie hatte ein Glas in der Hand; **she's washing her hands** sie wäscht sich die Hände.

herb *noun* Kraut *das* (PL *die* Kräuter).

here *adverb* **1** (*in or at this place*) hier; **not far from here** nicht weit von hier; **here's my address** hier ist meine Adresse; **I want to stay here** ich möchte hier bleiben; **2** (*to this place*) hierher; **when Peter came here** als Peter hierher kam; **3 here they are!** da sind sie!; **Tom isn't here at the moment** Tom ist im Moment nicht da.

hero *noun* Held *der* (PL *die* Helden).

heroin *noun* Heroin *das*.

heroine *noun* Heldin *die* (PL *die* Heldinnen).

herring *noun* Hering *der* (PL *die* Heringe).

hers *pronoun* **1** (*for a masculine noun*) ihrer; **my coat is blue and hers is red** mein Mantel ist blau und

ihrer ist rot; **I took my hat and she took hers** ich nahm meinen Hut und sie nahm ihren; **2** (*for a feminine noun*) ihre; **I gave Ann my address and she gave me hers** ich habe Ann meine Adresse gegeben und sie hat mir ihre gegeben; **3** (*for a neuter noun*) ihr(e)s; **my bike is new but hers is old** mein Rad ist neu, aber ihrs ist alt; **4** (*for masculine/feminine/neuter plural nouns*) ihre; **I showed Emma my photos and she showed me hers** ich habe Emma meine Fotos gezeigt und sie hat mir ihre gezeigt; **5 the CDs are hers** die CDs gehören ihr; **it's hers** das gehört ihr.

herself *pronoun* **1** (*reflexive*) sich; **she's hurt herself** sie hat sich wehgetan; **2** (*stressing something*) selbst; **she said it herself** sie hat es selbst gesagt; **3 she did it by herself** sie hat es ganz allein gemacht.

hesitate *verb* zögern.

heterosexual *adjective* heterosexuell. *noun* Heterosexuelle *der/die* (PL *die* Heterosexuellen).

hi *exclamation* hallo!

hiccups *plural noun* **to have the hiccups** einen Schluckauf haben.

hidden *adjective* verborgen.

hide *verb* **1** sich verstecken; **she hid behind the door** sie hat sich hinter der Tür versteckt; **2 to hide something** etwas verstecken.

hi-fi *noun* Hi-Fi-Anlage *die* (PL *die* Hi-Fi-Anlagen).

high *adjective* 1 hoch; **how high is the wall?** wie hoch ist die Mauer?; **the wall is two metres high** die Mauer ist zwei Meter hoch; **the shelf is too high** das Regal ist zu hoch; (*the adjective 'hoch' loses its c when it has an ending, becoming hoher/hohe/hohes*) **a high tower** ein hoher Turm; **a high wall** eine hohe Mauer; **at high speed** mit hoher Geschwindigkeit; **a high voice** eine hohe Stimme; 2 **high winds** starker Wind.
adverb hoch.

high-heeled *adjective* hochhackig.

high jump *noun* Hochsprung *der*.

hijack *verb* **to hijack a plane** ein Flugzeug entführen.

hijacker *noun* Entführer *der* (PL *die* Entführer).

hike *noun* Wanderung *die* (PL *die* Wanderungen).

hilarious *adjective* lustig.

hill *noun* 1 (*large hill*) Berg *der* (PL *die* Berge); **you can see the hills** man kann die Berge sehen; 2 (*smaller*) Hügel *der* (PL *die* Hügel); **to walk up the hill** den Hügel hinaufgehen; 3 (*hillside*) Hang *der* (PL *die* Hänge); **the house on the hill** das Haus am Hang.

him *pronoun* (*in German this pronoun changes according to the function it has in the sentence or the preposition it follows*) 1 (*as a direct object in the accusative*) ihn; **I know him** ich kenne ihn; **I saw him last week** ich habe ihn letzte Woche gesehen; 2 (*after prepositions* +ACC) ihn; **he fought against him** er hat

gegen ihn gekämpft; **without him** ohne ihn; 3 (*as an indirect object or after verbs that take the dative*) ihm; **I gave him my address** ich habe ihm meine Adresse gegeben; **you must help him** du musst ihm helfen; 4 (*after prepositions* +DAT) ihm; **with him** mit ihm; 5 (*in comparisons*) er; **she's older than him** sie ist älter als er; 6 (*in the nominative*) er; **it was him** er war es.

himself *pronoun* 1 (*reflexive*) sich; **he's hurt himself** er hat sich wehgetan; 2 (*stressing something*) selbst; **he said it himself** er hat es selbst gesagt; 3 **he did it by himself** er hat es ganz allein gemacht.

Hindu *adjective* hinduistisch.

hip *noun* Hüfte *die* (PL *die* Hüften).

hippie *noun* Hippie *der* (PL *die* Hippies).

hire *noun* 1 Vermietung *die*; **car hire** *die* Autovermietung; 2 **for hire** zu vermieten.
verb mieten.

his *adjective* 1 (*before a masculine noun*) sein; **his brother** sein Bruder; 2 (*before a feminine noun*) seine; **his sister** seine Schwester; 3 (*before a neuter noun*) sein; **his house** sein Haus; 4 (*before a plural noun*) seine; **his children** seine Kinder; 5 (*with parts of the body*) der/die/das, die (*plural*); **he had a glass in his hand** er hatte ein Glas in der Hand; **he's washing his hands** er wäscht sich ←(DAT) die Hände.

△ NEW SPELLING: *See page xii*

pronoun 1 (*for a masculine noun*)
seiner; **my hat is red and his is blue**
mein Hut ist rot und seiner ist blau;
2 (*for a feminine noun*) seine; **I gave
him my address and he gave me
his** ich habe ihm meine Adresse
gegeben und er hat mir seine
gegeben; 3 (*for a neuter noun*)
sein(e)s; **my book is new but his is
old** mein Buch ist neu, aber seins ist
alt; 4 (*for masculine/feminine/
neuter plural nouns*) seine; **I've
invited my parents and Steve's
invited his** ich habe meine Eltern
eingeladen und Steve hat seine
eingeladen; 5 **the green car's his**
das grüne Auto gehört ihm; **it's his**
das gehört ihm.

history *noun* Geschichte *die*.

hit *noun* 1 (*song*) Hit *der* (PL die
Hits); **their latest hit** ihr neuester
Hit; 2 (*success*) Erfolg *der* (PL die
Erfolge); **the film is a huge hit** der
Film ist ein großer Erfolg.
verb 1 treffen ✧; **to hit the ball** den
Ball treffen; 2 **to hit your head on
something** sich ←(DAT) den Kopf an
etwas ←(DAT) stoßen; **I hit my head
on the door** ich habe mir den Kopf
an der Tür gestoßen; 3 prallen gegen
(+ACC) (PERF *sein*); **the car hit a wall**
das Auto ist gegen eine Wand
geprallt; 4 **to be hit by a car** von
einem Auto angefahren werden.

hitch *noun* Problem *das* (PL die
Probleme); **there's been a slight
hitch** ein kleines Problem ist
aufgetaucht.
verb **to hitch a lift** per Anhalter
fahren ✧ (PERF *sein*).

hitchhike *verb* per Anhalter
fahren ✧ (PERF *sein*); **we hitchhiked
to Heidelberg** wir sind per Anhalter
nach Heidelberg gefahren.

hitchhiker *noun* Anhalter *der* (PL
die Anhalter), Anhalterin *die* (PL die
Anhalterinnen).

HIV-negative *adjective* HIV-
negativ.

HIV-positive *adjective* HIV-positiv.

hobby *noun* Hobby *das* (PL die
Hobbys).

hockey *noun* Hockey *das*.

hockey stick *noun*
Hockeyschläger *der* (PL die
Hockeyschläger).

hold *verb* 1 halten ✧; **to hold
something in your hand** etwas in
der Hand halten; **can you hold the
torch?** kannst du die Taschenlampe
halten?; 2 (*be able to contain*)
fassen; **the jug holds a litre** der Krug
fasst einen Liter; 3 **to hold a
meeting** eine Versammlung
abhalten ✧ SEP; 4 **can you hold the
line, please?** bleiben Sie bitte am
Apparat; 5 **hold on!** (*wait*) warten
Sie!; (*on the phone*) bleiben Sie am
Apparat.
● **to hold on to something** (*to stop
yourself from falling*) sich an etwas
←(DAT) festhalten ✧ SEP.
● **to hold somebody up** (*delay*)
jemanden aufhalten ✧ SEP; **I was
held up at the dentist's** ich bin beim
Zahnarzt aufgehalten worden.
● **to hold something up** (*raise*) etwas
hochhalten ✧ SEP.

hold-up *noun* 1 Verzögerung *die* (P

✧ IRREGULAR VERB: *See the verb table in the centre of the dictionary*

die Verzögerungen); **2** (*traffic jam*)
Stau *der* (PL *die* Staus); **3** (*robbery*)
Überfall *der* (PL *die* Überfälle).

hole *noun* Loch *das* (PL *die* Löcher).

holiday *noun* **1** Ferien (*plural*),
Urlaub *der* (PL *die* Urlaube)
(*students, schoolchildren, and
families usually have 'Ferien'; people
in paid employment usually have
'Urlaub'*); **where are you going for
your holiday?** wo fahrt ihr in den
Ferien hin?; **have a good holiday!**
schöne Ferien!, schönen Urlaub!; **to
be away on holiday** auf Urlaub sein,
in Ferien sein; **to go on holiday** in
Urlaub fahren, in die Ferien fahren;
the school holidays die
Schulferien; **2** (*day off work*) freie
Tag *der* (PL *die* freien Tage); **I'm
taking two days' holiday next
week** ich nehme mir nächste Woche
zwei Tage frei; **3 public holiday** *der*
Feiertag; **Monday's a holiday**
Montag ist ein Feiertag.

Holland *noun* Holland *das*.

holy *adjective* heilig.

home *noun* **1 I was at home** ich war
zu Hause; **to stay at home** zu Hause
bleiben; **2 make yourself at home**
mach es dir bequem.
adverb **1** (*to home*) nach Hause;
Susie's gone home Susie ist nach
Hause gegangen; **on my way home**
auf dem Weg nach Hause; **to get
home** nach Hause kommen; **we got
home at midnight** wir sind um
Mitternacht nach Hause
gekommen; **2** (*at home*) zu Hause;
I'll be home in the afternoon ich
bin am Nachmittag zu Hause.

homeless *adjective* obdachlos; **the
homeless** die Obdachlosen.

homemade *adjective* selbst
gemacht Δ; **homemade biscuits**
selbst gebackene Kekse.

homeopathic *adjective*
homöopathisch.

homesick *adjective* **to be
homesick** Heimweh haben.

homework *noun* Hausaufgaben
(*plural*); **I did my homework** ich
habe meine Hausaufgaben gemacht;
my German homework meine
Deutschhausaufgaben.

homosexual *adjective*
homosexuell.
noun Homosexuelle *der/die* (PL *die*
Homosexuellen).

honest *adjective* ehrlich.

honestly *adverb* ehrlich.

honesty *noun* Ehrlichkeit *die*.

honey *noun* Honig *der* (PL *die*
Honige).

hood *noun* **1** Kapuze *die* (PL *die*
Kapuzen); **2** (*on a car*) Verdeck *das*
(PL *die* Verdecke).

hook *noun* **1** Haken *der* (PL *die*
Haken); **2 to take the phone off the
hook** das Telefon aushängen SEP.

hooligan *noun* Hooligan *der* (PL *die*
Hooligans).

hooray *exclamation* hurra!

hoover *verb* saugen; **I hoovered my
bedroom** ich habe mein
Schlafzimmer gesaugt.

Δ NEW SPELLING: *See page xii*

Hoover™ *noun* Staubsauger *der* (PL *die* Staubsauger).

hope *noun* Hoffnung *die* (PL *die* Hoffnungen); **to give up hope** die Hoffnung aufgeben.
verb 1 hoffen; **we hope you'll be able to come** wir hoffen, ihr könnt kommen; **I'm hoping to see you on Friday** ich hoffe, dich am Freitag zu sehen; 2 **I hope so** hoffentlich; **I hope not** hoffentlich nicht.

hopefully *adverb* hoffentlich; **hopefully, the film won't have started** hoffentlich hat der Film noch nicht angefangen.

hopeless *adjective* miserabel (*informal*); **I'm hopeless at geography** ich bin miserabel in Erdkunde.

horn *noun* 1 (*of an animal, instrument*) Horn *das* (PL *die* Hörner); 2 (*of a car*) Hupe *die* (PL *die* Hupen).

horoscope *noun* Horoskop *das* (PL *die* Horoskope).

horrible *adjective* 1 furchtbar; **the weather was horrible** das Wetter war furchtbar; 2 (*person*) gemein; **she's really horrible** sie ist richtig gemein; **he was really horrible to me** er war richtig gemein zu mir.

horror *noun* Entsetzen *das*.

horror film *noun* Horrorfilm *der* (PL *die* Horrorfilme).

horse *noun* Pferd *das* (PL *die* Pferde).

hospital *noun* Krankenhaus *das* (PL *die* Krankenhäuser); **in hospital** im Krankenhaus; **to be taken into hospital** ins Krankenhaus kommen.

hospitality *noun* Gastfreundschaft *die*.

host *noun* 1 Gastgeber *der* (PL *die* Gastgeber); 2 (*on a TV programme*) Moderator *der* (PL *die* Moderatoren).

hostage *noun* Geisel *die* (PL *die* Geiseln).

hostel *noun* **youth hostel** die Jugendherberge.

hostess *noun* 1 Gastgeberin *die* (PL *die* Gastgeberinnen); 2 (*on a TV programme*) Moderatorin *die* (PL *die* Moderatorinnen); 3 **air hostess** *die* Stewardess.

hot *adjective* 1 heiß; **be careful, the plates are hot** sei vorsichtig, die Teller sind heiß; **it's hot today** heute ist es heiß; 2 (*person*) **I'm very hot** mir ist sehr heiß; 3 (*spicy*) scharf; **the curry's too hot for me** das Curry ist mir zu scharf; 4 **a hot meal** ein warmes Essen.

hotel *noun* Hotel *das* (PL *die* Hotels)

hour *noun* Stunde *die* (PL *die* Stunden); **two hours later** zwei Stunden später; **we waited for two hours** wir haben zwei Stunden lang gewartet; **I've been waiting for hours** ich warte schon seit Stunden; **two hours ago** vor zwei Stunden; **to be paid by the hour** pro Stunde bezahlt werden; **every hour** jede Stunde; **half an hour** eine halbe Stunde; **a quarter of an hour** eine Viertelstunde; **an hour and a half** anderthalb Stunden.

house *noun* 1 Haus *das* (PL *die*

Häuser); **2 at somebody's house** bei jemandem; **I'm at Judy's house** ich bin bei Judy; **I'm going to Sid's house tonight** ich gehe heute Abend zu Sid; **I phoned from Jill's house** ich habe von Jill angerufen.

housewife *noun* Hausfrau *die* (PL *die* Hausfrauen).

housework *noun* Hausarbeit *die*; **he does the housework** er macht den Haushalt (*informal*).

hovercraft *noun* Luftkissenfahrzeug *das* (PL *die* Luftkissenfahrzeuge).

how *adverb* **1** wie; **how did you do it?** wie hast du das gemacht?; **how are you?** wie geht es dir?; **how many?** wie viele?; **how many brothers do you have?** wie viele Brüder hast du?; **how old are you?** wie alt bist du?; **how far is it?** wie weit ist es?; **how far is it to York?** wie weit ist es bis York?; **how long will it take?** wie lange dauert es?; **how long have you known her?** wie lange kennst du sie?; **2 how much?** wie viel?; **how much money do you have?** wie viel Geld hast du?; **how much is it?** wie viel kostet das?

however *adverb* **1** jedoch; **2** (*in questions*) **however did she do it?** wie hat sie das nur gemacht?; **3 however famous he is** wie berühmt er auch sein mag.

hug *noun* **to give somebody a hug** jemanden umarmen; **she gave me a hug** sie hat mich umarmt.

huge *adjective* riesig.

hum *verb* summen.

human *adjective* menschlich.

human being *noun* Mensch *der* (PL *die* Menschen).

humour *noun* Humor *der*; **to have a sense of humour** Humor haben.

hundred *number* hundert; **two hundred** zweihundert; **two hundred and ten** zweihundertzehn; **a hundred people** hundert Menschen; **about a hundred** um die hundert; **hundreds of people** hunderte von Menschen.

Hungary *noun* Ungarn *das*.

hunger *noun* Hunger *der*.

hungry *adjective* **to be hungry** Hunger haben; **I'm hungry** ich habe Hunger.

hunting *noun* Jagd *die*; **fox-hunting** *die* Fuchsjagd.

hurry *noun* **to be in a hurry** es eilig haben; **I'm in a hurry** ich habe es eilig; **there's no hurry** es eilt nicht. *verb* **1** sich beeilen; **I must hurry** ich muss mich beeilen; **hurry up!** beeil dich!; **2 he hurried home** er ging schnell nach Hause.

hurt *verb* **1 to hurt somebody** jemandem wehtun ✧ SEP; **you're hurting me!** du tust mir weh!; **that hurts!** das tut weh!; **2 my arm hurts** der Arm tut mir weh; **3 to hurt yourself** sich ←(DAT) wehtun ✧ SEP; **did you hurt yourself?** hast du dir wehgetan? *adjective* **1** (*in an accident*) verletzt; **three people were hurt** drei Menschen wurden verletzt; **2** (*in* *feelings*) gekränkt; **she felt hurt** sie fühlte sich gekränkt.

husband *noun* Ehemann *der* (PL *die* Ehemänner).

hymn *noun* Kirchenlied *das* (PL *die* Kirchenlieder).

hypermarket *noun* Großmarkt *der* (PL *die* Großmärkte).

hyphen *noun* Bindestrich *der* (PL *die* Bindestriche).

I i

I *pronoun* ich; **I have two sisters** ich habe zwei Schwestern.

ice *noun* Eis *das*.

ice cream *noun* Eis *das*; **two chocolate ice creams** zwei Schokoladeneis.

ice hockey *noun* Eishockey *das*.

ice rink *noun* Eisbahn *die* (PL *die* Eisbahnen).

ice-skating *noun* **to go ice-skating** Schlittschuh laufen ✧ (PERF *sein*).

icy *adjective* **1** vereist (*road*); **2** (*very cold*) eiskalt.

idea *noun* **1** Idee *die* (PL *die* Ideen); **what a good idea!** was für eine gute Idee!; **2 I've no idea** ich habe keine Ahnung.

ideal *adjective* ideal.

identical *adjective* identisch.

identification *noun* **1** Identifizierung *die*; **2** (*proof of identity*) Ausweispapiere (*plural*).

identity card *noun* Personalausweis *der* (PL *die* Personalausweise).

idiot *noun* Idiot *der* (PL *die* Idioten).

idiotic *adjective* idiotisch.

i.e. *abbreviation* d.h. (*das heißt*).

if *conjunction* **1** wenn; **if it rains** wenn es regnet; **if I won the lottery** wenn ich in der Lotterie gewinnen sollte; **if not** wenn nicht; **if only** wenn nur; **if only you'd told me** wenn du mir das nur gesagt hättest; **2 even if** selbst wenn; **even if it snows** selbst wenn es schneit; **3 if I were you** an deiner Stelle; **4** (*whether*) ob; **I wonder if he'll come** ich bin gespannt, ob er kommt; **as if** als ob.

ignore *verb* **1** ignorieren; **2** überhören (*what somebody says*).

ill *adjective* krank; **to fall ill, to be taken ill** krank werden; **I feel ill** ich fühle mich krank.

illegal *adjective* illegal.

illustration *noun* Illustration *die* (PL *die* Illustrationen).

image *noun* Bild *das* (PL *die* Bilder); ★ **he's the spitting image of his father** er ist das Ebenbild seines Vaters.

imagination *noun* Phantasie *die*.

imaginative *adjective* phantasievoll.

✧ IRREGULAR VERB: *See the verb table in the centre of the dictionary*

imagine *verb* sich ←(DAT) vorstellen; **imagine that you're very rich** stell dir vor, du bist sehr reich; **you can't imagine how hard it was** du kannst dir nicht vorstellen, wie schwer es war.

imitate *verb* nachahmen SEP.

immediate *adjective* 1 (*without delay*) unmittelbar; **2 the immediate family** die engste Familie.

immediately *adverb* 1 sofort; **I rang them immediately** ich habe sie sofort angerufen; **2 immediately before** unmittelbar davor; **immediately after** unmittelbar danach.

immigrant *noun* Einwanderer *der* (PL *die* Einwanderer), Einwanderin *die* (PL *die* Einwanderinnen).

immigration *noun* Einwanderung *die*.

impatience *noun* Ungeduld *die*.

impatient *adjective* 1 ungeduldig; **2 to be impatient with somebody** ungeduldig mit jemandem sein.

impatiently *adverb* ungeduldig.

importance *noun* Wichtigkeit *die*.

important *adjective* wichtig.

impossible *adjective* unmöglich; **it's impossible to find a telephone** es ist unmöglich, ein Telefon zu finden.

impressed *adjective* beeindruckt; **to be impressed by something** von etwas ←(DAT) beeindruckt sein.

impressive *adjective* eindrucksvoll.

improve *verb* 1 **to improve something** etwas verbessern; 2 (*get better*) besser werden; **the weather is improving** das Wetter wird besser.

improvement *noun* Verbesserung *die* (PL *die* Verbesserungen).

in *preposition* 1 in (+DAT *or*, *with movement into*, +ACC); **it is in my pocket** es ist in meiner Tasche; (*with movement*) **he put it in his pocket** er hat es in die Tasche gesteckt; **she sat in the sun** sie saß in der Sonne; **I read it in the newspaper** ich habe es in der Zeitung gelesen; **in Oxford** in Oxford; **in Germany** in Deutschland; **2 the biggest city in the world** die größte Stadt auf der Welt; **a house in the country** ein Haus auf dem Land; **in the street** auf der Straße; 3 (*wearing and with colours*) in (+DAT); **the girl in the pink shirt** das Mädchen im rosa Hemd; **4 in German** auf Deutsch; **5** (*time expressions*) in (+DAT); **in May** im Mai; **in 1994** (im Jahre) 1994; **in winter** im Winter; **in summer** im Sommer; **in the night** in der Nacht; **I'll phone you in ten minutes** ich rufe dich in zehn Minuten an; **she was ready in five minutes** sie war in fünf Minuten fertig; **6 in the morning** am Morgen; **at eight in the morning** um acht Uhr morgens; **7** (*among people or in literature*) bei (+DAT); **it's rare in children** das ist selten bei Kindern; **in Shakespeare** bei

△ NEW SPELLING: *See page xii*

Shakespeare; **in the army** beim Militär; **8 in time** rechtzeitig. *adverb* **1** (*inside*) hinein-, herein-, rein- (*informal*); (*Herein-, hinein-, and rein-* form prefixes to separable verbs. 'Herein-' is used with verbs like kommen, which have the sense of moving towards the speaker. 'Hinein-' is used with verbs like gehen, which have the sense of going away from the speaker. The informal 'rein-' can be used with either movement.) **to come in** hereinkommen ◇ SEP (PERF *sein*); **to go in** hineingehen ◇ SEP (PERF *sein*); **he was not allowed to go into the room** er durfte nicht ins Zimmer reingehen; **to run in** reinlaufen ◇ SEP (PERF *sein*) (*informal*); **2 to be in** da sein; **Mick's not in at the moment** Mick ist im Moment nicht da; **3** (*at home*) zu Hause; **4** (*indoors*) drinnen; **in here** hier drinnen; **in there** da drinnen.

include *verb* einschließen ◇ SEP; **service is included in the price** die Bedienung ist im Preis inbegriffen.

including *preposition*
1 einschließlich (+GEN); **everyone, including the children** alle, einschließlich der Kinder; **£50 including postage** fünfzig Pfund einschließlich Porto; **including Sundays** einschließlich sonntags; **2 not including Sundays** außer sonntags.

income *noun* Einkommen *das* (PL *die* Einkommen).

income tax *noun* Einkommensteuer *die* (PL *die* Einkommensteuern).

increase *noun* Erhöhung *die* (PL *die* Erhöhungen) (*in price, for example*). *verb* **1** steigen ◇ (PERF *sein*); **the price has increased by £10** der Preis ist um zehn Pfund gestiegen; **2** erhöhen (*salary*).

incredible *adjective* unglaublich.

incredibly *adverb* (*very*) unwahrscheinlich; **the film's incredibly boring** der Film ist unwahrscheinlich langweilig.

indeed *adverb* **1** (*to emphasize*) wirklich; **she's very pleased indeed** sie hat sich wirklich sehr gefreut; **2** (*certainly*) natürlich; **'can you hear the radio?' – 'indeed I can!'** 'kannst du das Radio hören?' – 'ja, natürlich!'; **3 thank you very much indeed** vielen herzlichen Dank.

indefinite article *noun* unbestimmte Artikel *der*.

independence *noun* Unabhängigkeit *die*.

independent *adjective* unabhängig; **independent school** *die* Privatschule.

India *noun* Indien *das*.

Indian *noun* **1** Inder *der* (PL *die* Inder), Inderin *die* (PL *die* Inderinnen); **2** (*a Native American*) Indianer *der* (PL *die* Indianer), Indianerin *die* (PL *die* Indianerinnen).

◇ IRREGULAR VERB: *See the verb table in the centre of the dictionary*

adjective **1** indisch; **he's Indian** er ist Inder; **2** (*Native American*) indianisch; **she's Indian** sie ist Indianerin.

indicate *verb* **1** zeigen auf (+ACC) (*a person or a thing*); **2** (*of a car or driver*) blinken.

indigestion *noun* Magenverstimmung *die* (PL *die* Magenverstimmungen).

individual *noun* Einzelne Δ *der/die* (PL *die* Einzelnen).
adjective **1** einzeln (*serving, contribution*); **2 individual tuition** *der* Einzelunterricht.

indoor *adjective* **an indoor swimming pool** ein Hallenbad; **indoor games** Spiele im Haus; (*in sports*) Hallenspiele.

indoors *adverb* drinnen; **it's cooler indoors** drinnen ist es kühler; **to go indoors** ins Haus gehen.

industrial *adjective* industriell.

industrial estate *noun* Industriegebiet *das* (PL *die* Industriegebiete).

industry *noun* Industrie *die* (PL *die* Industrien); **the car industry** die Autoindustrie.

inevitable *adjective* unvermeidlich.

inevitably *adverb* zwangsläufig.

inexperienced *adjective* unerfahren.

infant school *noun* Vorschule *die* (PL *die* Vorschulen).

infection *noun* Infektion *die* (PL *die* Infektionen); **eye infection** *die* Augeninfektion; **throat infection** *die* Halsentzündung.

infectious *adjective* ansteckend.

infinitive *noun* Infinitiv *der* (PL *die* Infinitive).

inflammable *adjective* feuergefährlich.

inflatable *adjective* **inflatable mattress** *die* Luftmatratze; **inflatable boat** *das* Schlauchboot.

influence *noun* Einfluss Δ *der* (PL *die* Einflüsse); **to be a good influence on somebody** einen guten Einfluss Δ auf jemanden haben.
verb beeinflussen.

inform *verb* informieren; **to inform somebody of something** jemanden über etwas ←(ACC) informieren.

informal *adjective* **1** zwanglos (*meal or event*); **2** ungezwungen (*language, tone*).

information *noun* Auskunft *die*; **where can I get information about flights to Berlin?** wo kann ich Auskunft über Flüge nach Berlin bekommen?

information desk, information office *noun* Auskunftsbüro *das* (PL *die* Auskunftsbüros).

information technology *noun* Informatik *die*.

ingredient *noun* Zutat *die* (PL *die* Zutaten).

Δ **NEW SPELLING:** *See page xii*

inhabitant *noun* Einwohner *der* (PL die Einwohner), Einwohnerin *die* (PL die Einwohnerinnen).

initials *plural noun* Initialen (*plural*).

injection *noun* Spritze *die* (PL die Spritzen).

injure *verb* verletzen.

injury *noun* Verletzung *die* (PL die Verletzungen).

ink *noun* Tinte *die* (PL die Tinten).

in-laws *noun* Schwiegereltern (*plural*).

innocent *adjective* unschuldig.

insane *adjective* 1 geisteskrank; 2 (*foolish*) wahnsinnig.

insect *noun* Insekt *das* (PL die Insekten); **insect bite** *der* Insektenstich.

insect repellent *noun* Insektenvertilgungsmittel *das*.

inside *noun* **on the inside** innen; **the inside of the oven is black** innen ist der Herd schwarz. *preposition* in (+DAT, *or, with movement towards a place,* +ACC); **inside the cinema** im Kino; **to go inside (the house)** ins Haus gehen. *adverb* drinnen; **she's inside, I think** ich glaube, sie ist drinnen.

inside out *adjective, adverb* (*clothing*) links.

insist *verb* darauf bestehen ◇; **if you insist** wenn du darauf bestehst; **to insist on doing something** darauf bestehen, etwas zu tun; **he insists on paying** er besteht darauf zu zahlen; **to insist that** ... darauf bestehen, dass ...; **Ruth insisted I was wrong** Ruth hat darauf bestanden, dass ich Unrecht hatte.

inspector *noun* 1 (*on a bus or train*) Kontrolleur *der* (PL die Kontrolleure), Kontrolleurin *die* (F die Kontrolleurinnen); 2 (*in the police*) Kommissar *der* (PL die Kommissare), Kommissarin *die* (PL die Kommissarinnen).

install *verb* installieren.

instalment *noun* (*of a story or serial*) Folge *die* (PL die Folgen).

instance *noun* **for instance** zum Beispiel.

instant *noun* Augenblick *der* (PL d Augenblicke); **come here this instant!** komm sofort her! *adjective* 1 Instant- (*coffee, tea*); 2 (*immediate*) sofortig.

instantly *adverb* sofort.

instead *adverb* 1 **Ted couldn't come, so I came instead (of him)** Ted konnte nicht kommen, also bi ich an seiner Stelle gekommen; 2 **instead of** statt (+GEN *or* +DAT); **bought a bike instead of a car** er hat ein Fahrrad statt eines Autos gekauft; **instead of cake I had cheese** statt Kuchen habe ich Käs genommen; **instead of playing tennis we went swimming** statt Tennis zu spielen, sind wir schwimmen gegangen.

instinct *noun* Instinkt *der* (PL die Instinkte).

◇ IRREGULAR VERB: *See the verb table in the centre of the dictionary*

institute *noun* Institut *das* (PL *die* Institute).

instructions *plural noun* Anweisung *die* (PL *die* Anweisungen); **follow the instructions on the packet** befolgen Sie die Anweisung auf der Packung; **'instructions for use'** 'Gebrauchsanweisung'.

instructor *noun* Lehrer *der* (PL *die* Lehrer), Lehrerin *die* (PL *die* Lehrerinnen); **my skiing instructor** mein Skilehrer.

instrument *noun* Instrument *das* (PL *die* Instrumente); **to play an instrument** ein Instrument spielen.

insulin *noun* Insulin *das*.

insult *noun* Beleidigung *die* (PL *die* Beleidigungen).
verb beleidigen.

insurance *noun* Versicherung *die* (PL *die* Versicherungen); **travel insurance** *die* Reiseversicherung.

intelligence *noun* Intelligenz *die*.

intelligent *adjective* intelligent.

intend *verb* beabsichtigen; **as I intended** wie beabsichtigt; **to intend to do something** beabsichtigen, etwas zu tun; **we intend to spend the night in Rome** wir beabsichtigen, in Rom zu übernachten.

intention *noun* Absicht *die* (PL *die* Absichten); **I have no intention of paying** ich habe nicht die Absicht zu zahlen.

interest *noun* **1** Interesse *das* (PL *die* Interessen); **to have lots of**

interests viele Interessen haben; **he has an interest in jazz** er hat Interesse an Jazz; **2** (*financial*) Zinsen (*plural*).
verb interessieren; **that doesn't interest me** das interessiert mich nicht.

interested *adjective* **to be interested in something** sich für etwas ←(ACC) interessieren; **Sean's interested in cooking** Sean interessiert sich für Kochen.

interesting *adjective* interessant.

interfere *verb* **1** **to interfere with something** (*to fiddle with it*) sich ←(DAT) an etwas ←(DAT) zu schaffen machen; **don't interfere with my computer!** mach dir nicht an meinem Computer zu schaffen!; **2** **to interfere in something** sich in etwas ←(ACC) einmischen SEP (*somebody else's affairs*).

interior designer *noun* Innenarchitekt *der* (PL *die* Innenarchitekten), Innenarchitektin *die* (PL *die* Innenarchitektinnen).

international *adjective* international.

Internet *noun* Internet *das*; **on the Internet** im Internet.

interpret *verb* (*act as an interpreter*) dolmetschen.

interpreter *noun* Dometscher *der* (PL *die* Dolmetscher), Dolmetscherin *die* (PL *die* Dometscherinnen).

interrupt *verb* unterbrechen ✧.

△ NEW SPELLING: *See page xii*

interruption *noun*
Unterbrechung *die* (PL *die* Unterbrechungen).

interval *noun* (*in a play or concert*)
Pause *die* (PL *die* Pausen).

interview *noun* **1** (*for a job*)
Vorstellungsgespräch *das* (PL *die* Vorstellungsgespräche); **to go for an interview** sich vorstellen SEP; **2** (*in a newspaper, on TV, or radio*)
Interview *das* (PL *die* Interviews).
verb interviewen (*on TV, radio*).

interviewer *noun* Interviewer *der* (PL *die* Interviewer), Interviewerin *die* (PL *die* Interviewerinnen).

into *preposition* **1** in (+ACC); **he's gone into the garden** er ist in den Garten gegangen; **I put the ball into the bag** ich habe den Ball in die Tasche getan; **we all got into the car** wir sind alle ins Auto eingestiegen; **to go into town** in die Stadt gehen; **to get into bed** ins Bett gehen; **to translate into German** ins Deutsche übersetzen; **to change pounds into marks** Pfund in Mark wechseln; **2** (*against*) gegen (+ACC); **he drove into the wall** er ist gegen die Wand gefahren; **3 to be into jazz** auf Jazz abfahren ✧ SEP (PERF *sein*) (*informal*).

introduce *verb* vorstellen SEP; **she introduced me to her brother** sie hat mich ihrem Bruder vorgestellt; **she introduced her brother to me** sie hat mir ihren Bruder vorgestellt; **can I introduce you to my mother?** darf ich Sie meiner Mutter vorstellen?

introduction *noun* (*in a book*)
Einleitung *die* (PL *die* Einleitungen).

invade *verb* einfallen ✧ SEP in (PERF *sein*) (+ACC).

invalid *noun* Kranke *der/die* (PL *die* Kranken);

invent *verb* erfinden ✧.

invention *noun* Erfindung *die* (PL *die* Erfindungen).

inverted commas *plural noun*
Anführungszeichen (*plural*);
in inverted commas in Anführungszeichen.

investigation *noun*
Untersuchung *die* (PL *die* Untersuchungen); **an investigation into the incident** eine Untersuchung des Vorfalls.

invisible *adjective* unsichtbar.

invitation *noun* Einladung *die* (PL *die* Einladungen); **an invitation to dinner** eine Einladung zum Abendessen.

invite *verb* einladen ✧ SEP; **Kirsty invited me to lunch** Kirsty hat mich zum Mittagessen eingeladen; **he's invited me out on Tuesday** er hat mich eingeladen, Dienstag mit ihm auszugehen; **they invited us round** sie haben uns zu sich eingeladen.

inviting *adjective* verlockend.

involve *verb* **1** erfordern; **it involves a lot of time** es erfordert viel Zeit; **2** (*include*) beteiligen; **the game will involve everybody** alle können sich an dem Spiel beteiligen; **to be involved in something** an etwas ←(DAT) beteiligt sein; **I am involved in the new project** ich bin an dem

neuen Projekt beteiligt;
3 (*implicate*) verwickeln; **to get
involved in something** in etwas
←(ACC) verwickelt werden; **two cars
were involved in the accident** zwei
Autos waren in den Unfall
verwickelt; **4 to get involved with
somebody** sich mit jemandem
einlassen ◇ SEP.

ran *noun* Iran *der*.

raq *noun* Irak *der*.

reland *noun* Irland *das*; **the
Republic of Ireland** die Republik
Irland.

rish *noun* **1** (*the language*)
Irisch *das*; **2** (*the people*) **the Irish**
die Iren.
adjective irisch; **he's Irish** er ist Ire;
she's Irish sie ist Irin.

rishman *noun* Ire *der* (PL *die* Iren).

rish Sea *noun* Irische See *die*.

rishwoman *noun* Irin *die* (PL *die*
Irinnen).

ron *noun* **1** (*for clothes*)
Bügeleisen *das* (PL *die* Bügeleisen);
2 (*the metal*) Eisen *das*.
verb bügeln.

roning *noun* Bügeln *das*; **to do the
ironing** bügeln.

roning board *noun*
Bügelbrett *das* (PL *die* Bügelbretter).

ronmonger's *noun*
Haushaltswarengeschäft *das* (PL *die*
Haushaltswarengeschäfte).

rregular *adjective* unregelmäßig.

rritable *adjective* reizbar.

irritate *verb* ärgern.

irritating *adjective* ärgerlich.

Islam *noun* Islam *der*.

Islamic *adjective* islamisch.

island *noun* Insel *die* (PL *die* Inseln).

isolated *adjective* **1** (*remote*)
abgelegen; **2** (*single*) einzeln;
isolated cases Einzelfälle.

Israel *noun* Israel *das*.

Israeli *noun* Israeli *der/die* (PL *die*
Iraelis).
adjective israelisch.

issue *noun* **1** (*something you
discuss*) Frage *die* (PL *die* Fragen);
a political issue eine politische
Frage; **2** (*of a magazine*)
Ausgabe *die* (PL *die* Ausgaben).
verb (*hand out*) ausgeben ◇ SEP.

it *pronoun* **1** (*as the subject*)
er (*standing for a masculine noun*),
sie (*standing for a feminine noun*),
es (*standing for a neuter noun*);
**'where's my key?' – 'it's in the
kitchen'** wo ist mein Schlüssel?' –
'er ist in der Küche; **'where's my
bag?'- 'it's in the living-room'**
'wo ist meine Tasche?' – 'sie ist im
Wohnzimmer'; **'how old is your
car?' – 'it's five years old'** 'wie alt
ist dein Auto?' – 'es ist fünf Jahre alt';
2 (*as the direct object, in the
accusative*) ihn (*standing for a
masculine noun*), sie (*standing for a
feminine noun*), es (*standing for a
neuter noun*); **'where's your
umbrella?' – 'I've lost it'** 'wo ist
dein Regenschirm?'- 'ich habe ihn
verloren'; **'have you seen my bag?' –**

Δ NEW SPELLING: *See page xii*

'I saw it in the kitchen' 'hast du meine Tasche gesehen?' – ' ich habe sie in der Küche gesehen'; **have you read his new book?' – 'I've just bought it'** 'hast du sein neues Buch gelesen?' – 'ich habe es gerade gekauft'; **3** to it ihm (*masculine*), ihr (*feminine*), ihm (*neuter*); **4 yes, it's true** ja, das stimmt; **it doesn't matter** das macht nichts; **5 who is it?** wer ist da?; **it's me** ich bins; **what is it?** was ist los?; **6 it's raining** es regnet; **it's Monday** es ist Montag; **it's two o'clock** es ist zwei Uhr; **7 of it** davon; **8 out of it** daraus.

Italian *noun* **1** (*the language*) Italienisch *das*; **2** (*person*) Italiener *der* (PL *die* Italiener), Italienerin *die* (PL *die* Italienerinnen). *adjective* **1** italienisch; **Italian food** die italienische Küche; **2 my Italian class** mein Italienischunterricht.

italics *noun* Kursivschrift *die*; **in italics** kursiv.

Italy *noun* Italien *das*.

itch *verb* **1 my back's itching** mein Rücken juckt; **2 this jumper itches** dieser Pullover kratzt.

item *noun* **1** Gegenstand *der* (PL *die* Gegenstände); **2** (*for sale in a shop*) Artikel *der* (PL *die* Artikel).

its *adjective* **1** sein (*for a masculine noun*), ihr (*for a feminine noun*), sein (*for a neuter noun*); **the dog has lost its collar** der Hund hat sein Halsband verloren; **the cat's in its basket** die Katze ist in ihrem Korb; **the horse is brown and its mane is black** das Pferd is braun und seine

Mähne ist schwarz; **2** (*for a plural noun*) seine (*standing for a masculine noun*), ihre (*standing for a feminine noun*), seine (*standing for a neuter noun*); **its toys** seine Spielsachen, ihre Spielsachen.

itself *pronoun* **1** (*reflexive*) sich; **the cat's washing itself** die Katze wäscht sich; **2 he left the dog by itself** er hat den Hund allein gelassen.

ivy *noun* Efeu *der*.

J j

jack *noun* **1** (*in cards*) Bube *der* (PL *die* Buben); **the jack of clubs** der Kreuzbube; **2** (*for a car*) Wagenheber *der* (PL *die* Wagenheber).

jacket *noun* Jacke *die* (PL *die* Jacken).

jackpot *noun* Jackpot *der* (PL *die* Jackpots); **to win the jackpot** das große Los ziehen.

jam *noun* **1** Marmelade *die* (PL *die* Marmeladen); **raspberry jam** *die* Himbeermarmelade; **2 traffic jam** *der* Stau.

January *noun* Januar *der*; **in January** im Januar.

Japan *noun* Japan *das*.

Japanese *noun* **1** (*the language*) Japanisch *das*; **2** (*person*) Japaner *der* (PL *die* Japaner),

Japanerin *die* (PL *die* Japanerinnen);
the Japanese die Japaner.
adjective japanisch.

jar *noun* 1 (*small*) Glas *das* (PL *die*
Gläser); **a jar of jam** ein Glas
Marmelade; 2 (*large*) Topf *der* (PL
die Töpfe).

javelin *noun* Speer *der* (PL *die*
Speere).

jaw *noun* Kiefer *der* (PL *die* Kiefer).

jazz *noun* Jazz *der*.

jealous *adjective* eifersüchtig; **to be
jealous of somebody** eifersüchtig
auf jemanden sein.

jeans *plural noun* Jeans (*plural*); **my
jeans** meine Jeans; **a pair of jeans**
ein Paar Jeans.

jelly *noun* 1 Gelee *das* (PL *die*
Gelees); 2 (*dessert*)
Götterspeise *die* (PL *die*
Götterspeisen).

jellyfish *noun* Qualle *die* (PL *die*
Quallen).

jersey *noun* 1 (*jumper*)
Pullover *der* (PL *die* Pullover); 2 (*for
football*) Trikot *das* (PL *die* Trikots).

Jesus *noun* Jesus *der*; **Jesus Christ**
Jesus Christus.

jet *noun* (*a plane*) Jet *der* (PL *die*
Jets).

Jew *noun* Jude *der* (PL *die* Juden),
Jüdin *die* (PL *die* Jüdinnen).

jewel *noun* Edelstein *der* (PL *die*
Edelsteine).

jeweller *noun* Juwelier *der* (PL *die*
Juweliere).

jeweller's *noun*
Juweliergeschäft *das*.

jewellery *noun* Schmuck *der*.

Jewish *adjective* jüdisch.

jigsaw *noun* Puzzlespiel *das* (PL *die*
Puzzlespiele).

job *noun* 1 (*paid work*) Stelle *die* (PL
die Stellen), Job *der* (PL *die* Jobs)
(*informal*); **a job as a secretary**
eine Stelle als Sekretärin; 2 (*a task*)
Arbeit *die* (PL *die* Arbeiten); **it's not
an easy job** das ist keine leichte
Arbeit; 3 **she made a good job of it**
sie hat es gut gemacht.

jobless *adjective* arbeitslos.

jog *verb* joggen ✧ (PERF *sein*).

join *verb* 1 (*become a member of*)
beitreten ✧ SEP (+DAT) (PERF *sein*);
I've joined the tennis club ich bin
dem Tennisklub beigetreten; 2 (*to
meet up with*) treffen ✧; **I'll join you
later** ich treffe euch später.
● **to join in** 1 mitmachen SEP; **Kylie
never joins in** Kylie macht nie mit;
2 **to join in something** bei etwas
←(DAT) mitmachen SEP; **won't you
join in the game?** willst du bei dem
Spiel nicht mitmachen?

joint *noun* 1 (*of meat*) Braten *der* (PL
die Braten); **a joint of beef** ein
Rinderbraten; 2 (*in your body*)
Gelenk *das* (PL *die* Gelenke).

joke *noun* Witz *der* (PL *die* Witze); **to
tell a joke** einen Witz erzählen.
verb Witze machen; **you must be
joking!** du machst wohl Witze!

joker *noun* (*in cards*) Joker *der* (PL
die Joker).

△ NEW SPELLING: *See page xii*

journalism *noun*
Journalismus *der*.

journalist *noun* Journalist *der* (PL *die* Journalisten), Journalistin *die* (PL *die* Journalistinnen); **Sean's a journalist** Sean ist Journalist.

journey *noun* 1 (*a long one*) Reise *die* (PL *die* Reisen); **on our journey to Italy** auf unserer Reise nach Italien; 2 (*shorter; to work or school*) Fahrt *die* (PL *die* Fahrten); **bus journey** *die* Busfahrt.

joy *noun* Freude *die* (PL *die* Freuden).

judge *noun* 1 (*in court*) Richter *der* (PL *die* Richter); 2 (*in sporting events*) Schiedsrichter *der* (PL *die* Schiedsrichter); 3 (*in a competition*) Preisrichter *der* (PL *die* Preisrichter).
verb schätzen (*time or distance*).

judo *noun* Judo *das*; **he does judo** er macht Judo.

jug *noun* Krug *der* (PL *die* Krüge).

juice *noun* Saft *der*; **two orange juices please** zwei Orangensaft bitte.

juicy *adjective* saftig.

jukebox *noun* Jukebox *die* (PL *die* Jukeboxes).

July *noun* Juli *der*; **in July** im Juli.

jumble sale *noun* Basar *der* (PL *die* Basare).

jump *noun* Sprung *der* (PL *die* Sprünge); **parachute jump** *der* Fallschirmsprung.
verb springen ✧ (PERF *sein*).

jumper *noun* Pullover *der* (PL *die* Pullover).

June *noun* Juni *der*; **in June** im Juni.

jungle *noun* Dschungel *der*.

junior *adjective* jünger; **junior school** *die* Grundschule; **the juniors** (*at primary school*) die Grundschüler, die Grundschülerinnen.

junk *noun* Trödel *der*.

junk food *noun* ungesunde Essen *das*.

just *adverb* 1 (*very recently*) gerade; **to have just done something** etwas getan haben; **Tom has just arrived** Tom ist gerade angekommen; 2 **to be just doing something** gerade dabei sein, etwas zu tun; **I'm just doing the food** ich bin gerade dabei, Essen zu machen; 3 **just before midday** kurz vor Mittag; **just after 4 o'clock** kurz nach vier Uhr; 4 (*only*) nur; **just for fun** nur zum Vergnügen; **he's just a child** er ist doch nur ein Kind; **just me and Justine are coming** nur ich und Justine kommen; 5 **just a minute!** einen Moment!; 6 **just coming!** ich komme schon!; 7 (*exactly*) **just as** genauso wie; **he's got just as many friends** er hat genauso viele Freunde.

justice *noun* Gerechtigkeit *die*.

✧ IRREGULAR VERB: *See the verb table in the centre of the dictionary*

K k

kangaroo *noun* Känguru △ *das* (PL *die* Kängurus).

karate *noun* Karate *das*.

kebab *noun* Kebab *der* (PL *die* Kebabs).

keen *adjective* **1** (*enthusiastic or committed*) begeistert; **he's a keen photographer** er ist ein begeisterter Fotograf; **you don't seem too keen** du scheinst nicht gerade begeistert zu sein; **2 to be keen on** mögen ✧; **I'm not keen on fish** ich mag Fisch nicht; **3 to be keen on doing** (*or* **to do**) **something** etwas gerne tun.

keep *verb* **1** behalten ✧; **you can keep the book** du kannst das Buch behalten; **to keep a secret** ein Geheimnis für sich behalten; **2 will you keep my seat?** können Sie meinen Platz freihalten?; **3 to keep somebody waiting** jemanden warten lassen; **4** (*store*) aufbewahren SEP; **can I keep my watch in your desk?** kann ich meine Uhr in deinem Schreibtisch aufbewahren?; **where do you keep saucepans?** wo hast du die Töpfe?; **5** (*not throw away*) aufheben ✧ SEP; **I kept all his letters** ich habe alle seine Briefe aufgehoben; **6 to keep on doing something** etwas weiter tun; **she kept on talking** sie hat weitergeredet; **keep straight on** weiter geradeaus gehen; **7 to keep on doing something** (*time after time*) dauernd etwas tun; **he keeps on ringing me up** er ruft mich dauernd an; **8** (*maintain*) halten ✧; **to keep the food warm** das Essen warm halten; **to keep a promise** ein Versprechen halten; **9** (*stay*) bleiben ✧ (PERF *sein*); **to keep calm** ruhig bleiben; **to keep out of the sun** im Schatten bleiben.

kerb *noun* Randstein *der*.

kettle *noun* Kessel *der* (PL *die* Kessel); **to put the kettle on** Wasser aufsetzen.

key *noun* **1** (*for a lock*) Schlüssel *der* (PL *die* Schlüssel); **bunch of keys** *das* Schlüsselbund; **2** (*on a piano or keyboard*) Taste *die*.

keyboard *noun* (*for a computer*) Tastatur *die* (PL *die* Tastaturen).

keyring *noun* Schlüsselring *der* (PL *die* Schlüsselringe).

kick *noun* **1** (*from a person or a horse*) Tritt *der* (PL *die* Tritte); **to give somebody a kick** jemandem einen Tritt geben; **2** (*in football*) Schuss △ *der* (PL *die* Schüsse); ★ **to get a kick out of doing something** etwas nur zum Spaß tun. *verb* **1 to kick somebody** jemandem einen Tritt geben; **2 to kick the ball** den Ball schießen. ● **to kick off** anstoßen ✧ SEP.

kick-off *noun* Anstoß *der*.

kid *noun* (*child*) Kind *das* (PL *die* Kinder); **Dad's looking after the kids** Vati passt auf die Kinder auf.

kidnap *verb* entführen.

△ NEW SPELLING: *See page xii*

kidney *noun* Niere *die* (PL *die* Nieren).

kill *verb* 1 töten (*an animal*); 2 (*murder*) umbringen ◇ SEP; **he killed the girl** er brachte das Mädchen um; 3 **she was killed in a car accident** sie kam bei einem Autounfall ums Leben.

killer *noun* Mörder *der* (PL *die* Mörder), Mörderin *die* (PL *die* Mörderinnen).

kilo *noun* Kilo *das* (PL *die* Kilo); **a kilo of sugar** ein Kilo Zucker; **ten marks a kilo** zehn Mark das Kilo.

kilogram *noun* Kilogramm *das*.

kilometre *noun* Kilometer *der* (PL *die* Kilometer).

kilt *noun* Kilt *der* (PL *die* Kilts).

kind *noun* 1 Art *die* (PL *die* Arten); **this kind of book** diese Art Buch; **all kinds of people** alle möglichen Leute; 2 (*brand*) Sorte *die* (PL *die* Sorten). *adjective* nett; **she was very kind to me** sie war sehr nett zu mir.

kindness *noun* Freundlichkeit *die*.

king *noun* König *der* (PL *die* Könige); **the king of hearts** der Herzkönig.

kingdom *noun* Königreich *das* (PL *die* Königreiche); **the United Kingdom** das Vereinigte Königreich.

kipper *noun* Räucherhering *der* (PL *die* Räucherheringe).

kiss *noun* Kuss ∆ *der* (PL *die* Küsse); **to give somebody a kiss** jemandem einen Kuss geben. *verb* küssen; **kiss me!** küss mich!;

we kissed each other wir haben uns geküsst.

kit *noun* 1 (*of tools*) Werkzeug *das*; 2 (*in a box*) **a tool kit** ein Werkzeugkasten; 3 (*clothes*) Sachen (*plural*); **where's my football kit?** wo sind meine Fußballsachen?; 4 (*for making a model, a piece of furniture, etc.*) Bausatz *der* (PL *die* Bausätze).

kitchen *noun* Küche *die* (PL *die* Küchen); **the kitchen table** der Küchentisch.

kitchen foil *noun* Alufolie *die*.

kitchen roll *noun* Küchenrolle *die* (PL *die* Küchenrollen).

kite *noun* Drachen *der*; **to fly a kite** einen Drachen steigen lassen.

kitten *noun* Kätzchen *das* (PL *die* Kätzchen).

kiwi fruit *noun* Kiwi *die* (PL *die* Kiwis).

knee *noun* Knie *das* (PL *die* Knie); **on (your) hands and knees** auf allen vieren.

kneel *verb* knien; **to kneel (down)** sich hinknien SEP.

knickers *plural noun* Schlüpfer *der* (PL *die* Schlüpfer); **two pairs of knickers** zwei Schlüpfer.

knife *noun* Messer *das* (PL *die* Messer). *verb* einstechen ◇ SEP auf (+ACC); (*kill*) erstechen ◇.

knight *noun* (*in chess*) Springer *der* (PL *die* Springer).

knit *verb* stricken.

◇ IRREGULAR VERB: *See the verb table in the centre of the dictionary*

knitting *noun* Strickerei *die*.

knob *noun* 1 (*on a door or walking stick*) Knauf *der* (PL *die* Knäufe); 2 (*control on a radio or machine*) Knopf *der* (PL *die* Knöpfe); 3 **knob of butter** *das* Butterklümpchen.

knock *noun* Schlag *der* (PL *die* Schläge); **a knock on the head** ein Schlag auf den Kopf; **a knock at the door** ein Klopfen an der Tür. *verb* 1 (*to bang*) stoßen ◇; **I knocked my arm on the table** ich habe mir den Arm am Tisch gestoßen; 2 **to knock on something** an etwas ←(ACC) klopfen.

● **to knock down** 1 (*in a traffic accident*) anfahren ◇ SEP (*a person*); 2 (*to demolish*) abreißen ◇ SEP (*an old building*).

● **to knock out** 1 (*to make unconscious*) bewusstlos △ schlagen ◇; 2 (*in sport, to eliminate*) k.o. schlagen ◇.

knot *noun* Knoten *der* (PL *die* Knoten); **to tie a knot** einen Knoten machen.

know *verb* 1 (*know a fact*) wissen ◇; **do you know where Tim is?** weißt du, wo Tim ist?; **I know they've moved house** ich weiß, dass sie umgezogen sind; **yes, I know** ja, weiß ich; **you never know!** man kann nie wissen!; **I know how to get to town** ich weiß, wie man in die Stadt kommt; 2 (*be personally acquainted with*) kennen ◇; **do you know the Jacksons?** kennst du die Jacksons?; **all the people I know** alle Leute, die ich kenne; **I don't know his mother** ich kenne seine Mutter

nicht; 3 **to know how to do something** etwas tun können; **Steve knows how to make potato salad** Steve kann Kartoffelsalat machen; **Liz knows how to mend it** Liz kann es reparieren; 4 **to know about** Bescheid wissen über (+ACC) (*items in the news*); 5 **to know about** sich auskennen ◇ SEP mit (*machines, cars, etc.*); **Lindy knows about computers** Lindy kennt sich mit Computern aus; 6 **to get to know somebody** jemanden kennen lernen △.

knowledge *noun* Wissen *das*.

Koran *noun* Koran *der*.

kosher *adjective* koscher.

L l

lab *noun* Labor *das* (PL *die* Labors).

label *noun* Etikett *das* (PL *die* Etikette).

laboratory *noun* Labor *das* (PL *die* Labors).

lace *noun* 1 (*for a shoe*) Schnürsenkel *der* (PL *die* Schnürsenkel); **to tie your laces** sich ←(DAT) die Schnürsenkel binden; 2 (*fabric or trimming*) Spitze *die*.

ladder *noun* 1 (*for climbing*) Leiter *die* (PL *die* Leitern); 2 (*in your tights*) Laufmasche *die* (PL *die* Laufmaschen).

ladies noun (*lavatory*)
Damentoilette *die* (PL *die*
Damentoiletten); (*on a sign*)
'**Ladies**' 'Damen'.

lady noun Dame *die* (PL *die* Damen);
ladies and gentlemen meine
Damen und Herren.

lager noun helle Bier *das* (PL *die*
hellen Biere), Helle *das* (PL *die*
Hellen) (*informal*); **a lager, please**
ein Helles bitte.

laid-back adjective gelassen.

lake noun See *der* (PL *die* Seen); **Lake
Geneva** der Genfer See.

lamb noun Lamm *das* (PL *die*
Lämmer); **leg of lamb** *die*
Lammkeule.

lamp noun Lampe *die* (PL *die*
Lampen).

lamp-post noun
Laternenpfahl *der* (PL *die*
Laternenpfähle).

lampshade noun
Lampenschirm *der* (PL *die*
Lampenschirme).

land noun 1 (*when at sea*) Land *das*;
2 (*property*) Grundstück *das*; **piece
of land** *das* Grundstück.
verb 1 (*plane, passenger*) landen
(PERF *sein*); 2 (*leave a ship*) an Land
gehen.

landing noun 1 (*between flights of
stairs*) Treppenabsatz *der* (PL *die*
Treppenabsätze); (*passage*)
Treppenflur *der*; 2 (*of a plane or
ship*) Landung *die* (PL *die*
Landungen).

landlady noun 1 (*of a house or
room*) Vermieterin *die* (PL *die*

Vermieterinnen); 2 (*of a pub*)
Gastwirtin *die* (PL *die*
Gastwirtinnen).

landlord noun 1 (*of a house or room*)
Vermieter *der* (PL *die* Vermieter);
2 (*of a pub*) Gastwirt *der* (PL *die*
Gastwirte).

lane noun 1 (*small road*) Weg *der*
(PL *die* Wege); 2 (*of a motorway*)
Spur *die* (PL *die* Spuren).

language noun 1 (*German, Italian,
etc.*) Sprache *die* (PL *die* Sprachen);
foreign language *die*
Fremdsprache; 2 (*way of speaking*)
Ausdrucksweise *die*; **bad language**
Kraftausdrücke (*plural*).

lap noun 1 Schoß *der* (PL *die*
Schöße); 2 (*in races*) Runde *die* (PL
die Runden).

laptop noun Laptop *der* (PL *die*
Laptops).

larder noun Speisekammer *die* (PL
die Speisekammern).

large adjective groß.

last adjective letzter/letzte/letztes;
last week letzte Woche; **for the last
time** zum letzten Mal; **last night**
gestern Nacht.
adverb 1 (*in final position*) als
Letzter/als Letzte/als Letztes; **Rob
arrived last** Rob kam als Letzter an;
2 **at last!** endlich!; 3 (*most
recently*) zuletzt; **I last saw him in
May** ich habe ihn zuletzt im Mai
gesehen.
verb dauern; **the film lasted two
hours** der Film dauerte zwei
Stunden.

late *adjective, adverb* 1 spät; **I'm late** ich bin spät dran; **we were five minutes late** wir haben uns fünf Minuten verspätet; **they arrived late** sie sind zu spät angekommen; **to be late for something** zu spät zu etwas ←(DAT) kommen; **we were late for the party** wir kamen zu spät zur Party; 2 **to be late** (*of a bus or train*) Verspätung haben; **the train was an hour late** der Zug hatte eine Stunde Verspätung; 3 (*late in the day*) spät; **we got up late** wir sind spät aufgestanden; **the chemist is open late** die Apotheke hat bis spät auf; **late last night** gestern spät in der Nacht; **too late!** zu spät!

lately *adverb* in letzter Zeit.

later *adverb* später; **I'll explain later** ich erkläre es später; **see you later!** bis später!

latest *adjective* 1 neuester/neueste/ neuestes; **the latest news** die neuesten Nachrichten; 2 **at the latest** spätestens.

Latin *noun* Latein *das*.

laugh *noun* Lachen *das*; **to do something for a laugh** etwas aus Spaß machen.
verb 1 lachen; **everybody laughed** alle haben gelacht; **to laugh about something** über etwas ←(ACC) lachen; 2 **to laugh at somebody** jemanden auslachen SEP; **they'll only laugh at me** sie lachen mich bestimmt aus.

launderette *noun* Waschsalon *der* (PL *die* Waschsalons).

lavatory *noun* Toilette *die* (PL *die* Toiletten); **to go to the lavatory** auf die Toilette gehen.

lavender *noun* Lavendel *der*.

law *noun* 1 Gesetz *das* (PL *die* Gesetze); **to break the law** gegen das Gesetz verstoßen; 2 **it's against the law** das ist verboten; 3 (*subject of study*) Jura (*plural*).

lawn *noun* Rasen *der* (PL *die* Rasen).

lawnmower *noun* Rasenmäher *der* (PL *die* Rasenmäher).

lawyer *noun* Rechtsanwalt *der* (PL *die* Rechtsanwälte), Rechtsanwältin *die* (PL *die* Rechtsanwältinnen).

lay *verb* 1 (*put*) legen; **she laid the cards on the table** sie legte die Karten auf den Tisch; 2 **to lay the table** den Tisch decken.

lay-by *noun* Parkplatz *der* (PL *die* Parkplätze).

layer *noun* Schicht *die* (PL *die* Schichten).

lazy *adjective* faul.

lead[1] *noun* 1 (*when you are ahead*) Führung *die*; **to be in the lead** in Führung liegen; **Baxter's in the lead** Baxter liegt in Führung; **to take the lead** in Führung gehen; 2 (*electric*) Schnur *die* (PL *die* Schnüre); 3 (*for a dog*) Leine *die* (PL *die* Leinen); **on a lead** an der Leine; 4 (*role*) Hauptrolle *die* (PL *die* Hauptrollen); 5 (*an actor*) Hauptdarsteller *der* (PL *die* Hauptdarsteller), Hauptdarstellerin *die* (PL *die* Hauptdarstellerinnen).

△ NEW SPELLING: *See page xii*

verb 1 führen; **the path leads to the sea** der Weg führt zum Meer; **to lead by three points** mit drei Punkten führen; 2 **to lead the way** vorangehen ◇ SEP (PERF *sein*); 3 **to lead to something** zu etwas ←(DAT) führen (*an accident or problems, for example*).

lead² *noun* (*metal*) Blei *das*.

leader *noun* 1 (*of a political party*) Vorsitzende *der/die* (PL die Vorsitzenden); 2 (*of an expedition or group*) Leiter *der* (PL die Leiter), Leiterin *die* (PL die Leiterinnen); 3 (*in a competition*) Erste *der/die* (PL die Ersten); 4 (*of a gang*) Anführer *der* (PL die Anführer), Anführerin *die* (PL die Anführerinnen).

lead singer *noun* Leadsänger *der* (PL die Leadsänger), Leadsängerin *die* (PL die Leadsängerinnen).

leaf *noun* Blatt *das* (PL die Blätter).

leaflet *noun* 1 (*with instructions*) Merkblatt *das* (PL die Merkblätter); 2 (*for advertising*) Reklameblatt *das* (PL die Reklameblätter).

leak *noun* 1 (*in a roof, tent*) undichte Stelle *die* (PL die undichten Stellen); 2 **gas leak** der Gasausfluss △; 3 (*in a boat*) Leck *das* (PL die Lecks). *verb* (*of a bottle or a roof*) undicht sein.

lean *adjective* (*meat*) mager. *verb* 1 **to lean on something** sich an etwas ←(ACC) lehnen; **he leaned against the door** er hat sich gegen die Tür gelehnt; 2 sich lehnen; **she was leaning out of the window** sie

lehnte sich aus dem Fenster; 3 **to lean forward** sich vorbeugen SEP.

leap year *noun* Schaltjahr *das* (PL die Schaltjahre).

learn *verb* lernen; **to learn German** Deutsch lernen; **to learn (how) to drive** Auto fahren lernen.

learner *noun* 1 Lerner *der* (PL die Lerner); **to be a fast learner** schne\[ll\] lernen; 2 (*beginner*) Anfänger *der* (PL die Anfänger), Anfängerin *die* (P\[L\] die Anfängerinnen).

least *adjective, pronoun* 1 wenigster/wenigste/wenigstes; **to have least time** am wenigsten Zeit haben; **Tony has the least money** Tony hat das wenigste Geld; 2 (*the slightest*) geringster/geringste/geringstes; **I haven't the least idea** ich habe nicht die geringste Ahnung. *adverb* 1 am wenigsten; **I like the blue shirt least** ich mag das blaue Hemd am wenigsten; 2 **the least expensive hotel** das billigste Hotel\; 3 **at least** (*at a minimum*) mindestens; **at least twenty people** mindestens zwanzig Leute; 4 **at least** (*at any rate*) wenigstens; **she's a teacher, at least I think she is** sie ist Lehrerin, glaube ich wenigstens.

leather *noun* Leder *das*; **leather jacket** *die* Lederjacke.

leave *noun* Urlaub *der*; **three days\' leave** drei Tage Urlaub. *verb* 1 (*go away*) gehen ◇ (PERF *sein*); (*by car*) fahren ◇ SEP (PERF *sein*); (*a train or bus*) abfahren ◇ SE\[P\]

◇ **IRREGULAR VERB:** *See the verb table in the centre of the dictionary*

PERF *sein*); **they're leaving tomorrow evening** sie fahren morgen Abend; **we left at six** wir sind um sechs Uhr gegangen; **the train leaves Munich at ten** der Zug fährt um zehn Uhr von München ab; **2** (*go away from or go out of*) verlassen ✧; **I left the office at five** ich habe das Büro um fünf verlassen; **he left his wife** er hat seine Frau verlassen; **3** (*deposit or allow to remain in the same state*) lassen ✧; **you can leave your coats in the hall** Sie können Ihre Mäntel in der Diele lassen; **to leave the door open** die Tür offen lassen; **leave it until tomorrow** lass es bis morgen; **4 to leave somebody something** jemandem etwas hinterlassen ✧ (*a message or money*); **he didn't leave a message** er hat keine Nachricht hinterlassen; **5** (*not do*) stehen lassen ✧ Δ; **leave the washing up** lass den Abwasch stehen; **6** (*forget*) vergessen ✧; **he left his umbrella on the train** er hat seinen Regenschirm im Zug vergessen; **7 be left** übrig sein (PERF *sein*); **there are two pancakes left** zwei Pfannkuchen sind noch übrig; **I don't have any money left** ich habe kein Geld mehr übrig; **we have ten minutes left** wir haben noch zehn Minuten Zeit.

ecture *noun* **1** (*at university*) Vorlesung *die* (PL *die* Vorlesungen); **2** (*public*) Vortrag *der* (PL *die* Vorträge).

eek *noun* Lauch *der*.

eft *noun* **on the left** links; **to drive on the left** links fahren; **on my left**

links von mir.
adverb links; **turn left at the church** an der Kirche links abbiegen.
adjective linker/linke/linkes; **his left foot** sein linker Fuß.

left-hand *adjective* **the left-hand side** die linke Seite.

left-handed *adjective* linkshändig.

leg *noun* **1** Bein *das* (PL *die* Beine); **my left leg** mein linkes Bein; **to break your leg** sich ←(DAT) das Bein brechen; **2** (*in cooking*) Keule *die* (PL *die* Keulen); **leg of lamb** die Lammkeule; ★ **to pull somebody's leg** jemanden auf den Arm nehmen.

leggings *plural noun* Leggings (*plural*).

leisure *noun* Freizeit *die*; **in my leisure time** in meiner Freizeit.

lemon *noun* Zitrone *die* (PL *die* Zitronen).

lemonade *noun* Limonade *die* (PL *die* Limonaden).

lemon juice *noun* Zitronensaft *der* (PL *die* Zitronensäfte).

lend *verb* leihen ✧; **to lend something to somebody** jemandem etwas leihen; **I lent Judy my bike** ich habe Judy mein Rad geliehen; **will you lend it to me?** kannst du es mir leihen?

length *noun* Länge *die* (PL *die* Längen).

lens *noun* **1** (*in a camera*) Objektiv *das* (PL *die* Objektive); **2** (*in spectacles*) Brillenglas *das* (PL *die* Brillengläser); **3 contact lenses** Kontaktlinsen (*plural*).

Lent *noun* Fastenzeit *die*.

lentil *noun* Linse *die* (PL die Linsen).

less *pronoun, adjective, adverb* weniger (*'weniger' never changes*); **Ben eats less** Ben isst weniger; **less time** weniger Zeit; **less than** weniger als; **less than three hours** weniger als drei Stunden; **you spent less than me** du hast weniger als ich ausgegeben; **less and less** immer weniger.

lesson *noun* (*class*) Stunde *die* (PL die Stunden); **German lesson** *die* Deutschstunde; **driving lesson** *die* Fahrstunde.

let¹ *verb* 1 (*allow*) lassen ✧; **to let somebody do something** jemanden etwas tun lassen; **she lets me drive her car** sie lässt mich mit ihrem Auto fahren; **the police let us through** die Polizei hat uns durchgelassen; **let me in** lass mich herein; 2 (*as a suggestion or a command*) **let's go!** gehen wir!; **let's not talk about it** reden wir nicht mehr darüber; **let's eat out** essen wir im Restaurant.

● **to let off** 1 hochgehen lassen ✧ (*fireworks*); 2 (*to excuse from*) befreien von (+DAT) (*homework*).

let² *verb* (*to rent out*) vermieten; **'flat to let'** 'Wohnung zu vermieten'.

letter *noun* 1 Brief *der* (PL die Briefe); **a letter for you from Delia** ein Brief für dich von Delia; 2 (*of the alphabet*) Buchstabe *der* (PL die Buchstaben).

letter box *noun* Briefkasten *der* (PL die Briefkästen).

lettuce *noun* Salat *der*; **two lettuces** zwei Kopf Salat.

level *noun* Höhe *die*; **at eye level** in Augenhöhe.
adjective 1 eben (*ground or floor*); 2 (*horizontal*) waagerecht (*shelf*); 3 (*at the same height*) auf gleicher Höhe; **to be level with the ground** auf gleicher Höhe mit dem Boden sein.

level crossing *noun* Bahnübergang *der* (PL die Bahnübergänge).

lever *noun* Hebel *der* (PL die Hebel).

liar *noun* Lügner *der* (PL die Lügner), Lügnerin *die* (PL die Lügnerinnen).

liberal *adjective* 1 tolerant; 2 (*in politics*) liberal; **the Liberal Democrats** *die* Liberaldemokraten.

Libra *noun* Waage *die*; **Sean's Libra** Sean ist Waage.

librarian *noun* Bibliothekar *der* (PL die Bibliothekare), Bibliothekarin *die* (PL die Bibliothekarinnen).

library *noun* Bibliothek *die* (PL die Bibliotheken); **public library** *die* öffentliche Bücherei.

licence *noun* 1 (*for a TV*) Genehmigung *die* (PL die Genehmigungen); 2 (*driving licence*) Führerschein *der* (PL die Führerscheine).

lick *verb* lecken.

lid *noun* Deckel *der* (PL die Deckel).

lie *noun* Lüge *die* (PL die Lügen); **to tell a lie** (*or* **lies**) lügen ✧.
verb 1 (*to be stretched out*) liegen ✧

✧ IRREGULAR VERB: *See the verb table in the centre of the dictionary*

he's lying on the sofa er liegt auf dem Sofa; **my coat lay on the bed** mein Mantel lag auf dem Bett; **2 to lie down** (*for a rest*) sich hinlegen SEP; **I'm going to lie down for a little** ich lege mich ein bisschen hin; **3** (*tell lies*) lügen ✧.

lie-in *noun* **to have a lie-in** ausschlafen ✧ SEP.

life *noun* Leben *das* (PL die Leben); **all her life** ihr ganzes Leben lang; **full of life** voller Leben; **that's life!** so ist das Leben!

life-style *noun* Lebensstil *der* (PL die Lebensstile).

lift *noun* **1** Aufzug *der* (PL die Aufzüge); **let's take the lift** fahren wir mit dem Aufzug; **2** (*a ride*) **to give somebody a lift to the station** jemanden zum Bahnhof mitnehmen ✧ SEP; **Khaled's giving me a lift** Khaled nimmt mich mit; **would you like a lift?** möchtest du mitfahren?
verb hochheben ✧ SEP; **he lifted the box** er hob die Kiste hoch.

light *noun* **1** Licht *das*; **will you turn the light on?** kannst du das Licht anmachen?; **to turn off the light** das Licht ausmachen; **are your lights on?** hast du Licht an?; **2** (*in the street*) Straßenlampe *die* (PL die Straßenlampen); **3** (*a lamp*) Lampe *die* (PL die Lampen); **4 traffic lights** die Ampel (*singular*); **the lights are green** die Ampel ist grün; **5** (*for a cigarette*) **have you got a light?** hast du Feuer?
adjective **1** (*not dark*) hell; **a light blue dress** ein hellblaues Kleid; **it**

gets light at six es wird um sechs hell; **2** (*not heavy*) leicht; **a light coat** ein leichter Mantel; **a light breeze** eine leichte Brise.
verb **1** anzünden SEP (*the fire, a match, the gas*); **we lit a fire** wir zündeten ein Feuer an; **2 to light a cigarette** sich ←(DAT) eine Zigarette anzünden.

light bulb *noun* Glühbirne *die* (PL die Glühbirnen).

lighter *noun* Feuerzeug *das* (PL die Feuerzeuge).

lightning *noun* Blitz *der*; **flash of lightning** der Blitz; **to be struck by lightning** vom Blitz getroffen werden.

like[1] *preposition, conjunction* **1** wie; **like me** wie ich; **like a duck** wie eine Ente; **like I said** wie gesagt; **what's it like?** wie ist es?; **what was the weather like?** wie war das Wetter?; **2 like this/that** so; **3** ähnlich (+DAT); **to look like somebody** jemandem ähnlich sehen; **Cindy looks like her father** Cindy sieht ihrem Vater ähnlich.

like[2] *verb* **1** mögen ✧; **I like vegetables** ich mag Gemüse; **I don't like meat** ich mag Fleisch nicht; **I like Dürer best** ich mag Dürer am liebsten; **2 to like doing something** etwas gerne tun; **Mum likes reading** Mutti liest gerne; **3 I would like …** ich möchte gerne …; **would you like a coffee?** möchten Sie einen Kaffee?; **what would you like to eat?** was möchten Sie essen?; **yes, if you like** ja, wenn du willst; **4 I like**

△ NEW SPELLING: *See page xii*

the dress das Kleid gefällt mir; **how do you like it?** wie gefällt es dir?

likely *adjective* wahrscheinlich; **she's likely to phone** wahrscheinlich ruft sie an.

lime *noun* Kalk *der.*

limit *noun* Grenze *die* (PL *die* Grenzen); **speed limit** *die* Geschwindigkeitsbeschränkung.

limp *noun* **to have a limp** hinken.

line *noun* 1 Linie *die* (PL *die* Linien); **a straight line** eine gerade Linie; **to draw a line** eine Linie ziehen; 2 (*in writing*) Zeile *die* (PL *die* Zeilen); **six lines of text** sechs Zeilen Text; 3 (*railway*) Bahnlinie *die* (PL *die* Bahnlinien) (*from one place to another*); **on the line** (*the track*) auf der Strecke; 4 (*a queue of people or cars*) Schlange *die* (PL *die* Schlangen); **to stand in line** Schlange stehen; 5 (*telephone*) Leitung *die* (PL *die* Leitungen); **the line's bad** die Verbindung ist schlecht; **hold the line, please** bitte bleiben Sie am Apparat. *verb* füttern (*a coat*).

linen *noun* Leinen *das;* **a linen jacket** eine Leinenjacke.

lining *noun* Futter *das* (PL *die* Futter).

link *noun* Verbindung *die* (PL *die* Verbindungen); **what's the link between the two?** was für eine Verbindung besteht zwischen den beiden? *verb* verbinden ✧ (*two places*); **the two towns are linked by a railway line** die beiden Städte sind durch eine Bahnlinie miteinander verbunden.

lion *noun* Löwe *der* (PL *die* Löwen).

lip *noun* Lippe *die* (PL *die* Lippen).

lip-read *verb* von den Lippen lesen ✧.

lipstick *noun* Lippenstift *der* (PL *die* Lippenstifte).

liquid *noun* Flüssigkeit *die* (PL *die* Flüssigkeiten). *adjective* flüssig.

list *noun* Liste *die* (PL *die* Listen).

listen *verb* 1 zuhören SEP; **I wasn't listening** ich habe nicht zugehört; **to listen to somebody** jemandem zuhören; **you're not listening to me** du hörst mir nicht zu; 2 **to listen to something** etwas ←(ACC) hören; **to listen to the radio** Radio hören.

listener *noun* (*to the radio*) Hörer *der* (PL *die* Hörer), Hörerin *die* (PL *die* Hörerinnen).

litre *noun* Liter *der* (PL *die* Liter); **a litre of milk** ein Liter Milch.

litter *noun* (*rubbish*) Abfall *der.*

litter bin *noun* Abfalleimer *der* (PL *die* Abfalleimer).

little *adjective, pronoun* 1 (*small*) klein; **a little boy** ein kleiner Junge; **a little break** eine kleine Pause; 2 (*not much*) wenig; **we have very little time** wir haben sehr wenig Zeit; 3 **a little** ein wenig; **we have a little left** wir haben ein wenig übrig; 4 **just a little, please** nur ein bisschen, bitte; **it's a little late** es ist ein bisschen spät;

✧ IRREGULAR VERB: *See the verb table in the centre of the dictionary*

a little more ein bisschen mehr; **a little less** ein bisschen weniger; ★ **little by little** nach und nach.

live¹ *verb* **1** (*in a house or town*) wohnen; **she lives in York** sie wohnt in York; **we live in a flat** wir wohnen in einer Wohnung; **2** (*be or stay alive, spend one's life*) leben; **we're living in the country now** wir leben jetzt auf dem Land; **they live on fruit** sie leben von Obst; **they live apart** sie leben getrennt.

live² *adjective, adverb* **1** live (*broadcast*); **a live programme** eine Livesendung; **live music** *die* Livemusik; **a broadcast live from Wembley** eine Übertragung live aus Wembley; **to broadcast a concert live** ein Konzert live senden; **2** (*alive*) lebend.

lively *adjective* lebhaft.

liver *noun* Leber *die* (PL *die* Lebern).

living *noun* Lebensunterhalt *der*; **to earn a living** sich ←(DAT) seinen Lebensunterhalt verdienen.

living room *noun* Wohnzimmer *das* (PL *die* Wohnzimmer).

load *noun* **1** (*on a lorry*) Ladung *die* (PL *die* Ladungen); **a (lorry-)load of bricks** eine Ladung Ziegelsteine; **2 a bus-load of tourists** ein Bus voll Touristen; **3 loads of** massenhaft (*informal*); **loads of tourists** massenhaft Touristen; **they've got loads of money** die haben einen Haufen Geld (*informal*).
verb **1** beladen ✧ (*a vehicle*);

2 to load a camera einen Film einlegen SEP.

loaf *noun* Brot *das* (PL *die* Brote); **a loaf of white bread** ein Weißbrot.

loathe *verb* hassen; **I loathe getting up early** ich hasse es, früh aufzustehen.

local *noun* **1** (*a pub*) Stammkneipe *die* (PL *die* Stammkneipen); **2 the locals** (*people*) die Einheimischen. *adjective* **1** hiesig; **the local library** die hiesige Bücherei; **2 local newspaper** *die* Lokalzeitung.

lock *noun* Schloss △ *das* (PL *die* Schlösser). *verb* abschließen ✧ SEP (*a door, room, or bicycle*); **have you locked the door?** hast du abgeschlossen?

lodger *noun* Untermieter *der* (PL *die* Untermieter), Untermieterin *die* (PL *die* Untermieterinnen).

loft *noun* Dachboden *der* (PL *die* Dachböden).

log *noun* **1** Baumstamm *der* (PL *die* Baumstämme); **2** (*as firewood*) Holzscheit *das* (PL *die* Holzscheite); **a log fire** ein offenes Feuer.

lollipop *noun* Lutscher *der* (PL *die* Lutscher).

London *noun* London *das*.

Londoner *noun* Londoner *der* (PL *die* Londoner), Londonerin *die* (PL *die* Londonerinnen).

lonely *adjective* einsam; **to feel lonely** sich einsam fühlen.

△ NEW SPELLING: *See page xii*

long *adjective, adverb* **1** lang; **a long film** ein langer Film; **a long day** ein langer Tag; **it's five metres long** es ist fünf Meter lang; **the film is an hour long** der Film dauert eine Stunde; **2 a long time** lange; **he stayed for a long time** er ist lange geblieben; **I've been here for a long time** ich bin schon lange hier; **a long time ago** vor langer Zeit; **this won't take long** das dauert nicht lange; **3 how long?** wie lange?; **how long have you been here?** wie lange sind Sie schon hier?; **long ago** vor langer Zeit; **4 a long way** weit; **it's a long way to the cinema** bis zum Kino ist es weit; **5 all night long** die ganze Nacht; **6 no longer** nicht mehr; **he doesn't work here any longer** er arbeitet nicht mehr hier.
verb **to long to do something** sich danach sehnen, etwas zu tun; **I'm longing to see you** ich sehne mich danach, dich zu sehen.

long jump *noun* Weitsprung *der*.

longlife milk *noun* H-Milch *die*.

loo *noun* Klo *das* (PL *die* Klos) (*informal*).

look *noun* **1** (*a glance*) Blick *der* (PL *die* Blicke); **to take a look at somebody** einen Blick auf jemanden werfen; **2** (*a tour*) **to have a look at the school** sich ←(DAT) die Schule ansehen; **to have a look round the town** sich ←(DAT) die Stadt ansehen; **3 to have a look for** suchen.
verb **1** sehen ✧; **to look out of the window** aus dem Fenster sehen; **I**

wasn't looking ich habe nicht hingesehen; **2 to look at** ansehen ✧ SEP; **he looked at the girl** er hat das Mädchen angesehen; **to look at something** sich ←(DAT) etwas ansehen; **I'm looking at the photos** ich sehe mir die Fotos an; **3** (*to seem*) aussehen ✧ SEP; **she looks sad** sie sieht traurig aus; **the salad looks delicious** der Salat sieht köstlich aus; **to look like** aussehen wie; **what does the house look like?** wie sieht das Haus aus?; **4** (*resemble*) **to look like somebody** jemandem ähnlich sehen; **she looks like her aunt** sie sieht ihrer Tante ähnlich; **they look like each other** sie sehen sich ähnlich.

● **to look after 1** sich kümmern um (+ACC); **Dad's looking after the children** Vati kümmert sich um die Kinder; **2** aufpassen SEP auf (+ACC) (*luggage*).

● **to look for** suchen; **I'm looking for my keys** ich suche meine Schlüssel.

● **to look forward to** sich freuen auf (+ACC) (*a party or a trip, for example*).

● **to look out** (*to be careful*) aufpassen SEP; **look out, it's hot!** pass auf, das ist heiß!

● **to look up** nachschlagen ✧ SEP (*in a dictionary or directory*); **he's looking it up in the dictionary** er schlägt es im Wörterbuch nach.

loose *adjective* **1** (*screw or knot*) locker; **2** (*garment*) weit; **3 loose change** *das* Kleingeld; ★ **I'm at a loose end** ich habe nichts zu tun.

lorry *noun* Lastwagen *der* (PL *die* Lastwagen).

lorry driver *noun*
Lastwagenfahrer *der* (PL *die* Lastwagenfahrer).

lose *verb* 1 verlieren ✧; **we lost** wir haben verloren; **we lost the match** wir haben das Spiel verloren; **Sam's lost his watch** Sam hat seine Uhr verloren; 2 **to get lost** sich verlaufen ✧; **we got lost in the woods** wir haben uns im Wald verlaufen; 3 **to lose weight** abnehmen ✧ SEP.

loss *noun* Verlust *der* (PL *die* Verluste).

lost property *noun* Fundsachen (*plural*).

lot *noun* 1 **a lot** viel; **Wilbur eats a lot** Wilbur isst viel; **I spent a lot** ich habe viel ausgegeben; **he's a lot better** es geht ihm viel besser; **a lot of** viel; **a lot of coffee** viel Kaffee; 2 (*many*) **a lot of** viele; **a lot of books** viele Bücher; 3 **lots of** eine Menge (*informal*); **lots of people** eine Menge Leute.

lottery *noun* Lotterie *die* (PL *die* Lotterien); **to win the lottery** in der Lotterie gewinnen.

loud *adjective* 1 laut; **in a loud voice** mit lauter Stimme; 2 **to say something out loud** etwas laut sagen.

loudly *adverb* laut.

loudspeaker *noun* Lautsprecher *der* (PL *die* Lautsprecher).

lounge *noun* 1 (*in a house*) Wohnzimmer *das* (PL *die* Wohnzimmer); 2 (*in a hotel or an airport*) Halle *die* (PL *die* Hallen); **departure lounge** *die* Abflughalle.

love *noun* 1 Liebe *die*; **for love** aus Liebe; 2 **to be in love with somebody** in jemanden verliebt sein; **she's in love with Jake** sie ist in Jake verliebt; 3 **Gina sends her love** Gina lässt grüßen; **with love from Charlie** herzliche Grüße von Charlie; 4 (*in tennis*) null.
verb 1 lieben (*a person*); **I love you** ich liebe dich; 2 sehr gerne mögen ✧ (*a place or food*); **she loves London** sie mag London sehr gerne; **Wayne loves chocolate** Wayne mag Schokolade sehr gerne; 3 **to love doing something** etwas sehr gerne tun; **I love dancing** ich tanze sehr gerne; 4 **I'd love to come** ich würde sehr gerne kommen.

lovely *adjective* schön; **a lovely dress** ein schönes Kleid; **we had lovely weather** wir hatten schönes Wetter; **we had a lovely day** es war sehr schön.

low *adjective* 1 niedrig; **a low table** ein niedriger Tisch; **at a low price** zu einem niedrigen Preis; 2 (*not loud*) leise; **in a low voice** mit leiser Stimme.

lower *adjective* (*not as high*) tiefer.
verb senken.

luck *noun* 1 Glück *das*; **good luck!** viel Glück!; **with a bit of luck** wenn wir Glück haben; 2 **bad luck!** so ein Pech!

luckily *adverb* zum Glück; **luckily for them** zu ihrem Glück.

△ NEW SPELLING: *See page xii*

lucky *adjective* **1 to be lucky** Glück haben; **we were lucky** wir haben Glück gehabt; **2 to be lucky** (*bringing luck*) Glück bringen; **it's supposed to be lucky** es soll Glück bringen; **my lucky number** meine Glückszahl.

luggage *noun* Gepäck *das*; **my luggage is in the boot** mein Gepäck ist im Kofferraum.

lump *noun* **1** Klumpen *der* (PL die Klumpen); **2** (*of sugar or butter*) Stück *das* (PL die Stücke).

lunch *noun* Mittagessen *das* (PL die Mittagessen); **to have lunch** zu Mittag essen; **we had lunch in Oxford** wir haben in Oxford zu Mittag gegessen.

lunch break *noun* Mittagspause *die* (PL die Mittagspausen).

lunch hour, lunch time *noun* Mittagszeit *die*.

lung *noun* Lungenflügel *der*; **lungs** die Lunge (*singular*).

luxurious *adjective* luxuriös.

lyrics *plural noun* Text *der*.

M m

mac *noun* Regenmantel *der* (PL die Regenmäntel).

macaroni *noun* Makkaroni (*plural*).

machine *noun* **1** Maschine *die* (PL die Maschinen); **2** (*a slot machine*) Automat *der* (PL die Automaten).

mackerel *noun* Makrele *die* (PL die Makrelen).

mad *adjective* **1** verrückt; **she's completely mad!** sie ist total verrückt!; **2** (*angry*) wütend; **to be mad at somebody** wütend auf jemanden sein; **3 to be mad about something** ganz verrückt auf etwas ←(ACC) sein; **she's mad about horses** sie ist ganz verrückt auf Pferde.

madman *noun* Verrückte *der* (PL die Verrückten).

madness *noun* Wahnsinn *der*.

magazine *noun* Zeitschrift *die* (PL die Zeitschriften); (*with mostly photos*) Magazin *das* (PL die Magazine).

magic *noun* Zauber *der*; (*conjuring tricks*) Zauberei *die*. *adjective* **1** Zauber-; **magic wand** *der* Zauberstab; **2** (*great*) super (*informal*).

magician *noun* **1** (*wizard*) Zauberer *der* (PL die Zauberer); **2** (*conjurer*) Zauberkünstler *der* (PL die Zauberkünstler).

magnifying glass *noun* Lupe *die* (PL die Lupen).

maiden name *noun* Mädchenname *der* (PL die Mädchennamen).

mail *noun* Post *die*.

mail order *noun* Bestellung per Post *die*; **to buy something by mail**

order etwas bei einem Versandhaus bestellen; **mail order catalogue** *der* Versandhauskatalog.

main *adjective* Haupt-; **main entrance** *der* Haupteingang.

mainly *adverb* hauptsächlich.

main road *noun* Hauptstraße *die* (PL *die* Hauptstraßen).

major *adjective* 1 (*important*) groß; 2 (*serious*) schwer; **a major accident** ein schwerer Unfall.

Majorca *noun* Mallorca *das*.

majority *noun* Mehrheit *die*.

make *noun* Marke *die* (PL *die* Marken); **the make of a car** die Automarke.
verb 1 machen; **to make a meal** Essen machen; **I made breakfast** ich habe Frühstück gemacht; **she made her bed** sie hat ihr Bett gemacht; **to make somebody happy** jemanden glücklich machen; **it makes you tired** das macht einen müde; 2 herstellen SEP; **they make computers** sie stellen Computer her; **'made in Germany'** 'in Deutschland hergestellt'; 3 **he made me wait** er ließ mich warten; **she makes me laugh** sie bringt mich zum Lachen; 4 verdienen; **he makes forty pounds a day** er verdient vierzig Pfund pro Tag; **to make a living** seinen Lebensunterhalt verdienen; 5 (*force*) zwingen ◇; **to make somebody do something** jemanden zwingen, etwas zu tun; **she made him give the money back** sie hat ihn gezwungen, das

Geld zurückzugeben; 6 (*the verb 'make' is often translated by a more specific verb*) **to make a cake** einen Kuchen backen; **to make a phone call** telefonieren; **to make a dress** ein Kleid nähen; 7 **to make friends with somebody** sich mit jemandem anfreunden SEP; 8 **I can't make it tonight** ich kann heute Abend nicht kommen; 9 **two and three make five** zwei und drei ist fünf.

● **to make something up** 1 etwas erfinden ◇; **she made up an excuse** sie hat eine Ausrede erfunden; 2 **to make it up** (*after a quarrel*) sich versöhnen; **they've made it up again** sie haben sich wieder versöhnt.

make-up *noun* 1 Make-up *das*; **I don't wear make-up** ich trage kein Make-up; 2 **to put on your make-up** sich schminken; **Jo's putting on her make-up** Jo schminkt sich.

male *adjective* 1 männlich; **male voice** *die* Männerstimme; 2 **male animal** *das* Männchen; **male rat** *das* Rattenmännchen; 3 **male student** *der* Student.

male chauvinist *noun* Chauvi *der* (PL *die* Chauvis) (*informal*).

man *noun* 1 Mann *der* (PL *die* Männer); **an old man** ein alter Mann; 2 (*the human race*) der Mensch.

manage *verb* 1 leiten (*a business, team*); **she manages a travel agency** sie leitet ein Reisebüro; 2 (*cope*) zurechtkommen ◇ SEP (PERF *sein*); **I can manage** ich komme schon zurecht; **3 to manage to do something** es schaffen, etwas zu tun; **he managed to push the door open** er hat es geschafft, die Tür aufzustoßen; **I didn't manage to get in touch with her** ich habe es nicht geschafft, sie zu erreichen.

management noun
1 Management das (PL die Managements); **management course** der Managementkurs;
2 Leitung die.

manager noun 1 (of a company or bank) Direktor der (PL die Direktoren); 2 (of a shop or restaurant) Geschäftsführer der (PL die Geschäftsführer); 3 (in football) Trainer der (PL die Trainer); 4 (in entertainment) Manager der (PL die Manager).

manageress noun (of a shop or restaurant) Geschäftsführerin die (PL die Geschäftsführerinnen).

mania noun Manie die (PL die Manien).

maniac noun Wahnsinnige der/die (PL die Wahnsinnigen); **she drives like a maniac** sie fährt wie eine Wahnsinnige.

man-made adjective **man-made fibre** die Kunstfaser.

manner noun 1 **in a manner of speaking** mehr oder weniger;
2 **manners** Manieren (plural); **to have good manners** gute Manieren haben; **it's bad manners to talk like that** es gehört sich nicht, so zu reden.

mantelpiece noun Kaminsims der (PL die Kaminsimse).

manual noun Handbuch das (PL die Handbücher).

manufacture verb herstellen SEP.

manufacturer noun Hersteller der (PL die Hersteller).

many adjective, pronoun 1 viele; **does she have many friends?** hat sie viele Freunde?; **we didn't see many people** wir haben nicht viele Leute gesehen; **not many** nicht viele; **many of them forgot** viele haben es vergessen; **there were too many people** es waren zu viele (Leute) da; **how many?** wie viele?; **how many were there?** wie viele waren da?; **how many sisters have you got?** wie viele Schwestern hast du?; **how many are there left?** wie viele sind übrig geblieben?; **I've never had so many presents** ich habe noch nie so viele Geschenke bekommen; 2 (a lot) **so many** so viel; **I have so many things to do** ich habe so viel zu tun; 3 (as much as) **as many as** so viel wie; **take as many as you like** nimm so viel wie du willst; 4 (too much) **that's far too many** das ist viel zu viel.

map noun 1 Karte die (PL die Karten); 2 (of a town) Stadtplan (PL die Stadtpläne).

marathon noun Marathonlauf der (PL die Marathonläufe).

marble noun 1 Marmor der;
2 (for playing) Murmel die (PL die Murmeln); **to play marbles** Murmeln spielen.

March noun März der; **in March** im März.

march noun Marsch der (PL die Märsche).
verb marschieren (PERF sein).

mare noun Stute die (PL die Stuten).

margarine noun Margarine die.

margin noun Rand der (PL die Ränder).

marijuana noun Marihuana das.

mark noun 1 (at school) Note die (PL die Noten); **I got a good mark in German** ich habe eine gute Note in Deutsch bekommen; 2 (stain) Fleck der (PL die Flecke); 3 (German money) Mark die (PL die Mark).
verb 1 korrigieren; **the teacher marks our homework** die Lehrerin korrigiert unsere Hausaufgaben; 2 (in sports) decken.

market noun Markt der (PL die Märkte).

marketing noun Marketing das.

marmalade noun Orangenmarmelade die.

maroon adjective kastanienbraun.

marriage noun 1 Ehe die; 2 (wedding) Hochzeit die (PL die Hochzeiten).

married adjective 1 verheiratet; **they've been married for twenty years** sie sind seit zwanzig Jahren verheiratet; 2 **married couple** das Ehepaar.

marry verb 1 **to marry somebody** jemanden heiraten; **she married a Frenchman** sie hat einen Franzosen geheiratet; 2 **to get married**

heiraten; **they got married in July** sie haben im Juli geheiratet.

marvellous adjective wunderbar.

marzipan noun Marzipan das.

mascara noun Wimperntusche die.

masculine noun (in German and other grammars) männlich.

mash verb stampfen.

mashed potatoes plural noun Kartoffelbrei der (singular).

mask noun Maske die (PL die Masken).

mass noun 1 **a mass of** eine Menge; 2 **masses of** massenhaft (informal); **they've got masses of money** sie haben massenhaft Geld; **there's masses left over** es ist massenhaft übrig geblieben; 3 (religious) Messe die (PL die Messen); **to go to mass** zur Messe gehen.

massage noun Massage die (PL die Massagen).

massive adjective riesig.

master verb 1 meistern; 2 **to master a language** eine Sprache beherrschen.

mat noun 1 (doormat) Matte die (PL die Matten); 2 (to put under a hot dish) Untersetzer der (PL die Untersetzer); 3 **table mat** das Platzdeckchen.

match noun 1 (for lighting) Streichholz das (PL die Streichhölzer); **box of matches** die Streichholzschachtel; 2 (in sports)

Spiel das (PL die Spiele); **football match** das Fußballspiel; **to watch the match** das Spiel sehen; **to win the match** das Spiel gewinnen; **to lose the match** das Spiel verlieren. *verb* passen zu (+DAT); **the jacket matches the skirt** die Jacke passt zu dem Rock.

mate noun Freund der (PL die Freunde); **I'm going to the pub with my mates** ich gehe mit meinen Freunden in die Kneipe.

material noun 1 (*fabric, also information*) Stoff der (PL die Stoffe); 2 (*substance*) Material das (PL die Materialien).

mathematics noun Mathematik die.

maths noun Mathe die (*informal*); **I like maths** ich mag Mathe gerne; **Anna's good at maths** Anna ist gut in Mathe.

matter noun **what's the matter?** was ist los? *verb* 1 **that's what matters most** das ist am wichtigsten; **it matters a lot to me** es ist mir sehr wichtig; **does it really matter?** ist das wirklich so wichtig?; 2 **it doesn't matter** es macht nichts; **it doesn't matter if it rains** es macht nichts, wenn es regnet; 3 **you can write it in German or English, it doesn't matter** du kannst es auf Deutsch oder Englisch schreiben, das ist egal; 4 **to matter to somebody** jemandem etwas ausmachen SEP; **does it matter to you if I leave earlier?** macht es dir etwas aus, wenn ich früher gehe?

mattress noun Matratze die (PL d Matratzen).

May noun Mai der; **in May** im Ma

may verb 1 **she may be ill** vielleic ist sie krank; **we may go to Spain** wir fahren vielleicht nach Spanien; 2 (*expressing permission*) dürfen ◆ **may I close the door?** darf ich die Tür zumachen?

maybe adverb vielleicht; **maybe they've got lost** vielleicht haben s sich verlaufen.

May Day noun der Erste Mai.

mayonnaise noun Majonäse △ d

mayor noun Bürgermeister der (P die Bürgermeister), Bürgermeister die (PL die Bürgermeisterinnen).

me pronoun (*in German this prono changes according to the function i has in the sentence or the prepositi it follows*) 1 (*as a direct object in t accusative*) mich; **she knows me** sie kennt mich; 2 (*after a preposition that takes the accusati* mich; **they left without me** sie sin ohne mich abgefahren; **wait for m** warte auf mich!; 3 (*as an indirect object or following a verb that take the dative*) mir; **can you give me your address?** kannst du mir dei Adresse geben?; **he helped me** er hat mir geholfen; 4 (*after a preposition that takes the dative*) mir; **she never talks to me** sie re nie mit mir; 5 (*in comparisons*) th me als ich; **she's older than me** ist älter als ich; 6 (*in the nominative*) ich; **it's me** ich bin's **not me** ich nicht.

meal noun 1 Essen das (PL die Essen); **to cook a meal** Essen kochen; 2 **to go for a meal** essen gehen.

mean verb 1 (signify) bedeuten; **what does that mean?** was bedeutet das?; 2 (intend to say) meinen; 3 **what do you mean?** was meinst du?; **that's not what I meant** das habe ich nicht gemeint; 4 **to mean to do something** etwas tun wollen; **I meant to phone my mother** ich wollte meine Mutter anrufen; 5 **to be meant to do something** etwas tun sollen; **she was meant to be here at six** sie sollte um sechs hier sein.
adjective 1 (with money) geizig; 2 (unkind) gemein; **she's really mean to her brother** sie ist richtig gemein zu ihrem Bruder; **what a mean thing to do!** das ist gemein!

meaning noun Bedeutung die (PL die Bedeutungen).

means noun 1 Mittel das (PL die Mittel); **means of transport** das Verkehrsmittel; 2 **a means of** eine Möglichkeit; **a means of earning money** eine Möglichkeit, Geld zu verdienen; 3 **by means of** mit Hilfe (+GEN); 4 **by all means!** selbstverständlich!

meantime adverb **for the meantime** einstweilen; **in the meantime** in der Zwischenzeit.

measles noun Masern (plural).

measure verb messen ◇.

measurements plural noun Maße (plural); **the measurements of the**

room die Maße des Zimmers; **my measurements** meine Maße.

meat noun Fleisch das.

mechanic noun Mechaniker der (PL die Mechaniker), Mechanikerin die (PL die Mechanikerinnen).

mechanical adjective mechanisch.

medal noun Medaille die (PL die Medaillen); **the gold medal** die Goldmedaille.

media noun **the media** die Medien (plural).

medical noun 1 ärztliche Untersuchung die (PL die ärztlichen Untersuchungen); 2 **to have a medical** sich untersuchen lassen.
adjective 1 medizinisch; 2 ärztlich (examination, treatment).

medicine noun 1 (drug) Medikament das (PL die Medikamente); 2 (subject of study) Medizin die; **she's studying medicine** sie studiert Medizin; 3 **alternative medicine** die Alternativmedizin.

Mediterranean noun **the Mediterranean (Sea)** das Mittelmeer.

medium adjective mittlerer/mittlere/mittleres.

medium-sized adjective mittelgroß.

meet verb 1 (by chance) treffen ◇; **I met Rosie at the baker's** ich habe Rosie beim Bäcker getroffen; 2 (by appointment) sich treffen mit (+DAT); **I'll meet you outside the cinema** ich treffe mich mit dir vor dem Kino; 3 sich treffen; **we're**

△ NEW SPELLING: See page xii

meeting at six wir treffen uns um sechs; **4** (*get to know*) kennen lernen△; **I met a German girl last week** ich habe letzte Woche eine Deutsche kennen gelernt; **5 I've never met Oskar** ich kenne Oskar nicht; **6** (*off a train or bus, for example*) abholen SEP; **my dad's meeting me at the station** mein Vater holt mich vom Bahnhof ab.

meeting *noun* **1** (*by arrangement*) Treffen *das* (PL die Treffen); **2** (*in business*) Besprechung *die* (PL die Besprechungen); **she's in a meeting** sie ist in einer Besprechung; **3** (*by chance, in sports*) Begegnung *die* (PL die Begegnungen).

melon *noun* Melone *die* (PL die Melonen).

melt *verb* **1** schmelzen ✧ (PERF *sein*); **the snow has melted** der Schnee ist geschmolzen; **2** (*in cookery*) zerlassen ✧ (*butter, fat*); **melt the butter in a saucepan** Butter im Topf zerlassen.

member *noun* Mitglied *das* (PL die Mitglieder).

Member of Parliament *noun* Abgeordnete *der/die* (PL die Abgeordneten).

membership *noun* Mitgliedschaft *die*.

membership card *noun* Mitgliedskarte *die* (PL die Mitgliedskarten).

membership fee *noun* Mitgliedsbeitrag *der* (PL die Mitgliedsbeiträge).

memorize *verb* **to memorize something** etwas auswendig lernen.

memory *noun* **1** (*of a person*) Gedächtnis *das*; **you have a good memory** du hast ein gutes Gedächtnis; **2** (*of the past*) Erinnerung *die* (PL die Erinnerungen); **I have good memories of our stay in Italy** ich habe schöne Erinnerungen an unseren Urlaub in Italien; **3** (*of a computer*) Speicher *der*.

mend *verb* **1** reparieren; **2** (*by sewing*) ausbessern SEP.

mental *adjective* **1** geistig; **2 mental illness** die Geisteskrankheit; **mental hospital** die psychiatrische Klinik.

mention *verb* erwähnen.

menu *noun* **1** (*in a restaurant*) Speisekarte *die* (PL die Speisekarten); **2** (*in computing*) Menü *das* (PL die Menüs).

meringue *noun* Baiser *das* (PL die Baisers).

merit *noun* **1** Verdienst *das* (PL die Verdienste); **2** (*good feature or advantage*) Vorzug *der* (PL die Vorzüge).

merry *adjective* **1** fröhlich; **Merry Christmas** fröhliche Weihnachten; **2** (*from drinking*) angeheitert.

mess *noun* **1** Durcheinander *das*; **my papers are in a complete mess** meine Unterlagen sind ein einziges Durcheinander; **what a mess!** was für ein Durcheinander!; **2 to mak**

✧ **IRREGULAR VERB:** *See the verb table in the centre of the dictionary*

a mess Unordnung machen; **3 to
clear up the mess** aufräumen SEP.

• **to mess about** herumalbern SEP;
stop messing about! hör auf
herumzualbern!

• **to mess about with something** mit
etwas ←(DAT) herumspielen SEP; **it's
dangerous to mess about with
matches** es ist gefährlich, mit
Streichhölzern herumzuspielen.

• **to mess something up 1** etwas
durcheinander bringen △ ✧; **you've
messed up all my papers** Sie haben
meine Unterlagen völlig
durcheinander gebracht; **2** (*make
dirty*) etwas schmutzig machen;
3 (*botch*) etwas verpfuschen.

message *noun* **1** Nachricht *die* (PL
die Nachrichten); **a telephone
message** eine telefonische
Nachricht; **2 to give somebody a
message** jemandem etwas
ausrichten SEP.

messy *adjective* **1** (*dirty*) **it's a
messy job** das ist ein dreckiger Job;
2 he's a messy eater er bekleckert
sich beim Essen; **3 her writing's
really messy** sie hat eine furchtbare
Schrift; **4** (*untidy*) **she's very
messy** sie ist sehr unordentlich.

metal *noun* Metall *das* (PL *die*
Metalle).

meter *noun* **1** (*electricity, gas, taxi*)
Zähler *der* (PL *die* Zähler); **to read
the meter** den Zähler ablesen ✧
SEP; **2 parking meter** *die* Parkuhr.

method *noun* Methode *die* (PL *die*
Methoden).

Methodist *noun* Methodist *der* (PL
die Methodisten), Methodistin *die*
(PL *die* Methodistinnen).

metre *noun* Meter *der* (PL *die*
Meter).

metric *adjective* metrisch.

microphone *noun* Mikrofon *das*
(PL *die* Mikrofone).

microscope *noun* Mikroskop *das*
(PL *die* Mikroskope).

microwave (oven) *noun*
Mikrowellenherd *der* (PL *die*
Mikrowellenherde).

midday *noun* Mittag *der*; **at
midday** mittags.

middle *noun* **1** Mitte *die*; **in the
middle of the room** in der Mitte des
Zimmers; **in the middle of June**
Mitte Juni; **in the middle of the
night** mitten in der Nacht; **2 to be
in the middle of doing something**
gerade dabei sein, etwas zu tun;
**when she phoned I was in the
middle of washing my hair** als sie
anrief, war ich gerade dabei, mir die
Haare zu waschen.

middle-aged *adjective* mittleren
Alters; **a middle-aged lady** eine
Dame mittleren Alters.

middle-class *adjective* der
Mittelschicht; **a middle-class family**
eine Familie der Mittelschicht.

Middle-East *noun* **the Middle
East** der Nahe Osten.

midge *noun* Mücke *die* (PL *die*
Mücken).

midnight *noun* Mitternacht *die*; **at
midnight** um Mitternacht.

△ NEW SPELLING: *See page xii*

Midsummer's Day *noun*
Sommersonnenwende *die*.

might *verb* 1 'are you going to
phone him?' – 'I might' 'rufst du
ihn an?' – 'vielleicht'; **I might invite
Jo** vielleicht lade ich Jo ein; **he
might have forgotten** vielleicht hat
er es vergessen; 2 **she might be
right** sie könnte Recht haben.

mike *noun* (*microphone*) Mikro *das*
(PL *die* Mikros) (*informal*).

mild *adjective* mild.

mile *noun* 1 Meile *die* (PL *die* Meilen)
(*Germans use kilometres for
distances; to convert miles to
kilometres, multiply by 8 and divide
by 5*); **it's ten miles to Oxford** es
sind sechzehn Kilometer bis Oxford;
2 **it's miles better** das ist viel besser.

milk *noun* Milch *die*; **full-cream
milk** *die* Vollmilch; **skimmed milk**
die Magermilch; **semi-skimmed
milk** *die* fettarme Milch.
verb melken.

milk chocolate *noun*
Milchschokolade *die*.

milkman *noun* Milchmann *der* (PL
die Milchmänner).

milk shake *noun*
Milchmixgetränk *das* (PL *die*
Milchmixgetränke).

millimetre *noun* Millimeter *der* (PL
die Millimeter).

million *noun* Million *die* (PL *die*
Millionen); **a million people** eine
Million Menschen; **two million
people** zwei Millionen Menschen.

millionaire *noun* Millionär *der* (PL
die Millionäre), Millionärin *die* (PL
die Millionärinnen).

mince *noun* Hackfleisch *das*.

mind *noun* 1 Sinn *der*; **it never
crossed my mind to ask them for
help** es kam mir überhaupt nicht in
den Sinn, sie um Hilfe zu bitten;
2 Meinung *die*; **to change your
mind** seine Meinung ändern; **I've
changed my mind** ich habe meine
Meinung geändert; 3 **to make up
your mind to do something** sich
entschließen ✧, etwas zu tun; **I can't
make up my mind which dress to
wear** ich kann mich nicht
entschließen, welches Kleid ich
anziehe; 4 **I've made up my mind**
ich habe mich entschieden.
verb 1 aufpassen SEP auf (+ACC); **can
you mind my bag for me?** können
Sie auf meine Handtasche
aufpassen?; **could you mind the
baby for ten minutes?** könntest du
zehn Minuten auf das Baby
aufpassen?; 2 **do you mind closing
the door?** würden Sie bitte die Tür
zumachen?; 3 **do you mind if …?**
würde es Ihnen etwas ausmachen SEP,
wenn …?; **do you mind if I open the
window?** würde es Ihnen etwas
ausmachen, wenn ich das Fenster
aufmache?; **I don't mind** es macht
mir nichts aus; **I don't mind the heat**
die Hitze macht mir nichts aus;
4 **never mind** macht nichts.

mine[1] *noun* Bergwerk *das* (PL *die*
Bergwerke); **coal mine** *das*
Kohlenbergwerk.

mine[2] *pronoun* 1 (*for a masculine*

noun) mein; **she took her coat and I took mine** sie hat ihren Mantel genommen und 2 ich habe meinen genommen; **2** (*for a feminine noun*) meine; **she gave me her address and I gave her mine** sie hat mir ihre Adresse gegeben und ich habe ihr meine gegeben; **3** (*for a neuter noun*) meins; **her dress is red and mine is blue** ihr Kleid ist rot und meins ist blau; **4** (*for masculine/feminine/neuter plural nouns*) meine; **she showed me her photos and I showed her mine** sie hat mir ihre Fotos gezeigt und ich habe ihr meine gezeigt; **5 a friend of mine** ein Freund von mir; **it's mine** das gehört mir.

miner *noun* Bergarbeiter *der* (PL *die* Bergarbeiter).

mineral water *noun* Mineralwasser *das*.

minibus *noun* Kleinbus *der* (PL *die* Kleinbusse).

minimum *noun* Minimum *das* (PL *die* Minima); **a minimum of** ein Minimum von.
adjective Mindest-; **the minimum age** das Mindestalter; **minimum wage** *der* Mindestlohn.

miniskirt *noun* Minirock *der* (PL *die* Miniröcke).

minister *noun* **1** (*in government*) Minister *der* (PL *die* Minister), Ministerin *die* (PL *die* Ministerinnen); **2** (*of a church*) Geistliche *der/die* (PL *die* Geistlichen).

ministry *noun* Ministerium *das* (PL *die* Ministerien).

mint *noun* **1** (*herb*) Minze *die* (PL *die* Minzen); **2** (*sweet*) Pfefferminzbonbon *der* (PL *die* Pfefferminzbonbons).

minus *preposition* minus (+GEN); **seven minus three is four** sieben minus drei ist vier; **it was minus ten this morning** es war minus zehn heute Morgen.

minute[1] *noun* **1** Minute *die* (PL *die* Minuten); **I'll be ready in two minutes** ich bin in zwei Minuten fertig; **it's five minutes' walk from here** es ist fünf Minuten zu Fuß von hier; **2** Moment *der*; **just a minute!** einen Moment bitte!; **3 in a minute** gleich.

minute[2] *adjective* winzig; **the bedrooms are minute** die Schlafzimmer sind winzig.

miracle *noun* Wunder *das* (PL *die* Wunder).

mirror *noun* Spiegel *der* (PL *die* Spiegel); **he looked at himself in the mirror** er hat sich im Spiegel betrachtet.

misbehave *verb* sich schlecht benehmen ◇.

miserable *adjective* **1** unglücklich; **he was miserable without her** er war unglücklich ohne sie; **2 I feel really miserable today** ich fühle mich heute richtig elend; **3** mies; **it's miserable weather** das Wetter ist mies; **she gets paid a miserable salary** sie bekommt ein mieses Gehalt.

△ NEW SPELLING: See page xii

miss *verb* 1 verpassen; **she missed her train** sie hat ihren Zug verpasst; **I missed the film** ich habe den Film verpasst; **to miss an opportunity** eine Gelegenheit verpassen; 2 nicht treffen ✧; **the stone missed me** der Stein hat mich nicht getroffen; **the ball missed the goal** der Schuss ging am Tor vorbei; **missed!** nicht getroffen!; 3 versäumen; **he's missed his classes** er hat den Unterricht versäumt; 4 vermissen (*a person or thing*); **I miss you** ich vermisse dich; **she's missing her sister** sie vermisst ihre Schwester; **I miss England** ich vermisse England.

Miss *noun* Fräulein *das*; **Miss Jones** Fräulein Jones, Frau Jones (*adult women are usually addressed as 'Frau', whether or not they are married*).

missing *adjective* 1 fehlend; **she's found the missing pieces** sie hat die fehlenden Teile gefunden; **the missing link** das fehlende Glied; 2 **to be missing** fehlen; **there's a plate missing** ein Teller fehlt; **there are three forks missing** drei Gabeln fehlen; 3 **to go missing** verschwinden ✧ (PERF *sein*); **several things have gone missing lately** mehrere Sachen sind kürzlich verschwunden; 4 **three children are missing** drei Kinder werden vermisst.

missionary *noun* Missionar *der* (PL die Missionare), Missionarin *die* (PL die Missionarinnen).

mist *noun* Nebel *der*.

mistake *noun* 1 Fehler *der* (PL die Fehler); **spelling mistake** *der* Rechtschreibfehler; **you've made lots of mistakes** du hast viele Fehler gemacht; 2 **to make a mistake** (*be mistaken*) sich irren; **sorry, I made a mistake** Entschuldigung, ich habe mich geirrt; 3 **by mistake** aus Versehen.
verb **I mistook you for your brother** ich habe dich mit deinem Bruder verwechselt.

mistaken *adjective* **to be mistaken** sich täuschen; **you're mistaken** du täuschst dich.

mistletoe *noun* Mistel *die* (PL die Misteln).

misty *adjective* dunstig; **a misty morning** ein dunstiger Morgen.

misunderstand *verb* missverstehen △ ✧; **I misunderstood** ich habe es missverstanden.

misunderstanding *noun* Missverständnis △ *das* (PL die Missverständnisse); **there's been a misunderstanding** da liegt ein Missverständnis vor.

mix *noun* Mischung *die* (PL die Mischungen); **a good mix** eine gute Mischung; **cake mix** *die* Backmischung.
verb 1 vermischen; **mix the ingredients together** die Zutaten vermischen; **mix the cream into the sauce** die Sahne in die Soße rühren; 2 **to mix with** verkehren mit (+DAT); **she mixes with lots of interesting people** sie verkehrt mit vielen interessanten Leuten.

✧ IRREGULAR VERB: *See the verb table in the centre of the dictionary*

to mix up 1 durcheinander bringen △ ✧; **you've mixed up all the papers** du hast alle Unterlagen durcheinander gebracht; **you've got it all mixed up** du hast alles durcheinander gebracht; **2** (*confuse*) verwechseln; **I get him mixed up with his brother** ich verwechsele ihn mit seinem Bruder.

mixed *adjective* **1** bunt; **a mixed programme** ein buntes Programm; **2** gemischt; **a mixed salad** ein gemischter Salat.

mixture *noun* Mischung *die* (PL *die* Mischungen); **it's a mixture of jazz and rock** es ist eine Mischung aus Jazz und Rock.

moan *verb* (*complain*) jammern; **stop moaning!** hör auf zu jammern!

mobile home *noun* Wohnwagen *der* (PL *die* Wohnwagen).

mobile phone *noun* Mobiltelefon *das* (PL *die* Mobiltelefone), Handy *das* (PL *die* Handys).

mock *noun* (*mock exam*) Übungsprüfung *die* (PL *die* Übungsprüfungen). *verb* sich lustig machen über (+ACC); **stop mocking me** hör auf, dich über mich lustig zu machen.

model *noun* **1** Modell *das* (PL *die* Modelle); **his car is the latest model** sein Auto ist das neueste Modell; **a model of Westminster Abbey** ein Modell von der Westminsterabtei; **2** (*fashion*

model) Mannequin *das* (PL *die* Mannequins); **she's a model** sie ist Mannequin.

model aeroplane *noun* Modellflugzeug *das* (PL *die* Modellflugzeuge).

model railway *noun* Minieisenbahn *die* (PL *die* Minieisenbahnen).

modem *noun* Modem *der* (PL *die* Modems).

modern *adjective* modern.

modernize *verb* modernisieren.

modern languages *noun* neuere Sprachen (*plural*).

modest *adjective* bescheiden.

modify *verb* abändern SEP.

moisture *noun* Feuchtigkeit *die*.

moisturizer *noun* Feuchtigkeitscreme *die*.

mole *noun* **1** (*animal*) Maulwurf *der* (PL *die* Maulwürfe); **2** (*on the skin*) Leberfleck *der* (PL *die* Leberflecke).

moment *noun* **1** Moment *der* (PL *die* Momente); **at any moment** jeden Moment; **at the moment** im Moment, im Augenblick; **at the right moment** im richtigen Moment; **2** Augenblick *der* (PL *die* Augenblicke); **wait a moment!** einen Augenblick!; **3 he'll be ready in a moment** er ist gleich fertig.

monarchy *noun* Monarchie *die*.

Monday *noun* **1** Montag *der*; **on Monday** am Montag; **I'm going to**

see him on Monday ich sehe ihn am Montag; **see you on Monday!** bis Montag!; **every Monday** jeden Montag; **last Monday** letzten Montag; **next Monday** nächsten Montag; **2 on Mondays** montags; **the museum is closed on Mondays** das Museum ist montags geschlossen.

money *noun* Geld *das*; **I don't have enough money** ich habe nicht genug Geld; **to make money** Geld verdienen.

monitor *noun* (*of a computer*) Monitor *der* (PL *die* Monitoren).

monkey *noun* Affe *der* (PL *die* Affen).

monotonous *adjective* eintönig.

monster *noun* Ungeheuer *das* (PL *die* Ungeheuer).

month *noun* Monat *der*; **in the month of May** im Mai; **this month** diesen Monat; **next month** nächsten Monat; **last month** letzten Monat; **for three months** drei Monate lang; **every month** jeden Monat; **every three months** alle drei Monate; **in two months' time** in zwei Monaten; **at the end of the month** am Monatsende.

monthly *adjective* monatlich; **monthly payment** *die* monatliche Zahlung; **monthly ticket** *die* Monatskarte.

monument *noun* Denkmal *das* (PL *die* Denkmäler).

mood *noun* **1** Laune *die* (PL *die* Launen); **to be in a good mood**

gute Laune haben; **to be in a bad mood** schlechte Laune haben; **2 I'm not in the mood** ich habe keine Lust dazu; **I'm not in the mood for working** ich habe keine Lust zum Arbeiten.

moon *noun* Mond *der* (PL *die* Monde); **by the light of the moon** im Mondschein; ★ **to be over the moon** im siebten Himmel sein (*literally: to be in seventh heaven*).

moonlight *noun* Mondschein *der*; **by moonlight** im Mondschein.

moped *noun* Moped *das* (PL *die* Mopeds).

moral *noun* Moral *die*; **the moral of the story** die Moral der Geschichte. *adjective* moralisch.

morals *noun* Moral *die*.

more *adverb* **1** (*followed by an adjective*) (*in German the ending '-er' is added to the adjective to show the comparative*) **more interesting** interessanter; **the book's more interesting than the film** das Buch ist interessanter als der Film; **more difficult** schwieriger; **more slowly** langsamer; **more easily** einfacher; **books are getting more and more expensive** Bücher werden immer teurer; **2 not any more** (*no longer*) nicht mehr; **she doesn't live here any more** sie wohnt nicht mehr hier. *adjective* **1** mehr (*'mehr' never changes*); **more friends** mehr Freunde; **more ... than** mehr ... als; **they have more money than we do** sie haben mehr Geld als wir; **2 no more** kein; **there's no more milk**

es ist keine Milch mehr da; **3** (*of something you have already*) noch; **would you like some more cake?** möchtest du noch etwas Kuchen?; **a few more glasses** noch ein paar Gläser.
pronoun **1** mehr; **he eats more than me** er isst mehr als ich; **no more, thank you** nichts mehr, danke; **2** (*of something you have already*) noch; **we need three more** wir brauchen noch drei; **any more?** noch etwas?; **3 more and more** immer mehr; **it takes more and more time** es beansprucht immer mehr Zeit; **4 more or less** mehr oder weniger; **it's more or less finished** es ist mehr oder weniger fertig.

morning *noun* **1** Morgen *der* (PL *die* Morgen); **in the morning** am Morgen; **this morning** heute Morgen; **tomorrow morning** morgen früh; **yesterday morning** gestern Morgen; **on Friday morning** am Freitagmorgen; **2 in the morning** (*regularly*) morgens; **she doesn't work in the morning** sie arbeitet morgens nicht; **on Friday mornings** freitagmorgens; **at six o'clock in the morning** um sechs Uhr morgens; **3** (*as opposed to afternoon*) Vormittag *der* (PL *die* Vormittage); **I spent the whole morning waiting for him** ich habe den ganzen Vormittag auf ihn gewartet.

Moscow *noun* Moskau *das*.

Moslem *noun* Moslem *der* (PL *die* Moslems), Moslime *die* (PL *die* Moslimen).

mosque *noun* Moschee *die* (PL *die* Moscheen).

mosquito *noun* Mücke *die* (PL *die* Mücken); **mosquito bite** *der* Mückenstich.

most *adjective, pronoun* **1** (*followed by a plural noun*) die meisten; **most children like chocolate** die meisten Kinder mögen Schokolade; **most of my friends** die meisten von meinen Freunden; **2** (*followed by a singular noun*) der meiste/die meiste/das meiste; **they've eaten most of the ice-cream** sie haben das meiste Eis gegessen; **3 the most** (*followed by a noun or a verb*) am meisten; **I've got the most time** ich habe am meisten Zeit; **4 most of the time** die meiste Zeit; **most of them** die meisten.
adverb **1** (*followed by an adjective*) (*in German the ending '-(e)st' is added to the adjective to show the superlative*) **the most interesting film** der interessanteste Film; **the most exciting story** die spannendste Geschichte; **the most boring book** das langweiligste Buch; **2** am meisten; **the noise bothers me most** der Lärm stört mich am meisten; **3** (*very*) höchst; **it's most unlikely** es ist höchst unwahrscheinlich.

moth *noun* **1** Nachtfalter *der* (PL *die* Nachtfalter); **2** (*clothes moth*) Motte *die* (PL *die* Motten).

mother *noun* Mutter *die* (PL *die* Mütter); **Kate's mother** Kates Mutter.

△ NEW SPELLING: *See page xii*

mother-in-law *noun*
Schwiegermutter *die* (PL *die*
Schwiegermütter).

Mother's Day *noun* Muttertag *der*
(PL *die* Muttertage).

motor *noun* Motor *der* (PL *die*
Motoren).

motorbike *noun* Motorrad *das* (PL
die Motorräder).

motorcyclist *noun*
Motorradfahrer *der* (PL *die*
Motorradfahrer), Motorradfahrerin
die (PL *die* Motorradfahrerinnen).

motorist *noun* Autofahrer *der* (PL
die Autofahrer), Autofahrerin *die* (PL
die Autofahrerinnen).

motor racing *noun*
Autorennen *das.*

motorway *noun* Autobahn *die* (PL
die Autobahnen).

mouldy *adjective* schimmelig.

mountain *noun* Berg *der* (PL *die*
Berge); **in the mountains** in den
Bergen.

mountain bike *noun*
Mountainbike *das* (PL *die*
Mountainbikes).

mountaineer *noun*
Bergsteiger *der* (PL *die* Bergsteiger),
Bergsteigerin *die* (PL *die*
Bergsteigerinnen).

mountaineering *noun*
Bergsteigen *das*; **to go
mountaineering** Bergsteigen gehen.

mountainous *adjective* gebirgig.

mouse *noun* Maus *die* (PL *die*
Mäuse) (*also for a computer*).

moustache *noun* Schnurrbart *der*
(PL *die* Schnurrbärte).

mouth *noun* 1 (*of a person*)
Mund *der* (PL *die* Münder); 2 (*of an
animal*) Maul *das* (PL *die* Mäuler);
3 (*of a river*) Mündung *die* (PL *die*
Mündungen).

mouthful *noun* (*food*) Happen *der*
(PL *die* Happen) (*informal*).

mouth organ *noun*
Mundharmonika *die* (PL *die*
Mundharmonikas); **to play the
mouth organ** Mundharmonika
spielen.

move *noun* 1 (*to a different house*)
Umzug *der* (PL *die* Umzüge); 2 (*in a
game*) Zug *der* (PL *die* Züge); **your
move!** du bist am Zug!
verb 1 sich bewegen; **she didn't
move** sie hat sich nicht bewegt; 2 **to
move up** vorrücken SEP (PERF *sein*);
move up a bit rücken Sie etwas vor;
3 wegnehmen ✧ SEP; **can you move
your bag, please?** können Sie Ihre
Handtasche bitte wegnehmen?; 4 **to
move something somewhere else**
etwas woandershin stellen; **I've
moved the chest into the cellar** ich
habe die Truhe in den Keller gestellt;
5 (*car*) fahren ✧ (PERF *sein*);
6 (*traffic*) vorwärtskommen ✧ SEP
(PERF *sein*); 7 (*driver*) wegfahren ✧
SEP; **could you move your car,
please?** würden Sie bitte Ihr Auto
wegfahren?; 8 **to move forward**
(*person*) vorrücken SEP (PERF *sein*);
(*vehicle*) vorwärts fahren ✧ (PERF
sein); 9 (*move house*) umziehen ✧
SEP (PERF *sein*); **we're moving on
Tuesday** wir ziehen am Dienstag

✧ IRREGULAR VERB: *See the verb table in the centre of the dictionary*

um; **they've moved to London** sie sind nach London umgezogen; **10 to move away** (*live somewhere else*) wegziehen ◇ SEP (PERF *sein*); **11 to move in** einziehen ◇ SEP (PERF *sein*); **she's moving in with friends** sie zieht bei Freunden ein.

movement *noun* Bewegung *die* (PL die Bewegungen).

movie *noun* Film *der* (PL die Filme); **to go to the movies** ins Kino gehen.

moving *adjective* **1** fahrend; **a moving car** ein fahrendes Auto; **2** (*emotionally*) ergreifend.

mow *verb* mähen.

mower *noun* Rasenmäher *der* (PL die Rasenmäher).

MP *noun* Abgeordnete *der/die* (PL die Abgeordneten).

Mr *noun* Herr *der*; (*in an address*) **Mr Angus Brown** Herrn Angus Brown; (*in a letter*) **Dear Mr Brown** Sehr geehrter Herr Brown.

Mrs *noun* Frau *die*; **Mrs Mary Hendry** Frau Mary Hendry; (*in a letter*) **Dear Mrs Hendry** Sehr geehrte Frau Hendry.

Ms *noun* Frau *die* (*there is no direct equivalent to 'Ms' in German, but 'Frau' may be used whether the woman is married or not*).

much *adjective, adverb, pronoun* **1** viel; **she doesn't eat much for breakfast** sie isst nicht viel zum Frühstück; **much more** viel mehr; **much quicker** viel schneller; **we**

don't have much time wir haben nicht viel Zeit; **2 not much** nicht viel; **'do you have a lot of work?'** – **'no, not much'** 'hast du viel Arbeit?' – ' nein, nicht viel'; **3 so much** so viel; **I have so much to do** ich habe so viel zu tun; **you shouldn't have given me so much** du hättest mir nicht so viel geben sollen; **4 as much as** so viel; **take as much as you like** nimm so viel du willst; **5 too much** zu viel △; **she gets too much money from her parents** sie bekommt zu viel Geld von ihren Eltern; **that's far too much** das ist viel zu viel; **6 how much?** wie viel? △; **how much is it?** wie viel kostet es?; **how much do you want?** wie viel möchten Sie?; **how much money do you need?** wie viel Geld brauchst du?; **7** (*greatly*) sehr; **he loved her very much** er hat sie sehr geliebt; **too much** zu sehr; **so much** (so) sehr; **we liked it so much** es hat uns sehr gefallen; **8** (*often*) oft; **I don't watch television much** ich sehe nicht oft fern; **we don't go out much** wir gehen nicht oft aus; **9 thank you very much** vielen Dank.

mud *noun* Schlamm *der*.

muddle *noun*
1 Durcheinander *das*; **2 to be in a muddle** durcheinander sein.

mug *noun* Becher *der* (PL die Becher); **a mug of milk** ein Becher Milch.
verb **to mug somebody** jemanden überfallen ◇; **to be mugged** überfallen werden.

multiplication *noun* Multiplikation *die*.

multiply *verb* multiplizieren; **six multiplied by four** sechs multipliziert mit vier.

mum, mummy *noun* Mutti *die* (PL *die* Muttis); **Tom's mum** Toms Mutti; **I'll ask my mum** ich frage die Mutti.

mumps *noun* Mumps *der*.

Munich *noun* München *das*.

murder *noun* Mord *der* (PL *die* Morde).
verb ermorden.

murderer *noun* Mörder *der* (PL *die* Mörder), Mörderin *die* (PL *die* Mörderinnen).

muscle *noun* Muskel *der* (PL *die* Muskeln).

muscular *adjective* muskulös.

museum *noun* Museum *das* (PL *die* Museen); **to go to the museum** ins Museum gehen.

mushroom *noun* Pilz *der* (PL *die* Pilze), Champignon *der* (PL *die* Champignons); **mushroom salad** *der* Champignonsalat.

music *noun* Musik *die*; **pop music** *die* Popmusik; **classical music** *die* klassische Musik.

musical *noun* Musical *das* (PL *die* Musicals).
adjective **1** **musical instrument** *das* Musikinstrument; **2** **they're a very musical family** sie sind eine sehr musikalische Familie.

musician *noun* Musiker *der* (PL *die* Musiker), Musikerin *die* (PL *die* Musikerinnen).

Muslim *noun* Moslem *der* (PL *die* Moslems), Moslime *die* (PL *die* Moslimen).

mussel *noun* Muschel *die* (PL *die* Muscheln).

must *verb* **1** müssen ✧; **we must leave now** wir müssen jetzt gehen; **you must learn the vocabulary** du musst die Vokabeln lernen; **2** (*with a negative*) dürfen ✧; **you mustn't do that** das darfst du nicht tun; **3** (*expressing probability*) müssen ✧; **you must be tired** ihr müsst müde sein; **it must be five o'clock** es muss fünf Uhr sein; **he must have forgotten** er muss es vergessen haben.

mustard *noun* Senf *der* (PL *die* Senfe).

mutter *verb* murmeln.

my *adjective* **1** (*before a masculine noun*) mein; **my brother** mein Bruder; **they don't like my dog** sie mögen meinen Hund nicht; **2** (*before a feminine noun*) meine; **my sister** meine Schwester; **3** (*before a neuter noun*) mein; **that's my new car** das ist mein neues Auto; **we can go in my car** wir können mit meinem Auto fahren; **4** (*before masculine/feminine/neuter plural nouns*) meine; **my children** meine Kinder; **5** (*with parts of the body*) der/die/das (*plural:* die); **I had a glass in my hand** ich hatte ein Glas in der Hand; **I'm washing my hands** ich wasche mir die Hände.

✧ IRREGULAR VERB: *See the verb table in the centre of the dictionary*

myself *pronoun* **1** (*reflexive and after a preposition taking the accusative*) mich; **I've cut myself** ich habe mich geschnitten; **I've addressed the letter to myself** ich habe den Brief an mich adressiert; **2** (*reflexive and after a preposition taking the dative*) mir; **I've hurt myself** ich habe mir wehgetan; **I said to myself** ich habe mir gesagt; **3** (*stressing something*) selbst; **I said it myself** ich habe es selbst gesagt; **4 by myself** allein.

mysterious *adjective* rätselhaft.

mystery *noun* **1** Rätsel *das* (PL *die* Rätsel); **2** (*book*) Krimi *der* (PL *die* Krimis) (*informal*).

mythology *noun* Mythologie *die* (PL *die* Mythologien).

N n

nail *noun* (*on your finger or toe, also metal*) Nagel *der* (PL *die* Nägel). *verb* nageln.

nailbrush *noun* Nagelbürste *die* (PL *die* Nagelbürsten).

nailfile *noun* Nagelfeile *die* (PL *die* Nagelfeilen).

nail polish *noun* Nagellack *der*.

nail polish remover *noun* Nagellackentferner *der*.

name *noun* **1** Name *der* (PL *die* Namen); **I've forgotten her name** ich habe ihren Namen vergessen;

what's your name? wie heißt du?; **my name's Joy** ich heiße Joy; **2** (*of a book or film*) Titel *der* (PL *die* Titel).

napkin *noun* Serviette *die* (PL *die* Servietten).

nappy *noun* Windel *die* (PL *die* Windeln).

narrow *adjective* schmal; **a narrow street** eine schmale Straße.

nasty *adjective* **1** (*mean*) gemein; **that was a nasty thing to do** das war gemein; **2** (*unpleasant, bad*) scheußlich; **that's a nasty job** das ist eine scheußliche Arbeit; **a nasty smell** ein scheußlicher Geruch.

nation *noun* Nation *die* (PL *die* Nationen).

national *adjective* national.

national anthem *noun* Nationalhymne *die* (PL *die* Nationalhymnen).

nationality *noun* Nationalität *die* (PL *die* Nationalitäten).

national park *noun* Nationalpark *der* (PL *die* Nationalparks).

natural *adjective* natürlich.

naturally *adverb* natürlich.

nature *noun* Natur *die*.

nature reserve *noun* Naturschutzgebiet *das* (PL *die* Naturschutzgebiete).

naughty *adjective* unartig.

△ NEW SPELLING: *See page xii*

navy *noun* Marine *die*; **my uncle's in the navy** mein Onkel ist bei der Marine.

navy-blue *adjective* marineblau.

near *adjective* 1 nah(e); 2 (*the superlative of nah(e) is der/die/das nächste*) **the nearest park** der nächste Park; **the nearest bank** die nächste Bank; **the nearest shop** das nächste Geschäft.
preposition nahe an (+DAT); **near (to) the station** nahe am Bahnhof.
adverb 1 nah(e) (*in spoken German 'nah' is more common*); **they live quite near** sie wohnen ganz nah; 2 **to come nearer** näher kommen.

nearly *adverb* fast; **nearly empty** fast leer.

neat *adjective* 1 (*well organized, tidy*) ordentlich; **a neat room** ein ordentliches Zimmer; 2 adrett (*clothes or the way you look*).

necessarily *adverb* **not necessarily** nicht unbedingt.

necessary *adjective* nötig; **if necessary** falls nötig.

neck *noun* 1 (*of a person*) Hals *der* (PL *die* Hälse); 2 (*of a garment*) Kragen *der* (PL *die* Kragen).

necklace *noun* Halskette *die* (PL *die* Halsketten).

need *noun* **there's no need, I've already done it** das ist nicht nötig, ich habe es schon gemacht; **there's no need to wait** du brauchst nicht zu warten.
verb 1 brauchen; **we need bread** wir brauchen Brot; **everything you need** alles, was man braucht; 2 (*to have to*) müssen ✧; **I need to go to the bank** ich muss zur Bank gehen; 3 (*with a negative*) **you needn't wait** du brauchst nicht zu warten.

needle *noun* Nadel *die* (PL *die* Nadeln).

negative *noun* (*of a photo*) Negativ *das* (PL *die* Negative).

neighbour *noun* Nachbar *der* (PL *die* Nachbarn), Nachbarin *die* (PL *die* Nachbarinnen); **we're going round to the neighbours'** wir besuchen die Nachbarn.

neighbourhood *noun* Nachbarschaft *die*; **in our neighbourhood** in unserer Nachbarschaft.

neither *conjunction* 1 **neither ... nor** weder ... noch; **I have neither the time nor the money** ich habe weder die Zeit noch das Geld; 2 **neither do I** ich auch nicht; **'I don't like fish'** – **'neither do I'** 'ich mag keinen Fisch' – 'ich auch nicht'; **'I didn't like the film'** – **'neither did Kirsty'** 'mir hat der Film nicht gefallen' – 'Kirsty hat er auch nicht gefallen'.
pronoun keiner von beiden/keine von beiden/keins von beiden; **'which do you like?'** – **'neither'** 'welches gefällt dir?' – 'keins von beiden'.

nephew *noun* Neffe *der* (PL *die* Neffen).

nerve *noun* Nerv *der* (PL *die* Nerven); 1 **to lose your nerve** die Nerven verlieren; **you've got a nerve!** du hast Nerven! (*informal*);

✧ IRREGULAR VERB: *See the verb table in the centre of the dictionary*

2 what a nerve! so eine Frechheit!;
★ **he gets on my nerves** er geht mir
auf die Nerven (*informal*).

nervous *adjective* **1** (*afraid*)
ängstlich; **to feel nervous about
something** Angst vor etwas ←(DAT)
haben; **2** (*highly strung*) nervös
(*person*).

net *noun* Netz *das* (PL die Netze).

Netherlands *noun* Niederlande
(*plural*); **in the Netherlands** in den
Niederlanden.

nettle *noun* Nessel *die* (PL die
Nesseln).

neutral *noun* (*neutral gear*)
Leerlauf *der*; **to be in neutral** im
Leerlauf sein.
adjective neutral.

never *adverb* **1** nie; **Ben never
smokes** Ben raucht nie; **I've never
told him** ich habe es ihm nie gesagt;
never again nie wieder; **2** noch nie;
**'have you ever been to Spain?' –
'no, never'** 'warst du schon mal in
Spanien?' – 'nein, noch nie'; **3 never
mind** macht nichts.

new *adjective* neu; **have you seen
their new house?** hast du ihr neues
Haus gesehen?

news *noun* **1** (*new information*)
Nachricht *die* (PL die Nachrichten);
I've got good news ich habe gute
Nachrichten; **2 a piece of news**
eine Neuigkeit; **any news?** was gibt
es Neues?; **3** (*on TV or the radio*)
Nachrichten (*plural*); **we saw it on
the news** wir haben es in den
Nachrichten gesehen.

newsagent *noun*
Zeitungshändler *der* (PL die
Zeitungshändler).

newspaper *noun* Zeitung *die* (PL
die Zeitungen).

newsreader *noun*
Nachrichtensprecher *der* (PL die
Nachrichtensprecher),
Nachrichtensprecherin *die* (PL die
Nachrichtensprecherinnen).

New Year *noun* Neujahr *das*;
Happy New Year! ein gutes neues
Jahr!

New Year's Day *noun*
Neujahr *das*.

New Year's Eve *noun*
Silvester *der*.

New Zealand *noun*
Neuseeland *das*.

next *adjective* **1** nächster/nächste/
nächstes; **the next train leaves at
ten** der nächste Zug fährt um zehn
ab; **next week** nächste Woche; **next
Thursday** nächsten Donnerstag;
next year nächstes Jahr; **next time I
see you** nächstes Mal, wenn ich
dich sehe; **2** (*following*) **next
please!** der Nächste bitte/die
Nächste bitte; **the next thing** das
Nächste; **the next day** am nächsten
Tag; **the letter arrived the next day**
der Brief kam am nächsten Tag an;
3 the week after next übernächste
Woche; **4** (*next-door*) nebenan; **I'm
in the next room** ich bin nebenan.
adverb **1** (*afterwards*) **what
did he say next?** was hat er danach
gesagt?; **2** (*now*) als Nächstes; **what**

shall we do next? was machen wir als Nächstes?; **3** next to neben (+DAT, *or* +ACC *with movement towards a place*); **the house next to the baker's** das Haus neben dem Bäcker; **I sat down next to her** ich habe mich neben sie gesetzt.

next door *adverb* nebenan; **they live next door** sie wohnen nebenan; **the girl next door** das Mädchen von nebenan.

nice *adjective* **1** (*pleasant*) schön; **we had a nice evening** wir haben einen schönen Abend verbracht; **Brighton's a nice town** Brighton ist eine schöne Stadt; **we had nice weather** wir hatten schönes Wetter; **2 to have a nice time** sich amüsieren; **have a nice day!** viel Spaß!; **3** (*attractive to look at*) hübsch; **that's a nice dress** das ist ein hübsches Kleid; **4** (*kind, friendly*) nett (*person*); **she's really nice** sie ist wirklich nett; **5 to be nice to somebody** nett zu jemandem sein; **she's been very nice to me** sie war sehr nett zu mir; **6** (*tasting good*) gut; **it tastes nice** es schmeckt gut.

niece *noun* Nichte *die* (PL *die* Nichten).

night *noun* **1** (*after bedtime*) Nacht *die* (PL *die* Nächte); **during the night** während der Nacht; **Sunday night** Sonntag Nacht; **it's cold at night** nachts ist es kalt; **to stay the night** über Nacht bleiben; **I stayed the night at Emma's** ich habe bei Emma übernachtet; **2** (*before you go to bed*) Abend *der*

(PL *die* Abende); **what are you doing tonight?** was macht ihr heute Abend?; **one night** eines Abends; **tomorrow night** morgen Abend; **I met Greg last night** ich habe Greg gestern Abend getroffen; **on Friday night** am Freitagabend; **see you tonight!** bis heute Abend!

night club *noun* Nachtklub *der* (PL *die* Nachtklubs).

nightie *noun* Nachthemd *das* (PL *die* Nachthemden).

nightmare *noun* Alptraum *der* (PL *die* Alpträume).

nil *noun* (*in sport*) null; **they won four-nil** sie haben vier zu null gewonnen.

nine *number* neun.

nineteen *number* neunzehn.

ninety *number* neunzig.

ninth *number* neunter/neunte/ neuntes; **on the ninth floor** im neunten Stock; **on the ninth of June** am neunten Juni.

no *adverb* nein; **I said no** ich habe nein gesagt; **no thank you** nein danke.
adjective **1** kein; **we've got no bread** wir haben kein Brot; **no problem!** kein Problem!; **2** (*on a notice*) 'no smoking' 'Rauchen verboten'; 'no parking' 'Parken verboten'.

nobody *pronoun* niemand; **'who's there?' – 'nobody'** 'wer ist da?' – 'niemand'; **there's nobody in the kitchen** es ist niemand in der

---

◇ **IRREGULAR VERB:** *See the verb table in the centre of the dictionary*

Küche; **nobody was at home**
niemand war zu Hause.

nod *verb* nicken; **he nodded in
agreement** er hat zustimmend
genickt.

noise *noun* Lärm *der*; **to make a
noise** Lärm machen.

noisy *adjective* laut.

none *pronoun* **1** (*not one*)
keiner/keine/keins; **none of us**
keiner von uns/ keine von uns; **'how
many students failed the exam?'** –
'none' 'wie viele Schüler sind durch
die Prüfung gefallen?' – 'keine';
none of the boys knows him keiner
der Jungen kennt ihn; **2 there's
none left** es ist nichts mehr übrig.

nonsense *noun* Unsinn *der*; **to talk
nonsense** Unsinn reden;
nonsense! Unsinn!

non-stop *adjective* durchgehend
(*train*); Nonstop- (*flight*).
adverb ununterbrochen;
she talks non-stop sie redet
ununterbrochen.

noon *noun* Mittag *der*; **at (twelve)
noon** um zwölf (Uhr mittags).

no-one *pronoun* niemand; **'who's
there?'** – **'no-one'** 'wer ist da?' –
'niemand'; **there's no-one in the
kitchen** es ist niemand in der
Küche; **no-one was at home**
niemand war zu Hause.

nor *conjunction* **1 neither … nor**
weder … noch; **I have neither the
time nor the money** ich habe weder
die Zeit noch das Geld; **2 nor do I**
ich auch nicht; **'I don't like fish'** –

'nor do I' 'ich mag keinen Fisch' –
'ich auch nicht'; **nor do we** wir
auch nicht.

normal *adjective* normal.

normally *adverb* **1** (*usually*)
normalerweise; **2** (*in a normal way*)
normal.

north *noun* Norden *der*; **in the
north** im Norden.
adjective nördlich, Nord-; **the north
side** die Nordseite; **north wind** *der*
Nordwind.
adverb **1** (*towards the north*) nach
Norden; **to travel north** nach
Norden fahren; **2 north of London**
nördlich von London.

North America *noun*
Nordamerika *das*.

northeast *noun* Nordosten *der*.
adjective **in northeast England** in
Nordostengland.

Northern Ireland *noun*
Nordirland *das*.

North Pole *noun* Nordpol *der*.

North Sea *noun* **the North Sea** die
Nordsee.

northwest *noun* Nordwesten *der*.
adjective **in northwest England** in
Nordwestengland.

Norway *noun* Norwegen *das*.

Norwegian *noun* **1** (*person*)
Norweger *der* (PL *die* Norweger),
Norwegerin *die* (PL *die*
Norwegerinnen); **2** (*language*)
Norwegisch *das*.
adjective norwegisch.

△ NEW SPELLING: *See page xii*

nose *noun* Nase *die* (PL *die* Nasen); **to blow your nose** sich ←(DAT) die Nase putzen.

not *adverb* **1** nicht; **not on Sundays** sonntags nicht; **not all alone!** nicht ganz allein!; **not bad** nicht schlecht; **not at all** überhaupt nicht; **not yet** noch nicht; **Sam didn't phone** Sam hat nicht angerufen; **I hope not** hoffentlich nicht; **2 not a** kein/keine; **he's not a specialist** er ist kein Fachmann; **not a bit** kein bisschen.

note *noun* **1** (*a short letter*) Zettel *der* (PL *die* Zettel) (*informal*), Brief *der* (PL *die* Briefe); **2** (*in a class*) Notiz *die* (PL *die* Notizen); **to take notes** sich ←(DAT) Notizen machen; **3** (*a banknote*) Schein *der* (PL *die* Scheine); **a ten-pound note** ein Zehnpfundschein; **4** (*in music*) Note *die* (PL *die* Noten).

notebook *noun* Notizbuch *das* (PL *die* Notizbücher).

notepad *noun* Notizblock *der* (PL *die* Notizblöcke).

nothing *pronoun* nichts; **'what did you say?' – 'nothing'** 'was hast du gesagt?' – 'nichts'; **nothing special** nichts Besonderes; **nothing new** nichts Neues; **I saw nothing** ich habe nichts gesehen; **there's nothing left** es ist nichts mehr übrig.

notice *noun* **1** (*a sign*) Anschlag *der* (PL *die* Anschläge); **2** (*an advertisement*) Anzeige *die* (PL *die* Anzeigen); **3** (*advance warning*) Ankündigung *die*; **4 don't take any notice of her** nimm keine Notiz von ihr; **5 at short notice** kurzfristig. *verb* bemerken; **I didn't notice anything** ich habe nichts bemerkt.

notice board *noun* Anschlagbrett *das* (PL *die* Anschlagbretter).

nought *noun* Null *die* (PL *die* Nullen).

noun *noun* Substantiv *das* (PL *die* Substantive).

novel *noun* Roman *der* (PL *die* Romane).

novelist *noun* Romanautor *der* (PL *die* Romanautoren), Romanautorin *die* (PL *die* Romanautorinnen).

November *noun* November *der*; **in November** im November.

now *adverb* **1** jetzt; **where is he now?** wo ist er jetzt?; **from now on** von jetzt an; **2 he left just now** er ist gerade eben gegangen; **I saw her just now in the corridor** ich habe sie gerade eben im Gang gesehen; **3 do it right now!** mach es sofort!; **4 now and then** hin und wieder.

nowhere *adjective* nirgends; **there's nowhere to park** man kann nirgends parken.

nuclear *adjective* Kern-; **nuclear power** *die* Kernenergie; **nuclear power station** *das* Kernkraftwerk.

nude *noun* **in the nude** nackt. *adjective* nackt.

nuisance *noun* **it's a nuisance** das ist ärgerlich; **what a nuisance!** wie ärgerlich!

✧ IRREGULAR VERB: *See the verb table in the centre of the dictionary*

numb *adjective* **1** (*with cold*) gefühllos; **2** (*emotionally*) benommen.

number *noun* **1** (*of a house, telephone, or account*) Nummer *die* (PL *die* Nummern); **I live at number five** ich wohne Nummer fünf; **my new phone number** meine neue Telefonnummer; **2** (*a written figure*) Zahl *die* (PL *die* Zahlen); **3** (*amount*) Anzahl *die*; **the number of visitors** die Anzahl der Besucher.

number plate *noun* Nummernschild *das* (PL *die* Nummernschilder).

nun *noun* Nonne *die* (PL *die* Nonnen).

nurse *noun* Krankenschwester *die* (PL *die* Krankenschwestern); **Janet's a nurse** Janet ist Krankenschwester.

nursery *noun* **1** (*for children*) Kindertagesstätte *die* (PL *die* Kindertagesstätten); **2** (*for plants*) Gärtnerei *die* (PL *die* Gärtnereien).

nursery school *noun* Kindergarten *der* (PL *die* Kindergärten).

nut *noun* **1** Nuss △ *die* (PL *die* Nüsse); **2** (*for a bolt*) Mutter *die* (PL *die* Muttern).

nylon *noun* Nylon *das*.

O o

oak *noun* Eiche *die* (PL *die* Eichen).

oar *noun* Ruder *das* (PL *die* Ruder).

oats *noun* Hafer *der*; **porridge oats** Haferflocken (*plural*).

obedient *adjective* gehorsam.

obey *verb* **1** gehorchen (+DAT); **to obey somebody** jemandem gehorchen; **2 to obey the rules** sich an die Vorschriften halten ✧.

object *noun* **1** (*thing*) Gegenstand *der* (PL *die* Gegenstände); **2** (*aim*) Zweck *der*; **3** (*in grammar*) Objekt *das* (PL *die* Objekte). *verb* etwas dagegen haben ✧; **if you don't object** wenn Sie nichts dagegen haben.

objection *noun* Einwand *der* (PL *die* Einwände).

observe *verb* beobachten.

obsessed *adjective* besessen; **she's really obsessed with her diet** sie ist von ihrer Schlankheitskur ganz besessen.

obstinate *adjective* starrsinnig.

obtain *verb* erhalten ✧.

obvious *adjective* eindeutig.

obviously *adverb* **1** (*of course*) natürlich; **2** (*looking at something*) offensichtlich; **the house is**

obviously empty das Haus steht offensichtlich leer.

occasion *noun* Gelegenheit *die* (PL *die* Gelegenheiten); **on special occasions** zu besonderen Gelegenheiten.

occasionally *adverb* gelegentlich.

occupation *noun* Beruf *der* (PL *die* Berufe).

occupied *adjective* 1 (*taken*) besetzt; **the seat is occupied** der Platz ist besetzt; 2 (*lived in*) bewohnt.

occur *verb* 1 **to occur to somebody** jemandem einfallen ◇SEP (PERF *sein*); **it occurs to me that …** mir fällt ein, dass …; 2 **it never occurred to me** darauf wäre ich nie gekommen; 3 (*happen*) sich ereignen.

ocean *noun* Ozean *der* (PL *die* Ozeane).

o'clock *adverb* **at ten o'clock** um zehn Uhr; **it's three o'clock** es ist drei Uhr.

October *noun* Oktober *der*; **in October** im Oktober.

odd *adjective* 1 (*strange*) komisch; **that's odd, I'm sure I heard the bell** das ist komisch, ich habe es bestimmt klingeln gehört; 2 (*number*) ungerade; **three is an odd number** drei ist eine ungerade Zahl; 3 **the odd one out** die Ausnahme.

odds and ends *plural noun* Kleinkram *der*.

of *preposition* 1 von (+DAT); (*instead of translating 'of' with 'von', the*

genitive case can be used) **the parents of the children** die Eltern von den Kindern, die Eltern der Kinder; **the name of the flower** der Name der Blume; **it's very kind of you** das ist sehr nett von Ihnen; 2 (*with quantities 'of' is not translated*) **a kilo of tomatoes** ein Kilo Tomaten; **a bottle of milk** eine Flasche Milch; **the three of us** drei; 3 **of it/them** davon (*things*); **of them** von ihnen (*people*); **how many of them didn't pay?** wie viele von ihnen haben nicht gezahlt?; **Ray has four cars but he's selling three of them** Ray hat vier Autos, aber er verkauft drei davon; **half of it** die Hälfte davon; **we ate a lot of it** wir haben viel davon gegessen; 4 **the sixth of June** der sechste Juni; 5 **made of** aus; **a bracelet made of silver** ein Armband aus Silber.

off *adverb, adjective, preposition* 1 (*switched off*) aus; **is the telly off?** ist der Fernseher aus?; **to turn off the lights** das Licht ausmachen SEP; 2 (*electricity, water, gas*) abgestellt; **the gas and electricity were off** Gas und Strom waren abgestellt; **to turn off the tap** den Wasserhahn zudrehen SEP; 3 **to be off** (*to leave*) gehen ◇ (PERF *sein*); (*in a vehicle*) fahren ◇ (PERF *sein*); **I must be off** ich muss gehen; 4 **on my day off** an meinem freien Tag; **to take three days off work** sich ←(DAT) drei Tage frei nehmen; **we were given two days off school** wir hatten zwei Tage schulfrei; **to be off sick** wegen Krankheit fehlen; **Maya's off school today** Maya fehlt heute in der

◇ IRREGULAR VERB: *See the verb table in the centre of the dictionary*

Schule; **5** (*cancelled*) abgesagt; **the match is off** das Spiel ist abgesagt worden; **6 '20% off shoes'** 'Schuhe 20% reduziert'.

offence *noun* **1** (*crime*) Straftat *die* (PL *die* Straftaten); **2 to take offence** beleidigt sein; **he takes offence easily** er ist schnell beleidigt.

offer *noun* **1** Angebot *das* (PL *die* Angebote); **job offer** *das* Stellenangebot; **2 on special offer** im Sonderangebot.
verb anbieten ◇ SEP (*a present, a reward, or a job*); **he offered her a chair** er bot ihr einen Stuhl an; **to offer to do something** anbieten, etwas zu tun; **he offered to drive me to the station** er hat angeboten, mich zum Bahnhof zu fahren.

office *noun* Büro *das* (PL *die* Büros); **he's still at the office** er ist noch im Büro.

office block *noun* Bürohaus *das* (PL *die* Bürohäuser).

official *adjective* offiziell.

off-licence *noun* Wein- und Spirituosenhandlung *die* (PL *die* Wein- und Spirituosenhandlungen).

often *adverb* **1** oft; **he's often late** er kommt oft zu spät; **how often?** wie oft?; **2 more often** öfter; **couldn't you come more often?** könntest du nicht öfter kommen?

oil *noun* **1** (*crude oil*) Öl *das*; **2 olive oil** *das* Olivenöl; **suntan oil** *das* Sonnenöl.

ointment *noun* Salbe *die* (PL *die* Salben).

okay *adjective* **1** okay (*informal*); **tomorrow at ten, okay?** morgen um zehn, okay?; **is it okay if I don't come till Friday?** ist es okay, wenn ich erst Freitag komme?; **2** (*person*) in Ordnung; **Daisy's okay** Daisy ist in Ordnung; **3** (*nothing special, not ill*) ganz gut; **the film was okay** der Film war ganz gut; **I've been ill but I'm okay now** ich war krank, aber jetzt geht es mir ganz gut; **'how are you?' – 'okay'** 'wie geht's?' – 'ganz gut'; **4 it's okay by me** mir ist es recht.

old *adjective* **1** (*not young, not new, previous*) alt; **an old man** ein alter Mann; **an old lady** eine alte Dame; **an old tree** ein alter Baum; **old people** alte Leute; **bring some old clothes** bring ein paar alte Sachen mit; **I've only got their old address** ich habe nur ihre alte Adresse; **2** (*talking about age*) **how old are you?** wie alt bist du?; **James is ten years old** James ist zehn Jahre alt; **3 a two-year-old child** ein zweijähriges Kind; **4 my older sister** meine ältere Schwester; **she's older than me** sie ist älter als ich; **he's a year older than me** er ist ein Jahr älter als ich.

old age *noun* Alter *das*.

old age pensioner *noun* Rentner *der* (PL *die* Rentner), Rentnerin *die* (PL *die* Rentnerinnen).

old-fashioned *noun* altmodisch.

olive *noun* Olive *die* (PL *die* Oliven).

△ NEW SPELLING: *See page xii*

olive oil *noun* Olivenöl *das* (PL *die* Olivenöle).

Olympic Games, Olympics *plural noun* Olympische Spiele (*plural*).

omelette *noun* Omelett *das* (PL *die* Omelette); **a cheese omelette** ein Käseomelett.

on *preposition* 1 auf (+DAT, *or* +ACC *with movement towards a place*); **it's on the desk** es ist auf dem Schreibtisch; 2 (*attached to*) an (+DAT, *or* +ACC *with movement towards a place*); **on the wall** an der Wand; 3 **on the beach** am Strand; **on the right/left** rechts/links; 4 (*in expressions of time*) **on March 21st** am 21. März; **he's arriving on Tuesday** er kommt am Dienstag an; **it's shut on Sundays** es ist sonntags geschlossen; **on rainy days** an Regentagen; 5 (*for buses, trains, etc.*) **to go on the bus** mit dem Bus fahren; **I met Jackie on the train** ich habe Jackie im Zug getroffen; **let's go on our bikes** fahren wir mit dem Rad; 6 **on TV** im Fernsehen; **on the radio** im Radio; **on video** auf Video; 7 **on holiday** in den Ferien. *adjective* 1 (*switched on*) **to be on** an sein; **the lights are on** das Licht ist an; **is the radio on?** ist das Radio an?; 2 (*happening*) **what's on TV?** was gibt's im Fernsehen?; **what's on this week at the cinema?** was läuft diese Woche im Kino?

once *adverb* 1 einmal; **I've tried once already** ich habe es schon einmal versucht; **try once more** versuch es noch einmal; **once a day**

einmal täglich; 2 **more than once** mehrmals; 3 **at once** (*immediately*) sofort; **the doctor came at once** der Arzt kam sofort; 4 **at once** (*at the same time*) gleichzeitig; **I can't do two things at once** ich kann nicht zwei Sachen gleichzeitig machen.

one *number* (*when counting*) eins; (*with a noun*) ein; **one son** ein Sohn; **one apple** ein Apfel; **if you want a biro I've got one** falls du einen Kugelschreiber brauchst, habe ich einen; **at one o'clock** um ein Uhr.
pronoun 1 einer/eine/eins; **I saw the photos, can I have one of them?** ich habe die Fotos gesehen, kann ich eins davon haben?; 2 **this one** dieser/diese/dieses; **I'd prefer that bike, but this one's cheaper** ich würde lieber das Rad haben, aber dieses ist billiger; 3 **that one** der da/die da/das da; **'which video?'** – **'that one'** 'welches Video?' – 'das da'; 4 **which one?** welcher/welche/welches?; **'my foot's hurting'** – **'which one?'** 'mir tut der Fuß weh' – 'welcher?'; **'she borrowed a skirt from me'** – **'which one?'** 'sie hat sich einen Rock von mir geliehen' – 'welchen?'; 5 (*you*) man; **one never knows** man kann nie wissen.

one's *adjective* sein/seine/sein; **one pays for one's car** man zahlt für sein Auto.

oneself *pronoun* 1 (*reflexive*) sich; **to wash oneself** sich waschen; 2 (*stressing something*) selbst; **one**

has to do everything oneself man muss alles selbst machen.

one-way street *noun* Einbahnstraße *die* (PL *die* Einbahnstraßen).

onion *noun* Zwiebel *die* (PL *die* Zwiebeln).

only *adjective* 1 einziger/einzige/ einziges; **the only free seat** der einzige freie Platz; **the only thing you could do** das Einzige, was du machen könntest; 2 **an only child** ein Einzelkind.
adverb, conjunction 1 nur; **they've only got two bedrooms** sie haben nur zwei Schlafzimmer; **Anne's only free on Fridays** Anne ist nur freitags frei; **there are only three left** es sind nur noch drei übrig; **I'd walk, only it's raining** ich würde zu Fuß gehen, nur regnet es; 2 (*very recently*) gerade erst; **he's only just got the message** er hat die Nachricht gerade erst bekommen; 3 (*barely*) gerade noch; **we've only just made it on time** wir sind gerade noch rechtzeitig angekommen.

onto *preposition* auf (+ACC).

open *noun* **in the open** im Freien.
adjective 1 offen; **the door's open** die Tür ist offen; **the baker's is not open** die Bäckerei ist nicht geöffnet; 2 **in the open air** im Freien.
verb 1 aufmachen SEP; **can you open the door for me?** kannst du mir die Tür aufmachen?; **the bank opens at nine** die Bank macht um neun auf; 2 (*open up*) sich öffnen; **the door opened slowly** die Tür öffnete sich langsam.

opera *noun* Oper *die* (PL *die* Opern).

operation *noun* 1 Operation *die* (PL *die* Operationen); 2 **to have an operation** operiert werden.

opinion *noun* Meinung *die* (PL *die* Meinungen); **in my opinion** meiner Meinung nach.

opinion poll *noun* Meinungsumfrage *die* (PL *die* Meinungsumfragen).

opportunity *noun* Gelegenheit *die* (PL *die* Gelegenheiten); **to have the opportunity of doing something** die Gelegenheit haben, etwas zu tun.

opposite *noun* Gegenteil *das* (PL *die* Gegenteile); **no, quite the opposite** nein, ganz im Gegenteil.
adjective 1 entgegengesetzt (*direction*); **she went off in the opposite direction** sie ging in die entgegengesetzte Richtung; 2 (*facing*) gegenüberliegend; **in the house opposite** im gegenüberliegenden Haus.
adverb gegenüber; **they live opposite** sie wohnen gegenüber.
preposition gegenüber (+DAT); **opposite the station** gegenüber dem Bahnhof.

optician *noun* Optiker *der* (PL *die* Optiker), Optikerin *die* (PL *die* Optikerinnen).

option *noun* Wahl *die*; **we have no option** wir haben keine andere Wahl.

optional *adjective* auf Wunsch erhältlich; **optional subject** *das* Wahlfach.

△ NEW SPELLING: *See page xii*

or *conjunction* **1** oder; **English or German?** Englisch oder Deutsch?; **today or Tuesday?** heute oder Dienstag?; **2** (*in negatives*) noch; **I don't have a cat or a dog** ich habe weder eine Katze noch einen Hund; **not in June or July** weder im Juni noch im Juli; **3** (*or else*) sonst; **phone Mum, or she'll worry** ruf Mutti an, sonst macht sie sich Sorgen.

oral *noun* (*an exam*) Mündliche *das* (*informal*); **my German oral** mein Deutschmündliches.

orange *noun* (*the fruit*) Orange *die* (PL *die* Orangen); **orange juice** *der* Orangensaft.
adjective orange ('*orange' never changes*); **my orange socks** meine orange Socken.

orchestra *noun* Orchester *das* (PL *die* Orchester).

order *noun* **1** (*sequence*) Reihenfolge *die* (PL *die* Reihenfolgen); **in the right order** in der richtigen Reihenfolge; **in the wrong order** nicht in der richtigen Reihenfolge; **in alphabetical order** in alphabetischer Reihenfolge; **2** (*in a restaurant, café, or shop*) Bestellung *die* (PL *die* Bestellungen); **3** '**out of order**' 'außer Betrieb'; **4 in order to do something** um etwas zu tun.
verb **1** (*in a restaurant or a shop*) bestellen; **we ordered soup** wir haben Suppe bestellt; **have you ordered?** haben Sie schon bestellt?; **2** bestellen (*a taxi*).

ordinary *adjective* normal.

organ *noun* **1** (*the instrument*) Orgel *die* (PL *die* Orgeln); **2** (*of the body*) Organ *das* (PL *die* Organe).

organic *adjective* Bio- (*food*); **organic food** *die* Biokost.

organization *noun* Organisation *die* (PL *die* Organisationen).

organize *verb* **1** organisieren; **2** veranstalten (*a conference or festival*).

original *adjective* **1** ursprünglich; **the original plan was better** der ursprüngliche Plan war besser; **2** originell; **it's a really original novel** das ist ein wirklich origineller Roman.

originally *adverb* ursprünglich; **originally we wanted to go by car** ursprünglich wollten wir mit dem Auto fahren.

other *adjective* **1** anderer/andere/anderes; **we took the other road** wir haben die andere Straße genommen; **where are the others?** wo sind die anderen?; **the other two cars** die anderen beiden Autos; **2 give me the other one** gib mir den anderen/die andere/das andere (*the translation of 'the other one' depends on the gender of the noun it refers to*); **3 the other day** neulich; **4 every other week** jede zweite Woche; **5 somebody or other** irgendjemand; **something or other** irgendetwas; **somewhere or other** irgendwo; **6 any other questions?** sonst noch Fragen?

✧ IRREGULAR VERB: *See the verb table in the centre of the dictionary*

otherwise *adverb, conjunction*
sonst.

ought *verb* (*'ought' is usually
translated by the subjunctive of
'sollen'*) **I ought to go** ich sollte
eigentlich gehen; **they ought to
have known the address** sie
hätten die Adresse kennen sollen;
**you oughtn't to have any
problems** du solltest keine
Probleme haben.

our *adjective* 1 (*before a masculine
noun*) unser; **our father** unser
Vater; 2 (*before a feminine noun*)
unsere; **our mother** unsere Mutter;
3 (*before a neuter noun*) unser; **our
house** unser Haus; 4 (*before
masculine/feminine/neuter plural
nouns*) unsere; **our parents** unsere
Eltern; 5 (*with parts of the body*)
der/die/das (*plural:* die); **we'll go
and wash our hands** wir waschen
uns die Hände.

ours *pronoun* 1 (*for a masculine
noun*) unserer; **their garden's
bigger than ours** ihr Garten ist
größer als unserer; 2 (*for a feminine
noun*) unsere; **their kitchen is
smaller than ours** ihre Küche ist
kleiner als unsere; 3 (*for a neuter
noun*) unsers; **their child is younger
than ours** ihr Kind ist jünger als
unsers; 4 (*for plural nouns*) unsere;
**they've invited their friends and
we've invited ours** sie haben ihre
Freunde eingeladen und wir haben
unsere eingeladen; 5 **the green car
is ours** das grüne Auto gehört uns;
it's ours es gehört uns; **a friend of
ours** ein Freund von uns.

ourselves *pronoun* 1 (*reflexive*)
uns; **we introduced ourselves** wir
haben uns vorgestellt; 2 (*for
emphasis*) selbst; **in the end we did
it ourselves** schließlich haben wir
es selbst gemacht.

out *adverb* 1 (*outside*) draußen; **it's
cold out there** es ist kalt da
draußen; **they're out in the garden**
sie sind draußen im Garten; 2 **to go
out** hinausgehen ✧ SEP (PERF *sein*),
rausgehen ✧ SEP (PERF *sein*)
(*informal*); **to go out shopping**
einkaufen gehen; 3 **get out!** raus!
(*informal*); 4 **the ball is out** der Ball
ist aus; 5 (*absent*) **to be out** nicht
da sein; **Mr Barnes is out** Herr
Barnes ist nicht da; 6 **to go out** (*for
an evening or to the theatre or
cinema*) ausgehen ✧ SEP (PERF *sein*),
weggehen ✧ SEP (PERF *sein*)
(*informal*); **are you going out this
evening?** gehst du heute Abend
weg?; **to be going out with
somebody** mit jemandem gehen;
Alison's going out with Danny now
Alison geht jetzt mit Danny; 7 **to ask
somebody out** jemanden
einladen ✧ SEP; **he's asked me out**
er hat mich eingeladen; 8 (*light,
fire*) aus; **are all the lights out?** ist
das Licht aus?
preposition **out of** aus (+DAT); **to go
out of the room** aus dem Zimmer
gehen; **he threw it out of the
window** er hat es aus dem Fenster
geworfen; **to drink out of a glass**
aus einem Glas trinken; **she took the
photo out of her bag** sie hat das
Foto aus der Tasche genommen.

outdoor *adjective* (*activity or sport*) im Freien; **outdoor games** Spiele im Freien.

outdoors *adverb* draußen; **to go outdoors** nach draußen gehen.

outing *noun* Ausflug *der* (PL *die* Ausflüge); **to go on an outing** einen Ausflug machen.

outline *noun* (*of an object*) Umriss *der* (PL *die* Umrisse).

out-of-date *adjective* 1 (*no longer valid*) ungültig; **my passport's out of date** mein Pass ist ungültig; 2 (*old-fashioned*) altmodisch (*clothes, music*).

outside *noun* Außenseite *die*; **it's blue on the outside** auf der Außenseite ist es blau. *adjective* Außen-. *adverb* draußen; **it's cold outside** es ist kalt draußen. *preposition* vor (+DAT); **I'll meet you outside the cinema** ich treffe mich vor dem Kino mit dir.

oven *noun* Ofen *der* (PL *die* Öfen); **to put something in the oven** etwas in den Ofen tun.

over *preposition* 1 (*above*) über ←(DAT); **there's a mirror over the sink** über dem Waschbecken hängt ein Spiegel; 2 (*involving movement*) über (+ACC); **he threw the ball over the wall** er hat den Ball über die Mauer geworfen; 3 **over here** hier drüben; **the food is over here** das Essen ist hier drüben; 4 **over there** da drüben; **she's over there** sie ist da drüben; 5 (*more than*) über; **it will cost over**

a hundred pounds es wird über hundert Pfund kosten; **he's over sixty** er ist über sechzig; 6 (*during*) über (+ACC); **over Christmas** über Weihnachten; **over the weekend** übers Wochenende; 7 (*finished*) zu Ende; **when the meeting's over** wenn die Besprechung zu Ende ist; **it's all over** es ist vorbei; 8 **over the phone** am Telefon; **to ask someone over** jemanden einladen ✧ SEP; **to come over** herüberkommen ✧ SEP; **come over on Saturday** komm am Samstag zu uns herüber; 9 **all over the place** überall; **I've been looking for it all over** ich habe überall danach gesucht.

overtake *verb* überholen.

overtime *noun* **to work overtime** Überstunden machen.

overweight *adjective* **to be overweight** Übergewicht haben.

owe *verb* schulden; **I owe him ten pounds** ich schulde ihm zehn Pfund.

owing *adjective* 1 (*outstanding*) ausstehend; **there's five pounds owing** fünf Pfund stehen aus; 2 **owing to** wegen (+GEN); **owing to the snow** wegen des Schnees.

owl *noun* Eule *die* (PL *die* Eulen).

own *adjective* 1 eigen; **my own computer** mein eigener Computer; **I've got my own room** ich habe mein eigenes Zimmer; 2 **on your own** allein; **Annie did it on her own** Annie hat es allein gemacht. *verb* besitzen ✧.

✧ IRREGULAR VERB: *See the verb table in the centre of the dictionary*

owner *noun* Besitzer *der* (PL *die* Besitzer), Besitzerin *die* (PL *die* Besitzerinnen).

oxygen *noun* Sauerstoff *der*.

ozone layer *noun* Ozonschicht *die*.

P p

pace *noun* 1 (*a step*) Schritt *der* (PL *die* Schritte); 2 (*the speed you walk at*) Tempo *das* (PL *die* Tempos).

Pacific *noun* the Pacific (Ocean) der Pazifik.

pack *noun* 1 Packung *die* (PL *die* Packungen); 2 **pack of cards** *das* Kartenspiel.
verb 1 packen (*your case*); **I haven't packed yet** ich habe noch nicht gepackt; **I'll pack my case tonight** ich packe meinen Koffer heute Abend; 2 einpacken SEP (*clothes, shoes, etc.*); **have you packed my red shirt?** hast du mein rotes Hemd eingepackt?

package *noun* Paket *das* (PL *die* Pakete).

packed lunch *noun* Lunchpaket *das* (PL *die* Lunchpakete).

packet *noun* 1 Päckchen *das* (PL *die* Päckchen); **a packet of tea** ein Päckchen Tee; 2 (*box*) Schachtel *die* (PL *die* Schachteln); 3 (*bag*) Tüte *die* (PL *die* Tüten); **a packet of crisps** eine Tüte Chips.

pad *noun* (*of paper*) Block *der* (PL *die* Blöcke).

page *noun* Seite *die* (PL *die* Seiten); **on page seven** auf Seite sieben.

pain *noun* Schmerz *der* (PL *die* Schmerzen); **to be in pain** Schmerzen haben; **I've got a pain in my leg** ich habe Schmerzen im Bein; ★ **Eric's a real pain (in the neck)** Eric geht einem richtig auf den Wecker (*informal*).

painful *adjective* schmerzhaft.

paint *noun* Farbe *die* (PL *die* Farben); **'wet paint'** 'frisch gestrichen'.
verb malen (*a picture*); streichen ✧ (*a room*); **to paint a room pink** ein Zimmer rosa streichen.

paintbrush *noun* Pinsel *der* (PL *die* Pinsel).

painter *noun* Maler *der* (PL *die* Maler), Malerin *die* (PL *die* Malerinnen).

painting *noun* (*picture*) Gemälde *das* (PL *die* Gemälde); **a painting by Picasso** ein Gemälde von Picasso.

pair *noun* 1 Paar *das* (PL *die* Paare); **a pair of socks** ein Paar Socken; 2 **a pair of scissors** eine Schere; 3 **a pair of trousers** eine Hose; **a pair of knickers** eine Unterhose; 4 **to work in pairs** paarweise arbeiten.

Pakistan *noun* Pakistan *das*.

palace *noun* Palast *der* (PL *die* Paläste).

pale *adjective* blass ∆; **to turn pale** blass werden; **pale green** zartgrün.

palm *noun* **1** (*of your hand*) Handfläche *die* (PL *die* Handflächen); **2** (*a palm tree*) Palme *die* (PL *die* Palmen).

pan *noun* **1** (*saucepan*) Topf *der* (PL *die* Töpfe); **a pan of water** ein Topf Wasser; **2** (*frying-pan*) Pfanne *die* (PL *die* Pfannen).

pancake *noun* Pfannkuchen *der* (PL *die* Pfannkuchen).

panel *noun* **1** (*for a discussion*) Diskussionsrunde *die*; (*for a quiz*) Rateteam *das*; **2** (*a piece of wood*) Tafel *die* (PL *die* Tafeln).

panic *noun* Panik *die*.
verb in Panik geraten ◇; **don't panic!** keine Panik!

pantomime *noun* Märchenvorstellung *die* (PL *die* Märchenvorstellungen).

pants *plural noun* Unterhose *die* (PL *die* Unterhosen).

paper *noun* **1** Papier *das*; **a sheet of paper** ein Blatt Papier; **2 paper hanky** *das* Papiertaschentuch; **3 paper cup** *der* Pappbecher; **4** (*newspaper*) Zeitung *die* (PL *die* Zeitungen); **it was in the paper** es stand in der Zeitung; **5 papers** (*documents*) Unterlagen (*plural*).

paperback *noun* Taschenbuch *das* (PL *die* Taschenbücher).

paperclip *noun* Büroklammer *die* (PL *die* Büroklammern).

paper towel *noun* Papierhandtuch *das* (PL *die* Papierhandtücher).

parachute *noun* Fallschirm *der* (PL *die* Fallschirme).

parade *noun* Umzug *der* (PL *die* Umzüge).

paragraph *noun* Absatz *der* (PL *die* Absätze); **'new paragraph'** 'Absatz'.

paralysed *adjective* gelähmt.

parcel *noun* Paket *das* (PL *die* Pakete).

pardon *noun* **I beg your pardon** (*as an apology*) Entschuldigung!; **pardon?** wie bitte?

parent *noun* Elternteil *der*; **parents** Eltern (*plural*); **my parents live in Germany** meine Eltern wohnen in Deutschland; **parents' evening** *der* Elternabend.

park *noun* **1** Park *der* (PL *die* Parks); **theme park** *der* (thematische) Freizeitpark; **2 car park** *der* Parkplatz.
verb **1** parken; **you can park outside the house** du kannst vor dem Haus parken; **2 to find somewhere to park** einen Parkplatz finden.

parking *noun* Parken *das*; **'no parking'** 'Parken verboten'.

parking meter *noun* Parkuhr *die* (PL *die* Parkuhren).

parking space *noun* Parklücke *die* (PL *die* Parklücken).

parking ticket *noun* Strafzettel *der* (PL *die* Strafzettel).

parliament *noun* Parlament *das* (PL *die* Parlamente).

parrot *noun* Papagei *der* (PL *die* Papageien).

◇ IRREGULAR VERB: *See the verb table in the centre of the dictionary*

parsley *noun* Petersilie *die*.

part *noun* **1** Teil *der* (PL *die* Teile); **part of the garden** Teil des Gartens; **the last part of the book** der letzte Teil des Buches; **2** **that's part of your job** das gehört dazu; **3 to take part in something** an etwas ←(DAT) teilnehmen ◇ SEP; **4** (*spare part*) Teil *das* (PL *die* Teile) (*for a machine or an engine*); **5** (*a role in a play*) Rolle *die* (PL *die* Rollen).

particular *adjective* besonderer/besondere/besonderes; **nothing in particular** nichts Besonderes.

particularly *adverb* besonders; **not particularly interesting** nicht besonders interessant.

partly *adverb* teilweise.

partner *noun* Partner *der* (PL *die* Partner), Partnerin *die* (PL *die* Partnerinnen).

part-time *adjective* Teilzeit-; **part-time work** *die* Teilzeitarbeit. *adverb* **to work part-time** Teilzeit arbeiten.

party *noun* **1** (*small, private*) Party *die* (PL *die* Partys), Feier *die* (PL *die* Feiern); **a Christmas party** eine Weihnachtsfeier; **to have a birthday party** eine Geburtstagsparty machen; **2** (*more formal, in the evening*) Gesellschaft *die* (PL *die* Gesellschaften); **we've been invited to a party at the Smiths' house** wir sind zu einer Gesellschaft bei Smiths eingeladen worden; **3** (*group*) Gruppe *die* (PL *die* Gruppen); **a party of schoolchildren** eine Gruppe

Schulkinder; **4** (*in politics*) Partei *die* (PL *die* Parteien).

party game *noun* Gesellschaftsspiel *das* (PL *die* Gesellschaftsspiele).

pass *noun* **1** (*to let you in*) Ausweis *der* (PL *die* Ausweise); **2 bus pass** *die* Buskarte; **3** (*over the mountains*) Pass △ *der* (PL *die* Pässe); **4** (*in an exam*) **to get a pass in maths** die Mathematikprüfung bestehen.
verb **1** (*walk past*) vorbeigehen ◇ SEP (PERF *sein*) an (+DAT) (*a place or building*); **we passed your house** wir sind an deinem Haus vorbeigegangen; **2** (*drive past*) vorbeifahren ◇ SEP (PERF *sein*) an (+DAT) (*a place or building*); **3** (*overtake*) überholen (*a car*); **4** (*give*) reichen; **could you pass me the sugar please?** könnten Sie mir bitte den Zucker reichen?; **5** (*time*) vergehen ◇ (PERF *sein*); **the time passed slowly** die Zeit verging langsam; **6** bestehen ◇ (*an exam*); **to pass an exam** eine Prüfung bestehen; **did you pass in German?** hast du die Deutschprüfung bestanden?

passenger *noun* **1** (*in a plane or ship*) Passagier *der* (PL *die* Passagiere); **2** (*in a train or bus*) Fahrgast *der* (PL *die* Fahrgäste); **3** (*in a car*) Mitfahrer *der* (PL *die* Mitfahrer).

Passover *noun* Passah *das*.

passport *noun* Reisepass △ *der* (PL *die* Reisepässe), Pass △ *der* (PL *die* Pässe).

password noun Kennwort das (PL die Kennwörter).

past noun Vergangenheit die; **in the past** in der Vergangenheit.
adjective 1 (recent) letzter/letzte/letztes; **in the past few weeks** in den letzten paar Wochen; 2 (over) vorbei; **winter is past** der Winter ist vorbei.
preposition, adverb 1 **to walk past something** an etwas ←(DAT) vorbeigehen ✧ SEP (PERF sein); **we went past the school** wir sind an der Schule vorbeigegangen; **to go past** vorbeifahren ✧ (PERF sein); 2 (after) nach (+DAT); **it's just past the post office** es ist kurz nach der Post; 3 (talking about time) **ten past six** zehn nach sechs; **half past four** halb fünf; **a quarter past two** Viertel nach zwei.

pasta noun Nudeln (plural); **I don't like pasta** ich mag keine Nudeln.

pastry noun 1 (for baking) Teig der; 2 (cake) Gebäck das.

path noun Weg der (PL die Wege); (very narrow) Pfad der (PL die Pfade).

pathetic adjective (useless, hopeless) jämmerlich.

patience noun 1 Geduld die; 2 (card game) Patience die.

patient noun Patient der (PL die Patienten), Patientin die (PL die Patientinnen).
adjective geduldig.

patiently adverb geduldig.

patio noun Terrasse die (PL die Terrassen).

pattern noun 1 (on wallpaper or fabric) Muster das (PL die Muster); 2 (dressmaking, knitting) Schnitt der (PL die Schnitte).

pause noun Pause die (PL die Pausen).

pavement noun Bürgersteig der (PL die Bürgersteige); **on the pavement** auf dem Bürgersteig.

paw noun Pfote die (PL die Pfoten).

pawn noun (in chess) Bauer der (PL die Bauern).

pay noun (wage) Lohn der (PL die Löhne); (salary) Gehalt das (PL die Gehälter).
verb 1 zahlen; **I'm paying** ich zahle; **to pay cash** bar zahlen; **to pay by credit card** mit Kreditkarte zahlen; **they pay £8 an hour** sie zahlen acht Pfund pro Stunde; **to pay by cheque** mit Scheck zahlen; 2 bezahlen ('bezahlen' is used when you pay a person, a bill or for something); **to pay for something** etwas bezahlen; **Tony paid for the drinks** Tony hat die Getränke bezahlt; **it's all paid for** es ist alles bezahlt; 3 **to pay somebody back** (money) jemandem Geld zurückzahlen SEP; 4 **to pay attention** aufpassen SEP; 5 **to pay a visit to somebody** jemanden besuchen.

payment noun 1 Bezahlung die (of sum, bill, debt, or fine); 2 Zahlung die (PL die Zahlungen) (of interest, tax, or fee).

pay phone noun Münzfernsprecher der (PL die Münzfernsprecher).

✧ IRREGULAR VERB: See the verb table in the centre of the dictionary

PC *noun* (*computer*) PC der (PL die PC).

pea *noun* Erbse die (PL die Erbsen).

peace *noun* Frieden der.

peaceful *adjective* friedlich.

peach *noun* Pfirsich der (PL die Pfirsiche).

peak period (*for holidays*) Hauptferienzeit die (PL die Hauptferienzeiten).

peak rate *noun* (*for phoning*) Höchsttarif der (PL die Höchsttarife).

peak time *noun* (*for traffic*) Stoßzeit die (PL die Stoßzeiten).

peanut *noun* Erdnuss △ die (PL die Erdnüsse).

peanut butter *noun* Erdnussbutter △ die.

pear *noun* Birne die (PL die Birnen).

pearl *noun* Perle die (PL die Perlen).

pebble *noun* Kieselstein der (PL die Kieselsteine).

peculiar *adjective* komisch.

pedal *noun* Pedal das (PL die Pedale).
verb (*on a bike*) **to pedal off** (mit dem Rad) wegfahren ✧ (PERF *sein*).

pedestrian *noun* Fußgänger der (PL die Fußgänger), Fußgängerin die (PL die Fußgängerinnen).

pedestrian crossing *noun* Fußgängerüberweg der (PL die Fußgängerüberwege).

pedestrian precinct *noun* Fußgängerzone die (PL die Fußgängerzonen).

pee *noun* **to have a pee** pinkeln (*informal*).

peel *noun* Schale die (PL die Schalen).
verb schälen (*fruit, vegetables*).

peg *noun* **1** (*hook*) Haken der (PL die Haken); **2 clothes peg** der Kleiderhaken; **3** (*for a tent*) Pflock der (PL die Pflöcke).

pen *noun* (*ball-point*) Kugelschreiber der (PL die Kugelschreiber); **felt pen** der Filzstift.

penalty *noun* **1** (*a fine*) Geldstrafe die (PL die Geldstrafen); **2** (*in football*) Elfmeter der (PL die Elfmeter).

pence *plural noun* Pence (*plural*).

pencil *noun* Bleistift der (PL die Bleistifte); **to write in pencil** mit Bleistift schreiben.

pencil case *noun* Federmäppchen das (PL die Federmäppchen).

pencil sharpener *noun* Bleistiftanspitzer der (PL die Bleistiftanspitzer).

penfriend *noun* Brieffreund der (PL die Brieffreunde), Brieffreundin die (PL die Brieffreundinnen); **my German pen-friend is called Heidi** meine deutsche Brieffreundin heißt Heidi.

penis *noun* Penis der (PL die Penisse).

△ NEW SPELLING: *See page xii*

penny *noun* Penny *der* (PL *die* Pence).

pension *noun* Rente *die* (PL *die* Renten).

pensioner *noun* Rentner *der* (PL *die* Rentner), Rentnerin *die* (PL *die* Rentnerinnen).

people *plural noun* 1 Leute (*plural*), Menschen (*plural*); ('*Menschen*' *is used in a more formal context*); **most people round here** die meisten Leute hier; **several people** verschiedene Leute; **nice people** nette Leute; **all the people in the world** alle Menschen auf der Welt; **a crowd of people** eine Menschenmenge; 2 (*when you're counting them*) Personen (*plural*); **for ten people** für zehn Personen; **how many people have you invited?** wie viele Personen hast du eingeladen?; 3 **people say that** … man sagt, dass …

pepper *noun* 1 (*spice*) Pfeffer *der*; 2 (*vegetable*) Paprikaschote *die* (PL *die* Paprikaschoten).

peppermill *noun* Pfeffermühle *die* (PL *die* Pfeffermühlen).

peppermint *noun* (*plant*) Pfefferminze *die*; **peppermint tea** *der* Pfefferminztee.

per *preposition* pro (+ACC); **ten pounds per person** zehn Pfund pro Person.

per cent *adverb* Prozent *das*; **sixty per cent of students** sechzig Prozent der Studenten.

percentage *noun* Prozentsatz *der* (PL *die* Prozentsätze).

percussion *noun* Schlagzeug *das*; **to play percussion** Schlagzeug spielen.

perfect *adjective* 1 perfekt; **she speaks perfect English** sie spricht perfekt Englisch; 2 (*ideal*) herrlich (*day or weather*).

perfectly *adverb* 1 (*absolutely*) vollkommen; 2 (*faultlessly*) perfekt.

perform *verb* 1 spielen (*a piece of music or a part*); 2 singen ◇ (*a song*); 3 **to perform a play** ein Theaterstück aufführen SEP.

performance *noun* 1 (*playing or acting*) Darstellung *die* (PL *die* Darstellungen); **his performance as Hamlet** seine Darstellung des Hamlet; 2 (*show or film*) Vorstellung *die* (PL *die* Vorstellungen); **the performance starts at eight** die Vorstellung fängt um acht Uhr an; 3 (*of a play or opera*) Aufführung *die* (PL *die* Aufführungen).

performer *noun* Künstler *der* (PL *die* Künstler), Künstlerin *die* (PL *die* Künstlerinnen).

perfume *noun* Parfüm *das* (PL *die* Parfüme).

perhaps *adverb* vielleicht; **perhaps he's missed the train** vielleicht hat er den Zug verpasst.

period *noun* 1 (*length of time*) Zeit *die* (PL *die* Zeiten); **trial period** *die* Probezeit; 2 (*a portion of time*) Zeitraum *der*; **a two-year period**

◇ IRREGULAR VERB: *See the verb table in the centre of the dictionary*

ein Zeitraum von zwei Jahren;
3 (*in school*) Stunde *die* (PL *die*
Stunden); **4** (*menstruation*)
Periode *die* (PL *die* Perioden).

perm *noun* Dauerwelle *die* (PL *die*
Dauerwellen).

permanent *adjective* **1** ständig;
2 fest (*job or address, for example*).

permanently *adverb* **1** dauernd;
2 to be permanently employed fest
angestellt sein.

permission *noun* Erlaubnis *die*; **to
get permission to do something**
Erlaubnis zu etwas ←(DAT) erhalten.

permit *noun* Genehmigung *die* (PL
die Genehmigungen).
verb **1** erlauben; **to permit
somebody to do something**
jemandem erlauben, etwas zu tun;
smoking is not permitted Rauchen
ist nicht gestattet; **2 weather
permitting** bei entsprechendem
Wetter.

person *noun* **1** Person *die* (PL *die*
Personen); **there's still room for
one more person** wir haben noch
Platz für eine Person; **2 in person**
persönlich.

personal *adjective* persönlich.

personality *noun*
Persönlichkeit *die* (PL *die*
Persönlichkeiten).

personally *adverb* persönlich;
personally, I'm against it
persönlich bin dagegen.

perspiration *noun* Schweiß *der*.

persuade *verb* überreden; **to
persuade somebody to come**
jemanden überreden zu kommen.

pessimistic *adjective*
pessimistisch.

pest *noun* **1** (*greenfly, for example*)
Schädling *der* (PL *die* Schädlinge);
2 (*annoying person*) Nervensäge *die*
(PL *die* Nervensägen) (*informal*).

pet *noun* **1** Haustier *das* (PL *die*
Haustiere); **do you have a pet?**
habt ihr Haustiere?; **a pet dog** ein
Hund; **2 Julie is teacher's pet** Julie
ist der Liebling des Lehrers.

petrol *noun* Benzin *das* (PL *die*
Benzine); **to fill up with petrol**
tanken; **to run out of petrol** kein
Benzin mehr haben.

petrol station *noun* Tankstelle *die*
(PL *die* Tankstellen).

pharmacy *noun* Apotheke *die* (PL
die Apotheken).

pheasant *noun* Fasan *der* (PL *die*
Fasane).

phone *noun* Telefon *das* (PL *die*
Telefone); **she's on the phone** sie
telefoniert; **I was on the phone to
Sophie** ich habe mit Sophie
telefoniert; **you can book by phone**
du kannst telefonisch buchen.
verb **1** telefonieren; **while I was
phoning** während ich telefonierte;
2 to phone somebody jemanden
anrufen ✧ SEP; **I'll phone you
tonight** ich rufe dich heute Abend
an.

phone book *noun* Telefonbuch
das (PL *die* Telefonbücher).

△ NEW SPELLING: *See page xii*

phone box *noun* Telefonzelle *die* (PL *die* Telefonzellen).

phone call *noun* 1 Anruf *der* (PL *die* Anrufe); **to get a phone call** einen Anruf erhalten; 2 **to make a phone call** ein Telefongespräch führen; **phone calls are free** Telefongespräche sind gebührenfrei.

phone card *noun* Telefonkarte *die* (PL *die* Telefonkarten).

phone number *noun* Telefonnummer *die* (PL *die* Telefonnummern).

photo *noun* Foto *das* (PL *die* Fotos); **to take a photo** ein Foto machen; **to take a photo of somebody** ein Foto von jemandem machen.

photocopier *noun* Fotokopiergerät *das* (PL *die* Fotokopiergeräte).

photocopy *noun* Fotokopie *die* (PL *die* Fotokopien). *verb* fotokopieren.

photograph *noun* Fotografie *die* (PL *die* Fotografien); **to take a photograph** ein Foto machen. *verb* fotografieren.

photographer *noun* Fotograf *der* (PL *die* Fotografen), Fotografin *die* (PL *die* Fotografinnen).

photography *noun* Fotografie *die*.

physics *noun* Physik *die*.

physiotherapist *noun* Physiotherapeut *der* (PL *die* Physiotherapeuten), Physiotherapeutin *die* (PL *die* Physiotherapeutinnen).

physiotherapy *noun* Physiotherapie *die*.

piano *noun* Klavier *das* (PL *die* Klaviere); **to play the piano** Klavier spielen; **piano lesson** *die* Klavierstunde.

pick *noun* **to take your pick** sich ←(DAT) etwas aussuchen SEP. *verb* 1 (*to select*) wählen; **he picked his words carefully** er wählte seine Worte mit Bedacht; 2 (*choose for oneself*) sich ←(DAT) aussuchen SEP; **pick any book** such dir irgendein Buch aus; 3 **to pick a team** eine Mannschaft aufstellen; 4 pflücken (*fruit*); **to pick strawberries** Erdbeeren pflücken.

● **to pick up** 1 (*lift*) (in die Hand) nehmen ✧; **he picked up the papers** er hat die Unterlagen genommen; 2 (*collect*) abholen SEP; **I'll pick you up at six** ich hole dich um sechs Uhr ab; **I'll pick up the keys tomorrow** ich hole die Schlüssel morgen ab.

pickpocket *noun* Taschendieb *der* (PL *die* Taschendiebe).

picnic *noun* Picknick *das* (PL *die* Picknicke); **to have a picnic** ein Picknick machen.

picture *noun* 1 Bild *das* (PL *die* Bilder); 2 **to go to the pictures** (*the cinema*) ins Kino gehen.

pie *noun* 1 (*sweet*) Kuchen *der* (PL *die* Kuchen); **apple pie** *der* Apfelkuchen; 2 (*savoury*) Pastete *die* (PL *die* Pasteten).

piece *noun* 1 (*a bit*) Stück *das* (PL *die* Stücke); **a big piece of cheese**

✧ IRREGULAR VERB: *See the verb table in the centre of the dictionary*

ein großes Stück Käse; **2** (*that you fit together*) Teil *das* (PL *die* Teile); **the pieces of a jigsaw** die Teile von einem Puzzle; **to take something to pieces** etwas in Einzelteile zerlegen; **3 piece of furniture** *das* Möbelstück; **a piece of information** eine Information; **a piece of luck** ein Glücksfall; **4** (*coin*) Stück *das* (PL *die* Stücke); **a five-pence piece** ein Fünf-Pence-Stück.

pierce *verb* **1** durchstechen ◇ SEP; **2 to have pierced ears** Löcher in den Ohrläppchen haben.

pig *noun* Schwein *das* (PL *die* Schweine).

pigeon *noun* Taube *die* (PL *die* Tauben).

pigtail *noun* Zopf *der* (PL *die* Zöpfe).

pile *noun* **1** (*a neat stack*) Stapel *der* (PL *die* Stapel); **a pile of plates** ein Stapel Teller; **2** (*a heap*) Haufen *der* (PL *die* Haufen).

● **to pile something up** (*neatly*) etwas aufstapeln SEP; (*in a heap*) etwas auftürmen SEP.

pill *noun* Pille *die* (PL *die* Pillen).

pillow *noun* Kopfkissen *das* (PL *die* Kopfkissen).

pilot *noun* Pilot *der* (PL *die* Piloten), Pilotin *die* (PL *die* Pilotinnen).

pimple *noun* Pickel *der* (PL *die* Pickel).

● **pin** *noun* **1** (*for sewing*) Stecknadel *die* (PL *die* Stecknadeln); **2 a three-pin plug** ein dreipoliger Stecker.

● **to pin up 1** hochstecken SEP (*a hem*); **2** anschlagen ◇ SEP (*a notice*).

PIN *noun* (*personal identification number*) Geheimnummer *die*.

pinball *noun* Flippern *das*; **to play pinball** flippern; **pinball machine** *der* Flipper.

pinch *noun* (*of salt, for example*) Prise *die* (PL *die* Prisen).
verb **1** kneifen ◇; **she pinched my arm** sie hat mich in den Arm gekniffen; **2** klauen; **somebody's pinched my bike** jemand hat mein Rad geklaut.

pine *noun* Kiefer *die* (PL *die* Kiefern); **pine furniture** Kiefernmöbel (*plural*).

pineapple *noun* Ananas *die* (PL *die* Ananas).

ping-pong *noun* Tischtennis *das*; **to play ping-pong** Tischtennis spielen.

pink *adjective* rosa (*'rosa' never changes*); **pink hats** rosa Hüte.

pip *noun* (*in a fruit*) Kern *der* (PL *die* Kerne).

pipe *noun* **1** (*for gas or water*) Rohr *das* (PL *die* Rohre); **2** (*for smoking*) Pfeife *die* (PL *die* Pfeifen); **he smokes a pipe** er raucht Pfeife.

Pisces *noun* Fische (*plural*); **Amanda is Pisces** Amanda ist Fisch.

pitch *noun* Platz *der* (PL *die* Plätze); **football pitch** *der* Fußballplatz. *verb* **to pitch a tent** ein Zelt aufstellen SEP.

△ NEW SPELLING: *See page xii*

pity noun 1 (*feeling sorry for somebody*) Mitleid *das*; 2 **what a pity!** wie schade!; **it would be a pity to miss the beginning** es wäre schade, den Anfang zu verpassen.
verb **to pity somebody** jemanden bemitleiden.

place noun 1 Ort *der* (PL *die* Orte); **Salzburg is a wonderful place** Salzburg ist ein schöner Ort; **in place** an Ort und Stelle; 2 **all over the place** überall; 3 (*a space*) Platz *der* (PL *die* Plätze); **a place for the car** ein Platz für das Auto; **is there a place for me?** gibt es Platz für mich?; **will you keep my place?** kannst du mir den Platz freihalten?; **to change places** die Plätze tauschen; 4 (*spot*) Stelle *die* (PL *die* Stellen); **this is a good place to stop** das ist eine gute Stelle zum Halten; 5 (*in a race*) Platz *der* (PL *die* Plätze); **to gain first place** den ersten Platz belegen; 6 **at your place** bei dir; **we'll go round to Zafir's place** wir gehen zu Zafir; 7 **to take place** stattfinden ✧ SEP; **the competition will take place at four** der Wettbewerb findet um vier Uhr statt.
verb (*upright*) stellen; (*lying flat*) legen.

plain noun Ebene *die* (PL *die* Ebenen).
adjective 1 einfach; **plain food** einfaches Essen; 2 (*unflavoured*) Natur-; **plain yoghurt** *der* Naturjoghurt; 3 (*not patterned*) einfarbig; **plain curtains** einfarbige Vorhänge.

plait noun Zopf *der* (PL *die* Zöpfe).

plan noun Plan *der* (PL *die* Pläne); **we've made plans for the summer** wir haben Pläne für den Sommer gemacht; **to go according to plan** nach Plan gehen; **everything went according to plan** alles ist nach Plan gegangen.
verb 1 **to plan to do something** etwas vorhaben ✧ SEP; **we're planning to leave at eight** wir haben vor, um acht abzufahren; 2 (*make plans for, organize, design*) planen; **she's planning a trip to Italy** sie plant eine Reise nach Italien.

plane noun Flugzeug *das* (PL *die* Flugzeuge); **we went by plane** wir sind geflogen.

planet noun Planet *der* (PL *die* Planeten).

plant noun Pflanze *die* (PL *die* Pflanzen); **a house plant** eine Topfpflanze.
verb pflanzen.

plaster noun 1 (*sticking plaster*) Pflaster *das* (PL *die* Pflaster); 2 (*for walls*) Verputz *der*; 3 Gips *der*; **to have your leg in plaster** das Bein in Gips haben.

plastic noun Plastik *das*; **plastic bag** *die* Plastiktüte.

plate noun Teller *der* (PL *die* Teller).

platform noun 1 (*in a station*) Bahnsteig *der* (PL *die* Bahnsteige); 2 **the train is arriving at platform six** der Zug fährt auf Gleis sechs ein; 3 (*for lecturing or performing*) Podium *das* (PL *die* Podien).

play noun (*in the theatre*) Stück *das* (PL *die* Stücke); **television play** *das*

Fernsehspiel; **we are putting on a play by Brecht at school** wir führen ein Stück von Brecht in der Schule auf.

verb **1** spielen; **the children are playing with a ball** die Kinder spielen Ball; **they play the piano and the guitar** sie spielen Klavier und Gitarre; **who's playing Hamlet?** wer spielt Hamlet?; **to play tennis** Tennis spielen; **they were playing cards** sie haben Karten gespielt; **2** (*in sport*) **to play somebody** gegen jemanden spielen; **Italy are playing Germany** Italien spielt gegen Deutschland; **3** spielen (*a tape, CD, or record*); **play your new CD** spiele mal deine neue CD.

player *noun* **1** Spieler *der* (PL *die* Spieler), Spielerin *die* (PL *die* Spielerinnen); **football player** *der* Fußballspieler; **2** (*in the theatre*) Schauspieler *der* (PL *die* Schauspieler), Schauspielerin *die* (PL *die* Schauspielerinnen).

playground *noun* Spielplatz *der* (PL *die* Spielplätze); **school playground** *der* Schulhof.

playgroup *noun* Kindergarten *der* (PL *die* Kindergärten).

playing field *noun* Sportplatz *der* (PL *die* Sportplätze).

pleasant *adjective* angenehm.

please *adverb* bitte; **two coffees, please** zwei Kaffee bitte; **could you turn the TV off, please?** könntest du bitte den Fernseher ausmachen?

pleased *adjective* **1** erfreut; **I'm really pleased!** das freut mich wirklich!; **2 she was pleased with her present** sie hat sich über ihr Geschenk gefreut; **3 pleased to meet you!** freut mich!

pleasure *noun* **1** (*amusement*) Vergnügen *das*; **2** (*joy*) Freude *die*; **to get a lot of pleasure out of something** viel Freude an etwas ←(DAT) haben.

plenty *pronoun* **1** (*lots*) viel; **he's got plenty of money** er hat viel Geld; **2** (*enough*) genug; **that's plenty!** das ist genug!; **we've got plenty of time left** wir haben noch genug Zeit.

plot *noun* (*of a film or novel*) Handlung *die*.

plug *noun* **1** (*electrical*) Stecker *der* (PL *die* Stecker); **2** (*in a bath or sink*) Stöpsel *der* (PL *die* Stöpsel); **to pull out the plug** den Stöpsel herausziehen.

plum *noun* Pflaume *die* (PL *die* Pflaumen); **plum tart** *der* Pflaumenkuchen.

plumber *noun* Installateur *der* (PL *die* Installateure).

plural *noun* Mehrzahl *die*, Plural *der*; **in the plural** in der Mehrzahl, im Plural.

plus *preposition* plus (+DAT); **three children plus a baby** drei Kinder und ein Baby.

p.m. *abbreviation* nachmittags (*for times up to 6 p.m.*); abends (*for times after 6 p.m.*); **at two p.m.** um zwei Uhr nachmittags, um vierzehn Uhr; **at nine p.m.** um neun Uhr abends, um einundzwanzig Uhr (*in German you usually express times after*

△ NEW SPELLING: *See page xii*

midday in terms of the 24-hour clock).

pocket *noun* Tasche *die* (PL *die* Taschen).

pocket money *noun* Taschengeld *das*.

poem *noun* Gedicht *das* (PL *die* Gedichte).

poet *noun* Dichter *der* (PL *die* Dichter), Dichterin *die* (PL *die* Dichterinnen).

poetry *noun* Dichtung *die*.

point *noun* 1 (*tip*) Spitze *die* (PL *die* Spitzen); **the point of a nail** die Spitze eines Nagels; 2 (*a tiny mark or dot*) Punkt *der* (PL *die* Punkte); 3 (*in time*) Zeitpunkt *der* (PL *die* Zeitpunkte); **at that point** zu diesem Zeitpunkt; **to be on the point of doing something** gerade etwas tun wollen; 4 **that's not the point** darum geht es nicht; **there's no point phoning, he's out** es hat keinen Sinn anzurufen, er ist nicht da; **what's the point?** wozu?; 5 **that's a good point!** das stimmt!; **the point is** … es geht darum …; 6 **point of view** *der* Standpunkt; **from my point of view** von meinem Standpunkt aus; 7 **her strong point** ihre Stärke; 8 (*in scoring*) Punkt *der* (PL *die* Punkte); **to win by fifteen points** mit fünfzehn Punkten Vorsprung gewinnen; 9 (*in decimals*) **6 point 4** sechs Komma vier (*in German, a comma is used for the decimal point*).
verb 1 hinweisen ◇ SEP auf (+ACC); **a notice pointing to the station** ein Schild, das auf den Bahnhof

hinweist; 2 (*with your finger*) zeigen auf (+ACC); **he pointed at Tom** er zeigte auf Tom.

pointless *adjective* sinnlos; **it's pointless to keep on ringing** es ist sinnlos, dauernd zu klingeln.

poison *noun* Gift *das* (PL *die* Gifte). *verb* vergiften.

poisonous *adjective* giftig.

Poland *noun* Polen *das*.

pole *noun* 1 (*for a tent*) Stange *die* (PL *die* Stangen); 2 (*for skiing*) Stock *der* (PL *die* Stöcke); 3 **the North Pole** der Nordpol.

Pole *noun* (*a Polish person*) Pole *der* (PL *die* Polen), Polin *die* (PL *die* Polinnen).

police *noun* **the police** die Polizei; **the police are coming** die Polizei kommt.

police car *noun* Streifenwagen *der* (PL *die* Streifenwagen).

policeman *noun* Polizist *der* (PL *die* Polizisten).

police station *noun* Polizeiwache *die* (PL *die* Polizeiwachen).

policewoman *noun* Polizistin *die* (PL *die* Polizistinnen).

polish *noun* 1 (*for furniture*) Politur *die*; 2 (*for shoes*) Schuhcreme *die*; 3 (*for the floor*) Bohnerwachs *das*. *verb* 1 polieren (*furniture, silver*); 2 **to polish your shoes** seine Schuhe putzen.

◇ IRREGULAR VERB: *See the verb table in the centre of the dictionary*

Polish noun (language)
Polnisch das.
adjective polnisch.

polite adjective höflich; **to be polite
to somebody** höflich zu jemandem
sein.

political adjective politisch.

politician noun Politiker der (PL die
Politiker), Politikerin die (PL die
Politikerinnen).

politics noun Politik die.

polluted adjective verschmutzt.

pollution noun
Verschmutzung die.

polo-necked adjective Rollkragen-;
a polo-necked jumper ein
Rollkragenpullover.

pond noun Teich der (PL die Teiche).

pony noun Pony das (PL die Ponys).

ponytail noun Pferdeschwanz der
(PL die Pferdeschwänze).

poodle noun Pudel der (PL die
Pudel).

pool noun 1 (swimming pool)
Schwimmbecken das (PL die
Schwimmbecken); 2 (pond)
Tümpel der (PL die Tümpel);
3 (puddle) Lache die (PL die
Lachen); 4 (game) Poolbillard das;
5 **the football pools** das Toto; **to do
the pools** Toto spielen.

poor adjective 1 arm; **a poor country**
ein armes Land; **a poor family** eine
arme Familie; 2 **poor Tanya's failed
her exam** die arme Tanya ist durch
die Prüfung gefallen; 3 (bad)

schlecht; **that's a poor result** das
ist ein schlechtes Ergebnis; **the
weather was pretty poor** das Wetter
war ziemlich schlecht.

pop noun Popmusik die; **pop
concert** das Popkonzert; **pop star**
der Popstar; **pop song** der Schlager.
● **to pop into: I'll just pop into the
bank** ich gehe kurz auf die Bank.

popcorn noun Puffmais der.

pope noun Papst der (PL die Päpste).

poppy noun Mohn der.

popular adjective beliebt.

population noun Bevölkerung die
(PL die Bevölkerungen).

porch noun Vorbau der (PL die
Vorbauten).

pork noun Schweinefleisch das;
pork chop das Schweinekotelett.

porridge noun Haferbrei der.

port noun 1 Hafen der (PL die
Häfen); 2 (wine) Portwein der (PL
die Portweine).

porter noun 1 (at a station or an
airport) Gepäckträger der (PL die
Gepäckträger); 2 (in a hotel)
Portier der (PL die Portiers).

portion noun (of food) Portion die
(PL die Portionen).

portrait noun Porträt das (PL die
Porträts).

Portugal noun Portugal das.

Portuguese noun 1 (language)
Portugiesisch das; 2 (a person)
Portugiese der (PL die Portugiesen),

Portugiesin *die* (PL *die* Portugiesinnen).
adjective portugiesisch.

posh *adjective* vornehm; **a posh area** eine vornehme Gegend.

position *noun* 1 Platz *der* (PL *die* Plätze); 2 (*situation*) Lage *die* (PL *die* Lagen); 3 (*status, job*) Stellung *die* (PL *die* Stellungen).

positive *adjective* 1 (*sure*) sicher; **I'm positive he's left** ich bin mir sicher, dass er gegangen ist; 2 (*enthusiastic*) positiv; **her reaction was very positive** ihre Reaktion war sehr positiv.

possessions *plural noun* Sachen (*plural*); **all my possessions are in the flat** alle meine Sachen sind in der Wohnung.

possibility *noun* Möglichkeit *die* (PL *die* Möglichkeiten).

possible *adjective* möglich; **it's possible** es ist gut möglich; **if possible** wenn möglich; **as quickly as possible** so schnell wie möglich.

possibly *adverb* 1 (*maybe*) möglicherweise; **'will you be at home at midday?' – 'possibly'** 'bist du mittags zu Hause?' – 'möglicherweise'; 2 **how can you possibly believe that?** wie kannst du das nur glauben?; **I can't possibly arrive before Thursday** ich kann unmöglich vor Donnerstag ankommen.

post *noun* 1 (*jar*) Post *die*; **to send something by post** etwas per Post schicken; (*letters*) **is there any post for me?** ist Post für mich

gekommen?; 2 (*a pole*) Pfosten *der* (PL *die* Pfosten); 3 (*a job*) Stelle *die* (PL *die* Stellen).
verb **to post a letter** einen Brief abschicken SEP.

postbox *noun* Briefkasten *der* (PL *die* Briefkästen).

postcard *noun* Postkarte *die* (PL *die* Postkarten).

postcode *noun* Postleitzahl *die* (PL *die* Postleitzahlen).

poster *noun* 1 (*for decoration*) Poster *das* (PL *die* Poster); **I've bought an Oasis poster** ich habe ein Poster von Oasis gekauft; 2 (*advertising*) Plakat *das* (PL *die* Plakate); **I saw a poster for the concert** ich habe ein Plakat für das Konzert gesehen.

postman *noun* Briefträger *der* (PL *die* Briefträger).

post office *noun* Post *die*; **the post office is on the right** die Post ist au der rechten Seite.

postpone *verb* verschieben ✧; **we've postponed the meeting until next week** wir haben die Besprechung auf nächste Woche verschoben.

postwoman *noun* Briefträgerin *die* (PL *die* Briefträgerinnen).

pot *noun* 1 (*jar*) Topf *der* (PL *die* Töpfe); **a pot of honey** ein Topf Honig; 2 (*teapot*) Kanne *die* (PL *die* Kannen); 3 **the pots and pans** die Töpfe und Pfannen.

✧ IRREGULAR VERB: *See the verb table in the centre of the dictionary*

potato noun Kartoffel die (PL die Kartoffeln); **fried potatoes** Bratkartoffeln (plural); **mashed potatoes** der Kartoffelbrei.

potato crisps plural noun Kartoffelchips (plural).

pottery noun 1 (craft) Töpferei die; 2 (objects) Töpferwaren (plural).

pound noun 1 (money) Pfund das (PL die Pfunde); **fourteen pounds** vierzehn Pfund; **three marks to the pound** drei Mark für ein Pfund; **a five pound note** ein Fünfpfundschein; 2 (in weight) Pfund das; **two pounds of apples** zwei Pfund Äpfel.

pour verb 1 gießen ✧ (liquid); **he poured milk into the pan** er hat Milch in den Topf gegossen; 2 eingießen ✧ SEP (a drink); **to pour the tea** den Tee eingießen; **I poured him a drink** ich habe ihm zu trinken eingegossen; 3 (with rain) **it's pouring** es gießt.

poverty noun Armut die.

powder noun 1 Pulver das (PL die Pulver); 2 (for face or body) Puder der (PL die Puder).

power noun 1 (electricity) Strom der; **a power cut** eine Stromsperre; 2 (energy) Energie die; **nuclear power** die Kernenergie; 3 (strength) Kraft die; 4 (over other people) Macht die; **to be in power** an der Macht sein.

powerful adjective (strong) stark; (influential) mächtig.

power station noun Kraftwerk das (PL die Kraftwerke).

practical adjective praktisch.

practice noun 1 (for sport) Training das; **hockey practice** das Hockeytraining; 2 Übung die; **to do your piano practice** Klavier üben; **to be out of practice** außer Übung sein.

practise verb 1 üben (an instrument, exercise, or skill); **to practise the piano** Klavier üben; 2 anwenden SEP (a language); **a week in Berlin to practise my German** eine Woche in Berlin, um mein Deutsch anzuwenden; 3 (in sport) trainieren; **the team practises on Wednesday** die Mannschaft trainiert Mittwoch.

praise verb loben; **to praise somebody for something** jemanden für etwas ←(ACC) loben.

pram noun Kinderwagen der (PL die Kinderwagen).

prawn noun Garnele die (PL die Garnelen).

pray verb beten.

prayer noun Gebet das (PL die Gebete).

precinct noun **shopping precinct** das Einkaufszentrum; **pedestrian precinct** die Fußgängerzone.

precisely adverb genau; **at eleven o'clock precisely** um genau elf Uhr.

prefer verb 1 vorziehen ✧ SEP; **I prefer Anna to her sister** ich ziehe Anna ihrer Schwester vor; 2 **to prefer to do something** etwas lieber tun; **I prefer to stay at home** ich bleibe lieber zu Hause.

∆ NEW SPELLING: See page xii

pregnant *adjective* schwanger.

prejudice *noun* Vorurteil *das* (PL *die* Vorurteile); **to fight against racial prejudice** gegen Rassenvorurteile ankämpfen.

prejudiced *adjective* **to be prejudiced** voreingenommen sein.

prep *noun* Hausaufgaben (*plural*); **my English prep** meine Englischhausaufgaben.

preparation *noun* Vorbereitung *die* (PL *die* Vorbereitungen); **in preparation for something** in Vorbereitung auf etwas ←(ACC); **our preparations for Christmas** unsere Weihnachtsvorbereitungen.

prepare *verb* 1 vorbereiten SEP; **to prepare somebody for something** jemanden auf etwas ←(ACC) vorbereiten; 2 **to be prepared for the worst** sich auf das Schlimmste gefasst machen.

prepared *adjective* bereit; **I'm prepared to pay half** ich bin bereit, die Hälfte zu zahlen.

preposition *noun* Präposition *die* (PL *die* Präpositionen).

prep school *noun* private Grundschule *die*.

prescription *noun* Rezept *das* (PL *die* Rezepte); **on prescription** auf Rezept.

present *noun* 1 (*a gift*) Geschenk *das* (PL *die* Geschenke); **to give somebody a present** jemandem ein Geschenk machen; 2 (*the time now*) Gegenwart *die*;

in the present (tense) in der Gegenwart; 3 **that's all for the present** das ist vorläufig alles. *adjective* 1 (*attending*) anwesend; **Mr Blair is not present** Herr Blair ist nicht anwesend; **to be present at something** bei etwas ←(DAT) anwesend sein; **fifty people were present at the funeral** fünfzig Personen waren bei der Beerdigung anwesend; 2 (*existing now*) gegenwärtig; **the present situation** die gegenwärtige Lage; 3 **at the present time** zur Zeit. *verb* 1 überreichen (*a prize*); 2 (*introduce*) vorstellen SEP; 3 (*on TV, radio*) moderieren (*a programme*).

presenter *noun* (*on TV*) Moderator *der* (PL *die* Moderatoren Moderatorin *die* (PL *die* Moderatorinnen).

president *noun* Präsident *der* (PL *die* Präsidenten), Präsidentin *die* (P *die* Präsidentinnen).

press *noun* **the press** die Presse. *verb* 1 (*to push*) drücken; **press here!** hier drücken!; 2 drücken au (+ACC) (*a button or switch*); **she pressed the button** sie hat auf den Knopf gedrückt.

press conference *noun* Pressekonferenz *die* (PL *die* Pressekonferenzen).

pressure *noun* Druck *der*; **to put pressure on somebody** jemanden unter Druck setzen.

pressure group *noun* Interessengruppe *die* (PL *die* Interessengruppen).

⬦ IRREGULAR VERB: *See the verb table in the centre of the dictionary*

pretend *verb* **to pretend that** ... so tun, als ob ...; **he's pretending not to hear** er tut so, als ob er nicht hört.

pretty *adjective* hübsch; **a pretty dress** ein hübsches Kleid. *adverb* ziemlich; **it was pretty silly** das war ziemlich blöd.

prevent *verb* **to prevent somebody from doing something** jemanden daran hindern, etwas zu tun; **there's nothing to prevent you from leaving** niemand kann dich daran hindern wegzugehen.

previous *adjective* **1** (*earlier*) früher (*years, opportunity, or job*); **2** (*immediately preceding*) vorig; **on the previous Tuesday** am vorigen Dienstag.

price *noun* Preis *der* (PL die Preise); **the price per kilo** der Preis pro Kilo; **CDs have gone up in price** CDs sind im Preis gestiegen; **what is the price of this?** was kostet das?

price list *noun* Preisliste *die* (PL die Preislisten).

price ticket *noun* Preisschild *das* (PL die Preisschilder).

prick *verb* stechen ◇; **to prick your finger** sich in den Finger stechen.

pride *noun* Stolz *der*.

priest *noun* Priester *der* (PL die Priester).

primary school *noun* Grundschule *die* (PL die Grundschulen).

primary (school) teacher *noun* Grundschullehrer *der* (PL die Grundschullehrer),

Grundschullehrerin *die* (PL die Grundschullehrerinnen).

prime minister *noun* Premierminister *der* (PL die Premierminister), Premierministerin *die* (PL die Premierministerinnen).

prince *noun* Prinz *der* (PL die Prinzen).

princess *noun* Prinzessin *die* (PL die Prinzessinnen).

principal *noun* (*of a college*) Direktor *der* (PL die Direktoren), Direktorin *die* (PL die Direktorinnen). *adjective* (*main*) Haupt-.

principle *noun* Prinzip *das* (PL die Prinzipien); **on principle** im Prinzip; **that's true in principle** im Prinzip stimmt das.

print *noun* **1** (*letters*) Druck *der*; **in small print** klein gedruckt; **2** (*a photo*) Abzug *der* (PL die Abzüge); **colour print** der Farbabzug.

printer *noun* (*for a computer*) Drucker *der* (PL die Drucker).

print-out *noun* Ausdruck *der* (PL die Ausdrucke).

prison *noun* Gefängnis *das* (PL die Gefängnisse); **in prison** im Gefängnis.

prisoner *noun* Gefangene *der/die* (PL die Gefangenen).

private *adjective* **1** Privat-, privat; **private school** die Privatschule; **private property** das Privateigentum; **to have private**

lessons Privatstunden nehmen;
2 in private privat.

prize *noun* Preis *der* (PL *die* Preise);
to win a prize einen Preis
gewinnen.

prize-giving *noun*
Preisverleihung *die* (PL *die*
Preisverleihungen).

prizewinner *noun* Gewinner *der*
(PL *die* Gewinner), Gewinnerin *die*
(PL *die* Gewinnerinnen).

probable *adjective* wahrscheinlich.

probably *adverb* wahrscheinlich.

problem *noun* Problem *das* (PL *die*
Probleme); **it's a serious problem**
das ist ein ernstes Problem; **no
problem!** kein Problem!

process *noun* **1** Prozess △ *der* (PL *die*
Prozesse); **2 to be in the process of
doing something** dabei sein, etwas
zu tun.

produce *noun* (*food*) Erzeugnisse
(*plural*).
verb **1** herstellen SEP (*goods, food*);
2 vorzeigen SEP (*a ticket, document*);
I produced my passport ich habe
meinen Pass vorgezeigt; **3** erzeugen
(*interest, tension*); **it produces heat**
es erzeugt Wärme; **4 to produce a
film** einen Film produzieren; **5 to
produce a play** ein Theaterstück
inszenieren.

producer *noun* (*of a film or
programme*) Produzent *der* (PL *die*
Produzenten).

product *noun* Produkt *das* (PL *die*
Produkte).

production *noun* **1** (*of a film or an
opera*) Produktion *die* (PL *die*
Produktionen); **2** (*of a play*)
Inszenierung *die* (PL *die*
Inszenierungen); **a new production
of Hamlet** eine neue Inszenierung
von Hamlet; **3** (*by a factory*)
Produktion *die*.

profession *noun* Beruf *der* (PL *die*
Berufe).

professional *noun* **1** (*a trained
person*) Fachmann *der* (PL *die*
Fachleute); **2** (*in sport*) Profi *der* (PL
die Profis).
adjective **1** professionell (*work,
sportsman*); **a professional
footballer** ein professioneller
Fußballer; **2** beruflich (*career,
success*); **she's a professional
singer** sie ist Sängerin von Beruf.

professor *noun* Professor *der* (PL
die Professoren), Professorin *die* (PL
die Professorinnen).

profile *noun* Profil *das* (PL *die*
Profile).

profit *noun* Gewinn *der* (PL *die*
Gewinne).

profitable *adjective* rentabel.

program *noun* **computer program**
das Programm.

programme *noun* **1** (*for a play or a
event*) Programm *das* (PL *die*
Programme); **2** (*on TV or radio*)
Sendung *die* (PL *die* Sendungen).

progress *noun* **1** Fortschritt *der* (PL
die Fortschritte); **to make progress**
Fortschritte machen; **2 to be in
progress** im Gange sein.

◇ IRREGULAR VERB: *See the verb table in the centre of the dictionary*

project noun 1 (*at school*) Arbeit die (PL die Arbeiten); 2 (*a plan*) Projekt das (PL die Projekte); **a project to build a bridge** ein Brückenbauprojekt.

promise noun Versprechen das (PL die Versprechen); **to make somebody a promise** jemandem ein Versprechen geben; **to keep a promise** ein Versprechen halten; **it's a promise!** ganz bestimmt! verb **to promise something** etwas versprechen ✧; **I've promised to ring my mother** ich habe versprochen, meine Mutter anzurufen.

promote verb **to be promoted** (*in football*) aufsteigen ✧ SEP (PERF sein); (*at work*) befördert werden.

promotion noun 1 Beförderung die; 2 (*in football*) Aufstieg der; 3 (*in advertising*) Reklame die.

pronoun noun Pronomen das (PL die Pronomen).

pronounce verb aussprechen ✧ SEP; **you don't pronounce the 'c'** das 'c' spricht man nicht aus.

pronunciation noun Aussprache die.

proof noun Beweis der (PL die Beweise); **there's no proof that …** es gibt keine Beweise dafür, dass …

propaganda noun Propaganda die.

propeller noun Propeller der (PL die Propeller).

proper adjective 1 (*correct, real, genuine*) richtig; **the proper answer** die richtige Antwort; **he's not a proper doctor** er ist kein richtiger Arzt; 2 (*decent*) anständig; **I need a proper meal** ich brauche ein anständiges Essen; 3 **in its proper place** an Ort und Stelle.

properly adverb 1 richtig; 2 (*decent*) anständig.

property noun 1 (*your belongings*) Eigentum das; 2 (*land, premises*) Besitz der; **'private property'** 'Privatbesitz'; 3 (*house*) Haus das (PL die Häuser).

propose verb 1 (*suggest*) vorschlagen ✧ SEP; 2 (*marriage*) **he proposed to her** er hat ihr einen Heiratsantrag gemacht.

protect verb schützen; **to protect somebody from something** jemanden vor etwas ←(DAT) schützen.

protection noun Schutz der.

protein noun Protein das (PL die Proteine).

protest noun 1 Beschwerde die (PL die Beschwerden); **to make a protest** eine Beschwerde einlegen SEP; 2 (*disapproval*) Protest der (PL die Proteste); **in protest against something** aus Protest gegen etwas ←(ACC). verb protestieren; **to protest about something** gegen etwas ←(ACC) protestieren.

Protestant noun Protestant der (PL die Protestanten), Protestantin die (PL die Protestantinnen). adjective protestantisch.

△ NEW SPELLING: *See page xii*

protest march *noun*
Protestmarsch *der* (PL *die*
Protestmärsche).

proud *adjective* stolz; **to be proud
about something** stolz auf etwas
←(ACC) sein.

prove *verb* beweisen ✧.

provide *verb* zur Verfügung stellen.

provided, providing *conjunction*
vorausgesetzt; **provided it doesn't
rain** vorausgesetzt, es regnet nicht.

prune *noun* Backpflaume *die* (PL *die*
Backpflaumen).

psychiatrist *noun* Psychiater *der*
(PL *die* Psychiater), Psychiaterin *die*
(PL *die* Psychiaterinnen).

psychological *adjective*
psychologisch.

psychologist *noun*
Psychologe *der* (PL *die*
Psychologen), Psychologin *die* (PL
die Psychologinnen).

psychology *noun* Psychologie *die*.

PTO *abbreviation* b.w. (*bitte
wenden*).

pub *noun* Kneipe *die* (PL *die*
Kneipen) (*informal*).

public *noun* **the public** die
Öffentlichkeit; **in public** in aller
Öffentlichkeit.
adjective öffentlich.

public holiday *noun* gesetzliche
Feiertag *der* (PL *die* gesetzlichen
Feiertage); **January 1st is a public
holiday** der erste Januar ist ein
gesetzlicher Feiertag.

publicity *noun* **1** Publicity *die*;
2 (*advertising*) Werbung *die*.

public school *noun*
Privatschule *die* (PL *die*
Privatschulen).

public transport *noun* öffentliche
Verkehrsmittel (*plural*).

publish *verb* veröffentlichen.

publisher *noun* **1** Verleger *der* (PL
die Verleger), Verlegerin *die* (PL *die*
Verlegerinnen); **2** (*company*)
Verlag *der* (PL *die* Verlage).

pudding *noun* (*dessert*)
Nachtisch *der* (PL *die* Nachtische);
**for pudding we've got
strawberries** zum Nachtisch gibt es
Erdbeeren.

puddle *noun* Pfütze *die* (PL *die*
Pfützen).

puff *noun* (*of smoke*) Wölkchen *das*
(PL *die* Wölkchen).

puff pastry *noun* Blätterteig *der*.

pull *verb* **1** ziehen ✧; **to pull a cart**
einen Wagen ziehen; **2** ziehen an
(+DAT); **to pull a rope** an einem Seil
ziehen; **he pulled a letter out of his
pocket** er hat einen Brief aus der
Tasche gezogen; ★ **he's pulling
your leg!** er nimmt dich auf den Arm
(*literally: he's picking you up in his
arms*).
● **to pull down 1** herunterziehen ✧
SEP; **2** (*demolish*) abreißen ✧ SEP (*a
building*).
● **to pull in** (*at the roadside*) an den
Straßenrand fahren ✧ (PERF *sein*).

pullover *noun* Pullover *der* (PL *die*
Pullover).

pump *noun* Pumpe *die* (PL *die*
Pumpen); **bicycle pump** *die*

Fahrradpumpe.
verb pumpen.
- **to pump up** aufpumpen SEP.

punch *noun* **1** (*in boxing*)
Faustschlag *der* (PL *die*
Faustschläge); **2** (*drink*) Bowle *die*
(PL *die* Bowlen).
verb **1 he punched me in the
stomach** er hat mich in den Magen
geboxt; **2** lochen (*a ticket*).

punctual *adjective* pünktlich.

punctuation *noun*
Interpunktion *die*.

punctuation mark *noun*
Satzzeichen *das* (PL *die*
Satzzeichen).

puncture *noun* (*flat tyre*)
Reifenpanne *die* (PL *die*
Reifenpannen).

punish *verb* bestrafen.

punishment *noun* Strafe *die* (PL *die*
Strafen).

pupil *noun* Schüler *der* (PL *die*
Schüler), Schülerin *die* (PL *die*
Schülerinnen).

puppet *noun* Puppe *die* (PL *die*
Puppen).

puppy *noun* junge Hund *der* (PL *die*
jungen Hunde); **a boxer puppy** ein
junger Boxer.

pure *adjective* rein.

purple *adjective* lila (*'lila' never
changes*).

purpose *noun* **1** Zweck *der* (PL *die*
Zwecke); **what's the purpose of it?**
was hat das für einen Zweck?; **2 on
purpose** absichtlich; **she did it on**

purpose das hat sie absichtlich
getan; **he closed the door on
purpose** er hat die Tür absichtlich
zugemacht.

purr *verb* schnurren.

purse *noun* Portemonnaie *das* (PL
die Portemonnaies).

push *noun* **to give something a
push** etwas schieben ✧.
verb **1** schubsen; **he pushed me** er
hat mich geschubst; **2** (*to press*)
drücken auf (+ACC) (*a bell or button*);
**3 to push somebody to do
something** jemanden zu etwas
drängen; **his teacher is pushing him
to sit the exam** sein Lehrer drängt
ihn, die Prüfung zu machen; **4 to
push your way through the crowd**
sich durch die Menge drängen.
- **to push something away** etwas
wegschieben ✧ SEP; **she pushed her
plate away** sie schob ihren Teller
weg.

pushchair *noun* Sportwagen *der*
(PL *die* Sportwagen).

put *verb* **1** (*place generally*) tun ✧;
put some milk in your tea tu etwas
Milch in den Tee; **you can put the
butter in the fridge** du kannst die
Butter in den Kühlschrank tun; **2** (*lay
flat*) legen; **she put the pencil on the
desk** sie hat den Bleistift auf den
Schreibtisch gelegt; **3** (*place
upright*) stellen; **where did you put
my bag?** wo hast du meine
Handtasche hingestellt?; **4** (*write*)
schreiben ✧; **put your address
here** schreiben Sie Ihre Adresse
hierhin.
- **to put away** wegräumen SEP; **put**

away your things räume deine Sachen weg.

- **to put back 1** zurücklegen SEP, zurückstellen SEP, zurücktun SEP (*the translation of 'put back' depends on the way it is done: if it's placed lying down, use 'zurücklegen', if placed upright use 'zurückstellen' and if it could be either, use 'zurücktun'*); **I put it back in the drawer** ich habe es in die Schublade zurückgetan; **2** (*postpone*) verschieben ✧; **the meeting has been put back until Thursday** die Besprechung ist auf Donnerstag verschoben worden.

- **to put down** (*lying down*) hinlegen SEP; (*upright*) hinstellen SEP; **where can I put the vase down?** wo kann ich die Vase hinstellen?

- **to put off 1** (*postpone*) verschieben ✧; **he's put off my lesson till Thursday** er hat meine Stunde auf Donnerstag verschoben; **2** (*turn off*) ausmachen SEP; **don't forget to put off the lights** vergiss nicht, das Licht auszumachen; **3 to put somebody off something** jemandem die Lust an etwas ←(DAT) verderben ✧; **it really put me off my food** das hat mir wirklich die Lust am Essen verdorben; **4 to put somebody off doing something** jemanden davon abbringen ✧ SEP, etwas zu tun; **don't be put off** lass dich nicht davon abbringen.

- **to put on 1** anziehen ✧ SEP (*clothes*); **I'll just put my shoes on** ich ziehe nur schnell meine Schuhe an; **2** auflegen SEP (*a CD or record*); **I'm putting on Oasis** ich lege Oasis auf; **3** (*switch on*) anmachen SEP (*a light or the heating*); **could you put the lamp on?** kannst du die Lampe anmachen?

- **to put out 1** (*put outside*) hinaustun ✧ SEP, raustun ✧ SEP (*informal*); **have you put the rubbish out?** hast du den Müll rausgetan?; **2** ausmachen SEP (*a light or cigarette*); **I've put the lights out** ich habe das Licht ausgemacht; **3 to put out your hand** die Hand ausstrecken SEP.

- **to put up 1** heben ✧ (*your hand*); **2** aufhängen SEP (*a picture or poster*); **I've put up some posters in my room** ich habe ein paar Poster in meinem Zimmer aufgehängt; **3** anschlagen ✧ SEP (*a notice*); **4** erhöhen (*the price*); **they've put up the fare** sie haben den Fahrpreis erhöht; **5** (*for the night*) **friends put me up** ich habe bei Freunden übernachtet; **can you put me up on Friday?** kann ich Freitag bei euch übernachten?

- **to put up with something** etwas aushalten ✧ SEP; **I don't know how she puts up with it** ich weiß nicht, wie sie das aushält.

puzzle *noun* (*jigsaw*) Puzzle *das* (PL *die* Puzzles).

puzzled *adjective* verdutzt.

pyjamas *plural noun* Schlafanzug *der* (PL *die* Schlafanzüge); **a pair of pyjamas** ein Schlafanzug; **where are my pyjamas?** wo ist mein Schlafanzug?

✧ IRREGULAR VERB: *See the verb table in the centre of the dictionary*

Q q

qualification *noun* **1** (*ability, experience*) Qualifikation *die* (PL *die* Qualifikationen); **2** (*on paper*) Zeugnis *das* (PL *die* Zeugnisse).

qualified *adjective* **1** ausgebildet; **she's a qualified ski instructor** sie ist eine ausgebildete Skilehrerin; **2** (*having a degree or a diploma*) Diplom-; **a qualified engineer** ein Diplomingenieur.

quality *noun* Qualität *die*; **good quality products** Waren von guter Qualität.

quantity *noun* Menge *die* (PL *die* Mengen).

quarrel *noun* Streit *der* (PL *die* Streite); **to have a quarrel** Streit haben.
verb sich streiten ✧; **they're always quarrelling** sie streiten sich dauernd.

quarter *noun* **1** Viertel *das* (PL *die* Viertel); **a quarter of the price** ein Viertel des Preises; **three quarters of the class** drei Viertel der Klasse; **it's a quarter past ten** es ist Viertel nach zehn; **it's a quarter to ten** es ist Viertel vor zehn; **2 we meet at quarter to eight** wir treffen uns um Viertel vor acht; **3 a quarter of an hour** eine Viertelstunde; **4 three quarters of an hour** eine Dreiviertelstunde; **5 an hour and a quarter** eineinviertel Stunden.

queen *noun* **1** Königin *die* (PL *die* Königinnen); **2** (*in chess, cards*) Dame *die* (PL *die* Damen).

question *noun* Frage *die* (PL *die* Fragen); **to ask somebody a question** jemandem eine Frage stellen; **I asked her a question** ich habe ihr eine Frage gestellt; **it's out of the question** das kommt nicht in Frage.
verb befragen (*a person*).

question mark *noun* Fragezeichen *das* (PL *die* Fragezeichen).

questionnaire *noun* Fragebogen *der* (PL *die* Fragebögen).

queue *noun* (*of people, cars*) Schlange *die* (PL *die* Schlangen); **to stand in a queue** Schlange stehen; **a queue of cars** eine Autoschlange.

quick *adjective* schnell; **to have a quick lunch** schnell etwas zu Mittag essen; **it's quicker on the motorway** auf der Autobahn geht es schneller; **to have a quick look at something** sich ←(DAT) schnell etwas ansehen; **be quick!** mach schnell!

quickly *adverb* schnell; **I'll just quickly phone my mother** ich rufe schnell meine Mutter an.

quiet *adjective* **1** (*silent*) still; **to keep quiet** still sein; **please keep quiet** sei bitte still; **2** (*not loud*) leise; **the children are very quiet** die Kinder sind ganz leise; **in a quiet voice** mit leiser Stimme; **3** (*peaceful*) ruhig; **a quiet street** eine ruhige Straße.

△ NEW SPELLING: *See page xii*

quietly adverb 1 (speak, move) leise; **he got up quietly** er ist leise aufgestanden; 2 (read or play) ruhig; **to sit quietly** ruhig sitzen.

quilt noun Steppdecke die (PL die Steppdecken).

quite adverb 1 (fairly) ziemlich; **it's quite cold outside** es ist ziemlich kalt draußen; **quite often** ziemlich oft; **quite a few** ziemlich viele; **quite a few of our friends came** ziemlich viele unserer Freunde sind gekommen; **quite a few people** ziemlich viele Leute; **that's quite a good idea** das ist eine ganz gute Idee; 2 (completely) völlig; **it was quite amazing** es war einfach fantastisch; **not quite** nicht ganz; **she's not quite ready** sie ist noch nicht ganz fertig; 3 genau; **I don't quite know what he wants** ich weiß nicht genau, was er will; **quite !** genau!

quiz noun Quiz das (PL die Quiz).

quotation noun (from a book) Zitat das (PL die Zitate).

quotation marks plural noun Anführungszeichen (plural); **in quotation marks** in Anführungszeichen.

quote noun 1 (from a book) Zitat das (PL die Zitate); 2 (estimate) Kostenvoranschlag der (PL die Kostenvoranschläge). verb zitieren.

R r

rabbi noun Rabbi der (PL die Rabbis).

rabbit noun Kaninchen das (PL die Kaninchen).

race noun 1 (a sports event) Rennen das (PL die Rennen); **cycle race** das Radrennen; 2 **to have a race** (running) um die Wette laufen ◇ (PERF sein); (swimming) um die Wette schwimmen ◇ (PERF sein); 3 (an ethnic group) Rasse die (PL die Rassen).

racetrack noun Rennbahn die (PL die Rennbahnen).

racial adjective rassisch, Rassen-; **racial discrimination** die Rassendiskriminierung.

racing car noun Rennwagen der (PL die Rennwagen).

racing driver noun Rennfahrer der (PL die Rennfahrer).

racism noun Rassismus der.

racist noun Rassist der (PL die Rassisten), Rassistin die (PL die Rassistinnen). adjective rassistisch.

racket noun 1 (for tennis) Schläger der (PL die Schläger); **my tennis racket** mein Tennisschläger; 2 (noise) Krach der.

radiator noun Heizkörper der (PL die Heizkörper).

◇ IRREGULAR VERB: *See the verb table in the centre of the dictionary*

radio *noun* Radio *das* (PL *die* Radios); **to listen to the radio** Radio hören; **to hear something on the radio** etwas im Radio hören.

radioactive *adjective* radioaktiv.

radio station *noun* Rundfunkstation *die* (PL *die* Rundfunkstationen).

radish *noun* Radieschen *das* (PL *die* Radieschen).

rag *noun* Lumpen *der* (PL *die* Lumpen).

rage *noun* Wut *die*; **to fly into a rage** in Wut geraten ✧ (PERF *sein*); **she's in a rage** sie ist wütend; ★ **it's all the rage** das ist der letzte Schrei (*literally: it's the last scream*).

rail *noun* 1 (*for a train*) Schiene *die* (PL *die* Schienen); 2 (*the railway*) **to go by rail** mit der Bahn fahren; 3 (*on a balcony, bridge, or stairs*) Geländer *das* (PL *die* Geländer).

rail card *noun* Bahnpass △ *der* (PL *die* Bahnpässe).

railing(s) *noun* Geländer *das* (PL *die* Geländer).

railway *noun* 1 (*the system*) Bahn *die*; **the railways** die Bahn; 2 **railway line** (*from one place to another*) *die* Bahnstrecke; 3 **on the railway line** (*the track*) auf dem Gleis.

railway carriage *noun* Eisenbahnwagen *der* (PL *die* Eisenbahnwagen).

railway station *noun* Bahnhof *der* (PL *die* Bahnhöfe).

rain *noun* Regen *der*; **in the rain** im Regen.
verb regnen; **it's raining** es regnet; **it's going to rain** es wird regnen.

rainbow *noun* Regenbogen *der* (PL *die* Regenbogen).

raincoat *noun* Regenmantel *der* (PL *die* Regenmäntel).

rainy *adjective* regnerisch.

raise *verb* 1 (*lift up*) hochheben ✧ SEP; 2 (*increase*) erhöhen (*prices*); 3 **to raise money for something** Geld für etwas aufbringen ✧ SEP.

raisin *noun* Rosine *die* (PL *die* Rosinen).

rally *noun* 1 (*a meeting*) Versammlung *die* (PL *die* Versammlungen); 2 (*for cars*) Rallye *die* (PL *die* Rallyes); 3 (*in tennis*) Ballwechsel *der* (PL *die* Ballwechsel).

rambler *noun* Wanderer *der* (PL *die* Wanderer), Wanderin *die* (PL *die* Wanderinnen).

rambling *noun* Wandern *das*.

range *noun* 1 (*a choice*) Auswahl *die*; **a wide range of travel brochures** eine große Auswahl an Reiseprospekten; 2 **a range of subjects** verschiedene Fächer; **in a range of colours** in verschiedenen Farben; 3 **a computer in this price range** ein Computer in dieser Preislage; **that's out of my price range** das kann ich mir nicht leisten.

rap *noun* Rap *der* (*music*).

rape noun Vergewaltigung die (PL die Vergewaltigungen).
verb vergewaltigen.

rare adjective 1 selten; **a rare bird** ein seltener Vogel; 2 englisch gebraten (*steak*).

rarely adverb selten.

rash noun Ausschlag der (PL die Ausschläge).
adjective voreilig.

raspberry noun Himbeere die (PL die Himbeeren); **raspberry jam** die Himbeermarmelade.

rat noun Ratte die (PL die Ratten).

rate noun 1 (*a charge*) Gebühren (*plural*); **postage rates** Postgebühren; 2 **are there special rates for children?** gibt es Sonderpreise für Kinder?; **at reduced rates** zu ermäßigten Preisen; 3 **rate of exchange** der Wechselkurs; 4 **rate of pay** der Lohnsatz; 5 (*a level*) Rate die (PL die Raten); **a high cancellation rate** eine hohe Absagerate; 6 **at any rate** auf jeden Fall.

rather adverb 1 lieber; **I'd rather wait** ich warte lieber; **I'd rather you didn't go** es wäre mir lieber, wenn du nicht gingst; 2 ziemlich; **I'm rather busy** ich habe ziemlich viel zu tun; **I've got rather a lot of shopping to do** ich muss noch ziemlich viel einkaufen; 3 **rather than** eher als; **in summer rather than winter** eher im Sommer als im Winter.

rave noun (*party*) Fete die (PL die Feten) (*informal*).

raw adjective roh.

razor noun Rasierapparat der (PL die Rasierapparate).

razor blade noun Rasierklinge die (PL die Rasierklingen).

RE noun Religionsunterricht der.

reach noun Reichweite die; **out of reach** außer Reichweite; **within reach** leicht ereichbar; **to be within easy reach of Munich** von München aus leicht erreichbar sein.
verb 1 ankommen ✧ SEP (PERF *sein*) an (+DAT) (*a place or point*), ankommen ✧ SEP (PERF *sein*) in (+DAT) (*a town or country*); **when you reach the station** wenn du am Bahnhof ankommst; 2 kommen ✧ (PERF *sein*) zu (+DAT) (*an agreement, a conclusion*); **to reach a decision** zu einer Entscheidung kommen; 3 **to reach for something** nach etwas ←(DAT) greifen ✧.

react verb reagieren.

reaction noun Reaktion die (PL die Reaktionen).

read verb 1 lesen ✧; **what are you reading at the moment?** was liest du zur Zeit?; **I'm reading a detective novel** ich lese einen Krimi; 2 **to read out** vorlesen ✧ SEP; **he read out the list to the students** er hat die Liste den Studenten vorgelesen.

reading noun 1 (*action*) Lesen das; 2 (*reading matter*) Lektüre die; **some easy reading for the holidays** eine leichte Lektüre für die Ferien.

ready adjective 1 fertig; **supper's not ready yet** das Essen ist noch nicht

---

✧ IRREGULAR VERB: *See the verb table in the centre of the dictionary*

fertig; **we are not quite ready** wir sind noch nicht ganz fertig; **are you ready to leave?** seid ihr fertig?; (*on a journey*) seid ihr reisefertig?; **to get ready** sich fertig machen; **I'm getting ready to play tennis** ich mache mich zum Tennisspielen fertig; **I was getting ready for bed** ich war gerade dabei, ins Bett zu gehen; **2 to get something ready** (*complete*) etwas fertig machen, etwas vorbereiten SEP (*a room or food*); **I'll get your room ready** ich bereite dein Zimmer vor.

real *adjective* **1** (*genuine*) echt; **it's a real diamond** das ist ein echter Brillant; **he's a real coward** er ist ein echter Feigling; **2** (*true*) richtig; **is that her real name?** ist das ihr richtiger Name?; **3** (*not imagined*) wirklich; **it's a real pity you can't come** es ist wirklich schade, dass du nicht kommen kannst.

realistic *adjective* realistisch.

realize *verb* wissen ◇; **I hadn't realized** das wusste ich nicht; **I didn't realize he was French** ich habe nicht gewusst, dass er Franzose ist; **do you realize what time it is?** weißt du, wie viel Uhr es ist?

really *adverb* **1** wirklich; **the film was really good** der Film war wirklich gut; **really?** wirklich?; **2 not really** eigentlich nicht.

reason *noun* Grund *der* (PL *die* Gründe); **for that reason** aus diesem Grund; **the reason why I phoned** der Grund meines Anrufs.

reasonable *adjective* vernünftig.

receipt *noun* Quittung *die* (PL *die* Quittungen).

receive *verb* erhalten ◇.

receiver *noun* Hörer *der* (PL *die* Hörer); **to pick up the receiver** den Hörer abnehmen ◇ SEP.

recent *adjective* **1** kürzlich erfolgter/kürzlich erfolgte/ kürzlich erfolgtes; **the recent closure** die kürzlich erfolgte Schließung; **2 in recent years** in den letzten Jahren.

recently *adverb* **1** (*at a time not long ago*) kürzlich; **2** (*over the recent period*) in letzter Zeit.

reception *noun* **1** Rezeption *die* (PL *die* Rezeptionen); **he's waiting at reception** er wartet in der Rezeption; **2** Empfang *der* (PL *die* Empfänge); **a big wedding reception** ein großer Hochzeitsempfang; **3 to get a good reception** gut aufgenommen werden.

receptionist *noun* **1** Empfangsdame *die* (PL *die* Empfangsdamen); **2** (*in a doctor's surgery*) Sprechstundenhilfe *die* (PL *die* Sprechstundenhilfen).

recipe *noun* Rezept *das* (PL *die* Rezepte).

reckon *verb* glauben; **I reckon it's a good idea** ich glaube, das ist eine gute Idee.

recognize *verb* erkennen ◇.

recommend *verb* empfehlen ◇; **can you recommend a dentist?** kannst du mir einen Zahnarzt

△ NEW SPELLING: *See page xii*

empfehlen?; **I recommend the fish soup** ich empfehle die Fischsuppe.

record noun **1** Rekord der (PL die Rekorde); **it's a world record** das ist ein Weltrekord; **record sales** Verkaufsrekorde; **2** (of events) Aufzeichnung die (PL die Aufzeichnungen); **on record** aufgezeichnet; **to keep a record of something** sich ←(DAT) etwas notieren; **3** (music) Platte die (PL die Platten); **a Miles Davis record** eine Platte von Miles Davis; **4 records** (office files) Unterlagen (plural); **I'll just check your records** ich prüfe nur Ihre Unterlagen.
verb (on tape) aufnehmen ✧ SEP; **I'm recording it on cassette** ich nehme es auf Kassette auf.

recorder noun **1** Blockflöte die (PL die Blockflöten); **to play the recorder** Blockflöte spielen; **2 cassette recorder** der Kassettenrekorder; **video recorder** der Videorekorder.

recording noun (on tape or CD) Aufnahme die (PL die Aufnahmen); (on video) Aufzeichnung die (PL die Aufzeichnungen).

record player noun Plattenspieler der (PL die Plattenspieler).

recover verb sich erholen; **she's recovered now** sie hat sich wieder erholt.

recovery noun (from an illness) Erholung die; **to make a good recovery** sich gut erholen.

recycle verb recyceln.

red adjective rot; **a red car** ein rotes Auto; **to go red** rot werden; **to have red hair** rote Haare haben.

Red Cross noun **the Red Cross** das Rote Kreuz.

redcurrant noun Johannisbeere die (PL die Johannisbeeren); **redcurrant jelly** das Johannisbeergelee.

redecorate verb (with paint) neu streichen ✧; (with wallpaper) neu tapezieren; **they've redecorated the kitchen** sie haben die Küche neu gestrichen.

redo verb noch einmal machen.

reduce verb **1 to reduce prices** die Preise herabsetzen SEP; **2 to reduce speed** die Geschwindigkeit verringern.

reduction noun **1** (in price) Ermäßigung die (PL die Ermäßigungen); **2** (in speed or number) Verringerung die.

redundant adjective **to be made redundant** entlassen werden.

referee noun (in sport) Schiedsrichter der (PL die Schiedsrichter), Schiedsrichterin die (PL die Schiedsrichterinnen).

reference noun Referenz die (PL die Referenzen); (for a job) **she gave me a good reference** sie hat mir gute Referenzen ausgestellt.

reference book noun Nachschlagewerk das (PL die Nachschlagewerke).

refill verb nachfüllen SEP.

✧ IRREGULAR VERB: *See the verb table in the centre of the dictionary*

reflect *verb* spiegeln; **to be reflected** sich spiegeln.

reflection *noun* 1 (*in a mirror or on water*) Spiegelung *die* (PL *die* Spiegelungen); **to see your reflection in the mirror** sich im Spiegel sehen; 2 (*thought*) Überlegung *die*; **on reflection** nach nochmaliger Überlegung.

reflexive *adjective* **a reflexive verb** ein reflexives Verb.

refreshing *adjective* erfrischend.

refrigerator *noun* Kühlschrank *der* (PL *die* Kühlschränke).

refugee *noun* Flüchtling *der* (PL *die* Flüchtlinge).

refund *noun* Rückzahlung *die* (PL *die* Rückzahlungen). *verb* zurückerstatten SEP.

refusal *noun* 1 Weigerung *die* (PL *die* Weigerungen); 2 (*for a job*) Absage *die* (PL *die* Absagen); **to get a refusal** eine Absage bekommen.

refuse *noun* (*rubbish*) Abfall *der*. *verb* sich weigern; **I refused** ich habe mich geweigert; **he refuses to help** er weigert sich zu helfen.

regards *plural noun* Grüße (*plural*); **regards to your parents** viele Grüße an deine Eltern; **Nat sends his regards** Nat lässt grüßen.

reggae *noun* Reggae *der*.

region *noun* Gebiet *das* (PL *die* Gebiete).

regional *adjective* regional.

register *noun* (*in school*) Anwesenheitsliste *die* (PL *die* Anwesenheitslisten), Klassenbuch *das* (PL *die* Klassenbücher) (*kept by the teacher, it also contains notes about students' achievements*). *verb* 1 eintragen ◆ SEP (*a name*); 2 (*report*) anmelden SEP.

registered letter *noun* Einschreiben *das* (PL *die* Einschreiben).

registration number *noun* Autonummer *die* (PL *die* Autonummern).

regret *verb* bedauern.

regular *adjective* regelmäßig; **regular visits** regelmäßige Besuche.

regularly *adverb* regelmäßig.

regulation *noun* Vorschrift *die* (PL *die* Vorschriften).

rehearsal *noun* Probe *die* (PL *die* Proben).

rehearse *verb* proben.

reheat *verb* aufwärmen SEP.

reject *verb* ablehnen SEP.

related *adjective* verwandt; **we're not related** wir sind nicht verwandt.

relation *noun* Verwandte *der/die* (PL *die* Verwandten).

relationship *noun* Beziehung *die* (PL *die* Beziehungen); **I have a good relationship with my parents** ich habe eine gute Beziehung zu meinen Eltern.

△ NEW SPELLING: *See page xii*

relative *noun* Verwandte *der/die* (PL *die* Verwandten).

relatively *adverb* relativ.

relax *verb* entspannen; **I'm going to relax and watch telly tonight** heute Abend entspanne ich und sehe fern.

relaxed *adjective* entspannt.

relaxing *adjective* entspannend.

relay race *noun* Staffel *die* (PL *die* Staffeln).

release *noun* (*a film, CD, or book*) **1** Neuerscheinung *die* (PL *die* Neuerscheinungen); **this week's new releases** die neuen Filme der Woche; **2** (*of a prisoner or hostage*) Freilassung *die* (PL *die* Freilassungen).
verb **1** herausbringen ✧ SEP (*a record, film, or video*); **2** freilassen ✧ SEP (*a person*).

reliable *adjective* zuverlässig.

relief *noun* Erleichterung *die*; **what a relief!** da bin ich aber erleichtert!

relieve *verb* stillen (*pain*).

relieved *adjective* erleichtert; **I was relieved to hear you'd arrived** es hat mich erleichtert zu hören, dass du angekommen bist.

religion *noun* Religion *die* (PL *die* Religionen).

religious *adjective* religiös.

rely *verb* **1** (*trust*) **to rely on somebody** sich auf jemanden verlassen ✧; **I'm relying on your help for Saturday** ich verlasse mich darauf, dass du mir am Samstag hilfst; **2** (*be dependent on*) **to rely on** angewiesen sein auf (+ACC).

remain *verb* (*be left over*) übrig bleiben ✧ Δ (PERF *sein*); (*stay*) bleiben ✧ (PERF *sein*).

remark *noun* Bemerkung *die* (PL *die* Bemerkungen); **to make remarks about something** Bemerkungen über etwas ←(ACC) machen.

remarkable *adjective* bemerkenswert.

remarkably *adverb* bemerkenswert.

remember *verb* **1** sich erinnern an (+ACC) (*a person or an occasion*); **I don't remember** daran kann ich mich nicht erinnern; **do you remember the holiday in Italy?** erinnerst du dich noch an die Ferien in Italien?; **2 I can't remember his number** seine Nummer fällt mir nicht ein; **3 to remember to do something** daran denken ✧, etwas zu tun; **remember to lock the door** denk daran abzuschließen; **I remembered to bring the CDs** ich habe daran gedacht, die CDs mitzubringen.

remind *verb* **1** erinnern; **to remind somebody to do something** jemanden daran erinnern, etwas zu tun; **remind your mother to pick me up** erinnere deine Mutter daran, mich abzuholen; **he reminds me of my brother** er erinnert mich an meinen Bruder; **2 oh, that reminds me ...** dabei fällt mir ein, ...

remote *adjective* abgelegen.

✧ IRREGULAR VERB: *See the verb table in the centre of the dictionary*

remote control noun 1 (for a car or plane) Fernsteuerung die (PL die Fernsteuerungen); 2 (for TV or video) Fernbedienung die (PL die Fernbedienungen).

remove verb 1 entfernen (a stain, mark, or obstacle); 2 ausziehen ✧ SEP (clothes).

renew verb verlängern (a passport or licence).

rent noun Miete die (PL die Mieten). verb mieten; **Simon's rented a flat** Simon hat eine Wohnung gemietet.

reorganize verb umorganisieren.

repair noun Reparatur die (PL die Reparaturen). verb reparieren; **to get something repaired** etwas reparieren lassen; **we've had the television repaired** wir haben unseren Fernseher reparieren lassen.

repay verb zurückzahlen SEP.

repeat noun Wiederholung die (PL die Wiederholungen). verb wiederholen.

repeatedly adverb wiederholt.

repetitive adjective eintönig.

replace verb ersetzen.

reply noun Antwort die (PL die Antworten); **I didn't get a reply to my letter** ich habe keine Antwort auf meinen Brief bekommen; **there's no reply** niemand antwortet. verb antworten; **I still haven't replied to the letter** ich habe immer noch nicht auf den Brief geantwortet.

report noun 1 (of an event) Bericht der (PL die Berichte); 2 (school report) Zeugnis das (PL die Zeugnisse). verb 1 melden (a problem or an accident); **we've reported the theft** wir haben den Diebstahl gemeldet; 2 sich melden; **I had to report to reception** ich musste mich an der Rezeption melden; 3 (in the news) berichten; **to report on the strike** über den Streik berichten.

reporter noun Reporter der (PL die Reporter), Reporterin die (PL die Reporterinnen).

represent verb 1 darstellen SEP (a word, a thing, an idea); 2 verteten ✧ (a group or company).

representative noun Vertreter der (PL die Vertreter), Vertreterin die (PL die Vertreterinnen).

republic noun Republik die (PL die Republiken).

reputation noun 1 Ruf der; **to have a good reputation** einen guten Ruf haben; 2 **she has a reputation for honesty** sie gilt als ehrlich.

request noun Bitte die (PL die Bitten); **at my mother's request** auf Bitte meiner Mutter. verb bitten ✧; **to request something** um etwas ←(ACC) bitten.

rescue noun Rettung die; **rescue operation** die Rettungsaktion; **to come to somebody's rescue** jemandem zu Hilfe kommen. verb retten; **they rescued the dog** sie haben den Hund gerettet.

rescue party *noun*
Rettungsmannschaft *die* (PL *die*
Rettungsmannschaften).

research *noun* 1 Forschung *die*;
for research into Aids für die
Aidsforschung; 2 **to do research**
forschen.
verb **to research into something**
etwas erforschen.

resemblance *noun*
Ähnlichkeit *die* (PL *die*
Ähnlichkeiten).

reservation *noun* (*a booking*)
Reservierung *die* (PL *die*
Reservierungen); **to make a
reservation (for a room)** (ein
Zimmer) reservieren lassen.

reserve *noun* 1 Reserve *die* (PL *die*
Reserven); **we have a few in
reserve** wir haben ein paar in
Reserve; 2 **nature reserve** *das*
Naturschutzgebiet; 3 (*for a match*)
Reservespieler *der* (PL *die*
Reservespieler), Reservespielerin
die (PL *die* Reservespielerinnen).
verb reservieren; **this table is
reserved** dieser Tisch ist reserviert.

resident *noun* Bewohner *der* (PL *die*
Bewohner), Bewohnerin *die* (PL *die*
Bewohnerinnen).

residential *adjective* Wohn-; **a
residential area** eine Wohngegend.

resign *verb* 1 (*from your job*)
kündigen; 2 (*from an official post*)
zurücktreten ✧ SEP.

resignation *noun* 1 Kündigung *die*
(PL *die* Kündigungen); 2 (*from an
official post*) Rücktritt *der*.

resist *verb* widerstehen ✧ (+DAT)
(*an offer or temptation*).

resit *verb* wiederholen (*an exam*).

resort *noun* 1 (*for holidays*) **holiday
resort** *der* Urlaubsort; **ski resort**
der Skiurlaubsort; **seaside resort**
das Seebad; 2 **as a last resort** als
letzter Ausweg.

respect *noun* Respekt *der*.
verb respektieren.

respectable *adjective* anständig.

responsibility *noun*
Verantwortung *die* (PL *die*
Verantwortungen).

responsible *adjective*
1 verantwortlich; **he was
responsible for the accident** er war
für den Unfall verantwortlich; **I'm
responsible for booking the rooms**
ich bin für die Zimmerreservierung
verantwortlich; 2 (*reliable*)
verantwortungsbewusst ∆; **he's not
very responsible** er ist nicht sehr
verantwortungsbewusst.

rest *noun* 1 **the rest** der Rest; **the
rest of the day** der Rest des Tages;
the rest of the bread der Brotrest,
der Rest von dem Brot; 2 (*the others*)
the rest die Übrigen; **the rest have
gone home** die Übrigen sind nach
Hause gegangen; 3 Erholung *die*;
**he's going to the mountains for a
rest** er fährt zur Erholung ins
Gebirge; **ten days' rest** zehn Tage
Erholung; **to have a rest** sich
ausruhen SEP; 4 (*a short break*)
Pause *die* (PL *die* Pausen); **to stop for
a rest** eine Pause machen.
verb (*have a rest*) sich ausruhen SEP.

✧ IRREGULAR VERB: *See the verb table in the centre of the dictionary*

restaurant *noun* Restaurant *das* (PL *die* Restaurants).

restful *adjective* erholsam.

restless *adjective* unruhig.

restrain *verb* zurückhalten ✧ SEP.

result *noun* 1 Ergebnis *das* (PL *die* Ergebnisse); **the exam results** die Prüfungsergebnisse; 2 **as a result** infolgedessen; **as a result we missed the train** infolgedessen haben wir den Zug verpasst.

retire *verb* 1 (*from work*) aufhören zu arbeiten; (*civil servant, teacher, soldier*) sich pensionieren lassen; **she retires in June** sie lässt sich im Juni pensionieren; 2 **to be retired** nicht mehr arbeiten.

retirement *noun* Ruhestand *der*; **since his retirement** seitdem er in den Ruhestand gegangen ist.

return *noun* 1 (*coming back*) Rückkehr *die*; **the return journey** die Rückreise; 2 **by return of post** postwendend; 3 **in return for** für; **in return for his help** für seine Hilfe; 4 **in return** dafür; ★ **many happy returns!** herzlichen Glückwunsch zum Geburtstag.
verb 1 (*come back*) zurückkommen ✧ SEP (PERF *sein*); **he returned ten minutes later** er kam zehn Minuten später zurück; **to return from holiday** aus den Ferien zurückkommen; 2 (*go back*) zurückgehen ✧ SEP (PERF *sein*); (*drive*) zurückfahren ✧ SEP (PERF *sein*); **we are planning to return in the evening** wir wollen am Abend zurückfahren; 3 (*to give back*)

zurückgeben ✧ SEP; **Gemma's never returned the video** Gemma hat das Video nie zurückgegeben.

return fare *noun* Preis für eine Rückfahrkarte *der*; (*for a flight*) Preis für einen Rückflugschein *der*.

return ticket *noun* Rückfahrkarte *die* (PL *die* Rückfahrkarten); (*for a flight*) Rückflugschein *der* (PL *die* Rückflugscheine)

reveal *verb* enthüllen.

reverse *verb* 1 (*in a car*) rückwärts fahren ✧ (PERF *sein*); 2 **to reverse the charges** ein R-Gespräch führen.

review *noun* (*of a book, play, or film*) Kritik *die* (PL *die* Kritiken). *verb* rezensieren (*a book, play, or film*).

revise *verb* 1 lernen (*for an exam*); **Tessa's busy revising for her exams** Tessa lernt jetzt für ihre Prüfung; 2 wiederholen; **to revise maths** Mathe wiederholen.

revision *noun* Wiederholung *die*.

revolting *adjective* eklig.

revolution *noun* Revolution *die* (PL *die* Revolutionen).

reward *noun* Belohnung *die* (PL *die* Belohnungen). *verb* belohnen.

rewind *verb* zurückspulen SEP (*a cassette or video*).

rhubarb *noun* Rhabarber *der*.

rhyme *noun* Reim *der* (PL *die* Reime).

rhythm noun Rhythmus der (PL die Rhythmen).

ribbon noun Band das (PL die Bänder).

rice noun Reis der; **rice pudding** der Milchreis.

rich adjective **1** reich; **they are very rich** sie sind sehr reich; **2 the rich** die Reichen.

rid adjective **to get rid of something** etwas loswerden ✧ SEP (PERF sein) (informal); **we got rid of the car** wir sind das Auto losgeworden.

riddle noun Rätsel das (PL die Rätsel).

ride noun Fahrt die (PL die Fahrten); **to go for a ride (on a bike)** eine Fahrt machen; **to go for a ride (on a horse)** reiten gehen ✧ (PERF sein). verb **1 to ride a bike** Rad fahren ✧ Δ (PERF sein); **can you ride a bike?** kannst du Rad fahren?; **I've never ridden a bike** ich bin noch nie Rad gefahren; **2 to ride (a horse)** reiten ✧ (PERF sein); **I've never ridden a horse** ich bin noch nie auf einem Pferd geritten.

ridiculous adjective lächerlich.

riding noun Reiten das; **to go riding** reiten gehen.

riding school noun Reitschule die (PL die Reitschulen).

right noun **1** (not left) rechte Seite die; **on the right** auf der rechten Seite; **on my right** rechts von mir; **2** (to do something) Recht das (PL die Rechte); **to have the right to something** ein Recht auf etwas ←(ACC) haben; **the right to work** das Recht auf Arbeit; **you have no right to say that** du hast kein Recht, das zu sagen.
adjective **1** (not left) rechter/rechte/ rechtes; **my right hand** meine rechte Hand; **2** (correct) richtig; **the right answer** die richtige Antwort; **is this the right address?** ist das die richtige Adresse?; **3 to be right** (of a person) Recht haben; **you see, I was right** siehst du, ich hatte Recht; **4 you were right not to say anything** du hattest Recht, nichts zu sagen; **5 the clock is right** die Uhr geht richtig; **6 yes, that's right** ja, das stimmt; **is that right?** stimmt das?
adverb **1** (direction) rechts; **turn right at the lights** biege an der Ampel rechts ab; **2** (correctly) richtig; **you're not doing it right** du machst das nicht richtig; **3** (completely) ganz; **right at the bottom** ganz unten; **right at the beginning** ganz am Anfang; **4** (exactly) genau; **right in the middle** genau in der Mitte; **5 right now** sofort; **6** (okay) gut; **right, let's go** gut, gehen wir.

right-hand adjective **on the right-hand side** rechts.

right-handed adjective rechtshändig.

ring noun **1** (on the phone) **to give somebody a ring** jemanden anrufen ✧ SEP; **2** (for your finger) Ring der (PL die Ringe); **3** (circle) Kreis der (PL die Kreise); **4 there was a ring at the door** es hat geklingelt.

✧ IRREGULAR VERB: See the verb table in the centre of the dictionary

verb 1 (*a bell or phone*) klingeln; **the phone rang** das Telefon hat geklingelt; 2 (*phone*) anrufen ✧ SEP; **I'll ring you tomorrow** ich rufe dich morgen an; 3 **to ring for a taxi** ein Taxi rufen.

● **to ring back** zurückrufen ✧ SEP; **I'll ring you back later** ich rufe dich später zurück.

● **to ring off** auflegen SEP.

ring road *noun* Ringstraße *die* (PL die Ringstraßen).

rinse *verb* spülen.

riot *noun* Aufstand *der* (PL die Aufstände).

rioting *noun* Unruhen (*plural*).

rip *verb* zerreißen ✧.

ripe *adjective* reif; **are the tomatoes ripe?** sind die Tomaten reif?

rip-off *noun* **it's a rip-off** das ist Nepp (*informal*).

rise *noun* 1 Anstieg *der*; **a rise in temperature** ein Temperaturanstieg; 2 **pay rise** *die* Gehaltserhöhung.
verb 1 (*the sun*) aufgehen ✧ SEP (PERF *sein*); 2 (*prices*) steigen ✧ (PERF *sein*).

risk *noun* Risiko *das* (PL die Risiken); **to take a risk** ein Risiko eingehen.
verb riskieren; **he risks losing his job** er riskiert es, seine Stelle zu verlieren.

river *noun* Fluss △ *der* (PL die Flüsse).

road *noun* 1 Straße *die* (PL die Straßen); **the road to London** die Straße nach London; 2 **the baker's**

is on the other side of the road die Bäckerei ist auf der anderen Straßenseite; 3 **across the road** gegenüber; **they live across the road from us** sie wohnen bei uns gegenüber.

road accident *noun* Verkehrsunfall *der* (PL die Verkehrsunfälle).

road map *noun* Straßenkarte *die* (PL die Straßenkarten).

roadside *noun* **by the roadside** am Straßenrand.

road sign *noun* Straßenschild *das* (PL die Straßenschilder).

roadworks *plural noun* Straßenarbeiten (*plural*).

roast *noun* Braten *der* (PL die Braten).
adjective gebraten; **roast potatoes** Bratkartoffeln; **roast beef** *der* Rinderbraten.

rob *verb* 1 berauben (*a person*); 2 ausrauben SEP (*a bank*).

robber *noun* Räuber *der* (PL die Räuber).

robbery *noun* Raub *der* (PL die Raube); **bank robbery** *der* Bankraub.

rock *noun* 1 (*a big stone*) Felsen *der* (PL die Felsen); 2 (*the material*) Fels *der*; 3 (*music*) Rock *der*; **rock band** *die* Rockband; **to dance rock and roll** Rock'n'Roll tanzen.

rock climbing *noun* Klettern *das*; **to go rock climbing** zum Klettern gehen.

rock star *noun* Rockstar *der* (PL *die* Rockstars).

rocky *adjective* felsig.

rod *noun* **a fishing rod** eine Angel.

role *noun* Rolle *die* (PL *die* Rollen); **to play the role of Hamlet** die Rolle des Hamlet spielen.

roll *noun* **1** Rolle *die* (PL *die* Rollen); **a roll of film** eine Rolle Film; **a toilet roll** eine Rolle Toilettenpapier; **2 bread roll** *das* Brötchen, *die* Semmel (*South German*). *verb* rollen (PERF *sein*).

roller *noun* **1** (*for hair*) Lockenwickler *der* (PL *die* Lockenwickler); **2** (*for paint*) Rolle *die* (PL *die* Rollen).

rollerblades *plural noun* Inlineskates (*plural*), Inliners (*plural*).

roller skates *plural noun* Rollschuhe (*plural*).

Roman Catholic *adjective* römisch-katholisch.

romantic *adjective* romantisch.

roof *noun* Dach *das* (PL *die* Dächer).

roof rack *noun* Gepäckträger *der* (PL *die* Gepäckträger).

room *noun* **1** Zimmer *das* (PL *die* Zimmer); **she's in the other room** sie ist im anderen Zimmer; **a three-room flat** eine Dreizimmerwohnung; **2** (*space*) Platz *der*; **enough room for two** genug Platz für zwei; **very little room** wenig Platz; **to make room** Platz machen.

root *noun* Wurzel *die* (PL *die* Wurzeln).

rope *noun* Seil *das* (PL *die* Seile).

rose *noun* Rose *die* (PL *die* Rosen).

rot *verb* verfaulen (PERF *sein*).

rotten *adjective* verfault.

rough *adjective* **1** (*scratchy*) rau ∆; **2** (*vague*) grob (*plan or estimate*); **3 a rough idea** eine vage Vorstellung; **4** (*stormy*) stürmisch; **a rough sea** eine stürmische See; **5** (*difficult*) **to have a rough time** es schwer haben; **6 to sleep rough** im Freien schlafen.

roughly *adverb* (*approximately*) ungefähr; **roughly ten per cent** ungefähr zehn Prozent; **it takes roughly three hours** es dauert ungefähr drei Stunden.

round *noun* Runde *die* (PL *die* Runden); **a round of talks** eine Gesprächsrunde; **a round of drinks** eine Runde. *adjective* rund; **a round table** ein runder Tisch. *preposition* **1** um (+ACC); **round the city** um die Stadt; **round my arm** um meinen Arm; **they were sitting round the table** sie haben um den Tisch gesessen; **it's just round the corner** es ist gleich um die Ecke; **2 to go round a museum** ein Museum besuchen. *adverb* **1 to go round to somebody's house** jemanden besuchen←(DAT); **2 to invite somebody round** jemanden zu sich←(DAT) einladen ✧ SEP; **we invited Sally round for lunch** wir haben Sally zum Mittagessen eingeladen; **3 to look round the shops** sich in den Geschäften umsehen ✧ SEP; **4 all the year round** das ganze Jahr hindurch.

roundabout *noun* **1** (*for traffic*) Kreisverkehr *der*; **2** (*in a fairground*) Karussell *das* (PL *die* Karussells).

route *noun* **1** (*that you plan*) Route *die* (PL *die* Routen); **the best route is via Calais** die beste Route ist über Calais; **2 bus route** *die* Linie.

row¹ *noun* **1** Reihe *die* (PL *die* Reihen); **in the front row** in der ersten Reihe; **in the back row** in der letzten Reihe; **2 in a row** hintereinander; **four times in a row** viermal hintereinander. *verb* (*in a boat*) rudern (PERF *sein/haben*); **we rowed across the lake** wir sind über den See gerudert; **he rowed us across the lake** er hat uns über den See gerudert.

row² *noun* **1** (*a quarrel*) Krach *der* (*informal*) (PL *die* Kräche); **to have a row** Krach haben; **they've had a row** sie haben Krach gehabt; **I had a row with my parents** ich habe Krach mit meinen Eltern gehabt; **2** (*noise*) Krach *der*; **they were making a terrible row** sie haben einen furchtbaren Krach gemacht.

rowing *noun* Rudern *das*; **to go rowing** rudern gehen.

rowing boat *noun* Ruderboot *das* (PL *die* Ruderboote).

royal *adjective* königlich; **the royal family** die königliche Familie.

rub *verb* reiben ✧; **to rub your eyes** sich ←(DAT) die Augen reiben.

● **to rub something out** etwas ausradieren SEP.

rubber *noun* **1** (*an eraser*) Radiergummi *der* (PL *die* Radiergummis); **2** (*material*) Gummi *der*; **rubber soles** Gummisohlen.

rubbish *noun* **1** (*for the bin*) Müll *der*; **2** (*nonsense*) Quatsch *der* (*informal*); **you're talking rubbish!** du redest Quatsch. *adjective* blöd; **the film was rubbish** der Film war blöd; **they're a rubbish band** sie sind eine blöde Band.

rubbish bin *noun* Mülleimer *der* (PL *die* Mülleimer).

rucksack *noun* Rucksack *der* (PL *die* Rucksäcke).

rude *adjective* **1** unhöflich; **that's rude** das ist unhöflich; **2** unanständig; **a rude joke** ein unanständiger Witz.

rug *noun* **1** Teppich *der* (PL *die* Teppiche); **2** (*a blanket*) Decke *die* (PL *die* Decken).

rugby *noun* Rugby *das*.

ruin *noun* (*remains*) Ruine *die* (PL *die* Ruinen); **in ruins** in Trümmern. *verb* **1** ruinieren; **you'll ruin your jacket** du ruinierst dir die Jacke; **2** verderben ✧ (*day, holiday*); **it ruined my evening** das hat mir den Abend verdorben.

rule *noun* **1** Regel *die* (PL *die* Regeln); **the rules of the game** die

Spielregeln; **as a rule** in der Regel;
2 (*administrative*) Vorschrift *die*
(PL *die* Vorschriften); **according to
the school rules** nach den
Schulvorschriften.

ruler *noun* Lineal *das* (PL *die*
Lineale); **I've lost my ruler** ich habe
mein Lineal verloren.

rumour *noun* Gerücht *das* (PL *die*
Gerüchte).

run *noun* **1** (*in games, sport, and for
fitness*) Lauf *der* (PL *die* Läufe); **to
go for a run** einen Lauf machen,
joggen (PERF *sein*); **2** (*of a play*)
Laufzeit *die*; **3** (*in skiing*)
Abfahrt *die* (PL *die* Abfahrten);
4 in the long run auf lange Sicht.
verb **1** laufen ✧ (PERF *sein*); **I ran ten
kilometres** ich bin zehn Kilometer
gelaufen; **he ran across the pitch**
er ist über das Spielfeld gelaufen;
2 (*run fast*) rennen ✧ (PERF *sein*);
Kitty ran for the bus Kitty rannte,
um den Bus zu kriegen; **3** (*drive*)
fahren ✧; **I'll run you home later**
ich fahre dich später nach Hause;
4 (*organize*) veranstalten (*a course
or competition*); **who's running this
competition?** wer veranstaltet
diesen Wettbewerb?; **5** (*manage*)
leiten (*a business*); **she's been
running the firm for years** sie leitet
die Firma schon seit Jahren; **to
run a shop** ein Geschäft führen;
6 (*a train or a bus*) fahren ✧ (PERF
sein); **the buses don't run on
Sundays** sonntags fahren keine
Busse; **7 to run a bath** ein Bad
einlaufen lassen.
● **to run away** weglaufen ✧ SEP (PERF
sein).

● **to run into something** gegen etwas
←(ACC) fahren ✧ (PERF *sein*); **the car
ran into a tree** das Auto ist gegen
einen Baum gefahren.

● **to run out of something: we've run
out of bread** wir haben kein Brot
mehr; **I'm running out of money** ic
habe kaum noch Geld.

● **to run somebody over** jemanden
überfahren ✧; **he nearly got run
over** er ist beinahe überfahren
worden.

runner *noun* Läufer *der* (PL *die*
Läufer), Läuferin *die* (PL *die*
Läuferinnen).

runner-up *noun* Zweite *der/die* (PL
die Zweiten).

running *noun* (*for exercise*)
Laufen *das*, Jogging *das*.
adjective **1 running water**
fließendes Wasser; **2 three days
running** drei Tage hintereinander;
to win three times running dreimal
hintereinander gewinnen.

runway *noun* **1** (*for take-off*)
Startbahn *die* (PL *die* Startbahnen);
2 (*for landing*) Landebahn *die* (PL
die Landebahnen).

rush *noun* (*a hurry*) **to be in a rush**
in Eile sein; **sorry, I'm in a rush**
Entschuldigung, ich bin in Eile.
verb **1** (*hurry*) sich beeilen; **I must
rush!** ich muss mich beeilen;
2 (*run*) rasen (PERF *sein*); **she rushed
out** sie raste raus (*informal*);
3 Louise was rushed to hospital
Louise ist schnellstens ins
Krankenhaus gebracht worden.

✧ IRREGULAR VERB: *See the verb table in the centre of the dictionary*

rush hour noun Stoßzeit die (PL die Stoßzeiten); **in the rush hour** während der Stoßzeit.

Russia noun Russland Δ das.

Russian noun 1 (a person) Russe der (PL die Russen), Russin die (PL die Russinnen); 2 (the language) Russisch das. adjective russisch; **he's Russian** er ist Russe.

rust noun Rost der.

rusty adjective rostig.

rye noun Roggen der.

S s

Sabbath noun 1 (Jewish) Sabbat der (PL die Sabbate); 2 (Christian) Sonntag der (PL die Sonntage).

sack noun 1 Sack der (PL die Säcke); 2 **to get the sack** rausgeschmissen werden (informal). verb **to sack somebody** jemanden rausschmeißen ◇ SEP (informal).

sad adjective traurig.

saddle noun Sattel der (PL die Sättel).

sadly adverb 1 traurig; **she looked at me sadly** sie hat mich traurig angesehen; 2 (unfortunately) leider.

safe adjective 1 (out of danger) sicher; **to feel safe from something** sich vor etwas ←(DAT) sicher fühlen;

2 she's safe sie ist in Sicherheit; **3** (not dangerous) ungefährlich; **the path is safe** der Weg ist ungefährlich; **it's not safe** das ist gefährlich.

safety noun Sicherheit die.

safety belt noun Sicherheitsgurt der (PL die Sicherheitsgurte).

safety pin noun Sicherheitsnadel die (PL die Sicherheitsnadeln).

Sagittarius noun Schütze der; **Kylie's Sagittarius** Kylie ist Schütze.

sail noun Segel das (PL die Segel).

sailing noun Segeln das; **to go sailing** segeln.

sailing boat noun Segelboot das (PL die Segelboote).

sailor noun Seemann der (PL die Seeleute).

saint noun Heilige der/die.

sake noun 1 **for your mother's sake** deiner Mutter zuliebe; 2 **for heaven's sake** um Gottes willen.

salad noun Salat der (PL die Salate); **tomato salad** der Tomatensalat.

salad dressing noun Salatsoße die (PL die Salatsoßen).

salary noun Gehalt das (PL die Gehälter).

sale noun 1 (selling) Verkauf der (PL die Verkäufe); **the sale of the house** der Verkauf des Hauses; **'for sale'** 'zu verkaufen'; **2 the sales**

der Ausverkauf; **I bought it in the sales** ich habe es im Ausverkauf gekauft.

sales assistant *noun* Verkäufer *der* (PL *die* Verkäufer), Verkäuferin *die* (PL *die* Verkäuferinnen).

salesman *noun* Verkäufer *der* (PL *die* Verkäufer).

saleswoman *noun* Verkäuferin *die* (PL *die* Verkäuferinnen).

salmon *noun* Lachs *der* (PL *die* Lachse).

salt *noun* Salz *das*.

salty *adjective* salzig.

same *adjective* **the same** der gleiche/die gleiche/das gleiche; **she said the same thing** sie hat das gleiche gesagt; **her birthday's the same day as mine** sie hat am gleichen Tag Geburtstag wie ich; **at the same time** zur gleichen Zeit; **their car's the same as ours** sie haben das gleiche Auto wie wir. *adverb* **1 the same** gleich; **the two bikes look the same** die beiden Fahrräder sehen gleich aus; **2 all the same** trotzdem.

sample *noun* Muster *das* (PL *die* Muster); **a free sample** ein unverkäufliches Muster, eine Warenprobe.

sand *noun* Sand *der*.

sandal *noun* Sandale *die* (PL *die* Sandalen); **a pair of sandals** ein Paar Sandalen.

sandwich *noun* Sandwich *das* (PL *die* Sandwichs), belegte Brot *das* (PL *die* belegten Brote); **ham sandwich** *das* Schinkenbrot.

sanitary towel *noun* Damenbinde *die* (PL *die* Damenbinden).

Santa Claus *noun* der Weihnachtsmann.

sarcastic *adjective* sarkastisch.

sardine *noun* Sardine *die* (PL *die* Sardinen).

satchel *noun* Ranzen *der* (PL *die* Ranzen).

satellite *noun* Satellit *der* (PL *die* Satelliten).

satellite dish *noun* Satellitenschüssel *die* (PL *die* Satellitenschüsseln).

satellite television *noun* Satellitenfernsehen *das*.

satisfactory *adjective* befriedigend.

satisfied *adjective* zufrieden.

satisfy *verb* befriedigen.

satisfying *adjective* **1** befriedigend; **2 a satisfying meal** ein sättigendes Essen.

Saturday *noun* **1** Samstag *der* (PL *die* Samstage), Sonnabend *der* (*North German*) (PL *die* Sonnabende); **on Saturday** am Sonnabend/am Samstag; **I'm going out on Saturday** ich gehe Sonnabend aus; **see you on Saturday!** bis Samstag!; **every Saturday** jeden Samstag; **last**

✧ IRREGULAR VERB: *See the verb table in the centre of the dictionary*

Saturday vorigen Sonnabend; **next Saturday** nächsten Sonnabend; **2 on Saturdays** samstags, sonnabends (*North German*); **the museum is closed on Saturdays** das Museum ist sonnabends/ samstags geschlossen; **to have a Saturday job** sonnabends/ samstags arbeiten.

sauce *noun* Soße *die* (PL *die* Soßen).

saucepan *noun* Kochtopf *der* (PL *die* Kochtöpfe).

saucer *noun* Untertasse *die* (PL *die* Untertassen).

sausage *noun* Wurst *die* (PL *die* Würste).

save *verb* 1 retten (*life*); **to save somebody's life** jemandem das Leben retten; **the doctors saved his life** die Ärzte haben ihm das Leben gerettet; 2 sparen (*money*); **I've saved £60** ich habe sechzig Pfund gespart; **I cycle to school to save money** ich fahre mit dem Rad zur Schule, um Geld zu sparen; **we'll take a taxi to save time** um Zeit zu sparen, nehmen wir ein Taxi; 3 (*on a computer*) speichern; 4 (*stop*) abwehren SEP (*a shot*); **to save a penalty** einen Elfmeter abwehren.
● **to save up** sparen; **I'm saving up for a car** ich spare auf ein Auto.

savings *plural noun* Ersparnisse (*plural*).

savoury *adjective* (*not sweet*) pikant.

sax *noun* Saxophon *das* (PL *die* Saxophone).

saxophone *noun* Saxophon *das* (PL *die* Saxophone); **to play the saxophone** Saxophon spielen.

say *verb* 1 sagen; **what did you say?** was hast du gesagt?; **she says she's tired** sie sagt, dass sie müde ist; **he said to wait here** er hat gesagt, wir sollen hier warten; **they say** man sagt; 2 **to say something again** etwas wiederholen; 3 **that's to say** das heißt.

saying *noun* Redensart *die* (PL *die* Redensarten); **it's just a saying** das ist so eine Redensart; **as the saying goes** wie man so sagt.

scale *noun* 1 (*of a map or model*) Maßstab *der* (PL *die* Maßstäbe); 2 (*extent*) Ausmaß *das* (PL *die* Ausmaße); **the scale of the disaster** das Ausmaß der Katastrophe; 3 (*in music*) Tonleiter *die* (PL *die* Tonleitern).

scales *noun* Waage *die* (PL *die* Waagen); **bathroom scales** die Personenwaage.

scandal *noun* 1 Skandal *der* (PL *die* Skandale); 2 (*gossip*) Klatsch *der* (*informal*).

Scandinavia *noun* Skandinavien *das*.

Scandinavian *adjective* skandinavisch.

scar *noun* Narbe *die* (PL *die* Narben).

scarce *adjective* knapp.

scare *noun* 1 Schrecken *der* (PL *die* Schrecken); **to give somebody a scare** jemandem einen Schrecken einjagen SEP; 2 (*general alarm*)

△ NEW SPELLING: *See page xii*

Panik *die* (PL *die* Paniken); **to cause a scare** eine Panik auslösen; **3 bomb scare** *die* Bombendrohung. *verb* **to scare somebody** jemanden erschrecken; **you scared me!** du hast mich erschreckt!

scared *adjective* **1 to be scared** Angst haben; **I'm scared** ich habe Angst; **to be scared of something** vor etwas ←(DAT) Angst haben; **he's scared of dogs** er hat vor Hunden Angst; **2 to be scared of doing something** sich nicht trauen, etwas zu tun; **I'm scared of telling him the truth** ich traue mich nicht, ihm die Wahrheit zu sagen.

scarf *noun* **1** (*silky*) Tuch *das* (PL *die* Tücher); **2** (*long, warm*) Schal *der* (PL *die* Schals).

scary *adjective* unheimlich.

scene *noun* **1** (*of an incident or event*) Schauplatz *der* (PL *die* Schauplätze); **to be on the scene** am Schauplatz sein; **the scene of the crime** der Tatort; **2** (*world*) **the music scene** die Musikszene; **on the fashion scene** in der Modewelt; **3** (*argument*) Szene *die* (PL *die* Szenen); **to make a scene** eine Szene machen.

scenery *noun* **1** (*landscape*) Landschaft *die*; **2** (*in the theatre*) Bühnenbild *das*.

schedule *noun* Programm *das* (PL *die* Programme).

scheme *noun* Projekt *das* (PL *die* Projekte).

scholarship *noun* Stipendium *das* (PL *die* Stipendien).

school *noun* Schule *die* (PL *die* Schulen); **at school** in der Schule; **to go to school** zur Schule gehen.

schoolbook *noun* Schulbuch *das* (PL *die* Schulbücher).

schoolboy *noun* Schüler *der* (PL *die* Schüler).

schoolchildren *plural noun* Schulkinder (*plural*).

schoolfriend *noun* Schulfreund *der* (PL *die* Schulfreunde), Schulfreundin *die* (PL *die* Schulfreundinnen).

schoolgirl *noun* Schülerin *die* (PL *die* Schülerinnen).

science *noun* Wissenschaft *die* (PL *die* Wissenschaften).

science fiction *noun* Sciencefiction △ *die*.

scientific *adjective* wissenschaftlich.

scientist *noun* Wissenschaftler *der* (PL *die* Wissenschaftler), Wissenschaftlerin *die* (PL *die* Wissenschaftlerinnen).

scissors *plural noun* Schere *die* (PL *die* Scheren); **a pair of scissors** eine Schere.

scooter *noun* **1** (*motor scooter*) Motorroller *der* (PL *die* Motorroller); **2** (*for a child*) Roller *der* (PL *die* Roller).

score *noun* Spielstand *der* (PL *die* Spielstände); **the score was three two** es stand drei zu zwei. *verb* **1 to score a goal** ein Tor schießen ◇; **2 to score three**

◇ IRREGULAR VERB: *See the verb table in the centre of the dictionary*

points drei Punkte erzielen; **3** (*keep score*) zählen.

Scorpio *noun* Skorpion *der*; **Neil is Scorpio** Neil ist Skorpion.

Scot *noun* Schotte *der* (PL *die* Schotten), Schottin *die* (PL *die* Schottinnen); **the Scots** die Schotten.

Scotland *noun* Schottland *das*; **from Scotland** aus Schottland; **Pauline's from Scotland** Pauline kommt aus Schottland; **to Scotland** nach Schottland.

Scots *adjective* schottisch.

Scotsman *noun* Schotte *der* (PL *die* Schotten).

Scotswoman *noun* Schottin *die* (PL *die* Schottinnen).

Scottish *adjective* schottisch; **he's Scottish** er ist Schotte.

scout *noun* Pfadfinder *der* (PL *die* Pfadfinder).

scrambled eggs *noun* Rührei *das*.

scrap *noun* Stück *das* (PL *die* Stücke); **a scrap of paper** ein Stück Papier.

scrapbook *noun* Album *das* (PL *die* Alben).

scrape *verb* **1** schaben (*potatoes or carrots*); **2** (*remove dirt or paint*) abkratzen SEP; **3** (*damage*) verschrammen.

scratch *noun* (*on your skin or a surface*) Kratzer *der* (PL *die* Kratzer); **★ to start from scratch** von vorn anfangen ✧ SEP.

verb (*scratch yourself*) sich kratzen; **to scratch your head** sich am Kopf kratzen.

scream *noun* Schrei *der* (PL *die* Schreie).
verb schreien ✧.

screen *noun* **1** Bildschirm *der* (PL *die* Bildschirme) (*of a TV or computer*); **on the screen** auf dem Bildschirm; **2** (*in the cinema*) Leinwand *die* (PL *die* Leinwände).

screw *noun* Schraube *die* (PL *die* Schrauben).
verb schrauben.

screwdriver *noun* Schraubenzieher *der* (PL *die* Schraubenzieher).

scribble *verb* kritzeln.

scrub *verb* scheuern (*a saucepan or the floor*); **to scrub your nails** sich ←(DAT) die Nägel bürsten.

sculptor *noun* Bildhauer *der* (PL *die* Bildhauer), Bildhauerin *die* (PL *die* Bildhauerinnen); **Rebecca's a sculptor** Rebecca ist Bildhauerin.

sculpture *noun* Skulptur *die* (PL *die* Skulpturen).

sea *noun* Meer *das* (PL *die* Meere), See *die*; **by the sea** am Meer, an der See.

seafood *noun* Meeresfrüchte (*plural*); **I love seafood** ich esse Meeresfrüchte sehr gern.

search *verb* **1** absuchen SEP; **I've searched my desk but I can't find the letter** ich habe meinen Schreibtisch abgesucht, aber ich

kann den Brief nicht finden;
2 durchsuchen; **they searched the building for him** sie haben das Gebäude nach ihm durchsucht;
3 suchen; **to search for something** nach etwas ←(DAT) suchen; **I've been searching everywhere for my scissors** ich habe überall nach meiner Schere gesucht.

seasick *adjective* **to be seasick** seekrank sein.

seaside *noun* **at the seaside** am Meer.

season *noun* **1** Jahreszeit *die* (PL *die* Jahreszeiten); **the four seasons** die vier Jahreszeiten; **2** (*period of social or sporting activity*) Saison *die* (PL *die* Saisons); **the tennis season** die Tennissaison; **off-season prices** Preise außerhalb der Saison; **3 strawberries are not in season at the moment** jetzt ist nicht die richtige Zeit für Erdbeeren.

season ticket *noun* Dauerkarte *die* (PL *die* Dauerkarten).

seat *noun* **1** Sitz *der* (PL *die* Sitze); **the front seat** (*in a car*) der Vordersitz; **the back seat** der Rücksitz; **take a seat** nehmen Sie Platz (*formal*); setz dich (*informal*); **2** (*on a bus, in the theatre, etc.*) Platz *der* (PL *die* Plätze); **to book a seat** einen Platz reservieren; **can you keep my seat?** kannst du mir meinen Platz freihalten?

seatbelt *noun* Sicherheitsgurt *der* (PL *die* Sicherheitsgurte).

second *noun* Sekunde *die* (PL *die* Sekunden); **can you wait a second?** kannst du eine Sekunde warten?
adjective **1** zweiter/zweite/zweites; **for the second time** zum zweiten Mal; **2 the second of July** der zweite Juli.

secondary school *noun* **1** höhere Schule *die* (PL *die* höheren Schulen) (*Germans define the type of secondary school*); **2** Gymnasium *das* (PL *die* Gymnasien) (*grammar school, from age 10 to 19 when Abitur is taken*); **3** Realschule *die* (PL *die* Realschulen) (*from age 10 to 16, less academic than a Gymnasium*).

secondhand *adjective, adverb* gebraucht; **a secondhand bike** ein gebrauchtes Fahrrad; **secondhand car** *der* Gebrauchtwagen; **I bought it secondhand** ich habe es gebraucht gekauft.

secondly *adverb* zweitens.

secret *noun* Geheimnis *das* (PL *die* Geheimnisse); **to tell somebody a secret** jemandem ein Geheimnis verraten; **in secret** heimlich.
adjective geheim; **a secret plan** ein geheimer Plan; **to keep something secret** etwas geheim halten.

secretary *noun* Sekretär *der* (PL *die* Sekretäre), Sekretärin *die* (PL *die* Sekretärinnen); **the secretary's office** das Sekretariat.

secretly *adverb* heimlich.

sect *noun* Sekte *die* (PL *die* Sekten).

section *noun* Teil *der* (PL *die* Teile).

security *noun* Sicherheit *die*.

⬦ IRREGULAR VERB: *See the verb table in the centre of the dictionary*

security guard *noun* Wächter *der* (PL *die* Wächter), Wächterin *die* (PL *die* Wächterinnen).

see *verb* 1 sehen ✧; **I saw Lindy yesterday** ich habe Lindy gestern gesehen; **have you seen the film?** hast du den Film gesehen?; **I can't see anything** ich kann überhaupt nichts sehen; 2 **to go and see** nachsehen ✧ SEP; **I'll go and see** ich sehe nach; 3 (*visit*) besuchen; **why don't you come and see us in the summer?** warum besucht ihr uns nicht im Sommer?; 4 **to see somebody home** jemanden nach Hause begleiten; 5 **see you!** tschüs! (*informal*); **see you on Saturday!** bis Samstag!; **see you soon!** bis bald!

• **to see to something** sich um etwas ←(ACC) kümmern; **Jo's seeing to the drinks** Jo kümmert sich um die Getränke.

seed *noun* Samen *der* (PL *die* Samen).

seem *verb* 1 scheinen ✧; **his story seems odd to me** seine Geschichte kommt mir komisch vor; **he seems shy** er scheint schüchtern zu sein; **the museum seems to be closed** das Museum scheint geschlossen zu sein; 2 **it seems (that)** ... anscheinend ...; **it seems he's left** anscheinend ist er weggegangen; **it seems that there are problems** anscheinend gibt es Probleme.

select *verb* auswählen SEP.

self-confidence *noun* Selbstbewusstsein △ *das*; **she doesn't have much self-confidence** sie hat sehr wenig Selbstbewusstsein.

self-employed *adjective* **to be self-employed** selbstständig △ sein; **my parents are self-employed** meine Eltern sind selbstständig.

selfish *adjective* egoistisch.

self-service *adjective* **a self-service restaurant** ein Selbstbedienungsrestaurant.

sell *verb* 1 verkaufen; **to sell something to somebody** jemandem etwas verkaufen; **I sold him my bike** ich habe ihm mein Rad verkauft; **the house sold for a million** das Haus wurde für eine Million verkauft; 2 **the concert's sold out** das Konzert ist ausverkauft; **the tickets sold out very quickly** die Karten waren schnell ausverkauft.

sell-by date *noun* Verfallsdatum *das* (PL *die* Verfallsdaten).

Sellotape™ *noun* Tesafilm™ *der*. *verb* **to sellotape something** etwas mit Tesafilm kleben.

semi *noun* Doppelhaushälfte *die* (PL *die* Doppelhaushälften).

semi-detached house *noun* Doppelhaushälfte *die* (PL *die* Doppelhaushälften).

semi-final *noun* Halbfinale *das* (PL *die* Halbfinale).

send *verb* schicken; **to send something to somebody** jemandem etwas schicken; **I sent her a present for her birthday** ich habe ihr zum Geburtstag ein Geschenk geschickt.

● **to send somebody back** jemanden zurückschicken SEP.

● **to send something back** etwas zurückschicken SEP.

sender *noun* Absender *der* (PL *die* Absender).

senior citizen *noun* Senior *der* (PL *die* Senioren), Seniorin *die* (PL *die* Seniorinnen).

sensational *adjective* sensationell.

sense *noun* **1** (*common sense*) Verstand *der*; **2** (*faculty*) Sinn *der* (PL *die* Sinne); **sense of smell** *der* Geruchssinn; **sense of touch** *der* Tastsinn; **to have a sense of humour** Humor haben; **she has no sense of humour** sie hat keinen Sinn für Humor; **3** (*meaning*) Sinn *der*; **this sentence makes no sense** dieser Satz ergibt keinen Sinn; **it doesn't make sense to do that** es ist Unsinn, das zu machen; **it makes sense to collect her first** es ist sinnvoll, sie erst abzuholen.

sensible *adjective* vernünftig; **be sensible** sei vernünftig; **that's a sensible suggestion** das ist ein vernünftiger Vorschlag.

sensitive *adjective* empfindlich; **for sensitive skin** für empfindliche Haut.

sentence *noun* **1** (*words*) Satz *der* (PL *die* Sätze); **2** (*prison*) Strafe *die* (PL *die* Strafen); **the death sentence** die Todesstrafe.
verb verurteilen; **to be sentenced to death** zum Tode verurteilt werden; **to sentence somebody to a year in prison** jemanden zu einem Jahr Gefängnis verurteilen.

separate *adjective* **1** extra ('*extra*' *never has an ending*); **a separate pile** ein extra Stapel; **she wrote it on a separate sheet of paper** sie hat es auf ein anderes Blatt Papier geschrieben; **the drinks are separate** die Getränke gehen extra; **2** (*different*) verschieden; **two separate problems** zwei verschiedene Probleme; **3 they have separate rooms** sie haben getrennte Zimmer.
verb **1** trennen; **2** (*a couple*) sich trennen.

separately *adverb* **1** extra; **2** getrennt; **they live separately** sie leben getrennt.

separation *noun* Trennung *die* (PL *die* Trennungen).

September *noun* September *der*; **in September** im September.

sequel *noun* Folge *die* (PL *die* Folgen).

sergeant *noun* **1** (*in the police*) Polizeimeister *der* (PL *die* Polizeimeister), Polizeimeisterin *die* (PL *die* Polizeimeisterinnen); **2** (*in the army*) Feldwebel *der* (PL *die* Feldwebel).

serial *noun* **1** Fortsetzungsgeschichte *die* (PL *die* Fortsetzungsgeschichten); **2** (*on TV or radio*) Serie *die* (PL *die* Serien).

series *noun* Serie *die* (PL *die* Serien); **television series** *die* Fernsehserie.

✧ IRREGULAR VERB: *See the verb table in the centre of the dictionary*

serious *adjective* 1 ernst; **a serious discussion** eine ernste Unterhaltung; **to be serious about something** etwas ernst nehmen; **are you serious?** ist das dein Ernst?; 2 schwer (*accident or mistake*).

seriously *adverb* 1 im Ernst; **seriously, I have to go now** im Ernst, ich muss jetzt gehen; **seriously?** im Ernst?; 2 **to take somebody seriously** jemanden ernst nehmen; 3 (*gravely*) schwer; **she is seriously ill** sie ist schwer krank.

serve *noun* (*in tennis*) Aufschlag *der* (PL *die* Aufschläge); **it's my serve** ich habe Aufschlag. *verb* 1 (*in tennis*) aufschlagen ✧ SEP; **Becker is serving** Becker schlägt auf; 2 servieren; **can you serve the vegetables, please?** können Sie bitte das Gemüse servieren?; ★ **it serves him right** das geschieht ihm recht.

service *noun* 1 (*in a restaurant, shop, etc.*) Bedienung *die*; **service is included** inklusive Bedienung; 2 (*from a company or firm to a customer*) Service *der*; 3 **the emergency services** der Notdienst; 4 (*church service*) Gottesdienst *der* (PL *die* Gottesdienste); 5 (*of a car or machine*) Wartung *die* (PL *die* Wartungen).

service charge *noun* Bedienung *die*; **there is no service charge** die Bedienung wird nicht extra berechnet.

service station *noun* Tankstelle *die* (PL *die* Tankstellen).

serviette *noun* Serviette *die* (PL *die* Servietten).

session *noun* Sitzung *die* (PL *die* Sitzungen).

set *noun* 1 (*for playing a game*) Spiel *das* (PL *die* Spiele); **chess set** *das* Schachspiel; 2 **train set** *die* Spielzeugeisenbahn; 3 (*in tennis*) Satz *der* (PL *die* Sätze).
adjective 1 fest (*hours, habits*); **a set date** ein festes Datum; **at a set time** zu einer festgesetzten Zeit; 2 **set menu** *das* Menü.
verb 1 festlegen SEP (*a date, time*); 2 aufstellen SEP (*a record*); 3 **to set the table** den Tisch decken; **to set an alarm clock** einen Wecker stellen; **I've set my alarm for seven** ich habe meinen Wecker auf sieben gestellt; 4 **to set your watch** seine Uhr richtig stellen; 5 (*sun*) untergehen ✧ SEP;
● **to set off** aufbrechen ✧ SEP (PERF *sein*); **we're setting off at ten** wir brechen um zehn auf; **they set off for Vienna yesterday** sie sind gestern nach Wien aufgebrochen.
● **to set off something** 1 etwas auslösen SEP (*an alarm, reaction*); 2 etwas abbrennen ✧ SEP (*a firework*); 3 etwas explodieren lassen (*a bomb*).
● **to set out** aufbrechen ✧ SEP (PERF *sein*); **they set out for Hamburg at ten** sie sind um zehn nach Hamburg aufgebrochen.

settee *noun* Sofa *das* (PL *die* Sofas).

△ NEW SPELLING: *See page xii*

settle *verb* 1 bezahlen (*a bill*);
2 lösen (*a problem*); 3 beilegen SEP
(*an argument*).

seven *number* sieben; **Rosie's
seven** Rosie ist sieben.

seventeen *number* siebzehn; **I'm
seventeen** ich bin siebzehn.

seventh *adjective*
siebter/siebte/siebtes; **on the
seventh floor** im siebten Stock; **the
seventh of July** der siebte Juli.

seventies *plural noun* **the
seventies** die Siebzigerjahre △; **in
the seventies** in den
Siebzigerjahren.

seventieth *adjective*
siebzigster/siebzigste/siebzigstes;
it's her seventieth birthday es ist
ihr siebzigster Geburtstag.

seventy *number* siebzig; **my
granny's seventy** meine Oma ist
siebzig.

several *adjective, pronoun*
1 mehrere; **I've read several of her
novels** ich habe mehrere ihrer
Romane gelesen; 2 **I've seen her
several times** ich habe sie
mehrmals gesehen.

sew *verb* nähen.

sewing *noun* Nähen *das*; **I like
sewing** ich nähe gern.

sewing machine *noun*
Nähmaschine *die* (PL *die*
Nähmaschinen).

sex *noun* 1 (*gender*) Geschlecht *das*
(PL *die* Geschlechter); 2 (*sexuality*)
Sex *der*.

sex education *noun*
Aufklärungsunterricht *der*.

sexism *noun* Sexismus *der*.

sexist *adjective* sexistisch; **sexist
remarks** sexistische Bemerkungen.

sexual *adjective* sexuell.

sexual harassment *noun*
sexuelle Belästigung *die*.

sexuality *noun* Sexualität *die*.

sexy *adjective* sexy.

shabby *adjective* schäbig.

shade *noun* 1 Ton *der* (PL *die* Töne);
a shade of green ein Grünton;
2 Schatten *der*; **in the shade** im
Schatten.

shadow *noun* Schatten *der* (PL *die*
Schatten).

shake *verb* 1 (*tremble*) zittern; **I was
shaking with fear** ich zitterte vor
Angst; 2 **to shake something** etwas
schütteln; **to shake your head**
(*meaning no*) den Kopf schütteln;
3 **to shake hands with somebody**
jemandem die Hand geben ✧; **she
shook hands with me** sie hat mir
die Hand gegeben; **we shook hands**
wir gaben uns die Hand.

shaken *adjective* erschüttert; **I was
shaken by the news** die Nachricht
hat mich erschüttert.

shall *verb* **shall I come with you?**
soll ich mitkommen?; **shall we stop
now?** sollen wir jetzt aufhören?

shallow *adjective* flach; **stay in the
shallow end of the pool** bleib am
flachen Ende des Beckens.

✧ IRREGULAR VERB: *See the verb table in the centre of the dictionary*

shambles *noun* Chaos *das*; **it was a total shambles!** es war ein völliges Chaos!

shame *noun* 1 Schande *die*; **the shame of it!** was für eine Schande!; 2 **what a shame!** wie schade!; **it's a shame she can't come** schade, dass sie nicht kommen kann.

shampoo *noun* Shampoo *das* (PL die Shampoos), Schampon *das* (PL die Schampons); **I bought some shampoo** ich habe Shampoo gekauft.

shamrock *noun* Klee *der*.

shandy *noun* Radler *der* (PL die Radler) (*South German*), Alsterwasser *das* (PL die Alsterwasser) (*North German*).

shape *noun* Form *die* (PL die Formen).

share *noun* 1 Anteil *der* (PL die Anteile); **your share of the money** dein Anteil am Geld; **he paid his share** er hat seinen Anteil gezahlt; 2 (*in a company*) Aktie *die* (PL die Aktien).
verb teilen; **I'm sharing a room with Lucy** ich teile ein Zimmer mit Lucy.

sharp *adjective* 1 (*knife*) scharf; **this knife isn't very sharp** dieses Messer ist nicht sehr scharf; 2 (*pointed*) spitz; **a sharp pencil** ein spitzer Bleistift; 3 **a sharp bend** eine scharfe Kurve; 4 (*clever*) clever.

shave *verb* 1 (*have a shave*) sich rasieren; 2 **to shave your legs** sich ←(DAT) die Beine rasieren; 3 **to shave off your beard** den Bart abrasieren SEP.

shaver *noun* Rasierapparat *der* (PL die Rasierapparate); **electric shaver** *der* Elektrorasierer.

shaving cream *noun* Rasiercreme *die* (PL die Rasiercremes).

shaving foam *noun* Rasierschaum *der*.

she *pronoun* sie; **she's a student** sie ist Studentin; **she's a very good teacher** sie ist eine sehr gute Lehrerin.

shed *noun* Schuppen *der* (PL die Schuppen).

sheep *noun* Schaf *das* (PL die Schafe).

sheepdog *noun* Schäferhund *der* (PL die Schäferhunde).

sheet *noun* 1 (*for a bed*) Laken *das* (PL die Laken); 2 **a sheet of paper** ein Blatt Papier; **a blank sheet** ein leeres Blatt; 3 (*of glass or metal*) Platte *die* (PL die Platten); ★ **to be as white as a sheet** leichenblass △ sein.

shelf *noun* 1 (*in the home or a shop*) Regal *das* (PL die Regale); **a set of shelves** ein Regal; 2 (*in an oven*) Schiene *die* (PL die Schienen).

shell *noun* 1 (*of an egg or a nut*) Schale *die* (PL die Schalen); 2 (*seashell*) Muschel *die* (PL die Muscheln).

shellfish *noun* 1 Schalentier *das* (PL die Schalentiere); 2 (*in cookery*) Meeresfrüchte (*plural*).

shelter *noun* Schutz *der*; **in the shelter of** im Schutz (+GEN); **to take**

shelter from the rain sich unterstellen SEP.

sherry *noun* Sherry *der* (PL *die* Sherrys).

Shetland Islands *noun* Shetlandinseln (*plural*).

shift *noun* Schicht *die* (PL *die* Schichten); **the night shift** die Nachtschicht; **to be on night shift** Nachtschicht haben.
verb **to shift something** etwas verrücken.

shifty *adjective* verschlagen; **he looks shifty** er sieht verschlagen aus; **a shifty-looking guy** ein verschlagener Typ.

shine *verb* scheinen ✧; **the sun is shining** die Sonne scheint.

shiny *adjective* glänzend.

ship *noun* Schiff *das* (PL *die* Schiffe).

shipyard *noun* Werft *die* (PL *die* Werften).

shirt *noun* 1 (*man's*) Hemd *das* (PL *die* Hemden); 2 (*woman's*) Bluse *die* (PL *die* Blusen).

shiver *verb* zittern.

shock *noun* 1 Schock *der* (PL *die* Schocks); **to get a shock** einen Schock bekommen; **it gave me a shock** das hat mir einen Schock versetzt; 2 **electric shock** *der* Schlag.
verb (*upset*) erschüttern; (*cause scandal*) schockieren.

shocked *adjective* schockiert.

shocking *adjective* schockierend.

shoe *noun* Schuh *der* (PL *die* Schuhe); **a pair of shoes** ein Paar Schuhe.

shoelace *noun* Schnürsenkel *der* (PL *die* Schnürsenkel).

shoe polish *noun* Schuhcreme *die* (PL *die* Schuhcremes).

shoe shop *noun* Schuhgeschäft *das* (PL *die* Schuhgeschäfte).

shoot *verb* 1 (*fire*) schießen ✧; **to shoot at somebody** auf jemanden schießen; **she shot him in the leg** sie hat ihm ins Bein geschossen; **he was shot in the arm** er wurde am Arm getroffen; 2 (*kill, execute*) erschießen ✧; **he was shot by terrorists** er wurde von Terroristen erschossen; 3 (*in football, hockey*) schießen ✧; 4 **to shoot a film** einen Film drehen.

shop *noun* Geschäft *das* (PL *die* Geschäfte), Laden *der* (PL *die* Läden); **shoe shop** *das* Schuhgeschäft; **to go round the shops** einen Ladenbummel machen.

shop assistant *noun* Verkäufer *der* (PL *die* Verkäufer), Verkäuferin *die* (PL *die* Verkäuferinnen).

shopkeeper *noun* Ladenbesitzer *der* (PL *die* Ladenbesitzer), Ladenbesitzerin *die* (PL *die* Ladenbesitzerinnen).

shoplifter *noun* Ladendieb *der* (PL *die* Ladendiebe), Ladendiebin *die* (PL *die* Ladendiebinnen).

✧ IRREGULAR VERB: *See the verb table in the centre of the dictionary*

shoplifting *noun*
Ladendiebstahl *der*.

shopping *noun* 1 Einkäufe (*plural*);
can you put the shopping away?
kannst du die Einkäufe wegräumen?;
2 (*activity*) Einkaufen *das*;
shopping is fun Einkaufen macht
Spaß; **to go shopping** einkaufen
gehen.

shopping trolley *noun*
Einkaufswagen *der* (PL *die*
Einkaufswagen).

shop window *noun*
Schaufenster *das* (PL *die*
Schaufenster).

short *adjective* 1 kurz; **a short dress**
ein kurzes Kleid; **she has short hair**
sie hat kurze Haare; 2 **a short break**
eine kurze Pause; **to go for a short
walk** einen kurzen Spaziergang
machen; **it's a short walk from the
bus stop** es ist nicht weit zu Fuß von
der Bushaltestelle; 3 **to be short of
something** knapp mit etwas ←(DAT)
sein; **we're a bit short of money at
the moment** wir sind im Moment
etwas knapp mit Geld; **we're getting
short of time** wir sind knapp mit der
Zeit.

shortage *noun* Mangel *der*.

shortbread *noun*
Buttergebäck *das*.

shortcrust pastry *noun*
Mürbeteig *der*.

short cut *noun* Abkürzung *die* (PL
die Abkürzungen).

shortly *adverb* gleich; **shortly
before I left** kurz bevor ich ging;
shortly after kurz danach.

shorts *plural noun* Shorts (*plural*);
a pair of shorts ein Paar Shorts; **my
red shorts** meine roten Shorts.

short-sighted *adjective*
kurzsichtig; **I'm short-sighted** ich
bin kurzsichtig.

shot *noun* 1 (*from a gun*)
Schuss △ *der* (PL *die* Schüsse);
2 (*a photo*) Aufnahme *die* (PL *die*
Aufnahmen).

should *verb* 1 sollen ✧ (*'should' is
usually translated by the imperfect
subjunctive of 'sollen'*); **you should
ask Simon** du solltest Simon fragen;
the potatoes should be ready now
die Kartoffeln sollten jetzt fertig
sein; 2 (*'should have' is translated by
'hätte sollen'*) **you should have told
me** du hättest es mir sagen sollen;
I shouldn't have stayed ich hätte
nicht bleiben sollen; **you shouldn't
have said that** das hättest du nicht
sagen sollen; 3 (*'should' meaning
'would' is translated by 'würde'*)
I should forget it if I were you an
deiner Stelle würde ich es vergessen;
4 **I should think** ich würde sagen;
I should think he's forgotten ich
würde sagen, er hat's vergessen;
5 **this should be enough** das
müsste eigentlich reichen.

shoulder *noun* Schulter *die* (PL *die*
Schultern).

shoulder bag *noun*
Umhängetasche *die* (PL *die*
Umhängetaschen).

shout *noun* Schrei *der* (PL *die*
Schreie).
verb 1 schreien ✧; **stop shouting!**

hör auf zu schreien !; **2** (*call*)
rufen ◇; **he shouted at us to come
back** er rief uns zu, wir sollten
zurückkommen.

show *noun* **1** (*on stage*) Show *die* (PL
die Shows); **we went to see a show**
wir haben eine Show gesehen; **2** (*on
TV, radio*) Sendung *die* (PL *die*
Sendungen); **3** (*exhibition*)
Ausstellung *die* (PL *die*
Ausstellungen); **fashion show** *die*
Modenschau.
verb **1** zeigen; **to show something
to somebody** jemandem etwas
zeigen; **I'll show you my photos** ich
zeige dir meine Fotos; **to show
somebody how something works**
jemandem zeigen, wie etwas
funktioniert; **he showed me how to
make pancakes** er hat mir gezeigt,
wie man Pfannkuchen macht; **2 it
shows!** das sieht man !
• **to show off** angeben ◇ SEP.

shower *noun* **1** (*in a bathroom*)
Dusche *die* (PL *die* Duschen); **to have
a shower** duschen; **2** (*of rain*)
Schauer *der* (PL *die* Schauer).

show-jumping *noun*
Springreiten *das*.

show-off *noun* Angeber *der* (PL *die*
Angeber), Angeberin *die* (PL *die*
Angeberinnen).

shriek *verb* kreischen.

shrimp *noun* Krabbe *die* (PL *die*
Krabben).

shrink *verb* **1** schrumpfen (PERF
sein); **2** (*clothes*) einlaufen ◇ SEP
(PERF *sein*); **my sweater has shrunk**
mein Pullover ist eingelaufen.

Shrove Tuesday *noun*
Fastnachtsdienstag *der*.

shrug *verb* **to shrug your shoulders**
die Achseln zucken.

shuffle *verb* **to shuffle the cards**
die Karten mischen.

shut *adjective* zu; **the shops are
shut** die Geschäfte haben zu.
verb zumachen SEP; **can you shut
the door please?** kannst du die Tür
bitte zumachen?; **the shops shut at
six** die Geschäfte machen um sechs
zu.
• **to shut up** den Mund halten ◇
(*informal*); **shut up !** halt den
Mund !

shuttlecock *noun* Federball *der*
(PL *die* Federbälle).

shy *adjective* schüchtern.

shyness *noun* Schüchternheit *die*.

Sicily *noun* Sizilien *das*.

sick *adjective* **1** (*ill*) krank; **2 to be
sick** (*vomit*) sich übergeben ◇; **I
was sick several times** ich habe
mich mehrmals übergeben; **3 I feel
sick** mir ist schlecht; **4** übel; **a sick
joke** ein übler Witz; **5 to be sick of
something** etwas satt haben; **I'm
sick of staying at home every day**
ich habe es satt, jeden Tag zu Hause
zu sitzen.

sickness *noun* Krankheit *die* (PL *die*
Krankheiten).

side *noun* **1** Seite *die* (PL *die* Seiten);
on the other side of the street auf
der anderen Straßenseite; **on the
wrong side** auf der falschen Seite;

◇ IRREGULAR VERB: *See the verb table in the centre of the dictionary*

I'm on your side (*I agree with you*) ich bin auf deiner Seite; **2** (*edge*) Rand *der* (PL die Ränder) (*of a pool, river*); **at the side of the road** am Straßenrand; **3** (*team*) Mannschaft *die* (PL die Mannschaften); **the winning side** die siegreiche Mannschaft; **she plays on our side** sie spielt bei uns mit; **4 to take sides** Partei ergreifen ✧; **he always takes sides against her** er ergreift immer gegen sie Partei; **5 side by side** nebeneinander.

sideboard *noun* Anrichte *die* (PL die Anrichten).

sideburns *noun* Koteletten (*plural*).

side-effect *noun* Nebenwirkung *die* (PL die Nebenwirkungen).

side street *noun* Seitenstraße *die* (PL die Seitenstraßen).

sieve *noun* Sieb *das* (PL die Siebe).

sigh *noun* Seufzer *der* (PL die Seufzer).
verb seufzen.

sight *noun* **1** Anblick *der*; **it was a marvellous sight** es war ein herrlicher Anblick; **2 at first sight** auf den ersten Blick; **3** (*eyesight*) **to have poor sight** schlechte Augen haben; **to know somebody by sight** jemanden vom Sehen kennen; **out of sight** außer Sicht; **to lose sight of somebody** jemanden aus den Augen verlieren; **4 the sights** die Sehenswürdigkeiten; **to see the**

sights die Sehenswürdigkeiten besichtigen.

sightseeing *noun* Sightseeing *das*; **to do some sightseeing** einige Sehenswürdigkeiten besichtigen.

sign *noun* **1** (*notice*) Schild *das* (PL die Schilder); **there's a sign on the door** da hängt ein Schild an der Tür; **2** (*trace, indication*) Zeichen *das* (PL die Zeichen); **3** (*of the zodiac*) Sternzeichen *das* (PL die Sternzeichen); **what sign are you?** was für ein Sternzeichen bist du? *verb* **1** unterschreiben ✧; **to sign a cheque** einen Scheck unterschreiben; **2** (*using sign language*) sich durch Zeichen verständigen.

● **to sign on** sich arbeitslos melden.

signal *noun* Signal *das* (PL die Signale).

signature *noun* Unterschrift *die* (PL die Unterschriften).

significant *adjective* bedeutend.

sign language *noun* Zeichensprache *die* (PL die Zeichensprachen).

signpost *noun* Wegweiser *der* (PL die Wegweiser).

silence *noun* Stille *die*.

silent *adjective* still.

silk *noun* Seide *die* (PL die Seiden). *adjective* Seiden-; **a silk blouse** eine Seidenbluse.

silky *adjective* seidig.

△ NEW SPELLING: *See page xii*

silly *adjective* dumm; **it was a really silly thing to do** das war wirklich dumm.

silver *noun* Silber *das*.
adjective Silber-; **a silver medal** eine Silbermedaille.

similar *adjective* ähnlich; **it looks similar to my old bike** es sieht so ähnlich wie mein altes Rad aus.

similarity *noun* Ähnlichkeit *die* (PL die Ähnlichkeiten).

simple *adjective* einfach.

simply *adverb* einfach.

sin *noun* Sünde *die* (PL die Sünden).

since *preposition* 1 seit (+DAT); (*notice that German uses the present tense for an action starting in the past and still going on in the present*) **I have been in Berlin since Saturday** ich bin seit Samstag in Berlin; **since when?** seit wann?; 2 (*with a negative the perfect tense is used*) **I haven't seen her since Monday** ich habe sie seit Montag nicht gesehen. *conjunction* 1 seit; **since I have known him** seit ich ihn kenne; **since I've been learning German** seitdem ich Deutsch lerne; 2 (*because*) da; **since it was raining, the match was cancelled** da es regnete, wurde das Spiel abgesagt.
adverb seitdem; **I haven't seen him since** ich habe ihn seitdem nicht mehr gesehen.

sincere *adjective* aufrichtig.

sincerely *adverb* **Yours sincerely** Mit freundlichen Grüßen.

sing *verb* singen ✧.

singer *noun* Sänger *der* (PL die Sänger), Sängerin *die* (PL die Sängerinnen).

singing *noun* 1 Singen *das*; **a singing lesson** eine Singstunde; 2 **I like singing** ich singe gern.

single *noun* 1 (*ticket*) einfache Fahrkarte *die* (PL die einfachen Fahrkarten); **a single to Munich, please** eine einfache Fahrkarte nach München bitte; 2 (*record, CD*) Single *die* (PL die Singles).
adjective 1 (*not married*) allein stehend △; **a single woman** eine allein stehende Frau; (*on forms*) ledig; 2 (*just one*) einzig; **I haven't had a single reply** ich habe keine einzige Antwort bekommen; 3 **not a single one** kein Einziger/keine Einzige/kein Einziges △; 4 **single room** *das* Einzelzimmer; **single bed** *das* Einzelbett.

single parent *noun* allein Erziehende △ *der/die* (PL die allein Erziehenden); **she's a single parent** sie ist allein erziehende Mutter; **a single-parent family** eine Einelternfamilie.

singles *plural noun* (*in tennis*) Einzel *das* (PL die Einzel); **the women's singles** das Dameneinzel; **the men's singles** das Herreneinzel.

singular *noun* Einzahl *die*; **in the singular** in der Einzahl.

sink *noun* Spülbecken *das* (PL die Spülbecken).
verb sinken ✧ (PERF *sein*).

✧ IRREGULAR VERB: See the verb table in the centre of the dictionary

sir *noun* Herr *der* (PL *die* Herren); (*in German,' Sir' is usually not translated*) **would you like another one, sir?** möchten Sie noch eins?; **yes, sir** ja, mein Herr.

sister *noun* Schwester *die* (PL *die* Schwestern); **my sister's ten** meine Schwester ist zehn.

sister-in-law *noun* Schwägerin *die* (PL *die* Schwägerinnen).

sit *verb* 1 (*to sit down*) sich setzen; **you can sit on the sofa** ihr könnt euch aufs Sofa setzen; **sit on the floor** setz dich auf den Boden; 2 (*to be sitting*) sitzen ✧; **Leila was sitting on the sofa** Leila saß auf dem Sofa; **to sit on the floor** auf dem Boden sitzen; 3 **to sit an exam** eine Prüfung machen.

● **to sit down** sich setzen; **he sat down on the chair** er setzte sich auf den Stuhl; **do sit down** setzen Sie sich.

sitcom *noun* Situationskomödie *die* (PL *die* Situationskomödien).

site *noun* 1 **building site** *die* Baustelle; 2 **camping site** *der* Campingplatz; 3 **archaeolological site** *die* archäologische Stätte.

sitting room *noun* Wohnzimmer *das* (PL *die* Wohnzimmer).

situated *adjective* **to be situated** liegen ✧; **the house is situated in a small village** das Haus liegt in einem kleinen Dorf.

situation *noun* 1 (*location*) Lage *die* (PL *die* Lagen);

2 (*circumstances*) Situation *die* (PL *die* Situationen).

six *number* sechs; **Harry's six** Harry ist sechs.

sixteen *number* sechzehn; **Alice is sixteen** Alice ist sechzehn.

sixth *adjective* sechster/sechste/sechstes; **on the sixth floor** im sechsten Stock; **on the sixth of July** am sechsten Juli.

sixty *number* sechzig; **she's sixty** sie ist sechzig.

size *noun* 1 Größe *die* (PL *die* Größen); **it depends on the size of the house** es kommt auf die Größe des Hauses an; 2 **what size is the window?** wie groß ist das Fenster?; 3 (*in clothes*) Größe *die* (PL *die* Größen); **what size do you take?** welche Größe haben Sie?; 4 (*of shoes*) Schuhgröße *die* (PL *die* Schuhgrößen); **I take a size thirty-eight** ich habe Schuhgröße achtunddreißig.

skate *noun* 1 (*an ice skate*) Schlittschuh *der* (PL *die* Schlittschuhe); 2 (*a roller skate*) Rollschuh *der* (PL *die* Rollschuhe). *verb* 1 (*ice-skate*) Schlittschuh laufen ✧ (PERF *sein*); 2 (*roller-skate*) Rollschuh laufen ✧ (PERF *sein*).

skateboard *noun* Skateboard *das* (PL *die* Skateboards).

skateboarding *noun* Skateboardfahren *das*; **to go skateboarding** Skateboard fahren ✧ (PERF *sein*).

skating *noun* 1 (*on ice*) Schlittschuhlaufen *das*; **to go**

△ NEW SPELLING: *See page xii*

skating Schlittschuh laufen ✧ (PERF *sein*); 2 (*roller-skating*) Rollschuhlaufen *das*; **to go roller-skating** Rollschuh laufen ✧ (PERF *sein*).

skating rink *noun* 1 (*ice rink*) Eisbahn *die* (PL *die* Eisbahnen); 2 (*for roller-skating*) Rollschuhbahn *die* (PL *die* Rollschuhbahnen).

sketch *noun* 1 Skizze *die* (PL *die* Skizzen); 2 (*comedy routine*) Sketch *der* (PL *die* Sketche).

ski *noun* Ski *der* (PL *die* Skier). *verb* Ski fahren ✧ (PERF *sein*); **he can ski** er kann Ski fahren.

ski boot *noun* Skistiefel *der* (PL *die* Skistiefel).

skid *verb* schleudern (PERF *sein*); **the car skidded** das Auto ist geschleudert.

skiing *noun* Skifahren *das*; **to go skiing** Ski fahren ✧ (PERF *sein*).

ski lift *noun* Skilift *der* (PL *die* Skilifte).

skin *noun* Haut *die* (PL *die* Häute).

skinhead *noun* Skinhead *der* (PL *die* Skinheads).

skinny *adjective* dünn.

skip *noun* (*for rubbish*) Container *der* (PL *die* Container). *verb* 1 auslassen ✧ SEP (*a meal, part of a book*); **I skipped a few chapters** ich ließ ein paar Kapitel aus; 2 **to skip a lesson** ein Stunde schwänzen (*informal*).

skirt *noun* Rock *der* (PL *die* Röcke); **a long skirt** ein langer Rock; **a tight skirt** ein enger Rock; **a mini-skirt** ein Minirock.

sky *noun* Himmel *der* (PL *die* Himmel).

skyscraper *noun* Wolkenkratzer *der* (PL *die* Wolkenkratzer).

slam *verb* zuknallen SEP; **she slammed the door** sie hat die Tür zugeknallt; **the door slammed** die Tür ist zugeknallt.

slang *noun* Slang *der* (PL *die* Slangs).

slap *noun* Klaps *der* (PL *die* Klapse); (*in the face*) Ohrfeige *die* (PL *die* Ohrfeigen). *verb* **to slap somebody** (*across the face*) jemanden ohrfeigen; (*on the bottom*) jemandem einen Klaps geben.

sledge *noun* Schlitten *der* (PL *die* Schlitten).

sledging *noun* **to go sledging** Schlitten fahren ✧ (PERF *sein*).

sleep *noun* Schlaf *der*; **you need more sleep** du brauchst mehr Schlaf; **I had a good sleep** ich habe gut geschlafen; **to go to sleep** einschlafen ✧ SEP (PERF *sein*); **he's gone back to sleep** er ist wieder eingeschlafen. *verb* schlafen ✧; **she's sleeping** sie schläft.

sleeping bag *noun* Schlafsack *der* (PL *die* Schlafsäcke).

sleeping pill *noun* Schlaftablette *die* (PL *die* Schlaftabletten).

✧ IRREGULAR VERB: See the verb table in the centre of the dictionary

sleepy *adjective* **to be sleepy** schläfrig sein; **he was getting sleepy** er wurde schläfrig.

sleet *noun* Schneeregen *der*.

sleeve *noun* Ärmel *der* (PL die Ärmel); **a long-sleeved jumper** ein Pullover mit langen Ärmeln; **a short-sleeved shirt** ein Hemd mit kurzen Ärmeln; **to roll up your sleeves** die Ärmel hochkrempeln.

slice *noun* Scheibe *die* (PL die Scheiben); **a slice of bread** eine Scheibe Brot.
verb **to slice something** etwas in Scheiben schneiden ◇.

slide *noun* 1 (*photo*) Dia *das* (PL die Dias); 2 (*hairslide*) Haarspange *die* (PL die Haarspangen); 3 (*for sliding down*) Rutschbahn *die* (PL die Rutschbahnen).

slight *adjective* klein; **there is a slight problem** es gibt ein kleines Problem.

slightly *adverb* etwas.

slim *adjective* schlank.
verb abnehmen ◇ SEP; **I'm slimming** ich mache eine Schlankheitskur.

sling *noun* Schlinge *die* (PL die Schlingen); **to have your arm in a sling** den Arm in der Schlinge haben.

slip *noun* 1 (*mistake*) Fehler *der* (PL die Fehler); 2 (*petticoat*) Unterrock *der* (PL die Unterröcke).
verb 1 (*slide*) ausrutschen SEP (PERF *sein*); 2 **it slipped my mind** es ist mir entfallen.
● **to slip up** einen Fehler machen.

slipper *noun* Hausschuh *der* (PL die Hausschuhe).

slippery *adjective* glatt.

slope *noun* Hang *der* (PL die Hänge).

slot *noun* Schlitz *der* (PL die Schlitze).

slot machine *noun* 1 (*vending machine*) Automat *der* (PL die Automaten); 2 (*games machine*) Spielautomat *der* (PL die Spielautomaten).

slow *adjective* 1 langsam; **the service is a bit slow** die Bedienung ist etwas langsam; 2 (*of a clock or watch*) **to be slow** nachgehen ◇ SEP (PERF *sein*); **my watch is slow** meine Uhr geht nach.
● **to slow down** langsamer werden.

slowly *adverb* langsam; **he got up slowly** er ist langsam aufgestanden; **can you speak more slowly, please?** können Sie bitte etwas langsamer sprechen?

sly *adjective* gerissen (*a person*);
★ **on the sly** heimlich.

smack *noun* Klaps *der* (PL die Klapse).
verb **to smack somebody** jemandem einen Klaps geben ◇.

small *adjective* klein; **a small dog** ein kleiner Hund.

smart *adjective* 1 (*well-dressed, posh*) elegant; **a smart restaurant** ein elegantes Restaurant; 2 (*clever*) clever.

smash *noun* (*collision*) Zusammenstoß *der* (PL die Zusammenstöße).

verb 1 (*break*) zerschlagen ✧; **they smashed a window pane** sie haben eine Fensterscheibe zerschlagen; 2 (*get broken*) zerbrechen ✧ (PERF *sein*); **the plate smashed** der Teller ist zerbrochen.

smashing *adjective* klasse (*informal*).

smell *noun* Geruch der (PL die Gerüche); **a nasty smell** ein scheußlicher Geruch; **a smell of gas** ein Gasgeruch.
verb 1 riechen ✧; **I can't smell anything** ich kann nichts riechen; **to smell of perfume** nach Parfüm riechen; 2 (*smell bad*) stinken ✧; **the drains smell** der Abfluss stinkt.

smelly *adjective* 1 stinkend; **her smelly dog** ihr stinkender Hund; 2 **to be smelly** stinken ✧.

smile *noun* Lächeln das.
verb lächeln; **to smile at somebody** jemanden anlächeln SEP.

smoke *noun* Rauch der.
verb rauchen; **she doesn't smoke** sie raucht nicht.

smoking *noun* 'no smoking' 'Rauchen verboten'; **to give up smoking** mit dem Rauchen aufhören.

smooth *adjective* 1 glatt; **a smooth surface** eine glatte Oberfläche; 2 (*person*) aalglatt.

smug *adjective* selbstgefällig.

smuggle *verb* **to smuggle something** etwas schmuggeln.

smuggler *noun* 1 Schmuggler der (PL die Schmuggler), Schmugglerin die (PL die Schmugglerinnen); 2 **drugs smuggler** der Drogenschmuggler.

snack *noun* Snack der (PL die Snacks).

snail *noun* Schnecke die (PL die Schnecken).

snake *noun* Schlange die (PL die Schlangen).

snap *noun* (*card game*) Schnippschnapp das (PL die Schnippschnapp).
verb 1 (*break*) brechen ✧ (PERF *sein*); 2 **to snap something** etwas zerbrechen ✧; 3 **to snap your fingers** mit den Fingern schnalzen.

snapshot *noun* Schnappschuss ∆ der (PL die Schnappschüsse).

snarl *verb* knurren.

snatch *verb* 1 entreißen ✧; **to snatch something from somebody** jemandem etwas entreißen; **she had her bag snatched** man hat ihr die Handtasche entrissen; 2 **he snatched it out of my hand** er hat es mir aus der Hand gerissen.

sneak *verb* 1 **to sneak in** sich hineinschleichen ✧ SEP; **to sneak out** sich hinausschleichen ✧ SEP; 2 **to sneak on somebody** jemanden verpetzen (*informal*).

sneeze *verb* niesen.

sniff *verb* schnüffeln.

snob *noun* Snob der (PL die Snobs).

✧ IRREGULAR VERB: *See the verb table in the centre of the dictionary*

snobbery *noun* Snobismus *der*.

snooker *noun* Snooker *das*.

snore *verb* schnarchen.

snow *noun* Schnee *der*.
verb schneien; **it's snowing** es
schneit.

snowball *noun* Schneeball *der* (PL
die Schneebälle).

snowman *noun* Schneemann *der*
(PL *die* Schneemänner).

so *conjunction, adverb* **1** so; **he's so
lazy** er ist so faul; **not so** nicht so;
**our house is a bit like yours, but not
so big** unser Haus ist so ähnlich wie
eures, aber nicht so groß; **2 so much**
so sehr; **I hate it so much** ich hasse
es so sehr; **3 so much** so viel; **I have
so much work** ich habe so viel
Arbeit; **4 so many** so viele; **we've
got so many problems** wir haben
so viele Probleme; **5** (*therefore*) also;
**he got up late, so he missed his
train** er ist spät aufgestanden, also
hat er den Zug verpasst; **so what
shall we do?** also, was machen wir?;
6 so what? na und?; **7** (*also*) **so do
I, so did I** ich auch; **'I live in Leeds' –
'so do I'** 'ich wohne in Leeds' – 'ich
auch'; **I liked the film and so did he**
ich fand den Film gut und er auch; **so
am I** ich auch; **so do we** wir auch; **;**
8 I think so ich glaube schon;
9 I hope so hoffentlich.

soak *verb* einweichen SEP.

soaked *adjective* patschnass △;
★ **to be soaked to the skin**
patschnass sein.

soap *noun* **1** Seife die (PL *die* Seifen);
2 (*soap opera*) Seifenoper *die* (PL *die*
Seifenopern).

soap powder *noun*
Seifenpulver *das*.

sober *adjective* nüchtern.
● **to sober up** nüchtern werden ✧
(PERF *sein*).

soccer *noun* Fußball *der*.

social *adjective* **1** sozial; **social
problems** soziale Probleme;
2 gesellschaftlich (*engagement,
ambition*); **social engagements**
gesellschaftliche Verpflichtungen;
social class die gesellschaftliche
Schicht; **3** (*sociable*) gesellig
(*evening, person*).

socialism *noun* Sozialismus *der*.

socialist *noun, adjective*
Sozialist *der* (PL *die* Sozialisten),
Sozialistin *die* (PL *die*
Sozialistinnen).

social security *noun*
1 Sozialhilfe *die*; **to be on social
security** Sozialhilfe bekommen;
2 (*the system*) Sozialversicherung
die.

social worker *noun*
Sozialarbeiter *der* (PL *die*
Sozialarbeiter), Sozialarbeiterin *die*
(PL *die* Sozialarbeiterinnen).

society *noun* Gesellschaft *die* (PL
die Gesellschaften).

sociology *noun* Soziologie *die*.

sock *noun* Socke *die* (PL *die* Socken);
a pair of socks ein Paar Socken.

socket *noun* (*power point*)
Steckdose *die* (PL *die* Steckdosen).

sofa *noun* Sofa *das* (PL *die* Sofas).

sofa bed *noun* Schlafcouch *die* (PL *die* Schlafcouchs).

soft *adjective* **1** weich; **2 a soft option** eine bequeme Lösung; ★ **to have a soft spot for somebody** eine Vorliebe für jemanden haben.

soft drink *noun* alkoholfreie Getränk *das* (PL *die* alkoholfreien Getränke).

soft toy *noun* Stofftier *das* (PL *die* Stofftiere).

software *noun* Software *die*.

soil *noun* Erde *die*.

solar energy *noun* Sonnenenergie *die*.

soldier *noun* Soldat *der* (PL *die* Soldaten).

solicitor *noun* **1** (*dealing with lawsuits*) Rechtsanwalt *der* (PL *die* Rechtsanwälte), Rechtsanwältin *die* (PL *die* Rechtsanwältinnen); **2** (*dealing with property or documents*) Notar *der* (PL *die* Notare), Notarin *die* (PL *die* Notarinnen).

solid *adjective* **1** (*not flimsy*) stabil; **a solid structure** ein stabiler Bau; **2** massiv; **a table made of solid oak** ein Tisch aus massiver Eiche; **solid silver** massives Silber.

solo *noun* Solo *das* (PL *die* Solos); **guitar solo** *das* Gitarrensolo. *adjective* Solo-; **a solo act** eine Solonummer. *adverb* solo.

soloist *noun* Solist *der* (PL *die* Solisten), Solistin *die* (PL *die* Solistinnen).

solution *noun* Lösung *die* (PL *die* Lösungen).

solve *verb* lösen.

some *adjective, adverb* **1** (*followed by a singular noun*) etwas; **would you like some salad?** möchtest du etwas Salat?; **can you lend me some money?** kannst du mir etwas Geld leihen?; **have you got some bread?** (*some is often not translated*) hast du Brot?; **2** (*followed by a plural noun*) (*a few*) ein paar; **I've bought some apples** ich habe ein paar Äpfel gekauft; **3** (*followed by a plural noun*) (*a certain number but not all*) einige; **some of his films are too violent** einige von seinen Filmen sind zu brutal; **4** (*referring to something that has been mentioned*) **'would you like tea?'** – **'thanks, I've got some'** 'möchten Sie Tee?' – 'nein danke, ich habe schon welchen'; **he's eaten some of it** er hat etwas davon gegessen; **I'd like some** ich möchte etwas; (*with a plural noun*) ich möchte welche; **5** (*certain people or things*) manche; **some people think he's right** manche Leute glauben, dass er Recht hat; **6 some day** eines Tages.

somebody, someone *pronoun* jemand; **there's somebody in the garden** da ist jemand im Garten.

somehow *adverb* irgendwie; **I've got to finish this essay somehow** ich muss diesen Aufsatz irgendwie fertig schreiben.

♦ IRREGULAR VERB: *See the verb table in the centre of the dictionary*

something *pronoun* **1** etwas; **there's something I've got to tell you** ich muss dir etwas erzählen; **something new** etwas Neues; **something interesting** etwas Interessantes; **there's something wrong** irgendetwas stimmt nicht; **2 their house is really something!** ihr Haus ist einfach Klasse!

sometime *adverb* irgendwann; **give me a ring sometime next week** ruf mich irgendwann nächste Woche an.

sometimes *adverb* manchmal; **I sometimes take the train** manchmal fahre ich mit der Bahn.

somewhere *adverb* **1** (*in a place*) irgendwo; **I've left my bag somewhere here** ich habe meine Handtasche hier irgendwo liegen lassen; **2** (*to a place*) irgendwohin; **I'd like to go somewhere warm** ich möchte irgendwohin fahren, wo es warm ist.

son *noun* Sohn *der* (PL *die* Söhne).

song *noun* Lied *das* (PL *die* Lieder).

son-in-law *noun* Schwiegersohn *der* (PL *die* Schwiegersöhne).

soon *adverb* **1** bald; **we'll soon be on holiday** wir haben bald Ferien; **see you soon!** bis bald!; **2 as soon as she arrives** sobald sie ankommt; **as soon as possible** so bald wie möglich; **3 it's too soon** es ist zu früh.

sooner *adverb* **1** früher; **we should have started sooner** wir hätten früher anfangen sollen; **sooner or later** früher oder später; **2 I'd sooner wait** ich würde lieber warten.

soprano *noun* Sopran *der* (PL *die* Soprane).

sore *noun* wunde Stelle *die* (PL *die* wunden Stellen). *adjective* **1** (*inflamed*) wund; **to have a sore throat** Halsschmerzen haben; **2 he has a sore leg** ihm tut das Bein weh; **my arm's sore** mir tut der Arm weh; ★ **it's a sore point** das ist ein wunder Punkt.

sorry *adjective* **1 I'm really sorry** es tut mir wirklich Leid △; **sorry to disturb you** es tut mir Leid, dass ich dich störe; **I'm sorry I forgot your birthday** es tut mir Leid, dass ich deinen Geburtstag vergessen habe; **I'm sorry, were closing** es tut mir Leid, aber wir machen jetzt zu; **2 sorry!** Entschuldigung!; **3 sorry?** wie bitte?; **4 I feel sorry for him** er tut mir Leid △.

sort *noun* Art *die* (PL *die* Arten); **a sort of dance music** eine Art Tanzmusik; **what sort of car have you got?** was für ein Auto hast du?; **all sorts of people** alle möglichen Leute; **for all sorts of reasons** aus allen möglichen Gründen.
● **to sort something out 1** Ordnung schaffen ✧ in (+DAT) (*papers, desk, room, possessions*); **I must sort out my room tonight** ich muss heute Abend in meinem Zimmer Ordnung schaffen; **2** klären (*a problem, arrangement*); **Liz is sorting it out** Liz klärt es.

so-so *adjective* so lala (*informal*); **'how was the film?' – 'so-so'** 'wie war der Film?'- 'so lala'.

soul *noun* **1** Seele *die* (PL *die* Seelen); **2** (*music*) Soul *der*.

sound *noun* **1** (*noise*) Geräusch *das* (PL *die* Geräusche); **2** (*of voices, laughter, bell*) Klang *der*; **the sound of her voice** der Klang ihrer Stimme; **I can hear the sound of voices** ich kann Stimmen hören; **3 without a sound** lautlos; **4** (*volume*) Lautstärke *die*; **to turn the sound down** leiser stellen. *verb* **1 it sounds easy** es hört sich einfach an; **2 it sounds as if she's happy** sie scheint glücklich zu sein.

sound asleep *adverb* **to be sound asleep** fest schlafen ✧.

sound effect *noun* Geräuscheffekt *der* (PL *die* Geräuscheffekte).

soundtrack *noun* Soundtrack *der* (PL *die* Soundtracks).

soup *noun* Suppe *die* (PL *die* Suppen); **mushroom soup** *die* Pilzsuppe.

soup plate *noun* Suppenteller *der* (PL *die* Suppenteller).

soup spoon *noun* Suppenlöffel *der* (PL *die* Suppenlöffel).

sour *adjective* sauer.

south *noun* Süden *der*; **in the south** im Süden. *adjective* Süd-, südlich; **the south side** die Südseite; **south wind** *der* Südwind.

adverb **south of Berlin** südlich von Berlin; **they went south** sie sind nach Süden gefahren.

South Africa *noun* Südafrika *das*.

South America *noun* Südamerika *das*.

southeast *noun* Südosten *der*. *adjective* **in southeast England** in Südostengland.

South Pole *noun* Südpol *der*.

southwest *noun* Südwesten *der*. *adjective* **in southwest England** in Südwestengland.

souvenir *noun* Souvenir *das* (PL *die* Souvenirs).

soya *noun* Soja *die*.

space *noun* **1** (*room*) Platz *der*; **there's enough space** es ist genug Platz da; **we've got enough space for two** wir haben genug Platz für zwei; **2** (*gap*) Zwischenraum *der* (PL *die* Zwischenräume); **to leave a large space between lines** einen großen Zwischenraum zwischen den Zeilen lassen; **3** (**parking**) **space** *die* Lücke; **4** (*outer space*) Weltraum *der*; **in space** im Weltraum.

spacecraft *noun* Raumschiff *das* (PL *die* Raumschiffe).

spade *noun* **1** Spaten *der* (PL *die* Spaten); **2** (*in cards*) Pik *das*; **the queen of spades** die Pikdame.

Spain *noun* Spanien *das*; **from Spain** aus Spanien; **to Spain** nach Spanien.

✧ IRREGULAR VERB: *See the verb table in the centre of the dictionary*

Spaniard *noun* Spanier *der* (PL *die* Spanier), Spanierin *die* (PL *die* Spanierinnen).

spaniel *noun* Spaniel *der* (PL *die* Spaniels).

Spanish *noun* 1 (*language*) Spanisch *das*; **I'm learning Spanish** ich lerne Spanisch; **2 the Spanish** (*people*) die Spanier. *adjective* spanisch; **Pedro is Spanish** Pedro ist Spanier.

spare *adjective* Extra-; **we have a spare ticket** wir haben eine Extrakarte. *verb* **to have time to spare** Zeit haben; **can you spare a moment?** hast du einen Moment Zeit?

spare room *noun* Gästezimmer *das* (PL *die* Gästezimmer).

spare time *noun* Freizeit *die*; **in my spare time** in meiner Freizeit.

spare wheel *noun* Reserverad *das* (PL *die* Reserveräder).

sparkling *adjective* **sparkling mineral water** Mineralwasser mit Kohlensäure; **sparkling wine** *der* Schaumwein.

sparrow *noun* Spatz *der* (PL *die* Spätze).

speak *verb* 1 sprechen ✧; **do you speak German?** sprechen Sie Deutsch?; **spoken German** gesprochenes Deutsch; **to speak to somebody about something** mit jemandem über etwas ←(ACC) sprechen; **she's speaking to Mike about it** sie spricht mit Mike

darüber; **2 who's speaking?** (*on the phone*) wer ist am Apparat?

speaker *noun* 1 (*on a music system*) Lautsprecher *der* (PL *die* Lautsprecher); **2** (*at a public lecture*) Redner *der* (PL *die* Redner), Rednerin *die* (PL *die* Rednerinnen).

special *adjective* 1 besonderer/besondere/besonderes; **on special occasions** bei besonderen Anlässen; **2 special offer** *das* Sonderangebot.

specialist *noun* Fachmann *der* (PL *die* Fachleute), Fachfrau *die* (PL *die* Fachfrauen).

specially *adverb* 1 besonders; **not specially** nicht besonders; **it's specially good for babies** es ist besonders gut für Babys; **2** (*specifically*) speziell; **I made this cake specially for you** ich habe diesen Kuchen speziell für dich gebacken.

spectacles *noun* Brille *die* (PL *die* Brillen).

spectacular *adjective* spektakulär.

spectator *noun* Zuschauer *der* (PL *die* Zuschauer), Zuschauerin *die* (PL *die* Zuschauerinnen).

speech *noun* Rede *die* (PL *die* Reden); **to make a speech** eine Rede halten.

speed *noun* 1 Geschwindigkeit *die* (PL *die* Geschwindigkeiten); **at top speed** mit Höchstgeschwindigkeit; **what speed was he doing?** wie schnell ist er gefahren?; **2** (*gear*) Gang *der* (PL *die* Gänge); **a twelve-speed bike** ein Rad mit zwölf Gängen.

△ NEW SPELLING: *See page xii*

• **to speed up 1** beschleunigen (*a car*); **2** (*of a person, car*) schneller werden.

speeding *noun* zu schnelle Fahren *das*; **he was fined for speeding** er hat wegen zu schnellen Fahrens einen Strafzettel bekommen.

speed limit *noun* Geschwindigkeitsbeschränkung *die*.

spell *noun* **1** (*of time*) Weile *die*; **for a spell** eine Weile; **2 cold spell** *die* Kälteperiode; **sunny spells** sonnige Wetterabschnitte.
verb **1** (*in writing*) schreiben ✧; **how do you spell it?** wie schreibt man das?; **how do you spell your surname?** wie schreibt man Ihren Nachnamen?; **2** (*out loud*) buchstabieren.

spelling *noun* Rechtschreibung *die*; **spelling mistake** *der* Rechtschreibfehler.

spend *verb* **1** ausgeben ✧ SEP (*money*); **I've spent all my money** ich habe mein ganzes Geld ausgegeben; **2** verbringen ✧ (*time*); **we spent three days in Munich** wir haben drei Tage in München verbracht; **she spends her time reading** sie verbringt ihre Zeit mit Lesen.

spice *noun* Gewürz *das* (PL *die* Gewürze).

spicy *adjective* scharf; **he doesn't like spicy food** er mag kein scharfes Essen.

spider *noun* Spinne *die* (PL *die* Spinnen).

spill *verb* verschütten; **I've spilled my wine on the carpet** ich habe meinen Wein auf dem Teppich verschüttet.

spinach *noun* Spinat *der*.

spire *noun* Kirchturm *der* (PL *die* Kirchtürme).

spirit *noun* **1** (*energy*) Energie *die*; **2 in the right spirit** mit der richtigen Einstellung.

spirits *noun* **1** (*alcohol*) Spirituosen (*plural*); **2 to be in good spirits** guter Laune sein.

spit *verb* **1** spucken; **2 to spit something out** etwas ausspucken SEP; **spit it out!** spuck es aus!

spite *noun* **1 in spite of** trotz (+GEN); **we decided to go in spite of the rain** wir beschlossen trotz des Regens zu gehen; **2** (*nastiness*) Boshaftigkeit *die*; **to do something out of spite** etwas aus Boshaftigkeit tun.

spiteful *adjective* gehässig.

splash *noun* **1** (*noise*) Platsch *der*; **2 splash of colour** *der* Farbfleck.
verb bespritzen.

splendid *adjective* herrlich.

split *verb* **1** (*with an axe or a knife*) spalten; **to split wood** Holz spalten; **2** (*come apart*) zerreißen ✧ (PERF *sein*); **the lining has split** das Futter ist zerrissen; **3** (*divide up*) teilen; **they split the money between**

them sie haben das Geld untereinander geteilt.

● **to split up 1** (*a group or crowd*) sich auflösen SEP; **2** (*a couple*) sich trennen; **she's split up with her husband** sie hat sich von ihrem Mann getrennt; **she's split up with Sam** sie hat mit Sam Schluss gemacht (*informal*).

spoil *verb* verderben ✧; **it completely spoiled our evening** das hat uns den Abend völlig verdorben; **to spoil sombody's fun** jemandem den Spaß verderben.

spoiled *adjective* verwöhnt; **a spoiled child** ein verwöhntes Kind.

spokesman *noun* Sprecher *der* (PL *die* Sprecher).

spokeswoman *noun* Sprecherin *die* (PL *die* Sprecherinnen).

sponge *noun* Schwamm *der* (PL *die* Schwämme).

sponge cake *noun* Rührkuchen *der* (PL *die* Rührkuchen).

sponsor *noun* Sponsor *der* (PL *die* Sponsoren).
verb sponsern.

spooky *adjective* gruselig; **a spooky story** eine gruselige Geschichte.

spoon *noun* Löffel *der* (PL *die* Löffel); **a spoon of sugar** ein Löffel Zucker; **soup spoon** *der* Suppenlöffel; **teaspoon** *der* Teelöffel.

spoonful *noun* Löffel *der* (PL *die* Löffel).

sport *noun* **1** Sport *der*; **to be good at sport** gut im Sport sein; **my favourite sport** mein Lieblingssport; **2** (*in games*) **to be a good sport** ein guter Verlierer sein.

sports bag *noun* Sporttasche *die* (PL *die* Sporttaschen).

sports car *noun* Sportwagen *der* (PL *die* Sportwagen).

sports centre *noun* Sportzentrum *das* (PL *die* Sportzentren).

sports club *noun* Sportverein *der* (PL *die* Sportvereine).

sportsman *noun* Sportler *der* (PL *die* Sportler).

sportswear *noun* Sportbekleidung *die*.

sportswoman *noun* Sportlerin *die* (PL *die* Sportlerinnen).

spot *noun* **1** (*pattern in fabric*) Punkt *der* (PL *die* Punkte); **a red shirt with black spots** ein rotes Hemd mit schwarzen Punkten; **2** (*on your skin*) Pickel *der* (PL *die* Pickel); **I've got spots** ich habe Pickel; **to be covered in spots** völlig verpickelt sein; **3** (*stain*) Fleck *der* (PL *die* Flecke); **you've got a spot on your shirt** du hast einen Fleck auf dem Hemd; **4** (*spotlight*) Scheinwerfer *der* (PL *die* Scheinwerfer); (*in the home*) Spot *der* (PL *die* Spots); **5 on the spot** (*immediately*) wir machen es Ihnen auf der Stelle; **6** (*at hand*) **on the spot** zur Stelle; **7** (*at the same place*) **on the spot** an Ort

△ NEW SPELLING: *See page xii*

und Stelle.
verb entdecken; **he spotted his friend in the crowd** er entdeckte seinen Freund in der Menge.

spotlight *noun* **1** Scheinwerfer *der* (PL *die* Scheinwerfer); **2** (*in the home*) Spot *der* (PL *die* Spots).

spotty *adjective* (*pimply*) pickelig.

sprain *noun* Verstauchung *die* (PL *die* Verstauchungen).
verb **to sprain your ankle** sich ←(DAT) den Fuß verstauchen.

spray *noun* (*spray can*) Spray *das* (PL *die* Sprays).
verb sprühen.

spread *noun* Brotaufstrich *der*; **cheese spread** *der* Streichkäse.
verb **1** (*of news or a disease*) sich verbreiten; **2** streichen ✧ (*butter, jam, glue*).

spreadsheet *noun* (*on a computer*) Tabellenkalkulation *die*.

spring *noun* **1** (*the season*) Frühling *der* (PL *die* Frühlinge); **in the spring** im Frühling; **spring flowers** Frühlingsblumen; **2** (*made of metal*) Feder *die* (PL *die* Federn); **3** (*providing water*) Quelle *die* (PL *die* Quellen).

springtime *noun* Frühjahr *das*; **in springtime** im Frühjahr.

spring water *noun* Quellwasser *das*.

sprint *noun* Sprint *der* (PL *die* Sprints).
verb rennen ✧ (PERF *sein*).

sprinter *noun* Sprinter *der* (PL *die* Sprinter), Sprinterin *die* (PL *die* Sprinterinnen).

sprout *noun* (*Brussels sprout*) Rosenkohl *der*; **he likes sprouts** er mag Rosenkohl.

spy *noun* Spion *der* (PL *die* Spione), Spionin *die* (PL *die* Spioninnen).
verb **to spy on somebody** jemandem nachspionieren SEP; **he's spying on me** er spioniert mir nach.

squabble *verb* sich zanken.

square *noun* **1** (*shape*) Quadrat *das* (PL *die* Quadrate); **2** (*in a town or village*) Platz *der* (PL *die* Plätze); **the village square** der Dorfplatz.
adjective quadratisch; **a square box** eine viereckige Schachtel; **three square metres** drei Quadratmeter; **the room is four metres square** das Zimmer ist vier mal vier Meter; ★ **to go back to square one** noch einmal von vorn anfangen.

squash *noun* **1** (*drink*) Saft *der*; **orange squash** *der* Orangensaft; **2** (*sport*) Squash *das*.
verb zerquetschen.

squeak *verb* **1** (*door, hinge*) quietschen; **2** (*person, animal*) quieken.

squeeze *verb* **1** **to squeeze somebody's hand** jemandem die Hand drücken; **2** drücken (*toothpaste*).

stab *verb* stechen ✧; **to stab somebody** (*kill*) jemanden erstechen ✧.

✧ IRREGULAR VERB: *See the verb table in the centre of the dictionary*

stable *noun* Stall *der* (PL *die* Ställe). *adjective* stabil.

stack *noun* **1** Stapel *der* (PL *die* Stapel); **2 stacks of** ein Haufen; **she's got stacks of CDs** sie hat einen Haufen CDs.

stadium *noun* Stadion *das* (PL *die* Stadien).

staff *noun* **1** (*of a company*) Personal *das*; **2** (*in a school*) Lehrkräfte (*plural*).

stage *noun* **1** (*for a performance*) Bühne *die* (PL *die* Bühnen); **on stage** auf der Bühne; **2** (*phase*) Phase *die* (PL *die* Phasen); **at this stage of the project** in dieser Phase des Projekts; **at this stage it's hard to say** im Augenblick ist es schwer zu sagen.

staggered *adjective* (*amazed*) verblüfft.

stain *noun* Fleck *der* (PL *die* Flecke). *verb* beflecken.

stainless steel *noun* Edelstahl *der*; **a stainless steel sink** ein Spülbecken aus Edelstahl.

stair *noun* **1** (*step*) Stufe *die* (PL *die* Stufen); **2 the stairs** die Treppe (*singular*); **I met her on the stairs** ich habe sie auf der Treppe getroffen.

staircase *noun* Treppe *die* (PL *die* Treppen).

stale *adjective* alt.

stalemate *noun* (*in chess*) Patt *das* (PL *die* Patts).

stall *noun* **1** (*at a market or fair*) Stand *der* (PL *die* Stände); **2** (*in a theatre*) **the stalls** das Parkett.

stammer *noun* **to have a stammer** stottern.

stamp *noun* Briefmarke *die* (PL *die* Briefmarken). *verb* **1** frankieren (*a letter*); **2 to stamp your foot** mit dem Fuß aufstampfen.

stamp album *noun* Briefmarkenalbum *das* (PL *die* Briefmarkenalben).

stamp collection *noun* Briefmarkensammlung *die* (PL *die* Briefmarkensammlungen).

stand *verb* **1** stehen ✧; **several people were standing** viele Leute standen; **we stood outside the cinema** wir haben vor dem Kino gestanden; **2** (*bear*) ausstehen ✧ SEP; **I can't stand her** ich kann sie nicht ausstehen; **I can't stand waiting** ich kann es nicht ausstehen, wenn man warten muss; **3** (*keep going*) aushalten ✧ SEP; **I can't stand it any longer** ich halte es nicht mehr aus. *noun* (*in a stadium*) Tribüne *die* (PL *die* Tribünen).
● **to stand for something** (*be short for*) bedeuten; **UN stands for United Nations** UN bedeutet United Nations.
● **stand up** aufstehen ✧ SEP (PERF *sein*); **everybody stood up** alle standen auf.

standard *noun* **1** (*level*) Niveau *das*; **of high standard** von hohem Niveau; **2 standard of living**

der Lebensstandard; **3 she sets herself high standards** sie stellt hohe Ansprüche an sich selbst.
adjective normal; **the standard size** die Normalgröße.

staple *noun* Heftklammer *die* (PL *die* Heftklammern).
verb heften; **to staple the pages together** die Seiten zusammenheften.

stapler *noun* Hefter *der* (PL *die* Hefter).

star *noun* 1 (*in the sky*) Stern *der* (PL *die* Sterne); 2 (*person*) Star *der* (PL *die* Stars); **he's a film star** er ist ein Filmstar.
verb **to star in a film** in einem Film die Hauptrolle spielen; **starring** ... in der Hauptrolle ...

stare *verb* 1 starren; **what are you staring at?** was starrst du so?; 2 **to stare at somebody** jemanden anstarren SEP; **he's staring at the wall** er starrt die Wand an.

start *noun* 1 Anfang *der*; **at the start** am Anfang; **at the start of the film** am Anfang des Films; **from the start** von Anfang an; **we knew from the start that it was dangerous** wir wussten von Anfang an, dass es gefährlich war; 2 **to make a start on something** mit etwas ←(DAT) anfangen ✧ SEP; **I've made a start on my homework** ich habe mit meinen Hausaufgaben angefangen; 3 (*of a race*) Start *der* (PL *die* Starts).
verb 1 anfangen ✧ SEP; **the film starts at eight** der Film fängt um acht an; **I've started the book** ich habe das Buch angefangen; **to start**

doing something anfangen, etwas zu tun; **I've started learning Spanish** ich habe angefangen, Spanisch zu lernen; **to start crying** anfangen zu weinen; 2 **to start a business** ein Geschäft gründen; 3 **to start a car** ein Auto starten; **she started the car** sie hat das Auto gestartet; 4 **the car won't start** das Auto springt nicht an.

starter *noun* (*first course*) Vorspeise *die* (PL *die* Vorspeisen).

starve *verb* verhungern; **I'm starving!** ich bin schon am Verhungern!

state *noun* 1 Zustand *der* (PL *die* Zustände); **the house is in a very bad state** das Haus ist in einem sehr schlechten Zustand; 2 (*country*) Staat *der* (PL *die* Staaten); **the state** der Staat; 3 **the States** (*USA*) die Staaten; **they live in the States** sie leben in den Staaten.
verb 1 erklären (*intention, reason*); 2 angeben ✧ SEP (*an address, income, a reason*).

stately home *noun* Schloss △ *das* (PL *die* Schlösser).

statement *noun* Erklärung *die* (PL *die* Erklärungen).

station *noun* 1 Bahnhof *der* (PL *die* Bahnhöfe); **at the railway station** am Bahnhof; **bus station** *der* Busbahnhof; 2 **police station** *die* Polizeiwache; 3 **radio station** *der* Rundfunksender.

stationer's *noun* Schreibwarengeschäft *das* (PL *die* Schreibwarengeschäfte).

✧ IRREGULAR VERB: See the verb table in the centre of the dictionary

statistics *noun* (*subject*)
Statistik *die*; **the statistics** (*figures*)
die Statistik.

statue *noun* Statue *die* (PL *die*
Statuen).

stay *noun* Aufenthalt *der* (PL *die*
Aufenthalte); **our stay in Cologne**
unser Aufenthalt in Köln; **enjoy your
stay!** einen schönen Aufenthalt!
verb **1** bleiben ◇ (PERF *sein*); **I'll stay
here** ich bleibe hier; **how long are
you staying?** wie lange bleibst du?;
2 (*spend the night*) **you can stay
with us** du kannst bei uns
übernachten; **to stay the night with
friends** bei Freunden übernachten;
3 (*be temporarily lodged*) wohnen;
where are you staying? wo wohnst
du?; **I'm staying in a hotel** ich
wohne im Hotel; **4** (*be on a visit*)
sein ◇ (PERF *sein*); **I'm going to stay
with my sister this weekend** ich bin
am Wochenende bei meiner
Schwester; **I stayed in Munich for a
couple of days** ich war ein paar
Tage in München.
● **to stay in** zu Hause bleiben ◇ (PERF
sein); **I'm staying in tonight** heute
Abend bleibe ich zu Hause.

steady *adjective* **1** fest; **a steady job**
eine feste Stelle; **2** gleichmäßig; **at a
steady pace** mit gleichmäßiger
Geschwindigkeit; **3** (*hand, voice*)
ruhig; **to hold something steady**
etwas ruhig halten; **4** (*dependable*)
zuverlässig.

steak *noun* Steak *das* (PL *die* Steaks);
steak and chips Steak mit Pommes
frites.

steal *verb* stehlen ◇.

steam *noun* Dampf *der*.

steel *noun* Stahl *der*.

steep *adjective* steil; **a steep slope**
ein steiler Hang.

steeple *noun* (*spire*) Kirchturm *der*
(PL *die* Kirchtürme).

steering wheel *noun*
Lenkrad *das* (PL *die* Lenkräder).

step *noun* **1** Schritt *der* (PL *die*
Schritte); **to take a step forwards**
einen Schritt nach vorn machen; **to
take a step backwards** einen
Schritt zurück machen; **2** (*stair*)
Stufe *die* (PL *die* Stufen);
● **to step back** zurücktreten ◇ SEP
(PERF *sein*).
● **to step forward** vortreten ◇ SEP (PERF
sein).

stepbrother *noun* Stiefbruder *der*
(PL *die* Stiefbrüder).

stepdaughter *noun*
Stieftochter *die* (PL *die* Stieftöchter).

stepfather *noun* Stiefvater *der* (PL
die Stiefväter).

stepladder *noun* Trittleiter *die* (PL
die Trittleitern).

stepmother *noun* Stiefmutter *die*
(PL *die* Stiefmütter).

stepsister *noun* Stiefschwester *die*
(PL *die* Stiefschwestern).

stepson *noun* Stiefsohn *der* (PL *die*
Stiefsöhne).

stereo *noun* Stereoanlage *die* (PL *die*
Stereoanlagen).

sterling *noun* Sterling *der*; **in
sterling** in Pfund (Sterling).

△ NEW SPELLING: *See page xii*

stew *noun* Eintopf *der* (PL *die* Eintöpfe).

steward *noun* Steward *der* (PL *die* Stewards).

stewardess *noun* Stewardess Δ *die* (PL *die* Stewardessen).

stick *noun* 1 Stock *der* (PL *die* Stöcke); 2 **hockey stick** *der* Hockeyschläger.
verb 1 (*with glue*) kleben; 2 (*put*) tun ✧; **stick them on my desk** tu sie auf meinen Schreibtisch.

sticker *noun* Aufkleber *der* (PL *die* Aufkleber).

sticky *adjective* 1 klebrig; **I've got sticky hands** ich habe klebrige Hände; 2 **a sticky label** ein Aufkleber.

sticky tape *noun* Klebestreifen *der*.

stiff *adjective* 1 steif; **to feel stiff** steif sein; (*after exercise*) Muskelkater haben; **to have a stiff neck** einen steifen Hals haben; 2 **to be bored stiff** sich zu Tode langweilen; 3 **to be scared stiff** furchtbare Angst haben.

still *adjective* 1 **sit still!** sitz still!; **keep still!** halt still!; 2 **still mineral water** Mineralwasser ohne Kohlensäure.
adverb 1 noch; **do you still live in London?** wohnst du noch in London?; **I've still not finished** ich bin immer noch nicht fertig; **he's still working** er arbeitet noch; 2 (*nevertheless*) trotzdem; **I told her not to, but she still did it** ich habe

es ihr verboten, aber sie hat es trotzdem gemacht; 3 **better still** noch besser.

sting *noun* Stich *der* (PL *die* Stiche).
verb stechen ✧.

stink *noun* Gestank *der*.
verb stinken ✧; **it stinks of fish in here** es stinkt hier nach Fisch.

stir *verb* rühren.

stitch *noun* 1 (*in sewing, surgical*) Stich *der* (PL *die* Stiche); 2 (*in knitting*) Masche *die* (PL *die* Maschen); 3 (*pain*) Seitenstechen *das*.

stock *noun* 1 (*in a shop*) Warenbestand *der*; **to have something in stock** etwas auf Lager haben; **to be out of stock** ausverkauft sein; 2 (*supply*) Vorrat *der* (PL *die* Vorräte); **I always have a stock of pencils** ich habe immer einen Bleistiftvorrat; 3 (*for cooking*) Brühe *die*; **chicken stock** die Hühnerbrühe.
verb (*in a shop*) führen; **they don't stock books** sie führen keine Bücher.

stock cube *noun* Brühwürfel *der* (PL *die* Brühwürfel).

stocking *noun* Strumpf *der* (PL *die* Strümpfe).

stomach *noun* Magen *der* (PL *die* Mägen).

stomach-ache *noun* Magenschmerzen (*plural*); **to have stomach-ache** Magenschmerzen haben.

✧ IRREGULAR VERB: *See the verb table in the centre of the dictionary*

stone *noun* Stein *der* (PL *die* Steine); **stone wall** *die* Steinmauer.

stool *noun* Hocker *der* (PL *die* Hocker).

stop *noun* Haltestelle *die* (PL *die* Haltestellen); **bus stop** *die* Bushaltestelle.
verb **1** halten ✧; **does the train stop in Stuttgart?** hält der Zug in Stuttgart?; **2 to stop somebody/ something** jemanden/etwas anhalten ✧ SEP; **the police stopped the car** die Polizei hielt den Wagen an; **3** (*cease*) aufhören SEP; **the noise has stopped** der Lärm hat aufgehört; **to stop doing something** aufhören, etwas zu tun; **he's stopped smoking** er hat aufgehört zu rauchen; **she never stops asking questions** sie hört nie auf, Fragen zu stellen; **stop it!** hör auf!; **4 to stop somebody doing something** jemanden daran hindern, etwas zu tun; **I can't stop her ringing him** ich kann sie nicht daran hindern, ihn anzurufen; **5** (*prevent*) verhindern (*an accident, a crime*).

stopwatch *noun* Stoppuhr *die* (PL *die* Stoppuhren).

store *noun* (*shop*) Geschäft *das* (PL *die* Geschäfte); **department store** *das* Kaufhaus.
verb **1** aufbewahren SEP; (*in a warehouse*) lagern; **2** (*on a computer*) speichern.

storey *noun* Stockwerk *das* (PL *die* Stockwerke); **a four-storey house** ein vierstöckiges Haus.

storm *noun* **1** Sturm *der* (PL *die* Stürme); **2** (*thunderstorm*) Gewitter *das* (PL *die* Gewitter).

stormy *adjective* stürmisch.

story *noun* Geschichte *die* (PL *die* Geschichten); **to tell a story** eine Geschichte erzählen.

stove *noun* (*cooker*) Herd *der* (PL *die* Herde).

straight *adjective* **1** gerade; **a straight line** eine gerade Linie; **2 to have straight hair** glatte Haare haben.
adverb **1** (*in direction*) **straight ahead** geradeaus; **to go straight ahead** geradeaus gehen; **2** (*immediately, directly*) sofort; **straight away** sofort; **he went straight to the doctor's** er ging sofort zum Arzt.

straightforward *adjective* einfach.

strain *noun* Stress △ *der*; **the strain of the last few weeks** der Stress in den letzten Wochen; **to be a strain** anstrengend sein.
verb **1** zerren (*a muscle*); **2** verrenken (*your arm, back*); **he's strained his back** er hat sich ←(DAT) den Rücken verrenkt.

strange *adjective* seltsam; **his strange behaviour** sein seltsames Verhalten.

stranger *noun* Fremde *der/die* (PL *die* Fremden).

strap *noun* **1** (*on a case, bag, camera*) Riemen *der* (PL *die* Riemen); **2** (*on a garment*) Träger *der* (PL *die* Träger);

3 (*of a watch*) Armband *das* (PL *die* Armbänder).

strapless *adjective* trägerlos.

straw *noun* **1** (*for drinking*) Strohhalm *der* (PL *die* Strohhalme); **2** (*the material*) Stroh *das*; **straw hat** *der* Strohhut.

strawberry *noun* Erdbeere *die* (PL *die* Erdbeeren); **strawberry jam** *die* Erdbeermarmelade.

stray *adjective* **a stray dog** ein streunender Hund.

stream *noun* Bach *der* (PL *die* Bäche).

street *noun* Straße *die* (PL *die* Straßen); **I met Simon in the street** ich habe Simon auf der Straße getroffen.

streetlamp *noun* Straßenlampe *die* (PL *die* Straßenlampen).

street map *noun* Stadtplan *der* (PL *die* Stadtpläne).

streetwise *adjective* gewieft.

strength *noun* Kraft *die* (PL *die* Kräfte).

stress *noun* Stress △ *der*. *verb* betonen; **to stress the importance of something** die Wichtigkeit von etwas betonen.

stretch *verb* **1** (*garment, shoes*) sich dehnen; **this jumper has stretched** der Pullover hat sich gedehnt; **2 to stretch your legs** sich ←(DAT) die Beine vertreten ✧.

stretcher *noun* Trage *die* (PL *die* Tragen).

stretchy *adjective* elastisch.

strict *adjective* streng.

strike *noun* Streik *der* (PL *die* Streiks); **to go on strike** in den Streik treten ✧ (PERF *sein*); **to be/go on strike** streiken. *verb* **1** (*hit*) schlagen ✧; **the clock struck six** die Uhr schlug sechs; **2** (*be/go on strike*) streiken.

striker *noun* **1** (*in football*) Stürmer *der* (PL *die* Stürmer), Stürmerin *die* (PL *die* Stürmerinnen); **2** (*person on strike*) Streikende *der/die* (PL *die* Streikenden).

string *noun* **1** (*for tying*) Schnur *die* (PL *die* Schnüre); **2** (*on a musical instrument*) Saite *die* (PL *die* Saiten).

strip *noun* Streifen *der* (PL *die* Streifen). *verb* **1** (*undress*) sich ausziehen ✧ SEP; **2** (*remove paint from*) abbeizen SEP.

strip cartoon *noun* Comicstrip △ *der* (PL *die* Comicstrips).

stripe *noun* Streifen *der* (PL *die* Streifen).

striped *adjective* gestreift.

stroke *noun* **1** (*style of swimming*) Stil *der* (PL *die* Stile); **2** (*medical*) Schlaganfall *der* (PL *die* Schlaganfälle); **to have a stroke** einen Schlaganfall bekommen; ★ **a stroke of luck** ein glücklicher Zufall; **to have a stroke of luck** Glück haben. *verb* streicheln.

✧ IRREGULAR VERB: *See the verb table in the centre of the dictionary*

strong adjective **1** (person, drink, feeling) stark; **2** (sturdy) stabil (furniture); **strong shoes** feste Schuhe.

strongly adverb **1** (believe, oppose) fest; **2** (support) nachdrücklich; **3** (advise, recommend) dringend; **4 she smelt strongly of garlic** sie hat stark nach Knoblauch gerochen.

struggle noun Kampf der (PL die Kämpfe); **the struggle for freedom** der Kampf für die Freiheit; **it's been a struggle** es war ein Kampf. verb **1** (to obtain something) kämpfen; **to struggle to do something** kämpfen, um etwas zu tun; **she struggled for a place** sie kämpfte um einen Platz; **2** (physically, in order to escape or reach something) sich wehren; **3** (have difficulty in doing something) sich abmühen SEP; **they are struggling to pay the rent** sie mühen sich ab, ihre Miete zu zahlen; **he's struggling with his homework** er müht sich mit seinen Hausaufgaben ab.

stub noun **cigarette stub** die Kippe. **to stub out** ausdrücken SEP.

stubborn adjective stur.

stuck adjective **1** (jammed) **it's stuck** es klemmt; **the drawer's stuck** die Schublade klemmt; **2 to get stuck** (person) stecken bleiben △ ◇ (in a lift, traffic jam, or place).

stud noun **1** (on clothes) Niete die (PL die Nieten); **2** (on a boot) Stollen der (PL die Stollen);

3 (earring) Ohrstecker der (PL die Ohrstecker).

student noun **1** (at college or university) Student der (PL die Studenten), Studentin die (PL die Studentinnen); **2** (at school) Schüler der (PL die Schüler), Schülerin die (PL die Schülerinnen).

studio noun **1** (film, TV) Studio das (PL die Studios); **2** (artist's) Atelier das (PL die Ateliers).

study verb **1** lernen; **he's busy studying for his exams** er lernt fleißig für seine Prüfung; **2** studieren; **she's studying medicine** sie studiert Medizin.

stuff noun (things, personal belongings) Zeug das (informal); **we can put all that stuff in the attic** wir können das ganze Zeug auf den Boden bringen; **you can leave your stuff at my house** du kannst dein Zeug bei mir lassen. verb **1** (shove) stopfen; **she stuffed some things into a suitcase** sie hat ein paar Sachen in einen Koffer gestopft; **2** füllen (vegetables, turkey); **stuffed peppers** gefüllte Paprikaschoten.

stuffing noun (in cooking) Füllung die (PL die Füllungen).

stuffy adjective (airless) stickig.

stunned adjective sprachlos.

stunning adjective toll (informal).

stunt noun (in a film) Stunt der (PL die Stunts).

stuntman noun Stuntman der (PL die Stuntmen).

△ NEW SPELLING: *See page xii*

stupid *adjective* blöd; **that was really stupid** das war so blöd; **I did something stupid** ich habe etwas Blödes gemacht.

stutter *noun* **to have a stutter** stottern.
verb stottern.

style *noun* **1** Stil *der* (PL *die* Stile); **style of living** *der* Lebensstil; **he has his own style** er hat seinen eigenen Stil; **2** (*fashion*) Mode *die*; **it's the latest style** das ist die neueste Mode.

subject *noun* **1** Thema *das* (PL *die* Themen); **the subject of my talk** das Thema meiner Rede; **2** (*at school*) Fach *das* (PL *die* Fächer); **my favourite subject is biology** mein Lieblingsfach ist Biologie.

subscription *noun* Abonnement *das* (PL *die* Abonnements); **to take out a subscription to a magazine** eine Zeitschrift abonnieren.

subsidize *verb* subventionieren.

subsidy *noun* Subvention *die* (PL *die* Subventionen).

substance *noun* Substanz *die* (PL *die* Substanzen).

substitute *noun* (*in sport*) Ersatzspieler *der* (PL *die* Ersatzspieler), Ersatzspielerin *die* (PL *die* Ersatzspielerinnen).
verb ersetzen.

subtitled *adjective* mit Untertiteln.

subtitles *plural noun* Untertitel (*plural*).

subtract *verb* abziehen ✧ SEP.

suburb *noun* Vorort *der* (PL *die* Vororte); **a suburb of Edinburgh** ein Vorort von Edinburgh; **in the suburbs of London** in den Londone Vororten.

suburban *adjective* Vorort-; **a suburban train** ein Vorortzug.

subway *noun* (*underpass*) Unterführung *die* (PL *die* Unterführungen).

succeed *verb* gelingen ✧ (PERF *sein*); **we've succeeded in contacting her** es ist uns gelungen, sie zu erreichen.

success *noun* Erfolg *der* (PL *die* Erfolge); **a great success** ein großer Erfolg.

successful *adjective* **1** erfolgreich; **he's a successful writer** er ist ein erfolgreicher Schriftsteller; **2 to be successful in doing something** etwas mit Erfolg tun.

successfully *adverb* mit Erfolg.

such *adjective, adverb* **1** so; **they're such nice people** das sind so nette Leute; **I've had such a busy day** ich habe so einen hektischen Tag gehabt; **it's such a long way** es ist so weit; **it's such a pity** es ist so schade; **2 such a lot of** (*followed by a singular noun*) so viel; **they've got such a lot of money** sie haben so viel Geld; **3 such a lot of** (*followed by a plural noun*) so viele; **she's got such a lot of problems** sie hat so viele Probleme; **4 such as** wie; **in big cities such as Glasgow** in großen Städten wie Glasgow;

5 there's no such thing so etwas gibt es nicht.

suck *verb* lutschen; **to suck your thumb** am Daumen lutschen.

sudden *adjective* plötzlich; ★ **all of a sudden** plötzlich.

suddenly *adverb* plötzlich; **he suddenly started to laugh** plötzlich hat er angefangen zu lachen; **suddenly the light went out** plötzlich ging das Licht aus.

suede *noun* Wildleder *das*; **suede jacket** *die* Wildlederjacke.

suffer *verb* leiden ✧; **to suffer from asthma** an Asthma leiden.

sufficiently *adverb* genug.

sugar *noun* Zucker *der*; **do you take sugar?** nimmst du Zucker?

suggest *verb* vorschlagen ✧ SEP; **he suggested I should speak to you about it** er hat vorgeschlagen, dass ich mit dir darüber sprechen soll.

suggestion *noun* Vorschlag *der* (PL *die* Vorschläge); **to make a suggestion** einen Vorschlag machen.

suicide *noun* Selbstmord *der* (PL *die* Selbstmorde); **to commit suicide** Selbstmord begehen.

suit *noun* 1 (*man's*) Anzug *der* (PL *die* Anzüge); 2 (*woman's*) Kostüm *das* (PL *die* Kostüme).
verb 1 (*be convenient*) passen (+DAT); **does Monday suit you?** passt Ihnen Montag?; 2 (*look good on*) stehen ✧ (+DAT); **hats suit her** ihr stehen Hüte gut.

suitable *adjective* 1 geeignet; **to be suitable for something** für etwas geeignet sein; **it's suitable for children** es ist für Kinder geeignet; 2 (*convenient*) passend; **at a suitable time** zur passenden Zeit; **Saturday is the most suitable day for me** Samstag passt mir am besten; 3 (*for a social occasion*) angemessen (*clothes*).

suitcase *noun* Koffer *der* (PL *die* Koffer).

sulk *verb* schmollen.

sum *noun* 1 Summe *die* (PL *die* Summen); **a sum of money** eine Geldsumme; 2 (*calculation*) Rechenaufgabe *die* (PL *die* Rechenaufgaben).
● **to sum up** zusammenfassen SEP.

summarize *verb* zusammenfassen SEP.

summary *noun* Zusammenfassung *die* (PL *die* Zusammenfassungen).

summer *noun* Sommer *der* (PL *die* Sommer); **in summer** im Sommer; **summer clothes** *die* Sommerkleidung; **the summer holidays** die Sommerferien.

summertime *noun* Sommer *der*; **in summertime** im Sommer.

summit *noun* Gipfel *der* (PL *die* Gipfel).

sun *noun* Sonne *die* (PL *die* Sonnen); **in the sun** in der Sonne.

sunbathe *verb* sich sonnen.

△ NEW SPELLING: *See page xii*

sunblock *noun* Sun-Block-Creme *die* (PL *die* Sun-Block-Cremes).

sunburned *adjective* **to get sunburned** einen Sonnenbrand bekommen.

Sunday *noun* 1 Sonntag *der* (PL *die* Sonntage); **on Sunday** am Sonntag; **I'm going to the cinema on Sunday** ich gehe (am) Sonntag ins Kino; **see you on Sunday!** bis Sonntag!; **every Sunday** jeden Sonntag; **last Sunday** vorigen Sonntag; **next Sunday** nächsten Sonntag; 2 **on Sundays** sonntags; **the museum is closed on Sundays** das Museum ist sonntags geschlossen.

sunflower *noun* Sonnenblume *die* (PL *die* Sonnenblumen); **sunflower oil** *das* Sonnenblumenöl.

sunglasses *plural noun* Sonnenbrille *die* (PL *die* Sonnenbrillen).

sunlight *noun* Sonnenlicht *das*.

sunny *adjective* sonnig; **a sunny day** ein sonniger Tag; **sunny intervals** Aufheiterungen.

sunrise *noun* Sonnenaufgang *der* (PL *die* Sonnenaufgänge).

sunscreen *noun* Sonnenschutzcreme *die* (PL *die* Sonnenschutzcremes).

sunset *noun* Sonnenuntergang *der* (PL *die* Sonnenuntergänge).

sunshine *noun* Sonnenschein *der*.

sunstroke *noun* Sonnenstich *der* (PL *die* Sonnenstiche); **to get sunstroke** einen Sonnenstich bekommen.

suntan *noun* Bräune *die*; **to have a suntan** braun sein; **to get a suntan** braun werden.

suntan lotion *noun* Sonnenmilch *die*.

suntan oil *noun* Sonnenöl *das*.

super *adjective* klasse (*informal*) (*'klasse' never changes*); **we had a super time** es war wirklich klasse.

supermarket *noun* Supermarkt *der* (PL *die* Supermärkte).

supernatural *adjective* übernatürlich.

superstitious *adjective* abergläubisch.

supervise *verb* beaufsichtigen.

supper *noun* Abendessen *das* (PL *die* Abendessen); **I had supper at Sandy's** ich war bei Sandy zum Abendessen.

supplement *noun* 1 (*to newspaper*) Beilage *die* (PL *die* Beilagen); 2 (*to fare*) Zuschlag *der* (PL *die* Zuschläge).

supply *noun* 1 (*stock*) Vorrat *der* (PL *die* Vorräte); 2 **to be in short supply** knapp sein.
verb 1 stellen; **the school supplies the books** die Schule stellt die Bücher; 2 (*deliver*) liefern; **to supply somebody with something** jemandem etwas liefern.

supply teacher *noun* Aushilfslehrer *der* (PL *die* Aushilfslehrer), Aushilfslehrerin *die* (PL *die* Aushilfslehrerinnen).

⬦ IRREGULAR VERB: *See the verb table in the centre of the dictionary*

support *noun* Unterstützung *die*;
in support zur Unterstützung.
verb 1 (*back up*) unterstützen; **her
teachers have really supported
her** die Lehrer haben sie sehr
unterstützt; **to support somebody
financially** jemanden finanziell
unterstützen; 2 **Will supports
Chelsea** Will ist ein Chelsea-Fan;
what team do you support? für
welche Mannschaft bist du?; 3 (*keep,
provide for*) ernähren; **to support a
family** eine Familie ernähren.

supporter *noun* 1 Fan *der* (PL *die*
Fans); **she's a Manchester United
supporter** sie ist ein Manchester-
United-Fan; 2 (*of a party or cause*)
Anhänger *der* (PL *die* Anhänger),
Anhängerin *die* (PL *die*
Anhängerinnen).

suppose *verb* annehmen ◇ SEP;
I suppose she's forgotten ich
nehme an, sie hat es vergessen.

supposed *adjective* **to be
supposed to do something** etwas
tun sollen; **you were supposed to
be here at six** du solltest um sechs
hier sein.

sure *adjective* 1 sicher; **are you
sure?** bist du sicher?; **are you sure
you saw her?** bis du sicher, dass du
sie gesehen hast?; 2 **sure!** klar!

surely *adverb* doch sicherlich;
surely she hasn't forgotten sie hat
es doch sicherlich nicht vergessen.

surface *noun* Oberfläche *die* (PL *die*
Oberflächen).

surfboard *noun* Surfbrett *das* (PL
die Surfbretter).

surfing *noun* Surfen *das*.

surgeon *noun* Chirurg *der* (PL *die*
Chirurgen), Chirurgin *die* (PL *die*
Chirurginnen).

surgery *noun* 1 **to have surgery**
operiert werden; 2 (*doctor's*)
Praxis *die* (PL *die* Praxen); **the
dentist's surgery** die
Zahnarztpraxis; 3 (*surgery hours*)
Sprechstunde *die*.

surname *noun* Nachname *der* (PL
die Nachnamen).

surprise *noun* Überraschung *die*
(PL *die* Überraschungen); **what a
surprise!** was für eine
Überraschung!

surprised *adjective* überrascht; **I
was surprised to see her** ich war
überrascht, sie zu sehen.

surprising *adjective* überraschend.

surround *verb* umgeben;
surrounded by umgeben von (+DAT);
she was surrounded by friends sie
war von Freunden umgeben.

survey *noun* Umfrage *die* (PL *die*
Umfragen).

survive *verb* überleben.

survivor *noun*
Überlebende *der/die* (PL *die*
Überlebenden).

suspect *noun* Verdächtige *der/die*
(PL *die* Verdächtigen).
adjective verdächtig.
verb verdächtigen.

suspend *verb* 1 **to be suspended**
(*from school*) vom Unterricht
ausgeschlossen werden; 2 (*from a*

team) sperren; **to suspend a player for four weeks** einen Spieler für vier Wochen sperren.

suspense *noun* Spannung *die*.

suspicious *adjective*
1 misstrauisch △; **to be suspicious of somebody** jemandem misstrauen; **2** (*suspicious looking*) verdächtig.

swallow *noun* (*bird*) Schwalbe *die* (PL *die* Schwalben).
verb schlucken.

swan *noun* Schwan *der* (PL *die* Schwäne).

swap *verb* tauschen; **do you want to swap?** willst du tauschen?; **he swapped his bike for a computer** er hat sein Rad gegen einen Computer getauscht; **we swapped seats** wir tauschten die Plätze.

swear *verb* (*use bad language*) fluchen.

swearword *noun* Kraftausdruck *der* (PL *die* Kraftausdrücke).

sweat *noun* Schweiß *der*.
verb schwitzen.

sweater *noun* Pullover *der* (PL *die* Pullover).

Swede *noun* Schwede *der* (PL *die* Schweden), Schwedin *die* (PL *die* Schwedinnen).

Sweden *noun* Schweden *das*; **from Sweden** aus Schweden; **to Sweden** nach Schweden.

Swedish *noun* (*the language*) Schwedisch *das*.

adjective schwedisch; **he's Swedish** er ist Schwede; **she's Swedish** sie ist Schwedin.

sweep *verb* fegen.

sweet *noun* **1** Bonbon *der* (PL *die* Bonbons); **2** (*dessert*) Nachtisch *der* (PL *die* Nachtische).
adjective **1** süß; **I try not to eat sweet things** ich versuche nichts Süßes zu essen; **she looks really sweet in that hat** sie sieht richtig süß mit dem Hut aus; **2** (*kind*) lieb; **she's a really sweet person** sie ist wirklich ein sehr lieber Mensch; **how sweet of him** wie lieb von ihm.

sweetcorn *noun* Mais *der*.

swell *verb* (*part of the body*) anschwellen ♦ SEP (PERF *sein*).

swim *noun* **to go for a swim** schwimmen gehen ♦ (PERF *sein*).
verb schwimmen ♦ (PERF *sein*); **can he swim?** kann er schwimmen?; **to swim across a lake** über einen See schwimmen.

swimmer *noun* Schwimmer *der* (PL *die* Schwimmer), Schwimmerin *die* (PL *die* Schwimmerinnen); **she's a strong swimmer** sie ist eine gute Schwimmerin.

swimming *noun* Schwimmen *das*; **to go swimming** schwimmen gehen

swimming cap *noun* Badekappe *die* (PL *die* Badekappen).

swimming costume *noun* Badeanzug *der* (PL *die* Badeanzüge).

♦ IRREGULAR VERB: *See the verb table in the centre of the dictionary*

swimming pool *noun*
Schwimmbecken *das* (PL *die*
Schwimmbecken).

swimming trunks *noun*
Badehose *die* (PL *die* Badehosen).

swimsuit *noun* Badeanzug *der* (PL
die Badeanzüge).

swing *noun* Schaukel *die* (PL *die*
Schaukeln).

Swiss *noun* (*person*) Schweizer *der*
(PL *die* Schweizer), Schweizerin *die*
(PL *die* Schweizerinnen); **the Swiss**
die Schweizer.
adjective schweizerisch; **she is
Swiss** sie ist Schweizerin.

switch *noun* (*for a light, radio, etc*).
Schalter *der* (PL *die* Schalter).
verb (*change*) wechseln; **to switch
places** die Plätze wechseln.
● **to switch something off** etwas
ausschalten SEP.
● **to switch something on** etwas
anschalten SEP.

Switzerland *noun* die Schweiz;
from Switzerland aus der Schweiz;
in Switzerland in der Schweiz; **to
Switzerland** in die Schweiz.

swollen *adjective* geschwollen.

swop *verb* SEE **swap**.

syllabus *noun* Lehrplan *der* (PL *die*
Lehrpläne); **to be on the syllabus**
auf dem Lehrplan stehen.

symbol *noun* Symbol *das* (PL *die*
Symbole).

sympathetic *adjective*
verständnisvoll.

sympathize *verb* **to sympathize
with somebody** mit jemandem
mitfühlen SEP; **I sympathize with
you** ich kann mit Ihnen mitfühlen.

sympathy *noun* Mitleid *das*.

symptom *noun* Symptom *das* (PL
die Symptome).

synthesizer *noun* Synthesizer *der*
(PL *die* Synthesizers).

synthetic *adjective* synthetisch.

syringe *noun* Spritze *die* (PL *die*
Spritzen).

system *noun* System *das* (PL *die*
Systeme).

T t

table *noun* Tisch *der* (PL *die* Tische);
to lay the table den Tisch decken;
to clear the table den Tisch
abräumen SEP.

tablecloth *noun* Tischdecke *die* (PL
die Tischdecken).

tablespoon *noun* Esslöffel △ *der*
(PL *die* Esslöffel); **a tablespoon of
flour** ein Esslöffel Mehl.

tablet *noun* Tablette *die* (PL *die*
Tabletten).

table tennis *noun*
Tischtennis *das*.

tackle *verb* **1** (*in football or hockey*)
angreifen ◇ SEP; **2** angehen ◇ SEP
(PERF *sein*) (*a job or a problem*).

tact *noun* Takt *der*.

tactful *adjective* taktvoll; **that wasn't very tactful** das war nicht sehr taktvoll.

tail *noun* 1 Schwanz *der* (PL *die* Schwänze); 2 **'heads or tails?' – 'tails'** 'Kopf oder Zahl?'- 'Zahl'.

take *verb* 1 nehmen ◇; **he took a sweet** er nahm einen Bonbon; **take my hand** nimm meine Hand; **I took the bus** ich habe den Bus genommen; **do you take sugar?** nimmst du Zucker?; 2 (*with time*) dauern; **it takes two hours** es dauert zwei Stunden; 3 (*react to*) aufnehmen ◇ SEP; **he took the news calmly** er hat die Nachricht gelassen aufgenommen; 4 (*take to a place*) bringen ◇; **I'm taking Jake to my parents** ich bringe Jake zu meinen Eltern; **I must take the car to the garage** ich muss das Auto in die Werkstatt bringen; **to take somebody home** jemanden nach Hause bringen; 5 **to take something up(stairs)** etwas heraufbringen ◇ SEP; **could you take the towels up?** könntest du die Handtücher heraufbringen?; 6 **to take something down(stairs)** etwas herunterbringen ◇ SEP; **Cheryl's taken the cups down** Cheryl hat die Tassen heruntergebracht; 7 (*carry with you*) mitnehmen ◇ SEP; **she's taken some of the files home** sie hat einige der Akten mit nach Hause genommen; **I'm taking my Walkman** ich nehme meinen Walkman mit; **I'll take him next time** nächstes Mal nehme ich ihn mit; 8 annehmen ◇ SEP (*a credit card or a cheque*); **do you take cheques?** nehmen Sie Schecks an?; 9 machen (*an exam, a holiday, or a photo*); **she's taking her driving test tomorrow** sie macht morgen ihre Fahrprüfung; **to take a holiday** Ferien machen; 10 (*need*) brauchen **it takes a lot of courage** dazu braucht man viel Mut; **it takes me at least two hours to read it** ich brauche mindestens zwei Stunden, um es zu lesen; 11 haben ◇ (*clothes size*); **what size do you take?** welche Größe haben Sie?

- **to take something apart** etwas auseinander nehmen Δ ◇.
- **to take something back** etwas zurückbringen ◇ SEP.
- **to take off** 1 (*plane*) abfliegen ◇ SEP (PERF *sein*); 2 ausziehen ◇ SEP (*clothes, shoes*); **take your jacket off** zieh die Jacke aus; **to take your clothes off** sich ausziehen; 3 abziehen ◇ SEP (*money*); **he took five pounds off the price** er hat fünf Pfund vom Preis abgezogen.
- **to take out something** (*from a bag or pocket*) etwas herausnehmen ◇ SEP; **Eric took out his wallet** Eric nahm seine Brieftasche heraus.
- **to take somebody out** jemanden einladen ◇ SEP; **to take somebody out for a meal** jemanden zum Essen einladen ◇ SEP.

takeaway *noun* 1 (*meal*) Essen zum Mitnehmen *das* (PL *die* Essen zum Mitnehmen); **an Indian takeaway** ein indisches Essen zum Mitnehmen; 2 (*where you buy it*) Restaurant mit Straßenverkauf *das* (PL *die* Restaurants mit Straßenverkauf).

◇ IRREGULAR VERB: *See the verb table in the centre of the dictionary*

take-off noun (of a plane)
Abflug der (PL die Abflüge).

talent noun Talent das (PL die
Talente); **to have a talent for
painting** ein Talent zum Malen
haben.

talented adjective talentiert; **he's
really talented** er ist wirklich
talentiert.

talk noun 1 (a chat) Gespräch das
(PL die Gespräche); **we had a serious
talk about it** wir hatten ein ernstes
Gespräch darüber; 2 Vortrag der (PL
die Vorträge); **she's giving a talk on
Hungary** sie hält einen Vortrag über
Ungarn.
verb 1 reden; **to talk to somebody**
mit jemandem reden; **we talked
about football** wir haben über
Fußball geredet; **what's he talking
about?** wovon redet er?; **we'll talk
about it later** darüber reden wir
später; **they're always talking** sie
reden immer; 2 **to talk to
somebody on the phone** mit
jemandem telefonieren.

tall adjective 1 groß; **she's very tall**
sie ist sehr groß; **I'm 1.7 metres tall**
ich bin ein Meter siebzig groß;
2 hoch (building or tree).

tampon noun Tampon der (PL die
Tampons).

tan noun Bräune die; **to have a tan**
braun sein; **to get a tan** braun
werden.

tank noun 1 (for petrol or water)
Tank der (PL die Tanks); 2 **fish tank**
das Aquarium; 3 (army) Panzer der
(PL die Panzer).

tanned adjective braun.

tap noun Wasserhahn der (PL die
Wasserhähne); **to turn on the tap**
den Wasserhahn aufdrehen SEP; **to
turn off the tap** den Wasserhahn
zudrehen SEP; **the hot tap** der
Warmwasserhahn.
verb klopfen; **to tap on the door** an
die Tür klopfen.

tap-dancing noun
Stepptanzen das.

tape noun 1 Kassette die (PL die
Kassetten); **my tape of the Stones**
meine Kassette von den Stones; **I've
got it on tape** ich habe es auf Band;
2 **sticky tape** der Klebestreifen.
verb aufnehmen ◇ SEP; **I want to
tape the film** ich will den Film
aufnehmen.

tape measure noun
Metermaß das (PL die Metermaße).

tape recorder noun
Tonbandgerät das (PL die
Tonbandgeräte).

target noun Ziel das (PL die Ziele).

tart noun Kuchen der (PL die
Kuchen); **apple tart** der
Apfelkuchen.

tartan adjective Schotten-; **a tartan
skirt** ein Schottenrock.

task noun Aufgabe die (PL die
Aufgaben).

taste noun 1 Geschmack der (PL die
Geschmäcke); **a taste of onions** ein
Zwiebelgeschmack; **she's got no
taste** sie hat keinen Geschmack;
2 **in bad taste** geschmacklos.
verb 1 schmecken; **the soup tastes**

△ NEW SPELLING: See page xii

horrible die Suppe schmeckt furchtbar; **2 to taste of something** nach etwas ←(DAT) schmecken; **it tastes of garlic** es schmeckt nach Knoblauch; **3** (*try a little*) probieren; **do you want to taste?** möchtest du mal probieren?

tasty *adjective* schmackhaft.

tattoo *noun* Tätowierung *die* (PL *die* Tätowierungen); **he's got a tattoo on his arm** er hat eine Tätowierung am Arm.

Taurus *noun* Stier *der*; **Josephine's Taurus** Josephine ist (ein) Stier.

tax *noun* Steuer *die* (PL *die* Steuern) (*on goods, income*).

taxi *noun* Taxi *das* (PL *die* Taxis); **to go by taxi** mit dem Taxi fahren; **to take a taxi** ein Taxi nehmen.

taxi driver *noun* Taxifahrer *der* (PL *die* Taxifahrer), Taxifahrerin *die* (PL *die* Taxifahrerinnen).

taxi rank *noun* Taxistand *der* (PL *die* Taxistände).

tea *noun* **1** Tee *der* (PL *die* Tees); **a cup of tea** eine Tasse Tee; **to have tea** Tee trinken; **2** (*evening meal*) Abendessen *das* (PL *die* Abendessen).

teabag *noun* Teebeutel *der* (PL *die* Teebeutel).

teach *verb* **1** beibringen ✧ SEP; **she's teaching me to drive** sie bringt mir das Autofahren bei; **2 to teach yourself something** sich ←(DAT) etwas beibringen ✧ SEP; **I taught myself Italian** ich habe mir Italienisch beigebracht; **3 that'll**

teach you ! das wird dir eine Lehre sein !; **4** unterrichten; **her mum teaches maths** ihre Mutter unterrichtet Mathematik.

teacher *noun* Lehrer *der* (PL *die* Lehrer), Lehrerin *die* (PL *die* Lehrerinnen).

teaching *noun* Unterrichten *das*.

team *noun* Mannschaft *die* (PL *die* Mannschaften); **football team** *die* Fußballmannschaft.

teapot *noun* Teekanne *die* (PL *die* Teekannen).

tear¹ *noun* (*a rip*) Riss ∆ *der* (PL *die* Risse).
verb **1** zerreißen ✧; **she tore up my letter** sie hat meinen Brief zerrissen; **2** reißen ✧ (PERF *sein*); **the net has torn** das Netz ist gerissen; **be careful, it tears easily** sei vorsichtig, es reißt leicht.

tear² *noun* (*when you cry*) Träne *die* (PL *die* Tränen); **to be in tears** in Tränen aufgelöst sein; **to burst into tears** in Tränen ausbrechen.

tease *verb* **1** necken (*a person*); **2** quälen (*an animal*).

teaspoon *noun* Teelöffel *der* (PL *die* Teelöffel); **a teaspoon of vinegar** ein Teelöffel Essig.

teatime *noun* (*evening meal*) Abendessenszeit *die* (PL *die* Abendessenszeiten); **it's teatime !** es gibt Abendessen !

tea towel *noun* Geschirrtuch *das* (PL *die* Geschirrtücher).

technical *adjective* technisch.

✧ IRREGULAR VERB: *See the verb table in the centre of the dictionary*

technical college *noun*
Fachhochschule *die* (PL *die* Fachhochschulen).

technician *noun* Techniker *der* (PL *die* Techniker), Technikerin *die* (PL *die* Technikerinnen).

technique *noun* Technik *die* (PL *die* Techniken).

techno *noun* (*music*) Techno *der*.

technology *noun*
1 Technologie *die*; **2 information technology** *die* Informatik.

teddy bear *noun* Teddybär *der* (PL *die* Teddybären).

teenage *adjective* **1** Teenage-;
2 they have a teenage son sie haben einen Sohn im Teenageralter;
3 (*films, magazines, etc.*) für Teenager; **a teenage magazine** eine Zeitschrift für Teenager.

teenager *noun* Teenager *der* (PL *die* Teenager); **a group of teenagers** eine Gruppe von Teenagern.

teens *plural noun* **the teens** die Teenagerjahre; **he's in his teens** er ist ein Teenager.

tee-shirt *noun* T-Shirt *das* (PL *die* T-Shirts).

telephone *noun* Telefon *das* (PL *die* Telefone); **on the telephone** am Telefon.
verb anrufen ◇ SEP; **I'll telephone the bank** ich rufe die Bank an.

telephone box *noun*
Telefonzelle *die* (PL *die* Telefonzellen).

telephone call *noun*
Telefongespräch *das* (PL *die* Telefongespräche).

telephone directory *noun*
Telefonbuch *das* (PL *die* Telefonbücher).

telephone number *noun*
Telefonnummer *die* (PL *die* Telefonnummern).

televise *verb* im Fernsehen übertragen ◇; **they're televising the match** sie übertragen das Spiel im Fernsehen.

television *noun* **1** Fernsehen *das*; **I saw it on television** ich habe es im Fernsehen gesehen; **2 to watch television** fernsehen ◇ SEP; **I'm watching television** ich sehe fern.

television programme *noun*
Fernsehsendung *die* (PL *die* Fernsehsendungen).

tell *verb* **1** sagen; **to tell somebody something** jemandem etwas sagen; **if she asks, tell her** sag's ihr, wenn sie fragt; **2 to tell somebody to do something** jemandem sagen, er/sie soll etwas tun; **he told me to do it myself** er hat mir gesagt, ich soll es selbst machen; **she told me not to wait** sie hat mir gesagt, ich soll nicht warten; **3** (*explain*) **can you tell me how to do it?** kannst du mir sagen, wie man das macht?; **4** erzählen (*a story*); **tell me about your holiday** erzähl mir von deinen Ferien; **5** (*to see*) sehen ◇; **you can tell it's old** man sieht, dass es alt ist; **I can't tell them apart** ich kann sie nicht unterscheiden.

△ NEW SPELLING: *See page xii*

telly *noun* **1** (*set*) Fernseher *der* (PL *die* Fernseher); **2 to watch telly** fernsehen ◇ SEP; **I saw her on telly** ich habe sie im Fernsehen gesehen.

temp *noun* Aushilfskraft *die* (PL *die* Aushilfskräfte).

temper *noun* **to lose your temper** wütend werden.

temperature *noun* **1** Temperatur *die* (PL *die* Temperaturen); **what is the temperature?** wie viel Grad sind es?; **2 to have a temperature** Fieber haben.

temporary *adjective* vorübergehend.

temptation *noun* Versuchung *die* (PL *die* Versuchungen).

tempted *adjective* versucht; **I'm really tempted to come** ich bin wirklich versucht zu kommen.

tempting *adjective* verlockend.

ten *number* zehn; **Harry's ten** Harry ist zehn.

tend *verb* **to tend to do something** dazu neigen, etwas zu tun.

tender *adjective* **1** (*loving*) zärtlich; **2** (*painful*) empfindlich.

tennis *noun* Tennis *das*; **to play tennis** Tennis spielen.

tennis ball *noun* Tennisball *der* (PL *die* Tennisbälle).

tennis court *noun* Tennisplatz *der* (PL *die* Tennisplätze).

tennis player *noun* Tennisspieler *der* (PL *die* Tennisspieler), Tennisspielerin *die* (PL *die* Tennisspielerinnen).

tennis racket *noun* Tennisschläger *der* (PL *die* Tennisschläger).

tenor *noun* Tenor *der* (PL *die* Tenöre).

tenpin bowling *noun* Bowling *das*.

tense *noun* Zeit *die*; **the present tense** das Präsens; **in the future tense** im Futur.
adjective gespannt.

tent *noun* Zelt *das* (PL *die* Zelte).

tenth *number* zehnter/zehnte/ zehntes; **on the tenth floor** im zehnten Stock; **the tenth of April** der zehnte April.

term *noun* (*in school*) Halbjahr *das* (PL *die* Halbjahre); (*at university*) Semester *das* (PL *die* Semester).

terminal *noun* **1** (*at an airport*) Terminal *der* (PL *die* Terminals); **2 bus terminal** *die* Endstation; **3** (*computer terminal*) Terminal *das* (PL *die* Terminals).

terrace *noun* **1** (*outside a house*) Terrasse *die* (PL *die* Terrassen); **2** (*row of houses*) Häuserreihe *die* (PL *die* Häuserreihen); **3 the terraces** (*at a stadium*) die Ränge (*plural*).

terrible *adjective* furchtbar.

terribly *adverb* **1** (*very*) sehr; **not terribly clean** nicht sehr sauber; **2** (*badly*) furchtbar; **I played terribly** ich habe furchtbar gespielt.

terrific *adjective* **1** irre (*informal*); **a terrific amount** eine irre Menge; **2 terrific!** super! (*informal*).

◇ **IRREGULAR VERB:** *See the verb table in the centre of the dictionary*

terrified *adjective* verängstigt; **to be terrified** furchtbare Angst haben.

terrorism *noun* Terrorismus *der*.

terrorist *noun* Terrorist *der* (PL *die* Terroristen), Terroristin *die* (PL *die* Terroristinnen).

test *noun* 1 (*in school*) Klassenarbeit *die* (PL *die* Klassenarbeiten); **we've got a maths test tomorrow** wir schreiben morgen eine Mathearbeit; 2 (*medical check, trial*) Test *der* (PL *die* Tests); **eye test** *der* Sehtest; **blood test** *die* Blutprobe; 3 **driving test** *die* Fahrprüfung; **she's taking her driving test on Friday** sie macht am Freitag ihre Fahrprüfung; **he passed his driving test** er hat seine Fahrprüfung bestanden. *verb* (*in school*) prüfen; **can you test me?** kannst du mich abfragen?

test tube *noun* Reagenzglas *das* (PL *die* Reagenzgläser).

text *noun* Text *der* (PL *die* Texte).

textbook *noun* Lehrbuch *das* (PL *die* Lehrbücher).

Thames *noun* **the Thames** die Themse.

than *conjunction* als; **they have more money than we do** sie haben mehr Geld als wir; **more than forty** mehr als vierzig; **more than thirty years** mehr als dreißig Jahre.

thank *verb* 1 **to thank somebody for something** sich bei jemandem für etwas ←(ACC) bedanken; 2 **thank you** danke; **thank you for looking after the children** danke, dass du auf die Kinder aufgepasst hast.

thanks *plural noun* 1 Dank *der*; **thanks a lot!** vielen Dank!; **many thanks** vielen Dank; 2 **no thanks** nein danke; **thanks for your letter** danke für deinen Brief; 3 **thanks to** dank (+DAT); **it was thanks to him that we made it** dank ihm haben wir es geschafft.

thank you *adverb* danke; **thank you very much for the cheque** herzlichen Dank für den Scheck; **no thank you** nein danke; **a thank-you letter** ein Dankbrief.

that *adjective* 1 dieser/diese/dieses; **that boy** dieser Junge; **that woman** diese Frau; **that house** dieses Haus; 2 **that one** der da/die da/das da; **'which cake would you like?'** – **'that one, please'** 'welchen Kuchen möchten Sie?' – 'den da, bitte'; **I like all the dresses but I'm going to buy that one** mir gefallen alle Kleider, aber ich kaufe das da. *adverb* so; **it's not that easy** es ist nicht so einfach. *pronoun* 1 das; **what's that?** was ist das?; **who's that?** wer ist das?; **where's that?** wo ist das?; **is that Mandy?** ist das Mandy?; 2 das; **did you see that?** hast du das gesehen?; **that's my bedroom** das ist mein Schlafzimmer; 3 (*in relative clauses*) der/die/das (*depending on the gender of the noun 'that' refers to*); **the train that's leaving now** der Zug, der jetzt abfährt; **the flower that I picked** die Blume, die ich gepflückt habe; **the car that's red** das Auto, das rot ist. *conjunction* dass △; **I knew that he was lying** ich wußte, dass er log.

△ NEW SPELLING: *See page xii*

the *definite article* **1** der/die/das (*the article changes according to the gender of the noun*); (*before a masculine noun*) **the dog** der Hund; (*before a feminine noun*) **the cat** die Katze; (*before a neuter noun*) **the car** das Auto; **2** (*before all plural nouns*) die ; **the windows** die Fenster.

theatre *noun* Theater *das* (PL *die* Theater); **to go to the theatre** ins Theater gehen.

their *adjective* ihr; (*plural*) ihre; **their son** ihr Sohn; **their daughter** ihre Tochter; **their car** ihr Auto; **their presents** ihre Geschenke.

theirs *pronoun* **1** ihrer (*when standing for a masculine noun*); **our garden's smaller than theirs** unser Garten ist kleiner als ihrer; **2** ihre (*when standing for a feminine noun*); **your flat is bigger than theirs** deine Wohnung ist größer als ihre; **3** ihrs (*when standing for a neuter noun*); **our car was cheaper than theirs** unser Auto war billiger als ihrs; **4** ihre (*when standing for a plural noun*); **our children are older than theirs** unsere Kinder sind älter als ihre; **5 the yellow car's theirs** das gelbe Auto gehört ihnen; **it's theirs** das gehört ihnen.

them *pronoun* **1** (*as a direct object in the accusative*) sie; **I know them** ich kenne sie; **I don't know them** ich kenne sie nicht; **2** (*after prepositions* +ACC) sie; **it's for them** das ist für sie; **3** (*as an indirect object or following a verb that takes the dative*) ihnen; **I told them a story** ich habe

ihnen eine Geschichte erzählt; **4** (*to them*) ihnen; **I gave them my address** ich habe ihnen meine Adresse gegeben; **5** (*after prepositions* +DAT) ihnen; **I'll go with them** ich gehe mit ihnen mit; **6** (*in comparisons*) **he's older than them** er ist älter als sie.

themselves *pronoun* **1** sich; **they enjoyed themselves** sie haben sich amüsiert; **2** (*for emphasis*) selbst; **the boys can do it themselves** die Jungen können es selbst machen.

then *adverb* **1** (*next*) dann; **I get up and then I make the bed** ich stehe auf und dann mache ich das Bett; **I went to the post office and then the bank** ich bin zur Post und dann auf die Bank gegangen; **2** (*at that time*) damals; **we were living in York then** wir haben damals in York gewohnt; **3** (*in that case*) dann; **then why worry?** warum machst du dir dann Sorgen?; **4 since then** seitdem; **5 from then on** von da an.

theory *noun* **1** Theorie *die* (PL *die* Theorien); **2 in theory** theoretisch.

there *adverb* **1** (*in a fixed location*) da; **up there** da oben; **down there** da unten; **in there** da drin; **stay there** bleib da; **2 over there** da drüben; **she's over there with Mark** sie ist da drüben mit Mark; **3** (*with movement to a place*) dahin; **put it there** leg es dahin; **we're going there on Tuesday** wir fahren am Dienstag dahin; **4** (*further away*) dort; **I've seen photos of Oxford but I've never been there** ich habe Fotos von Oxford gesehen, aber ich

⬦ IRREGULAR VERB: *See the verb table in the centre of the dictionary*

war noch nie dort; **5 there is** (*there exists*) da ist, es ist; **there's a cat in the garden** da ist eine Katze im Garten; **there's enough bread** es ist genug Brot da; **no, there's not enough** nein, es ist nicht genug da; **6 there is** es gibt; **there's only one hospital in this town** in dieser Stadt gibt es nur ein Krankenhaus; **7 there are** da sind, es sind; **there were lots of people in town** es waren viele Leute in der Stadt; **8 there are** (*there exist*) es gibt; **there are lots of museums here** es gibt hier viele Museen; **9** (*when drawing attention*) da; **there they are!** da sind sie!; **there's the bus coming!** da kommt der Bus!

therefore *adverb* deshalb.

thermometer *noun* Thermometer *das* (PL *die* Thermometer).

these *adjective* diese; **these glasses** diese Gläser. *pronoun* die; **these are cheaper** die sind billiger.

they *pronoun* **1** sie; **'where are the knives?'** – **'they're in the drawer'** 'wo sind die Messer?' – 'sie sind in der Schublade'; **2** man; **they say** man sagt.

thick *adjective* dick; **a thick layer of butter** eine dicke Schicht Butter.

thief *noun* Dieb *der* (PL *die* Diebe), Diebin *die* (PL *die* Diebinnen).

thin *adjective* dünn.

thing *noun* **1** (*an object*) Ding *das* (PL *die* Dinge); **they have lots of nice things** sie haben viele schöne Dinge;

she told me some strange things sie hat mir ein paar seltsame Dinge erzählt; **that thing next to the hammer** das Ding da neben dem Hammer; **2 things** (*belongings*) Sachen (*plural*); **you can leave your things in my room** du kannst deine Sachen in meinem Zimmer lassen; **3 the best thing to do is …** am besten wäre es …; **4** (*subject, affair*) Sache *die* (PL *die* Sachen); **the thing is, I've lost her address** die Sache ist die, ich habe ihre Adresse verloren; **5 how are things?** wie geht's?

think *verb* **1** (*believe*) glauben; **do you think they'll come?** glaubst du, sie kommen?; **no, I don't think so** nein, ich glaube nicht; **I think so** ich glaube schon; **I think he's already paid** ich glaube, er hat schon gezahlt; **2** denken ✧; **I'm thinking about you** ich denke an dich; **what are you thinking about?** woran denkst du?; **3 what do you think of that?** was halten Sie davon?; **I don't think much of her proposal** ich halte nicht viel von ihrem Vorschlag; **4 what do you think of my new jacket?** wie findest du meine neue Jacke?; **5** (*remember*) **to think to do something** daran denken, etwas zu tun; **he didn't think of locking the door** er hat nicht daran gedacht, die Tür abzuschließen; **6** (*to think carefully*) nachdenken ✧ SEP; **he thought for a moment** er hat einen Moment lang nachgedacht; **think about it!** denk darüber nach!; **7 I've thought it over carefully** ich habe es mir genau überlegt;

△ NEW SPELLING: *See page xii*

third

ENGLISH–GERMAN

8 (*imagine*) sich ←(DAT) vorstellen SEP; **just think, we'll soon be in Spain!** stell dir nur vor, bald sind wir in Spanien!; **I never thought it would be like this** ich habe mir nie vorgestellt, dass es so sein würde.

third *noun* Drittel *das* (PL *die* Drittel); **a third of the population** ein Drittel der Bevölkerung. *adjective* dritter/dritte/drittes; **on the third floor** im dritten Stock; **on the third of March** am dritten März.

thirdly *adverb* drittens.

Third World *noun* Dritte Welt △ *die*.

thirst *noun* Durst *der*.

thirsty *adjective* durstig; **to be thirsty** Durst haben; **I'm thirsty** ich habe Durst; **we were all thirsty** wir hatten alle Durst.

thirteen *number* dreizehn; **Ahmed's thirteen** Ahmed ist dreizehn.

thirty *number* dreißig.

this *adjective* **1** dieser/diese/dieses; **this boy** dieser Junge; **this flower** diese Blume; **this car** dieses Auto; **at the end of this week** Ende dieser Woche; **2 this morning** heute Morgen; **this evening** heute Abend; **this afternoon** heute Nachmittag; **3 this one** der/die/das; (*with more emphasis*) dieser/diese/dieses; **if you need a pen you can have this one** wenn du einen Kugelschreiber brauchst, kannst du den haben; **I'll take this one** ich nehme diesen. *pronoun* **1** das; **can you hold this?** kannst du das festhalten?; **what's**

this? was ist das?; **2 this is my sister Carla** (*in introductions*) das ist meine Schwester Carla; **3 this is Tracy speaking** (*on the phone*) hier spricht Tracy.

thistle *noun* Distel *die* (PL *die* Disteln).

those *adjective* diese; **those books** diese Bücher. *pronoun* die da; **if you need more knives you can take those** wenn du mehr Messer brauchst, kannst du die da nehmen.

though *conjunction* obwohl; **though it's cold** obwohl es kalt ist. *adverb* aber; **it was a good idea, though** es war aber eine gute Idee.

thought *noun* Gedanke *der* (PL *die* Gedanken).

thousand *number* **1** tausend; **a thousand** eintausend; **three thousand** dreitausend; **2 thousands of** Tausende von; **there were thousands of tourists in Venice** Tausende von Touristen waren in Venedig.

thread *noun* Faden *der* (PL *die* Fäden). *verb* einfädeln (*a needle*).

threat *noun* Drohung *die* (PL *die* Drohungen); **is that a threat?** soll das eine Drohung sein?

threaten *verb* drohen (+DAT); **he threatened her** er hat ihr gedroht; **to threaten to do something** damit drohen, etwas zu tun.

three *number* drei; **Oskar's three** Oskar ist drei.

✧ IRREGULAR VERB: *See the verb table in the centre of the dictionary*

three-quarters *noun*
Dreiviertel *das*.
adverb **three-quarters full** drei
viertel Δ voll.

thrilled *adjective* **to be thrilled** sich
wahnsinnig freuen.

thriller *noun* Thriller *der* (PL *die*
Thriller).

thrilling *adjective* spannend.

throat *noun* Hals *der* (PL *die* Hälse);
to have a sore throat
Halsschmerzen haben.

through *preposition* **1** (*across, via*)
durch (+ACC); **through the forest**
durch den Wald; **the train goes
through Leeds** der Zug fährt durch
Leeds; **through the window** durch
das Fenster; **2 to let somebody
through** jemanden durchlassen ♦
SEP; **the police let us through** die
Polizei ließ uns durch; **3 I know
them through my cousin** ich kenne
sie über meinen Vetter.

throw *verb* **1** werfen ♦; **I threw the
letter in the bin** ich habe den Brief
in den Mülleimer geworfen; **2 to
throw something to somebody**
jemandem etwas zuwerfen ♦ SEP;
throw me the ball wirf mir den Ball
zu; **to throw something at
somebody** etwas nach jemandem
werfen.

● **to throw something away** etwas
wegwerfen ♦ SEP; **I'm throwing
away the old newspapers** ich werfe
die alten Zeitungen weg.

● **to throw somebody out** jemanden
rauswerfen ♦ SEP.

● **to throw something out** etwas
wegwerfen ♦ SEP (*rubbish*).

thumb *noun* Daumen *der* (PL *die*
Daumen).

thunder *noun* Donner *der*; **peal of
thunder** *der* Donnerschlag.

thunderstorm *noun* Gewitter *das*
(PL *die* Gewitter).

Thursday *noun* **1** Donnerstag *der*
(PL *die* Donnerstage); **on Thursday**
(am) Donnerstag; **I'm leaving on
Thursday** ich fahre am Donnerstag
ab; **see you on Thursday** bis
Donnerstag; **every Thursday** jeden
Donnerstag; **last Thursday** vorigen
Donnerstag; **next Thursday**
nächsten Donnerstag; **2 on
Thursdays** donnerstags; **the
museum is closed on Thursdays**
das Museum ist donnerstags
geschlossen.

thyme *noun* Thymian *der*.

tick *verb* **1** (*clock, watch*) ticken;
2 (*on paper*) abhaken SEP.

ticket *noun* **1** (*for an exhibition,
theatre, or cinema*) Karte *die* (PL *die*
Karten); **two tickets for the concert**
zwei Karten für das Konzert; **2** (*for
the underground, a bus, or a train*)
Fahrkarte *die* (PL *die* Fahrkarten); **a
plane ticket** ein Flugschein, ein
Ticket; **3** (*for left luggage, parking*)
Schein *der* (PL *die* Scheine); **4** (*for a
lottery or raffle*) Los *das* (PL *die*
Lose); **5 parking ticket** *der*
Strafzettel.

ticket office *noun* (*at a station*)
Fahrkartenschalter *der* (PL *die*
Fahrkartenschalter).

tickle *verb* kitzeln.

tidy *adjective* ordentlich.
verb aufräumen SEP; **I'll tidy (up) the kitchen** ich räume die Küche auf.

tie *noun* 1 (*necktie*) Krawatte *die* (PL die Krawatten); 2 (*in a match*) Unentschieden *das*.
verb 1 binden✧; **to tie your shoelaces** sich ←(DAT) die Schnürsenkel binden; 2 **to tie a knot in something** einen Knoten in etwas ←(ACC) machen; 3 (*in a match*) **we tied two all** wir haben zwei zu zwei gespielt.

tiger *noun* Tiger *der* (PL die Tiger).

tight *adjective* (*close-fitting*) eng; **the skirt's a bit tight** der Rock ist etwas eng; **these shoes are too tight** diese Schuhe sind zu eng; **she was wearing tight jeans** sie hatte enge Jeans an.

tightly *adverb* fest.

tights *plural noun* Strumpfhose *die* (PL die Strumpfhosen); **a pair of purple tights** eine lila Strumpfhose.

tile *noun* 1 (*on a floor*) Fliese *die* (PL die Fliesen); 2 (*on a wall*) Kachel *die* (PL die Kacheln); 3 (*on a roof*) Ziegel *der* (PL die Ziegel).

till[1] *preposition, conjunction* 1 bis; **they're staying till Sunday** sie bleiben bis Sonntag; **till then** bis dann; **till now** bis jetzt; 2 (*when 'till' is followed by a noun it is usually translated as 'bis zu' +DAT*) **till the evening** bis zum Abend; 3 **not till** erst; **she won't be back till ten** sie kommt erst um zehn zurück; **we**

won't know till Monday wir werden erst am Montag Bescheid wissen.

till[2] *noun* Kasse *die* (PL die Kassen); **please pay at the till** bitte zahlen Sie an der Kasse.

time *noun* 1 (*on the clock*) Zeit *die*; **it's time for breakfast** es ist Zeit zum Frühstücken; 2 **what time is it?** wie viel Δ Uhr ist es?; **at what time does it start?** um wie viel Uhr fängt es an?; **ten o'clock German time** zehn Uhr, deutsche Zeit; 3 **on time** pünktlich; 4 (*an amount of time*) Zeit *die*; **we've got lots of time** wir haben viel Zeit; **I haven't got time now** ich habe jetzt keine Zeit; **there's no time left to do it** dafür bleibt keine Zeit mehr; **from time to time** von Zeit zu Zeit; **for a long time** lange; 5 (*moment*) Moment *der* (PL die Momente); **this isn't a good time to discuss it** das ist kein guter Moment, um sich darüber zu unterhalten; **at the right time** im richtigen Moment; **for the time being** im Moment; **any time now** jeden Moment; 6 **at times** manchmal; 7 (*in a series*) Mal *das* (PL die Male); **eight times** achtmal; **for the first time** zum ersten Mal; **the first time I saw you** das erste Mal, als ich dich sah; **three times a year** dreimal jährlich; 8 **three times two is six** drei mal zwei ist sechs; 9 **to have a good time** sich amüsieren; **we had a really good time** wir haben uns richtig gut amüsiert; **have a good time!** viel Vergnügen!

timetable *noun* 1 (*in school*) Stundenplan *der* (PL die

✧ **IRREGULAR VERB:** *See the verb table in the centre of the dictionary*

Stundenpläne); **2** (*for trains or buses*) Fahrplan *der* (PL *die* Fahrpläne); **bus timetable** *der* Busfahrplan.

tin *noun* Dose *die* (PL *die* Dosen); **a tin of tomatoes** eine Dose Tomaten.

tinned *adjective* in Dosen; **tinned peas** Erbsen in Dosen.

tin opener *noun* Dosenöffner *der* (PL *die* Dosenöffner).

tiny *adjective* winzig.

tip *noun* **1** (*end*) Spitze *die* (PL *die* Spitzen); **2** (*money*) Trinkgeld *das*; **3** (*useful hint*) Tipp △ *der* (PL *die* Tipps) (*informal*).
verb (*give money*) ein Trinkgeld geben ◇ (+DAT); **we tipped the waiter** wir haben dem Kellner ein Trinkgeld gegeben.

tired *adjective* **1** müde; **I'm tired** ich bin müde; **you look tired** du siehst müde aus; **2 to be tired of something** etwas satt haben; **I'm tired of London** ich habe London satt; **I'm tired of watching TV every evening** ich habe es satt, jeden Abend fernzusehen.

tiring *adjective* ermüdend.

tissue *noun* (*a paper hanky*) Papiertaschentuch *das* (PL *die* Papiertaschentücher).

tissue paper *noun* Seidenpapier *das*.

title *noun* Titel *der* (PL *die* Titel).

to *preposition* **1** (*to a country or town*) nach; **to go to London** nach London fahren; **the motorway to**

Italy die Autobahn nach Italien; **they're going to Switzerland** sie fahren in die Schweiz; **2** (*to the cinema, theatre, school, office*) in (+ACC); **I'm going to school** ich gehe in die Schule; **she's gone to the office** sie ist ins Büro gegangen; **we want to go to town** wir wollen in die Stadt gehen; **3** (*to a wedding, party, university, the toilet*) auf (+ACC); **she's gone to the toilet** sie ist auf die Toilette gegangen; **4** (*addressed or attached to*) an (+ACC); **a letter to my parents** ein Brief an meine Eltern; **5 give the book to her** gib ihr das Buch; **he said to me that …** er hat mir gesagt, dass …; **6** (*to somebody's house, a particular place, or person*) zu (+DAT); **I went round to Paul's house** ich bin zu Paul nach Hause gegangen; **we're going to the Browns' for supper** wir gehen zu Browns zum Abendessen; **I'm going to the dentist tomorrow** morgen gehe ich zum Zahnarzt; **7** (*talking about the time*) **it's ten to nine** es ist zehn vor neun; **from eight to ten** von acht bis zehn; **from Monday to Friday** von Montag bis Freitag; **8** (*in order to*) um … zu (+ *infinitive*); **he gave me some money to buy a sandwich** er hat mir Geld gegeben, um ein Sandwich zu kaufen; **9** (*in verbal phrases with the infinitive*) zu; **I have nothing to do** ich habe nichts zu tun; **have you got something to eat?** hast du etwas zu essen?

toast *noun* **1** Toast *der* (PL *die* Toasts); **two slices of toast** zwei Scheiben Toast; **2** (*to your health*)

Toast *der* (PL *die* Toasts); **to drink a toast to somebody** auf jemanden trinken.

toaster *noun* Toaster *der* (PL *die* Toaster).

tobacco *noun* Tabak *der*.

tobacconist's *noun* Tabakladen *der* (PL *die* Tabakläden).

today *adverb* heute; **today's her birthday** sie hat heute Geburtstag.

toe *noun* Zeh *der* (PL *die* Zehen).

toffee *noun* Karamell Δ *der*.

together *adverb* 1 zusammen; **we did it together** wir haben es zusammen gemacht; 2 (*at the same time*) gleichzeitig; **they all left together** sie sind alle gleichzeitig weggegangen.

toilet *noun* Toilette *die* (PL *die* Toiletten); **she's gone to the toilet** sie ist auf die Toilette gegangen.

toilet paper *noun* Toilettenpapier *das*.

toilet roll *noun* Rolle Toilettenpapier *die* (PL *die* Rollen Toilettenpapier).

token *noun* 1 (*for a machine or game*) Marke *die* (PL *die* Marken); 2 (*voucher*) Gutschein *der* (PL *die* Gutscheine); **gift token** *der* Geschenkgutschein.

toll *noun* Gebühr *die* (PL *die* Gebühren).

tomato *noun* Tomate *die* (PL *die* Tomaten); **tomato salad** *der* Tomatensalat; **tomato sauce** *die* Tomatensoße.

tomorrow *adverb* 1 morgen; **I'll do it tomorrow** ich mache es morgen; **tomorrow afternoon** morgen Nachmittag; **tomorrow morning** morgen früh; **tomorrow night** morgen Abend; 2 **the day after tomorrow** übermorgen.

tone *noun* (*on an answerphone, of a voice, or letter*) Ton *der* (PL *die* Töne).

tongue *noun* Zunge *die* (PL *die* Zungen); **to stick your tongue out at somebody** jemandem die Zunge herausstrecken; ★ **it's on the tip of my tongue** es liegt mir auf der Zunge.

tonic *noun* Tonic *das* (PL *die* Tonics); **a gin and tonic** ein Gin Tonic.

tonight *adverb* 1 (*this evening*) heute Abend Δ; **I'm going out with my friends tonight** ich gehe heute Abend mit meinen Freunden weg; 2 (*after bedtime*) heute Nacht Δ.

tonsillitis *noun* Mandelentzündung *die*; **Ahlem's got tonsillitis** Ahlem hat eine Mandelentzündung.

too *adverb* 1 zu; **it's too expensive** es ist zu teuer; **too often** zu oft; 2 **too much** zu viel; **I've spent too much** ich habe zu viel ausgegeben; **too many** zu viele; 3 (*as well*) auch; **Karen's coming too** Karen kommt auch; **me too!** ich auch!

tool *noun* Werkzeug *das* (PL *die* Werkzeuge).

tool kit *noun* Werkzeug *das*.

tooth *noun* Zahn *der* (PL *die* Zähne);

to brush your teeth sich ←(DAT) die Zähne putzen.

toothache *noun* Zahnschmerzen (*plural*).

toothbrush *noun* Zahnbürste *die* (PL *die* Zahnbürsten).

toothpaste *noun* Zahnpasta *die* (PL *die* Zahnpasten).

top *noun* 1 (*highest part*) Spitze *die* (PL *die* Spitzen) (*of a tree*); 2 **at the top of** oben auf (+DAT); **at the top of the ladder** oben auf der Leiter; **it's on top of the chest of drawers** es liegt oben auf der Kommode; 3 **at the top** oben; **there are four rooms at the top** oben sind vier Zimmer; **from top to bottom** von oben bis unten; 4 (*of a container, jar, or box*) Deckel *der* (PL *die* Deckel); 5 (*of a mountain*) Gipfel *der* (PL *die* Gipfel); 6 (*a lid*) Kappe *die* (PL *die* Kappen) (*of a pen*); Verschluss △ *der* (PL *die* Verschlüsse) (*of a bottle*); 7 (*of a garment*) Oberteil *das* (PL *die* Oberteile); 8 (*in sport*) **the top of the table** die Tabellenspitze; ★ **and on top of all that** obendrein; ★ **it was a bit over the top** es war leicht übertrieben.
adjective oberster/oberste/oberstes (*step or floor*); **on the top floor** im obersten Stockwerk.

topic *noun* Thema *das* (PL *die* Themen).

torch *noun* Taschenlampe *die* (PL *die* Taschenlampen).

torn *adjective* zerrissen.

tortoise *noun* Schildkröte *die* (PL *die* Schildkröten).

torture *noun* 1 Folter *die* (PL *die* Foltern); 2 **the exam was torture** die Prüfung war die Hölle (*informal*).
verb quälen.

Tory *noun* Konservative *der/die* (PL *die* Konservativen).

total *noun* 1 (*number*) Gesamtzahl *die* (PL *die* Gesamtzahlen); 2 (*result of addition*) Summe *die* (PL *die* Summen).
adjective gesamt.

totally *adverb* völlig.

touch *noun* 1 (*contact*) **to get in touch with somebody** sich mit jemandem in Verbindung setzen; **to stay in touch with somebody** mit jemandem in Verbindung bleiben; 2 **we've lost touch** wir haben keinen Kontakt mehr miteinander; **I've lost touch with Peter** ich habe keinen Kontakt mehr mit Peter; 3 (*a little bit*) **a touch of salt** eine Spur Salz; **it was a touch embarrassing** es war ein bisschen peinlich.
verb 1 berühren; 2 (*get hold of*) anfassen SEP; **don't touch that** fass das nicht an.

touched *adjective* gerührt.

touching *adjective* rührend.

tough *adjective* 1 hart; **she's had a tough time** sie hat eine harte Zeit hinter sich; **a tough guy** ein harter Kerl; 2 zäh; **the meat's tough** das Fleisch ist zäh; 3 fest (*material, shoes, etc*).; 4 **tough luck!** Pech!; **tough, you're too late** so'n Pech, du bist zu spät dran.

tour noun 1 Besichtigung die (PL die Besichtigungen); **a tour of the city** eine Stadtbesichtigung; **we did a tour of the castle** wir haben das Schloss besichtigt; 2 **guided tour** die Führung; 3 **package tour** die Pauschalreise; 4 (by a band or theatre group) Tournee die (PL die Tournees); **to go on tour** auf Tournee gehen.
verb (performer) auf Tournee sein ✧ (PERF sein); **they're touring America** sie sind auf Tournee in Amerika.

tour guide noun Reiseleiter der (PL die Reiseleiter), Reiseleiterin die (PL die Reiseleiterinnen).

tourism noun Tourismus der.

tourist noun Tourist der (PL die Touristen), Touristin die (PL die Touristinnen).

tourist information office noun Fremdenverkehrsbüro das (PL die Fremdenverkehrsbüros).

tournament noun Turnier das (PL die Turniere); **tennis tournament** das Tennisturnier.

tow verb **to be towed away** abgeschlepppt werden ✧ (PERF sein).

towards preposition zu (+DAT); **she went off towards the lake** sie ist zum See gegangen; **to come towards somebody** auf jemanden zukommen ✧ SEP (PERF sein).

towel noun Handtuch das (PL die Handtücher).

tower noun Turm der (PL die Türme).

tower block noun Hochhaus das (PL die Hochhäuser).

town noun Stadt die (PL die Städte); **to go into town** in die Stadt gehen.

town centre noun Stadtmitte die (PL die Stadtmitten).

town hall noun Rathaus das (PL die Rathäuser).

toy noun Spielzeug das.

toyshop noun Spielzeuggeschäft das (PL die Spielzeuggeschäfte).

trace noun Spur die (PL die Spuren); **there was no trace of the thieves** es fehlte jede Spur von den Dieben.
verb 1 (find) finden ✧; 2 (follow) verfolgen; 3 (copy) durchpausen SEP.

tracing paper noun Pauspapier das.

track noun 1 (for sport) Bahn die (PL die Bahnen); **cycling track** die Radrennbahn; **racing track** (for cars) die Rennstrecke; 2 (a path) Weg der (PL die Wege); 3 (song) Stück das (PL die Stücke); **this is my favourite track** das ist mein Lieblingsstück.

track suit noun Trainingsanzug der (PL die Trainingsanzüge).

tractor noun Traktor der (PL die Traktoren).

trade noun 1 (a profession) Gewerbe das; 2 (skill, craft) Handwerk das; **to learn a trade** ein Handwerk erlernen.

✧ IRREGULAR VERB: See the verb table in the centre of the dictionary

trade union *noun*
Gewerkschaft *die* (PL *die*
Gewerkschaften).

tradition *noun* Tradition *die* (PL *die*
Traditionen).

traditional *adjective* traditionell.

traffic *noun* Verkehr *der*.

traffic jam *noun* Stau *der* (PL *die*
Staus).

traffic lights *plural noun*
Ampel *die* (PL *die* Ampeln).

traffic warden *noun*
Hilfspolizist *der* (PL *die*
Hilfspolizisten), Politesse *die* (PL *die*
Politessen).

tragedy *noun* Tragödie *die* (PL *die*
Tragödien).

tragic *adjective* tragisch.

trailer *noun* Anhänger *der* (PL *die*
Anhänger).

train *noun* Zug *der* (PL *die* Züge);
he's coming by train er kommt mit
dem Zug; **I met her on the train** ich
habe sie im Zug getroffen; **the train
for York** der Zug nach York.
verb **1** (*for a career*) ausbilden SEP;
2 she's training to be a nurse sie
lässt sich als Krankenschwester
ausbilden; **3** (*in sport*) trainieren;
the team trains on Wednesdays die
Mannschaft trainiert mittwochs.

trainer *noun* **1** (*of an athlete or
horse*) Trainer *der* (PL *die* Trainer),
Trainerin *die* (PL *die* Trainerinnen);
2 trainers Trainingsschuhe
(*plural*).

training *noun* **1** (*for a career*)
Ausbildung *die*; **2** (*for sport*)
Training *das*.

train ticket *noun* Fahrkarte *die* (PL
die Fahrkarten).

train timetable *noun*
Bahnfahrplan *der* (PL *die*
Bahnfahrpläne).

tram *noun* Straßenbahn *die* (PL *die*
Straßenbahnen).

tramp *noun* Landstreicher *der* (PL
die Landstreicher), Landstreicherin
die (PL *die* Landstreicherinnen).

transfer *noun* Abziehbild *das* (PL
die Abziehbilder).

transform *verb* verwandeln.

transistor *noun* Transistor *der* (PL
die Transistoren).

translate *verb* übersetzen; **to
translate something into German**
etwas ins Deutsche übersetzen.

translation *noun* Übersetzung *die*
(PL *die* Übersetzungen).

translator *noun* Übersetzer *der* (PL
die Übersetzer), Übersetzerin *die* (PL
die Übersetzerinnen).

transparent *adjective*
durchsichtig.

transport *noun* Transport *der* (PL
die Transporte); **the transport of
goods** der Warentransport; **public
transport** öffentliche
Verkehrsmittel (*plural*).

trap *noun* Falle *die* (PL *die* Fallen).

travel *noun* Reisen *das*; **foreign
travel** Auslandsreisen (*plural*).
verb reisen (PERF *sein*).

△ NEW SPELLING: *See page xii*

travel agency *noun*
Reisebüro *das* (PL *die* Reisebüros).

travel agent's *noun*
Reisebüro *das* (PL *die* Reisebüros).

traveller *noun* 1 Reisende *der/die*
(PL *die* Reisenden); 2 (*gypsy*)
Zigeuner *der* (PL *die* Zigeuner),
Zigeunerin *die* (PL *die*
Zigeunerinnen).

traveller's cheque *noun*
Reisescheck *der* (PL *die*
Reiseschecks).

tray *noun* Tablett *das* (PL *die*
Tabletts).

tread *verb* **to tread on something**
auf etwas ←(ACC) treten ✧ (PERF *sein*);
she trod on my foot sie ist mir auf
den Fuß getreten.

treasure *noun* Schatz *der* (PL *die*
Schätze).

treat *noun* 1 **I took them to the
circus as a treat** ich habe ihnen
eine besondere Freude gemacht und
sie in den Zirkus eingeladen;
2 (*food*) Leckerbissen *der* (PL *die*
Leckerbissen).
verb 1 behandeln; **he treats his dog
well** er behandelt seinen Hund gut;
the doctor who treated you der
Arzt, der dich behandelt hat; 2 **to
treat somebody to something**
jemandem etwas spendieren; **I'll
treat you to an ice cream** ich
spendiere euch ein Eis.

treatment *noun* Behandlung *die*
(PL *die* Behandlungen).

tree *noun* Baum *der* (PL *die* Bäume).

tremble *verb* zittern.

trend *noun* 1 (*a fashion*) Trend *der*
(PL *die* Trends); 2 (*a tendency*)
Tendenz *die* (PL *die* Tendenzen).

trendy *adjective* modern.

trial *noun* (*in court*) Prozess △ *der*
(PL *die* Prozesse).

triangle *noun* Dreieck *das* (PL *die*
Dreiecke).

trick *noun* 1 (*a joke*) Streich *der* (PL
die Streiche); **to play a trick on
somebody** jemandem einen Streich
spielen; 2 (*a knack or by a conjuror*)
Trick *der* (PL *die* Tricks); **there must
be a trick to it** da muss ein Trick
dabei sein.
verb hereinlegen SEP; **he tricked
me!** er hat mich hereingelegt!

tricky *adjective* verzwickt; **it's a
tricky situation** das ist eine
verzwickte Situation.

trim *verb* schneiden ✧ (*hair*).

trip *noun* 1 Reise *die* (PL *die* Reisen);
a trip to Florida eine Reise nach
Florida; **he's going on a business
trip** er macht eine Geschäftsreise;
2 (*a day out*) Ausflug *der* (PL *die*
Ausflüge); **a day trip to France** ein
Tagesausflug nach Frankreich.
verb (*to stumble*) stolpern (PERF
sein); **Nicky tripped over a stone**
Nicky ist über einen Stein gestolpert.

trolley *noun* 1 (*for shopping*)
Einkaufswagen *der* (PL *die*
Einkaufswagen); 2 (*for luggage*)
Kofferkuli *der* (PL *die* Kofferkulis).

trombone *noun* Posaune *die* (PL *die*
Posaunen).

✧ IRREGULAR VERB: *See the verb table in the centre of the dictionary*

troops *plural noun* Truppen (*plural*).

trophy *noun* Trophäe *die* (PL *die* Trophäen); (*in competitions*) Pokal *der* (PL *die* Pokale).

trot *verb* traben (PERF *sein*).

trouble *noun* 1 (*general difficulties*) Ärger *der*; **to make trouble** Ärger machen; **to get into trouble** Ärger bekommen; **we had trouble with the travel agency** wir hatten Ärger mit dem Reisebüro; 2 (*problem*) Problem *das* (PL *die* Probleme); **the trouble is, I've lost his phone number** das Problem ist, dass ich seine Telefonnummer verloren habe; **Steph's in trouble** Steph hat Probleme; **what's the trouble?** was ist los?; **it's no trouble!** das ist kein Problem; 3 (*difficulty, effort*) Mühe *die*; **to have trouble doing something** Mühe haben, etwas zu tun; **I had trouble finding a seat** ich hatte Mühe, einen Platz zu finden; **it's not worth the trouble** das ist nicht der Mühe wert.

trousers *plural noun* Hose *die* (PL *die* Hosen); **my old trousers** meine alte Hose; **a new pair of trousers** eine neue Hose.

trout *noun* Forelle *die* (PL *die* Forellen).

truck *noun* Lastwagen *der* (PL *die* Lastwagen).

true *adjective* 1 wahr; **a true story** eine wahre Geschichte; 2 **is that true?** stimmt das?; **it's true she's absent-minded** das stimmt, sie ist sehr vergesslich.

trump *noun* Trumpf *der* (PL *die* Trümpfe); **hearts are trumps** Herz ist Trumpf.

trumpet *noun* Trompete *die* (PL *die* Trompeten).

trunk *noun* 1 (*of a tree*) Stamm *der* (PL *die* Stämme); 2 (*of an elephant*) Rüssel *der* (PL *die* Rüssel).

trust *noun* Vertrauen *das*. *verb* 1 (*believe*) **to trust somebody** jemandem vertrauen; 2 (*rely on*) **you can trust him** man kann sich auf ihn verlassen.

truth *noun* Wahrheit *die*.

try *noun* Versuch *der* (PL *die* Versuche); **it's my first try** es ist mein erster Versuch; **to have a try** es versuchen; **give it a try!** versuch's doch mal! *verb* 1 versuchen; **to try to do something** versuchen, etwas zu tun; **I'm trying to open the door** ich versuche, die Tür aufzumachen; 2 (*taste*) probieren.
● **to try something on** etwas anprobieren SEP (*a garment*).

T-shirt *noun* T-Shirt *das* (PL *die* T-Shirts).

tube *noun* 1 Tube *die* (PL *die* Tuben); 2 (*the Underground*) **the Tube** die U-Bahn.

Tuesday *noun* 1 Dienstag *der* (PL *die* Dienstage); **on Tuesday** (am) Dienstag; **I'm going to the cinema on Tuesday** ich gehe Dienstag ins Kino; **see you on Tuesday!** bis Dienstag!; **every Tuesday** jeden Dienstag; **last Tuesday** vorigen Dienstag; **next Tuesday** nächsten

△ NEW SPELLING: *See page xii*

Dienstag; **2 on Tuesdays** dienstags; **the museum is closed on Tuesdays** das Museum ist dienstags geschlossen.

tuition noun **1** Unterricht der; **piano tuition** der Klavierunterricht; **2 extra tuition** Nachhilfestunden (plural).

tulip noun Tulpe die (PL die Tulpen).

tumble-drier noun Wäschetrockner der (PL die Wäschetrockner).

tuna noun Thunfisch der.

tune noun Melodie die (PL die Melodien).

tunnel noun Tunnel der (PL die Tunnel); **the Channel Tunnel** der Eurotunnel.

turkey noun Pute die (PL die Puten).

Turkey noun die Türkei; **from Turkey** aus der Türkei; **in Turkey** in der Türkei; **to Turkey** in die Türkei.

Turkish noun (language) Türkisch das.
adjective türkisch; **he is Turkish** er ist Türke; **she is Turkish** sie ist Türkin.

turn noun **1** (in a game) **it's your turn** du bist an der Reihe; **whose turn is it?** wer ist an der Reihe?; **it's Jane's turn** Jane ist an der Reihe; **2 to take turns** sich abwechseln; **to take it in turns to do something** abwechselnd etwas tun; **3** (in a road) Kurve die (PL die Kurven); **to take a right/left turn** nach rechts/links abbiegen.
verb **1** drehen; **turn the key to the**
right dreh den Schlüssel nach rechts; **turn your chair round** dreh deinen Stuhl herum; **2** (person, car) abbiegen ◇ SEP (PERF sein); **turn left at the next set of lights** biegen Sie an der nächsten Ampel links ab; **3** (become) werden ◇ SEP (PERF sein); **she turned red** sie ist rot geworden.

● **to turn back** umkehren SEP (PERF sein).

● **to turn off 1** (from a road) abbiegen ◇ SEP (PERF sein); **2** (switch off) ausmachen SEP (a light, an oven, a TV, or radio); zudrehen SEP (a tap); abstellen SEP (gas, electricity, or water); ausschalten SEP (an engine).

● **to turn on** anmachen SEP (a TV, radio, or light); aufdrehen SEP (a tap); anschalten SEP (an oven); anlassen ◇ SEP (an engine).

● **to turn out 1 to turn out well** gut ausgehen ◇ SEP (PERF sein); **the discussions turned out badly** die Gespräche sind schlecht ausgegangen; **it all turned out all right in the end** am Ende ging alles gut aus; **2 it turned out that I was right** es stellte sich heraus, dass ich Recht hatte.

● **to turn up 1** (to arrive) aufkreuzen SEP (PERF sein); **they turned up an hour later** sie sind eine Stunde später aufgekreuzt; **2** (to make louder) lauter machen.

turquoise adjective türkis.

turtle noun Schildkröte die (PL die Schildkröten).

TV noun Fernsehen das; **I saw her on TV** ich habe sie im Fernsehen gesehen.

◇ IRREGULAR VERB: *See the verb table in the centre of the dictionary*

tweezers *noun* Pinzette *die* (PL *die* Pinzetten).

twelfth *number* zwölfter/zwölfte/ zwölftes; **on the twelfth floor** im zwölften Stock; **the twelfth of May** der zwölfte Mai.

twelve *number* **1** zwölf; **Tara's twelve** Tara ist zwölf; **2 at twelve o'clock** um zwölf Uhr.

twenty *number* zwanzig; **Marie's twenty** Marie ist zwanzig; **twenty-one** einundzwanzig.

twice *adverb* **1** zweimal; **I've asked him twice** ich habe ihn zweimal gefragt; **twice a day** zweimal täglich; **2 twice as much** doppelt so viel.

twin *noun* Zwilling *der* (PL *die* Zwillinge); **Helen and Tim are twins** Helen und Tim sind Zwillinge; **her twin sister** ihre Zwillingsschwester. *verb* **Richmond is twinned with Konstanz** Richmond und Konstanz sind Partnerstädte.

twist *verb* **1** (*bend out of shape*) verbiegen ✧; **2** verdrehen (*words, meaning*); **3 to twist your ankle** sich ←(DAT) den Knöchel verrenken.

two *number* zwei; **Ben's two** Ben ist zwei; **two by two** zu zweit.

type *noun* Art *die*; **what type of computer is it?** welche Art Computer ist es? *verb* (*on a typewriter*) Schreibmaschine schreiben ✧, tippen (*informal*); **I'm learning to type** ich lerne Schreibmaschine schreiben; **I'm just typing some**

letters ich tippe gerade ein paar Briefe.

typewriter *noun* Schreibmaschine *die* (PL *die* Schreibmaschinen).

typical *adjective* typisch.

tyre *noun* Reifen *der* (PL *die* Reifen).

U u

ugly *adjective* hässlich △.

UK *noun* (*United Kingdom*) Vereinigte Königreich *das*.

Ulster *noun* Ulster; **from Ulster** aus Ulster.

umbrella *noun* Regenschirm *der* (PL *die* Regenschirme).

umpire *noun* Schiedsrichter *der* (PL *die* Schiedsrichter), Schiedsrichterin *die* (PL *die* Schiedsrichterinnen).

UN *noun* (*United Nations*) UN (*plural*).

unable *adjective* **to be unable to do something** etwas nicht tun können; **he's unable to come** er kann nicht kommen.

unavoidable *adjective* unvermeidlich.

unbearable *adjective* unerträglich.

unbelievable *adjective* unglaublich.

uncertain *adjective* 1 (*not sure*) **to be uncertain whether** … sich ←(DAT) nicht sicher sein, ob …; 2 (*unpredictable*) ungewiss △ (*future or result*).

uncle *noun* Onkel *der* (PL *die* Onkel).

uncomfortable *adjective* 1 unbequem (*shoes, chair, or journey*); 2 unangenehm (*situation, heat*).

unconscious *adjective* (*out cold*) bewusstlos △.

under *preposition* 1 (*underneath*) unter (+DAT, *or* +ACC *when there is movement towards a place*); **the dog's under the bed** der Hund ist unter dem Bett; **the ball rolled under the bed** der Ball ist unter das Bett gerollt; 2 **under there** da drunter; **perhaps it's under there** vielleicht ist es da drunter; 3 (*less than*) unter (+DAT); **under £20** unter zwanzig Pfund; **children under five** Kinder unter fünf.

under-age *adjective* **to be under-age** minderjährig sein.

undercooked *adjective* nicht gar.

underestimate *verb* unterschätzen.

underground *noun* (*railway*) U-Bahn *die* (PL *die* U-Bahnen); **I saw her on the underground** ich habe sie in der U-Bahn gesehen; **shall we go by underground?** fahren wir mit der U-Bahn? *adjective* unterirdisch (*cave*);

underground car park *die* Tiefgarage.

underline *verb* unterstreichen ✧.

underneath *preposition* unter (+DAT, *or* +ACC *when there is movement towards a place*); **it's underneath the newspaper** es ist unter der Zeitung; **I put it underneath the newspaper** ich habe es unter die Zeitung gelegt. *adverb* darunter; **check underneath** sieh darunter nach.

underpants *plural noun* Unterhose *die* (PL *die* Unterhosen); **my underpants** meine Unterhose.

underpass *noun* Unterführung *die* (PL *die* Unterführungen).

understand *verb* verstehen ✧; **do you understand?** verstehst du?; **I couldn't understand what he was saying** ich konnte ihn nicht verstehen; **I can't understand why she doesn't want to see him** ich kann nicht verstehen, warum sie ihn nicht sehen will.

understandable *adjective* **that's understandable** das ist verständlich.

understanding *noun* Verständnis *das*. *adjective* verständnisvoll.

underwear *noun* Unterwäsche *die*.

undo *verb* aufmachen SEP.

undone *adjective* **to come undone** aufgehen ✧ SEP (PERF *sein*).

undress *verb* **to get undressed** sich ausziehen ✧ SEP.

✧ IRREGULAR VERB: *See the verb table in the centre of the dictionary*

unemployed *noun* **the unemployed** die Arbeitslosen (*plural*).
adjective arbeitslos.

unemployment *noun* Arbeitslosigkeit *die*.

unexpected *adjective* unerwartet.

unexpectedly *adverb* (*to happen, arrive*) überraschend.

unfair *adjective* unfair; **it's unfair on young people** es ist jungen Leuten gegenüber unfair.

unfashionable *adjective* unmodern.

unfasten *verb* aufmachen SEP.

unfit *adjective* nicht fit; **I'm terribly unfit** ich bin nicht sehr fit.

unfortunate *adjective* unglücklich.

unfortunately *adverb* leider.

unfriendly *adjective* unfreundlich.

ungrateful *adjective* undankbar.

unhappy *adjective* 1 unglücklich; 2 (*not satisfied*) unzufrieden; **to be unhappy about something** mit etwas unzufrieden sein.

unhealthy *adjective* ungesund.

uniform *noun* Uniform *die* (PL *die* Uniformen).

union *noun* (*trade union*) Gewerkschaft *die* (PL *die* Gewerkschaften).

Union Jack *noun* **the Union Jack** die britische Nationalflagge.

unique *adjective* einzigartig.

unit *noun* 1 (*for measuring, for example*) Einheit *die* (PL *die* Einheiten); 2 (*in a kitchen*) Einbauschrank *der* (PL *die* Einbauschränke); 3 (*a department*) Abteilung *die* (PL *die* Abteilungen); **the research unit** die Forschungsabteilung.

United Kingdom *noun* Vereinigte Königreich *das*.

United Nations *noun* Vereinte Nationen (*plural*).

United States (of America) *plural noun* Vereinigte Staaten (von Amerika) (*plural*).

universe *noun* Universum *das*, Weltall *das*.

university *noun* Universität *die* (PL *die* Universitäten); **to go to university** auf die Universität gehen.

unkind *adjective* unfreundlich.

unknown *adjective* unbekannt.

unleaded petrol *noun* bleifreie Benzin *das*.

unless *conjunction* es sei denn; **unless he does it** es sei denn, er macht es; **unless you write** es sei denn, du schreibst.

unlike *adjective* 1 im Gegensatz zu (+DAT); **unlike me, she hates dogs** im Gegensatz zu mir hasst sie Hunde; 2 **it's unlike her to be late** es sieht ihr gar nicht ähnlich, zu spät zu kommen.

unlikely *adjective* unwahrscheinlich.

unload *verb* 1 ausladen ◇ SEP (*luggage, car*); 2 entladen ◇ (*lorry*).

unlock *verb* aufschließen ◇ SEP.

unlucky *adjective* **1 to be unlucky** (*person*) Pech haben; **I was unlucky, the shop was shut** ich hatte Pech, das Geschäft war zu; **2** (*bringing bad luck*) Unglücks-; **thirteen is an unlucky number** dreizehn ist eine Unglückszahl; **it's unlucky** es bringt Unglück.

unnecessary *adjective* unnötig.

unpack *verb* auspacken SEP; **I'm just unpacking my rucksack** ich packe gerade meinen Rucksack aus; **I'll just unpack and then come down** ich packe nur noch aus und dann komme ich runter.

unpaid *adjective* unbezahlt.

unpleasant *adjective* unangenehm.

unplug *verb* **to unplug the lamp** den Stecker von der Lampe herausziehen ◇ SEP.

unpopular *adjective* unbeliebt.

unreasonable *adjective* uneinsichtig; **he's being really unreasonable** er ist so uneinsichtig.

unreliable *adjective* unzuverlässig; **he's unreliable** er ist unzuverlässig.

unsafe *adjective* gefährlich (*wiring, for example*).

unsatisfactory *adjective* unbefriedigend.

unscrew *verb* aufschrauben SEP.

unshaven *adjective* unrasiert.

unsuccessful *adjective* **1** erfolglos; **an unsuccessful attempt** ein erfolgloser Versuch; **2 to be unsuccessful** keinen Erfolg haben; **I tried, but I was unsuccessful** ich habe es versucht, aber ich hatte keinen Erfolg.

unsuitable *adjective* unpassend.

untidy *adjective* unordentlich; **the house is always untidy** das Haus ist immer unordentlich.

until *preposition, conjunction* **1** bis; **until Monday** bis Montag; **until now** bis jetzt; **until then** bis dahin; **2** (*when 'until' is followed by a noun it is usually translated as 'bis zu'* +DAT) **until the tenth** bis zum Zehnten; **until the morning** bis zum Morgen; **3 not until** erst; **not until September** erst im September; **it won't be finished until Friday** es wird erst Freitag fertig sein.

unusual *adjective* ungewöhnlich; **an unusual face** ein ungewöhnliches Gesicht.

unwilling *adjective* **to be unwilling to do something** etwas nicht tun wollen.

unwrap *verb* auspacken SEP.

up *preposition, adverb* **1** (*out of bed*) **to be up** auf sein △ ◇ (PERF *sein*); **Liz isn't up yet** Liz ist noch nicht auf; **I was up late last night** ich war gestern bis spät auf; **2 to get up** aufstehen ◇ SEP (PERF *sein*); **we got up at six** wir sind um sechs aufgestanden; **3** (*higher up*) auf (+DAT, *or* +ACC *when there is movement towards a place*); **up on the roof** auf

◇ IRREGULAR VERB: *See the verb table in the centre of the dictionary*

dem Dach; **4 up here** hier oben; **up there** da oben; **to go up** (*upstairs*) nach oben gehen; **I went up** ich bin nach oben gegangen; **5 to go up the road** die Straße entlanggehen ✧ SEP (PERF *sein*); **it's further up the road** es ist weiter die Straße entlang; **6 to go up the hill** (*on foot*) hinaufgehen ✧ SEP (PERF *sein*); (*in a vehicle*) hinauffahren ✧ SEP (PERF *sein*); (*in spoken German the prefix 'rauf-' is most common*) **does the bus go up the hill?** fährt der Bus den Berg rauf?; **7 to come up** heraufkommen ✧ SEP (PERF *sein*), raufkommen ✧ SEP (PERF *sein*) (*informal*); **8** (*wrong*) **what's up?** was ist los? (*informal*); **what's up with him?** was ist mit ihm los?; **9 up to** bis; **up to here** bis hier; **up to last week** bis zur letzten Woche; **10 she came up to me** sie kam auf mich zu; **11 what's she up to?** was hat sie vor?; **12 it's up to you** (*it's for you to decide*) das hängt von dir ab; (*it concerns only you*) das ist deine Sache; ★ **time's up!** die Zeit ist um.

upheaval *noun* Unruhe *die* (PL *die* Unruhen).

upper-class *adjective* der Oberschicht; **an upper-class family** eine Familie der Oberschicht.

upright *adjective* aufrecht; **put it upright** stell es aufrecht; **to stand upright** aufrecht stehen.

upset *noun* **stomach upset** *die* Magenverstimmung.
adjective **1** (*annoyed*) ärgerlich; **he's upset** er ist ärgerlich; **2** (*distressed*) bestürzt; (*sad*) betrübt.
verb **to upset somebody** (*hurt*) jemanden kränken; (*annoy*) jemanden ärgern.

upside down *adjective* verkehrt herum.

upstairs *adverb* **1** oben; **Mum's upstairs** Mutti ist oben; **2** (*with movement*) nach oben; **to go upstairs** nach oben gehen.

up-to-date *adjective* **1** (*in fashion*) modern; **2** (*information*) aktuell.

upwards *adjective* nach oben.

urgent *adjective* dringend.

US *noun* USA (*plural*).

us *pronoun* uns; **she knows us** sie kennt uns; **they saw us** sie haben uns gesehen; **with us** mit uns.

USA *noun* USA (*plural*).

use *noun* **1** Gebrauch *der*; **instructions for use** *die* Gebrauchsanweisung (*singular*); **2 it's no use** es hat keinen Zweck; **it's no use phoning** es hat keinen Zweck anzurufen.
verb benutzen; **we used the dictionary** wir haben das Wörterbuch benutzt; **to use something to do something** etwas zu etwas ←(DAT) benutzen; **I used a towel to dry myself** ich habe ein Handtuch zum Abtrocknen benutzt.
● **to use up 1** aufbrauchen SEP (*food*); **2** verbrauchen (*money*).

used *adjective* **1 to be used to something** an etwas ←(ACC) gewöhnt sein; **I'm used to cats** ich bin an Katzen gewöhnt; **I'm not used to it!**

ich bin nicht daran gewöhnt!; **I'm not used to eating in restaurants** ich bin nicht daran gewöhnt, in Restaurants zu essen; **2 to get used to something** sich an etwas ←(ACC) gewöhnen; **you'll soon get used to the new car** du wirst dich schnell an das neue Auto gewöhnen; **I've got used to living here** ich habe mich daran gewöhnt, hier zu wohnen; **you'll get used to it** du wirst dich schon daran gewöhnen.
verb **they used to live in the country** sie haben früher auf dem Land gewohnt; **she used to smoke** sie hat früher geraucht.

useful *adjective* nützlich.

useless *adjective* **1** unbrauchbar; **this knife's useless** dieses Messer ist unbrauchbar; **you're completely useless!** du bist wirklich zu nichts zu gebrauchen!; **2** nutzlos (*advice, information, or facts, for example*); **useless knowledge** nutzloses Wissen; **3** (*pointless*) zwecklos.

user-friendly *adjective* benutzerfreundlich.

usual *adjective* **1** üblich; **it's the usual problem** es ist das übliche Problem; **as usual** wie üblich; **2 it's colder than usual** es ist kälter als gewöhnlich.

usually *adjective* normalerweise; **I usually leave at eight** normalerweise gehe ich um acht weg.

V v

vacancy *noun* **1** (*in a hotel*) **'vacancies'** 'Zimmer frei'; **'no vacancies'** 'belegt'; **2 job vacancy** die freie Stelle.

vacant *adjective* frei.

vaccination *noun* Impfung die (PL die Impfungen).

vacuum *verb* saugen; **I'm going to vacuum my room** ich sauge mein Zimmer.

vacuum cleaner *noun* Staubsauger der (PL die Staubsauger).

vagina *noun* Vagina die (PL die Vaginen).

vague *adjective* vage.

vain *adjective* eitel; **in vain** vergeblich.

Valentine's Day *noun* Valentinstag der (PL die Valentinstage).

valid *adjective* gültig.

valley *noun* Tal das (PL die Täler).

valuable *adjective* wertvoll.

value *noun* Wert der (PL die Werte). *verb* schätzen.

van *noun* Lieferwagen der (PL die Lieferwagen).

vandal *noun* Rowdy der (PL die Rowdies).

$\diamond$ IRREGULAR VERB: *See the verb table in the centre of the dictionary*

vandalism *noun*
Wandalismus △ *der*.

vandalize *verb* mutwillig zerstören.

vanilla *noun* Vanille *die*; **vanilla ice cream** *das* Vanilleeis.

vanish *verb* verschwinden ✧ (PERF *sein*).

variety *noun* 1 Abwechslung *die* (*in a routine, diet, or style*); **for the sake of variety** zur Abwechslung; 2 (*kind*) Sorte *die* (PL *die* Sorten); **a new variety of apple** eine neue Apfelsorte; 3 (*assortment*) Auswahl *die*.

various *adjective* verschieden; **there are various ways of doing it** man kann es auf verschiedene Art und Weise machen.

vary *verb* 1 (*become different*) sich ändern; 2 **it varies a lot** es ist sehr unterschiedlich; 3 (*make different*) ändern (*a programme or method*).

vase *noun* Vase *die* (PL *die* Vasen).

VAT *noun* Mehrwertsteuer *die* (PL *die* Mehrwertsteuern).

VCR *noun* Videorecorder *der* (PL *die* Videorecorder).

VDU *noun* Bildschirm *der* (PL *die* Bildschirme).

veal *noun* Kalbfleisch *das*.

vegan *noun* Veganer *der* (PL *die* Veganer), Veganerin *die* (PL *die* Veganerinnen).

vegetable *noun* Gemüse *das*; **fresh vegetables** frisches Gemüse.

vegetarian *noun* Vegetarier *der* (PL *die* Vegetarier), Vegetarierin *die* (PL *die* Vegetarierinnen).
adjective vegetarisch.

vehicle *noun* Fahrzeug *das* (PL *die* Fahrzeuge).

vein *noun* Vene *die* (PL *die* Venen).

velvet *noun* Samt *der*.

vending machine *noun* Automat *der* (PL *die* Automaten).

verb *noun* Verb *das* (PL *die* Verben).

verdict *noun* Urteil *das* (PL *die* Urteile).

verge *noun* 1 (*roadside*) Bankette *die* (PL *die* Banketten); 2 **to be on the verge of doing something** im Begriff sein, etwas zu tun; **I was on the verge of leaving** ich war im Begriff zu gehen.

version *noun* Version *die* (PL *die* Versionen).

versus *preposition* gegen (+ACC); **Arsenal versus Chelsea** Arsenal gegen Chelsea.

very *adverb* sehr; **it's very difficult** es ist sehr schwer; **very much** sehr viel.
adjective 1 **the very person I need!** genau der Mann, den ich brauche; genau die Frau, die ich brauche; **the very thing he's looking for** genau das, was er sucht; **in the very middle** genau in der Mitte; 2 **at the very end** ganz am Ende; **at the very front** ganz vorne.

vest *noun* Unterhemd *das* (PL *die* Unterhemden).

△ NEW SPELLING: *See page xii*

vet noun Tierarzt der (PL die Tierärzte), Tierärztin die (PL die Tierärztinnen); **she's a vet** sie ist Tierärztin.

via preposition über (+ACC); **we're going to Frankfurt via Brussels** wir fahren über Brüssel nach Frankfurt.

vicar noun Pfarrer der (PL die Pfarrer).

vicious adjective **1** bösartig (dog); **2** brutal (attack).

victim noun Opfer das (PL die Opfer).

victory noun Sieg der (PL die Siege).

video noun **1** (film, cassette) Video das (PL die Videos); **to watch a video** ein Video ansehen; **I've got it on video** ich habe es auf Video; **it's out on video** das gibt's als Video; **2** (video recorder) Videorecorder der (PL die Videorecorder).
verb aufzeichnen SEP; **I'll video it for you** ich zeichne es für dich auf.

video camera noun Videokamera die (PL die Videokameras).

video cassette noun Videokassette die (PL die Videokassetten).

video game noun Videospiel das (PL die Videospiele).

video recorder noun Videorecorder der (PL die Videorecorder).

video shop noun Videothek die (PL die Videotheken).

Vienna noun Wien das; **to Vienna** nach Wien.

view noun **1** Aussicht die; **a room with a view of the lake** ein Zimmer mit Aussicht auf den See; **2** (opinion) Meinung die (PL die Meinungen); **in my view** meiner Meinung nach; **point of view** der Standpunkt.

viewer noun Zuschauer der (PL die Zuschauer), Zuschauerin die (PL die Zuschauerinnen).

vile adjective ekelhaft.

villa noun Villa die (PL die Villen).

village noun Dorf das (PL die Dörfer).

vine noun Weinrebe die (PL die Weinreben).

vinegar noun Essig der.

vineyard noun Weinberg der (PL die Weinberge).

violence noun Gewalt die.

violent adjective **1** gewalttätig (person, film, behaviour); **2** heftig (jolt, punch).

violin noun Geige die (PL die Geigen); **to play the violin** Geige spielen.

violinist noun Geiger der (PL die Geiger), Geigerin die (PL die Geigerinnen).

virgin noun Jungfrau die (PL die Jungfrauen).

Virgo noun Jungfrau die; **Robert's Virgo** Robert ist Jungfrau.

virtual reality noun virtuelle Realität die.

virus noun Virus das (PL die Viren).

✧ IRREGULAR VERB: *See the verb table in the centre of the dictionary*

visa *noun* Visum *das* (PL *die* Visa).

visit *noun* Besuch *der* (PL *die* Besuche); **I was in Berlin on a visit to friends** ich war in Berlin bei Freunden zu Besuch; **my last visit to Germany** mein letzter Deutschlandbesuch.
verb **1** besuchen (*a person*);
2 besichtigen (*a building, town*).

visitor *noun* **1** Besucher *der* (PL *die* Besucher), Besucherin *die* (PL *die* Besucherinnen); **2 we've got visitors tonight** wir haben heute Abend Besuch; **3** (*in a hotel*) Gast *der* (PL *die* Gäste).

visual *adjective* visuell.

vital *adjective* unbedingt erforderlich; **it's vital to book** man muss unbedingt buchen.

vitamin *noun* Vitamin *das* (PL *die* Vitamine).

vivid *adjective* lebhaft (*colours, memory*); **to have a vivid imagination** eine lebhafte Phantasie haben.

vocabulary *noun* Wortschatz *der*.

vocational *adjective* beruflich.

vodka *noun* Wodka *der* (PL *die* Wodkas).

voice *noun* Stimme *die* (PL *die* Stimmen).

volcano *noun* Vulkan *der* (PL *die* Vulkane).

volleyball *noun* Volleyball *der*; **to play volleyball** Volleyball spielen.

volume *noun* **1** Lautstärke *die*; **could you turn down the volume?**
könntest du etwas leiser stellen?;
2 (*book*) Band *der* (PL *die* Bände).

voluntary *adjective* **1** freiwillig; **a voluntary worker** ein freiwilliger Helfer, eine freiwillige Helferin;
2 to do voluntary work für einen wohltätigen Zweck arbeiten.

volunteer *noun* Freiwillige *der/die* (PL *die* Freiwilligen).
verb **to volunteer to do something** sich anbieten, etwas zu tun.

vote *verb* wählen; **to vote for somebody** jemanden wählen.

voucher *noun* Gutschein *der* (PL *die* Gutscheine).

vowel *noun* Vokal *der* (PL *die* Vokale).

vulgar *adjective* vulgär.

W w

wage(s) *noun* Lohn *der* (PL *die* Löhne).

waist *noun* Taille *die* (PL *die* Taillen).

waistcoat *noun* Weste *die* (PL *die* Westen).

waist measurement *noun* Taillenweite *die*.

wait *noun* Wartezeit *die*; **an hour's wait** eine Stunde Wartezeit.
verb **1** warten; **they're waiting in the car** sie warten im Auto; **she kept me waiting** sie hat mich warten lassen; **2 to wait for somebody** auf jemanden warten; **wait for me**

△ NEW SPELLING: *See page xii*

warte auf mich; **to wait for something** auf etwas ←(ACC) warten; **we waited for a taxi** wir haben auf ein Taxi gewartet; **3 to wait for somebody to do something** darauf warten, dass jemand etwas tut; **I'm waiting for him to ring** ich warte darauf, dass er anruft; **4 I can't wait to open it** ich kann's kaum erwarten, es aufzumachen.

waiter noun Kellner der (PL die Kellner); **waiter!** Herr Ober!

waiting room noun Wartezimmer das (PL die Wartezimmer); (at a station) Warteraum der (PL die Warteräume).

waitress noun Kellnerin die (PL die Kellnerinnen); **waitress!** Fräulein!

wake verb **1** wecken (somebody); **Jess woke me at six** Jess hat mich um sechs geweckt; **2** aufwachen SEP (PERF sein); **I woke (up) at six** ich bin um sechs aufgewacht; **wake up!** wach auf!

Wales noun Wales das; **from Wales** aus Wales; **to Wales** nach Wales.

walk noun **1** Spaziergang der (PL die Spaziergänge); **to go for walk** einen Spaziergang machen; **we'll go for a little walk round the village** wir machen einen kleinen Spaziergang durchs Dorf; **2 to take the dog for a walk** mit dem Hund spazieren gehen ◇ (PERF sein); **3 it's about five minutes' walk from here** es ist ungefähr fünf Minuten zu Fuß von hier.
verb **1** (go, not run) gehen ◇ (PERF sein); **he walks very slowly** er geht

sehr langsam; **I'll walk to the bus stop with you** ich gehe mit dir zur Bushaltestelle; **2** (on foot rather than by car or bus) zu Fuß gehen ◇ (PERF sein); **it's not far, we can walk** es ist nicht weit, wir können zu Fuß gehen; **3** (walk around) spazieren gehen ◇ Δ (PERF sein); **we walked around the old town** wir sind in der Altstadt spazieren gegangen; **4** (move on foot) laufen ◇ (PERF sein); **to learn to walk** laufen lernen; **the child can't walk yet** das Kind kann noch nicht laufen.

walking noun (hiking) Wandern das; **to go walking** wandern (PERF sein).

walking distance noun **to be within walking distance** zu Fuß zu erreichen sein; **it's within walking distance of the sea** man kann das Meer zu Fuß erreichen.

walkman™ noun Walkman™ der (PL die Walkmen).

wall noun **1** (inside a building) Wand die (PL die Wände); **there's a picture on every wall** an jeder Wand hängt ein Bild; **2** (outside) Mauer die (PL die Mauern).

wallet noun Brieftasche die (PL die Brieftaschen).

wallpaper noun Tapete die (PL die Tapeten).

walnut noun Walnuss Δ die (PL die Walnüsse).

wander verb **to wander around town** durch die Stadt bummeln

---

◇ **IRREGULAR VERB:** See the verb table in the centre of the dictionary

(PERF *sein*); **to wander off**
weggehen ✧ SEP (PERF *sein*).

want *verb* 1 wollen ✧; **do you want
to come?** willst du mitkommen?;
what do you want to do? was willst
du machen?; **I don't want to bother
him** ich will ihn nicht stören;
2 (*more polite*) mögen ✧ ('*ich
möchte' is much politer than 'ich
will*'); **do you want some more
coffee?** möchtest du noch Kaffee?;
I want two pounds of apples please
ich möchte gern zwei Pfund Äpfel
('*möchte gern' is particularly used
when shopping*).

war *noun* Krieg *der* (PL *die* Kriege).

wardrobe *noun*
Kleiderschrank *der* (PL *die*
Kleiderschränke).

warm *adjective* 1 warm; **a warm
coat** ein warmer Mantel; **it's warm
today** heute ist es warm; **I'll keep
your dinner warm** ich halte dir das
Essen warm; **it's warm inside**
drinnen ist es warm; **I am warm** mir
ist warm; 2 (*friendly*) herzlich; **a
warm welcome** ein herzlicher
Empfang.
verb wärmen; **to warm the plates**
die Teller wärmen.
● **to warm up** 1 (*weather*) warm
werden; 2 (*an athlete*) sich
aufwärmen SEP; 3 (*to heat up*)
aufwärmen SEP; **I'll warm the soup
up for you** ich wärme dir die Suppe
auf.

warmth *noun* Wärme *die*.

warn *verb* 1 warnen; **I warn you, it's
expensive** ich warne dich, es ist
teuer; **to warn somebody not to do
something** jemanden davor

warnen, etwas zu tun; **she warned
me not to let him drive** sie hat mich
davor gewarnt, ihn fahren zu lassen;
2 **he warned me to lock the car** er
hat mich ermahnt, das Auto
abzuschließen.

warning *noun* Warnung *die* (PL *die*
Warnungen).

wash *noun* **to give something a
wash** etwas waschen ✧; **to have a
wash** sich waschen.
verb 1 waschen ✧; **I've washed your
jeans** ich habe deine Jeans
gewaschen; 2 (*have a wash*) sich
waschen ✧; **to get washed** sich
waschen; 3 **to wash your hands**
sich ←(DAT) die Hände waschen; **I
washed my hands** ich habe mir die
Hände gewaschen; **to wash your
hair** sich ←(DAT) die Haare waschen;
4 **to wash the dishes** abwaschen ✧
SEP.
● **to wash up** abwaschen ✧ SEP.

washbasin *noun*
Waschbecken *das* (PL *die*
Waschbecken).

washing *noun* Wäsche *die*; **to do
the washing** Wäsche waschen.

washing machine *noun*
Waschmaschine *die* (PL *die*
Waschmaschinen).

washing powder *noun*
Waschpulver *das*.

washing-up *noun* Abwasch *der*; **to
do the washing-up** den Abwasch
machen.

washing-up liquid *noun*
Spülmittel *das* (PL *die* Spülmittel).

△ NEW SPELLING: *See page xii*

wasp *noun* Wespe *die* (PL *die* Wespen).

waste *noun* Verschwendung *die*; **it's a waste of time** das ist eine Zeitverschwendung.
verb verschwenden.

waste-bin *noun* Mülltonne *die* (PL *die* Mülltonnen).

waste-paper basket *noun* Papierkorb *der* (PL *die* Papierkörbe).

watch *noun* Uhr *die* (PL *die* Uhren); **my watch is fast** meine Uhr geht vor; **my watch is slow** meine Uhr geht nach.
verb **1** (*to look at*) sich ←(DAT) ansehen ✧ SEP; **I was watching a film** ich habe mir einen Film angesehen; **2 to watch TV** fernsehen ✧ SEP; **3** (*keep a check on, look after*) achten auf (+ACC); **watch the children** achte auf die Kinder; **4** (*to be careful*) aufpassen SEP; **watch you don't spill it** pass auf, dass du es nicht verschüttest; **watch out!** pass auf!; **5** (*observe*) beobachten; **they were being watched** sie wurden beobachtet.

water *noun* Wasser *das*.
verb gießen ✧ (*plants*).

waterfall *noun* Wasserfall *der* (PL *die* Wasserfälle).

watering can *noun* Gießkanne *die* (PL *die* Gießkannen).

waterproof *adjective* wasserdicht.

water-skiing *noun* Wasserskifahren *das*; **to go water-skiing** Wasserski fahren.

wave *noun* **1** (*in the sea*) Welle *die* (PL *die* Wellen); **2** (*with your hand*) **to give somebody a wave** jemandem zuwinken SEP; **she gave him a wave from the bus** sie winkte ihm vom Bus zu.
verb **1** (*with your hand*) winken; **2** (*flap*) schwenken (*a flag, for example*).

wax *noun* Wachs *das*.

way *noun* **1** (*a route or road*) Weg *der* (PL *die* Wege); **the way to town** der Weg in die Stadt; **we asked the way to the station** wir haben gefragt, wie man zum Bahnhof kommt; **on the way back** auf dem Rückweg; **on the way** unterwegs; **to be in the way** im Weg sein; **to be in somebody's way** jemandem im Weg sein; **to get out of the way** aus dem Weg gehen; **2 to lose your way** sich verlaufen ✧; (*in a car*) sich verfahren ✧; **3 'way in'** 'Eingang'; **'way out'** 'Ausgang'; **4** (*direction*) Richtung *die* (PL *die* Richtungen); **which way did he go?** in welche Richtung ist er gegangen?; **this way** in diese Richtung; **5** (*side*) **the right way up** richtig herum; **the wrong way round** falsch herum; **the other way round** andersherum; **6** (*distance*) **it's a long way** es ist weit weg; **we still had a little way to go** wir mussten noch ein kleines Stück gehen; **7** (*manner*) Art und Weise *die*; **my way of learning German** meine Art und Weise, Deutsch zu lernen; **he does it his way** er macht es auf seine Art und Weise; **I've done it the wrong way** ich habe es falsch gemacht; **in a way**

✧ **IRREGULAR VERB:** *See the verb table in the centre of the dictionary*

in gewisser Weise; **8 no way!** auf keinen Fall!; **9 by the way** übrigens.

we *pronoun* wir; **we're going to the cinema tonight** wir gehen heute Abend ins Kino.

weak *adjective* **1** (*feeble*) schwach; **in a weak voice** mit schwacher Stimme; **2** dünn (*coffee or tea*).

wealthy *adjective* reich.

weapon *noun* Waffe *die* (PL *die* Waffen).

wear *noun* **children's wear** *die* Kinderkleidung; **sports wear** *die* Sportkleidung.
verb tragen ✧, anhaben ✧ SEP (*informal*); **she often wears red** sie trägt oft Rot; **Tamsin's wearing her jeans** Tamsin hat ihre Jeans an.

weather *noun* **1** Wetter *das*; **what's the weather like?** wie ist das Wetter?; **in fine weather** bei schönem Wetter; **the weather is terrible** das Wetter ist furchtbar; **2 in wet weather** wenn es regnet; **the weather was cold** es war kalt.

weather forecast *noun* Wettervorhersage *die*; **the weather forecast says it will rain** der Wettervorhersage zufolge soll es regnen.

wedding *noun* Hochzeit *die* (PL *die* Hochzeiten).

Wednesday *noun* **1** Mittwoch *der* (PL *die* Mittwoche); **on Wednesday** (am) Mittwoch; **I'm going to the cinema on Wednesday** ich gehe Mittwoch ins Kino; **see you on Wednesday!** bis Mittwoch!; **every**

Wednesday jeden Mittwoch; **last Wednesday** vorigen Mittwoch; **next Wednesday** nächsten Mittwoch; **2 on Wednesdays** mittwochs; **the museum is closed on Wednesdays** das Museum ist mittwochs geschlossen.

weed *noun* Unkraut *das*.

week *noun* Woche *die* (PL *die* Wochen); **last week** vorige Woche; **next week** nächste Woche; **this week** diese Woche; **for weeks** wochenlang; **a week today** heute in einer Woche; **in three weeks' time** in drei Wochen.

weekday *noun* **on weekdays** wochentags.

weekend *noun* Wochenende *das* (PL *die* Wochenenden); **last weekend** voriges Wochenende; **next weekend** nächstes Wochenende; **they're coming for the weekend** sie kommen übers Wochenende; **I'll do it at the weekend** ich mache es am Wochenende; **have a nice weekend!** ein schönes Wochenende!

weigh *verb* **1** wiegen ✧; **to weigh something** etwas wiegen; **to weigh yourself** sich wiegen; **2 how much do you weigh?** wie viel wiegst du?; **I weigh 50 kilos** ich wiege fünfzig Kilo.

weight *noun* **1** Gewicht *das* (PL *die* Gewichte); **2 to put on weight** zunehmen ✧ SEP; **3 to lose weight** abnehmen ✧ SEP.

weird *adjective* seltsam.

welcome *noun* **1 they gave us a warm welcome** sie haben uns herzlich empfangen; **2 welcome to Oxford!** herzlich willkommen in Oxford!
adjective willkommen; **you're welcome any time** du bist immer willkommen; **'thank you!' – 'you're welcome!'** 'danke!' – 'bitte!'.
verb begrüßen; **to welcome somebody** jemanden begrüßen.

well *adverb* **1 to be well** gesund sein; **I'm very well, thank you** danke, es geht mir gut; **get well soon!** gute Besserung!; **2** gut; **Terry played well** Terry hat gut gespielt; **it's well paid** es wird gut bezahlt; **well done!** gut gemacht!; **3 as well** auch; **Kevin's coming as well** Kevin kommt auch; **4** na ja; **well, never mind** na ja, macht nichts; **5** gut; **it may well be that …** es ist gut möglich, dass …; **very well then, you can go** also gut, du kannst gehen.

well-behaved *adjective* artig.

well-done *adjective* durchgebraten (*steak*).

wellington (boot) *noun* Gummistiefel *der* (PL *die* Gummistiefel).

well-known *adjective* bekannt.

well-off *adjective* wohlhabend.

Welsh *noun* **1 the Welsh** (*people*) die Waliser (*plural*); **2** (*language*) Walisisch *das*.
adjective walisisch; **he's Welsh** er ist Waliser; **she's Welsh** sie ist Waliserin.

Welshman *noun* Waliser *der* (PL *die* Waliser).

Welshwoman *noun* Waliserin *die* (PL *die* Waliserinnen).

west *noun* Westen *der*; **in the west** im Westen.
adjective West-; **the west side** die Westseite; **west wind** *der* Westwind; **west of** westlich von; **it's west of Munich** es liegt westlich von München.
adverb nach Westen.

western *noun* (*film*) Western *der* (PL *die* Western).

West Indian *noun* Westinder *der* (PL *die* Westinder), Westinderin *die* (PL *die* Westinderinnen).
adjective westindisch.

West Indies *plural noun* die Westindischen Inseln (*plural*); **in the West Indies** auf den Westindischen Inseln.

wet *adjective* **1** nass △; **we got wet** wir sind nass geworden; **2 a wet day** ein regnerischer Tag.

whale *noun* Wal *der* (PL *die* Wale).

what *pronoun, adjective* **1** (*in questions*) was; **what did you say?** was hast du gesagt?; **what's she doing?** was macht sie?; **what did you buy?** was hast du gekauft?; **what is it?** was ist das?; **what's the matter?** was ist los?; **what's happened?** was ist passiert?; **what?** was?; **2 what's your address?** wie ist Ihre Adresse?; **what's her name?** wie heißt sie?; **what was it like?** wie war's?; **3** (*asking for an amount*) wie viel △;

at what time? um wie viel Uhr?; **4** (*that which*) was (*relative pronoun*); **she told me what had happened** sie hat mir gesagt, was passiert ist; **do what I tell you** tu, was ich dir sage; **5** (*which*) welcher/welche/welches; **what country is it in?** in welchem Land ist es?; **what colour is it?** welche Farbe hat es?; **what make is it?** welche Marke ist es?; **6 what for?** wozu?

wheat *noun* Weizen *der*.

wheel *noun* Rad *das* (PL *die* Räder); **the spare wheel** das Reserverad; **the steering wheel** das Lenkrad.

wheelbarrow *noun* Schubkarre *die* (PL *die* Schubkarren).

wheelchair *noun* Rollstuhl *der* (PL *die* Rollstühle).

when *adverb* wann; **when is she arriving?** wann kommt sie an?; **when's your birthday?** wann hast du Geburtstag?
conjunction **1** (*with the past*) als; **I was out shopping when you rang** ich war beim Einkaufen, als du anriefst; **2** (*with the present or future*) wenn; **when she comes I'll ring** wenn sie kommt, rufe ich an.

where *adverb, conjunction* wo; **where do you live?** wo wohnst du?; **where are you going?** wo gehst du hin?; **I don't know where they live** ich weiß nicht, wo sie wohnen.

whether *conjunction* ob; **I don't know whether he's back** ich weiß nicht, ob er schon zurück ist.

which *adjective, pronoun*
1 welcher/welche/welches; **which CD did you buy?** welche CD hast du gekauft?; **2 which (one)** welcher/welche/welches (*depending on the gender of the noun the question refers back to*); **I met your brother' – 'which one?'** 'ich habe deinen Bruder getroffen' – 'welchen?'; **'I met your sister' – 'which one?'** 'ich habe deine Schwester getroffen' – 'welche?'; **'have you seen my book?' - 'which one?'** 'hast du mein Buch gesehen?' – 'welches?'; **3** (*relative pronoun*) der/die/das (*depending on the gender of the noun 'which' refers to*); (*plural*) die; **the film which is showing now** der Film, der gerade läuft; **the lamp which is on the table** die Lampe, die auf dem Tisch steht; **the book which I lent you** das Buch, das ich dir geliehen habe; **the books which I've read** die Bücher, die ich gelesen habe.

while *noun* **for a while** eine Weile; **she worked here for a while** sie hat eine Weile hier gearbeitet; **after a while** nach einer Weile.
conjunction während; **you can make some coffee while I'm finishing my homework** du kannst Kaffee kochen, während ich meine Hausaufgaben fertig mache.

whip *noun* Peitsche *die* (PL *die* Peitschen).
verb schlagen ✧ (*cream*); **whipped cream** *die* Schlagsahne.

whisky *noun* Whisky *der* (PL *die* Whiskys).

△ NEW SPELLING: *See page xii*

whisper *noun* Flüstern *das*; **in a whisper** im Flüsterton.
verb flüstern.

whistle *noun* Pfeife *die* (PL *die* Pfeifen).
verb pfeifen ✧.

white *noun* Weiß *das*; **egg white** *das* Eiweiß.
adjective weiß; **a white shirt** ein weißes Hemd.

white coffee *noun* Kaffee mit Milch *der* (PL *die* Kaffees mit Milch).

Whitsun *noun* Pfingsten *das* (PL *die* Pfingsten).

who *pronoun* 1 (*in questions*) wer; **who wants some chocolate?** wer möchte Schokolade?; 2 (*in the accusative*) wen; **who did you ring?** wen hast du angerufen?; 3 (*in the dative*) wem; **who did you give it to?** wem hast du es gegeben?; 4 (*relative pronoun*) der/die/das (*depending on the gender of the noun 'who' refers to*); (*plural*) die; **my boy friend who lives in Liverpool** mein Freund, der in Liverpool wohnt; **my girl friend who lives in Berlin** meine Freundin, die in Berlin wohnt; **the child who's staying with us** das Kind, das bei uns wohnt; **the friends who are coming to see us tonight** die Freunde, die heute Abend kommen.

whole *noun* **the whole of the class** die ganze Klasse; **the whole of Germany** ganz Deutschland; **on the whole** im Großen und Ganzen.
adjective ganz; **the whole family** die ganze Familie; **the whole morning** den ganzen Morgen; **the whole time** die ganze Zeit; **the whole world** die ganze Welt.

wholemeal *adjective* Vollkorn-; **wholemeal bread** *das* Vollkornbrot.

whom *pronoun* 1 den/die/das; (*plural*) die; **the man whom I saw** der Mann, den ich sah; **the woman whom I saw** die Frau, die ich sah; **the child whom I saw** das Kind, das ich sah; 2 (*in the dative*) dem/der/dem; (*plural*) denen; **the girl to whom I wrote** das Mädchen, dem ich geschrieben habe; 3 (*in questions*) wen; **whom did you see?** wen haben Sie gesehen?; 4 **to whom did you give it?** wem haben Sie es gegeben?

whose *pronoun, adjective* 1 (*in questions*) wessen; **whose is this jacket?** wessen Jacke ist das?; **whose shoes are these?** wessen Schuhe sind das?; 2 **whose is it?** wem gehört das?; **I know whose it is** ich weiß, wem es gehört; 3 (*as a relative pronoun*) dessen/deren/dessen (*depending on the gender of the noun 'whose' refers to*); (*plural*) deren; **the man whose car I'm buying** der Mann, dessen Auto ich kaufe; **the woman whose bag I found** die Frau, deren Tasche ich gefunden habe; **the girl whose sister I know** das Mädchen, dessen Schwester ich kenne; **the people whose children he teaches** die Leute, deren Kinder er unterrichtet.

why *adverb* 1 warum; **why did she phone?** warum hat sie angerufen?; **why not?** warum nicht?; 2 **that's**

✧ IRREGULAR VERB: *See the verb table in the centre of the dictionary*

why I don't want to come darum will ich nicht kommen.

wicked *adjective* **1** (*bad*) böse; **2** (*brilliant*) geil (*informal*).

wide *adjective* **1** breit; **it's a very wide road** es ist eine sehr breite Straße; **the shelf is 30 cm wide** das Regal ist dreißig Zentimeter breit; **wide screen** *das* Breitbild; **2** groß; **a wide range** eine große Auswahl. *adverb* **the door was wide open** die Tür stand weit offen.

wide awake *adjective* hellwach.

widow *noun* Witwe *die* (PL *die* Witwen).

widower *noun* Witwer *der* (PL *die* Witwer).

width *noun* Breite *die*.

wife *noun* Ehefrau *die* (PL *die* Ehefrauen).

wig *noun* Perücke *die* (PL *die* Perücken).

wild *adjective* **1** wild; **wild animals** wilde Tiere; **2** (*crazy*) verrückt (*idea, party, person*); **3 to be wild about something** scharf auf etwas ←(ACC) sein.

wildlife *noun* Tierwelt *die*; **a programme on wildlife in Africa** eine Sendung über die afrikanische Tierwelt.

wildlife park *noun* Wildpark *der* (PL *die* Wildparks).

will *verb* **1** (*in German the present tense is often used to express future actions and intentions*) **I'll wait for you at the bus stop** ich warte an der Bushaltestelle auf dich; **he'll be pleased to help you** er hilft dir gern; **that won't be a problem** das ist kein Problem; **I'll phone them at once** ich rufe sie sofort an; **2** (*the German future tense is used when firm intention is stressed, when referring to the more distant future and when some doubt about the future is expressed*) werden ✧; **he will definitely come** er wird ganz bestimmt kommen; **she'll probably ring before leaving** sie wird wahrscheinlich anrufen, bevor sie geht; **3** (*in questions and requests*) **will you have some more tea?** möchten Sie noch Tee?; **will you help me?** hilfst du mir?; **'will you write to me?' – 'of course I will!'** 'schreibst du mir?' – 'ja, natürlich'; **'he won't like it' – 'yes he will'** 'es wird ihm nicht gefallen' – 'doch'; **4** wollen ✧; **he won't help us** er will uns nicht helfen; **the car won't start** das Auto will nicht anspringen.

willing *adjective* **to be willing to do something** bereit sein, etwas zu tun; **I'm willing to pay half** ich bin bereit, die Hälfte zu zahlen.

willingly *adverb* gern.

win *noun* Sieg *der* (PL *die* Siege); **our win over Everton** unser Sieg über Everton.
verb **1** gewinnen ✧; **we won!** wir haben gewonnen!; **2 to win a prize** einen Preis bekommen.

wind¹ *noun* Wind *der* (PL *die* Winde).

wind² *verb* **1** wickeln (*a wire or rope, for example*); **2** aufziehen ✧ SEP (*a clock*).

△ NEW SPELLING: *See page xii*

wind instrument *noun*
Blasinstrument *das* (PL *die*
Blasinstrumente).

window *noun* 1 Fenster *das* (PL *die*
Fenster); **to look out of the window**
aus dem Fenster sehen; 2 (*in a shop*)
Schaufenster *das* (PL *die*
Schaufenster).

windscreen *noun*
Windschutzscheibe *die* (PL *die*
Windschutzscheiben).

windscreen wiper *noun*
Scheibenwischer *der* (PL *die*
Scheibenwischer).

windy *adjective* windig; **it's windy
today** heute ist es windig.

wine *noun* Wein *der* (PL *die* Weine);
a glass of white wine ein Glas
Weißwein.

wing *noun* Flügel *der* (PL *die* Flügel).

wink *verb* **to wink at somebody**
jemandem zuzwinkern SEP.

winner *noun* Sieger *der* (PL *die*
Sieger), Siegerin *die* (PL *die*
Siegerinnen).

winning *adjective* siegreich.

winnings *plural noun* Gewinn *der*.

winter *noun* Winter *der* (PL *die*
Winter); **in winter** im Winter.

wipe *verb* 1 abwischen SEP; **I'll just
wipe the table** ich wische schnell
den Tisch ab; **to wipe your nose** sich
←(DAT) die Nase abwischen; 2 **to wipe
the floor** den Boden wischen; 3 **to
wipe your feet** sich ←(DAT) die
Schuhe abtreten SEP.
● **to wipe up** abtrocknen SEP (*dishes*).

wire *noun* Draht *der* (PL *die* Drähte);
electric wire *die* Leitung.

wise *adjective* weise.

wish *noun* 1 Wunsch *der* (PL *die*
Wünsche); **to make a wish** sich
←(DAT) etwas wünschen; **make a
wish!** wünsch dir was!; 2 **best
wishes on your birthday** alles Gute
zum Geburtstag; 3 (*in a letter*) **with
best wishes** mit freundlichen
Grüßen.
verb 1 **I wish she were here** ich
wünschte, sie wäre hier; 2 **to wish
for something** sich ←(DAT) etwas
wünschen; 3 **to wish somebody a
happy Christmas** jemandem frohe
Weihnachten wünschen; **I wished
him happy birthday** ich habe ihm
alles Gute zum Geburtstag
gewünscht.

with *preposition* 1 mit (+DAT); **with
me** mit mir; **with pleasure** mit
Vergnügen; **he went on holiday with
his friends** er ist mit seinen
Freunden in die Ferien gefahren; **a
girl with red hair** ein Mädchen mit
roten Haaren; 2 (*at the house of*) bei
(+ACC); **we're staying the night with
friends** wir übernachten bei
Freunden; 3 vor (+DAT); **to shiver
with cold** vor Kälte zittern; **to
tremble with fear** vor Angst zittern;
4 **I haven't got any money with me**
ich habe kein Geld dabei.

without *preposition* ohne (+ACC);
without you ohne dich; **without a
sweater** ohne einen Pullover;
without knowing ohne zu wissen.

✧ IRREGULAR VERB: *See the verb table in the centre of the dictionary*

witness *noun* Zeuge *der* (PL *die* Zeugen), Zeugin *die* (PL *die* Zeuginnen).

witty *adjective* geistreich.

woman *noun* Frau *die* (PL *die* Frauen); **a woman friend** eine Freundin; **a woman doctor** eine Ärztin.

wonder *noun* Wunder *das* (PL *die* Wunder); **it's no wonder you're tired** es ist kein Wunder, dass du müde bist.
verb 1 sich fragen; **I wonder why she did that** ich frage mich, warum sie das getan hat; 2 **I wonder who?** wer wohl?; **I wonder where Jake is** wo Jake wohl ist?; 3 (*in polite requests*) **I wonder if you could tell me ...?** könnten Sie mir vielleicht sagen ...?

wonderful *adjective* wunderbar.

wood *noun* Holz *das*; **the lamp is made of wood** die Lampe ist aus Holz.

wooden *adjective* Holz-, hölzern; **wooden toys** *das* Holzspielzeug.

woodwork *noun* (*craft*) Tischlerei *die*.

wool *noun* Wolle *die*.

word *noun* 1 Wort *das* (PL *die* Wörter) (*the plural 'Wörter' is used when the words are unrelated*); **a long word** ein langes Wort; **what's the German word for 'window'?** wie heißt 'window' auf Deutsch?; **I've learned ten German words today** ich habe heute zehn deutsche Wörter gelernt; **words in the dictionary** Wörter im Wörterbuch; 2 Wort *das* (PL *die* Worte) (*the plural*

'Worte' *is used when the words are connected in a text or conversation*); **he wanted to say a few words** er wollte nur ein paar Worte sagen; **in other words** mit anderen Worten; **to have a word with somebody** mit jemandem sprechen; 3 (*promise*) Wort *das*; **to keep your word** sein Wort halten; **he broke his word** er hat sein Wort gebrochen; 4 **the words of a song** der Text von einem Lied.

word processing *noun* Textverarbeitung *die*.

word processor *noun* Textverarbeitungssystem *das*.

work *noun* Arbeit *die*; **I enjoy my work** meine Arbeit macht mir Spaß; **she's looking for work** sie sucht Arbeit; **I've got some work to do** ich habe noch etwas Arbeit; **he's out of work** er hat keine Arbeit; **to be off work** nicht arbeiten; **Ben's off work** (*sick*) Ben ist krank; **to go to work on the tube** mit der U-Bahn zur Arbeit fahren.
verb 1 arbeiten; **she works in an office** sie arbeitet in einem Büro; **Mum works as a dentist** Mutti ist Zahnärztin; **he works part-time** er arbeitet halbtags; 2 (*to operate*) sich auskennen ◇ SEP mit; **can you work the video?** kennst du dich mit dem Videorecorder aus?; 3 (*function*) funktionieren; **the washing machine's not working** die Waschmaschine funktioniert nicht; 4 (*a plan or idea*) klappen; **that worked really well** das hat prima geklappt.

● **to work out 1** (*understand*) verstehen ✧; **I can't work out why** ich kann nicht verstehen, warum; **2** (*exercise*) trainieren; **3** (*to go well*) klappen; **4** (*calculate*) ausrechnen SEP (*a sum*); **I'll work out how much it would cost** ich rechne aus, wie viel es kosten würde; **5** (*solve*) lösen (*a problem*).

worker *noun* Arbeiter *der* (PL *die* Arbeiter), Arbeiterin *die* (PL *die* Arbeiterinnen).

work experience *noun* Praktikum *das* (PL *die* Praktika); **to do work experience** ein Praktikum machen.

working-class *adjective* der Arbeiterschicht; **a working-class family** eine Familie der Arbeiterschicht.

workshop *noun* Werkstatt *die* (PL *die* Werkstätten).

world *noun* Welt *die*; **the biggest tree in the world** der größte Baum der Welt; **all over the world** auf der ganzen Welt; **the Western world** die westliche Welt.

World Cup *noun* **the World Cup** die Weltmeisterschaft.

world war *noun* Weltkrieg *der* (PL *die* Weltkriege); **the Second World War** der Zweite Weltkrieg.

worm *noun* Wurm *der* (PL *die* Würmer).

worn out *adjective* **1** (*person*) erschöpft; **2** (*clothes or shoes*) abgetragen.

worried *adjective* **1** besorgt; **his worried parents** seine besorgten Eltern; **2 to be worried about somebody** sich ←(DAT) um jemanden Sorgen machen; **we're worried about Susan** wir machen uns um Susan Sorgen.

worry *noun* Sorge *die* (PL *die* Sorgen).
verb sich ←(DAT) Sorgen machen; **don't worry!** keine Sorge!; **don't worry about it** mach dir darum keine Sorgen.

worrying *adjective* beunruhigend.

worse *adjective* **1** (*more unpleasant*) schlimmer (*problem, pain, illness*); **things couldn't be worse** es kann nicht schlimmer kommen; **2** (*less good*) schlechter; **it was even worse than the last time** es war noch schlechter als letztes Mal; **to get worse** schlechter werden; **the weather's getting worse** das Wetter wird schlechter; **she's getting worse** (*in health*) es geht ihr schlechter.

worst *adjective* **1** (*most unpleasant*) schlimmster/schlimmste/ schlimmstes; **the worst** der/die/das Schlimmste; **it was the worst day of my life** es war der schlimmste Tag meines Lebens; **if the worst comes to the worst** wenn es zum Schlimmsten kommt; **2** (*least good*) schlechtester/schlechteste/ schlechtestes; **it's his worst film** das ist sein schlechtester Film; **French is my worst subject** in Französisch bin ich am schlechtesten.

worth *adjective* **to be worth** wert sein; **how much is it worth?** wie viel ist es wert?; **it's worth buying**

✧ IRREGULAR VERB: *See the verb table in the centre of the dictionary*

das lohnt sich zu kaufen; **it's worth it** das lohnt sich; **it's not worth it** es lohnt sich nicht.

would *verb* **1 would you like something to eat?** möchtest du etwas essen?; **what would you like?** was möchten Sie?; **2 I wouldn't do it** ich würde das nicht machen; **I would buy it, but I haven't got any money at the moment** ich würde es kaufen, aber ich habe zur Zeit kein Geld; **I'd like to go to the cinema** ich würde gern ins Kino gehen; **she said she'd help us** sie hat gesagt, sie würde uns helfen; **that would be a good idea** das wäre ein gute Idee; **if we had asked her she would have helped us** wenn wir sie gefragt hätten, hätte sie uns geholfen; **4 he wouldn't answer** er wollte nicht antworten; **the car wouldn't start** das Auto wollte nicht anspringen.

wound *noun* Wunde *die* (PL *die* Wunden).
verb verwunden.

wrap *verb* einwickeln SEP; **I'm going to wrap (up) my presents** ich wickele meine Geschenke ein; **could you wrap it for me please?** können Sie es bitte in Geschenkpapier einwickeln?

wrapping paper *noun* Geschenkpapier *das*.

wreck *noun* **1** Wrack *das* (PL *die* Wracks); **2 I feel a wreck** ich bin völlig kaputt.
verb **1** zerstören (*a building or machinery*); **2** kaputtfahren ✧ SEP (*a car*); **3** verderben ✧ (*a party, holidays*); **it completely wrecked**

my evening das hat mir den Abend völlig verdorben; **4** zunichte machen (*plans*).

wrestler *noun* Ringer *der* (PL *die* Ringer), Ringerin *die* (PL *die* Ringerinnen).

wrestling *noun* Ringen *das*.

wrist *noun* Handgelenk *das* (PL *die* Handgelenke).

write *verb* schreiben ✧; **to write to somebody** jemandem schreiben; **I'll write her a letter** ich schreibe ihr einen Brief; **to write to a firm** an eine Firma schreiben.
● **to write down** aufschreiben ✧ SEP; **I wrote down her name** ich schrieb ihren Namen auf; **she wrote it down for me** sie hat es mir aufgeschrieben.

writer *noun* Schriftsteller *der* (PL *die* Schriftsteller), Schriftstellerin *die* (PL *die* Schriftstellerinnen).

writing *noun* Schrift *die*.

wrong *adjective* **1** (*not correct*) falsch; **the wrong answer** die falsche Antwort; **it's the wrong address** das ist die falsche Adresse; **2 you've got the wrong number** Sie haben sich verwählt; **3 to be wrong** (*be mistaken*) sich irren; **I must have been wrong** ich muss mich geirrt haben; **4** (*out of order*) **to be wrong** nicht stimmen; **there's something wrong** etwas stimmt nicht; **5** (*dishonest*) unrecht; **it's wrong to make him pay for it** es ist unrecht, dass er dafür zahlen muss; **he's wrong** er hat Unrecht; **you're quite wrong there, cars pollute the**

environment da haben Sie aber Unrecht, Autos verschmutzen die Umwelt; **6 what's wrong?** was ist los?
adverb **1** (*false*) falsch; **he's got it wrong** er hat es falsch gemacht; **2 to go wrong** (*break*) kaputtgehen ◇ SEP (PERF *sein*) (*informal*); **3 to go wrong** schief gehen ∆ ◇ (*plan*).

X x

xerox™ *noun* Fotokopie *die* (PL *die* Fotokopien).
verb fotokopieren.

X-ray *noun* Röntgenaufnahme *die* (PL *die* Röntgenaufnahmen); **to have an X-ray** geröntgt werden ◇ (PERF *sein*).
verb röntgen; **they X-rayed her ankle** sie haben ihren Knöchel geröntgt.

Y y

yacht *noun* **1** (*sailing boat*) Segelboot *das* (PL *die* Segelboote); **2** (*large luxury boat*) Jacht *die* (PL *die* Jachten).

yawn *verb* gähnen.

year *noun* **1** Jahr *das* (PL *die* Jahre); **six years ago** vor sechs Jahren; **the whole year** das ganze Jahr; **2 they lived in Moscow for years** sie haben jahrelang in Moskau gewohnt; **3 to be seventeen years old** siebzehn Jahre alt sein; **a two-year-old child** ein zweijähriges Kind; **4** (*in school*) Klasse *die* (PL *die* Klassen) (*in German secondary schools the years go from the 'fünfte Klasse' to the 'dreizehnte Klasse'*); **I'm in Year 10** (*in Britain*) ich gehe in die zehnte Klasse; **he'll be in Year 11** (*in Britain*) er kommt in die elfte Klasse.

yellow *adjective* gelb.

yes *adverb* **1** ja; **yes please** ja bitte; **'is Tom in his room?' – 'yes, he is'** 'ist Tom im Zimmer?' – 'ja'; **2** (*answering a negative*) doch; **'you don't want to come with us, do you?' – ' yes, I do!'** 'du willst nicht mitkommen?' – 'doch!'; **'you haven't finished, have you?' – 'yes, I have'** 'Sie sind noch nicht fertig, oder?' – 'doch!'.

yesterday *adverb* **1** gestern; **I saw her yesterday** ich habe sie gestern gesehen; **yesterday afternoon** gestern Nachmittag; **yesterday morning** gestern früh; **2 the day before yesterday** vorgestern.

yet *adverb* **1** not yet noch nicht; **it's not ready yet** es ist noch nicht fertig; **2** (*in questions*) schon; **has she mentioned it yet?** hat sie es schon erwähnt?

yoghurt *noun* Joghurt *der* (PL *die* Joghurt).

◇ IRREGULAR VERB: *See the verb table in the centre of the dictionary*

yolk noun Eigelb das (PL die Eigelbe).

you pronoun 1 (as the subject of the sentence and in comparisons) du (familiar form, singular); Sie (polite form, singular and plural); ('du' is the familiar way of talking to family members, close friends, and people of your own age; 'Sie' is more polite) **do you want to go to the cinema tonight?** möchtest du heute Abend ins Kino gehen?; **can you tell me where the station is, please?** können Sie mir bitte sagen, wo der Bahnhof ist?; **he's older than you** er ist älter als du, er ist älter als Sie; 2 (the object form of 'du' and 'Sie', in the dative) dir (familiar form, singular); Ihnen (polite form, singular and plural); **I'll lend you my bike** ich leihe dir mein Rad; **I'll write to you** ich schreibe Ihnen; **I'll come with you** ich komme mit Ihnen mit; 3 (the object form of 'du' and 'Sie', in the accusative) dich (familiar form, singular); Sie (polite form, singular and plural); **I saw you** ich habe dich gesehen, ich habe Sie gesehen; 4 (as the subject of the sentence) ihr (familiar form, plural); **do you all want to come?** wollt ihr alle kommen?; 5 (the object form, in the accusative and the dative) euch; **I'll invite you all!** ich lade euch alle ein!; **I'll give it to you later** ich gebe es euch später.

young adjective jung; **young people** junge Leute; **he's younger than me** er ist jünger als ich; **Tessa's two years younger than me** Tessa ist zwei Jahre jünger als ich.

your adjective 1 (familiar form, singular) dein; (this is the familiar way of talking to family members, close friends, and people of your own age; 'Ihr' is more polite) **I met your brother** ich habe deinen Bruder getroffen; **I met your sister** ich habe deine Schwester getroffen; **I drove your car** ich bin mit deinem Auto gefahren; **I know your brothers** ich kenne deine Brüder; 2 (familiar form, plural) euer; **your brother** euer Bruder; **your sister** eure Schwester; **your car** euer Auto; **your friends are waiting downstairs** eure Freunde warten unten; 3 (polite form, singular and plural) Ihr; **your brother** Ihr Bruder; **your sister** Ihre Schwester; **your car is in the garage** Ihr Auto ist in der Garage; **you can all bring your friends** Sie können alle Ihre Freunde mitbringen.

yours pronoun 1 (familiar form, singular) deiner/deine/deins; (this is the familiar way of talking to family members, close friends, and people of your own age, 'Ihrer/Ihre/Ihrs' is more polite) **my brother's younger than yours** mein Bruder ist jünger als deiner; **my sister is older than yours** meine Schwester ist älter als deine; **I enjoyed that book – is it yours?** das Buch hat mir gefallen – ist es deins?; **my shoes are more expensive than yours** meine Schuhe sind teurer als deine; 2 (familiar form, plural) euer/eure/eures; **my children are younger than yours** meine Kinder sind jünger als eure; 3 (polite form, singular and

△ NEW SPELLING: See page xii

plural) Ihrer/Ihre/Ihrs; **his father must be older than yours** sein Vater muss älter als Ihrer sein; **4 she's a friend of yours** sie ist eine Freundin von Ihnen; **these books are yours** diese Bücher gehören Ihnen; **5** (*in letters*) **Yours sincerely** Mit freundlichen Grüßen.

yourself *pronoun* **1** (*when translated by a reflexive verb in German*) dich; (*formal*) sich; **ask yourself** frage dich, fragen Sie sich; **2** (*as a reflexive dative pronoun*) dir; (*formal*) sich; **did you hurt yourself?** hast du dir wehgetan?, haben Sie sich wehgetan?; **3** (*for emphasis*) selbst; **did you do it yourself?** hast du es selbst gemacht?; **4 all by yourself** ganz allein.

yourselves *pronoun* **1** euch; (*formal*) sich; **make yourselves comfortable** macht es euch gemütlich, machen Sie es sich gemütlich; **2** (*for emphasis*) selbst; **did you do it yourselves?** habt ihr es selbst gemacht?; **3 by yourselves** allein.

youth hostel *noun* Jugendherberge *die* (PL *die* Jugendherbergen).

Yugoslavia *noun* Jugoslawien *das*; **in the former Yugoslavia** im ehemaligen Jugoslawien.

Z z

zany *adjective* verrückt.

zebra *noun* Zebra *das* (PL *die* Zebras).

zebra crossing *noun* Zebrastreifen *der* (PL *die* Zebrastreifen).

zero *noun* Null *die* (PL *die* Nullen).

zigzag *verb* **1** im Zickzack laufen ✧(PERF *sein*); **2** (*in a car*) im Zickzack fahren ✧(PERF *sein*).

zip *noun* Reißverschluss △ *der* (PL *die* Reißverschlüsse).

zodiac *noun* Tierkreis *der*; **the signs of the zodiac** die Sternzeichen (*plural*).

zone *noun* Zone *die* (PL *die* Zonen).

zoo *noun* Zoo *der* (PL *die* Zoos).

zoom lens *noun* Zoomobjektiv *das* (PL *die* Zoomobjektive).

✧ IRREGULAR VERB: *See the verb table in the centre of the dictionary*

USEFUL LISTS

Deutschland

DEUTSCHLAND	GERMANY
Bundesland	**State**
Baden-Württemberg	Baden-Württemberg
Bayern	Bavaria
Berlin	Berlin
Brandenburg	Brandenburg
Bremen	Bremen
Hamburg	Hamburg
Hessen	Hessen
Mecklenburg-Vorpommern	Mecklenburg-West Pomerania
Niedersachsen	Lower Saxony
Nordrhein-Westfalen	North Rhine-Westphalia
Rheinland-Pfalz	Rhineland-Palatinate
Saarland	Saarland
Sachsen	Saxony
Sachsen-Anhalt	Saxony-Anhalt
Schleswig-Holstein	Schleswig-Holstein
Thüringen	Thuringia

Europa

Reykjavik ISLAND

Europäisches
Nordmeer

NORWEGEN SCHWEDEN FINNLAND

Oslo Stockholm Helsinki

Tallinn ESTLAND

RUSSLAND

Moskau

SCHOTTLAND

NORDIRLAND

Nordsee

Ostsee

Riga LETTLAND

LITAUEN
Wilna

REPUBLIK
IRLAND

Dublin GROSSBRITANNIEN

DÄNEMARK
Kopenhagen

RUSSLAND

Minsk

WALES

ENGLAND

Hamburg

Amsterdam Berlin

POLEN

WEISSRUSSLAND

London

Ärmelkanal

NIEDERLANDE

DEUTSCHLAND

Warschau

Kiew

Brüssel
BELGIEN

Bonn

LUXEMBURG

Prag

UKRAINE

Atlantischer
Ozean

Paris

LIECHTENSTEIN

TSCHECHISCHE
REPUBLIK

München

Wien SLOWAKEI

FRANKREICH

Bern
SCHWEIZ

Bratislava
Budapest

MOLDAWIEN

Chişinău

ÖSTERREICH

UNGARN

SLOWENIEN Ljubljana

RUMÄNIEN

Mailand

Zagreb Belgrad

Bukarest

MONACO

SAN MARINO

BOSNIEN – HERZEGOWINA

PORTUGAL

Lissabon

Madrid ANDORRA

Sarajevo

BULGARIEN

SPANIEN

Korsika

ITALIEN

JUGOSLAWIEN

Sofia

Skopje

Ibiza

Menorca

Rom

ALBANIEN MAZEDONIEN

Mallorca

Sardinien

Tirana

GRIECHENLAND

TÜRKEI

0   200 400 600 800 km

Athen

0 100 200 300 400 500 Meilen

Sizilien

Mittelmeer

Kreta

EUROPA	EUROPE
Land	**Country**
Albanien	Albania
Andorra	Andorra
Belgien	Belgium
Bosnien-Herzogowina	Bosnia-Herzegovina
Bulgarien	Bulgaria
Dänemark	Denmark
Deutschland	Germany
Estland	Estonia
Finnland	Finland
Frankreich	France
Griechenland	Greece
Großbritannien	United Kingdom; Great Britain
England	England
Nordirland	Northern Ireland
Schottland	Scotland
Wales	Wales
Kroatien	Croatia
Island	Iceland
Italien	Italy
Jugoslawien	Yugoslavia
Lettland	Latvia
Liechtenstein	Liechtenstein
Litauen	Lithuania
Luxemburg	Luxembourg

EUROPA	EUROPE
Land	**Country**
Mazedonien (Ehmalige Jugoslawische Republik Mazedonien)	FYROM (Former Yugoslav Republic of Macedonia)
Monaco	Monaco
Moldawien	Moldavia
Niederlande	Netherlands
Norwegen	Norway
Österreich	Austria
Polen	Poland
Portugal	Portugal
Republik Irland	Republic of Ireland
Rumänien	Romania
Russland	Russia
San Marino	San Marino
Schweden	Sweden
Schweiz	Switzerland
Slowakei	Slovakia
Slowenien	Slovenia
Spanien	Spain
Tschechische Republik	Czech Republic
Türkei	Turkey
Ukraine	Ukraine
Ungarn	Hungary
Weißrussland	Belarus

NUMBERS

null	0	einundzwanzig	21
eins	1	zweiundzwanzig	22
zwei	2	dreiundzwanzig	23
drei	3	vierundzwanzig	24
vier	4	fünfundzwanzig	25
fünf	5	sechsundzwanzig	26
sechs	6	siebenundzwanzig	27
sieben	7	achtundzwanzig	28
acht	8	neunundzwanzig	29
neun	9		
zehn	10		
elf	11	dreißig	30
zwölf	12	vierzig	40
dreizehn	13	fünfzig	50
vierzehn	14	sechzig	60
fünfzehn	15	siebzig	70
sechzehn	16	achtzig	80
siebzehn	17	neunzig	90
achtzehn	18		
neunzehn	19	hundert	100
zwanzig	20	tausend	1 000
		eine Million	1 000 000

DATES

am ersten Januar	on January 1st
der erste Januar	the 1st of January
zweite (2.)	2nd
dritte (3.)	3rd
vierte (4.)	4th
fünfte	5th
sechste	6th
siebte	7th
achte	8th
neunte	9th
zehnte	10th
elfte	11th
zwölfte	12th
dreizehnte	13th
vierzehnte	14th
fünfzehnte	15th
sechzehnte	16th
siebzehnte	17th
achtzehnte	18th
neunzehnte	19th
zwanzigste	20th
einundzwanzigste	21st
dreißigste	30th

IMPORTANT DATES

Feiertag	public holiday
Fasching/Fastnacht	carnival time
Heiligabend	Christmas Eve
Karfreitag	Good Friday
Maifeiertag	May Day
Neujahr	New Year
Ostern	Easter
Pfingsten	Whitsun
Silvester	New Year's Eve
Weihnachten	Christmas
1. Weihnachtstag	Christmas Day
2. Weihnachtstag	Boxing Day

DAYS

Montag	Monday
Dienstag	Tuesday
Mittwoch	Wednesday
Donnerstag	Thursday
Freitag	Friday
Samstag/Sonnabend	Saturday
Sonntag	Sunday

MONTHS

Januar	January
Februar	February
März	March
April	April
Mai	May
Juni	June
Juli	July
August	August
September	September
Oktober	October
November	November
Dezember	December

SEASONS

der Winter	winter
der Frühling	spring
der Sommer	summer
der Herbst	autumn

NOTES

NOTES

NOTES

NOTES